A COMMENTARY ON

LIVY

BOOKS VI–X

For Tony Woodman

A COMMENTARY ON
LIVY
BOOKS VI–X

S. P. Oakley

Volume IV
Book X

CLARENDON PRESS · OXFORD

OXFORD

UNIVERSITY PRESS

Great Clarendon Street, Oxford OX2 6DP

Oxford University Press is a department of the University of Oxford.
It furthers the University's objective of excellence in research, scholarship,
and education by publishing worldwide in

Oxford New York

Auckland Cape Town Dar es Salaam Hong Kong Karachi
Kuala Lumpur Madrid Melbourne Mexico City Nairobi
New Delhi Shanghai Taipei Toronto

With offices in

Argentina Austria Brazil Chile Czech Republic France Greece
Guatemala Hungary Italy Japan Poland Portugal Singapore
South Korea Switzerland Thailand Turkey Ukraine Vietnam

Oxford is a registered trade mark of Oxford University Press
in the UK and in certain other countries

Published in the United States
by Oxford University Press Inc., New York

© S. P. Oakley 2005

British Library Cataloguing in Publication Data
Data available

Library of Congress Cataloging in Publication Data
A commentary on Livy, Books VI–X / S. P. Oakley.
Includes bibliographical references and index.
Contents: v. 1. Introduction and Book VI.
1. Livy. Ab urbe condita. Libri 6–10. 2. Rome—History—
Republic, 265–30 B.C.—Historiography. 3. Punic Wars—
Historiography. I. Title.
PA6459.03 1996 937'.02'92—dc20 96-17028

Typeset by SPI Publisher Services, Pondicherry, India
Printed in Great Britain on acid-free paper by
Antony Rowe Ltd., Chippenham

ISBN 978–0–19–927256–3 (Hbk.) 978–0–19–923785–2 (Pbk.)

1 3 5 7 9 10 8 6 4 2

Preface

THIS volume completes my commentary on Livy books vi–x and includes *addenda* and *corrigenda* that reflect what I have learnt about books vi–viii over the last seven years; it remains my intention to publish a revised text, but only after a break of a few years to work on other subjects. The whole tyepscript has been read and greatly improved by Dr J. Briscoe, Dr L. A. Holford-Strevens (whose copy-editing has again removed several mistakes), and Professor A. J. Woodman, and the commentary on chapters 32–47 by Professor C. S. Kraus. Most of my textual notes were scrutinized and improved by the late Professor W. S. Watt, some by Professor M. D. Reeve; Professor M. H. Crawford performed a similar service for some of the longer historical notes. Once again Dr N. Hopkinson kindly read the book in proof. A term's sabbatical leave funded by the Arts and Humanities Research Board hastened the completion of the book. I owe special thanks to my wife, Ruth, who has allowed me to be preoccupied for weeks on end with Livy. Reaching the end of the four volumes, I have come to realize that there are many things that I could have done better or differently. Some of my regrets will be obvious from the *addenda* and *corrigenda*. Here I shall mention only my two different versions of the author/date system of reference, which no one likes and for which I must absolve my copy-editors of responsibility. One thing I do not regret is publishing with Oxford University Press: once again I thank Hilary O'Shea for publishing the commentary that I wished to write, and Lavinia Porter and her colleagues for seeing these last two volumes through the press. Like many others who work on the Latin historians I have received much support and encouragement from Tony Woodman, in return for which the dedication of this book is a small offering.

S.P.O.

University of Reading
October 2003

Contents

List of Figures

Abbreviations

CIE	*Corpus inscriptionum Etruscarum*
CIL	*Corpus inscriptionum Latinarum*
CSEL	*Corpus scriptorum ecclesiasticorum Latinorum*
Daremberg and Saglio	C. Daremberg and E. Saglio, *Dictionnaire des antiquités* (Paris, 1877–1919)
D.H.	Dionysius of Halicarnassus (almost invariably referring to the *Roman Antiquities*)
D.S.	Diodorus Siculus
F.C.	*Fasti Capitolini*
FGrH	F. Jacoby (ed.), *Die Fragmente der griechischen Historiker* (Berlin, 1923–30; Leiden 1940–58)
F.T.	*Fasti triumphales*
H–S	J. B. Hofmann and A. Szantyr, *Lateinische Grammatik: Syntax und Stilistik* (Munich, 1965)
I.G.	*Inscriptiones Graecae*
I.I.	*Inscriptiones Italiae* (almost invariably referring to vol. xiii. 1 [1947], xiii. 2 [1963], or xiii. 3 [1937])
ILLRP	A. Degrassi (ed.), *Inscriptiones Latinae liberae rei publicae* (vol. i., ed. 2) (Florence, 1963–5)
ILS	H. Dessau (ed.), *Inscriptiones Latinae selectae* (Berlin, 1892–1916)
K.	C. S. Kraus, *Livy* ab urbe condita *book vi* (Cambridge, 1994)
K–S	R. Kühner and C. Stegmann, *Ausführliche Grammatik der lateinischen Sprache: Satzlehre* (Hanover, 1914)
L.	Livy
L–S–J	H. G. Liddell, R. Scott, and H. S. Jones, *A Greek–English Lexicon*[9] (Oxford, 1940)
ORF	H. Malcovati (ed.), *Oratorum Romanorum fragmenta*[4] (Turin, 1976)
PG	*Patrologia Graeca*
PL	*Patrologia Latina*
RE	*Real-Encyclopädie der classischen Altertumswissenschaft* (Stuttgart, 1893–1980)
SEG	*Supplementum epigraphicum Graecum* (Leiden and then Amsterdam, 1923–)
TLL	*Thesaurus linguae Latinae* (Leipzig, later Leipzig and Stuttgart, and later Munich 1901–)

W–M   the final edition of H. J. Müller's revision of Weissenborn's comm. (book i^9 [1908], book ii^8 [1894], book iii^6 [1900], books iv–v^6 [1896], books vi–viii^6 [1924, further revised by O. Rossbach], books ix–x^5 [1890], book xxi^{10} [1921, further revised by O. Rossbach], book xxii^9 [1905], book xxiii^8 [1907], books $xxiv$–xxv^5 [1895], book xxvi^5 [1911], books $xxvii$–xxviii^4 [1910], books $xxix$–xxx^4 [1899], books $xxxi$–xxxiv^3 [1883], books $xxxv$–xxxvi^3 [1903], books $xxxvii$–xxxviii^3 [1907], books $xxxix$–xlii^3 [1909], books $xliii$–xliv^2 [1880], books xlv and fragments^2 [1881])

[x] in connection with a lexical note means that concordances (or indexes or lexica) to L., Sallust, Valerius Maximus, Velleius Paterculus, Curtius, Tacitus, Florus, *SHA*, Ammianus, and the fragments of the Roman historians have been checked.

[*] in connection with a lexical note means that the concordance (or indexes or lexica) to Ennius, Caesar, Cato, *agr.*, Celsus, Cicero, Columella, Curtius, Florus, Germanicus, Grattius, Horace, Juvenal, Livy, Lucilius, Lucretius, Manilius, Mela, Nepos, Persius, Petronius, Phaedrus, Plautus, the elder and younger Plinys, Propertius, Quintilian, Sallust, the younger Seneca, Silius, Statius, Suetonius, Tacitus, Terence, Tibullus, Valerius Flaccus, Valerius Maximus, Varr. *rust.*, Velleius Paterculus, Virgil, and the fragments of the Roman historians have been checked.

Editions of Livy

Editions, commentaries, and translations of book ix are referred to by the name of their author alone (with the exception of W–M):

Alschefski	C. F. S. Alschefski, edn. of books vi–x (Berlin, 1843)
Briscoe	J. Briscoe, edn. of books xxxi–xl (Sttutgart, 1991)
Conway	the contributions of R. S. Conway to the edn. of Walters
Crévier	J. B. L. Crévier, edn. of Livy (Paris, 1735–42)
Doering	F. W. Doering, revision of Stroth's edn. of Livy (Gotha, 1801–19; books vi–x, 1805)
Drakenborch	A. Drakenborch, edn. of Livy (Leiden and Amsterdam, 1738–46)
Foster	B. O. Foster, edn. and trans. of books viii–x (Cambridge, Mass., and London [Loeb], 1926)
Gelenius	See Rhenanus
Hertz	M. Hertz, edn. of books i–x (Leipzig, 1857)
Heusinger	K. Heusinger, *Titus Livius Römische Geschichte übersetzt mit kritischen und erklärenden Anmerkungen* (book x is contained in the second of the five volumes) (Brunswick, 1821)

Abbreviations

Luterbacher	F. Luterbacher, edn. of book x (Leipzig, 1892)
Madvig and Ussing	J. N. Madvig and J. L. Ussing, edn. of books vi–x (Copenhagen, 1861)
Madvig and Ussing²	J. N. Madvig and J. L. Ussing, second edn. of books vi–x (Copenhagen, 1875)
McDonald	A. H. McDonald, edn. of books xxxi–xxxv (Oxford, 1965)
H. J. Müller (ed.)	Müller's fifth edn. of Weissenborn's comm. on books ix–x (Berlin [Weidmann], 1890)
M. Müller	M. Müller's revision of Weissenborn's edn. of books vii–xxiii (Leipzig [Teubner], 1905)
Ogilvie	R. M. Ogilvie, edn. of books i–v (Oxford, 1974)
Rhenanus (or Gelenius)	Beatus Rhenanus and Sigismundus Gelenius, edn. of Livy (Basel [Froben], 1535)
Ruperti	G. E. Ruperti, comm. on Livy (Göttingen, 1807–9)
Stroth	F. A. Stroth, edn. of Livy (Gotha, 1793–4)
Walters	W. C. F. Walters (and R. S. Conway), edn. of books vi–x (Oxford, 1919)
Weissenborn (ed.)	W. Weissenborn, edn. of books vii–xxiii (Leipzig [Teubner], 1853)
Weissenborn (ed.²)	W. Weissenborn, edn. of books vii–xxiii² (Leipzig [Teubner], 1868)
Weissenborn (*Komm.*)	W. Weissenborn, comm. on books vi–x (Berlin [Weidmann], 1854)
Weissenborn (*Komm.³*)	W. Weissenborn, comm. on books ix–x³ (Berlin [Weidmann], 1869)
Weissenborn (*Komm.⁴*)	W. Weissenborn, comm. on books ix–x⁴ (Berlin [Weidmann], 1877)

Other bare references to the names of scholars are usually to editors preceding Crévier and Drakenborch, and may be elucidated from Drakenborch's commentary.

Other modern works

With the exception of commentaries on Latin and Greek authors, these are cited according to the Harvard system. The fuller bibliographical details of these shortened references may be elucidated from the bibliography (where I have also listed the commentaries and some editions which I cite).

Fragments, ancient authors for whom there is no recognized division into chapters, and authors for whom it is helpful to quote the page number of an edn., are cited according to the numeration or page of the following editions: the fragments of the Greek comic poets of Kassel and Austin (Berlin and New York, 1983–); Greek historians of Jacoby (*FGrH*); Roman republican drama (except Ennius) of Ribbeck³ (Leipzig, 1897–8); the Roman historians of Peter (Leipzig: vol. i, 1914²; vol. ii, 1906); the surviving fragments of *iurisprudentia antehadriana* of Bremer (Leipzig, 1896–1901); the fragments of Roman poetry of both Blänsdorf (Stuttgart, 1992) and Courtney (Oxford, 1993); the *grammatici Latini* of Keil (Leipzig, 1857–70) or (for fragments of grammarians) Funaioli (Leipzig, 1907); the *agrimensores* of Thulin (Leipzig, 1913); the *anthologia Latina* (including the *carmina epigraphica*) of Riese and Bücheler (Leipzig, 1886–1906); the Latin glossaries of Goetz *et al.*, *Corpus glossariorum Latinorum* (Leipzig, 1888–1923); Apuleius of Hildebrand (Leipzig, 1842); Asconius and Σ on Cicero of Stangl (Vienna, 1912); Ausonius of Green (Oxford, 1991); Augustus of Malcovati (Turin, 1928); Cato (apart from the *origines* and oratorical fragments) of Jordan (Leipzig, 1860); Calpurnius Flaccus of Håkanson (Stuttgart, 1978); Cicero of Watt (Oxford, 1958: letters) and C. F. W. Müller (Leipzig, 1898: other prose works); Ennius of Skutsch (Oxford, 1985: *annales*), Jocelyn (Cambridge, 1967: *scaenica*), and Vahlen² (Leipzig, 1903: other fragments); Festus of Lindsay (Leipzig, 1913); Fronto of van den Hout² (Leipzig, 1988); Livy of W–M; Lydus of Wünsch (Lepizig, 1903); Nonius of Lindsay (Leipzig, 1903); Seneca of Haase (Leipzig, 1902); Sallust of Maurenbrecher (Leipzig, 1891–3); Suetonius of Roth (Leipzig, 1862); and Varro's *Menippean satires* of Bücheler (ed. 6, W. Heraeus, Berlin, 1922; Astbury's edition [Leipzig, 1985] uses the same numeration).

Sigla

The following *sigla* are used for the primary witnesses:

D	=	Florence, Laur. S. Marco 326. S. xi
L	=	Leiden, Bibl. der Rijksuniversiteit, B.P.L. 6A. S. xi
M	=	Florence, Laur. plut. lxiii. 19. S. $x^{med.}$
O	=	Oxford, Bodl. Auct. T. I. 24, s.c. 20631. S. xi^I
P	=	Paris, B.N.F. lat. 5725. S. $ix^{med.}$
R	=	Vat. lat. 3329. S. x
T	=	Paris, B.N. lat. 5726. S. ix^I
U	=	Uppsala, Universiteitsbibl. C 908. S. x
Zb	=	Vatican, Borgh. lat. 368. S. $xv^{3/4}$
Zs	=	Siena, Bibl. Com. K V 14. S. xv^I
Zt	=	Turin, Bibl. Naz. E III 17 S. $xv^{3/4}$

N	=	the lost Nicomachean archetype of all these witnesses
Π	=	the lost parent of PUOZbZtZs, of which OZbZtZs are in differing ways contaminated
λ	=	the lost parent of TRLD (Λ, the lost parent of H = London, B.L. Harley 2672 and λ, cannot be reconstructed for book x, as H is not available)
θ	=	the lost parent of RLD
Z	=	the lost parent of ZsZbZt

Other extant or lost witnesses to which reference is occasionally made:

A	=	London, B.L. Harley 2493. S. xiii
A^c	=	corrections to the above of an authorship that cannot certainly be identified
A^p	=	corrections by Petrarch to the above
A^v	=	corrections by Valla to the above
F	=	Paris, B.N.F. lat. 5724 (S. $ix^{4/4}$), a descendant of P
Gr	=	Leiden, Bibl. der Rijksuniversteit, Gronovianus 1. S. xii
u	=	completion of U from 38. 9 onwards
Zr	=	the editio princeps (Rome, 1469 or early 1470), quite closely related to Zs
χ	=	the lost parent of A^p, Paris, B.N.F. Lat. 5690^c (S. xiv), El Escorial R I 4 (S. xiv), and Florence, Riccardianus 485 (S. xiv). χ, which probably derives from a contaminated copy of M, is the source of several plausible conjectures.

For full discussion of these and other mss, and for a stemma, see vol. i, pp. 152–327.

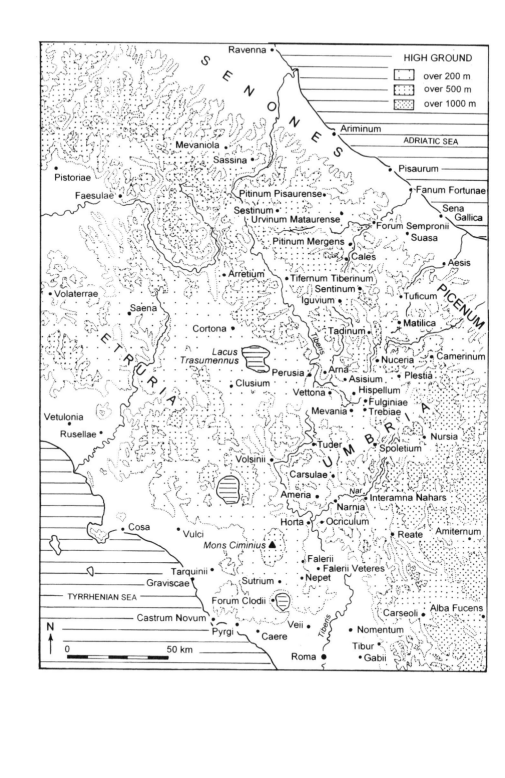

HIGH GROUND

over 200 m
over 500 m
over 1000 m

Ravenna

ADRIATIC SEA

S E N O N E S

Ariminum

Pisaurum

Fanum Fortunae

Mevaniola

Sassina

Pistoriae

Faesulae

Pitinum Pisaurense

Sestinum

Urvinum Mataurense

Sena Gallica

Forum Sempronii

Suasa

Pitinum Mergens

Cales

Aesis

Arretium

Tifernum Tiberinum

Sentinum

Iguvium

Tuficum

PICENUM

Volaterrae

Saena

Cortona

Matilica

Tadinum

E T R U R I A

Lacus Trasumennus

Perusia

Arna

Nuceria

Camerinum

Asisium

Plestia

Clusium

Vettona

Hispellum

Tiberis

Mevania

Fulginiae

Trebiae

Vetulonia

Rusellae

Nursia

Tuder

U M B R I A

Spoletium

Volsinii

Carsulae

Ameria

Nar.

Interamna Nahars

Horta

Narnia

Ocriculum

Reate

Amiternum

Cosa

Vulci

Mons Ciminius ▲

Falerii

Falerii Veteres

Carseoli

Alba Fucens

Tarquinii

Graviscae

Sutrium

Nepet

TYRRHENIAN SEA

Forum Clodii

Castrum Novum

Veii

Tiberis

Nomentum

Pyrgi

Caere

Tibur

Gabii

Roma

N

0   50 km

BOOK X

Historical Introduction

THE ROMAN STATE *c*.300 BC[1]

BECAUSE of the successful wars of conquest which L. describes in books vii–x, the size of the Roman state had grown from *c*.2,005 km² in the mid-340s to *c*.5,525 km² in the mid-330s and to *c*.6,285 km² by 300, and, with further successful warfare, was to grow to *c*.15,295 km² by the mid-280s.[2] Although the figures recorded by L. and others are unreliable, its population must have grown proportionately, until deaths in the Samnite Wars and the dispersal of citizens in colonies at the end of the fourth and the beginning of the third centuries provided some check.[3] For 300 an estimate of 90,000 free adult males is not unreasonable (ix. 19. 2 n.), and in addition to this free population there were increasing numbers of slaves.[4] How many of these Romans and their slaves lived in the city itself is not known; but the fact that the city grew greatly in size in the period around 300 is shown by the construction of aqueducts in 312 (ix. 29. 6 n.) and 272 (ix. 17. 8 n.).

All Roman citizens had full rights in private and public law and were expected, if required, to serve in the army; but in another important respect they fell into two categories. The right to vote in elections was possessed by those who came from old Roman territory (which included Gabii and other settlements incorporated in the sixth and fifth centuries) and from the Latin towns of Tusculum, Lanuvium, Aricia, Nomentum, and Pedum.[5] It was not possessed by others (hence known as *ciues sine suffragio*), whose *patriae* had been

---

[1] The purpose of this section is to provide a brief general historical analysis that places in context evidence and arguments that may be found scattered in individual notes throughout the commentary, notes which given the nature of commentaries are sometimes rather antiquarian in their perspective. Evidence for most of the assertions made here can be found either in these notes, to which frequent reference is made, or in the other references; but for a few general statements about well-known factors or institutions in Roman history, no evidence is cited.

[2] For these approximate estimates see Afzelius (1942) 136–81.

[3] Those who settled in Latin colonies lost their Roman citizenship. On colonization, see below.

[4] Discussed below.

[5] For the incorporation of these states see vol. ii, pp. 542–4; perhaps Lavinium should be added to their number: see viii. 11. 3 n.

conquered in recent times. The most notable of these *ciuitates sine suffragio* were the Campanian towns of Capua (including her satellites Casilinum, Calatia, and Atella), Cumae, Acerrae, and Suessula; others included Formiae, Fundi, Arpinum, Frusino and most of the Hernican towns, and (perhaps) some of the Aequi.[6]

Like almost all other states in the ancient world, republican Rome had an economy that was primarily agrarian: the vast majority of the population earned their living from working land which they owned. Some of these farmers will have lived in the city itself; some in outlying farmsteads, hamlets, villages, or towns; and a few will have had both country- and town-dwellings. However, by 300 a significant number of dwellers in the city itself must have earned their livelihood from shopkeeping and other 'industries';[7] and doubtless they, and perhaps farmers too (during slack periods in their year), picked up extra work elsewhere, for instance helping in the construction of Rome's public buildings.[8]

The most obvious reason for a farmer to leave his land was to visit a market, either in a nearby town or village,[9] or in Rome itself.[10] Other reasons for those who did not live in Rome to visit the city included the annual elections to magistracies,[11] festivals of various kinds,[12] and the games (21. 13, 47. 3, viii. 20. 1, and 40. 2 nn.). Festivals and the games were the only forms of leisure organized by the state (or indeed by anyone) for the masses; the latter, for which a large proportion of the state was gathered together, provided notable occasions for celebration and display (x. 47. 3 n.). Men who owned property, however, were required to serve in the legions (vol. ii, pp. 452–5), and, during the first thirty years of their adulthood, military service will have taken them from their farms for far longer than any visits to the elections or to games; for, after the need to farm the land, warfare, to which we shall return below, is the single most important factor in Roman history in this period.

---

[6] See vol. ii, pp. 544–59. On Aequan *ciuitas sine suffragio* see 1. 3 n.

[7] L. refers to such people at viii. 20. 4 (n.) (329 BC); it is not clear whether this notice rests ultimately on an authentic memory or only on annalistic reconstruction. That they were recruited to the army, as some of L.'s sources implied, is very doubtful.

[8] For this practice see Brunt (1980) (concerned with later times but with arguments that must be true also for this epoch).

[9] For *nundinae* and *conciliabula* see vii. 15. 13 (n.), which, however, may derive from Livian or annalistic reconstruction rather than good testimony.

[10] For the integration of market-days into the Roman calendar, see ix. 46. 1–15 n.

[11] The date of these was probably not fixed in this period; see viii. 20. 3 n.

[12] L. tends to mention only exceptional festivals (see e.g. vii. 28. 8 and viii. 33. 20 nn. on *supplicationes*) and not the regular celebrations held on fixed days throughout the year.

The population of Rome that had the right to vote was divided and classified in three ways.[13] The oldest was a division into thirty *curiae*, a system of organization that went back to the regal period; but the practice of assembling the people by *curiae* seems to have been largely obsolete by 300 (and even more so by the end of the Republic and early principate, from which period most of our evidence dates), except for the ratification of adoption among patrician clans (for which purpose it was known as the *comitia calata*) and the passing of the *lex curiata de imperio* at the time of elections (for which purpose it was known as the *comitia curiata*). In books vi–x and our other evidence for the period the *curiae* are mentioned only in this last context (ix. 38. 15 n.).

At each census the population was organized on a timocratic basis into *centuriae* ('centuries'), and, when assembled by centuries, was called the *comitia centuriata*. This assembly had strong military connotations: it was known sometimes as the *exercitus*;[14] a century was the name of the smallest unit in the Roman army; and the assembly met on the Campus Martius, the military exercise ground on the left bank of the Tiber, and never in the city itself (reflecting a taboo on bringing the army into the city). The assembly was probably instituted at the time of the introduction of the hoplite phalanx and reflects a phase of Rome's history in which power in the state was vested in the propertied classes, who elected men who would lead both army and state.[15] The centuriate assembly was reformed in the mid-third century, so that the centuries were aligned with the tribes. Unfortunately, our evidence for the workings of both the reformed assembly and earlier version(s) of it is inadequate. If L. (i. 43. 1–13) and D.H. (iv. 16. 1–18. 3) are to be believed, the assembly originally comprised 193 centuries, of which a majority would be given by the votes of the cavalry (eighteen centuries) and first class (eighty centuries), whose view it therefore reflected on those occasions when the matter on which a vote was taken concerned the interests of the upper class as a whole;[16] unfortunately, their evidence is likely to derive from annalistic and antiquarian reconstruction and may not be reliable. Nevertheless, since the reformed assembly, of which a

[13] For Roman assemblies see esp. Taylor (1966); Lintott (1999) 40–64 provides a briefer and more up-to-date account.

[14] See xxxix. 15. 11 and other evidence cited by Lintott (1999: 55 n. 72).

[15] For the centuries and the early organization of Rome's hoplite phalanx see viii. 8. 3–14 n. The censorship was instituted only in the mid-fifth century, perhaps in 443 (iv. 8. 2–7); but earlier censuses had been conducted by consuls (47. 2 n.).

[16] Emphasized by L., §§ 10–11. When a majority had been reached, the other centuries were not called to vote.

partial description is provided by Cicero (*rep*. ii. 39), was certainly weighted in favour of the propertied classes, it seems likely that this must have been true earlier.[17] In which case, from early times, and certainly in our period, a century could comprise more than one hundred men, and the centuries into which the lower classes were assigned contained many more men than those into which the upper classes were assigned. Throughout the Republic the centuriate assembly was always assembled for the election of curule magistrates and censors[18] and for votes on war (vi. 21. 5 n.). However, its timocratic bias must have made it seem somewhat old-fashioned by the mid-fourth century, and, although it may originally have been used for passing much of Rome's legislation,[19] it was so used only very rarely in the late third, second, and first centuries, and probably quite rarely in our period.

Since the early Republic the populace had been organized also on a tribal basis, each tribe comprising those who were domiciled in a tract of the *ager Romanus* (vi. 5. 8 n.). As the *ager* expanded with conquest, so new tribes were added: ultimately there were to be thirty-five, and in our period the Ufentina and Falerna (318: ix. 20. 6 n.) and the Aniensis and Teretina (299: 9. 14 n.) took the number to first thirty-one, then thirty-three. The fact that the number of tribes was always odd may suggest that from early times they had been used as voting districts, and by our period the tribal assembly was the assembly summoned most often in a year. That was because, with the patricians absent, it was the only assembly over which tribunes of the plebs could preside, and the tribunes had increasingly come to introduce most of Rome's new legislation:[20] they were elected by it and passed their legislation and held capital trials through it. Presided over by tribunes, the tribal assembly was known as the *concilium plebis*; it has generally, and probably rightly, been believed that there was a separate assembly, known as the *comitia tributa*, over which dictators, consuls, and praetors could preside.[21] In general the tribal assembly had less bias towards the rich than the *comitia centuriata*.[22]

[17] It is highly unlikely that the centuriate assembly was more democratic before the mid-third century.

[18] L. occasionally describes scenes at election-time, and more often in book x than in earlier books; unfortunately his evidence is unreliable (see esp. 9. 10–13 n.). His account of elections in books ii–x ought to reflect the workings of the unreformed *comitia centuriata*, but whether it always does is disputed; see e.g. 22. 1 n.

[19] Two caveats: (*a*) this legislation is unlikely to have been extensive in quantity; and (*b*) we cannot be certain that in the fifth century the *comitia curiata* was not used for passing it.

[20] For the role of the tribunes see below.

[21] But the existence of this has been disputed; see vii. 16. 7–8 n. with *addendum*.

[22] Note that all the tribes seem always to have voted: see viii. 37. 11 n.

However, with the growth of the city of Rome the four urban tribes (ix. 46. 14 n.) developed a disproportionately large population, and freedmen were regularly assigned to them even when they lived in the country. The issues at stake in the tribal reforms of Ap. Claudius Caecus (in 312) and Fabius Rullianus (in 304) are not entirely clear, but it is virtually certain that the question of enrolment in the urban and rural tribes was one of them (ix. 46. 11 n.).

Again as in most other ancient states, the central governmental apparatus of the Roman Republic was by modern standards remarkably small.[23] All its officials were elected annually. In 300 BC they comprised two consuls, who were the chief executive magistrates of the state, summoned the senate when they were in Rome, presided at the Latin festival and on other occasions, sometimes passed legislation,[24] and, above all, commanded Rome's armies; a praetor, who was in charge of Rome's legal affairs, deputized for the consuls in the senate in their absence, and sometimes commanded troops (22. 7 n., *addendum* to vi. 34. 1–42. 14 n.); two curule aediles, who were responsible for organizing the *ludi Romani* and for state prosecutions that did not involve a capital charge (23. 11–12 n., *addendum* to vi. 42. 13–14 n.); eight quaestors, who assisted the consuls and performed other administrative tasks in the city and on campaign;[25] ten tribunes of the plebs, who protected plebeians against coercion by curule magistrates, acted as guardians of the constitution (ix. 33. 5 n.), conducted state-prosecutions that involved a capital charge (a function related to that previously mentioned) (*addendum* to vi. 1. 6 n.), and introduced new legislation, perhaps by 300 most new legislation; and two plebeian aediles, who assisted the tribunes of the plebs, administered the plebeian games (23. 13 n.), and performed duties similar to those of the curule aediles (*addendum* to vi. 42. 13–14 n.). These last two offices (unlike the others, not technically magistracies) were inherited by the whole state from the plebeians, who had once been only a faction inside the state.[26] From time to time a pair of censors, who normally held office for eighteen months, was appointed to register the property-ratings of citizens and to scrutinize membership of the senate (vol. i, pp. 48–50, ix. 29. 5–11, 30. 1 nn.). Religious affairs were administered by priests, who held office for life and

---

[23] Mommsen (1887–8) remains a fundamental collection of evidence and arguments for anyone considering Roman magistracies and other aspects of the constitution. There are numerous briefer accounts; by far the best in English is Lintott (1999).

[24] This has become controversial: it is discussed below.

[25] In books vi–x L. refers to a quaestor only at 32. 9.

[26] For the Struggle of the Orders and the extent of plebeian success, see below.

whose numbers exceeded those of the annually elected magistrates: the most important priestly colleges were the *xuiri sacris faciundis*, the *augures*, and the *pontifices* (6. 3–9. 2, vi. 42. 1 nn.). In addition, in recent years a dictator and *magister equitum* had been appointed in time of crisis—usually to take charge of a military campaign,[27] but sometimes for another task, such as holding the elections (vol. ii, p. 22);[28] military tribunes were elected (or appointed) each year (however, their duties were entirely military rather than civil) (vii. 5. 9, ix. 30. 3 nn.); prefects were elected or appointed to administer justice and oversee Roman rule in Rome's *ciuitates sine suffragio* (vol. ii, pp. 555–6); and minor officials such as *iiiuiri coloniis deducendis* were elected when needed (vol. i, pp. 52–3, vi. 16. 6 n.). These officials were supported by various permanent officials (*apparitores*), from whose number—anonymous lictors apart—only one man is mentioned in our sources for this period: Cn. Flavius, who was a *scriba* (ix. 46. 1 n.). The senate, which met regularly[29] and consisted of curule magistrates, ex-curule magistrates, and other citizens of senior status,[30] gave advice to magistrates; we shall see that its role and importance were enhanced in this period.[31]

The Second and Third Samnite Wars revealed two weaknesses in the Roman magisterial system then in place. One was an occasional shortage of magistrates with *imperium* to command armies; the other was the difficulty of making sure that the best general was in command when needed.[32] These problems had occurred much less frequently before 366, partly because Rome's wars were smaller in scale, but partly too because of the election of six consular tribunes, with iteration unrestricted.

The first problem was the more pressing. The traditional remedy for this was to appoint a dictator *rei gerundae causa*, and in the years before 300 such dictators were appointed in 315, 314, 310/9, 302/1.[33] However, after 300 there seems to have been a reluctance to appoint them,[34] and Q. Hortensius, appointed at the time of the Third

---

[27] See below.

[28] However, see below on the demise of the dictatorship *rei gerundae causa*.

[29] How regularly we do not know.

[30] On recruitment to the senate see ix. 30. 1 n.

[31] Below, p. 15.

[32] For the steps taken to counteract these weaknesses see esp. Loreto (1993) 35–77.

[33] The dictator of 313 was almost certainly *claui figendi causa*: see ix. 28. 2–8 n.

[34] Perhaps because in these more democratic times the power of a dictator was felt to be too overweening, perhaps because the power of the office was blunted by the *lex Valeria de prouocatione* of 300 (9. 3–6 n.). If the office was indeed regulated by the *lex Valeria*, then the first explanation may also account for the need for this law. See further the *addendum* to vi. 16. 3 n.

Secession of the Plebs in 287, is the only man known to have held the office between 301 and Q. Fabius Maximus Verrucosus in 217. The demise of the dictatorship was doubtless made easier because by 300 the Romans had developed a more satisfactory substitute: the prorogation of the *imperium* of consuls into the following year, by making them proconsuls. This device was used first in 327/6, when a political crisis caused a delay in the election of the consuls, when, because of this, the dictator appointed had to be *comitiorum habendorum causa* (viii. 23. 12, and 13–17 nn.), and when, especially in this crisis, it was absurd to remove Q. Publilius Philo from the prosecution of the Neapolitan War, which he had nearly finished. It was used next in 307, when the *imperium* of Q. Fabius Maximus Rullianus, consul in 308 was continued. In the climactic years of the Third Samnite War, when (for whatever reason) the Romans had decided not to appoint dictators, it was used again: both consuls for 297 had their commands prorogued into 296; one of the consuls for 296 had his command prorogued into 295 (the other was elected praetor); and one of the consuls for 292 had his command prorogued into 291.[35]

In the Third Samnite War Rome fought on more fronts, and with larger forces, than ever before and even prorogation did not provide sufficient commanders: in 295 a further four men, who had not held office in 296, were made propraetors (so-called *priuati cum imperio*), an innovative device that was to be used again later in the third century (see nn. on 26. 15, 29. 3, viii. 23. 12 with *addendum*).

The second weakness was a potential lack of continuity in command. For the system of annual magistracies, especially with the ban on iteration introduced in 342,[36] meant that, even in a crisis, Rome's most able commander could not hold office. This was not unusual in ancient states, in many of which the offices of magistrate and general were not distinguished, and reflection on it may have been a regular τόπος in criticism of states like Rome and Athens (ix. 18. 13–16 n.). It is uncertain how strongly it would have been felt at Rome *c*.300: since all holders of office had served in the army and would not have been elected without demonstrating their fundamental competence in war, many Romans may have thought that not always having their best general in command was a small price to pay for the annual rotation of magistrates. Nevertheless, before 300 the dictatorship was available in a crisis to bring an important and trusted man to supreme command. Other devices that could bring a successful general to office, or

---

[35] For the evidence see viii. 23. 12 n.
[36] On this see below, p. 15.

keep him at the head of an army, were the suspension of the Genucian plebiscite banning iteration (a device often used in the Second and Third Samnite Wars and the Pyrrhic War: see vol. ii, pp. 24–5), pro-rogation (just discussed), the appointment of *priuati cum imperio* (again, discussed above: the four men appointed in 295 had held con-sulships in 305, 302/1, and 298), and the election of a consul to the praetorship of the following year (not attested before 295 but used for 295, 293, and 292: see 22. 9 n.). For the later years of the third century and for the second century we have ample evidence for consulars serving as legates or military tribunes (ix. 30. 3 n.), and this was another device which kept good commanders involved in the making of decisions; in our period it is attested for L. Postumius Megellus in 293 (46. 16 n.) and for Fabius Rullianus in 292.[37] As a result of these devices Fabius Rullianus was consul II in 310/9, consul III in 308, and proconsul in 307 and then consul IV in 297, proconsul in 296, and consul V in 295; P. Decius Mus was consul III in 297, proconsul in 296, and consul IV in 295; L. Volumnius Flamma was consul II in 296 and proconsul in 295; and L. Postumius Megellus was propraetor in 295 (a *priuatus cum imperio*), consul II in 294, a legate in 293, and consul III in 291.

The political structures of the Roman state may be analysed in this way because they had reached some stability after an extended period of unrest and political evolution, known as the Struggle of the Orders, the climactic phase of which occupied approximately the second third of the fourth century.[38]

Before 367/6 government and magisterial office were largely in the hands of the patrician families, who had consolidated their position in the second third of the fifth century and who based their right to rule primarily on their claim exclusively to be able to mediate between the gods of the Roman state and man. Since they met strong political opposition even in the mid-fifth century, they could have maintained their more or less exclusive position for so long only because of the support of large numbers of clients or other retainers who were to varying degrees beholden to them (vi. 18. 5 n.).

Whatever they may have been called earlier, by 367/6 the oppo-nents of the patricians were called plebeians. Their membership represented a coalition of interests. On one hand there were the poor, who wanted legislation that would improve their welfare; on the other hand there were the richer plebeians, who saw no reason why

---

[37] For the sources see *MRR* i. 182.

[38] For the Struggle of the Orders in the early fourth century, see vol. i, pp. 365–76.

they should be excluded from the political offices to which they aspired and for which they had the aptitude. Each year the plebeian organization elected their ten tribunes of the plebs, to look after their interests and to lead the campaign against the patrician state.

In 368–366 the plebeians won a decisive victory, on both fronts (vi. 34. 1–42. 14 n.). In the interests of the poor progressive legislation was passed in 367/6 to ameliorate their lot, and it was followed by further legislation on debt in the 350s and 340s (vol. i, pp. 659–61), and by the abolition of the form of debt-bondage known as *nexum* in either 326 or 313 (viii. 28. 1–9 n.).

To benefit the richer leading plebeians, in 368 the priestly college of *duouiri sacris faciundis* was reorganized as *decemuiri sacris faciundis* and plebeians were admitted to it (vi. 42. 1 n.). This college was less important than the two other great colleges, the pontificate and the augurate, but the admission of plebeians to it marked the beginning of the end for patrician claims exclusively to mediate between man and god. A year or so later, in 367/6, in another major victory for the plebeians, the constitution of the state was reorganized. For a generation six consular tribunes had been the chief annual executive magistrates of the state, and in most years these colleges of consular tribunes were dominated by patricians (vol. i, pp. 367–76 with *addendum*). Henceforth they were to be replaced by five new magistrates: the consuls (the chief executive magistrates of the state),[39] the praetor, and the two curule aediles. As before, a dictator and *magister equitum* could be appointed in emergencies,[40] and two censors were appointed from time to time. One of the posts of consul was open to plebeians, and, after a few years, a system developed in which the curule aediles of one year were patrician, of the next plebeian (vii. 1. 6); at first the praetorship was the exclusive preserve of the patricians. In some years during the 350s and 340s the patricians managed to capture both consulships (vol. ii, pp. 19–22); but in general the thirty years after 366 saw the patrician magistrates in retreat and the steady advance of the plebeians: in 356 C. Marcius Rutilus (vii. 16. 1 n.) became the first plebeian dictator (vii. 17. 6); in 351 he became the first plebeian censor (vii. 22. 7–10); in 342 the Genucian plebiscites probably guaranteed that henceforth one consul in each year should be plebeian (vi. 34. 1–42. 14 n., vol. ii, pp. 18–27); in 339 a *lex Publilia* guaranteed that one censor should always be plebeian (viii. 12. 16 n.);

---

[39] On the vexed question of whether the consulate had existed before the consular tribunate, see vii. 3. 5 n.

[40] Whether or not this was agreed between patricians and plebeians in 367/6, it is a fact that dictators continue to be appointed.

and in 336 Q. Publilius Philo became the first plebeian praetor (viii. 15. 9).

With these victories the Struggle of the Orders, at least in so far as it concerned the plebeian aristocracy, was in large part over. Of major battles, only admission to the exclusively patrician priesthoods remained—something that was important in a society in which religion and politics were so indissolubly fused, but probably less important than admission to the curule magistracies, which carried with them the right to command armies and to preside on state occasions. This took more than a generation from 337, and in the event the plebeian elite acquiesced in admission by means of the Ogulnian rogation of 300 to the two most important priestly colleges, the pontificate and augurate (6. 3–9. 2 n.). Plebeians were never allowed to be *interreges*, or to hold some other priesthoods, which however declined in political (if not social) importance, partly because they were not open to plebeians (below, p. 85).[41]

The Ogulnian rogation was another important victory, but already by then a new governing class, often called the patricio-plebeian nobility,[42] was emerging, a class that continued to dominate Roman politics, albeit with various vicissitudes and changes in its composition, until the end of the Republic, some 250 years later.[43] For patricians some of the cachet of their old blue blood must have remained; but the number of patrician *gentes* was in decline, and marriage between patricans and plebeians must have been increasingly common.[44] For patrician and plebeian alike status now came largely from the holding of office and from achievement in office.[45]

The corporate security of the new governing class rested largely on their success in war: the steady stream of Roman victories and growth of Roman power proved to the populace at large that the government of the state was in good hands.[46] Like wealthy aristocrats in other ancient states, virtually all young nobles, when not *tribuni militum*, will have served in the cavalry, and the reorganization of the *transuectio equitum* by Fabius Rullianus in 304 provided an occasion

---

[41] What one may regard as more minor advances of the plebeians were the gaining of the right for the plebeian censor to complete the *lustrum* (*per.* xiii; in 280 Cn. Domitius Calvinus was the first to do this) and the election *c.*254 of Ti. Coruncanius as the first plebeian *pontifex maximus* (see *per.* xviii and *MRR* i. 210).

[42] For the term *nobilis* see vi. 37. 11 n.

[43] For the emergence of this class see above all Hölkeskamp (1987) and, in summary form, (1993) = (2004) 11–48.

[44] For such marriages see 23. 4 n.

[45] For the implications of this for Rome's aggressive warfare, see below, p. 21.

[46] This point is made well by Hölkeskamp (1993: 26 = 2004: 28).

on which the younger members of the governing class could parade their martial talent (ix. 46. 15 n.).

The tendency of noble families to advertise their prestige to the people, so marked in the second and first centuries, seems to have begun early. In this way nobles competed with each other, but this competition, taken as a whole, served further to advertise the virtues of the class. Something of the ideology of a noble family in this period is revealed by the inscription on the tomb of L. Scipio Barbatus (*cos.* 298) (11. 10 n.), which lists the offices that he had held and describes him as a *fortis uir sapiensque*, an expression redolent of Greek aristocratic καλοκἀγαθία.[47] The desire publicly to proclaim one's wisdom is shown by the *cognomen* of the plebeian P. Sempronius Sophus (*cos.* 304), a noted jurist (ix. 33. 5 n.), and, from a somewhat later period, the 'summa sapientia' possessed by another plebeian, L. Caecilius Metellus (*cos.* I 251), at least according to his son's laudation as recorded by Plin. *nat.* vii. 140.[48] Other Romans called themselves, or allowed themselves to be called, Maximus (ix. 46. 15 n.). We may point also to triumphs,[49] building (especially, but not exclusively, of temples) that would in future be associated with the builders,[50] the construction of grandiose tombs (if the well-known tombs of the Scipiones were typical), and (in three cases) the erection of equestrian statues (viii. 13. 9 n.).[51]

The determination of nobles, again so characteristic of later republican political practice, to secure the holding of office in each generation must have begun early.[52] As one would expect when plebeians had been admitted to the consulship within living memory, the plebeian nobility *c.*300 was more permeable to outsiders than it was later to become, as is shown by the following figures.[53] In the decade

[47] See Wölfflin (1890) 121 and Till (1970) 280–1. However, some qualification is necessary: Scipio was a patrician.

[48] Pliny's record may not be reliable.

[49] See *addendum* to vol. i, pp. 56–7.

[50] Building is discussed further below. Temples vowed in this period are listed at vii. 28. 4 n. For construction named after magistrates note the Maeniana (viii. 13. 1 n.), the Via Appia (ix. 29. 6 n.), the Aqua Appia (ix. 29. 6 n.), and the Via Valeria (ix. 43. 25 n.).

[51] It is reasonable to ask how different the ideology of the new patricio-plebeian nobility was from that of the old patrician aristocracy. One answer is that claims to have privileged access to the mind of the gods became less important, another that the expansion of Rome and her riches gave the elite increased opportunity for more lavish display.

[52] Again, it is reasonable to ask whether this characteristic is so very different from that of the old patrician aristocracy: even within the ranks of the blue-blooded one could distinguish oneself further by service to the state.

[53] I gauge access to nobility solely by the criterion of a family reaching the consulship (or dictatorship) since we have little good evidence for the names of praetors or curule aediles in this period (see vol. i, pp. 50–2). Even if nobility was conferred by the holding of curule office, as it may very well have been (vi. 37. 11 n.), this analysis still retains its interest.

312–301 ten different plebeians held eleven consulships:[54] four (P. Decius Mus [I 312, II 308], C. Marcius Rutilus [310/9], M. Fulvius Curvus [305], L. Genucius Aventinensis [303]) were descended from men who had held the consulship before; one (Decius) held the office twice;[55] and six new men emerged. In the decade 300–291 nine different plebeians held ten consulships: four (P. Decius Mus [III 297, IV 295], M. Atilius Regulus [294], D. Junius Brutus Scaeva [292], and C. Junius Brutus Bubulcus [the younger] [291]) were descended from men who had held the consulship before;[56] two were iterating (in addition to Decius, note L. Volumnius Flamma [I 307, II 296]); and five new men emerged. It may be significant that three descendants of consulars held office at the end of this period, in 294, 292, and 291, suggesting that the first two generations of plebeian consuls had now produced heirs eager for office. Thereafter it was to become harder for plebeians whose ancestors had not held the consulship or dictatorship to reach these offices:[57] between 290 and 281 five plebeians of consular descent held the consulship,[58] one plebeian who was not of consular descent but who had himself held the office before, but only four men who were the first in their family to hold this office;[59] then between 280 and 271 the plebeian consulship was held by three men who were descended from consular families but had not themselves held the office before, six men who had themselves held the office before, and only one, Ti. Coruncanius in 280, who was the first in his family to reach this office.[60]

---

[54] Note that 309 and 301 are dictator-years. There was a plebeian suffect consulship in 305 (ix. 44. 15 n.).

[55] Note too that C. Junius Bubulcus held the office in 317 and 311.

[56] Note too that M. Fulvius Paetinus and Cn. Fulvius Centumalus, probably brothers, were almost certainly related collaterally to the consuls of 322 and 305.

[57] Since these consuls do not feature in books vi–x, I do not cite their names, which may easily be found in *MRR*.

[58] I assume that M. Claudius Marcellus (filiation unknown), *cos.* 287, and C. Claudius M. f. C. n. Canina, *cos.* I 285, II 273, were the sons of the first known Marcellus, M. Claudius C. f. C. n. Marcellus, *cos.* 331 (for the Marcelli this assumption is made also at *MRR* i. 186). Forty-two years is a long gap between the consulates of father and son (for instance the intervals between the first consulships of Fabius Rullianus and Fabius Gurges, and of L. Papirius Cursor father and son, are respectively twenty-eight and thirty-one years) but not impossible (C. Marcius Rutilus senior was *cos.* I in 357, his son forty-five years later in 310/9, Cn. Domitius Calvinus was consul in 332, his homonymous son forty-five years later in 283). If this assumption is wrong, my figures will need slight adjustment.

[59] To whom Q. Hortensius, *dict.* 287, should be added; and C. Canina, if the argument of the previous note is wrong.

[60] Analysis of this kind is carried out much less easily for patricians, for two very different reasons. First, there are some men who cannot be placed securely on the family trees of the patrician *gentes* (e.g. Q. Aemilius Barbula [I 317, II 311], L. Postumius Megellus [I 305], P. Sulpicius Saverrio [304], Ser. Cornelius Lentulus [303], and M. Aemilius Paullus [302/1]). Secondly, despite the difficulties we have with men such as these, it is reasonable to hold that,

The rise of the patricio-plebeian nobility coincides with the rise of many of the political structures and practices which served to regulate aristocratic competition and magisterial power and which are so familiar from the period in which this nobility dominated Roman politics. As mentioned above, already from the Genucian rogations of 342 iteration in the consulship within a ten- (or eleven-)year period had been banned:[61] initially this allowed an increasing number of both plebeians and patricians to hold the new magistracies established in 367/6; later, when fewer new families joined the nobility, it allowed more competition within the ranks of the nobles.

The senate increased in importance in this period. Its early history is obscure, because L. and other writers dependent on the annalistic tradition regularly but implausibly suggest that between 500 and 350 it functioned in the same manner as it was to function between 218[62] and 133.[63] However, the Ovinian plebiscite, which must have been passed by the censorship of Ap. Claudius Caecus in 312 at the very latest, established rules that controlled its composition and ensured that eligible plebeians were enrolled in it (ix. 30. 1 n.). Partly because of this, partly because the state's increasing size demanded a deliberative body of greater consequence, and partly because most magistrates had only one or two years in office, in which it was not in their interests to offend their peers, the senate took an increasingly important role in the direction of affairs. Its status may be reflected in the legislation reported by L. for 304 at ix. 46. 7 (n.), in which anyone who wished to dedicate required either its permission or that of a majority of the tribunes.[64] Throughout the middle Republic there are occasional examples of magistrates who were prepared to carry out their designs despite the strong disapproval of their peers. In the period 312–294 Ap. Claudius Caecus (ix. 29. 5–11 n.) and L.

---

after 150 years of republican political activity, most patrician office-holders *c.*300 were descended from men who had held magistracies of some kind. Nevertheless, although competition was less intense among the patricians, some families that are known to have continued to exist failed to reach the consulship for many years. The Verginii (23. 4 n.) and the Julii, who sink without trace between a dictatorship in 352 (vii. 21. 9 n.) and a consulship in 267 (*F.C.*, *F.T.*), and then again until a praetorship in 208 (xxvii. 21. 5), provide good examples.

   [61] For the lifting of the ban under certain circumstances, see p. 10.

   [62] A date chosen because it is the first year for which L.'s text returns, not because it is of any significance in itself.

   [63] See Appendix 2.

   [64] The argument of this paragraph rests largely on general considerations. Were it right to have confidence in the detailed evidence of L.'s text, this too could be used; but for the difficulties of using it see Appendix 2 (where, however, it is suggested that much of the evidence from book x, which more strongly supports the argument adopted here, is more likely to be sound than that from the earlier books).

Postumius Megellus (37. 6–12, ix. 44. 2 nn.) provide two such examples; whether their behaviour suffices to show that the control of the senate *c*.300 was not quite what it was later to become is uncertain.

Our understanding of the end of the Struggle of the Orders and of the rise of the patricio-plebeian nobility, and indeed of the whole history of the middle Republic, would be enhanced greatly if we had better evidence for the role and constitutional position of the tribunate of the plebs.[65] Before 366 the tribunes had protected plebeians against overweening force on the part of the patrician magistrates, and this protective function (now exercised also against plebeian holders of curule office) continued until the end of the Republic. However, the tribunate also had a long history of promulgating plebeian decrees, and it is particularly vexing that our evidence does not allow us to be certain when, and by what means, legislation passed in the *concilium plebis* became binding on the whole state. At viii. 12. 15 n. with *addendum* it is suggested that the easiest way to account for our discrepant testimony is to argue that before the *leges Publiliae* of 339 tribunician legislation sometimes became binding on the whole state if it received *patrum auctoritas* ('the consent of the patricians'); that this procedure was formalized in 339; and that after the *lex Hortensia*, passed in the aftermath of the Third Secession of 287, it became binding on the whole state, whether or not it had received *patrum auctoritas*. The *leges Publiliae* are an important landmark in the Struggle of the Orders: for from 327/6 onwards we have evidence for tribunes' introducing measures which affected the whole state (and not just the plebeians), which were not obviously partisan,[66] and which were often introduced at the behest of the senate (see viii. 12. 15 n. with *addendum*; 23. 12 n.). It is a fact that in the middle and late Republic down to Sulla (for the constitutional practices of which books xxi–xlv provide by far our best evidence) most new legislation was introduced by tribunes, generally after consideration by the senate. This may be explained in part by the radical earlier history of the tribunate (in Roman minds the office may have been associated with innovation) and in part by the fact that the consuls and most of the praetors were away for most of the year commanding armies or governing provinces. What is certain is that the practice has its origins in our period.[67]

---

[65] For the changing role of the tribunate in this period see esp. Hölkeskamp (1988*b*) = (2004) 49–83.

[66] Doubtless, however, each law had its opponents, as is the case with any new law.

[67] For the view of Sandberg that only tribunes, and not curule magistrates, had the power to legislate, see Appendix 3.

This co-operation between senate and tribunes is the clearest sign that the heat had gone out of the Struggle of the Orders, that the dominant collective body of Roman statesmen was the mixed senate and not the assembled patricians. For the nobility, among whom were the patricians, were hardly likely to cooperate closely with the tribunes if the tribunate was still viewed as the chief office of a dangerously radical institution. A further sign of this is the fact that many tribunes went on to hold curule office: from our period M'. Curius Dentatus (ix. 17. 8 n.), P. Sempronius Sophus (ix. 33. 5 n.), Q. Ogulnius Gallus (x. 6. 3 n.), Cn. Ogulnius (x. 6. 3 n.), and (perhaps) Cn. Flavius are striking examples (the first three became consuls, the others at least aediles).[68] The aspiration to join the ranks of the nobility was a powerful incentive for not using one's period as tribune to introduce legislation that aimed to subvert the foundations of the power of this nobility.

Yet vestiges of the old role of the tribunes always remained, strong enough to flare up during the career of C. Flaminius (*tr. pl.* 232),[69] and fully to be ignited by Ti. Gracchus and the *populares* of the late Republic. They were not themselves members of the senate, at least until the Atinian plebiscite;[70] they were approached by consuls or praetors after decrees of the senate with all the caution and politeness that one would use towards the head of an alien state;[71] they developed a role as guardians of the constitution (ix. 33. 5 n.) and took to harrying those magistrates who, they believed, abused their power;[72] and, in an extension of this, they initiated prosecutions on captal charges—which were often against ex-magistrates (*addendum* to vi. 1. 6 n.).

Once they were admitted to the highest offices of state the plebeian nobles had less incentive to concern themselves with the problems of the poor. How extensive these problems were it is hard to be certain. Apart from the abolition of *nexum*, we hear of no legislation to help the poor between 342 and the Third Secession of 287. Since it is scarcely credible that the reforms of 342 removed the conditions that

---

[68] It is not certain that Flavius was tribune; see ix. 46. 1–15 n.

[69] For the sources see *MRR* i. 225.

[70] For the plebiscite see Gell. xiv. 8. 2; Badian (1996: 202–4) plausibly argues that it was passed after 168. For criticism of the senate by tribunes see e.g. xxii. 34. 3, xxvii. 21. 2, xxxi. 6. 4–5. Although these passages relate to a later period, it is a reasonable conjecture that, if tribunes criticized the senate in the late third century, they were even more likely to have done so in the late fourth and early third century, for which period L. provides less good evidence.

[71] See Badian (1996) 206.

[72] From our period see ix. 33. 3–34. 26, 42. 3, x. 37. 6–12; examples from the later books of L. include xxix. 37. 17.

created poverty at Rome, this may be explained in three ways: (*a*) the heavy programme of colonization effected in the period after 334 (vol. iii, pp. 663–5) alleviated the problem by allowing the poor a fresh start;[73] (*b*) our sources, fascinated by the Samnite War, have omitted to record political action at Rome affecting the poor; and (*c*) our sources are not misleading, but the upper class did little (colonization and abolition of *nexum* apart) to help the poor. The first explanation is likely to contain much truth; whether the third is preferable to the second, it is hard to say.

If the governing class did not do enough for the poor, they were made to pay for their neglect in 287, when the plebs seceded to the Janiculum, citing the burden of debt among their grievances.[74] What legislation (if any) affecting indebtedness was passed in its aftermath we do not know, but certainly in bringing back the plebs the plebeian dictator, Q. Hortensius, passed legislation that compelled patricians henceforth to be bound by plebiscites.[75] No more than in 342 is it likely that in 287 the conditions that created poverty were removed by legislation: however, after this the nobility, doubtless aided greatly by the expansion of the Roman Empire and its revenues, did not allow unrest among the poor to get out of hand until the tribunate of Ti. Gracchus in 133.

The legislation on plebiscites in 287 has sometimes been viewed as marking a climactic moment or the end of the Struggle of the Orders, changing the nature of the tribunate of the plebs for ever from a radical institution to part of the governmental apparatus of the state.[76] This view seems unlikely and has not been espoused in the interpretation of the end of the Struggle of the Orders given above, since it involves rejecting the *lex Publilia* of 339, and since it does not account for the tribunician legislation which L. records in books viii–x. Rather, even if the indebtedness of the plebs in this year points to continuing economic ills, the *lex Hortensia* on plebiscites should be viewed as an isolated episode, occurring long after the plebeian elite had won most of their battles.[77]

---

[73] Compare the remarks of Harris (1990: 501–3).

[74] This indebtedness occurred despite the establishment of Latin colonies at Venusia in 291 and Hadria in 289.

[75] Our sources for this Third Secession are not good. Most revealing for the economic conditions of the time is *per.* xi 'plebs propter aes alienum post graues et longas seditiones ad ultimum secessit in Ianiculum, unde a Q. Hortensio dictatore deducta est; isque in ipso magistratu decessit'. Other sources, the most important cited at viii. 12. 15 n., refer to the law on plebiscites.

[76] Thus the study of the tribunate by Bleicken (1955).

[77] This is the interpretation of Hölkeskamp (1988*b* = 2004: 49–83).

If one views the changes in Roman politics in the period 367–287 from the perspective of the curule magistracies, one sees a steady erosion of their powers in favour of both people and senate. As regards the people, Millar (1989: 144–7 = 2002: 98–103) has argued that the early middle Republic was more democratic than has generally been believed; and indeed the right of the *concilium plebis* to legislate for the whole people, even if the curule magistrates and other senators disliked the legislation, was largely accepted by 300, and was soon finally to be accepted, and some of the prerogatives of magisterial power were removed in favour of the people (see e.g. vii. 16. 7–8 n. [on magisterial *seuocatio*], ix. 30. 3 n. [on the right to nominate military tribunes], 46. 7 n. [on dedications of temples], and x. 9. 3–6 [on *prouocatio*]). The enhanced power of the people in the second third of the fourth century is symbolized by the rebuilding of the comitium, perhaps on the lines of a Greek ἐκκλησία, associated with C. Maenius (viii. 13. 1 n.).[78] Yet by the late fourth century the advance of democracy and of popular rights had largely stalled: note in particular the considerations advanced above with regard both to the tribunes[79] and to the failure to introduce either significant legislation to ameliorate the lot of the poor or a more equitable system of voting. For, although the initial gains at magisterial expense were made by the tribunes and the assembly of the plebs, ultimately the major beneficiary of the decline in magisterial power was the senate. Its increasing authority has already been illustrated, and it should be stressed that many of the tribunician laws of this period, especially the Ovinian plebiscites and the laws on iteration, served to enhance its power: the tribunes regulated the workings of Roman politics as much for the nobility itself as for the people. A century and a half later Polybius was famously to term Rome's constitution 'mixed', and it is hard to think that, had he lived *c*.300, his verdict would have been very different, although he would probably have found the people somewhat more assertive and the emergent senate somewhat less powerful.

Livy's hero Q. Fabius Maximus Rullianus (viii. 18. 4 n.) stands in many respects at the heart of the new patricio-plebeian nobility and symbolizes the epoch in which the Roman constitution approached its 'classical' form: his career typified the military excellence on which the security of the new governing class rested (at Sentinum he won one of the most important battles ever fought by republican

---

[78] Scholars often point to the redesign of the comitium in this context: see e.g. Millar (1989) = 146 (2002) 101 and Curti (2000) 77–8.

[79] This is an important point, and it is fair to note that Millar (1989: 144 = 2002: 96–7) takes a different view of the tribunate.

Rome); although scion of a famous patrician family, he married a daughter to a plebeian[80] and had a political alliance with P. Decius Mus, the leading plebeian consular of his generation (vol. iii, pp. 671–2); his position in the newly emergent senate is shown by the fact that he was *princeps senatus*, as his father had been before him, and his son was to become after him; and his unwillingness to countenance radical reform that might undermine the established social order is shown by his opposition while censor to the reforms of Ap. Claudius Caecus (ix. 46. 10–15 nn.).

Once the democratic fires of the plebeian elite burnt less brightly, warfare became the main catalyst for social and economic change at Rome. The Romans went to war with extraordinary frquency, virtually every year between 343 and 242 (x. 1. 4 n.). They were generally successful in their fighting, as is made clear on the one hand by the the cult of Victoria *c*.300 (29. 14 n.) and on the other by the speed with which peninsular Italy was conquered between *c*.345 and 264, and they were able to benefit from it in various ways, all of which effected changes in the economy.

First, land confiscated from defeated opponents led to the expansion of the state. It could be used for settling colonists in either Latin or Roman colonies or in viritane allotments. As we have seen, impoverished citizens of Rome could be given a new start by this process, and the dangers of social unrest averted. More wealthy citizens, too, probably made use of this land by increasing their estates and the amount of *ager publicus* that they used for pasturage.[81]

Secondly, booty from conquered peoples greatly increased the financial resources of the Roman state. This allowed the construction of a series of public works, of a magnitude that surpassed anything that had occurred previously in Roman history.[82] This in turn gave enhanced opportunities for employment to those who lived in the city, and led to growth in its population.

Third, large numbers of captured slaves began to transform the Roman economy,[83] increasing the population of the city itself and providing labour to work the estates of the rich (thereby compensating for the loss of *nexi*) and perhaps even those of only modest means.

---

[80] See the anecdote quoted at vol. iii, p. 557.

[81] Note the prosecutions mentioned at 13. 14 and 23. 13 (nn.).

[82] Significant public works that may be added to those listed above (p. 13 n. 50) include the temple of Concordia dedicated in 304 (ix. 46. 6), the works carried out in the aedileship of the Ogulnii (23. 12–13 nn.), and the work on the Via Appia in 293 (47. 4 n.). For a consolidated list of all construction in this period known from our literary sources, see Oakley (1993) 33–5.

[83] For captured slaves see 14. 21 n.; see also vii. 16. 7 n.

Once freed, these slaves became *libertini*, a class over whose classification there were political arguments even by the late fourth century (ix. 46. 11 n.).

How far Rome was consciously 'imperialistic' in this period it is hard to say (even though the ideology of Victoria must imply some self-conscious reflection on the expanding empire): doubtless she was sometimes attacked by her enemies before she attacked them (but it is remarkable that, Campania apart, in books viii–x L. records no battle on *ager Romanus*), and doubtless she sometimes regarded herself as the injured party, even though a disinterested observer might regard her as the aggressor. Yet to guess at the conscious intentions of the Roman people, senate, and magistrates is less important than to appreciate the structures which drove them to war. With annual warfare an expectation, with revenue and land from it fuelling the Roman economy, and with success in it becoming ever more important in politics and hence encouraging aggression on the part of Rome's commanders,[84] it is easy to see why Rome expanded so aggressively and so fast.[85]

The economic changes brought about by warfare potentially threatened the political culture of the state. As regards the governed, the increasing population of the city of Rome itself, and the increasing distance from the city of some of the rural peasantry in the newly annexed lands (making visits to Rome difficult), put a strain on the old ideal, by which power in the state resided with those who possessed landed property;[86] and the process by which small free-holdings in the *ager Romanus* were replaced by the large estates of the rich, worked by slaves, had probably begun. As for the governing class, the increasing wealth and prestige derived from successful warfare allowed greater opportunities for self-advertisement, which in turn raised the stakes in competition for office. In more developed form, these were among the factors that ultimately were to lead to the collapse of the Republic, when a constitution and political practices that had evolved to administer a comparatively small city-state

---

[84] This point is made well by Harris (1990: 505).

[85] For fuller exposition of these themes see Harris (1990) and Oakley (1993). The best starting-point for consideration of Roman imperialism is Harris (1979), as discussed by North (1981).

[86] If one ignores the *ciues sine suffragio*, whose ties will have been mostly with their native city or tribe, even in 300 most Romans will have lived within 50 km, that is, two days' walk, of the city, and so will have had relatively easy access to markets and political, religious, and social events in it; but already some members of the Teretina tribe must have lived further away, and in 290, with the confiscation of territory from the Sabines, some of it 120 km from Rome, this phenomenon was to increase greatly.

ceased to evolve sufficiently to cope with the burden of a vast empire. However, in the third century the effects of these processes were well controlled by the nobility: the urban plebs was not allowed to exert itself as a political force (ix. 46. 11 n.); the status of the rural peasantry was aggressively maintained;[87] and the ambitions of individual aristocrats were controlled.

L.'s narrative reveals less about culture than about warfare and politics. How far Rome was Hellenized *c*.300 BC, it is not easy to say, in part because Hellenic culture is itself difficult to define: since we know far more about the Greeks than about any of the other Mediterranean peoples in the period 500–300 BC, the Romans and (perhaps) the Egyptians excepted, it is tempting to view from a Greek perspective many practices which the Greeks shared with, for example, the Phoenicians of Carthage and the Italian cities. Nevertheless, the expansion of the Roman state into southern Italy must have brought the Romans into increasing contact with Magna Graecia. We hear only of her awkward relations with Tarentum (vol. ii, pp. 680–2, 780); but there must have been much political contact with other cities that our sources do not record, and numerous commercial links in which they were not interested. Some Greek influences on Rome can be detected even in our meagre sources, and even before the late fourth century: for instance, the religious innovations of the *decemuiri* (before 368 *duumuiri*) *sacris faciundis* (vi. 42. 1 n.) and scenic performances at the games (vii. 2. 4–13 nn.). However, *c*.300 we do find increasing evidence for Greek practices at Rome: for example, the cultivation of abstract deities such as Salus (ix. 43. 25 n.), Fors Fortuna (46. 14 n.), and Concordia (ix. 46. 6 n.); the adoption of the cult of Aesculapius and perhaps with it the practice of Greek medicine (47. 7 n.); the cult of Victoria modelled on that of Νίκη (29. 14 n.); the use of laurels and palms at the games (47. 3 n.); the use of Greek *cognomina* (vii. 21. 6, ix. 33. 3 nn.); and (if they be genuine) the *sententiae* of Ap. Claudius Caecus, which seem to show some knowledge of Greek (ix. 29. 5–11 n.). The first Roman known to have spoken Greek is L. Postumius Megellus, *cos.* I 305 BC, and prominent in book x (ix. 44. 2 n.).[88] The extent to which Greek

[87] The tribal assembly was never reformed so as to reflect the fact that the population of the more demotic urban tribes was greater than that of the rural tribes; and adjustments to the *comitia centuriata* still left far greater power with the wealthy.

[88] One should add here Plin. *nat*. xxxiv. 26 'inuenio et Pythagorae et Alcibiadi (*sc.* statuas) in cornibus comitii positas, cum bello Samniti Apollo Pythius iussisset fortissimo Graiae gentis et alteri sapientissimo simulacra celebri loco dicari' and the report of the same story at Plut. *Numa* 8. 20. Pythagoras was an important figure in Magna Graecia, but the precise interpreta-

thought affected Roman political institutions cannot now be ascertained, but the Romans must have been aware of the ideological conflicts in Greek cities between the rich and the poor, dressed up as they were as conflicts between aristocracy and oligarchy on the one hand and democracy on the other; it is extremely likely that the temple of Concordia built in 304 by Cn. Flavius reflects the influence of Homonoia (ix. 46. 6 n.); and, as noted above, the redesign of the comitium and forum in the late first century may reflect designs found in the western Greek cities.[89] It is in this period too that some Roman families may have begun to construct ancestries for themselves that connected them to Greek and other myth (9. 2, ix. 33. 1 nn.) and the Roman foundation legend seems first to have developed.[90]

ROMAN EXPANSION AND CONQUEST

Introductory

The purpose of this section is twofold: (*a*) to provide an overview of Rome's wars in the period covered by book x, and (*b*) to offer a brief introduction to the Umbrians and Sabines (the former mentioned only intermittently by L.; the latter almost entirely, but perhaps wrongly, ignored by him) and Rome's wars against them, which are therefore discussed at greater length than the wars against other peoples. Less is said about the fighting against the Abruzzese tribes than about that against other peoples, because an overview of Roman fighting against them has been provided already in the excursus at vol. iii, pp. 345–7.[91] Dates and references to L. are regularly given; for fuller discussion, and for the evidence of other sources, one should consult the introductory notes in the commentary to the campaigns and foreign affairs of each year. For the dynamics of Roman imperialism, see above, pp. 20–1.

tion of these statues is difficult and disputed: see e.g. Wallace (1990) 289 and Wiseman (2000*a*) 299.

[89] On Hellenization at Rome in this period see further Starr (1980) 48–51, Wallace (1990), Gruen (1992) 227–30, and Wiseman (1991) 115–16 and (2000*a*) 299.

[90] See Wiseman (1991), the clearest statement of views discussed at 23. 1–10, 23. 12, 37. 15, 46. 7 nn. This is not strictly a manifestation of Hellenism but may conveniently be mentioned in the context of the rapidly changing culture of Rome in this period.

[91] A more appropriate position for such a discussion. The Umbrians too could have been discussed in the commentary on book ix (they appear first in 310/9), but it is preferable to combine discussion of them with that of the Sabines: here as elsewhere consistency is not to be attained, because Rome's wars, other than the Samnite, do not always neatly fit the boundaries of L.'s books.

The Samnites[92]

Just as the Second Samnite War (327 or 326–304) had dominated the end of book viii and all of book ix, so the Third Samnite War (298–290) dominates book x and will have dominated much of the lost book xi. It is wrong to think naïvely in terms of firm territorial boundaries, but by the end of the Second Samnite War Rome seems to have gained mastery, whether by incorporation of territory or by alliance, of the valley of the Liri and of all territory south of the Via Latina, which ran from Interamna Lirenas through Cales to Capua. Latin colonies at Cales (viii. 16. 13–14 n., 334), Fregellae (viii. 22. 1–2 n., 328), Suessa Aurunca (ix. 28. 7, 313), and Interamna Lirenas (ix. 28. 8 n., 312) had all been established by the end of the war, and the establishment of another Latin colony at Sora is described at x. 1. 1–2 (303). When the war began Rome controlled Capua on the Campanian plain; by the end of it she controlled the whole plain including Nola (ix. 28. 5–6, 313) and Nuceria Alfaterna (ix. 41. 3 n., 308) and had established a Latin colony at Saticula (313: see ix. 28. 2–28. 8 n.), to watch the Caudine Samnites. However, the lower Volturno valley, the territory of the Aurunci and the Sidicini, and Campania were all still vulnerable to Samnite incursions, of which we read of several in our sources for the Third Samnite War (x. 16. 1–21. 12 n.). Whether, and how securely, Rome controlled Atina and the valley of the Melfa during this period is uncertain: L. records that Atina was captured by Rome in 313 (ix. 28. 6 n.) but later that Rome raided its territory in 293 (x. 39. 5); perhaps the town changed hands more than once. Likewise it is unclear how firm was Rome's control of the Monti Trebulani in the lower valley of the Volturno; but the Latin colonies at Cales and Saticula flanked these mountains to the west and east, and we have some evidence that by the end of the war she controlled Allifae (ix. 38. 1, 310/9) and perhaps Trebula Balliensis (x. 1. 3 [n.], 303),[93] which would have given her a firm grip the area.[94]

There is no evidence that during the period covered by book x Rome confiscated any more Samnite territory, but in the Third Samnite War her armies seem to have been able to penetrate into Samnium more deeply and more regularly than in the Second War:

---

[92] On the Samnites see vol. ii, pp. 274–84; the most vivid account of the Third Samnite War remains Salmon (1967) 255–79.

[93] However, it is disputed to which Trebula L. here refers.

[94] Note, however, a probable reference to the Samnite capture of Caiatia in 306 (ix. 43. 1 [n.]).

we read of Roman attacks on Samnite territory in every year of the war. At the end of the war Rome's dominance was confirmed by her confiscation of land in the upper valley of the Volturno: Venafrum, Allifae, and the surrounding area were incorporated with *ciuitas sine suffragio*,[95] and the Latin colony of Aesernia was established in 263.

Apulia and Lucania

In the Second Samnite War Rome had developed a second front against the Samnites, regularly sending armies to the central and southern Adriatic seaboard (see vol. ii, pp. 649–51, ix. 1. 1–16. 19 n., and introductory notes to 318, 317, 315, 314, 310/9, and 307); and her presence in the area was confirmed by the establishment of a Latin colony at Luceria, perhaps in 315 (ix. 26. 1–5). For 302/1 L. (x. 2. 1–3) reports an excursion as far as the south coast of Italy that was connected in some way with the arrival of Cleonymus. She was less active in Lucania, although L. in 317 (ix. 20. 9) reports an expedition deep into Lucania. Our sources for the Third Samnite War mention the Apulians just once (x. 15. 1–2, 297), but it is reasonable to suppose that Roman armies regularly operated from Apulia against the Samnites. As for Lucania, L. reports an alliance in 298 between Rome and the Lucani that led to the Third Samnite War (x. 11. 11–12. 3 n.), Roman involvement in Lucanian affairs in 296 (18. 8), and the presence of Lucanian troops in the Roman army (33. 1 n. [a doubtful notice], 294). Despite the alliance, it is unlikely that Lucanian relations with Rome were always friendly: we have the enigmatic reference in the *elogium* of Scipio Barbatus (11. 10, 12. 3–13. 1 nn.) to his subjugation of the whole of Lucania, and Rome established the Latin colony of Venusia on the Apulian and Lucanian border in 291. Moreover, our sources for the 280s and 270s are full of references to fighting in southern Italy.

The Aequi and the Abruzzese peoples[96]

In 306 BC the Romans built the Via Valeria (ix. 43. 25 n.) from Rome to Tibur and thence up the valley of the Aniene. This construction was associated with much military and diplomatic activity, recounted in the final chapters of book ix and the opening chapters of book x. The Aequi rebelled and fought Rome in 304, 302/1, 300, and 299 (for

---

[95] See Fest. 262, quoted at vol. ii, p. 553.
[96] For a fuller overview of Roman relations with the tribes of the Abruzzo see ix. 29. 1–5 n.

this war see ix. 45. 1–18 n.). Of the tribes who occupied the central mountains of Italy beyond the Aequi, the Marsi, Marrucini, Paeligni, and Frentani made a treaty with Rome in 304 (ix. 45. 18), and the Vestini in 302/1 (x. 3. 1). After these treaties these tribes did not fight Rome again until the Social War, with the sole exception of some unrest among the Marsi in 302/1 (x. 1. 7–5. 14 n.) and perhaps in 295 (*uir. ill.* 32. 1). Rome secured the route of the Via Valeria by establishing Latin colonies at Alba Fucens (x. 1. 1–2 n.) and Carseoli (x. 3. 2 n.).

The Etruscans

Rome fought various Etruscan cities in the war of 311–308. There then followed a few years of peace, but in 302/1 fighting broke out again and L. mentions fighting against the Etruscans in 299, 298, 296, 295, 294, and 293; he also mentions some unrest in 297. In the war of 311 L. refers often to the Etruscan *nomen* collectively but specifically mentions that thirty-year *indutiae* were agreed with Perusia, Cortona, and Arretium in 310/9 (ix. 37. 12); that Perusia was captured later in 310/9 (a rather doubtful notice) (ix. 40. 18–20); that there was fighting against Volsinii and Tarquinii in 308 (ix. 41. 6); and that the whole *nomen* agreed *indutiae annuae* in 308 (ix. 41. 7). However, many of these notices have been disputed by modern scholars. In book x he refers to Roman involvement in an internal dispute at Arretium in 302/1 (3. 2, 5. 13), the presence of Caerites on the Roman side in 302/1 (4. 9), hostile action against Rusellae in 302/1 (4. 5) and its capture in 294 (37. 3), against Volaterrae in 298 (12. 4), against Clusium in 295 (26. 7–15,[97] 27. 4–5, 30. 1–2), against Perusia in 295 (30. 1–2, 31. 1–3), against Falerii in 293 (46. 12), an agreement of *indutiae* with Volsinii, Perusia, and Arretium in 294 (37. 4–5), and with Falerii in 293 (46. 12). The import of references to Roman troops on Faliscan land in 298 (12. 7) and 295 (26. 15, 27. 5) is not entirely clear, but they probably suggest that Falerii was friendly to Rome before 293 (cf. 45. 6).

It is hard to draw conclusions from this: the absence of any reference to hostility from Tarquinii and Caere may point to their remaining friendly with Rome in this period, but Arretium, Clusium, and Perusia plainly enjoyed an uneasy relationship with her, the threat of hostilities always being present. It is clear that in the 290s the Roman

---

[97] Where, however, for Clusium one should probably understand Camerinum; see 24. 1–31. 7 n.

legions were able to penetrate Etruria far more easily than ever before.

Umbria[98]

Conveniently, but somewhat artificially, the territory of the Umbrians may be divided into four parts. First the settlements in the valley of the Tiber. The western extremity of Umbria was bounded by the Tiber, and the southernmost Umbrian town was Ocriculum (ix. 41. 20 n.), which overlooked the confluence of the Tiber and the Nera. Only 15 km north of Ocriculum but a little to the east of the Tiber was Ameria (modern Amelia); further up the valley of the Tiber were first Tuder (Todi), and then Perusia (Perugia, ix. 37. 12 n.) and A(ha)rna (Civitella d'Arno, x. 25. 4 n.). Second, the settlements of the lower valley of the Nera, Narnia (Narni, x. 9. 8 n.) and Interamna Nahars (Terni). Third, the valley of the Clitumnus and other streams, which runs from Spoletium (Spoleto) in the south, past Trebiae (Trevi), Fulginiae (Foligno), Mevania (Bevagna, ix. 41. 13 n.), Hispellum (Spello), and Asisium (Assisi), to join the Tiber just south of Perusia. In the west only rolling hills divide these settlements from those of the valley of the Tiber; in the south higher but passable hills and mountains divide Spoletium from the valleys of the Tiber and Nera. Fourth, the settlements in the mountains to the north and north-east of Fulginiae: these include Iguvium (Gubbio) and Nuceria (Nocera Umbra) in the valleys of tributaries of the Tiber and much more distant Camerinum (Camerino, ix. 36. 7 n.), Sentinum (Sassoferrato, x. 27. 1 n.), and Sassina (Sarsina) in valleys which flow into the Adriatic. South of Camerinum and east of Fulginiae and Spoletium Umbrian territory borders on that of the Sabines.

Our sources record fighting between Rome and the Umbrians in the following years:

310/9 In his campaign north of the Ciminian Forest Fabius Rullianus forges an alliance with Camerinum (ix. 36. 7 [n.]). The campaign, in which, according to L., Perusia on the Etrusco-Umbrian border first makes terms with Rome (ix. 37. 12, D.S. xx. 35. 4–5) and is then captured (ix. 40. 18–20), arouses unrest among some of the Umbri (see ix. 37. 1, 37. 11), who later in the year are defeated in battle (ix. 39. 4).

---

[98] For pre-Roman and early republican Umbria see especially the recent synthesis by Bradley (2000).

308 The Umbrians raise an army and threaten to march on Rome. The Romans, under Fabius Rullianus, defeat them easily at Mevania. Ocriculum makes an alliance with Rome (ix. 41. 8–20). D.S. xx. 44. 8 mentions merely a hostile Roman march through Umbrian territory.

303 The Romans attack Umbrian rebels who are based in a cave (x. 1. 4–6).

300 The Romans attack Nequinum (x. 9. 8–9).

299 The Romans capture and colonize Nequinum (x. 10. 1–5, *F.T.*).

296 Together with the Etruscans, Gauls, and Samnites, the Umbrians form a great coalition against Rome (x. 18. 2).[99]

295 Before their victory at Sentinum, the Romans suffer a reverse, probably in the territory of Camerinum. The Etruscans and Umbrians were probably absent from the battle at Sentinum, after which the Perusini were defeated by Rome (x. 30. 1).

283 The Tarentines persuade some Etruscans, Umbrians, and Gauls to rise up against Rome (Dio fr. 39. 2).

266 The Romans defeat Sassina (*per*. xv, *F.T.*).

Our knowledge of how the non-Roman and non-Greek peoples of Italy governed themselves in the late fourth and early third centuries is so poor that it is perhaps rash to generalize from silence, but from the evidence presented above it is a reasonable deduction that the Umbrian peoples were not united by any strong central government and that they did not present a strong united force to counter the menace of Rome: witnesss the manner in which Rome had separate dealings with Camerinum, Ocriculum, Nequinum, and Sassina.[100]

Our sources imply that in 310/9, when the Umbrians fought Rome for the first time, they were provoked to take up arms against Rome by the march of Fabius Rullianus beyond the Ciminian Wood; and, since the annalists have not bothered to invent an Umbrian attack on Rome, this may well have been the truth. Certainly it is easy to see that, when Umbrian territory lay so close to Perusia (which was sometimes regarded as Umbrian rather than Etruscan: see ix. 37. 11 n.), an attack on the city, such as that made by Fabius Rullianus, could have roused the Umbrians to fight. Textual corruption at ix. 39. 4 (n.) makes it difficult to determine how serious the fighting was

---

[99] Against the view of Beloch (1926: 443), that the Umbrians were not at war with Rome, see 24. 1–31. 7 n.

[100] For this view see e.g. Afzelius (1942) 177, Bradley (2000) *passim*, and Bandelli (2002) 64.

in this year. That the area near Perusia had been involved in the fighting is suggested by the events of the following year, when there was fighting at Mevania. Since at the end of this second campaign Ocriculum made, or was forced to make, an alliance with Rome, it is likely that many of the settlements between and around Ocriculum and Mevania, that is the Umbrian heartland, were involved in the battle lost by the Umbrians. That Ocriculum was tied closely to Rome is significant: it was the Umbrian settlement closest to Rome, and therefore the settlement which the Romans would most wish to see obedient to their wishes.

For forty years thereafter relations between Rome and the Umbrians were not tranquil, although it is only occasionally that we can glimpse some of the results of these tensions. For five years L. tells us nothing, perhaps because the Umbrians had been disheartened by their defeat in 308. Then, in 303, we learn about the Roman attack on the cave: precisely what lies behind this notice is uncertain, but it is likely to reflect fighting in the area of Ocriculum and Nequinum. The Roman attack on Nequinum in 300 and 299 follows on logically from her operations against Ocriculum. With the fall of Nequinum and its colonization as Narnia Rome gained control of the southern end of the fertile *conca Ternana*; and, although Narnia was separated by quite high hills from the Umbrian heartland, it would in future be much easier for the Romans to respond to difficulties in Umbria. The nature of the treaty which Camerinum enjoyed with Rome makes it likely to have remained a Roman ally throughout this period, therefore making it even more difficult for the Umbrians to unite themselves. When the Etruscans, Samnites, Gauls, and Umbrians allied, Camerinum would have been faced with grave difficulties in defending itself, and it is not surprising that the Romans seem to have fought one (unsuccessful) battle in its territory; nevertheless, we do not read of its capture. In the aftermath of Sentinum it is likely that several Umbrian communities were forced to submit themselves to Rome, but, sadly, L. provides no details. As for the period after 293, the year in which book x stops, it is most unlikely that there was unrest only in 283 and 266, but our defective evidence allows us to say little about Umbrian relations with Rome in this period. However, it is worth observing that, just as Ocriculum, the most southerly Umbrian state, was the first to come under Rome's sway, so Sassina, the most northerly, was the last.

Military conquest was followed by the confiscation of land, at dates not recorded but perhaps as early as the aftermath of Sentinum, and by colonization. Latin colonies were established at Narnia in 299

(x. 10. 5), at Ariminum, on the coast to the north of Umbria in 268, and at Spoletium, in the Umbrian heartland, in 241. The construction of a road, the Via Flaminia, followed, being begun in either 223, when C. Flaminius was consul for the first time, or 220, when he was censor.

The Sabines

The Sabines occupied an ill-defined territory that divided Latin and Umbrian lands.[101] On the western side of the Tyrrhenian–Adriatic watershed this comprised the valley of the Tiber due north of Rome, the rolling hills to the east of this valley, perhaps the lower reaches of the valley of the Aniene,[102] the valley of the Velino around Reate, and the upper reaches of the Nera valley around Nursia; on the eastern side of the watershed it embraced Amiternum (39. 2 n.) and the uppermost reaches of the Aterno valley. Although in a rhetorical passage L. has a passing reference (ix. 38. 7) to the possibility of the Samnites' marching through Marsic and Sabine territory to join the Etruscans, our only evidence for hostility between the Sabines and Rome comes (*a*) in the *elogium* of Ap. Claudius Caecus (quoted in full at vol. iii, p. 352), which states that Appius 'Sabinorum et Tuscorum exercitum fudit' (presumably in his second consulship of 296); (*b*) at *uir. ill.* 34. 5 'Sabinos, Samnitas, Etruscos bello domuit', which is likely to reflect the same tradition as that found in the *elogium*; and (*c*) in our sources for 290, in which year M'. Curius Dentatus is said to have defeated Samnites, Sabines, and the Praetutii of the eastern Abruzzo and to have incorporated the Sabines as *ciues sine suffragio* (see esp. *per.* xi, Vell. i. 14. 6 'M'. Curio Dentato et Rufino Cornelio consulibus Sabinis sine suffragio data ciuitas',[103] Frontin. *strat.* i. 8. 4, Flor. i. 10(15). 2–3 'sed Curio Dentato consule omnem eum tractum, qua Nar Anio fontes Velini, Hadriano tenus mari igni ferroque uastauit. qua uictoria tantum hominum, tantum agrorum redactum in potestatem ut in utro plus esset nec ipse posset aestimare qui uicerat' [the reference to conquest as far as the coast suggests that Dentatus defeated the Praetutii as well as the Sabines], *uir. ill.* 33. 1–3; also e.g. Cic. *Cat. mai.* 55, Val. Max. iv. 3. 5). To these one may add perhaps L.'s report of the capture of Amiternum (x. 39. 2

---

[101] For their territory see now Crawford (2003) 60.
[102] See Crawford loc. cit.
[103] Velleius (i. 14. 7) states that the Sabines were given the full citizenship in 268. For discussion of Roman policy towards the Sabines in the period after their conquest by Dentatus, see e.g. Frank (1911) 367–73, Brunt (1969), and Humbert (1978) 234–43.

'Amiternum oppidum de Samnitibus ui cepit'), which one would have assumed to refer to the Sabine town had L. not explicitly mentioned the Samnites.[104]

Beloch (1904/5: 269–70 and 1926: 434) well posed the question of whether the occupants of so large a stretch of territory were likely to have capitulated to Rome in just one campaign.[105] Thinking that this was improbable, and pointing to *rebellauerant* in the passage from the *periocha* just cited, he argued that Rome did not fight just one major Sabine campaign in 290 but had been fighting the Sabines on and off since 304, and that confusion in our sources between the Sabine and Samnite peoples obscures this fact.

The evidence adduced by Beloch, and also by his pupil Bruno, and their interpretation of it, are best considered on a year-by-year basis.[106]

304 The triumph over the Samnites which *F.T.* ascribe to Sulpicius Saverrio was in fact over the Sabines.[107]

If the rest of the evidence adduced by Beloch were compelling, this conjecture too could be right; but there is no particular reason to think that *F.T.* are wrong. Nevertheless, if the Trebula given *ciuitas sine suffragio* in 303 was Trebula Suffenas, and if Trebula Suffenas was Sabine (as Pliny implies: see x. 1. 3 n.), then the Aequan War of this year may have involved some of the Sabines on the borders of Aequan territory. (Beloch, however, argues for fighting against different Sabines: see next paragraph.)

303 The Trebula incorporated with *ciuitas sine suffragio* was Sabine Trebula Mutuesca.[108]

Since the only evidence that Rome had fought in the area of Trebula Mutuesca comes from Beloch's speculative reconstruction of the events of 304, Trebula Balliensis (Samnite) and especially Trebula Suffenas (Aequan or, if Sabine, from a very different part of Sabine territory) are more plausible identifications: see x. 1. 3 n.

300 The Roman attack on Nequinum (later called Narnia) must have involved fighting aginst the Sabines, who occupied the valley of the Tiber south of Narnia. Stephanus, *ethn. s.u.* Narnia, an entry which draws on D.H., calls the city Samnite, by which Sabine is meant.[109]

---

[104] For the difficult topographical problems posed by our evidence for the campaigns of this year, see 38. 1–46. 16 n.   [105] See also Bruno (1906) 72 n. 1.

[106] See also Bruno's list (1906: 114–15). This evidence is discussed also in the introductory notes in the commentary to the campaigns of this year.

[107] See Beloch (1926) 424.

[108] See Beloch (1926) 425–6.

[109] See Beloch (1904/5) 270, (1926) 426, and Bruno (1906) 12–16.

This is one of the more compelling parts of Beloch's thesis: even though Stephanus is not the most reliable of sources, it is easy to see that Narnia could have been regarded as Sabine by some writers.

299 Nequinum fell to Rome in this year. That fighting against the Sabines continued is shown by *F.T.*, where the notice of a triumph over the Samnites is a mistake for one over the Sabines.[110]

Beloch's suggestion would remove the very real difficulty caused by *F.T.*'s recording a triumph over the Samnites in the year before L. and D.H. record the outbreak of the Third Samnite War: see further 10. 1–11. 8 n.

298 The victory over the Samnites which L. and *F.T.* ascribe to Cn. Fulvius Centumalus was in fact over the Sabines.[111]

Our sources for this year are desperately confused: no interpretation of them is certain, but Beloch's hypothesis does no more to dispel the confusion than several others; see further 12. 3–13. 1 n.

296 The victory of Ap. Claudius Caecus over the Sabines, recorded by both *elogium* and the author of the *de uiris illustribus*, should be referred to this year: L. was wrong to think that the Etruscans joined forces with the Samnites rather than the Sabines, and his absurd story of how Decius Mus drove a Samnite army out of Samnium is another pointer to his mistake on this matter.[112]

Beloch's argument has some force: there is no reason to reject these victories over the Sabines, and they are more likely to have happened in 296 than in any other year. Whether it follows, however, that there was no fighting against the Samnites in Etruria is doubtful: see 16. 1–21. 12 n.

295 At the battle of Sentinum Fabius Rullianus and Decius Mus must have faced an alliance of Gauls, Etruscans, and Umbrians with the Sabines and not the Samnites. Although L. and other Latin sources are supported by Duris, Duris too could easily have confused Sabines and Samnites. The defeat which L. (x. 30. 3) states that the Paeligni inflicted on the retreating Samnites was in fact inflicted on the Sabines.[113]

See discussion below.

294 L. (x. 36. 16–17) describes a Samnite attack on Interamna Lirenas, where the Roman legions later passed the winter, but Interamna Lirenas has been confused with Interamna Nahars

---

[110] See Beloch (1904/5) 271, (1926) 426, and Bruno (1906) 12–16.
[111] See Beloch (1904/5) 277 and (1926) 431–2 and 438.
[112] See Beloch (1904/5) 275–6, (1926) 432–3, and Bruno (1906) 31–2.
[113] See Beloch (1904/5) 276–7, (1926) 433–4, and Bruno (1906) 36 n. 2, 44.

(Terni), an Umbrian town on the borders of Sabine territory. It follows that the version of events which L. reports from Quadrigarius (37. 13) was largely correct, except that Quadrigarius should have stated that Regulus fought Sabines as well as Etruscans in this year. The notice in *F.T.* of Atilius' triumph over both Etruscans and Samnites is due to confusion between Samnites and Sabines.[114]

This hypothesis, although far from certain, does help to explain the difficulties in L.'s sources for this year. The postulated confusion between Interamna Nahars and Interamna Lirenas goes against L.'s explicit reference to the latter but would explain a feature of his narrative for 293. See further 32. 1–37. 16 n.

293 L. describes Amiternum (x. 39. 2), attacked by Sp. Carvilius Maximus, as Samnite; in fact Carvilius attacked the Sabine town of this name. Likewise Cominium, the scene of one of the two major battles of this year, may have been the site in the territory of the Aequiculi and not a Samnite settlement.[115]

The strength of this hypothesis lies in L.'s statement (39. 1) that Sp. Carvilius Maximus joined his legions at Interamna and then attacked Amiternum. For the only Amiternum known to us is the Sabine settlement. Moreover, with regard to the hypothesis that L. or his sources confused Interamna Nahars with Interamna Lirenas, a march to Amiternum from Interamna Nahars would have been very much easier than from Interamna Lirenas. For difficulties in this hypothesis, see below and 38. 1–46. 16 n.

290 Since the events of this year fall outside those covered by books vi–x, and since no one doubts that M'. Curius Dentatus triumphed over the Sabines, there is no need for full discussion of Beloch's view that in this year Rome fought only Sabines and not Samnites. It may be observed only that, since there was fighting against the Samnites in 292 and 291, there is no obvious reason why it should not have continued into 290.[116]

Although few scholars writing in the last fifty years have taken much notice of Beloch's thesis, it is not as absurd as may appear at first sight. Like several of his other bold ideas, it explains some oddities in our evidence: it would be surprising if the Sabines had capitulated in just one year; it is likely that the capture of Nequinum provoked hostilities among the Sabines; it accounts for the evidence from our sources for Ap. Claudius Caecus; it explains the capture of

---

[114] See Beloch (1904/5) 273, (1926) 431, and Bruno (1906) 52–60.
[115] See Beloch (1904/5) 273–4, (1926) 430–1, and Bruno (1906) 71–3.
[116] See Beloch (1904/5) 271–3 and (1926) 428–30.

Amiternum in 293; it would explain the very difficult reference to the Samnites in *F.T.* for 299. Nor was Beloch (1926: 426–8) fanciful in explaining the postulated confusion between Sabine and Samnite as due to misinterpretation of the root *Safin-*, since both words were derived from this root;[117] and, although the application of the theory to 304, 303, and 294 is less convincing, it is hard after reading his and Bruno's work not to be convinced that Rome was at war, at least intermittently, with the Sabines in the 290s. Just conceivably they could be right, too, to argue that there were no Samnite armies at Sentinum and that the battle of Cominium was not fought on Samnite soil; but the notions that at Sentinum the terror of the coalition facing Rome came because the Samnites had joined forces with Gauls, Etruscans, and Umbrians, and that in 293 Carvilius joined Papirius Cursor in winning a great victory over the Samnites, appear to be embedded so deeply in L. and our other sources that I should be reluctant to reject them.[118]

---

[117] See recently Dench (1995), esp. 204–5.

[118] For an early and full examination of Beloch's hypothesis, rejecting some of his and Bruno's more extreme arguments but accepting the possibility of confusion between Sabine and Samnite, see Costanzi (1919) 177–94.

Commentary

1. 1–11. 10. *Between the Second and Third Samnite Wars*

303 BC

1. 1–6. *Foreign affairs*

L.'s account of 303 BC presents comparatively few problems. The Second Samnite War had ended the previous year, and now Rome's energies were concentrated for the most part in consolidating and administering gains made in the final stages of that conflict.

The colonization of Sora and Alba Fucens (§§ 1–2) is recorded also by Velleius (i. 14. 5), who agrees with L.'s date. The strategic position of Sora at the south end of the Val Roveto meant that the town had been the focus of much fighting between Rome and the Samnites: most recently it had been stormed by the Samnites in 306 (ix. 43. 1) and retaken by Rome in 305 (ix. 44. 16). The establishment of a Latin colony on the site must have been intended to secure it permanently for Rome, and we have no reason to think that Sora ever again changed hands. Indeed, if the evidence of 14. 4 (297) and 33. 7–10 (294) is reliable (which is admittedly doubtful), then it soon became an important base for operations against the Samnites. In many ways the colonization of Alba was a bolder move. Among existing Latin colonies only Luceria was more distant from the *ager Romanus* or from the territory of *ciues sine suffragio*, and the colony was Rome's first settlement in the Abruzzo. It served three important purposes: to help control the eastern territory of the Aequi, on the extreme edge of which it was founded; to watch over the neighbouring Marsi, who had just made peace with Rome (ix. 45. 18) after at least eight years of hostilities (ix. 29. 1–5 n.); and to help keep open for Roman armies the important route through the Abruzzo to the Adriatic.

Rome had gained, or regained, control of Arpinum in 305 (ix. 44. 16 n.), and the incorporation of the town as a *ciuitas sine suffragio* (§ 3) shows her employing one of her customary methods for organizing conquered territory and expanding her own state. As regards the Trebula incorporated at the same time as a *ciuitas sine suffragio*, there

35

is some doubt as to the Trebula to which L. refers (§ 3 n.); but, if the standard view that he refers to Aequan or Sabine Trebula Suffenas is correct, then the Romans were organizing territory conquered in the previous year (ix. 45. 1–18 n.). For reasons already given (ix. 42. 10–43. 24 n.), the view of D.S. (xx. 80. 4), that Frusino was mulcted of territory in 306, is to be rejected in favour of L.'s evidence (§ 3) that the land was taken in this year. L. omits to mention that the town was incorporated as a *ciuitas sine suffragio*, but this is an obvious deduction from Fest. 262, where it is listed as a *praefectura*. With Aletrium, Ferentinum, and Verulae conspicuously loyal (ix. 42. 11, 43. 23), with Latin colonies at Fregellae and Sora, and with Frusino and Arpinum incorporated as *ciuitates sine suffragio*, Rome now had a grip of iron on the strategically vital zone around the confluence of the Liri and the Sacco.

If, as is possible (1. 7–5. 14 n.), Rome was involved in operations against Tarentum in this year, then it was not so devoid of military activity as L. believed (§ 4). He records just one campaign, an expedition against some Umbrian brigands based in a cave (§§ 4–6). Our general ignorance of the process by which Rome won control of Sabine and Umbrian territory (see above, pp. 27–34) makes it hard to place this in context; but there is no reason to doubt the basic outline of the report. Conceivably, its details may bear some relationship to what actually happened, but their invention would have been easy (thus Harris [1971] 63).

For the events of this year, see further Salmon (1967) 255–6, Harris loc. cit., and Humbert (1978) 217–20.

1. 1. L. Genucio: (15). Otherwise unknown; *chron. ann.* 354 gives him the *cognomen* Aventinensis, which suggests that he was a descendant—perhaps a grandson—of either L. Genucius M. f. Cn. n. Aventinensis (*cos.* I 365, II 362: see vii. 1. 7 n. with *addendum*) or Cn. Genucius M. f. M. n. Aventinensis (*cos.* 363: see vii. 3. 3 n.).
Ser. Cornelio: (206). A fragment of *F.C.* (. . . *C*]*n. f. Cn. n. Lentulus*) shows that this man was a Lentulus. His relationship to the consul of 327 (viii. 22. 8 n.) is unclear.
ab externis ferme bellis otium fuit: for this phrasing see vii. 27. 1 n. *ferme* is inserted because of what L. tells us in §§ 4–6.
Soram: for the town see vii. 28. 6 n. M has the unidiomatic *ad Soram* for *Soram*, on the basis of which Alschefski tentatively conjectured *at Soram*, and Weissenborn *ac Soram*; but the sense given by these conjectures is so poor that it is preferable to believe that Πλ have the truth.

Albam: the remains of Alba (called Alba Fucens at Ptol. *geog.* iii. 1. 50 and Charis. *Gramm. Lat.* i. 106 after the Fucine Lake, from the northern-western edge of which it is just 5 km distant), the Roman bulwark in western Abruzzo, are to be found at Albe, 6 km north of the modern centre of Avezzano. The strategic situation of the colony was excellent: it stood on a hill of 966 m; and, although this hill is not especially prominent in an area of high mountains (it is dwarfed by M. Velino [2487 m], which towers over it to the north), it offers a site that is both accessible and defensible. Its location at the extreme eastern edge of Aequan territory placed it conveniently on the line of the Via Valeria (whose construction had been begun in 306 [ix. 43. 25 n.]), enabled it to impede communications between Marsi and Aequi, and gave it access to some of the best arable land in the area. Even after the Belgian excavations have uncovered much of the centre of the town, the site continues to be dominated by its massive polygonal defensive walls (FIG. 1). Rather than being Aequan, these were probably built when the Latin colony was founded. For the excavations at Alba see e.g. Mertens (1969) and Du Ruyt (1982); further publications are listed by Coarelli and La Regina (1984: 333–4), who at pp. 62–98 provide an excellent introduction to the site.

deductae: see vi. 16. 6 n.

1–2. sex milia colonorum scripta . . . eo quattuor milia hominum missa: for notices of the number of men sent into colonies, see viii. 16. 14 n.

in Aequos: L.'s statement that Alba was founded on Aequan territory is supported by App. *Han.* 39. 167 and Ptol. *geog.* iii. 1. 50. By contrast Silius (viii. 507) and Paulus (Fest. 4) state or imply that it was Marsic; Pliny (*nat.* iii. 106) distinguishes the Albenses from both Aequi and Marsi; and Strabo (v. 3. 7 [C 235] and v. 3. 13 [C 240]) calls it Latin but neighbouring the Marsi. If territorial boundaries between Italian tribes had been rational, all the land around the Fucine Lake would have been Marsic; but this evidence is accounted for best if one assumes that L. is right: Pliny's evidence would be explained by postulating that Alba's former status as a Latin colony separated it from neighbouring tribes, Strabo's by the former Latin status of the town and by the fact that Aequan territory formed part of Latium Adiectum, and Silius' and Paulus' by a mistake on their part caused by the proximity of Alba to Marsic territory. If this is right, then the Aequi will have controlled all the mountains to the west of the Fucine Lake, the Marsi those to the south and east.

FIG. 1 Walling of the Latin colony at Alba Fucens

However, one may wonder whether the border between these two tribes was ever firm. See further Mommsen, *CIL* ix, p. 370, Hülsen, *RE* i. 1300, and Crawford (2003) 60.

2. Sora agri Volsci fuerat sed possederant Samnites: for ethnographical notices of this kind, see viii. 22. 2 n.

3. Arpinatibus: see ix. 44. 16 n.
Trebulanisque: unfortunately L. does not specify which of the five settlements in Italy known to have been called Trebula was incorporated with *ciuitas sine suffragio* (they are listed, with brief comments, by Philipp, *RE* viA. 2283–5). He can hardly have meant the sites near Quadri in the Samnite Sangro valley (unlikely to have been controlled by Rome at this date) or near Maddaloni on the eastern edge of the Campanian plain (Maddaloni, near Calatia, had probably been incorporated long since), but the other three have each had supporters.
    The least likely is Trebula Mutuesca, near Sabine Monteleone (championed by Beloch [1926: 425] and Afzelius [1942: 174–5]). This would fit in well with Beloch's argument that in this period Rome was engaged in a Sabine War (he noted that the town was not very far from the northern territory of the Aequi);[1] but his view that it might have been captured by Rome in the campaign of 304 depends on his speculative conjecture that the Sabines were fought in that campaign.
    Mommsen (*CIL* x, p. 442) (tentatively) and De Sanctis (1907–64: ii. 338–9) argued for Trebula Balliensis (modern Treglia): since nearby Caiatia seems to have seen fighting in 307 (ix. 43. 1 n.), this view could be right. If it is, it would follow that Rome now controlled the Monti Trebulani; but Caiatia was not incorporated in the Roman state, and a different policy for two settlements so close to each other would be a little surprising.
    Most scholars (e.g. Adcock [1928: 608], Taylor [1960: 56 n. 35], Toynbee [1965: i. 153 n. 7], and Humbert [1978: 218–19]) plump for Trebula Suffenas at Ciciliano near Tibur. The evidence pertaining to this settlement was assembled fully by Taylor (1956: esp. 9–14). It is mentioned in the literary sources only at Plin. *nat.* iii. 107 'Sabinorum ... Trebulani qui cognominantur Mutuesci et qui Suffenates', where it is assigned to the fourth Augustan region; but the ascription of the town to the Sabines need not rule out a site in the neighbourhood of Tibur, since Tibur itself is listed by Pliny as Sabine and placed in the

---

[1] For discussion of this see above, p. 31.

fourth region.[1] The large number of inscriptions found around Ciciliano proves the existence of an ancient settlement (see conveniently Coarelli [1982] 117–20); that it was called Trebula is suggested by the frequent appearance of the name Trebulanus both on inscriptions (e.g. *CIL* xiv. 3513) and in the *Fasti* (*CIL* vi. 29681), which Taylor has shown to originate from the site at Ciciliano. It seems likely too that *tebulae sue* in our report of the now lost *CIL* xiv. 3492 (which begins 'M. Vettius M. l. Cissus apparitor Xuir VIuir Aug. tebulae sue . . .') refers to Trebula Suffenas. The Peutinger Table, moreover, mentions a Treblae between Praeneste and Carseoli ('preneste xi treblis xv carsulis'), which is far more easily equated with a Trebula at Ciciliano (which is on a direct route from Praeneste to Carseoli) than Trebia, modern Trevi (which is far off any direct route). The existence of a Trebula at Ciciliano would also fit in well with Martial's reference to Trebula at v. 71. 1. Even if the town was Sabine rather than Aequan,[2] the incorporation of a settlement close to Tibur fits in very well with the series of Aequan Wars being waged at this time by Rome, and there is no difficulty in believing that Rome could have captured the town in 304.[3]

ciuitas data: for *ciuitas sine suffragio*, see vol. ii, pp. 544–54.

Frusinates: Frusino, modern Frosinone, lies in the valley of the Sacco south of the Hernican towns of Ferentinum (from which it is 10 km distant), Aletrium (9 km distant), and Verulae (8 km distant), and north of Volscian Fabrateria (8 km distant). From its hill-top position it overlooks the route of the Via Latina to its south, the road from the Sacco to Sora to its north, and the middle Liri valley to its east. This position has doubtless encouraged the growth of the modern town, and to-day it is one of the provincial capitals of Lazio. Whether ancient Frusino ever achieved such local dominance is unclear: the special references to it in L. and D.S. xx. 80. 4 may indicate a certain importance in the late fourth century BC; but the small scale of its amphitheatre suggests that in the principate it was of no great size. With the sole exception of this amphitheatre, ancient remains are not to be found: they have been obliterated by modern

---

[1] See also the banter at Catull. 44. 1–5.

[2] A view put forcefully by Crawford (2003: 60).

[3] Taylor's suggestion that uniquely among the Aequan settlements Trebula wished to be incorporated with *ciuitas sine suffragio* (contrast ix. 45. 5–8) seems somewhat improbable: *ciuitas sine suffragio* is best viewed as an aggressive instrument of Roman imperialism (see vol. ii, pp. 544–59), and, if L.'s sources referred to Trebula Suffenas, they are likely to have done so because it was the prospective administrative centre of a large area of southern Aequan territory that was incorporated in the Roman state after the campaign of 304. See further Humbert (1978) 218 n. 38.

development. For the appearance of Frusino in Festus' list of *prae-fecturae* (262. 14–15), see above, p. 36.

We have seen that Frusino lay equidistant from both Hernican and Volscian settlements, and it is not certain to which people it belonged. Since our passage seems to suggest that it was not a Hernican town, most scholars have regarded it as Volscian; see e.g. Mommsen, *CIL* x. p. 554, Nissen (1883–1902) ii. 655, Weiss, *RE* vii. 188, and Humbert (1978) 219–20. However, at D.S. xx. 80. 4 Frusino is linked with Anagnia, and it is possible, therefore, to argue that it was one of the rebel Hernican communities (thus Salmon [1967] 248 n. 3). Yet it is surely rather artificial to try to draw a firm boundary between these culturally indistinct peoples.

In addition to Mommsen, Nissen, and Weiss, see also Coarelli (1982) 203–4.

tertia parte agri damnati: for the regular Roman practice of mulcting territory from conquered foes, see viii. 1. 3 n. with *adden-dum*.

compertum: see ix. 16. 10 n.

capitaque coniurationis: see vi. 6. 4–5, viii. 19. 13 nn.

quaestione . . . habita: for these *quaestiones*, see viii. 18. 1–13 n. with *addendum*.

uirgis caesi ac securi percussi: for the punishment and L.'s expression, see vii. 19. 3 n. Despite the neuter *capita*, the participles are put in the masculine by a not uncommon *constructio ad sensum*, for which cf. Ter. *eun.* 645–6 'quin etiam insuper scelu', postquam ludificatust uirginem, | uestem omnem miserae discidit' and Cic. *fam.* i. 9. 15 'illa furia muliebrium religionum, qui non pluris fecerat Bonam Deam quam tris sorores, impunitatem est . . . adsecutus' (both cited, with other parallels, at K–S i. 27). For an analogous construction see 19. 22 n.

4. tamen ne prorsus imbellem agerent annum, parua expedi-tio in Vmbria⟨m⟩ facta est: for the idea, cf. esp. Plb. xxxii. 13. 6 (on the Dalmatian War of 157) . . . τούς τε κατὰ τὴν Ἰταλίαν ἀνθρώπους οὐκ ἐβούλοντο κατ' οὐδένα τρόπον ἀποθηλύνεσθαι διὰ τὴν πολυχρόνιον εἰρήνην; also Flor. i. 19(ii. 3). 2 'quippe iam Ligures, iam Insubres Galli, nec non et Illyrii lacessebant . . . deo quodam incitante adsidue, ne robiginem ac situm scilicet arma sentirent' and perhaps Liv. xxxix. 1. 2 (where however L. does not explicitly state that the Ligurians were fought just because there were no wars in the East). The regularity of Rome's warfare during her rise to hegemony in Italy is a remarkable phenomenon: for the period 343–293 L. records some fighting every year except 331 and 328, and there can be strong doubts about only 320 (especially) and 319 (see ix. 1. 1–16. 19 n.); for the period after the end of book x (292–264) 288, 287, and 285 are the only years for which no fighting is recorded, and for these years our sources are very inadequate. After 264 the pattern continued with continuous fighting in the First Punic War. The final clause in our passage probably expresses *uoluntas fati* rather than the intentions of the Romans (for such clauses see vii. 1. 7 n., with *addendum*); but, if it were accurately to represent Roman attitudes in 303, it would provide remarkable testimony to Roman aggressiveness. In general on annual warfare at Rome, see Harris (1979) 9–10, 256–7, Oakley (1993) 14–16, and Raaflaub (1996) 290–2.

The correction *Vmbriam*, found first in L, but not adopted by Walters, is necessary because *in* must here govern the accusative: cf. Curt. vii. 2. 26 'rex . . . expeditionem parat in Arachosios', Suet. *Dom.* 2. 1 'expeditionem . . . in Galliam Germaniasque . . . incohauit', and see *TLL* v. 2. 1627. 11–14. For *imbellem . . . annum* see ix. 45. 10 n. **nuntiabatur:** see vii. 19. 6 n.

5. cum signis: L. does not use this expression elsewhere, but by it he appears to mean that it was not just a detachment which reached the cave but the full army.

ex eius loci obscuro is the conjecture of Watt (2002: 184) for **N**'s *ex eo loco obscuro*. Two difficulties have been found with the paradosis: Madvig (1877: 221) held that, whereas the preceding *eam speluncam* exhibits a normal use of the demonstrative, the use of resumptive *eo* with an adjective (*obscuro*) providing fresh information about the cave (here termed *loco*) is awkward and solecistic; Watt additionally objected that, when the Romans were themselves in the cave, they can hardly have been attacked from it.

Madvig's objection is not quite decisive. Pettersson (1930: 138–9) countered it by adducing some twoscore passages from L. which (he claimed) were analogous or parallel to what the paradosis offers here; in most a noun is picked up by another noun of similar meaning that is qualified by resumptive *is* or *hic*, just as in our passage *speluncam* is picked up by *eo loco*. Although all but one of these passages are not truly parallel, since they do not provide an adjective equivalent to *obscuro*, at xxxii. 4. 3–4 'namque Thaumaci . . . *loco alto* siti sunt *in ipsis faucibus*, imminentes quam Coelen uocant Thessaliae; *quae* transeunti *confragosa loca* implicatasque flexibus uallium uias ubi uentum ad hanc urbem est, repente uelut maris uasti sic uniuersa panditur planities ut . . .' *quae* and *confragosa loca* do function in much the same way as *eo* and *loco obscuro* in our passage. But if Madvig's objection can be circumvented, it is harder to refute that of Watt. To do so one would have to argue (*a*) that *ex* has a causal sense and that one should translate 'because of that gloomy place many wounds were received', or (*b*) that *in eam speluncam penetratum . . . est* may be translated 'the Romans made their way as far as the cave' (note the rubric 'to make one's way or penetrate into or as far as' at *OLD s.u.* 2[a]); but this interpretation of *ex* gives very awkward sense (as the translation shows; for emendation to give a better causal phrase, see below), and almost all the passages cited at *OLD* 2(a) suggest penetration into something, and in the only one that does not (Curt. iv. 9. 4 'praeter Armeniam penetrat ad Tigrin') *ad* is used and not *in*.

Therefore the text is probably corrupt. Choice of remedy depends on the weight which one gives to Madvig's objection. Madvig himself, followed by several more recent editors, deleted *eo*, but it is not quite clear what *ex loco obscuro* would mean: Foster translated it 'in the murk', which is an imprecise paraphrase; more accurate would be 'from the dark place' (which, if Watt's observation is right, would have to mean that the Romans were attacked from a further dark recess in the cave), but the resulting sense is not pointed. Point would be given by understanding *ex* as causal and translating 'as a result of the darkness of the place', but the Latin for this is *ex loci obscuro* (*obscuro* being used as a substantive: cf. xli. 2. 6 and see *TLL* ix. 2. 169. 12–32) and not *ex loco obscuro*. Accordingly Watt's conjecture (translate: 'and in consequence of the darkness of the place many wounds were received') has been adopted; as he points out, the corruption could have been made by a copyist who expected the usual ablative, and not a genitive, after *ex*.[1]

utraeque fauces congestis lignis accensae: for this method of flushing men out of a cave, cf. Tac. *ann.* xiv. 23. 2 'dux Romanus . . . ora et exitus specuum sarmentis uirgultisque completos igni exurit' and Amm. xxiv. 4. 30.

6. euadere tendunt: see vi. 38. 7 n.

---

[1] Since Pettersson has shown that Madvig's objection is not quite decisive, I tentatively canvass *in eo loco obscuro*: it need not be an objection that *in* has already appeared thrice in §§ 4–5 (see vol. i, pp. 725–7), but explanation of why *in* should have been corrupted to *ex* is harder. *et ex* [*eo*] *loci obscuro* would also be possible but postulates a harder corruption. Walters adopted *ex ea loco obscuro* from OZ (but *obscuro loco* O¹ [a slip corrected by the scribe] and *in* for *ex* Zs; Walters knew only the evidence of O) and punctuated . . . *ex ea, loco obscuro,* . . . ; but (*a*) the isolated testimony of OZ has no authority, (*b*) the apposition is awkward, and (*c*) the sense given by *ex* is difficult.

302/1 BC

1. 7–5. 13. *Foreign affairs*

L.'s long account of this year is full of difficulties. Some of these concern the two dictatorships of the year: L. makes both C. Junius Bubulcus and M. Valerius Corvus dictator in 302, but *F.C.* and *F.T.* (quoted below) have only Bubulcus as dictator in 302 and make Corvus dictator instead in 301, which is one of the four dictator-years, of which L. as usual takes no notice.[1] The easiest resolution of this discrepancy is to argue that L. is correct and that the person responsible for creating the dictator-years transferred the dictator-ship of Corvus to 301, the newly created Varronian dictator-year. Bruno (1906: 9) argued that the two dictatorships which L. records for 302/1 reveal the unreliability of his narrative; but this phenomenon may be paralleled (e.g. in 321 [ix. 7. 12–14 n.] and 320 [ix. 15. 9–10 n.]), and the diversity of fronts on which Rome was fighting could have forced the appointment of extra commanders. After this year *dictatores rei gerundae causa* were appointed more rarely, and disquiet at the successive appointments in 302/1 may have hastened the demise of the office. However, if one of the dicta-torships should be rejected, it is more likely to be that of Valerius, since his holding of the office is adorned with a long and implausible account of an Etruscan campaign.

L. refers to Roman dealings with the Aequi (1. 7–9), Cleonymus (2. 1–15), the Vestini (3. 1), the Marsi (3. 2–5), and the Etruscans (3. 2, 3. 6–5. 13); it will be easiest to discuss each in turn but in a different order.

The Aequi. L.'s report (1. 7–9) of the campaign and triumph of Junius Bubulcus is supported by *F.T.* for 302:

> *C. Iunius C. f. C. n. Bubulcus Brutus II, an. CDLI*
> *dict(ator), de Aequeis III k. Sext.*

This campaign takes its place in a series of Aequan campaigns between 304 and 300 (see also 9. 7–9, ix. 29. 1–5, and 45. 1–18 nn.). We may well believe that the insurrection was caused by the coloniza-tion of Alba and that Bubulcus put it down within a week; certainly there is no reason to follow Bandel (1910: 110) in regarding it as a

---

[1] For the view that the dictator-years are invented, see vol. i, pp. 104–5. For the problem of who was *magister equitum* to Corvus, see 3. 3–4 n.

doublet of the campaign of 304. If the Latin colony at Carseoli was established in this year and not in 298 (contrast 3. 2 [n.] with 13. 1), then it would provide a second good explanation of Aequan unrest.[1] Not but what Rome's ever-tightening grip on the route up the Aniene valley to the Fucine Lake would in itself have provided a strong motive for renewed rebellion.

The view of L. and *F.T.* that C. Junius Bubulcus was in command of the Roman force which defeated the Aequi is supported by the fact that he dedicated the temple of Salus in this year (1. 9 n.). His nomination as dictator was probably occasioned by the absence elsewhere of the consuls.

The Marsi. L.'s report (3. 2–5) of a campaign against the Marsi led by M. Valerius Maximus is supported by the entry in *F.T.* for 301:

> M. Valer[i]us M. f. M. n Cor[uus] an. CDLII
> IV, dict(ator) II, [de] Etrusceis et [Ma]rseis
> X k. De[cem]br.

We have seen already that L.'s view that the Marsi rebelled because of the foundation of the Latin colony at Carseoli on their territory is difficult, since Carseoli lay on Aequan land; and Beloch (1926: 422–3) deemed it impossible that they should have rebelled so soon after making peace in 304 (ix. 45. 18). Yet the rebellion may have been limited, and the foundation of Alba Fucens very close to Marsic territory in the previous year may have incited some of the Marsi to war (see De Sanctis [1907–64] ii. 341 n. 6). Besides, L.'s reference (3. 5) to the capture of the obscure sites Milionia, Plestina, and Fresilia suggests that at least the outline of his report is authentic (for the argument, see vol. i, pp. 63–7). The triumph recorded by L. (5. 13)

---

[1] Bruno (1906: 1–5) and Beloch (1926: 422–3) argue that the victory over the Marsi which L. gives to M. Valerius Corvus for 302/1 was in reality identical with the victory over the Aequi which he gives to him for 300 (9. 7): to increase the glory of Valerius some annalist transferred the details of this later victory to 302/1 but, mistakenly thinking that Carseoli was in Marsic territory, he turned it into a Marsic War; and, having done this, he referred to the renewal of the treaty that the Marsi had made in 304. Their objections to L.'s account are based on (*a*) his mistakenly placing Carseoli in Marsic territory, (*b*) his having two dictatorships in 302/1, (*c*) his having victories won by M. Valerius Corvus over the Aequi (if one accepts [*a*]) in two successive years. However, although (*a*) is a tolerably attractive argument (but note that the foundation of Alba so close to Marsic territory provides a motive for a Marsic rebellion [see below] and that Milionia [3. 5 n.] is described elsewhere as Samnite—perhaps conceivable for a Marsic site [the Fucine Lake is not far from the Sangro valley], but rather less so for an Aequan one), (*b*) is less cogent, since the Romans had two dictators in a year on other occasions (see above), and (*c*) is weaker still, since it depends on the speculations of (*a*) and since there is no obvious reason why a Roman should not fight the same enemy twice in successive years. These readjustments, therefore, are conceivable but far from probable.

and *F.T.* has often been doubted, but, whatever happened in Etruria, there is no reason to believe that the Marsic successes of Valerius were inferior to those won by Bubulcus at the expense of the Aequi.

The Vestini. L.'s notice (3. 1) that the Vestini agreed a treaty with Rome in this year is not to be doubted; but we do not know why they did not join the other tribes of the Abruzzo in making this agreement in 304. In general on Rome's relations with the Abruzzese tribes, see ix. 29. 1–5 n.

The Etruscans. This year also saw the return of hostilities with the Etruscans, for the first time since 308. L. reports two variant traditions about the fighting: in both the campaign had its origin in the appeal of the aristocratic Cilnii of Arretium to Rome for help after they had been driven from power. The authenticity of these references to the Cilnii has been questioned, on the ground that the fame of Maecenas in L.'s own generation led to a gratuitous insertion of the clan into the events of 302/1 (see Harris [1971] 64–5); but we know that the family was old (3. 2 n.), and there is no strong reason for suspicion.

L. reports his second, and unfavoured, version briefly and without adornment (5. 13):

habeo auctores sine ullo memorabili proelio pacatam ab dictatore Etruriam esse seditionibus tantum Arretinorum compositis et Cilnio genere cum plebe in gratiam reducto.

The other, however, is given an extended and elaborate narrative. We learn how, after the dictator had returned to Rome to take the auspices, the master of the horse was ambushed and defeated (3. 6–8). The dictator then takes emergency measures (4. 1–3) but on returning to his army he finds it avid for revenge, with the delinquent troops punished (4. 4); he therefore moves into the territory of Rusellae (4. 5). There then follows a long section (4. 6–11) in which an enemy ambush is exposed, and this leads into an account of a major Roman victory (4. 12–5. 11). The Etruscans sue for peace and are given *indutiae* for two years; the dictator triumphs (5. 12).

L.'s brief version exposes his longer version as the product of annalistic elaboration and invention;[1] we may note that the motif of the dictator returning to consult the auspices recurs at viii. 30. 2,

---

[1] Since Valerius Corvus is involved, Valerius Antias has often been regarded as the inventor (see e.g. W–M on 5. 13 and J. Jahn [1970] 99). This may be right, but not every invention involving a Valerius should be blamed on Antias (see vol. i, p. 91).

another passage replete with such elaboration. Since *F.C.* and *F.T.* make Valerius Corvus dictator in the dictator-year 301 and not in 302 (see above), it is conceivable that this long tale was invented at the same time as the dictator-years, and that L.'s narrative has been influenced by an account which recognized the dictator-years. It is theoretically possible that the shorter version too was invented,[1] but there is no good reason to doubt that the Romans were involved at Arretium in this year. The report of the triumph of Valerius Corvus over the Etruscans in *F.T.* proves only that they were based on a source which also included this invention, and not that the triumph itself is authentic. Nevertheless, it is not impossible that *F.T.* were correct to record that Valerius really did triumph over both Marsi and Etruscans: the major fighting had taken place in Marsic territory, but, since he had also accomplished his Etruscan operation success-fully, this was included in the triumph. The absence of any notice of a battle against the Etruscans might then explain the inventions in L.'s longer version.

Despite the general inauthenticity of L.'s longer narrative, some items in it could perhaps have originated in an unadorned version and hence be reliable. The reference to the two-year *indutiae* (5. 12) is the detail most likely to be sound, but Harris may be correct to defend also the reference to Roman involvement in the territory of Rusellae, and Costanzi wished to accept the notice of a Roman reverse.

The argument of Steinbauer (1998: 273–6), that the statement in an Etruscan funeral inscription (the transcription of which is preserved in the Vatican and which she discusses) that an Etruscan woman called Larthi Cilnei left Arretium in her youth refers to the unrest of this year, is possible but far from certain. Steinbauer would also refer to the events of this year the *elogium* from Tarquinii (edited by Torelli [1975: 39, nos. 3 and 4]) in which A. Spurinna '[A]rretium bello seruili u[exatum liberauit]'; this seems less probable, since in the same inscription Spurinna is said to have taken nine towns from the Latins and it is not easy to find an occasion *c*.300 BC when he could have done this.[2]

For scepticism about L.'s main version of the Etruscan campaign, see further e.g. Münzer (1891) 32–3, Bruno (1906) 5–7, Bandel (1910) 112, Costanzi (1919) 166–7, Beloch (1926) 423, Afzelius

---

[1] See e.g. Bruno (1906) 7.
[2] For the text of the inscription and discussion of Torelli's own dating of it to the 350s, see vol. ii, p. 9 n. 13.

(1942) 175 (these last two holding that the narrative is a retrojection of the campaign of M. Valerius in 299); Harris (1971: 63–5) looks more kindly on some of the details.

Cleonymus. According to D.S. (xx. 104. 1–105. 3), our best source, Cleonymus, the rest of whose career is summarized at 2. 1 n., was sent by Sparta in 303 to help her daughter-city Tarentum, which was facing hostilities from not only the Lucanians (regular foes of the cities of Magna Graecia) but also Rome. The expedition was one of Sparta's most ambitious military undertakings in this period, and D.S.'s long report of it may be summarized as follows.

After enlisting 5,000 mercenaries at Taenarum in Laconia, Cleonymus sailed to Tarentum, where he recruited another 5,000 mercenaries, 20,000 Tarentine foot-soldiers, and 2,000 Tarentine cavalry. Most of the cities of Magna Graecia, with the notable exception of Metapontum, and some of the Messapians came over to his side (104. 2). The Lucanians yielded to this force, made peace with Tarentum and Cleonymus, and were persuaded to attack Metapontum. This compelled the Metapontines to agree terms with Cleonymus (which included the handing over of 600 talents of silver and 200 maidens of noble birth), and then he took up residence in the city,[1] where he behaved dissolutely. After considering an attack on Agathocles in order to free the Sicels, he sailed to Corcyra, which he captured and used as a base to await developments in Greece (104. 3–4). There he rejected overtures for an alliance from both Demetrius Poliorcetes and Cassander and instead, leaving a garrison at Corcyra, sailed back to Italy, where he had heard that Tarentum and some other states had defected. At first things went well for him: he captured a barbarian (i.e. non-Greek) town which D.S. does not name, enslaved its inhabitants, and ravaged the countryside (105. 1); and then he captured an otherwise unknown town called Triopium (Τριόπιον) and took 3,000 prisoners. However, in an attack on his camp by night two hundred of his troops were killed and a thousand captured (105. 2), and around the same time a storm destroyed twenty of his ships which were at anchor near his camp. After this he withdraw to Corcyra (105. 3).[2] Athen. xiii. 84, p. 605 D–E, who cites Duris (*FGrH* 76 F 18) for the story that Cleonymus took girls from Metapontum as hostages and the *Antilais* of Epicrates (fr. 4

---

[1] Here D.S., who suggests that Cleonymus as well as the Lucanians attacked Metapontum, is not easy to understand. I follow the reconstruction of De Sanctis (1907–64: ii. 346).

[2] Braccesi (1990: 21) conjectures that, after his break with Tarentum, Cleonymus used revenue from Corcyra to pay for his mercenaries.

K–A) for his reputation as a lover, is our only other source for these events.

About the exploits of Cleonymus in this year, 302/1, D.S. tells us nothing, but L. presents us with variant versions of what happened in southern Italy: some of his sources held that, after Cleonymus had captured Thuriae (but for the disputed name of this site see 2. 1 n.) in the Sallentine peninsula, the Roman consul M. Aemilius routed his forces in battle, drove him back to his ships, and restored Thuriae to its old inhabitants (2. 1–2); other sources (2. 3) held that Cleonymus sailed from Italy before he had to fight the Romans (L. does not make it clear whether these sources also mentioned the capture of Thuriae). L. then adds (4–15) that Cleonymus sailed up the Adriatic to the Veneto, where he disembarked his forces into smaller boats suitable for the marshes of that district, and ravaged some of the territory of Patavium. However, after being driven back by the Patavini, he departed from the Adriatic, having achieved nothing except the loss of four-fifths of his fleet. For many years the outcome of this fighting was commemorated at Patavium.

Our only other sources for the expedition of Cleonymus are Trog. *prol.* xv 'Cleonymi deinde Spartani res gestae Corcyrae et Illyrico et in Italia: cui ablata Corcyra' and Polyaen. viii. 19, which refers to Cleonymus' designs on Apollonia and Dyrrachium, and to the escape of a Titus whom Cleonymus had imprisoned. Braccesi (1990: 97–8) may be right to suggest that Cleonymus lost control of Corcyra when Cassander attacked the island in 299/8 (D.S. xxi. 2. 1).

The narratives of L. and D.S. may be harmonized in two diverse ways. Since D.S. explicitly dates his narrative to 303 and L. his to 302/1, one possibility is to combine their evidence and argue that Cleonymus sailed thrice to Italy: twice in 303, as D.S. states, and once in 302/1, as L. states.[1] Alternatively, one may argue that in 303 D.S. gives Cleonymus too much to do, that Cleonymus is unlikely to have crossed the Adriatic thrice, and that D.S. has combined into one account the events of the two years (303 and 302/1), something that he is known to have done on several other occasions (see vol. i, p. 108 with *addendum*).[2] On this interpretation Cleonymus will have passed the winter of 303/2 in Corcyra and attacked Triopium in 302/1. This interpretation of D.S. is likely to be right but cannot quite be proved: if Cleonymus sailed from Laconia early in 303 and

---

[1] Thus e.g. Klinger (1884) 56.
[2] Thus e.g. De Sanctis (1907–64) ii. 345 n. 1, Costanzi (1919) 208, Wuilleumier (1939) 95 n. 8, Marasco (1980) 43 n. 44, and Braccesi (1990) 16. Salmon (1967: 252) suggests that already in 304 Cleonymus was in Italy; this too is possible.

swiftly overawed the Lucanians and Metapontines, it is just conceivable that in that year he was able to do all that D.S. says that he did.

If one leaves on one side the likelihood of compression, there is no reason to reject the outline of the account presented by D.S., even though his description of the dissolute behaviour of Cleonymus at Metapontum may be exaggerated. As for L., his introductory comment at 2. 1 'eodem anno classis Graecorum Cleonymo duce Lacedaemonio ad Italiae litora adpulsa Thurias urbem in Sallentinis cepit' suggests ignorance of Cleonymus' campaigns in 303 and implies that he and his sources knew little about him; even so, it is conceivable that the notice of the capture of the mysterious Thuriae (2. 1 n.) is genuine. Of his two versions, the second is probably to be preferred to his first,[1] since the Roman annalistic tradition is more likely to have invented a Roman victory than to have ignored one; but quite possibly both versions are inventions, the first being an improvement on the second.[2] By placing the consul M. Aemilius in charge of Rome's forces, L.'s first version has the merit of giving Aemilius a command in this year. By placing the dictator Junius Bubulcus, who is said also to have commanded against the Aequi, in command, his second version presents a double command for Junius which may seem unlikely; but for this period our sources are so unreliable as to who commanded where (see vol. i, pp. 67–72) that no campaign should be rejected simply because one distrusts the name of the Roman commander said to have been involved in it.[3] If one accepts that some of D.S.'s narrative refers to 302/1 and is prepared to give some credence to L., then the barbarians whom D.S. makes attack Cleonymus could have included the Romans as well as the Sallentini and other natives of southern Italy; if one prefers L.'s second version, then the barbarians were natives of southern Italy, and Cleonymus did not actually fight against the Romans. If L. referred to Thurii rather than Thuriae (see 2. 1 n.), then Cleonymus perhaps captured the city at the same time as he took control of Metapontum.

L.'s account of Cleonymus' visit to the Veneto probably derives from a local Paduan or a lost Greek tradition rather than from the Roman annalistic tradition.[4] Although some of the details may be

---

[1] See e.g. Münzer, *RE* x. 1029–30.

[2] For this view see De Sanctis (1907–64) ii. 346–7.

[3] Frederiksen (1968a: 227) suggested that L.'s account may stem from annalists combining Greek sources with Roman *fasti*; but if all L.'s material derived solely from Roman sources, that would perhaps explain why it is so jejune.

[4] Braccesi (1990: 59–60) speculates that the account of the battle between the Paduans and the forces of Cleonymus derives ultimately from a lost Paduan epic.

exaggerated or romanticized, there is once again no compelling reason to doubt the outline of the story.[1] L. does not record whither Cleonymus sailed from the Veneto, but, if he really did lose most of his ships, that might explain the notice in Trogus about his losing control of Corcyra.

D.S.'s statement (xx. 104. 1: κατὰ δὲ τὴν Ἰταλίαν Ταραντῖνοι πόλεμον ἔχοντες πρὸς Λευκανοὺς καὶ Ῥωμαίους ἐξέπεμψαν πρεσβευτὰς εἰς τὴν Σπάρτην . . .), that the Romans were fighting the Tarentines, is not entirely surprising. Although the two cities had fought only once before (at Naples in 327–326), they had long been suspicious of each other, not least because Tarentum had tended to take the side of the Samnites against Rome;[2] and, whatever truth lies behind notices of Roman involvement in the Sallentine peninsula in 307 (ix. 42. 4–9 n.) and at Silvium in 306 (ix. 42. 10–43. 24 n.), her increasing power in southern Italy must have led to tensions with Tarentum. However, despite D.S., it must remain uncertain whether in these years Roman and Tarentine forces ever fought each other: if they did, it is surprising that there is no record of such an engagement in L. (a war with Tarentum is not something which his annalistic sources are likely to have ignored); and the mere presence in 302/1 (or threatened presence in 303) of a Roman force in southern Italy campaigning in the manner suggested by L.'s second version is perhaps sufficient to account for the notice in D.S. Several scholars have dated to this year the treaty between Rome and Tarentum recorded by Appian (*Samn.* 7. 1), a view which is possible but far from certain.[3]

The statement of D.S. that the Romans and Lucani were on the same side is unexpected but perhaps not to be rejected: Rome would

[1] Braccesi (1990: 37–8, 85–98 and *passim*) argues that L., with his focus on Padua, has failed to realize that Cleonymus was allied to the Gauls, that the foreign mercenaries that he is said to have recruited at D.S. xx. 104. 2 were Gauls who had already served in southern Italy (for such mercenaries see vol. i, pp. 363–4), that his and the Gauls' common purpose in the Veneto was to sack the sanctuary at the *fons Aponi*, that § 14 'nulla regione maris Hadriatici prospere adita' suggests that he attacked Illyrian settlements on his voyage up the Adriatic, and that he retreated after the battle of Ipsus which had shifted the balance of power in the Hellenistic world. It is possible that Cleonymus did not arrive in the Veneto by accident, and in principle it must be correct to seek to place his exploits in the wider context of Hellenistic history; but none of these speculations can be established or even made probable. However, it is difficult to argue against Braccesi's suggestion (pp. 35–8) that Cleonymus, with his band of mercenaries, is unlikely to have been frightened of pirates.

[2] On Romano-Tarentine relations see viii. 25. 7, ix. 14. 1 nn. and vol. ii, p. 780 (but at viii. 25. 7 n. too sceptical an approach is taken to the evidence for Roman involvement with Cleonymus).

[3] For discussion and other possibilities see viii. 25. 7 n. (where add De Sanctis [1907–64: ii. 347], Beloch [1912–27: iv. 1. 202], Costanzi [1919: 165–6], and Braccesi [1990: 19] to the list of those who favour dating the treaty to this year).

have been glad of any opportunity to divide the Samnites from their Oscan-speaking kinsmen. See further 11. 11–12. 3 n.

On Cleonymus in Italy see further Niebuhr (1837–44) iii. 270–3, Rospatt (1856), Klinger (1884) 54–6, De Sanctis (1907–64) ii. 344–8, Tillyard (1908) 205–10, Beloch (1912–27) iv. 1. 202–3, Costanzi (1919) 206–12, Wuilleumier (1939) 94–6, Dell (1967) 351–2, Giannelli (1974) 358–69, Marasco (1980) 38–48, David (1981) 121–3, Urso (1998) 69–103 (but with highly speculative chronological rearrangement, after the manner of Sordi discussed at vol. iii, pp. 651–2), Braccesi (1990) 15–98, and Forsythe (1999) 106–9.

7. M. Liuio Dentre: (11). M. Denter is the first Livius certainly recorded as holding curule office (*Fast. Hydat.* and *chron. pasch.* make a Drusus *magister equitum* to Papirius Cursor in the dictator-year 324, but the authenticity of this notice is extremely doubtful [viii. 29. 9 n.]. A L. Livius is recorded by L. as tribune of the plebs in either 321 or 320 [8. 13]). Apart from his consulship in this year, M. Denter is known only for his election in 300 as one of the four first plebeian *pontifices* (9. 2) and for his alleged role at Sentinum (as the *pontifex* who read out the prayer of *deuotio*, and as pro-praetor appointed by Decius just before his death: see 28. 14, 29. 3, *uir. ill.* 27. 3). His relationship to the later Drusi and to the famous Salinator is uncertain, but Münzer (1999: 207–9), in a discussion of the early members of the family, suggested that he was the son of the Drusus who may have been *magister equitum* in 324.

⟨**M.**⟩ **Aemilio:** (116). **N** offers no *praenomen* for Aemilius, and we must choose between supplying *M.* (from D.S. xx. 106. 1) or *L.* (from Cassiodorus). To follow Cassiodorus would give a man otherwise unknown. To follow D.S., with most scholars, would allow our man to be identical with the M. Aemilius L. f. L. n. Paullus (L. [3. 3] provides the *praenomen* and *cognomen*, *F.C.* the filiation) appointed *magister equitum* later in the year. Even though it is unusual to find the consul of the year appointed *magister equitum* (see ix. 15. 9–10 n.), this is the most economical way of reconciling the evidence. Apart from his activities in this year Aemilius is unknown; the filiation of M. Aemilius M. f. L. n. Paullus, whom *F.C.* record as consul for 255, suggests that he was the son of the *magister equitum*, despite the forty-six year gap between their holding of office; see Münzer (1999) 149.

expugnare adorti: see vi. 2. 8 n.

uelut arcem suis finibus impositam: Gemoll (1890–8: ii. 16) well compared Hor. *carm.* iv. 14. 11–12 'arces | Alpibus impositas tremendis'.

8. adfectis rebus: see vi. 3. 2 n.
tumultus: see vii. 9. 6 n.
C. Iunius Bubulcus: see ix. 20. 7 n.

9. ⟨is⟩ cum: this attractive supplement is due to T^c; the omission of *is* after -*us* would have been easy, and after the introduction of a name L. often begins a new sentence with resumptive *is* (see e.g. ix. 21. 1–2 'consules exitu anni non consulibus ab se creatis . . . ceterum dictatori L. Aemilio legiones tradiderant. is cum L. Fuluio magistro equitum Saticulam oppugnare adortus . . .'). Weissenborn (ed.²) tentatively suggested *qui* as an alternative supplement, but it is less easy to see why it should have been omitted. Walters and Pettersson (1930: 44) have rightly argued that it is not absolutely necessary to emend, but the resulting improvement to the sense justifies the change.

M. Titinio: (11). Otherwise unknown.

primo congressu: see viii. 29. 12 n.

die octauo: see ix. 45. 17 n.

triumphans in urbem cum redisset: see vi. 4. 1 n.

quam consul uouerat censor locauerat, dictator dedicauit: the temple of Salus was dedicated on the Nones of August (for the abundant testimony see Degrassi, *I.I.* xiii. 2, p. 492). If L. is stating that Bubulcus triumphed and dedicated the temple on the same day (as Degrassi held), then he is almost certainly wrong, since *F.T.* (see above) record that he triumphed on the Kalends of August. However, it is very doubtful whether he does in fact say this, since (*a*) it is hard to think that L., even if his concentration wandered, believed that a Roman commander could find the time in one day both to hold a triumph (which included a celebratory meal) and to dedicate a temple, and (*b*), given the characteristic compression of L.'s periodic writing, *die octauo* may modify just *triumphans in urbem cum redisset*. Normally, our ignorance of when the Roman year began and of how the Roman calendar was functioning makes it difficult to use the evidence of dates in *F.T.*; but here, if the interpretation of L. just expounded is correct, *F.T.* seem to corroborate what L. implies: Bubulcus stayed in office after his triumph to dedicate his temple.

It was indeed normal for dedications at Rome to be performed by the man responsible for the initial vow (e.g. 33. 9 [n.], v. 22. 7, xxiii. 30. 13–14 and 31. 9, xxxiv. 53. 3, 53. 4, xxxv. 9. 6, xl. 52. 1–2, xlii. 10. 5, xlv. 15. 10) or, if he was dead, by his son (e.g. 46. 7, ii. 42. 5, xxix. 11. 13, xl. 34. 4, 34. 5–6).[1] If the desired dedicator was not holding

---

[1] As Orlin (1997: 172–3) has observed, only for xxix. 11. 13 (the younger Marcellus dedicating a temple in 205 vowed by his father first in 222) do we know for certain that the man who

office when the time for the ceremony came, then he could be created a *duumuir* for the purpose (vi. 5. 8 n.);[1] these practices are very similar to those employed for the *locatio* of a temple. Temples often took several years to build, and the gap between vow in 311 and dedication in 302/1 is not particularly long (contrast some of the intervals listed above). See in general Orlin (1997) 162–89; also ix. 46. 6–7 n. for the rules governing permission to dedicate.

For the vow and *locatio* of the temple of Salus, see ix. 31. 1–32. 12 (311) and 43. 25 (306) nn.

2. 1–15. *Cleonymus.* L.'s account of the adventures of Cleonymus begins simply: his first version of his involvement with Rome comprises just three short sentences, his second just one. However, when he comes to recount Cleonymus' visit to the Veneto, his writing expands in the manner of his more elaborate military narrative. A longer, periodic sentence (§ 4) takes Cleonymus from southern Italy to the Veneto; another periodic sentence, the structure of which is made unclear by textual corruption, leads to his men exploring the terrain (§§ 5–6). The pillaging of the Greeks and the response of the locals bring forth a series of verbs in the historic present (§ 8 'expugnant', 'inflammant', 'agunt', 'procedunt', § 9 'diuidunt', § 10 'coguntur', 'obsistunt', § 11 'indicant', § 12 complent', 'circumuadunt', § 13 'reuertuntur'). Finally, in characteristically Livian fashion (see vol. i, pp. 127–8), the whole narrative is rounded off with the implications of this victory for later periods: the *rostra* of the Greek ships are displayed in a temple of Juno, and an annual re-enactment of the naval victory is instituted.

L. came from Patavium, and his decision to tell the story of the mishaps of Cleonymus in the Veneto presumably owed much to *pietas* towards his *patria* and his interest in its institutions. A similar

---

made the original vow was dead, but this is very likely to have been the case for 46. 7 (L. Papirius Cursor, who vowed the temple dedicated by his son in 293, had last held office in 310/9), and likely enough for ii. 42. 5 (A. Postumius, who in 499 or 496 vowed the temple dedicated by his son in 484, last appears in our sources in 493 [D.H. vi. 69. 3: the notice may well be invented]), and xl. 34. 5–6 (M'. Acilius Glabrio, who in 191 vowed the temple dedicated by his son in 181, last appears in our sources in 187 [xxxviii. 46. 10]); only for xl. 34. 4 [181] is it less likely, although still conceivable (the man who made the vow, L. Porcius Licinus, *cos.* 184, was alive in 183 [xxxix. 54. 2] but could have died in the next two years). For dedications performed by someone other than the man who made the original vow, or his son, see e.g. xxiii. 21. 7, xxxiv. 53. 5, and xxxvi. 36. 5.

[1] However, Orlin (1997: 174–5) observes that the office of *iiuir* seems generally to have been held by young men: generals who had made vows on campaign tended to wait until their next magistracy before making a dedication. He notes xxiii. 30. 14 and 31. 9 as an exception to his rule; one should probably add xxxv. 9. 6 and xlv. 15. 10.

interest in Patavium at i. 1. 1–3, where he tells the story of Antenor's settling in the region even before he tells the story of Rome, and at fr. 43 = Plut. *Caes*. 47. 3–6 (cf. Obsequ. 65), where he tells how on the day of the battle of Pharsalus C. Cornelius, taking the auspices at Patavium, announced first the fact that a battle was taking place and then its outcome. In the extant parts of the history the only other references to Patavium are at xli. 27. 3–4.

2. 1. Cleonymo duce: (3, *s.u*. Kleonymos). Cleonymus was a Spartan prince who never became king, because succession in the Agiad line passed from his father Cleomenes to his nephew Areus, the son of his elder brother Acrotatus (Plut. *Pyrrh*. 26. 16, Paus. iii. 6. 2–3). According to Pausanias, Cleonymus seemed βίαιος καὶ μοναρ-χικός, and, after slighting him by passing over his claims, the Spartans had to work hard to keep him happy; entrusting him with a command in Italy may have been one attempt to do so. Of his other activities before setting off on this expedition we know nothing. Likewise, of his career in the years after he had returned from Italy we have only isolated glimpses: in 293 he was at the head of a Spartan army in Boeotia (Plut. *Dem*. 39. 1–2); in 279 he refused to make a truce with the Messenians and thereby stopped them from joining the resistance to the Gauls at Delphi (Paus. iv. 28. 3); c.278 he besieged Troezen (Frontin. *strat*. iii. 6. 7, Polyaen. ii. 29. 1). At some point in the 270s his wife Chilonis left him for his great-nephew Acrotatus, the son of his rival Areus (Plut. *Pyrrh*. 26. 17–18). He had abandoned Sparta for Pyrrhus by 274 (Plut. *mor*. 219f, *Pyrrh*. 26. 20; on Cleonymus and Pyrrhus see further Plut. *Pyrrh*. 26. 15–20, 27. 1–3, 10), when he helped Pyrrhus in his attack on Edessa (Polyaen. ii. 29. 2). Then in 273 Pyrrhus invaded Sparta in an attempt to place him on the throne; this is probably the year in which Cleonymus captured Zarax on the east Laconian coast (Paus. iii. 24. 1). His hatred of Sparta had become such that he made his son Leonidas swear to ruin it (Paus. iii. 6. 7). We have no evidence for his career after 273 or for the date of his death.

On Cleonymus and his times see further Marasco (1980) (*index s.u*.), David (1981) 119–32, and Cartledge and Spawforth (1989) 29–34.

Thurias: L.'s references to this town or settlement are a notorious *crux*, in part because the mss leave us uncertain as to what he actually wrote. Here **N** had *thurios* (with *trurios* [T] and *durior* [θ] showing that λ was corrupt), but in § 2 it read *thuriae*. Note also ix. 19. 4 'adiuncta omni ora Graecorum inferi maris a Thuriis (*thuris* **N**)

Neapolim et Cumas'. Broadly speaking, there have been three different appoaches to the problem.

(*a*) To argue that L. was referring to an otherwise obscure site in the Sallentine peninsula called Thuriae. This has the advantage of accounting for **N**'s reading in § 2 and avoids postulating a geographical error on L.'s part but the disadvantages of not explaining the ms. reading here[1] and of introducing a place that is probably otherwise unknown with a name that differs only slightly from a place (Thurii) that is very well known.

However, in this context an oddity in the mss of Strabo needs to be considered. At vi. 3. 6 (C 282), in his description of the Sallentine peninsula, we read in standard editions: ἐπὶ δὲ τῷ ἰσθμῷ μέσῳ Οὐρία (Cluverius: θυρέαι Αω¹: θυραῖαι nB), ἐν ᾗ βασίλειον ἔτι δείκνυται τῶν δυνατῶν τινος. εἰρηκότος δ' Ἡροδότου Ὑρίαν (Cluverius: Οὐρίαν *codd.*) εἶναι ἐν τῇ Ἰαπυγίᾳ, κτίσμα Κρητῶν τῶν πλανηθέντων ἐκ τοῦ Μίνω στόλου τοῦ εἰς Σικελίαν, ἤτοι αὐτὴν δεῖ δέχεσθαι ἢ τὸ Οὐερητόν. The reference to Herodotus is to vii. 17. 2, where his mss read: Ὑρίην (D), Ὑρηδίην (A¹B), or Ὑρηλίην (AᶜC); see also Steph. Byz. *ethn. s.u.* Ὑρία: ἔστιν Ὑρία πρὸς τῇ Ἰαπυγίᾳ, Κρητῶν κτίσμα. Ἡρόδοτος ἑβδόμῃ. For our purposes the plausibility of the second of Cluverius' conjectures matters less:[2] editors adopt it to bring the mss of Strabo into line with those of Herodotus.[3] Editors adopt Cluverius' first conjecture because it is easier to understand how Strabo thought that a place called Οὐρία rather than a place called Θυρέαι could have been the same as the Hyria of Herodotus, and because corruption of *O* to *Θ* is easy enough to postulate. Yet it is striking that both the mss of Strabo and (in § 2) those of L. mention a place in the Sallentine peninsula called Thureae or Thuriae; and, although Strabo's etymologizing would be odd, it is not impossible that he could have argued that the Hyria of Herodotus was either Thureae or Veretum. For these reasons, it is just conceivable that the mss of Strabo are right and that Cluverius is wrong; in which case we have powerful support for this approach to L.'s evidence. This line of argument was espoused by e.g. Rospatt (1856: 75–6), who mentioned the evidence of Strabo's mss, and Pais (1908: 127–34).[4]

---

[1] But the text must be corrupt in at least one of § 1 or § 2, and it is easy enough to argue that the corruption is here.

[2] But note the conjecture of Weissenborn, reported below, which is based on it.

[3] It is worth observing, however, that the mss of Herodotus could be corrupt.

[4] Pais considered equating Thuriae with the Turenum of the *tabula Peutingeriana* and suggested that Thuriae was a colony of Thurii; neither hypothesis is compelling. He also thought that in the inscription δαμόσιον Θουρίōν δαμόσιον Βρενδεσίνōν, found on a *caduceus* near Brindisi and published by Mommsen (1868), Θουρίōν referred to the men of Thuriae. If Thuriae

(*b*) To argue that L. was referring to Thurii, the well-known pan-Hellenic colony established in 443 BC on the site of Sybaris. The advantages of this are that it fits with the reading of **N** here; that it allows L. to refer to by far the best-known settlement in southern Italy with a name beginning in *Thur-*, and avoids postulating a reference to an obscure settlement; and that twenty years later, in 282, Rome is known to have been on friendly terms with Thurii and to have helped her against Tarentum and the Samnites, Lucani, and Bruttii. The disadavantages are that Thurii, situated on the instep of southern Italy, was not *in Sallentinis*; that it does not account for the ms. reading in § 2; that an alliance existing in 282 did not certainly exist in 302/1; and that, if in 302/1 the Romans were fighting at a major site such as Thurii, L.'s failure to mention Tarentum, the dominant power in the region, becomes even more extraordinary. However, none of these objections is decisive: for example, it is easy enough to argue that L.'s knowledge of the geography of southern Italy was poor and that in § 2 the mss are corrupt, and that the reference to Thurii was an annalistic falsification. This line of argument was espoused by Beloch (1926: 435–6).

(*c*) To emend L.'s text to either *Rudias . . . Rudiae* (Doujat) or *Vriam . . . Vria* (Weissenborn, *Komm.*, who was also attracted by Doujat's conjecture). The advantages of this approach are that it avoids postulating a geographical error on L.'s part and that it makes L. refer to a site that is otherwise attested (but for difficulties with regard to the evidential basis of Weissenborn's *Uriae*, see above). Its principal disadvantage is that it requires two emendations to L.'s text; another is that, although L.'s reference to Thurii at ix. 19. 4 may have been prompted by his knowledge that Thurii was friendly to Rome in 282, it does not allow it to have been prompted by this episode (contrast [*a*] and [*b*]).

Either (*a*) or (*b*) seems preferable to (*c*), but it is hard to choose between them.

in Sallentinis: see ix. 42. 4 n.

2. proelio uno: see viii. 29. 12 n.

ueteri cultori: for *uetus* used in the context of old and long-established occupants, cf. e.g. xxviii. 28. 6 'Capuam Tuscis ueteribus cultoribus ademptam' and Virg. *ecl.* 9. 4 'ueteres migrate coloni'.

3. in quibusdam annalibus inuenio: see vii. 18. 10 n.

existed, this is quite possible; but there is nothing odd about Thurii appearing in conjunction with Brundisium.

4. Brundisii promunturium: Braccesi (1990: 30–1) suggests that, since there is no headland at Brindisi, L. means the Capo S. Maria di Leuca.

importuosa Italiae litora: for ancient comment on the lack of harbours on Italy's Adriatic coast cf. Stb. vii. 5. 10 τὸν μὲν οὖν παράπλουν ἅπαντα τὸν Ἰλλυρικὸν σφόδρα εὐλίμενον εἶναι συμβαίνει καὶ ἐξ αὐτῆς τῆς συνεχοῦς ἠόνος καὶ ἐκ τῶν πλησίον νήσων, ὑπεναντίως τῷ Ἰταλικῷ τῷ ἀντικειμένῳ, ἀλιμένῳ ὄντι. See further Horden and Purcell (2000) 139.

Found earlier only at Sall. *Iug.* 17. 5, *importuosus* ('harbourless') is nevertheless reasonably common throughout subsequent Latin (see e.g. Tac. *ann.* iv. 67. 2 and xii. 20. 1) and must have been the regular word for describing a coast without harbours.

Illyrii Liburnique et Histri: in the classical period Histri occupied the land around Trieste and the western part of the Istrian peninsula, the Liburni the eastern part of the Istrian peninsula and the northern end of the Dalmatian coast. L. probably uses *Illyrii* as a generic term for the tribes of the north-eastern coast of the Adriatic.

gentes ferae et magna ex parte latrociniis maritimis infames: for Illyrian piracy, cf. xl. 18. 4 (complaints against the Histri made by the Tarentines and Brundisini in 182–181 BC), 42. 1–2 (allegations made against Gentius in 180 BC), Plb. ii. 8. 1–3, 8 (general comments on Illyrian piracy at the time of the First Illyrian War), D.S. xvi. 5. 3 (on colonies established by Dionysius the Younger of Syracuse against piracy [however, D.S. does not make it clear whether the pirates were Illyrian or Italian]), Stb. vii. 5. 6 (C 315) (with specific reference to the Ardiaei), 5. 10 (C 317) (references to the Illyrians in general), Dio fr. 49. 2 (with specific reference to the Ardiaei at the time of Rome's First Illyrian War), and App. *Ill.* 3. 7 (with specific reference to the Liburni). However, it is not easy to distinguish either the attacks on shipping perpetrated by the Illyrian tribes from their other plundering raids (see Plb. ii. 5. 1–2 and note e.g. the attack by land on Mothone described at Paus. iv. 35. 5–7), or the attempts of the Romans to stop these attacks from their Illyrian and Dalmatian Wars. Illyrian piracy is discussed by Ormerod (1924) esp. 166–82 and most fully by Dell (1967), who doubts whether in the period before Rome's First Illyrian War it was of much significance.

5–6. expositis paucis qui loca explorarent, cum audisse[n]t tenue praetentum litus esse, quod transgressis stagna ab tergo sint inrigua aestibus maritimis; agros [haud procul] proximos campestres cerni, ulteriora colles uideri esse; ⟨haud procul⟩ ostium fluminis praealti quo circumagi naues

in stationem tutam ⟨possent⟩ uidisse (Meduacus amnis erat): eo inuectam classem subire flumine aduerso iussit: this lemma gives a readable text of a very difficult passage that is full of textual problems to which there is no certain solution. Translate: 'when he had disembarked a few men to explore the terrain and had heard ⟨from them⟩ that a narrow beach was stretched out in front, behind which (if crossed) there were lagoons filled by the tides of the sea, that low-lying land was observed next to this, that the land which was further away seemed to consist of hills, that not far off they had seen the estuary of a deep river into which ships might be sailed to a safe anchorage (the river was the Brenta), he ordered his fleet to be sailed there against the current of the river'. These are the difficulties posed by the mss:

(*a*) For *expositis* in MΠ, λ had *ibi expositis*, which gives excellent sense. However, the connecting adverb is hardly necessary; and, since λ is the least authoritative of the descendants of **N**, it is probably unwise to accept its readings when the united testimony of M and Π offers acceptable sense.

(*b*) Emendation to *audisset* seems unavoidable: this *cum*-clause explains the main clause *eo . . . iussit* and therefore should have Cleonymus as its subject; and the scouts of Cleonymus explored with their eyes and not with their ears. The emendation is reported by Gebhardus from Vatican Pal. Lat. 873 and is found also in all witnesses to χ except Paris 5690.

(*c*) The easiest interpretation of the *quod*-clause is to explain it as a relative clause qualifying *litus*, in which case no emendation of *sint* is necessary, since L. regularly uses primary subjunctives where a historic would be expected and since he is reporting a fact that he knew to be true.[1]

(*d*) For *ab tergo* Weissenborn (*Komm.*) conjectured *ab terra* and Leutsch (1855: 125), followed by H. J. Müller, *ex aduerso*; but *ab tergo* is acceptable: the perspective is that of one standing on the ship and looking towards the shore and the lagoons behind it.

(*e*) In *haud procul proximos*, offered by the paradosis, either *haud*

---

[1] However, it has caused difficulties. If (as some interpreters have preferred) it be viewed as introducing a continuative clause parallel to *tenue praetentum litus esse* and *agros haud procul proximos campestres cerni*, then one would expect *esse* rather than *sint*. Grammar could then be restored in one of three ways: by emending *sint* to *esse*, a conjecture ascribed wrongly by Walters to Gronovius (but this sentence already has sufficient *esses*); by following Gronovius in deleting *sint* and understanding *esse* from *tenue praetentum litus esse* (*sint* could conceivably have been interpolated by a scribe who took *quod . . . maritimis* as a relative clause with *litus* as its antecedent); or by emending *sint* to *sita* with F. C. Wolff (1826: 3–4). However, even if this view of the clause is correct, L. may not have been worried by strict grammar.

procul or *proximos* is redundant, and, although the paradosis is not impossible, a more pointed text can be produced by emendation. Walters, who had persuaded himself that the reading of O (. . . *maritimis, haud procul agro pax parta. Iunium Bubulcum dictatorem missum in Sallentinos proximos campestres* . . . : the interpolation comes from § 3) could have authority, suggested that *procul* ended a page in the archetype and hence invited the interpolation of extra words; he therefore deleted *proximos*. However, as Madvig (1860: 186 = 1877: 221–3) pointed out, L. carefully distinguishes the land (*agros*) that the scouts had observed to be near (*proximos*) and flat (*campestres*) from that which was further (*ulteriora*) and seemed (*uideri esse*) to consist of hills (*colles*); and the change to the neuter *ulteriora* elegantly reflects the scouts' lack of certainty about what was in the distance.[1] Weissenborn (*Komm.*), followed by E. Wolff (1896: 1228), transposed *haud procul* to a position before *esse ostium* (Weissenborn) or between *esse* and *ostium* (Wolff).[2] These conjectures give *haud procul* proper force: after a description of the plains nearby and the hills further away, there is now a report of a harbourage in the vicinity.

(*f*) Weissenborn (ed.) punctuated after *uideri* (an articulation that goes back to O); but this may encourage the unwary reader to take *uideri* in the sense of *cerni*, and as one then has to supply *esse*, the sense of *ulteriora colles uideri* is defective. The conventional punctuation with a semi-colon after *esse* gives impeccable sense, and, if *possint* or *possent* is supplied (see below), *esse* is not needed to construe the following *ostium . . . uidisse*.

(*g*) As just stated, the decision as to whether to punctuate before or after *esse* affects the interpretation of *ostium . . . uidisse*. If one punctuates before *esse*, then the relative clause introduced by *quo*, which will qualify the estuary as affording shelter, needs a verb in the pluperfect subjunctive, and this is easily provided by emending *uidisse* (Mλ) to *uidissent* (the Rome edn. of 1472; *uidisset* already in Π). If one punctuates after *esse*, then *ostium* may be taken as the object of *uidisse* (*eos* being understood as its subject) and either *possent* (thus Madvig, giving the correct tense) or *possint* (thus the Paris edn. of 1510, giving the primary subjunctive for which L. has a penchant) inserted as the verb of the relative clause.[3]

---

[1] See also Pettersson (1930) 25.

[2] This at least is how Walters interprets Wolff's '*haud procul* scheint in der Hs. um eine Zeile zu hoch verirrt zu haben'.

[3] Walters punctuated with a semi-colon between *uideri* and *esse* but also accepted the supplement *possint* and deleted *uidisse* ('uoce *uidisse* seclusa ut glossema quod ii necessarium putauerint qui *esse* cum *uideri* coniungebant quodque uocem *possint* extruserit'). This solution is both uneconomical and vulnerable to the objection to *ulteriora colles uideri* raised in (*f*).

(*h*) Luterbacher (who otherwise followed Madvig) proposed *ostium⟨que⟩*, a conjecture that is elegant but hardly needed at the end of a string of accusatives and infinitives in asyndeton.

(*i*) Zingerle (1889: 987) proposed the elegant and palaeographically very easy conjecture *Meduacus amnis ⟨is⟩ erat*. He compared xxiv. 48. 13 'Carthaginienses . . . extemplo ad Galam in parte altera Numidiae (Maesuli ea gens uocatur) regnantem legatos mittunt', but closer parallels are provided by e.g. xlii. 43. 9 'nouus deinde praetor (Ismenias is erat, uir nobilis ac potens'), xliv. 26. 8 'Bylazora (Paeoniae is locus est)', and other passages to be found at Packard (1968) ii. 1332–3. This may well be right.

The best discussion of this passage remains Madvig's, to which this note owes much.

5. aestibus: on the tides of the Adriatic in the Veneto see Stb. v. 1. 5 (C 212) μόνα γὰρ ταῦτα τὰ μέρη σχεδόν τι τῆς καθ' ἡμᾶς θαλάττης ὁμοιοπαθεῖ τῷ ὠκεανῷ, καὶ παραπλησίους ἐκείνῳ ποιεῖται τάς τε ἀμπώτεις καὶ τὰς πλημμυρίδας, ὑφ' ὧν τὸ πλέον τοῦ πεδίου λιμνοθαλάττης γίνεται μεστόν.
stagna: the lagoons of the Veneto; cf. Stb. v. 1. 5 (C 212) ἑλῶν.
colles: the Colli Euganei; see Braccesi (1990: 43).

6. stationem . . . Meduacus amnis erat: the course of the Meduacus, modern Brenta, has changed since antiquity: see Philipp's map at *RE* xviii. 1. 2183. On the harbourage at the mouth of the river see Stb. v. 1. 7 (C 213) (*sc.* Παταούιον) ἔχει δὲ θαλάττης ἀνάπλουν ποταμῷ διὰ τῶν ἑλῶν φερομένῳ σταδίων πεντήκοντα καὶ διακοσίων ἐκ λιμένος μεγάλου· καλεῖται δ' ὁ λιμὴν Μεδόακος ὁμωνύμως τῷ ποταμῷ and Plin. *nat.* iii. 121 '(*sc.* faciunt) Aedronem Meduaci duo ac fossa Clodia'.

7. Patauinorum: the site of Patavium, modern Padova (Padua), has been occupied at least since the eighth century BC. Of its early history our literary sources tell us little (if one leaves aside legends concerning Antenor [see above for L.'s version], this is the first episode in which it appears). The town was given Roman citizenship in 49 BC by Julius Caesar. L. is its best-known ancient citizen, followed by Thrasea Paetus and Asconius. The archaeological evidence from the site is collected in AA.VV. (1976) and (1977). See also Philipp, *RE* xviii. 4. 2115–16 and Mangani *et al.* (1981) 126–30, 140–7.

8. hominum pecudumque praedas: see vi. 31. 8 n.

et . . . procedunt: W–M (on this passage and also on v. 20. 8 and xxiv. 15. 5) argue that in sentences in which two or more clauses in asyndeton are followed by a clause introduced by *et*, the clause introduced by *et* should be taken closely with the clause which precedes it, the meaning of which it extends; they cite iv. 3. 7, v. 16. 6, xxiv. 21. 3, and 33. 6. Neither here nor elsewhere is their interpretation inevitable.

dulcedine praedae: see ix. 38. 2 n.

9. Patauium . . . eos: for the plural pronoun following a singular place-name, see vi. 3. 2 n.

effusa populatio: 'widespread pillaging'. For the expression cf. [x] xxiii. 40. 8, xxxi. 41. 7, xxxii. 31. 1; also ii. 64. 4, ix. 31. 6, xxi. 57. 3, xxii. 3. 9, xxii. 12. 9, and xli. 10. 2 'ubi cum effuse popularentur'.

altero: 'the other'. Some scholars have emended the text because they either doubt this sense or dislike the iteration *altera . . . altera . . . altero*: Gronovius (followed by Foster) proposed *alio*, Burman *auio*, Freudenberg (1854–62: ii. 14) *ulteriore*, and H. J. Müller (in W–M) *diuerso*. Since iteration is so common in L. (see vol. i, pp. 725–7), it is not an argument for emendation, and the conjectures of Burman, Freudenberg, and Müller are improbable as regards both sense and (in the case of Müller's) palaeography, but Gronovius' is diplomatically easy, gives good sense, and may be what L. wrote, especially if he knew or imagined that there were more than two ways to the camp.

10. paucis: N had *paruis*. Although this can be construed with the following *custodibus interemptis*, the resulting sense is very poor (either 'after the small guards had been killed' or 'after the unimportant guards had been killed'). There have been three approaches to emendation.

(*a*) U (for the innovations of which see vol. i, p. 299) has *paruas*. Although amongst modern editors this has been adopted by only Madvig and Ussing, it is quite attractive, in that *paruas* would refer back to the *leuiora* of § 7 'leuiora nauigia' (for the use of *paruus* to describe ships cf. e.g. xxxv. 51. 4, Cic. *Quir.* 20, *Att.* x. 11. 4); however, L. did not need to tell us twice that the boats into which the troops of Cleonymus had unloaded themselves were small.

(*b*) *prius*, found in A[c1] and reported by Drakenborch from the first

---

[1] It is not attested in any other witness to χ.

hand of C, was supported by Novák (see H. J. Müller [1884: 104]); with it one could translate *in naues prius custodibus interemptis impetus factus* as 'after the guards had first been killed, an assault was made on the ships'. Although *prius*, used quite regularly by L. in ablatives absolute (e.g. at vii. 7. 8, xxii. 6. 4, 11. 4, xxvii. 10. 2, xxix. 9. 6, xxxii. 13. 10, 25. 1, xxxiii. 29. 9), is generally found between the noun and the verb (or vice versa), in some passages it comes immediately before the ablative absolute: e.g. xxxvii. 7. 6 'prius Scipione conuento . . .', 45. 6 'prius Eumene conuento . . .', xxxviii. 3. 7 'his territi, prius ab Rhodo et Athenis legationibus excitis . . .'. That *prius* would be redundant hardly matters (it is equally redundant in many of the passages listed above), and this reading could be right.

(*c*) Others have proposed alternative adjectives or participles in the masculine ablative plural. Zr (followed by Walters and Foster) has *ignaris*, Weissenborn (*Komm.*) conjectured *paucis* (championed again by Zingerle [1889: 987–8]), Harant (1880: 64) *sparsis*, and Heraeus (1901: 376) *raris*. Of these conjectures *ignaris* is diplomatically improbable and would state the obvious (L. did not need to spell out that the guards did not know that they were about to be killed); *sparsis* and *raris* (the second being the easier corruption to explain; for something similar see vi. 1. 2 n.) would imply that there were guards 'here and there', which is possible; but *paucis* is both diplomatically easy (for corruption of *paucus* to *paruus* see Ov. *Pont.* iii. 1. 60 and Sidon. *carm.* v. 353) and would refer back to § 8 'leui praesidio'. With hesitation (as [*a*] and [*b*] are not certainly wrong) I have adopted it.[1]

in terra: as K–S i. 348 observe, the plain ablative *terra* would be more usual; but they themselves quote xxxvii. 29. 5 'trepidatumque cum periculo et in mari et in terra foret, ni . . .' (which is closely analogous), and one may add xxii. 19. 7 'tumultusque prius in terra et castris quam ad mare et ad naues est ortus' (which is parallel).

prosperum aeque: for the combination of *prosperus* and *aequus/-ue* cf. 8. 10 and viii. 13. 6 'aeque prospero euentu'.

palatos: see vii. 8. 6 n.

circumuenti . . . caesique: for this coupling see viii. 35. 11 n.

11. pars capti: this use of *pars* without a preceding distributive word such as *pars* itself, *quidam*, or *alii* is aptly termed *nachträgliche Beschränkung* by W–M, who (in their notes ad loc. and on iii. 61. 9 [on the Roman cavalry] 'concitant equos permittuntque in hostem

---

[1] That this reading could be interpreted in the wrong way (not that there were only a few guards who were all killed, but that only a few of the guards were killed) is not a decisive objection to it.

pedestri iam turbatum pugna, et perruptis ordinibus elati ad nouissi-
mam aciem, pars liberi spatio circumuecti, iam fugam undique
capessentes plerosque a castris auertunt') cite xxxvi. 17. 9 'refuger-
unt in iuga montium, pars Heracleae incluserunt sese'. Both these
passages (but not ours) could be explained by postulating an ellipse
of *pars*, which at *TLL* x. 1. 456. 1–7 is illustrated by Sall. *Iug.* 31. 10,
hist. fr. (P. Ryl. 473) 28. 7, Tac. *hist.* ii. 100. 3, and iv. 68. 4 but without reference to L. W–M also compare a similar usage with *alii* at iii.
37. 8 'et iam ne tergo quidem abstinebatur; uirgis caedi, alii securi
subici' and iv. 33. 11.

regemque Cleonymum: W–M rightly point out that Cleonymus
was not actually a king of Sparta. Braccesi (1990: 60) suggests that
this was an exaggeration caused by the influence of local epic on L.'s
account, but L. may simply have made a mistake (cf. Plin. *nat.* vii.
109 'Lysandro . . . rege'). For *rex* used of royal personages other than
a king, see *OLD s.u.* 6(a), but all the passages cited there are poetical.

**12. fluuiatiles naues, ad superanda uada stagnorum apte pla-
nis alueis fabricatas:** with these flat-bottomed ships (ancestors of
the gondola) compare those built by Suetonius Paulinus for his
attack on Anglesey (Tac. *ann.* xiv. 29. 3): 'nauesque fabricatur plano
alueo aduersus breue et incertum' (perhaps a verbal reminiscence of
this passage); also *ann.* ii. 6. 2. For *fabricare* with *apte* and *ad* and the
accusative cf. i. 10. 5 'fabricato ad id apte ferculo'.

naues . . . timentes: for the personification of *naues* W–M on xxvii.
31. 3 'classis . . . laeta' cite several parallels, including xxxvi. 20. 5
'trepidae . . . naues'.

circumuadunt: for this verb see ix. 40. 13 n.

13. fugientesque in altum acrius quam repugnantes: Koch
(1861: 7) commented 'quando acris fuga quomodo defendi possit
nescio, scribendum esse censeo: *fugientesque in altum uerius quam
repugnantes*'; but *acer* qualifies *fuga* at Virg. *georg.* iii. 141–2, and L.
himself uses it to qualify *concursus* (xxi. 59. 8, xlii. 53. 9), which like
fuga implies swift movement.

14. rostra . . . fixa: for the display of *rostra* in a temple see viii. 14. 12
n., for this use of *figere* vi. 29. 9 n.

multi supersunt qui uiderunt Pataui: L. implies that by his time
the *rostra* no longer survived but that he knew people who had seen
them.

15. monumentum naualis pugnae eo die quo pugnatum est quotannis sollemne certamen nauium in oppidi medio exercetur: for games at Padua see also Tac. *ann.* xvi. 21. 1 and Dio lxii. 26. 4. Wiseman (1989: 137 = 1994: 36) cites all three passages to illustrate the holding of games to celebrate the origins and ancestral achievement of a city.

If, as seems reasonably certain, L. refers to an event already established before his lifetime, then this is the earliest mock sea-battle in Italy of which we have knowledge. Whether slaves or criminals were used, and whether actual killing took place, we do not know. For displays that were probably similar cf. Auson. xvi (*Mos.*) 208–19 on mock battles staged in Campania to celebrate the naval victories of Augustus and Claud. xvii. 331–2 on displays that Claudian hopes will mark the assumption of the consulate for 399 by Mallius Theodorus. Better known are the sea-battles involving slaves, convicts, and real deaths put on (usually at Rome) by Julius Caesar between 'Tyrians' and 'Egyptians' in 46 BC (Suet. *Caes.* 39. 4, 44. 1, App. *ciu.* ii. 102. 423), by Sex. Pompeius in 40 BC at Rhegium (Dio xlviii. 19. 1), by Augustus between 'Athenians' and 'Persians' in 2 BC (*res gest.* 23, Vell. ii. 100. 2, Tac. *ann.* xii. 56. 1, Mart. *spect.* 28. 1–2, Suet. *Aug.* 43. 1, Dio lv. 10. 7), by Gaius (perhaps) in AD 38 (Dio lix. 10. 5), by Claudius on the Fucine Lake between 'Sicilians' and 'Rhodians' in AD 52 (Mart. *spect.* 28. 11, Tac. *ann.* xii. 56. 1–3, Suet. *Claud.* 21. 6–7, Dio lx. 33. 3–4), by Nero between 'Athenians' and 'Persians' in AD 57 or 58 (Suet. *Nero* 12. 1, Dio lxi. 9. 5) and perhaps between unknown contestants in AD 64 (Mart. *spect.* 28. 11, Suet. *Nero* 27. 2 [cf. Tac. *ann.* xv. 37. 1–2], Dio lxii. 15. 1), by Titus between 'Corinthians' and 'Corcyraeans' and 'Athenians' and 'Syracusans' in AD 80 (Mart. *spect.* 24–6, 28, Suet. *Tit.* 7. 3, Dio lxvi. 25. 3), by Domitian perhaps in AD 89 (Suet. *Dom.* 4. 2 and 5, Dio lxvii. 8. 2–4), by Elagabal (*SHA* xviii. 23. 1), and perhaps by Philippus Arabs (Aur. Vict. *Caes.* 28. 1). Note too Hor. *epist.* i. 18. 61–4 (on mock battles of Actium staged privately by Lollius on his own estate). For further discussion see Bernert, *RE* xvi. 1970–4, Coleman (1990) 70–2 and (1993), and Wiedemann (1992) 89–90.

sollemne certamen, adopted by e.g. Ruperti, H. J. Müller, and M. Müller but rejected by J. Walker (1822: 85) and not even cited by Walters, is Crévier's conjecture for **N**'s *sollemni certamine*: *monumentum* would make a much less satisfactory subject for *exercetur* ('is performed') than *sollemne certamen*.

in flumine oppidi medio: thus M: *flumine in oppidi medio* λ: *in oppidi medi medio* P¹: *in oppidi medio* PᶜUZ: *in oppido medio* O or Oᶜ.

Walters adopted the reading of P^{c}UZ: presumably he would have argued that a scribe or reader who felt that the fact that the commemorative mock battle took place on water needed to be spelt out inserted *flumine* into M and λ (perhaps by way of a marginal variant in **N**). In fact, there is no reason to take exception to the word: its absence would leave readers wondering how the Paduans managed to re-enact the battle, and its differing position in M and λ and its omission in Π could be explained by its omission by **N**^{1} and its restoration by **N**^{c} in an ambiguous position, where it was missed by Π. An alternative but perhaps less economical explanation is that the reading of M or λ stood in **N**, that Π omitted *flumine* by mistake, and that either M or λ changed the position of *in*.

The readings of M and λ are both possible, but that of M is preferable. Although L. seems to use *flumine* in the sense postulated by the reading of λ at xliv. 31. 10 'nauem conscendit et flumine Barbanna nauigat in lacum Labeatium' (where however it is conceivable that the sense is instrumental), he uses *in flumine* at xxiv. 44. 8 'nauium longarum species in flumine Tarracinae quae nullae erant uisas' and xxvi. 7. 9 'nauis in flumine Vulturno comprehensas'. And although the combination of *in* with substantivized *medio* and a dependent genitive is found once in L. (i. 57. 9 'Lucretiam . . . in medio aedium sedentem'), it is far more stylish to have *medio* as an adjective with dependent genitive: cf. the passages cited at K–S i. 444–5 and *TLL* viii. 582. 68–77 (which include xxviii. 6. 2 'altera (*sc.* arx) urbis media est') and add v. 54. 4 'regionem Italiae mediam' (adduced by W–M). For M being alone in the truth, see vol. i, pp. 321–2 with *addendum*.

3. 1. *Treaty with the Vestini.* L. separates his lengthy accounts of the campaigns of Cleonymus and of Roman fighting against the Marsi and in Etruria with this brief and unadorned sentence.
Vestinis: see viii. 29. 1 n.
petentibus amicitiam ictum est foedus: see vii. 19. 4, ix. 20. 7–8 nn.

3. 2–13. *Fighting against the Marsi and in Etruria.* When L. writes (§ 2) 'multiplex . . . exortus terror' because of hostile movements among the Marsi and Etruscans, and (§ 3) that a dictator was appointed, he encourages his readers to imagine that these will be campaigns in which Roman arms are sorely stretched. However, the Marsi offer little resistance: they are beaten in just one battle, and the campaign against them is dispatched in just two sentences (§ 5).

The opening of the campaign against the Etruscans makes a striking contrast. In L. the return to Rome of a dictator to retake the auspices (3. 6) is often a prelude to some unfortunate event (see esp. the events of 325/4 [viii. 30. 1–36. 12 n.], referred to in § 8, in which Fabius Rullianus fights the Samnites against the express command of his dictator and then quarrels with him), and on this occasion several detachments left in the care of the *magister equitum* are ambushed and lose their standards, with panic ensuing at Rome (4. 1). However, then L. springs a surprise: the dictator finds that the *magister equitum* has the situation entirely under control and that the army is keen to do battle again with the enemy. L. gives his account of the following battle at Rusellae individuality by dwelling on two features: first, the attempt of the Etruscans to ambush the Romans (§§ 6–11), and second the manner in which the dictator delays sending reinforcements to his legate, who is withstanding the full brunt of the Etruscan attack (4. 12–5. 8). L. emphasizes the skill with which the Romans spot the Etruscan ruse, and the triumphant words which he gives the legate (4. 10 'ite igitur, dicite . . . detegant nequiquam conditas insidias: omnia scire Romanum nec magis iam dolo capi quam armis uinci posse') look back not just to the earlier ambush but also to the Caudine Forks: now the Romans do not fall for such stratagems. The dictator's delay is caused by a desire to wear down the enemy (5. 5): 'quam maxime uolt fatigari hostem ut integris adoriatur uiribus fessos' (where note the emphasis on *integris* and the final *fessos*); and the success of his plan is brought out in § 8 'integri accepere pugnam nec ea ipsa longa aut anceps fuit', where *integri* looks back to § 5.

    L. uses several familiar devices to enliven the episode: historic presents (4. 6 'temptant', § 8 'inclamat', § 9 'iubet', § 12 'mittit', 5. 1 'iubet', 5. 3 'urgent', 'hortantur', 'uidet', 'retentat', 'iubet', § 4 'nuntiant', 'cernit', § 7 'inuehitur', 'offundit', § 9 'repetunt', 'cedunt', 'conglobantur', § 10 'conscendit', § 11 'euadunt'), verbs at the head of the clause (5. 3 'urgent', § 10 'haerent'), and short sentences (5. 3, 8–10). It is rounded off with an account of the terms made with the Etruscans and with a reference to the dictator returning to Rome in triumph (see vol. i, p. 127). Then, in characteristic fashion, L. appends a variant version that he found in his sources. The focus on the dictator throughout the episode but especially in 5. 13 makes for an easy transition to the account of his election in § 14. By giving much more space to the battle in which the Romans were victorious than to the one in which they were defeated L. lessens the significance of the defeat.

    See further Bruckmann (1936) 34–6.

2. Arretinorum: see ix. 32. 1 n.

seditionibus: our other sources for civil unrest in Etruscan cities all mention slaves: note the *bellum seruile* at Arretium mentioned on the *elogium* from Tarquinii discussed above (p. 47), the revolt at the obscure Oinarea ([Aristot.] *mir. ausc.* 94); and the revolt that led to the Roman conquest of Volsinii in 264 (Val. Max. ix. 1. *ext.* 2, Flor. i. 16(21), *uir. ill.* 36. 1–2, Zon. viii. 7. 4–8). Whether this evidence suffices to prove that *c.*300 such revolts were endemic in Etruscan society is uncertain. See further Heurgon (1964) 59–61.

Rome's support for the Cilnii (cf. 5. 13) conforms to her general policy of supporting oligarchies against democracies (see vol. ii, pp. 557–8); for the possibility that this support ensured that generally she was on good terms with Arretium, see ix. 32. 1 n.

nuntiabatur: see vii. 19. 6 n.

Cilnium, the reading of PO (-*lmi-* O) ZbZt, is certainly what L. wrote and stood in Π; UZs have *licinium* (based on 5. 13) (prefaced by *per* in U); M¹(?)λ had the dittography *ciuium cilnium*; and Mᶜ has *ciuium cilicium*. See also Winkler (1890–2) ii. 18–19.

Only here and at 5. 13 do we have an explicit reference in a reasonably reliable source to the power of the Cilnii of Arretium in republican times. Maecenas, however, was certainly descended from the family: Augustus (*epist.* fr. 47 = Macrob. *Sat.* ii. 4. 12) calls him *lasar Arretinum* and *Cilniorum smaragde*, and Tacitus (*ann.* vi. 11. 2) refers to him as Cilnius Maecenas. Inscriptions show that Tacitus was mistaken in imagining that Cilnius and not Maecenas was the *nomen* of the great equestrian, but it is clear that he must have been related closely to the Cilnii, and it is often argued that his mother was a Cilnia. On several occasions the poets refer to Maecenas' descent from princes: Hor. *serm.* i. 6. 1–2, *carm.* i. 1. 1 'Maecenas atauis edite regibus', iii. 29. 1 'Tyrrhena regum progenies', and Prop. iii. 9. 1 'Maecenas eques Etrusco de sanguine regum'; and these allusions probably reflect his relationship to the blue-blooded Cilnii. Even without the career of Maecenas, Silius Italicus, a competent antiquarian, might have known that the Cilnii had once been the dominant family in Arretium; but it was surely because of Maecenas that at vii. 29 he invented a Cilnius from Arretium.[1] The Cilnii survived long there, and their name is found on several inscriptions and Arretine sherds; see *CIL* xi. 1857–8, 6700, 183, *CIE* i. 408–9, Ihm (1898) 125. See further Münzer, *RE* iii. 2545–6, Kappelmacher, *RE* xiv. 208, Stein (1927) 196 n. 3, Harris (1971) 320–1 and index *s.u.* Cilnii, Maggiani (1986), and Steinbauer (1998).

---

[1] On the same principle a Tullius of Arpinum is invented at viii. 404–5.

simul Marsos agrum ui tueri, in quem colonia Carseoli deducta erat quattuor milibus hominibus scriptis: for the Marsi, see viii. 6. 8 n. The remains of Carseoli are to be found at Civita. This hill lies mid-way between Arsoli and Carsóli, 3 km to the east of the Aniene/Turano watershed; it overlooks the main route—that taken by the Via Valeria—from Rome to the Fucine Lake and the central Apennines. The site is readily defensible (albeit not impregnable) and is surrounded by good arable land. Although the fields at Civita are full of fragments of Roman tile and pottery, virtually no structures now survive from the ancient town.

This notice causes two difficulties. First, L.'s view that the Latin colony of Carseoli was established on Marsic territory is wrong. As he himself recognizes at 13. 1, and as Pliny (*nat*. iii. 107) states, this was Aequan territory: the land of the Marsi probably began only at the Fucine Lake. Second, L. records the foundation of Carseoli also at 13. 1 (298).

Attempts to remove these difficulties by emendation are unconvincing. Sigonius, supported by F. C. Wolff (1826: 4–5), conjectured *a Marsis agrum ui teneri*, which could be interpreted as meaning that the Marsi were assisting the Aequi; but this is forced, and it is easier to believe that L. made a mistake. Wolff additionally proposed *deducenda* for *deducta*; this would remove the chronological difficulty, but the use of the gerundive with no hint of obligation would be unwelcome, and again it is probably easier to accept that L. has created an unfortunate doublet by combining sources.[1]

If the text is sound, it is impossible to make a certain decision between the two dates of foundation. Given the mistake about the tribe in whose territory Carseoli lay, the later notice may seem preferable; but Vell. i. 14. 5 'tunc Sora atque Alba deductae coloniae et Carseoli post biennium', our only other evidence for the date of foundation, either supports the date of 302/1 (if Velleius was counting inclusively) or suggests that our passage has placed the foundation just one year too soon (if he counted exclusively). These three passages are the only references to Carseoli in our sources for the Roman conquest of Italy.

For Carseoli and the problem of its date of foundation see further Bruno (1906) 3–4 (in favour of the date given in our passage), Pfeiffer and Ashby (1905) (the fullest account of the physcial remains, with references to descriptions of the site made at a time when more of it

---

[1] Another conjecture which would remove the doublet is Conway's tentative idea that we should supply *quattuor post annos* between *deducta* and *quattuor*; but nowhere else does L. tell us that a colony was going to be founded several years later.

was preserved), Säflund (1935) 74–7, Ward-Perkins (1964) 18–20, Coarelli and La Regina (1984) 60–2, and Gatti and Onorati (1991). For the 4,000 colonists see viii. 16. 14 n.

Walters adopts Conway's suggestion of deleting *erat* and inserting *est* after *colonia* (perhaps because *erat* is omitted by L, and PU insert *est* after *scriptis*). This conjecture is unnecessary: although PU could alone preserve a vestige of the truth, the paradosis gives excellent sense, and L has no authority on its own (even R does not agree with it).

3–4. L. states simply that he prefers to believe that Aemilius Paullus was *magister equitum* and not Fabius Maximus (the famous Rullianus: see viii. 18. 4 n.); although he does not mention any discrepancy in his sources, it is plain that he found one. Perhaps some sources made Paullus hold the post, others Maximus. Or perhaps some sources had a notice similar to that found in *F.C.* for 301:

> [Q. Fabius] M. f. N. n. Maxi[mus Rullianus II abd(icauit)] mag(ister)
> [eq(uitum). In e(ius) l(ocum) f(actus) e(st)]
> [M. Ai]milius L. f. L. [n. Paullus mag(ister eq(uitum)]

A certain resolution of these difficulties is not to be had. The notice in *F.C.* may be no more than a rationalization of two discrepant notices, in which case we must choose one man or the other, and the younger Paullus is the more plausible candidate for the post. On the other hand, there is no reason why there should not have been two *magistri equitum* in a dictatorship (for instance, the first holder of the office may have fallen ill), and it is possible that *F.C.* reflect what happened and that L. and/or his sources have misunderstood this.

Whatever one may think of L.'s romantic defence of his hero at §§ 7–8, it would be very surprising, as he says here, if the old and experienced Fabius had served in a post normally held by a young man. Just conceivably the fact that Corvus was both senior to Fabius and perhaps—at least until Sentinum—the more distinguished man may explain Fabius' willingness to serve. Another possibility is that the tradition wrongly recorded Fabius Rullianus rather than the young Fabius Gurges (14. 10 n.) as *magister equitum*, and that *F.C.* adapted its filiation accordingly.[1] L.'s argument that the fact that Valerius and Fabius shared the *cognomen* Maximus may have encouraged the tradition to have interpolated Fabius as *magister equitum* perhaps reads more oddly to logical modern eyes (one would

---

[1] Tentatively suggested by Walt (1997: 283).

have thought it more likely that the identical *cognomina* would have led to doubt as to who was dictator) than it would have done to ancient.[1]

3. tumultus: see vii. 9. 6 n.
M. Valerius Maximus: the famous Corv(in)us; for the difficulties involved in reconstructing his career, see vii. 26. 2 n.
sibi legit: see vii. 19. 10 n.
M. Aemilium Paullum: see 1. 7 n.

4. ea aetate: for the expression cf. iii. 35. 3 'demissa iam in discrimen dignitas ea aetate iisque honoribus actis stimulabat Ap. Claudium'.
cognomine is the reading of Π, perhaps from conjecture. M has *cōs nomine*, and λ had *cōs cognomine*, but the context shows that *consulis* is quite impossible. Probably **N¹** had M's *cōs nomine* and correction of it led to variants reflected in the reading of λ. For this phenomenon see vol. i, pp. 316–20.

5. proelio uno: for this τόπος see viii. 29. 12 n.
fundit. compulsis: see ix. 42. 6 n.
Milioniam, Plestinam, Fresiliam: the site of none of these places is known.
parte agris multatis: see viii. 1. 3 n.
foedus restituit: for this treaty see ix. 20. 7–8 (n.) and 45. 18.

6. auspiciorum repetendorum: see viii. 30. 2 n. and *addendum*.

7. signis aliquot omissis: see vii. 13. 4 n.
foeda militum caede ac fuga: for *foeda* qualifying *fuga* ('shameful flight') add i. 12. 6, xxii. 31. 5, xxvi. 41. 19, xxx. 6. 6, Cic. *Att.* ix. 10. 6, *Phil.* iii. 24, Luc. iv. 713–14, Val. Fl. vi. 723 (*e conj.*), and Front. p. 206. 4 to the passages cited at *TLL* vi. 1000. 2–3. For the coupling of *caedes* and *fuga* see ix. 24. 13 n.

7–8. qui terror . . . adduci potuisset: it is not absurd of L. to suggest that Fabius' fame as a warrior makes it unlikely that he suffered a reverse from an ambush when foraging. His implication that Fabius might not have fought back because the dictator had banned

---

[1] For the difficulties which L.'s lack of logic caused early interpreters, see Drakenborch's note.

fighting is less probable: foraging was necessary, and foragers had to protect themselves. In general, this passage offers some typical romantic psychologizing from L., who shows a touching confidence in the ability of humans (and esp. his heroes) to learn from their mistakes: at viii. 30. 1–36. 12 (n.) he made much of the quarrel between Rullianus and Papirius Cursor. See further Chaplin (2000) 111–12.

For *terror* used in the context of a Roman defeat, Bruckmann (1936: 340) compares v. 28. 7–8.

7. cognomen suum aequauit is not necessarily inconsistent with ix. 46. 15, where L. explains that Fabius received his *cognomen* not from his military exploits but from his censorship in 304: the military exploits of Fabius justified the *cognomen* which he had gained for other reasons.

tum maxime: Madvig (1860: 187–8 = 1877: 223–4) saw that *tum* is anomalous: 'quoniam particulae *tum* sic in comparando (post *si quis alius*) additae nullum omnino exemplum est nec, quid agat, intellegitur'; he therefore deleted it, and Seyffert (1861: 76) conjectured *cum* for it. However, the anomaly is perhaps more likely to have been perpetrated by L. than by a scribe: there is no difficulty with *tum* itself, which picks up *si*; and L. uses *tum maxime* twice elsewhere (admittedly in different circumstances, as in each case *cum* precedes): i. 8. 2 'cum cetero habitu se augustiorem, tum maxime lictoribus duodecim sumptis fecit' and xxi. 19. 1 'haec derecta percontatio ac denuntiatio belli magis ex dignitate populi Romani uisa est quam de foederum iure uerbis disceptare, cum ante, tum maxime Sagunto excisa'. Against Seyffert it may be observed that elsewhere L. uses *cum maxime* in the sense 'at this particular time', which is inapposite here. With *maxime* L. puns on the name Maximus.

bellicis laudibus: see ix. 16. 12 n.

4. 1–2. For the exaggerated panic at Rome after a defeat see ix. 38. 9 n. For the practical response to this defeat compare esp. L.'s account of the Roman response to Hannibal's march on the city in 211 (xxvi. 9. 9): 'praesidia in arce, in Capitolio, in muris, circa urbem, in monte etiam Albano atque arce Aefulana ponuntur'; also iii. 5. 4 (after a Roman defeat in 464) 'uigiliae in urbe, stationes ante portas praesidiaque in muris disposita, et, quod necesse erat in tanto tumultu, iustitium per aliquot dies seruatum'. In pointed contrast stand v. 39. 2 (after the Allia, in a part of the text in which L. goes out of his way to show how the Romans were behaving in an un-Roman manner) 'cum praegressi equites (*sc.* Gallici) . . . non stationem pro portis

excubare, non armatos esse in muris rettulissent' and Plut. *Cam.* 22.
1. For the *iustitium*, mass levy, and guards for the city, see vii. 9. 6 n.
with *addendum*; for the *uigiliae* see *addendum* to viii. 8. 1 n.; for the
expression *iustitium indictum* see vii. 6. 12 n.

1. maiorem quam res erat terrorem exciuit: 'gave rise to . . . a
greater alarm than the situation warranted' (Foster); for the idiom,
cf. iv. 56. 8 'quae ubi tumultu maiore etiam quam res erat nuntiantur
Romam' and xxv. 30. 12 'regiae opes, quarum fama maior quam res
erat'. I have not been able to parallel the expression *terrorem excire*
elsewhere [x].

ut exercitu deleto: although used quite often by L. (i. 54. 7, xxiv.
45. 11, xxix. 32. 3, xxxiv. 39. 8, 10, 52. 10), only rarely elsewhere does
ut modify an ablative absolute. Before him it is found at Cic. *Att.* ii.
18. 3 (twice), Caes. *Gall.* iii. 18. 8 and *ciu.* ii. 13. 2; after him at e.g.
Vell. ii. 12. 1 and Amm. xiv. 7. 4. For the coupling with *ita* W–M well
compare the analogous ii. 52. 2 'tamquam Veiis captis, ita pauidi
Veientes ad arma currunt'. See further viii. 14. 6 n. and Lease (1928)
352.[1]

2. uigiliae uicatim [ex]actae: for night-watches in the city, organized in times of crisis, compare with our passage esp. xxxii. 26. 17
(reaction to a threatened revolt amongst slaves) 'itaque et Romae
uigiliae per uicos seruatae, iussique circumire eas minores magistratus'; also e.g. iii. 5. 4 (quoted above), 6. 9 (an Aequan and Volscian
attack in 463), xxxix. 14. 10, 16. 13 (the reaction to the Bacchanalian
affair), Cic. *Cat.* i. 1, and Sall. *Cat.* 30. 7 (response to the threat of
Catiline).

    The *uici* were the streets of Rome (for the surviving names see e.g.
Platner and Ashby [1929] 570–80, L. Richardson [1992] 421–30, and
Steinby [1993–2000] v. 155–201); and so *uicatim* means 'street by
street' (see *OLD s.u.* [a], and contrast ix. 13. 7 n.).

    For *exactae* Madvig (*ap.* Madvig and Ussing 1877: 224 n. 1) pro-
posed *actae*, on the ground that *uigilias agere* or *agitare* was the usual
idiom (see Cic. *IIVerr.* iv. 93, Curt. iv. 13. 10, and Tac. *ann.* xi. 18.
3). Despite Walters's assertion that the conjecture is unnecessary,
exactae is difficult to parallel: our passage is listed at *OLD s.u.* 5(a)
under the rubric 'to achieve, execute, complete (a task)', but it has
little similarity to the others listed there, among which is Hor. *carm.*

---

[1] However, Lease was wrong to claim xl. 12. 13 (where *ut* introduces a final clause) as an
instance of the phenomenon.

iii. 30. 1 'exegi monumentum aere perennius'. It would have been better to have listed it under 8(b) 'to exact, enforce the performance of (a task)', where e.g. xlv. 36. 3 'exacta acerbe munia militiae' is rightly to be found; our passage would then mean 'the setting up of watches in the streets was enforced'. Yet even this is rather awkward, and it is better to follow Madvig. Although the appearance of *ex-* in **N** has no very obvious diplomatic explanation, the corruption of a simple verb into a compound is not difficult to parallel (see e.g. vi. 33. 1 n. on the corruption of *spectare* to *exspectare*).[1]

arma tela: the asyndeton is paralleled at xxix. 4. 2 and xxxvi. 18. 1 (where Briscoe rightly defends the paradosis and cites further parallels). For the coupling, see vi. 6. 14 n.

3. omnia spe tranquilliora: see vi. 25. 11 n.

4. cohortes: see vii. 39. 7 n.

extra uallum sine tentoriis: for this punishment, cf. Plb. vi. 38. 3 . . . ἔξω κελεύει τοῦ χάρακος καὶ ἀσφαλείας ποιεῖσθαι τὴν παρεμβολήν, Val. Max. ii. 7. 15 (on men ransomed from Pyrrhus) ' . . . neue quis eorum intra castra tenderet, neue locum extra adsignatum uallo aut fossa cingeret, neue tentorium ex pellibus haberet', Frontin. (?) *strat.* iv. 1. 18, 19 'Otacilius Crassus consul eos, qui ab Hannibale sub iugum missi redierant, tendere extra uallum iussit, ut inmuniti adsuescerent periculis et aduersus hostem audentiores fierent', and 21 (Corbulo in the orient; cf. Tac. *ann.* xiii. 36. 3). See further Fischer (1914) 144.

destitutas: *destituo* is used regularly of those who have been placed in a position of ignominy; cf. e.g. ii. 12. 8 'ante tribunal regis destitutus', vii. 13. 3 (figurative), xxiii. 10. 5 '(Hannibal) . . . Decium Magium . . . ante pedes destitutum causam dicere iussit', and see *TLL* v. 1. 762. 22–38.

5. inde: since L. had previously written (3. 6) 'tum in Etruscos uersum bellum', and since Rusellae is in Etruria, Klinger (1884: 6–7) thought L.'s use of this adverb loose; but the contrast is probably with *in tutiorem locum*.

castra . . . promouit: see ix. 37. 2 n.

agrum Rusellanum: Rusellae, modern Roselle (which lies about 8 km north by north-east of Grosseto), was one of the more powerful

---

[1] Alternatively one may conjecture that the writer of an early copy changed *actae* into *exactae* because his eye had caught *exercitus* in the line above, or (as Professor Watt suggested to me) one could conjecture *ex⟨templo⟩ actae* and postulate omission of *-templo*.

Etruscan cities but in our surviving evidence for the Roman conquest of Italy is mentioned only here and at 37. 3. Since no authentic information about the campaigns of Tarquinius Priscus can have survived into the period in which the history of Rome was written, the notice at D.H. iii. 51. 4 of the Rusellani joining the inhabitants of Clusium, Arretium, and Volaterrae in attacking Rome during the reign of Tarquinius Priscus must be an invention of D.H. or (just conceivably) earlier tradition; by contrast, the report at Liv. xxviii. 45. 18 (the only other passage in which he mentions them) of their help in the construction of the fleet with which Scipio invaded Africa is credible. Massive defensive walls from *c*.550 BC survive at the site. See further Philipp, *RE* iA. 1236, Scullard (1967) 133–5, and Torelli (1982) 268–75.

6. summam . . . uirium spem: i.e. *spem quam uires dabant* (the genitive is subjective); cf. iii. 11. 2 'neque suum cuique ius modum faciebat, sed uirium spe et manu obtinendum erat quod intenderes'.
in aperto certamine . . . insidiis: for this contrast see viii. 36. 9 n.

7. semiruta: for L.'s predilection for compounds in *semi-*, see ix. 6. 1 n.
Cn. Fuluius: (88). Cn. Fulvius Cn. f. Cn. n. Maximus Centumalus (the filiation is provided by *F.C.* for 263 and *F.T.* for 298) was to become consul in 298 (11. 1), when he fought against Samnites and Etruscans (12. 3–13. 1 n.), propraetor in 295, when he commanded a reserve force kept near Rome and then defeated Etruscan forces (26. 15, 30. 1–2), and dictator *claui figendi causa* in 263 (*F.C.*), when as an elder statesman he was well suited to this ceremonial office. He was the fourth Fulvius to reach the consulship: see viii. 38. 1 (L. Curvus), ix. 44. 15 (M. Curvus Paetinus), and x. 9. 9 (M. Paet[in]us), with nn. ad locc. Centumalus bears the *praenomen* of his father, and therefore may have been his first son. However, M. Paet(in)us was also Cn. f. Cn. n., and therefore may have been his younger brother, who, however, beat his senior sibling to the consulship. If so, possible parallels for this phenomenon are provided by Cn. and L. Cornelius L. f. L. n. Lentulus (*coss.* 201 and 199) and T. and L. Quinctius Flamininus (*coss.* 198 and 192; for the ambiguous evidence on these two last see Badian [1971] 110–11). However, since these Fulvii bear different *cognomina*, it is possible that they were not brothers; and it is possible too (as it is in the case of the Lentuli) that the man who became consul second was in fact the third brother in the family, the first (who had also borne the father's *praenomen*) having died young

before the birth of the third. On these Fulvii and the arrival of the family in the Roman *nobilitas* see Brunt (1982) 2; for the *cognomen* Maximus see ix. 46. 15 n.

legatus: see vii. 7. 1 n.

8. pastorum unus: a 'classical' writer, such as Caesar or Cicero, would almost certainly have written *unus ex* (or *de*) *pastoribus*; but there are many exceptions to this rule, both in L. (cf. e.g. xxvi. 12. 16, 33. 11, xxx. 42. 20) and in pre-Ciceronian and post-Augustan writers. See further W–M on xxiv. 28. 1 and K–S i. 426–7.

9. Caerites: since Caere had not been at war with Rome since 353 (vii. 19. 6–20. 8), the Caerites could perhaps have been serving as allies in the Roman army (see 18. 4 n.). Therefore, although this whole detail—like the rest of the scene—is almost certainly an invention, L. (or a source) has taken care to make it seem plausible.

manipulos: see viii. 8. 3–14 n.

mouere: *mouere se* is printed in some older editions and Madvig emended to the middle *moueri* (for the usage see vii. 14. 8 n.), which is read by W–M. However, the reading of **N** (retained by Walters) is probably right: although none of the passages listed by Drakenborch or at *TLL* viii. 1546. 29–39 and *OLD s.u.* 6(b) is precisely parallel, some of them provide not too distant analogies; cf. e.g. xxi. 32. 1, 39. 6 'Hannibal mouit ex Taurinis', xxii. 1. 1 'Hannibal ex hibernis mouit', xxiii. 1. 1, and xxxviii. 41. 2 (where the subject is part of the Roman army) 'prius explorato saltu quam mouerent'.

adtendere animum: 'to pay attention'. This idiomatic coupling is common in Latin (*TLL* ii. 1119. 57–79, *OLD s.u. attendo* 1), but not found elsewhere in L.; indeed, he uses *attendo* elsewhere only at xxvii. 47. 3.

10. sonum linguae . . . pastoralia esse: quite as much as moderns, the ancients were attuned to, and snobbish about, standard and non-standard accents and vocabulary (see Quint. i. 5. 56, where he mentions Pollio's famous jibe about L.'s *Patauinitas*); for comment on rustic accents cf. e.g. Cic. *de orat.* iii. 42 'rustica uox et agrestis quosdam delectat', [Virg.] *mor.* 29–30 'modo rustica carmina cantat | agrestique suum solatur uoce laborem', and Hil. *in psalm.* 65. 3 (*PL* ix, p. 425). It seems unlikely, however, that *c.*300 BC, when many town-dwellers worked in the country, the difference between rural and urban accents in Etruscan would have been so very marked, and our passage may reflect later conditions; see Frayn (1984) 68–9 and

Adams (2003) 168 'this anecdote seems to impose on early Etruscan speech the sort of model that was later applied in certain quarters to Latin'. That a too smart imitation of shepherd's clothing (for which see ix. 36. 6 n.) could have been detected is perhaps more likely.

ite . . . dicite: for this idiom, see ix. 24. 9 n.

omnia scire Romanum nec magis iam dolo capi quam armis uinci posse: this looks back in the first instance to the ambush at 3. 6, but there is also a wider reference back to the tale of the Caudine Forks (see ix. 1. 1–16. 19 n.).

11. consederant: see ix. 24. 5 n.
consurrectum: see ix. 25. 8 n.
prolata signa: see ix. 32. 5 n.

5. 1. signa ferri . . . iubet: see ix. 14. 5 n.

2. accidens clamor: see viii. 24. 11 n.
ira ab accepta nuper clade stimulabat: for the prepositional phrase dependent on *ira* cf. the analogous construction at ii. 51. 6 'ex hac clade atrox ira'; for the coupling of *ira* and *stimulare*, see vii. 32. 3 n.; for anger as a motive spurring on troops, see vol. iii, p. 21 and ix. 13. 3 n.

3. urgent . . . signiferos: see viii. 11. 7, ix. 13. 2 nn.
ocius: see vii. 26. 6 n.
sensim: see viii. 8. 11 n.

5. fretus: the infinitive or accusative and infinitive are found only rarely after *fretus*, and, in addition to our passage, only Curt. vii. 7. 31, Stat. *Theb.* iv. 182, vi. 23, and *carm. epigr.* 279. 10–11 are listed at *TLL* vi. 1319. 1–5.

6. lente procedunt: for this expression cf. [x] Caes. *ciu.* i. 80. 1 and Frontin. *strat.* ii. 3. 6; also Curt. iv. 7. 15 (with *incedere*).
ad impetum capiundum: see viii. 30. 6 n.
signa: see viii. 11. 7 n.
interualla: see viii. 8. 5 n.
permitti: see viii. 30. 6 n.

7. emissus eques: for cavalry charges being used to shock the enemy see vi. 29. 2 n.; for L.'s language here see vii. 15. 4 n.
libero cursu: for the expression cf. [x] iv. 33. 7 'et alii concitati equi

libero cursu ferunt equitem in hostem'; it is used in a rather different context at Curt. v. 1. 30.

equestrem procellam: *procella* and *tempestas* are often used metaphorically in Latin; for this expression, cf. [x] xxix. 2. 11, xxx. 18. 4, xxxv. 5. 9, xxxviii. 41. 14, and Tac. *hist.* iii. 53. 2. The image of a sudden Mediterranean squall is very apt for a cavalry charge; Briscoe (on xxxv. 5. 9) suggests that the expression was 'military jargon'.

subitum pauorem offundit: the coupling *pauorem offundere* appears to be unique to this passage, but cf. *terrorem offundere* at xxii. 19. 6 (with the conjecture of Walch [1815] 157), xxviii. 29. 9, xxxix. 15. 4, and Phaedr. ii. 4. 11, and *metum offundere* at Tac. *ann.* xi. 20. 1. The development of this figurative use of *offundere* is well illustrated by Plin. *epist.* iii. 9. 16 'solet dicere Claudius Restitus . . . numquam sibi tantum caliginis tantum perturbationis offusum, quam cum praerepta et extorta defensioni suae cerneret, in quibus omnem fiduciam reponebat'. See further *TLL* ix. 532. 37–46.

8. ita uniuersa requies data est: a precise parallel for the use of *uniuersus* in the sense of 'complete' or 'absolute' is not easily found. Most of the Livian instances assembled by Gronovius and Drakenborch are used with words like *bellum* and *dimicatio* and tend to contrast a part with the whole, and none of the passages with which ours is listed in *OLD* (*s.u.* 5) seems precisely parallel. Wachendorf (1864: 12–14) thought that the sentence needs some word or phrase to balance *paene circumuentis* and boldly suggested emendation to ⟨fort⟩una uersa, and Watt (2002: 184) suggested *uniuersa ⟨pugna inclinata⟩* or *uniuersa ⟨re mutata⟩*; but, if change is needed, it would be better to adopt *uniuersis*, proposed by a friend of Gronovius. However, the paradosis may probably stand: the Latin is a little unusual, but not impossibly far removed from passages such as xxii. 12. 10 'neque uniuerso periculo summa rerum committebatur'.

nec ea ipsa longa aut anceps: 'nor was it (*sc.* the fighting) either drawn-out or of doubtful outcome'. *ea* picks up *pugna* and is in turn reinforced by *ipsa*; cf. (for *ipsa*) e.g. vii. 2. 4 and xxxviii. 21. 4 'scuta longa, ceterum ad amplitudinem corporis parum lata et ea ipsa plana, male tegebant Gallos'. *ea*, found in Campano's Rome edn. of 1470, is not attested in any primary ms.: M or MᶜZs¹λ omit it; M¹ (in the view of Walters) had *a*;[1] P¹Zb have *ex*; PᶜOZs; and U has *nec hec ex*.

---

[1] On my microfilm I can detect merely a gap slightly larger than one would expect between *nec* and *ipsa*; but it is possible that there was an erasure.

However, it gives good sense and accounts well for the readings of M¹ and P¹, which must be the most primitive in the uneliminable mss; by contrast Walters's tentative suggestion to read either *nec ea* or *nec haec* with *ipsa* deleted does not account for the ms. readings. For *anceps* see vi. 22. 3 n.

9. inferentibus . . . signa: see viii. 11. 7 n.

10. haerent fugientes in angustiis portarum: L. tells us quite often that large numbers of troops impeded themselves by becoming crowded in a gateway: xxx. 5. 10, xxxi. 24. 15, xxxiv. 15. 8, xliv. 31. 9; also xxxiv. 46. 10–47. 1. The appearance of the motif here is due to his own or his sources' reconstruction, based on the realities of ancient warfare. For the similar τόπος of troops being prevented from flight because of their large numbers, see viii. 26. 3 and ix. 23. 16 nn. See also Klinger (1884) 8.

11. pandere uiam fugae: although *pandere* is found often enough in prose, *pandere uiam* may be poetical: in *TLL* x. 1. 196. 81–197. 12 only four other instances of it are cited from prose (41. 9, iv. 15. 5, Tac. *hist.* ii. 4. 1, and Flor. i. 18[ii. 2]. 3; it is perhaps significant that all these instances are in history) but six from verse (first Virg. *Aen.* vi. 96–7 and xii. 626), and for *iter pandere* eight instances are cited from verse but none from prose. For *uia fugae* cf. 35. 19, Cic. *Caecin.* 44, Frontin. *strat.* ii. 6. 5, Just. xi. 14. 4, and Yardley (2003) 42.
plures inermes quam armati: a sign that they had no intention of fighting.

12. fractae iterum Etruscorum uires: this remark looks back to ix. 39. 11 'ille primum dies fortuna uetere abundantes Etruscorum fregit opes' (n.), which refers to the victory of Fabius Rullianus over the Etuscans in 310/9.
annuo stipendio et duum mensum frumento: see ix. 41. 6–7 n.
ut de pace legatos mitterent Romam: see viii. 36. 12 n.
pax negata, indutiae biennii datae: see ix. 41. 6–7 n.

13. triumphans in urbem rediit: for the expression see vi. 4. 1 n.; for the parallel notice in *F.T.*, see above, p. 45.
habeo auctores: see viii. 4. 10 n.
Cilnio: for the textual problem and the interesting corruptions in the mss, see vol. i, p. 318. On the Cilnii and Arretium, see 3. 2 n.

5. 14. *The consular elections*

There is no reason to doubt that Valerius was consul in 300 (if he did indeed triumph, his success is likely to explain his election [see further ix. 41. 1 n.]), but the variants that L. reports here make it difficult to reconstruct the circumstances in which he was elected. There would seem to be the following possibilities:

(*a*) Valerius triumphed, resigned office as was normal for a dictator after a triumph when he had no further duties to perform, and was elected consul, with the elections held by one of the consuls for 302/1 in the normal manner. If this is correct, L.'s words *consul ex dictatura factus M. Valerius* should not be taken literally, and L.'s main version is correct, his alternative version wrong.

(*b*) Valerius held the elections himself, since the consuls were detained by warfare. In which case, L.'s words could be taken literally but Valerius went against normal custom in presiding over his own election (see vii. 25. 2 n. with *addendum*). On this view L.'s main version is again correct, his alternative version wrong.

(*c*) Valerius' dictatorship extended beyond the consular year, and for this reason he held the elections himself (L.'s alternative version again being in error). Again L.'s phrase could be taken literally, but again Valerius would have gone against normal custom. The late date of the triumph in *F.T.* (21 November) may support this but does not certainly do so because we do not know the date at which the consular year began in this period (see viii. 20. 3 n.); nor can we be sure of the constitutional position of a dictator *rei gerundae causa* after the resignation of consuls who had appointed him.[1]

(*d*) Valerius resigned his office after his triumph but during the consular year. Because the consuls did not manage to hold the elections, they were held by an *interrex*, as some of L.'s sources suggested. If this is right, then L.'s main version is wrong, his alternative version correct.

(*e*) Valerius carried on his dictatorship after the consular year (on the implications of which see [*c*] above), resigning after his triumph but before the elections, which were therefore held by *interreges*. Again, on this view L.'s main version is wrong, his alternative version correct.

Although the vagueness of the notice concerning the *interregnum* does not much enhance its claims to authenticity (see also vol. i, p.

---

[1] One may wonder whether this was a contributory factor in the demise of the dictatorship after Valerius resigned his office: see *addendum* to vi. 16. 3 n.

46), there is no obvious reason for it to be invented, and therefore (*d*) or (*e*) is perhaps the most likely to be right. See further J. Jahn (1970: 98–9) and Loreto (1993: 167 and 190), who both favour (*e*).

14. atque adeo etiam: the idiomatic use of *adeo* after *atque* ('and what is more') is very common in Latin (K–S ii. 17–18, *TLL* i. 612. 58–613. 42), but L. avails himself of it only here. The coupling *adeo etiam*, in which two intensifying particles are placed together to give extra force, is much rarer, but to the four other passages cited at *TLL* v. 2. 953. 13–20 add *per.* 50, Curt. ix. 4. 7, Sen. *ben.* i. 2. 5, ii. 1. 4, *epist.* 94. 43, and Plin. *nat.* xx. 131. For *atque adeo etiam* cf. Varr. *ling.* viii. 10 and *SHA* xxiv. 29. 3.

absentem: see vii. 26. 12 n. with *addendum*.

tradidere is Duker's conjecture, accepted by all modern editors, for **N**'s *credidere*, which gives inferior sense and cannot adequately be paralleled. *tradere* is used regularly by L. in the context of the citation of sources: cf. e.g. xxi. 46. 10, xli. 27. 2, xlv. 40. 1 and esp. *tradidere quidam* at iv. 46. 11 and xlv. 3. 3. For the corruption of a part of *tradere* to a part of *credere* cf. e.g. Ov. *am.* iii. 4. 22 (*tradita* PYSω: *credita* ς).

Appuleio Pansa: (24). Q. Appuleius Pansa, the first Appuleius known to have held curule office, is otherwise unknown. Our sources spell the name variously with one or two 'p's. There is no certainty which form L. would have used or indeed whether he would have been consistent; the spelling adopted here is that of *F.T.* (for 26), which were contemporary with him.

300 BC

6. 1–2. *External and internal affairs*

2. aduersae belli res is found in the Froben (Basle) edn. of 1535 and is reported by Drakenborch from the first hand of Dresden Dc 126; **N** had *aduersa belli res*; and Gronovius deleted *res*. Although the expression *aduersa res* is not in itself difficult (cf. e.g. iv. 55. 5 'ea aduersa ciuitatis res uires tribuniciae actioni adiecit'), a plural would be more stylish, and it is best to emend. Gronovius' deletion postulates an easy corruption through perseveration and could be right: for the substantivized use of neuter adjectives with dependent partitive genitive see vi. 32. 5 n.; for *aduersus* in this construction cf. ix. 3. 1 'aduersa montium'. However, it is better to emend to *aduersae*: the

corruption postulated is very easy; iteration of a word is not unexpected in L. (vol. i, pp. 725–7); *aduersae res* is found at v. 51. 8, xxv.
1. 6, xxvi. 37. 2, xxx. 30. 10, xxxv. 2. 2, and xxxvii. 45. 12; and, as
Duker first noted, there is a good analogy for dependent *belli* at iii. 9.
1 'secundaeque belli res extemplo urbanos motus excitauerunt'. U
has *aduersi belli res* (probably by conjecture: see vol. i, p. 299 with
addendum), which is possible but less attractive. See further Häggström (1874) 65–6.

Romae quoque plebem quietam [et] exonerata[m deductam]
in colonias multitudo praestabat: *et exoneratam deductam* is the
reading of MPTR¹L, which must be archetypal. The easiest remedy
is to read *deducta* for *deductam* (thus UOZRᶜD), which was for long
accepted by editors: with it the plebs are said to be quiescent and
unburdened of the worries caused by overcrowding; we may compare the use of *exonero* at 21. 5 'ceterum parte curae exonerarunt
senatum L. Volumni consulis litterae'. However, it is more pointed
to make L. refer to the *multitudo* being unburdened or discharged
into colonies, and this sense is given by the deletions of Madvig
(1860: 188–9 = 1877: 224) accepted in the lemma; cf. e.g. xxiv. 29. 1
'quae legatio peropportuna uisa ad multitudinem inconditam ac
tumultuosam exonerandam ducesque eius ablegandos', Sen. *dial*. xii.
7. 4 'alios nimia superfluentis populi frequentia ad exonerandas uires
emisit', Tac. *hist*. v. 2. 2 'multitudinem ducibus Hierosolymo ac Iuda
proximas in terras exoneratam', and Tert. *anim*. 30 'sollemnes . . .
migrationes, quas ἀποικίας appellant, consilio exonerandae populari-
tatis in alios fines examina gentis eructant'. This explanation
requires one to believe either that *deducta* (the technical term) was
written as a variant reading or gloss above *exonerata* in **N**, then both
participles were corrupted into the accusative through perseveration
from *quietam*, and an *et* was inserted to expedite the sense; or that,
after *exonerata* was corrupted to *exoneratam*, *et* and *deducta* were
inserted and then *deducta* was corrupted to *deductam*. Also possible is
exonerata et deducta: this gives less taut phrasing than Madvig's conjecture but is diplomatically a little easier.[1] See further vol. i, pp.
316–20 (on doublets of the kind postulated by Madvig's conjecture)
and Winkler (1890–2) ii. 19.

---

[1] H. J. Müller (in W–M) conjectured *ut exoneratam deducta*: changing *et* to *ut* is at first sight
easy, but this is a facile approach to the *crux*.

6. 3–9. 2. *The Ogulnian plebiscite*

Literary analysis. L.'s account of the debate which accompanied the passing of the Ogulnian plebiscite balances his account (vi. 34. 1–42. 14 nn.) of the similar debate which accompanied the passing of the Licinio-Sextian plebiscites: that debate occurs just before the end of book vi, this in an almost symmetrical position just after the beginning of book x; there L. gives a long speech (40. 1–41. 12) to Ap. Claudius Crassus, the leading patrician protagonist, here (7. 3–8. 12) to the plebeian P. Decius Mus; and, by stating (7. 2) that almost the same arguments were used as on the earlier occasion, he encourages a reading of this episode with reference to that in book vi. A comparison of the two episodes makes clear that a final resolution of the religious issues at stake between the patricians and plebeians is now possible: Ap. Claudius Crassus had denied that the gods would tolerate plebeians taking the auspices, but now, by pointing to numerous plebeian successes, Decius is able to answer this challenge (something that would have been impossible for the opponents of Ap. Crassus in 368, when few plebeians had held any significant office); and, quite apart from the examples which Decius adduces, contemplation of L.'s own narrative of events between 366 and 300 shows that he has an unanswerable case. Early in this episode (6. 11) L. states that on this occasion the patricians strove less hard because they had grown used to being defeated in contests of this kind. This comment encourages his readers to concentrate less on the drama of a predictable contest but rather on the long speech of Decius (7. 2–8. 12), which sums up an epoch of Roman history.[1]

    L.'s own attitude to the politics of the episode is characteristically ambiguous. As on other occasions, he criticizes adversely the behaviour of the tribunes of the plebs, stating that they settled on their plebiscite simply because other attempts to cause trouble had failed (6. 3–4); but he was no lover of aristocratic pride, and the speech of Decius is a resounding rebuke to patrician exclusiveness.

    The episode is dominated by the speech of Decius, which provides its emotional core; as so often, its lasting outcome is narrated very swiftly. For these techniques, see vol. i, p. 127.

Historical analysis. The historical kernel of this long episode is L.'s report that the tribunes Q. and Cn. Ogulnius carried a plebiscite which allowed plebeians admission to the pontificate and to the augurate, and that the nine men whom he lists at 9. 2 were made

---

[1] For this interpretation see further Lipovsky (1981) 72–6 and Levene (1993) 233.

pontiffs and augurs. Although the only other reference to this plebiscite is the rather imprecise allusion to it at Lyd. *mag.* i. 45 (part of a list of Roman constitutional developments) καὶ πάλιν ὁ δῆμος προεχειρίσατο πέντε μὲν οἰωνοσκόπους, τέσσαρας δὲ ἱεροφάντας, so many plebeians are attested as pontiffs and augurs in the years after 300 that there is no doubt about the essential correctness of the information which L. supplies, even though he presents the episode with much rhetorical colour.[1] This expansion of the pontificate and the augurate to accommodate the admission of plebeians finds a good parallel in the earlier (368 BC) expansion of the duumvirate into the decemvirate (see below).

The reasons why the plebeian elite wanted access to the pontificate and augurate may readily be conjectured. Although the major Roman priesthoods were much less important than either the annual elective curule magistracies or the dictatorship or the censorship (most obviously, priests did not command armies), nevertheless in a society in which religion and politics were for the most part indivisible they carried much prestige and not inconsiderable power, over both of which ambitious plebeians saw no reason why there should be patrician monopoly, and in which they themselves would wish to share. The patrician monopoly in holding the major priesthoods had been broken even before the passing of the Licinio-Sextian rogations had allowed plebeians access to the consulate: in 368 the *duumuiri sacris faciundis* were increased to a college of ten, made up equally of patricians and plebeians (vi. 42. 1 n.). Yet these priests did not have the importance of the pontiffs and augurs, who wielded far more power than is apparent from the few references to them in L. The power of the pontiffs is revealed in the struggles involving Cn. Flavius (ix. 45. 1–15 n.), that of the augurs in their ability to detect a *uitium* in the auspices which accompanied the election or nomination of a magistrate, or his departure for war, or his holding of a legislative assembly. In plebeian minds there must always have lurked the suspicion that patrician augurs might use this power against them, a suspicion that would only be increased if, as some scholars argue (see *addendum* to vi. 41. 5 n.), augurs now had the right to adjudicate on *auspicia* taken for the *concilium plebis*. L.

---

[1] This is the view of almost all modern scholars: see the very full bibliography at Hölkeskamp (1988a) 52 n. 3. Beloch (1922: 126 and 1926: 349–50) argued that the episode belongs rather to 296, when the Ogulnii were curule aediles, on the ground that, unlike tribunes, curule aediles then had the *ius agendi cum populo*; but it is doubtful if aediles had this power, and there are several earlier instances of tribunes foisting controversial measures on the patricians. For minor difficulties caused by L.'s account of the development of the pontificate and augurate, see 6. 6–8 n.

(viii. 23. 14–17) records such suspicions in 327/6, when the plebeian dictator M. Claudius Marcellus was made to resign on the ground that he was *uitio creatus*; and, although the theme does not reappear in his (or anyone else's) account of events between 326 and 300, that does not mean that there was no plebeian disquiet: we know very little about political life in this period.

That the plebeians waited so long for admission to these priesthoods, when they had had access to all the major magistracies for more than a generation (the consulship since 366, the dictatorship since 356, the censorhip since 351, and the praetorship since 336) reflects the fact that these offices were of less importance than the curule magistracies; but it reflects too the peculiar tenacity with which the patricians justified their exclusive right to mediate between god and man: although Ti. Coruncanius became the first plebeian *pontifex maximus c.*255 (*per.* xviii) and C. Mamilius became the first Curio Maximus in 209 (xxvii. 8. 1–3), a post which he held to his death in 174 (xli. 21. 8), no plebeian was ever a Salian priest, a major *flamen*, or (if Cicero [*dom.* 38] is right) *rex sacrorum.*[1]

There is no reason to doubt that in the political life of Rome the Ogulnian plebiscite was of major importance and caused a major controversy, to which L. was right to devote much space. However, the political crisis seems hardly to have been comparable to those of 367 and 342, when in very different circumstances the Licinio-Sextian and Genucian plebiscites had been passed. Then an alliance of the plebeian elite and the impoverished masses had forced through packages of diverse measures which addressed the grievances of each: economic relief was forthcoming for the masses, and access to political honours for the elite (see above, pp. 10–18 and vol. i, pp. 366–7). By 300 an influx of booty from Rome's successful warfare and the availability of land in Latin colonies had helped to ameliorate the economic deprivations of the poor, and the Ogulnii offered rewards only for the elite.[2] L. (6. 9) states that they stirred up both the masses and the elite and, although he probably had no good evidence for this statement, he is likely to be right (many plebeians

---

[1] However, restrictions on the activity of *flamines* meant that these positions would not have attracted men who wished to command armies. Cicero's statement involves a difficulty: at xxvii. 6. 16 L. records the death of the *rex sacrorum* M. Marcius, and we have no evidence that any of the Marcii were patrician. To reconcile our evidence we must choose between rival arguments: that Cicero's statement should be rejected; or that in the 150 years after the death of Marcius the patricians reasserted their claim to the office; or that Marcius was in fact a patrician. The first is perhaps the least difficult. For discussion and bibliography see Szemler (1972) 174–5.

[2] Rightly stressed by Hölkeskamp (1987: 197).

must have been interested in the political struggle, even if they were not themselves going to become priests); but the state was not threatened with revolutionary change.

It is noteworthy that the plebeians adlected to the more important college of pontiffs had all held the consulship. By contrast, of the men adlected to the augurate, only Marcius (if he is indeed to be equated with Marcius Rutilus) is known to have held curule office;[1] however, all were from families from which at least one man had reached the consulate.

It does not follow from acceptance of the historicity of the Ogulnian plebiscite that all the details of L.'s account are authentic. The alleged opposition of Ap. Claudius Caecus to the measure is viewed by some scholars as part of his opposition to the tenets of the newly emergent patricio-plebeian nobility, but it corresponds so closely to the anti-plebeian Claudian stereotype regular in L. and D.H., that one should have grave doubts about accepting it:[2] for discussion see vol. iii, pp. 370–2. Doubtful too is L.'s statement (9. 1) that the measure was at first thwarted by the intercession of other tribunes:[3] even though as early as the first half of the third century the tribunate had increasingly become part of the political establishment (see above, pp. 16–17), intercession of tribune against tribune (except in support of individuals) is very rare before 133;[4] and here the only conceivable reason, and not a very likely one, that any tribune should have made such an intercession against the wider interests of his class was reliance on the patronage of patrician families opposed to the law. Moreover, such intercession is a regular τόπος of the invented political narratives of L. and D.H. (even before 367, when it is quite unthinkable) and is associated particularly with the patrician Claudii.[5]

As for P. Decius Mus, already twice consul and with C. Junius Bubulcus the leading plebeian of his day, he may have been a passionate supporter of the plebiscite, and the memory of his support for it may have survived until the beginnings of the annalistic tradition; but one cannot be certain that either L. or an annalist, aware of his importance in the forthcoming Third Samnite War and desirous of further enhancing his role in the events of this period, did not invent his part in this episode. Even if Decius did support the Ogulnii, it is

---

[1] Unless P. Aelius Paetus is identical with the consul of 337, which is doubtful: see 9. 2 n.
[2] Thus, rightly, Hölkeskamp (1988a) 63.
[3] Thus, rightly, Hölkeskamp (1987) 142 n. 12 and (1988a) 63–4.
[4] See further vi. 35. 6 n. (where this passage should have been cited).
[5] See vol. iii, p. 359.

singularly unlikely that any precise details of what he said survived to
be used by L. and his annalistic predecessors. Like other speeches in
the extant books of L., the speech of Decius is his own creation; and,
if its arguments seem perceptive and penetrating, that is due more to
the imaginative sympathy of L.'s masterly rhetoric than to the reliability of his sources.[1] Schönberger (1960: 222) has argued that here
the insistence of Decius on plebeian virtue looks forward to his own
crowning act of virtue on the field of Sentinum; he also points out
(p. 220) that it is possible to view Appius and Decius as opposites of
each other: the former controversial and self-seeking, the latter harmonious in his co-operation with his patrician colleagues, especially
Fabius Rullianus. This opposition is found again at 25. 11–26. 7.

See further De Sanctis (1907–64) ii. 223–4, Beloch (1926) 349–51,
Altheim (1938*b*) 280–1, Ferenczy (1976) 191, Develin (1978–9)
11–12, Hölkeskamp (1987) 140–2 and (1988*a*), and Cornell (1989)
398.

3. ne undique tranquillae res essent: for final clauses of this kind,
see vii. 1. 7 n. with *addendum*. For *tranquillae res* see viii. 17. 6 n.
certamen iniectum: for the expression cf. esp. xxvii. 6. 2 'certamine inter tribunos dictatoremque iniecto'; also xxi. 54. 4, xxvi. 36.
11, and xxxiv. 4. 15. Analogous expressions may be found at *TLL* vii.
1. 1614. 41–75.
Q. et Cn. Ogulniis: (5) and (2). Cn. Ogulnius and Q. Ogulnius L. f.
A. n. Gallus (the *cognomen* is given by *F.C.* for 269 and 257 and by
Zonaras, the filiation by *F.C.* for 257) shared office again in 296,
when as curule aediles they conducted prosecutions, carried out
building, and, most famously, placed at the *ficus Ruminalis* a statue of
Romulus and Remus being suckled by the she-wolf (23. 11–12 n.).
The two men were probably brothers. Of Gnaeus we know nothing
more, but Quintus had a notable career: in 292 he was at the head of
the embassy to bring Aesculapius to Rome (see 47. 7 n.); in 273 he
went on an embassy to Ptolemy (D.H. xx. 14. 1, Val. Max. iv. 3. 9);
in 269 he was consul, when he fought against the Samnites (D.H. xx.
17. 1–2 and esp. Zon. viii. 7. 1); and in 257 he was appointed dictator
for the Latin festival (*F.C.*), an appointment appropriate for someone who by then was a very senior statesman indeed. The two
embassies suggest that Quintus was interested in Greek culture; and,
since the *xuiri sacris faciundis* were responsible for introducing

---

[1] The point of view rejected here is stated explicitly by Lübtow (1955: 87): 'Die Argumente
stimmen sichtlich mit der historischen Wahrheit überein und müssen als echt und wertvoll
anerkannt werden'. See also 7. 3 n.

several Greek cults into Rome, Münzer, *RE* xvii. 2064 and (1999) 84, plausibly suggested that he belonged to this college. For further discussion of the career of Q. Ogulnius and of his significance, see e.g. Altheim (1938a) 144–9, Hölkeskamp (1988a) 65, and D'Ippolito (1986) 71–6 and (1988) 157–8. For an overview of the place of the Ogulnii in the politics of the third and second centuries BC, see Briscoe on xxxiii. 36. 5 and esp. Münzer (1999) 81–7; for discussion of Münzer's view that they had a long-term alliance with the Fabii, see vol. iii, p. 673.

4. criminandorum patrum: see vi. 5. 3 n.

5. consulares triumphalesque plebeios: for the coupling of *consularis* and *triumphalis* cf. v. 39. 13 'senes triumphales consularesque', Calp. *decl.* 8, Tac. *ann.* iii. 30. 2 'multos triumphalium consulariumque', and Apul. *apol.* 18. In our passage *consulares triumphalesque* is taken as substantival at *OLD s.u. triumphalis* 2(a) and by Woodman and Martin on Tac. loc. cit. (in which *triumphalium* and *consularium* are certainly substantival); but at v. 39. 13 and Apul. loc. cit. *consularis* and *triumphalis* are adjectives, and therefore it seems more likely that *plebeios* is the substantive here.
promiscua: see vii. 17. 7 n.

6–8. *The proposal to increase the number of augurs and pontiffs.* The information provided by L. about the early history of the augurate and pontificate is difficult and controversial.[1] With regard to the augurate, scholars have debated the correctness of four of L.'s statements: (*a*) that there were originally three augurs, each representing a Romulean tribe; (*b*) that the total number of augurs should always have been divisible by three; (*c*) that the total number of augurs should always have been an odd number; and (*d*) that four augurs were in office prior to the passing of the Ogulnian rogation (L. himself is doubtful about this last statement).

L.'s view that there were originally three augurs, one per Romulean tribe, is supported by Cic. *rep.* ii. 16 'nam et ipse (*sc.* Romulus) . . . urbem condidit auspicato, et omnibus publicis rebus instituendis, qui sibi ⟨ad⟩essent in auspiciis, ex singulis tribubus singulos cooptauit augures' and D.H. ii. 22. 3 (where Romulus decrees that there should be three *haruspices*, or rather augurs, at public sacrifices,

---

[1] The fullest discussion of these difficulties is that of Hölkeskamp (1988a), with whom I am in agreement on all significant matters. Other discussions are cited in the footnotes that follow.

one from each tribe).[1] Both Cicero and D.H. state that Romulus founded the augurate; L. does not actually do this, although it is a possible deduction from § 7 that this was his view.[2] Furthermore, although L.'s doubts about the evidence which he reports makes it impossible for us to know for certain what was the official complement of augurs in 300, the first two republican expansions about which we are informed led to a total divisible by three: after the passing of the Ogulnian rogation the college was expanded to nine; after the reform of Sulla (for which see *per*. lxxxix) the colleges of both pontiffs and augurs were enlarged to fifteen.[3] Further support comes from *lex col. Gen.* (Crawford [1996] i. 402, no. 25) § 67, where three augurs and three pontiffs are prescribed for the colony: Roman colonies seem to have retained some primitive features of the Roman constitution. This evidence shows beyond any reasonable doubt that several (perhaps even most) ancient antiquarians shared L.'s views on the original composition of the augurate. And, with the proviso that much of what our sources tell us about the Romulean tribes is an antiquarian construct,[4] it is quite tempting to follow those modern scholars who accept these views.[5]

However, four texts provide discrepant evidence. In the case of two the discrepancy is not serious. According to L.'s Canuleius (iv. 4. 2) 'pontifices augures Romulo regnante nulli erant; ab Numa Pompilio creati sunt'; but, although this reflects a tradition that the augurate, like several other religious institutions, was established by Numa rather than by Romulus, it does not contradict the view that augurs were originally three in number. According to Cicero (*leg. agr.* ii. 96) Rullus proposed in 63 BC that his colony at Capua should have ten augurs: but by 63 many traditional republican rules were being violated, and Capua was not Rome.

More serious difficulties are posed by Cic. *rep.* ii. 26 (on Numa)

---

[1] Note also the analogous view that the vestal virgins were recruited on the basis of two *per* Romulean tribe: see Fest. 468 (quoted below, p. 93).

[2] But see below for a discrepant view that he expresses in book iv. Holzapfel (1902: 239) and Wissowa (*RE* ii. 2316) argued that augury at least must have been as old as the Roman state, citing passages such as i. 18. 6 'sicut Romulus augurato urbe condenda regnum adeptus est' and the famous account of the augury of Romulus at Enn. *ann.* 72–91. This may well be correct, but it passes belief that passages of this kind rest on any secure testimony.

[3] The increase in both colleges to sixteen under Caesar (Dio xlii. 51. 4) is easily viewed as an aberrant Caesarian innovation.

[4] For further discussion of the Romulean tribes see § 7 n.

[5] They include Marquardt (1881–5: iii. 241, 398–9), Wissowa, *RE* ii. 2316–17, and Hölkeskamp (1988a) *passim*. Following the work of older scholars on early Roman legends and rituals, Hölkeskamp argues (pp. 54–7) that the number three and its multiples had a special significance for the Romans (he adduces many examples: note e.g. the thirty *curiae*, the three *flamines maiores*, and the late establishment of *iiiuiri epulones*); there may be some truth in this.

'idemque Pompilius et auspiciis maioribus inuentis ad pristinum numerum duo augures addidit, et sacris e principum numero pontifices quinque praefecit', and by L.'s statement ([c] above) that there were four augurs at the time of the passing of the Ogulnian rogation. Cicero's testimony about Numa may be harmonized by arguing that, if the king is added to the number of five augurs, then there would be six augurs, a total divisible by three.[1] This argument is vulnerable to the objection that, if one applies the same logic to the reign of Romulus one would have a total of four augurs.[2] This in turn would mean abandoning the view that the total number of augurs should always have been divisible by three. Nevertheless, it is quite an attractive explanation of the text and allows the view that from regal times until 300 the complement of augurs was six.

Wissowa resolved the difficulties of our passage by holding that the notion that five augurs were added in 300 was 'eine willkürliche Annahme', but since the names of the new plebeian augurs which L. gives at 9. 2 are all quite acceptable (see nn. ad loc.), it is hard to believe that they are invented; and since they are five in number, it is hard to avoid the conclusion that there were four existing patrician augurs. It is better to accept L.'s view that in 300 death had reduced the number of augurs to four from their official complement of six.

Those who are not satisfied by these explanations may follow Valeton (1891: 410) in abandoning the view that the total number of augurs was divisible by three (one could argue that it was a false antiquarian construct) and replacing it with one in which there was an enlargement from four to nine in 300 and then to fifteen under Sulla.[3] With such defective evidence it is unwise to be dogmatic, but I prefer to accept L.'s explanation.

With regard to the pontificate scholars have debated whether L. is correct to state that prior to the passing of the rogation there were four pontiffs in office, and that after its passing there were eight. The only source to refer to the number of pontiffs in office before the Ogulnian rogation is Cic. *rep.* ii. 26 (quoted above), where the number given is five. This may reflect a sound tradition about the regal period, and L. may be right that there were only four pontiffs

---

[1] For this argument see e.g. Marquardt (1881–5: iii. 241) and Mommsen (1887–8: ii. 21 n. 6).

[2] This was pointed out by Holzapfel (1902: 239). Since both Romulus and Numa were figures of myth, this may not seem to matter; but, if Romulus too was to be counted as an augur, and the total number of augurs had to be divisible by three, then the makers of these antiquarian constructs were rather careless.

[3] Bleicken (1957: 363–4), mainly concerned with the history of the pontificate, also argues that the normal complement of augurs was only four before the passing of the Ogulnian rogation.

prior to the passing of the Ogulnian rogation,[1] but the decrease in number would be surprising. Another difficulty is that for the period covered by books xxi–xlv, that is 218–167 BC, Bardt (1871: 8–17) established that the complement of pontiffs was nine—four patricians and five plebeians. Therefore, if L. is right that the total after the passing of the rogation was eight (four patricians, four plebeians),[2] at some point between 300 and 218 the college must have been enlarged by the adlection of an extra plebeian: a motive for this reform would be provided by the desire to bring the composition of the pontificate in line with that of the augurate.[3] However, if such harmonization had not already happened, one might have expected it to occur at the time of the major reform of the Ogulnii. Therefore, even though it involves postulating a mistake on L.'s part, several scholars have argued that there were in fact nine pontiffs after the passing of the Ogulnian plebiscite.[4]

Among them are those who, noting that three is the number of pontiffs prescribed in *lex col. Gen.* loc. cit., that according to Cicero (*agr.* ii. 96) Rullus proposed a colony at Capua with six pontiffs, and that there were nine priests in 218 and afterwards, go further and argue that the total complement of pontiffs was parallel in size to that of the augurs and always divisible by three; that the evidence of Cic. *rep.* ii. 26 is compatible with this view if the king himself made a sixth pontiff;[5] and that there were six and not four pontiffs before the

[1] On this point alone Bleicken (1957: 364) agrees with L.

[2] L.'s view is accepted by e.g. Münzer, *RE* xvii. 2065.

[3] Mommsen (1887–8: ii. 22 n. 1) considered this possibility; see also Herzog (1884–91) i. 279 n. 1 and De Martino (1972–90) i. 386.

[4] In addition to those whose views are discussed in the next paragraph, these scholars include Herzog (1884–91: i. 279 n. 1) (as an alternative to the argument noted above), A. Bouché-Leclercq, in Daremberg and Saglio vii. 1. 567, De Sanctis (1907–64: ii. 223), and Bleicken (1957: 363–4). De Sanctis argued that there were five patrician pontiffs before the passing of the Ogulnian plebiscite and four new plebeians after it, and that at some point between 300 and 218, on the death of a patrician pontiff, a law was passed that a fifth plebeian should be co-opted. Bleicken argues that five plebeian pontiffs were adlected in 300. If he were right, the mistaken view that only four plebeians were adlected, found also at Lyd. *mag.* i. 45 (quoted above), must have occurred at some earlier point in the annalistic tradition: quite apart from the evidence of Lydus, the fact that L.'s text mentions the adlection of four new pontiffs and later gives four names, shows that he himself is hardly likely to have been responsible for a mistake of this kind. Bleicken also argued that the term *pontifex minor* (*fast. Praen.* for 1 January [*I.I.* xiii. 2, pp. 110–11], Fest. 160, Macrob. *Sat.* i. 15. 9–19) shows that originally there were two pontiffs and that the number had been doubled by 300; but there may well have been more than one *pontifex minor* (see xxii. 57. 3, Cic. *har.* 12, passages which Bleicken does not satisfactorily explain away), and Bleicken has to reject Cicero's statement (*rep.* ii. 26) that Numa established five pontiffs. For a fuller refutation of Bleicken's views, which are accepted in part by Szemler, *RE* Suppl. xv. 341, see Hölkeskamp (1988a) 53–4.

[5] For the king as pontiff see Zosim. iv. 36. 3–5 (admittedly not a text of much authority on republican matters).

passing of the Ogulnian plebiscite.[1] Any such argument involves postulating a mistake of some kind on L.'s part, but one may mitigate it by suggesting that before the rogation was passed the college of pontiffs had an official complement of six and that L. and his sources ignored either two vacancies[2] or one vacancy and the *pontifex maximus*, who would make a sixth member of the college before 300 and a ninth after 300.[3] The second alternative also allows the later plebeian majority in the pontificate to be explained: it occurred at the time of the election of the first plebeian *pontifex maximus*, Ti. Coruncanius. That it need not involve special pleading to argue that simultaneously there were vacancies in the pontificate and augurate is shown by the occurrence of similar vacancies after Cannae and in 213, 211, 203, 196, 180, 174, and 170;[4] as Hölkeskamp observes, the existence of vacancies among both the augurs and the pontiffs may have suggested to the Ogulnii that the time was ripe for the promulgation of their rogation. I incline to accept this approach, as it has the merit of harmonizing the numbers of pontiffs and augurs, just as they are harmonized at Cic. *rep*. ii. 26.

6. cum . . . numerum: L.'s phrasing implies that even before the Ogulnii made their proposal a decision had been taken to increase the number of augurs and pontiffs. This may accurately reflect the events of 300.

ea tempestate: see vii. 26. 15 n.

7. tres antiquae tribus, Ramnes, Titienses, Luceres: almost all that our sources tell us about the so-called Romulean tribes is based on antiquarian speculation rather than good evidence that survived from regal times to the historical period.

That the Ramnes or Ramnenses were named after Romulus and the Titienses after Tatius was generally believed (see i. 13. 8, Enn. *ann*. i. fr. lix, *ap*. Varr. *ling*. v. 55 [quoted below], Cic. *rep*. ii. 14, *uir. ill*. 2. 11), but there was much diverse speculation about the etymology of the name Luceres. L. himself (i. 13. 8) ventures no opinion; Cicero, Junius (*ap*. Varr. *ling*. v. 55), Varro himself (*ap*. Serv. *Aen*. v. 560), Ps.-Ascon. (p. 227) (in his first version) and *Σ* Pers. 1. 20 (in his first version) derive it from Lucumo, whom Cicero describes as 'qui

---

[1] For a strong statement of this view see Marquardt (1881–5: iii. 241–4).
[2] For this view see e.g. Mommsen (1887–8) ii. 21 n. 6 and Siber, *RE* xxi. 156.
[3] For this view see Latte (1960a) 197 and Hölkeskamp (1988a) 59.
[4] For this point and the full evidence, see Hölkeskamp (1988a) 61.

Romuli socius in Sabino proelio occiderat'; Plutarch (*Rom*. 20. 2), the author of the *de uiris illustribus* (2. 11), [Ascon.] 227 (in his third version) and (in his other version) Σ Pers. 1. 20 from *lucus*; and Paulus (Fest. p. 106) 'a Lucero, Ardeae rege, qui auxilio fuit Romulo aduersus Tatium bellanti', also recorded as the second derivation at [Ascon.] 227. The names are listed in the order found here also at i. 13. 8, 36. 2, Cic. *rep*. ii. 14, and *uir. ill*. 2. 11 but in the order Titie(nse)s, Ramne(nse)s, and Luceres in all the passages of Varro cited in this note and at Cic. *rep*. ii. 36, Prop. iv. 1. 31, Fest. 468 and 484, and [Ascon.] 227. This second order is likely to have been official and inherited: the Ramne(nse)s were probably put first after someone decided that Romulus had to take precedence over T. Tatius.

D.H. (ii. 7. 2–3) held that the tribes were organized by Romulus immediately after he had established his kingdom, Paulus (Fest. 106) together with his later co-regent T. Tatius, Cicero (*rep*. ii. 14) after the death of Tatius. Cicero and D.H. state that at the same time Romulus established the curiate organization, dividing each tribe into ten *curiae*. For those ancients who accepted the etymology of the Titie(nse)s from T. Tatius, and who thought that some *curiae* were named after raped Sabine women (ix. 38. 15 n.), D.H.'s view was obviously impossible. That this tribal organization was based on a division of land was stated by D.H. and also by Varro (*ling*. v. 55 'ager Romanus primum diuisus in partis tres, a quo tribus appellata Titiensium, Ramnium, Lucerum. nominatae, ut ait Ennius [*ann*. i, fr. lix], Titienses ab Tatio, Ramnenses ab Romulo, Luceres, ut ait Iunius ab Lucumone; sed omnia haec uocabula Tusca, ut Volnius, qui tragoedias Tuscas scripsit, dicebat'); elsewhere (iv. 14. 2) D.H. refers to the tribes' being γενικαί. Varro (*ling*. v. 81 and 89) explains the expressions *tribuni militum* and *miles* by stating that each *tribus* supplied one tribune and a thousand (*mille*) men to an original legion of three thousand. According to L. in our passage and to Fest. 468 (taken over almost verbatim at Paul. Fest. 475) 'SEX VESTAE SACERDOTES constitutae erant, ut populus pro sua quaque parte haberet ministram sacrorum, quia ciuitas Romana in sex est distributa partes: in primos secundosque Titienses, Ramnes, Luceres', in the early Republic augurs and vestal virgins, respectively, were recruited on the basis of two per Romulean tribe.[1]

This is in fact L.'s first reference to the tribes. In his account of

---

[1] However, this evidence on the vestals is not easy to square with another antiquarian view, that Servius Tullius or Tarquinius Priscus added two extra priestesses to the existing four established by Numa (see D.H. ii. 67. 1, iii. 67. 2, Plut. *Numa* 10. 1); for discussion see e.g. Holzapfel (1902) 240.

Romulus himself he mentions their names, but only in the context of the equestrian centuries (i. 13. 8); and at i. 36. 2–7 he comments that Tarquinius Priscus, wishing to add to the strength of Rome's cavalry but prevented by the augur Attus Navius from adding any extra centuries or changing the names of the centuries, instead doubled the size of these centuries (§ 7) '. . . ut mille et octingenti equites in tribus centuriis essent. posteriores modo sub iisdem nominibus qui additi erant appellati sunt; quas nunc quia geminatae sunt sex uocant centurias'.[1] Likewise at *uir. ill.* 2. 11 the names refer only to the centuries and the tribes are not mentioned. This threefold division of the cavalry is reflected in Virgil's account of the *lusus Troiae* (*Aen.* v. 551–74; see also Serv. *Aen.* v. 560). The link between the centuries and the tribes, implicit in L., is made explicit at Fest. 484 'TURMAM equitum dictam esse ait Curiatius quasi terimam, quod ter deni equites ex tribus tribubus Titiensium, Ramnium, Lucerum fiebant'.

The only certain fact about these tribes is that in the middle and late Republic the names Ramne(nse)s, Titie(nse)s, and Luceres were still used of six of the eighteen equestrian centuries in the *comitia centuriata*: see i. 43. 9 'sex item alias centurias, tribus ab Romulis institutis, sub iisdem quibus inauguratae erant nominibus fecit' (referring back to the increase in number under Tarquinius Priscus which L. had just mentioned in the passage cited above) and the references to the *sex suffragia* (*uel sim.*) at Cic. *rep.* ii. 39 and Fest. 452.[2] However, it is reasonable to postulate that these names were inherited from the regal period and that the appearance of the number six as a significant number in the organization of the cavalry, vestals, and augurs reflects a sixfold division of the Roman state towards the end of the regal period. It is a little bolder, but still quite reasonable, to argue that our sources are right to hold that this number of six was reached by dividing three earlier tribes and that Rome was once divided into three tribes and thirty *curiae* (for the vestigial role of the *curiae* in the Republic, see ix. 38. 15 n.).[3] However, none of these further inferences is certain: the whole notion of three tribes may be merely an antiquarian construct, perhaps based on the names of the equestrian centuries.[4] Since Romulus

---

[1] For this tale see also Cic. *rep.* ii. 36, D.H. iii. 71. 1–5, Val. Max. i. 4. 1 (dependent on L.), Fest. 168–70, *uir. ill.* 6. 7, Zon. vii. 8. 8–10.

[2] For succinct discussion of the place of these six centuries in the constitution see conveniently Momigliano (1966*b*: 17–18) = (1969) 379–82.

[3] For the pattern of division by three in Rome's early institutions, see above, p. 89.

[4] For a clear statement of this view, see Poucet (1967) 361, 371, 405, and *passim*.

himself is a mythological and antiquarian construct, the alleged connection of the tribal organization with him must be bogus, reflecting the not uncommon tendency among ancient states to ascribe as much as possible of their constitutions to mythical founders. The commonly accepted etymologies of the Ramnes and Titienses may therefore be dismissed, and it is apparent that the ancients had no idea why the Luceres were so called; Volnius (*ap.* Varr. *ling.* v. 55, cited above), followed by e.g. Ogilvie, held that all three names were Etruscan.

For further discussion see Ogilvie on i. 13. 6–8, to whose bibliography add e.g. Holzapfel (1902), Momigliano (1963) 108–9 = (1966*a*) 572–3 = (1989*b*) 93–4 and (1984) 427 = (1989*a*) 104–5 = (1989*b*) 41–2, Poucet (1967) 333–410 (a very full treatment), Skutsch (1985) 252–3, and Cornell (1995) 114–15.

8. pari: 'equal', even though in § 7 *imparem* means 'odd'.

9. iuxta . . . quam . . .: strictly illogical comparative clauses introduced by *quam* are quite common in Latin, and depend on a variety of expressions (see K–S ii. 460 and H–S 593). However, this use of *iuxta* is rare: the only parallel cited for it at *TLL* vii. 2. 749. 37–9 is Front. 189. 13–14 'existimationi tuae famaeque iuxta quam meae consultum'; in using it L. and Fronto were perhaps influenced by analogous constructions with *citra*, *extra*, *supra*, and *ultra*, but with these the comparative clause is rather more logical.
uolgari: for *uolgare* in the context of the admission of plebeians to a patrician prerogative, cf. iv. 1. 3. For the use of the verb in a religious context, cf. 23. 10.

10. simulabant . . . clades ueniat: in his account of 362 L. (vii. 6. 10–11) had made the patricians claim that the defeat of L. Genucius was due to gods vindicating their own auspices.

11. minus autem tetendere, adsueti in tali genere certaminum uinci: for the idea that the patricians had no real stomach for the fight, cf. iv. 5. 4 (Canuleius speaking) 'nec nunc erit certamen, Quirites; animos uestros illi temptabunt semper, uires non experientur'.
et cernebant aduersarios non, id quod olim uix sperauerint, adfectantes magnos honores sed omnia in quorum spem dubiam erat certatum adeptos, multiplices consulatus censurasque et triumphos: the comma after *non* is due to Madvig

(1860: 189 = 1877: 224–5), who well remarked: 'pondus orationis est in *adfectantes*. Olim plebeii vix adfectare se honores, hoc est petere posse, speraverant; tunc iam adepti erant'; previously editors had placed the comma after *id*. Perthes (1863: 30–2) objected without cogency that readers would naturally take *id* with *non* and held that one should rather delete *id quod olim uix sperauerint* as a gloss on *omnia . . . certatum*. One may grant that the repetition *sperauerint . . . spem* does not display L.'s writing at its most elegant, but it is hard to see why anyone should have wished to pen a gloss of this kind, and there is a good parallel at xliv. 27. 3 'quod uix sperauerat ipse posse contingere'. For *sperauerint* Madvig, *ap.* Madvig and Ussing, conjectured *sperauerant*, but in support of the paradosis W–M compared vii. 4. 4, and L. often uses primary subjunctives in passages where they are illogical; see Conway (1901) 187–97. *certatum* is the reading of M; after Πλ add *tamen*, which would have to mean 'had acquired them all the same despite the struggle to stop them' but doubtless intruded from 7. 1 'certatum tamen'. For M alone in the truth, see vol. i, pp. 321–4.

According to *TLL* iii. 896. 36–42 L. was the first author to use *certare* with *in* and the accusative; other early instances include 19. 5, iv. 4. 12, Prop. iii. 1. 13, and Sen. *contr.* ii. 7. 1. For *multiplices consulatus censurasque et triumphos* cf. Vell. ii. 127. 1 'M. Agrippa et . . . Statilio Tauro, quibus nouitas familiae haud obstitit quominus ad multiplices consulatus triumphosque et complura eueherentur sacerdotia'.

7. 1. suadenda dissuadendaque lege: see vi. 36. 7 n.
inter Ap. Claudium . . . et inter P. Decium: the repetition of *inter* is illogical and found only here in L. It is not uncommon, however, in Cicero (e.g. *leg. agr.* ii. 89 and *Lael.* 95 'quid inter popularem . . . et inter constantem'), and there are a few examples elsewhere (e.g. Hor. *serm.* i. 7. 11–13 and Prop. ii. 31. 15–16 'deinde inter matrem deus ipse interque sororem | . . . sonat'). See further K–S i. 580, H–S 217, and *TLL* vii. 1. 2147. 75–2148. 3.

For Ap. Claudius see ix. 29. 5–11 (introductory note), for P. Decius Mus ix. 29. 3 n.
ferunt suggests that L. found an account of this debate in at least some of his sources.

2. cum . . . disseruissent: for the debate on the *leges Liciniae Sextiae* see vi. 34. 1–42. 14 nn.

7. 3–8. 12. *The speech of Decius Mus.* The most notable feature of this speech is that it begins in *oratio obliqua* but then at 7. 9 moves into *oratio recta*; for this technique see vol. i, p. 119. Ullmann (1927: 79–80) analysed it as follows:

7. 3–5 *prooemium: principium a nostra persona*
    7. 6–8. 12 *tractatio*
        (*a*) 7. 6–8 *religiosum*
        (*b*) 7. 9–12 *dignum*
        (*c*) 8. 1–4 *iustum*
        (*d*) 8. 5–8 *ciuile*
        (*e*) 8. 9–11 *aequum*
    8. 12 *conclusio.*

Although the divisions suggested at 7. 9 (the point at which Decius turns to direct speech), 7. 12, and 8. 11 are just, elsewhere L.'s transitions are (as so often) less rigid and more subtle than Ullman allows.

3–7. In these sections Decius varies his focus between public and private, and between himself and his father. In §§ 3–4 he claims that his father seemed *purus piusque* to the gods and as acceptable a consul for devotion as T. Manlius, his patrician colleague. Since this Decius was able to make public sacrifices on behalf of the Roman people (§ 5 'eundem ... faceret'), it was absurd to say that he could not have been co-opted correctly (*rite*) into a priesthood. Decius then considers himself (§ 5 'suas', 'se'), and argues that it was wrong to think either that the gods found the prayers of Ap. Claudius more effective than his own or that Appius was more pious in private than he. This argument has particular point to L.'s readers, who have already been told that in changing the rituals at the Ara Maxima Appius had committed a notable instance of impiety (see ix. 29. 9–11 [n.]). Decius then turns (§§ 6–7) to a general consideration of all those plebeian commanders who had made public prayers on behalf of the state.

3. rettulisse parentis sui speciem: 'recalled [see *OLD s.u. refero* 18–19] the appearance [or 'spectacle'] [see *OLD s.u. species* 1, 3–4] of his father'. For *speciem referre* cf. Apul. *met.* xi. 3. 3 'eius mirandam speciem ad uos etiam referre conitar'. Since Decius will die at Sentinum emulating the death of his father (see esp. 28. 12–15, 30. 9), it is hardly surprising that here and later at 13. 13 L. keeps his father in the minds of readers. See further Schönberger (1960) 222.
qualem eum multi qui in contione erant uiderant: since the elder Decius Mus died in 340 and this *contio* allegedly takes place thirty-six years later in 300, *multi* could refer only to a minority of

those present—but it would be a mistake to imagine that L. had any good evidence that Decius really spoke words such as these.

incinctum Gabino cultu: see viii. 9. 9 n.

super telum stantem: see viii. 9. 5 n.

pro populo Romano ac legionibus Romanis: see viii. 9. 8 n.

T. Manlius collega eius: the famous Torquatus, a patrician, for whom see vii. 4. 4 n.

5. id esse periculum ne: see ix. 17. 15 n.

minus audirent: Gemoll (1890–8: ii. 16) compared Hor. *carm.* i. 2. 27–8 'minus audientem | carmina Vestam'.

castius . . . religiosius: see vii. 20. 4 n.

6–7. paenitere . . . paenitere: see vi. 37. 9 n.

6. uotorum quae pro re publica nuncupauerint: when a Roman magistrate set out for war, he went first to the Capitol where he took the auspices and made vows to Jupiter; then, having put on his *paludamentum* (for which see ix. 5. 13–14 [n.]), he made his ritual crossing of the *pomerium*, escorted by the crowd (see vii. 30. 21 [n.]). The regular expression for the taking of these vows was *uota nuncupare*. L. refers often to this process, especially in his later books, several times using the formulaic ablative absolute *uotis nuncupatis*: for a full description of it see esp. xlii. 49. 1–2 'per hos forte dies P. Licinius consul, uotis in Capitolio nuncupatis, paludatus ab urbe profectus est. semper quidem ea res cum magna dignitate ac maiestate †quaeritur†; praecipue conuertit oculos animosque cum ad magnum nobilemque aut uirtute aut fortuna hostem euntem consulem prosequuntur. contrahit enim non officii modo cura sed etiam studium spectaculi, ut uideant ducem suum, cuius imperio consilioque summam rem publicam tuendam permiserunt'; also iv. 32. 8, xxxi. 14. 1, xli. 10. 7, 11, 13, 27. 3, xlv. 39. 11 (twice), and Caes. *ciu.* i. 6. 6. At xxi. 63. 7 and 9 and xli. 10. 5 L. refers to the avoidance of these rituals; at *Phil.* iii. 11 Cicero refers to their perversion. At vii. 40. 4 L. makes Valerius Corvus say something about the actual content of the vows which he made when he set out to confront rebel Roman soldiers: 'deos . . . immortales, milites, uestros publicos meosque ab urbe proficiscens ita adoraui ueniamque supplex poposci ut mihi de uobis concordiae partae gloriam non uictoriam darent'. See further Marshall (1984) 121–3 and Bell (1997) 12.

7. numerarentur . . . coeptae sint; numerarentur triumphi: these two clauses are each equivalent to the protasis of a conditional clause; for the construction see vi. 18. 7 n. (where this passage should have been cited).

numerarentur triumphi: counting triumphs recorded by L. and others after the beginning of book vii (the date at which he records the admission of plebeians to the consulship), one finds about fifteen celebrated by patricians and about fourteen celebrated by plebeians. These figures must be qualified with 'about', because L. admits that he was not certain about the identity of some *triumphatores*. For the names of all known *triumphatores* in this period, and a comparison of L.'s evidence with that of *F.T.* and other sources, see *addendum* to vol. i, pp. 55–6.

ductu et auspicio: see viii. 31. 1 n. (where this passage should have been cited).

res geri coeptae sint: *sint* is Duker's conjecture for **N**'s *sunt*; the *oratio obliqua* requires a subjunctive, and L. often affects primary subjunctives in contexts in which Cicero would have preferred a historic. At first sight it is a little surprising that L. did not write just *res gestae sint* (the other instance [xxviii. 33. 5] of *rem gerere* after *coepi* listed at *TLL* iii. 1426. 66–7 is not at all similar). However, he has just referred to the vows taken by magistrates when they depart for war, and here he continues this train of thought by implying that wars under the plebeians were begun with favourable auspices; then he turns from the beginning of wars to their end, and refers to plebeian triumphs.

iam ne nobilitatis quidem suae plebeios paenitere: this statement is rendered somewhat enigmatic by two ambiguities: *plebeios* could refer either to the plebeians as a whole or merely to those who had gained nobility; and *paenitere* with a negative could mean either 'not regret' (of an action) or 'be satisfied'. The context, however, makes it hard to believe that *plebeios* refers to plebeian nobles: they would hardly regret their own elevation, and, once ennobled, there was no more of *nobilitas* to be sought. It is less clear whether one should translate 'now the plebeians were satisfied with their nobility' (with the implication that what they desired was admission to the priesthoods) or 'now the plebeians did not regret their own nobility' (with the implication that no longer did the plebeians feel embarrassed by their leaders). The latter is probably to be preferred, as allowing a pointed recall of disasters such as that described at vii. 6. 7–12. For the term *nobilitas* see vi. 37. 11 n.

8. repens bellum: for this expression cf. [x] iv. 14. 2 (the expression *repentinum bellum* seems never to be found).

9–12. Decius argues that it is ridiculous to say that those who had held curule office and triumphed should not be allowed to perform the duties of priests and augurs. For general treatments of the rituals of the Roman triumph, to several of which Decius here refers, see e.g. Marquardt (1881–5) ii. 582–90, Ehlers, *RE* viiA. 493–511, Warren (1970), Versnel (1970), and Weinstock (1971) 64–79. L. devotes most space to these rituals in the speech which he gives M. Servilius Geminus at xlv. 37. 1–39. 20.

9. If **eos uiros** is sound, as it may be, then it is the subject of *pontificalia atque auguralia insignia adicere*, and we should translate 'that those men, whom you have honoured with curule chairs [etc.] . . ., whose houses you have made stand out among others with the spoils of the enemy nailed to them, add the emblems of the priest-hood and augurship (*sc.* to the emblems which they have gained from the honours that you have already given to them)'. However, although *adicere* is found twice elsewhere in this context (see below), there seems to be no precise parallel to the formulation found in the mss (Tac. *Agr.* 9. 6 is closest). Therefore, Walters may have been right to commend *eis uiris*, found in three of the four witnesses to χ (not Esc. R. I 4), which (despite the need to supply *uos* from the relative clause as subject of the main clause) would give an easier sequence of thought; translate: 'that *to* those men, whom you have honoured with curule chairs [etc.] . . ., whose houses you have made stand out among others with the spoils of the enemy nailed to them, ⟨you⟩ add the emblems of the priesthood and augurship'.

sellis curulibus, toga praetexta: for the coupling together of the curule chair and the *toga praetexta*, usually as symbols of office, cf. i. 8. 3, ii. 54. 4 'fasces, praetextam, curulemque sellam', vii. 1. 5 'tres patricios magistratus curulibus sellis praetextatos', xxvii. 8. 8, xxxi. 11. 11 (as explained by e.g. Briscoe ad loc.), and Cic. *IIVerr.* v. 36, *Cluent.* 154, Plin. *pan.* 59. 2, Flor. i. 7(13). 10, and (perhaps) Flor. i. 1(5). 6. For the curule chair, the official seat of kings, the annual magistrates, dictators, censors, and *flamines* see vol. i, pp. 479 with *addendum* and 528. The *toga praetexta*, which was white with a purple stripe, was worn by local as well as Roman magistrates; L. uses it here with reference to curule magistracies (for which see e.g. Ov. *Pont.* iv. 9. 42 'praetextam fasces aspiciamque tuos', Vell. ii. 65. 3 'uidit hic annus Ventidium . . . consularem praetextam iungentem praetoriae'). See further Mommsen (1887–8) i. 418–23.

tunica palmata et toga picta et corona triumphali laureaque: all refer to the garb of the *triumphator*, to which L. turns after mentioning the symbols of curule office. Walters places a comma after *palmata*, which obscures this point. It also obscures the fact that *tunica palmata* and *toga picta* are regularly coupled: see e.g. xxx. 15. 11, Flor. i. 1(5). 6, *SHA* xx. 4. 4 (quoted below), xxiii. 8. 5, and xxvi. 13. 3 (and note too the coupling of *tunica palmata* and *toga purpurea* at xxxi. 11. 11). That they were the clothes of *triumphatores* (and hence could be used as symbols of a triumph) is plain from our passage and Flor. loc. cit., and from passages in which they are mentioned individually in the context of triumphs (for the *tunica palmata* cf. e.g. Serv. *ecl.* 10. 27 [quoted below]; for the *toga picta* cf. e.g. Luc. ix. 177, Juv. 10. 38–9, Front. p. 15. 11, App. *Lib.* 66. 297; also Suet. *Nero* 25. 1 and Dio lxiii. 20. 3). In the Principate the terminology became less precise, and there are several references to the *toga palmata* (see e.g. Mart. vii. 2. 8, Apul. *apol.* 22 [both in the context of triumphs], and Ehlers, *RE* viiA. 505). The actual appearance of the *toga picta* and *tunica palmata* are discussed at Fest. 228. 18–25 (a rather obscure passage) 'picta quae nunc toga dicitur, purpurea ante uocitata est, eaque erat sine pictura. eius rei argumentum est ⟨. . .⟩ pictum in aede Vertumni, et Consi, quarum in altera M. Fuluius Flaccus, in altera L. (T. *codd.*) Papirius Cursor triumphantes ita picti sunt. tunica autem palmata a latitudine clauorum dicebatur, quae nunc a genere picturae appellatur.'

Although worn in the Republic only for triumphs and the games (see Tert. *cor.* 13, quoted and discussed below), the Romans believed that earlier these clothes had been the peculiar adornment of their kings (see e.g. D.H. iii. 61. 1, 62. 1, iv. 74. 1, vi. 95. 4, and the other passages cited by Mommsen [1887–8] i. 411 n. 2); their presentation to foreign rulers (xxx. 15. 11, xxxi. 11. 11, Tac. *ann.* iv. 26. 2) was a sign that the Romans recognized them as kings (see e.g. Versnel [1970] 64, 74, 76–7 and Warren [1970] 59).

One may also argue that the *triumphator* was dressed in the clothes of Jupiter himself. Prime evidence for this view comes from § 10 'Iouis Optimi Maximi ornatu', with which cf. Juv. x. 38 'tunica Iouis' (referring to the games rather than a triumph, but we have seen that the same clothes were worn by the magistrate presiding at the games), Serv. *ecl.* x. 27 'aether autem est Iuppiter. unde etiam triumphantes, qui habent omnia Iouis insignia, sceptrum, palmatam —unde ait Iuuenalis "in tunica Iouis"—faciem quoque de rubrica inlinunt instar coloris aetherii' and, perhaps, Suet. *Aug.* 94. 6 (in a dream Augustus appears to his father 'cum fulmine et sceptro exuuiisque Iouis Optimi Maximi ac radiata corona, super laureatum currum'). At least before the late principate, new garb seems not to have been made for each individual *triumphator* but rather existing garb was brought out from the temple of Jupiter on the Capitol,[1] a fact which reinforces the idea that these clothes were in some way the property of Jupiter: see Tert. *cor.* 13 'hoc uocabulum (*sc.* Etruscarum) est coronarum, quas gemmis et foliis ex auro quercinis ab Ioue insignes ad deducendas tensas cum palmatis togis sumunt' (the text of this passage is disputed, but it is certain that Tertullian refers to Jupiter and to the games [note *tensas*], and very likely that he refers to the removal of a crown of oak-leaves made of gold from the head of the cult statue), *SHA* xviii. 40. 8 'praetextam et pictam togam numquam nisi consul accepit, et eam quidem quam de Iouis templo sumptam alii quoque accipiebant aut praetores aut consules', xx. 4. 4 'palmatam tunicam et togam pictam primus Romanorum priuatus suam propriam habuit, cum ante imperatores etiam uel de Capitolio acciperent uel de Palatio', xxviii. 7. 4–5 (where the author states that *te manet Capitolina palmata* [i.e. the *tunica palmata* taken from the Capitoline temple] was a regular address to new consuls; if he is right, then this formula will have been inherited from the Republic, when consuls were able to celebrate triumphs).[2] Note too that the face of the *triumphator* was painted red like the cult statue of Capitoline Jupiter: see Plin. *nat.* xxxiii. 111–12, xxxv. 157, Plut. *quaest. Rom.* 98 = *mor.* 287d, Serv. loc. cit., Serv. *auct. ecl.* 6. 22 'quod robeus color deorum sit: unde et triumphantes facie miniata, et in Capitolio Iuppiter in quadrigis miniatus', Isid. *orig.* xviii. 2. 6, and Tzetz. *epist.* 97 and *chil.* 13. 37–8.[3]

The view that the *triumphator* represented Jupiter has been argued fully by Versnel (1970: 56–93), who cites eighteen previous scholars who had accepted it. Objections to it have been made by e.g. Warde Fowler (1916), Reid (1916) 177–82, and Deubner (1934). Their most important argument, that the *triumphator* is nowhere explicitly described as the impersonation of Jupiter, may suggest that by the middle and late Republic and the Principate a *triumphator* was not regarded as impersonating Jupiter (even though the alleged dream of

---

[1] Perhaps, in the Principate from the imperial residence on the Palatine too: see *SHA* xx. 4. 4 (quoted below), where however the author may be mistaken.

[2] However, *triumphatores* probably had some special insignia that they could wear at the games: see v. 41. 2 (of the senior senators awaiting death at the hands of the Gauls) 'qui eorum curules gesserant magistratus ut in fortunae pristinae honorumque ac uirtutis insignibus morerentur, quae augustissima uestis est tensas ducentibus triumphantibusue, ea uestiti medio aedium eburneis sellis sedere'. This passage comes from a part of book v replete with annalistic and Livian invention and can hardly reflect the conditions of *c.*390 but may reflect those of the late Republic (see Mommsen and Weinstock, cited on 47. 3 n.).

[3] For the colour of the cult statue of Jupiter see also Plin. *nat.* xxxv. 157.

Augustus, and expressions such as *ornatus Iouis* [on which see below], come close to an explicit equation of *triumphator* with Jupiter). However, the triumph could still have had its prehistoric origin in such an impersonation: although many elements of the impersonation still survived in the classical period, the original meaning of the ceremony had been forgotten. It is argued also that in the procession of the games the carrying of the statue of Jupiter and the appearance of the presiding magistrate in triumphal garb would mean that there were two Jupiters on view, but this is rightly dismissed by Versnel as dependent on modern notions of logic and consistency. As for our passage, to suggest that *ornatu Iouis Optimi Maximi* refers only to clothing borrowed from the temple of Jupiter and not to the actual clothes of the cult statue (thus e.g. Warde Fowler, pp. 154–5, Reid, pp. 177–8, and Deubner, p. 319) gives a forced interpretation of the genitive in L., Juvenal, and the first passage of Servius; rather, the *triumphator* probably borrowed them on the day of his triumph. Versnel rightly points out that the uncertainty as to whether the garb of a *triumphator* was modelled on that of a king or on Jupiter may be resolved by postulating that on festive occasions the kings of Rome wore garb associated with Jupiter.

For the garb of the *triumphator* see esp. Marquardt (1881–5) ii. 586–7 and (1886) ii. 542–4. For discussion of the evidence for the connection between *triumphatores* and Jupiter, see, in addition to the works cited, e.g. Warren (1970) 57–62 and Weinstock (1971) 67–8.

corona triumphali laureaque: our sources do not allow us to distinguish with absolute confidence between the various crowns and garlands on show at the Roman triumph. Here L. appears to distinguish the laurels worn by the *triumphator* from his triumphal crown, by which he presumably means the large gold crown held over his head. His terminology, however, is unusual: normally the crown that was worn was termed *triumphalis*. For the large triumphal crown, which Juvenal (10. 39–42) says was too heavy to be worn and which in the triumphal procession was carried by a slave who stood in the triumphal chariot behind the *triumphator*, see also e.g. Plin. *nat.* xxxiii. 11, Juv. loc. cit., and Zon. vii. 21. 9. This is presumably the crown mentioned at Tert. *cor.* 13 (quoted above). For the triumphal laurels, see e.g. Tib. ii. 5. 5, Ov. *am.* ii. 12. 1, *cons. Liu.* 334, Firm. *math.* vi. 30. 26. For the *corona triumphalis* as something that could be worn see Val. Max. iii. 7. 1e, v. 1. 10, and perhaps Plin. *nat.* xxii. 6. Different again are the triumphal crowns presented by subdued states (e.g. Gell. v. 6. 5 and Fest. 504. 25–7). See further Ehlers, *RE* viiA. 506 and Versnel (1970) 56 n. 4 and 73–7.

domos spoliis hostium adfixis: *spolia* might be taken from an enemy whom one had killed either in single combat (vii. 9. 6–10. 14, 10. 11 nn.) or in the normal course of battle; the legendary L. Siccius Dentatus is said (see e.g. Val. Max. iii. 2. 24; for other sources and discussion see further Oakley [1985] 409 and Rawson [1990] 160 = [1991] 584) to have taken eight *spolia* in single combat and twenty-eight on other occasions. Both the private soldier and the commander (who, even if he himself had killed no one, had a right to retain token spoil) displayed *spolia* on their door-posts; with our passage, cf. e.g. xxxviii. 43. 11, Plb. vi. 39. 10, Cic. *Phil.* ii. 68, Tib. i. 1. 54, Prop. iii. 9. 26, Ov. *trist.* iii. 1. 33–4, Plin. *nat.* xxxv. 7, Sil. vi. 434–5, 445–6, Plut. *C. Gracch.* 15. 1, and Suet. *Nero* 38. 2.[1] In Rome's militaristic society possession of *spolia* conveyed considerable prestige: Cato made a speech (*ORF* fr. 97 = Serv. auct. *Aen.* iv. 244) *ne spolia figantur nisi de hoste capta*; and in the crisis after Cannae those who had spoils affixed to their houses were recruited to the senate during the Hannibalic War (xxiii. 23. 6). Note too that Ap. Claudius Caecus is said to have argued that those who had disgraced themselves in the fighting against Pyrrhus should not be allowed back inside the *uallum* until they had each brought back *bina spolia* (Val. Max. ii. 7. 15, Frontin. (?) *strat.* iv. 1. 18). See further Lammert, *RE* iiiA. 1843–5 and Rawson (1990) 159–61 = (1991) 583–5.

insignia adicere: for the expression and the idea cf. Tac. *Agr.* 9. 6 'adiecto pontificatus sacerdotio' and Plin. *epist.* x. 13 'rogo dignitati, ad quam me prouexit indulgentia tua, uel auguratum uel septem-uiratum, quia uacant, adicere digneris'. Analogous is Tac. *hist.* i. 77. 3 'sed Otho pontificatus auguratusque honoratis iam senibus cumulum dignitatis addidit'.

10. qui Iouis Optimi Maximi ornatu decoratus, curru aurato per urbem uectus in Captolium ascenderit, is ⟨non⟩ conspicietur cum capide ac lituo, ⟨non⟩ capite uelato uictimam caedet auguriumue ex arce capiet?: the supplements were proposed by Weissenborn (respectively, ed. and ed.²); *conspicietur* was conjectured by Madvig for **N**'s *conspiciatur*.

N's text renders this sentence barely intelligible. In § 9 Decius asked whether any god or man could have thought it unbecoming that a man who had triumphed and held curule office should add a

---

[1] Note, however, that Marcellus seems to have hung his *spolia opima* on a tree and then dedicated them to Jupiter Feretrius; see esp. Plut. *Marc.* 8. 2. For this practice see also Virg. *Aen.* xi. 5–11 and Luc. i. 136–8. A commander might also deposit *spolia* in a temple (see vi. 4. 2–3 n.), and spoil not claimed by any individual might be burnt (see viii. 1. 6 n.).

priesthood or an augurship to his honours, and the implied answer to his question was 'no god or man'. In § 10, in which *qui . . . ascenderit* continues the reference to the triumph, he contrasts the triumph, and esp. its religious aspects, with the symbols and practice of the pontiffs and augurs, and he ought to ask a similar question. However, if one adopts the paradosis, the implied answer to the question, 'Should a man who has been adorned in the clothes of Jupiter Optimus Maximus and carried through the city in a chariot of gold be seen with a vase and staff?' is 'No, he should not' rather than the expected 'Yes, he should.' Weissenborn (*Komm.*) glossed *is conspiciatur . . .* with 'kann wenn es richtig es . . . nur ironisch genommen werden', but this defence is desperate. Another difficulty is that, although *caedet* and *capiet* are co-ordinate in construction with *conspiciatur*, they are not co-ordinate in tense.

Madvig, *ap.* Madvig and Ussing, suggested reading ⟨*non*⟩ *conspicietur* for *conspiciatur*. Later (1877: 225–6) he rejected this on the grounds that (*a*) the corruption to the subjunctive was not explained; (*b*) the sense of (§ 9) *cui . . . indignum uideri potest* should be felt in § 10; and (*c*) a second *non* would have to be supplied before *uictimam*. Of these objections, (*a*) is not serious (an *e* could accidentally be changed to an *a* by any scribe), (*b*) is unnecessary (the indignant question is quite intelligible even if it is not connected to § 9), but (*c*) has force (the articulation of *is* ⟨*non*⟩ *conspicietur cum capide ac lituo, capite uelato, uictimam caedet auguriumue ex arce capiet?*, the text printed by Madvig and Ussing, is awkward). The conjecture of Weissenborn's adopted in the lemma answers (*c*) and places *non* in a more convincing position than before *uictimam* (the anaphora of *non* is in L.'s manner; see vol. i, p. 729).

No restoration of this passage can be regarded as certain and plausible alternatives to that adopted are (i) keeping *conspiciatur* ('should he not be seen?') and emending to *caedat* and *capiat* ('should he not sacrifice . . . should he not take?'), with addition of the two supplements; (ii) adopting Walters's *qui . . . ascenderit, is* ⟨*non*⟩ *conspiciatur cum capide ac lituo,* ⟨*cum*⟩ *capite uelato uictimam caedet auguriumue ex arce capiet?* In this second conjecture, which has the merit of allowing one to retain the tenses transmitted by the paradosis,[1] the supplied *cum* is the temporal conjunction.[2]

[1] Weissenborn's alternative conjecture *qui . . . ascenderit, is* ⟨*non*⟩ *conspiciatur cum capide ac lituo, capite uelato* ⟨*si*⟩ *uictimam caedet auguriumue ex arce capiet?* also has this merit but allows the implication that on some occasions plebeians might sacrifice without a *capis* and *lituus*.

[2] Dr Holford-Strevens observes that *cum* could also be supplied before *uictimam*. This would remove the awkwardness by which the second *cum* is not parallel to the first.

Other conjectures. A simple solution, found first in the Froben edn. (Basle) of 1531 and

Iouis optimi maximi ornatu decoratus: see § 9 n. above.

curru aurato: for the chariot of the *triumphator* which was inlaid with gold cf. e.g. Cic. *red. sen.* 28 (where the allusion to a triumph is implicit), Hor. *epod.* 9. 21–2, Prop. i. 16. 3, Ov. *am.* i. 2. 42, Sen. *contr.* x. 1. 8, and Flor. i. 1(5). 6. For full discussion of the decorations on the chariot see Ehlers, *RE* viiA. 503–4; also ix. 40. 20 n.

per urbem uectus in Capitolium ascenderit: after going to the Circus Flaminius (see e.g. xxxix. 5. 17, xlv. 39. 14), the triumphal procession entered the city at the Porta Triumphalis (see e.g. Cic. *Pis.* 55, Jos. *bell. Jud.* vii. 130) and went to the temple of Jupiter Optimus Maximus on the Capitol (e.g. Cic. *II Verr.* v. 77, Dio xliii. 21. 2 and lx. 23. 1), where the *triumphator* dedicated his crown (Zon. vii. 21. 11, Tzetz. *epist.* 107, p. 86) and there was a festival (e.g. xlv. 39. 13, Zon. loc. cit). Sites traversed on the way included the Velabrum (Suet. *Caes.* 37. 2), the Sacra Via (Prop. ii. 1. 34, iii. 4. 22, Hor. *carm.* iv. 2. 35 [with Porphyrio's comment]), and the forum (Cic. *II Verr.* v. 77, Ov. *Pont.* ii. 1. 42, Zon. vii. 21. 11, Dio xliv. 49. 3). See further Ehlers, *RE* viiA. 496 and 510.

cum capide ac lituo: *capis* could refer to any small bowl but was associated particularly with pontiffs (see e.g. Cic. *nat.* iii. 43 'docebo meliora me didicisse de colendis diis immortalibus iure pontificio et more maiorum capedunculis his, quas Numa nobis reliquit . . . quam . . .', Prisc. *inst.* vi. 67 [*gramm. Lat.* ii, p. 251] 'capis uasis est genus pontificalis, diminutiue capidula', and Fest. 292 '⟨PATELLAE⟩ . . . item sacris fa⟨ciendis apta⟩ . . . uelut capidul⟨ae⟩' [the supplements derived in part from the epitome of Paulus]).

The *lituus* was a curved staff carried by augurs that symbolized their office. The fullest description of it, including an explanation of its relationship to the trumpet called *lituus*, is to be found at Cic. *diu.* i. 30 'quid? lituus iste uester, quod clarissimum est insigne auguratus, unde uobis est traditus? nempe eo Romulus regiones direxit tum

---

adopted by e.g. Luterbacher, is to emend *caedet* and *capiet* to *caedat* and *capiat* and interpret all three subjunctives as jussive. This is possible, but with a question in § 9 and another question in § 11, the rhetoric of the passage is more effective if § 10 too is a question. Up to the late nineteenth century many editors read *si* for *is* (first printed in the Mainz edn. of 1519) and then *caedat* and *capiat*. With this text *si* depends upon (§ 9) *cui deorum hominumue indignum uideri potest*; but the change from accusative and infinitive to conditional clause is very awkward, and no recent editor has believed that L. wrote thus. Madvig finally came to favour *cui deorum hominumue indignum uideri potest . . . eos uiros, quos . . ., quorum . . ., pontificalia atque auguralia insignia adicere, ⟨ut⟩ qui . . . ascenderit, is conspiciatur cum capide ac lituo, capite uelato uictimam caedens auguriumue ex arce capiens?* In other words, he removed the question mark after *adicere* in § 9, supplied *ut* before *qui Iouis*, and emended *caedet* and *capiet* to *caedens* and *capiens*. The result restores sense, and one could construct a hypothesis which accounted for the corruption; but his earlier suggestion was perhaps closer to the mark.

cum urbem condidit. qui quidem Romuli lituus, id est incuruum et
leuiter a summo inflexum bacillum, quod ab eius litui quo canitur
similitudine nomen inuenit, cum situs esset in curia Saliorum quae
est in Palatio eaque deflagrauisset, inuentus est integer'; see also Liv.
i. 18. 7 'augur . . . dextra manu baculum sine nodo aduncum tenens,
quem lituum appellarunt', 18. 8, Cic. *nat.* ii. 9, iii. 14, *diu.* i. 31 (continuing the passage quoted above), Virg. *Aen.* vii. 187, Val. Max. i. 8.
11, Gell. v. 8. 6–11 (with fuller discussion of the similarities of the
augural staff and the trumpet), *Gloss.* ii. 124. 5 and v. 368. 35–6. Like
L. (above § 9), Apuleius (*apol.* 22) specifically terms it an *insigne* of
augurs. See further Ogilvie on i. 18. 7 (arguing for a Hittite origin for
the *lituus*).

     In this passage M has *cum li capide ac tuo*; P(= PUOZ) had *cum
lituo* (-*ua* U), and λ just *cum*. M's reading is obviously nonsense; with
a small adjustment λ's can be made to give sense, but interpolation of
capide and *lituo* is improbable; P's reading is grammatical but cannot
be right: the *lituus* was a symbol of an augur and not also of a pontiff,
and the structure of the sentence demands a reference to both
pontiffs and augurs. If **N**'s exemplar had *cum capide ac lituo*, found
first in the Milan edn. of 1478, then all the variants may be explained:
N¹ omitted *capide ac*, which was supplied in the margin (or above the
line) by **N**ᶜ; P copied the reading of **N**¹ but ignored that of **N**ᶜ;
Λ (whose reading doubtless is reflected λ) tried to make sense of the
reading of **N**¹ but produced only a progressive corruption; μ (whose
reading reappears in M) inserted the correction in the wrong place,
splitting *lituo* (this would have been particularly easy if a line in **N**¹
ended with *cum li-*). For variants of this kind in **N**, see vol. i, pp.
319–20. However, *ac* is odd, as it suggests that the same person may
be both pontiff and augur, a very rare phenomenon (see 9. 2 n.).
Perhaps one should consider reading *cum capide aut lituo*.

capite uelato uictimam caedet: when dealing with the gods a
Roman would often cover his head, a practice illustrated nicely by
the behaviour of L. Vitellius, as reported at Suet. *Vit.* 2. 5 'primus C.
Caesarem adorare ut deum instituit, cum reuersus ex Syria non aliter
adire ausus esset quam capite uelato circumuertensque se, deinde
procumbens' and contrasted by Varro, *ap.* Macr. *Sat.* iii. 6. 17, with
the practice of sacrificing *Graeco ritu* at the Ara Maxima with the
head uncovered. For this practice when sacrificing compare with our
passage Serv. *Aen.* ii. 166 'uelato capite sacrificans' and Macr. loc.
cit. For the practice in performance of religious rituals other than
sacrifice see e.g. viii. 9. 5, Cic. *nat.* ii. 10, Flor. i. 9(14). 3 (*deuotio*),
Liv. i. 18. 7 and 36. 5 (augurs), 32. 6 (*fetiales*), Cato, *orig.* fr. 18 =

Serv. *Aen.* v. 755 (ritual foundation of a city), Cic. *dom.* 124 (*conse-cratio* of possessions), Ov. *fast.* iii. 363 (prayer to Juppiter), D.H. xii. 16. 4 (prayer), and Serv. *Aen.* iv. 374 (marriage by *confarreatio*). It was held by some that the practice of covering the head was instituted by Aeneas: see e.g. Varr. loc. cit., D.H. xii. 16. 1–2, Plut. *quaest. Rom.* 10 = *mor.* 266c–e, Fest. 432. For further discussion of the ritual see the works cited by R. G. Nisbet on Cic. *dom.* 124 and Bömer on Ov. *fast.* iii. 363.

auguriumue ex arce capiet?: in the city of Rome augural observation took place above all on the *arx*; cf. iv. 18. 6, Cic. *off.* iii. 66, Varr. *ling.* v. 47, vii. 8, Val. Max. viii. 2. 1, Paul. Fest. 15 and 17 'AUGURACULUM appellabant antiqui, quam nos arcem dicimus, quod ibi augures publice auspicarentur' (but for other augural sites see Varr. *ling.* v. 52, with Linderski [1986] 2277 n. 518). L. may be thinking in particular of their role at the inauguration of priests: see i. 18. 6–10 (esp. § 6 'deductus in arcem'), where he describes the practice in the context of the inauguration of Numa Pompilius. See further Magdelain (1968) 60 n. 4 and Linderski (1986) 2257–8.

11. ⟨in⟩ imaginis titulo: for the *imagines* of office-holders see vol. i, pp. 28–30 with *addenda*. Flower (1996: 151–6) notes that references to them are found quite often in emotional appeals; however, none of the passages that she cites (which include i. 47. 4, iii. 58. 2, 72. 4, and Tac. *ann.* iv. 35. 2) is very similar to ours. For the *titulus* of an *imago* see *addendum* to viii. 40. 4 n.

The supplement, which is due to Luterbacher (who suggested that it could be placed alternatively before *cuius*) after Wesenberg (1870/1: 37) (who placed it before *titulo*) expedites the sense of the passage; *in* could easily have fallen out before *im-*.

12. pace dixerim deum: for this 'old ritual formula . . . by which a speaker sought to forestall any divine objection to his words' (Ogilvie on iii. 19. 7), cf. xxxviii. 46. 12, Ov. *am.* iii. 2. 60 'pace loquar Veneris, tu dea maior eris', *met.* vii. 704–5 'liceat mihi uera referri | pace deae', and Amm. xvi. 12. 12. Decius uses it here lest what he is about to say with regard to the priesthoods of these gods should seem offensive to them. The surviving evidence does not allow Ogilvie's view, that the use of this idiom in addresses to human beings (for which see e.g. iii. 19. 7 'C. Claudi pace et P. Valeri mortui loquar', Ter. *eun.* 466, Cic. *de or.* i. 76, Vell. i. 17. 3, and Sen. *nat.* iii. 11. 4; also Vell. i. 7. 4) is a later development, to be established. In addition to Ogilvie, see Hofmann (1951) 131, Bömer on Ov. *met.* vii. 704, and *TLL* x. 1. 865. 28–35, 865. 73–866. 7.

populi Romani beneficio: see vi. 40. 20 n.

dignatione means 'the repute in which we are held' (*TLL* v. 1. 1133. 27–39 [where, however, the gloss *patricia* beside *dignatione* in our passage is quite wrong], *OLD s.u.* 2), as J. Walker (1822: 86) saw.

8. 2. decemuiros . . . interpretes: according to L., a concession gained in 368; see vi. 42. 2 n.

3. nec aut tum . . . et nunc . . .: the disjunction *aut . . . et . . .* in the paradosis makes an anacoluthon which can be removed by emendation. The easiest conjecture is to delete *aut* with the Froben (Basle) edn. of 1535; but one could also change *et nunc* to *aut nunc* and the following *non ut* to *ut* (thus Gronovius: the sense would be 'neither then was any harm done to the patricians . . . nor now has the tribune added five places to the college of augurs and four to the college of pontiffs so that . . . but rather so that . . .'; but this postulates a less economical corruption). However, more recent editors are probably right to leave the text unchanged, since (*a*) the anacoluthon is not difficult (after saying 'neither then was any harm done to the patricians' Decius, instead of saying 'nor now has the tribune added', says rather the more emphatic 'and now the tribune has added'), and (*b*) analogous anacolutha after *aut* are found elsewhere; see *TLL* ii. 1572. 56–72 and K–S ii. 107. Among the passages listed in *TLL* is xxxviii. 26. 7 (on the Gauls) 'nec aut (aut *del. Vielhaber*) procurrere quisquam ab ordinibus suis, ne nudarent undique corpus ad ictus, audebant, et stantes quo densiores erant hoc plura, uelut destinatum petentibus, uolnera accipiebant', where the combination *nec aut . . . et* is precisely parallel to that in our passage. However, in our passage the presence of *nunc* balancing *tum* makes the disjunctive *aut* rather easier, and in their recent editions Briscoe and Walsh may well be right to accept Vielhaber's conjecture.

tribunus, uir fortis ac strenuus: Decius refers to one tribune, despite 6. 4–6, where we are told that the law was introduced by two tribunes. Of the two brothers Ogulnius (6. 3 n.), Q. Gallus became the more important.

   uir fortis ac strenuus is an appellation generally reserved by L. for plebeians, whether by chance or design it is not entirely clear. See esp. iv. 3. 16 (Canuleius speaking) 'utrum tandem non credidimus fieri posse, ut uir fortis ac strenuus, pace belloque bonus, ex plebe sit . . .?' (he goes on to mention three kings who had a plebeian origin),

5. 5 (Canuleius says that an opportunity should be given to *uiris s. et f.*), 35. 9 (speculation from the tribunes on whether the plebeians could produce a *uir f. ac s.*), v. 12. 8 (tribunes state that government should now be transferred from failed patricians to plebeian *uiros f. ac s.*, xxii. 35. 7 (of new men passed over), and xxxviii. 47. 5 (of tribunes of the plebs). Other passages which support this pattern are i. 34. 6 (on the opportunities for new men in the new state of Rome), xxiii. 3. 6 (used by the Campanian Pacuvius Calavius of Campanian *noui homines*), xxxviii. 41. 3, 49. 8 (both of the plebeian Q. Minucius Thermus, who died fighting bravely). L. uses the coupling in four other passages. Three, in which it is used of foreigners (xxi. 4. 4 [on the young Hannibal] and xxiii. 15. 10 [on Hannibal's view of the Nolan L. Bantius], and xxx. 14. 8 [Scipio describing the actions of Masinissa]), hardly affect the argument outlined above. The fourth (xxviii. 40. 4 [Fabius Verrucosus on the future Africanus]), may be held to contradict it, but perhaps the epithet suggests that Scipio was using popular methods of which Fabius disapproved.

Apart from this last passage, L. never uses *strenuus*, even without co-ordinate *fortis*, to describe a patrician or a *nobilis*; see iii. 47. 2 (of the wronged Verginius on himself), vi. 34. 11 (on the tribune of the plebs L. Sextius), viii. 8. 16 (of a brave centurion not over-endowed with physical strength; the use of the word in a military context is regular: see below on Sallust), 22. 8 (of Greeks being a *gens lingua magis strenua quam factis*; this is an inversion of the regular use of the word in a military context), xxiv. 15. 6 and 16. 11 (on the actions of Gracchus' *uolones*). A passage which proves the rule is x. 19. 8, where the plebeian Volumnius says to Ap. Claudius Caecus: 'quam mallem . . . tu a me strenue facere quam ego abs te scite loqui didicissem'.

The usage of other writers is not so clear-cut. Santoro L'hoir makes a reasonable case for seeing popular resonances in the two instances of *strenuus* in Cicero's speeches (*Phil.* ii. 78, viii. 11). However, in Sallust popular ideology is suggested most obviously at *Cat.* 20. 7 'strenui boni, nobiles atque ignobiles' (where the following contrast suggests that *strenui* is in opposition to *boni*) and *Iug.* 85. 50, where Marius associates being *strenuus* with *uirtus* (regularly claimed as their own by *noui homines* and contrasted with the claims of birth: see vii. 32. 14 n.); but he also uses the word in many other contexts, esp. military (e.g. *Cat.* 58. 1, 60. 4, *hist.* iv. 7).

See further Klinger (1884) 13 n. 1, Moore (1989) 17–19, and Santoro L'hoir (1990) 224–7; also Ogilvie on iv. 3. 16 and Woodman on Vell. ii. 88. 2.

adicit is Duker's conjecture, accepted by most editors, for **N**'s *adiecit.* If the paradosis is right, it must be an archaic spelling of the present (see Leumann [1977] 128), not the perfect; for the notion of completion is inappropriate in the context of a measure on which voting has still to take place, and the continuous sense ('is adding') provided by the present is preferable. Cf. 37. 14 n.

4. homines plebeii: see vi. 36. 11 n.
pro parte uirili: see vi. 11. 5 n.

5. noli erubescere . . . habere: *erubescere* with dependent infinitive is attested earlier only at Virg. *ecl.* 6. 2 'nostra neque erubuit siluas habitare Thalea'; it is found also at xlii. 41. 2, xlv. 35. 5, and then quite frequently in later authors. A dependent accusative and infinitive is found first at xlv. 38. 7. See further *TLL* v. 1. 822. 69–823. 16.

6. principem nobilitati⟨s⟩ uestrae: for such a description of the first man in a family to become a *nobilis* cf. esp. Cic. *Brut.* 53 'L. Bruto illi nobilitatis uestrae principi' (like the following passage addressed to M. Brutus); also (with *auctor* for *princeps*) *Tusc.* iv. 2 'L. Brutus . . . auctor nobilitatis tuae' and (with *consulatus* for *nobilitatis*) *fin.* ii. 61 'P. Decius princeps in ea familia consulatus'. Somewhat less close are other passages in which Cicero comments that an individual was the first to bring the consulship into his family (*diu.* i. 51, *off.* i. 138, and *Phil.* ix. 4). See further Gelzer (1969) 34.

N read *nobilitati*. The dative dependent on *princeps* is defended by Drakenborch as analogous to *adiutor consiliis* or *imperator Romanis*, but it is very rare (only Auson. xxvi. 163–4 'Milesius Thales sum, aquam qui principem | rebus creandis dixi, ut uates Pindarus' is cited at *TLL* x. 2. 1276. 42), and the emendation adopted, which is found in all witnesses to χ, is very easy.

Sabinam aduenam . . . Attium Clausum seu Ap. Claudium: (321). All ancient authorities agreed that the Claudii were a Sabine family which had migrated to Rome, but Suet. *Tib.* 1. 1 offers rival accounts of the migration: in one they came at the time of Romulus' co-regent, Titus Tatius, in the other in the sixth year of the Republic. For other sources that mention this migration, and modern discussion of it, see vol. iii, p. 358. The Sabine name of the first Appius Claudius is variously given as Attus, Attius, or (at Suet. *Tib.* 1. 1) Atta Clausus. He was said to have been consul in 495 BC (ii. 21. 5, D.H. vi. 23. 1) and features prominently in the (almost entirely invented) accounts of the politics of this period that are offered by L. and (esp.) D.H., in which he is given the extreme anti-plebeian attitudes that are so characteristic of the annalistic portrayal of the early Claudii (of the passages listed at vol. iii, p. 358, those from book ii of L. down to 44. 6 and from books v–ix. 1 of D.H. refer to this Appius). In the copy of the *elogium* from the Augustan forum (*CIL* i². p. 199 no. 31 = vi. 1279 = *I.I.* xiii. 3. no. 67) he is said to have been quaestor as well as consul; but this is simply an invention so as to give him a *cursus honorum* (apart from the consulship, the quaestorship was the only republican magistracy in existence in the 490s). See further Wiseman (1979) 59–76.

ne fastidieris . . . accipere: *fastidire* is found with dependent infinitive first here in Latin, then at Ov. *rem.* 304, Sen. *contr.* iv. *praef.* 2, and in several later writers. A dependent accusative and infinitive is found at vi. 41. 2. See further *TLL* vi. 311. 52–69.

Siesbye, *ap.* Madvig and Ussing, supplied *tu* before *ne*; the conjecture makes the text more pointed but is hardly necessary.

7. superbos: for patrician pride see vi. 14. 3 n.

8. L. Sextius: see vi. 34. 11 and, in general, 34. 1–42. 14 nn.
C. Licinius Stolo primus magister equitum: for Stolo, see vi. 34. 5 n.; for the mastership of the horse of 368, see vi. 39. 3 n. with *addendum*, where it is argued that the honour more probably belonged to C. Licinius Calvus.
C. Marcius Rutilus primus et dictator et censor: for Marcius see vii. 16. 1 n. L. records his dictatorship of 356 at vii. 17. 6–10, his censorship of 351 at vii. 22. 7–10.
Q. Publilius Philo, primus praetor: for Philo see vii. 21. 6 n.; for his praetorship in 337 see viii. 15. 9.

9. uos solos gentem habere: the expression *gentem habere* is unusual: the only parallel cited at *TLL* vi. 1848. 17–22 is Papin. *dig.* xxii. 3. 1 'quotiens quaereretur, genus uel gentem quis haberet necne, eum probare oportet'. Foster translates 'that you alone are of noble birth', and for *gens* having a sense akin to 'rank' one may compare Hor. *serm.* ii. 5. 15 'sine gente'. However, here L. almost certainly refers to membership of a *gens* or 'clan' (to use the word which is perhaps the least inapposite English equivalent) and 'that you alone have (i.e. "belong to") a clan' is better.

Most modern scholars reject the implications of this passage and use the word *gens* of plebeian as well as patrician families. For this view see e.g. Kübler, *RE* vii. 1180 'Es gab sowohl patrizische wie plebeiische Gentes' (however, he argued that plebeian *gentes* were

formed after patrician ones), Richard (1978) 181–4 (with large
bibliography), and Momigliano (1984: 421 = 1989*a*: 99 = 1989*b*: 37):

There is no firm evidence to show that in Rome only the aristocracy was
organized by *gentes*. Even less do we know of a time in which the *gentes* could
be identified with that special type of hereditary aristocracy which was
known as the patriciate. The isolated polemical utterance attributed in Livy
to his patrician opponents by a plebeian of the fourth century B.C., 'uos
(patricios) solos gentem habere' ('that you (patricians) alone have a clan')
(Livy x. 8. 9), cannot be turned into a statement of fact, 'plebeii gentes non
habent' ('plebeians do not have clans'), as modern students are apt to do. At
best the sentence represents Livy's notion of archaic Roman society.

However, this standard view needs to be weighed against the philological evidence, carefully assessed long ago by Radin (1914), five
aspects of which suggest that the notion expressed by Decius may
not be eccentric.[1]

(*a*) *gens* is qualified by the adjective *plebeius* just once, and at that in
an author of the second century AD (Suet. *Tib.* 1. 1 'patricia gens
Claudia—fuit enim et alia plebeia . . .', where the usage is made much
easier by the preceding *patricia*).

(*b*) It is qualified regularly by *patricius*. Particularly interesting are
the following passages: iii. 27. 1 'L. Tarquinium, patriciae gentis',
33. 10 'L. Sestium, patriciae gentis uirum', vi. 11. 2 'patriciae gentis
uiro . . . M. Manlio Capitolino', vii. 1. 2 'patres praeturam Sp. Furio
M. filio Camillo, aedilitatem Cn. Quinctio Capitolino et P. Cornelio
Scipioni, suarum gentium uiris, . . . ceperunt', 39. 12 (on T.
Quinctius) 'patriciae hic uir gentis erat', viii. 18. 8 'Cornelia ac Sergia,
patriciae utraque gentis', Sall. *Iug.* 95. 3 'Sulla gentis patriciae nobilis
fuit', *hist.* iv. 1 'Cn. Lentulus, patriciae gentis', Val. Max. iv. 3. 4 'Cn.
Marcius patriciae gentis adulescens', Plin. *nat.* xi. 244 'M. Corani ex
patricia gente'.[2] Note that in these passages L. and other authors do
not write *L. Sestium, uirum patricium* (*uel sim.*), but rather incorporate
the word *gens* into their expression. Of equal interest is Gell. x. 20. 5
'"plebem" autem Capito in eadem definitione seorsum a populo
diuisit, quoniam in populo omnis pars ciuitatis omnesque eius
ordines contineantur, "plebes" uero ea dicatur, in qua gentes ciuium

---

[1] Professor C. J. Smith kindly drew my attention to Radin's article. In the following paragraphs Radin's material is reworked, with the addition of only a small amount of extra evidence. At first sight the treatment of the philological evidence by Kübler, *RE* vii. 1180–1, who
reaches the opposite conclusion, appears to be full and thorough, but (as Radin observed) in
many of the passages which he adduces neither the word *gens* nor *gentilis* occurs.

[2] Less interesting instances of the coupling of *gens* and *patricius* may be found at x. 15. 9,
Juv. 10. 332 (where, however, Juvenal is wrong to describe Silius as patrician), Suet. *Tib.* 1. 1
(quoted above), and Aur. Vict. *Caes.* 39. 7.

patriciae non insunt': here, in the context of a legal definition, Capito couples *gentes* and *patriciae*. With this passage one should compare Gell. xvii. 21. 27 'lege Licinii Stolonis consules creari ex plebe coepti, cum antea ius non esset nisi ex patriciis gentibus fieri consulem', where Gellius chooses not to balance *patriciis gentibus* with *plebeiis gentibus*.

(*c*) At vi. 40. 3–4 in the context of the adlection of the Claudii to the patricians *gens* is used of both the Claudii and the patricians in general. Compare also x. 15. 9.

(*d*) L. uses the expression *ius gentium* in the context of the erosion of patrician privileges (see vii. 6. 11 n., adding a reference to iv. 4. 4).

(*e*) At *TLL* vi. 1847. 51–1848. 3, where passages in which *gens* is used of a particular family or clan are helpfully listed, the names in question are largely patrician;[1] and, if one takes account of evidence written before the death of Augustus, one finds the word used of plebeians only at Cic. *IIVerr.* i. 115 (the Minucii), *dom.* 116 (referring to the adoption of Clodius by Fonteius) 'non suae genti Fonteiae, sed Clodiae, quam reliquit' (where the context is heavily sarcastic), *leg.* ii. 55 (of the Popillii), Catull. 79. 2–3 (of Catullus' own family, but in a context in which he almost certainly alludes to the patrician *gens* Claudia), Varr. *rust.* i. 2. 9 'eiusdem gentis C. Licinius', and ii. 4. 1–2 (twice of the family of Tremellius Scrofa).[2] To these passages one should probably add those in which *gentilis* is used with reference to a family, esp. in legal contexts (see e.g. [Cic.] *Her.* i. 23, Cic. *inu.* ii. 148 [and some of the other sources for *lex xii tab.* 5. 4–5 listed at Crawford (1996) 640], *de or.* i. 176 [which may, but does not certainly, imply that the plebeian Marcelli belonged to the *gens* Claudia], *top.* 29, Paul. Fest. 83, and *TLL* vi. 1867. 6–58).[3] With the possible exception of xxxix. 19. 5 'gentis enuptio' (referring to a reward granted to the freedwoman Faecenia Hispala, who had provided information about the celebration of the rites of Bacchus),[4] L. himself nowhere uses *gens* with reference to plebeians.[5] If one takes account of the usage of writers of the first and early second century AD, a few more passages can be added: see Vell. ii. 11. 3 (the

---

[1] I do not cite the passages where *gens* is used of patrician families: about forty-five were assembled by Radin.

[2] I have added some references to those adduced in *TLL*, most collected from other parts of the same entry on *gens*. At Cic. *Phil.* xiii. 27 'Saxam uero Decidium . . . hominem deductum ex ultimis gentibus' the following *ciuem* suggests that *gentibus* refers to Saxa's alleged foreign extraction, to which Cicero elsewhere refers.

[3] However, it is conceivable that *gentilis* was used with wider reference than *gens*.

[4] On this famously difficult passage see Watson (1974), with a summary of earlier views.

[5] Meyer, *TLL* loc. cit. 78, is wrong to suggest that iii. 58. 5 is used of the (here plebeian) Verginii.

Domitii and Caecilii), Val. Max. iv. 4. 9 (Aelii), ix. 2. 1 (Lutatii), Plin. *nat*. vii. 100 (the Porcii), xvii. 7 (the Licinii), Sil. iv. 495 (the Sempronii Gracchi), Tac. *ann*. xv. 23. 2 (Domitii, in a context which refers also to the Julii and Claudii), Suet. *Nero* 50 (Domitii), as well as several references to the Flavian family.[1] Note also the use of *gens* in two epigraphic texts, the so-called *laudatio Turiae* (*CIL* vi. 1527. 22) and the *s.c. de Cn. Pisone patre* 76–80 'recte et ordine facturos, qui qu|andoq(ue) familiae Calpurniae essent, quiue eam familiam cognatione | adfinitateue contingerent, si dedissent operam, si quis eius gentis aut quis eo | rum, qui cognatus adfinisue Calpurniae familiae fuisset, mortuos esset, lugend|us esset, ne . . .'.[2]

This evidence shows that several writers (esp. L.) instinctively thought that belonging to a *gens* was a patrician prerogative; and, since there is no obvious reason for the invention of such a notion in the late Republic or early Principate, this is likely to reflect an idea that goes back at least to the middle Republic. Whether the idea was then universally accepted or was merely a claim made by patricians in the Struggle of the Orders, our ignorance about exactly what a *gens* was, and how it functioned, makes it hard to say: it is certainly possible that it was a generally accepted view that only patricians had *gentes*; but, since Decius plainly contests both the claim which he ascribes to the patricians before this clause and the one that he ascribes to them immediately after it, our passage may be a pointer that patrician claims in this respect had always been controversial.

By the late Republic the view that to belong to a *gens* was a patrician prerogative must have changed, or else writers of Latin were prepared to used the term *gens* more loosely, since (as we have seen) some writers of the first century BC (occasionally), and some writers of the post-Augustan period (more often) use it in the context of plebeians.

The fact that religious matters are mentioned so often in the context of *gentes* (see e.g. i. 26. 13 [Horatii], v. 46. 2 [Fabii], ix. 29. 9 [Potitii], Ov. *Pont*. ii. 2. 107 [Valerii], Tac. *ann*. xv. 23. 2 [Julii, Claudii, Domitii]), suggests that religious rituals played an important part in uniting members of a *gens*. This perhaps explains why L. uses the expression *ius gentium*: it is easy to see how these rituals might be thought to be polluted by the intermarriage between patricians and

---

[1] I do not include Suet. *Aug*. 2. 1, as in the same sentence in which Suetonius refers to the Octavii as a *gens* he mentions their adlection to the patricians.

[2] This second passage is awkward (see Eck *et al*. [1996] 196): it is unclear why *gens* is used once and *familia* thrice; but it may be noteworthy for the argument of this note that the inscription twice refers to the *familia Calpurnia* (this expression is used again in l. 81) but not to the *gens Calpurnia*.

plebeians that resulted from the Canuleian plebiscite; and such an attitude probably lies behind L.'s story of Verginia's exclusion from the shrine of Pudicitia Patricia (see 23. 3–10 n.). However, it remains mysterious how exactly these rituals of private individual families could be thought to be polluted by admission of the plebeians to the auspices of the state as consuls, pontiffs, and augurs.

The view that patricians alone belonged to *gentes* is taken seriously by e.g. De Martino (1953: 40–1 = 1979: 65–6), Giuffrè (1970), and Guarino (1975: 158–60) but with arguments different from those used here and not always convincing.

10. aeque prosperum: see 2. 10 n.

porroque erit. en umquam: thus Mλ: *porroque erit quire* (*quiī̄* U) *numquam* PU: *porroque erit qui reum* (*renum* Zt) *quam* ZbZt: *porroque erit qui ne* (*an* Zs^c) *umquam* Zs: O def. Some sense can be made of these readings in the Π mss, if one reads *porroque erit, Quirites* with the *codex Klockianus*, which derives from P via F (vol. i, p. 315). However, quite apart from the failure of this reading to appear in M or λ, an address to the *Quirites* anticipating that in § 11 is unwanted in the middle of this address to the patricians.

en umquam fando audistis: L. uses similar phrasing at iv. 3. 10 'en umquam creditis fando auditum esse . . .'. For *en umquam* see ix. 10. 5 n.

patricios primo esse factos non de caelo demissos: for the proverb see vii. 12. 13 n.

patrem ciere: 'to call on a father by name'. In this passage Decius (*a*) states that patricians were merely people who could name their fathers, (*b*) implies that this meant that they were freeborn, and (*c*) hints at a derivation of *patricius* from *patrem ciere*. For (*a*) and (*b*) cf. Cinc. *ap.* Fest. 277. 2–3 'PATRICIOS, Cincius ait in libro de comitiis, eos appellari solitos qui nunc ingenui uocentur', D.H. ii. 8. 3, Plut. *quaest. Rom.* 58 = *mor.* 278d, *Rom.* 13. 3. D.H. and Plutarch also mention different etymologies, as does Isid. *orig.* ix. 3. 25. I have found no parallel for (*c*). See further Mommsen (1887–8) iii. 14.

11. filius meus: almost certainly L. was thinking of P. Decius Mus, *RE* no. 17, who was consul in 279, when he was defeated by Pyrrhus at Ausculum; that the consul of 279 was the son of the Decius who speaks here is stated explicitly by Cicero (*Tusc.* i. 89 and *fin.* ii. 61) and by Zonaras (viii. 5. 2). Our sources disagree as to whether or not he devoted himself in that battle, dying in the same manner as his grandfather and father were alleged to have done; for the view that he tried to devote himself but was thwarted by Pyrrhus, see vol. ii, pp. 478–9. However, Cavallaro (1976: 271–8) has argued that the fragments of *F.C.* show that the consul of 279 had a grandfather called Decimus. If both Cavallaro and *F.C.* are correct, he could not be the son of our Decius; for fuller discussion, see vol. ii, p. 477 n. 3. A further difficulty is that, according to *uir. ill.* 36. 2, a Decius Mus was involved in the capture of Volsinii (which took place in 265 and 264, years in which other sources make men of other families consuls); it is uncertain whether this report is reliable and, if it is, whether the Decius was the consul of 279.

12. ego . . . censeo: for *censeo* see vi. 41. 12 n. For the use of the first-person pronoun when a speaker gives his opinion at the end of a deliberative speech, cf. vi. 18. 14, xxi. 3. 6, xxii. 60. 27, xxiv. 8. 18, xxviii. 42. 22, and xxxiv. 4. 21.
quod bonum faustum felixque sit uobis ac rei publicae: for this expression see viii. 25. 10 n.
uti rogas: for this expression see vi. 38. 5 n.

9. 1. ille tamen dies intercessione est sublatus: for the doubtful authenticity of this notice, see 6. 3–9. 2 and vi. 35. 6 nn.

2. creantur: in later years, until the *lex Domitia* of 104 BC introduced partial election to the priesthoods (see *MRR* i. 559), new priests were appointed by co-option. However, the procedure followed in 300 is not quite certain. In the context of the appointment of magistrates *creare* is normally used by L. and others to mean 'elect', and it is conceivable that at this important new juncture in the history of the priesthoods there was popular voting. Nevertheless, *creare* is sometimes found in contexts where there was no election (note esp. xxiii. 21. 7 [of pontiffs] and xxv. 2. 2, xxvii. 36. 5, and xxxix. 45. 8 [augurs]; perhaps also vi. 41. 9), and therefore Wissowa (*RE* ii. 2318) and Münzer (1999: 171) were probably correct to imply that the usual process occurred in this year; this is suggested also by 6. 6 'adlegerentur'.
suasor legis: see vi. 36. 7 n.
P. Sempronius Sophus: see ix. 33. 5 n.
C. Marcius Rutulus . . . C. Marcius: see ix. 33. 1 n.
M. Liuius Denter: see 1. 5 n.
C. Genucius: (3). Otherwise unknown, but probably related quite closely to one or more of L. Genucius (*tr. pl.* 342: vii. 42. 1 n.), L. Genucius (*cos.* I 365: vii. 1. 7 n.), Cn. Genucius (*cos.* 363: vii. 3. 1 n.),

and L. Genucius (*cos.* 303: 1. 1 n.). In *F.C.* the *cognomen* Augurinus is given to T. Genucius L. f. L. n. (*cos.* and *xuir* 451), Cn. Genucius M. f. M. n. (*cos. tr.* I 399, II 396) and in *chron. ann.* 354 (*F.C.* not extant) to M. Genucius (*cos.* 445). Since there is no reason to believe that any Genucius held the augurate before our man, these *cognomina* must be invented. The same phenomenon is found among the Minucii, with the exception that for them some later bearers of the *cognomen* are known; for discussion of it, see below. For possible other retrojections of *cognomina* see ix. 16. 13, 20. 1 nn.

P. Aelius Paetus: (100). This man is generally identified with the consul of 337 (viii. 15. 1 n.), who seems also to have been *magister equitum* in 321 (ix. 7. 13): see e.g. Klebs, *RE* i. 526, *MRR* i. 172, and Hölkeskamp (1988*a*) 64. But the gap of thirty-three years between consulate and augurate is long, and Beloch (1926: 351) was right to be doubtful. However, if our Paetus was not the consul of 337, he was almost certainly his son, in which case the L. Paetus, plebeian aedile in 296 (x. 23. 13 n.), was probably his brother. For later Aelii as augurs, see viii. 15. 1 n.

M. Minucius Faesus: (42). Otherwise unknown. The augurate of this man was celebrated by the family's later use of the *cognomen* Augurinus (see e.g. Gell. vi. 19. 2 for a tribune of 187 or 184 and Crawford [1974] 273–6 for two moneyers of the 130s) and by the *lituus* appearing on the coins of these moneyers (see Crawford loc. cit.).[1] In lists of magistrates M. Minucius (*cos.* I 497, II 491), P. Minucius (*cos.* 492), L. Minucius P. f. M. n. Esquilinus (*cos.* or *cos. suff.* 458, *xuir* 450), and Ti. Minucius (*cos.* 305) are given the *cognomen* Augurinus (for the evidence see most conveniently *F.C.* for 458 and 451 and *MRR* i. 12, 17, 47, 166), but that any Minucius was an augur before our man is extremely improbable. For a comparable phenomenon involving the Genucii, see above. The use of the *cognomen* by the later Minucii mentioned above, and perhaps also by otherwise unknown descendants of C. Genucius, may have encouraged

---

[1] For the adoption of a *cognomen* in consequence of the success of a member of the family in gaining priestly office, compare the *cognomina* Rex adopted by the Marcii after M. Marcius the *rex sacrorum* (on whom see above, p. 85), Curio adopted by the C. Scribonius who was elected *curio maximus* in 174 (xli. 21. 9) and by his descendants, Epulo of C. Cestius Epulo (an Augustan *uiiuir epulo*, on whom see *CIL* vi. 1374), and (perhaps surprisingly, because the family was patrician) Flamininus adopted by a branch of the Quinctii after an ancestor had become *flamen dialis* (for this man see Badian [1971] *passim*; the most important testimony to him is the *apex* on the coins issued by a T. Flamininus in 126, for which see Crawford [1974] 291). In the case of Scribonius there is an anticipation, which may be compared with that found for the Genucii and Minucii, in that Scribonius is given the *cognomen* at xxxiii. 42. 10 (for the text see Briscoe's n.). This practice is discussed by Münzer (*RE* xv. 1955 and 1999: 79) and Alföldi (1966) 719.

annalists and antiquarians to foist it on members of the family who lived in the fifth and fourth centuries.

That these *cognomina* were employed first by the new augurs of 300 is quite possible (if men of this time could call themselves Barbatus, Maximus, or Philippus, there is no obvious reason why they should not call themselves Augurinus) but cannot be proved. We may note here the intriguing argument of Wiseman (1991: 118–19, 1996: 70 = 1998: 103), who suggests that the augurs Minucius and Genucius based their claim to office on the alleged prophetic tradition of their families; he interestingly points to the play on Μηνύκιος and μήνυσις in D.H.'s account of the exploits of an earlier member of the family (xii. 4. 3, 4. 6); suggests that this etymology of the name was invented *c*.300; and points to possible parallel claims of the Marcii with regard to both the prophet Marcius and to Marsyas (see ix. 33. 1 n.), and of the Publicii with regard to the prophet Publicius (but see below on T. Publilius).

C. Marcius is the only one of the augurs of 300 whose name is to be found in the fragmentary remains of the list of augurs at *ILS* 9338, where *C. Marcius C. f. Rutilus* is preserved, together with the name of one of the consuls of this year (M. Valerius Corvinus). If, as seems probable, he is the C. Marcius Rutilus just mentioned, he held two priesthoods concurrently (thus e.g. Münzer [1999] 62 and 80). Although Wissowa (1912: 492–3) and Szemler (1972: 190 and 1974) have shown that in the Republic this phenomenon was always very rare, and that it is attested most often when a pontiff or augur was also a *decemuir sacris faciundis*, nevertheless, Q. Fabius Maximus Verrucosus provides a certain parallel from the third century for a man concurrently being a member of both pontificate and augurate (see xxiii. 21. 7, xxx. 26. 7, 10, Szemler [1972] 72 and [1974] 74); T. Otacilius Crassus may provide a second parallel from the same period;[1] Julius Caesar almost certainly added the augurate to his existing post of *pontifex maximus* in 47 (for the evidence see Szemler [1972] 156 and [1974] 75); and Badian (1968: 31–3 and 39–40) has made a good case for believing that Sulla held both offices. For L.'s failure to repeat the *cognomen* cf. vii. 17. 11, where in a list of *interreges* Q. Servilius Ahala and M. Fabius Ambustus seem to appear once with their *cognomen* and once without it. The equation of

---

[1] See xxvi. 23. 8 'T. Otacilius Crassus pontifex . . . mortuus erat' and xxvii. 6. 15 'C. Seruilius pontifex factus in locum T. Otacili Crassi, Ti. Sempronius Ti. filius Longus augur factus in locum T. Otacili Crassi'. However, in the second passage the second *T. Otacili Crassi* may be due to perseveration from the first: for discussion see the critical apparatus of standard editions and Szemler (1972) 73 and (1974) 76.

the two C. Marcii is doubted by Wissowa (1912: 493 n. 2) (mildly) and Beloch (1926: 351); but the filiation in *ILS* loc. cit. shows that, if the Marcius who was made augur in this year was not the consul of 310/9, the only other possibility is his son; and it is easier to believe that the father held both posts.

T. Publi⟨li⟩us: (9). Haplographic corruption of *Publilius* to *Publius* is easy and common, and, since there was no Roman family called Publius, this restoration by Glareanus is very probable; he made the same conjecture at vii. 21. 6. Wiseman (1996: 69 = 1998: 103) has suggested that one could restore *Publicius*; he points to the seer Publicius mentioned by Cicero (*diu.* i. 115, ii. 113) and suggests that this Publicius made claims about the prophetic powers of his family (compare Wiseman's views on the Minucii, discussed above). The emendation is possible but diplomatically less probable than Glareanus'. Beloch (1926: 479) conjectured (quite attractively, but with no possibility of proof) that our man was the son of the famous Q. Publilius Philo (see vii. 21. 6 n.).

9. 3–6. *The* lex Valeria de prouocatione

The structure of the passage. L.'s general meaning is easier to explain than the organization of the passage in which he has expressed it. Initially he states that a *lex Valeria de prouocatione* was introduced that was *diligentius sancta* ('more carefully enacted' or 'protected'), the unexpressed object of comparison being previous laws on *prouo-catio*. To these he now turns, mentioning that this was the third such law and that its two predecessors had been introduced by the same family. He then conjectures (§ 4 'reor') that the reason for renewing the law so often was that the resources of the few had prevailed over the freedom of the plebs. Then, abruptly, he mentions the *lex Porcia*. The reason for this can be elicited from § 4 'tamen', to which the preceding part of the paragraph is concessive: although the third *lex Valeria* was more carefully protected, it was only the *lex Porcia* which provided real support for citizens against scourging, because it was sanctioned *graui poena*. From this one concludes that the third *lex Valeria* did not in fact carry a heavy penalty; and in §§ 5–6, which contrast with *graui poena*, L. confirms this by stating that its sanction against a magistrate who scourged or killed against *prouocatio* was simply the utterance *improbe factum*.

Prouocatio: *general problem.* Virtually everything connected with *prouocatio ad populum* has been disputed by modern scholars. Of the views to be discussed in this note the least controversial is that L., even though he is not supported by any other ancient testimony, was right to hold that a *lex Valeria* dealing with *prouocatio* was passed in this year.[1] Although our sources provide a reasonable number of references to the concept of *prouocatio* and to the legislation by which it was introduced, and although L. refers to it several times in his early books, interpretation of the concept is made very difficult by the fact that we are informed of only four occasions between 323 BC and the end of the Republic (that is the period for which our evidence is more reliable) in which recourse was had to it: two concern disputes in which the *pontifex maximus* fines a magistrate (see xxxvii. 51. 1–6 and xl. 42. 8–11); the third concerns a dispute between the *pontifex maximus* and another priest (Fest. 462–4, a passage that is very defective); and the fourth refers to the appeal of Rabirius when prosecuted for *perduellio* by Labienus in 63 (see Suet. *Iul.* 12). In this note discussion will be restricted to the following problems raised by this passage of L.: (*a*) the nature and meaning of *prouocatio*; (*b*) the date of its introduction; and (*c*) the relationship of the law of 300 to the *leges Porciae* and other later republican developments. It will be convenient first to quote Cic. *rep.* ii. 53–4, the longest ancient account of legislation on *prouocatio*:

idem (*sc.* P. Valerius Publicola) . . . legem ad populum tulit eam quae centuriatis comitiis prima lata est, ne quis magistratus ciuem Romanum aduersus prouocationem necaret neue uerberaret. (54) prouocationem autem etiam a regibus fuisse declarant pontificii libri, significant nostri etiam augurales itemque ab omni iudicio poenaque prouocari licere indicant xii tabulae conpluribus legibus, et quod proditum memoriae est, xuiros qui leges scripserint sine prouocatione creatos, satis ostendit reliquos sine prouocatione magistratus non fuisse, Lucique Valeri Potiti et M. Horati Barbati, hominum concordiae causa sapienter popularium, consularis lex sanxit ne qui magistratus sine prouocatione crearetur, neque uero leges Porciae, quae tres sunt trium Porciorum ut scitis, quicquam praeter sanctionem attulerunt noui.[2]

---

[1] But for doubts about even this see Cloud (1984: 1369–72), who argues that all three of the Valerian laws on *prouocatio* should be rejected, and (1998) 47–8. His argument that the failure of Cicero to mention this law in his *de re publica* shows that it must have been invented by Valerius Antias after the publication of the *de re publica* in the late 50s BC has the merit of drawing attention to the absence of attestation in Cicero. However, it is far from certain that Valerius Antias wrote after the publication of the *de re publica*; and, if the law had already been anticipated in the annalistic tradition by the laws of 509 and 449, then there would not be much of interest to be said about it (Cicero finds little to say about the *leges Porciae*, which he mentions simply because of the stiffer sanctions which they enacted).

[2] Cloud (1984: 1372–3) argues that, since in this passage Cicero associates *prouocatio* with *popularis* politics, his source is likely to have been the *popularis* Licinius Macer. It is conceivable that Cicero used Macer as a source (although one may wonder if he really needed to

Prouocatio: *nature and meaning*. Whatever its original nature, by the late Republic and L.'s own day *prouocatio* was regarded as the right of appeal to the people in face of coercion (that is the use of lictors to inflict summary punishment on individuals, often by scourging or execution) from a curule magistrate (in addition to the passage of Cicero just quoted see e.g. ii. 8. 2, 29. 10–12, 55. 5–7, iii. 55. 5, 56. 5–13, iv. 13. 11, viii. 33. 8) and as an important component of the *libertas* of the humble (see e.g. iii. 45. 8 'tribunicium auxilium et prouocationem plebi Romanae, duas arces libertatis tuendae', 55. 4 'consularem legem de prouocatione, unicum praesidium libertatis', 56. 5–13, esp. §§ 5–6 '"prouoco" . . . audita uox una uindex libertatis', Cic. *de or*. ii. 199 'prouocationem, patronam illam ciuitatis ac uindicem libertatis'). Hence those who had proposed laws introducing it could be deemed 'popular' politicians: see Cic. *Luc*. 13 'leges populares de prouocationibus'. Only the dictatorship, at least in its original form, which had been defunct since the beginning of the third century, was regarded by annalists as not having been subject to *prouocatio* (vi. 16. 3 n. with *addendum*).

Among modern discussions of *prouocatio* the most fundamental division is between Mommsen with his followers and others. Mommsen famously argued that *prouocatio* lay at the heart of Roman system of criminal justice:[1] after the prosecuting magistrate— whether quaestor, *iiuir*, tribune, or aedile[2]—had pronounced the defendant guilty, the defendant made an appeal to the people (*prouocatio*), who decided on his fate in an assembly that was the last stage of the judicial process. The best evidence for his reconstruction is to be found in Cicero's view (quoted above) that the Twelve Tables allowed appeal *ab omni iudicio poenaque*, at Cic. *leg*. iii. 27 'deinceps igitur omnibus magistratibus auspicia et iudicia dantur, iudicia, ut esset populi potestas, ad quam prouocaretur, auspicia, ut multos inutiles comitiatus probabiles impedirent morae',[3] and in the version

---

consult any source in detail to compose this paragraph), but 'hominum concordiae causa sapienter popularium' shows that he does not wish his views to be associated with the contemporary popular ideology espoused by the likes of Macer.

[1] Mommsen (1899) 151–74 is his final treatment of the subject. His most notable follower in modern times has been Jones (1972: 1–44). For brief summaries of Mommsen's position and the evidence on which it is based, see Kunkel (1962) 18–21 and Jolowicz and Nicholas (1972) 305–8.

[2] For prosecutions by the last three see, respectively, vi. 20. 12 n., *addendum* to vi. 1. 8, and x. 23. 11–13 n.

[3] This passage looks back to iii. 6 'iusta imperia sunto, isque ciuis modeste ac sine recusatione parento; magistratus nec oboedientem et noxium ciuem multa uinculis uerberibusue coherceto, ni par maiorue potestas populusue prohibessit, ad quos prouocatio esto'. This earlier passage offers little support to the Mommsenian position, implying that *prouocatio* was a response to magisterial *coercitio*.

of the trial of Horatius under Tullus Hostilius in which Horatius is pronounced guilty by the prosecuting *duumuiri* and then successfully appeals (*prouocare*) to the people,[1] a legend which could be viewed as an archetypal model for this procedure.[2] However, in the *de re publica* Cicero may have misinterpreted the Twelve Tables, drawing an inference about *prouocatio* even though it was not mentioned in the Tables themselves;[3] the sense of the passage of the *de legibus* is obscure, but he perhaps means no more than that trials were to be held before the people;[4] and fatal for Mommsen's interpretation is the fact that we have numerous notices of Roman criminal trials but a reference to *prouocatio* only in that of Rabirius, which was so eccentric that it should hardly be taken as typical of any republican procedure (see vi. 20. 12 n.).[5]

Noting that in the context of laws on *prouocatio* L. and others refer to magisterial coercion, most modern scholars have rejected Mommsen's interpretation, arguing that *prouocatio* was not a procedure fundamental to the whole Roman system of justice and that tribunes of the plebs, aediles, and other prosecuting magistrates took their cases directly to the people before any appeal. Rather, it was the right to appeal to the people in face of magisterial coercion.[6] Several have argued that it had its origin in the Struggle of the Orders in an extra-legal appeal to the bystanding crowd,[7] who either did, or did

---

[1] See i. 26. 7–12, viii. 33. 8, Cic. *Mil.* 7, and Fest. 380. That D.H. iii. 22. 6 tells the story differently (Tullus entrusts the judgement to the people without Horatius' making an appeal) does not necessarily invalidate this evidence: D.H. or his source(s) could have altered the standard version of the tale.

[2] Mommsen's interpretation is also compatible with the late republican view of *prouocatio* as a bastion of liberty. The passages in which the people pronounce on the fines imposed by the *pontifex maximus* are also compatible with it but susceptible to a more convincing interpretation (see below).

[3] Note the vagueness of his *indicant*: perhaps he misinterpreted a reference to an appeal to a higher magistrate. For this view of Cicero's evidence see e.g. Heuss (1944) 117, Kunkel (1962) 30, and Brunt (1988) 522 'Cicero avers (*de rep.* ii. 54) that the right of appeal was . . . attested by several laws in the XII Tables; but if that had been the case, it is unintelligible that so much later legislation was necessary.'   [4] Thus Kunkel (1962) 20–1.

[5] Brecht (1939) and Heuss (1944: esp. 105–6) provided the first notable challenges to Mommsen's doctrine. Kunkel (1962) reconsidered afresh the whole history of the republican system of criminal justice: for consideration of his views see Brunt (1964) and Jolowicz and Nicholas (1972) 308–17. Against Jones's attempt to reassert Mommsen's views, see e.g. Brunt (1974).

[6] But for the view of Humbert that originally *prouocatio* was not a popular right, see below.

[7] See e.g. Bleicken (1959: 345–63), who argues that the rudimentary *prouocatio* of the fifth century should be viewed in the same social and political context as the tribunician trials in the *concilium plebis* (listed conveniently in Ogilvie's note on ii. 35. 5; see also *addendum* to vi. 1. 6 n.): by means of *prouocatio* individual plebeians could appeal to the plebs as a body; by means of the trials the plebeians could punish their patrician opponents who had threatened plebeians. However, the connection between *prouocatio* and tribunician trials need not be quite as close as he postulates.

not, protect the person who made the appeal,[1] and that it was later instituted formally by one of the *leges Valeriae* as the right of appeal to the appropriate assembly of the people.[2] This interpretation would explain even better than Mommsen's why in the late Republic *prouocatio* was associated so strongly with liberty; and, if L.'s accounts of *prouocatio* in the early Republic have any basis in reality,[3] it would explain several of them: both a plebeian threatened by Ap. Claudius' lictors and Volero Publilius appeal to the crowd in this way, and the appeals are accepted (ii. 27. 12, 55. 4–10); Ap. Claudius the decemvir appeals, and the appeal is rejected (iii. 56. 6–57. 6).[4] Its weaknesses are that it does not coincide with the usage of *prouocare/ -atio* in private law, that for the period before 300 L.'s narrative is unlikely to be very reliable, and that it does not fit with the few attested cases of *prouocatio* from the third and second centuries.[5]

Cloud, while still rejecting Mommsen's views, propounds a very different thesis. Basing his interpretation on the regular use of *prouocare* to mean 'challenge' (vi. 42. 5 n.), he suggests that *prouocatio* had its origin in a legal challenge, finding evidence for this in Gaius' use of the verb in his account (iv. 16) of the formula for the *legis actio sacramento in rem*, and in the practice of settling a dispute between two people who were more or less equal in status by means of a challenge (*prouocatio*) with a wager (*sponsio*) before a private judge. Although the people has replaced the private judge, and the parties are no longer equal (because one is a magistrate with powers of co-ercion and the other is not), and there is no wager, the procedure of

[1] Lintott has argued that it is related closely to *quiritatio*, the practice by which a Roman in difficulties or in face of a criminal misdemeanour might cry out to neighbours and bystanders for assistance, often using some form of the expression *fidem implorare* (viii. 32. 11 n.).

[2] The *comitia centuriata* for capital trials, the *comitia tributa* (or *concilium plebis*) for fines.

[3] However, this is doubtful: it is perhaps just conceivable that a dim memory of such crowd-scenes survived to be elaborated by L. and his sources (thus Lintott [1972: 230–1]), but it would be rash to argue that an accurate memory of the particular occasions survived until the time of the annalists. For discussion of them see, in addition to Lintott, Heuss (1944) 111–14 and Bleicken (1959) 332–3.

[4] Like the appeal of Ap. Claudius, that made at viii. 33. 8 by Fabius Ambustus on behalf of Fabius Rullianus against the dictator Papirius Cursor differs from these scenes in books ii and iii in that it is made by a patrician. For discussion of it see n. ad loc. with *addendum*.

[5] In general see Cloud (1998); also Magdelain (1990) 567–9. In addition to these objections, Cloud (1998: 32–4), arguing against e.g. Lintott (1972: 232–3), also doubts whether *prouoco*, if it was used in the sense of 'call out' (which it sometimes has in early Latin), would have gener-ated the expression *ad populum prouocare* rather than *populum prouocare* for the name of the procedure. However, as Dr Holford-Strevens points out, if the standard cry was not *prouoco populum* but merely *prouoco*, then this absolute use might in time be interpreted as an intransi-tive verb, so that when it became necessary, after formalization of the procedure, to distinguish appeals to the people from other appeals, *ad populum prouocare* and *prouocatio ad populum* would naturally be used rather than *populum prouocare* or *prouocatio populi*.

prouocatio ad populum, he argues, is essentially similar to *sponsione prouocare*, in that the magistrate is challenged to contest the validity of his action before the people in their role as judge. The strengths and weaknesses of this interpretation are largely the converse of that discussed in the previous paragraph: although it involves dismissing the references to *prouocatio* in the early books of L., 'challenge' is both a regular meaning of *prouocatio* and is found in other legal contexts in which these words are used, and it fits the cases involving the *pontifex maximus* particularly well (the arguments between the *pontifex maximus* and magistrates are much closer in form to the kind of dispute settled by the procedure of *sponsione prouocare* than to the violent scenes of early Roman history in which L. alleges that *prouocatio* occurred).[1] If this view of the origin of *prouocatio ad populum* is right, it is still possible to regard its introduction as democratic: to protect the liberty of individuals in the face of magisterial coercion the procedure was adapted from private law; and a magistrate would be subject to a challenge if he tried to coerce in an unacceptable manner.[2]

In several passages L. couples the notion of *prouocatio* with that of *appellatio* to the tribunes of the plebs: see ii. 55. 4–5, iii. 55. 5, viii. 33. 8, and xxxvii. 51. 4. On the view of those who regard *prouocatio* as originating in plebeian self-help, an appeal by *prouocatio* to the people and by *appellatio* to the tribunes may be seen as more or less the same, the appeal to the people reinforcing that to the tribunes, whose power was grounded in popular support; this interpretation fits well with the evidence of the early books of L.[3] However, if Cloud is right, and the origins of *prouocatio* are to be sought in private law rather than in plebeian self-help, then originally the two notions must have been quite distinct.[4] That this means rejecting the evidence from books ii–viii is not a particular difficulty;[5] for the passage in book xxxvii a compromise position may be effected: after the introduction of *prouocatio*, the tribunes as guardians of the constitution (ix. 33. 5 n.) will have had an interest in seeing that the law was properly upheld.

[1] These cases are marginalized by Bleicken (1959: 341–5 and *RE* xxiii. 2462) and Lintott (1972), who hardly mentions them; their importance has been asserted by e.g. Martin (1970: 78–83) and Cloud (1998: 37–40). They support the testimony of D.H. (v. 19. 4) on the alleged *lex Valeria* of 509 that there was *prouocatio* against fining as well as physical coercion.

[2] Cloud (1998: 45) exaggerates the difficulties which the democratic associations of *prouocatio* pose for his theory.

[3] See e.g. Staveley (1954) 416–17, Bleicken (1959) 347–8, and Lintott (1972) 233–4.

[4] Humbert (1988) *passim* likewise views the two as distinct, although he regards the securing of the right of *prouocatio* as a prime achievement of the tribunate.

[5] We have seen that its reliability is at best dubious.

Whatever interpretation of *prouocatio* one adopts, it is clear that what was prohibited by one or more *leges Valeriae* was not magisterial coercion in itself but magisterial coercion *aduersus prouocationem*.

Prouocatio: date of introduction. We have seen that several sources state that *prouocatio* was employed by Horatius in the reign of Tullus Hostilius, and reference to *prouocatio* under the kings is made more generally at Cic. *rep.* ii. 54 (quoted above) and Sen. *epist.* 108. 31. It is one thing to argue that the story of Horatius may have served as a legendary model for middle and late republican procedure, quite another that any good evidence survived even to the middle Republic about the nature of legal proceedings in the regal period. Therefore it is not a weakness of most modern explanations of the origin of *prouocatio* that they regard it as republican in origin.[1]

In claiming that the law of 300 was preceded by two other *leges Valeriae* L. follows the orthodox view of the Roman historical tradition. The first was said to have been passed in 509 by P. Valerius Publicola,[2] the second by L. Valerius Potitus and M. Horatius Barbatus in 449, after the end of the decemvirate.[3] Quite apart from the undue prominence of the Valerii in our sources for early Roman history,[4] the alleged existence of three laws on *prouocatio* strains credulity.[5]

The reports in our sources of the law of 509 are vulnerable to three arguments: most of what Roman annalists and antiquarians record about this year is fictitious; there was little point in the Romans creating magistrates who had powers of *coercitio* if in the same year in which these magistracies were created their powers were curbed by *prouocatio*; and, if *prouocatio* in its later form was already recognized,

---

[1] The most eloquent statement of the opposing point of view is by Humbert (1988: 435–42), who, as well as arguing strongly in favour of the evidential value of the story of Horatius as an archetype of later *prouocatio*, accepts that there was *prouocatio* under the kings.

[2] See ii. 8. 2 (with no mention of the provisions of the law), Cic. *rep.* ii. 53 (quoted above), D.H. v. 19. 4 (the law allowed appeal against threatened execution, scourging, or fining), Val. Max. iv. 1. 1 (giving the same information as Cicero), Plut. *Publ.* 11. 3 (the law allowed appeal to the people from the consuls), Pompon. *dig.* i. 2. 2. 16 'lege lata factum est ut ab eis (*sc.* consulibus) prouocatio esset neue possent in caput ciuis Romani animaduertere iniussu populi: solum relictum est illis ut coercere possent et in uincula publica duci iuberent', and *uir. ill.* 15. 5.

[3] See iii. 55. 5–6 (restoration of the law of 509, which had been repealed by the decemvirs and addition of the provision 'ne quis ullum magistratum sine prouocatione crearet') and Cic. *rep.* ii. 54 (quoted above).

[4] For the problem see vol. i, p. 91.

[5] For the opposite point of view see Develin (1978) 48–9.

the creation of the tribunate of the plebs in 493 would have been much less likely.[1] Those who wish to believe in the historicity of the law may counter by arguing that the annalistic tradition has recorded the law rightly but has misunderstood its terms. Humbert (1988: 442–68), for example, argues that, reaffirming regal practice, the law gave the consuls the right to take a case to the *comitia centuriata*. This right was established more for the convenience of the consuls, who were not bound to avail themselves of it, than for the accused; later, however, the idea of *prouocatio* was taken up by the early tribunes of the plebs as part of their campaign to curb the power of the patrician magistrates. This position cannot finally be refuted, but the ascription to the first year of the Republic of what was later to become a fundamental popular right looks very suspicious, and indeed in the Roman historical tradition much that is unhistorical is ascribed to P. Valerius Publicola.[2]

The second law on *prouocatio* is rejected by most scholars, but it is harder to marshal decisive arguments against it.[3] The view of Cicero that the Twelve Tables guaranteed appeal to the people *ab omni iudicio poenaque* may be cited in its favour,[4] and it is conceivable that in 449, with the tribunate in existence, a consular law on *prouocatio* could have served to support a right of appeal to the people now championed strongly by the tribunes. This argument would have more force if the models of either Humbert[5] or those who believe that *prouocatio*, like tribunician *appellatio*, had its origin in plebeian

---

[1] These points are made well by Bleicken (1955: 113–14).

[2] For the view that the law of 509 was invented so that *prouocatio* should appear older than the tribunate of the plebs, see p. 134.

[3] Note the indecision of e.g. Ogilvie on iii. 55. 3, Bauman (1973: 34), and Cloud (1998: 46–7). For recent arguments in favour of accepting the law see Develin (1978) 53–4, Humbert (1988) 468–84, and Cornell (1995) 276–7.

[4] The view that the Twelve Tables allowed capital trials to be held only in the *comitia centuriata* and hence guaranteed the right of *prouocatio* is sometimes cited in this context. The evidence on which this view is based, among which note esp. Cic. *Sest.* 65 'cum et sacratis legibus et XII tabulis sanctum esset ut ne cui priuilegium inrogari liceret neue de capite nisi comitiis centuriatis rogari' and *leg.* iii. 11 'priuilegia ne inroganto; de capite ciuis nisi per maximum comitiatum ollosque, quos censores in partibus populi locassint, ne ferunto' is assembled fully by A. D. E. Lewis and M. H. Crawford in Crawford (1996) 696–701. However, most scholars dismiss this testimony, for two different reasons: (*a*) if Lewis, Crawford and the earlier scholars whom they cite are correct, then Cicero's evidence is so influenced by his own experiences at the hands of Clodius in 58, that it is worthless; (*b*) several scholars who accept that the Twelve Tables contained a ban on capital trials taking place in an assembly other than the *comitia centuriata* have argued that the Tables were prohibiting the trials conducted by tribunes in the *concilium plebis* (see esp. Heuss [1944] 115–16, Bleicken [1959] 352–6, and Kunkel [1962] 31).

[5] Humbert argues that the law of 449 forced consuls to take to the people appeals that had tribunician backing.

self-help are right, but could be valid also with Cloud's.[1] Nevertheless, the duplication of the law of 300 remains very suspicious, and the specific extra provision of the law reported by L. and Cicero is particularly hard to accept, since numerous *dictatores rei gerundae causa* were appointed between 449 and 302/1.[2] This provision may have been invented by the annalists to explain how affairs returned to normal after the decemvirate, during which (in their view) *prouocatio* had been suspended.[3]

L. does not explain how the law of 300 was (§ 3) 'diligentius sanctam'. Indeed, given his belief in the traditions about the laws of 509 and 449, it may have been hard for him to add any extra liberties which were established by it, and it is not surprising that his explanation of why it was necessary is vague (§ 4): 'causam renouandae saepius haud aliam fuisse reor quam quod plus paucorum opes quam libertas plebis poterat'.[4] If there had been no previous statutory recognition of *prouocatio*, then the *lex Valeria* of 300 may well

---

[1] Another view is that of Staveley (1954), followed by Ogilvie on iii. 55. 3, who accepted the testimony of Cic. *rep*. ii. 54 and argued that *prouocatio* did exist in 449 as part of a compromise between the patricians and plebeians: in return for giving up trials in the *concilium plebis* the right of *prouocatio ab omni iudicio poenaque* to the whole *populus* in the *comitia centuriata* was established, and in capital cases the consuls could voluntarily choose to employ the judgement of the people rather than their own *coercitio*. However, if *prouocatio* was viewed as a popular right, then it is not easy to see that Roman politics and constitutional practice could have coped for 149 years with the uncertainty of a system in which it existed but was not binding on the consuls. If one accepts the evidence of Cicero, it is better to follow Lintott (1972: 235) and argue that the Twelve Tables did no more than recognize that *prouocatio* in its early, uninstitutionalized form was a fact of life.

An oddity of the argument of Bleicken (1959: 357) that, as a result of the provisions of the Twelve Tables, *prouocatio* (in what he regarded as its primitive form) and trials before the *concilium plebis* declined, is that it is entirely compatible with the passing in 449 of the *lex Valeria* institutionalizing *prouocatio*, a law that he rejects.

[2] The argument that the provision applied only to newly created magistracies and not to the dictatorship, the traditional date for the establishment of which was 501 (ii. 18. 5), is unconvincing: each naming of a dictator created a magistrate not subject to *prouocatio*. Cloud (1998: 46–7) inclines to reject the law of 449 but suggests in passing that his view of *prouocatio* as in origin a method of solving a dispute between equals would invalidate the objection based on the dictatorship, postulating that it would legitimate quarrels such as that in 217 between the dictator Fabius Verrucosus and Minucius, his *magister equitum*, who had been given a power equal to his; but (*a*) the elevation of Minucius in 217 to equality with the dictator seems to have been without precedent, and (*b*) it is unlikely that the only people who could make use of *prouocatio ad populum* were colleagues of the dictators, consular tribunes, and consuls in office. If Cloud's view is right, then *prouocatio* must early on have moved away from being a contest of equals.

[3] After the passage quoted above Cic. *rep*. ii. 54 continues 'et quod proditum memoriae est, xuiros qui leges scripserint sine prouocatione creatos, satis ostendit reliquos sine prouocatione magistratus non fuisse'; see also Liv. iii. 32. 6, 33. 9, 36. 4, and 41. 7.

[4] This vagueness may be used as another argument against the authenticity of the two earlier laws: see e.g. Heuss (1944) 115 n. 142, Staveley (1954) 414, and Bleicken (1959) 346.

have had the import ascribed by our sources to the law of 509:[1] the protection of the rights of individuals against magisterial coercive force may be seen as a notable advance in the safeguarding of the liberty of individuals,[2] and the passing of the law may have marked a further stage in the controlling of the *imperium* of the old 'patrician' magistracies and the ending of the Struggle of the Orders.[3] It has been argued that it was passed so as to counterbalance the Ogulnian plebiscite: the plebeian elite was granted access to the priesthoods, the plebeian rank and file the right of *prouocatio*; this view is possible but our (admittedly limited) evidence does not make it compelling.[4] The similar view, that the *lex Valeria* was passed because the tribunes, increasingly integrated into the system of government, no longer guaranteed plebeian liberty, is less attractive:[5] although some individual tribunes may have been lacking in courage, there is no reason to believe that tribunes in general ceased to protect the poor against unjust magisterial activity. It is more likely that the *lex Valeria* helped to define more clearly the grounds on which tribunes could reasonably act.

If a law on *prouocatio* really had been passed in 449, then the law of 300 may have been connected with the dictatorship, which went into decline after this year.[6] Indeed, it is perhaps possible, if the explanation of the provision *ne quis magistratum ullum sine prouocatione creared* given above is not correct, that it belonged originally to the

---

[1] Cloud (1998: 46 n. 58) observes that at Cic. *rep.* ii. 53 both scourging and execution are seen as separate acts (note *neue*) but in our passage scourging is coupled more closely with execution (note *-que*). He suggests that the fact that the alleged terms of the law of 509 imposed more restrictions on magistrates than those of the law of 300 is another reason for disbelief in it. However, the difference in phrasing may not be significant: *-que* can be disjunctive (see ix. 19. 3 n.); *-ue* appears in our passage in the description of the *lex Porcia*; and, above all, L. is not precise in his use of technical terms.

[2] Several scholars have noted that the laws of *prouocatio* are more likely to have benefited those engaging in political activity than common criminals, whom no one would have wished to see protected against magisterial coercion. See e.g. Kunkel (1962) 29.

[3] It is worth noting that the *lex Valeria* is unique among the progressive legislation of the period 366–289, most of which was initiated by tribunes of the plebs or plebeian dictators, in being initiated by a consul and a patrician.

[4] In an extreme version of this thesis Ferenczy (1976: 191) argued that Ap. Claudius Caecus was the main instigator of the law of 300, on the grounds that his natural instincts were to champion the poor against the oligarchy, and that he would have wanted a measure to counterbalance the Ogulnian plebiscite, which favoured the *nobiles*; but we know nothing about Appius' view of *prouocatio*, and we should be cautious about viewing Roman politics solely from the perspective of one man, and at that not the most distinguished Roman of his day.

[5] For this view see e.g. Heuss (1944) 119, Magdelain (1990) 570–1, and Cloud (1998) 47. Preferable is the view of Humbert (1988: 484–8), who argues that the law compelled consuls for the first time to respect *prouocatio*, even when it was not supported by tribunician *appellatio*, but regards this as a victory for the tribunes rather than a sign of their weakness.

[6] For the evidence see the *addendum* to vi. 16. 3 n.

law of 300 and was retrojected wrongly by our sources to the law which they held to have been passed in 449.[1]

The absence of instances of *prouocatio* in our sources for the period after 300 needs explanation. Bleicken (1959: 356–63) held that due to the changes in society effected by the ending of the Struggle of the Orders it had become largely irrelevant and that the appeal to the plebs to take action against aggressive magistrates had been replaced by tribunician prosecutions of malefactors against the state. Even if one does not wish to argue with Bleicken for a close connection between *prouocatio* and the justice dispensed by the *concilium plebis*, it is possible that the *lex Valeria* and its sanction of *improbe factum* was so respected by magistrates in their dealings with (especially) the well-to-do, that the only instances of *prouocatio* about which we hear are those cases involving the *pontifex maximus* and another member of the governing class (the *prouocatio* of an ordinary plebeian arraigned on a criminal charge is hardly likely to have attracted much notice). Yet it is conceivable that the absence of instances of *prouocatio* is simply a quirk of our sources, who do not reflect what really happened in third- and second-century Rome: if there were no instances of magisterial transgression the *leges Porciae* would have been unnecessary.[2]

The leges Porciae *and other late republican developments.* By some later date it must have been felt that the *lex Valeria* did not provide a strong enough deterrent against magistrates and it was modified by

---

[1] Establishing the date at which the law on *prouocatio* was introduced gave Cloud (1998) needless difficulties. Although he inclined to accept the date of 300 offered by our passage, he also canvassed the possibility that all three *leges Valeriae de prouocatione* may be annalistic fabrications (see above, p. 121 n. 1), and that *prouocatio* was introduced first in the early second century. His interpretation of the two certainly historical instances of *prouocatio* (in which a magistrate clashes with a *pontifex maximus* who denies that his magisterial duties are compatible with his religious duties) may be one reason why he was uncomfortable with the date of 300. On Cloud's preferred view of these as challenges between more or less equal parties, they may suggest that in the first quarter of the second century *prouocatio* was still in transition between something akin to *sponsione prouocare* and its late republican form—and that is awkward 111 years after its introduction. However, if one places less stress than he does on the idea of a challenge between equals, and if one views the *pontifex maximus* as a superior coercing an inferior, then these cases are much closer to the idea of coercion suggested by the *lex Valeria*.

[2] Lintott (1972: 238–46) and Humbert (1988: 488–98) examine incidents in which our sources may have omitted to record that *prouocatio* played a part. The best evidence for a such trial before the people relates to the execution in 270 BC of the rebel Campanian garrison at Rhegium after a vote of the people; see D.H. xx. 16. 1, Oros. iv. 3. 5 (where note 'populi iussu'). Val. Max. ii. 7. 15 can be reconciled with these passages if one argues that the tribune (M. Fulvius Flaccus) who objected to the execution was responsible for ensuring that the matter was decided by trial.

the *leges Porciae*.[1] At *rep*. ii. 54 (quoted above) Cicero, whose testimony we have no reason to doubt, tells us that there were three *leges Porciae*.[2] However, elsewhere he and all other authors (including L. here) refer to just one *lex Porcia*: see § 4, Cic. *IIVerr*. v. 163 'o lex Porcia legesque Semproniae' (in the context of the illegal scourging of a Roman citizen by Verres), *Rab. perd*. 8 'de ciuibus contra legem Porciam uerberatis', 12 'Porcia lex uirgas ab omnium ciuium Romanorum corpore amouit', *Corn. ap*. Ascon. 61 'Porciam, principium iustissimae libertatis', Sall. *Cat*. 51. 21–2 'sed, per deos immortales, quam ob rem in sententiam non addidisti uti prius uerberibus in eos animaduorteretur? an quia lex Porcia uetat?', and [*Cic*.] 5. Since all but two of these passages refer to protection from scourging, and since there was a tendency to refer to just one *lex Porcia*, the most important (perhaps the first) of the *leges Porciae* probably strengthened the protection of Roman citizens against scourging. L.'s comments in §§ 4–5 do not make it entirely clear how this law differed from the *lex Valeria* of 300, but an obvious interpretation of his remarks is that the sanction *improbe factum* in the *lex Valeria* was replaced by a *grauis poena* (presumably the threat of a heavy fine or a capital prosecution). Alternatively, a/the *lex Valeria* may have banned scourging only as a prelude to execution (esp. if *-que* in our passage is significant);[3] a/the *lex Porcia* any scourging *contra prouocationem*.[4]

The identity of the Porcius or Porcii who promulgated this and the other two laws is uncertain. Fest. 266–8: 'PRO SCAPULIS cum dicit Cato, significat pro iniuria uerberum. nam complures leges erant in ciues rogatae, quibus sanciebatur poena uerberum. his significat prohibuisse multos suos ciues in ea oratione quae est contra

---

[1] For the *leges Porciae* see esp. Martin (1970) 87–91 and Lintott (1972) 249–53, which supersede Bleicken, *RE* xxiii. 2447–50; also Brunt (1964) 447–8 and Lovisi (1999) 208–17. Martin shows that there is no evidence for Bleicken's contention that a *lex Porcia* introduced the right of exile for those condemned on a capital charge.

[2] Cicero is doubted by Bauman (1973: 46–7) and Cloud (1984: 1375), who hold that there was just one *lex Porcia*; but it is hard to find a plausible motive for the invention of the two extra *leges Porciae* (contrast the three alleged Valerian laws, which are part of the wider problem of the undue prominence of the Valerii in our sources for early Rome). Bauman's view that the existence of three Porcian laws was 'evidently a Porcian claim to numerical parity with the Valerii' trivializes the workings of Roman politics and historiography.

[3] Thus e.g. Lovisi (1999) 199–200. She finds confirmation of this in the famous story of M'. Curius Dentatus' punishment of the man who failed to respond to the call of the levy (Varr. *ap*. Non. p. 28, Val. Max. vi. 3. 4); but one may conjecture other reasons why Curius chose to sell and not to kill the man.

[4] Martin wondered whether a *lex Porcia* banned all flogging and execution of Roman citizens rather than flogging and execution *aduersus prouocationem*. Lintott rightly observes that the legend on the coin of the moneyer Laeca (for whom see below) suggests otherwise.

M. Caelium (*ORF* 8 fr. 117): "si em percussi, saepe incolumis abii; praeterea pro republica, pro scapulis atque aerario multum rei publicae profuit"' is in several respects obscure and hard to translate;[1] but since a *lex Porcia* was connected with scourging, and since in this fragment Cato is saying that he protected the shoulders of citizens from scourging, it has been argued that as either praetor in 198 or consul in 195 Cato passed a *lex Porcia* which protected citizens from scourging.[2] This is possible, but, since praetorian legislation was unusual, and since the absence of a reference to this law in our good sources for Cato's consulship is surprising, Cato perhaps merely supported legislation in which citizens were protected from scourging. In which case the legislation may have been introduced by other Porcii contemporary with Cato, such as P. Porcius Laeca (*tr. pl.* 199, *pr.* 195) or L. Porcius Licinus (*pr.* 193).[3]

That this or another Porcius Laeca was responsible for at least one of the *leges Porciae* is made virtually certain by a coin issued in 110 or 109 BC by the moneyer P. Porcius Laeca (see FIG. 2, also Crawford [1974] 313–14 and plate xl). On its reverse this depicts a figure in *paludamentum* with right hand raised to give an order, a lictor with one rod in his right hand and two in his left, and a figure in a toga gesturing protectively with his right hand, and bears the legend *PROVOCO*.[4] The contrast on the coin between military and civilian dress shows that the *lex Porcia* in question guaranteed the right of *prouocatio* to Roman citizens anywhere, a deduction confirmed by a famous passage of Cicero (*IIVerr.* v. 158–68), which reveals that in the early first century BC *prouocatio* was valid in the provinces, and by the *lex repetundarum* (Crawford [1996] no. 1) § 78, which shows that *prouocatio* was granted to Latins, a privilege that would have conferred much benefit only if it was efficacious outside Rome.

The import of the third *lex Porcia* is less easily deduced, but, since at Numantia in 134–133 Scipio is said (*per.* lvii) to have punished Roman citizens in his army with *uites* but allies with *uirgae*, and since Livius Drusus in 122 proposed a law forbidding the flogging of Latins even on military service (Plut. *C. Gracch.* 9. 5), it perhaps gave Roman citizens rights *militiae* as well as *domi*.[5]

---

[1] I have quoted Lindsay's text, which is essentially that of the *codex Farnesianus*. Paul. Fest. 267 adds nothing.

[2] See e.g. Lintott (1972) 249.

[3] See Astin (1978) 22.

[4] For this description see e.g. Martin (1970: 88), Lintott (1972: 250), and Crawford, who refute Bleicken (1959: 362).

[5] It could have been one of the laws 'quae . . . rem militarem impedirent' abrogated in 109 (Ascon. p. 54).

FIG. 2. Obverse of *denarius* of P. Porcius Laeca
minted in 110 or 109 BC and celebrating *prouocatio*

The *leges Porciae* show that protection from magisterial coercion
remained a political issue in the first two-thirds of the second
century. Thereafter it was thrust more firmly into the political lime-
light by the tribunates of the Gracchi: Ti. Gracchus may have proposed a law allowing appeal from the judgement of a *quaestio* (see
Plut. *Ti. Gracch.* 16. 1); M. Fulvius Flaccus probably tried to introduce a law giving it to allies (a plausible interpretation of Val. Max.
ix. 5. 1); and C. Gracchus, in response to the execution of supporters
of his brother by the consuls of 132 acting under the authority of the
senate, certainly passed a *lex Sempronia* which seems to have
reaffirmed the laws on *prouocatio* and made it illegal for citizens to be
executed on the judgement of any *quaestio* that had been set up by
consuls without a prior vote of the populace.[1] Against this law the
ideology of the so-called *senatus consultum ultimum* was diametrically
opposed, and many of the great conflicts in the final seventy years of

---

[1] For this law see Cic. *IIVerr.* v. 163, *Rab. perd.* 12, *Cat.* iv. 10 (with Σ Ambr. p. 271 and Σ
Gron. p. 289), and perhaps *Cluent.* 151 and Plut. *C. Gracch.* 4. 2; the other passages cited by
Rotondi (1912: 309–10) as evidence for this *lex Sempronia* do not mention it by name. For the
political context of the law see e.g. Bleicken (1959) 363–6, Martin (1970) 91–2, and Brunt
(1988) 225.

republican history came about when its provisions were broken by the likes of Opimius and Cicero.[1]

The retrojection of the *lex Valeria* to (probably) 449, 509, and the regal period is part of the general phenomenon by which our sources' presentation of early Roman political history is coloured by the events of the late Republic.[2] If the scenes in books ii and iii in which *prouocatio* appears have no basis in reality (as Cloud's model requires), their invention may have been inspired by scenes in the forum in the late Republic; if some dim memory of the use of *prouocatio* in the fifth century did survive to the time of the annalists, it is likely to have been elaborated on the basis of such scenes. Martin (1970: 95) has noted that a possible motive for the retrojection of the *lex Valeria* to 509 or the regal period was to remove it from the Struggle of the Orders and hence the credit for its introduction from the plebeian leaders, to whom later *populares* looked back. Some scholars have suggested that Valerius Antias is likely to have been responsible for the retrojection,[3] but one may suspect that an idea so deep-rooted originated rather earlier: the ascription of laws to Valerius Publicola reflects an urge to believe that important republican institutions had always been present in its constitution.

For further discussion of all or some of the matters considered in this note see e.g. Rotondi (1912) 190, 204, 235–6, 268–9, Heuss (1944) 104–24, Staveley (1954), Bleicken (1955) 110–20, (1959), *RE* xxiii. 2444–63, Kunkel (1962) esp. 21–33, Brunt (1964) and (1988) 222–5, 522–3, Ogilvie on ii. 8 and iii. 55. 5, Lintott (1968) 161–4, (1972), (1999) 147–62, Martin (1970), Jolowicz and Nicholas (1972) 305–17, Jones (1972) 1–44, Bauman (1973), Ferenczy (1976) 190–3, Astin (1978) 21–3, Develin (1978) 45–55, Amirante (1983), Cloud (1984) and (1998), Humbert (1988), Drummond (1989) 219–21, Magdelain (1990) 567–88, Cornell (1995) 276–7, and Lovisi (1999) 184–218.

3–4. diligentius sanctam . . . sanxit: *sancire* has a wide range of meaning in legal contexts, for example 'ratify', 'enact', 'make an offence punishable'. It is modified by *diligenter* also at Cic. *inu.* ii. 146 (in the context of penalties), *leg. agr.* i. 13, *Pis.* 90, and *leg.* ii. 37; note also Cic. *IIVerr.* iii. 20 'legem . . . acutissime ac diligentissime scrip-

---

[1] *prouocatio* makes its final appearance in our sources for the Republic in 44 BC, when Antony proposed to introduce it for those convicted of *uis* or *maiestas* in the *quaestiones perpetuae*, a proposal to which Cicero took strong exception (*Phil.* i. 21).

[2] See esp. Martin (1970) 94–6.

[3] See e.g. Staveley (1954) 414 and (with particular reference to the possible invention of the law of 300) Cloud (1984) 1368–9 and (1998) 47.

tam . . . scripta lex ita diligenter . . . ita diligenter sunt iura constituta'. These parallels suggest that 'more carefully enacted' is the primary meaning; but, since both the first of these parallels and *sanxit* here appear in the context of penalties, the sense 'more carefully protected' must also be present, hinting at the *sanctio* familiar from some charters of the late Republic and early principate (for a good example see *lex Irn.* ch. 96 [González (1986) 181]). Citing Cic. *rep.* ii. 54 (note too *sanxit* here), Bispham (1997: 128) notes that the *leges Porciae* are the first laws for which a *sanctio* is attested. If one limits one's search to the noun *sanctio*, this is true, but in this context it is hard to regard 'Valeria lex . . . nihil ultra quam "improbe factum" adiecit' as referring to anything other than a *sanctio*; see also *sanciebatur* in Fest. 266–8 (quoted above, pp. 131–2), referring to several laws earlier than the *leges Porciae*. In general on *sanctiones*, see the survey of Bispham (1997: 128–48), with further bibliography on p. 128.

Alschefski's conjecture *sancienda* for *sanctam* is possible but unnecessary.

4. reor: see viii. 40. 4 n.
paucorum: see vi. 14. 12 n.
opes: see ix. 42. 4 n.

5. 'improbe factum': 'improperly performed'. *improbus* often combines the ideas of being incorrect and morally unacceptable; cf. Gell. xv. 13. 11 = *xii tab.* viii. 11 (Crawford [1996] 690–1, where other less full sources are cited) 'qui se sierit testarier libripensue fuerit, ni testimonium fariatur (*codd.*: fatiatur *Schoell*: fateatur *Ernout–Meillet*), improbus intestabilis esto'. For the combination with *facere* see viii. 10. 12 n. and perhaps add *amprufid facus estud* in l. 30 of the *lex Osca tabulae Bantinae* (see Crawford and Coleman in Crawford [1996] 291). The consequences for a magistrate of being informed that one's action was *improbe factum* are nowhere specified but would certainly have included a blow to his public reputation (thus e.g. Cloud [1998] 47) and may have left him exposed to a censorial *nota* (thus Amirante [1983] 23–4) or prosecution (Crawford and Coleman loc. cit.). See further Lovisi (1999) 198–9.

6. uinclum . . . legis: the genitive is subjective 'restraint provided by the law'; for the expression cf. iv. 4. 10 and 13. 11.
nunc uix serio ita minetur quisquam is the (conjectural) reading of the *codex Klockianus*, now defective in this passage but reported by Drakenborch (see vol. i, p. 315). L. means that in his day the rebuke

improbe factum seemed ludicrously weak. W–M suggest that *uix* is taken better with *quisquam* than with *serio* 'now hardly anyone would threaten seriously in this way', but in view of iv. 25. 13 'parua nunc res et uix serio agenda uideri possit' and xxxix. 42. 12 'et cum is uixdum serio adnuisset' it should perhaps be taken with both.

For *uix serio ita* M has *uix seruos ero ita*, P¹ *uixsum r serio ita*, Pᶜ *uixsum serio ita*, U *uix si summo serio ita*, OZT *uix seruo ita*, and θ *uix seru ita*. Unless the reading of the *codex Klockianus* is wrong, and L. referred to a slave or slaves in this passage, as some of the mss suggest, then the easiest explanation of the diverse corruptions in the mss is that **N** had something like *serio* (or a corruption of it) and *seruo* as variants (as Walters notes, this is suggested particularly by the reading of M; for variants in **N**, see vol. i, pp. 316–20). Among other conjectures *uix serio suis ita* (Pighius) is similar in meaning to that adopted but gives less taut Latin (however, it may seem more attractive if one rejects the notion of variants in **N**); *uix si summa* (= *summa supplicia*) *serio ita* (Doujat) is barely intelligible;[1] and *uix si summas poenas* (Gronovius, tentatively) is too far from the paradosis. Several scholars have sought to retain a form of *seruus*. Haupt (1842: 474 = 1875–6: i. 150) argued that M has more or less what L. wrote (*seruos* being an equivalent to *seruus*); but 'now a slave would hardly threaten his master in this way' is absurd, since L., a traditionalist, is unlikely to have approved of any insubordination from slave towards master. *uix seruos* (i.e. *seruus* = παιδαγωγός) *puero* (H. J. Müller) lessens the absurdity, but L.'s imagination is unlikely to have strayed to tutors and their pupils. If a reference to a slave is to be retained, it is preferable to have *seruo* in the dative and to paraphrase L.'s meaning as 'now the tame *improbe factum* would hardly be said to a slave, even though one might have thought it would be more efficacious said to someone who was totally in the power of his or her master'. Conjectures on these lines include *uix seruo herus ita* (Salvinius); *uix seruo serio ita* (Alschefski, anticipating Niemeyer [1890: 710]), which gives better sense than that previously mentioned, in which *herus* would be redundant; and the conjecture in OZT, which could be explained by the hypothesis of variants in **N** and which gives sense that is even tauter and better ('now hardly anyone would threaten a slave in this way'). This reading could be right, but *serio* is supported by the parallels quoted above, and the general application of L.'s point is somewhat weakened by the introduction of a reference to a slave.

---

[1] To be fair to Doujat, he was trying to take account of U's reading (known to him through Gronovius' reports of its descendants Gr and Gb).

For L.'s view of the degeneration of Roman society and his disapproval of many of the customs of his own day see vi. 12. 5 n.

9. 7–9. *Foreign affairs*

Neither the notice of fighting against the Aequi nor that of the
Roman attack on Nequinum (supported implicitly by Steph. Byz.
ethn. [*s.u.* Νηκούια] Νηκούια, πόλις Ὀμβρικῶν. Διονύσιος ἑπτακαιδεκάτῳ
Ῥωμαϊκῆς ἀρχαιολογίας. τὸ ἐθνικὸν Νηκουιάτης) presents any difficulty.
This was Rome's last Aequan campaign, and it fits into the sequence
of hostilities which began in 304 (see ix. 29. 1–5 and 45. 1–18 nn.).
The colonization of Nequinum as Narnia guarantees that the town
fell in these years, and we have no reason to doubt that the Roman
assault began in 299. The advance on it follows the excursion into
Umbria in 303 (1. 4–6) and the alliance with Ocriculum in 308 (ix. 41.
20); see in general pp. 27–30 above, De Sanctis (1907–64) ii. 348,
Harris (1971) 65, and Bradley (2000) 113–15. L. reports these events
briefly and with very little elaboration.

9. 7. haudquaquam memorabile: see vii. 10. 5 n.
**cum praeter animos feroces nihil ex antiqua fortuna haber-
ent:** see ix. 43. 5 n.

8. Appuleius: see 5. 14 n.
Vmbria: see above, pp. 27–30.
Nequinum was captured and colonized by the Romans in 299 (10.
1–5). Since the name of the site reminded the Romans of the ill-
omened adjective *nequam*, they renamed it Narnia (whence modern
Narni), after the nearby river Nar, the modern Nera (see 10. 5 and
Steph. Byz. *ethn. s.u.* Ναρνία [quoted below, p. 153]); for this practice
of renaming, see ix. 27. 14 n. Later, Narnia was one of the colonies
which refused to supply extra manpower to Rome in 209 BC (xxvii. 9.
7), but the most exciting period of her early history came in AD 69,
when Vitellius attempted to use the town as a bulwark against the
advancing Flavian troops (Tac. *hist.* iii. 58. 1–79. 2).

Narnia lies in a splendidly strategic position, on a high hill which
controls the narrow gorge of the part of the Nera valley which links
the Tiber valley around Horta (Orte) and Ocriculum (Otricoli) to the
plain of Interamna Nahars (Terni). Ancient authors often comment
on the site. With L.'s remarks here compare Sil. viii. 457–8, Mart. vii.
93. 1–2 'Narnia, sulphureo quam gurgite candidus amnis | circuit,
ancipiti uix adeunda iugo', Claud. xxviii. 515 'celsa dehinc patulum

FIG. 3 Fragments of the original walls of
the colony at Narnia near the cathedral

prospectans Narnia campum', Serv. *Aen.* vii. 517, and Procop. *bell.* v.
17. 8–11.

A few Roman antiquities are visible in the modern town, including
a small stretch of *opus quadratum* near the cathedral that may date
from the foundation of the republican colony (see FIG. 3).

See further Philipp, *RE* xvi. 1734–6 and Gaggiotti *et al.* (1980)
47–9.

arduus is the reading of Π; Μλ have the doublet *arduus altus*. This
doublet may be explained by postulating either that in **N** *altus* and
arduus stood as alternative readings or that one was a gloss on the
other (although it is not easy to see why either word should have
required explanation), and that, while the scribe of Π correctly chose
just one reading, those of μλ conflated both. (Alternatively, the
conflation was found already in **N**, and Π's reading is a conjecture;
but, since **N** is known to have had variants, this is perhaps less likely.) We must therefore choose between the two adjectives, and it
seems clear that Π was right: *altus* is a banalization of *arduus* (which
L. uses twenty-four times elsewhere). See further vol. i, pp. 316–20,
Welz (1852) 13–14, and Winkler (1890–2) ii. 19.

nunc: see vii. 39. 16 n.

nec ui nec munimento capi poterat: for Roman interest in the different ways in which a town might be captured, see vi. 3. 10 n.; for L.'s commenting on how the geographical position of a town made it easy or difficult to capture, see ix. 26. 1–2 n.

9. eam infectam rem: see ix. 32. 6 n.

M. Fuluius Paetus: (96). M. Fulvius Cn. f. Cn. n. Paet(in)us (*F.T.* record the filiation in full and the *cognomen* in extended form, the fragments of *F.C.* some of the filiation) is not known apart from his activities in this year. Whether he was related to L. Fulvius L. f. L. n. Curvus (*cos.* 322 [viii. 38. 1 n.]) and his son M. Fulvius L. f. L. n. Curvus Paetinus (*cos. suff.* 305 [ix. 44. 15 n.]) is unclear, but for a possible relationship to Cn. Fulvius Cn. f. Cn. n. Maximus, the consul of 298, see 4. 7 n. For the variation in spelling between Paetus and Paetinus, see vii. 1. 2 n.

T. Manlius Torquatus: (81). Otherwise unknown, and not enough of *F.C.* survives to give his filiation; Münzer, *RE* xiv. 1207, suggested that he was the grandson of the famous Torquatus (vii. 4. 4 n.), and the son of the son of Torquatus executed before the Veseris (viii. 7. 1 n.); he could also have been a son born to the great Torquatus in his old age. The T. Manlius T. f. T. n. Torquatus who was censor in 247 may well have been his grandson.

9. 10–13. *Elections to the curule aedileship for 299*

The evidence provided by L. makes it impossible to be certain who held the curule aedileship in 299.[1] On his testimony Macer and Tubero (the latter perhaps using Macer as a source: see 9. 10. n.) held that, although all the centuries wished to elect Fabius Rullianus to the consulship, he refused election on the grounds that the circumstances did not justify it and that an urban magistracy would suit him and the state better; he was therefore elected curule aedile. However, Piso held that Cn. Domitius Calvinus and Sp. Carvilius Maximus were aediles in this year.

---

[1] Both L.'s use of *in eum annum* in § 10 straight after § 9 'M. Fuluius Paetus T. Manlius Torquatus noui consules' and his reference at 11. 9 to Fabius Rullianus as curule aedile show that L. describes the aedilician elections for 299. The status of § 14 'eo anno' is less clear. At 9. 14–10. 1: 'haec Romae gesta. ceterum ad Nequinum . . .' there may be a contrast between the internal and external affairs of 299. However, it is also possible that all of 9. 10–14 may refer to 300; in which case Broughton (*MRR* i. 172) and Taylor (1960: 56) would be in error in holding that at 9. 14 L. refers to the censors of 300 under 299.

The testimony of both Piso (or at least what L. claims for Piso) and Macer and Tubero can be challenged. It is not absolutely certain that in 299 the agreement by which patricians and plebeians held the curule aedileship in alternate years was in force (see further vii. 1. 6 with n. and *corrigendum*); but, if it was (as the appearance of plebeian curule aediles in 296, and the virtually certain appearance of a patrician in 295, suggest), then Piso as reported by L. must be wrong to have plebeian curule aediles in an odd-numbered year of the third century. Yet since there is no obvious reason why he or a source should have invented the names of Domitius and Carvilius (both unimportant),[1] it is easier to believe that he made an inadvertent slip, either by recording plebeian aediles as curule or (more probably) by placing the aedileship of Domitius and Carvilius in the wrong year.[2] If one desires entirely to absolve Piso from error, one may argue that these slips were made by L.

A further reason for trying to save Piso's evidence is the frailty of that offered by Macer. When an older and a younger annalist are in conflict, the older should generally be regarded as more reliable, since as the annalistic tradition progressed errors and fabrications were more likely than corrections to establish a place in it. Moreover, whereas Piso had no obvious motive for inventing the names that he presents, Macer records the election of the most famous Roman of the day (Fabius Rullianus) and of the bearer of a name greatly celebrated in the Samnite Wars (Papirius Cursor): these are precisely the kind of men whose careers the late annalists liked to embroider. Furthermore, although iteration in the aedileship is attested in this

---

[1] Even if Piso meant to refer to the well-known Sp. Carvilius C. f. Maximus, this Carvilius rose to fame only in 293, and there was no need to invent a magistracy for him in 299. If Piso was the source or ultimate source of Plin. *nat.* xxxiii. 17 (quoted at vol. iii, pp. 602–3), in which the defeat of Domitius by Cn. Flavius in the aedilician elections of 304 is recorded, he may have thought it worth noting the year in which Domitius was finally elected to this magistracy; but (*a*) it is far from clear that Piso was Pliny's source or ultimate source (see vol. iii, pp. 606–7), and (*b*) this is hardly a motive for fabrication of information which was not available.

[2] Raimondi (1995*b*: 152) suggests that the confusion may have been caused by Piso's omission of two consular years a little earlier (see ix. 44. 3–4); but this theory could work only if Piso was adding information on the aediles that was calculated by intervals of years ('six years later' rather than 'in the consulship of . . .'), and this seems improbable. Radke (1991: 70–2), concerned to reconcile the alleged notice at Mart. Cap. iii. 261 that Ap. Claudius Caecus started the use of the letter *G* with that at Plut. *quaest. Rom.* 54 = *mor.* 277d, in which the invention is ascribed to a Sp. Carvilius, suggested ingeniously but very implausibly that the notice about the election of Carvilius should be referred to 304 BC, and that Carvilius was a replacement for the colleague of Flavius who was sick in this year (ix. 46. 9): Appius, he argues, will have influenced Carvilius, as he is known to have influenced Flavius. Unfortunately, the passage of Martianus Capella mentions only that Appius was averse to the letter *Z* (see vol. iii, p. 354), and Radke does not attempt to explain L.'s notice concerning Domitius, who cannot have been the sick colleague, since Pliny states that he failed to achieve election for 304.

period (vol. iii, p. 352), it is hard to believe that Fabius Rullianus returned to this post twenty-nine years after he had first held it. Wilful perversion of the evidence on the part of Macer therefore seems quite likely, a possibility strengthened by the implausibility of some of the notice relating to Fabius' alleged activities as aedile (11. 9 [n.]). L. himself (§ 13) charitably thought that confusion over two men who bore the *cognomen* Maximus, one involved in the consular elections, the other in the aedilician, may have led Macer astray and to the invention of the *fabula*. However, if some of Macer's credit is to be saved it is preferable to follow Münzer, *RE* vi. 1807, in suggesting that it may have been Rullianus' son, Gurges, who was aedile and that Macer or a source failed to realize this (Gurges was almost certainly curule aedile in 295 [31. 9 n.] but we have seen that iteration in this office was possible); but Macer or his source will still have been responsible for inventing the tale about the consular elections.

That we are dealing here with an annalistic invention will seem all the more plausible when it is noted that our passage is the first in a series of greatly elaborated episodes involving the possible or actual election of Fabius Rullianus to a magistracy. Analysis of these episodes will show once again (cf. 6. 3–9. 2 n.) just how much fictional material has attached itself to both Fabius Rullianus and Ap. Claudius in the political narratives of book x.

At 13. 5–13 (the elections for the consulate of 297) L. tells us that Rullianus was on the point of being elected, when he objected that he was both ineligible (for no one could be consul within ten years of a previous tenure of that magistracy) and too old. The tribunes of the plebs, however, encouraged the populace to ignore his modesty; and accordingly Fabius both was elected and ensured the election of his old ally P. Decius Mus as his colleague (this last a theme we shall meet again).[1] Several motifs in this later episode recall our passage: on both occasions L. describes Fabius as *non petentem*; on both occasions he is the unanimous choice of the centuries (9. 10, 13. 5, 13. 13); and on both occasions the motif of external danger is important: in our passage it is a reason why Fabius will not stand, but at 13. 5 it impels his election. The impression that 13. 5–13 is invented is

---

[1] Suda α 3435 Ἀπομαχομένου, ἀνθισταμένου, παραιτουμένου. ἀπομαχομένου δὲ τοῦ Φαβίου καὶ πολλὰς ποιουμένου δεήσεις, ἵνα τῆς ἀρχῆς ἀπολυθείη (referring to Fabius' refusal to countenance election) and π 306 Παραγγέλλοντα: δεχόμενον τὴν ἀρχήν. ὁ δὲ Φάβιος λαβὼν τὴν ἀρχὴν Πόπλιον ἀποδείκνυσιν ὕπατον, οὐδ' αὐτὸν παραγγέλλοντα τὴν ἀρχήν (referring to the election of Decius [the Suda misunderstands the meaning of παραγγέλλοντα, which is equivalent to *profitentem*]) probably derive from a lost portion of D.H. and must refer either to these elections or to those for 295; see the full discussion of Favuzzi (1999). That L.'s version is found also in another writer merely shows that the inventions in his account go back to his annalistic sources.

strengthened by the fact that Fabius may in fact have been eligible for the consulship in this year, having been consul last in 308, exactly ten years previously.[1]

Much the same applies to x. 15. 7–12, the elections for 296, which on this occasion were being held by Fabius himself. Once again we meet the motif of the spontaneous election of Fabius by all the centuries (§ 7). On this occasion, however, Ap. Claudius, in the stereotypical guise of the patrician reactionary, wants an all-patrician college. Fabius' reaction will by now be unsurprising ([§ 9] 'Fabius primo de se eadem fere quae priore anno dicendo abnuere'). There follows a scene of picturesque invented detail, in which the patricians beg him to help them rescue the consulate from the plebeians; this may be compared with the protestations of the tribunes the year before (13. 8–9). Finally Fabius relents to the extent that he states that he is prepared to allow two patricians to be elected so long as he is not one of them. In the event L. Volumnius, a plebeian, was elected with Appius, and the *nobiles* concluded that Fabius was afraid of having Appius as a colleague. As Forni (1953: 188–90) points out, the surprising conclusion to L.'s tale hardly fits the words which he gives to Fabius and suggests that his account of the episode is unreliable.[2] Here we may see very clearly how clashes between Appius and Fabius have deliberately been given prominence in L.'s narrative; and this is doubtless one reason why the roles of each have been made more prominent elsewhere.

L.'s account of internal Roman politics in 295 is extremely complicated and is discussed more fully at 24. 1–31. 7 n.; here we need examine only 22. 1–9, the account of the elections for that year, in which motifs appear that are by now familiar. When he was about to hold the elections Volumnius Flamma warns the populace of the great danger that was threatening; consequently (22. 1) 'nemini dubium erat quin Q. Fabius omnium consensu destinaretur', and once again all the centuries make him consul together with L. Volumnius himself. It is no surprise to find that (22. 2) 'Fabi oratio fuit, qualis biennio ante'; but, as in the elections for 297, he is persuaded to change his mind on condition that Decius is made his

---

[1] However, a difficulty for this argument is that by the second century the ten-year rule on iteration was interpreted as a gap of ten whole years between the holding of the office: see vol. ii, p. 25 n. 69. Stewart (1998: 173), following Broughton (*MRR* i. 175 n. 1), states with undue confidence that 'the incident belongs to 295'.

[2] Forni's principal contention, that this was the year in which M'. Curius Dentatus as tribune successfully opposed the attempt of Appius as *interrex* to procure the election of two patricians (see Cic. *Brut.* 55), could be right only if L. has omitted to record an *interregnum*. It is safer to admit that we do not know the year in which this clash occurred.

colleague. Again, as in the elections for 297, Fabius introduces the motif of his age: (22. 3) 'id senectuti suae adminiculum fore . . . nouo imperii socio uix iam adsuescere senilem animum posse'. Volumnius approves of all this, delivers a solemn sermon on the merits of concord between the consuls, and duly oversees the election of Fabius and Decius.[1]

The regular occurrence of these motifs in L.'s narrative of the Third Samnite War is in itself noteworthy,[2] but it suggests also that the account of the aedilician elections for 299 presented by Licinius Macer and Aelius Tubero is a literary invention. It is an attractive theory that Macer was responsible for most of the annalistic elaboration in the passages analysed above (we know that he was quite capable of inventing extra magistracies for the protagonists of his history [see vol. i, p. 92]).[3] However, given the nature of our evidence, it is incapable of proof, and others, not least L. himself, probably played their part.

For scepticism concerning L.'s account of the involvement of Rullianus in the elections of this year, see Münzer, *RE* vi. 1807–8 and Forsythe (1994) 347; for this scepticism extended also to L.'s account of the elections for 297–295 see Klinger (1884) 15–16, 21–3, and 26 (who argued for invention by Licinius Macer), Develin (1985) 149–52, Raimondi (1995*b*)[4] and Walt (1997) 283. Stewart (1998:

---

[1] The episode then ends with the following details (22. 8–9): 'his agendis dies est consumptus. postridie ad praescriptum consulis et consularia et praetoria comitia habita. consules creati Q. Fabius et P. Decius, Ap. Claudius praetor, omnes absentes'. Part of this may be plausible invention; but why Fabius was absent the day after he had spoken to the assembly is not made clear, and this may be an authentic detail that has been merged unsuccessfully with the surrounding annalistic invention.

[2] The motif of Fabius Rullianus' refusing an election appears also at *uir. ill.* 32. 2, where he is said to have refused a second censorhip, and at Val. Max. iv. 1. 5 (cf. Polyaen. viii. 15), where he is alleged to have recommended to the people that they should not elect his son consul (see 14. 10 n.).

[3] For a different opinion, see the views of Raimondi analysed in the next footnote.

[4] Raimondi pays particular attention to 13. 5–13, suggesting that this scene is modelled on Marius' election to the consulship of 102, which is described at Plut. *Mar.* 14. 12–14. She argues that the annalist responsible for the invention was critical of Marius and created this account of Rullianus' sincere behaviour to contrast with the insincerity of Marius, and that Rullianus' legalistic behaviour resembles that of another legalist, Sulla, who refused election to the consulship of 79 (App. *ciu.* i. 103. 480). She further argues that the annalist responsible for the invention cannot have been Macer, since Macer is unlikely to have been critical of Marius, and since Macer's inventions, as revealed (in her opinion) by the present passage, are a defence of Marius (Rullianus' suggestion that he be kept in reserve for a *bellicosior annus* reflecting Macer's view that the behaviour of Marius was more altruistic).

In general, one should be very cautious in claiming to find precise echoes of events from the period 133–31 BC in annalistic narratives as mediated to us by L., D.H., and others (see vol. i, p. 88). However, there certainly are similarities between L. and Plutarch: compare § 5 'cum illustres uiri consulatum peterent' with μετιόντων δὲ πολλῶν καὶ ἀγαθῶν τὴν ὑπατείαν, 'non

172–4) optimistically inclines to accept most of the material relating to the elections of 297 and 295 that L. presents, Loreto (1992–3: 348–50) all of it.

10. non petentem: so long as the presiding magistrate was agreeable, there was nothing unusual about the election of someone who had not made an earlier *professio*; cf. 22. 2–9 and Suda π 306 (P. Decius Mus elected consul for 295), xxvi. 18. 7 (P. Scipio professes for the command in Spain only on the day of the election), 22. 2–13 (Marcellus and Valerius Laevinus elected consuls for 210), and Plut. *Aem.* 10. 3–5 (Aemilius Paullus elected consul for 168). See further vi. 37. 4, vii. 22. 7 nn., and Staveley (1972) 146 n. 260.

omnes . . . centuriae: cf. 11. 4, 15. 7, v. 13. 3, xxiv. 9. 3, xxvi. 22. 13, xxvii. 21. 4, and xxviii. 38. 6. L. records the fact that all centuries, by which he means all those that voted before a majority was reached, elected a candidate to emphasize the high esteem in which Fabius was held; and for his hero P. Scipio he has a hyperbolic variation on the theme: (xxvi. 18. 9) 'iussi deinde inire suffragium ad unum omnes non centuriae modo, sed etiam homines P. Scipioni imperium esse in Hispania iusserunt'. Naturally a unanimous election by the centuries was something about which one might boast—on behalf of either oneself (Cic. *imp. Pomp.* 2) or someone else (xxix. 22. 5 and Cic. *Sull.* 91).[1]

ipsum auctorem . . . differendi in bellicosiorem annum: whatever doubts one may have about the reality of this scene, interventions and speeches of this kind do seem to have occurred during elections, particularly after the *praerogatiua* had voted; cf. e.g. 15. 7–12, 22. 1–8, xxiv. 7. 12–9. 3, and xxvi. 22. 2–15. Even if these scenes rest on annalistic invention, the authors probably invented along the lines of what might possibly have happened at the elections.

Macer Licinius: see vii. 9. 4 n. with *addendum* for Licinius Macer and vi. 18. 4 n. for the inversion of *nomen* and *cognomen*.

---

petentem' with μὴ δεομένου, and 'recusantem' with παραιτεῖσθαι τὴν ἀρχὴν φάσκοντος, and, although these could be coincidental, Raimondi's suggestion that the behaviour of Rullianus reflects events involving Marius and Sulla may be right. However, even if it is right, it need not follow that Macer was not responsible for the initial invention: Macer's attitude to Marius may not have been entirely favourable (we do not know what he thought about the end of Saturninus); and, although he was strongly opposed to the policies of Sulla, he may have thought that declining the consulship of 79 was the one good thing that Sulla did. Raimondi's explanation of the motivation of Macer's inventions with regard to the aedileship of Rullianus is implausibly complex.

[1] Note too Cic. *dom.* 142, where Cicero claims that all the centuries voted for his recall.

Tubero: (150) or (156). It is disputed whether the Tubero to whom L. refers here and at iv. 23. 1–3 was L. Aelius Tubero, the friend of Cicero (thus e.g. Soltau and Badian), or, as more scholars believe (e.g. Peter, Bowersock, Ogilvie, and Wiseman) his son Quintus, the jurist. We are quite well informed about both men.[1]

Lucius served as senior legate on the staff of Quintus Cicero in Asia in 61–58 (Cic. *Q.fr.* i. 1.10 [quoted below]); met Cicero in Macedon in 58 (Cic. *Planc.* 100); and served on the Pompeian side in the civil war, during which he was involved in a quarrel with Q. Ligarius that is very well documented, most fully in Cicero's *Pro Q. Ligario* and in the (not always reliable) comments of the Gronovian scholiast on this speech. At *Lig.* 1 Cicero describes Tubero as a *propinquus*, which almost certainly implies a relationship by marriage.[2] At *Lig.* 21 Cicero tells us that he and Tubero were educated together in the same house, had shared their military *contubernium*, were connected by marriage, and had been friends all their lives; besides, he says, they shared common *studia*, by which he probably means an interest in philosophy and other literary pursuits. These statements allow the conjecture that the date of Lucius's birth was not far removed from that of Cicero in 106 BC, and that, like Cicero, he saw military service in the Social War. That Lucius wrote history is guaranteed by Cic. *Q.fr.* i. 1. 10 'quamquam legatos habes eos qui ipsi per se habituri sint rationem dignitatis tuae. de quibus honore et dignitate et aetate praestat Tubero, quem ego arbitror, praesertim cum scribat historiam, multos ex suis annalibus posse deligere quos uelit et possit imitari'.

We meet Quintus first in 49: when he was ill, his father wished to land their boat in Africa but was prevented by Ligarius and others (Caes. *ciu.* i. 31. 3, *Σ* Gron. p. 291 St.). In 48 he fought with the Pompeians at Pharsalus, and in 44 he prosecuted Ligarius before Caesar. We do not know when he was born, but he can hardly have been younger than sixteen when in 48 he fought with the Pompeians at Pharsalus; this would give 64 BC as a *terminus ante quem* for his birth. According to Pomponius (*dig.* i. 2. 2. 46) he studied as a youth

---

[1] On the basis of an uneliminable ms. reading at Gell. x. 28. 1 'K. Tubero in *historiarum* primo' (*K. Tubero* Fγ: *Tubero* δ) Unger (1891: 320–1) argued that the historian was called Caeso. Even though the ms. reading is inexplicable (*K*, a symbol used to indicate a new chapter, is sometimes interpolated into mediaeval mss, but its presence here alone in those of Gellius would be surprising), it seems unwise to use this isolated testimony to postulate a third Tubero. See further Holford-Strevens (2003) 316, who discusses this passage in the context of other names which Gellius has recorded wrongly.

[2] However, the comment of *Σ* Gron. on this passage, that Tubero had married a sister of Cicero, is probably no more than the deduction of the scholiast or one of his predecessors: if Cicero had had a sister who was married to Tubero, we should read of her elsewhere in his voluminous writings.

with Ofilius and abandoned oratory in favour of jurisprudence after his failure to secure the conviction of Ligarius; we have no reason to reject either statement. From Pompon. *dig.* i. 2. 2. 51 we may deduce that he married a daughter of the great jurist Ser. Sulpicius Rufus. We do not know what magistracies Quintus held, but the consulship was not among them. Nevertheless, two of his sons were consuls: Quintus Aelius Tubero as suffect in 11 BC, Sex. Aelius Catus as *ordinarius* in AD 4. D.H., the dates of whose residence in Italy are uncertain but who published the first book of his *Roman antiquities* twenty-two years after Augustus had brought peace (i.e. in 10 or 9 BC), dedicated his first treatise on Thucydides to a Quintus Aelius Tubero, to whom he refers at §§ 1, 25, 35, 55 and at *Amm.* ii. 1. Most scholars think that the dedicatee of Dionysius was Quintus, and indeed if Quintus had written a history, it would have been appropriate to dedicate a treatise on Thucydides to him; but we cannot be certain that the dedicatee was not the suffect consul of 11 BC. All our other testimonia for Quintus relate to his prosecution of Ligarius or to his writings.

It has been argued that Quintus is nowhere clearly attested as having written history and that, even if he did write a history, he was too young to have been the writer used by L. The second argument is more easily dismissed. We have seen that he must have been born before 64, which would make him only five years older than L., who was born in 59. But if his father was born around 106, then he could easily have been born earlier, perhaps around 75. If he was born in 75, he would have been 27 at Pharsalus; he could have married in the 40s in time to have a son who was suffect consul in 11; and he could have lived long enough to receive a dedication from Dionysius of Halicarnassus. He could have written his history *c*.40–35 BC, when he would have been between thirty-five and forty. And he may have been even older than this. Gellius (i. 22. 7) tells us that Cicero regarded Quintus Tubero as the equal of his ancestors in jurisprudence: since it is hard to see that this Quintus Tubero can be anyone other than the son of Lucius, he must have been old enough for Cicero, who died in 43, to respect.

The first argument may appear paradoxical, since Peter assigned all the historical fragments of Tubero to Quintus, and since his *praenomen* appears in frr. 6 (= iv. 23. 1–3), 10A, and 11; but the ascription of fr. 10A depends on an uncertain conjecture of Reifferscheid; fr. 11 could be from a work of jurisprudence; and at iv. 23. 1, where Ogilvie prints 'Antias et Q. Tubero', most of the mss are corrupt (*Antias et Q. Tubero* UZ: *antiates Q. Tubero* V: *antias et q̄*

tuuō M: *antiasset q̄. itubero* H: *ancias et q. tuuero* P: *acias et q. tubero*
O). From a palaeographical point of view the easiest solution to this
textual problem is that L. wrote what is found in UZ: note in particular that, an anagrammatic corruption of -*s et* apart, V, which is
independent of **N**, has this. This reading may be a conjecture; but the
readings of P and O show that what stood in Π was not very
different.[1] Nevertheless, a disadvantage of the reading of UZ is that
it introduces a *praenomen*, something that L. employs elsewhere in
his citation of sources only at xxi. 38. 3 'L. Cincius Alimentus, qui
captum se ab Hannibale scribit', where the fact that Cincius took part
in the events described may put this passage in a different class. Even
if one argues that L. wished to give Tubero a second name to balance
the two names that he had given to Macer and Antias, it remains
the case that the reading of OZ, although attractive, introduces an
oddity, and that in general the evidence for Quintus having written a
history is less good than is usually believed.

If one conjectures that all our fragments of the historical writings
of Tubero come from the work of one man, whichever Tubero he
may have been (this conjecture is not certain, but it would be surprising if L. and D.H., at least, were using different authors, and it is
not invalidated by the statement of D.H. [i. 7. 3] that he used Aelii,
since in the following words he refers also to Gellii and Calpurnii),
we may argue that, since fr. 3 refers to Romulus, fr. 4 to Servius
Tullius, fr. 6 to 434 BC, fr. 7 to 300–299 BC, fr. 8 to 256 BC and fr. 9 to
the death of Regulus at some point after 255, this work must have
covered at least the period from Romulus to 255; and, since fr. 2
seems to relate to the Trojan horse, it may have begun with the sack
of Troy and the flight of Aeneas from Troy. Fr. 4 on Servius Tullius
came from book i, and if in the chapter heading of Gell. vii. 4 a very
easy conjecture of Gronovius (*nonae* for *nouae*) is right, then fr. 9 on
Regulus came from book ix. If a book of Tubero was roughly equivalent in length to a book of L., this would show that Tubero wrote at
approximately half the length that L. did. From fr. 14, the chronological context of which is unfortunately irrecoverable, we learn that
Tubero reached at least book xiv, which, if the conjecture of
Gronovius mentioned above is correct, should fall somewhere in the
Hannibalic War or its aftermath. If frr. 10A and 11 are rightly

---

[1] The rival conjecture of Unger (1891: 321), *Antias atque Tubero*, would be a harder corruption to explain and would introduce *atque* before a *t*, which L. employs elsewhere only at iii. 9.
7, xxi. 7. 8, and (perhaps) xxv. 27. 8 (where the text is uncertain); he uses *ac* before *t* on 159
occasions.

ascribed to this work (which is very doubtful: see above), they would show that it continued to the time of Julius Caesar.

In fr. 6 L. states that Tubero recorded the same information as Valerius Antias; in fr. 7 that he recorded the same information as Licinius Macer. This evidence allows the conjecture that Tubero used the works of Antias and Macer, just as L. used the works of Antias, Macer, Quadrigarius, and Tubero himself. If this attractive conjecture is right, then Tubero's history will have been a blend of earlier *annales*, just like those of L. and Dionysius. However, the conjecture is not certain: on both occasions Tubero and the other annalist may have a common lost source, for instance Cn. Gellius.

From the fragments themselves we can learn little about Tubero's historical techniques. In fr. 6 L. records that he reported the *libri lintei* differently from Macer: this may suggest that he was capable of independent research, something that we do not find in his successor L. From frr. 8 and 9 on Regulus we can learn that he was quite happy to include the kind of sensational content that we associate with Q. Curtius Rufus or with lost writers such as Clitarchus and Phylarchus. From fr. 2 we may perhaps deduce that he took a rationalizing view of the Trojan War, or at least of the wooden horse. Anything further that is said about the nature of Tubero's history must be largely speculative, based on the use of him by L. and D.H.[1]

See further Lachmann (1822–8) i. 40–1, ii. 26–7, Unger (1891)

---

[1] It is tempting to argue that Catilinarian allusions may have been a feature of his history: for some possible examples, see ii. 4. 4–7 with D.H. v. 7. 1–5 (when such allusions are found in both L. and D.H., they must go back to a common source; and, unless one is prepared to date Valerius Antias to the 50s BC, no other source known to have been used by L. or D.H. wrote after 63) and *addendum* to vii. 38. 4–42. 7 n.; but (*a*) if Lucius was the Tubero whose work was used by L. and D.H., he could have written his Catilinarian allusions into his account of early Roman history only between 63 and 61, when he departed for Asia with his history published or in progress; (*b*) this, and the uncertain evidence for the history of Quintus, makes one look hard at the alleged instances of Catilinarian allusions and the examples cited above are not certain (Ogilvie on ii. 4 is rightly cautious); and (*c*) some more certain Catilinarian allusions could easily be the work of L. himself (see vol. i, pp. 483–4).

Ogilvie argued that, since D.H. dedicated his first treatise on Thucydides to him, Quintus is likely to have had an interest in Thucydides. He therefore suggested that various passages of Livy which seem to recall Thucydides derive directly from Tubero, and by the same token he might have added similar passages in Dionysius. However, quite apart from the fact that we cannot be quite certain either that Quintus wrote history or that he was the dedicatee of D.H., Lucian's *quomodo sit historia conscribenda* shows that many Greek writers of the imperial period regularly tried to imitate Thucydides (among extant writers note D.H. and Dio), and among Latin writers Quintus' contemporary Sallust owes an obvious debt to him. Therefore, while it is possible that Tubero was particularly interested in Thucydides, we cannot rule out the possibility that Thucydidean echoes in Livy come either from other annalists who had read Thucydides' work or even (despite Seneca's comments at *contr.* ix. 1. 14) from Livy himself.

For Wiseman's argument that Tubero was responsible for 'correcting' the black portrait of the Claudii allegedly painted by Valerius Antias, see vol. iii, pp. 666–8.

318–21, Soltau (1894), Bremer (1896–1901) i. 358–63 (for Quintus as jurist), Peter (1906–14) i, pp. ccclxvii–ccclxxiii, Klebs, *RE* i. 534–5, 537–8, Bowersock (1965) 129–30, Ogilvie (1965) 16–17, Badian (1966) 22–3, Malcovati (1976) i. 527–8 (for the oratorical fragments of Quintus), and Wiseman (1979) esp. 135–9.
bellicosiorem annum: for the expression see ix. 45. 10 n.

11. nec petentem tamen: 'but still not standing for election'. For *tamen* preceded by a negative see *OLD s.u.* 2(b); for *tamen* after the participle cf. iv. 21. 3.
L. Papirio Cursore: Macer probably referred to the younger Cursor, *cos.* I 293 (38. 1 n.), but conceivably to his father, *cos.* I 326 (viii. 12. 2 n.).

12. id ne pro certo ponerem: for this use of *ponere* see 18. 7.
uetustior annalium auctor: for phrases of this kind used of Piso and Fabius Pictor, see vol. i, p. 18 n. 17 with *addendum*.
Piso: see ix. 44. 3 n.
Cn. Domitium Cn. filium Caluinum: (45). Cn. Domitius Cn. f. Cn. n. Domitius Calvinus Maximus (the *cognomen* Maximus is found in *F.C.* for 283 and 280, the full filiation in *F.C.* for 280), son (Plin. *nat.* xxxiii. 17) of the consul of 332 (viii. 17. 5 n.), had already tried to be elected to the aedileship of 304, when he suffered a *repulsa* at the hands of Cn. Flavius (ix. 46. 1–15 n.). His subsequent career was more successful, including the consulship of 283, when he fought the Celts, and a censorship and dictatorship in 280.
    Since this is one of the few passages in which L. gives the filiation of office-holders, and since in fr. 27 Piso gives the filiation of Cn. Flavius, Klinger (1884: 16) reasonably suggested that this may have been a characteristic of his *annales*.
Sp. Caruilium Q. filium Maximum: (8). Otherwise unknown, unless L. meant to refer to the celebrated Sp. Carvilius C. f. C. n. Maximus, *cos.* I 293. See further 39. 1 n., where the family is discussed, and Vishnia (1996) 437. For the *cognomen* Maximus, used also by Domitius (see above), see ix. 46. 15 n.

13. id credo cognomen errorem . . . fecisse: the argument recalls 3. 4; here L. is more logical.
fabulam: see vii. 6. 6 n.

9. 14. *Censorship*

For this censorship, see Cram (1940) 84, *MRR* i. 172, and Suolahti (1963) 235–8.

9. 14. lustrum conditum: see 47. 2 n.

P. Sempronio Sopho et P. Sulpicio Sauerrione: for these men see ix. 33. 5 and 45. 1 nn.[1]

tribusque additae duae: for L.'s regular reporting of additions to the tribes, see vi. 5. 8 n.

Aniensis: as its name implies, this tribe was established on land in the Aniene valley (vii. 9. 6 n.), taken from the Aequi during the wars of 304–300; see further Taylor (1960) 56–7 and Humbert (1978) 218.

Tere[n]tina: for the name of this tribe, see Fest. 498 'TERETINATIBUS a flumine Terede dicti existimantur, et syllaba eius tertia mutata, et pro Terede Teram scribi debuisse'. The location, however, of the Teretina is disputed. Mommsen (1857 = 1905–13: vii. 280–2) argued that the mysterious *Terede* referred to the Trerus or Sacco; and he was followed by Beloch (1926: 33, 417, 585–6), who held that the tribe was established on land recently confiscated from Frusino (see 1. 3). But Taylor (1960: 57–9) rightly rejected this hypothesis, since Frusino was placed in the Oufentina after it was enfranchised, and it is therefore probable that Roman territory in the Sacco valley was placed in the Oufentina from the start. Noting that Minturnae and Sinuessa were placed in the Teretina, she convincingly argued that the territory of this tribe is likely to have consisted of land confiscated from the Aurunci after their final defeat in 314.

As Mommsen (locc. citt.) and Ritschl (1859 = 1866–79: iv. 760–1) saw, the spelling *Teretina* is guaranteed by Fest. loc. cit., *CIL* iii. 4464, and the Greek transliteration at Jos. *ant*. xiv. 10. 10, 13, 19 (= 219, 229, 238). The same corruption is found at Cic. *Planc*. 21 'Teretinam (*TE*: -entinam *cett*.)'. Walters's defence of the paradosis therefore fails.

haec Romae gesta: see viii. 17. 12 n.

---

[1] Mλ actually read *p. sulpicio sopho et p. sempronio auerrione*; Π *p. sulpicio sauerrione* (but *seu-Zb, -ertione* Zt, and *p. sulpicio sopho uerione* Zs). The truth was restored by early editors. For corruptions of this kind see ix. 6. 12 n. Whether Π acquired *sauerrione* from a variant in **N**, by omitting *opho et p. sempronio* from the reading of Mλ and joining the remaining *s* with *auerrione*, or by conjecture, is uncertain; if it is a conjecture, it is a very good one, since *auerrione* was read by **N** also at ix. 45. 1.

10. 1–11. 8. *Foreign affairs*

With L.'s narrative for this year we may compare Plb. ii. 19. 1–4 on the Gauls:

ἐν αἷς ἔτη τριάκοντα μείναντες ἐμπεδῶς, αὖθις γενομένου κινήματος ἐκ τῶν Τρανσαλπίνων, δείσαντες μὴ πόλεμος αὐτοῖς ἐγερθῇ βαρύς, ἀπὸ μὲν αὐτῶν ἔτρεψαν τὰς ὁρμὰς τῶν ἐξανισταμένων, δωροφοροῦντες καὶ προτιθέμενοι τὴν συγγένειαν, ἐπὶ δὲ Ῥωμαίους παρώξυναν καὶ μετέσχον αὐτοῖς τῆς στρατείας. (2) ἐν ᾗ τὴν ἔφοδον ποιησάμενοι διὰ Τυρρηνίας, ὁμοῦ συστρατευσαμένων σφίσι Τυρρηνῶν, καὶ περιβαλόμενοι λείας πλῆθος ἐκ μὲν τῆς Ῥωμαίων ἐπαρχίας ἀσφαλῶς ἐπανῆλθον. (3) εἰς δὲ τὴν οἰκείαν ἀφικόμενοι καὶ στασιάσαντες περὶ τὴν τῶν εἰλημμένων πλεονεξίαν τῆς τε λείας καὶ τῆς αὐτῶν δυνάμεως τὸ πλεῖστον μέρος διέφθειραν. (4) τοῦτο δὲ σύνηθές ἐστι Γαλάταις πράττειν, ἐπειδὰν σφετερίσωνταί τι τῶν πέλας, καὶ μάλιστα διὰ τὰς ἀλόγους οἰνοφλυγίας καὶ πλησμονάς.

and *F.T.*:

> *M. Fuluius Cn. f. Cn. n. ann. CD[LIV*
> *Paetinus co(n)s(ul) de Samnitibus*
> *Nequinatibusque VII k. Oct.*

The establishment of the tribes Aniensis and Teretina, reported by L. in his section on domestic affairs (9. 14), marked further consolidation of recently conquered territory. The Aniensis lay on what had once been Aequan territory in the Aniene valley (for the Aequan Wars of 304–300 see 1. 7–5. 14, 9. 7–9, ix. 29. 1–5, 45. 1–18 nn.). The Teretina, if correctly located by Taylor (9. 14 n.), strengthened Rome's presence in the strategically important zone north-west of Campania.

L.'s report of the Roman capture of Nequinum and colonization of the site as Narnia is supported by *F.T.*, and is universally and rightly accepted by scholars. Although there is no particular reason to disbelieve the details which he (10. 1–3) gives of how the town was captured (namely, that two Nequinates who had houses next to the wall made a tunnel through which Roman troops were admitted), we should recognize that invention of them would have been easy.[1]

The notices in L. and Polybius referring to the Etruscans and Gauls clearly have a common ultimate origin: both mention an agreement between the two powers, Gallic hunger for land, and an attempt

---

[1] They are rejected by e.g. Harris (1971: 65).

to assuage this by financial inducements. Although Polybius' reports on the Gallic Wars are not always reliable (see vol. i, pp. 360–5), the fact that he mentions a somewhat embarrassing raid on Roman territory, which L. ignores, points to his superiority for this year. Therefore it is likely that he was correct to state that the Cisalpine Gauls were under pressure from their Transalpine kinsmen but managed to deflect this with the raid on Rome. Although Polybius refers only briefly to Etruscan involvement (§ 2), L. states that the Gauls were not so much planning to raid Roman territory as to settle on Etruscan land, and that the Etruscans had to buy them off. One may argue that the two accounts are not incompatible and should be combined: the Gauls first threaten Etruria, but are then directed to Rome; on this argument L.'s failure to mention the attack on Rome will be due to either late annalistic or his own patriotic chauvinism. However, whereas Polybius will have taken his account from an early annalist and probably from Fabius Pictor, L.'s version looks very much as though it has been garbled by later annalists, and it is perhaps preferable to reject it outright.[1] This would allow one to argue that the Etruscans, the deterioration of whose relationship with Rome is marked by the fighting of 302/1, helped plan the raid on Rome. This joint expedition is thus the precursor of the great combined anti-Roman armies of 296–295.

Beloch, Salmon, and Harris have argued that L.'s report (11. 1–2) of the accidental death of the Roman consul T. Manlius Torquatus is an invention which was designed to obscure the reality of a Roman defeat. This argument may be correct; but (*a*) L.'s report cannot certainly be refuted, and (*b*) Polybius does not mention any battle between Rome and the Etruscans and Gauls. L.'s account of the operations of M. Valerius Maximus in Etruria are narrated in a bland and pro-Roman way; but there is no compelling reason to doubt that he did operate there, even if he achieved no great success.[2]

For the Gallic and Etruscan War see further Klinger (1884) 63–4, Bruno (1906) 16–18, De Sanctis (1907–64) ii. 350, Beloch (1926) 439–40, Salmon (1967) 257, and Harris (1971) 65–6.

Since the Picentes bordered on the territory of the Gallic Senones, L.'s notice (10. 12) of a Romano-Picentine alliance forged in a year in which the Gauls were stirring seems particularly credible. The view

---

[1] However, Costanzi (1919: 168 n. 4) would accept from L.'s account the report of the Gauls' being dissatisfied with their payment; this, he suggests, explains their failure to attack Rome between 299 and the campaign of Sentinum.

[2] For the opposite view, see Bruno (1906: 18).

of De Sanctis (1907–64: ii. 350) that this alliance precipitated the Gallic invasion of Roman territory is possible but not certain.

Evaluation of L.'s report of a rumour of a Samnite War would be difficult even if we did not have to take account of other testimony: such rumours could easily be invented by the annalists as padding for their narratives, and several seem rather improbable (see vi. 29. 9 n.); and yet there is no absolutely compelling reason to reject the notice. However, the matter is made very much more complicated by the report in *F.T.* that Fulvius triumphed over the Samnites. Various solutions to this problem have been espoused.

(*a*) To argue with Mommsen (*CIL* i¹, pp. 16–17) that L.'s notice of a *fama* conceals the fact that there was fighting against the Samnites in this year. If this is correct, then Frontin. *strat*. i. 11. 2 (quoted at 12. 3–13. 1 n.), in which a Fulvius is said to have fought the Samnites, could refer to this year. However, it goes against the view of L. and D.H. that the Third Samnite War began only in 298 (11. 10–13. 13 n.),[1] and it is hard to see why L. and his sources should have ignored the fighting.

(*b*) To reject outright the notice in *F.T.* (thus Münzer, *RE* vii. 269); but this fails to explain the error.

(*c*) To hold that the notice in *F.T.* is a doublet of the Fulvian triumphs of 305 or 298 (thus De Sanctis [1907–64] ii. 348 n. 1, Salmon [1967] 257 n. 1); this explanation is possible, but will not appeal to those who reject the notion that doublets played an important part in the formation of the historical tradition (see vol. i, pp. 102–4).

(*d*) To argue with Beloch (1904/5: 271 and 1926: 426) and Bruno (1906: 12–16) that the Samnites have here been erroneously substituted for the Sabines: Fulvius not only took Nequinum, but also defeated the Sabines, who occupied territory between Rome and Nequinum. This ingenious suggestion is supported by Steph. Byz. *ethn. s.u.* Ναρνία, πόλις Σαυνιτῶν, ἀπὸ τοῦ παραρρέοντος ποταμοῦ Νάρνου, ὡς Διονύσιος ὀκτωκαιδεκάτῳ Ῥωμαϊκῆς ἀρχαιολογίας. Whether or not one accepts Beloch's general view of Roman relations with the Sabines in this period (see above, pp. 30–4), this is perhaps the most economical solution to the problem posed by *F.T.*

---

[1] Mommsen also referred to this year the notices in Frontin. *strat*. i. 6. 1–2 of a Fulvius Nobilior fighting against Lucani (quoted at 12. 3–13. 1 n.); but (*a*) whatever one thinks of the veracity of L.'s notice (11. 11–12. 3 n.) of Rome's alliance with the Lucani in 298, this would introduce the added complication that Roman forces had in fact been fighting in Lucania a year previously; (*b*) a reasonably plausible context for these notices of Frontinus may be found in 298. See further Bruno (1906: 12–16) (but her attempt to refer the notices in Frontinus to the campaigns of Fulvius Curvus in 322 is not attractive).

10. 1. ceterum: resumptive, as though 9. 10–14 were a digression; see viii. 3. 8 n.

segni obsidione: for the expression cf. v. 46. 1; also 11. 7 n.

1–3. specu . . . cuniculo: *specus* can mean a man-made pit or tunnel (*OLD s.u.* 2[a]) and hence can have a meaning virtually identical with that of *cuniculus* (for their use in close proximity cf. Quint. [?] *decl. min.* 255. 9).

1–2. ad stationes Romanas . . . inde ad consulem deducti: see *addendum* to viii. 8. 1 and ix. 24. 3 nn.

2. moenia et muros: Madvig (1860: 190 = 1877: 227) deleted *et muros* as tautologous; but, since the tautology is not unparalleled (Virg. *Aen.* ix. 196 'muros et moenia Pallantea'), and since there is no obvious motive for interpolation, the paradosis should probably stand. For *murus* and *moenia* used in the same sentence but not co-ordinate, see several of the passages cited at *TLL* viii. 1327. 15–22; for variation between *murus* and *moenia*, see ix. 28. 5 n. See further Giers (1862) 8–9.

3. nec aspernanda res uisa: for the expression cf. xxv. 23. 12–13 '. . . ad Marcellum rem defert. haud spernenda uisa' and perhaps also x. 40. 9 'qui rem haud spernendam rati'.

obses retentus: see vi. 30. 4 n.

5. colonia . . . a flumine Narnia appellata: for a similar comment cf. Procop. *bell.* v. 17. 8 ποταμὸς δὲ Νάρνος τὸν τοῦ ὄρους παραρρεῖ πρόποδα, ὃς καὶ τὴν ἐπωνυμίαν τῇ πόλει παρέσχεν. The Nera rises in the Monti Sibillini on the Umbrian–Picene border and flows into the Tiber below Horta (Orte); for the naming of Narnia, see 9. 9 n.

It is surprising that L. does not actually mention the name of the river Nera, since in other passages in which he uses *appellari* in this way—with or without *a(b)*—the reason for the naming is usually spelt out more clearly; cf. e.g. i. 3. 3 'urbem . . . nouam ipse aliam sub Albano monte condidit quae ab situ porrectae in dorso urbis Longa Alba appellata', 13. 5 'Quirites a Curibus appellati', iv. 8. 7 'Papirium Semproniumque . . . censui agendo populus suffragiis praefecit. censores ab re appellati', xxxii. 4. 5 'ab eo miraculo Thaumaci appellati'. (xxiii. 28. 10 'urbem a propinquo flumine Hiberam appellatam' is not parallel, as the Ebro had just been men-tioned in § 9.) It follows that conjectures like *a ⟨Nare⟩ flumine* (Zr) or better (as it would explain the corruption more easily) *a flumine*

⟨*Nare*⟩ (Weissenborn [ed.], tentatively) may very well be on the right lines; but I have not emended, as L. may have expected his readers to know the name of the Nera.

exercitus cum magna praeda Romam reductus: for this method of closing an episode, see vol. i, p. 127.

6. indutias: see x. 5. 12 and 6. 2.
⟨**t**⟩**alia:** Walters glossed **N**'s *alia*: '*sc*. quam Gallicum bellum'; but in this context it could refer only to the Etruscans' doing something other than preparing for a war with Rome, which would be nonsense, and his comparison of the idiom *aliud agens* (for *neglegens*) is inapposite. Glareanus' simple conjecture *talia* has been generally accepted in all other modern editions; and, although it does not give quite such good sense as plain *id*, its diplomatic ease makes it almost inevitable.

7. socios ex hostibus facere: for *ex* used with *facere* or *fieri* to denote movement or transition from one state to another, cf. i. 35. 3 'et Tatium non ex peregrino solum sed etiam ex hoste regem factum', xxii. 30. 6 'laetus . . . dies ex admodum tristi . . . factus', xxiv. 10. 10 'ex muliere Spoleti uirum factum'. For an analogous usage with *habere* see 19. 7 'quod ex muto atque elingui facundum etiam consulem haberent'. Further parallels are cited at Vahlen (1907–8) ii. 137–8, K–S i. 18, and *TLL* v. 2. 1100. 26–1101. 9.

8. infitias eunt: see vi. 40. 4 n.

11. non tam quia . . . quam quia: see viii. 19. 3 n.
efferatae gentis: see vii. 10. 3 n.

12. sine labore ac periculo: see vi. 24. 7 n.
paratam: since *labore* is coupled much more regularly with *partus* than *paratus* (see esp. Cic. *de or*. ii. 210 'magno illa labore, magnis periculis esse parta' [where, however, *uirtute parata* precedes]; also e.g. Ter. *Phorm*. 45–6, *eun*. 399 'labore alieno magno partam gloriam', Cic. *S. Rosc*. 88, Lucr. v. 869, Planc. *ap*. Cic. *fam*. x. 4. 2, Val. Max. viii. 7. *ext*. 15, and Juv. 16. 52–3), and since corruption of *parta* to *parata* could have occurred so easily, it is quite tempting to emend to *partam* (a conjecture reported by Sigonius from one of his mss and by Gebhardus from Vat. Pal. lat. 873). However, the temptation should probably be resisted: *parare* quite often means 'obtain', 'get', 'acquire' (see *OLD s.u.* 3), and the paradosis is paralleled at xxx. 36. 11 'Scipionem exspectatio successoris uenturi ad paratam alterius

labore ac periculo finiti belli famam sollicitaret' and perhaps Sil. xiv. 583–4 'pelagique labore parata | . . . gaudia' (where, however, the text is hard to understand and may be corrupt: see Delz's apparatus). See further F. Walter (1892) 624.

fama: see vi. 21. 9 n.

Gallici tumultus: see vii. 9. 6 n.

minus cunctanter: perhaps alluding to the fact that Rome often preferred to grant *indutiae* rather than a *foedus*; see ix. 20. 7–8, 41. 6–7 nn.

Picenti populo: this is the first appearance of the Picentes in our sources for the Roman conquest of Italy. Their chief settlements were Firmum and Asculum, and their proximity to the Gallic Senones, who were hostile (26. 7 n.), made them a useful ally for Rome. They are mentioned next at 11. 7–8 but then not until our sources (*per.* xv, *F.T.*, Flor. i. 14[19]. 1–2, Eutrop. ii. 16) for the wars of 269–268, in which they were conquered by Rome. The status of Picenum after its conquest is not entirely clear: many Picentes were exported to the hinterland of the Gulf of Paestum (see e.g. Stb. v. 4. 13 [C 251], Plin. *nat.* iii. 70), and plainly large tracts of territory were confiscated, on which the Latin colony of Firmum was founded in 264 and on which Flaminius in his tribunate of 232 was able to establish viritane allotments (see *MRR* i. 225, and esp. Plb. ii. 21. 7). The standard view that the remaining Picentes were incorporated as *ciues sine suffragio* is not implausible given Rome's incorporation of the Sabines and Praetutii but rests on no explicit testimony; for the *praefecturae* mentioned at Caes. *ciu.* i. 15. 1 could have been established to administer Roman settlers, and Asculum remained independent until the Social War. See esp. Toynbee (1965) i. 386; also Beloch (1926) 474–6, Taylor (1960) 64–5, Humbert (1978) 237–8, 243–4, Bandelli (2002) 70. The Picentes have given their name to the famous prehistoric culture of the central Adriatic seaboard; for the archaeology of the area see Naso (2000).

11. 1. prouincia Etruria is attested among the primary mss only in MZbZt (the two last by contamination from a descendant of M, as the coincidence against them of PUOZs shows), but without these words the sentence makes no sense, and there is no doubt that L. wrote them. For true readings found in M alone, see vol. i, pp. 321–2 with *addendum*.

sorte ⟨e⟩uenit: for this expression see vii. 6. 8 n. **N** read *uenit* for *euenit* (an easy haplography after *sorte*); the truth is restored in UOZT^cD^c.

circumagendo equo: see viii. 7. 10. n.

equo effusus: *effundo* is regular in the sense of 'cause to fall' from a horse, chariot, or the like; for the middle usage found here, cf. e.g. xxvii. 19. 10, xxx. 12. 1 'Syphax . . . equo grauiter icto effusus', Virg. *Aen.* x. 893, and see *TLL* v. 2. 222. 61–4.

2. quo uelut omine belli accepto deos pro se commisisse bellum: for the idea that the death of a leader pointed to the will of the gods, cf. i. 23. 4; for the idea of 'receiving an omen', see ix. 14. 8 n.; for L.'s language here, cf. xxi. 40. 11 'sed ita forsitan decuit, cum foederum ruptore duce ac populo deos ipsos sine ulla humana ope committere ac profligare bellum . . .'.

memorantes: see vi. 9. 3 n.

3. Romae cum desiderio uiri tum incommoditate temporis tristis nuntius fuit; [ut] patres ab iubendo dictatore consulis subrogandi comitia ex sententia principum habita deterruerunt: this passage, in which **N** had *deterruerint*, is obscure, but it is not certain how much of the obscurity is due to textual corruption, and how much to L. himself. The principal difficulty is that, despite Drakenborch's defence, *ut . . . deterruerint* is not logically consecutive upon *Romae . . . fuit*. A second difficulty is that it is not entirely clear how the *principes* persuaded the senate not to appoint a dictator. The deletion of *ut* and the emendation to *deterruerunt* adopted in the lemma are both due to Gronovius and remove the first difficulty: if *ut* intruded into the text as a result of dittography after *fuit*, consequential change to *deterruerint* could very easily have occurred. The second difficulty may be elucidated if one postulates that L. (who writes in a compressed manner but may well have found something similar in his sources) imagined that most senators wanted M. Valerius to be appointed dictator but were deterred by the *principes*, who correctly foresaw that the appointment of M. Valerius to a suffect consulship (and hence *imperium*) could be managed through a by-election.[1] *deterruerint* is a strong word; presumably the *patres* were frightened by the odium that would be incurred by recourse to a magistracy that could be regarded as undemocratic, especially when the electoral assemblies were likely to make such recourse

---

[1] Those who do not accept this explanation may prefer to follow Dr Holford-Strevens in postulating a lacuna before *ut*. *Exempli gratia* he suggests the following supplement: *Romae cum desiderio uiri tum incommoditate temporis tristis nuntius ⟨fuit; sed tantum populus ab omni pauore a⟩fuit ut patres ab iubendo dictatore consulis subrogandi comitia ex sententia principum habita deterruerint.*

unnecessary. Whether this account of Roman politics in the aftermath of the death of Manlius is reliable is another matter, since there is reason to think that after 300 appointments to dictatorships became controversial (see below).

Weissenborn (ed.[2]) tried to heal the corruption by inserting *tam* before *tristis*, but then the consecutive clause would be illogical: one would expect L. to say that the Romans appointed a dictator. Walters printed an elaborate transposition of his own, which required reorganization of the whole passage: *Romae cum desiderio uiri tum incommoditate temporis tristis nuntius fuit. consulis subrogandi comitia ex sententia principum habita: M. Valerium consulem omnes [sententiae] centuriae[que] dixere, ut patres ab iubendo dictatore deterruerint, quem senatus dictatorem dici iussurus fuerat.* But, despite the fact that *ut* and *deterruerint* are retained, the transposition is diplomatically extremely uneconomical, obscures the relationship between *M. Valerium . . . consulem* and *quem . . . fuerat*, and introduces an inelegant and potentially confusing variation between *patres* and *senatus*.

For suffect consulships, of which this is the second that is attested reasonably securely, see ix. 44. 15 n.

11. 3–4. ab iubendo dictatore . . . dictatorem dici iussurus fuerat: see vi. 11. 10 n.

4. M. Valerium: for the career of M. Valerius Corvus and the difficulties posed by our evidence for it, see vii. 26. 2 n.

omnes [sententiae] centuriae[que]: as Walters saw, the deletions of Cobet (1882: 104) are right: (*a*) *omnes centuriae* is a regular expression (9. 10 n.), but *omnes sententiae centuriaeque* is unparalleled; (*b*) although *sententia* can be used of the vote (or 'opinion') of a century or tribe (see e.g. viii. 37. 11, Cic. *leg. agr.* ii. 26), the coupling with *centuriae* makes translation on these lines almost impossible; (*c*) even if one understands *omnes sententiae* as the 'votes of everyone', the expression remains awkward, and the idea is expressed much more naturally at xxvi. 18. 9 (quoted at 9. 10 n.).[1] *sententiae* could have intruded into the text as a perseveration from *ex sententia*, or as a dittographic corruption of *centuriae*, or as a variant reading which has been incorporated into the text as a doublet. Whichever of these explanations is correct, the appearance of *sententiae* in the text before *centuriae* would have made consequential interpolation of -*que* very

---

[1] If one adopts the transposition of H. J. Müller and reads *omnes centuriae sententiaeque* (with the result that the view of the centuries is mentioned before that of individuals), this interpretation becomes easier; but the other difficulties remain.

likely. For doublets and dittographic corruptions, see vol. i, pp. 316–20.

quem senatus dictatorem dici iussurus erat: for this kind of comment, see vi. 6. 6 n.; for doubts as to whether it was still acceptable to appoint a dictator, see *addendum* to vi. 16. 3 n., where this passage is discussed in a footnote.

in Etruriam ad legiones proficisci: expressions of this kind were to become part of L.'s stock phrasing. Cf. esp. xxvii. 22. 4 'ut pro praetore in Etruriam ad duas legiones succederet C. Calpurnio'; also (for this coupling of *in* and *ad*) x. 18. 9, 25. 15–16, xxii. 11. 6, xxxvii. 2. 12, and see Oakley (1983) 218.

5. aduentus: add this passage to those cited by Woodman on Vell. ii. 75. 1 (Cic. *imp. Pomp.* 13, 30, Vell. ii. 50. 4, 75. 1, *pan.* iv. 25. 3, vi. 5. 2, 19. 4) to illustrate the notion that the mere arrival of a famous general quietened the enemy, a regular τόπος of panegyric. For a similar idea see vi. 2. 9 n.

timorque ipsorum obsidioni similis esset: for the *comparatio compendiaria* see ix. 18. 11 n.

6. elicere ad certamen: see vi. 31. 7 n.

7. segnius: for the coupling of *segne* and *bellum*, cf. 12. 4, xxiii. 26. 1, 35. 1; also xxxv. 3. 1. Note too 10. 1 (n.).
in uicem: see ix. 43. 17 n.
fama . . . exorta est: see vi. 21. 9 n.
arma . . . spectare: see ix. 10. 5 n.

11. 9. *Shortage of food*

The uncertainty as to whether Fabius Rullianus really was curule aedile in this year or whether this was an invention of Macer or his source (see 9. 10–13 n.) makes interpretation of this passage difficult. Since notices concerning shortages of food are known to have been recorded in the Pontifical Tables (Cato, fr. 77 = Gell. ii. 28. 6), and since L.'s somewhat dismissive *ut scripsere quibus aedilem fuisse eo anno Fabium Maximum placet* could refer just to *uentumque ad inopiae ultimum foret* rather than the shortage of food itself, this notice, like others in L. and D.H. (for which see vol. i, pp. 58–9 and 733) may have been archival and stood in all or most of L.'s sources; in which case the annalists invented only the energetic intervention of Rullianus. On the other hand, it is possible too that the whole notice is a fiction invented by Macer or his source.

The view of Klinger (1884: 17) that the words just quoted show that L. has changed his main source is possible but not certain: those who held that Fabius was aedile may also have had accounts of foreign affairs similar to 10. 1–11. 8.

9. sollicitam ciuitatem habuit: i.e. *ciuitatem sollicitabat*. For the idiom, cf. xxxiv. 36. 3 'omnem oram . . . infestam habenti', xxxix. 29. 9 'uias . . . pascuaque publica infesta habuerant', and see K–S i. 296–7.

aedilem: at least from the late third century oversight of the corn-supply was one of the duties of the aediles: see e.g. xxiii. 41. 7, xxvi. 10. 2, xxx. 26. 5–6, xxxi. 4. 5–6, 50. 1, xxxviii. 35. 5 (in the second passage L. refers to the plebeian aediles; in the first he is not specific; in the others he refers to the curule aediles), Cic. *off.* ii. 58, *leg.* iii. 7, Mommsen (1887–8) ii. 502–3, and Rickman (1980) 34–6. Already in the fourth and early third centuries they may very well have been entrusted with this responsibility, but there is no text which proves this: we can neither date nor authenticate the statement of Pliny (*nat.* xviii. 15) that 'M'. Marcius aedilis plebis primum frumentum populo in modios assibus datauit'; and, in view of our analysis of L.'s sources for this episode, Rickman (pp. 34–5) was far too optimistic when he held that 'the first undisputed example of a curule aedile taking action with regard to the *annona* is Q. Fabius Maximus in 299', since the intervention of Fabius Rullianus may have been invented by an annalist on the model of what aediles did in the late Republic.

On the duties of curule aediles see further *addendum* to vi. 42. 13–14 n.

qualis . . . talis . . . fuisset: for the idea of the great general's being equally efficient in civil administration, see Woodman on Vell. ii. 113. 1 'accipe . . . tantum in bello ducem quantum in pace uides principem'.

298 BC

11. 10. Interregnum

The *elogium* of Appius (quoted at vol. iii, p. 352) records that he was thrice *interrex* but does not state the years in which he performed this office. According to Cicero (*Brut.* 55 [quoted ibid.]), Appius as *interrex* attempted to secure the election of an all-patrician college of consuls but was thwarted by M'. Curius Dentatus, then tribune of the plebs. Several scholars (e.g. Niccolini [1934: 77–8], Ferenczy

[1976: 179], Wiseman [1979: 89], MacBain [1980: 356 and 365], and Loreto [1991*b*] 70–2), trying to combine the evidence of Cicero and L., have placed the clash between Appius and Dentatus in this year, but Mommsen (1864–79: i. 312) pointed out that the anecdote should not be referred to this *interregnum*, since the first *interrex* could not hold elections.[1] There is no reason to doubt the historicity of L.'s notice. For further discussion, and agreement with Mommsen, see e.g. Münzer, *RE* iii. 2683, Garzetti (1947) 213 n. 7 = (1996) 52 n. 171, and Forni (1953) 188.

11. 10. interregnum initum: for this expression see vi. 1. 8 n.
traditur: cf. ix. 36. 2 n.
Ap. Claudius: see ix. 29. 5–11 n.
P. Sulpicius: almost certainly P. Sulpicius Saverrio, for whom see ix. 45. 1 n.
creauit: see vol. ii, pp. 21–2 with *addendum*.
L. Cornelium Scipionem: (343). Apart from his consulship in this year, L. tells us that Scipio served as a legate of Fabius Rullianus in 297 (14. 14), as a propraetor, perhaps appointed by Rullianus, in 295 (25. 11, 26. 7–13, 29. 5), and as a legate of Papirius Cursor in 293 (40. 7, 41. 9, 41. 12–14). Either he, or his father, or the dictator of 306 is likely to have been the Cornelius Barbatus who was *pontifex maximus* in 304 (see below and ix. 46. 6 n.). His main claim to fame is that he was the first Scipio to be buried in the family tomb beside the Via Appia, and that the *elogium* from this tomb still survives in the Museo Pio-Clementino of the Vatican (*ILLRP* 309):

[*L. Cornelio*](*s*) *Cn. f. Scipio*
. . . .
. . . .
Cornelius Lucius Scipio Barbatus⟨—⟩Gnaiuod patre
prognatus, fortis uir sapiensque—quoius forma uirtutei parisuma
fuit,—consol, censor, aidilis quei fuit apud uos.—Taurasia, Cisauna
Samnio cepit,—subigit omne Loucanam opsidesque abdoucit.

See also FIGS. 4–5.[2] The lettering, language, and content of this inscription are extremely controversial. For long the *communis opinio*

---

[1] Loreto suggests that the information provided by Cicero is compatible with our passage, apparently on the ground that Cicero affirms that Appius did not hold an election; but (*a*) if it was an inviolable rule that the first *interrex* could not hold an election, it seems unlikely that even Appius would have tried to hold one, and especially one that was controversial, and (*b*) we can be certain only that Appius, on the occasion described by Cicero, did not effect the election of two patricians, not that he oversaw no election.

[2] I reproduce the text from *ILLRP*. There is a different photograph of the inscription at Flower (1996) pl. 7.

Fig. 4 The *elogium* of L. Scipio Barbatus, left-hand side

Fig. 5 The *elogium* of L. Scipio Barbatus, right-hand side

of scholars, founded on linguistic, epigraphic, and art-historical arguments, was that it dated from the late third century at the earliest, and was therefore not the original memorial to Scipio, who must have died in the first or second quarter of the third century, perhaps as late as 260.[1] However, recently several scholars have argued for a date of composition in the second third of the third century.[2]

While it is important for students of Latin epigraphy and the Latin language to know whether the inscription provides a genuine example of how Latin was written in the mid-third century, the precise date of the inscription matters rather less for the historian of fourth- and third-century Rome: even if it was engraved *c*.200, it is still by far our earliest testimony to this period of Roman history. As for the authenticity of the information included on the inscription, although it would perhaps have been easier to include exaggerations in an inscription cut *c*.200, it would still have been possible to distort the facts *c*.260.

The dates of the aedileship and censorship to which the *elogium* refers are not known, but, since we have no secure example of a man holding the curule aedileship after his consulship, Scipio is likely to have been aedile before 298, and our knowledge of other censorships in this period suggests that he held this office in either 289, 283, or 280.

The interpretation of *Taurasia, Cisauna | Samnio cepit,—subigit omne Loucanam opsidesque abdoucit* involves several difficulties. First it is disputed whether *Samnio* is accusative ('he took Taurasia, Cisauna, and Samnium') or dative ('he took Taurasia ⟨and⟩ Cisauna from Samnium'). The former gives a tricolon in asyndeton and reads more easily (see further e.g. Wachter [1987] 308–9 and Radke [1991] 73). However, the latter avoids the awkwardness of either translating *Samnio* as 'territory of the Samnites' or postulating that Scipio captured a site with the improbable name 'Samnium' and makes a better contrast with the following *omne*.[3] A clear decision on this matter is not possible. Second, while Taurasia can be placed with some confidence in the valley of the Tammaro near the later

---

[1] Wölfflin (1890: esp. 122) has been influential. The extreme of scepticism was reached by Fay (1920: 164–71), who implausibly argued that the inscription was forged at the behest of Metellus Scipio in the first century BC.

[2] See Wachter (1987) 301–42, Radke (1991), and Flower (1996) 159–84. Other discussions of the content of the *elogium* include La Regina (1968) and (1989) 390–6, Till (1970) 279–82, Silvestri (1978), Innocenti Prosdocimi (1980/1), and Marcotte (1985). An early rebuttal of Fay was provided by Frank (1921).

[3] Silvestri (1978: 178) argues for interpretation as an ablative. For arguments against the existence of a site called 'Samnium' see Patterson (1985).

sites of Ligures Baebiani and Corneliani (see xl. 38. 3–9, with Patterson [1988] esp. 149–50), Cisauna is not known.[1] Third, it is disputed whether *Loucanam* is equivalent to *Lucaniam*[2] and whether the Lucani implied by the word are the same as the well-known people who lived in the hinterland of Paestum.[3] Fourth, the year in which Scipio performed these military exploits is not stated: since the exploits of which Roman magistrates were most proud were those performed *suis auspiciis* (see e.g. Plin. *nat.* vii. 140 on L. Caecilius Metellus), one would assume that it referred to 298 when Scipio fought as consul, were it not for the glaring discrepancy with L.'s account of this year. That the *elogium* refers to the events of another year (e.g. 297 or 293 when he was a legate or 295 when he was propraetor) is a conceivable but unattractive view.[4] Whatever the truth, the inscription does more than any other piece of evidence to cast doubt on L.'s evidence for the Samnite Wars. This matter is discussed further at 12. 3–13. 1 n.

The genealogy of the first Scipiones cannot certainly be established. For P. Cornelius Scipio, the first man attested as bearing the *cognomen*, see vi. 1. 8 n.; for his sons P. and L. Scipio see vii. 1. 2 and 21. 4 nn.; for P. Scipio Barbatus, *dict.* 306, perhaps the son of one of the preceding, see ix. 44. 1 n. Note too that *chron. ann.* 354 gives the consulship of 328 to a Barbatus (see viii. 22. 1 n. with important *addendum*) and that L. states (ix. 46. 6) that a Barbatus was *pontifex maximus* in 304. If the chronographer is right (which is far from certain: L. gives the consulship to a P. Cornelius Scapula), if the *pontifex maximus* was not our man, and if this Barbatus or these Barbati is/are not otherwise unknown, then he or they could be either the dictator of 306 or conceivably the Gnaeus whom the inscription mentions as the father of our Barbatus (for this Gnaeus see also *F.C.* for 260, 259, and 254 and *F.T.* for 259 and 253). This Gnaeus is otherwise unknown, but could have been a son of the P. or L. Scipio of book vii.

---

[1] Long ago Lachmann (1822–8: i. 73 n. 22) argued that Cisauna derived from *cis* + *Aufidum*. Silvestri (1978: *passim*), developing a similar argument, held that Taurasia Cisauna was one place (*Cisauna* being a form akin to *Cisalpina* and meaning 'on this side of Samnium'). Radke (1991: 74–5), taking account of the objections of Innocenti Prosdocimi (1980/1: 13–23), argued that it derives from *cis*- and *amnis*. Without new evidence these speculations can be neither established nor disproved.

[2] For this view see Silvestri (1978) 170–1.

[3] Despite the difficulties involved in reconciling this with the evidence from L. and D.H., this seems to be the easiest interpretation. For La Regina's view that these Lucani were to be found near Monte Pallano, see vol. iii, p. 654; for Marcotte's view that they were a people near Cales, see 12. 3–13. 1 n.

[4] It is considered by Luterbacher in his textual note.

Flower (1996: 177) very tentatively considers the possibility that our man was the first to bear the *cognomen* Scipio, but there is no compelling reason to believe that the *cognomen* has been wrongly ascribed to all the men just listed. What is certain is that virtually all known later Scipiones can be shown to descend from him, and that the dominating position of his tomb in the family vault (for the construction of which he may have been responsible) reflects his position as their ancestor.

The relationship of his immediate descendants is depicted stemmatically in Fig. 6. This stemma allows us to see, what is borne out by the rest of the republican evidence, that the only *praenomina* found in the family were Publius, Lucius, and Gnaeus (whether a male Scipio ever had the problem of having to name a fourth son we do not know): see Mommsen (1860) 178 = (1864–79) i. 16.[1] For a stemma see Münzer, *RE* iv. 1430.

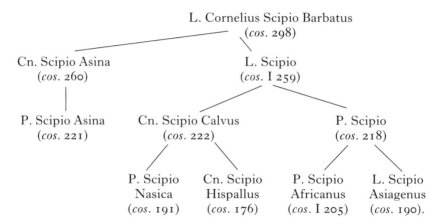

FIG. 6 The immediate descendants of Scipio Barbatus

Cn. Fuluium: see x. 4. 7 n.

---

[1] The only exception is the praetor of 176 (*RE* no. 348; cf. 35), whom L. (xli. 15. 5; cf. xli. 14. 5 and Cic. *de or.* ii. 260) calls M. Cornelius Scipio Maluginensis, and who is the first Maluginensis to appear in our sources for Roman history since Ser. Maluginensis (vi. 6. 3 n. with *addendum*) in 361 (vii. 9. 3). Despite the almost unparalleled brilliance of the career of Ser. Maluginensis, later generations of the family may have failed in politics, to reappear in our sources only this one time. The name is perhaps explicable if the praetor had been adopted from the Maluginenses by a Scipio; if the converse had happened, one might have expected M. Cornelius Maluginensis Scipio (like Q. Caecilius Metellus Pius Scipio Nasica), but in either case he could hardly have been called M. Cornelius Maluginensis Cornelianus. In the fifth and fourth centuries there were several Marci Cornelii Maluginenses.

11. 11–23. 13. *The opening years of the Third Samnite War*

11. 11–12. 3. *The alliance with the Lucani and the outbreak of the Third Samnite War*

D.H. xvii/xviii. 1. 1–3. 1 provides an important narrative parallel to L.'s own. Many details in the two accounts are similar: the Lucanians send ambassadors to Rome (Liv. 11. 11~ D.H. 1. 1); they admit their previous wrongdoings—an allusion to viii. 25. 3 and 27. 2–11—against Rome (11. 12~1. 2); they offer hostages (11. 12~1. 2); the senate agrees to make a treaty (12. 1~1. 3); and *fetiales* (πρέοβεις in D.H.) are sent, but are rebuffed (12. 2~2. 3). D.H.'s account, however, is more extensive than L.'s: he has a longer description of the origins of the conflict between the Samnites and Lucanians, including the point that for a while the Lucanians tried to fight the Samnites on their own (1. 1–2); he records that the people ratified the alliance with the Lucanians (1. 3); he records the pronouncement of the Roman envoys (1. 4); the reply of the Samnites, who point out that the Lucanians were only recent friends of Rome (2. 1); a further retort by the Romans, who claim that the terms of the peace of 304 compelled the Samnites to yield to Rome's will (2. 2); an account of the Samnite vote for war (2. 3); and then an authorial comment (3. 1) reminiscent of Thucydides, in which D.H. notes that for the Romans the alliance with the Lucanians served only as a pretext for going to war, their real worry being the power which might accrue to the Samnites if they defeated the Lucani.

Nevertheless, despite the greater length of D.H., the two narratives are so close in content that there can be little doubt that both authors were using the same, or very similar, sources. D.H. was prone to introducing greatly elaborated speeches into his history; but little of his material here comes into this category, and it is clear that he represents the common source more faithfully (although the allusion to Thucydides' discussion of real and alleged causes is probably his own work).[1] L., however, has abbreviated it, and his comment at 12. 2 on the brusque handling of the Roman *fetiales* by the Samnites suggests that he has also given the tale a more pro-Roman slant.

A strong case can be made for believing that the basic outline of the events reported by L. and D.H. is sound, and that a Roman alliance with some of the Lucani led to the outbreak of the Third Samnite War. If this is right, whereas the Samnites may not have sought a war

---

[1] For such allusions in Greek and Roman historiography, see vol. i, p. 85.

against Rome when they attacked the Lucani, the Romans seem deliberately to have sought another Samnite War by allying themselves with the latter. D.S. (xx. 104. 1) implies that already in 302/1 the Romans were co-operating with some of the Lucani (1. 7–5. 14 n.): this earlier co-operation may not have involved a formal treaty,[1] but may have opened the way for the agreement of this year; alternatively, the new treaty of 298 may have been with a different section of the tribe and may have had a specifically anti-Samnite purpose. We hear of the Lucani next in 296, when Fabius Rullianus was dispatched to sort out to Rome's satisfaction an internal crisis in their government (x. 18. 8).

However, even if this basic outline of events is sound, there is little reason to have any confidence in the details given by either L. or D.H., which show all the hallmarks of stereotypical annalistic invention; in particular, we should note the similarities with the events alleged by L. for 343 (vii. 29. 3–31. 12 n.), when, after a hasty *entente* with Capua, envoys sent to the Samnites were similarly rebuffed and the First Samnite War began.

See further Bruno (1906) 18–21, De Sanctis (1907–64) ii. 351, Beloch (1926) 436–7, and Salmon (1967) 257–8.

11. perlicere . . . ad societatem armorum: L. rather affects this use of *perlicere*; cf. esp. xxi. 19. 6 'in societatem perlicerent', xxxvii. 18. 1, xlii. 37. 2, xliii. 18. 3; note too Just. xxii. 5. 5, xxxviii. 3. 1. For *societas armorum* cf. ii. 22. 3 and xxi. 60. 4. See further Yardley (2003) 45, 56.

ad bellum cogere: 'eine mehr dichterische Verbindung' according to W–M; but numerous analogies from prose are cited at *TLL* iii. 1528. 62–1529. 11 (cf. e.g. Sall. *Iug.* 85. 3 and Nep. *Them.* 4. 4).

12. satis superque: a common idiomatic expression; to the instances cited by Fordyce on Catull. 7. 2, add Cic. *Q. Rosc.* 11, *Flacc.* 66, *har. resp.* 18, Tac. *ann.* i. 40. 1, and iv. 38. 1. L. particularly affected the idiom with dependent partitive genitive (see e.g. ii. 42. 6, xxv. 32. 6, xxviii. 29. 7, xxxiv. 34. 6, xxxvii. 55. 2, xli. 25. 8). That it was acceptable in high poetry is shown by Virg. *Aen.* ii. 642.

omnia . . . uiolent: an ironical comment given the numerous years in which the Lucanians were to fight Rome in the 280s and 270s.

ferre ac pati: for the coupling, cf. e.g. xxvii. 34. 14, Mart. v. 80. 5,

---

[1] By contrast, Giannelli (1974: 361–3) argues that the Romans and Lucanians were allied against Tarentum in 303 but then abandoned their alliance by making separate peaces. If the notice in D.S. is sound, this is possible.

xii. 26. 8; elsewhere the two verbs are often used in close proximity and with similar meaning; see xxviii. 29. 5, Plaut. *Aul.* 88, and Cic. *S. Rosc.* 145.

nomen Romanum uiolent: for the expression *nomen uiolare* cf. Cic. *Arch.* 19, *Sest.* 59, Sil. iii. 366, Tac. *hist.* iii. 80. 2, and *SHA* xviii. 9. 4 'tantum uiolari nomen'.

13. Lucanos: more emotive than *se*; see vii. 30. 6 n.
in fidem accipiant: see vii. 29. 3–31. 12 n.; this passage should have been adduced on p. 288.
uim atque iniuriam: for this coupling see vii. 31. 3 n.
quamquam bello . . . suscepto: Lease (1929: 349) notes that L. is the first extant author to modify an ablative absolute with *quamquam*; but, although iv. 53. 1 and xxxi. 41. 7 do illustrate this phenomenon, neither in our passage nor in xxxvi. 6. 3 and xlii. 46. 8, which he also cites, should *quamquam* be taken closely with the ablative absolute. See further viii. 14. 6 n.

12. 1–3. For Roman procedures for declaring war in this period, see vii. 32. 1–2 n.

1. ad unum omnes: see vi. 33. 12 n.
foedus: see ix. 20. 8 n.
resque ⟨re⟩petendas: since *res petere* is not used as an equivalent to *res repetere*, *repetendas*, found first in U, is a certain restoration. For emendations in U see vol. i, p. 299 with *addendum*.

2. fetiales: for the *fetiales* see vii. 32. 1–2 n. Loreto (1991–2: 250) argues that D.H. (xvii/xviii. 1. 4) was right to make the Romans send an embassy and not *fetiales* and that we have here an early instance of the new Roman method of declaring war by means of an embassy rather than *fetiales*. A compromise is possible: D.H. xv. 7. 6 (on the outbreak of the Second Samnite War) suggests that *fetiales* accompanied the embassy, and this may be how the change to the new method of declaring war began.
qui . . . iuberent: the Roman order is reminiscent of the similar order which L. makes them give to the Samnites in 343, and it meets with an equally ferocious response; see vii. 31. 8–12.
concilium: see vii. 31. 11 n.

3. et patres censuerunt et populus iussit: see vi. 22. 4 n. Outside Tacitus, who rather affected it, *censere* is not found very often with a noun (as opposed to pronoun) as its direct object; *censere bellum*, however, is found also at xxxviii. 46. 11 and Claud. xxi. 327. See further *TLL* iii. 795. 10–24 and Goodyear on Tac. *ann.* ii. 83. 3.

12. 3–13. 1. *Fighting in Etruria and against the Samnites*

L., who provides the only extended narrative of the campaigns of this year, states that L. Cornelius Scipio, after being allotted the province of Etruria, fought an indecisive engagement at Volaterrae and with-drew to the territory of Falerii; from there he ravaged the Etruscan countryside but did not attack any of the cities. In the meantime, Cn. Fulvius defeated the Samnites in battle and captured Bovianum and Aufidena. This account is generally clear[1] (note § 4 'Scipioni' and § 9 'Cn. Fului consulis', each at the head of sections dealing with their exploits)[2] and notable for its lack of elaboration and literary adorn-ment; in particular, the *clara pugna* of Fulvius is dispatched with no explanation of why it was *clara*. One may therefore suspect that just as in the preceding section (11. 11–12. 3 n.), L. abbreviates what he found in his sources. Perhaps because of its brevity L.'s narrative has a superficial appearance of plausibility; but there is no harder task in the historical criticism of book x than attempting to reconcile it with our other testimony for this year.

Foremost amongst this is the epitaph of Scipio (quoted and dis-cussed at 11. 10 n.). This is our only early epigraphic document for the Samnite Wars; and, although its precise date is controversial, it is still earlier than any of L.'s sources, and there is no compelling reason to believe that it includes extensive invention. However, in it we find no mention of any campaigning in Etruria undertaken by Scipio, but only in Samnium and Lucania; moreover, this fighting in Samnium takes place at Cisauna and Taurasia and not at Aufidena and Bovianum, where L. makes Fulvius fight. It is perhaps possible that this epitaph could refer to other years in Scipio's career, but (as argued at 11. 10 n.) one would expect it to refer to what he had achieved when fighting under his own auspices as consul. The expression *subigit omne Loucanam* poses another problem, since L.,

---

[1] However, although it seems likely that L. intended his readers to think that Bovianum was captured in this year, his language at 12. 9 leaves the matter somewhat doubtful.

[2] Perhaps one should start a new paragraph at § 4 'Scipioni' rather than, with Walters, at § 3 'consules'; alternatively one could place 12. 9–13. 1 in the same paragraph as 12. 3–8. Here and elsewhere all divisions are artificial, as L. did not write with modern paragraphing in mind; but W–M's division, with 11. 11–12. 8 as one paragraph, 12. 9 as a second, and 13. 1–13 as a third is unattractive: the first paragraph is too long, and the swift termination of the second separates 13. 1 'Fuluius consul de Samnitibus triumphauit' from the account of his exploits.

supported by D.H., has just described the agreement of an alliance between the Lucani and Rome; but one could perhaps argue that Samnite pressure in Lucania caused the Romans to fight there, or that *subigit* refers to the alliance.[1]

F.T. record the triumph of Fulvius to which L. refers at 13. I:

> *Cn. Fuluius Cn. f. Cn. n. Maxim(us) an. CDLV*
> *Centumalus co(n)s(ul) de Samnitibus*
> *Etrusceisque idibus Nou.*

but they further complicate matters by suggesting that Fulvius fought in Etruria as well as in Samnium; L. had placed only Scipio in Etruria.

Further evidence may come from Frontinus; see *strat.* i. 6. 1–2:

Fuluius Nobilior, cum ex Samnio in Lucanos exercitum duceret et cognouisset a perfugis hostes nouissimum agmen eius adgressuros, fortissimam legionem primo ire, ultima sequi iussit impedimenta. ita factum pro occasione amplexi hostes diripere sarcinas coeperunt: Fuluius legionem, de qua supra dictum est, quinque cohortes in dextram uiae partem direxit, quinque ad sinistram, atque ita praedationi intentos hostes explicato per utraque latera milite clausit ceciditque.

(2) Idem, hostibus tergum eius in itinere prementibus, flumine interueniente non ita magno, ut transitum prohiberet, moraretur tamen rapiditate, alteram legionem in occulto citra flumen conlocauit, ut hostes paucitate contemptas audacius sequerentur: quod ubi factum est, legio, quae ob hoc disposita erat, ex insidiis hostem adgressa uastauit

and i. 11. 2:

Fuluius Nobilior, cum aduersus Samnitium numerosum exercitum et successibus tumidum paruis copiis necesse haberet decertare, simulauit unam legionem hostium corruptam a se ad proditionem imperauitque ad eius rei fidem tribunis et primis ordinibus et centurionibus, quantum quisque numeratae pecuniae aut auri argentique haberet conferret, ut repraesentari merces proditoribus posset; se autem his qui contulissent pollicitus est consummata uictoria ampla insuper praemia daturum; quae persuasio Romanis alacritatem attulit et fiduciam, unde etiam praeclara uictoria commisso statim bello parata est.

It is not wholly clear to which Fulvius and to which year these passages refer. Four Fulvii are said to have fought against the Samnites: L. Fulvius Curvus in 322 (viii. 38. 1–40. 5 n.), his son M. Curvus in 305 (ix. 44. 5–16 n.), M. Fulvius Paetinus in 299 (but only

---

[1] For this argument see Innocenti Prosdocimi (1980/1) 9–10 and Radke (1991) 75–6.

if *F.T.* are right: see above, p. 151), and the consul for this year.[1] The *cognomen* Nobilior, however, is attested elsewhere first for the consul for 255, Ser. Fulvius M. f. M. n. Paetinus Nobilior (see *F.C.* for 255 and *F.T.* for 254). It is therefore reasonable to argue that the *cognomen* has been retrojected by Frontinus or a source to one of the four Fulvii listed above. Münzer, *RE* vii. 264, not implausibly referred all three anecdotes to our consul; but it would be unwise to rule out a reference to the others, since (*a*) L. suggests that in 322 there was fighting in Apulia (and hence perhaps Lucania) and records (viii. 38. 13–16) that the Samnites were distracted by their desire for booty,[2] and (*b*) we do not know where the consul for 299 fought (if indeed he did fight the Samnites). If, however, one or more of these anecdotes did refer originally to the events of this year, then they are compatible with L.'s evidence but not with the epitaph of Scipio, since they place Fulvius precisely where the epitaph places Scipio.

It is at once evident that the events of 298 cannot be reconstructed with any certainty, and we must remember that in the matter of the correct assignation of provinces the tradition was often muddled (see vol. i, pp. 67–72). It is also clear, however, that, if (as seems most probable but is unfortunately not quite certain) the *elogium* refers to the events of 298, then primacy must be given to its testimony, and no reconstruction should carry conviction unless it is compatible with its evidence. By contrast, L.'s narrative seems very much less authoritative. The account of the fighting in Etruria contains little or nothing that could not have been invented; and the brief reference to the Samnite War is problematic: although it is quite possible that a Roman raid up the Sangro valley led to the capture of Aufidena, it is rather improbable that Bovianum should have fallen in 298. L. records assaults on it on no fewer than five occasions in books ix and x (of which four were successful), but only those of 305 and 293 carry conviction (see ix. 24. 1–28. 2 n.): if the Romans had taken this town, one would have expected hostilities to have come to a swift close, but in 298 the war was only beginning.[3] Therefore, when one faces the

---

[1] In addition, we should note that Frontin. *strat.* ii. 5. 9 (quoted below, p. 270) refers to the activities of a Cn. Fulvius in the territory of Falerii. The *praenomen* shows that this is a reference to the consul of 298, and the anecdote could relate to this year (see Beloch [1926] 438); but he was stationed in Etruria during the Sentinum campaign of 295 (26. 15, 30. 1–3), and it is perhaps a little more likely that the anecdote refers to that year.

[2] L. makes A. Cornelius Cossus, the dictator for 322, command in this campaign; but in this he is probably wrong; see viii. 38. 1–40. 5 n.

[3] Bruno (1906: 24 n. 2), De Sanctis (1907–64: ii. 353), Beloch (1926: 438), and Salmon (1967: 261) all suggest confusion with the capture of Bovianum in 305 by M. Fulvius Curvus; here, at least, the notion of a doublet does seem a real possibility.

central difficulty, that it is very hard to square the evidence of the *elogium* with that from L. but much easier with that from *F.T.*, an over-elaborate defence of L. (who has ignored a major achievement of Fulvius and the main achievement of Scipio) seems unwise.

The following possibilities and combinations of evidence present themselves.

(*a*) The most conservative approach (adopted by e.g. Münzer, *RE* iv. 1488–90, Frederiksen [1968*a*] 226, and La Regina [1989] 390–6) is to argue that our evidence should be combined: both consuls fought together in both Samnium and Etruria, but only Fulvius triumphed, because of his more important victories. In Samnium Fulvius will have fought more or less where L. places him (i.e. in central Samnium), whereas Scipio will have fought on the eastern and south-eastern borders, where the *elogium* records his successes. One could then argue that, although the part of Etruria in which Fulvius fought is unknown, Scipio fought in Etruria where L. states, near Volaterrae and Falerii. L. will have erred only in dividing up the provinces between the consuls. This approach involves two difficulties: (i) it is incompatible with Frontin. *strat*. i. 6. 1, where Fulvius is found on the Samnite–Lucanian border (but this objection will fall if it can be argued that Frontinus refers to fighting in another year); (ii), more seriously, it does nothing to explain away the difficulties which we have noted in L.'s account, and it would be surprising if at one time Rome had concentrated all her forces in one area.

(*b*) A variant of this approach is that espoused by Marcotte (1985: 736–42), who argued that both consuls fought in both provinces and that, after their Samnite campaigns (which in the case of Fulvius were where L. places him, in the case of Scipio where the *elogium* places him) they joined forces in the Lucania of the *elogium* and of Frontinus, by which we should think not of the hinterland of Paestum but rather of a small territory near Cales. This approach has the merit of removing the contradiction between the *elogium* and Frontinus and L. and D.H.; but the evidence for a Lucania near Cales is not good.[1]

(*c*) One could try to rescue L.'s account by suggesting that he has placed the wrong consul in the wrong province. Fulvius will then have fought at Volaterrae and Scipio in Samnium. But, quite apart

---

[1] For these Lucani Marcotte cites 33. 1, xxv. 19. 6, Ps.-Scymn. 246, and *CIL* x. 1. 3917 (probably from Cales) where there is a reference to an *ager Lucanus*. The reference to the *cohors Lucana* at 33. 1 is undeniably awkward (even though the Lucani were allied to Rome at this time), but despite the best efforts of Marcotte all the other passages could refer to the Lucania of Paestum. See further La Regina (1989: 393).

from the problem of Frontinus, this involves two difficulties: (i) the *elogium* does not record fighting at Bovianum and Aufidena, and (ii) *F.T.* places Fulvius in both spheres of action. (One might argue that, if the references to the capture of Bovianum and Aufidena are rejected as inventions, then this approach will seem more plausible; but the evidence of *F.T.* cannot so easily be circumvented.)

(*d*) A more radical version of (*c*) would be to reject both L.'s account of the fighting in Samnium and the notion of *F.T.* that Fulvius fought there. On this approach there were only two campaigns: that of Fulvius in Etruria and that of Scipio around eastern and south-eastern Samnium. This is broadly the position of Beloch (1905/6: 277 and 1926: 431–2, 438), who, however, argues that Fulvius fought against Sabines as well as Etruscans and accounts for the notice in *F.T.* with his hypothesis that in the tradition Samnites have been substituted for Sabines; for discussion of this, see pp. 30–4 above.

(*e*) Bruno (1906: 21–3) and Salmon (1967: 260–1) rejected the evidence from both L. and *F.T.* which relates to Etruria and argued that Fulvius attacked central Samnium, while Scipio operated in the east and south-east.[1] But such a reconstruction rashly dismisses the strong evidence for fighting in Etruria in this year.

(*f*) Mommsen (*CIL* i¹, pp. 16–17) accounted better for the evidence of *F.T.* by holding that, while Scipio fought on the eastern and south-eastern borders of Samnium, Fulvius fought first in Samnium and then in Etruria. This position would allow one to accept something of L.'s account of the campaign in central Samnium.

To conclude: a sure reconstruction of the events of this year cannot easily be made, but there is little reason to have confidence in L.'s narrative. As observed already (vol. i, pp. 67–72), the survival of this inscription and L.'s general unreliability in the matter of consular provinces are the main reasons to question the basic reliability of his evidence for the period of the Samnite Wars.

These uncertainties make it hard to interpret the Roman strategy in this year, but Scipio's campaigns on the southern and eastern borders of Samnium will have been greatly facilitated by Rome's new Lucanian allies; and doubtless his presence gave the Lucanians

---

[1] Bruno argued (more confidently as regards Fulvius) that the Etruscan victory given by *F.T.* to Fulvius and by L. to Scipio reflects their exploits as propraetor in 295 (24. 1–31. 7 n.), which in the case of Fulvius was transferred to the year in which he was consul so as to increase his glory. Mazzarino (1966: ii. 289), in a variant of this approach, held that the annalistic tradition gave Scipio a victory at Volaterrae to compensate for ignoring his successes in Samnium. These arguments are very improbable.

some security against possible Samnite reprisals. Scipio's campaign also set a pattern of Roman involvement on the southern flank of the Samnites, which was to be continued in the next two years and was to culminate in the colonization of Venusia in 291. We have seen, however, that L.'s view that the Romans made major inroads into central Samnium is unlikely to be sound. The Etruscan campaign continued the pattern of rather desultory fighting which had been the norm since the outbreak of hostilities in 302/1: only in 296 and 295, when Etruscan, Samnite, Gallic, and Umbrian forces joined, was the warfare to become fierce and dangerous to Rome.[1]

3. consules . . . obuenerunt: see ix. 12. 9 n.
quisque: see vii. 9. 7 n.

4. segne bellum: see 11. 7 n.
et simile prioris anni militiae exspectanti: for the previous year see 11. 4–7.
Volaterras: this is the only appearance of Volaterrae, modern Volterra, in our sources for the Roman conquest of Italy. Situated on a commanding hill between the rivers Cecina and Esa, Volaterrae had become by the late fifth century the most powerful city in northwestern Etruria. Numerous antiquities survive on the site, including the remains of Etruscan fortifications. See further Enking and Radke, *RE* ixA. 721–40, Scullard (1967) 146–51, and Torelli (1982) 252–63.

5. magna utrimque caede: standard Livian phrasing; see vii. 11. 7 n.
nox incertis qua data uictoria esset. lux insequens uictorem uictumque ostendit: for this idea see vii. 33. 15 n. For *qua* with the meaning 'to which side', cf. i. 27. 6 'qua Fortuna rem daret, ea inclinare uires' and, from the parallels cited by W–M on that passage, iv. 37. 9 'clamor indicium . . . fuit qua res inclinatura esset', x. 28. 1 'necdum discrimen Fortuna fecerat qua datura uires esset'.[2] These parallel passages suggest that in ours *Fortuna* should be understood as giving victory.[3]

---

[1] Costanzi (1919: 201) argues that the Romans are unlikely to have penetrated as far as Volaterrae in 298. This view, however, seems arbitrary—which is not to say that L.'s narrative is trustworthy.

[2] For *Fortuna* coupled with *uires dare* in this passage one may perhaps compare Cic. *de or.* ii. 342 and Luc. v. 505–6.

[3] This implication would not be present if one accepts Stroth's *inclinata* for *data*, but the conjecture is unnecessary.

reliquerunt: Heusinger's *reliquerant* may be correct, but L. sometimes employs a perfect where one would expect a pluperfect; see ix. 21. 4 n.

6. profectione: the agreement of MPλ in reading *professione* makes it virtually certain that this was the reading of **N**. However, *profectione*, found only in UOZ, and therefore probably a conjecture, gives far more pointed sense, and is supported by vii. 33. 17 'quem terrorem non pugnae solum euentu sed nocturna profectione confessi sunt'.

uacuis: either *castris* or *eis*, with which *uacuis* is to be construed, must be supplied from *castra*.

et trepide: *et* was omitted by Π but is needed to make clear that there were two reasons why much booty was found: it was a fixed summer camp (hence much had collected inside it) and it was deserted very quickly (without the Etruscans' having time to remove much).

7. Faliscum . . . Faleriis: for Falerii see vi. 4. 4 n.
cum modico praesidio reliquisset, expedito agmine . . .: see vi. 3. 5 nn.

8. ferro ignique uastantur: see vii. 30. 15 n.
uastum: see 34. 6 n.
castellis etiam uicisque: for the coupling, see ix. 38. 1 n. (and note in particular xxxv. 21. 10 'Minucius . . . ex agro Pisano in Ligures profectus castella uicosque eorum igni ferroque peruastauit').
urbibus oppugnandis temperatum: against the proposal to insert *ab* before *urbibus*, the paradosis may be defended by e.g. ii. 16. 9 'nec magis post proelium quam in proelio caedibus temperatum est'; see further K–S i. 754.[1]

9. clara pugna: it is curious that L. says so little about a *pugna* which he calls *clara*; for the expression, see ix. 37. 11 n.
haudquaquam ambiguae uictoriae: in contrast to the outcome of Scipio's battle at Volaterrae. For *ambiguae* in this context, see vii. 7. 7 n.
Bouianum: see ix. 28. 1 n.
Aufidenam: Samnite and Roman Aufidena are almost certainly to be sought at Castel di Sangro, whence come *CIL* ix. 2801 and 2803,

---

[1] Walters ascribes this proposal to M. Müller, but I have not been able to trace the place of publication.

both of which mention Aufidena. The town lies beside the Roman road from Aesernia to Sulmo and is dominated by the craggy Rocca, which rises at its north-eastern extremity and commands the Sangro valley at the point where it begins to tighten into a much more narrow gorge. Interspersed with the mediaeval ruins on the summit of the Rocca are several fragments of Samnite polygonal walling; the best preserved of these runs down the northern face of the summit.

Since the Roman name survives in the name of the modern village of Alfedena, which lies 9 km upstream, and since the major Samnite fortified centre of the Curino lies in the *comune* of Alfedena, several scholars have argued that Samnite and Roman Aufidena must have been there (see e.g. Mommsen, *CIL* ix, p. 259, Hülsen, *RE* ii. 2288, and Salmon [1967] index *s.u.*); but there are no Roman remains at Alfedena, and there is no difficulty in believing that the name migrated between antiquity and the Middle Ages (compare the case of Capua). See further Balzano (1923), Coarelli and La Regina (1984) 260–1, La Regina (1989) 395–6, and Oakley (1995) 73–7.

ui cepit: see vi. 3. 10 n.

13. 1. Carseolos: this notice repeats information given already at 3. 2 (302/1); see the n. ad loc. and 1. 7–5. 14 n.

de is a certain correction in UOZ for **N**'s *eos de. eos* arose as a dittography of *cos̄*; see Winkler (1890–2) ii. 20.

Aequicolorum: it is a nice question whether the Aequicoli (sometimes spelt Aequiculi) should be distinguished from the Aequi, whom L. mentions on numerous occasions. Other references to the Aequicoli in literary texts may be found at i. 32. 5, Vitr. viii. 3. 20, Virg. *Aen.* vii. 747, Ov. *fast.* iii. 93, Val. Max. ii. 7. 7 (thus the obvious emendation of the paradosis; but the epitome of Julius Paris refers to the Aequi), Plin. *nat.* iii. 107 'Aequiculanorum Cliternini, Carseolani' (note the reference to Carseoli), 108, xxv. 86, Sil. viii. 369, Suet. *Vit.* 1. 3, Serv. *Aen.* vii. 746, x. 14, *uir. ill.* 5. 4 (parallel to Liv. i. 32. 5), and Paris x. 1. In addition, D.S. refers to Αἰκικλοί at xiv. 98. 5 and 117. 4 ὑπ' Αἰκουλανῶν τῶν νῦν Αἰκικλῶν καλουμένων, and D.H. uses this form at ii. 72. 2 (elsewhere he refers always to Αἰκανοί). For references in inscriptions see *TLL* i. 1007. 2–54. The evidence may be explained in two ways.

(*a*) The form Aequiculi was used to refer to that portion of Aequan territory which was not incorporated in the Roman state until the Social War (hence the modern name Cicolano; for pre-Roman and republican settlement in the Cicolano see Grossi [1984]). This derives some support from the passage of D.S. quoted (despite his reference to an otherwise unattested form *Aequulanus*), but, put as a rule in this extreme form, its fatal weakness is that the form Aequicoli is used in contexts where the form Aequi would have been expected (e.g. by Ovid and Valerius Maximus) and twice of Carseoli, which was a Latin colony and therefore no longer under Aequan control. Nevertheless, if one argues that the distinction between Aequi and Aequicoli had become somewhat vague by the Augustan period, this explanation is attractive. See further Salmon (1982) 9.

(*b*) The two forms were always interchangeable (thus Ogilvie on i. 32. 5). The weakness of this is that it does not explain why L. and D.H. so regularly refer, respectively, to Aequi and Αἰκανοί, the only exceptions being in antiquarian contexts (in which category it is possible to include our passage). It is certainly possible, but (*a*) is perhaps preferable.

13. 2–13. *Rumours of an Etruscan and Samnite alliance and the elections for 297*

After the comparative brevity of his account of 298 L.'s narrative becomes more expansive. The rumour (§ 2) that the Etruscans and Samnites were enlisting huge forces anticipates the longer descriptions of battles involving the joint forces of these peoples that will follow in the rest of the book. It is impossible to be certain whether the rumour was true (as it may have been: if huge armies were being conscripted, the Romans would probably have heard about the fact), whether (if true or false) it really did reach Rome at the time of the elections, or whether (if a fiction) it was invented by L. or his sources, as they invented other rumours (vi. 21. 9 n.); but by recounting it at the time of the elections L. both neatly combines external and internal affairs and provides strong motivation for his long account (§§ 5–13) of the election of Fabius Rullianus to the consulship. This begins with the comparatively low-key indirect speech of §§ 6–7, 9, and 10, but in §§ 12–13 direct speech brings the episode to a more lively climax (for this technique, see vol. i, p. 119).

For the doubtful historicity of L.'s three reports in this book of Fabius' trying to refuse election, see 9. 10–13 n.

2. fama exorta: for the expression again see vi. 21. 9 n.

3. principes Etruscorum: see vi. 2. 2 n. with *addendum*
increpari is a conjecture in the Basle (Froben) edn. of 1531 for **N**'s *increpare*. The passive is needed to balance the preceding *uexari*: the

magistrates of the Samnites were not criticizing others or being criticized by the Etruscans (either of which could be implied by the active infinitive) but, like the chiefs of the Etruscans, were being criticized by their own people.

4. pari: Madvig (1860: 190–1 = 1877: 227–8) conjectured ⟨*im*⟩*pari*, arguing that after their previous victories the Romans could hardly have regarded themselves as *haudquaquam par* to their enemies. However, the prospect of a coalition of Gauls, Etruscans, and Samnites (a threat which did materialize in 297) might explain Roman fears. Besides, some rhetorical exaggeration is appropriate in the context of a *fama* which led to the election of Fabius Rullianus to the consulship. Freudenberg (1854–62: ii. 14) less cogently argued that the Romans, frightened by the *fama*, thought that the coming battle would be in no way comparable (*haudquaquam pari*) to that in which Fulvius had just been involved but a much more serious affair. For L.'s sentiment here, cf. iii. 5. 13 'multitudinem (*sc.* Aequorum) praedam agentem quae inciderit in Quinctium nequaquam pari defunctam esse caede'. For the coupling of *haudquaquam* with *par*, see vii. 10. 6 n.

5–8. studia . . . studia: see vii. 19. 5 n.

6. For protestations from a politician that he is too old for office or political strife, see vi. 22. 7 n.
nec corporis nec animi uigorem: see ix. 16. 12 n.
nimia: for the coupling of *nimius* with *fortuna* in the context of a surfeit, or threatened surfeit, of good fortune, cf. [x] v. 21. 15 '(Camillus) dicitur . . . precatus esse ut si cui deorum hominumque nimia sua fortuna populique Romani uideretur, ut eam inuidiam lenire quam minimo suo priuato incommodo publicoque populi Romani liceret' (with Ogilvie's note), xlv. 41. 6 'mihi quoque ipsi nimia iam fortuna uideri, eoque suspecta esse', and Tac. *ann.* iv. 39. 1 'Seianus nimia fortuna socors'. Note also its coupling with *felicitas* (add e.g. Vell. i. 6. 2, Val. Max. i. 5. 2, Flor. i. 47 [iii. 12]. 7 to the passages cited at *TLL* vi. 433. 18–19); and, at one further remove, passages such as iv. 14. 20 'fragilitatis humanae, cuius nimia in prosperis rebus obliuio est'.

7. succreuisse . . . consurgentes: the image is of young trees growing up beneath mature specimens. Although *succresco* is not rare in Latin, it is used only here by L.
nec honores . . . uiros: *sententiae* of this kind are quite rare in L.'s

work (see vi. 36. 12 n.); here Fabius is made to reinforce his point with an elegant chiasmus.

8. acuebat: the initial position of the verb emphasizes the effect the speech of Fabius had in sharpening the enthusiasm of the populace.

uerecundia legum is easy to understand ('deference to the laws') but perhaps unparalleled as an expression.

legem recitari iussit, qua intra decem annos eundem con-sulem refici non liceret: the law was one of the Genucian plebiscites of 342 (vii. 42. 2). If, as seems to be the case in this period, men were allowed to hold the consulship ten years after they had last held it,[1] then the reference to the law here is surprising: Fabius had been consul last in 308, that is exactly ten years before 297 (301 is a dictator year). L. is quite correct (§ 9) to make the tribunes imply that they could procure any exemption which might be needed: the rules had often been broken in the Second Samnite War and were to be broken again in 295, when the election of Fabius and Decius was quite clearly against standard constitutional procedure. If there is any truth in L.'s notice about an attempt to have Fabius elected consul for 296 (15. 7–12), there was an unsuccessful attempt to set aside the law only a year after the events described here. For full discussion and bibliography, see vol. ii, pp. 24–5 with *addendum*.

For a magistrate reciting, or ordering the recitation of, a law see ix. 33. 6 n.; for *refici* see vi. 35. 10 n.

9. prae strepitu is a combination found also at ii. 27. 8, viii. 33. 2, and xxii. 5. 3 but in no other author.

tribunique plebis . . . solueretur: for parallels to the role given to the tribunes here see esp. App. *Lib.* 112. 528–33 (the people wish to elect Scipio Aemilianus, even though he is under age, to the consul-ship of 147. When the consuls refuse to accept his candidature, one of the tribunes threatens to use his intercession against their conduct of the elections; finally the senate instruct the tribunes to suspend the law on age of candidature for a year) and *Hisp.* 84. 363–5 (the people wish to elect Aemilianus, who is still too young to hold the office [this is a mistake on Appian's part: the difficulty was not Scipio's age but his iteration of the consulship, which was forbidden in this period], to his second consulship of 134; the senate instructs the tribunes to suspend the law). For the tribunes as guardians of the constitution see ix. 33. 5 n.

---

[1] However, it is awkward that by the second century a gap of eleven years had become normal: see vol. ii, p. 25 n. 69.

10. ferri rogitans: Walters and Conway (1918: 112–13) pointed out that *rogitans* is otiose and that its position (after one part of an indirect question and before its continuation) is unusual; they therefore deleted it. Although I have found no parallel for L.'s word-order, the paradosis is hardly objectionable and may stand.
fraus fieret: see vii. 16. 9 n.

11. iam regi leges, non regere: for the idea of laws ruling cf. Hdt. vii. 104. 4–5 and Plat. *rep.* 563 D; note too Plin. *pan.* 65. 1. I have not found a precise parallel for the notion of the laws being ruled. For *regi . . . regere* cf. Sall. *Iug.* 1. 5.
suffragia inibat: see vi. 38. 4 n.
intro uocata: although this expression is used only here of centuries being called to vote in the *comitia centuriata*, note the analogous *Σ* Bob. *ad* Cic. *in Clod. et Cur.*, p. 90. 5 'cum centuriae . . . introducerentur'. Elsewhere it is used of the *comitia tributa*: 24. 18, xl. 42. 10, xlv. 36. 7, *CIL* i². 583. 72 = Crawford (1996) p. 72 (the *lex repetundarum*), Cic. *or.* fr. A vii. 31, and Ascon. *Corn.* p. 57. 16, in which at trials and legislative assemblies the tribes were called successively to vote (vi. 38. 5 n. with *addendum*), at first in the Comitium but after 145 in the forum, in which an area of assembly must have been fenced off (see Taylor [1966] 23–5). There is no reason to follow Mommsen (1887–8: iii. 399), who did not believe that there was successive voting in the *comitia tributa*, in thinking that in L. the expression has lost its meaning and is used simply as a general term for voting. Nor does this expression prove that here L. and his annalistic sources had in mind the voting-procedure of the revised *comitia centuriata* (thus Klinger [1884] 23), although this view is possible. See further Lintott (1992) 150 and Humm (1999) 641–2.

12. consensu . . . uictus: for the expression, and for a republican politician retreating in face of the consensus of senate or people (a course of action generally approved, since it avoided an escalation of conflict), cf. ii. 57. 4, iii. 52. 10, v. 9. 8, xxxi. 20. 6, Vell. ii. 32. 1; note also (for the expression) xxiv. 27. 3, [Sen.] *Oct.* 485, Tac. *hist.* i. 35. 1, and (for the idea) Cic. *Phil.* iii. 2.
dei approbent: for this prayer cf. Cic. *fam.* ii. 15. 2 and 18. 3 (in both passages, as here, the expression is coupled with *agere*); also xxxvi. 7. 21, Cic. *IIVerr.* v. 49, and *Att.* vi. 6. 1 (all cited by Hickson [1993: 52–3]).
quod: in an attempt to account for M's *quid* Weissenborn (ed.²) conjectured *quidquid*; the conjecture gives quite acceptable sense, but it

is easier to believe that *quod*, the reading of Πλ, stood in **N**, and that
M corrupted it by perseveration after *inquit*.

agitis acturique estis: for the polyptoton see vi. 26. 5 n. with *addendum*.

13. dignum parente suo: for references to the elder Decius in this
book see 7. 3 n.; for Roman approval of sons who lived up to the
repute of their fathers, see vii. 10. 3 n. with *addendum*.

13. 14. *Aedilician prosecutions*

For the role of the aediles in the middle Republic, see 23. 11–13 n.

14. quod plus quam quod lege finitum erat agri possiderent:
for the law restricting *possessio* of *ager publicus*, see vol. i, pp. 654–9;
for *possiderent*, see vi. 5. 4 n.

uinculumque ingens immodicae cupiditati[s] iniectum est:
although **N**'s *immodicae cupiditatis* may be explained as an objective
genitive, it is awkward and not easily paralleled. Drakenborch
adduced 41. 3 'iis uinculis fugae obstricti erant', but there *fugae* is
even harder, and Gemoll was probably right to delete it (see n. ad
loc.); and I can add only Cic. *Phil.* xiii. 20 '(D. Brutus) . . . Mutinam
. . . illi exultanti tamquam frenos furoris iniecit', which is not a very
close analogy. Therefore it is preferable to follow both Drakenborch's *Portugallicus* and Gronovius in reading *immodicae cupiditati*,
which has the merit of restoring the common construction *inicere
aliquid alicui* (for which see *TLL* vii. 1. 1612. 54–65).

297 BC

14. 1–15. 6. *Foreign affairs*

L.'s narrative for this year presents comparatively few problems, in
part (one may fear) because there is no parallel material with which it
may be compared. On his notice (14. 3) that envoys from Sutrium,
Nepet, and Falerii reported that the Etruscans were suing for peace,
Harris (1971: 67) may have been correct to remark: 'Such a notice
may have been an attempt to fill a gap in a year when Etruria was
known not to have been assigned to either of the consuls, and the
legati . . . may be a subsidiary fiction'; but we have no reason to doubt
L.'s view that both consuls fought solely in Samnium, and hence
Etruria is likely to have been quiescent.

Fabius Rullianus is said to have marched into Samnium from the territory of Sora (14. 4), fought and won a battle near the Matese (§§ 6–21), and captured the otherwise unknown Cimetra (15. 6). Any route which takes one from Sora to the region of the Matese is bound to be rather convoluted; but, if this geographical information is sound, Rullianus may have marched from Sora into the Melfa valley, over the Forca d'Acero into the Sangro valley, down to the territory of Aufidena, over an easy pass into the Volturno valley, and hence to the Matese. Alternatively, he may have marched to Atina, over the pass between the Melfa and Volturno valleys which lies between S. Biagio Saracinisco and Filignano, to the Volturno between Venafrum and Aesernia, and thence to the Matese. But L.'s geographical indications may very well be erroneous.[1]

Decius is said to have started from the territory of the Sidicini (14. 4) and to have fought an Apulian army at Maleventum (15. 1–2). Although the route from the territory of the Sidicini to Maleventum is easy (to Vairano, and then down the broad Volturno and Calore valleys), the appearance of an Apulian army at Maleventum is somewhat surprising, especially as L. has told us nothing of Apulian hostility to Rome since ix. 20. 7 (317). It is easy, however, to conjecture either that the Apulians were divided as to whether they should ally themselves with Rome or the Samnites, or that, frightened either by Rome's increasing power or by Samnite intimidation, they had abandoned their Roman alliance and had sent an army to help the Samnites; perhaps they were roused by Scipio's campaign in 298.[2] Whatever motive one ascribes to them, Decius' campaign may be viewed as part of a pattern of Roman warfare in south-east Italy, which began in 298 and continued until the end of the Third Samnite War. Since Decius' expedition took him further from Rome, it is not surprising that it was Fabius who returned to hold the elections (15. 7–12). L. may even imply (16. 2) that Decius stayed with his troops throughout the winter, in which case it is quite likely that he was based in Apulia. Salmon (1967: 262) went so far as to argue that he started his campaign of 297 from an Apulian base (in his view L.'s reference to the Sidicini hides Teanum Sidicinum, which has been confused with Teanum Apulum); this is possible, but we have seen that sense can be made of L.'s narrative without resort to such an interpretation.

[1] Salmon (1967: 261) calls them 'mere supposition based on the usual pattern of western operations'; but L. has not previously shown any familiarity with a 'usual pattern'.

[2] Costanzi suggests that the Apulians came from Venusia, a conjecture which it is impossible either to refute or to affirm. Against Wuilleumier's view (1939: 97–8) that they were encouraged by Tarentum, see Marasco (2002) 128–9.

As several scholars have noted, the fact that neither Fabius nor Decius triumphed suggests that any victories which they won were not of great significance; hence it is unlikely that they made inroads deep into central Samnium. For the events of this year, see also Bruno (1906) 25–7, De Sanctis (1907–64) ii. 353, Costanzi (1919) 195–7, Beloch (1926) 439, and Salmon (1967) 261–2.

L. launches the episode (§§ 1–3) with a powerful periodic sentence (for the technique, see vol. i, p. 134). Then, after three sections (§§ 4–6) describing the joint operations of the consuls, he turns to describe their individual achievements: *Fabius* in § 7 serves as a heading which picks up *profecti consules* (§ 4), and is in turn picked up by *P. Decius* at 15. 1. Always faced with the problem of making the long succession of Roman victories interesting, L. here focuses attention on the surprising resistance offered by the Samnites to Fabius (§§ 9–10). We are then told of the two tactics to which Fabius resorted in his attempt to break this resistance, a cavalry charge and a ruse whereby some of his men were to appear in the rear of the enemy (§§ 9–10); and we await their outcome. The cavalry are unsuccessful, frightening the Romans themselves quite as much as the Samnites (§§ 15–16). Indeed, the Samnites stand as firm as before (compare § 16 'immota' with § 10 'nulla ex parte . . . moueri'), and the growth of their confidence is emphasized by the initial position of *creuit* in § 17. To stay on even terms with them the Romans have to bring forward their second line. At this point comes the peripeteia (§ 18): the Roman troops appear behind the enemy, and the enemy disperse in panic, thinking that the army of Decius had appeared. In general, L.'s account of the end of the battle is swift, and he makes surprisingly little attempt to build up tension before the peripeteia. The battle fought by Decius at Maleventum is then described in a matter-of-fact way (15. 1–2), as is the remainder of the campaign (§§ 3–6).

14. 1. consules noui, Q. Fabius Maximus quartum et P. Decius Mus tertium: for Fabius see viii. 18. 4 n., for Decius ix. 28. 8 n. This was the second time in which these men had been elected together as consuls: for the phenomenon see ix. 1. 1 n.

2. et uter ad utrum bellum dux idoneus magis esset: the doubling of interrogative pronouns or particles is quite common in both Latin and Greek; cf. e.g. ii. 21. 4, xxx. 42. 18 '. . . commemorantium ex quantis opibus quo recidissent Carthaginiensium res', Cic. *Mil.* 23 'reliquum est . . . ut nihil iam quaerere aliud debeatis nisi uter utri insidias fecerit', W–M on xxvi. 13. 16, Kühner and Gerth (1898–1904) i. 521–2, and K–S ii. 497.

For *magis* following the word which it modifies, cf. 36. 5 'impigre magis', v. 42. 5, xxi. 8. 9, and see *TLL* viii. 69. 73–80.

3. Sutrio et Nepete et Faleriis: see vi. 3. 2, 4. 4, 9. 3 nn.

auctores concilia Etruriae populorum de petenda pace haberi: *concilia* for N's *concilii* is a conjecture found in D^c and adopted by e.g. W–M and M. Müller. Walters, dissenting on the ground that the indirect statement was impossible after *auctores*, commended Conway's *habiti*, considered deletion of *haberi*, and finally printed *concilii* and obelized *haberi*. However, sense is restored so easily by *concilia* that it seems rash not to adopt it; the indirect statement is indeed rare but may be paralleled at ii. 48. 8 'auctores sumus tutam ibi maiestatem Romani nominis fore'.[1] The corruption to *concilii* could have been made by a scribe who thought that the word ought to be governed by *auctores*.

belli molem: see vii. 29. 5 n.

4. Soranum: see vii. 28. 6 n.

Sidicinum: see vii. 29. 4 n.

5. effuso agmine: *effusum agmen* is quite a common stock Livian phrase; cf. ii. 59. 8, v. 44. 3, xxi. 25. 8, xxxvii. 34. 2, xlii. 65. 2, xliv. 39. 8. *effusus* literally means 'spread wide', but it quite often approaches to the sense 'rapid' (see *TLL* v. 2. 221. 1–3); 'rapid' is certainly more apt than 'widespread' at xxi. 25. 8, xxxvii. 34. 2, and xlii. 65. 2, and it is possible in our passage. *agmen effundere* is found also at [x] Sil. ii. 151, xii. 576, and [Quint.] *decl.* 13. 4.

6. explorant: see viii. 30. 3 n. (where this passage might have been cited).

non fefellere . . . instructi: see viii. 20. 5 n.

ad Tifernum: see ix. 44. 6 n.

7. impedimentis in locum tutum remotis praesidioque modico imposito: for the removal of baggage cf. viii. 38. 8 and see *addendum* to viii. 11. 11 n. For the expression *praesidium modicum* see vi. 3. 5 n.

quadrato agmine: see vii. 29. 6 n.

---

[1] In the instances of this construction cited at *OLD s.u.* 5(a) *auctor* is used in a rather different sense.

praedictas: when referring to something just mentioned L. and earlier writers normally used expressions like *(sic)ut ante dictum est* (Packard [1968] i. 415). *praedico* is used in this way first here and occasionally by later writers; cf. e.g. Manil. iii. 174, Vell. ii. 107. 1, and see further Krebs and Schmalz (1905–7) ii. 351, K–S i. 771, Goodyear on Tac. *ann.* i. 60. 2, and *TLL* x. 2. 563. 13–29. For cross-references in general see Woodman and Martin on Tac. *ann.* iii. 18. 1.

9. omnium Samnitium populis: for the transferred epithet see ix. 19. 2 n.

summae rerum: see vi. 22. 9 n.

augebat, almost certainly a conjecture, is found in Zb and Zr: PU are defective; MOZtZs^c have *angebat*, Zs^1 *agebant*, and Tθ *agebat*. Although *angebat animos*, printed by Walters, is in itself an acceptable expression (see *TLL* ii. 48. 32–5), it should mean something like 'was distressing them' (or 'their spirits'), and this does not suit the context: we have been told in § 8 that the Samnites join the battle *maiore animo* and shall soon be told that their fighting causes some difficulties to the Romans; and the knowledge that a decisive battle was at hand was as likely to raise the Samnites' morale as make them anxious. For *animos augere*, a very common expression, see *TLL* ii. 1350. 13–29.

quoque aperta pugna: I have followed Walters in retaining the reading of the paradosis against *aperta quoque pugna*, a standardizing conjecture made in the second Froben (Basle) edn. of 1535, for two reasons. First *quoque* may modify the whole clause. Secondly, even if this first argument is wrong, Shackleton Bailey (1956: 175) has argued that 'writers on Latin syntax underestimate the frequency with which this particle [*sc. quoque*] precedes the word it qualifies', and there are parallels for what the mss offer here in several other writers, notably Curtius; cf. e.g. vi. 6. 5 'et ille se quidem spolia Persarum gestare dicebat, sed cum illis quoque mores induerat'.[1] See

---

[1] From L. one may cite iv. 41. 3 'itaque ne ab se imperatoria consilia neu consulares artes exquirerent, quae pensitanda quoque magnis animis atque ingeniis essent', xxii. 14. 15 'haec uelut contionanti Minucio circumfundebatur tribunorum equitumque Romanorum multitudo, et ad aures quoque militum dicta ferocia euoluebantur', xxv. 16. 10–11 'omnium populorum praetoribus, qui ad Poenum in illo communi Italiae motu descissent, persuasisse ut redirent in amicitiam Romanorum, quando res quoque Romana . . . in dies melior atque auctior fieret'. However, these passages make less convincing parallels: at iv. 41. 3, if Ogilvie is right to take *quoque* with *pensitanda*, there may be no instance of the idiom at all, and, if he is wrong, Reiz's *magnis quoque* for *quoque magnis* is an easy conjecture; and at xxii. 14. 15 and xxv. 16. 10–11 the interlaced word-order is very much easier than what the mss offer here.

further Riemann (1885) 242 n. 2, F. Walter (1892) 624, Krebs and Schmalz (1905–7) 468–9, and K–S ii. 54.

10. Maximum filium: (112). This is L.'s first reference to Q. Fabius Q. f. M. n. Maximus Gurges, the son of Rullianus (viii. 18. 4 n.). The name *Gurges*, characteristically Roman in its offensiveness, is explained at Macr. *Sat*. iii. 13. 6 'Gurgitem a deuorato patrimonio cognominatum' (with reference also to later compensating virtues); we cannot be certain whether this explanation is correct or merely a guess. Gurges appears next in 295, when he prosecuted some *matronae* for *stuprum* and used the resulting *aes multaticium* to build a temple of Venus; though L. omits to mention the office which he held, there can be little doubt that it was the curule aedileship (31. 9 n.). An anecdote in Valerius Maximus (iv. 1. 5) relates to the election of Gurges to the consulship: 'Fabius uero Maximus, cum a se quin-quies et a patre, auo, proauo maioribusque suis saepenumero con-sulatum gestum animaduerteret, comitiis quibus filius eius summo consensu consul creabatur, quam potuit constanter cum populo egit ut aliquando uacationem huius honoris Fabiae genti daret, non quod uirtutibus filii diffideret—erat enim inluster—sed ne maximum imperium in una familia continuaretur. quid hac moderatione efficacius aut ualentius, quae etiam patrios adfectus, qui potentissimi habentur, superauit?'[1] Given the almost insatiable desire of Roman aristocratic families for the glory of office, it is singularly unlikely that there is any truth in this tale. Valerius himself clearly had no idea to which election it related: *continuaretur* may perhaps point to the elections for 294 (Rullianus was consul for the fifth time in 295); but since he seems to imply that the protests of Rullianus were of no avail (note *summo consensu*), it perhaps related originally to the elections for 292, when Gurges was elected consul for the first time. This election is noted by L. at 47. 5, but without any comment. Gurges must then have featured prominently in the lost book xi, but the surviving sources (*per*. xi [and the new fragment which may come from book xi], D.H. xvii/xviii. 4. 4–6, Dio fr. 36. 30–1, Zon. viii. 1. 11–14) for the years 292–291 are rather confused, and a coherent reconstruction of his activities is not possible. We are told that Gurges was defeated by the Samnites and criticized strongly for this at Rome; that he was rescued by his father, who defended him and

---

[1] At Polyaen. viii. 15 a Q. Fabius is said to have told the populace that he was too old to go on campaign and thereby to have secured the election of his son; this is probably another fanciful anecdote relating to Rullianus and Gurges, but the father could conceivably be the grandson (or great-grandson) of Rullianus, the celebrated Verrucosus.

went out to help him in the campaign; and that together they defeated the Samnites. A proconsular command followed in 291, in which Gurges was prevented by the jealous consul Postumius Megellus from taking Cominium; *F.T.* record that he triumphed in this year. A second consulship followed in 276, in which he triumphed over the Samnites, Lucanians, and Bruttians (*F.T.*). Three years later he was one of the three ambassadors sent to Ptolemy Philadelphus (D.H. xx. 14. 1–2, Val. Max. iv. 3. 9). Gurges was elected consul for the third time in 265, but he died from a wound incurred during the successful campaign against Volsinii (Flor. i. 16[21], Zon. viii. 7. 4–8). Pliny (*nat.* vii. 133) tells us that he succeeded his father (in whose honour he had given a funeral banquet [*uir. ill.* 32. 4]) as *princeps senatus*. Münzer provides a full and penetrating discussion of his career at *RE* vi. 1798–1800.

W–M correctly noted that the reference to *Maximum filium* is unusual; we would have expected *Quintum filium*, as at xxii. 23. 8 'misso Romam Quinto filio'. The closest parallels which I have noted are xlv. 34. 8 'missas cum Scipione Nasica Maximoque filio copias' (but Paullus' son had been adopted into the Fabii Maximi) and Cic. *Arch.* 6 'Q. Metello illi Numidico et eius Pio filio'.

M. Valerium: if, as seems likely, L. is referring to M. Valerius Maximus, *cos.* I 312 and the son of Corvus (ix. 28. 8 n.), then *iuuenes* (§ 12) is in this case only barely apt. It is possible that L. was referring to another M. Valerius (perhaps the son of M. Maximus), but the whole scene may be the product of Livian or annalistic invention, the name of a well-known noble being added to give verisimilitude.
tribunos militum: see vii. 26. 3 n.

11. si quando umquam: see vi. 42. 12 n.
gloriam inuictam: see 10. 4 n.

12. in impetu . . . equitum: for cavalry charges in L.'s early battle-scenes see vi. 29. 2 n.
nominatim: see viii. 39. 4 n.
nunc . . . nunc: see ix. 18. 15 n.

13. †quando, ne ea quoque temptata uis proficeret†: since no entirely cogent emendation of this vexed passage has yet been produced, Walters was right to obelize.

Hell (1870: 14–15), followed by Walters, drew attention to the extremely otiose repetition *uis proficeret . . . si nihil uires iuuarent* and argued that the words in the lemma should be deleted. The conjecture gives excellent sense, and certainly one may wish that L. had not written a sentence involving such a repetition. However, I hesitate to adopt it since it is not easy to see how the words intruded into the text.[1]

Even if Hell's divination of an interpolation be wrong, it is hard to extract good meaning from these words. The sense required is something on the lines of *si forte ne ea quidem uis proficeret* (the formulation of Madvig [1860] 191 = [1877] 228–9); but this cannot be obtained from the paradosis, since *ne . . . quoque* is not used by L. as an equivalent to *ne . . . quidem* and since *quando* cannot introduce such a fear concerning the future.[2] Indeed, the clause *ne . . . proficeret* may be translated only by something like 'lest that attempt at force should succeed', which is precisely the opposite of the sense required.

Sense can be restored by following some *recentiores* in removing *quando* (Drakenborch reports its omission in Dresden Dc 126; other late mss change *quando ne* to *nec*) and by introducing a negative into the *ne*-clause. Harant (1880: 67) proposed *uix* for *uis* with the further consequential change of *proficeret* to *proficerent*;[3] this is diplomatically easy,[4] but *ea* would refer only to *laudibus* and *promissis* and not to the forthcoming charge of the cavalry. Much better is Madvig's ⟨*parum*⟩ *proficeret*: there are good parallels for it at iv. 43. 5, vii. 31. 10, xxxii. 22. 7, and xxxviii. 9. 7 'id cum per conloquia principum succedens murum parum proficeret . . .', and it is easy to postulate the omission of *parum* before *pro-*. However, it is not easy to explain why anyone should have inserted *quando*.

Madvig therefore preferred to integrate his *ne ea quoque temptata uis* ⟨*parum*⟩ *proficeret* into the rest of the sentence by supplying *timeri poterat* between *proficeret* and *consilio*, and this approach has been followed by later scholars: Wesenberg (1870/1: 38) and Brakman (1928: 68–9) thought *periculum erat* (or *esset*) and *fieri poterat* respectively an improvement on *timeri poterat* (alternatively, in Madvig's conjecture Wesenberg suggested changing *poterat* to *posset* and

---

[1] Dr Holford-Strevens suggests to me that they may have been added by somebody who, not having read further than *si nihil uires iuuarent*, wrongly supposed that the cavalry charge had already failed and that he was expressing the notion 'when not even that use of force, when put to the test, did any good'. This is not impossible, but it would have been a very imprudent reader who interpolated before finishing reading the sentence.

[2] Pettersson (1930: 128 n. 2) thought that the text was sound but that, if emendation were required, *quidem* could be substituted for *quoque* (an idea that had occurred earlier to Doering). This emendation alone will not work, for the reasons given above.

[3] Drakenborch reports *uix* from Holkham 344 and its descendant Leiden, Lips. 28.

[4] Harant also suggested the transposition *ne quando ea quoque temptata uix proficere⟨n⟩t*; but *quando* would then suggest a cavalry charge in the indefinite future rather than the one with which he was immediately concerned.

placing *parum* after *proficeret*). These supplements give adequate sense, but none has any especial probability; Professor Watt (*per litteras*) suggested *quando* ⟨*timebat*⟩ *ne ea quoque temptata uis* ⟨*parum*⟩ *proficeret*, which is simpler than any of them.

Other scholars have emended in a different manner. Seyffert (1861: 76) proposed *[qua]* ⟨*metue*⟩*ndo, ne* ⟨*non*⟩ *ea quoque temptata uis proficeret*; Weissenborn (*Komm.*³) a lacuna between *quando* and *ne*, later (ed.²) suggesting that it could be filled with *periculum erat* or *timendum erat*; H. J. Müller *quandoque ea quoque temptata uis* ⟨*non semper*⟩ *proficeret*, but *non semper* is feeble; Luterbacher ⟨*incertus*⟩ *quantum ea quoque temptata uis proficeret*, which is bold and quite attractive; and Conway *secum quaerendo num ea quoque temptata uis proficeret*, which is far from the paradosis and goes badly with *ratus*.[1]

grassandum: see vi. 5. 4 n.

ratus: for L.'s use of *ratus* in his periods, see vol. i, p. 134.

consilio: a similar stratagem is recommended at Onas. 22. 2–4.

14. Scipionem: see 11. 10 n.

legatum: see vii. 7. 1 n.

hastatos: for the *hastati*, see viii. 8. 3–14 nn. The weakening of the front line by the removal of these troops may account for the difficulties experienced at § 17.

primae legionis: see 18. 3–4 n.

ostendere: see ix. 35. 2 n.

15. euecti: see ix. 40. 12 n.

16. turmas: see viii. 7. 1 n.

immota: much of our evidence [*] for the distribution of the choice adjective *immotus* supports the view of W–M and *TLL* vii. 1. 497. 55 that it was poetical. Apart from heavy attestations in Vitruvius (eight times), the younger Seneca (fourteen times), Columella (eight times), and Tacitus (fifteen times), it is found only sporadically in prose: xxi. 55. 10 'tamen in tot circumstantibus malis mansit aliquamdiu immota acies' (a usage very similar to that in our passage), xxiii. 24. 7, fr. 60, Sen. *contr.* ix. 2. 8, Vell. ii. 6. 3, Plin. *nat.* viii. 49, xvi. 230, xvii. 222, Quint. xi. 3. 79, 158, Plin. *epist.* ii. 17. 16, *pan.* 82. 2. By contrast, the adjective is common in poetry: there are fourteen instances in Virgil, eleven in Ovid, four in Manilius, nine in Seneca,

---

[1] Walters for his part wondered whether *quando* hid *uerendo* or *timendo* (compare Seyffert's conjecture).

twelve in Lucan, eight in Valerius Flaccus, nine in Statius; see also
Germ. 19, 436, Calp. Sic. 4. 99, Sil. xiv. 276, and Mart. v. 31. 5.
Since many of the instances in Columella are used in the technical
sense of 'unmoved' (i.e. 'unploughed') land, it is tempting to argue
that *immotus* was a poetical word which gained increasing currency
in prose throughout the first century AD: used by Livy when it had
been avoided by Cicero, Caesar, Varro, Nepos, and Sallust, it was
employed on a modest scale by the elder Seneca, Velleius, the Plinys,
and Quintilian; the younger Seneca and Tacitus rather affected it,
but the style of both, and esp. the latter, shows the influence of the
poets. However, this argument takes no account of the evidence of
Vitruvius, whose employment of the word is not really confined to
technical matters: note e.g. v. 3. 1 'et corpora propter uoluptatem
inmota patentes habent uenas' and vi. 1. 9 'serpentibus . . . quae . . .
per brumalia autem et hiberna tempora ab mutatione caeli refriger-
atae, inmotae sunt stupore'.

acies . . . perrumpi: for this particular expression cf. [x] xxxiii. 8.
14, Virg. *Aen.* ix. 513, Vell. ii. 112. 6, Tac. *hist.* ii. 44. 1, Curt. viii. 14.
18, and Frontin. *strat.* ii. 4. 2 (derivative from our passage); naturally *perrumpere* is used in many similar contexts.

inritum inceptum: the first appearance of what was to become a
favourite Livian coupling (some fourteen instances in all, twelve
between xxiv. 19. 7 and xxxviii. 6. 4). Cf. also Curt. iii. 1. 17, and see
32. 5 n.

17. frons prima: i.e. the *hastati*; see viii. 8. 6 n. for the expression.
fiducia sui: see vii. 33. 5 n.
ni secunda acies iussu consulis in primum successisset: the
secunda acies was the *principes*; for the advancing and retreating lines
of the manipular army see viii. 8. 3–14 (with nn.).

in primum is used as the equivalent of *in primam aciem*; cf. esp. ii.
46. 7 'sic in primum infestis hastis prouolant duo Fabii', iii. 62. 8
'equites . . . prouolant in primum'; also xxv. 21. 6 'prima legio et
sinistra ala in primo instructae', xxxvi. 18. 2 'leuis armaturae partem
. . . in primo locauit'; and, slightly different, x. 41. 6 'arma signaque
per turbidam lucem in primo ('in the van') apparebant'. Drakenborch has a full discussion of the idiom.

18. et ⟨in⟩ tempore [inpro]uisa ex montibus signa: the paradosis
is *et* (cett.: *eo* U) *tempore inprouisa* (MOZ [but *imp-* ZtZs]λ: *in se uisa*
P: *uisa* U) *ex montibus signa*, which presents various difficulties. First,
the meaning of *tempore* is uncertain. The translations 'at that time' or

'at the right time' (i.e. ἐν καιρῷ) in themselves would give reasonable sense, but here the first is impossible (unless we emend to ⟨eo⟩ *tempore*), and the second rather awkward: although plain *tempore* (or *tempori* in the older spelling) is occasionally found in this sense (e.g. Cic. *fam.* vii. 18. 1, *off.* iii. 58), *in tempore, tempore ipso, tempore in ipso*, or *in ipso tempore* would be much more normal and idiomatic (for the first see e.g. xxxiv. 41. 2 'defecissetque ab Romanis ulterior Hispania, ni P. Cornelius raptim traducto exercitu Hiberum dubiis sociorum animis in tempore aduenisset', and Packard [1968] ii. 1138; for the expressions with *ipso*, which are not found in L., see *TLL* vii. 2. 333. 46–59). Second, although the expression *inprouisa ex montibus signa* in the sense 'the unexpected appearance of the standards coming from the mountains' is perhaps just possible in itself (it is compressed but perhaps not too compressed for L.), it does not go well with *tempore* (or whatever it is emended to), and the whole sentence would be smoother if there were a verb or participle (such as *uisa*) qualifying *signa* and balancing *sublatus* (which can refer only to *clamor*).

Therefore numerous conjectures have been proposed, in all of which the perfect passive participle *uisa* is extracted from *improuisa*. U (for the innovations of which, see vol. i, p. 299 with *addendum*) has *eo tempore uisa*. The postulated corruption can be explained (*impro* arising by anagrammatic corruption from a dittography of *-mpore*), and the resulting sense is also quite attractive; but one really needs the connecting particle, and a better conjecture would be *et ⟨eo⟩ tempore uisa*. Very similar in approach is *et ⟨in⟩ tempore uisa* (Weissenborn, *Komm.*), which I have adopted, as it restores the standard Livian idiom. Alternatively, J. Perizonius suggested *et tempore ipso uisa*, Drakenborch (anticipating Luterbacher) *et tempore in ipso uisa* (both these conjectures give good sense and are palaeographically easier than that of Weissenborn, but since elsewhere L. does not use *ipso* in this idiom, neither is likely to be right),[1] Heraeus (1893: 78) *et ⟨in⟩ tempore procul uisa* (but *procul* does not quite fit with *proximos* in § 14), and Cornelissen (1889: 191–2), ingeniously, *et tendere in se uisa* (but the opportune appearance of the standards from the mountains needs to be signalled by a phrase like *in tempore*).[2]

Dr Holford-Strevens acutely objects that all these conjectures

---

[1] xxii. 61. 14 'quo in tempore ipso' is different.

[2] I relegate some less successful conjectures to a footnote: *et tempore, ecce, uisa* (Klockius), *eodem tempore uisa* (Gronovius), *et tempore uisa* (Wesenberg [1870/1] 38), *et tempore uno ferri uisa* (Novák [1894] 117–18), *et tempore uno pro⟨ferri⟩ uisa* (M. Müller, who shows that *uno tempore* is Livian, but not that it is apt here), and *et tempore inferri uisa* (Conway, *dubitanter*).

involve a somewhat abrupt change of focus from the Romans (*et in tempore* uel sim.), to the Samnites (*uisa*), to the Romans again (*sublatus*). Therefore, if *tempore* or the like is to be retained, he would prefer to emend *inprouisa* to something like ⟨*inlata*⟩ *inprouiso*. This is certainly attractive; but the change of focus does not seem to me so awkward, and I have adopted the conjecture of Weissenborn, as it restores standard Livian idiom.

non uero tantum metu: L.'s sequence of thought here is slightly unusual but quite comprehensible: the Samnites quite correctly feared that they might be attacked by the troops whom they had just noticed, but they were deluded into unnecessary fear by Fabius' shout that these troops were the approaching army of Decius.

20. fugae formidinisque: see vii. 37. 16 n.

maxime[que] territos: N's text is obviously corrupt. Good sense may be restored either by deleting -*que* (the Froben [Basle] edn. of 1531) or by emending to *maximeque terr⟨u⟩it ⟨e⟩os* (Weissenborn [ed.], *dubitanter*); the deletion is easier.

integro intactoque: for this nearly pleonastic coupling, cf. [x] 27. 9, 36. 3, v. 38. 6, Curt. v. 6. 5, Sil. x. 63–4, Sic. Flacc. p. 108, Just. xxv. 2. 5, and see Yardley (2003) 60.

21. et: Madvig (1860: 191 = 1877: 229) proposed *sed*; but *et* can have an adversative sense; cf. e.g. xxxiv. 29. 9 'Dexagoridas miserat ad legatum Romanum traditurum se urbem; et cum ad eam rem tempus et ratio conuenisset, a Gorgopa proditor interficitur' (adduced by W–M on xxxiv. 42. 6), and see *TLL* v. 2. 893. 4–894. 3, Pettersson (1930) 156–7 (with numerous Livian parallels), and *OLD s.u.* 14.

in fugam dissipati sunt: see viii. 39. 8 n.

minor caedes quam pro tanta uictoria fuit: for the expression cf. Tac. *hist.* v. 15. 2 'minor tamen quam pro tumultu caedes'; for the construction with *quam pro* see vii. 7. 5 n.; for *uictoria fuit* see vii. 8. 7 n.

capti octingenti ferme et triginta: this is the first in a remarkable series of notices which record enslavements in the period 297–293 BC; other such notices may be found at 14. 21, 15. 6, 17. 4, 17. 8, 18. 8, 19. 22, 20. 15, 29. 17, 31. 4, 31. 7, 34. 3, 37. 3, 39. 3, 39. 4, 42. 5, 43. 8, 45. 11, 45. 14, and 46. 12. These give a total of about 69,000 enslaved for these five years. To them one may add D.H. xvii/xviii. 5. 1, where 6,200 men are said to have surrendered their arms at Venusia in 291 BC (and hence were probably taken prisoner). Although the authenticity of no individual notice can be proved, and although some may be due to annalistic or Livian invention (for the possibility of duplications in L.'s account of 296, which would affect several notices, see 16. 1–21. 12 n.), the general authenticity of information of this kind is made more likely by the facts that this series begins only in the second half of book x, that is in the most reliable portion of the pentad, and that for previous Roman history precise figures are to be found only at ix. 42. 8 (307 BC) and 44. 7 (305 BC), and D.S. xx. 80. 2 (306 BC), all of which refer to a period only ten years earlier than our passage. For this reason it is tempting to believe that a substantial portion of L.'s information goes back to records made in the 290s. If so, the figures bear witness to the increasing importance of slavery in Roman society during our period (see also vii. 16. 7 n.): after *nexum* was abolished and debt-bondage became less common (viii. 28. 1–9 n.), slaves were replacing citizens as labour on the larger estates. For full tabulation and discussion of this evidence, see Oakley (1993) 24–5; also Harris (1979) 59 and Cornell (1989) 388–9.

octingenti (or rather *dccc*) is found in P^c. MP^{1}OT have *accc*, ZbZt *ccc*, Zs *tricenti*, and θ *dcccxxx* (this last still with *ferme et triginta* following), but Drakenborch saw that in our mss *a* is a regular corruption of ɪɔ. For similar corruptions see 15. 6 (M has the truth, but other mss read *accc* or *cccc*), 29. 18, 33. 6, 34. 3, 36. 14 and at 46. 5 nn. See further Heraeus (1885) 52 and Winkler (1890–2) ii. 20.
signa militaria capta tria et uiginti: see vii. 37. 16 n.

15. 1. Maleuentum: see ix. 27. 14 n.
extractos . . . ad certamen: see viii. 29. 11 n.

2. plus fugae fuit quam caedes: see ix. 24. 13 n.
duo milia . . . caesa: see vii. 17. 9 n.

4. quadraginta et quinque (or *xl et v*) is given by M and Π, and was probably the reading of **N**; λ had *et quadraginta et quindecim* (or *et xl et xv*). The usual word-order would be *quinque et quadraginta*, which was conjectured and printed by Walters; but W–M had already adduced seven Livian passages which defend the paradosis: xxi. 22. 4 'sed aptae instructaeque remigio triginta et duae quinqueremes erant et triremes quinque', xxvii. 29. 8 'octoginta erant et tres naues', xxxv. 1. 10, xl. 50. 6, xli. 13. 5, xlii. 27. 3, and xlv. 43. 5.
loca . . . in quibus Deci castra fuerunt, alterius consulis sex et octoginta: I have been unable to parallel this enumeration of the number of camp-sites on enemy soil.

fuere . . . fuerunt: for the two different forms of the third person plural of the perfect used in close proximity, W–M well compare 25. 5 and iv. 59. 10.

5. multo illis insigni⟨ti⟩ora: 'much more remarkable than these'. N's *multo aliis* cannot be translated and must be corrupt. Most editors have restored sense by adopting the minimal change *multo illis* (reported by Drakenborch from several *recentiores*). Walters proposed and printed *multo ali⟨a ill⟩is*, but the separation of *multo* from *insigni⟨ti⟩ora* would then become more awkward; *multa alia* (found in many early editions) is another possibility.

It is doubtful whether L. would have used the form *insignior* (from *insignis*): it is attested only here in his extant books; in other writers of the Augustan age and earlier it is attested only at Germ. 213 (the instances at [Cic.] *Her.* iv. 36 and Nep. *Ages.* 3. 2 are due to conjectures); and at vi. 16. 8 and xl. 59. 3 L. himself prefers to use the periphrasis *magis insignis*. By contrast, the form *insignitior* (from *insignitus*) stood in **N** at iv. 4. 5, vii. 6. 6, 15. 10, and viii. 13. 1. See further Neue and Wagener (1892–1905) ii. 254 and *TLL* vii. 1902. 1. 4–8.
uastitatis circa: see vi. 15. 7, ix. 15. 1 nn.

6. Cimetram is the reading of Mλ. Walters considered the spelling *Gimetram* (Π) to be possible, but the agreement of M and λ suggests that the *C* was archetypal. The location of Cimetra is quite unknown, and the suggestion of Salmon (1967: 262) that the -*etra* ending points to a site in the middle Liri valley is entirely speculative.
capta . . . triginta: see 14. 21 n. for the figure for enemy captured, vii. 17. 9 n. for a general discussion of casualty figures.

15. 7–12. *The elections for 296*

This episode probably has little basis in fact, resting almost entirely on annalistic invention (for an analysis, see 9. 10–13 n.). L. has written it well: note the periodic sentence which introduces the scheming of Ap. Claudius (§§ 7–8), the careful division of the action into stages (§ 9 *primo* . . . § 10 *silentio facto*), the forceful initial position of the historic infinitives *circumstare* and *orare* (§ 9), the depiction of the confusion around the curule chair (§ 9; see further vol. i, p. 479), and the call to silence with which Fabius restores order (§ 10).

15. 7. comitiorum causa Romam profectus: for the phrasing, see viii. 20. 1 n.

omnes centuriae: see 9. 10 n.

8–12. For interventions in the consular elections, see 9. 10 n.
nobilitatis . . . nobilitas: see vi. 37. 11 n.

8. Ap. Claudius: see ix. 29. 5–11 n.
uir acer et ambitiosus: the coupling seems to be unparalleled. For *ambitiosus* of men desirous of election see e.g. [Cic.] *Her.* ii. 5 and [Q. Cic.] *comm. pet.* 24; for the noun *ambitio* see vii. 15. 12–13 n. See further Hellegouarc'h (1963) 210–11.
cum suis tum totius nobilitatis uiribus incubuit ⟨ut⟩: for the expression cf. esp. Val. Max. ii. 9. 9 'omnibus uiribus incubuerunt ut digni ciuibus uiderentur'; also Tac. *hist.* ii. 10. 2 'et propria ui Crispus incubuerat delatorem fratris sui peruertere'.

The supplement, found first in UOZ, is obviously correct (*ut* could easily have fallen out after *-uit*); for the construction cf. (in addition to the passage of Valerius Maximus) Cic. *fam.* x. 19. 2, Ov. *Pont.* i. 9. 27–8, and see *TLL* vii. 1. 1074. 32–40.

9. primo is picked up not by the usual *deinde* but by *silentio facto*; Walters's tentative proposal to delete the word is unattractive.
priore anno: see 13. 5–13 on the elections for 297.
ut ex caeno plebeio consulatum extraheret: for the image (not uncommon and very appropriate to political invective), cf. e.g. Cic. *Vat.* 17 'unus tu emersus e caeno', Lucr. iii. 77 'ipsi se in tenebris uolui caenoque queruntur', Petron. 119. 58 'hoc mersam caeno Romam somnoque iacentem', *anth. Lat.* 472. 7 'idcirco uirtus medio iacet obruta caeno', and see Otto (1890) 63. *caenum* is found only here in L.
maiestatem: for the majesty of the consulate see ix. 5. 14 n.
patriciis gentibus: for the expression see 8. 9 n.

10. silentio facto: for L.'s love of dramatic silences, see vii. 10. 1 n.
media: see viii. 13. 3 n.
studia: for the use of this word in political contexts, see vii. 19. 5 n.
facturum enim se fuisse . . . ut . . .: the construction is heavy and almost tautologous; but there are good parallels at e.g. xxxvi. 29. 9 'non facturum ut insultet aduersis rebus eorum' (there would be another in L. at vi. 42. 13 were the paradosis sound in that passage; but see n. ad loc.) and Cic. *Cat.* iii. 7 'negaui me esse facturum ut de periculo publico non ad consilium publicum rem integram deferrem', and this use of *facio* is quite common in Latin; see *TLL* vi. 105. 47–106. 37.

nomina reciperet: see ix. 46. 2 n.

11. nunc ('but now, as it is' or just 'as it is'; cf. Greek νῦν δέ) is used quite often to mark a return to reality after a wish or hypothetical condition; cf. e.g. xxi. 40. 1–4 'si eum exercitum, milites, educerem in aciem quem in Gallia mecum habui, supersedissem loqui apud uos . . . nunc, quia ille exercitus, Hispaniae prouinciae scriptus, ibi cum fratre Cn. Scipione meis auspiciis rem gerit . . . pauca uerba facienda sunt', xxxii. 21. 1 'forsitan ego quoque tacerem, si priuatus essem; nunc praetori uideo aut non dandum concilium legatis fuisse aut non sine responso eos dimittendos esse', Cic. *Att.* xi. 2. 3, and see W–M on xxii. 39. 3 (with many Livian instances), Krebs and Schmalz (1905–7) ii. 179 (with further bibliography), and *OLD s.u.* 11.

suam rationem . . . non habiturum: for *rationem habere*, see vi. 37. 4 n. For *suam*, cf. iv. 7. 9 'principes plebis ea comitia malebant, quibus non haberetur ratio sua', Cic. *Att.* viii. 9. 4 (*meam*), and *fam.* xvi. 12. 3, passages which protect the paradosis against emendation to *sui* with ZtZr.

cum contra leges futurum sit: see 13. 8 n.

pessimo exemplo: for the stigma attached to presiding over one's own election, see vii. 25. 2 n.

12. L. Volumnius: see ix. 42. 2 n.

priore inter se consulatu inter se comparati: in 307; see ix. 42. 2–9. For the phenomenon of a consular college being re-elected, see ix. 1. 1 n.

eloquentia ciuilibusque artibus haud dubie praestantem: for Appius' reputation for eloquence, see vol. iii, pp. 353–4. For *ciuiles artes* compare the more common *pacis artes*, for which see Heubner on Tac. *hist.* i. 8. 1.

296 BC

16. 1–21. 12. *Foreign affairs*

L. and parallel narratives. Stripped of some of its numerous embellishments, L.'s account may be summarized as follows. The commands of Q. Fabius Rullianus and P. Decius Mus, the consuls of 297, were prorogued for six months. Decius remained in Samnium, where he drove the army of the Samnites out of their own country, and forced it to flee to Etruria and to beg the Etruscans, who had been quiescent in 297, to join the war (16. 1–8). Murgantia, Romulea, and

Ferentinum were then taken from the Samnites (17. 1–10). L.'s main source made Decius responsible for the capture of these cities; but it was stated *in quibusdam annalibus* that Ferentinum and Romulea had been taken by Fabius, and only Murgantia by Decius; in other sources these successes were ascribed to the consuls, Ap. Claudius Caecus and L. Volumnius Flamma; and in others to Volumnius alone (17. 11–12).

In the meantime, a coalition of Etruscans, Gauls, Samnites, and Umbrians under the leadership of the Samnite Gellius Egnatius had assembled against Rome, and Appius, to whom the province of Etruria had been assigned, was struggling to contain the forces of the Etruscans (18. 1–7). Therefore his colleague, who had just taken three Samnite forts, marched to support him. His departure did not leave southern Italy denuded of Roman troops: the proconsul Fabius Rullianus was sorting out a factional dispute among the Lucani, while Decius was left fighting in Samnium (18. 8–9). After a quarrel over whether or not Appius had requested this aid (L. [18. 7] found three *annales* which stated that he had but did not feel able to pronounce for certain on the matter), the consuls together defeated the enemy force (18. 9–19. 22), and in the battle Appius vowed a temple to Bellona (19. 17 n.).

While the two consuls were in Etruria, the Samnites raided the territory of Vescia and the *ager Falernus*; but they were defeated by the swift return of Volumnius, and their leader Staius Minatius was captured (20. 1–16). But the departure of Volumnius from Etruria led to a resurgence of the coalition under Gellius Egnatius, which in turn led to panic and a *iustitium* at Rome. These fears were assuaged by the victory of Volumnius in Campania (21. 1–6), but, in response to the raid on northern Campania, the decision was taken to send Roman colonies to Minturnae and Sinuessa (21. 7–10). L.'s account of the year ends with further gloomy news from Etruria about the strength of the enemy coalition; Appius consequently passed the winter in the region (21. 11–15).

Only two of the other sources with which L.'s narrative may be compared provide information unquestionably independent of it. One is the Augustan *elogium* of Ap. Claudius Caecus (see vol. iii, p. 352), in which we find 'complura oppida de Samnitibus cepit; Sabinorum et Tuscorum exercitum fudit'; the other is *uir. ill.* 34. 5 (again referring to Appius) 'Sabinos, Samnitas, Etruscos bello domuit'. Dio fr. 35. 27 refers to the altercation between Appius and his fellow consul L. Volumnius Flamma but could derive from L.

L.'s sources. For the events of this year L. says more than usual about his sources: at 17. 11–12 he reveals knowledge of three versions of the capture of Murgantia, Romulea, and Ferentinum different from the version which he recounts at 17. 1–10; and by mentioning at 18. 6 that three *annales* recorded that Appius had written to Volumnius he implies that he knew of at least one source which did not record this.

Now a slight oddity of L.'s narrative is that he twice narrates the gathering storm in Etruria, at first in general terms (16. 2–17. 1) and then with specific reference to the part played by Gellius Egnatius (18. 1–3). Making use of the information which L. provides at 17. 11–12, and particularly the report that some sources ascribed to Volumnius the capture of the three Samnite sites mentioned above, Klinger (1884: 27) acutely suggested that L. may narrate the events of the year twice. After reporting the development of the coalition against Rome in the north (16. 1–8), L. follows the source(s) which assigned the capture of the aforementioned strongholds to Decius (17. 1–10) but reports other versions at the end of his narrative (17. 11–12). In consultation of one of these, Klinger suggests, he found a stirring version of the quarrel between Appius and Volumnius, which he decided to follow. In order to place this in its context, L. narrated some of the preliminaries to this tale that he had found in this source but seems not to have realized that he was in fact reporting events which he had already described. This explains why at 18. 1–3 he again returns to events in the north, this time mentioning Gellius Egnatius as the Samnite leader: if he was not named in the version which L. consulted first, he may have thought that he was now recording different events. He then states (18. 8) that Volumnius had captured three *castella* in Samnium, but these *castella* were in fact the same as Murgantia, Romulea, and Ferentinum.[1] Only then does Volumnius march to the north and quarrel with Appius, leaving Fabius in Lucania and Decius in Samnium.

In the absence of any of L.'s sources the rightness of this analysis cannot finally be demonstrated, but its attractions are obvious. Klinger is likely to be wrong only if (*a*) L. himself was responsible for inventing some of the content of 16. 2–8, 18. 1–2, and 21. 2, returning thrice to the worry caused by the events in Etruria as a deliberate artistic ploy to emphasize the worsening military situation facing Rome (despite her successes in Samnium) in the build-up to Sentinum (see further Lipovsky [1981] 157–8); and (*b*) the *tria castella* said to have been captured by Volumnius at 18. 8 were not Murgantia, Romulea, and Ferentinum.

[1] For this interpretation of the *tria castella* see also W–M ad loc. and Bruno (1906) 28 n. 1.

Klinger (p. 28) also observed how similar to each other in content are 18. 1–3 and 21. 2, in both of which passages the Umbrians and Gauls are mentioned in the same context as Gellius Egnatius, suggesting that L. had twice taken the same material from one source. However, it is more likely either that these two passages reflect the account of the same event in two different sources or that in the second passage L. deliberately returned to Gellius Egnatius for the reason given in the previous paragraph.

*Prorogation and the coalition against Rome.*We have no reason to doubt L.'s report of the prorogations of the commands of Fabius and Decius:[1] with heavy fighting continuing in Samnium, with a powerful coalition forming in Etruria and Umbria,[2] and with Rome's being required to send troops to Lucania, there was need for more than two commanders and armies in the field. Indeed, Rome had never before found so powerful a coalition of Italians ranged against her, and 296 was clearly the year which saw the formation of the grand alliance which fought Rome at Sentinum.[3]

L.'s view that the military might of the Romans under Decius drove Gellius Egnatius and his Samnite army out of Samnium has long and rightly been dismissed as an absurdity: Gellius will have marched north to help foster the incipient coalition in Etruria and Umbria, and the Romans were either taken by surprise or powerless to stop him.[4] L. limits the membership of this coalition to Etruscans, Gauls, Samnites, and Umbrians, but both the *elogium* and the author of the *de uiris illustribus* record that Appius defeated the Sabines; and it is quite probable that in the period after 303 the Umbrians were supported by the Sabines in their hostility towards Rome (see above, pp. 30–4). Although an alliance between the neighbouring Etruscans, Umbrians, and Sabines is hardly surprising, the Etruscans were natural partners of neither the Gauls (against whose presence on their north-eastern flank they had been struggling for decades) nor the Samnites (against whom they had once fought in

---

[1] However, the prorogation for only six months is surprising: see 16. 1 n.

[2] Salmon (1967: 264 n. 3) tried to establish precisely which Etruscan cities were fighting Rome in 296 by transferring to this year L.'s notice (ix. 32. 1) that all the Etruscan cities except Arretium rose against Rome in 311; but such arbitrary handling of the sources is unhelpful.

[3] However, the Etruscans and Gauls had already allied for a raid on Roman territory in 299; see 10. 1–11. 8 n.

[4] We cannot reconstruct with any probability the route taken by the Samnite army in its march north: De Sanctis (1907–64: ii. 354) held that it passed through Paelignian territory and up the Aterno valley, W–M (on 16. 2) and Salmon (1967: 264) that it passed through Marsic territory.

Campania);[1] and the alliance may well have been difficult to organize and never very stable. Indeed, we cannot tell whether the full coalition was formed at the beginning of the year, or only later: at 16. 6 L. makes the Samnites allude to the Gauls, and at 18. 2 he records that Gallic and Umbrian contingents reinforced the Samnites and Etruscans in the major battle against Appius and Volumnius; but the Gauls and Umbrians feature neither in his account of the fighting nor in the brief parallel notices, and at 21. 2 and 14 he suggests that their forces were mobilized only later in the year. But, even if the authenticity of 21. 11–15 (where Ap. Claudius reports to Rome that the armies of the allied Etruscans, Gauls, Samnites, and Umbrians was so large that it could not fit into one camp) is doubtful, the campaign of Sentinum in 295 guarantees that by the end of the year massive forces were allied together.

Fighting in Etruria. The coalition forming to the north of Rome could draw on vast reserves of manpower, and L. must have been right to stress the gravity of the threat which it posed to the Romans (who, it should be remembered, were still deeply involved in fighting around Samnium and its borders). In particular, we may well believe that Appius faced great difficulties in trying to protect the interests of Rome and her Etruscan and Umbrian allies: the vow to Bellona guarantees the report in our sources that he fought a major engagement against the Etruscans, Samnites, and Sabines; and the need to make the vow suggests that the battle was hard-fought and desperately close. If, as L. states, the Romans were victorious, their victory did no more than stall the build-up of enemy power.

It is harder to be certain whether L. and Dio were correct to hold that for this engagement Appius was joined by Volumnius and a second consular army. On the one hand, L.'s reports (18. 5–7, 21. 11–15) of the difficulty which Appius had in holding the situation on his own seem entirely credible (although the derogatory aspersions cast on his military ability at 18. 5–6, 19. 8 and later at 25. 6–9 are part of a standard annalistic τόπος; see vol. iii, p. 359). On the other, there was plenty to occupy Volumnius in the south; the alleged union with the forces of Appius would require us to believe that Volumnius started the campaigning season in Samnium, then marched to Etruria, and then marched back to Samnium;[2] and L.'s narrative of

---

[1] But see p. 32 for the view of Beloch (1926: 432) that the Samnites had no part in the alliance of this year.

[2] The difficulties involved in accepting this are well pointed out by Bruno (1906: 30); see also Costanzi (1919) 197–8.

the meeting of the two consuls is full of the most obvious Livian and annalistic elaboration. Nevertheless, it is perhaps safer to accept the outline of L.'s notice: most of his sources held that Volumnius did march north, and, since two consular armies were needed against the same coalition at Sentinum, they may have been needed a year earlier. If the *tria castella* captured by Volumnius at 18. 8 are indeed Murgantia, Romulea, and Ferentinum, then another possibility may be conceivable: these towns were captured by either Fabius or (much more probably) Decius, and Volumnius began the year fighting in the north with Appius and only later went to Samnium. The tale of the letters would then be an annalistic fiction, perhaps to blacken the name of Appius, perhaps to provide a link with the Etruscan campaign after the capture of the *tria castella* had wrongly been ascribed to Volumnius.

Samnium. L.'s account of the fighting in Samnium is very much harder to interpret than that which relates to Etruria, largely because of the difficulties which his sources gave him over the assignation of consular provinces. Nevertheless, both the obscurity of Murgantia, Romulea, and Ferentinum and the fact that all L.'s sources seem to have recorded their capture provide a strong indication that this particular information is reliable. We do not know, however, in which part of Samnium these sites lay,[1] nor can we be certain which commander captured them. Of L.'s four versions, two may reasonably be dismissed. In one Fabius Rullianus is said to have captured some of these sites; but he is a hero whose deeds are often embellished, and the fact that he is recorded (18. 8) as having been in Lucania for at least part of the campaigning season is another powerful reason for rejecting this variant. In the other the credit is shared between the two consuls; but this notice is reminiscent of Fabius Pictor's failure to divide the consular provinces for 294 (32. 1–37. 16 n.), and, given the strength of the northern coalition, it is improbable that Appius left Etruria.[2] Whether L.'s main source is correct in ascribing these successes to Decius, or we should follow the variant

---

[1] However, the attempt of Beloch (1926: 439) and Salmon (1967: 263) to identify them with settlements in the region of Venusia has some merits (see 17. 3, 6, and 9 nn.); if it were correct, then it would strengthen the claims of Decius to have been the commander who captured them, since he fought in the Apulian area in 297 and may have passed the winter there (14. 1–15. 6 n.). It would also provide a continuation of the strategy adopted in 298 and 297 of attacking the Samnites from the south-east.

[2] It is true that the *elogium* does refer to the capture of Samnite *oppida* by Appius; but (*a*) this may be a relic of the tradition to which L. alludes, or (*b*) it may be a misplaced reference to the events of 295, when Appius operated on the borders of Samnium (31. 3–7).

which ascribed them to Volumnius, it is very hard to say; but, since Decius must have campaigned somewhere, and since numerous other activities of Volumnius in this year are recorded, L.'s main narrative should perhaps be accepted. If Volumnius' first campaign of the year was in Etruria, as was mentioned above as a possibility, then the version which ascribes the capture of these sites to Decius must be preferred.

This uncertainty also makes it difficult to establish the whereabouts of Volumnius throughout this year. There seems no reason to doubt that at the end of the year he countered a Samnite raid on northern Campania,[1] and we have seen that immediately before this he is likely to have been in Etruria. What is hardest to determine is whether he fought in Samnium before going to Etruria, as L. implies that he did at 18. 8, and, if so, whether, as Klinger and others have argued, the *tria castella* which he is said to have captured were Murgantia, Romulea, and Ferentinum. If the *tria castella* were not these strongholds, then it becomes much more likely that Volumnius did begin the year campaigning in Samnium (presumably in a different area from Decius).[2]

As for the Samnites, at the beginning of the year their energies will have been consumed in defending their territory against Decius and Volumnius and in establishing their army under Gellius Egnatius in Etruria; but it is certainly credible that later in the year they seized the opportunity offered by the absence of substantial Roman forces to make a major raid on Campania. The report (21. 3–6) of the calling of a *iustitium* at Rome when both consuls were away and the Samnites were threatening also seems entirely credible; and the likely authenticity of the notice is enhanced by the fact that L. claimed to know the name of the praetor who called the *iustitium* and, for only the second time, its precise duration. Northern Campania had suffered from such raids at the end of the Second Samnite War (ix. 44. 5, 305 BC), and doubtless the Romans hoped that by creating two citizen colonies they could strengthen the defences of the area; but there was another raid on the area of Vescia 295 (31. 1–5) and on Campania in 292 (Zon. viii. 1. 11).[3]

---

[1] According to Salmon (1967: 264) he was joined in Campania by Fabius Rullianus; but L. (20. 2) thought that the prorogued command of Rullianus had terminated.

[2] The supposition of Salmon (1967: 263) that Volumnius was sent initially to northern Campania may be correct but rests on no evidence.

[3] Costanzi (1919: 198) argues, not implausibly, that the Samnite raid on Campania was a diversion from their gathering of forces further north.

The Lucani. The alliance between Rome and at least some of the Lucani, which had been established since 298 (11. 11–12. 3 n.), meant that the Samnites were threatened on their southern flank and were largely encircled by the territory of Rome or her allies. It is thus easy both to understand why Rome should have been disturbed by reports of political unrest in Lucania and to accept L.'s notice (18. 8) that Fabius Rullianus was dispatched to sort it out. Our sources do not mention any further engagement with the Lucani until M'. Curius Dentatus defeated them in 290 (*MRR* i. 184); this should not, however, be taken to imply that they did not waver in their allegiance to Rome during this five-year period.[1]

Apart from her capture of a few Samnite strongholds, this was a year in which Rome made little military progress. Nor did her adversaries achieve actual military success; but the establishment of their alliance was of the highest importance and posed a very major threat. Perhaps it was obvious even at the time that 295 would be a year of great importance for the future of Italy.

On the events of this year, see further Klinger (1884) 26–30, Bruno (1906) 27–32, De Sanctis (1907–64) ii. 353–5, Münzer, *RE* iii. 2684, iv. 2282–3, ixA. 880–1 (this last with H. Gundel), Costanzi (1919) 197–9, Beloch (1926) 432–3, 439, Salmon (1967) 262–4, and Harris (1971) 67–9.

16. 1–17. 12. *P. Decius Mus in Samnium.* In this episode L. describes how the successes of Decius in Samnium force the Samnite army to leave Samnium and to forge an alliance with the Etruscans (16. 2–8). Decius is therefore able to win easy successes at Murgantia (17. 1–6), Romulea (17. 6–8), and Ferentinum (17. 9–10), only the last being defended. Since there was no Samnite army for the Romans to fight and Samnite resistance was feeble, L. is able to describe these assaults swiftly. The episode is notable for two brief bursts of *oratio recta* (17. 2, 5–6), which contrast with the *oratio obliqua* used earlier by the Samnites (16. 4–8) and in which Decius urges his troops to capture the Samnite bases, and also for the response of the Roman troops, which illustrates the *caritas* (17. 3) that they felt for their leader. The focus on Decius throughout this episode prepares for his death at Sentinum.

16. 1. prorogato ... imperio: see viii. 23. 12 n.; nowhere else are we told that such a prorogation was limited to six months (although

---

[1] However, Costanzi (1919: 198) may be right to suggest that the activities of Fabius were limited to towns on the Samnite/Lucanian border.

Publilius Philo's prorogation in 326 was *quoad debellatum cum Graecis esset).* This does not mean that this detail should be rejected, but L.'s account of the division of provinces in this year between consuls and proconsuls has so many difficulties that the possibility of a mistake should be kept in mind.

2. insequenti . . . anno: see vi. 11. 1 n.
pro consule: for the spelling see *addendum* to viii. 23. 12 n.

2–3. expulit . . . pulsi: see 24. 14 n.

3. mixtis terrore precibus: see ix. 22. 10 n.
principum Etruriae concilium: see vi. 2. 2 n.

4. suismet ipsorum uiribus: see vii. 9. 8 n.
molem belli: see vii. 29. 5 n.

5. haud magni momenti . . . auxilia: the Campani, Volsci, Hernici, Aequi, and the Etruscans themselves had all fought Rome at some point during previous Samnite Wars. *haud magni momenti* is attributive, qualifying *auxilia.* The examples of this use of *momenti* listed at *TLL* viii. 1393. 9–13 include Plin. *nat.* xx. 79 'heliam [a variety of cabbage] . . . nullius in medicina momenti' and Tac. *hist.* iii. 8. 1 'magni momenti locum obtinuit'.
quod pax seruientibus grauior quam liberis bellum esset: for the equation of peace with servitude cf. Cic. *Phil.* xii. 14, xiii. 2, Sall. *hist.* i. 55. 25, and Tac. *hist.* ii. 17. 1; note also viii. 21. 6 and Cic. *Phil.* ii. 113 'pax est tranquilla libertas, seruitus postremum malorum omnium, non modo bello, sed morte etiam repellendum'.

6. opulentissimum: see ix. 36. 11 n.
armis, uiris: for the juxtaposition of these words, see viii. 5. 3 n.
inter ferrum et arma natos: see ix. 9. 11 n.
feroces . . . aduersus Romanum populum: for the *ferocia* of the Gauls, see vii. 23. 6 n. For the construction, cf. e.g. i. 25. 7 'is . . . aduersus singulos ferox' and Tac. *hist.* iii. 69. 4 'miles Vitelli aduersus pericula ferox'; these parallels show that ⟨*odio*⟩ *aduersus* (Geist [1877] 258) is unnecessary.
suopte ingenio: for this expression cf. 42. 6, i. 18. 4, 25. 1, xxv. 18. 2, xxix. 6. 2, Varr. *rust.* ii. 8. 1, and see further vi. 15. 12 n. and Neue and Wagener (1892–1905) ii. 374.
Romanum populum: see viii. 23. 6 n.

quem captum a se auroque redemptum: L. tells the tale at v. 32. 6–49. 7; our passage does not necessarily contradict L.'s account in book v of how Camillus prevented the Gauls making off with the gold, since he is probably writing loosely here. See also ix. 4. 16 n.
memorent: see vi. 9. 3 n.

7. si sit animus . . . qui: Harant (1880: 67) attractively proposed *si is sit animus . . . qui*: for *is* (or the semantically similar *idem*) qualifying *animus* and pointing to a following relative clause, cf. xxi. 40. 6 'erit igitur in hoc certamine is uobis illisque animus qui uictoribus et uictis esse solet', 41. 10, xxiv. 8. 18, and xxvi. 33. 9. However, what the mss offer is not certainly wrong. For *si sit animus* cf. vi. 27. 8 'si sit animus plebi memor patrum libertatis'.
Porsinnae: at ii. 9. 1–14. 9 L. tells how Lars Porsinna (or Porsenna) of Clusium had besieged Rome in 508.
cis Tiberim: before the demise of Veii Etruscan territory had reached the Tiber; hence the Roman expression *trans Tiberim*, often equivalent to 'abroad' (viii. 14. 5 n.).
pro . . . de: for the juxtaposition of these prepositions W–M on xxi. 41. 14 'non de possessione Siciliae ac Sardiniae . . . sed pro Italia uobis est pugnandum' cite Tac. *Agr.* 26. 2 'securi pro salute de gloria certabant'.
intolerando Italiae regno: for the notion of hegemony in Italy, see viii. 23. 9 n.

8. instructum armis stipendio: in other words the Etruscans would not have to pay for the help of the Samnites; contrast their difficulties with the Gauls, as described at 10. 6–12. Luterbacher suggested *subsidio* for *stipendio*; but this does not fit in well with the general tone of the Samnites' speech (they have come to stir up the Etruscans to war, not to bring them help in time of special need), and the asyndeton which it removes is not particularly awkward.

17. 1. urebat: the metaphor is particularly apt with *bellum*, since the burning of crops and buildings was regular in ancient warfare. Cf. especially xxvii. 29. 9 'Philippus implorantibus Achaeis auxilium tulit, quos . . . Machanidas tyrannus Lacedaemoniorum finitimo bello urebat', 39. 9 'Punici belli, quo duodecimum annum Italia urebatur', and xxviii. 43. 21; also analogous metaphorical uses of *urere* with other expressions, e.g. at Vell. ii. 77. 1 'populi, quem grauis urebat infesto mari annona' (on which see Woodman's note).
comperit per exploratores: see viii. 30. 3 n.

aduocato consilio: see ix. 2. 15 n.

2. uicatim: see ix. 13. 7 n.
circumferentes bellum: see vi. 29. 6 n.

3. adprobantibus cunctis: see vi. 6. 16 n.
Murgantiam: L. mentions many obscure sites whose locality is now unknown. R. Kiepert, in H. Kiepert (1894–1910) xx. 3, suggested that Murgantia should be sought at Castelmanno, near S. Bartolomeo in Galdo in the Valfortore (for this view see also Philipp, *RE* xvi. 660). Salmon (1967: 263) preferred to place the site in Apulia, mentioning the area known to-day as Le Murghe and places in that area called Murgia. The truth will never be known without the discovery of new evidence.
agrestibus populationibus: see ix. 2. 9 n.
uno die ui atque armis urbem caperent: see vi. 3. 10 n.

4. duo milia . . . captique: for this figure see 14. 21 n.; for general discussion of casualty figures also vii. 17. 9 n.
capta est: with *caperent* in § 3 and *captique* earlier in this sentence the iteration may appear harsh. If emendation is required, the best conjecture is *parta est* (Novák [1894] 118), which gives excellent sense. Deletion of *capta est* with Gronovius is possible but less economical; and *facta est* (Weissenborn, *Komm.*) is feeble. However, as Wesenberg (1870/1: 38) emphasized, L. was not very sensitive to iteration (see further vol. i, pp. 725–7), and the paradosis may probably stand.

5. uoltis uos pro uirtute spes gerere?: literally 'Do you wish to carry hopes that correspond to your courage?'; Foster has 'Will your expectations not be equal to your courage?' However, *uis* and *uoltis* can have the force almost of a command; cf. e.g. Hor. *serm.* ii. 6. 92 'uis tu homines urbemque feris praeponere siluis?', Sen. *epist.* 58. 23 'uis tu non timere ne semel fiat quod cotidie fiat!', and 88. 41 'non uis cogitare quantum temporis tibi auferat mala ualetudo . . .?', and see discussions of the idiom at Madvig (1871–84) ii. 198, K–S ii. 505, and H–S 461–2, 467. Madvig was the first to see that our sentence is a question.

spes gerere is an expression that is rare (only 25. 4 'exercitu . . . plus fiduciae ac spei gerente', *carm. epigr.* 787. 53, and Rufin. *hist.* v. 1. 3, p. 403. 11 are cited for it at *TLL* vi. 1934. 36–8) but provides an apt image here, since booty was carried.

6–8. The idea that booty has to be sold because of its cumbersome nature is surprisingly hard to parallel, but cf. 20. 16 'coactique uendere praedam ne alibi quam in armis animum haberent'. These passages are discussed at vi. 2. 12 n. Contrast the behaviour of the Samnites at 20. 4–13.

6. inlicite . . . agmen: merchants would quite naturally follow an army in the hope of trade; cf. e.g. Sall. *Iug.* 44. 5, 45. 2, Fest. 103. 17 'lixae, qui exercitum sequuntur quaestus gratia . . .'. For *inlicere* used in a neutral or favourable sense, see Goodyear on Tac. *ann.* ii. 37. 1.
uos labor haud maior . . . manet: for the transitive use of *manere*, the following passages from pre-Antonine writers of prose are listed at *TLL* viii. 291. 11–292. 37: 35. 10, ii. 40. 9, xxvi. 13. 18, xlii. 66. 3, xliv. 25. 2, Cic. *Phil.* xiii. 45, Mela ii. 20, Sen. *dial.* vi. 24. 5, x. 15. 2, *epist.* 78. 6, Curt. vi. 10. 32, ix. 4. 18, Quint. *inst.* vi. 1. 19, Quint. (?) *decl. min.* 345. 14, [*decl. mai.*] 3. 2, Frontin. (?) *strat.* iv. 1. 17, Plin. *epist.* ii. 10. 7, vi. 13. 6, *pan.* 55. 10, Suet. *Iul.* 14. 1, and *Tib.* 67. 2. This comparatively meagre haul should be contrasted with the strong attestation of the usage in Plautus and Terence (a dozen examples, including e.g. *aul.* 680 and *Phorm.* 480) and its frequent employment in later poetry. This distribution suggests that the usage had been regular in the third and second centuries BC but fell into desuetude in the first and later, being used only as a choice expression, particularly by L. and the poets. See also K–S i. 257 and Tränkle (1968) 116–17.

7. Romuleam: in our sources for the Samnite Wars Romulea is mentioned elsewhere only at Steph. Byz. *ethn. s.u.* Ῥωμυλία, which he describes as a τῶν ἐν Ἰταλίᾳ Σαννιτῶν πόλις; doubtless Stephanus drew this information from D.H.'s now lost narrative of this year. The itineraries, however, refer to a Sub Romula between Aeclanum and Aquilonia, which may be placed with some confidence near Bisaccia; it is not unlikely that this was the site to which L. refers. See further Mommsen, *CIL* ix p. 121, Beloch (1926) 439, Philipp, *RE* iA. 1073–4, and Salmon (1967) 263.
tormentis: vi. 9. 2 n.
in moenia: for the construction with *in* see vii. 36. 12 n.; for variation between *murus* and *moenia* see ix. 28. 5 n.

8–9. captum oppidum ac direptum est: ad duo milia et trecenti occisi et sex milia hominum capta, et miles ingenti praeda potitus; quam uendere sicut priorem coactus, Ferentinum

**inde, quamquam nihil quietis dabatur, tamen summa alacri-
tate ductus:** the punctuation of this passage is that suggested to me
by Profesor Watt and is similar to that of Drakenborch (who placed
a colon after *potitus*). As conventionally punctuated (with a comma
after *potitus* and a semi-colon after *coactus*; thus e.g. Madvig and
Ussing), it has been regarded as posing two difficulties, to which a
third may be added.

(*a*) The ellipse of *est* with *coactus*, depriving the relative clause of a
main verb. The limits within which the auxiliary could be omitted
from Latin perfect passives are perhaps impossible adequately to
define, but this difficulty has been overstated, since Wesenberg
(1870/1: 38) has adduced many passages where a similar ellipse is
found in a relative clause (including e.g. 21. 8, 30. 4, 33. 6, and vi. 1.
11 [twice]). Therefore, even if the difficulty were not removed by the
punctuation adopted, there would probably be no need for *coactus*
⟨*est*⟩ (Drakenborch's *codex Portugallicus*; the reading was considered
a possibility by Madvig, *ap.* Madvig and Ussing).

(*b*) The ellipse of *est* with *ductus*. Such ellipses are common enough
when the verb comes at the end of its clause (thus *occisi* and *capta* in
this lemma), and Baehrens (1913: 268) lists several instances offered
by the mss of L. Not all are acceptable, and he himself describes the
instance here as harsh. However, since its harshness comes not from
the ellipse itself, which is not abnormal, but from the combination of
ellipse in main and relative clause and from the consideration noted
below under (*c*), there is probably no need to emend to either *ductus*
⟨*est*⟩ (an alternative conjecture of Madvig, loc. cit.), or ⟨*est*⟩ *ductus*
(Walters).[1]

(*c*) The continuation of *miles* as subject after *Ferentinum inde*,
which may seem somewhat awkward, but is made much easier with
heavy punctuation after *potitus*.

If emendation is required, I should prefer to write either ⟨*exercitus*⟩ *ductus* or *ductus* ⟨*exercitus*⟩ (of these the first provides the more
usual Livian word-order, but the second is perhaps better, as it
postulates an omission which is particularly easy to explain). The
result would be standard Livian phrasing, cf. esp. v. 19. 9 'inde ad
Veios exercitus ductus', viii. 1. 4 'inde uictor exercitus Satricum
contra Antiates ductus', xl. 34. 13 'inde in Sardiniam exercitus
ductus', xlii. 63. 12 'inde Thebas exercitus ductus' (all with *inde*);
also ii. 65. 7 'Antium et Romanus exercitus ductus', iv. 47. 5 'postero

[1] One cannot use weight of parallels to choose between these conjectures, since there is
only one parallel passage in L. (xxiii. 10. 7 'est ductus'), and that on its own should hardly be
decisive.

die ad Labicos ductus exercitus oppidumque . . . captum ac direptum est', vi. 9. 12 'Sutrio recepto restitutoque sociis Nepete exercitus ductus', 29. 6, 33. 8, ix. 10. 6, xxi. 12. 3, and xxxviii. 15. 1. See also vii. 15. 5 n., on similar ellipses with deponent verbs.

Ferentinum: not a reference to the well-known Hernican town (vii. 9. 1 n.) but to a Samnite or south Italian site, as Stephanus (*ethn. s.u.*) confirms with an entry for Φερεντῖνος which includes the words πόλις Σαυνιτῶν ἐν Ἰταλίᾳ and a reference to D.H. xvii. The speculative argument of Beloch (1926: 439) and Salmon (1967: 263) that we should equate Ferentinum with Forentum (ix. 20. 9 n.) has the merit of placing the site quite close to where the itineraries place Romula.

8. captum . . . ac direptum est: see vi. 32. 9 n.
ad duo milia et trecenti occisi et sex milia hominum capta: for the use of *ad* with a numeral in the nominative see ix. 42. 8 n.; for the figure for enemy captured see 14. 21 n.; and for general discussion of casualty figures see vii. 17. 9 n.

10. ibi plus laboris ac periculi fuit: see vi. 24. 7, ix. 21. 6 nn.
adsuetus praedae: L. and Virgil are the first authors to use forms which are certainly dative after *assuesco*; cf. e.g. v. 48. 3 'gens umorique ac frigori adsueta', xxi. 16. 5, and *Aen.* vii. 490. (In several earlier passages forms are employed which could be either dative or ablative.) See further K–S i. 381–2 and *TLL* ii. 908. 57–909. 11, 910. 5–17.

11–12. *The variants in L.'s sources.* These are discussed at pp. 199–200 above.

11. oppugnatarum urbium decori: see ix. 22. 9 n.
in quibusdam annalibus: see vii. 18. 10 n.
trahitur: see ix. 28. 6 n.

12. L. Volumnio: N had *P. Volumnius*, but Sigonius rightly restored the *praenomen* which Volumnius is given elsewhere.

18. 1–19. 22. *Appius and Volumnius in Etruria.* The first part of the episode is built around speeches: the brusque greeting of Appius in *oratio recta* (18. 11); the dignified reply of Volumnius in *oratio obliqua* (18. 12);[1] the dismissal of Appius in *oratio recta* (18. 13); a

---

[1] It may be significant that L. never uses his *cognomina* Flamma Violens.

second dignified reply, again in *oratio obliqua*, from Volumnius; the
plea of the legates and tribunes to the consuls in *oratio obliqua* (19.
1–4); the notice of long speeches given in the assembly (here L. may
ignore speeches in his sources) (19. 5); the rebuttal of Appius by
Volumnius (19. 6–9), with the climactic put-down of Appius by
Volumnius in *oratio recta* and introduced at the end of a periodic
sentence; the cry of the troops (19. 10); the request of Volumnius, in
oratio recta, that they should leave him in no doubt as to what they
want (19. 11); and finally the great roar of the troops which brings the
enemy out to battle (19. 12).

Since L.'s sources left him uncertain as to whether or not Appius
had summoned Volumnius (18. 7), he was unable to say (18. 10)
whether Appius was genuinely surprised at the arrival of his colleague or was merely dissembling. However, throughout this first
part of the episode he implies that Appius was in the wrong: he
stresses his unsatisfactory performance as a commander (18. 5–6),
the good cheer with which his troops greet Volumnius (18. 10), and
the desire of his legates and tribunes that Volumnius should stay
(19. 1–4); he describes Volumnius (19. 6) as 'causa superior', and he
notes (19. 10–13) the approval which he gained from the troops of
Appius' army. Finally, Appius decides to fight only lest he lose face
(19. 13).

The fact that neither side was ready for battle is the novelty in L.'s
description of the ensuing contest in the second part of the episode
(19. 14–22). He describes the fighting briefly, the main focus of his
interest being the transformation of Appius, who after making a vow
to Bellona (given prominence in § 17 by being placed in *oratio recta*)
suddenly becomes a warlike figure. Inspired by Bellona and his
leadership, his troops burst through the ditch and rampart of the
enemy camp, whereas Volumnius is able only to attack more conventionally at the gate (19. 21–2). The report (19. 22) of Samnite
casualties rounds off an episode notable for the large quantity of
annalistic and Livian elaboration to be found in it.

18. 1. cum . . . gererentur: the mss here offer *dum . . . gererentur*.
Instances of *dum* with the imperfect subjunctive in purely temporal
contexts have been found in the mss of several authors (see Riemann
[1885] 298–9, K–S ii. 377–8, H–S 613–14), but it is not entirely clear
whether L. should be numbered among those for whom the construction is admissible. Of the instances listed by K–S, at ii. 47. 5 M^1
has *cum* and not *dum*, and this may be correct; and at iv. 25. 9, xxiv.
40. 10, and xxxix. 49. 8 the *dum*-clause is not purely temporal. This

leaves only i. 40. 7 'dum intentus in eum se rex totus auerteret, alter elatam securim in caput deiecit, relictoque in uolnere telo ambo se foras eiciunt', where Gronovius (followed by Ogilvie) made the easy change of *cum* for *dum*. The absence of good parallels makes defence of the paradosis difficult in our passage, for which Gronovius again proposed *cum* for *dum* and Walters *geruntur* for *gererentur*. Both conjectures give good sense. That of Walters offers an expression which is much more common in L. (ix. 32. 1 n.), and he adduced xxix. 23. 1, where the first stage of the corruption which he postulates is to be found in the Codex Puteanus. That of Gronovius, which I prefer, has parallels at xxxiii. 36. 1 'cum haec in Graecia Macedoniaque et Asia gererentur . . .', xlii. 64. 1 'cum haec in Boeotia gererentur, Perseus . . .', and xlv. 11. 1 '⟨cum⟩ haec gererentur, Antiochus . . .' (where the supplement of Grynaeus seems necessary).

cuiuscumque ductu auspicioque: see viii. 31. 1 n.

Gellius Egnatius: (9). L. refers to Egnatius also at 19. 14, 21. 2, and 29. 16 (explicitly) and at 19. 16 (implicitly). He was presumably the architect of the grand alliance in the north, between Etruscans, Samnites, and Gauls. Beloch (1926: 128) arbitrarily argued that he was a retrojection of the Marius Egnatius of the Social War (for whom see e.g. *per.* lxxv, Vell. ii. 16. 1, App. *ciu.* i. 40. 181, 41. 183, 45. 199). See further viii. 39. 12 n. and Münzer, *RE* v. 1994–5.

ex Samnitibus: for this attributive usage, W–M (on iv. 28. 3) cite iv. 13. 1 'Sp. Maelius ex equestri ordine', 28. 3 'Vettius Messius ex Volscis', and xxxix. 11. 4 'anum Aebutiam ex Auentino'. Add xxxix. 12. 1, and many of the passages listed at *TLL* v. 2. 1096. 6–62 are also comparable.

2. traxerat contagio . . . sollicitabantur: L. employs a medical image: the use of *contagio* of disease needs no illustration; for *trahere* of disease xxv. 26. 8 and Ov. *met.* i. 190–1 'cuncta prius temptata, sed inmedicabile corpus | ense recidendum est, ne pars sincera trahatur' are cited at *OLD s.u.* 2(e); for *sollicitare* cf. Hor. *serm.* ii. 2. 43. For the idea cf. also i. 15. 1 'belli Fidenatis contagione inritati Veientium animi'.

3. qui tumultus repens postquam est Romam perlatus: there is a striking parallel for L.'s phrasing at xxi. 26. 1 'qui tumultus repens postquam est Romam perlatus et Punicum insuper Gallico bellum auctum patres acceperunt . . .'; note also xxi. 57. 1 'Romam tantus terror ex hac clade perlatus est ut . . .'. For the concept of *tumultus* see vii. 9. 6 n.

est Romam perlatus is the reading of M: P^cUOZbZt have *Romam perlatus est*, P¹Zsλ *Romam perlatus* (without *est*). This unusual division of the mss suggests that *est* was originally absent from the text of N and restored only in its margin. If so, P¹Zs may have the more 'honest' Π-reading, and P^cUOZbZt may have tried to repair the text by insertion of *est* (for difficulties of this kind, see vol. i, pp. 311–14). Editors, however, rightly reject their position of *est* in favour of M's text: (*a*) it is very strongly supported by xxi. 26. 1 (quoted above); (*b*) elsewhere L. places *est* after *perlatus* only at xxi. 57. 1 (quoted above) but before it in five passages (Packard [1968] iii. 872–3).[1]

3–4. cum legione secunda ac tertia . . . duae Romanae legiones secutae, prima et quarta: in book x L. gives legions their official numbers for the first time; cf. 27. 10–11 'aduersus Samnites Q. Fabius primam ac tertiam legionem pro dextro cornu, aduersus Gallos pro sinistro Decius quintam et sextam instruxit; secunda et quarta cum L. Volumnio pro consule in Samnio gerebant bellum' and the reference to the third legion at 29. 13; note too that D.H. (xx. 1. 4–5) does the same in his account of Ausculum. These passages anticipate L.'s practice in the later decades, where legions are regularly given their numbers (e.g. xxii. 27. 10–11, xxvii. 41. 9, 42. 2, xxxiv. 46. 12, xl. 41. 2–3: see further Marquardt [1881–5] ii. 380 n. 7, Ritterling, *RE* xii. 1205, and Paul on Sall. *Iug.* 38. 6). From this book one should perhaps cite also 14. 14 'hastatos primae legionis', 25. 11 'relicta secunda legione ad Clusium . . . ipse (*sc.* Q. Fabius) ad consultandum de bello rediit', and 43. 3 'D. Brutum Scaeuam legatum cum legione prima et decem cohortibus alariis . . . ire aduersus subsidium hostium iussit'; but in these passages L. may be using *primus* and *secundus* somewhat loosely, meaning no more than the first or second of the two legions which were in a consul's army: for a parallel see xxxiv. 15. 3, as interpreted by Briscoe (1981: 36 n. 8).

The appearance of such notices in book x and in book xx of D.H. is probably another indication of the richer sources which L. and D.H. had at their disposal for this period (see vol. i, pp. 38–72). However, it is worrying that sometimes this information may appear contradictory and hard to use in tracing the movements of a legion, as the following table suggests:

---

[1] However, the force of this second argument is greatly reduced if one considers all instances of the participle *perlatus* with the auxiliary.

Legio	year	location
I	296	Etruria/Umbria (with Ap. Claudius: 18. 4)
	295	Etruria/Umbria (with Fabius: 27. 10)
II	296	Samnium (with Volumnius: 18. 3)
	296/5	Etruria/Umbria (with Scipio: 25. 11)
	295	Samnium (with Volumnius: 27. 11)
III	296	Samnium (with Volumnius: 18. 3)
	295	Etruria/Umbria (with Fabius: 27. 10, 29. 13)
IV	296	Etruria/Umbria (with Appius: 18. 4)
	295	Samnium (with Volumnius: 27. 11)
V	295	Etruria/Umbria (with Decius: 27. 10)
VI	295	Etruria/Umbria (with Decius: 27. 10)

Note in particular that *secunda* at 25. 11 seems to contradict the information given at 27. 10–11 and 29. 13 (Fabius is hardly likely to have changed in mid-campaign the legions which he commanded). However, one possible explanation of this discrepancy has just been given; another is that after their defeat in early 295 the second legion returned to Rome and was then used by Volumnius; a third is that at this time legions were renumbered each year; and a fourth is that L.'s account at 25. 11 derives from an unreliable source.[1] For further discussion see Loreto (1989–90) 623–4.

By the late third century the legions were divided among the consuls by lot (see e.g. xxii. 27. 10–11 and xlii. 32. 5); this practice may well have begun in our period.

3. primo quoque tempore: see vi. 3. 2 n. (but the expression is not used here of instructions to a magistrate).

4. sociorum duodecim milia: this is the first time that L. gives the number of allies serving in the Roman army. One may perhaps compare 26. 14 'Campanisque mille equitibus delectis' and 29. 12 'Campanorum alam, quingentos fere equites', but these passages do not give the total number of allies serving. There are casual or implicit references to the help of allies at 4. 9 and ix. 40. 17. Twelve thousand men was the equivalent of two legions: the figure can neither be confirmed or rejected, but it certainly seems quite possible. It provided a substantial force, but still under half the number of troops which L. claims that the Romans had in the field during this year. The number of allies serving in the Roman army is next recorded for Ausculum (D.H. xx. 1. 8; he refers to an army of 70,000,

---

[1] However, Brunt (1971: 647 n. 1) too easily assumes that all figures of this kind must have been invented.

of which 20,000 men were supplied by Rome). In the later third and second centuries, when Rome had many more Italian allies, the proportion of allies to Romans serving in the army varied within the approximate range 1:1 (the ratio retrojected at viii. 8. 14 to give the size of the Latin army in 340) to 2:1; see Brunt (1971) 677–86. For the historical implications of Rome's use of allied manpower, see Oakley (1993) 16–18 (with further bibliography).

5. spectantes . . . arma: see ix. 10. 5 n.
quam quod: Allen (1864–74: i. 24) proposed *quam quo.* His parallels show that this would be quite acceptable, but other parallels show that there is nothing wrong with the paradosis; cf. e.g. xxxii. 12. 5 'pars magis quia locus fugae deerat quam quod animi satis esset ad pugnam cum substitissent, ab hoste . . . circumuenti sunt' and xlv. 10. 12.
ductu: see viii. 31. 1 n.
scite: L. often singles out the *inscitia* of generals for opprobrium; see vi. 30. 6 n. At 19. 8, however, we learn that Appius did speak *scite.*
fortunate: a good general made his own fortune; see vi. 27. 1 n.

6. temporibus iniquis: see ix. 17. 15 n.
spes: i.e. that the incompetence of Appius would allow them to beat the Romans.
iam prope erat: according to *OLD, s.u. prope* 5(c) and 7(a), *prope est ut* is found first in L., who particularly affects it in combination with *iam*; cf. ii. 23. 14 'iam prope erat ut ne consulum quidem maiestas coerceret iras hominum', 65. 6, iii. 41. 2, xxi. 39. 6, xxviii. 39. 7, and xl. 32. 5. To the instances from other authors cited in *OLD*, add Plin. *pan.* 6. 2.
ut nec duci milites nec militibus dux fideret: see vi. 12. 11, vii. 39. 9 nn.

7. in trinis annalibus inuenio: see vii. 18. 10 n.
piget tamen in certo ponere: 'but it displeases to count as certain'. L. is unable to vouch for the information that he has just mentioned, since it was the point at issue between the two consuls; but *piget* implies too that he would rather this information were not true, because, if it were true, it would bring shame to the consuls (for this attitude and *piget* see further viii. 18. 2, ix. 18. 4 nn.). *in certo* is M. Müller's conjecture for **N**'s *incertum ponere.* The paradosis is not quite impossible: it can be translated 'but it displeases to state an uncertainty', which gives acceptable grammar (cf. Cic. *fat.* 12

'quoniam certum in Fabio ponitur, natum esse eum Canicula ori-
ente') and tolerable sense.[1] However, emendation will give *piget*
proper point: improved sense would be given by *ut certum* (Walch
[1815] 35–6); better sense still and a corruption easier to explain by
either *id certum* (F. Büttner [1819] 47–8),[2] for the sense of which v.
35. 3 'hanc gentem Clusium Romamque inde uenisse comperio: id
parum certum est, solamne an ab omnibus Cisalpinorum Gallorum
populis adiutam' may be cited as generally analogous, or *incertum*
⟨*pro certo*⟩ (tentatively suggested to me by Professor Watt); but a
corruption even easier to explain (*in* omitted after -*n*) and still more
point by Müller's *in certo* (adopted also by Walters). Strictly speaking, this cannot be paralleled in either L. or any other author: but iv.
23. 3 'sit inter cetera uetustate cooperta hoc quoque in incerto
positum' is very close (it differs from our passage merely by having
incerto rather than *certo*); viii. 6. 3 'exanimatum auctores quoniam
non omnes sunt, mihi quoque in incerto relictum sit' is analogous;
and xxxiv. 5. 3 'in dubio poneret' may be compared for *ponere* with *in*
and the ablative. For L.'s use of *ponere* in this context cf., in addition
to iv. 23. 3, 9. 12 'id ne pro certo ponerem'.[3]

consules populi Romani: the coupling of *populi Romani* with *consul* is redundant, but *populi Romani* serves to draw attention to the
dignity of the office of consul; cf. Cic. *leg. agr.* ii. 41 'hic ego consul
populi Romani non modo nihil iudico sed ne quid sentiam quidem
profero'. Here it particularly emphasizes L.'s disappointment that
Roman chief magistrates have behaved in a way that ill befitted their
office. Compare xxxix. 32. 10–11 'clamitantibus aduersariis et maiore
parte senatus meminisse eum debere se prius consulem populi
Romani quam fratrem P. Claudi esse', where Ap. Claudius was said
to be degrading the office of consul by campaigning for his brother.
iam iterum: the two men ought by now have built up a relationship
of mutual trust.

8. iam refers back to § 3.
tria castella ceperat: see ix. 45. 17 n.
ad tria . . . captum: see 14. 21 n. for the figure for enemy captured,
vii. 17. 9 n. for general discussion of casualty figures.

---

[1] J. Walker (1822: 88) explains it as 'pro certo affirmare id, quod incertum est', which would
make it seem somewhat more pointed than it really is.

[2] Thus anticipating Kiehl, *ap.* Bisschop *et al.* (1852) 96–7.

[3] This last passage suggests that *pro certo* is a possible conjecture in our passage, but the
corruption would be harder to explain (contrast the parablepsy postulated by Watt's conjecture). Crévier's *certum* gives unpointed sense (hence Büttner's improvement).

eius is used because plural numerals are quite often regarded by Latin authors as singular entities; cf. xxi. 59. 8 'ab neutra parte sescentis plus peditibus et dimidium eius equitum cecidit', xxx. 12. 5 'non plus quinque milia occisa, minus dimidium eius hominum captum est', xxxvi. 4. 5, and the passages from other authors assembled at K–S i. 62.

summa optimatium uoluntate: Rome generally supported oligarchic aristocracies in their struggles against the desires of the populace for greater democracy; see vol. ii, pp. 557–8. For the anachronistic *optimates*, see vi. 39. 6 n.: here, as often, L. applies a Roman term to the practice of another nation (see vi. 26. 5 n. with *addendum*).

pro consule: for the spelling see *addendum* to viii. 23. 12 n.

9. in Etruriam ad collegam pergit: see 11. 4 n. For *pergit* see vi. 12. 1 n.

10. quem . . . dissimulantem: the paradosis caused difficulties to earlier scholars, who proposed some violent emendations (see Drakenborch's note) but was explained correctly by F. C. Wolff (1826: 6–7); translate: 'whom all ⟨others⟩ greeted cheerfully as he arrived. I believe that Appius adopted his attitude [L. has already stated that Appius had denied sending any letter] in accord with his own understanding, being not unreasonably angry if he had written nothing but dissembling with a mean and ungrateful attitude if he had needed assistance'. For *animum habere* cf. Cic. *IIVerr.* ii. 113 'estne hic qui et animum in rem publicam habuit eius modi . . .?'

11. uix enim salute mutua reddita: see ix. 6. 12 n.
'Satin salue': see vi. 34. 8 n.
ut prouincia excederes: this comment reflects later notions of consular provinces; see 37. 7 n.

12. falsae: 'forged'. For both the expression and anxiety about the possibility of letters' being forged, cf. xl. 23. 7, Cic. *Flacc.* 39, *ad Brut.* 5. 3–4, Tac. *ann.* v. 4. 2, and Ulp. *dig.* xlviii. 10. 25. See also Gell. xv. 22. 2.

13. neque te quisquam moratur: see viii. 35. 8 n.
huc ('hither'), found in all witnesses to χ, gives better sense than **N**'s *hic* ('here').

19. 1. Appiano exercitu: see vi. 9. 11 n.

acci[pi]endum: this easy correction of **N**'s reading (which makes no sense) is found first in O.

2. obsistere atque obtestari is the reading of Πλ. M. Müller, W–M, Walters, and Foster all follow M in omitting *atque*. This is undoubtedly more dramatic (it gives a forceful asyndeton with chiasmus) and may be correct. However, the reading of Πλ has a close analogy at ii. 10. 3 'obsistens obtestansque deum et hominum fidem testabatur' (note also that *obsistere* is regularly connected with another verb in L. and others; see *TLL* ix. 2. 229. 49–52).

rem publicam prodat: i.e. by putting his personal feud with Appius before the common good. For the association of the idea of betrayal with that of desertion (*desertori*), see ix. 4. 14 n.

3. eo rem adductam ut: for *rem adducere* cf. [x] esp. v. 30. 6 'eo . . . rem adducerent ut . . .', xxv. 8. 11 'ubi iam eo consuetudinis adducta res est ut . . .', xlii. 12. 6 'eo rem prope adductam ut aditus ei in Achaiam daretur'; also xxiv. 15. 7, xxv. 8. 11, xxxv. 11. 1, Tac. *Agr.* 36. 1. Note too x. 27. 7 'ad discrimen summa rerum adducta'. For other authors, see *TLL* i. 601. 75–81.

omne rei bene aut secus gestae decus dedecusque ad L. Volumnium sit delegatum: for this construction after *delegare*, see ix. 13. 11 n.; for the genitive qualified by a perfect passive participle dependent on *decus* see ix. 22. 9 n.; for the disjunctive use of *-que*, see ix. 19. 3 n. *omne* is found in various *recentiores* (see Drakenborch) for *omni* (MΠ), which cannot be translated, and *omnis* (λ), which is less pointed, though championed by Pettersson (1930: 106 n. 2).

5. restitantes is the reading of Πλ; M has *resistantes*. Although *resistentes*, which is found in all witnesses to χ, would be somewhat easier, it is much less likely to have been corrupted than *restitantes*, and vii. 39. 14 'atque honorem aut ubi restitaret mortem ni sequeretur denuntiantes' perhaps suffices to protect the reading of Πλ. For *restitare* see vi. 7. 2 n.

in quam ante paucis certatum uerbis fuerat: *ante paucis* is a conjecture, found first in Tᶜ and perhaps made by Lupus, for *inter paucos*. There is nothing wrong with *inter paucos* in itself: Gronovius defended it as referring to the 'comites et proximos utriusque', W–M as referring back to the *legati tribunique* of § 1. However, *longiores* leads one to expect an adjective qualifying *uerbis*, and this the paradosis conspicuously fails to supply; indeed, the bare *uerbis* might

have been expected to stand in antithesis to *factis*. Jenicke, *ap.*
Weissenborn (ed.), suggested *in quam inter paucos ⟨paucis⟩ certatum
uerbis fuerat*, but the conjecture of T^c avoids the inelegant *paucos
paucis*.

6. eloquentiam: for the eloquence of Appius, see ix. 29. 5 n.

7. cauillans: see ix. 34. 1 n.
sibi acceptum referre . . . debere: 'that they (i.e. the troops) ought
to give the credit to him'. The metaphor comes from banking, in
which *acceptum* was the technical term for a receipt or the receipt side
of the account; see *TLL* i. 321. 56–322. 21 and *OLD s.u.* For the construction here, cf. Cic. *IIVerr.* i. 102 '. . . cum tot tibi nominibus
acceptum Curtii referrent'.
ex . . . haberent: for the construction see 10. 7 n.
muto atque elingui: a regular coupling and a forceful way of saying
'dumb'; cf. Val. Max. v. 3. *ext.* 3 'nonne ingeniosum et garrulum
populum mutum atque elinguem hac postulatione reddidissent?',
Suet. *Vit.* 6, Gell. v. 9. 2, and the other passages listed at *TLL* v. 2.
390. 84–391. 7.
hiscere: see vi. 16. 3 n.
orationes serere: the root meaning of *serere* is strongly felt: previously Volumnius could hardly utter anything; now he can string
words into speeches.[1]

8. quam mallem: for the expression cf. xxii. 49. 3 '"quam mallem,
uinctos mihi traderet!"' (an ironical exclamation). There are numerous analogies in which *quam uellem* is used: in the following passages
it is separated by *inquit* (*uel sim.*) from the rest of the sentence to
which it belongs, like *quam mallem* here: Cic. *fin.* iii. 10 '"quam
uellem" inquit "te ad Stoicos inclinauisses!"', Curt. iii. 12. 26 'motus
ergo rex constantia pueri (*sc.* Darei filii) Hephaestionem intuens,
"quam uellem" inquit "Darius aliquid ex hac indole hausisset!"',
Suet. *Nero* 10. 2, Apul. iii. 12. 3, 20. 1, and vi. 4. 4.
condicionem ferre: 'he made a proposal'. W–M note that *ferre* is
used in the sense of *offerre*, as it quite often is with *condicio* (*TLL* iv.
136. 12–20, vi. 1. 547. 27–30).
strenue: for the connotations of this word in plebeian ideology, see
8. 3 n.

---

[1] W–M gloss *serere* 'durch kunstreiche Verknüpfung der Gedanken und Worte', but
kunstreiche seems an exaggeration.

orator . . . imperator: Volumnius emphasizes his point by assonance and word-play.

9. Volumnius could not possibly have made an offer of this kind, and W–M need not have wondered whether any reality underlies L.'s notice.

12. tantus est clamor exortus: adjectives of quantity regularly attract *esse* both as copula and auxiliary; here *est* has been pulled away from *exortus* and splits *tantus clamor*. See further Adams (1994*b*) 19–24 and 35–6. Troops shouted both to show their assent to a proposition (vii. 35. 2 n.) and when they charged into battle (viii. 38. 10 n.); hence the enemy thought that they would soon be attacked.
in aciem descendunt: see ix. 14. 7 n.
signa canere . . . iussit: standard Livian phrasing; cf. 20. 9, 40. 14, xxiii. 16. 12, xxvii. 14. 2 'signa inde canere iussit', xxxiv. 39. 13 'Quinctius . . . receptui canere iussit'; for the omission of an object for *iussit*/subject for *canere*, see also vii. 36. 9, ix. 14. 5 nn.; for the tone of *signa canere* see *addendum* to vii. 40. 9 n.
uexilla efferri: see viii. 11. 7 n.

13. ferunt: L. does not vouch for the authenticity of this malicious remark.
ne suae quoque legiones Volumnium sequerentur: L. seems to imagine that Appius' legions might have behaved like troops in the civil wars of the first century BC.

14. satis commode: for this combination cf. xxxiv. 3. 5 and xlii. 38. 10.
Gellius Egnatius: see 18. 1 n.

15. ductu aut imperio: for this coupling cf. Cic. *har.* 3; xl. 52. 5, Plaut. *Amph.* 196, Curt. vi. 3. 2 are rather different, since in these passages *ductu* and *imperio* are coupled with *auspicio*. See also viii. 31. 1 n.

16. uelut sorte quadam: *uelut sorte* is an easy conjecture, found first in Zr, for *uelut forte* (Mλ) or *et ut forte* (Π): although L. very often uses *forte* and sometimes couples it with *uelut* or *quadam* (but never with both together), he never uses it as the noun governed or governing in an ablative absolute. The sentence may be translated thus: 'and, as though a lot were changing the opponent to which each was accustomed, the Etruscans came face to face with Volumnius, the

Samnites, delaying a little because their commander was absent, with Appius'. For the expression *uelut sorte quadam* see vi. 21. 2 (n.), where this passage should have been cited (but neither in that passage, nor in those cited to illustrate it, is *sorte* found in an ablative absolute).

17. dicitur not only suggests that a vow or speech of Claudius was found in one or more of L.'s sources but may also warn readers that they should not have total confidence that his sentiments were reported accurately by these sources. Cf. vi. 40. 2 and see Forsythe (1999) 79–81.

ita . . . ita: a striking instance of iteration; in general, see vol. i, pp. 725–7 with *addendum*.

inter prima signa: for Appius' behaviour cf. 41. 7 'consul . . . clamitans inter prima signa', xxix. 2. 10 'L. Manlium inter prima signa hortantem'; for the expression *prima signa*, see viii. 11. 7 n.

manibus ad caelum sublatis: for the use of this gesture in prayers see 36. 11, vi. 20. 10 nn.

Bellona: for this goddess of war see viii. 9. 6 n.[1] The temple vowed by Appius was dedicated on 3 June: see *fast. Venus.* ad diem 'Bellon(ae) in cir(co) Flam(inio)' (*I.I.* xiii. 2, p. 58) and Ov. *fast.* vi. 201–8 'hac sacrata die Tusco Bellona duello | dicitur, et Latio prospera semper adest. | Appius est auctor, Pyrrho qui pace negata | multum animo uidit, lumine captus erat. | prospicit a templo summum breuis area Circum: | est ibi non paruae parua columna notae; | hinc solet hasta manu, belli praenuntia, mitti, | in regem et gentes cum placet arma capi'. The building of the temple is mentioned in the *elogium* of Appius (quoted at vol. iii, p. 352) and an interesting detail about it is found at Plin. *nat.* xxxv. 12 'uerum clupeos in sacro uel publico dicare priuatim primus instituit, ut reperio, Appius Claudius, [qui consul cum P. Seruilio fuit anno urbis CCLVIIII].[2] posuit enim in Bellonae aede maiores suos, placuitque in excelso spectari in titulos honorum legi, decora res'. Since L. does not mention the dedication, it may well have occurred after 293.

In addition to Ovid and *fast. Venus.* locc. citt., Serv. *auct. Aen.* ix. 52 attests to the fact that the temple of Bellona stood near what was later the Circus Flaminius, presumably at one of its ends (cf. Ovid, l. 205 and contrast l. 209 'altera pars Circi custode sub Hercule tuta

---

[1] Massa-Pairault (2001: 103–5) tries unsuccessfully to connect the vow of Appius with the *euocatio* of a Sabine god.

[2] I reproduce the standard Teubner text of Mayhoff. Even if Urlichs's deletion is wrong and Pliny himself made a mistake, there is little doubt that he refers to Ap. Claudius Caecus.

est'); and Coarelli has shown that it may be identified with the so-called *tempio sconosciuto* at its south-eastern end, next to the temple of Apollo. The senate often met in the temple, its position outside the *pomerium* making it a suitable venue for returning generals to address their peers; see Bonnefond-Coudry (1989) 137–60, with a full list of passages that includes e.g. xxxvi. 39. 5, xli. 6. 4, xlii. 9. 2, 21. 6, 28. 2, and 36. 2.

See further Coarelli (1965–7), Wiseman (1974) 14–17, L. Richardson (1992) 57–8, and Ziolkowski (1992) 18–19.

duis: the only other instance in L. of a form of the present subjunctive of *dare* in *dui-* is at xxii. 10. 3, part of the vow of a *uer sacrum* made by the *pontifex maximus*. By his time these forms had long been archaic, and in both these passages he uses them for deliberate effect. They are found often in Plautus and Terence, occasionally in quotations from old laws (see e.g. Paul. *Fest.* p. 247), and in prayers at Cato, *agr.* 141. 3, Pac. *trag.* 219, but only very rarely in Cicero and later authors, and then always in prayers or wishes expressed to the gods: see Cic. *Cat.* i. 22 'utinam tibi istam mentem di immortales duint!',[1] Tac. *ann.* iv. 38. 3 (in a prayer uttered by Tiberius) 'deos et deas ipsas precor . . . ut . . . intelligentem humani diuinique iuris mentemduint', Aurel. *ap.* Front. p. 61. 1 (where in a joke grapes are viewed as gods), and Apul. *apol.* 64 'at tibi, Aemiliane, pro isto mendacio duit deus iste superum et inferum commeator utrorumque deorum malam gratiam . . .'.[2] Similar forms are found for third conjugation compounds of *do*, such as *perdo*. For a fuller account of the evidence see Neue and Wagener (1892–1905) iii. 311–12 and *TLL* v. 1. 1659. 78–1660. 19.

ast, found only here in L., was originally a continuative particle, usually extending a protasis introduced by *si*: see e.g. Plaut. *Capt.* 683–4 'si ego hic peribo, ast ille ut dixit non redit, | at erit mi hoc factum mortuo memorabile', *lex col. Gen.* (Crawford [1996] 25, p. 400) 61. 7–8 'si quis in eo uim faciet, ast eius uincitur, dupli damnas esto', Fest. p. 260 (quoting a law of 'Servius Tullius') 'si parentem puer uerberauit, ast olle plorassit [parens *del.* C. O. *Müller*], puer diuis parentum sacer esto'. It is also found introducing a simple adverbial clause, for example in the four instances in Cic. *leg.* iii. 9–11, of which the first is 'ast quando duellum grauius, discordiae ciuium escunt,

---

[1] *duint* is found in B.L. Add. 47678 (*olim* Holkham Hall 387), and, although various other readings are found in other mss, it must be what Cicero wrote.

[2] To these passages one should perhaps add Cic. *Phil.* x. 13 'quod di duint!', where Halm's conjecture *di duint* may explain the ms. variants *di dent*, *dicit*, and *didicit*, which *di dent* fails to do, even though it gives aceptable Latin.

oenus ne amplius sex menses, si senatus creuerit, idem iuris quod duo consules teneto'. Apart from the passage of Plautus quoted, these usages are found only in laws or Cicero's archaizing reconstruction of laws. Whether the second usage would have been recognized in archaic Latin is very doubtful.

ast has no etymological connection with the adversative particle *at* but as early as Plaut. *Merc.* 245–6 'atque oppido hercle bene uelle illi uisu' sum, | ast non habere quoi commendarem capram' is found as an artificial substitute for it. This usage is attested on a few other occasions in early Latin and several times in the mss of Cicero's *ad Atticum*, from the text of which it is emended away by many editors, including Shackleton Bailey (see his note on i. 16. 17; also Reid [1899] 311). The Augustan and later poets adopted *ast* as a very convenient alternative for *at*, usually placing it before a vowel and a pronoun (most often *ego*); see e.g. Hor. *epod.* 15. 24, Virg. *Aen.* i. 46, and vii. 308.

The use of *ast* in our passage to introduce an apodosis appears to be unparalleled: L. was probably trying to give further archaic colour to this brief speech of Appius but did not understand the circumstances in which *ast* had once been used. He is influenced by (*a*) a recollection of the archaic use of *ast* after a *si*-clause (but he seems not to have realized that in this *ast* introduces a second protasis rather than an apodosis), (*b*) the use of *ast ego* in the poets, and (*c*) the construction (*quod*) *si . . . at*, which he himself affected (see ix. 1. 8 n.).

See further e.g. *TLL* ii. 942. 31–944. 33, Nettleship (1889) 329, Reid (1899) 311–12, Krebs and Schmalz (1905–7) i. 211, K–S ii. 88–9, Austin (i. 46, ii. 467) and Fordyce (vii. 308) on Virg. *Aen.* locc. citt., H–S 489, Skutsch on Enn. *ann.* 93.

uoueo: for vows of temples in battle, and the success which they bring to the Romans, see vii. 28. 4 n. with *addendum*.

18. et ipse collegae et exercitus uirtutem aequauit ducis; ⟨et duces⟩ imperatoria opera exsequuntur et milites ne ab altera parte prius uictoria incipiat adnituntur: on any interpretation of these words Appius, who had previously been shy of fighting, is said to equal the bravery of his colleague; but the rest of the sentence brings a difficulty: without emendation *imperatoria opera exsequuntur* ('they perform the duties of commanders') lacks a subject (which can hardly be extracted out of the following *milites*, since, with Appius now fighting properly, the troops are hardly likely to be said to be performing the duties of commanders) and has no obvious connection to what precedes.

The least promising line of conjecture is to follow Walters's tentative suggestion that *imperatoria opera exsequuntur milites* could be deleted as a corruption of a gloss (the gloss which he suggests, *imperatoria opera exaequant*, is unlikely to have been penned by anyone).

The simplest way of restoring sense is to punctuate with a full stop after *aequauit* and to read *duces* for *ducis*, so that it may serve as subject of *exsequuntur* (thus F^c and other *recentiores*, for which see Drakenborch's note; before Weissenborn this was the modern vulgate); on this interpretation the troops of Appius have shown bravery in being willing to fight. Translate: 'And he equalled the bravery of his colleague and of his troops. The leaders perform the duties of commanders and the troops . . .'. This could be right, but it is not obvious that as yet Appius' troops have shown very much bravery. Moreover, the asyndeton before *duces* is quite harsh, although this second objection could be removed by reading ⟨*et*⟩ *duces*, as Geist (1877: 259) tentatively suggested. Gronovius read *duces* with the full stop before it but suggested emendation of *aequauit* to *aequarunt*. With this conjecture *exercitus* is plural, and both armies are said to emulate each other's bravery; but this emendation and interpretation make L.'s thought rather contorted.

Others, still changing *ducis* to *duces* and punctuating strongly after *aequauit*, introduce a supplement between *exercitus* and *aequauit*. Thenn (1877: 440–1) commended *exercitus* ⟨*exercitus*⟩ *uirtutem*, the reading of Munich Clm 15731, which is impossibly ugly and has no authority. Doujat proposed *exercitus* ⟨*ipsius*⟩ *uirtutem*, which gives satisfactory sense (it is preferable to have Appius' army imitating his bravery than vice versa), but there are better ways of achieving this sense.[1] Heusinger proposed *exercitus uirtutem* ⟨*alterius*⟩, arguing that *alterius* was corrupted into the *ad-* of *adaequauit* found in O and some *recentiores*; although the diplomatic argument is unattractive (O has no authority), the conjecture gives good sense, and is much more elegant than that found in the Munich ms. Hertz proposed *exercitus* ⟨*alterius exercitus*⟩ *uirtutem*, which gives the same good sense as Heusinger's conjecture but is diplomatically easier; although it is inelegant, it is not ruled out by Thenn's objection that *alterius* is redundant.

Alternatively, one may retain *ducis*, punctuate strongly after it, and introduce a supplement after this punctuation: F. C. Wolff (1826: 6–7), anticipating Luterbacher, suggested *duces imperatoria*, Weissenborn (*Komm.*) ⟨*et duces*⟩ *imperatoria*, and Walters tentatively

---

[1] Doujat also read ⟨*ad*⟩*aequauit*.

⟨*iam et duces*⟩ *imperatoria*. All provide the required connection with what precedes and allow an elegant contrast between the leaders (Appius and Volumnius now acting like commanders) and their troops; if one of them is right, the corruption in the mss could have been caused by haplography (in the case of Luterbacher's conjecture) or something similar to *saut du même au même* (*duces* being very similar to *ducis*). A possible disadvantage of Weissenborn's and Walters's conjectures is that they introduce *et . . . et* into successive sentences; but iteration is so common in L. (see vol. i, pp. 725–7) that this hardly matters. Since the asyndeton is rather harsh, and since *iam* strikes a note that is rather too knowing, Weissenborn's conjecture is preferable to the other two. Choice between it and Hertz's conjecture is difficult, but as it allows retention of *ducis* it is diplomatically a little easier.

For an idea quite similar to that found here cf. xxxix. 31. 9 'et equites praetoris eximia uirtute et equitum pedites accensi sunt'. For the expression perhaps compare also formulations such as vi. 12. 11 'nec dux legiones nec Fortuna fefellit ducem' and parallel passages cited ad loc.

For rivalry between two armies or wings of an army see ix. 40. 8–11 n.

fundunt fugantque: see 30. 7 n.

20. recruduit: see vi. 18. 1 n.
Sabellarum: see viii. 1. 6 n.

21. a uictoribus is the reading of P^cUOZs: *auiatoribus* P¹ZbZt (*ama-* Zt): *ausiatoribus* λ: *ausiatoribus iam pugnatoribus* M. For full discussion of the mss readings, see vol. i, p. 318. There seems to be little doubt that **N** had either *auiatoribus* or *ausiatoribus* and *pugnatoribus* as variants. *pugnatoribus* is unintelligible, but *au(s)iatoribus* is plainly a corruption of *a uictoribus*, which L. must have written.
ipse is contrastive: Volumnius urges on his troops by taking the standards himself to the gates of the enemy camp, Appius by telling them that they are victorious with Bellona.
accenderet: M¹P¹λ have *accenderant* and M^cUOZ *accenderat*, but syntax requires *accenderet*, a subjunctive co-ordinate with *inferret* and conjectured first in the Paris edn. of 1510.

22. castra capta direptaque: see vi. 29. 8, 32. 9 nn.
praeda . . . militi concessa est: stock Livian language, see vi. 13. 6 n.

septem ... capti: see 14. 21 n. for the figure for enemy captured, vii. 17. 9 n. for general discussion of casualty figures.

20. 1–16. *The Samnite attack on Campania.* L. rounds off the foreign affairs of this year with an account of another Roman victory. In § 2 the report of Volumnius' hearing of the Samnite raid provides a link with the previous episode (for the technique see vol. i, p. 126). More easily won than the previous encounter, in which Ap. Claudius and Volumnius had defeated a combined army of Etruscans and Samnites, the campaign does not tempt L. to produce one of his more dramatic narratives. Rather, he focuses on the careful preparations of Volumnius (§§ 5–7), which contrast sharply with the disorganization of the Samnites (§§ 8–13); by making the Romans sell their booty at the end of the campaign (§ 16) Volumnius does not let his troops make the same mistake as the Samnites, who had become encumbered by it. L. pays particular attention to the time of night and day in which the battle takes place: the Samnites plan to set out in the night at the third watch (§ 6), Volumnius moves his forces close to the enemy camp a little before dawn (§ 8), and he attacks as dawn breaks (§ 9). Another carefully placed detail concerns the Samnite *signa*: in § 8 these are the first to set out; and in § 14 L. describes their return. Central to the episode are the short dramatic sentences in § 9: 'tempus adgrediendi aptissimum uisum est; et iam lux appetebat; itaque signa canere iussit agmenque hostium adgreditur'. L. adds to the vividness of the narrative by using his much-favoured technique of splitting a scene into its component parts (§ 10 'pars ... pars', § 12 'partim ... partim': see vol. i, p. 137); throughout many of the main verbs in the episode (esp. in §§ 1–6) are in the vivid historic present; and in §§ 15–16 the episode is rounded off with L.'s notice of enemy killed and captured and of the recovery of booty.

20. 1. per Vescinos: N's *per Vestinos* makes for excellent grammar but extremely difficult geography: the Vestini inhabited the lands around the Gran Sasso some way north of Samnium (in between lay the territory of the Paeligini); it would have been extraordinary for the Samnites to start an attack on Campania by marching through their territory. Therefore all recent editors adopt Sigonius' *per Vescinos* (for another example of the very easy corruption, see viii. 11. 5 n.). When a tribe is mentioned expressions of this kind are commonplace (e.g. xxi. 38. 7 'non in Taurinos sed per Salassos'), but Vescia was a settlement and not a tribe, and I have found no parallel for *per Vescinos* meaning 'through the land of the Vescini' (Foster's translation). The following solutions to this difficulty seem possible: (*a*) that the confusion between Vescia and the Vestini is due to L. himself and not to later copyists of his work: this would explain the Latin, but has the grave demerits that on other occasions L. seems to have known perfectly well where the territory of the Vestini was and that he specifically refers to colonies being sent to the territory of Vescia at 21. 7–8; (*b*) emendation of *per Vestinos* to something like *per Vescinum saltum*: this has the demerit that the corruption is not very easily explained (although stranger corruptions are to be found in most ms. traditions; and, if *saltum* was omitted, then *Vescinum* could have been changed to *uestinos* and then *uescinos*); (*c*) emendation to *per Vescinum*: but, although *Sabinum* and *Picenum* provide analogies for this substantivized usage, it is worrying that there is no parallel elsewhere; and (*d*) emendation to *per Vescinos* ⟨*agros*⟩ (cf. 21. 7): although *ager* already occurs quite often in this passage, this is perhaps the easiest conjecture.

Falernumque agrum: for the *ager Falernus* see viii. 11. 13 n.

2. magnis itineribus: see viii. 30. 12 n.
fama: see vi. 21. 9 n.

3. in Calenum agrum . . . Caleni: for Cales see viii. 16. 2 n. *agrum* was omitted by Π (thus PUZ; O def.); but, as the combination of M and λ is likely to point to the reading of **N** and the unnecessary ellipse makes Π's reading patently inferior, Walters was wrong to adopt it. See also Pettersson (1930) 112–13.
tantum iam praedae hostes trahere: *praedam/-as trahere* is found at Sil. x. 374, Tac. *ann.* iii. 20. 2, and iv. 48. 1; for the formulation found here, in which *praeda* is found in the genitive, cf. xxix. 35. 5.

4. dimicationi is the reading of Πλ, *dimicationibus* (adopted by Walters) that of M. *dimicationi* gives slightly better sense ('nor should they commit such a burdened detachment to battle' [i.e. against Volumnius, of whose imminent return they may have heard] as opposed to 'nor should they commit such a burdened detachment to battles' [but one would have expected one decisive battle against Volumnius to have been in the mind of the Samnite commanders]).

5. uagos praedatores in agris palantes: N's *in agros* is ungrammatical and must be emended to either *in agro* (thus F, followed by Walters), or *in agris* (Sigonius), or *per agros*. The last would give good sense and a very regular idiom (see vii. 8. 6 n.), but is uneconomical. The other two conjectures are diplomatically easy, but *in agris* is clearly preferable, as it alone may be paralleled in L.; cf. i. 11. 1 'Romana legio . . . palatos in agris oppressit' and iv. 55. 4 'alios palantes in agris caesos'. For the coupling with *uagus* see vii. 17. 8 n. **excipiant:** thus Πλ: *inc-* M¹: *interc-* Mᶜχ. Although *intercipiant* is an intelligent attempt by Mᶜ to make sense of the reading of M¹, the use of *intercipere* in this context cannot be paralleled, and Walters was wrong to adopt what is plainly a progressive corruption. By contrast, *excipiant* is very much the *mot juste* in this context; cf. e.g. vii. 11. 7 'palati a consule Poetelio . . . excepti', xxii. 32. 2 'carpentes agmen palatosque excipientes', and xxiii. 26. 8 '. . . ut palantes exciperent'.

6. Volturnum flumen is the Volturnus, modern Volturno, the third largest (after the Tiber and Arno) of the rivers that flow in peninsular Italy from the Apennines into the Tyrrhenian Sea. It rises in the heart of Samnite territory beneath the Mainarde near the abbey of San Vincenzo al Volturno, is joined by other tributaries which flow from the mountains around Aesernia, and then flows past the Samnite settlements at Venafrum, Rufrae, Allifae, Combulteria, Telesia (where it is joined by its largest tributary, the Calor [modern Calore]), and Caiatia, to Casilinum and the sea at Volturnum. Most Samnite territory on the Tyrrhenian side of Italy is drained by it or its tributaries; for settlement in its valley, see conveniently Oakley (1995) 18–72, for a fuller description of its middle and lower valley, vol. ii, p. 283.

The closest that the Volturno comes to Cales is at Casilinum, 11 km away as the crow flies. However, L. does not specify exactly where the Samnites had camped, and it is unlikely that he had very precise information on this matter.

7. propinquitate nimia: for the expression cf. v. 54. 4.

8. ad castra accessit: see viii. 36. 2 n.
Oscae linguae: Oscan, to which this is L.'s only reference, and Latin were both Italic languages but not mutually intelligible. Oscan was spoken by the Samnites and their kinsmen in Campania and Lucania; the tribes of the Abruzzo spoke a similar language. As Oscan-speakers from Campania would have been serving in the Roman army, and as many of those living at or near Cales (a Latin colony founded in an Oscan-speaking area) would have been bilingual, Volumnius would have had no difficulty in finding men to understand what the Samnites were saying; but it is quite likely that

this notice concerning Volumnius' use of spies derives from the imaginative reconstructions of L. or his annalistic sources rather than from authentic testimony that survived from 296 itself. For the interaction of Latin and Oscan see Adams (2003) 112–59.

nocturna trepidatione: for the expression see ix. 24. 8 n. L. normally refers to the panic induced by night in contexts where darkness compounded another reason for fear. Since there is here no other reason for the Samnites to be afraid, Foster was probably correct to translate *trepidatione* in a somewhat weakened sense as 'confusion'.

infrequentia armatis signa: for *infrequentia . . . signa* see vii. 8. 6 n. The desertion of the standards was a typical piece of indiscipline; cf. viii. 34. 10.

inter ipsos: N had *inter alios*, but one wants a reference not to 'others' but to 'one another'. Crévier therefore suggested *inter se* or *inter ipsos*, Hell (1870: 15, anticipating H. J. Müller) *inter illos*, Weissenborn (*Komm.*⁴) *inter turbatos*, Madvig (1877: 229 n. 1) *inter ullos*, and Walters deletion of *inter alios*. Crévier's *inter se* gives excellent sense but postulates an improbable corruption. The conjectures of Weissenborn and Walters are uneconomical (and, besides, *turbatos* does not give quite the required sense; see above on *nocturna trepidatione*). Those of Madvig and Hell are economical, but reciprocal *inter ullos* and *inter illos* are not attested either in L. or (perhaps) any other author (for what is possible see *TLL* vii. 1. 2140. 39–2144. 47). Crévier's *inter ipsos* is diplomatically a little harder but gives excellent sense (see *TLL* 2144. 16–34 and Packard [1968] iii. 1259).

9. lux appetebat: cf. [x] Caes. *Gall.* vii. 82. 2, Curt. vii. 8. 3, viii. 6. 16, ix. 4. 25, Tac. *ann.* iv. 51. 3, Amm. xx. 7. 6, and see viii. 38. 3 n. **itaque** is used by L. quite regularly after a clause containing *iam*; cf. 46. 1, xxii. 19. 11, xxv. 41. 8, xxxv. 8. 1, 16. 1, 41. 1–2; *igitur* is found in the same context at v. 19. 1–2. See Wölfflin (1864) 5 = (1933) 2. **signa canere iussit:** see 19. 12 n.

10. addere gradum: 'hurried along'; the idiom may be paralleled at iii. 27. 7, xxvi. 9. 5, Plaut. *Trin.* 1010 'adde gradum, adpropera', Luc. iv. 759–60 (of horses), and Plin. *epist.* vi. 20. 12. Certainly analogous is Petron. 23. 3 'cursum addite'; probably analogous is Virg. *georg.* i. 513 '(quadrigae) addunt in spatia' (where see Mynors's note for the difficulties of text and interpretation), which is imitated at Sil. xvi. 372–3 'iamque fere medium euecti certamine campum | in spatio addebant'. The limited distribution of the expresson in extant Latin makes its tone difficult to gauge, but, despite the Plautine instance, it was probably less colloquial than the modern English 'step on it'.

inter cunctationem: a phrase used four times by L. (cf. esp. xxi. 56. 4 'qui . . . inter cunctationem ingrediendi [*sc.* flumen] ab hostibus oppressi'; also xxiv. 19. 10, xxvii. 15. 16), but which I have not been able to parallel in other writers.

caedesque ac tumultus: for the coupling cf. xxiii. 26. 8, xxxii. 26. 8, and Cic. *Sull.* 54; also xxi. 48. 1 and Tac. *hist.* v. 15. 2 'minor tamen quam pro tumultu caedes'. Contrast xxv. 25. 9 'refractisque foribus cum omnia terrore ac tumultu streperent, a caedibus tamen temperatum est'.

12. arma in sarcinis deligata: W–M compare Tac. *hist.* iv. 35. 2 'arma in uehiculis'.

13. memorandum . . . facinus: this coupling is rare, and the only parallel which I have found [x] is Amm. xxiii. 5. 18; much more common is *memorabile facinus*, for which see [x] xxiii. 7. 6, xxiv. 22. 16, xxxviii. 24. 2, xl. 40. 9, Ter. *heaut.* 314, Sall. *Cat.* 4. 4, Tac. *Agr.* 28. 1, *hist.* i. 44. 2, Apul. *met.* viii. 22. 1 (also Mela i. 38). For *facinus* with a positive sense, see viii. 24. 9 n.
hortantemque: see ix. 27. 11 n.

14. proeliumque iam profligatum integratum est: for the expression *proelium profligare*, cf. [x] Tac. *ann.* xiv. 36. 2 (and see ix. 29. 1 n. for *bellum profligare*); for *proelium integrare* see vi. 24. 4 n.
nec diutius sustineri potuit: see vi. 32. 8 n.

15. caesa . . . capti: see 14. 21 n. for the figure for enemy captured, vii. 17. 9 n. for general discussion of casualty figures.
tribuni militum: L. calls Samnite officers by the Roman term. For this practice see vi. 26. 5 n. with *addendum*.
signa militaria triginta: see vii. 37. 16 n.
⟨et⟩ praeda: the paradosis offers what W–M call 'ein hartes Asyndeton'; Madvig, *ap.* Madvig and Ussing, commented 'dure omittitur *et* inter *quadringenti* et *praeda*'. M. Müller, rightly followed by Walters, was the first to place *et* in the text.
accitique edicto domini ad res suas noscendas recipiendasque praestituta die: for booty displayed so that its owners may recover it, cf. 36. 18 'Interamnam edicto dominis ad res suas noscendas recipiendasque reuocatis' (a good instance of L.'s repeating his phrasing), iv. 29. 4, xxiv. 16. 5, xxxv. 1. 12, all of which refer to the

recovery of property by Rome's allies. For Romans' recovering their own property from booty, see iii. 10. 1 'Lucretius . . . auget gloriam adueniens exposita omni in campo Martio praeda, ut suum quisque per triduum cognitum abduceret. reliqua uendita, quibus domini non exstitere', v. 16. 7, D.H. xi. 48. 3 (note also Liv. viii. 39. 15). For a lawyer's view on this matter, see Pompon. *dig.* xlix. 15. 20. 1 'uerum est expulsis hostibus ex agris quos ceperint dominia eorum ad priores dominos redire nec aut publicari aut praedae loco cedere: publicatur enim ille ager qui ex hostibus captus sit'. We may therefore presume that, despite the paucity of references in L., the procedure described at iii. 10. 1 was regular. See further vi. 2. 12 n. with *addendum* and Matthaei (1908) 244.

praestituta die: for the expression see vi. 4. 5 n. Before Madvig and Ussing it was conventional to place a full stop before, rather than after, these words, but Madvig's punctuation renders them much more pointed. He was probably correct to suggest (1877: 229 n. 1) that they refer to the day before which property should be claimed, as one would have expected more than one day to be put aside for the recovery of booty (of the passages cited above, iii. 10. 1, v. 16. 7, and xxiv. 16. 5 all imply that more than one day was spent in reclaiming property).

16. coactique uendere praedam: for the soldiers' being made to sell their booty, see 17. 6–8 n.

ne alibi quam in armis animum haberent: for the idea see ix. 23. 8 n.

21. 1–12. *The Roman reaction to the Samnite incursion.* L. emphasizes the seriousness with which the Samnite raid on Campania was taken at Rome, no doubt in part because, in preparation for his account of Sentinum, he wishes to make clear that Rome's military circumstances remained grave. However, he reports these matters without any significant dramatic elaboration. In §§ 11–12 he returns to the situation in northern Italy, but his elegant transition (11 'auertit ab eis') and his decision to report these events by means of a letter from Appius, allow him to keep the scene at Rome. Because of this brief section all of chapters 21 and 22 can be viewed as a seamless whole, and my rather artificial division at § 12 is made only for ease of exposition.

21. 1. tumultum: see vii. 9. 6 n.

2. Volumnianum exercitum: for the expression see vi. 9. 11 n.

concitam in arma: I have not been able to parallel this coupling [x]; but for *concire ad arma* see xxxi. 3. 5, 40. 9, and Vell. ii. 74. 2. For *concitare* with *in* (or *ad*) *arma*, see viii. 27. 9 n.

Gellium Egnatium: see 18. 1 n.

uocare . . . sollicitare is Gronovius' conjecture for **N**'s *uocari . . . sollicitari*. **N**'s readings imply that Gellius Egnatius, together with the Umbrians and Gauls, was being urged to rebel; but, since Gellius was already in northern Italy leading an army against Rome, this is very difficult to understand. With Gronovius' conjecture it is Gellius who urges the Umbrians and Gauls to rebel. Duker, whose conjecture was championed forcefully by F. C. Wolff (1826: 7–8), wished to retain *sollicitari*; this postulates a corruption more easily explained than Gronovius' conjecture (*uocare* corrupted because of the following *sollicitari*, rather than a double corruption of normal actives into less normal passives), but *et* before *Vmbros* becomes difficult (it would have to mean 'too', but, with *et* also preceding *Gallos*, the context leads one to expect that it will mean 'both'). Klinger (1884: 28 n. 1) wished to retain the passives because of the thematic similarity to 18. 1 'sollicitabantur', but he was wrong to think that his own analysis of the passage (for which see above, pp. 199–200) is incompatible with Gronovius' conjecture.

3–4. his nuntiis . . . P. Sempronius praeerat: for the *iustitium*, its duration, the levy, and the enrolment of *seniores*, see *addendum* to vi. 6. 14 n. and vii. 9. 6 n. This is the first recorded instance of the recruitment of *libertini*; a later example occurred in 90 during the Social War (*per.* lxxiv). During the Second Punic War *uolones* are attested as serving in the legions in 216–212 (xxii. 57. 11, xxiii. 14. 2, 35. 6, xxiv. 10. 3, 14. 3, 16. 6, 16. 9, xxv. 20. 4, 22. 3–4: Gracchus' famous recruits) and 207–205 (xxvii. 38. 10, xxviii. 10. 11, xxix. 5. 9). Other reports of *libertini* being conscripted refer to service in the fleet (xxii. 11. 8–9 [217], xli. 27. 3 [172]). The part played by the praetor in these affairs is akin to that of the *praefectus urbi* in earlier years (viii. 36. 1 n.) and should not be doubted. For the senate's role in commissioning levies, see vii. 19. 7 n.; for P. Sempronius Sophus see ix. 33. 5 n.; for the presence of the praetor in Rome see 22. 7 n.

3. indici: see vii. 6. 12 n.

4. defendendae urbis consilia: for the genitive of the gerund(ive) after *consilia*, see vi. 2. 1 n.

5. litterae: for the letter from the commander which led to a *supplicatio*, see viii. 30. 10 n.
populatores: see vii. 17. 8 n.

6. itaque et supplicationes ob rem bene gestam consulis nomine decernunt ⟨et⟩ iustitium remittitur quod fuerat dies duodeuiginti; supplicatioque perlaeta fuit: this is Walters's text and punctuation. The *et* before *iustitium* is reported by Drakenborch from Holkham 347. If one adopts it, as Madvig (1860: 192–3 = 1877: 229) has persuaded subsequent editors to do, then the first *et* reads much more comfortably ('and therefore they *both* vote *supplicationes* in the name of the consul because of the campaign which he had successfully conducted *and* revoke the *iustitium*'); with the reading in N this first *et* has to be taken to mean 'even', which is awkward. A slight disadvantage of this conjecture is that the *-que* after *supplicatio* becomes somewhat redundant; but this is not a strong argument for retaining the paradosis, and by printing a semi-colon rather than a comma before *supplicatioque* Walters makes the articulation of this part of the passage easier.
supplicationes . . . supplicatio: see vii. 28. 8, viii. 33. 20 nn.
consulis nomine: the correct technical expression; cf. iii. 63. 5 'senatus in unum diem supplicationes consulum nomine decreuit', xxvi. 21. 3 'cuius nomine . . . supplicatio decreta foret', xxviii. 9. 9 'et supplicatio amborum nomine et triumpho utrique decreto', Cic. *Cat.* iii. 15, *Phil.* xiv. 29, and see Halkin (1953) 107–8.
iustitium remittitur: for *iustitium remittere* cf. iii. 5. 14; on the rather more vivid *exuto iustitio* at Tac. *ann.* iii. 7. 1, see Woodman and Martin ad loc.
perlaeta: the adjective is attested only here [*]; at Curt. viii. 4. 20 (cited at *OLD s.u.*) *perlaetus* is Hedicke's plausible but not certain conjecture for *praefatus*. Nowhere else is *laetus* or one of its cognates found qualifying *supplicatio*.

7–10. *The foundation of the colonies at Minturnae and Sinuessa.* The foundation of these colonies is dated to 295 at Vell. i. 14. 6 'at Q. Fabio quintum Decio Mure quartum consulibus, quo anno Pyrrhus regnare coepit, Sinuessam Minturnasque missi coloni'. His evidence may be reconciled with our passage if one argues that the foundations were approved in 296 but established only in 295. Both colonies were small 'Roman' rather than larger 'Latin' colonies (note § 8 'ab colonis Romanis' and see vol. ii, p. 599), although notoriously L. does not always make a clear distinction between the two, tending to regard most colonies as Roman (see vol. i, pp. 341–3). Likewise, Velleius includes these foundations without comment in a list which consists largely of Latin colonies. Loreto (1991a: 291–2) suggested that § 10 'in agros' shows that the original intention of the senate was to send Latin and not Roman colonies; but colonists at Roman colonies also needed land. For the role of the senate in the sending of colonies, see vi. 21. 4 n. with *addendum*.

7. agitari coeptum: see vi. 1. 11 n.

circa Vescinum et Falernum agrum: for Vescia and the *ager Falernus*, see viii. 11. 5, 11. 13 nn. In fact, neither Sinuessa nor Minturnae lay in the *ager Falernus*, but, as L. states, Sinuessa bordered on it (it lay between the Mons Massicus and the sea, and the Mons Massicus marked the boundary of the *ager Falernus*).

deducerentur: see vi. 16. 6 n.

Liris fluuii: L.'s first reference to the well-known river, which rises in Marsic territory at Cappadocia just west of the Fucine Lake and flows into the Golfo di Gaeta at Minturnae (Marina di Minturno is the nearest modern village to its estuary); he refers to it also at xxvi. 9. 3 and 34. 8. Sora (vii. 28. 6 n.), Arpinum (ix. 44. 16 n.), Cereatae Marianae, Fregellae (viii. 22. 1 n.), Aquinum, Casinum (ix. 28. 8 n.), and Interamna Lirenas (ix. 28. 8 n.) were the largest ancient settlements close to the river; for some remarks on the strategic importance of the Liri valley during the Samnite Wars, see vol. ii, pp. 281–3. In antiquity the name Liris covered the whole course of the river; to-day it is called Liri for its course between Cappadocia and Casinum but, after it is joined by its tributary the Gari (known also as the Rapido) just below Casinum, it is called the Garigliano. The most famous reference in ancient literature to the Liri is Hor. *carm.* i. 31. 7–8 'rura quae Liris quieta | mordet aqua taciturnus amnis', to which Silius pays a graceful compliment (iv. 348–50) 'Liris . . . qui fonte quieto | dissimulat cursum ac nullo mutabilis imbri | perstringit tacitas gemmanti gurgite ripas'. At *Aen.* xi. 670 Virgil calls a Trojan Liris.

Minturnae . . . Sinope . . . Sinuessa: see viii. 10. 9, 11. 11 nn.

ubi Sinope dicitur Graeca urbs fuisse: for brief geographical comments of this kind in the context of the foundation of a colony, see viii. 22. 2 n.

9. tribunis plebis: for co-operation between the tribunes and the senate see above, pp. 16–17. For tribunician involvement in the establishing of colonies, see vi. 21. 4 n. with *addendum*.

negotium datum est, ut is the only instance in books vi–x of an expression often to be used by L. in his later books for the issuing of instructions by the senate to a magistrate; there are earlier instances at iii. 4. 9, v. 25. 8, and 48. 8. See further Packard (1968) iii. 463.

triumuiros: see vi. 21. 4 n.

colonis deducendis: *coloni⟨i⟩s*, reported by Drakenborch from Holkham 345, would give a reading more usually found in editions and mss of L., and may be right. However, it is safer to retain the paradosis: (*a*) inscriptions from the principate (see *TLL* iii. 1698. 28–30) show that *colonis* could be used as the dative and ablative plural of *colonia*, and L. too could have written in this way;[1] and (*b*), what is perhaps the more likely explanation, at *TLL* v. 1. 273. 53–80 there is listed a large number of passages in which *deducere* has as its object the colonists rather than the colonies in which they settled (e.g. xxxvii. 46. 10 'ad eos colonos deducendos' and 57. 8 'tria milia hominum sunt deducta'). For *deductio* see vi. 16. 6 n.

10. nec . . . rebantur: for the reluctance of colonists to go to some sites see ix. 26. 4 n.

12. iam castra bifariam facta esse: for the phrasing cf. xxii. 40. 5 'castris bifariam factis'.

21. 13–22. 9. *The elections for 295*

We have seen already (21. 1–12 n.) that it is somewhat artificial to divide this episode from 21. 1–12, and esp. §§ 11–12. L.'s account of the elections for 295 is one of the longest reports of elections in books ii–x, at the heart of which lies the attempt of Fabius Rullianus to refuse office (22. 2–3). Such refusals on Fabius' part are a theme of the book and of doubtful historicity (see 9. 10–13 n.); therefore, although in its scope and content this section prefigures many similar passages in books xxi–xlv, it may very well rest on no good evidential basis. The reflections of Volumnius (22. 4–7) on the dangers of discord between the consuls and on the lack of aptitude of Ap. Claudius for command form a link with the narrative of events earlier

---

[1] The testimony of Renaissance, mediaeval, and even late antique witnesses to L.'s text is of little consequence on such a matter; but note that at xli. 5. 9, where L. is certainly using the ablative plural of *colonia*, the 1531 Froben (Basle) edn., our only source for the text and deriving from the fifth-century Vienna 15, has *colonis*.

in the year; but they are unintentionally ironical, since in this year Fabius and Decius will finally quarrel.

13. ob haec (et iam appetebat tempus comitiorum) [causa]: scholars agree that L. states that Volumnius was recalled both because of the worrying news from the north (*ob haec*) and because of the need to hold the elections but disagree as to whether the paradosis needs emendation and as to how it should be punctuated.

If one accepts what **N** offers, then one must punctuate: *ob haec et (iam appetebat tempus) comitiorum causa* (thus e.g. Gronovius [who also suggested an emendation], Drakenborch, and Walters). This poses three difficulties: (*a*) it would have been very hard for ancient readers not to take *et* with the following *iam*; (*b*) L. nowhere else begins a parenthesis of this kind with unadorned *iam* (and *et* cannot be placed in the parenthesis to help out as it is needed to couple *ob haec* and *comitiorum causa*); (*c*) in the words of M. Müller, 'non puto Livium scripsisse *tempus* non addito *comitiorum*', and it is a fact that in each of the other seven passages (xxv. 2. 3 'consularium comitiorum iam appetebat tempus', xxviii. 10. 1, xxix. 10. 1, 38. 2, xxxvii. 47. 1, xxxix. 6. 1, 32. 5; cf. also xxxv. 8. 1 'comitiorum iam appetebat dies')[1] in which L. uses *tempus* with *appetere* in the context of the elections he always couples it with *comitiorum*.

The second of these difficulties would be removed by adopting either *nam* for *iam* with Madvig (1860: 193 = 1877: 229) or *iam ⟨enim⟩*, which was considered by Weissenborn, *Komm.*[4] Both proposals are possible, and Weissenborn's is quite attractive, since L. uses the coupling *iam enim* thirty-two times elsewhere, usually to introduce an explanatory parenthesis; see e.g. 20. 2, ix. 43. 2 'Marcio noui hostes— iam enim Anagninis Hernicisque aliis bellum iussum erat—decernuntur'. Neither proposal, however, lessens the third difficulty, which is most easily removed by deletion of *causa* with Gronovius (M. Müller suggested that *causa* could have been interpolated by a scribe who recalled such standard formulae as *comitiorum causa consul Romam reuocatus*). This proposal has other advantages, too: it frees *et* to serve in the parenthesis, thereby removing the first difficulty; and it gives excellent Livian idiom: cf. e.g. 20. 9 'tempus adgrediendi aptissimum uisum est, et iam lux adpetebat', xxviii. 37. 5 '. . . ubi commode hibernaturum se—et iam extremum autumni erat—censebat', and xxx. 4. 10 'deductisque nauibus—et iam ueris principium

---

[1] Also analogous is xxvii. 30. 17 'iam enim Nemeorum appetebat tempus'; and note the similar language at xli. 28. 4 'iam consularia comitia appetebant'.

erat— . . .'. For these reasons I have adopted it, despite the danger of imposing undue standardization on L.'s language.

As the parallels listed above show, the appearance of *appetebat tempus* (*comitiorum*) is the first instance of what was to become stock Livian language. Another instance of L.'s tendency towards stock phrasing is the appearance of *iam* in all the passages cited above, with the exception of xxviii. 10. 1.

ad suffragium . . . uocaret: see vi. 38. 4 n.

14. nec duce uno nec exercitu ⟨uno⟩: Walters and Conway (1918: 114) argued that there is no need to change the text, as *uno* may easily be understood with *exercitu* from its occurrence with *duce*. This is possible; but none of the passages which they cite seems truly parallel (perhaps ix. 28. 4 'se intra moenia . . . et Samnitium omnis multitudo et Nolana agrestis contulerat' is closest; but the ellipse of *multitudo* is rather easier). χ^1 had ⟨*uno*⟩ *exercitu*, but H. J. Müller's *exercitu* ⟨*uno*⟩ provides better word-order; he well compared 25. 13 'non suffecturum ducem unum nec exercitum unum aduersus quattuor populos'.

15. aduersus quattuor populos duces consules illo die deligi: 'consuls were to be chosen on that day as leaders against four peoples'. If the paradosis is corrupt, the best remedy for it is to delete *consules* as a gloss (Holford-Strevens, *per litteras*). However, although compressed, it may be explained as giving emphasis to *duces*, which stands in contrast to *quattuor populos*.[2]

ductor: see vii. 41. 4 n.

22. 1. nemini dubium erat quin Q. Fabius omnium consensu destinaretur: for this kind of comment in L., see vi. 6. 6 n.

N read *Fabius quintum*, but, as W–M say, '*quintum* im Sinne von "zum fünften Male" zu fassen, ist an dieser Stelle unpassend, obgleich das 5. Konsulat des Fabius wirklich folgt'; and one may add that a *praenomen* is required here. Accordingly they adopted *Q. Fabius*, which involves little more than a simple transposition; the reading was then known from Zr, but it is found also in ZbZt and

---

[1] But not Ricc. 485, and Esc. R I 4 has *uno duce* for *duce uno*.

[2] Other conjectures: OZbZt (reflecting E) read ⟨*et*⟩ *duces*, which allows one to take *duces* with *populos*; but L. nowhere takes any interest in the leaders of three of these peoples; R^c and Zs have *duos* for *duces* (an emendation that has ousted the reading of Z which Zs ought to have inherited), but, as there was nothing remarkable about the election of two consuls, L. would hardly have stressed the figure; and J. Perizonius conjectured *duces* ⟨*non*⟩ *consules*, which does not give a Roman manner of thought.

thus probably stood in Z.[1] This is preferable to Walters's *Q. Fabius quintum*.

eumque, a self-evidently right correction of **N**'s *cumque*, is found in OZbZtZs and therefore must have appeared in E, either in the text or as a correction.

praerogatiua[e]: originally the eighteen centuries of *equites* voted first in the *comitia centuriata* (i. 43. 11). Later, and certainly by the Hannibalic War, one of the thirty-five centuries of *iuniores* in the first property class was selected by lot (xxiv. 7. 12, Cic. *Phil*. ii. 82) to vote first and was called the *praerogatiua*. Its choice was announced before the other centuries voted and served as a guide (Cic. *Planc*. 49; see also Fest. 290, quoted below) and omen (Cic. *Mur*. 38, *diu*. i. 103, ii. 83; see also v. 18. 3 'omen' [referring back to 18. 1, discussed below] and ix. 38. 15 n.) for the election. For other references to it in the later books of L., see xxiv. 8. 9, 9. 3, xxvi. 22. 2, 22. 13, and xxviii. 9. 20. The date at which the change in the *praerogatiua* was introduced is not recorded. Modern scholars generally associate it with the reform of the *comitia centuriata* in the third quarter of the third century, after which the centuries were reorganized on a tribal basis; but one cannot exclude the possibility that there had been some reform at an earlier date that had paved the way for the practice of the late third century.

Since the *comitia centuriata* had not been reformed in the period covered by L.'s first decade, and since no source tells us what the term (if it was indeed used) denoted in this period, a certain explanation of L.'s use of it here and at v. 18. 1 'P. Licinium Caluum praerogatiua (**N**: -iuae *Sigonius*) tribunum militum non petentem creant (**N**: -at *Pantagathus*)' is not to be had. If one assumes that the two passages should be interpreted in the same way, then the following interpretations are possible.

(*a*) L. is guilty of anachronism and retrojects the conditions of the reformed *comitia centuriata* to the fourth and third centuries. If this is right, then we should read *praerogatiua* with Crévier in our passage (the corruption may be explained as an anticipation of *uocatae . . . centuriae*) and *creat* with Pantagathus at v. 18. 1. This interpretation is supported by L.'s reference to tribes at v. 18. 2 'iure uocatis tribubus'.

(*b*) An equestrian century was selected to vote first and was called

---

[1] I say probably, because Zs has *Fabius quintius*. Long before Zs T^c had restored the *praenomen* by reading *Fabius quintus* (a reading found also in R^c); but the inversion of *nomen* and *praenomen* is unwanted.

the *praerogatiua*. If this was the case, L. is not guilty of anachronism, but we should still read *praerogatiua* with Crévier in our passage and *creat* with Pantagathus at v. 18. 1.

(*c*) The eighteen equestrian centuries were collectively known as *praerogatiuae*. If this is right, then there is no need to emend in our passage, but Sigonius' *praerogatiuae* should be accepted at v. 18. 1. This view, adopted by W–M on our passage and by Ogilvie on v. 18. 1, gains some support from Fest. 290 'PRAEROGATIVAE centuriae dicuntur, ut docet Varro rerum humanarum lib. VI, quo rustici (quo rustici *Ursinus*: quae rus *cod. Farn.*) Romani, qui ignorarent petitores, facilius eos animaduertere possent. Verrius probabilius iudicat esse, ut, cum essent designati a praerogatiuis, in sermonem res uenirent populi de dignis indignisue et fierent ceteri diligentiores ad suffragia de his ferenda'; but, although Festus uses the plural *praerogatiuae*, it is far from clear that he is referring to the conditions of the mid-third century and earlier and not to the time of Varro, and he may have garbled what he found in Varro, using the plural loosely.

The evidence does not allow a confident choice between these possibilities (moreover, if in one passage L. and his sources had in mind the conditions of the reformed *comitia* but in the other wished to reflect archaic conditions, then a different interpretation would be needed for each passage); but the reference to the tribes at v. 18. 2 perhaps makes (*a*) more likely than any of the others, and I have emended accordingly.

For further discussion of either the *praerogatiua* in general or our passage in particular see Backmund (1874), Klinger (1884) 31–2, Mommsen (1887–8) iii. 398, Botsford (1909) 211–12, 226–7, Taylor (1957) 345–6 and (1966) 91–4, Ogilvie on v. 18. 1, Staveley (1972) 154–5, Stewart (1998) 43–6, and Mouritsen (2001) 99.
omnes centuriae: see 9. 10 n.

2. oratio: see 9. 10 n.
ad collegam P. Decium poscendum: if Decius had made no formal *professio*, that was not necessarily a problem; see 9. 10 n.
adminiculum: see vi. 1. 4 n.

3. censura duobusque consulatibusque: see 24. 1 n.

4–6. subscripsit orationi eius consul cum meritis P. Deci laudibus, tum quae ex concordia consulum bona quaeque ex discordia mala in administratione rerum militarium

euenirent memorando, (5) quam⟨que⟩ prope ultimum discrimen suis et collegae certaminibus nuper uentum foret admonendo: (6) Decium Fabiumque [ut] uno animo, una mente uiuere[nt]; esse praeterea uiros natos militiae, factis magnos, ad uerborum linguaeque certamina rudes: the mss pose several problems: one was noted by Duker, but more penetrating analysis was provided first by F. C. Wolff (1826: 9–10) and then, most clearly, by Madvig (1877: 230). The supplement adopted was made by Siesbye, *ap.* Madvig and Ussing[2] and Madvig (1877) 230, the deletions by Ussing.

The most important problem is the difficulty caused by Volumnius' offering advice to Fabius and Decius. If the paradosis were correct, the advice offered by Volumnius to Fabius and Decius in § 6 would interrupt a sequence in which Fabius addresses the people (§§ 2–3), Volumnius addresses the people (§§ 4–5), and Volumnius addresses the people again (§§ 6–7 'ea ingenia . . . creandos esse'); it would be strange that Volumnius should seek to advise the pair before they had even been elected; and it would be impertinent of him to advise men who were senior to him and had always operated in harmony. Therefore the text should certainly be emended so as to make *Decium . . . uiuerent* part of the advice given by Volumnius to the people.

Another problem concerns the structure of the sentence. Before *memorando* analysis of it is uncontroversial: in § 4 *subscripsit* ('he gave support to': see *OLD s.u.* 8[a]) introduces the reported speech of Volumnius; this is articulated by ablatives that are linked by *cum . . . tum . . .* and depend on this initial verb. *cum* introduces the first part of his speech, the praise of Decius (this is brief, and consists of just *meritis P. Deci laudibus*). In the second (introduced by *tum*) the consul dilates on the benefits of concord between consuls: *memorando* goes closely with *tum*, introduces the double indirect question *quae . . . quaeque . . . euenirent*, and balances *meritis laudibus*. Then, in the third, if one acquiesces in Volumnius' giving advice to Decius and Fabius in § 6, *quam prope . . . foret* in § 5 must likewise depend on *memorando*, being a further indirect question introduced by asyndeton.[1] However, as Duker noted, this structure is cumbersome and unwieldy (even if one adopts Siesbye's *quam⟨que⟩*), and several

---

[1] Were Luterbacher, who punctuated thus: . . . *memorando (—quam prope ultimum discrimen suis et collegae certaminibus nuper uentum foret?—) et monendo Decium* . . . correct, my 'must' would be wrong; but the question that he places in this parenthesis is exceedingly awkward, and (being rhetorical) would require *esse* for *foret*. This punctuation involves accepting the reading of M, on which see below.

scholars have emended the sentence so that *quam prope . . . foret* is construed with *admonendo* (Πλ).

A third problem is whether this reading of Πλ is right, or whether one should prefer M's *et monendo*. If M's reading were right, then *quam prope . . . foret* would have to depend on *memorando*.

Various conjectures eliminate the major difficulty:

(*a*) Ussing punctuated strongly after *admonendo* and read *Decium Fabiumque* [*ut*] *uno animo, una mente uiuere*[*nt*] in § 6. This gives very good sense: it allows *quam prope . . . foret* to depend on *admonendo*, and then, in a very Livian manner, the text glides into indirect statement. However, the conjecture was improved further by Siesbye, who read *quam⟨que⟩* earlier in the sentence, thereby removing an awkward asyndeton. If *admonendo* was mistakenly construed with what follows, then the consequential interpolation of *ut* and corruption of *uiuere* to *uiuerent* would have been very easy; and it need not matter that this conjecture is not compatible with the reading of M.

(*b*) Weissenborn (*Komm.*³) construed the sentence before *admonendo* in the same way as Ussing, but suggested supplying *ita uno animo* (or *consilio*) *rem gesturos* after *uiuerent*. Later (*Komm.*⁴), he improved this by adopting Siesbye's *quam⟨que⟩*. This solution gives good sense, but the comparative violence of the surgery tells against it.

(*c*) Harant (1880: 67–8) thought that Ussing's conjecture placed unwanted emphasis on the following *esse* (in his view the word-order would at first glance give the misleading implication that Volumnius was talking about men other than Decius and Fabius) and that it departed too far from N's reading (but see above); he therefore suggested *Decium Fabiumque, qui uno animo, una mente uiuerent*, and this is the reading which Walters adopted. Although the objection to the word-order is misplaced (*esse*, as often when in initial position, is asseverative), this conjecture is certainly easy (for the corruption of *ut* to *qui* Walters compared the reading of H at v. 51. 1 [*ut* > *qui*] and of Λ at vi. 4. 2 [*ut* > *quae*]; note also Λ's reading at vi. 15. 6 [*ut* > *quod*]) and is a viable alternative to those adopted.[1]

---

[1] Before those scholars Wolff conjectured *atque monendo Decius Fabiusque ut uno animo una mente uiuerent* 'and by advising (*sc.* the people) that Decius and Fabius lived (i.e. 'worked together') with one soul, one mind'. This can hardly be right: (i) it leaves in place the cumbersome structure discussed above; (ii) the position of *ut* after *Decius Fabiusque* is slightly awkward; (iii) the *ut*-clause can be taken only as an indirect command (precisely the sense Wolff was trying to avoid); and (iv) it introduces *atque* before a consonant (however, this last difficulty can easily be removed by adopting M's reading). F. Walter (1892: 524–5) proposed *atque monendo* without further change; but the problems of the passage are more deep-rooted.

5. prope ultimum discrimen: see vi. 42. 10 n.

6. una mente: for this coupling cf. e.g. Cic. *Flacc.* 96, *har.* 12, *Phil.* iv. 7, 8, vi. 2, vii. 22, and Apul. *Plat.* ii. 24.

esse praeterea uiros natos militiae, factis magnos, ad uerborum linguaeque certamina rudes: in antiquity the military man—a type which appealed much to L.'s nostalgic romanticism—was conventionally characterized as blunt of speech and uninterested in eloquence, the niceties of politics, and other civilian pursuits: cf. 24. 4 'in contione, ut inter militares uiros et factis potius quam dictis fretos, pauca uerba habita', ii. 56. 8 'rudis in militari homine lingua', Sall. *Iug.* 63. 3 '(Marius) . . . ubi primum aetas militiae patiens fuit, stipendiis faciundis, non Graeca facundia neque urbanis munditiis sese exercuit', Quint. xi. 1. 33 'simpliciora (referring to manner of speaking) militaris decent' (implying that military men should speak in the style expected of them), xi. 1. 45 (in front of *militares* and *rustici* one should not speak in the same way as in front of *eruditi*), Quint. (?) *decl.* 310. 1 'contemnunt hominem militarem nihil minus quam litibus idoneum', Tac. *Agr.* 9. 2 (Agricola an exception to the general rule—a fine general, but not unskilled in civilian pursuits) 'credunt plerique militaribus ingeniis subtilitatem deesse, quia castrensis iurisdictio secura et obtusior ac plura manu agens calliditatem fori non exerceat: Agricola naturali prudentia, quamuis inter togatos, facile iusteque agebat', Plut. *Caes.* 3. 4 (on Caesar, feigning the inability to write polished prose) αὐτὸς δ᾽ οὖν ὕστερον ἐν τῇ πρὸς Κικέρωνα περὶ Κάτωνος ἀντιγραφῇ παραιτεῖται, μὴ στρατιωτικοῦ λόγον ἀνδρὸς ἀντεξετάζειν πρὸς δεινότητα ῥήτορος εὐφυοῦς καὶ σχολὴν ἐπὶ τοῦτο πολλὴν ἄγοντος, Dio lxviii. 10. 2 (another exception: Trajan, after his first Dacian success) οὐ μέντοι, οἷα πολεμικὸς ἀνήρ, τἆλλα ἧττον διῆγεν ἢ καὶ ἧττον ἐδίκαζεν, ἀλλὰ τοτὲ μὲν ἐν τῇ ἀγορᾷ τοῦ Αὐγούστου, τοτὲ δ᾽ ἐν τῇ στοᾷ τῇ Λιουίᾳ ὠνομασμένῃ, πολλάκις δὲ καὶ ἄλλοθι ἔκρινεν ἐπὶ βήματος, Amm. xiv. 9. 1 'Ursicinus . . . bellicosus sane milesque semper et militum ductor, sed forensibus iurgiis longe discretus', and *SHA* xxx. 13. 4 (the author is surprised by the knowledge of Virgil shown by Diocletian, a *homo militaris*). For implied comparisons between the military man and another type, see 19. 7–8 (the argument between Ap. Claudius and L. Volumnius), Vell. i. 13. 1–4 (Scipio and Mummius), and Tac. *ann.* xiii. 2. 1 (Seneca and Burrus); for the appearance of the military man, see vii. 10. 7 n.; for the constrast between words and deeds, see vii. 32. 12 n.

ad . . . certamina rudes: *rudis* with *ad* and the accusative is attested first here in Latin; cf. also [x] xxi. 25. 6 'gens ad oppugnandarum

urbium artes rudis', xxiv. 48. 5, xxviii. 25. 8, Ov. *epist*. 11. 48, *Pont.*
iii. 7. 18, Curt. vi. 6. 9, viii. 2. 24, 7. 8, and Just. i. 1. 5. See further
K–S i. 439.

7. Since many of the early praetors (listed at vol. i, p. 50) are introduced to us by L. in military contexts, and since Appius himself is to
lead an army later in 295, Brennan (2000: 61–2; see also 31) suggests
with some reason that here and at vi. 42. 11 'praetore uno qui ius in
urbe diceret', L. is influenced by the later duties of the *praetor
urbanus* (note 'urbis ac fori') and is guilty of anachronism. However,
even in this period a praetor would often remain in Rome when the
consuls were at war: at 45. 4 and viii. 2. 1 there are explicit references
to the praetor's presiding in the senate (as often later: see e.g. xxiii.
22. 4, xxx. 22. 5), and at 21. 4–9 we learn that the praetor was in
Rome; and as the leading magistrate in the city it is likely that he
would have been much concerned with the civil law.
callidos: see ix. 46. 1 n.
iuris atque eloquentiae consultos: of the genitives which follow
consultus in its role as a substantivized or semi-substantivized masculine perfect passive participle, *iuris* is by far the most common (see
TLL iv. 585. 71–586. 36), but *eloquentiae* may be paralleled at *uir. ill.*
72. 2, and one finds also *boni* (Cato, *ORF* 58 = Gell. x. 3. 17, Apul.
Socr. 23), *disciplinae* (Col. xi. 1. 12), *iustitiae* (Cic. *Phil.* ix. 10), *legis*
(Σ Pers. 5. 90), and *sapientiae* (Hor. *carm.* i. 34. 2–3). See further
TLL 585. 5–11 and Nisbet and Hubbard on Hor. loc. cit.
urbi⟨s⟩ ac fori: N had *urbi ac fori*, which gives an impossible
coupling of a dative and a genitive; emendation to *urbis ac fori* (which
I have not noticed as a ms. reading or seen proposed as a conjecture,
but which is likely to be read by some *recentiores*) restores the genitive that is regular after *praeses*: cf. e.g. vi. 6. 15 'praesidem huius
consilii', xxiii. 48. 7 'praesides prouinciarum', Cic. *dom.* 141, *Sest.*
137, and many other passages. Editors (e.g. W–M, M. Müller,
Walters) read *urbi ac foro* with Fᶜ, Dᶜ, and (doubtless) many *recentiores*, but the coupling of *praeses* with the dative is not easily paralleled: only Aug. *cons. euang.* i. 25. 38 (*PL* xxxiv. 1059) '(*sc.* deos) . . .
rebus ad quemque proprie pertinentibus praesides esse uelint' and
Auson. xx. 1 'praeses Tritonia bellis' are cited at *TLL* x. 2. 870. 13;
and amongst the analogous formulations listed in Drakenborch's
note on xxxix. 47. 10 there is no parallel. Therefore, although *foro* is
a little more likely to have been corrupted to *fori* (by perseveration
from *urbi*) than *urbis* to *urbi*, it is preferable to restore the standard
idiom.

qualis Ap. Claudius esset: for Ap. Claudius as a jurisconsult, see vol. iii, p. 353.

praetores . . . creandos esse: the tone and import of Volumnius' remarks on Ap. Claudius are slightly ambiguous. The strong contrast between the praetorian and the consular *ingenium*, and between Appius as the representative of the one and Decius and Fabius as representatives of the other, would have been motivated a little better if L. had told us that Appius had designs on a continued consulship; as it is, Volumnius seems to be continuing the arguments of ch. 19. However, despite the somewhat disparaging tone, Volumnius was clearly recommending that Appius be elected into the praetorship.

8. ad praescriptum consulis: Foster translates 'by the direction of the consul'; but this implies that Volumnius merely fixed the day on which the voting took place; rather 'according to the recommendation of the consul', with reference to the people making the elections that Volumnius wanted.

This is the only occasion on which L. uses a part of *praescribere* or one of its cognates; for *ad praescriptum*, cf. Caes. *Gall*. i. 36. 1 and the other passages cited at *TLL* x. 2. 830. 47–50, to which add Apul. *apol.* 42 'ad praescriptum opinionis et famae'.

9. praetor: the practice of electing a retiring consul to the praetorship of the following year (a procedure, which, like prorogation, allowed him to continue with *imperium*) is found also for 294–293 (M. Atilius Regulus: see 45. 4), 293–292 (L. Papirius Cursor; see 47. 5), 284–283 (L. Caecilius Metellus Denter: see *per*. xii, Plb. ii. 19. 8), 258–257 (Atilius Caiatinus: see *F.T.*), and, perhaps, 281–280 (Q. Marcius Philippus: see Hemin. fr. 21 'tunc Marcius †praeco† primum proletarios armauit', in which passage the corrupt *praeco* is emended more easily to *praetor* than to *pro consule*). See further Brennan (2000) 76. For the praetorship in this period, see further ix. 41. 1 n. For elections to the praetorship being held on the same day as those for the consulship, see *addendum* to vii. 1. 6 n.

The *elogium* of Appius (quoted in vol. iii, p. 352) informs us that he was praetor twice, but the other year in which he held this office is not known (see ix. 29. 5–11 n.).

omnes absentes may seem surprising: although Ap. Claudius was absent, Decius may well have been in Rome, and Fabius certainly was in Rome (note his speech to the people at 22. 1–3). However, Sigonius well cited D.H. ix. 42. 3 Ἄππιον Κλαύδιον . . . πολλὰ ἀντειπόντα καὶ οὐδ᾽ εἰς τὸ πεδίον ἐλθεῖν βουληθέντα ἕνεκα τῶν ἀρχαιρεσίων, οὐδὲν ἧττον προὐβούλευσάν τε καὶ ἐψηφίσαντ᾽ ἀπόντα ὕπατον, which shows that *absens* may mean absent only from the electoral assembly. In general on election *in absentia* see vii. 26. 12 n. with *addendum*.

ex senatus consulto et scito plebis prorogatum in annum imperium est: for the senate's advising the plebs to vote for a prorogation, see viii. 23. 12 n.

Badian (1980/1: 99 n. 9), discussing L.'s use of the phrase *ex senatus consulto* ('in accordance with a decree of the senate'), writes, 'the *et* is unexpected, for the plebiscite actually prolonged his *imperium*, *ex SC*, and is not parallel to it. There is no reason to suspect the text and the inaccuracy must be accepted as an exception [*sc.* to L.'s normal usage in these matters]. Perhaps it is due to aesthetic reasons, the *et* being inserted to avoid the succession of two ablatives'. However, (*a*) L. may have regarded the actions of the senate and of the plebs as parallel (the senate issued its advice and the plebs voted); and (*b*) at vi. 22. 4 'ex senatus consulto populique iussu bellum Praenestinis indictum' and xxxv. 40. 5 'Vibonem colonia deducta est ex senatus consulto plebique scito' there are close analogies for the expression found here.

prorogatum in annum imperium est is the first appearance of what was to become one of L.'s standard formulations: the identical words are found next at xxvii. 22. 4 (where Luchs alone of modern editors has divined which mss give the correct word-order) and then on ten other occasions, almost invariably at the end of a sentence. There are numerous slight variations on the formula; see Packard (1968) iii. 1191–2.

23. 1–10. *Prodigies and the establishment of the cult of Pudicitia Plebeia Literary analysis.* L. ends his account of 296 with 'annalistic' material, by reporting first prodigies, and then aedilician activity. The brief account of the prodigies develops into a small dramatic episode, in which L. describes the establishment of the cult of Pudicitia Plebeia. The episode builds up to the direct speech (§§ 7–8) which is used by Verginia for the establishment of her cult (for the technique see vol. i, p. 119). It is rounded off by a brief account of the decline of the cult in later years. By mentioning (§ 4) that Verginia was the wife of Volumnius, the consul of 296, L. provides a link with the rest of his narrative of the year.

The prodigies. That L.'s brief comment (§ 1) 'eo anno prodigia multa fuerunt, quorum auerruncandorum causa supplicationes in biduum senatus decreuit' on the prodigies of 296 BC and his almost equally brief comment at 31. 8 on the prodigies of 295 BC are merely summaries of the more extensive material which was available in his sources is shown by Zon. viii. 1. 2–4 (which follows on his notice of the alliance between the Samnites and the Gauls [quoted at p. 269 below]):

ὃ οἱ Ῥωμαῖοι μαθόντες ἐς δέος κατέστησαν, καὶ σημείων πολλῶν ἐς τοῦτο αὐτοὺς ἐναγόντων. ἐν γὰρ τῷ Καπιτωλίῳ ἐκ τοῦ βωμοῦ τοῦ Διὸς αἷμα τρισὶν ἡμέραις, μιᾷ δὲ μέλι καὶ ἐν ἑτέρᾳ γάλα θρυλεῖται ἀναδοθῆναι, εἴ τῳ ταῦτα πιστά· καὶ ἐν τῇ ἀγορᾷ Νίκης τι ἄγαλμα χάλκεον ἱδρυμένον ἐπὶ βάθρου λιθίνου αὐτομάτως εὑρέθη κάτω ἑστὸς ἐπὶ γῆς· ἐτύγχανε δὲ ἐκεῖ ἀποβλέπον ὅθεν οἱ Γαλάται ἤδη ἐπῄεσαν. (§ 3) ταῦτ' οὖν καὶ ἄλλως ἐξεφόβει τὸν δῆμον, πλέον δ' ὑπὸ τῶν μάντεων κεκριμένα ἀπαίσια. Μάνιος δέ τις Τυρσηνὸς τὸ γένος ἐθάρσυνεν αὐτούς, εἰπὼν τήν τε Νίκην, εἰ καὶ κατέβη, ἀλλ' εἰς τὸ πρόσθεν προχωρήσασαν καὶ βεβαιοτέραν ἐπὶ τῆς γῆς ἱδρυθεῖσαν τὸ κράτος σφίσι προδηλοῦν τοῦ πολέμου· κἀκ τούτου καὶ θυσίας πολλὰς γενήσεσθαι τοῖς θεοῖς· τοὺς γὰρ βωμούς, καὶ μάλιστα τοὺς ἐν τῷ Καπιτωλίῳ, ἐν ᾧ τὰ νικητήρια θύουσιν, ἐν ταῖς εὐπραγίαις αὐτῶν, ἀλλ' οὐκ ἐν ταῖς συμφοραῖς κατ' ἔθος αἱμάττεσθαι. (§ 4) ἐκ μὲν οὖν τούτων ἀγαθόν τι σφᾶς ἔπειθε προσδοκᾶν, ἐκ δὲ τοῦ μέλιτος νόσον, ὅτι αὐτοῦ οἱ κάμνοντες δέονται, καὶ ἐκ τοῦ γάλακτος λιμόν· ἐς γὰρ τοσαύτην σιτοδείαν ἀφίξεσθαι ὥστε καὶ τὴν αὐτόφυτον τήν τε αὐτόνομον ζητῆσαι τροφήν.

Ὁ μὲν οὖν Μάνιος οὕτω τὰ τῶν σημείων ἡρμήνευσε, καὶ ἐπὶ τῶν πραγμάτων δ' ἐσύστερον τῆς αὐτοῦ μαντείας ἐκβάσης, σοφίας ἐκομίσατο δόξαν καὶ προγνώσεως.

To which may be added a fragment from Zonaras' source, Dio (36. 28):

ὅτι ὁ ὅμιλος περὶ τῆς μαντείας παραχρῆμα μὲν οὔθ' ὅπως πιστεύσῃ οὔθ' ὅπως ἀπιστήσῃ αὐτῷ εἶχεν· οὔτε γὰρ ἐλπίζειν πάντα ἐβούλετο, ὅτι μηδὲ γενέσθαι πάντα ἤθελεν, οὔτ' αὖ ἀπιστεῖν ἅπασιν ἐτόλμα, ὅτι νικῆσαι ἐπεθύμει, ἀλλ' οἷα ἐν μέσῳ τῆς ταραχῆς καὶ τοῦ φόβου ὢν χαλεπώτατα διῆγεν. συμβάντων δ' αὐτῶν ὡς ἑκάστων καὶ τὴν ἑρμήνευσιν σφίσιν ἐκ τῆς τῶν ἔργων πείρας ἐφήρμοσαν, καὶ αὐτὸς σοφίας τινὰ δόξαν ἐς τὴν τοῦ ἀφανοῦς πρόγνωσιν προσποιεῖσθαι ἐπεχείρει.

This relates to § 4 of Zonaras. Since there are no dates in Zonaras, it is unclear whether the prophecy of Manius should be placed in 296 or 295; but note that it precedes his account of Sentinum, like L.'s notice here but unlike his notice at 31. 8. Plainly Dio and Zonaras present a version of these portents elaborated in the light of later events, namely the Roman victory at Sentinum and the *pestilentia* which L. mentions at 31. 8 and 47. 6–7; they or the Roman annalistic sources on which they drew may have been responsible for much of this elaboration, but some of it may go back to the third century itself.[1] On the statue of Victoria to which Zonaras here refers, and on the ideology of Victoria at Rome in the years around 295, see 29. 14 n. For prodigies in the annalistic tradition see vol. i, pp. 59–60; for L.'s selectivity in drawing on the material available to him, see vol. i, pp. 19–20 and 57.

Pudicitia Plebeia. In §§ 3–10 L. narrates that Verginia, excluded by the patrician *matronae* from the cult of Pudicitia Patricia on the ground that she was married to a plebeian, founded a rival cult of Pudicitia Plebeia; but this, he says, had fallen into desuetude by his own day. Our only other source for the tale, and our only other specific reference to the temple of Pudicitia Plebeia, is the fragmentary notice at Fest. p. 270: 'Plebeiae Pudicitiae sacellum in uico Longo est, quod cum Verginia, patriciae generis femina, conuiuio facto inter patres et plebem, no[. . .' (cf. Paul. Fest. p. 271 'Plebeiae Pudicitiae sacellum Romae ut sacra cetera colebatur'). *conuiuio facto inter patres et plebem*, if the text is sound,[2] adds a detail not found in L.; how far the rest of the tale would have corresponded to what L. tells it is impossible to say.

L.'s reference to the *sacellum* and cult of Pudicitia Patricia involves several difficulties. First, in our sources there is no other certain reference to either a *sacellum* or a cult of Pudicitia Patricia. Secondly, it is unclear what the relationship is between the cult and rituals which L. describes and a statue, perhaps of Pudicitia, that Festus, in a corrupt passage (p. 282), says was likewise to be found in the forum Boarium: 'Pudicitiae signum in foro Bouario est, ubi †familiana† aedes est (aedes est *Scaliger*: aedisset *cod.*) Herculis. eam quidam Fortunae esse existimant. item, uia Latina ad milliarium IIII (illi *cod.*) Fortunae muliebris, nefas est attingi, nisi ab ea quae semel nupsit' (abbreviated at Paul. Fest. 283).[3] If those who placed this

---

[1] For further discussion see Wiseman (1991) 122–3 and (1995*a*) 118–25; he tentatively speculates that a pit under the temple of Victoria on the Palatine may have been the repository of a human sacrifice used to propitiate the gods in the crisis of 296–295, that this was the context in which the death of Remus in the Roman foundation myth arose, and that the story in Zonaras reflects a bland reinterpretation of the expiatory rituals undertaken in these years. It is unlikely that we shall ever have the evidence either to confirm or to refute reconstructions of this kind.

[2] For *conuiuio* Gothofredus conjectured *conubio*, and Dr Holford-Strevens suggests *conuicio*.

[3] For *familiana aedisset* Scaliger conjectured *Aemiliana aedis est*, Mommsen (*CIL* i¹, p. 150) *familia edisset* or *familia sedisset*, Radke (*RE* xxiii. 1944) *effigies finitima aedi est*, and Palmer (1990: 237) *Flaminini aedis est*. Apart from that part of Scaliger's proposal which involves changing *aedisset* to *aedis est*, none of these conjectures is compelling.

statue near the temple of Hercules were right, then it must be connected with L.'s *sacellum*.[1]

---

[1] However, the fact that some ancients thought that the statue depicted Fortuna suggested to Wissowa that there may have been no cult of Pudicitia in the Forum Boarium separate from that of Fortuna in the temple allegedly built by Servius Tullius.

This temple was destroyed by fire in 213 BC, but rebuilt in the next year (xxiv. 47. 15, xxv. 7. 6, D.H. iv. 40. 7, Ov. *fast.* vi. 625–6). D.H. reports that inside it there was a wooden statue inlaid with gold, which was a representation of Servius himself and which miraculously survived the fire. Ovid too says that the statue survived the fire, beginning his tale by stating that it depicted a figure whose head was covered by a toga, and that this figure was Servius (*fast.* vi. 569–72): 'lux eadem, Fortuna, tua est, auctorque locusque; | sed superiniectis quis latet iste togis? | Seruius est, hoc constat enim: sed causa latendi | discrepat, et dubium me quoque mentis habet'. He then gives various explanations of why the figure of Servius had its head covered: one was that the goddess Fortuna had covered the head of Servius in shame at the circumstances of her affair with him (ll. 573–80); a second that it depicted the plebs grieving for him after his death (ll. 581–4); a third that a statue of Servius in his own temple of Fortuna was so horrified at the entrance into the temple of the parricide Tullia that it had asked to be covered (ll. 585–620). Pliny (*nat.* viii. 197), by contrast, identified the statue not with Servius but with Fortuna: 'Serui Tulli praetextae, quibus signum Fortunae ab eo dicatae coopertum fuerat, durauere ad Seiani exitum mirumque fuit neque diffluxisse eas neque teredinum iniurias sensisse annis quingentis sexaginta' (another reference to the remarkable way in which the statue had been preserved). This idea reappears in a fragment of Varro (*ap.* Non. p. 278), in which he gives the reason why some authorities rejected the identification of a statue with a king and preferred to identify it with Fortuna Virgo: 'VNDVLATVM, noue positum purum. Varro de Vita Populi Romani: "et a quibusdam dicitur esse Virginis Fortunae ab eo quod duabus undulatis togis est opertum, proinde ut non reges nostri undulatas et praetextatas togas soliti sint habere"'; comparison with Pliny shows that Varro was referring to the statue in the temple of Fortuna. It can now be seen that in Ovid's first explanation of the appearance of the statue the tale would run much more smoothly if the veiled figure was said to have been Fortuna herself. Clearly the figure on this old statue must have been so indistinct that it could be equated with either a male (Servius) or a female (Fortuna).

The temple of Fortuna was linked closely to that of Mater Matuta: both were said to have been founded by Servius Tullius, were situated next to each other (see esp. xxxiii. 27. 4; also xxiv. 47. 17 and xxv. 7. 6), and shared the same festal day, the Matralia (see *lux eadem* in Ovid, cited above). Just as the Matralia and the cult of Mater Matuta were associated particularly with *matronae* (Tertullian, *monogam.* 17, says that only *uniuirae* were entitled to place garlands on the statue of Mater Matuta), so too the temple of Fortuna had a connection with chastity and with *matronae*: at the end of his third explanation of the curious statue Ovid writes (ll. 617–22): 'ueste data tegitur; uetat hanc Fortuna moueri, | et sic e templo est ipsa locuta suo: | "ore reuelato qua primum luce patebit | Seruius, haec positi prima pudoris erit." | parcite, matronae, uetitas attingere uestes | (sollemni satis est uoce mouere preces)'. Here the veiled statue is specifically associated with the *pudor* of *matronae*, and a sign of the *pudor* of these *matronae* is that they do not touch the clothing depicted on the statue.

Given the association of the temple of Fortuna with the cult of *matronae* and with chastity, it is easy to conjecture that the old and mysterious statue with its head covered might have been regarded by some as a statue not of Servius nor of Fortuna but of the goddess Pudicitia; note that on coins which depict the later cult of Pudicitia established by Plotina (see e.g. Mattingly *et al.* [1923–] ii. 298), the goddess is shown with veiled head. This would explain the view reported by Festus in the second of the passages quoted above. It also suggests the possibility that there never was a *sacellum* of Pudicitia Patricia, merely a cult statue in the temple of Fortuna at which *matronae* worshipped.

All this is not necessarily fatal for the historicity of L.'s tale. First, as Champeaux has argued, Wissowa's speculations may be misguided: neither L. nor Festus suggests any doubt that the statue or *sacellum* of Pudicitia was near the temple of Hercules (it would have been easy to

Thirdly, the connection between chaste *matronae* and a cult statue of Fortuna recurs in what Festus (282 [quoted above]; cf. also D.H. viii. 56. 4, Tert. *monog.* 17, Serv. *auct. Aen.* iv. 19) tells us about the temple of Fortuna Muliebris on the Via Latina.[1] This temple of Fortuna Muliebris is said to have been founded in 488 BC by the wife and mother of Coriolanus after they had persuaded him to retire from Rome. Most sources call the wife of Coriolanus Volumnia (see e.g. ii. 40. 1, D.H. viii. 40. 1 and *passim*), but Plutarch calls the mother Volumnia (33. 5, 34. 1, 35. 1, 36. 1) and the wife Verginia;[2] one source (D.H. viii. 55. 5) says that the temple was dedicated by a Proculus Verginius, one of the consuls of 486. It is not easy to regard it as a coincidence that the names of the families Volumnia and Verginia are found twice in the context of the founding of a temple associated with Pudicitia.[3] Of the two tales, that of 488 is more suspect, since the story of Coriolanus relates to a very early episode in Roman history and has numerous other legendary features, and since the names Verginia and Volumnia could be a retrojection from 294 of the involvement of Verginia, wife of Volumnius, with Pudicitia (with whom the temple of Fortuna Muliebris was associated in our tale). However, our passage too is not above the suspicion of having a legendary origin: Palmer (1974: 124) rightly noted that in the famous tale of the end of the Decemvirate the name of Verginia is associated

mention that of Fortuna); both imply that it was in the open air, whereas the statue in the temple of Fortuna was certainly inside; and the certain associations with female chastity of the temple of Pudicitia on the Via Latina may have encouraged confusion with regard to the statue in the Forum Boarium. Therefore there may indeed have been two statues. Secondly, even if Wissowa was right, Verginia could simply have been excluded by patrician *matronae* from worship of the statue of Pudicitia in the temple of Fortuna. In which case, the only mistake of L. or his sources would have been to confuse worship at this statue with worship at a special shrine. Note too that Gagé well observed that it would be odd if Servius Tullius was associated with a patrician rather than a plebeian cult.

Palmer (1974: 121–3) held that one should not equate the statue of Fortuna with that of Pudicitia. He believed that the cult of Pudicitia Patricia was established by Fabius Rullianus in 331, the year in which as aedile he convicted 170 *matronae*, led by the patricians Cornelia and Sergia, on charges of poisoning. Although the notion (p. 122) that '[t]he guilt of the patrician women and the comparison with a plebeian secession [viii. 18. 12] suggest a relation to Pudicitia Patricia', has some attractions, Palmer does not engage with Wissowa's arguments, and his own speculation has no strong evidential basis.

[1] However, since *uniuirae* were there allowed to touch the statue (in contrast to what Ovid tells us about the statue in the temple founded by Servius), one wonders whether there has been some confusion in the description of the temples and cult-practices.

[2] Palmer (1974: 120 n. 29) observes that οὐεργινίω (33. 5) and οὐεργίαν (34. 1) in cod. N are emended more plausibly to, respectively, Οὐεργινία and Οὐεργινίαν than Οὐεργιλία and Οὐεργιλίαν, which most editors print.

[3] Thus, rightly, Palmer (1974) 120–1, 124.

with chastity (see e.g. iii. 44. 1–58. 11),[1] and in the context of Pudicitia the suggestion of *uirgo* implicit in the name is worrying.

These various considerations should make one suspicious with regard to what L. says about Pudicitia Patricia, but it remains possible that a cult of Pudicitia Plebeia was established in 296, and that it was connected with the house of Volumnius. Palmer (1974: 125–6) interestingly notes that an earlier Volumnius (*cos*. 461) is ascribed the *cognomen* Amintinus by *F.C.*, and that the Vicus Longus, where the shrine was established (§ 6), ran through the Pagus Amentinus. Although L. states that the cult of Pudicitia Plebeia had fallen into desuetude in his own day, and although his evidence may perhaps be supported by *ueterem* in Juv. 6. 308 'Pudicitiae ueterem cum praeterit aram', Palmer (1974: 137–59) makes a reasonable (albeit speculative) case for its revival from time to time in the imperial period and for the Christian church of S. Vitalis' having been founded on the site of the temple of Pudicitia Plebeia.

L. is probably correct to connect the origins of the cult with the Struggle of the Orders (it is hard to see how this should not be the case for a cult with such a title), but it is not easy to link the story which he tells in any meaningful way with the politics of the period.

See further Wissowa (1897 = 1904: 254–60) and (1912) 333–4, Platner and Ashby (1929) 433–4, Gagé (1960) 121–2, Radke, *RE* xxiii. 1942–5, Latte (1960a) 239 n. 3, Palmer (1974), Champeaux (1982–7) i. 281–3, 356, and F. Coarelli in Steinby (1993–2000) iv. 168–9.

23. 1. auerruncandorum: see viii. 6. 11 n.

causa is regular in the context of the procuration of prodigies; cf. e.g. xxv. 7. 9, xxvii. 23. 4, xxxii. 1. 13, 9. 4, xxxv. 21. 2, 21. 5, and other passages cited by Luterbacher (1904: 56). Contrast the use of *ob* found at 31. 8 (n.).

supplicationes: see vii. 28. 8 n.

2. uinum ac tus: wine and incense were very regularly used in supplication of the gods; cf. Plaut. *aul.* 24, Sall. *hist.* ii. 70. 3 (just incense), Sen. *dial.* v. 18. 1, Suet. *Aug.* 35. 3, *Tib.* 70. 3, Mart. ix. 1. 6 (just incense), Plin. *epist.* x. 96. 5 'qui negabant esse se Christianos aut fuisse, cum praeeunte me deos adpellarent et imagini tuae, quam

---

[1] The possibility of a connection between the two tales is developed further by Curti (2000: 86–8); but it may be optimistic to see more than coincidence in the facts that the earlier Verginia was lusted after by an Ap. Claudius and that the later was the daughter of a man who fell out with another Ap. Claudius.

propter hoc iusseram cum simulacris numinum adferri, ture ac uino supplicarent, praeterea male dicerent Christo . . . dimittendos putaui', and Apul. *apol.* 63. Particularly interesting is the passage of Pliny, in which the making of a supplication *ture ac uino* may be seen as an integral part of the process of establishing one's non-Christian religious orthodoxy. In explanation of the word *macte* Servius (*Aen.* ix. 641) writes: 'quotiens enim aut tus aut uinum super uictimam fundebatur, dicebant "mactus est taurus uino uel ture", hoc est cumulata est hostia et magis aucta'. For another Livian reference cf. xxiii. 11. 4 'tum dixit se oraculo egressum extemplo iis omnibus diuis rem diuinam ture ac uino fecisse'. See further Henzen (1874) 93 and Wissowa (1912) 399 and 412.

supplicatum iere frequentes uiri feminaeque: for *frequentes* in this context cf. iii. 63. 5 'populus iniussu et altero die frequens iit supplicatum'. For families supplicating cf. iii. 7. 7 'iussi cum coniugibus ac liberis supplicatum ire pacemque exponere deum', xxiv. 23. 1 'supplicauerunt cum coniugibus ac liberis'; the same idea is expressed more expansively at xxii. 10. 8 'supplicatumque iere cum coniugibus ac liberis non urbana multitudo tantum sed agrestium etiam, quos in aliqua sua fortuna publica quoque contingebat cura'. Perhaps cf. xxiv. 12. 15 'matronae supplicauere'.

L. quite often uses *ire* with the supine in *-um* of *supplicare*; cf. iii. 7. 7 (quoted above), 63. 5 (quoted below), vii. 28. 8 'non tribus tantum supplicatum ire placuit sed finitimos etiam populos', and xxii. 10. 8.

3. insignem supplicationem: *insignem* is emphasized by its prominent position at the head of the sentence; *supplicationem* links the story of Verginia to the account of the prodigies and their expiation in §§ 1–2.

in sacello Pudicitiae Patriciae: that *pudicitia* ('chastity') was one of the most hallowed traditional virtues of the Roman woman hardly needs illustration. In L. see above all the stories of Lucretia, who asks her husband (i. 58. 7): 'quid enim salui est mulieri amissa pudicitia?', and Verginia (see e.g. iii. 52. 4, quoted below). Stories on the theme are conveniently collected by Valerius Maximus (vi. 1) and Seneca in his *de matrimonio* (frr. 45–87). Amidst various witty tales told by Seneca note fr. 63 'L. Sullae, felicis si non habuisset uxorem. Metella coniunx palam erat impudica'. See also Treggiari (1991) 105–7.

quod, found in U and reported from Drakenborch from five *recentiores*, and doubtless found in many others, must be correct against N's *quae*, which presumably arose under the influence of the feminine *Pudicitiae*: proper meaning can be given to the sentence only if the antecedent of the relative clause is *sacello*. It is surprising that Walters went against most of his immediate predecessors in printing *quae*.

Foro Bouario: 'the area along the Tiber from the base of the Aventine to the base of the Capitoline, more precisely from the Velabrum . . . and Porta Trigemina . . . to Vicus Iugarius' (L. Richardson [1992] 162). The view that the Forum Bovarium (or Boarium) was originally Rome's cattle market rests principally upon the derivation of the name *boarium* from *bos* (Varr. *ling.* v. 146, Paul. Fest. 27 'boarium forum Romae dicebatur, quod ibi boues uenderentur'; Propertius [iv. 9. 19–20] slightly varies this by deriving it from the presence in the area of the cattle of Hercules, after he had killed Cacus); despite the facile nature of ancient etymologizing, the derivation could be correct. An alternative ancient view derived the name from a statue of an ox taken from Aegina and displayed in the forum (Ov. *fast.* vi. 477–8, Plin. *nat.* xxxiv. 10, Tac. *ann.* xii. 24. 1).

The Forum Boarium was especially connected with the cult of Hercules: on the slopes of the neighbouring Aventine he was said to have defeated Cacus, and in the forum itself the Ara Maxima (ix. 29. 9 n.) stood close to the temple which L. here mentions.

See further Hülsen, *RE* iii. 573–5, Platner and Ashby (1929) 223–4, Coarelli (1988) and in Steinby (1993–2000) ii. 295–7, and L. Richardson (1992) 162–4.

ad aedem rotundam Herculis: Macrobius (*Sat.* iii. 6. 10; cf. the almost identical words at Serv. *auct. Aen.* viii. 363) distinguishes two temples of Hercules Victor: 'Romae autem Victoris Herculis aedes duae sunt, una ad portam Trigeminam, altera in foro Boario'; the second of these must be the round temple mentioned in our passage. Other certain references to it are Plin. *nat.* x. 79 'Romae in aedem Herculis in foro Boario nec muscae nec canes intrant' (this phenomenon is mentioned also at Plut. *quaest. Rom.* 90 = *mor.* 285e and Solin. i. 10–11), xxxv. 19 (the temple contained a painting by Pacuvius), and the corrupt passage of Festus (282) quoted above; possible references include xl. 51. 6 and Plut. *praec. ger. reip.* 20 = *mor.* 816c. As Palmer notes, 'We do not know the year of foundation of this round temple, we do not know the anniversary of this round temple, and we do not know the epithet of Hercules of this round temple'; but it has been convincingly identified with the round temple near S. Maria in Cosmedin. See further Platner and Ashby (1929) 257–8, Palmer (1990) 237–9, L. Richardson (1992) 188–9, and F. Coarelli in Steinby (1993–2000) iii. 15.

4. Verginiam: (25). Known only from this story.

Auli: (5). This Aulus is otherwise unknown. The last Verginius known to have held office is L. Verginius Tricostus, *cos. tr.* 389 (vi. 1. 8 n.); thus the *gens* had not reached the consulship (or consular tribunate or dictatorship) for nearly a century, and it was never to do so again. It is just conceivable, however, that L. was mistaken in regarding Verginia as a patrician (plebeian Verginii appear to go back far into the fifth century; see e.g. iii. 11. 9, 25. 4, D.H. x. 2. 1, 6. 1 [on the tribune of 461] and Gundel, *RE* viiiA. 1508–9); in which case the cult of Pudicitia will have been established by a plebeian for plebeians.

patriciam plebeio nuptam: in the course of books vi–x the only other Roman marriages about which L. informs us are those of the patrician Fabiae sisters to the patrician Ser. Sulpicius and the plebeian Licinius Stolo (vi. 34. 5); however, Valerius Maximus (viii. 1. *abs.* 9, discussed at ix. 42. 10–43. 24 n.) tells us that a daughter of Fabius Rullianus married the plebeian Atilius Calatinus (or Caiatinus). L. perhaps implies that marriages between patrician women and plebeian men were rare; but after seventy years of plebeian consulates two Fabiae are hardly likely to have provided the only other examples, and, in addition to the Verginii, other declining patrician houses are likely to have allied themselves with up-and-coming plebeians. Perhaps patrician women who had married plebeians had traditionally been banned from this shrine, and Verginia, proud to be married to the consul of the year, was deliberately trying to flout this ban.

enupsisset: *enubere* is defined as follows at Isid. *diff.* app. 153 (Migne, *PL* lxxxiii p. 1327) 'inter nubere, enubere et denubere hoc interest, quod nubit ciuis ciui, enubit extraneo; denubit quae in manum uiri conuenit'. L. is the only extant Latin author to use the verb [*]: at iv. 4. 7 the context is again that of the marriage of patrician ladies to plebeians 'neque uestras filias sororesque enubere (*Rhenanus:* et nubere *codd.*) sinendo e patribus' (the conjecture of Rhenanus is obviously right); at xxvi. 34. 3 it is used of Campanian women leaving their families because of marriage. At xxxix. 19. 5 'gentis enuptio' (a conjecture in the *editio princeps*, to which the primary mss point), he has the only instance of *enuptio* in extant Latin (precisely what this expression means is unclear, although it must refer to the right of Faecenia to marry whom she chose; see also 8. 9 n.). *enubere* is attested also on a Moesian inscription of the second century AD (*CIL* iii. 7505). See further *TLL* v. 2. 614. 82–615. 10.

sacris arcuerant: for *arcere* used of refusing admission to a ritual or a sacred building, cf. e.g. Pac. *trag.* 305 'ut te ara arceam', Hor. *carm.*

iii. 1. 1 'odi profanum uolgus et arceo', Ov. *met.* vi. 209–10 'cultis |
arceor . . . aris', Luc. v. 139 'solitus templis arcere nocentis', Tac.
hist. iv. 82. 1, v. 8. 1, Lact. *inst.* ii. 4. 25, and some of the other
passages assembled at *TLL* ii. 443. 53–65.

iracundia muliebri: for L.'s views on women, see vi. 34. 7 n.

contentionem animorum: 'a fierce quarrel'; cf. Cic. *fam.* ii. 13. 2
'ex eo (*sc.* the different way in which Cicero and Ap. Claudius administered their province) quidam suspicati fortasse sunt animorum
contentione, non opinionum dissensione, me ab eo discrepare' and
Val. Max. ii. 1. 6 'quotiens uero inter uirum et uxorem aliquid iurgi
intercesserat in sacellum deae Viriplacae, quod est in Palatio,
ueniebant et ibi inuicem locuti quae uoluerant contentione animorum deposita concordes reuertebantur'; also Plin. *nat.* x. 83 (on
nightingales) 'certant inter se palamque animosa contentio est'.
Much more common, esp. in Cicero, is the expression *contentio
animi*, which can mean little more than 'exercise of the mind' (see e.g.
Cic. *Cael.* 39, *Brut.* 233, *Tusc.* ii. 58; but cf. e.g. *Sest.* 39 and Curt.
viii. 1. 33 for its use in a sense akin to that of *contentionem animorum*
here).

5. uni nuptam: the ideal of the wife who had been married to only
one husband is much celebrated in both the literary and, especially,
the inscriptional evidence of the late Republic and Principate.
Modern scholars conventionally call such women *uniuir(i)ae* (the
term is common on inscriptions [see e.g. *CIL* vi. 31711, xiv. 418], but
rare in literary texts, although note the passage of Tertullian quoted
below), but we find also *unicubae, uniiugae,* and *unimaritae,* and no
one term seems to have been technical. From the abundant evidence
note e.g. Val. Max. ii. 1. 3 'quae uno contentae matrimonio fuerant
corona pudicitiae honorabantur: existimabant enim eum praecipue
matronae sincera fide incorruptum esse animum qui depositae
uirginitatis cubile egredi nesciret, multorum matrimoniorum experi-
entiam quasi legitimae cuiusdam intemperantiae signum esse credentes', Sen. frr. 76–7 (esp. 'Porcia minor, cum laudaretur apud eam
quaedam bene morata quae secundum habebat maritum, respondit:
"felix et pudica matrona numquam praeterquam semel nubit"'),
carm. epigr. 643. 5 'uno contenta marito', 693. 4, 736. 3, and 968. 3.
The privileges of the *uniuira* about which we are informed included
the right to sacrifice at the shrine of *pudicitia* (mentioned in our
passage alone, although note the reference to the *corona pudicitiae*
at Val. Max. loc. cit.), to act as a *pronuba* (Fest. 282 'pronubae
adhibentur nuptis, quae semel nupserunt', Tert. *castit.* 13. 1 'denique

monogamia apud ethnicos ita in summo honore est, ut . . . uirginibus legitime nubentibus uniuira pronuba adhibeatur . . . item, ut in quibusdam sollemnibus et officiis prior sit uniuirae locus. certe Flaminica non nisi uniuira est; quae et flaminis lex est', Serv. auct. *Aen.* iv. 166 'Varro pronubam dicit quae ante nupsit et quae uni tantum nupta est'), to have first place at certain rituals (Tert. loc. cit.), and to touch the cult statue of Fortuna Muliebris (see above, p. 247). These religious privileges strongly suggest that the esteem in which *uniuirae* were held was not just a late republican phenomenon but went back to early Roman history; but the high divorce rate and the prevalence of remarriage for political and other reasons (e.g. death of husbands in illness or battle) must have made the aristocratic *uniuira* a comparatively rare phenomenon in late republican and early imperial Rome,[1] and this explains the lavish praise in some of the passages cited above. For other passages illustrating the esteem in which *uniuirae* were held, and for further bibliography and discussion, see e.g. Marquardt (1886) 42 n. 6, Bömer on Ov. *fast.* vi. 231, G. W. Williams (1958) 23–4, Courtney on Juv. 6. 231, Treggiari (1991) 232–7, and Evans Grubbs (1995) 69–70.

uere 'truly' is Doujat's conjecture.[2] *uero*, the reading of **N**, is found with the meanings 'honestly' and 'truly' quite often in early Latin, but only rarely after *c*.100 BC. At *OLD s.u.* 1–2 the only passage cited from this period that could plausibly have this sense is xxvii. 19. 12 '(Scipio) uocatum eum interrogat uelletne ad Masinissam reuerti. cum effusis gaudio lacrimis cupere uero diceret, tum . . .' (but, as W–M imply ad loc., *uero* is perhaps better taken in a confirmatory sense); to those adduced by C. F. W. Müller (1865: 48) one may add Curt. v. 2. 4, vi. 11. 21, and Gell. vii. 8. 5 (all instances of *uerone an falso* or the like) and Gell. xix. 1. 19.[3] While these parallels show that the paradosis is possible Latin, it is easier to believe that L. wrote something different. Madvig (*ap.* Madvig and Ussing and 1877: 230 n. 1) proposed *ex uero*, which is found at Sall. *Cat.* 8. 1, Hor. *serm.* ii. 2. 56, Ov. *am.* iii. 9. 4, *fast.* ii. 859, Sen. *dial.* vi. 25. 2, Tac. *ann.* iv. 43. 3, and xv. 68. 3. Although the corruption postulated by this conjecture would be easy to explain, it is best translated 'with good reason' or 'from fact', which would be rather ponderous here. Since

---

[1] It follows that there was no disgrace in remarriage, especially for a widow but also for a divorcée: see R. G. M. Nisbet (1978) 4–5 = (1995) 34–5.

[2] Anticipating Kiehl, *ap.* Bisschop *et al.* (1852) 97.

[3] At Cic. *leg.* i. 63 'uero facis et honeste et pie', also adduced in *OLD*, *uero* should be translated 'indeed'. The other passages cited by Müller are not parallel, in some because *uero* is not the reading of the mss, at Curt. ix. 2. 15 'cetera auditu maiora quam uero' because *uero* is substantival.

uere is very commonly used to mean 'truly', Doujat's conjecture is preferable.

6. Vico Longo: 'the street that crossed the valley between the Quirinal and the Viminal and joined the *alta semita* . . . inside the *porta Collina*' (Platner and Ashby [1929] 575). On this street was a temple of Febris (Val. Max. ii. 5. 6), an altar of Fortuna (Plut. *mor.* 323a = *fort. Rom.* 10; Plutarch refers to Τύχη Εὔελπις), and the surviving mediaeval church of S. Vitalis (*anon. descr. reg. urb.*, *PL* cxxvii, p. 358A). It is mentioned thrice at Anast. *uit. pont.* (*PL* cxxviii) 145, and in inscriptions at *CIL* vi. 9736 and perhaps also at vi. 10023. See further Platner and Ashby, loc. cit., Palmer (1974) esp. 125–9, 146–56, L. Richardson (1992) 425, and F. Coarelli in Steinby (1993–2000) v. 174–5.

ex ⟨extrema⟩ parte aedium quod satis esset loci modico sacello exclusit: the supplement is due to Fügner, *ap.* H. J. Müller (1890) 210. In the reading of the paradosis neither the meaning of *ex parte aedium* nor its connection to *exclusit* is immediately clear, and no precise parallel for it seems to be available:[1] in most of the passages with which ours is cited at *TLL* v. 2. 1269. 30–46 the verb must mean 'shut out' rather than 'separate off', which is the sense demanded here; and, where it is coupled with a part of *pars*, it usually has that part as its object. [Caes.] *Al.* 1. 4 'ut . . . hanc (*sc.* partem) . . . ab reliqua parte urbis excluderet' perhaps comes closest to our passage, but *ab reliqua parte* is much easier than our *ex parte aedium* because there is another part of *pars* to which it may relate. Foster translated, 'she shut off a part of her mansion, large enough for a shrine of moderate size', but by translating *ex parte aedium* as *partem aedium* he leaves the paradosis unexplained. Rather, if the paradosis were sound, we should have to translate 'out of part of her house she separated off what was sufficient space for a modest shrine', but it is not clear why L. should be writing of a part of a part. Fügner's conjecture, by contrast, gives excellent sense ('at the furthest end of her house she marked out [what was] enough space for a modest shrine'). For the expression compare the analogous i. 41. 4 'ex superiore parte aedium'.[2]

matrimoniis: is the reading of MP^cλ, and thus almost certainly stood in **N**; M^c has *matrimonuis*; P^1 *matrimonius*; and UZR^cD^c *matro-*

---

[1] *excludere* with *ex* and the ablative is not in itself objectionable: although it is attested only rarely in Latin (see *TLL* v. 2. 1272. 30–1, where [Quint.] *decl.* 13. 11 and Apul. *apol.* 100 are the earliest of the five other texts cited), numerous analogies can be mustered from other verbs compounded with *ex-*.

[2] Reporting Fügner's conjecture, Müller revealed that he had considered *ex parte ⟨postica⟩*; but this is not attractive.

nis (this last almost certainly a conjecture).[1] At *TLL* viii. 480. 45–481. 9 over fifty passages are collected in which *matrimonium* is said to be used, abstract for concrete, to mean 'wife' or 'husband'. Some of these are dubious: e.g. at Suet. *Gai*. 25. 1 (where Gaius has stolen for himself the wife of Piso at the time of Piso's nuptials) 'alii tradunt . . . edixisse matrimonium sibi repertum exemplo Romuli et Augusti' either sense is possible (and *matrimonium* would be well translated by 'match'). Others are somewhat ambiguous: e.g. Val. Max. vii. 2. *ext*. 1 'subsessor alieni matrimonii' (cf. ii. 1. 5 'subsessorum alienorum matrimoniorum') (where 'someone who has designs on another's wife' is the natural interpretation, but 'someone who has designs upon another's marriage' seems just possible), Plin. *nat*. xv. 136 'Liuiae Drusillae, quae postea Augusta⟨m⟩ matrimonii nomen accepit' (where editors seem to understand *matrimonii nomen* 'the name of her husband'; but the Latin is awkward and the text may be corrupt); [Quint.] *decl*. 2. 3 '. . . ut pater, cui matrimonium filiumque abstulerat incendium, residua senectutis alia consolaretur uxore' (where 'wife' is again the easiest translation but 'marriage' is possible), and Suet. *Aug*. 34. 2 'matrimoniorum crebra mutatione' (where 'with frequent changing of wives' is indeed the easiest translation, but 'with frequent changing of marriages' cannot quite be ruled out). Other passages, however, establish the usage beyond doubt: e.g. Tac. *ann*. ii. 13. 3 (on the thoughts of the Roman troops) 'matrimonia ac pecunias hostium praedae destinare', and Suet. *Iul*. 51 'ne prouincialibus quidem matrimoniis abstinuisse' (in the context of Caesar's adulterous affairs: 'marriages' is an impossible translation because Caesar contracted no provincial marriages). Doubtless the metonymical usage arose from the use of *matrimonium* in somewhat ambiguous passages such as those listed above.

Editors (e.g. W–M, Walters) have tended to emend to *matronis*; and against the reading of MP^{c}λ stands the fact that it would be the earliest attested instance of *matrimonium* used in this sense (the doubtful instances in Valerius Maximus come a full half-century later), and that L. uses *matrona* rather than *matrimonium* in §§ 3, 4, and 8. On the other hand, a usage acceptable to Tacitus and Pliny might very well have been acceptable to L., who may have sought variety in his phrasing; and it is not obvious why N should have been corrupted here. Therefore, with some hesitation, I retain the paradosis. See further Goodyear on Tac. *ann*. ii. 13. 3.

---

[1] Such an easy alteration could have been made four times independently, but the Z-witnesses could have been contaminated from a descendant of D.

7. hanc ego aram: for the position of *ego* see *addendum* to vii. 33. 17 n.

8. si quid potest: 'if in any way it is possible'; cf. Cic. *Att.* v. 13. 3 'deinde exhauri mea mandata maximeque si quid potest de illo domestico scrupulo quem non ignoras', *fam.* xvi. 19 'Demetrium redde nostrum, et aliud si quid potest boni', and (with personal *potestis* rather than impersonal *potest*) [Quint.] *decl.* 12. 11 'uos intus inplicitae, si quid potestis, admonete, animae'. Shackleton Bailey (1986: 322) conjectured *qua* for *quid*; this gives good sense but the parallels adequately defend the paradosis.

sanctius . . . castioribus: for the position of the comparatives after *quam*, see viii. 25. 12 n.

sanctitas was a wifely attribute (cf. *OLD s.u. sanctus* 4[a]), and hence *sanctus* and its cognates are found quite often in the context of *pudicitia*; cf. e.g. iii. 52. 4 'in ea urbe in qua nec pudicitia nec libertas sancta esset', Cic. *prou.* 24 'res sanctissimas, religionem et pudicitiam', *Phil.* ii. 69 'quid enim umquam domus illa uiderat nisi pudicum, quid nisi ex optimo more et sanctissima disciplina?', Val. Max. vi. 1. 6 'quam sanctam igitur in ciuitate nostra pudicitiam fuisse existimare debemus, in qua etiam institores libidinis tam seueros eius uindices euasisse animaduertimus?', viii. 15. 12 (where Valerius refers to a dedication designed to encourage *pudicitia* and to the choice of the *sanctissima femina*), Stat. *silu.* ii. 2. 144–5, Juv. 10. 298–9, Apul. *apol.* 69 'mulier sancte pudica', and 78 'feminam sanctissimam et pudicam'; note also xxxviii. 24. 10–11 and Cic. *fin.* ii. 73.

9. spectatae et quae nupta fuisset: for the combination of an adjective and relative clause with 'generic' subjunctive, see vi. 34. 11 n.

10. uolgata dein religio [a] pollutis, nec matronis solum sed omnis ordinis feminis; postremo in obliuionem uenit: *omnis ordinis feminis* presumably refers to women who were not *matronae* (being either divorced or not yet married).[1] The appearance of *matronis* in the context of *pollutae* is slightly surprising after what L. has just said about matronal rivalry in the matter of *pudicitia*, but he could mean that the cult was degraded by being opened to (amongst others) *matronae* who were ineligible (for instance, by having remarried after

---

[1] In the context of the Struggle of the Orders *omnis ordinis* may seem to be a reference to patricians; but it is unlikely that patrician women should have wished to visit this plebeian shrine. A reference to prostitutes (also possible in theory) is unnecessary, as it would needlessly senationalize the decline of the cult.

being widowed, or even after divorce). In which case one may try to translate the paradosis thus: 'the cult was then debased by those who were ceremonially impure—not only matrons but women of every station'. However, although an interpretation on these lines provides a satisfactory explanation of the presence of *matronis, uolgata* cannot easily mean 'debased'. Rather, one expects the meaning 'opened up' or 'made more widely available', which is well paralleled at xxxix. 8. 5 'initia erant quae primo paucis tradita sunt, dein uolgari coepta sunt per uiros mulieresque'. The simplest way to get this meaning is to delete *a* with Duker (thus Madvig and Ussing). Harant (1880: 68) proposed *est* for *a*, and H. J. Müller (1889a: 436) *cum* for *a* (for the construction he cited iii. 35. 6 and iv. 1. 3); these conjectures, too, are attractive (esp. Harant's), but the corruption postulated by Duker is marginally more likely (*a* might have been supplied by someone who thought that *pollutis* was in the ablative).[1] For *uolgata* see also 6. 9 n.

Strong punctuation is needed before *postremo* to bring out the three stages of the cult which L. delineates.

23. 11–13. *Aedilician activity*

This notice anticipates those in the 'annalistic' sections of L.'s later books, in which he quite often refers to the activities of first the curule and then the plebeian aediles (e.g. xxiii. 30. 16–17, xxv. 2. 6–10, xxviii. 10. 6–7, xxx. 39. 7–8, xxxiii. 25. 1–3, 42. 8–11, xxxix. 7. 8–10; also xxvii. 21. 9, xxix. 11. 12–13, xxxii. 7. 13–14 [in the last of these passages the curule aediles, unusually, are mentioned second]). These notices often refer just to the games (here mentioned only in the context of the plebeian aediles), but, in referring to prosecutions carried out by both sets of aediles, xxxviii. 35. 5–6 'et duodecim clipea aurata ab aedilibus curulibus P. Claudio Pulchro et Ser. Sulpicio Galba sunt posita ex pecunia qua frumentarios ob annonam compressam damnarunt; (§ 6) et aedilis plebi Q. Fuluius Flaccus duo signa aurata uno reo damnato—nam separatim accusauerunt— posuit; collega eius A. Caecilius neminem condemnauit'[2] is parallel to our passage.

Although there are a few references in other sources to the prosecutions and fining carried out by aediles, most of our evidence

---

[1] Müller also considered writing *et* for *a*, but this is more awkward.

[2] Since L. can hardly have imagined that the curule and plebeian aediles ever prosecuted in concert, *nam separatim accusauerunt* must refer to separate prosecutions by the two plebeian aediles. In which case the sense would perhaps be expedited if one emended *aedilis* to *aediles*; for the idiom see vi. 2. 8 n.

comes from the 'annalistic' sections of L., in which notices of this kind are reasonably common (albeit clustering in books x and xxx–xxxviii). For prosecutions by the curule aediles see 31. 9 (L. here omits to say that Fabius Gurges, who was conducting prosecutions for *stuprum*, was curule aedile, but the context makes this virtually certain), 33. 9 (a reference to *pecunia multaticia* procured by Postumius Megellus when aedile), 47. 4 (prosecution of *pecuarii*), viii. 18. 1–12 (prosecution of women on charge of poisoning: see n.), 22. 3 and Val. Max. viii. 1. *abs.* 7 (prosecution of M. Flavius on charge of *stuprum*), xxxi. 50. 2 (L. does not state the source of the *argentum multaticium* procured by the aediles), xxxv. 10. 11–12 (prosecution of *pecuarii*), 41. 9–10 (prosecution of *faeneratores*), xxxviii. 35. 5–6 (quoted above), Val. Max. vi. 1. 7 (Marcellus as curule aedile prosecutes C. Scantinius Capitolinus for trying to seduce Marcellus' own son; the same incident is told at Plut. *Marc.* 2. 5–8), Plin. *nat.* xxxiii. 19 (Flavius' prosecution of *faeneratores*), and Dio xxxix. 18 (Clodius prosecutes Milo *de ui*; cf. Cic. *Mil.* 40, *Vat.* 40–1, Ascon. 41). For prosecutions by the plebeian aediles see iii. 31. 5 (an ex-consul, on a capital charge; cf. D.H. x. 48. 3–4), xxv. 2. 9 (*matronae* prosecuted for *probrum*), xxvii. 6. 19, xxx. 39. 8, xxxiii. 25. 3 (in none of these last three passages does L. state the source of the *argentum multaticium* procured by the aediles), xxxiii. 42. 10 (prosecution of *pecuarii*; the same incident mentioned at xxxiv. 53. 4), xxxviii. 35. 6, Ov. *fast.* v. 283–94 (infringement of rules on pasturage; the same incident is reported at Fest. 276), Gell. x. 6. 1–4 (prosecution of Claudia for stating in public that she wished that her brother, P. Claudius Pulcher, could come back to life so that he could lose more of the populace in a second naval disaster; the same story is told, without mention of the aediles, at *per.* xix, Val. Max. viii. 1. *damn.* 4, Suet. *Tib.* 2. 3). For prosecutions in which L. does not state whether the aediles were curule or plebeian see 13. 14 (infringement of rules on possession of *ager publicus*), vii. 28. 9 (prosecution of *faeneratores*), xxiv. 16. 19 (a reference to *multaticia pecunia* procured as aedile by the father of Ti. Sempronius Gracchus). For other prosecutions likely to have been conducted by aediles, see vii. 16. 9 (Licinius Stolo in breach of his own agrarian law) and Val. Max. vi. 1. 8 (*stuprum*). From our passage onwards L. invariably tells us that the fines extracted by the aediles were used for public works (so also Ovid, Pliny, Plutarch, and Festus in the passages cited); and, as Briscoe notes, the phrase *aere multatic(i)o* is found on several inscriptions (e.g. *CIL* xiv. 2621). The absence of any reference to permission from the senate or people allows the inference that the aediles were able to order construction by virtue of their magisterial powers. For aedilician construction see Ziolkowski (1992) 258–60 (with reference to temples) and Trisciuoglio (1998) 134–6.

No source defines precisely either the powers of the curule and plebeian aediles as keepers of law and order in the middle and late Republic or the relationship of the two offices to each other. However, the following observations may be made: (*a*) the aediles conducted their prosecutions before either the *comitia tributa* (curule) or the *concilium plebis* (plebeian) (for the distinction between these assemblies, see vii. 16. 7–8 n. with *addendum*);[1] (*b*) except in the case of women, aediles rarely prosecute on capital charges (the case of M. Flavius is an obvious exception): the offences against which they most often took action were infringement of the rules governing usury, pasturage, and the use of the *ager publicus*; (*c*) the preponderance of references in L. to prosecution by the curule aediles (the senior of the two magistrates) suggests that in general they undertook prosecution for the more serious offences that fell within the competence of the aediles; (*d*) L., like other sources, generally refers to successful aedilician prosecutions: he and his annalistic sources were probably uninterested in most cases in which there was an acquittal (but xxxviii. 35. 6, quoted above, may be an exception); and (*e*) both curule and plebeian aediles tended to prosecute in pairs: for exceptions see 31. 9, 33. 9, viii. 18. 2–12 (in all of which L. may have suppressed the name of the less well-known aedile), xxxviii. 35. 6 (quoted above: L.'s explicit comment suggests that separate prosecutions were unusual), and Val. Max. viii. 1. *abs.* 7 (in the parallel passage to which, however, L. uses the plural *aedilibus*), and Val. Max. vi. 1. 7 and Plut. *Marc.* 2. 5–9 (on Marcellus' prosecution of his son's attempted seducer).

See further *addenda* to vi. 42. 13–14 n., Lintott (1968) 95–8, Jones (1972) 15–16 and 30, Briscoe on xxxi. 50. 2, Bauman (1974), and Garofalo (1989) esp. 86–167.

11. eodem anno: see vi. 4. 4 n.
Cn. et Q. Ogulnii: see 6. 3 n.

12. redactum est: see vii. 27. 8 n.
Iouemque in culmine cum quadrigis: in other words the Ogulnii erected a statue of Jupiter in a chariot on the ridge of the Capitoline temple; in republican Rome the chariot was the prerogative of gods

---

[1] Against the view that the people were involved in these trials only after *prouocatio*, see 9. 3–6 n.

and *triumphatores*. Mattingly (1945: 73–4) argued that the so-called *quadrigati* didrachms, on the reverse of which Jupiter is in a chariot driven by Victoria, issued by Rome *c.*225–214 (see Crawford [1974] 145–7, 715 and plates V and VI), depict this statue. If so, either Victoria has been added to the image on the coins or (more probably) L. omits to mention her presence on this sculpture.

Other literary sources make discussion of the statues on the roof of the temple of Jupiter Optimus Maximus more complicated. First, at *per.* xiv (278 BC) we read 'cum inter alia prodigia fulmine deiectum esset in Capitolio Iouis signum, caput eius per haruspices inuentum est'; the same story is told at Cic. *diu.* i. 16 and ii. 45, where, however, Cicero refers to a statue of Summanus on the roof of the temple. Since Summanus was an epithet of Jupiter in his guise as the god of lightning, his presence on the temple of Jupiter Optimus Maximus is explicable, and presumably L. or his epitomator has not given us his full name. It is easier to assume that there were two statues on the roof of the temple rather than that the statue of Jupiter in his *quadrigae* was regarded as a statue of Summanus.

Second, according to a story developed most fully at Plut. *Publ.* 13 but told or mentioned also at Plin. *nat.* viii. 161, xxviii. 16, xxxv. 157 'fictiles in fastigio templi eius quadrigas, de quibus saepe diximus', Fest. 340–2 (cf. Paul. Fest. 341), and Serv. *auct. Aen.* vii. 188, and, as Hubeaux saw, to be connected with other tales in which Rome's supremacy, especially over Veii, was prophesied, Tarquinius Superbus commissioned from Veii a terracotta chariot for the temple; the clay swelled up so much that the *quadrigae* could be extracted from the furnace only by removal of its top; and the Etruscan seers, regarding this as an omen of future empire, refused to hand over the *quadrigae*. However, at the next games at Veii the horses carrying the victorious charioteer charged to Rome and to the Capitol, where they ejected the charioteer at what was later called the Porta Ratumenna. After this omen they surrendered the *quadrigae*. Our evidence is not good enough for any sure reconcilation of this story with what L. tells us here. Pease (and others before him) argued that the Ogulnii merely added a statue of Jupiter to an existing terracotta *quadrigae*, but this is not what L., in a passage which appears to show him at his most reliable, states that they did. More plausibly, Andrén, Alföldi, and Weinstock argue that the statue of the Ogulnii replaced the earlier statue (but Alföldi was wrong to claim that the point is proved by the fact that the *quadrigae* of the Ratumenna tale was made of terracotta and the Ogulnian replacement of bronze: no source reveals the material out of which the Ogulnian *quadrigae* was made). However, since the historical credentials of an aetiological legend explaining the Porta Ratumenna and relating to events in the sixth century BC are at best dubious, rejection of the whole tale of Ratumenna must be a serious possibility.

There is an unproblematic reference to the statue at Plaut. *Trin.* 83–5. For other material placed on the temple, note L.'s references (xxxv. 10. 12 and 41. 10) to gilded shields' being put on its pediment. For a further reference to the roof of this temple see xxvii. 4. 11. Other chariots recorded as having been dedicated on the Capitol (see xxix. 38. 8, xxxv. 41. 10, xxxviii. 35. 4) need not have been placed on the roof or pediment.

For the phenomenon of statues on the roofs of temples see further xxvi. 23. 4 'in aede Concordiae Victoria, quae in culmine erat, fulmine icta' and esp. Plin. *nat.* xxxv. 158 'durant etiam nunc plerisque in locis talia (*sc.* fictilia) simulacra; fastigia quidem templorum etiam in urbe crebra et municipiis, mira caelatura et arte suique firmitate, sanctiora auro, certe innocentiora', which also illustrates how widespread were terracotta statues.

See further Pease on Cic. *diu.* i. 16, Platner and Ashby (1929) 298, Hubeaux (1950), Andrén (1960) 45, Alföldi (1965) 141 n. 5, Weinstock (1971) 54–9, Rawson (1981) 2–3 = (1991) 391, and G. Tagliamonte in Steinby (1993–2000) iii. 146.

ad ficum Ruminalem: most ancient sources place the *ficus Ruminalis* at the Lupercal or Cermalus on the lower slopes of the Palatine (see Varr. *ling.* v. 54, Ov. *fast.* ii. 411–22, Plut. *Rom.* 4. 1, *or. gent. Rom.* 20. 3–4); but Tacitus (*ann.* xiii. 58) places it in the Comitium, where Maxentius later erected statues to Mars and the twins (*CIL* vi. 33856), and Pliny (*nat.* xv. 77) states that the legendary augur Attus Navius effected a miraculous transfer of it from Lupercal to Comitium. Pliny's tale makes it a reasonable inference that the fig-tree in the Comitium was identical with the *ficus Navia* there mentioned by Festus (168, 170) in a damaged passage. The odd discrepancy in location, reflected in the story told by Pliny, may point to the twins' being honoured at both sites. The evidence does not allow us categorically to state at which site the Ogulnii erected their monument (which is almost certainly the site of the original fig-tree). Perhaps the Lupercal is marginally the more likely, since D.H. saw there a sculpture of the she-wolf and twins which he regarded as old (see next n.). In favour of the Comitium is the fact that, unlike the Palatine, it was not associated especially with the legend of the twins (and hence the location was less likely to have been invented); on the other hand, the view that the *ficus Ruminalis* was in the Comitium is not attested before *c.*65 AD. For other references to the tree, see e.g. i. 4. 5, Plut. *quaest. Rom.* 57 = *mor.* 278c–d, *fort. Rom.* 8 = *mor.* 320c, Fest. 326, 332, and perhaps Varr. *rust.* ii. 11. 5 (where the text is uncertain).

The derivation of the name Ruminalis is obscure. An ancient view that it derives from *ruma* or *rumis* (= 'teat', i.e. belonging to the she-wolf), for which see e.g. Varr. *rust.*, Plin., Plut. *Rom.* and *quaest. Rom.*, and Fest. locc. citt. and note also Non. 246 and Aug. *ciu.* iv. 11, is likely to have arisen under the influence of the Roman foundation-legend. Perhaps more probable, but still quite uncertain, is a connection with the goddess Rumina mentioned at Varr. *rust.* loc. cit. See further De Sanctis (1910) 77–85, Platner and Ashby (1929) 207–8, L. Richardson (1992) 151, F. Coarelli in Steinby (1993–2000) ii. 248–9, and Wiseman (1995a) 74–6.

simulacra infantium conditorum urbis sub uberibus lupae posuerunt: there is a well-known ambiguity in L.'s Latin: translate either 'they set up a statue of the infant founders of the city beneath the udders of the she-wolf' or, in an interpretation first expounded fully by Rayet (1884: 3), 'they placed statues of the infant founders of the city beneath the udders of the she-wolf', implying that a statue of the she-wolf was already in existence. The former translation is preferable: L.'s expression may be explained by his having the *infantes conditores* as the particular focus of his interest; and Carcopino was right to wonder whether L. would have used the verb *posuerunt* if he had meant the latter.

Since it would be unreasonable to doubt either that L.'s *infantes conditores* are Romulus and Remus or that his evidence for the creation of the Ogulnian monument was good, this passage provides our earliest attestation of the classical Roman foundation legend of Romulus, Remus, and the wolf which suckled them. Wiseman (1995a: 103–41) interestingly speculates that it was precisely in this period that several features of the legend were being developed (see further 23. 1–10, 37. 15, 46. 7 nn.).[1]

The she-wolf makes three, or perhaps four, appearances in the surviving remains of archaic Italian art: we have the famous bronze statue now kept in Rome in the Pinacoteca Capitolina in the Palazzo

---

[1] Rosenberg, *RE* iA. 1080, and Wiseman (1995a: 73–4) suggest that L.'s language may reflect that of the original inscription. This is possible but perhaps pushes the evidence too far and cannot easily be used of the rest of §§ 12–13. Wiseman additionally suggests that *infantium conditorum* may point to both twins', rather than just Romulus', being regarded as the founders of the city in 296. Yet *infantium conditorum* may simply be L.'s way of saying *Romuli et Remi* (so at Plin. *nat.* xv. 77 *conditores* varies an earlier reference to Romulus and Remus), and he may have had in mind the canonical version in which Remus too might be regarded as sharing in the foundation of the city before he was killed.

dei Conservatori, to which the figures of the twins were added in the fifteenth century (this is probably archaic and conceivably Etruscan, but when it first came to Rome there is no knowing: the *terminus ante quem* is the tenth century AD); an engraving on a Praenestine *cista* in the Ashmolean Museum, Oxford; the Praenestine mirror in the Antiquario Comunale, Rome; and perhaps a funerary stele in the Museo Civico Archeologico of Bologna (but it is disputed whether a wolf or large cat is depicted on this). These depictions allow us to conclude that the she-wolf was a reasonably familiar iconographic motif in this period, but, despite several attempts to connect her with Etruscan views of the underworld (for a summary see Holleman), they do not allow us to draw any safe conclusions about her ideological significance. Since the Praenestine mirror shows the she-wolf suckling twins, it is the most interesting of these depictions to compare with the Ogulnian monument; but Wiseman (1995*a*: 65–71) has shown that it is hard to interpret the rest of the engraving in accordance with the Roman foundation-legend. It is quite uncertain whether already in 296 BC the she-wolf was the symbol of Rome that she was later to become after the full development of the foundation-legend.[1]

Some scholars (including, recently, Dulière 54–62) equate the Capitoline and the Ogulnian she-wolves, arguing that the Ogulnii merely placed statues of Romulus and Remus beneath the Capitoline wolf. This view can be right only if the Capitoline she-wolf came to Rome before 296 and if the second, and less attractive, of the two translations considered above is correct.

Silver didrachms (for which see Crawford [1974] 137 and 714 and pl. I; a good illustration may be found also at Wiseman [1995*a*] 157), issued at some point between 269 and 266 BC, carry on their reverse a picture of the she-wolf suckling twins and plainly allude to the statue set up by the Ogulnii; since Q. Ogulnius Gallus was consul in 269, it is attractive to argue that the coins were issued in that year. Rome soon had other statues of both wolves and Romulus and Remus: xxii. 1. 11 'simulacra luporum' provides a *terminus ante quem* of 217 for at least one such statue; and we are told (Cic. *Cat.* iii. 19, *diu.* i. 19–20, ii. 45, 47, Dio xxxvii. 9. 1) that in 65 BC statues on the Capitol of the she-wolf and twins were damaged by lightning.[2] In view of these

---

[1] For the wolf as a symbol of Rome in L.'s narrative, see esp. 27. 9 (n.); note also the *denarius* issued by P. Satrienus in 77 BC, on which see Crawford (1974: 403–4 and pl. XLIX).

[2] The statue of the she-wolf damaged in 65 has sometimes been equated with the Capitoline she-wolf. This view can be correct only if the figures of Romulus and Remus were later placed under the archaic Capitoline wolf (in which case it need not be a difficulty that these figures were gilded [Cic. *Cat.* iii. 19] even though the Capitoline she-wolf is made of bronze); against

other statues, not all descriptions in classical literature of the she-wolf suckling the twins (which include i. 4. 6, Virg. *Aen.* viii. 630–4, and Ov. *fast.* ii. 413–20) necessarily reflect the Ogulnian monument. However, when D.H. (i. 79. 8) states that in his day there was a statue at the Lupercal of the she-wolf suckling the twins, χαλκᾶ ποιήματα παλαιᾶς ἐργασίας, the site of the statue and παλαιᾶς suggest that he may be referring to the monument (but see above for ancient uncertainty as to the site of the *ficus Ruminalis*).

The problems discussed in this note have generated a huge bibliography, which includes e.g. O. Rayet in Rayet (1884) i. iv. 1–8, Dieterich (1900) 204–7, Petersen (1908) and (1909), Soltau (1909) 121–4, De Sanctis (1910) esp. 71–7, Rosenberg, *RE* iA. 1080–3, Pease on Cic. *diu.* i. 20, Carcopino (1925) esp. 20–4, Dulière (1979) i. 21–64, Hollemann (1987), and Wiseman (1995*a*) 63–7; many earlier discussions are evaluated in Petersen's first article. For illustration of all four of the surviving artefacts that are mentioned in this note, see conveniently Wiseman (1995*a*) 64, 66, 68; the Capitoline she-wolf is illustrated also by Rayet, Carcopino, and Dulière, and at e.g. Cornell (1995) 61.

semitamque . . . strauerunt: this was the first section of the Via Appia (see ix. 29. 6 n.). Although the distance provided with a surface was no more than *c.*2 km, the cost will have been high. Note that as at 47. 4 (293), where the continuation of this work is recorded, L. explains how the work was financed. Resurfacing was necessary in 189, and it is interesting to note that the censors of that year provided only a surface of gravel (see xxxviii. 28. 3 [quoted at ix. 29. 6 n.]).

a Capena porta ad Martis: see vii. 23. 3 n.

strauerunt: see 47. 4, viii. 15. 8 nn.

13. L. Aelio Paeto: (99). Otherwise unknown, but probably the son of P. Aelius Paetus (viii. 15. 1 n.).

C. Fuluio Curuo: (45). Otherwise unknown, but his *cognomen* allows the possibility that he was the son of the consul of 322 (viii. 38. 1 n.) and the brother of the consul of 305 (ix. 44. 15 n.).

pecuariis: presumably these were owners of sheep or cattle who either were in possession of too much *ager publicus* (cf. 13. 14) or allowed too many from their flocks to graze on *ager publicus*. For similar prosecutions, see also 13. 14, 47. 4, xxxiii. 42. 10 (with Briscoe's note), xxxv. 10. 11–12, Ov. *fast.* v. 283–94, and Fest. 276.

---

it stands the fact that Cicero implies that both she-wolf and Romulus were severely damaged (note *uestigia* at *diu.* i. 20). It cannot be equated with the Ogulnian monument because the *ficus Ruminalis* was not on the Capitol (see above).

ludi facti: apart from [Ascon.] 217 'plebei ludi, quos exactis regibus pro libertate plebis fecerunt. an pro reconciliatione plebis post secessionem in Auentinum?', a passage of no great authority, no ancient source discusses the origin of the plebeian games. It is a reasonable conjecture that, like other plebeian institutions, they were set up to mirror and rival an institution of the patrician state, in this case the *ludi Romani*. They were administered by the plebeian aediles. This is L.'s first reference to them.[1] Its appearance in an 'annalistic' section of his work anticipates his regular practice in later books; from many examples see e.g. xxiii. 30. 17, xxv. 2. 10, xxvii. 6. 19, 21. 9, 36. 9, xxviii. 10. 7, xxix. 11. 12, 38. 8, xxx. 26. 11, and xxxi. 50. 3. The use of fines by aediles to finance expenditure at the games was probably regular but is attested explicitly only here and at Ov. *fast.* v. 277–330 (on the *Floralia*).[2]

pateraeque aureae: golden dishes were luxurious objects and hence suitable for dedication to the gods; for other such dishes in Greek and Roman temples see vi. 4. 3, *I.G.* ii². 1553–78 ('catalogus paterarum argentearum'), Cic. *diu.* i. 54 (Cicero here reports the theft of a golden dish from the temple of Heracles in Athens, but other sources for the tale refer to a golden crown), *nat.* iii. 84 (where the *paterae* may be presumed to be of gold), Plin. *nat.* xii. 94, and esp. Linders (1987). At xl. 59. 8 L. does not state of what metal the dish to which he refers was made.

ad Cereris: according to tradition the temple of Ceres, Liber, and Libera was built in 493 BC by Sp. Cassius (D.H. vi. 17. 2–3, 94. 3); it was sited at the western end of the Circus Maximus (see e.g. Vitr. iii. 3. 5). During the Struggle of the Orders the temple was very closely associated with the plebeian movement; and it was here that the property of those who had violated the sacrosanctity of the plebeian magistrates was placed (iii. 55. 7, D.H. vi. 89. 3, x. 42. 4). By 296 BC the plebeian movement had lost much of its revolutionary character, and the plebeian aedileship had largely become institutionalized as a step on the *cursus honorum* of *nobiles* and aspirants to *nobilitas*, but the use of the temple to receive a dedication from money acquired from aedilician prosecution is clearly a vestige of its old role in the Struggle of the Orders. And this vestige was to continue throughout the middle Republic (see e.g. xxvii. 6. 19, 36. 9 [where a fine may be conjectured], and xxxiii. 25. 3). On the temple see further Platner and Ashby (1929) 109–10, Le Bonniec (1958) 254–76, Briscoe on xxxiii. 25. 3, and F. Coarelli in Steinby (1993–2000) i. 260–1.

---

[1] However, games which L. at ii. 36. 1 calls *magni* are called *plebeii* at Val. Max. i. 7. 4.
[2] Perhaps add xxvii. 6. 19, where L.'s Latin is ambiguous.

24. 1–31. 15. *Sentinum*

24. 1–31. 7. *The Sentinum campaign and other foreign affairs*

GENERAL

The victory of Q. Fabius Rullianus in the battle of Sentinum, which dominates L.'s account of the events of 295, was one of the great turning-points in Rome's history, opening the way for her hegemony in peninsular Italy. The fame of the battle, which involved more troops than any previous encounter on Italian soil, spread even into the Greek world: later in the third century the Samian historian Duris would comment on its scale (*ap.* D.S. xxi. 6 = *FGrH* 76 F 56):

ὅτι ἐπὶ τοῦ πολέμου τῶν Τυρρηνῶν καὶ Γαλατῶν καὶ Σαμνιτῶν καὶ τῶν ἑτέρων συμμάχων ἀνῃρέθησαν ὑπὸ Ῥωμαίων Φαβίου ὑπατεύοντος δέκα μυριάδες, ὥς φησι Δοῦρις.[1]

Although L. does not claim that the battle was decisive,[2] by devoting so much space to it and to its preliminaries he shows that he appreciated its importance and significance.[3] This introductory note provides a general discussion and interpretation of his narrative. Its first part contains a survey of parallel narratives and sources, its second a literary analysis and interpretation of L.'s quite complex narrative, its third a discussion of the historicity of what L. and other writers say about the events of 295.

OTHER SOURCES

By far the longest surviving account of the events of this year is to be found in these chapters of L. The next longest is provided by Zonaras. His narrative for this part of the Samnite wars (which follows, without a break, his account of the campaign of C. Junius

---

[1] Cf. also the garbled recollection of Duris at Tzetz. *Lyc.* 1378 (probably derived from D.S.). Duris and other sources for Sentinum and the *deuotio* of Decius are discussed at length by Kornemann (1912: 20–30) in connection with the hypothesized pontifical *liber annalis*. For recent discussion of Duris' treatment of Sentinum, see Franco (2002), arguing that it was placed in his account of Agathocles.

[2] A reasonable position: fighting in Italy was to continue until 264 BC. For L.'s view of the significance of Sentinum see further Levene (1993) 234.

[3] Thus, rightly, Lipovsky (1981: 158–9).

Bubulcus in 311 [quoted at ix. 31. 1–32. 12 n.]) begins with this introductory comment (viii. 1. 2):

καὶ ἄλλοτε δὲ πολλάκις τοῖς Ῥωμαίοις πολεμήσαντες οἱ Σαυνῖται καὶ ἡττηθέντες οὐκ ἐφησύχασαν, ἀλλὰ καὶ συμμάχους ἄλλους τε προσλαβόμενοι καὶ Γαλάτας, ὡς καὶ πρὸς τὴν Ῥώμην αὐτὴν ἐλάσοντες ἡτοιμάζοντο. ὃ οἱ Ῥωμαῖοι μαθόντες ἐς δέος κατέστησαν . . .

Then, after his report of the prodigies of this time (quoted at 23. 1–10 n.), comes his narrative of the campaign of Sentinum (viii. 1. 5–7):

ὁ δὲ Οὐολούμνιος τοῖς Σαυνίταις πολεμεῖν ἐκελεύσθη, τοῖς δὲ Γαλάταις καὶ τοῖς ἄλλοις τοῖς μετ᾽ αὐτῶν ἀντικαταστῆναι ὕπατοι αἱρεθέντες ἐπέμφθησαν ὅ τε Ῥοῦλλος ὁ Φάβιος ὁ Μάξιμος καὶ ὁ Δέκιος ὁ Πούπλιος. οἳ πρὸς τὴν Τυρσηνίδα σπουδῇ ἀφικόμενοι, καὶ τὸ τοῦ Ἀππίου στρατόπεδον ἰδόντες διπλῷ σταυρώματι κατωχυρωμένον, τοὺς σταυροὺς ἀνέσπασάν τε καὶ διεφόρησαν, ἐν τοῖς ὅπλοις ποιεῖσθαι τὴν ἐλπίδα τῆς σωτηρίας τοὺς στρατιώτας διδάσκοντες. (§ 6) προσέβαλον οὖν τοῖς πολεμίοις· κἂν τούτῳ λύκος ἔλαφον διώκων εἰς τὸ μεταίχμιον εἰσπεσὼν αὐτὸς μὲν πρὸς τοὺς Ῥωμαίους ὁρμήσας διεξῆλθε καὶ αὐτοὺς ἐπεθάρσυνε, προσήκειν αὐτὸν νομίζοντας ἑαυτοῖς ὡς λυκαίνης θρεψαμένης τὸν Ῥωμύλον, καθάπερ ἱστόρηται· ἡ δ᾽ ἔλαφος πρὸς τοὺς ἑτέρους χωρήσασα κατεκόπη, καὶ τόν τε φόβον αὐτοῖς καὶ τὴν συντυχίαν τοῦ πάθους κατέλιπε. συμπεσόντων οὖν τῶν στρατευμάτων ὁ μὲν Μάξιμος ῥᾷον τοὺς κατ᾽ αὐτὸν ἐνίκησεν, ἡττῆτο δέ γε ὁ Δέκιος. ἐνθυμηθεὶς δὲ τὴν ἐπίδοσιν τοῦ πατρός, ἣν διὰ τὸ ἐνύπνιον ἐποιήσατο, ἑαυτὸν ὁμοίως ἐπέδωκε, μή τινι περὶ τῆς πράξεως κοινωσάμενος. (§ 7) ἄρτι δὲ ἔσφακτο καὶ οἱ συντεταγμένοι αὐτῷ τὸ μὲν ἐκείνου αἰδοῖ ὡς δι᾽ αὐτοὺς θανόντος ἐθελοντοῦ, τὸ δὲ καὶ ἐλπίδι τοῦ πάντως ἐκ τούτου κρατήσειν, τῆς τε φυγῆς ἐπέσχον καὶ τοῖς διώκουσι σφᾶς γενναίως ἀντικατέστησαν. κἂν τούτῳ καὶ ὁ Μάξιμος κατὰ νώτου τε αὐτοῖς προσέπεσε καὶ παμπόλλους ἐφόνευσεν· οἱ δὲ περιλειφθέντες ἀποδιδράσκοντες διεφθάρησαν. Μάξιμος δὲ Φάβιος τὸν μὲν τοῦ Δεκίου νεκρὸν κατέκαυσε σὺν τοῖς σκύλοις, τοῖς δὲ εἰρήνης δεηθεῖσι σπονδὰς ἐποιήσατο.

Although this account is probably independent of L., it offers nothing that is not found already in L. and at times reads like a summary of his narrative.[1]

Much more important, because it dates from the mid-second

---

[1] See Klinger (1884) 66–8. A possible exception to this conclusion is provided by Μάξιμος δὲ Φάβιος τὸν μὲν τοῦ Δεκίου νεκρὸν κατέκαυσε σὺν τοῖς σκύλοις, which does not quite correspond to what L. states at 29. 18–19. Klinger (p. 67) suggests that the discrepancy would be removed if in § 18 L. (or his source) had written not *collegae corpus* but *collegam, corpus*; but it is more likely that Zonaras has written loosely. The extent of the independence from L. of Dio (Zonaras' source) is discussed at vol. i, pp. 19–20 with *addendum*. Zonaras is quite likely to be independent of L. here because his preceding narrative and his ensuing narrative contain material not found in L.; see 23. 1–10 and 38. 1–46. 16 nn. His account of 294 poses exactly the same problem: see 32. 1–37. 16 n.

century BC, is the summary of the Sentinum campaign in the excursus which Polybius devoted to Rome's Gallic Wars (ii. 19. 5–6):

μετὰ δὲ ταῦτα πάλιν ἔτει τετάρτῳ συμφρονήσαντες ἅμα Σαυνῖται καὶ Γαλάται παρετάξαντο Ῥωμαίοις ἐν τῇ Καμερτίων χώρᾳ καὶ πολλοὺς αὐτῶν ἐν τῷ κινδύνῳ διέφθειραν. (6) ἐν ᾧ καιρῷ προσφιλονικήσαντες πρὸς τὸ γεγονὸς ἐλάττωμ᾽ αὐτοῖς Ῥωμαῖοι μετ᾽ ὀλίγας ἡμέρας ἐξῆλθον, καὶ συμβαλλόντες πᾶσι τοῖς στρατοπέδοις ἐν τῇ τῶν Σεντινατῶν χώρᾳ πρὸς τοὺς προειρημένους τοὺς μὲν πλείστους ἀπέκτειναν, τοὺς δὲ λοιποὺς ἠνάγκασαν προτραπάδην ἑκάστους εἰς τὴν οἰκείαν φυγεῖν.

Had it survived, Accius' play *Decius siue Aeneidae* would have been as important as any source: it would have revealed how the tale of Sentinum was told *c.*100 BC and taught us much about the influence of drama on historiography;[1] but the few remaining fragments (Acc. *praet.* 1–16) are of little importance for the student of L. or of the Samnite Wars.

Of the remaining sources the most important is Frontin. *strat.* ii. 5. 9, because it refers to a campaign at Falerii, which should probably be placed in this year:

Cn. Fuluius, cum in finibus nostris exercitus Faliscorum longe nostro maior castra posuisset, per suos milites quaedam procul a castris aedificia succendit, ut Falisci suos id fecisse credentes spe praedae diffunderentur.

Also independent of L. is the notice of the triumph of Fabius Rullianus in *F.T.*:

> *Q. Fabius M. f. N. n. Maximus an. CDLIIX*
> *Rullianus III, co(n)s(ul) V, de Samnitib(us)*
> *et Etrusceis, Galleis prid. non. Sept.*

The *de uiris illustribus* sometimes presents material independent of L. and refers to the events of this year in three passages: 27. 3–5 (on Decius) 'quarto consulatu cum Fabio Maximo, cum Galli, Samnites, Vmbri, Tusci contra Romanos conspirassent, ibi exercitu in aciem ducto et cornu inclinante exemplum patris imitatus aduocato Marco Liuio pontifice hastae insistens et solemnia uerba respondens se et hostes diis manibus deuouit. (§ 4) impetu in hostes facto uictoriam suis reliquit. (§ 5) corpus a collega laudatum magnifice sepultum est' (however, except for *hastae insistens* [for which cf. viii. 9. 5 (n.)],

---

[1] For the influence of drama on historiography, see *addenda*, below, pp. 478–9. For a very speculative (but not unattractive) reconstruction of it see Ribbeck (1887–92) i. 193–4; on the basis of l. 9 'fateor: sed saepe ignauauit fortem in spe exspectatio' he suggests that the two consuls disagreed on the conduct of the battle. Münzer, *RE* iv. 2284, wondered whether L. could have used the play as a source.

there is nothing here that could not derive from 28. 6–29. 20—which is not to say that it does derive from L.), 32. 1 (on Fabius) 'tertio de Gallis Vmbris Marsis atque Tuscis triumphauit' (a report of the triumph different from that in L. or *F.T.*) and 34. 4 (on Ap. Claudius) 'ne Fabius solus ad bellum mitteretur, contradixit' (which could derive from 25. 13–18). Otherwise, we have only passing references to the battle of Sentinum or to the *deuotio* of Decius in it[1] or brief accounts in later Latin writers who are unlikely to be independent of L.[2]

LITERARY ANALYSIS

24. 1–18. After opening the year (24. 1–2) by recording the entry into the consulship of Q. Fabius and P. Decius, men famous (note the emphatic final position of *clari*) both for their achievements and for the harmony of their earlier co-operation, L. springs a surprise (§ 2): the two men quarrelled over the assignment of provinces. He states that the patricians wished Fabius to be given the command in Etruria *extra sortem* but the plebeians demanded the drawing of lots. After an initial argument in the senate, the matter is referred to the people (§ 4). In the ensuing *contio* L. gives speeches in *oratio obliqua* to both consuls, first Fabius (§§ 5–7) and then, at somewhat greater length (§§ 8–17), Decius. After these speeches the episode is rounded off swiftly by Fabius' demanding that letters of Ap. Claudius from Etruria be read to the people, whereupon they promptly appoint him to the command *extra sortem*.[3]

25. 1–10. The following rush of people towards Fabius and the enthusiasm for enlistment in the war (25. 1) underline the pre-eminent qualities of Fabius as a general. In a brief section of direct speech (§§ 2–3) Fabius states that he will take only 4,000 men and 600 cavalry to Etruria: he is concerned more that all his troops shall enrich themselves than that he shall fight with a large army. To Fabius' reasoning the narrative voice assents (§ 4), stating that he set out *apto exercitu et eo plus fiduciae ac spei gerente*. On arrival at Aharna (§ 4), Fabius meets some troops of Ap. Claudius searching for wood.

---

[1] See e.g. Cic. *Tusc.* i. 89, *nat.* iii. 15, and Val. Max. v. 6. 6. Decius is usually mentioned together with his father.

[2] Frontin. *strat.* i. 8. 3, Flor. i. 12(17). 6–7, and Oros. iii. 21. 1–6. See also Ampel. 18. 6 (discussed below at p. 288 n. 2). Of these the most useful, because they may help to restore corruptions in L.'s mss (see 27. 6, 30. 5 nn.), are those of Frontinus and Orosius.

[3] The technique used here is a variation on that illustrated at vol. i, p. 127 n. 96.

He tells them to rip down their palisades: in future they will not be based in a camp, as it is more healthy for an army to be on the move (§§ 5–10). Although this episode is told also by Zonaras, his account of it is too brief to allow a comparison that reveals anything about L.'s literary techniques. However, note that in the brief exchange between Fabius and the troops of Appius, the imperious utterances of Fabius are put in *oratio recta*, those of the troops in *oratio obliqua*; this emphasizes the competence and authority of Fabius. As for Ap. Claudius, his stature as a commander, already low as a result of his unsatisfactory leadership in 296 (see above, p. 211), is diminished further by both the contrast with Fabius and the information (§ 9) that he became frightened when the palisade was demolished; he is sent back to Rome to perform his duties as praetor. Although the information which L. gives in the following pages may encourage a retrospective interpretation of 25. 1–11 in which Fabius appears over-confident, the enthusiasm of the Roman people, the confidence of Fabius in the number of troops needed, his decisive leadership at Aharna, and the approval of the narrative voice for his actions all serve as an omen for the war and point to success in it.

25. 11–26. 7. This section of L.'s narrative is the hardest to analyse, because he reports numerous discrepancies between his sources and makes it clear that the evidence which he had for the division of provinces between Fabius Rullianus and Decius Mus was extremely confused. In his main version (25. 11), L. states that Fabius himself returned to Rome, leaving Scipio at Clusium in command of the second legion. Some sources stated that he did this of his own accord, because the danger was greater than he had suspected; others held that he was summoned back by the senate; and a third group (whom by implication L. seems to have considered less reliable but whose views he none the less develops at greatest length) held that Appius had forced his return by pointing out the gravity of the war and suggesting that Fabius should be given either Decius or Volumnius as a colleague (25. 11–16).[1] However, Decius was made by some sources, probably again those of the third group, to recommend that the senate took no action until Fabius or one of his legates appeared in person (25. 17–18); and, when Fabius eventually did return, he did indeed choose Decius as his colleague (26. 1–4). Then L. adds two final notes on his sources. In the first (26. 5) he observes that some

---

[1] If at this point the author of the *de uiris illustribus* was using material independent of L., his notice at 34. 4 (quoted above) must go back to this group. It is too brief for a comparison with L. to be of much service.

sources stated that the consuls set out for Etruria with no argument over the assignment of provinces, a view which, if correct, would undermine all that he had written since 24. 1. In the second (26. 6) he observes that some sources stated that Appius had made violent accusations against Fabius, both while he was away on campaign and after his return, and that Decius had demanded that lots be drawn for the provinces.[1] Finally, he rounds off the section with a concluding remark: the sources are in harmony from the time when the consuls set off together on campaign.

The discrepancies in his sources made it difficult for L. to produce a coherent narrative. Above all, it is hard to discern whether Ap. Claudius was right to demand that a second commander and a *iustus exercitus* (25. 16) be appointed to support Fabius. L. (26. 1–3) gives Fabius a judicious reported speech in which he neither diminished nor exaggerated the danger facing Rome, implied that already he had sufficient forces at his disposal, but offered to take Decius as a colleague. And the authority and good sense of Fabius are emphasized by the deference shown towards him by Decius (25. 17–18) and the confidence shown by the people as Fabius and Decius set out for war (26. 4), which once again prefigures the ultimate Roman victory. Although L. refers explicitly to the hostility of Ap. Claudius towards Fabius only at the end of the section (26. 6), all this encourages one to read his opposition as no more than personal carping. Nevertheless, the fact remains that the consuls eventually set out with four legions (26. 14) and that, even with this force, the Romans only just had the resources to win the battle of Sentinum. Therefore, despite the lack of encouragement from the authorial voice, a reading of these chapters in which the confidence expressed by Fabius in ch. 25 is seen to be naïve, and Appius' criticism to be justified, is possible.

L. also makes it hard for his readers to decide the seriousness of the quarrel between Fabius and Decius, his narrative voice providing no clear guide through the multiplicity of variants that are reported. Although he chooses to start his account of the year by developing a version of events in which the dispute over who was to command in Etruria is given some prominence, and although he reports that other versions made the quarrel more serious and more extensive, he gives it as his personal opinion (24. 2 'reor') that it was inspired more by the Struggle of the Orders than the individuals themselves, and later, as we have seen, he emphasizes those versions in which Fabius and Decius acted in harmony (25. 17–26. 4). All this suggests that L.,

---

[1] But for difficulties in the interpretation of this passage, see 26. 6 n.

who had a tendency to romantic idealization of the great Roman leaders of the past, was uncomfortable with the idea that Fabius and Decius had quarrelled but nevertheless felt that he had to report the quarrel in order to do justice to his sources. Schönberger (1960: 224–5) is certainly right to note that, reading the episode from the perspective of Decius, its latter stages allow one to construct a picture of him as the ideal Roman noble, sublimating his own disappointment and harmonious in co-operation with his older colleague. As at 6. 3–9. 2 (n.), he is again contrasted with Ap. Claudius, whose interventions in the debate cause only disharmony. The story, as given by L., also shows Fabius forgiving Decius the affront to their friendship.

26. 7–15. At 25. 11 L. recorded that on his return to Rome Fabius Rullianus had left L. Scipio in charge of the second legion at Clusium. Now, as an interlude between the departure of the consuls for Umbria in § 6 and their arrival at 27. 1, he returns to Scipio and reports two versions of the events in which he was involved. In the first (26. 7–11) the Senones attacked the Roman camp, and, in an attempt to strengthen his position, Scipio marched his men to the top of a hill between his camp and the town of Clusium; but the hill was occupied already by the enemy, and Scipio's legion was cut to pieces. The consuls were nearby and learnt of the reverse from the sight of Gallic cavalry carrying Roman heads on their lances. In the second (26. 12) the disaster was smaller in scale, and inflicted by the Umbrians and not the Gauls. In this version the legate L. Manlius Torquatus and some *pabulatores* were surrounded and captured; but Scipio brought help from the Roman camp, the Umbrians were defeated, and the captives were freed.

Neither version is told at much length, perhaps because L. did not like describing Roman defeats, perhaps because this battle seemed insignificant when put beside the victory at Sentinum that was soon to follow. However, in §§ 14–15 L. underlines the consequences of the defeat: quite apart from the force of four legions with supporting cavalry, 1,000 Campanian cavalry, and Latin allies numbering even more than Romans which Rome had already sent to the north (the massive size of this force is brought out by the thirty-one-word *quod*-clause in which it is described), the Romans assembled two other armies under propraetors, whose movements were to affect the outcome of the ensuing battle (see 27. 5–6, 30. 1–3): Fulvius Centumalus was stationed in Faliscan territory, Postumius Megellus in the *ager Vaticanus*.

27. 1–29. 20. At 27. 1 'consules' looks back to 26. 7 'profecti ambo consules ad bellum sunt', and the narrative moves forward to the Battle of Sentinum itself, to which L. devotes this central and longest section of his account of events in 295. The consuls pitch camp in the territory of Sentinum, just four miles from their four enemies. These combine themselves in two camps (§ 2–3), the Samnites with the Gauls and the Etruscans with the Umbrians, and decide on the day on which they wish to fight: the main fighting will be left to the Samnites and the Gauls, while the Etruscans and Umbrians attack the Roman camp during the battle. L.'s style is crisp, urgent, and businesslike as he describes these preparations: he has four sentences in asyndeton, all containing past participles (*adiecti, indicta, delegata,* and *iussi*) shorn of accompanying auxiliary verbs.

However, in §§ 4–6 information procured from deserters allows the consuls, of whom Fabius is named, to order Fulvius and Postumius to attack Etruscan and Umbrian territory and hence to detach the Etruscans and (if a plausible emendation at 27. 6 is right) the Umbrians from the Gauls and Samnites. These sentences reveal the skill of Rullianus as a general and have consequences later in the campaign: L. remarks at § 11 that, if the Etruscans and Umbrians had been present at Sentinum, the Romans would have lost. With the enemy forces reduced, the consuls seize the initiative for themselves (§§ 6–7): for two days they try to provoke the enemy to battle, and then finally on the third day both sides lead out their forces. This is reflected in L.'s sentence structure: in § 6 'instare', a historic infinitive thrust to the beginning of its sentence, marks the instant response of the consuls, and introduces a series of five urgent sentences, in which with the small exception of § 6 'ut absentibus iis pugnaretur' only that running from *pauci* to *adducta* has any connection or subordination, and at that only slight. Again, the brisk action is reflected in the omission of the auxiliary after the perfect passive participles *actum* and *adducta*.

With the lines of battle drawn up L. pauses in §§ 8–9 to describe the appearance of a wolf chasing a deer: the deer is killed by the Gauls, the wolf given room by the Romans. Zonaras (viii. 1. 6) too mentions the appearance of these animals; and so long as he is not just giving a brief and bland summary of a longer narrative, Levene (1993: 235–6) may be right to suggest that the contrast between *lupo data inter ordines uia* and πρὸς τοὺς Ῥωμαίους ὁρμήσας διεξῆλθε may be due to L.'s changing what he found in his sources to make the Romans more actively pious, in allowing the wolf a free passage unmolested. After the wolf has passed through the Roman ranks an *antesignanus,* recognizing in it the emblematic animal of Rome's founder, claims the episode as a propitious omen: the killed deer foreshadows *fuga* and *caedes* coming to the Gauls, the untouched wolf victory for the Romans; and his claim is given prominence by being placed in direct speech. As so often in L., a religious theme is used to hint at which side will be victorious.[1]

For the account of the fighting itself, L.'s version may be compared with those found in Zonaras and the *de uiris illustribus*, both of which may be independent of it (see above, pp. 269–71). Although neither is sufficiently detailed for any firm conclusions to be drawn, they do suggest that, if they are indeed independent of L., he did not make any far-reaching changes to the account of the battle which he inherited from the late annalists. Note in the *de uiris illustribus* the similar description of the *deuotio* and the details that Fabius oversaw the burial of his colleague and delivered a funeral oration, in Zonaras many of the same details as in L.: the comparatively easy victory of Rullianus (which, unlike L., he describes before the *deuotio* of Decius), the difficulties of Decius, his *deuotio*, the restorative effect of the *deuotio*, the attack by Fabius on the rear of the troops facing the army of Decius, the search for the body of Decius, and the burning of the spoil. He differs from L. only in stating that Decius devoted himself without telling anyone about his action—an odd comment, not easily explained.

L. states (27. 10) that on the Roman right Fabius commanded the first and third legions against the Samnites and on the left Decius the fifth and sixth legions against the Gauls. Then he lets his account of the calm, rational, and decisive tactics employed by Fabius Rullianus frame his account of the frantic battle in which Decius was involved. In 28. 1 we are told that the battle was evenly matched, although it went differently on the two wings. In measured sentences Fabius (§§ 2–5) is described as conserving the strength of his troops until later in the day, believing that neither Samnites nor Gauls were able to fight with full vigour late in a battle. L.'s readers, doubtless

---

[1] In Roman thought an omen had to be claimed to be efficacious: see ix. 14. 8 n. Bayet (1962) offers a different interpretation. In his view the appearance of the wolf was a bad omen, which was compounded by the failure of the troops to kill the animal (for wolves which violated domestic space being regarded as omens he cites iii. 29. 9, xxxiii. 26. 9, xli. 9. 6, Obs. 27 [where the wolf escapes] and 49 [where the wolf is killed]). With the utterance reported by L. the *signifer* attempted to neutralize this omen, but he was not entirely successful, since the Romans still needed a *deuotio* and a vow to gain divine favour and win the battle. By contrast, the killing of the deer (an animal sacred in Gallic religion) by the Gauls may have been part of a propitiatory ritual. That this was the meaning of the tale in L.'s ultimate sources is just conceivable but unlikely; that L. himself viewed it in this way is very unlikely.

familar with the ethnographic τόπος that Celtic bodies wilted with prolonged exertion, have already met several battles in which Roman strength has outlasted that of the Gauls and Samnites; they may assent to Fabius' views and await the outcome. Formally the *oratio obliqua* in §§ 3–4 gives the reasons why Fabius was persuaded (*persuasum erat*) to adopt these tactics; but it may be read also as his explanation to, and encouragement of, his troops, to which § 4 'primaque eorum proelia plus quam uirorum, postrema minus quam feminarum esse' makes a ringing peroration.

With § 6 'ferocior Decius' the focus shifts to the other consul, and the adjective sets the tone for what follows. Those in L. who are *feroces* tend to act violently and impulsively, often with danger to themselves (vi. 23. 3 n.). The tactics of Decius contrast with those of Fabius, in that he begins the battle with all his might (note however the worryingly negative connotations of § 6 'effudit', used to describe this outpouring of force). Because the fighting among the infantry is indecisive, he turns to his cavalry (§ 6); and his exhortation to them in § 7 balances that given earlier by Fabius. In § 8 the trenchant four-word sentence 'bis auertere Gallicum equitatum' marks the high point of their success, but disaster follows, as the cavalry charge too far from their own forces and, fighting among the Gallic infantry, are driven back in panic-stricken flight by the sudden and unexpected appearance of Gallic chariots (§§ 8–10). In § 8 the cavalry come first in the sentence, and their over-long charge is reflected in the two participial cola that qualify them: they are left waiting as object of the sentence for something to happen to them. The turning-point at which the chariots appear is marked by the delayed subject *nouum pugnae genus*, with the separation of *nouum* from *genus* by hyperbaton emphasizing the surprise. *essedis carrisque* at the beginning of the next sentence swiftly explains the surprise, and another hyperbaton, *insolitos . . . equos*, underlines the inability of the Roman horse to cope with it. In § 10 the dramatic turn of events is emphasized by two short sentences with verbs (*dissipat, sternit*) juxtaposed[1] and in the historic present, by the complete lack of subordination, and by the ending of the second sentence with the delayed subject *improuida fuga*. Then § 11 'turbata', another verb put in the dramatic initial position, reflects a new stage in the downwards turn of the fortunes of the Romans: the flight of the cavalry is now affecting the solidity of their line of infantry.

Decius has to act. At first he exhorts his men, and the urgency of the situation is brought out by the three historic infinitives *uociferari*,

---

[1] For this technique see vol. ii, p. 121 n. 4.

obsistere, and *reuocare*, of which the first two are pushed forward to the beginning of their sentences. Then in §§ 12–13 a small periodic sentence leads up to a climactic utterance in direct speech: Decius proclaims that, like his father, he will devote himself. This brings the theme of the comparison of Decius to his father, latent throughout the book but occasionally made explicit (see 7. 3 n.), to its climax. In his account of the battle of the Veseris L. had foreshadowed the *deuotio* of the elder Decius (see viii. 6. 9–13); here, despite some similarities between the two battles (like his father, Decius is on the left wing [viii. 9. 2, x. 27. 10]; at first both battles are fought *aequis uiribus* [viii. 9. 3, x. 27. 11] but then begin to turn against the Romans; both battles are finally won through a combination of the *deuotio* of a Decius and the tactical skill of his fellow consul),[1] that of his son comes as a complete surprise. In two sentences Decius will be dead. The first (§ 14), which is unelaborate, describes his request to the pontiff M. Livius to say the words of devotion. The second (§§ 15–18), a period of splendid sweep and power, takes us through the extra words Decius adds to the prayer of devotion uttered by his father to a climax in a double main clause in which he charges into the enemy ranks and is killed.

Since in his account of the Veseris L. had already described the ritual of *deuotio* at great length and had included (viii. 9. 6–8) a long version of the prayer uttered by the elder Decius, it would have been otiose here to repeat the description. However, the extra words uttered by the younger Decius are significant. *Inter alia* he states that *fuga* and *caedes* will be with the enemy, thus picking up the theme of the omen of the wolf and the deer. The detail at *uir. ill.* 27. 3, that Decius stood on a spear as he uttered his prayer, conceivably suggests that some late annalistic sources had a fuller description of the ritual, which L. has abbreviated.

At 29. 1, the words 'uix humanae inde opis uideri pugna potuit' mark the turning-point of the episode, *uix humanae* emphasizing the divine assistance brought by the *deuotio*. With a series of six urgent historic infinitives L. contrasts the reaction of the two sides to the death of Decius, the contrast being pointed by § 1 'Romani' and § 2 'Galli'. Paradoxically (for one would have expected the death of a commander to produce a different reaction) the Romans regroup and

---

[1] For these similarities see Klinger (1884) 39–40; he notes too that on both occasions the body of the devoted Decius can be found only on the day after the battle (viii. 10. 10, x. 29. 19). Klinger suggests that these similarities occur because on both occasions L. was using the same source (Valerius Antias in his opinion); but we should not underestimate L.'s own desire to recall his narrative in book viii.

renew the battle; and in § 1 their renewed intent is marked by the hyperbaton *nouam . . . pugnam.* The Gauls, however, behave as though out of their minds, pointlessly hurling their javelins at the body of the dead consul; the futility of this is underlined by another hyperbaton, *uana . . . tela.* While Livius, appointed propraetor by Decius and entrusted with his lictors, urges on his men and explains to them how the *deuotio* is working (the language of § 4 recalling 28. 16), reinforcements arrive from the other Roman wing (note the emphatic *superueniunt* in § 5, marking their arrival). And the bizarre behaviour of the Gauls continues: when the Romans pick up javelins and hurl them at their *testudo,* they collapse in their formation, even though their bodies are unharmed (§§ 6–7). As Livius had said, the efficacy of Decius' vow that they should be called to the dead with him is seen by their deaths around his body: note the huge heap of corpses under which he is covered (29. 19). § 7 'haec in sinistro cornu Romanorum fortuna uariauerat' rounds off the description of the fighting in which the army of Decius was involved.

Schönberger (1960: 224) plausibly reads L.'s whole account of Decius' actions at Sentinum in the context of his disappointment at the beginning of the year at not being offered by the people the command against the enemy forces. L. portrays him (by implication) as wanting to show that the plebeians could do as well as the patricians (note the spirit of rivalry in his remarks at 28. 7) and as a Roman who was valiant and noble rather than just foolhardy and impetuous. Such an interpretation would explain some oddities in the account. After L.'s emphasis on the co-operative planning of the consuls before the battle (27. 5–6), the different tactics that they adopt may seem surprising. However, had L. made reference to a joint plan, then Decius would seem more rash in adopting tactics different from those of Fabius; as it is, he appears brave. Likewise, L. rather implausibly highlights the novelty of the Gallic attack with chariots (28. 9 n.), but by doing so he makes the cavalry charge of Decius seem less foolish. Hence also the swift and unannounced move to the *deuotio* and the sudden appearance of M. Livius at the side of Decius. Decius is shown to be ready for the final sacrifice if disaster strikes but not reliant upon it; he tries first to win the battle through bravery.[1] The way in which L. has shaped his account invites his readers to contrast the actions of Fabius and Decius; but he has written in such a way that the fault of Decius is not emphasized. And

---

[1] However, Chaplin (2000: 113), contrasting the behaviour of Fabius and Decius, suggests that, read beside the account of the planned *deuotio* at the Veseris, the unannounced *deuotio* at Sentinum points to the rashness of Decius.

this view is confirmed for us by the voices of the troops themselves at the triumph of Fabius (30. 9).

At 29. 8 L. returns to Fabius Rullianus, 'Fabius . . . cunctando extraxerat diem' recalling 28. 2 'extrahebaturque . . . certamen', and narrating events that happened at the same time as the *deuotio* of Decius and its aftermath (see 29. 12 n.). In the *postquam*-clause of § 8 the weakening of the Samnites and the ripeness of the time for a Roman charge is brought out by the triple *nec* in *nec clamor hostium nec impetus nec tela missa eandem uim habere uisa*; and, as the *postquam*-clause leads into an ablative absolute, a final clause (including another dependent ablative absolute), and then the main clause, the period and the Roman advance unfold together. But still the caution of Fabius contrasts with the earlier impetuosity of Decius: he orders the troops to advance gradually (§ 9 'sensim')[1] and unleashes his cavalry and the full force of his troops only when he sees that the enemy can no longer resist. Roman victory is now inevitable, and in §§ 10–16 L. narrates without much dramatic elaboration the flight of the Samnites, the slaughter of the Gauls, the vow of Fabius, the capture of the Samnite camp, and the death of Gellius Egnatius. The episode is then rounded off (§§ 17–20) with reports of casualties and enemy captured (25,000 enemy, 7,000 of the army of Decius, 1,700 of the army of Fabius; 8,000 enemy captured) and the burial of Decius.

30. 1–31. 7. Chapter 30 falls into four parts: in the first (§§ 1–2) L. returns to the fighting in Etruria and briefly reports the successes there of Cn. Fulvius, who ravages Etruscan territory and defeats Clusium and Perusia in battle. In the second (§ 3) L. tells us, again very briefly, that 5,000 Samnites returning in flight to their own country were assailed and defeated by the Paeligni as they passed through their land. In the third (§§ 4–7) he discusses variants in his sources: some had greatly inflated the size of the enemy army, had held that the Etruscans and Umbrians had fought in the battle, and had made the proconsul Volumnius and his army present alongside the consuls. Even though L. prefers the view of the majority of his sources, that Volumnius won a victory in Samnium at the Mons Tifernus, his reporting of these opinions that differed from his own serves further to emphasize the significance of Sentinum, something that is underlined by his initial remark (§ 4) 'magna eius diei, quo in Sentinati agro bellatum, fama est etiam uero stanti'. Throughout this section L. adopts the low-key style that he normally employs for such

---

[1] An adverb that L. has used once before to characterize Fabius in these later days of his career: see 24. 6 n.

discussion. In the fourth part of the chapter (§§ 8–10), which provides further rounding-off of the story, L. describes the return to
Rome of Fabius and the pageant that surrounded his triumph. His
reference to the opinion of the onlookers, that Decius had equalled
the glory of his father, is his final comment in book x on a man whose
career had been dominated by the shadow of his father; and his
remark (§ 10) that the rewards given to the troops from the booty of
Sentinum were *illa tempestate . . . haudquaquam spernenda* again
underlines the significance of the Roman victory.

After all this L.'s remark at 31. 1 that fighting still (*adhuc*) continued in Samnium and in Etruria comes as a surprise. L. describes
it briefly: after Samnites had raided both the region of Vescia and
Formiae and that of Aesernia and the valley of the Volturno, Ap.
Claudius was sent to Samnium with the army of Decius (§ 3); Appius
and Volumnius each pursue a part of the Samnite forces (§ 4); and,
after both Samnite and Roman forces are united (§ 5), the Romans
win a victory near the *ager Stellas* (§ 6). 16,300 Samnites are killed,
2,700 Romans, and a further 2,700 Samnites are captured (§ 7). In
Etruria the Perusini had again rebelled, and Fabius returned there
(§ 3), killing 4,000 of them and capturing 1,740. L. describes all this
briefly, placing his notice of the campaign of Fabius in between his
account of the fighting in Samnium.

For further discussion of the literary qualities of these chapters,
see esp. Schönberger (1960); also Lipovsky (1981) 157–63, Levene
(1993) 232–6, and Feldherr (1998) 85–92.

HISTORICAL DISCUSSION

The military situation confronting Rome. When the great year of
reckoning dawned, Rome was under pressure on two fronts—more
acutely in the north, where in the previous year Ap. Claudius (perhaps with the help of his fellow consul, L. Volumnius Flamma) had
only just managed to keep at bay the coalition of Etruscans, Gauls,
Umbrians, and Samnites, but also on the borders of Samnium and in
Campania, which had been raided by the Samnites in the previous
year (see 16. 1–21. 15 n.). L. (21. 11–15, 22. 9, 25. 4–9) seems to imply
that, until relieved by the new consul Fabius Rullianus, Ap. Claudius
stayed in the north with his army, which would mean that he spent the
winter of 296/5 away from Rome.[1] This is not implausible, since it

---

[1] But since we do not know at what time of year the consular year 295 began, this cannot be
stated for certain. For an alternative possibility, that in the winter of 296/5 L. Scipio was left in
charge of the Roman army in the north after Appius had returned to Rome, see below, p. 287.

would hardly be surprising if Rome had kept an army in the field to watch over her northern interests. These might well have included an alliance with the Umbrian town Camerinum: although most of the Umbrians were hostile to Rome,[1] Camerinum is said to have made an alliance with her in 310/9 (see ix. 36. 7 n.), which perhaps continued unbroken. Roman concern for the protection of Camerinum would explain the defeat which almost certainly occurred in her territory (see 26. 7–13, discussed below).[2] Although it is possible that some colonists had already arrived at Minturnae and Sinuessa, there is no evidence that a Roman army wintered on the borders of Samnium; but, if the Samnites could raid Campania in 296 when many of their troops were with Gellius Egnatius in the north, they could do so again in 295; and it must have been obvious at the beginning of the year that an army would be needed in Samnium.

Deferring discussion of the confusion in L.'s sources over the assignment of the northern command, we need note only that both the consuls marched to the north, and that Samnium was entrusted to L. Volumnius Flamma, whose command had been prorogued and who was now proconsul (22. 9, 30. 6). Since in this year the threat to Rome was so grave, there is no reason to doubt L.'s reports of other commanders being needed: Cn. Fulvius Centumalus and L. Postumius Megellus, both consulars, were given propraetorian commands as *priuati*,[3] and after Sentinum Ap. Claudius (who had become praetor straight after his consulship) had to take the army of Decius to the borders of Samnium (31. 1–7, discussed below).

L. states (26. 14, 27. 10–11) that each consul commanded two legions and that Volumnius had two legions with him in Samnium. If these legions were at their full strength of 4,200 men (see viii. 8. 3–14 n.), then they alone account for 25,200 men. And if Fulvius Centumalus and Postumius Megellus each had a legion (and it is not easy to see that they would have commanded a much smaller force), then the total rises to a staggering 33,600. Even if these legions were at only three-quarters or two-thirds strength, the total remains huge. Four of these legions (that is a notional 16,800 men) were with the consuls at Sentinum;[4] and, if L. was correct to state that the Latin

---

[1] Beloch (1926: 443) denied that the Umbrians were at war with Rome; but the cumulative weight of our sources for both 296 and 295 makes this position difficult to maintain.

[2] For the possibility of a Roman alliance with Camerinum in this year, see De Sanctis (1907–64) ii. 355–6 and Salmon (1967) 265.

[3] L. Cornelius Scipio Barbatus and M. Livius Denter are also recorded as acting as pro-praetors, but only in command of troops in the absence of a consul. For the propraetorian commands of this year see 25. 11, 26. 15, and 29. 3 nn.

[4] That all Rome's forces were at Sentinum (Humm [2001] 88) seems unlikely.

and allied force at Sentinum was as large as the Roman, then their army could have been as large as 33,600 infantry. Whatever one may think about these totals (which take no account of Rome's cavalry),[1] this must have been by far the largest force that Rome had ever assembled, a notable testimony to the scale of the war and to the militarism of Roman society.[2] Although the figure of 8,700 which L. gives for Roman and allied casualties at Sentinum is perhaps not very likely to go back to reliable testimony, it is at least plausible. As for the enemy numbers, L. emphasizes the great size of their forces (21. 12, 27. 2) but prefers not to give a precise figure; he does mention one figure at 30. 5 (n.), but then swiftly rejects it as an exaggeration; and textual corruption does not even allow us to be sure what this figure is.

Preliminaries to the campaign: the division of provinces. If the sources which L. mentions at 26. 5 were correct in holding that the consuls marched to the north without dispute over the division of provinces, then it follows that the narratives of all the other versions which L. mentions are likely to have been invented; and several arguments suggest that the sources mentioned at 26. 5 were correct: (*a*) the version of the tale in which Fabius and Decius went to war without any political haggling is the simplest and looks the most primitive; (*b*) if an account of a great political dispute was available to those annalists whose views are reported at 26. 5, it is surprising that they did not make use of it; (*c*) the Struggle of the Orders was a subject that attracted annalistic elaboration; (*d*) Appii Claudii are given a role in many of the most obviously invented scenes in annalistic accounts of the Struggle of the Orders; (*e*) the return of Fabius to Rome after he had set off for the war looks very dubious (see below); (*f*) Zonaras states that both consuls set out for the north, where they met the army of Ap. Claudius and ordered the dismantling of the double palisade with which it had surrounded itself.

If it is correct to argue that the political disputes which L. recounts, or to which he alludes, are the product of annalistic invention, it remains to attempt an explanation of the growth of the story.[3] An obvious approach is to conjecture that an annalist, mindful of the fact that Fabius was a patrician and Decius a plebeian, decided that his narrative would be enhanced if he inserted a dispute in the

---

[1] Bruno (1906: 37 n. 2) held that the Romans could not have put so many troops in the field.
[2] For the significance (and difficulties) of the fact that in this year the legions were numbered, see above 18. 3–4 n.
[3] My analysis here complements that at vol. i, pp. 79–80.

Struggle of the Orders into his account of the year of Sentinum.[1] Once invented, the tale offered good scope for elaboration, and particularly for a historian willing to make use of the idea that Fabius Rullianus returned to Rome. At least one annalist made Ap. Claudius responsible for the recall of Rullianus and offered an elaborate account of a dissension between the two men (25. 13, 26. 6); and, on a reasonable interpretation of 26. 6, this account also included the demand by Decius that lots should be cast for the province. Another annalist preferred to make Decius altruistically tell the senate that they should await the return of Rullianus before making any decisions; it is unclear whether this annalist recounted the initial dispute between Fabius and Decius of which L. tells at 24. 1–18.

These arguments are not certain, and it is possible to defend L.'s main narrative: the annalists to whom he refers at 26. 5 may have mistakenly or deliberately omitted the political disputes, either because they were embarrassed by them, or because they did not have space for them, or because they did not know of them;[2] and the narrative of Zonaras is so short that little weight should be placed on it. However, what we know of the practices of the later annalists makes this second approach to the sources rather less attractive than that outlined in the previous paragraph.[3]

Some of L.'s sources (30. 6–7) stated that the proconsul Volumnius was present at Sentinum alongside the two consuls; but as these seem to be the same writers who magnified the size of the Samnite army and who doubtless wished to magnify the size of the opposing Roman army, L. was probably correct to reject their view.[4]

Fabius Rullianus and the army of Ap. Claudius Caecus. There is no particular reason to doubt L.'s statement (25. 4) that the army of Ap. Claudius wintered near Aharna, but the historicity of the tale of the dismantling of the double palisade, found also at Zon. viii. 1. 5, is much more doubtful. Although it is not dependent on those annalistic narratives which recorded a quarrel between Fabius and Decius

---

[1] Whether the dubious return of Rullianus to Rome was already a part of the story, whether this putative annalist placed part of the dispute before Rullianus set out for Etruria, and part afterwards, or whether the dispute was later extended to include, and perhaps to explain, the return of Rullianus, are matters that require even freer conjecture.

[2] One must allow that some of the material added to the common stock by the later annalists may have been genuine.

[3] For this conclusion see also e.g. Bruno (1906) 33–5.

[4] See also Forsythe (1999) 55–6. For a different analysis of L.'s use of his sources here, see Klinger (1884) 33–8; his attempt to find similarities between the Cremera campaign and the defeat of Scipio is not convincing.

and a return to Rome by Fabius (we have seen that Zonaras records that both consuls met the army of Appius), and although it cannot finally be disproved, the idea that the Claudii were not suited for war is a common motif in annalistic narrative (see vol. iii, p. 359), and disputes between Fabius Rullianus and Ap. Claudius are a regular theme of this book, a theme which may owe more to annalistic elaboration than to the realities of politics in the years around 300 BC.

The return of Fabius Rullianus to Rome. L.'s statement at 25. 11 that Fabius Rullianus returned to Rome is one of the oddest features of his narrative of Sentinum.[1] It is possible that in the early months of 295 Fabius and other Romans believed that one consul and one consular army would suffice for the war in Etruria and Umbria, and that when Fabius found out that this view was mistaken he returned to collect more troops; and the fact that the annalists were uncertain of the correct explanation for his return (see 25. 11–18, summarized above) is not necessarily a reason for disbelieving it. However, we have seen already that it would be surprising if the Romans, after experiencing the coalition ranged against them in 296, had not realized the gravity of the war confronting them in 295; and just as the testimony of the unnamed annalists mentioned at 26. 5 casts much doubt on the political disputes alleged for this year, so also it casts much doubt on this abortive mission of Rullianus to the north. In the earliest version of the story there may have been just one departure from Rome, made by both consuls.

The defeat at Camerinum. The alleged return of Fabius may be connected in some way with the battle at either Clusium or Camerinum in which some of L.'s sources stated that the Romans were defeated. Polybius too (ii. 19. 5) records a reverse suffered by the Romans before their victory at Sentinum ἐν τῇ Καμερτίων χώρᾳ. He says that it was inflicted by a combined army of Samnites and Gauls; but, since his account is very summary, and since his main purpose in referring to the events of this year is to describe the Roman victory over the Samnites and Gauls at Sentinum, his reference to the Samnites may well be a mistake.

That this battle took place should not be doubted; the annalistic tradition was not wont to manufacture Roman defeats, and L.'s testimony receives decisive support from Polybius. However, it is not now possible to establish for certain whether it involved the

---

[1] Sometimes commanders return to Rome *auspiciorum repetendorum causa* (viii. 30. 2 n.); here L. makes no mention of such a reason.

Gauls or the Umbrians. Each of L.'s versions carries the hall-marks of annalistic elaboration: in the first the motif of no messenger surviving from the defeated army is a standard τόπος of a battle-scene, and the graphic picture of the Gauls carrying Roman heads on their horses may be no more than an ethnographic commonplace (see 26. 10 and 11 nn.); in the second we find a Roman reverse minimized and a Roman victory offered in compensation.[1] L.'s own reason for preferring the version in which the Gauls were involved and the Romans were defeated is hardly convincing (26. 13 'similius uero est a Gallo hoste quam Vmbro eam cladem acceptam, quod cum saepe alias tum eo anno Gallici tumultus praecipuus terror ciuitatem tenuit'), but his phrasing seems to imply that he found it in more of his sources, and the corroborating testimony of Polybius strongly suggests that he was right. Although Polybius, like L., probably depends on Roman sources, they were sources earlier than all those used by L. except Fabius Pictor.[2] It is possible, however, to go some way towards reconciling the two versions by suggesting that a combined army of Umbrians and Gauls attacked the Romans;[3] and this reconciliation could be made to square with either a reverse for Rome (L.'s first version) or a temporary reverse followed by a victory (L.'s second version).

L. reports that this defeat took place at Clusium; and his own testimony, perhaps supported by that of Frontinus (see below), shows that there was fighting at Clusium in 295. However, his statement that Clusium was known once as Camars (25. 11 'quod Camars olim appellabant') causes difficulty, since *Camers* (from which it is hard to distinguish *Camars*) is the adjective corresponding to the Umbrian town of Camerinum (ix. 36. 7 [n.]). Because of this, and because the battle of Sentinum probably took place in Umbria, and much closer to Camerinum than to Clusium, most scholars believe that L. is mistaken and was persuaded by (an) aberrant source(s) to transfer to Clusium a battle which in fact took place near Camerinum. The statement at 25. 11 may be explained as an attempt to account for references in other sources to *Camertes* (*uel. sim.*), such as that found in Polybius, and it is preferable to follow those scholars who place the battle at Camerinum.[4]

---

[1] For such practices in annalistic narrative, see vol. i, pp. 96–7.

[2] Whose work may perhaps have been consulted by both Polybius and L.

[3] Tentatively suggested by Harris (1971: 70).

[4] Thus e.g. Niebuhr (1837–44) iii. 377 n. 637, Luterbacher ad loc. (textual appendix), Bruno (1906) 35, De Sanctis (1907–64) ii. 355 n. 2, and Harris (1971) 70. Against this view see e.g. W–M, Werner (1963: 88–9), Pfiffig (1968: 328–9), and Firpo (2002). Werner objected on the inadequate grounds that Rullianus' province was Etruria not Umbria (but at this date a

If an important reason for Rome's keeping an army in the field in the winter of 296/5 was to protect Camerinum, then it is perhaps conceivable that the battle took place at the beginning of the year, and that Scipio had been given his propraetorian *imperium* to take charge of the camp after Ap. Claudius had returned to Rome. In which case L. may be right to place the battle before the arrival of the double consular army.[1] That this interpretation does not square with L.'s main version of events, in which Rullianus goes to Etruria and then puts Scipio in charge of the camp when he returns to Rome, need not be a difficulty: we have seen that this version involves many difficulties of its own.

However, another interpretation of the evidence has considerable attractions. It is tempting to reject the possibility that the defeat of the second legion under Scipio happened right at the beginning of the year and to suggest that Fabius Rullianus was in some way implicated in this disaster. That he should be absent in Rome at a time when a force of Gauls was threatening his army seems so improbable that one wonders whether the return to Rome was not invented by an annalist so that the victor at Sentinum might be exculpated, and whether this exculpation has not contributed to the confusion in the sources which L. records at 26. 7–13. In the words of Harris (1971: 71), 'the extensive confusion was what happened when a personage whose career was glorified in the account of at least one important annalist was responsible for a major defeat of a Roman army'.[2]

Whatever solution one adopts to these problems, it is most unlikely that Scipio Barbatus was killed in this engagement (as 26. 9–11 imply), since he reappears in L.'s narrative at 29. 5 (Sentinum), 40. 7, and 41. 9–14 (Aquilonia).

province did not have so precise a geographical definition) and that, if the battle had taken place at Camerinum, Polybius would have written Καμερίνων and not Καμερτίων (which seems improbable given the evidence for *Camers* or *Camars* used of Camerinum). Pfiffig, taking the details of L.'s account rather too literally, states that near Clusium there is no hill of the kind to which L. refers; he argues that the battle took place near Asisium, emending Frontin. *strat.* i. 8. 3 (which derives from L. but the mss of which refer to *icium* [emended to *Clusium* by Modius]) to reflect this view. Firpo challenges conventional opinion by holding not only that this battle took place at Clusium but that the battle of Sentinum also took place in the same area, where there are traces of the toponym. However, L. is clear (27. 1 n.) that the battle took place on the far side of the Apennines, and it is difficult to believe that the site of such an important battle could have been forgotten by the first century. Against his argument that a Roman alliance with Camerinum was useless, see *addendum* to ix. 35. 1–40. 21. Against his argument that a battle in the Marche would have led more swiftly to the overrunning of the Senones, one may observe that Rome always trod carefully when dealing with the Gauls and in 295 had the added distraction of a Samnite War.

[1] For this view see e.g. Münzer, *RE* vi. 1809.

[2] See also Bruno (1906) 38, Beloch (1926) 440, Mazzarino (1966) ii. 289, and Salmon (1967) 266 n. 1.

Therefore we may conclude that those of L.'s sources which stated that Fabius and Decius set out together for the war were probably correct, although it is an open question whether the reverse at Camerinum or Clusium occurred before or after they had arrived in Umbria. And, if one is determined to believe the tale of L. and Zonaras about Fabius' forcing Appius' army to uproot its camp, one should refer it to the time when both consuls arrived in Umbria.

Fulvius Centumalus and Postumius Megellus. L.'s report that Cn. Fulvius Centumalus and L. Postumius Megellus were sent respectively to the *ager Faliscus* and the *ager Vaticanus* is entirely credible: in such a great crisis, with both consuls away in the north, forces would have been needed to guard the approach from Etruria to the city. Since no other occasion is known on which a Furius is likely to have fought against the Faliscans, Frontin. *strat.* ii. 5. 9 (quoted above) should probably be referred to this campaign.[1] L.'s account of the movement of these forces at the time of the battle of Sentinum is discussed below.

The forces allied against Rome at Sentinum. Uncertainty as to how many enemies of Rome took the field makes consideration of the battle of Sentinum itself difficult. In his main narrative L. mentions Gauls, Samnites, Etruscans, and Umbrians but states that the last two were absent; Polybius concurs with this, referring only to Gauls and Samnites. At 30. 5, however, L. states that some of his sources recorded that the enemy forces at Sentinum were of a truly colossal size (exactly how colossal is not clear because of textual corruption) and implies that these sources included the Etruscans and Umbrians.[2] So also it is recorded at 30. 8, *F.T.*, and *uir. ill.* 32. 1 that Rullianus triumphed over the Etruscans as well as over the Samnites and Gauls. At *uir. ill.* loc. cit. the Marsi too are said to have been in the field; but as they are not mentioned in any of our other sources for Sentinum, it is very unlikely that they were involved.[3]

Since Polybius was writing only a summary of the campaign of Sentinum, his failure to mention the presence of the Etruscans and Umbrians is not necessarily decisive against L.'s second version; but it is hard to believe that this version is correct. If the Etruscans and

---

[1] Thus e.g. Bruno (1906) 23 n. 1.

[2] All four nations are mentioned at Ampel. 18. 6: it is impossible to determine whether this passage is independent of L.

[3] Just conceivably the notice in *uir. ill.* may be misplaced (by the author, a source, or the ms. tradition): Rullianus may have fought the Marsi in 308 (see ix. 41. 4).

Umbrians really were present at Sentinum, the Roman historical tradition is hardly likely to have lessened the danger facing Rome by subtracting them. Therefore it is much more likely that they were absent.[1] As for the explanation which L. gives for the absence of the Etruscans and Umbrians (the story of the Clusine deserters, the request to Fulvius and Postumius to ravage Etruscan and Umbrian territory, and the subsequent decision of the consuls to seize the initiative and fight), one may wonder whether the Roman forces at Sentinum were able to stay in close enough contact with those guarding the approaches to the city for the sequence of events to have been exactly as L. records it;[2] but it is hard to produce a decisive argument for or against its authenticity. As we shall see, the same uncertainty affects most of the details of the campaign.

The appearance of the Etruscans in the notices of the triumph of Rullianus in L., *F.T.*, and *uir. ill.* constitutes a more serious difficulty. Since L. tells us that after his triumph Rullianus returned to Etruria and defeated the Perusini (x. 31. 1–3), he may have misplaced his notice of Fabius' return to Rome and triumph, which one would have expected to come after, rather than before, the defeat of Perusia. But since L.'s triumphal notices are found customarily at the end of the year's campaigning, and since here the break with this practice is obvious and pointed, it would be a little surprising if he were wrong. Therefore it may be better to argue that the triumphal notice took account of some fighting, unreported by L., that occurred on the way to, or back from, Sentinum. Alternatively, one may wonder whether the victory of Fulvius, who could perhaps be regarded as having fought under the consul's auspices, was not incorporated in this notice.[3]

The omens. That the omen of the wolf and the deer really occurred is perhaps not very likely (one would have expected both creatures to stay well clear of the forces massed at Sentinum);[4] but the fact that Sentinum could generate stories of this kind is further witness to the magnitude of the struggle.

---

[1] Thus e.g. Bruno (1906) 40–1 and Harris (1971) 72; *contra* Firpo (2002) 97–8, arguing implausibly that L.'s narrative is influenced by the feeble performance of some of the Umbrians in the Social War.

[2] See Adcock (1928) 612.

[3] For the view that L. has wrongly placed the triumph of Fabius before his fighting in Etruria, see Klinger (1884: 44–5). For further discussion of the campaigns of Fabius and Fulvius in Etruria, see below, pp. 292–3.

[4] But not absolutely impossible: wolves and deer are both found in the central Apennines.

The course of the battle. Apart from the vow of a temple to Jupiter Victor, which we know to have been built (29. 14 n.), it is not easy to decide how many of the details in L. and other sources are credible. Although it is generally unwise to place too much reliance on the details of a battle-scene in L.'s first decade, it is conceivable that Sentinum should be regarded as a special case. L.'s unusually detailed account of the movement of Roman troops, and his know-ledge of the names of the legates and of the numbers of the legions may suggest that here his sources drew on good evidence. Besides, Sentinum comes from a period for which L. had increasingly good information, and the fame of the battle may have led to particular attention being paid to the preservation of details of it.

On the other hand, the very fame of Sentinum could have led to the invention of the elaborate account which we find in L. Even if the legionary numbers are sound, they could simply have been used as the basis for literary embellishment (as, for example, in L.'s detail about the use to which Fabius put the *principes* of the third legion [29. 13]); and the same could be true of the names of the *legati*. Moreover, two motifs in L.'s account look especially like annalistic elaborations: that of the younger Decius' being rasher and less prudent than the older and wiser Fabius, a motif that finds various parallels in the annalistic tradition and especially in the story of the contrasting temperaments of Camillus and L. Furius (see vi. 22. 6–27. 1 n.);[1] and that of Fabius' winning the day by initial delaying, which looks very like a retrojection of the behaviour of his great-grandson Verrucosus during the Hannibalic War.[2] One should therefore be sceptical about the reliability of L.'s account of the tactics employed by the Romans in this battle.[3]

In all the ancient historians reports of casualties are unreliable, and in writers like L. who were dependent upon the Roman annalistic tradition they are particularly unreliable. By his standards, L.'s reference to 25,000 enemy killed is quite modest: it may still be inflated, but is much less so than the 100,000 recorded by Duris, a writer who rivalled the annalists in his sensationalism.

It remains to consider the *deuotio* of Decius, described by Cornell (1995: 362) as '[t]his undoubtedly historical incident', but doubted

---

[1] However, the youth of Decius should not be exaggerated. As his father died in 340, by 295 he must have been at least forty-one years old (I ignore the dictator years), and perhaps con-siderably older.

[2] See vol. i, p. 99.

[3] This is the position of Münzer, *RE* vi. 1809. For L.'s surprising view that Gallic chariots confronted Rome with a new style of fighting, see 28. 8 n.

by other scholars.[1] The evidence for this *deuotio*, and also for that of Decius' father at the Veseris and his son at Ausculum has been discussed at vol. ii, pp. 477–86. Here it may be observed only that rejection both of L.'s account of the *deuotio* as a literary elaboration and of the notion of divine intervention in human affairs (both in general and in response to Roman vows) does not add up to proof that Decius did not devote himself at Sentinum. And indications that he did devote himself are provided by the fame of the Decii in later generations (which can hardly have arisen from nothing, and certainly did not arise from the fiasco of Ausculum) and perhaps by Dio fr. 40. 43 and Zon. viii. 5. 1–3, which record preparations by Pyrrhus against a possible *deuotio* at Ausculum.[2] And it is even possible that a *deuotio* by Decius could have inspired his troops. As for the details of the *deuotio*, it is conceivable that M. Livius Denter took over the command of the forces of Decius, and just conceivable that, if Decius' father had devoted himself at the Veseris and if before the battle Decius had considered following his example, Livius was ready for the role given him by L. and *uir. ill.*; but there is no reason to believe anything else that L. says. As we have seen, in the life of Decius in *uir. ill.*, which otherwise contains material remarkably similar to that found in L., there is one detail not in him, which may show that this account is independent of his; but, if so, it does not much enhance L.'s credibility: most of the details common to both writers could easily have been invented by a late annalist or annalists.

There is no particular reason to doubt that in the aftermath of the battle fleeing Samnites were killed by the Paeligni: the territory of the Paeligni lay between Sentinum and Samnium, and the Paeligni had been allies of Rome since 304 (ix. 45. 18; and see vol. iii, pp. 345–7).[3]

Fighting in Samnium and Campania. Nor are there any compelling reasons to doubt that there was fighting in this year against the

---

[1] See e.g. Pfiffig (1968) 329–30 and, most forcefully, Beloch (1926: 440–3), who argued that the *deuotiones* alleged for the Veseris and for Sentinum were no more than retrojections of the abortive *deuotio* at Ausculum. His argument that in 295 Decius was campaigning in Samnium cannot finally be refuted but is entirely arbitrary: whether or not Decius devoted himself, his subsequent fame must rest upon his death at Sentinum on the field of battle.

[2] However, for some difficulties in accepting the evidence of Dio and Zonaras, see vol. ii, pp. 477 n. 3 and 479.

[3] Bruno (1906: 31–2) argues that this detail must be an invention, on the ground that Roman sources would have had no reason to record what happened in the territory of the Paeligni; but the fate of Samnites just defeated at Sentinum would have been of great interest to the Romans, and, as Bruno herself admits, she argues in this way because the episode is an embarrassment to her view (on which see pp. 32–4 above) that the Samnites who fought at Sentinum were really Sabines (who would have had no reason to venture into Paelignian territory).

Samnites in and around Samnium, in which the Roman forces were led by Volumnius Flamma and Ap. Claudius.[1] Although much Samnite manpower was in the north with Gellius Egnatius, some troops must have remained to guard Samnium, and after so many years of fighting on the borders of Samnium, it is hardly surprising that there were further hostilities in this year. It is a little surprising to be told at 30. 7 that, in a year in which the Romans were so hard pressed on other fronts and in which one would not have expected them to plan a campaign in Samnium, Volumnius fought successfully at the Mons Tifernus in Samnium itself. However, L.'s report at 31. 1–7 of the defeat of the two Samnite raiding parties, one plundering the area around Aesernia, the other that around Vescia, may allow a conjectural explanation for this:[2] if Volumnius defeated the first force at the Mons Tifernus, which (if rightly interpreted as the Matese [ix. 44. 6 n.]) lies very close to Aesernia, his presence in Samnium would be explained.[3] The appearance in the south of Ap. Claudius with the army of Decius may also seem surprising, but would be possible if the battle of Sentinum took place near the beginning of the year and the Samnite raid near its end.[4]

Fighting in Etruria. As noted above, L. (27. 5) records that, as part of the Roman diversionary tactics during the campaign of Sentinum, Fulvius Centumalus and Postumius Megellus were ordered to attack the Etruscans, and in particular the territory and forces of Clusium.

---

[1] This could be the campaign in which Appius *complura oppida de Samnitibus cepit* (thus his *elogium*, quoted at vol. iii, p. 352): see La Regina (1989) 397 and Massa-Pairault (2001) 99–101. Klinger (1884: 44–5) may have been correct to argue that the Samnite casualties (16,000 killed, 2,700 captured), which suggest a very large force, are exaggerated.

[2] There is no reason why the report should not be trustworthy: raiding the Volturno valley and the northern fringes of Campania was an old Samnite habit.

[3] However, this conjecture would involve replacing L.'s view (that the two parties of marauding Samnites united in the *ager Stellas*) with the suggestion that it was only the two Roman detachments which met there, and this is not economical.

[4] Bruno (1906: 42–4), followed for the most part by Beloch (1926: 442–3), argued that L. was mistaken to record a campaign in Campania for both 296 and 295. In her view the Samnites attacked Campania late in 296 when Volumnius had returned to Rome to hold the elections and were defeated only in 295 when Volumnius returned to the area as proconsul. She therefore rejects any involvement of Ap. Claudius in these events. These objections are not absurd but equally are not compelling. Salmon (1967: 268–9), sympathetic to this view, suggested that L.'s account of events in Samnium in 295 has some similarities with his account of the campaign of 305, in which a Fulvius and Postumius were consuls, just as a Fulvius and the same Postumius were proconsuls in this year; but his argument for a doublet is rather arbitrary. He also wrote (p. 269 n. 1) 'Volumnius Flamma passes the winter of 296/295 in the field (Livy 10. 27. 11); he is reported to have done precisely this in in 307/306'. But (*a*) L. gives no indication at ix. 42. 3–5 that Volumnius passed the winter of 307/6 in the field: this statement rests on a conjecture which Salmon himself had made at p. 248; (*b*) it is not an obvious inference from 27. 11 that he passed the winter of 296/5 in the field.

L. makes no mention of Postumius, who may not have been involved in any serious fighting; but at 30. 1–2 he returns to Fulvius, whose base in the territory of Falerii was less far from Etruria,[1] saying that he ravaged Etruscan territory and defeated contingents from Perusia and Clusium, killing 3,000 of the enemy and capturing twenty of their standards. There is no good reason to doubt the notices of this campaign,[2] and the reference to these two Etruscan towns makes good sense: both were quite close to each other, Clusium lying to the western side of Lake Trasimene, Perusia not a very long way from its eastern shore; and it was an attack on precisely this area of Etruria (and also Umbria, whose western borders came close to Perugia) that was likely to have been most efficacious in drawing the Etruscan and Umbrian troops away from Sentinum.[3]

As we have seen, L. also reports (31. 1, 3) that after triumphing Fabius Rullianus returned to Etruria to fight and defeat the rebellious Perusini. The reappearance of the Perusini so soon after their defeat by Fulvius has suggested to some that this notice is a doublet of that at 30. 1–2.[4] This may be the case (we have seen that it is rather surprising to have Rullianus returning to Etruria after his triumph), but in a bid to maintain her independence Perusia perhaps defied Rome on more than one occasion in this year.[5]

The most important outcome of the fighting in the year of Sentinum was that never again were the Samnites and Rome's other southern enemies able to unite with the Etruscans, Umbrians, and Gauls in the north of the peninsula. For four years the Romans fought the Samnites and Etruscans on their own territories with increasing success, and then in 290, under M'. Curius Dentatus, they overran the whole of Sabine territory, turning it into *ager Romanus* and incorporating its inhabitants into the Roman state as *ciues sine suffragio*. The result of that campaign was that an unbroken corridor of *ager Romanus* stretched from the Tyrrhenian Sea to the Adriatic. As for the Gauls, although they were to threaten often in the third century (not least at Telamon in 225 and then under the command of Hannibal and Hasdrubal), the submission of the Umbrians to Rome in the years after 295 left them exposed to Roman attacks on their

---

[1] Pointed out by e.g. Münzer, *RE* xxii. 936.

[2] Beloch (1926: 444) rejects this campaign as a doublet of what Fulvius achieved in his consulship of 298; once again his argument is very arbitrary.

[3] News of an attack on more distant towns would have reached Sentinum more slowly.

[4] See e.g. Münzer, *RE* vi. 1810; also Harris (1971) 74.

[5] Beloch (1926: 444) was prepared to accept this notice, but his view that it was retrojected into annalistic accounts of the consulship of Fabius in 310/9 is not compelling (see vol. iii, p. 458).

own territory. Indeed, it is conceivable that it was in the aftermath of Sentinum that for the first time they ceded territory to Rome, the land on which the Roman colony of Sena Gallica was later founded.[1]

See further Bruno (1906) 33–44, De Sanctis (1907–64) ii. 355–9, Münzer, *RE* iii. 2684, iv. 2283–4, vi. 1808–10, vii. 264, xxii. 936, Beloch (1926) 440–4, Pfiffig (1968) 327–31, Salmon (1967) 265–8, Harris (1971) 69–74, and Bradley (2000) 115–16.

24. 1. Q. inde Fabius quintum et P. Decius quartum consulatum ineunt, tribus consulatibus censuraque collegae . . . clari: for Fabius see viii. 18. 4 n., for Decius ix. 28. 8 n. Fabius had held the consulship in 322, 310/9, 308, and 297, Decius in 312, 308, and 297. 308 and 297 were therefore the two previous years in which they had shared the office; their joint censorship (for which see ix. 46. 13–14 nn.) was in 304. For the same men to be elected thrice to the consulate was a phenomenon unique in republican history: see ix. 1. 1 n. **gloria . . . rerum:** *gloria rerum gestarum* would be a more usual expression, but cf. e.g. Cic. *diu.* ii. 22 and *fam.* vii. 3. 4.

2. ne perpetua esset: see vii. 1. 7 n. with *addendum*.
ordinum magis quam ipsorum inter se certamen interuenisse reor: that two of his heroes could have quarrelled did not correspond to L.'s romantic conception of history (for which see e.g. vi. 6. 3 n.). For *reor* see viii. 40. 4 n.

3. [in] Etruriam: *in* is quite impossible here and must be excised; Zingerle (1889: 988 n. 1) suggested that the corruption derived from the spelling *hetruriam*.
extra ordinem . . . extra sortem: see vi. 30. 3 n. with *addendum*.
ad sortem re⟨m⟩ uocaret: the paradosis *reuocaret* reads very awkwardly and cannot stand, not least because L. nowhere else uses *reuocare* intransitively.[2] Listov repaired the syntax with the diplo-

---

[1] For the conquest of Umbria, see above, pp. 27–30. According to L. (*per.* xi), Sena was founded after the victorious campaign of M'. Curius in 290, according to Polybius (ii. 19. 12) during the Gallic Wars of the mid-280s. The Polybian date comes in a period when the Romans were beginning to fight the Gauls on the Adriatic coast, but involves various difficulties; see e.g. Morgan (1972), esp. 314–16. De Sanctis (1907–64: ii. 358) pointed out that, if L. is right, the land could have been confiscated in this year; alternatively, it could have been taken by M'. Curius Dentatus in 290.

[2] Perhaps xxxvii. 32. 12 'ab hac uoce, uelut signo a praetore dato, ad diripiendam urbem passim discurrunt (*sc.* the Roman troops). Aemilius primo resistere et reuocare, dicendo captas non deditas diripi urbes' may count as an exception; but the context shows that one must understand *milites* (*uel sim.*) with *reuocare*.

matically easy conjecture ⟨rem⟩ *reuocaret,* on which Conway later proposed the variant *re⟨m⟩ uocaret* (adopted by Walters). Listov's conjecture is supported by the good parallel at Cic. *II Verr.* ii. 127 'res reuocatur ad sortem'; but Conway's postulates a corruption even easier to explain and lessens the iteration found at § 4 'reuocata res ad populum' (admittedly not a very important consideration in L.). For some other instances of *rem (re)uocare ad,* cf. Cic. *Cluent.* 136 and *dom.* 15; also Val. Max. ii. 7. 8 'coactus est . . . rem ad populum deuocare'.

4. certe: after outlining a difficulty in his sources, L., as so often, uses *certe* to introduce what was generally agreed; see vii. 9. 6 n.
contione: thus ZbZt and Ricc. 485. As MT have *contionem,* PUθ have or had *contentionem,* and Zs has *contentione,* the reading of **N** is unclear (esp. as the scribe of T, and perhaps even of M, could have changed *contentionem* in his exemplar into *contionem*). The truth may have been recovered first by χ, even though its other witnesses, apart from Ricc. 485, follow M.
militares uiros: see 22. 6 n.
factis potius quam dictis fretos: for this contrast, see vii. 32. 12 n.
pauca uerba habita: for *uerba habere* add e.g. Cic. *rep.* vi. 9, Quint. xi. 1. 37, [*decl.*] 7. 3, *SHA* xxviii. 5. 3 to the passages cited by Fletcher (1964: 19); *orationem habere* (26. 1, v. 3. 1, xlii. 14. 9, xliv. 37. 13, Cic. *Mur.* 61, *off.* ii. 48 etc.) is much more common.

5–6. L. gives Fabius four points in his reported speech: (*a*) that he should be allowed to continue the work which he had begun (§ 5); (*b*) that he should not have been asked to stand for office if his services were not going to be employed properly (§ 6); (*c*) that he had mistakenly favoured the election of a rival rather than a partner (§ 6) (these two points go closely together, but *sensim exprobrat* may perhaps mark an increased vehemence in Fabius' remarks); and (*d*) finally (*postremo*) that, if the people considered him worthy of the command, they should give it to him.

5. quam arborem conseuisset, sub ea legere alium fructum indignum esse: for this proverb see Otto (1890: 35), who compares Verg. *ecl.* 1. 72 'his nos conseuimus agros!' (where, however, in contrast to our passage, the surrounding context is itself agricultural: Meliboeus complains that soldiers and barbarians will reap the land which he has sowed) and several Greek expressions, including ἀλλότριον ἀμᾷς θέρος; note esp. *Eu. Io.* 4. 37 ἐν γὰρ τούτῳ ὁ λόγος ἐστὶν ἀληθινὸς ὅτι ἄλλος ἐστὶν ὁ σπείρων καὶ ἄλλος ὁ θερίζων. He also compares passages such as *SHA* xxx. 15. 3 'ego semper apros occido, sed alter utitur pulpamento'. The reference to the Ciminian wood continues the image; but here Fabius is (figuratively) planting trees, there he is (figuratively) cutting them down.

The correct *conseuisset* is found first in P^{c2} for **N**'s *conseruisset* (*conseruisset et* P¹).

For *indignum esse*, see vii. 17. 7 n.

se aperuisse Ciminiam siluam uiamque per deuios saltus . . . fecisse: for the march of Fabius through the Ciminian wood in 310/9, see in general ix. 35. 1–40. 21 (n.), and in particular ix. 36. 1 'silua erat Ciminia magis tum inuia atque horrenda quam nuper fuere Germanici saltus, nulli ad eam diem ne mercatorum quidem adita'. Fabius emphasizes his achievement by the verbal play *uiam . . . deuios.*

Romano bello is explained rightly by W–M as the equivalent of *Romanis ad bellum* ('for wars fought by the Romans'). The expression is unusual, and I have found no precise parallel: when an adjective derived from the name of a people qualifies *bellum* it normally refers to a war fought by Rome against that people (e.g. *bellum Punicum*).

6. id aetatis: the use of this adverbial accusative expression instead of *eius aetatis* is quite common (cf. e.g. xxvii. 19. 9 'quem cum percontaretur Scipio quis et cuias et cur id aetatis in castris fuisset', Cic. *S. Rosc.* 64, *Cluent.* 141, *de or.* i. 207). *aetatis* is used in this way also after *hoc* (e.g. Plaut. *Bacch.* 343), *illud* (e.g. Cic. *Phil.* viii. 5), and *istuc* (e.g. [Caes.] *Afr.* 22. 2); and note analogous formulations such as *id temporis* (i. 50. 8). See further K–S i. 306, Landgraf on Cic. *S. Rosc.* 64, H–S 47, and esp. C. F. W. Müller (1908) 164 (to whose comprehensive list of over thirty parallel passages I have been unable to add).

nimirum aduersarium se non socium imperii legisse sensim exprobrat et inuidisse Decium concordibus collegiis tribus: 'he increased his criticism by saying that it was clear that he had chosen an opponent rather than a colleague in command and that Decius was jealous of their three harmonious shared magistracies'. *sensim exprobrat* is somewhat awkward, since it interrupts the indirect speech which begins in § 5. For this reason Walters placed it in a parenthesis, but (*a*) the absolute use of *exprobrare* is not common (in L. I have found only ix. 6. 2 'circumstabant armati hostes, exprobrantes eludentesque'), and (*b*) *exprobrare* is found quite regularly introducing an indirect statement (e.g. at ii. 29. 6 'exprobrantibus

consulibus nihilo plus sanitatis in curia quam in foro esse', xxxiii. 35.
11, xlii. 38. 5, fr. 60, Plaut. *Capt.* 591, and Tac. *ann.* iv. 29. 3; further
parallels at *TLL* v. 2. 1801. 38–52).

sensim, a word much affected by L. (for its use in military contexts,
see viii. 8. 11 n.) may be translated either 'subtly' or 'gradually'; the
second is preferable and would imply some extra vehemence at this
point in Fabius' criticism (see above). Cf. ii. 45. 11 'totis castris
undique ad consules curritur; non iam sensim, ut ante, per centuri-
onum principes postulant, sed passim omnes clamoribus agunt' and
iv. 1. 2 'mentio sensim inlata . . . eo processit deinde ut . . .'.

7. nihil ultra quam ut: see viii. 27. 11 n.
si ⟨se⟩ dignum prouincia ducerent: *se*, which expedites the sense,
was supplied by the Milan edition of 1478; for its position after *si* see
Packard (1968) iv. 643.[1]
in senatus arbitrio se fuisse et in potestate populi futurum:
note the tactful contrast between *arbitrio* (used here of the senate but
elsewhere also of people and magistrates: see Packard [1968] i.
455–6) and *potestate* (a stronger word than *arbitrio*, reflecting the
constitutional power of the people).

8. patres: by 295 there were many plebeians in the senate, and so by
patres Decius must mean 'patricians'.
aditus: see vi. 35. 3 n.

9. uirtus: see vii. 32. 14 n.
peruicerit: *peruincere* is used regularly by L. and other authors of
'gaining one's objective' (see *OLD s.u.* 2[a] and *TLL* x. 1. 1877.
17–42, esp. 21–32 and 37–8 [for the dependent *ut*-clause]). Here,
however, the prefix *per-* may have special significance: the *aditus* to
honours had been blocked by the patricians, but plebeian virtue
found a way through. For the final clause after *peruincere* see K–S ii.
216–17.
arbitria . . . Fortunae: for the notion that the lot was in the hands of
Fortune, cf. viii. 16. 5 'et ne forte casu erraretur, petitum ab consulibus ut extra sortem Corui ea prouincia esset'; for the expression
arbitrium Fortunae ('the whim [or 'choice' or 'decision'] of Fortune'),

---

[1] Koch (1861: 7) further objected to the paradosis that Fabius was no longer concerned
about whether he should have Etruria *extra sortem* (the wish of the patricians in § 3) but rather
was reckoning that the people would appoint; he therefore proposed *qua se dignum prouincia
ducerent*; but (*a*) *prouincia* picks up *prouinciam* in § 3, and (*b*) §§ 5–6 make clear that Fabius
wanted the command in Etruria.

cf. xlii. 30. 6 and Sen. *dial.* vi. 10. 6 (both cited at *TLL* vi. 1189. 27–8).

paucorum: see vi. 14. 12 n.

10. omnes ante se consules sortitos prouincias esse: see *addendum* to vi. 30. 3 n.

11. ita eum de se deque re publica meritum esse ut . . .: for the sentiment cf. esp. Cic. *dom.* 7 'P. Lentulus consul optime de me ac re publica meritus'; for the coupling of *ita* with *meritus* see Cic. *dom.* 42, *Pis.* 75, and *Phil.* ix. 17 'cum Ser. Sulpicius . . . ita de re publica meritus sit, ut . . .' (in the first two passages there is no following consecutive clause). *de re publica meritus* is a common expression, esp. in Cicero; cf. iv. 32. 7, xxvi. 33. 7, Cic. *Flacc.* 81, *red. sen.* 8, *dom.* 85, 86, 131, *har.* 46, *Sest.* 21 etc. (in all but the first *meritus* is qualified by *bene* or *optime*).

gloriae quae . . . splendeat: I have not been able to parallel this expression; but *gloria* is found quite often in close proximity to *splendor* and cognate words: e.g. Cic. *Flacc.* 28, *Pis.* 57, *Cat. mai.* 8, *off.* i. 43, Tac. *hist.* i. 84. 3, and *SHA* xxix. 13. 3.

12. cum, obviously right, is found for **N**'s *cui* first in U. For successful emendation in U, see vol. i, p. 299 with *addendum*.

asperum ac difficile . . . superuacaneo atque inutili: for *congeries uerborum* in L.'s speeches, see vol. i, pp. 140–1; here these two expansive adjectival couplings balance each other.

13. quem ille obrutum ignem reliquerit, ita ut totiens nouum ex improuiso incendium daret: for the idea cf. Lucr. iv. 925–8 'quippe ubi nulla latens animai pars remaneret | in membris, cinere ut multa latet obrutus ignis, | unde reconflari sensus per membra repente | posset, ut ex igni caeco consurgere flamma?', Flor. i. 31(ii. 15). 15 '. . . cum interim iam diebus, iam noctibus, noua aliqua moles, noua machina, noua perditorum hominum manus quasi ex obruto incendio subita de cineribus flamma prodibat', iv. 2(ii. 13). 53, and perhaps also Hor. *carm.* ii. 1. 7 (where, however, Nisbet and Hubbard interpret differently). That the idea was more or less proverbial is suggested by our passage and by Flor. ii. 9(iii. 21). 9 'Cornelio Cinna Gaio Octauio consulibus male obrutum resurrexit incendium'. The idea is particularly common, and is certainly proverbial, in erotic contexts; see Gow and Page on Call. *anth. Pal.* xii. 139. 1–2 (their 1081–2). The proverb used by Decius thus balances that used by

Fabius in § 5. All the parallel passages cited above illustrate the use of *obruere* in the sense of 'smothering a fire'.

14. concessurum ... cedere ... cessurum: for the phenomenon of a simple verb used with a sense virtually identical with a preceding compound, see e.g. Kenney on Lucr. iii. 261, Diggle (1981) 18, Woodman and Martin on Tac. *ann.* iii. 29. 1, and esp. Wills (1996) 438–43 (all with further examples and bibliography). In L. note i. 9. 8–9 'conuenere ... uenit', 9. 11–12 'deferebant ... ferunt ... ferrent', and 10. 4–5 'occiso ... caesi'. Less commonly, the initial compound verb is a participle; see e.g. vi. 8. 1 'arreptum ... rapit'. However, in some passages in which a simple verb follows a compound, the force of the prefix in the compound is hardly felt; note 16. 2–3 'Decius ... Samnitium exercitum ... expulit finibus. Etruriam pulsi ...', i. 7. 4 'abegisse ... agens', and xxxiv. 14. 8 'auersos ... uerterit'.

Although § 15 *tulerit ... laturum* and in § 16 *dent ... daturi sint* are not parallel in structure to *cedere ... cessurum*, the sequence of three verbs each repeated a second time in the future participle is striking.
uerecundia ... maiestatis: see ix. 10. 7 n.
cum periculum, cum dimicatio: the second *cum* is omitted by Πλ; this reading is just possible, but the resulting asyndeton bimembre is very awkward. M reads *tum*, which does not itself make sense; but this may well be one of those passages where M has a reading superior to that in Πλ,[1] and it is very easy to follow Ricc. 485 and Zr and write *cum* for *tum*, which gives a characteristically Livian anaphora (see vol. i, p. 729).[2]

15. si nihil aliud is often used as an exact equivalent to the English 'if nothing else'; for examples with *certe* following, as it does here, cf. e.g. xxii. 29. 11 'si nihil aliud, gratorum certe nobis animorum gloriam dies hic dederit', Sen. *suas.* 2. 19, Sen. *nat.* v. 18. 11, *dial.* ix. 3. 3, Petron. 114. 11, and Quint. (?) *decl. min.* 247. 18. However, our passage is different, in that *nihil aliud* is the object of *tulerit* and *tulerit* and *illud* remove the ellipse normally inherent in the idiom. I have found no parallel for this: at Val. Max. v. 1. *ext.* 2 'si nihil aliud dignum honore memoriae gessisset, his tamen factis abunde se posteritati commendasset' *nihil aliud* is the object of *gessisset*, but then a different verb follows in the apodosis.

---

[1] One might object that *tum*'s presence in M is due to dittography after -*lum*; but it is quite as likely to have been omitted by haplography. Perhaps it was omitted from **N**[1] in this way and restored in **N**[c] as a marginal variant, where Π and λ failed to notice it.
[2] Further Italian witnesses probably have this reading, but the other three members of χ are not amongst them: they all follow M.

patres could mean 'senators' but is perhaps more likely to mean 'patricians'.

16. deosque: *-que* is quite regularly used with ellipse of *ceteri* (*uel sim.*) 'when proceeding from the particular to the general' (*OLD s.u.* 9[a], where several good parallels are cited). Cf. Plaut. *Capt.* 868 'Iuppiter te dique perdant' and 922 'Ioui disque ago gratias'. See also W–M ad loc. and on xxxv. 34. 1 'Quinctius legatique Corinthum redierunt'.

precari . . . dent: for the lot as manifestation of the will of the gods Bunse (2002: 421 n. 35) cites xxvii. 11. 11, Cic. *Phil.* iii. 26, and Fest. 382. See also Stewart (1998) 38–51 (on sortition and *auspicia*).

felicitatem: see vi. 27. 1 n.

17. id et natura aequum et ad famam populi Romani per-tinere: this text is due to Grynaeus in the first Froben (Basle) edn. of 1531; the mss have *et id . . .* Since L. quite often places conjunctive and disjunctive particles in positions that, strictly speaking, are illogical (see vii. 39. 10 n.), the paradosis may be sound; but it is more usual to find *et* moved backwards rather than forwards, and in his full discussion of the phenomenon Pettersson (1930: 1–24) offers no parallel. Therefore, unlike Walters, I have emended.

For *ad famam pertinere* cf. esp. Liv. xxviii. 44. 12 '. . . tamen ad dig-nitatem populi Romani famamque apud reges gentesque externas pertinebat . . .' and Cic. *IIVerr.* i. 22 'uos quod ad uestram famam existimationem salutemque communem pertinet, iudices, prospi-cite'; also Liv. xlv. 10. 5, Cic. *inu.* ii. 86, *Phil.* ix. 12, [Q. Cic.] *com. pet.* 49, and *SHA* xxvi. 24. 2.

18. intro uocarentur ad suffragium tribus: for *intro* see 13. 11 n., for *uocare ad suffragium* vi. 38. 4 n.

comitia habuit, the reading of **N**, involves three difficulties.

(*a*) *comitia habere* is the regular Latin expression for 'to hold (or 'preside over') an election', but here there is no election. However, a request to the *populus* to decide between the claims of two consuls for a command may be viewed as virtually the equivalent of an election; *comitia*, although it refers more often to an electoral assembly, is sometimes used of a legislative assembly (even without the qualify-ing *tributa*, *centuriata*, or *curiata*): from the passages cited by Farrell (1986: 417) see iii. 20. 6 and xxxi. 6. 3; and, although *comitium habere* is not found in either of these passages, it is a natural expression for presidency at an assembly.

(*b*) It has been doubted whether the consuls, rather than tribunes, ever presided over the tribes, but for arguments against this position see vii. 16. 7–8 n. with *addendum*.

(*c*) Here the tribes are asked to decide to which magistrate a command should be given. In most of the parallels for this tribunes certainly presided over the tribes: see esp. xxx. 27. 3–4 'consules iussi cum tribunis plebis agere ut . . . populum rogarent quem uellet in Africa bellum gerere. omnes tribus P. Scipionem iusserunt'; also xxix. 13. 7 'de Hispaniae imperio, quos in eam prouinciam duos pro consulibus mitti placeret latum ad populum est. omnes tribus eosdem L. Cornelium Lentulum et L. Manlium Acidinum pro consulibus, sicut priore anno tenuissent, obtinere eas prouincias iusserunt' (this could conceivably be, but is not likely to be, an exception to the rule of tribunician presidency), xxx. 41. 4, xxxi. 50. 10–11, xxxv. 20. 9–10,[1] and, from the late Republic, commands agreed by the people in response to tribunician measures (to be found conveniently by consulting Botsford [1909] index *s.u.* provinces). However, if one accepts the existence of a *comitia tributa* separate from what has traditionally been called the *concilium plebis*, then it is reasonable to suggest that in 295, when the role of the tribunes was less settled, one of the consuls presided over a matter which had been referred by the senate to the people; and there is no compelling reason why on this occasion Fabius, who had been elected first, should not have been the presiding consul.[2]

None of these difficulties gives sufficient reason to reject the paradosis. However, Walters and most other editors have printed *comitio abiit* (Ricc. 485 and A[p], and hence probably χ).[3] With this emendation Fabius is allowed the dramatic and assured gesture of walking out of the Comitium and leaving the tribes to their own devices, confident in the result of the vote. However, this reading causes three difficulties.

(*a*) One would have expected Fabius and Decius to have been addressing the tribes not in the Comitium but in the forum; only when voting began were the tribes called individually into the

---

[1] These passages are listed at Sandberg (2001) 137 n. 24. At xxvi. 18. 4–11 the *comitia centuriata* appoints the future Scipio Africanus to his command, *priuatus cum imperio*, in Spain: this assembly may have been used because the appointment was viewed as a proper election.

[2] That he would have been presiding on a matter in which his own interest was involved may be accounted a further difficulty but does not seem to be a compelling argument against this reconstruction.

[3] But not Esc. R I 4, and there is no correction in B.N.F. lat. 5690. The construction *comitio abiit* is legitimate, even though the omission of *ab* is rare (K–S i. 369–70).

Comitium. In the words of Taylor (1966: 130): '[t]here are allusions in Livy to statues, omens, floggings, seats of magistrates, burning of books on the Comitium; legates stand there, a *signifer* stops there. But there is not a reference either to a *contio* or a voting assembly held there.'

(*b*) Since there is a *concursus* towards Fabius at 25. 1, one must postulate that he has by then returned to the Comitium: it is simpler to follow **N** and keep him with the tribes all the time.

(*c*) The emendation leaves it unclear who was presiding in the assembly: perhaps Decius (the view of Rotondi [1912: 237], who optimistically counted this passage as evidence for the passing of a law), if it was the *comitia tributa*; perhaps the tribunes of the plebs (the view of W–M), who, however, are nowhere mentioned. The paradosis makes it quite clear that Fabius was presiding.

A further defence of the paradosis is this: if our passage does not reflect what happened in 295 but derives from annalistic or Livian invention (which is quite likely), then it may have been invented without proper regard for (later) constitutional practice.[1]

For these reasons it is hard to prefer the conjecture to the paradosis. Among recent discussions of this passage that of Humm (1999: 642) is preferable to those of Paananen (1993: 72–3) and Sandberg (2001: 87), who are not aware that the reading which they adopt is an emendation.

Ap. Claudi praetoris allatas ex Etruria litteras: see 21. 11–12.

25. 1. omnium ferme iuniorum: W–M rightly pointed out that L. exaggerates: a large Roman army was already in the field.

2. 'quattuor milia . . . peditum et secentos equites . . .': since the normal complement for a legion varied between 4,200 and 5,000+ and the normal complement of cavalry was 300 per legion (see vol. ii, pp. 465 and 475), Fabius seems to be stating that he will take with him one legion and a double complement of cavalry. When Fabius is trying to take only a small force, it is not clear why he looks for this double complement of cavalry.

hodierno et crastino die: for this expression see vii. 35. 5 n.; L. emphasizes these words by placing them at the head of their clause.

2–3. ducam . . . reducam: for this figure see ix. 1. 7–8 n. Following § 1 'duce' these words draw attention to Fabius' qualities as a leader.

---

[1] However, a similar argument could be used to defend the conjecture here rejected.

4. plus . . . spei gerente: see 17. 5 n.

Aharnam: the scanty remains of ancient Aharna, also spelt Arna, are to be found beneath modern Civitella d'Arno, which lies just east of the Tiber, some 8 km from Perusia, on the Etrusco-Umbrian border. In our sources for the Roman conquest of Italy this is the only mention of the settlement; other references to it in literary sources include Plin. *nat.* iii. 113, and Sil. viii. 456. See further Nissen (1883–1902) ii. 394, Hülsen, *RE* ii. 1201, Harris (1971) index *s.u.* Arna, and Gaggiotti *et al.* (1980) 147–8.[1]

pergit: see vi. 12. 1 n.

5. lignatores: the collection of wood for burning in fires was a regular duty of Roman troops when they were stationed in their camp; cf. e.g. xxii. 12. 8, xxv. 34. 4, xxvii. 27. 3, xxxviii. 25. 9, xl. 25. 4, 30. 9, xli. 1. 7, xliv. 40. 2, and Veg. *mil.* i. 22. 1. See further Fischer (1914) 10.

praegredi: lictors went in front of their magistrate; see e.g. ii. 18. 8, iii. 26. 11 'antecedentibus lictoribus', xxiv. 44. 10, Cic. *rep.* ii. 31, ii. 55, *Phil.* ii. 58, Sen. *contr.* ix. 2. 17, Plin. *pan.* 23. 3, and Mommsen (1887–8) i. 375. The phenomenon illustrated at vi. 34. 6 n., where lictors knock on a door in advance of the arrival of a magistrate, is very similar.

uiderunt . . . accepere: see 15. 4 n.

laeti atque alacres: the coupling is regular, although found only here in L.; to the passages listed by Gudeman in his note on Tac. *dial.* 23. 4 (his § 7), add [x] Cic. *Mur.* 49, Sen. *dial.* xii. 20. 1, *epist.* 20. 1, Quint. ii. 9. 2, and Apul. *met.* iii. 29. 6; also Cic. *ad Brut.* 5. 2.

6. 'ain tandem?': *ain?*, which is used only here by L., generally introduces a note of doubt or astonishment in response to something that has just been said. In the idiom found here *tandem* has its emphatic, asseverative sense ('really'); Gloss. iv. 13. 48 has the entry 'ai⟨n⟩ tandem: dicis uero'. *ain tandem?* is common in Plautus and Terence, is attested at *trag. pall.* 31, and is then found nine times in Cicero (to the Ciceronian passages cited at *TLL* i. 1460. 59–71 add *diu.* ii. 146, *rep.* i. 23, *leg.* i. 53, ii. 24, iii. 14). Its stylistic level can be gauged from its frequency in comedy, and from the fact that only one of the Ciceronian instances is found in a speech (*Planc.* 49; of the

---

[1] Firpo (2002: 122–3), to support his view that the battle of Sentinum took place near Clusium (see above, p. 287), argued that Arna lay in Tuscany, where the toponyms Arnano, Poggiodarno, and Poggio d'Arna are found; since Silius mentions Mevania in the same line and Hispellum in the next, the hypothesis may be dismissed.

other eight instances, six come from passages of dialogue in the philosophical treatises, two from the letters). Clearly this is one of the colloquial expressions which L. admitted into his speeches (for the principle see vol. i. p. 148); his coupling of the idiom with a plural verb (*habetis*) is unique, but we may compare the use of *agedum* as illustrated at vii. 9. 8 n.

7. in ingenti metu esse: see ix. 37. 11 n.
adfatim: see ix. 35. 4 n.

7–8. '... redite et uellite uallum'. redeunt ... uellentes uallum:
despite § 10, Fabius may be alluding to the τόπος (for which see ix. 23. 11 [n.], also spoken by Fabius) that it was better to protect oneself with arms rather than walls. The manner in which *redeunt ... uellentes uallum* picks up Fabius' words is striking, perhaps suggesting the automatic obedience of Roman troops to a consul whom they respect. For *uellere* in the context of the destruction of a *uallum*, see ix. 14. 9 n.

8. terroremque ... fecerunt: see ix. 38. 4 n.

10. mobiliorem is the easy conjecture of Doujat for **N**'s *nobiliorem*. Cornelissen (1889: 192) preferred *habiliorem*, with which both *habiliorem* and *salubriorem* would refer to *mutatione locorum*; but, as Walters saw, we have a balanced expression in which *itineribus* is picked up by *mobiliorem* and *mutatione locorum* by *salubriorem*.
salubriorem: the views of Fabius, the subject of *negabat*, coincide with those of military theorists, who regarded changes of camp as good for the health of an army; see Onas. 9. 1 and Veg. *mil*. iii. 2. 12 'si autumnali aestiuoque tempore diutius in isdem locis militum multitudo consistat, ex contagione aquarum et odoris ipsius foeditate uitiatis haustibus et aere corrupto perniciosissimus nascitur morbus, qui prohiberi non potest aliter nisi frequenti mutatione castrorum'.

11. secunda legione: see 18. 3–4 n.
Clusium: the first reference in books vi–x to the famous and old Etruscan town, modern Chiusi, which lies a little to the west of Lake Trasimene in the valley of the Chiana; cf. 26. 7, 26. 11, 27. 5, 30. 2. Previously L. mentioned it as the base of the legendary Lars Porsenna, who is said to have attacked Rome in 508 (see ii. 9. 1–14. 9; also many other sources), and as the city which in 390 appealed to Rome for help against the Gauls (v. 33. 1–6, 35. 4–37. 8; again, there are many other sources). In our sources for the Roman conquest of

Etruria it is mentioned only for this year, in the passages of L. cited above. If the information provided by L. at 27. 5 and 30. 2 is accurate, Clusium was at war with Rome, and we do not know when it was finally pacified. In later books L. refers to Clusium only at xxviii. 45. 18, where it is recorded as having assisted Rome in the Hannibalic War. See further Nissen (1883–1902) ii. 323–6, Hülsen, *RE* iv. 115–17, Scullard (1967) 151–6, and Torelli (1982) 308–14.

quod Camars olim appellabant: this statement is discussed above, pp. 286–7.

praepositoque castris L. Scipione pro praetore may be translated in two ways: either 'and after placing the propraetor L. Scipio in charge of the camp' or, more probably (with e.g. Mommsen [1887–8] i. 681 n. 2, Hölkeskamp [1987] 148–9, and Lintott [1999] 114 n. 95), 'and after placing L. Scipio in charge of the camp as propraetor'. If the former is correct, then one may presume that Scipio, for whom see 11. 10 n. and who is called a propraetor also at 26. 12, had already been created propraetor at Rome. However, if this were the case, it would perhaps be surprising that he did not have command of his own army as Fulvius and Postumius do at 26. 15. If the latter is correct, then Scipio is the first Roman attested as having been given propraetorian *imperium* by a consul. On propraetorian and proconsular commands see the full discussion at 26. 15 n. For the spelling *pro praetore* see *addendum* to viii. 26. 12 n.

12. nam in utrumque auctores sunt: see viii. 6. 3 n.

13. in senatu et apud populum: see vii. 11. 9 n.

14. periculum esse: for this idiom see ix. 17. 15 n.[1]

15. primo quoque tempore: see vi. 3. 2 n.

15–16. in Etruriam ad collegam . . . in Etruriam ad consulem: see 11. 4 n.

16. in suam prouinciam: presumably Samnium.
exercitu iusto consulari: i.e. two legions; for *iustus* see vi. 31. 6 n.

---

[1] There is no doubt that L. wrote *periculum*, reported by Drakenborch from Holkham 344 and its descendant Leiden, Lips. 28 and doubtless found in other *recentiores*. However, it is interesting that M¹P¹ alone have the most honest reading *periculos* (the corruption caused by perseveration from *populos*): Mᶜ has *periculo*, PᶜUZλ have *periculosum*, both progressive corruptions. This passage should be added to the list of errors shared by M and P/P¹ at vol. i, p. 311.

17. P. Decium censuisse ferunt, ut omnia integra ac libera Q. Fabio seruarentur, donec . . .: for the sentiment cf. Plin. *epist.* vii. 6. 14 'consules . . . omnia integra principi seruauerunt'; for the general run of the sentence cf. xli. 23. 17 'ego nihil noui censeo decernendum, seruandaque omnia integra donec ad certum redigatur uanusne hic timor noster an uerus fuerit'; for *omnia integra seruare* cf., in addition to Plin. loc. cit., also Anton. *ap.* Cic. *Att.* x. 8a. 2, and Planc. *ap.* Cic. *fam.* x. 21. 6; and for the coupling of *integer* and *liber*, used in various senses, cf. Cic. *Sull.* 86, *diu.* ii. 150, *nat.* ii. 31, *fam.* i. 9. 21, and Sen. *epist.* 94. 56. See also ix. 42. 10 'eam integram rem' (n.).

si per commodum rei publicae posset: regular phrasing in requests from the senate to a magistrate or a commander to a lieutenant; cf. xxii. 57. 1 'scribendumque consuli ut . . . primo quoque tempore, quantum per commodum rei publicae fieri posset, Romam ueniret', xxxi. 11. 1–2 'decreuerunt ut . . . ipse, si per commodum rei publicae posset, ad opprimendum Gallicum tumultum proficisceretur', xxxvii. 50. 6 'mandatum eidem ut si per commodum rei publicae facere posset, ut ad comitia Romam ueniret', Caes. *Gall.* v. 46. 4 'scribit Labieno, si rei publicae commodo facere posset, cum legione ad finis Neruiorum ueniat', and vi. 33. 5; also Caes. *Gall.* i. 35. 4. For *commodum rei publicae* in other contexts, add the following to the passages cited at *TLL* iii. 1927. 70–4 [x]: C. Gracch. *ORF* 30, Cic. *inu.* i. 68 (twice), *Caecil.* 64, *Sull.* 65, and *fam.* i. 1. 3.

legatis: of these the name of only L. Manlius Torquatus is known. For legates in early Roman history see vol. i, pp. 55–6 and vii. 7. 1 n.

18. quantisque administrandum copiis: for the ablative cf. Tac. *hist.* i. 10. 3 'bellum Iudaicum Flavius Vespasianus . . . tribus legionibus administrabat'.

26. 1. productus ad populum: see vi. 36. 10 n.
orationem habuit: see 24. 4 n.

2. ceterum . . . experti posse recalls Hom. *Il.* x. 242–3 εἰ μὲν δὴ ἕταρόν γε κελεύετέ μ' αὐτὸν ἑλέσθαι, | πῶς ἂν ἔπειτ' Ὀδυσῆος ἐγὼ θείοιο λαθοίμην . . .;
per tot collegia: see 24. 1 n.

3. sin . . . at . . .: see ix. 1. 8 n.
quid aliud mallet: Fabius allows for the possibility that Decius may like a separate command of his own (cf. 25. 16).

malit is the reading of P^{c}UZR^c; MP$^1\lambda$ have *mallit*, and the coincidence of these mss suggests that this stood in **N**. In which case, as
Walters observes, editors may choose between *malit* and *mallet*,
which was conjectured by Weissenborn (ed.). In favour of *malit*
stand diplomatic probability (it is a little easier to see why *malit* than
mallet should have been corrupted to *mallit*) and L.'s willingness to
employ in *oratio obliqua* the tense and mood which would have been
used in *oratio recta* (see vi. 39. 11 n.); but against it stands *darent* in
§ 2 and § 4, and for this reason I have followed Weissenborn.

4. arbitrium: a nice compliment to Fabius Rullianus, who at 24. 7
had said that he was *in arbitrio senatus . . . et in potestate populi*.
in Samnium uel: Madvig (*ap.* Madvig and Ussing and 1877: 211)
acutely observed that, since Rullianus had made it clear that he
would like Decius to come with him to Etruria, Decius ought to have
replied that he was very happy to go with Rullianus to Etruria.
Therefore, strictly speaking, the reference here to *Samnium* is not
appropriate, and Madvig suggested the deletion of *in Samnium uel*.
L.'s logic, however, does not always reach Madvigian standards of
precision, and I have therefore retained the paradosis, which is readily intelligible.[1]
tanta . . . uideretur: for a similar idea cf. xxix. 24. 11 'tantus
omnibus ardor erat in Africa traiciendi ut non ad bellum duci uiderentur sed ad certa uictoriae praemia'.
laetitia ac gratulatio: for this coupling cf. Cic. *IVerr.* 21, *IIVerr.*
iv. 74, *Flacc.* 98, *Pis.* 22, *Phil.* xiv. 12, Tac. *hist.* ii. 65. 1, Gell. iv. 18.
5; also Cic. *Sest.* 54 and Liv. xxx. 21. 1. For the use of these words in
the context of victory, cf. Caes. *ciu.* i. 74. 7; also Liv. viii. 33. 20.
praeciperetur . . . animis: see vii. 26. 8 n.

5. inuenio apud quosdam: see vi. 20. 4 n.

**6. sunt quibus ne haec quidem certamina exponere satis fuer-
it: adiecerunt et Appi criminationes de Fabio absente . . .:**
adiecerunt is D. Heinsius' conjecture for **N**'s *adiecerint*. The paradosis presents two difficulties.

(*a*) The asyndeton between *fuerit* and *adiecerint* is harsh: not only
is there no connecting particle between the two verbs, but *qui* has to

---

[1] Madvig further argued that, if one wished to retain the reference to Samnium, one would
have to read ⟨*uel*⟩ *in Samnium uel*, and H. J. Müller accordingly printed this. This view
is sufficiently refuted by a reference to *OLD s.u. uel* 2(b) '(w. omission of *uel* before the first
alternative)', where our passage is listed with many others.

be supplied from *quibus*. Any defence of this odd construction should begin from the numerous passages cited at K–S ii. 324, where a relative pronoun has to be supplied from an earlier use of the pronoun in a different case; see e.g. 29. 3 'Liuius, cui lictores Decius tradiderat iusseratque (for *et quem iusserat*) pro praetore esse' and Cic. *IIVerr.* iv. 64 'de quo et uos audistis et populus Romanus non nunc primum audiet et (*sc.* quod) in exteris nationibus usque ad ultimas terras peruagatum est', and Cic. *Vat.* 24 'M. Bibulum cuius inclusione contentus non eras, (*sc.* et quem) interficere uolueras, spoliaras consulatu, patria priuare cupiebas'; but even in the last passage, which is the hardest, the cumulative asyndeton and the presence of *M. Bibulum* (upon which the understood *quem* must depend) makes the construction much easier than in our passage.

(*b*) *fuerit* and *adiecerint* are in the perfect subjunctive, but in this context the present subjunctive is the tense which one would expect: see e.g. § 12, i. 4. 7 'sunt qui Larentiam uolgato corpore lupam inter pastores uocatam putent', 11. 9 'sunt qui . . . dicant', and many other examples in L. and others. The perfect subjunctive is sometimes used in contexts where the present is normal (see K–S i. 176–7), and *fuerit* itself is not especially awkward; it is the combination of the two perfect subjunctives in asyndeton which reads so strangely.

These difficulties suggest that the text is corrupt. H. J. Müller proposed *adiecerintque*, which removes the asyndeton and brings the passage into line with the others cited at K–S ii. 324; Walters ⟨qui⟩ *quibus*, which removes the asyndeton by turning *quibus . . . fuerit* into a relative clause independent of *sunt* ⟨qui⟩ *. . . adiecerint*. Müller's conjecture is preferable,[1] but neither removes the awkward double perfect subjunctive. For these reasons I have followed Drakenborch in adopting Heinsius' conjecture, which removes both anomalies, and have repunctuated so as to accommodate it; *adiecerunt* could easily have been corrupted to *adiecerint* by perseveration from *fuerit*.

haec quidem certamina exponere: Conway suggested, and Walters adopted, the deletion of *certamina*; but, although *certamina exponere* comes only six words after *certaminum . . . quae exposui*, iteration is so common in L. that it is most unwise to emend (see further vol. i, pp. 725–7).

praetoris: i.e. Appius.

---

[1] Walters must have wanted his conjecture to give the meaning 'there are those for whom it was not enough to describe these conflicts, who have added both . . .'; but it could be taken as giving 'there are some who have added to those who were content . . . [the statement] that . . .', which is very awkward.

ut suae quisque prouinciae sortem tueretur: Foster translates
'that each should attend to his allotted province', and this translation
is supported by the parallels for *sortem tueri* at ps.-Asc. *ad II Verr.* i.
34 'AC SORTE potuisti enim et debuisti, si nolles repudiare illam
sortem, aut susceptam tueri' and (in a non-political context) Ov.
epist. 17. 113 'sed sine (*sc.* me) quam tribuit sortem Fortuna tueri'
and by the similar locution at Virg. *Aen.* ix. 174–5 'omnis per muros
legio sortita periclum | excubat exercetque uices, quod cuique
tuendum est'. However, since L. has hitherto stated that the war in
Etruria and Umbria was given to Fabius *extra ordinem* or *extra
sortem* (24. 3, 18; cf. § 5 above), it is unclear what the *sors* of Decius
was. Various resolutions of the difficulty may be suggested, in
descending order of probability: (*a*) that we should understand that
the war in Samnium was the province of Decius (assigned without
sortition) and that he wished to be allowed to go to this and to leave
Fabius to fight on his own in the north, even if he was in difficulty (in
which case L., as so often, has been free in his use of technical
terms—and in this passage confusingly so); (*b*) we should translate
differently 'that each should see to the allotting of his province', i.e.
Decius calls for sortition; (*c*) *contentionemque aliam inter collegas*
refers to a second quarrel (after that mentioned earlier in the section)
between Decius and Appius and not to another quarrel between
Fabius and Decius (for praetors as colleagues of consuls see vii. 1. 6
n. with *addendum*; but the contrast between *praesentem consulem* and
Fabio absente tells against this).

    For the genitive *prouinciae* dependent on *sors*, cf. Cic. *II Verr.* i.
104, Vell. ii. 111. 4, and Tac. *ann.* xv. 19. 1.
quisque: see vii. 9. 7 n.

7. constare: for L.'s use of this verb in discussion of his sources see
vi. 16. 4 n. on *satis constat*.
Senones: this tribe was the closest of all the Gallic tribes to Rome,
settled on lands in the north-east of the Italian peninsula, around
Ariminum, Fanum, Pisaurum, and Sena Gallica. Being the closest to
Rome, it is not surprising that in the century or so after 390 the
Senones fought Rome more often than the other Gallic tribes. In
addition to their appearance here (and it may be conjectured that
they lie behind most of the earlier references in book x to the Gauls
[10. 6–12, 13. 3, 18. 2, 21. 2, 21. 14]), they are held by some of our
sources to have been responsible for the great Gallic invasion of 390
(v. 34. 5, 35. 3, D.S. xiv. 113. 3, Plut. *Cam.* 15. 2). In 283 they were
the first of the Gallic tribes to be subdued (*MRR* i. 188), after which

a Roman colony was established at Sena; in 232 C. Flaminius, as tribune, established viritane allotments on their land (*MRR* i. 225). See further Philipp, *RE* iiA. 1477, and J. H. C. Williams (2001) via index *s.u.*

oppugnaturi: for this use of the future participle see vi. 22. 9 n.

9. ut in re subita: generalizations of this kind are common in L. (see also vi. 34. 5, vii. 2. 4, ix. 13. 7, 22. 7 nn.); for those taking the form *ut in re(bus)*, with an adjective qualifying *re(bus)* cf. iv. 17. 8, xxii. 5. 1, xxiii. 14. 1, xxvi. 5. 7, 8. 2, xxviii. 28. 1, xxxvii. 5. 1, 11. 7, xlv. 36. 1; also v. 41. 1 and xxvii. 13. 2.

caesa ... circumuenta: for this coupling see viii. 35. 11 n.

10. ita ut nuntius non superesset: see vi. 28. 9 n.
quidam auctores sunt: see *addendum* to viii. 40. 1 n.

11. pectoribus equorum suspensa gestantes capita et lanceis infixa ouantesque moris sui carmine: for Gallic decapitation see also xxiii. 24. 11–12, Plb. iii. 67. 3 (beheading), Cn. Gell. fr. 26; and with our passage cf. esp. D.S. v. 29. 4–5 τῶν δὲ πεσόντων πολεμίων τὰς κεφαλὰς ἀφαιροῦντες περιάπτουσι τοῖς αὐχέσι τῶν ἵππων· τὰ δὲ σκῦλα τοῖς θεράπουσι παραδόντες ἡμαγμένα λαφυραγωγοῦσιν, ἐπιπαιανίζοντες καὶ ᾄδοντες ὕμνον ἐπινίκιον, καὶ τὰ ἀκροθίνια ταῦτα ταῖς οἰκίαις προσηλοῦσιν ὥσπερ οἱ ἐν κυνηγίοις τισὶ κεχειρωμένοι τὰ θηρία. τῶν δ' ἐπιφανεστάτων πολεμίων κεδρώσαντες τὰς κεφαλὰς ἐπιμελῶς τηροῦσιν ἐν λάρνακι, καὶ τοῖς ξένοις ἐπιδεικνύουσι σεμνυνόμενοι διότι τῆσδε τῆς κεφαλῆς τῶν προγόνων τις ἢ πατὴρ ἢ καὶ αὐτὸς πολλὰ χρήματα διδόμενα οὐκ ἔλαβε. φασὶ δέ τινας αὐτῶν καυχᾶσθαι διότι χρυσὸν ἀντίσταθμον τῆς κεφαλῆς οὐκ ἐδέξαντο, βάρβαρόν τινα μεγαλοψυχίαν ἐπιδεικνύμενοι· οὐ γὰρ τὸ μὴ πωλεῖν τὰ σύσσημα τῆς ἀρετῆς εὐγενές, ἀλλὰ τὸ πολεμεῖν τὸ ὁμόφυλον τετελευτηκὸς θηριῶδες and Stb. iv. 4. 5 (C197–8), where similar information is given, and where we are told that Posidonius was Strabo's source (doubtless he was also that of D.S.) and that the Romans put a stop to this practice of beheading. The abhorrence (explicit or implicit) which Greek and Roman writers had for this practice should be compared with their abhorrence for the human sacrifices which the Gauls were said to perpetrate. See further Last (1949) esp. 2–3 (on Gallic killing of humans) and Goldsworthy (1996) 271–6 (on beheading in battle).

For Gallic singing see vii. 10. 8 n.; for *ouantes* see vii. 13. 10 n.

12. L. Manlio Torquato: (77). Otherwise unknown. If this man really existed (and, although the events in which he is said to have been involved may have been invented by the annalists, it would be a little surprising if his existence was invented from nothing), he could have been the brother of the consul of 299; but there is no positive evidence that he was.

pro praetore: for the spelling see *addendum* to viii. 23. 12 n.

13. a Gallo hoste quam Vmbro: for the omission of the preposition, see viii. 31. 2 n.

cum saepe alias: in the two other passages in which L. employs *saepe alias* he couples it with *cum . . . tum . . .*; cf. xxv. 20. 7 'cum saepe alias tum paucis diebus ante expertus qualis sub inscio duce exercitus esset' and xxvii. 49. 2 'Hasdrubal . . . dux cum saepe alias memorabilis tum illa praecipue pugna' (where *praecipue* may be compared with *praecipuus* in our passage).

14. Campanisque mille equitibus delectis: for Campanian cavalry serving in the Roman army, see vol. ii, p. 556.

sociorum nominisque Latini: see viii. 3. 8 n.

15. in Falisco: for Falerii see vi. 4. 4 n.; for its likely stance towards Rome during the Sentinum campaign, see 24. 1–31. 7 n.

in Vaticano agro: in antiquity the term Vatican covered a wider area than that to-day under direct papal authority, including the Gianicolo, which was called the *mons Vaticanus* (see e.g. Cic. *Att.* xiii. 33. 4, Hor. *carm.* i. 20. 7, and Plin. *nat.* xviii. 20 with Liv. iii. 26. 8) and was notorious for the poverty of its land (Cic. *agr.* ii. 96) and for the poor quality of its wine (Mart. i. 18. 2, vi. 92. 3 etc.). See further Elter (1891), Platner and Ashby (1929) 546, Koch, *RE* viiiA. 490–3, and Nisbet and Hubbard on Hor. loc. cit.

Cn. Fuluius: see 4. 7 n.

L. Postumius Megellus: see ix. 44. 2 n.

pro praetores ambo: proconsular and propraetorian commands could be established in three ways: by prorogation, by delegation (see 29. 3 [n.]), or by the appointment of *priuati* by a popular vote. There is no reason to doubt the historicity of these two appointments, and, since Fulvius and Postumius had not held curule office in 296, they were plainly not prorogations; but scholars dispute into which of the two other categories they should be placed.

The only unambiguous report of a man being delegated propraetorian *imperium* by a magistrate in the period before the Second Punic War comes at 29. 3 'Liuius, cui lictores Decius tradiderat iusseratque pro praetore esse'. 25. 11, where L. mentions the appointment of L. Scipio to a pro-praetorian command [see also 26.

12] may very well provide another instance of the phenomenon, but L.'s writing is ambiguous (see n.): although he seems to imply that Scipio was appointed by Fabius Rullianus, he does not actually state this, and therefore leaves open the possibility that Scipio may have been appointed centrally at Rome. With regard to the historicity of these notices, there is no good reason to doubt that Scipio was a pro-praetor,[1] and, if Decius really did consecrate himself and perform a *deuotio*, then the notice about Livius could be true too.

Mommsen (1887–8: i. 682), Münzer, *RE* xxii. 936, and Brennan (2000: 77) have argued that Fulvius and Postumius too were appoint-ed in this way, receiving their powers by delegation from either the praetor (Mommsen, Münzer) or one of the consuls (Brennan). That before the Second Punic War no other parallels for such appoint-ments are known is likely to be due to the deficiency of our sources, since for the period after 218 BC there are several examples: see xxix. 6. 9 (205), where L. describes Scipio's legate Q. Pleminius, who was commanding forces in Italy from which Scipio was absent, as pro-praetor; xxxi. 3. 2 (201) 'decreuit . . . frequens senatus ut P. Aelius consul quem uideretur ei cum imperio mitteret, qui, classe accepta quam ex Sicilia Cn. Octauius reduceret, in Macedoniam traiceret. M. Valerius Laeuinus propraetor missus . . .' (an instance of a deputy being appointed for the period before a consul could take command); Sall. *Iug.* 36. 4 (110), where we learn that Sp. Postumius Albinus left his brother Aulus as propraetor in charge of the Roman forces in Africa (a parallel to the appointment of L. Scipio); and it is very likely that in 218 the consul P. Scipio sent his brother Cn. Scipio to Spain *pro praetore* (even if in subsequent years the appointment of Gnaeus was made at Rome).[2] Note also several passages listed by Mommsen (p. 681 n. 6), mostly from L.'s account of the Second Punic War, in which the urban praetor entrusts a *priuatus* with *imperium*. Analogous was the right of a magistrate with *imperium* to appoint someone to act *pro quaestore* in the absence of a regular quaestor (see Mommsen [1887–8] ii. 563).

Others (e.g. Kloft [1977: 99] and Hölkeskamp [1987: 149]),[3] hold

---

[1] Beloch (1926: 440) rejected the notice on the ground that the *elogium* of Scipio (for which see above, pp. 161–5) mentions no propraetorian command; but if Scipio's *imperium* was only delegated from a consul, it may not have been considered worth recording alongside the offices to which he had been elected.

[2] The sources are silent about the exact status of Gnaeus, but note *imperatores* at xxv. 32. 1 and στρατηγός at Plb. iii. 76. 1.

[3] Kloft observes without comment that there is no report of a popular vote; but it is easier to believe that L. did not record this than that the appointment was made without consultation of the people.

that Fulvius and Postumius were appointed by the senate and a popular vote. If this view is right, then they are the first men attested as having held such a command. The next attestations are for (*a*) M. Claudius Marcellus (proconsul in 215 after being praetor in 216: see *MRR* i. 255 and esp. xxiii. 30. 19), (*b*) P. Cornelius Scipio (proconsular command in Spain in 210: see xxvi. 18–20 and *MRR* i. 280), (*c*) L. Cornelius Lentulus and L. Manlius Acidinus (proconsular commands in Spain in 206: see *MRR* i. 299–300), (*d*) C. Cornelius Cethegus (proconsular command in Spain in 201: see *MRR* i. 320, where the appointment is rightly inferred), and (*e*) Cn. Cornelius Blasio and L. Stertinius (proconsular commands in Spain in 199: see *MRR* i. 328).[1] These commands were probably approved by the *concilium plebis* under the presidency of the tribunes, but L.'s evidence on this matter is not entirely consistent.[2]

A confident decision between these two possible modes of appointment is impossible, but, since these two commanders operated on their own away from the consuls and praetor, it is perhaps more likely that they were appointed by the senate and popular vote to their commands as *priuati cum imperio*.

See further viii. 23. 12 n. with *addendum* (on proconsuls and propraetors with prorogued *imperium*), Mommsen (1887–8) i. 680–2, Jashemski (1950) 6–7, 22–4 (on Cn. Scipio), Bleicken (1955) 48–9, Balsdon (1962) 134–5 (with extensive collection of evidence from the first century BC for the delegation of powers by magistrates), Kloft (1977) 98–9, Hölkeskamp (1987) 148–9, Loreto (1993) 49–51, Lintott (1999) 114, and Brennan (2000) 36–7 and 76–7.

27. 1–29. 20. THE BATTLE OF SENTINUM

27. 1. transgressos Appenninum, adopted by most modern editors, is Gronovius' conjecture for **N**'s *transgresso Appennino*, which is

---

[1] However, it is likely that after 218, for which year he was presumably given propraetorian *imperium* by his brother, Cn. Scipio commanded in Spain as *priuatus cum imperio* appointed by senate and popular vote.

[2] For (*d*) and (*e*) there are explicit references to the tribunes at xxx. 41. 4 and xxxi. 50. 10–11. On (*c*), for which L. writes (xxix. 13. 7, on the reappointment of these men) 'de Hispaniae imperio, quos in eam prouinciam duos pro consulibus mitti placeret latum ad populum est. omnes tribus eosdem L. Cornelium Lentulum et L. Manlium Acidinum pro consulibus, sicut priore anno tenuissent, obtinere eas prouincias iusserunt', it is very easy to infer tribunician presidency (although a reference to the *comitia tributa* is perhaps not impossible). On (*a*), for which L. writes 'populus iussit', tribunician presidency is not excluded, since L. very often uses *populus* loosely. On (*b*) xxvi. 18. 9 'omnes non centuriae modo sed etiam homines P. Scipioni imperium esse in Hispania iusserunt' seems to point to the *comitia centuriata*, but L., whose narrative concerning Scipio is often unreliable, could perhaps be wrong. See further Bleicken.

impossible since *transgredi* is not used in a passive sense. Emendation to *transgressi Appeninum* is ruled out by the word-order (thus, rightly, Madvig and Ussing). Walters obelized, stating that the corruption postulated by Gronovius' conjecture had not been satisfactorily explained; but if *transgressos* was corrupted to *transgresso* by the simple omission of one letter, then a consequential change to *Appeninum* is hardly difficult to posit.

in agrum Sentinatem: surviving inscriptions show that the site of Sentinum was at Sassoferrato, more precisely at the locality known now as Civita. The town lies in eastern Umbria in the valley of the Torrente Sentino (the name may not be old), which flows from the central Apennines into the Esino (the river of Iesi). Its fame rests on its role as host to the battle in this year: otherwise all that is known about its history in the republican period is that in 41 BC it was captured by Salvidienus Rufus during the Perusine War (Dio xlviii. 13. 2–6, App. *ciu.* v. 30. 116). It is mentioned at Stb. v. 2. 10 (C 227), Plin. *nat.* iii. 114, and Ptol. iii. 1. 46 (if one emends Κέντινον to Σέντινον). See further Bormann, *CIL* xi p. 838, Nissen (1883–1902) ii. 386, Philipp, *RE* iiA. 1508–9, and esp. Gaggiotti *et al.* (1980) 217–20 (with a description of the modern excavations).

The topographical evidence provided by L. and our other sources for the location of the battle is limited to (*a*) the statement (27. 1), which may be due to the plausible invention of L. or an earlier annalist, that the opposing camps were four Roman miles (about 6 km) apart, and (*b*) the implication that the terrain was suitable for use by Gallic chariots. This information does not allow us certainly to establish where in the vicinity of Sentinum the battle took place. Some antiquarians have suggested the ample plain of Fabriano, but Fabriano is not especially close to Sassoferrato. Others, looking for a site near Sassoferrato, have pointed to the plain south-west of it, but if L.'s *quattuor milium ferme* is reliable, this plain is not large enough. Sommella (1967: 35–47) has reviewed the various theories and argues not implausibly for a site 2 km north-west of Sassoferrato and 3 km south-west of the ancient site at Civitalba; he suggests that the battlefield was split by the Sanguerone, on the right bank of which the Gauls fought Decius and on the left bank of which the Samnites fought Fabius. As he points out, this would account for the impression gained from L. that the consuls fought what were almost separate battles. Only new evidence could resolve this problem.

2. ne unis castris miscerentur omnes: L. has already informed us (21. 12) that the enemy forces were too large to fit into one camp.

in aciem descenderet: see ix. 14. 7 n.

3. dies indicta pugnae: Madvig (1860: 417 n. 1 = 1877: 519 n. 1) proposed *dies inde dicta pugnae*, arguing (*a*) that *indicere* was not used in this way (whereas *diem dicere* is regular: see *TLL* v. 1. 1050. 11–18), and (*b*) that some connection with the previous sentence is desirable. The conjecture is attractive; but it is not certain, since (*a*) the expression *diem indicere* may be supported by other passages (most listed at *TLL* vii. 1. 1157. 45–8): i. 50. 6 'diem concilii . . . qui indixerit (*ΠΛ*: dixerit *M*)', xxvii. 30. 6 'concilioque ei locus et dies certa indicta', xxxvi. 6. 6 'nauibus eo ad diem indictum (*Bφ*: indictam *ψ*: dictum *Madvig*) concilio uenit', *SHA* xx. 11. 2 'non legitimo sed indicto senatus die', and *act. Arv.* Alex. B 5 (Henzen [1874] p. ccxx) (to which one may perhaps add xxxvi. 8. 2 'dies ad conueniendum . . . est dictus [*Bχ*: indictus *Mg*]),[1] and (*b*) the absence of a connective is not intolerable. See further Briscoe on xxxvi. 6. 6.

Samniti Gallisque: for the illogical change from singular to plural Drakenborch adduced the good parallels at ii. 45. 3 'Veiens hostis Etruscique', iii. 6. 3 'urbanos et agrestem', iv. 18. 5 'Faliscos . . . Veientem', xxiv. 9. 8, and xxx. 4. 7. Therefore there is no reason to emend *Samniti* to *Samnitibus* with F^c.

4. clam nocte: see ix. 16. 8 n.

5. Vaticano: Luterbacher suggested *Vaticano ⟨agro⟩*, but the ellipse given by the paradosis is not difficult; note the analogous omission involved in the expression *in Vaticano* (sc. *agro*) found at Plin. *nat.* iii. 54 and xviii. 20.

6. Etruscos ⟨et Vmbros⟩: Gundermann (1888: 366) proposed this supplement for two reasons. First, and more important, with § 3 'Etruscis Vmbri adiecti' and 'Etrusci Vmbrique iussi castra Romana oppugnare' preceding, and with § 11 'Etrusci et Vmbri' following, it seems a little odd that L. does not mention the Umbrians here. Secondly, Frontin. *strat.* i. 8. 3 'quibus adsecutis ad sua defendenda Etrusci Vmbrique deuerterunt', which almost certainly derives from L., includes a reference to the Umbrians. *et Vmbros* could easily have been omitted after the preceding *-os*. H. J. Müller (1889c: 48) rejected the supplement, arguing that Frontinus could have learnt about the Umbrians from elsewhere in the surrounding context.

---

[1] Ov. *fast.* i. 659 'lux haec indicitur', correctly cited at *TLL* loc. cit., is not truly parallel to what the paradosis offers in our passage because it has no equivalent to a noun dependent on *dies*.

7. summa rerum adducta: see 19. 3 n.
descensum in campum: see ix. 14. 7 n.

8–9. For interpretation of the omen of the wolf and the deer, see above, pp. 275–6.

8. inde diuersae ferae, cerua . . . lupus . . . deflexit: for the construction see vi. 2. 8 n.
data inter ordines uia: for the gap between the maniples see viii. 8. 5 n.

9. antesignanis: see viii. 11. 7 n.
illac . . . hinc . . . : translate: '"on that side," he said, "flight and slaughter attach themselves. From this side the victorious wolf of Mars, untouched and unblemished, has reminded us of the family [or 'race'] of Mars and of our founder"'. The coupling *illac . . . hinc* appears to be unique: no parallels are cited for it at either *TLL* vi. 2804. 31–2 or vii. 1. 334. 82–3, nor does *hac . . . illinc* appear to be attested anywhere.[1] Emendation of *illac* to *illinc* is impossible because *illinc* is unintelligible with *uertit*. *hac* could be written for *hinc*, but, since with *illac* preceding no scribe would have had a reason for either deliberately or accidentally changing *hac* to *hinc*, the conjecture should probably be resisted.
fuga . . . et caedes: for this coupling see ix. 24. 13 n.
uertit: is awkward. My translation 'attach themselves' assumes that L. uses the verb in the sense illustrated at ix. 38. 8 n. and *OLD s.u.* 17(b). However, in all the parallels for this usage the sense is completed with *in* governing an accusative of the people to whom the abstract concept is attaching, and it may be debated whether *illac* is equivalent. Yet, as the text stands, the alternative translation 'betake themselves' (*OLD s.u.* 12) is harder, since one would expect ⟨se⟩ *uertit* (in C. Gracch. *ORF* 61 'quo me miser conferam? quo uortam?' [cited for this intransitive usage in *OLD*] the preceding *me* makes all the difference); but perhaps *se* was omitted after -*es*.
integer et intactus: see 14. 20 n.
gentis nos Martiae . . . admonuit: for the association of the wolf with the foundation legend of Rome see 23. 12 (n.). Its role as a symbol of Rome is attested best on the coins produced by Papius in the Social War, for which see e.g. Sydenham (1952) 92 and 94 (nos. 628 and 641) and pl. 19. See further e.g. Bickerman (1969) 394–6.

---

[1] At *TLL* vii. 1. 334. 82–335. 2 *illac* in our passage is cited with Tert. *Val.* 26, which hardly seems comparable.

conditoris nostri: i.e. Romulus. 'Livy's treatment of the *conditores* allows us to identify further distinctions within that group. Not all of Rome's founders and foundations are equal. Romulus commands the greatest respect. He alone, for example, is often identified simply as *conditor, conditor noster,* and *conditor urbis*' (Miles [1988] 197 = [1995] 123).

10. dextro cornu Galli, sinistro Samnites constiterunt: for the phrasing see ix. 27. 8 n.
Q. Fabius . . . ⟨P.⟩ Decius: *Q.,* found in Mλ, is omitted by Π(= PUZ); *P.* is omitted by **N**. Since the omission of *praenomina* is very common in mss, since a scribe wishing to interpolate a *praenomen* is likely to have interpolated it also before *Decius,* and since *L. Volumnio* follows, I have accepted the reading of Mλ and supplied the balancing *P.* before *Decius.*

10–11. On the numbers of the Roman legions, see 18. 3–4 n.

11. pro consule: for the spelling see *addendum* to viii. 23. 12 n.
aequis uiribus: see vii. 33. 5 n.

28. 1. communis adhuc Mars belli erat: see vii. 8. 1 n.
qua Fortuna daret uires: see 12. 5 n.

2. arcebant magis quam inferebant pugnam: for this contrast see esp. Woodman's note on Vell. ii. 120. 1–2 'ultro Rhenum cum exercitu transgreditur; arma infert quae arcuisse pater et patria contenti erant', where together with our passage he cites iii. 8. 3 'non solum arcere bellum sed ultro etiam inferre', xxi. 21. 10, and 44. 3. Cf. also Cic. *Phil.* xiii. 14 'hoc (*sc.* exercitu) tu arcebis hostem, finis imperi propagabis' and Amm. xxix. 1. 2 'hoc obseruare principis iussu appositi, ut arcerent potiusquam lacesserent Persas'.
extrahebaturque in quam maxime serum diei certamen: amongst writers of military narrative the expressions *certamen, pugnam,* and *proelium extrahere* are affected above all by L.; cf. [x] iv. 41. 5, xxii. 59. 3, xxiii. 47. 4, xxvii. 27. 5, Curt. viii. 14. 28, Tac. *ann.* iv. 73. 4; note also *bellum extrahere* at iii. 2. 2, and xxv. 32. 6, and see *TLL* v. 2. 2068. 76–82. In all these passages *extrahere* has the sense 'draw out'. At 29. 8 'Fabius . . . ut ante dictum est . . . extraxerat diem' L., referring back to this passage, uses *extrahere* in a novel and arresting way, which combines the sense which it exhibits in our passage with the sense 'to waste time' (for which see Caes. *ciu.* i. 32.

3 'Catone . . . dies extrahente' and *TLL* 2069. 13–32); but Fabius was neither literally extending the day nor wasting time. For a parallel, albeit slightly less striking, see xxviii. 15. 3 'et ad id sedulo diem extraxerat Scipio ut sera pugna esset'.

3. ⟨et⟩ quos sustinere satis sit: the supplement is due to Dr Holford-Strevens; *sustinere* is found in F and various *recentiores* for **N**'s *sustineri*. The paradosis gives rise to two difficulties: (*a*) as Holford-Strevens observes, strict grammar demands that continuative *quos sustinere satis est* of direct speech should become *quos sustinere satis esse*; (*b*) the passive infinitive gives very awkward syntax. One may feel also (*c*) that the sentence would have more point than it has in the paradosis if the relative clause referred not to the Samnites and Gauls themselves but to their *impetus*. Holford-Strevens's conjecture deals with (*a*) and lessens the force of (*c*). If one is prepared to accept the grammatical anomaly, then *quem* (Koch [1861: 8]) for *quos* is attractive and gives the required point to the relative clause. Madvig, *ap*. Madvig and Ussing, conjectured *quo* (to be read with *sustineri*), but this is very awkward; later (1877: 231) he viewed Koch's conjecture with favour but suggested that the corruption to *quos* would be explained if L. had written *quom* (still with *sustineri*).

4. Gallorum . . . esse: for the notions that the Gauls expended all their fury in their first onslaught, and that their bodies were intolerant of heat, see vii. 12. 11 n. with *addendum*.
quidem etiam: see vii. 1. 6 n.
intolerantissima: see ix. 18. 1 n.
fluere: see vii. 33. 14 n.
primaque eorum proelia plus quam uirorum, postrema minus quam feminarum esse: the text has been variously garbled in the mss: MZsT have the truth; PU omit *proelia . . . feminarum*; and ZbZtθ place *esse* after *eorum*. No difficulty, however, is posed for the stemma if ZbZt adopted the reading of θ by contamination from descendants of D.

6. effudit has a sense here that embraces both the ideas 'let loose' and 'expended' or 'wasted'. For this second sense, a recognized but comparatively rare meaning of *effundere*, xxxviii. 17. 7 (on Galatians) 'si primum impetum, quem feruido ingenio et caeca ira effundunt, sustinueris . . .', Virg. *Aen*. v. 446 'Entellus uiris in uentum effudit', Curt. iv. 14. 13 'temeritas est, quam adhuc pro uirtute timuistis;

quae, ubi primum impetum effudit, uelut quaedam animalia emisso aculeo, torpet', and Sil. xvi. 339 'effusas primo certamine uires' are cited with our passage at *TLL* v. 2. 224. 72–84.

7. fortissimae iuuenum turmae: for the transferred epithet, see ix. 19. 2 n.; for the *turma* of cavalry, see viii. 7. 1 n.

proceres iuuentutis: for the expression see ix. 14. 16 n.; for *proceres* see ix. 18. 7 n.

in hostem is placed in an emphatic position before *ut*; whatever Fabius may do, Decius at least wishes to grapple with the enemy.

duplicem . . . incipiat: for rivalry between different wings, see ix. 40. 8–11 n.

8. euectos: see ix. 40. 12 n.

peditum is the conjecture of Madvig (1860: 193 = 1877: 231–2) for N's *equitum*. Even if one accepts Luterbacher's contention that *auertere* need mean only 'drove back' rather than 'put to flight', to be told that the Roman cavalry had twice driven back their Gallic counterparts, that on the second occasion they were *longius euecti*, and that now (*iam*) they were (still) fighting *inter media equitum agmina* seems very illogical. It is quite natural, however, that after putting to flight the cavalry they should turn their attention to the infantry and fight *inter media peditum agmina*. Weissenborn (ed.²) objected that, if they were *longius euecti*, they should not be in the middle of the ranks of the foot-soldiers; but L. may have imagined the infantry line of battle as far from where the cavalry were fighting. His other objection, that the Roman cavalry would not have met chariots among the infantry, has some force but is hardly decisive, since these chariots were about (§ 11) to charge against the Roman infantry. Luterbacher further objected that L. describes the Gallic troops as fighting in an *acies* and not an *agmen* (see §§ 11, 18, 29. 4, 11, 12); but this objection hardly seems cogent in view of 29. 13 'agmen' and other passages where *agmen* is virtually equivalent to *acies* (see viii. 30. 6 n.).

proelium cientes: see vii. 33. 12 n.

nouum pugnae . . . genus: as W–M and Pfiffig (1968: 330) rightly observe, L.'s comment is somewhat surprising, since one would have presumed that, after several previous battles against the Gauls, the Romans had already faced their chariots. That the Gauls did use chariots at Sentinum is likely enough, but it is just possible that this detail could be a piece of annalistic reconstruction.

9. insolitos eius tumultus Romanorum conterruit equos: *insolitos* is the reading of Zr; **N** (from which ZsZbZt do not diverge) had *insolitus*. Translate: '(the armed enemy) terrified the horses of the Romans, which were unused to such confusion'. Were **N**'s reading correct, one would have to translate: 'the unusual confusion which they (i.e. the armed enemy) caused terrified the horses of the Romans'; but *eius* is then very weak. The reading of Zr has the advantage of giving a hyperbaton which lends prominence and emphasis to both *insolitos eius tumultus* and *equos*.

The objective genitive after *insolitus* given by the conjecture in Zr is attested first at Sall. *Iug.* 39. 1, and then at *hist.* ii. 39, and conceivably at Curt. vii. 3. 13 (where, however, the paradosis probably needs emendation). It is found also with semantically related words, such as *insolens* and *insuetus*. See K–S i. 438 and *TLL* vii. 1. 1934. 2–3.

10. uelut lymphaticus pauor: see vii. 17. 3 n.
sternit: see vii. 24. 5 n.
equos uirosque: a standard Livian coupling. Here it means 'horses and riders' (so also probably at iii. 70. 6, xxi. 27. 5, xxiii. 5. 6, xxvi. 4. 8, and xxxi. 42. 1), but the *uiri* need not always be the riders of the *equi* (v. 37. 5, xxii. 52. 5, xxxvi. 19. 6). Note also *equi hominesque* at xxiv. 17. 7 and xxxv. 11. 7.
improuida fuga: the flight is *improuida*, because it heedlessly puts short-term above long-term safety. For this coupling I have found no parallel [x]; but for the general sense of the sentence, cf. xl. 58. 6 'itaque cum praecipiti fuga per rupes praealtas improuidi sternerentur ruerentque'.

11. turbata . . . signa: see vii. 33. 8 n.
antesignani: see viii. 11. 7 n.

12. uociferari: thus UT^c for **N**'s *uociferare*. Reasons for accepting the deponent form are given at vii. 12. 14 n.

13. datum hoc nostro generi est: for this kind of comment, cf. esp. 39. 14 'datum hoc forsitan nomini familiaeque suae, ut aduersus maximos conatus Samnitium opponerentur duces'; but note also passages such as Ter. *Eun.* 395–6 'est istuc datum | profecto ut grata mihi sint quae facio omnia'.
luendis: see ix. 9. 19 n.
piacula: see vi. 21. 7 n.
legiones . . . dabo: see viii. 6. 6 n.

mecum: in this context cf. 29. 4 'secum' and viii. 9. 8 'mecum'.
Telluri ac Dis Manibus: see viii. 9. 8 n.

14. M. Liuium: see 1. 7 n.
descendens in aciem: see ix. 14. 7 n.
praeire: see ix. 46. 6 n.
populi Romani Quiritium: see viii. 9. 8 n.

15. eodemque habitu: see viii. 9. 9 n.

16. secundum sollemnes precationes is ambiguous: it could
mean either 'according to the customary prayers' or 'after the customary prayers'. The second translation seems better, since *adiecis-
set* strongly suggests that the devotion of the younger Decius had
some elements added which were not found in the *deuotio* of his
father at the Veseris (see the following nn.).

Expressions like *sollemnes precationes* are quite common; cf. e.g.
xxxix. 15. 1–2, Cic. *Mur.* 1, and Stat. *silu.* iv. 3. 142, and see Appel
(1909) 207; but Appel's contention that *sollemnis* refers to the tone of
voice in which the *precatio* was delivered (rather than to its customary ritual nature) seems questionable.

formidinem ac fugam: in the account of the *deuotio* in book viii we
find 'terrore formidine morteque', and so *formidinem ac fugam* is
indeed an addition, as L. implies; but it is found in the formula
for the *deuotio* of the enemy quoted at Macr. *Sat.* iii. 9. 10. For the
coupling see further vii. 37. 16 n.

caedemque ac cruorem: this coupling is reasonably common but
more frequent in verse than prose; to the passages listed with ours
at *TLL* iv. 1244. 37–40, add e.g. Cic. *Phil.* iv. 11 'nullus ei ludus
uidetur esse iucundior quam cruor, quam caedes, quam ante oculos
trucidatio ciuium' and Petron. 123 l. 215 'arma, cruor, caedes, incen-
dia totaque bella'. The two nouns are very frequently found in close
proximity, esp. in Silius (e.g. v. 534). See further Wölfflin (1881)
49–50 = (1933) 255.

17. caelestium . . . iras: see vii. 2. 3 n.
tela arma: for this coupling see vi. 6. 14 n.

18. concitat equum: for the warrior riding to his death after a *deuotio*, cf. viii. 9. 19 n.
ipse infestis telis est interfectus: an emphatic series of long sylla-
bles and inversion of the more normal *interfectus est* underline this
climactic moment of narrative, as Decius rides to his death.

29. 1. humanae . . . opis: although the coupling of *ops* and *humana* is generally quite common, it is much affected by L. To the passages cited by Ogilvie on iii. 19. 10, add i. 16. 7, ii. 20. 12 'ibi nihil nec diuinae nec humanae opis dictator praetermittens' (the closest parallel to L.'s formulation here), vii. 30. 3, xxi. 40. 11. The expression is usually used in the context of a contrast, explicit or implicit, between humans and the divine.

quae res, often equivalent to *quod*, is used regularly by L.; cf. ii. 50. 7–8 'quo magis se hostis inferebat, cogebantur breuiore spatio et ipsi orbem colligere, quae res . . . paucitatem eorum insignem . . . faciebat', iv. 13. 5 'iam comitia consularia instabant, quae res necdum compositis eum maturisue satis consiliis oppressit', v. 47. 4, viii. 29. 2, xxviii. 3. 9, and other instances among the examples of the collocation to be found at Packard (1968) iv. 33–4.

terrori alias esse solet: see ix. 22. 7 n.

nouam de integro uelle instaurare pugnam: L. uses *de integro* more than any other author and affects the virtually redundant coupling of it with *nouus* or cognates, particularly in the context of a battle or war being renewed; cf. esp. xxxvii. 19. 5 'instauremus nouum de integro bellum' and (without *instaurare*) xxii. 5. 7 'et noua de integro exorta pugna est', xxiv. 16. 2, and xxx. 34. 12; also i. 19. 1, v. 5. 6, xxi. 21. 8. For *de integro* in the context of the renewal of war cf. also ix. 8. 6; for its use with *instaurare* cf. also Val. Max. viii. 1. *abs*. 4. In general, see *TLL* vii. 1. 2080. 44–65.

2. uelut alienata mente: 'almost out of their minds'. L. quite often tones down violent expressions of this kind (cf. ii. 12. 13 'uelut alienato ab sensu . . . animo' and xxv. 39. 4 'hostes . . . uelut alienatos sensibus', and see 28. 10 above and in general vii. 17. 3 n.), but his practice is not invariable; contrast e.g. iii. 48. 1 'decemuir alienatus ad libidinem animo'.

uana . . . tela: see vi. 12. 9 n.

in cassum: 'in vain', 'to no purpose'. This expression, sometimes written as one word, is formed from *in* and *cassus*, which can mean 'lacking', 'empty', and hence 'fruitless' or 'vain'. In prose it is rare, being attested elsewhere in pre-Antonine writers only at [*][x] ii. 49. 7, Sall. *hist*. iii. 48. 11, Sen. *dial*. x. 11. 1, Col. iv. 3. 5, 22. 7, and Tac. *ann*. i. 4. 2; note also its appearance at Front. p. 109. 8 and Apul. *apol*. 97 (it appealed to the archaizing taste of these writers) and at Just. xi. 15. 6, Dict. iii. 18, iv. 9, and in fourteen passages in Ammianus. In verse it is more common, esp. in epic: after its appearance at Plaut. *Poen*. 360, note five instances in Lucretius, seven instances in Virgil, *cons. Liu.* 75, Sen. *Ag.* 894, *Med.* 26, *Thy.* 1066, Luc. ii. 263, iv. 281, Val. Fl. ii. 54, Stat. *Theb.* i. 471, iii. 717, and Sil. x. 48–9. This suggests that between the times of Sallust and Tacitus the expression would have seemed poetical. Like other poeticisms, it was taken up by the historians (note its use by Justin, 'Dictys', and esp. Ammianus), and Columella too sometimes affects unusual vocabulary. For instances of the expression in later Latin see *TLL* iii. 522. 26–523. 24. For the combination with *uana*, to which it adds little, cf. Sil. loc. cit.

et nec pugnae meminisse nec fugae: for the construction here W–M compare xxix. 24. 10 'quidquid militum nauiumque in Sicilia erat, cum Lilybaeum conuenisset et nec urbs multitudinem hominum neque portus naues caperet . . .' and (slightly different) xxxix. 50. 2. When there is a gap between the ideas being disjoined and the initial co-ordinating conjunction, *nec . . . aut . . . aut* is perhaps more regular; see e.g. Caes. *Gall.* i. 22. 1 'cum mos a Labieno teneretur, ipse ab hostium castris non longius mille et quingentis passibus abesset, neque, ut postea ex captiuis comperit, aut ipsius aduentus aut Labieni cognitus esset . . .'. See further K–S ii. 47.

3. ex parte altera: see vi. 19. 1 n.

cui lictores Decius tradiderat iusseratque pro praetore esse: before *iusserat* one must understand *quem* from the preceding *cui*; see 26. 6 n. For the propraetorian *imperium* of Livius see 26. 15 n.; for the spelling *pro praetore* see *addendum* to viii. 23. 12 n.; for the lictors of those appointed *pro praetore* by a magistrate see xxix. 9. 6 and Mommsen (1887–8) i. 385–6.

4. Telluris Matris ac Deorum Manium: so also at viii. 9. 8 (n.) the Latins are devoted to Tellus and the Manes. For *Mater* as an epithet of Tellus cf. esp. Varr. *rust.* i. 1. 5 'Iouem et Tellurem: itaque, quod ii parentes magni dicuntur, Iuppiter pater appellatur, Tellus Terra mater'; also Virg. *Aen.* xi. 71, and Ov. *fast.* i. 671. Very closely comparable is the much more common appellation of Terra as *mater*; see e.g. viii. 6. 10, Varr. loc. cit., Ov. *fast.* ii. 719, Val. Max. i. 7. 3, and other evidence cited at *TLL* viii. 443. 6–16. In general on *Pater* and *Mater* as epithets of gods and goddesses, see viii. 9. 6 n., adding references to *TLL* viii. 442. 1–443. 60 (numerous instances of *mater*) and to viii. 1. 6 [Lua Mater]).

furiarum ac formidinis is a coupling which I have not been able to parallel (so also Wölfflin [1881: 60 = 1933: 262]).

5–13. cum subsidiis ex nouissima acie . . . principes: for the manipular tactic described here, see vii. 23. 7 and viii. 8. 3–14 nn.

5. L. Cornelius Scipio: see x. 11. 10 n.
C. Marcius: see ix. 33. 1 n.
subsidiis: see ix. 17. 15 n.
hortamen is found only here in L., and elsewhere in prose [*] only at Tac. *Germ.* 7. 2. Since the word is found several times in poetry (Ov. *met.* i. 277, Luc. vii. 736, Val. Fl. vi. 94, Stat. *Theb.* iv. 11 and viii. 157), it should probably be regarded as poetical, like many other nouns in -*men*. However, some caution is required in making this judgement, since the equivalent *hortamentum*, unlike the cognate *hortatio*, is not common, being found in prose at [*] vii. 11. 6, Sall. *Iug.* 98. 7, Tac. *hist.* iv. 18. 2, and then more commonly in later antiquity, starting with Gell. ix. 3. 4, xiii. 25. 21, Apul. *Socr.* 19, and in verse at Sil. v. 154.[1]

6. pede conlato: see vii. 33. 11 n.
collecta humi pila: these probably included enemy javelins; compare Sall. *Iug.* 58. 3, where the Romans are said to have re-used enemy *pila*.
testudinem: see 41. 14 n.

7. raris is Hertz's conjecture: Mλ have or had *uerarisque rutis*, Π(= PUZ) *uerutis* (*-erru-* P) (with *scuta plerisque* in ZbZt for the preceding *plerisque in scuta*). In view of similar corruptions elsewhere in books i–x (vol. i, pp. 316–20), these ms. readings are explained most easily if one postulates that *rarisque* (or *raris*: see below) and *uerutis* (= 'light javelins': see viii. 24. 13 n.) stood as variants in **N**, that in Mλ the two words have been conflated, and that in Π *rarisque* has been ignored (thus e.g. Hertz ad loc. and Madvig [1860: 18 = 1877: 19]). (In which case, *pace* Hertz, the manner in which *uerutis* is bisected in Mλ by *rarisque*, and its presence in Π, would make it likely that it stood in **N** before correction.) However, other explanations of the ms. variants are possible: *uerutisque raris* could have stood in an ancestor of **N** and have been corrupted to *uerarisque rutis* by a syllabic transposition (Π's reading would then have been caused by omission of *arisque* through *saut du même au même*); or one may postulate an omission.[2]

---

[1] But note also Liv. Andr. fr. iii 'hortamenta, flagella quibus aurigae utuntur cum equo hortantur. Aiax mastigophorus'.
[2] The tentative suggestion of Weissenborn (*Komm.*), that several words had fallen out of the text here, seems less probable, but note the conjectures of Drakenborch and Walters considered in the next paragraph.

Since *uerutum* is not a common word, and since its intrusion into the text is not easy to explain, one would have expected *uerutis* to be sound; but no reading with it gives good sense. If one adopts *uer(r)utis* from Π, the preceding *quibus plerisque* would refer to the majority of the javelins lying on the ground, most of which hit only the shields of the Gauls, and *uerutis* would contrast with *quibus plerisque* by means of adversative asyndeton. One could translate: 'After the majority of these had been planted in the shields ⟨of the Gauls⟩, but the light javelins actually in their bodies, the wedge of men was laid low . . .'.[1] However, the asyndeton is awkward and the resulting sense poor, since it is not clear why light javelins should have been especially efficacious in reaching the bodies. Alternatively, if the readings in **N** were caused by an omission, of *rutis* in Walters's opinion but much more probably of *rarisque* (its position in Mλ would be explained most easily if it was written in the margin with *ue-* ending one line and *-rutis* beginning the next), there would be a diplomatic explanation of Drakenborch's *rarisque uerutis* and Walters's *uerutisque raris*, conjectures which incorporate both words. The former is preferable since it retains *-que* in the position in which it is found in the mss; with it the preceding *quibus plerisque* would again refer to the majority of the javelins lying on the ground, most of which hit only the shields of the Gauls, and *-que* would have an adversative sense contrasting the few light javelins that did actually hit the bodies of the Gauls; translate 'After the majority of these had been planted in the shields ⟨of the Gauls⟩ but a few light javelins actually in their bodies, the wedge of men was laid low . . .'. Yet the contrast between *rarisque uerutis* and *quibus plerisque* would be a little awkward, and the success of the light javelins would remain very surprising. Pettersson (1930: 135–6) conjectured *uerutis rarisque*, with which both *plerisque* and *raris* are to be understood as distributing *uerutis*, and which postulates a corruption that could be explained in the same way. This conjecture is not vulnerable to the argument that *ueruta* should not be piercing armour when other projectiles have been unable to do this; but the collocation *quibus plerisque . . . uerutis* is impossibly awkward.

Therefore it is best to assume that at some point in the tradition *uerutis* has intruded, even though a motive for the intrusion is not

---

[1] Drakenborch reports X and other *recentiores* as having *uerutisque*. Adopted by e.g. Weissenborn (*Komm.*), this would have to be explained in a similar way but with the adversative sense supplied by *-que* rather than the asyndeton; however, it does not explain the position of *-que* in Mλ.

easily found.[1] If *rarisque*, an alternative conjecture of Hertz and adopted by e.g. Madvig and Ussing and by Foster, is right, then *-que* must have a sense that verges on the adversative; translate: 'After the majority of these had been planted in the shields ⟨of the Gauls⟩, and/but a few actually in their bodies, the wedge of men was laid low . . .'; but it is awkward. There is no such problem with *raris*, the conjecture of Hertz adopted in the lemma (and adopted previously by both H. J. and M. Müller); translate: 'After the majority of these had been planted in the shields ⟨of the Gauls⟩, but a few actually in their bodies, the wedge of men was laid low . . .'. This gives excellent sense (*plerisque* and *raris* distributing *quibus* and contrasting with each other through adversative asyndeton), and, as Heraeus (1893: 78) observed, finds a precise grammatical parallel at xxxiv. 39. 4 'itaque ex aduerso missa tela nulla in corporibus rara in scutis haerebant'. Its weakness is that it fails to account for *-que* in Mλ; but this perhaps intruded from *plerisque*, and the sense which *raris* gives is so good that I have adopted it.[2]

At xxxi. 34. 3 L. observes that projectiles such as javelins made only *rara . . . uolnera*; but for confusion caused by projectiles sticking in shields, see vii. 23. 9 n.

sternitur: see vii. 24. 5 n.

attoniti: see vii. 17. 3 n.

8. cunctando: the allusion to Q. Fabius Maximus Verrucosus, the famous *cunctator* and the grandson (or great-grandson) and most illustrious descendant of Rullianus, is the clearest indication in this episode that L. regards the tactics that Rullianus adopts as characteristic of his family, just as *deuotio* is a characteristic of Decii. For discussion of the Roman view that families had stock characteristics see vol. i, pp. 98–9.

9. praefectis equitum: although Roman cavalry (viii. 7. 1 n.) as well as allied (see e.g. xl. 31. 3) could be commanded by prefects, *alas* (used regularly of allied squadrons) shows that here L. was thinking of allied commanders. Since a squadron of Campanian cavalry is

---

[1] Perhaps it is a dittographic corruption of *plerisque in scuta*; or perhaps a scribe wrote it in the margin of his copy, remembering *ueruta* from viii. 24. 13. If one were desperate to save a reference to *ueruta*, one could argue that *pila* ousted *ueruta*, which was then restored in the margin but corrupted into the wrong case. But this sequence of corruption is highly improbable.

[2] Luterbacher conjectured *nec raris*, but this is diplomatically no improvement on *raris* (*nec* would hardly explain *uerutis* or *-que*) and would give very awkward sense, as it would virtually contradict the following *magna pars integris corporibus*.

mentioned again at § 12, W–M may have been right to suggest that L. thought that the Campanian cavalry was split into two.

ad latus Samnitium circumducere alas: 'to lead their squadrons around ⟨the side of the battlefield⟩ to face the flank of the Samnites'. Lines of battle were vulnerable to attack from the side, esp. from cavalry (note *transuersos* below).

in transuersos: see ix. 40. 12 n.

sensim: see viii. 8. 11 n.

signa inferre refers back to 28. 2 'arcebant magis quam inferebant pugnam'.

subsidiis: see ix. 17. 15.

commouere: see ix. 27. 10 n.

12. Galli testudine facta conferti stabant looks back to §§ 6–7, but is a little surprising, as L. there gives the impression that the Romans had begun to cut down the Gauls in the *testudo*. For this reason Weissenborn (ed.²) considered deletion of these words. However, § 8–§ 12 'stabant' should be seen as contemporaneous with the *deuotio* of Decius and its aftermath (like many other writers, L. finds it convenient for exposition to narrate successively events that had happened simultaneously): therefore Fabius and the Decians end up attacking the Gauls at more or less the same time. For *testudine* see 41. 14 n.

audita morte collegae is very similar in phrasing to viii. 10. 1 'audito euentu collegae', from the identical point in L.'s description of the battle at the Veseris.

Campanorum alam: see viii. 14. 1–12 n. (vol. ii, p. 556).

13. tertiae . . . legionis: cf. 27. 10–11 and see 18. 3–4 n.

agmen is virtually equivalent to the preceding *aciem*: see 28. 8, viii. 30. 6 nn.

14. Ioui Victori: although our sources say nothing about the building of this temple, references to a temple of Jupiter Victor in later periods of Roman history show that the vow of Fabius Rullianus was fulfilled. That its date of dedication was 13 April is shown by Ov. *fast.* iv. 621–2 'occupat Aprilis Idus cognomine Victor | Iuppiter: hac illi sunt data templa die' and *fast. Ant.* ad diem (Mancini [1921] 92; *I.I.* xiii. 2, pp. 8, 440).[1] Other references to the temple are at Jos.

---

[1] Since the epithets *Victor* and *Inuictus* are not the same, those scholars (e.g. Coarelli loc. cit.) who hold that Ov. *fast.* vi. 650 'Idibus (of June) Inuicto sunt data templa Ioui' refers to a different temple are likely to be right.

ant. Iud. xix. 4. 3 (248) (the consuls summon the senate to the temple after the assassination of Caligula), Dio xlvii. 40. 2 (the altar outside the temple struck by lightning in 43 BC), lx. 35. 1 (prodigy in AD 54), and perhaps Dio xlv. 17. 2 (prodigies in 43 BC, but the identity of the temple struck by lightning is not certain). The location of the temple is not certain: the view that it was on the Palatine rests on a late reference in the *Notitia urbis Romae*; the slightly more probable view that it was on the Quirinal depends on *ILLRP* 187, a dedication to Jupiter Victor found on that hill. See further Platner and Ashby (1929) 306–7, L. Richardson (1992) 227, Ziolkowski (1992) 91–4, and F. Coarelli in Steinby (1993–2000) iii. 161 (all with further bibliography).

With this dedication to Jupiter Victor we may compare other evidence which shows that in the years before Sentinum the Romans were beginning to take an interest in Victoria: in 305 a statue of Hercules, a god often associated with victory (23. 3 n.), was set up on the Capitol (ix. 44. 16 n.); in 294 Postumius Megellus dedicated his temple of Victoria, which he had vowed when curule aedile (33. 9 n.); in either 296 or 295 the falling to the ground of a statue of victory was regarded as a prodigy (see Zon. viii. 1. 2 [quoted above, p. 246]; we do not know when the statue was erected); and in 293 for the first time the Romans watched the games wearing garlands (a symbol of victory) (x. 47. 3 n.). From a slightly later period note the appearance of Hercules on the obverse of the silver didrachms of *c*.269 (discussed at x. 23. 12 n.) and the appearance of Roma on the obverse, and Victoria with palm branch and laurels on the reverse, of the didrachms struck in the First Punic War (Crawford [1974] 138–40, 714, and pl. I). Thereafter we have ample evidence for the adoption of Victoria as a symbol by both republican and imperial Rome: for the idea of the Romans as *inuicti* see vii. 10. 4 n.

The idea of Victoria was almost certainly adopted at Rome under the influence of Alexander the Great, who was called ἀνίκητος (ix. 18. 17 n.) and associated himself with the symbolism of Νίκη, and of the Diadochi, who in an attempt to legitimize their rule used similar symbolism. Weinstock (1957: 247) did not think that in the years around Sentinum it had yet become the potent symbol of later years. However, one may differ: in the years after 311 the Romans had regularly defeated the Samnites and Etruscans, as well as Hernici, Aequi, Umbri, Marsi, Paeligni, and Gauls. Well might they adopt Victoria as a symbol of their aggressive imperialism.

See Weinstock (1957) esp. 215–18, 247; also *id.*, *RE* viiiA. 2505–6 and (1971) 93–4, Crawford (1974) 714–15, and Harris (1979) 123–5.

spoliaque hostium: the vow is carried out at § 18.
uouisset: see vii. 28. 4 n. with *addendum*.

15. temptata ab exclusis turba suorum pugna: 'a stand was attempted by those who had been shut out because of the crowd of their own side'.

16. Gellius Egnatius: see 18. 1 n.

17. caesa . . . capta: for the figures for enemy captured, see 14. 21, for general discussion of casualty figures vii. 17. 9 n. There are less precise reports of enemy killed at Duris (*ap.* D.S. xxi. 6 = *FGrH* 76 F 56) and Plb. ii. 19. 6, both quoted above, pp. 268 and 270.
nec incruenta uictoria fuit: for this expression see vii. 8. 7 n.

18. ex P. Deci exercitu caesa septem milia, ex Fabi mille septingenti: for the first time in book x L. begins to give more detailed figures for Roman casualties: see also 31. 7 and 36. 15.
septingenti: here, at 33. 6, and at 34. 3 **N** had *acc* (*uel sim.*). Drakenborch's view that this is a corruption of *dcc* (i.e. *septingenti*) is the easiest and most economical explanation of this. For similar corruptions see 14. 21 n.
ad quaerendum collegae corpus: so too L. (viii. 10. 10) records that at the Veseris Manlius Torquatus sent men to search for the body of the elder Decius. For the expression cf. Tac. *ann.* i. 23. 1.
spolia hostium coniecta in aceruum Ioui Victori cremauit: for the burning of spoil see § 14 and the discussion at viii. 1. 6 n.

30. 1–3. CN. FULVIUS' CAMPAIGN AND THE SAMNITES'
DEFEAT BY THE PAELIGNI

30. 1 per eosdem dies: see vii. 18. 2 n.
ab Cn. Fuluio: M omits *ab*, a reading to which Walters ascribes *fort. recte*, citing viii. 15. 2 (of events in 337 BC) 'Aurunci, T. (tito *codd.*: a tito *ed. Med.* 1478) Manlio consule [i.e. 340 BC] in deditionem accepti, nihil deinde mouerunt' and xxx. 40. 7 'Cn. Lentulus consul cupiditate flagrabat prouinciae Africae, seu bellum foret, facilem uictoriam, seu iam finiretur, finiti tanti belli se (*codd.*: a se *J. Perizonius*) consule gloriam petens'. Although M sometimes stands alone in the truth against the other primary mss (see vol. i, pp. 321–2 with *addendum*), it is easier to regard its reading here as a mistake: (*a*) the reading of ΠΛ makes excellent sense (for the expression *res ab aliquo gesta*

[*est*] cf. e.g. iii. 3. 7 'ab altero consule res gesta egregie est' and vii. 26.
13 'cum Graecis a Camillo nulla memorabilis gesta res'); (*b*) viii. 15.
2 is not parallel to our passage because *Manlio consule* need be no
more than an indication of date, without stress on the agency of
Manlius; and (*c*) at xxx. 40. 7 the paradosis must be corrupt and
Perizonius' conjecture correct: Lentulus would get no glory if the
Second Punic War were finished when he was consul (which was in
fact what was to happen when Scipio Africanus concluded terms of
peace in this year) but only if the terms of peace were concluded by
him as consul (and not by Scipio).

For Fulvius see 4. 7 n.

pro praetore: see 26. 15, *addendum* to viii. 23. 12 nn.

Perusinorum: for Perusia see ix. 40. 18 n.

Clusinorum: for Clusium see 25. 11 n.

Paelignum . . . Paelignis: for the Paeligni see vii. 38. 1 n.; for
Roman relations with the Abruzzese tribes in this perod see ix. 29.
1–5 n.

2. signa militaria ad uiginti capta: for the capture of enemy
standards see vii. 37. 16 n.

3. circumuentum . . . caesi: for the coupling see viii. 35. 11 n.

30. 4–7. discrepant views on the size of the enemy
forces at sentinum

4. magna eius diei . . . fama: for the form of L.'s expression, cf.
perhaps Tac. *ann*. iii. 60. 3 'magnaque eius diei species fuit'.

stanti: for the dative participle see vii. 10. 6 n.

5. centum quadraginta milia trecentos triginta: the reading
adopted comes from Oros. iii. 21. 6 'Gallorum et Samnitium peditum CXL milia CCCXXX, equitum uero XLVII milia Liuius refert, et
carpentarios mille in armis contra aciem stetisse Romanis' (the apparatus in Zangemeister's edn. [*CSEL* v] leaves little doubt that this is
the paradosis). M has *x. cccxxx*, Π(= PZbZt) *xi cccxxx*, U *xi cccxxx*,
Zs *milia quadraginta et trecentum triginta*, T¹ *quadraginta tricentos
triginta milia*, Tᶜ *quadraginta milia trecentos triginta*, and θ *xl cccxxx*.
The corruption in L.'s mss, very common with numerals, and the
variation between them and those of Orosius (which may themselves be corrupt) does not allow the truth to be ascertained with
certainty.

To consider the reading of L.'s mss first. If the reading of T^1 diverges from that of T^c and θ because of a mistaken transposition that was corrected by T^c (an assumption which seems very reasonable), then λ must have read an abbreviation of *quadraginta milia trecentos triginta*. The reading of the Π mss is close to this, but PZbZtU have XI for XL, and PZbZt lack the suprascript stroke indicating that the numeral is a multiple of a thousand. As for M, it has neither the L nor the suprascript stroke. These readings allow the possibility that **N** too read an abbreviation of *quadraginta milia trecentos triginta* which was then corrupted by M and Π, and prior to Hertz many editors printed this. However, it is clear from earlier in the sentence that some of L.'s sources recorded an enormous figure for the size of the forces facing Rome at Sentinum, and in such a context 40,330 seems uncomfortably small: note that at ix. 27. 14 L. mentions that 30,000 enemy were killed or captured (at least according to his sources), at ix. 37. 11 that around 60,000 were killed or captured, and at ix. 43. 17 that 30,000 were killed. Furthermore, L. goes on to record a figure of 46,000 for the enemy cavalry, and he is unlikely to have thought that they had more cavalry than infantry.

Of conjectures that take no account of Orosius, the most plausible are *milia cccxxx* (Hertz, followed by Klinger [1884: 42–3], W–M and M. Müller).[1] This conjecture postulates that the initial XL, XI, or X of the mss are corruptions of the sign ∞ indicating that a numeral is a multiple of a thousand. The resulting figure of 330,000 would give an enormous army, far larger than any that could have been deployed in a battle in the ancient world, but perhaps not too large to be conceived in the imagination of L.'s sources. Niebuhr (1837–44: iii. 385 n. 647) conjectured *deciens centena milia*, Walters *sexiens centena milia*. As Niebuhr observed, it is conceivable that L.'s sources dared to write of such huge armies, but the corruptions postulated by these conjectures are more complex than that for those of Hertz and Madvig. Walters objected that Niebuhr's conjecture would give too high a proportion of infantry to cavalry (he compared the figures of Italian forces given at Plb. ii. 24), but in their desire to exaggerate L.'s sources may well have abandoned plausibility on such a mundane matter.

Since the manner in which we heal the textual corruption will affect our view of the historical techniques of the annalists,[2] there is

---

[1] The two last write the numeral out in full: whether L. did this here, and whether he was consistent on this matter, we cannot know.

[2] At vol. i, p. 97 I quoted this passage from Walters's text without making clear that *sexiens centena milia* was his conjecture.

quite a strong case for obelizing. However, I have preferred to adopt the reading of Orosius: it gives excellent sense, describing an army that is sufficiently large; and, if one postulates the loss of the initial *c*, the reading of L.'s mss could derive from it. Koehler (1860: 97–8) was perhaps the first to see that the text of Orosius, not properly edited in his day, could elucidate that of L.

equitum sex et quadraginta milia: if the mss of Orosius are correct in their report of the number of infantry, then they may very well be correct in their report of the number of cavalry. I retain the reading of **N** simply because it cannot be shown to be wrong, and the difference of 1,000 in a figure that is invented is of no great importance.

6. pro consule: for the spelling see *addendum* to viii. 23. 12 n.

7. in pluribus annalibus: for the expression, see vii. 18. 10 n.; for L.'s stating that he was following the majority view, see vi. 42. 5 n.
Tifernum: see ix. 44. 6 n.
fundit fugatque: the identical words are found seven times elsewhere in L. (i. 10. 4, ii. 31. 1, 33. 4, 53. 3, iii. 8. 6, v. 26. 7, xxix. 31. 7), always before a heavy or fairly heavy pause. The coupling of *fundere* and *fugare* is extremely common in military narrative: cf. also e.g. 19. 19, ix. 22. 6, 37. 10 and see Wölfflin (1881) 60 = (1933) 261–2, *TLL* vi. 1569. 1–6, and Ogilvie on ii. 31. 1. For the Livian affectation of the sentence ending with *-que* see Kraus (1992), esp. 325–6 (on Livy) and 328 (on other authors avoiding this particular expression).

30. 8–10. THE TRIUMPH OF FABIUS RULLIANUS

8–31. 3. Deciano exercitu . . . exercitu Deciano: see vi. 9. 11 n.

8. milites triumphantem secuti sunt: in a triumph the troops of the *triumphator*, led by their officers, followed his chariot: cf. e.g. vii. 13. 10, xlv. 40. 4, Prop. iv. 3. 68, Vell. ii. 67. 4. Since in the triumphal notices of his later books, which certainly go back to official documents (see 46. 2–8 n.), L. often comments on the presence or absence of the escorting army of the *triumphator* (presence: xxviii. 9. 10 [M. Livius Salinator], xxxiv. 52. 10, xxxvi. 40. 13, xxxix. 7. 3, xl. 43. 5, xlv. 40. 4; absence: xxviii. 9. 10 [C. Claudius Nero], xxxi. 49. 3, xxxvii. 46. 6), it is conceivable that this comment derives from official records. However, the troops are mentioned also at iii. 10. 4 and 29. 5, passages which are unlikely to rest on very good testimony; it would have been easy for L. or an annalist to reconstruct this scene; and here and at iii. 29. 5 reference to the troops is coupled with reference to their ribald jests, a topic with which L. was fascinated. See further Ehlers, *RE* viiA. 509.

9. inconditis militaribus: for these uncouth military songs see vii. 38. 3 n. The paradosis has caused difficulty: some *recentiores* have *inconditis militaribus ⟨iocis⟩* (cf. vii. 17. 5 'militaribus iocis'); Zr and other *recentiores* have *inconditis ⟨carminibus⟩ militaribus* (cf. iv. 20. 2 'carmina incondita'); H. J. Müller proposed and printed *inconditis militaribus ⟨carminibus⟩* (which postulates a corruption very easy to explain);[1] and Zingerle (1889: 988) proposed *inconditis militaribus ⟨uersibus⟩* (cf. iv. 53. 11 'inconditi uersus'; again, the corruption would be easy to explain). But the substantivized use of *incondita* presents no difficulties: it is used in this way almost certainly at vii. 10. 13 'inter carminum prope in modum incondita quaedam militariter ioculantes Torquati cognomen auditum' (where for the difficulties of the text see n. ad loc.) and certainly at e.g. Varro, *Men.* 363 'incondita cantare' and Virg. *ecl.* 2. 4–5 'haec incondita solus | . . . iactabat' (all cited at *TLL* vii. 1. 1002. 25–33); and the qualification with another adjective of a substantivized participle used in the plural is reasonably common (see K–S i. 230). See further Walters and Conway (1918) 5–6.

excitataque memoria parentis, aequata euentu publico priuatoque filii laudibus: 'and the memory of his parent was revived, being equalled by the renown of the son in both the success which he had brought to the state and in his private fate'. *aequata* is best taken as being co-ordinate in asyndeton to *excitata*, *laudibus* as an ablative dependent on *aequata*. *euentu* is ambiguous: it suggests (*a*) (*OLD s.u.* 1[a]) the 'outcome of a situation' (here, with the force of *publico* felt, the battles at the Veseris and the Sentinum); (*b*) (*TLL* v. 2. 1020. 46–60, *OLD* 3[a]) the death or fate of an individual (here, with the force of *priuato* felt, the deaths of the Decii; cf. viii. 10. 1 'audito euentu collegae' [of the elder Decius]), and (*c*) (*OLD* 1[b]) the fulfilment of a prayer (here that uttered by the Decii before their deaths). *excitata* is here translated as 'revived', but the verb is used also of the rousing of ghosts (*OLD s.u.* 3[d]), appropriate in a context recalling the elder Decius. For the expression *memoriam excitare* add Cic. *Sest.* 11 and *orat.* 35 to the passages cited at *TLL* v. 2. 1259. 39–42.

---

[1] Luterbacher proposed *inconditis militum carminibus*; but there is no difficulty with the combination of *inconditis* and *militaribus* given by H. J. Müller's conjecture, and this variation on it is diplomatically much harder.

Following Doujat, Drakenborch preferred to construe *laudibus* as a dative; but it is much more natural to say that the exploits of the father were later equalled by those of the son than that the exploits of the father equalled those of the son: the Romans were interested more in whether sons lived up to the reputations of their fathers than the converse, and the second interpretation seems almost to subtract from the glory of the son. Tanquil Faber proposed *aequatis* for *aequata*, which both is unnecessary and makes L. describe the son as being equalled by the father;[1] Walters implausibly took *filii laudibus* with *excitata*.

10. data ex praeda militibus aeris octogeni bini sagaque et tunicae: this is L.'s first notice of the donative to troops at the time of a triumph: for full discussion see 46. 2–8 and 13–15 nn. For the expression *data ex praeda militibus* see 46. 15 n. Presumably the garments were stripped off enemy soldiers who had been killed. Tunics were valuable for troops, and the Romans regularly demanded them as part of the price for *pax* or *indutiae*: see ix. 41. 6–7 n. For the *sagum* see vii. 34. 15 n.

illa tempestate: for similar reflections on the smaller scale of olden days, cf. 46. 2 'insigni, ut illorum temporum habitus, triumpho', i. 3. 3 'florentem . . . ut tum res erant atque opulentam urbem', 9. 7, 57. 1 'Rutuli . . . gens, ut in ea regione atque in ea aetate, diuitiis prae-pollens', ii. 7. 4, 50. 2, 63. 6, iii. 57. 7, iv. 13. 1, 45. 2, v. 13. 6, xxv. 24. 11, xxvi. 11. 8, xxvii. 6. 19, and xxxix. 6. 7–9. See further Häussler (1965) 408, Haehling (1989) 174 and, for L.'s general approval of the past in comparison with his own day, vi. 12. 5 n.

31. 1. his ita rebus gestis: *ita*, which does little more than reinforce *his*, is the reading of M; Π and λ have *itaque*, but 'therefore' gives inappropriate sense. L. uses *ita* after *his* in connecting ablatives absolute also at viii. 20. 10, xxi. 18. 1, xxvi. 51. 9, and xxxvi. 2. 1 (cf. perhaps xxxv. 35. 6); he uses *itaque* in this way at iv. 1. 5, where however it suits the context. For M alone in the truth see vol. i, p. 321 with *addenda*.

Perusinis: see ix. 37. 12 n.

2. Vescinum is Sigonius' conjecture, obviously correct, for **N**'s *Vestinum*. For Vescia see viii. 11. 5 n.; for the very easy corruption see also the discussion at 20. 1 n.

---

[1] Better sense is given by A. Perizonius' *aequatis euentu publico priuatoque filii ⟨patrisque⟩ laudibus*, but this postulates a double corruption.

Formianumque: see viii. 14. 10 n.

parte[m] alia[m]: this simple restoration is found first in U. For L.'s use of *parte alia* and *alia parte* see Packard (1968) i. 321–2 and iii. 765.

Aeserninum: this is the only reference in L. to Aesernia, modern Isernia. Since the colonization of its site by Rome in 263, Isernia has always been the most important settlement in the upper Volturno valley, and to-day it is one of the two provincial capitals of Molise. Its position is not esp. high (444 m), but is well suited for defence: it stands on a narrow neck of land between two tributaries of the Cavaliere, itself a tributary of the Volturno, and steep ravines protect its western, southern, and eastern flanks. The town lies on the main route from Latium and Campania to Bovianum and central Samnium (that which passes through Venafrum and then around the western edge of the Matese); it is well placed too for communication with Aufidena and other Samnite sites in the Sangro valley.

Given the excellent position of Aesernia, one might have expected it to have been a major settlement of the Samnites; but the polygonal walling found at various points on the periphery of the old town is probably to be connected with the later Latin colony, and, since no certain traces of Samnite occupation have yet been detected, the settlement may in fact have been founded by the Romans. However, Samnite forts are known from several neighbouring hills: in the west the massive settlement at Monte S. Paolo of Colli al Volturno is only 10 km away, and in the east, on the edges of the Matese, lie the Castello Riporso and Civitella of Longano. However, for Aesernia the most important of these Samnite settlements is that on La Romana, the hill which towers over Castel Romano (to-day a *frazione* of Isernia) and is the dominant topographical feature of the upper Volturno valley. This may have been pre-Roman Aesernia.

L. seems to imply that in 295 Aesernia was in Roman hands. After several years of fighting on the western borders of Samnium this is certainly possible; but, as the site was not to be colonized until 263 (Vell. i. 14. 8), his writing may be a little loose: perhaps he should have written that the Samnites raided the middle Volturno valley from the upper Volturno valley around Aesernia. Even if he is right, Aesernia is quite likely to have changed hands several times between 298 and 263.

For recent studies of Aesernia see Pasqualini (1966), Valente (1982), Viti (1982), Chouquer *et al.* (1987) 142–4, Terzani (1991*a*, 1991*b*, 1996); Samnite settlement in the area is discussed in Oakley (1995) 18–28 (with further bibliography).

Aeserninum is a certain and easy conjecture of Gronovius, restoring the adjective formed from Aesernia: M has *aesernium*, PUT (almost certainly giving the reading of Πλ) have *aeserunium*, ZbZt *aeser unicum* (a progressive corruption of the reading of Π), Zs *satricum* (a wild guess), and θ had *aesetrunium* (another progressive corruption). Luterbacher conjectured *Falernum* (for which see viii. 11. 14 n.), but it is easier to posit lack of precision in L.'s geography than textual corruption of this kind.

quaeque Vulturno adiace⟨n⟩t flumini: with **N**'s *adiacet* this clause cannot be translated. Gronovius saw that sense may be restored economically either by reading *adiacent* (reported by Drakenborch from M [erroneously] and the *codex Klockianus*) or by emending *quaeque* to *qua*. The former solution is diplomatically a little easier and gives better sense: since all the territory of Aesernia was close to the Volturno, the relative clause *qua Volturno adiacet flumini* would have no great point; but what L. tells us in § 5 allows the conjecture that the Samnites moved down the valley of the Volturno from Aesernia.[1]

For the dative with *adiacere* see vii. 12. 6 n.; for the Volturnus (Volturno), see 20. 6 n.

3. eos: Wesenberg (1870/1: 39) noted that *hos* would point the contrast better with *in Etruria*, but *eos* is not certainly wrong.

quattuor . . . decem: see 14. 21 n. for the figure for enemy captured, vii. 17. 9 n. for general discussion of casualty figures.

qui . . . concessa: see vi. 2. 12 n. with *addendum*.

4. redempti: for the first time L. states explicitly that the Romans did not sell captives into slavery but allowed their freedom to be bought. For later examples of this, cf. e.g. xxv. 23. 8–10, xxvi. 50. 10 (where the price of redemption was remitted), xxix. 6. 6–7, xxxii. 17. 2–3, 22. 10, and (perhaps) xlv. 42. 6–11.

5. praetor: for praetors commanding a Roman army, see the *addendum* to vii. 23. 3 n. (below, p. 557).

pro consule: for the spelling see *addendum* to viii. 26. 12 n.

agrum Stellatem: see ix. 44. 5 n.

et Samnitium omnes ⟨copiae⟩ is the conjecture of Madvig (1860: 193–4 = 1877: 232). MZbZtZs'λ have *et Samnitium omnes*; PU have

---

[1] Another possibility would be to retain *partem aliam* above and read *partem aliam [in] Aeserninam qua[que] Volturno adiacet flumini*; but this is less economical and gives less good sense.

ad Samnitium (*Samnium* U) *omnes,* and Zs^c has *et Samnitium omnes legiones.* Broadly speaking, approaches to emending the text may be divided into three categories.

The first involves postulating that *ad* in the Π mss goes back to a variant in **N**, in which case sense may be restored by emending P's *Samnitium.* The reading of U, a ms. which sometimes has an adventurous text, seems to reflect such an attempt at emendation; but in this context *Samnium* is far too imprecise, and it would be much better to introduce the name of a place. *ad Caiatiam omnes* (Conway) would allow the translation: 'the legions of the Samnites, of which one part was being pursued by the praetor Ap. Claudius, the other by the proconsul L. Volumnius, met on the *ager Stellas.* There all took up their position near Caiazzo, and Appius and Volumnius joined camps.' Since Caiatia is near the *ager Stellas* (see ix. 43. 1 n.), it may not be a fatal objection to this conjecture that it is not actually on it; since in this context *ad* was more likely to have been corrupted to *et* than vice versa, this approach is not unattractive.

Alternatively, one may argue that the failure of Mλ to read *ad* suggests that it is a corruption. Their own reading makes sense; but Madvig argued that the partitive genitive *Samnitium* was so awkward after *omnes,* that emendation was required.[1] With his conjecture we may translate: 'the legions of the Samnites, of which one part was being pursued by the praetor Ap. Claudius, the other by the proconsul L. Volumnius, met on the *ager Stellas.* There all the forces of the Samnites took up their position, and Appius and Volumnius joined camps.' This conjecture has the advantage over Conway's in that it allows a clear contrast, pointed by *et . . . et . . .,* between *Samnitium omnes copiae,* which settle together on the *ager Stellas* after being pursued separately by Appius and Volumnius, and the forces of Appius and Volumnius, which join camps. Similar conjectures, all of which introduce *legiones,* are: *et Samnitium legiones* (Ricc. 485, A^v), *et Samnitium legiones omnes* (ed. Med. 1480), and *et Samnitium omnes* ⟨*legiones*⟩ (Zs^c, anticipating H. J. Müller). Of these, that of Zs^c is

---

[1] The grammar is perhaps not impossible. In Latin there are unusual and irrational extensions of the partitive genitive (see H–S 56), and for its use after *omnis* the elder Gronovius adduced xxxi. 45. 7 'Attalus . . . et Macedonum fere omnibus et quibusdam Andriorum ut manerent persuasit' (but Madvig reasonably objected that *quibusdam* introduces a partitive notion that invalidates the parallel) and the younger xxiv. 32. 8 'ita Achradina quoque primo impetu capitur, praetorumque nisi qui inter tumultum effugerunt omnes interficiuntur'; but both these passages are easier than ours. F. Walter (1892: 624) added Ov. *met.* iv. 631 'hominum cunctis' and Tac. *ann.* xi. 22. 3 'cunctisque ciuium', which are certainly analogous (as are other passages cited at *TLL* iv. 1402. 44–60); but what was permissible with *cunctus,* whose neuter was often combined with a partitive genitive, was not necessarily permissible with *omnis.*

superior to that of A^v, because it is marginally easier to postulate the omission of *legiones* (*uel sim.*) than corruption of *legiones* to *omnes*;[1] and to that in the ed. Med. 1480, because it is easier to postulate that *legiones* fell out after *omnes* through homoioteleuton than before it for no obvious reason. Since the omission of *legiones* is more easily explained than that of *copiae*, it is diplomatically superior also to Madvig's; but, even though iteration is so common in L. (see vol. i, pp. 725–7), the repetition of *Samnitium legiones* jars, and it is difficult to believe that L. wrote in this way.

Professor Watt (*per litteras*) tentatively suggested a third approach: one could emend *Samnitium* to *Samnites*, explaining the corruption as caused by perseveration from the earlier instance of *Samnitium*. He would then read *ibi ad* ⟨name of place⟩ *et Samnites omnes*, but, if Mλ are nearer to the truth than Π, one could simply read *ibi et Samnites omnes*. There is little to choose between this approach and the conjecture of Madvig's that I have adopted. Dr Holford-Strevens suggests that, if one retains the reading of MZλ, one could delete *Samnitium*; this too gives good sense, but an omission is perhaps more likely than an intrusion.

6. hinc ira stimulante aduersus rebellantes totiens, illinc ab ultima iam dimicantibus spe: *illinc ab ultima iam dimicantibus spe*,

the reading of MZbZsλ (corrupted in Zt to *ab ultima dimicantibus iam spe*), was adopted by Walters and must have stood in **N**. It may be translated 'with those on that side now fighting as their last hope' and is probably what L. wrote. I hesitate for two reasons: (*a*) the modal or instrumental use of *a(b)* with *dimicare* seems to be unparalleled (see *TLL* v. 1. 1201. 55–7); (*b*) the only possible analogy in L. for this use of *a(b)* with *spe* is xxvii. 17. 5 'Scipio auidior etiam certaminis erat cum a (a *Sp*: ea *P and all witnesses to the Spirensian tradition other than Sp*) spe quam successus rerum augebat tum quod priusquam iungerentur hostium exercitus cum uno dimicare duce exercituque quam simul cum uniuersis malebat', where the text is uncertain.[2] In general on the difficulty of translating *a(b)*, see Munro on Lucr. i. 935.

Luterbacher, W–M, and Foster read *illinc ad ultimam iam dimicantibus spem*, which is the reading of PUT^c (although P^1 has *ab* for *ad*). This reading is grammatical, and, although its ms. authority is

---

[1] Although the reading of χ may not be quite right, this is yet another passage in which it has an intelligent conjecture; see vol. i, p. 182 with *addenda*.

[2] Although *ea* is not impossible, all editors read *a*.

much less good, it could perhaps have been a variant in **N**.[1] However, it makes L.'s thought extremely hard to understand and those who have adopted it diverge in their interpretation of it: 'Die Samniter, durch viele Niederlagen gedemütigt, kämpfen "bereits bis zur letzten Hoffnung", sich der römischen Herrschaft erwehren zu können' (Luterbacher), '*ad* = "im Hinblick auf", wie oft bei Livius; der gedanke ist: sie kämpften "für" ihre letzte Hoffnung' (W–M), 'while those on the other side were staking their last hopes on the conflict' (Foster, a translation which corresponds only approximately to the Latin).

Since L. ought to be saying that the *ultima spes* of the Samnites encouraged them to fight, I have considered deleting *ab*, which would allow the translation 'with those on that side fighting because of their last hope'; but this too is awkward.

Quite apart from uncertainties about the text, the imbalance of these two ablatives absolute leads to some awkwardness of expression. In the first, the abstract *ira* is subject, and the Samnites are mentioned in a present participle which depends on *aduersus*; in the second, the Samnites are themselves the subject of the ablative absolute, and the abstract *spe(m)* depends on either *dimicantibus* or *ab* or *ad*.

With our passage Klinger (1884: 45 n. 1) well compares iii. 2. 11 and 69. 10, in both of which the Romans are motivated by anger, their opponents by desperation. Contrast 41. 1, ii. 45. 14, and xxi. 11. 3 (all cited by W–M), in all of which *ira* and *spes* are said to act together as motivating forces. For *ira* inspiring troops see ix. 13. 3 n.

7. caesa ... septingenti: see 14. 21 n. for the figure of enemy captured, vii. 17. 9 n. for general discussion of casualty figures.

31. 8. *Prodigies*

annus ... pestilentia grauis: for *grauis* qualifying *annus* in the context of a pestilence, a usage akin to the transferred epithet, cf. Cic. *fam.* v. 16. 4 'hoc grauissimo et pestilentissimo anno'. More usually in this context *grauis* is found qualifying *pestilentia* (xxvii. 23. 6, xxxviii. 44. 7, and Caes. *ciu.* ii. 22. 1) or *tempus* (iii. 6. 2 'graue tempus [*Kalendis Sextilibus* precedes] et forte annus pestilens erat urbi agrisque', 8. 1, and xxxvii. 23. 2 [in this passage *grauis* also qualifies *locus*: see W–M's note]).

---

[1] But the reading of P¹ perhaps makes this less likely.

nam et . . . et: this formula is regular in the reporting of prodigies: see vii. 28. 7 n. with *addendum*.

et terra[m] multifariam pluuisse: for the prodigy of raining with earth cf. xxxiv. 45. 6 'et terra aliquotiens pluuit', xxxv. 21. 3–4 'nuntiatum est . . . Amiterni terra (*ψα, ed. Frob. 1535*: terram *Bφ*) pluuisse', xxxvii. 3. 3 'terra apud se pluuisse Tusculani nuntiabant', xlii. 20. 5 'nuntiatum erat . . . Auximi terra pluuisse', xlv. 16. 5 'Anagniae terra (*Grynaeus*: Anagnia terrae *V*) pluuerat'. See further Luterbacher (1904) 23, 49 and Krauss (1930) 57–8.

Walters accepted **N**'s *terram*. For taking this as the subject of the accusative and infinitive there is a probably analogous passage at xxviii. 27. 16 'lapides (*codd.*: -de Madvig, ap. *Madvig and Ussing²*: -dibus *Wesenberg [1870/1] 283*) pluere et fulmina iaci de caelo . . . uos portenta esse putatis' (where Wesenberg's conjecture is diplomatically difficult and Madvig's may be ruled out)[1] and possible analogies or parallels at xxxv. 21. 3–4 (see above for the ms. variants) and Cic. *diu.* ii. 58 'sanguinem (*codd.*: -ine *edd. plur.*) pluuisse senatui nuntiatum est'. For taking it as the object of *pluuisse* there may be analogies at xl. 19. 2 'in area Volcani et Concordiae sanguine (*ψα*: -nem *φ, Obsequens*) pluit' (where the coincidence of *φ* and Obsequens could perhaps point to the truth) and Cic. *diu.* ii. 58 (quoted above).[2] However, since in twenty-nine of the other thirty passages in which L. reports that it had rained with something unusual, he certainly or possibly places the unusual substance in the ablative (in twenty-four passages standard editions suggest that he does so; in two [xxxiv. 45. 6, xlv. 16. 5, both quoted above] *terra* is easily, and perhaps most naturally, taken as an ablative; at xxxxv. 21. 3–4 *terra* is a reading with ms. authority; at iii. 10. 6 'inter alia prodigia et carne [*VoMᶜHO*: carnem *M¹Π(=PUZgZs)Xθ*] pluit', *carne* is well attested in the mss; and at xl. 19. 2 [quoted above], *sanguine* is a reading with ms. authority;[3] the exception is xxviii. 27. 16 [quoted above]), it is easier to follow Wesenberg (1870/1: 39) and accept *terra*, a conjecture reported by Hearne from Oxford, Corpus Christi 7 (and doubtless found in other *recentiores*). With *multifariam* following, the -*m* could easily have arisen through dittography.

plerosque fulminibus ictos: for lightning which had struck

---

[1] Against Madvig note that on all the other occasions on which L. reports this prodigy (see vii. 28. 7 n.), except xxx. 38. 8 (where he uses the alternative expression *lapideus imber*), he uses the plural *lapidibus*. This passage is discussed by Kühnast (1872: 142) and Luterbacher (1904: 48), who do not persuade me that *lapides* must be the object of *pluere*.

[2] As Luterbacher notes, *saxa* is almost certainly subject at Stat. *Theb.* viii. 416–17 'stridentia funda | saxa pluunt'.

[3] In all three of the passages just mentioned I should accept the ablative.

humans or buildings regarded as a prodigy, cf. e.g. xxi. 62. 4, xxii. 1. 9 (like our passage, of soldiers being struck), xxv. 7. 8, xxvi. 23. 4, xxvii. 4. 11–12, xxxv. 9. 3, xxxvi. 37. 3, xxxvii. 3. 2, xli. 9. 5, xlii. 20. 5 (all with *fulmen* and *ictus* or a cognate); also i. 20. 7, xxxii. 1. 10, xxxiii. 26. 7–8, xl. 45. 3, and xlii. 20. 1. See further Luterbacher (1904) 22–3, 45–7 and Krauss (1930) 35–46.

in exercitu Ap. Claudi: Massa-Pairault (2001: 101) argues improbably that these prodigies should be connected with the religion of Capua (Appius had been fighting on the borders of Campania).

nuntiatum est: a ubiquitous feature of the lists of prodigies in L.'s later books, and especially those that (like the second prodigy in our passage, and perhaps also the first) come from districts other than Rome, is that they are announced: note the use of *nuntiare* also in several of the passages quoted above, and see Luterbacher (1904) 44–5. Among the other reports of prodigies in books i–x (listed at vol. i, pp. 59–60) one finds this only at iv. 21. 5 and v. 15. 1. Here as elsewhere annalistic material in book x resembles that in later books.

librique . . . aditi: a standard expression for consultation of the Sibylline oracles (on which see vii. 27. 1 n.), used by L. first at iii. 10. 7, then here, at 47. 6, xxi. 62. 6, xxii. 9. 9, 36. 6 'decemuiri libros adire atque inspicere iussi', and in eleven other passages. Sometimes L. uses *libros inspicere* (vii. 27. 1 [n.]), but passages such as xxii. 9. 9 and 36. 6 show that the approaching and inspection of the books were two separate ritual acts, one of which L. often omits to report.

ob haec and analogous expressions are regular in the reporting of prodigies; cf. iii. 29. 9, xxi. 62. 6, xxxii. 1. 14, xl. 45. 5 and other passages cited by Luterbacher (1904: 56). Contrast the use of *causa* found at 23. 1 (n.).

31. 9. *Aedilician prosecution and building of the temple of Venus*

Surprisingly L. omits to say that Fabius Gurges was curule aedile in this year, but the context makes this certain. For aedilician prosecutions see 23. 11–13, vii. 1. 6 nn.

9. eo anno: see vi. 4. 4 n.

Q. Fabius Gurges: see 14. 10 n.

matronas ad populum stupri damnatas: in republican times offences involving *stuprum*—which could then refer to any kind of sexual offence, including homosexuality and adultery: only after Augustus' *lex Julia* was it distinguished from adultery—were generally dealt with inside the family or by private prosecution rather than by the intervention of the magistrates of the state or of the plebs, and we know of only three other instances of public prosecution: that of M. Flavius in 328 (viii. 22. 3 'die dicta ab aedilibus crimine stupratae matrisfamiliae'; see viii. 22. 2–4 nn.); Marcellus' prosecution of a man who had made an advance towards his son (Val. Max. vi. 1. 7 [where the man is said to be a tribune of the plebs], Plut. *Marc.* 2. 5–8 [where the man is said to be a colleague, and Plutarch mistakenly imagines that the case took place before the senate]); and an aedilician prosecution in 213 (xxv. 2. 9) 'L. Villius Tappulus et M. Fundanius Fundulus, aediles plebeii, aliquot matronas apud populum probri accusarunt; quasdam ex eis damnatas in exsilium egerunt'. It is unclear why these cases were dealt with by aedilician rather than private prosecution, but it may be significant that in this year and in 213 a multiplicity of women were involved, thus perhaps suggesting organized behaviour that required the response of the state; and in prosecuting a tribune or aedile Marcellus may have thought it prudent to use his position as curule aedile. The case of Flavius is mysterious. See further Gardner (1986) 121–3 and Robinson (1995) 58.

ex quo multaticio aere: for *aes multaticium* see 23. 11–13 n. Walters unwisely followed F, a ms. of no authority, in omitting *quo*. He thereby removed an instance of an idiom rather affected by L.— to resume the narrative after a noun by using a second noun, different but related in sense, with a relative pronoun in agreement with it. Cf. e.g. vi. 10. 8 'militis autem non dati causam terrorem assiduum a Volscis fuisse, quam pestem adhaerentem lateri suo tot . . . bellis exhauriri nequisse', 35. 1 'uim aeris alieni, cuius . . . mali', vii. 25. 8 'decem legiones . . . quem nouum exercitum', and 25. 10 'Camillum, cui unico consuli'. See esp. Pettersson (1930) 133–5 (with these and many other Livian parallels); also K–S ii. 284 and Landgraf on Cic. *S. Rosc.* 37.

Veneris aedem: probably Rome's first temple of Venus. It is mentioned also at xxix. 37. 2 (which suggests that it lay on the Aventine side of the Circus Maximus) and perhaps at xli. 27. 9. Its date of dedication was 19 August: see *fast. Ant. mai.* ad diem (Mancini [1921] 108–9, *I.I.* xiii. 2, pp. 17, 497–8), *fast. Vall.* ad diem (*CIL* i². pp. 240, 325, *I.I.* xiii. 2, pp. 148–9), and Fest. p. 322. An alternative tradition about its vowing seems to be found at Serv. auct. *Aen.* i. 720 'dicitur etiam Obsequens Venus, quam Fabius Gurges post peractum bellum Samniticum ideo hoc nomine consecrauit, quod sibi fuerit obsecuta. hanc Itali †postuotam† dicunt', which suggests (although it does not actually state) that Fabius Gurges, either as consul in 292 or as proconsul in 291, vowed the temple when fighting the Samnites to encourage Venus to help him in battle. L.'s account of the origin of the temple is much to be preferred: (*a*) it is anchored in a secure and plausible chronological context; (*b*) when *matronae* had been convicted of *stuprum* the prosecuting aedile, or the collective Roman state, may well have thought that the goddess of love and sex needed appeasing (see also below).[1] If the building of the temple was started by Gurges in this year but the dedication took place only in 292 or 291, that may explain why Servius associates it with the fighting of these years. See further Platner and Ashby (1929) 552, L. Richardson (1992) 409, Ziolkowski (1992) 167–71, and E. Papi in Steinby (1993–2000) v. 118 (all with further bibliography).

When Fabius Verrucosus, the son or grandson of Gurges, vowed and dedicated a temple to Venus Erycina in 215 BC (xxiii. 30. 13–14, 31. 9), he was continuing a family association with this deity: see e.g. Palmer (1974: 135–6) and Münzer (1999) 77–8.[2]

The dedication to Venus in the context of sexual wrongdoing shows that the Roman deity was by this time equated with Greek Aphrodite. According to Ov. *fast.* iv. 157–60, the Romans acted in a similar way in 114, after the alleged sexual delinquency of three vestal virgins, when a temple was dedicated to Venus Verticordia (cf. Val. Max. viii. 15. 12).

quae prope Circum est: the Circus Maximus, principal site for Rome's games, runs between the Palatine and the Aventine hills. For a brief summary of its history see e.g. L. Richardson (1992) 84–7.

31. 10–15. *Reflections on the enduring bravery of the Samnites*

This paragraph, in which L. as narrator puts aside his more impersonal voice and addresses his readers, both concludes his account of 295 BC, the climactic year of the Samnite Wars, and emphasizes the importance of the events of the year. Although he occasionally makes favourable comments on Rome's foes, most notably Hannibal, this remarkable and extended tribute to the bravery of the Samnites has no real parallel in his work. However, his refusal in § 15 to accept that any reader could be bored by this unending series of campaigns finds a partial parallel at vi. 12. 2–6, where he also addresses his readers and admits that some of them may have had enough of the Volscian Wars.

---

[1] For similar vows see Orlin (1997) 19.

[2] But Palmer's view that in 331 Fabius Rullianus dedicated a temple to Pudicitia Patricia (a deity one might wish to associate with Venus) rests on no evidence; see above, p. 249.

10. quartum iam uolumen: L. introduces the Samnite Wars at vii. 29. 1. *uolumen* is regularly used of a papyrus-roll that corresponds to what in modern parlance is termed a book: see *OLD s.u.* 1(a) and note esp. xxxi. 1. 3 and Ov. *trist.* i. 1. 117 (of the fifteen books of the *metamorphoses*) 'ter quinque uolumina'.

annumque sextum et quadragesimum a M. Valerio A. Cornelio consulibus: Valerius and Cornelius were consuls in 343 (for them see vii. 19. 10, 26. 2 nn.). As elsewhere, L. takes no account of the four dictator years (333, 324, 309, and 301) and arrives at the figure of forty-six by inclusive counting of the campaigns of 343 and 294, the latter of which he was about to describe.

agimus may be translated simply 'discuss in writing' (thus *OLD s.u.* 40[a]); but there are no good parallels for this usage, and it seems more likely that L. views himself as performing the deeds about which he is writing; for the technique see Nisbet and Hubbard on Hor. *carm.* ii. 1. 18 and Courtney on Juv. 1. 163.

11–14. et ne . . . uictoriam malebant: as W–M note, *ne tot annorum clades utriusque gentis laboresque actos nunc referam* introduces a concessive contrast with *quibus nequiuerint tamen dura illa pectora uinci*, and the whole of *proximo anno . . . poterant* is concessive to *tamen . . . malebant*.

11. nequiuerint . . . uinci: the Samnites displayed some of the indomitability that was a prized characteristic of the Romans themselves (ix. 19. 9 n.).

dura illa pectora: for Samnite *duritia* see vii. 29. 5 n.

12. in Sentinati agro: see 27. 1–29. 20.

⟨in⟩ Paelignis: see 30. 3. Luterbacher's supplement is necessary: in a context like this L. seems always to place *in* before the name of an Italian tribe, and it is awkward to have to supply it from earlier in the sentence.

ad Tifernum: see 30. 7.

Stellatibus campis: see §§ 1–7. Conway wondered whether here too *in* has fallen out, but with the paradosis cf. e.g. xxii. 59. 15 'stratas Cannensibus campis legiones uestras' and xli. 18. 5 'campis Macris se eum exspectaturum'.

mixti alienis: the allies, present only at Sentinum of the Samnite defeats just mentioned, are listed at § 13.

quattuor exercitibus: as W–M observe, only three Roman armies fought the Samnites, since Ap. Claudius Caecus took over the army of P. Decius Mus (§ 3 above).

quattuor ducibus Romanis: probably Q. Fabius Rullianus and P. Decius Mus (Sentinum), L. Volumnius Flamma (Tifernum, *ager Stellas*), and Ap. Claudius Caecus (*ager Stellas*).
imperatorem . . . amiserant: see 29. 16.

13. stare: see vi. 1. 4 n.

14. adeo ne infeliciter quidem defensae libertatis taedebat et uinci quam non temptare uictoriam malebant: for the ἐπιφώνημα see vi. 41. 11 n. For the sentiment here cf. iv. 1. 4 'laeti ergo audiere patres . . . Volscos Aequosque ob communitam Verruginem fremere; adeo uel infelix bellum ignominiosae paci praeferebant' (where note *infelix* and the introductory *adeo*).

defensae libertatis is an instance of the so-called *ab urbe condita* construction in the genitive; cf. xxi. 16. 2, xxiii. 10. 10, 12. 9, and xxxviii. 56. 8 and (for parallels in earlier authors) see vi. 2. 9 n. and K–S i. 767.

15. longinquitatis: also used of the Samnite Wars at vii. 29. 1.
scribendo legendoque . . . gerentes: active engagement in affairs is regularly contrasted with both writing (e.g. Sall. *Cat.* 3. 2) and reading (e.g. Cic. *fam.* v. 12. 4). On L.'s use of gerunds as equivalent to present participles see vii. 39. 1 n. with *addendum*.

32. 1–47. 7. *The Third Samnite War continued*

294 BC

32. 1–37. 16. *Fighting in Samnium and Etruria*

The sources. Our evidence for the campaigns of this year shows particularly well the difficulties which L. and the annalists had in ascertaining the correct distribution of consular provinces. In his main narrative[1] L. records that, after a rumour that the Samnites were planning both to attack Campania and to cross once again into Etruria, both consuls were assigned Samnium as their province. Atilius Regulus set out at the beginning of the campaigning season and fought the enemy on the borders of Samnium; after an

---

[1] This paraphrase ignores the vast amount of 'plausible' detail with which these events are elaborated in L. Klinger (1884: 46–8) identifies Valerius Antias as L.'s main source; this is possible (and L. himself shows at 37. 13–14 that this source cannot have been Fabius Pictor or Quadrigarius), but he fails to show that Licinius Macer and Aelius Tubero are not possible too.

inconclusive engagement he retreated to the territory of Sora (32. 1–33. 7). The departure of Postumius Megellus was delayed by his illness, but, after dedicating the temple of Victoria, he joined his colleague at Sora (33. 8–10). From there each consul went his separate way to fight the Samnites. Megellus captured Milionia, Fertrum (or Feritrum), and several other strongholds (34. 1–14). Regulus, marching to protect Luceria from the Samnites, was involved in a major engagement in which victory came only after the very real threat of defeat and the vow of a temple to Jupiter Stator (35. 1–36. 15); on his return from Luceria he defeated the Samnite army which had been raiding Campania and had unsuccessfully attacked the Latin colony of Interamna Lirenas (36. 16–18); but at Rome he was refused a triumph (36. 19). Later in the season Megellus crossed over to Etruria, ravaged the territory of Volsinii, captured Rusellae, and forced Volsinii, Perusia, and Arretium to make peace (37. 1–5); L. then includes a full account of how he triumphed despite considerable opposition (37. 6–12).

At the end of his main narrative, however, he reports the views of Fabius Pictor and Claudius Quadrigarius (37. 13–16). Pictor recorded that both consuls had fought in Samnium and in the close and bloody battle at Luceria and also mentioned the vow to Jupiter Stator; he then recorded that the Roman army had crossed into Etruria, but he did not say whether it was commanded by both consuls or just one. Quadrigarius, by contrast, made Megellus command in Samnium and Apulia, but Regulus in Etruria; Regulus, he stated, had triumphed, but Megellus, after capturing several Samnite towns, had been defeated in Apulia, wounded, and driven back to Luceria.

With L. we may compare *F.T.*:

> *L. Postumius L. f. Sp. n. Megell(us), an. CDLIX*
> *co(n)s(ul) II, de Samnitib(us) VI k. Apr.*
> *M. Atilius M. f. M. n. Regulus co(n)s(ul) a. CDLIX*
> *de Volsonibus et Samnitib(us) V k. Apr.*

This evidence differs from L.'s main version in that both consuls triumph, and that it is Regulus, and not Megellus, who fights in both Samnium and Etruria. Despite some similarities (Regulus triumphing and in Etruria), this version is not easily equated with that of Quadrigarius, who, if L.'s summary is correct, limited Regulus to fighting in Etruria and did not allow Megellus a triumph;[1] but it is perhaps compatible with that of Fabius Pictor.

---

[1] However, note Beloch's explanation of the triumph recorded for Regulus over the Samnites, on which see below.

The other parallel sources are Frontin. *strat.* ii. 8. 11 (partly quoted at 36. 7 n.), Frontin. (?) *strat.* iv. 1. 29 (quoted at 36. 7 n.), and Zon. viii. 1. 8:

Τῷ δ' ἑξῆς ἔτει αὖθις τοῖς Σαυνίταις ἐπολέμησεν Ἀτίλιος Ῥήγουλος. καὶ μέχρι μέν τινος ἰσορρόπως ἐμάχοντο· εἶτα κρατησάντων τῶν Σαυνιτῶν αὖθις οἱ Ῥωμαῖοι ἀντεπεκράτησαν, καὶ ἑλόντες αὐτοὺς ὑπήγαγον ὑπὸ τὸν ζυγόν, καὶ οὕτως ἀφῆκαν.[1]

These are much less important. Since the narrative of Zonaras for 296 and 293 went back through Dio to at least one source independent of L., the same may be true for 294, even though all that he relates is found in L.[2] The Frontinian passages refer to the incident recounted at 36. 6–9; they add nothing to L. and may derive ultimately from him.

The Samnite War. Despite the difficult variants in our sources, it is still possible to draw some provisional conclusions about the nature of the fighting in this year. The construction of the temple of Jupiter Stator is a historical fact, and L.'s report of the vow is supported by Fabius Pictor; indeed, all three of L.'s main sources, Fabius Pictor, and Quadrigarius referred to a major battle at Luceria, and there is no reason to question this. Therefore at least one of the Roman consuls must have been fighting on the eastern borders of Samnium. Although L. (35. 1) holds that he had gone to this region to defend the Latin colony of Luceria from Samnite attack, the Romans may have been hoping to attack the Samnites from the east; but since they seem to have achieved little in this area, decision on this matter is perhaps not important.

L.'s view that Milionia, Fer(i)trum, and some other strongholds were taken from the Samnites derives support from the obscurity of their names: it is very hard to see why anyone intent on inventing sites for the Romans to capture would have picked these names. It is a difficulty that Milionia was probably Marsic (3. 5 n.), but perhaps the Samnites, marching up the Sangro valley, had overrun part of Marsic territory,[3] or the Romans had to fight the Marsi as well as the

---

[1] Zonaras' narrative of events in 294 extends only to . . . καὶ οὕτως ἀφῆκαν; some scholars (e.g Münzer, *RE* xvii. 938), perhaps misled by the unclear dating in Boissevain's edition of Dio, have believed that it continues further, but what follows clearly belongs to 293 (see 38. 1–46. 16 n.).

[2] See further pp. 268–9 above, where the same problem is discussed with regard to Zonaras' account of 295.

[3] Salmon (1967: 269) may have been correct in believing that the Romans wanted to stop the Samnites gaining access to the north via Marsic territory.

Samnites.[1] L.'s report of the Samnite attack on Interamna and their subsequent defeat cannot be confirmed by compelling arguments, but likewise there is no reason to disbelieve it.

The tough fighting against the Samnites in this year shows that, despite the victory at Sentinum, the Romans did not find it easy to penetrate into the heart of Samnium, and that the Samnites were still capable of putting major forces into the field. Only after the victories of 293 would Roman forces move more freely over Samnite territory.

The Etruscan War. All L.'s sources, and also *F.T.*, seem to have agreed that there was fighting in Etruria in this year; and L.'s main source and Fabius Pictor may have been correct to imply that it took place quite late in the year. Indeed, all the main details of L.'s account are unexceptional:[2] the attack on Volsinii is supported by *F.T.*; and the credibility of the alleged capture of Rusellae is enhanced by the fact that L. recounts the storming of no other major Etruscan town in books vi–x and therefore is not prone to including invented information of this kind.[3] These successes may have encouraged Perusia and Arretium to join Volsinii in making peace; and the absence of these towns from our notices of the fighting in 293 and 292 once again enhances the credibility of L.'s notice.

Never had Rome been so dominant in Etruria as she was at the end of 294: the victories of 295 had been followed up; her armies were freely penetrating the country; three major cities had been forced to make peace; and for the first time since 396 she had taken a major town. The rebellion of Falerii made this particular Etruscan War last until 292, but for these final years it was to be of considerably less significance.

The consular provinces. It is much harder to disentangle the confusion as to where each consul commanded in 294 than to discuss where the Romans were fighting. One has to decide whether it was because of carelessness or good evidence that Fabius Pictor made both consuls fight at Luceria; whether *F.T.* reflect a genuine tradition, or merely the combination of all available versions; whether L. singles out

---

[1] However, there is no good evidence for Marsic unrest at this time: for rejection of alleged fighting against them in 295, see above, p. 288. In his summary of Quadrigarius L. (37. 13) attributes to him the view that Postumius captured *aliquot urbes* in Samnium before being defeated at Luceria; it is just conceivable that the notice refers to this campaign.

[2] Thus, rightly, Harris (1971) 75.

[3] Although the report at ix. 40. 18–19 of the surrender of Perusia may be invented, L. does not there state that the town was captured.

Quadrigarius, who held views on the consular command diametrically opposed to those of his main narrative, because he was alone in holding such views; and whether Quadrigarius had any evidential basis for those views. These problems admit of no simple answer, but several points may be made in favour of L.'s main version: (*a*) Rome had not employed both consuls on the southern or eastern flank of Samnium since 317 (ix. 20. 9), a year in which the Samnite War was in abeyance: it would therefore be surprising were Fabius correct to have both consuls fighting at Luceria; (*b*) if the consuls did meet in the territory of Sora, it would have been sensible for one to move on to Apulia, and the other to fight on the northern borders of Samnium; (*c*) if Megellus stayed on the northern borders of Samnium, it would have been easy for him to move to Etruria from there; (*d*) it is much easier to believe that a triumph was invented for Regulus than that L.'s main source represented a tradition which had somehow lost this information; (*e*) although L.'s account of the triumph of Megellus is not devoid of difficulties, it is possible to argue that its detail is largely authentic (see 37. 6–12 n.); and (*f*) if, as seems likely (see vol. i, pp. 57–8), L.'s reports (quite frequent in book x) of which consul held the elections are authentic, then it should be noted Regulus is said to have held them in 294 (36. 18).

Nevertheless, it cannot be shown that Beloch (1904/5: 273–4 and 1926: 431) and Bruno (1906: 52–60) were wrong to follow Quadrigarius and to place Regulus in Etruria and Postumius in Samnium, where he was defeated at Luceria.[1] These scholars ingeniously explained the reference in *F.T.* to Regulus' triumphing over the Samnites by the hypothesis that in our tradition the Sabines have regularly been called Samnites: in their view Regulus could easily have moved from Etruria to the territory of the Sabines east of the Tiber, and the reference in L. (36. 16–18) to his operating at Interamna Lirenas is a mistake for Interamna Nahars, an Umbrian town close to the Sabine border. For fuller consideration of the hypothesis that Sabines have been confused with Samnites, see above, pp. 31–4.

On the events of this year, see further Bruno (1906) 45–60, Costanzi (1919) 180–5, Beloch (1926) 431 and 444, Münzer, *RE* xxii. 936–8, Salmon (1967) 269–70, Harris (1971) 74–6, and Loreto (1993) 186–7.

---

[1] However, Bruno's hypothesis (pp. 53–5) that L.'s account of the consuls' meeting in Samnium near Sora has been influenced by his account of 305, when Postumius was consul for the first time and when the Roman consuls seem to have united, is based on no good evidence.

32. 1–33. 7. *The Samnite attack on Regulus' camp.* The account of this year's campaigns is organized in such a way that we move from Regulus (32. 3–33. 7) to Megellus (33. 8–34. 14 n.), back to Regulus (35. 1–36. 19 n.), and back again to Megellus (37. 1–12 n.).

Because he had to describe so much fighting, L. needed to make his narrative varied and interesting. Here (see 32. 6–7, 33. 2, 5) he seizes on a motif that is relatively unusual (but see § 6 n.): all the fighting took place under the shroud of dense mist, so dense that the combatants could hear but not see their opponents. At the outset he introduces a surprise: despite all their defeats, the Samnites summoned the courage to attack the enemy camp, something which the Romans themselves would hardly dare to do (32. 5; the theme of Samnite boldness is met again at 33. 7, that of Roman caution at 33. 5). As so often, however, he describes in advance the outcome of the attack (32. 5): 'et quamquam non uenit ad finem tam audax inceptum, tamen haud omnino uanum fuit'; this allows his readers to concentrate not on the result of the story but on the way in which it is told. As he describes the Samnite attack L. employs the more graphic historic present (32. 7 'perueniunt'); then, as the Samnites break into the camp,[1] the pace quickens further with a series of short sentences and the fourfold omission of *esse* after verbs in the perfect passive (§ 8 'factus', § 9 'captum', 'occisus', and 'conclamatum'). For the fighting L. keeps his main verbs in the historic present, and characteristically marks out the stages of the action: first (33. 3 'primo') the Romans retreat, then (§ 3 'inde') the consul rallies them, then they begin to resist (§ 4 'primo'), then to advance (§ 4 'deinde'), but finally (§ 5 'inde') they do not dare to pursue the enemy. The exertion of the Romans is conveyed well by the series of main verbs and participles in § 4: ' conixi . . . resistunt . . . inferunt . . . urgent . . . impulsos . . . agunt . . . expellunt', and the peripeteia comes with the exhortation of the consul in § 3. L. ends this part of his narrative by recording the retreat of the Romans to the territory of Sora; his comment at 33. 6 on the *non infelix audacia* of the Samnites echoes 32. 5, and thereby frames the narrative.

32. 1. L. Postumius Megellus: see ix. 44. 2 n.
M. Atilius Regulus: (50). M. Atilius M. f. M. n. Regulus (the filiation is given by *F.T.*) is probably known only for his consulship in

---

[1] This may recall scenes in epic in which a hero breaks into the enemy camp; note esp. Hector in *Iliad* xii and Turnus in *Aeneid* ix (which, however, may have been written after this passage).

this year and his praetorship in 293 (45. 4);[1] but he was the son (conceivably the grandson) of the consul of 335 (viii. 16. 5 n.). For a probable son and other members of his family see the *addendum* to viii. 16. 5 n.

3. tenuit: for the use of *tenere* in medical contexts see *OLD s.u.* 10.
ita enim placuerat patribus: L. rather affects parenthetical expressions of this kind introduced by *ita enim*. For the sentiment here, cf. 39. 4 'Papirius nouo exercitu—ita enim decretum erat— scripto . . .', xxix. 13. 8, xxx. 27. 4; also ix. 23. 14, and see further Packard (1968) ii. 1340.

4. For **ubi** F. C. Wolff (1826: 12) conjectured *ibi*. Those who prefer to read *uastare* below may be attracted by this conjecture, but if *intrare* is rightly read, the sequence *ibi . . . ubi* may be held to underline the fact that the two armies met on the borders of Samnium *uelut ex composito*.

intrare [uastare] the deletion is due to Hertz. The mss have *intrare uastare* (Mλ[=T¹θ]), *uastare* (PUT^c), *intrare et uastare* (ZbZt), and *intrare nedum uastare* (Zs). The reading of Mλ must go back to **N** but is nonsense: either a connecting particle has been omitted; or it reflects variants conflated earlier in the transmission of the text; or this is one of those passages in which **N**'s base reading and an interlinear or marginal variant have been conflated by later scribes (see vol. i, pp. 316–20), in which case one must choose between *intrare* and *uastare*. Any solution to the *crux* will depend on one's view of whether or not Atilius managed to march into Samnium.

L.'s writing is more pointed if he makes the two armies face each other on the borders of Samnium. To achieve this one could adopt the reading of ZbZt or the more stylish *intrare ac uastare* (reported by Drakenborch from two *recentiores*). Better still, however, because **N** is known to have had variants, is Hertz's deletion of *uastare*, which was adopted by Winkler (1890–2: ii. 22–3) and Walters. It is supported by the good balance provided by *intrare* with *egredi* and

---

[1] However, if at Val. Max. viii. 1. *absol.* 9 the sole ms. of the epitome of Valerius Maximus by Julius Paris is right in stating that it was a M. Atilius, rather than an A. Atilius (thus the mss of Valerius Maximus), who was involved in an incident perhaps to be dated to 306 (on which see ix. 42. 10–43. 24 n.), and if the surname Calatinus (which is probably a mistake for Caiatinus) given by both Valerius Maximus and Paris could have been borne by a Regulus, then our man could have been a (or the) son-in-law of Fabius Rullianus. In which case it is interesting that Rullianus, the sole surviving consul for 295 and at the height of his fame, would have presided over his election to the consulship of this year (for the significance of the presidency at the elections, see vol. ii, p. 21). See also Münzer (1999) 57–8.

prohiberentur with *prohiberent*. Against it may be adduced 33. 7 'per agros suos', and 33. 10 'in Samnium ad castra collegae', which perhaps imply that Atilius did manage to penetrate into Samnium; but these can be explained if L.'s writing becomes a little loose later in the story, with 'Samnium' substituted for 'the borders of Samnium'.

Those who do not accept this explanation will read *uastare*; and it is plausible to argue that variants in **N** were conflated in Mλ, that PU represent Π, and that the Z mss have picked up readings with *intrare* by contamination (probably in Italy, but perhaps already in the lost E^c) from M or λ. See also Madvig (1860: 16–17 = 1877: 18), who argued for *uastare*.

5. castra castris conlata essent: see viii. 23. 9 n.

quod uix Romanus totiens uictor auderet, ausi Samnites sunt: for the idea see ix. 39. 6 n.

tantum . . . temeritatis: the hyperbaton emphasizes *temeritatis*.

inceptum . . . uanum: for the expression cf. xxxv. 47. 2, xxxvii. 27. 9, xliii. 1. 4, and xliv. 31. 7; see also 14. 16 n.

6. nebula erat: 'there was a mist'; this should perhaps be regarded as an instance of the *est locus* formula, for which see vii. 26. 2 n. There was mist at two famous battles in the middle Republic (Trasimene [xxii. 4. 6, 5. 3] and Magnesia [xxxvii. 41. 1–5]), and it is not impossible that there was an authentic record of it for 294 BC. However, it is probably easier to regard its appearance here as an annalistic (cf. Plut. *Publ.* 22. 5) or Livian invention.

ut . . . conspectu: the conditions created by the mist resemble those in a battle fought at night, for which see most famously Thuc. vii. 44. 1–2.

lucis usum eriperet: a precise parallel for this sense is not easily found, but Cicero couples *eripere* with figurative uses of *lux*; cf. *Sull.* 90 'lucisne hanc usuram eripere uis . . .?'; also *lucem eripere* at *S. Rosc.* 150, *Lucull.* ii. 30, 105, and *nat.* i. 6.

propinquo etiam congredientium inter se conspectu: there is a double contrast with the preceding colon: *conspectu* pointedly picks up *prospectu* (for such variation in the prefix of cognate words compare the passages cited at ix. 1. 7–8 n.) and, if the text is sound, *propinquo* is used in a pregnant sense to contrast with *extra uallum*. Translate 'but also with the removal of ⟨the possibility⟩ of their seeing at close quarters anyone whom they met'. However, ⟨ex⟩ *propinquo* (Fügner, *ap.* H. J. Müller [1890] 210) makes the contrast with *extra uallum* clearer and could be right.

7. uixdum satis certa luce et eam ipsam premente caligine:
'when daylight had hardly appeared and when fog took away what
light there was'. For *uixdum satis certa luce* see ix. 42. 7 n. For *premente caligine* cf. esp. Sen. *suas*. 1. 2 'taetra caligo fluctus premit'. Ov.
met. vii. 528–9 'caelum spissa caligine terras | pressit' is analogous;
compare too expressions such as *nox oppressit* (vii. 34. 11 n.).
premente . . . oppressis: see ix. 1. 7–8 n.

8. nec animi satis ad resistendum: for *animi satis* with *ad* and the
gerund(ive), cf. 43. 5 'Samnites . . . satis animi habuerunt ad prohibendos urbis aditu hostes', xxix. 21. 11, and xxxvi. 33. 4; also iv.
54. 5 and xxxii. 12. 5.
ab tergo castrorum decumana porta impetus factus: 'they
charged in by the decuman gate in the rear of the camp' (Foster). For
the ablative *decumana porta* (which combines the notion of both
'from' and 'by means of') compare e.g. iii. 51. 10 'porta Collina
urbem intrauere', xxvi. 10. 1 'Fuluius Flaccus porta Capena cum
exercitu Romam ingressus', xxvi. 37. 7, and xxvii. 37.

Between 32. 9 and 33. 6 L. mentions several features of the Roman
camp: the *porta decumana* here, the *quaestorium* (32. 9, 33. 6), the
praetorium (33. 1), and the *uia principalis* (33. 1): see n. on each.
Neither here nor anywhere else does he provide anything like a full
description of a Roman camp, but note xli. 2. 9–13, where again
several feaures are mentioned. Our only full literary source for
Roman castrametation in the republican period is Plb. vi. 26. 10–32.
8, but how some of the details in Polybius' account are to be interpreted, how the evidence derived from his account is to be compared
with the archaeological remains of Roman camps, and how it is to be
related to the account of Hyginus in his *de castrorum munitione* have
all been much disputed. A particular difficulty is that Polybius
describes half the camp of a double consular army of four legions (i.e.
how one consul and his two legions arranged themselves); his
arrangement therefore does not entirely apply for a singular consular
army. Here Atilius commands a singular consular army, and the
details of the camp which L. provides do not conform to the Polybian
description.

Convenient introductions to these problems are Kromayer and
Veith (1928) 342–6, Walbank's commentary on Plb. loc. cit., and
Keppie (1984) 36–8. Fabricius (1932) summarizes earlier scholarship, but not all his own contentions have gained general acceptance;
his plan of the Roman camp (p. 79) has been much reproduced, but
it is a plan of the camp adopted by half of a double consular army. In

our passage L. envisaged an arrangement in which the *praetorium* and *quaestorium* were either side of the assembly-area at the centre of the camp, close to, respectively, the *porta praetoria* and the *porta decumana*: see Kromayer and Veith, fig. 128; note also the discussion of Fischer (1914: 43–8).

The *porta decumana*, on the side of the camp opposite to the *porta praetoriana*, is mentioned quite often by our sources: see e.g. iii. 5. 5, Caes. *Gall.* vi. 37. 1, *ciu.* iii. 69. 2, 76. 1, Hyg. *mun.* 21, 56. For its position on the side of the camp not facing the enemy (*ab tergo* in our passage: see further Fischer [1914] 28–9), cf. Caes. *Gall.* ii. 24. 2, iii. 25. 2 (of a Gallic camp), *ciu.* iii. 96. 3, and Tac. *ann.* i. 66. 1.

9. quaestorium: for the *quaestorium* see xli. 2. 12, Plb. vi. 31. 1, and Hyg. *mun.* 18 'quaestorium dicitur quod aliquando quaestores ibi pedaturam acceperint; quod est supra praetorium in rigore portae quae a cohortibus decimis ibi tendentibus decimana est appellata. quaestorium minore esse debet latitudine quam praetorium, ut strigae statorum posticum praetorii proximi sint. in quo maxime legati hostium et obsides; et, si qua praeda facta fuerit, in quaestorio ponitur', 29, 39, 42, and 46. Here and at xxxiv. 47. 2–3 (where, however, the *quaestorium* is not mentioned) L. clearly places the quarters of the quaestor at the back of the camp near the *porta decumana*.
quaestorque: see vii. 23. 3 n.
L. Opimius Pansa: (12). Otherwise unknown. Münzer, *RE* xviii. 680, argued that the appearance of this man long before other Opimii are known points to his invention (the next Opimii in the historical record are the two moneyers of *c.*169–158 [Crawford (1974) 239–40], one of whom was probably the consul of 154); but the motive for such invention is not obvious.[1] Since the L. Opimius who was a member of the *consilium* of Cn. Pompeius Strabo in 89 belonged to the tribe Horatia (see *ILLRP* 515 = *CIL* i². 709), and since Aricia, incorporated into the Roman state in 338 (viii. 14. 3), was the leading town in this tribe, Taylor (1960: 239 and 290), tentatively, and Wiseman (1971: 16 and 185), more confidently, have argued that the family came from Aricia. This is quite attractive, but it is possible too that the domicile of the family changed between 294 and 89 and that our Opimius is not related to the member of Strabo's *consilium*.
conclamatum . . . ad arma: see vi. 28. 3 n.

---

[1] It would be far-fetched to suggest that an unsuccessful ancestor has been foisted on the opponent of C. Gracchus.

33. 1. Lucanam is most naturally interpreted as referring to a contingent of Lucanian troops who were serving with the Roman army: the Lucani had been allies of Rome since 298. Some scholars, however, reluctant to believe that at so early a date the Romans would have employed the untrustworthy Lucanians, have argued that L. refers to another people, either the inhabitants of the obscure Volscian Luca (viii. 18. 1 n.), whose existence is not certainly established (thus Salmon [1967: 194]) or a putative *ager Lucanus* near Cales (thus Marcotte [1985: 737], for discussion of whose views see 12. 3–13. 1 n.). Given that the whole narrative is of most doubtful authenticity, these questions are perhaps academic.

Suessanamque: see viii. 15. 4 n.

praetorium: the tent of the consul or commanding officer: see ix. 2. 12 n.

manipulos: see viii. 8. 3–14 n.

principali uia: the *uia principalis*, for which see Hyg. *mun.* 10, 11, 12, 14, 15, lay at a right-angle to the other main axis of the camp, which ran from the *porta praetoria*, through the *praetorium*, to the *porta decumana*. The troops assembled along it before going out through the *porta praetoria* to battle. See further Fischer (1914) 35 and 40–1 and Kromayer and Veith (1928) 344.

2. aptatis armis: see ix. 31. 9 n.

clamorem magis quam oculis noscunt hostem: for the idea W–M well cite xxii. 5. 4 'et erat in tanta caligine maior usus aurium quam oculorum'.

3. uociferaretur . . . rogitans: Walters and Conway (1918: 113) commended, and Walters adopted, Duker's deletion of *rogitans*, and indeed nowhere else does L. supplement *uociferari* with a verb like *rogitare*. Yet the paradosis seems harmless enough.

3–4. expulsi . . . impulsos . . . expellunt: see ix. 1. 7–8 n.

4. conixi . . . inferunt . . . urgent . . . impulsos . . . agunt . . . expellunt: with the progression of these verbs L. nicely shows how the Romans rallied.

et impulsos semel terrore eodem agunt quo coeperunt ⟨et⟩ expellunt extra portam uallumque: the supplement is due to Weissenborn (ed.²). The paradosis may be translated thus: 'and, having forced them back once and for all, they drive them on with the same fear with which they had begun ⟨to drive them⟩; ⟨and⟩ they force them out of the gate and rampart'; but the asyndeton between *agunt* and *expellunt* is very harsh.[1] Most editors follow Madvig (1860: 194 = 1877: 232–3), who deleted *agunt* and argued that something like *pellere* (from *impulsos*) should be supplied with *coeperunt*, but it is not easy to see how or why *agunt* should have been interpolated. Therefore, since *agunt* is not quite otiose between *impulsos* and *expellunt*, Weissenborn's much easier conjecture is to be preferred.[2]

Drakenborch reports *coeperant* for *coeperunt* from Holkham 346 and Vat. Pal. lat. 875 and 878. The reading may be correct, but L. sometimes employs a perfect where one would expect a pluperfect; see ix. 21. 4 n.

5. pergere ac persequi: a precise parallel for this coupling seems to be found only at Cic. *Brut.* 158, but cf. also xxxv. 30. 4.

turbida lux: for *turbidus* used of poor visibility caused by haze, cf. e.g. Lucr. iv. 168–71 'praeterea modo cum fuerit liquidissima caeli | tempestas, perquam subito fit turbida foede, | undique uti tenebras omnis Acherunta rearis | liquisse et magnas caeli complesse cauernas', Luc. x. 207 'sub Ioue temperies et numquam turbidus aer', and the other passages cited at *OLD s.u.* 2(b). At 41. 6, where this expression is used again, the context probably suggests that L. refers to poor visibility caused by dust rather than heat.

circa insidiarum: see vi. 15. 7, ix. 15. 1 nn.

6. stationis primae uigiliumque: for *stationes* and *uigiliae* see *addendum* to viii. 8. 1 n. *primae*, which does not relate very clearly to what L. wrote at 32. 7–8, has been suspected: Gemoll (1890–8: ii. 19) conjectured *prorutae*, H. J. Müller (1899: 13) *proximae* (*sc. hostibus, qui impetum fecerunt*). Nevertheless, the paradosis may be explained as referring to the foremost, i.e. outermost, guard-post; cf. xlii. 64. 4 'nequiquam primae stationes oppressae: tumultu ac terrore suo ceteros excitauerant' and xlv. 26. 9 'Antinous et Theodotus in primam stationem hostium inruperunt'. Conway, *ap.* Walters and Conway (1918) 114, deleted *uigiliumque* as a gloss on *stationis*, on the ground that no *uigiles* have been mentioned; but the *uigiles* may have been near the gate attacked by the enemy, and L.'s use of *uigilias* at 32. 7 might easily have suggested *uigiliumque* to him here.

---

[1] Further corruption perhaps lurks in *terrore eodem quo coeperunt*, an awkward expression that is not paralleled elsewhere in L.; but Alschefski's *ceperant* for *coeperunt* is unlikely to be right.

[2] Alternatives to it which would unite *eodem* with *quo coeperunt* are either *impulsos semel terrore eodem quo coeperunt agunt ⟨et⟩ expellunt* or *impulsos semel agunt terrore eodem quo coeperunt ⟨et⟩ expellunt* (for faulty word-order in **N**, see vol. i, p. 165).

periere ad septingentos triginta: see ix. 42. 8 n. For *septingentos* as the most probable interpretation of *acc* (*uel sim.*) in the mss, see 14. 21 n.

7. non infelix audacia: for the expression cf. *felix audacia* at Ov. *epist.* 18. 195 and Sidon. *epist.* i. 11. 6.
proferre . . . castra: 'advance their camp'; cf. [x] xxx. 29. 8 and Caes. *ciu.* i. 81. 4.
Soranum: for Sora see vii. 28. 6 n.

33. 8–34. 14. *Postumius Megellus at Milionia and Feritrum.* L. makes the Latin colony of Sora the link between his accounts of the first campaigns undertaken by Atilius Regulus and by Postumius Megellus: Regulus retreats to Sora (33. 7), and Megellus orders his troops to assemble at Sora (§§ 9–10). In this section L. describes the capture of first Milionia (34. 1–3), then Fer(i)trum (§§ 4–14), and then of other unnamed settlements (§ 14). Only the capture of Fer(i)trum is told at any length, with L. expanding his narrative to illustrate the care taken by the consul to establish that Fer(i)trum really had been abandoned before he sent his troops into the town. The scene is carefully visualized but, apart from a vivid series of verbs in the historic present (§ 6 'detinet', § 7' iubet', 'conspiciunt', § 8 'adequitant', 'conspiciunt', 'referunt', § 9 'circumducit', and 'iubet'), has little of stylistic note.

8. quarum rerum fama tumultuosior etiam quam res erant: it is quite tempting to follow Häggström (1874: 65) and adopt *erat* (PU) ('the rumour of these events, more startling even than the situation required'), which would align our passage with the idiom discussed at 4. 1 n. *etiam*, however, is much more pointed with the text of MZλ, which Foster well translated as 'the rumour of these events, more startling even than the events themselves'. For *fama*, see vi. 21. 9 n.

9. militibus edicto Soram iussis conuenire: see vii. 23. 3 n.
aedem Victoriae: 'Archaeological evidence now reveals why it [*sc.* the construction of the temple of Victoria] took so long. First, it was a very large and imposing building, even bigger than its later neighbour, the temple of Magna Mater. Second, the building programme evidently involved more than just the temple itself: the side of the Palatine overlooking the Forum Bovarium was built up with great terracing walls in opus quadratum, and it is probable that the programme included a new monumental approach, the Clivus Victoriae.

The effect must have been like the entrance to an acropolis, with a victory temple at the gate' (Wiseman [1995*b*] 4; cf. id. [1991] 120). Wiseman's view that the temple took a long time to construct is based on the reasonable, but not certain, surmise that Postumius was aedile before his first consulship in 305.[1] The temple was dedicated on 1 August (Degrassi, *I.I.* xiii. 2, p. 489, with evidence from the various *fasti*), and stood on the Palatine (xxix. 14. 14), where late republican myth retrojected a temple of Evander (D.H. i. 32. 5);[2] it gave its name to the *cliuus Victoriae* (Fest. 318). In 193 Cato dedicated a temple to Victoria Virgo, which stood near the temple of Postumius (xxxv. 9. 6, with Briscoe's note). For the interest in Victoria taken by the Romans in the years around 300, see 29. 14 n. For the precise site of the temple see Wiseman (1981) = (1987) 187–204 and Pensabene in Steinby (1993–2000) v. 149–50 (summarizing his earlier publications). See also Wissowa (1912) 139–40, Platner and Ashby (1929) 570, Latte (1960*a*) 234–5, and Ziolkowski (1992) 172–9.[3]

aedilis curulis: the date of Postumius' curule aedileship is not known.

ex multaticia pecunia faciendam curauerat: see 23. 11–13 n.

dedicauit: for the rules governing dedication see 1. 9, ix. 46. 6–7 nn. Our passage and xxxiv. 53. 4, supported by the doubtfully reliable testimony relating to the dedication of Flavius in 304 (ix. 46. 1–15 n.), suggests that it may have been normal for ex-aediles to dedicate the temples for the construction of which they had been responsible.

profectus, ab Sora: M has *profectusorā*, on the basis of which Hertz deleted *ab*; but the innocuous preposition is more likely to have been omitted by M than inserted by Π and λ.

ad uastandos agros urbesque oppugnandas: see viii. 29. 11 n.

34. 1. Milioniam: see 3. 5 n.

oppugnare adortus: see vi. 2. 8 n.

1–2. ui primo atque impetu, dein . . . opere ac uineis demum iniunctis muro cepit: for the importance attached by the Romans

---

[1] Ziolkowski suggests that the temple was vowed in 304 when Postumius was consul but that construction began only later when he was aedile.

[2] *Pace* Pensabene, a notice of this kind in D.H. hardly supports the view that there was a shrine to Victoria on this site even before Postumius constructed his temple.

[3] Noting that Postumius may have vowed another temple in this year (see 37. 1–15, esp. § 15), and thinking that this constituted a strange obsession with temples, Bruno (1906: 46 n. 2) wondered whether one of these notices should in fact be placed in 291; but (*a*) there is no obvious motive for the notice in our passage to have been placed in the wrong year, and (*b*) the vow recorded later by L. may have been made by the other consul (see above, pp. 345–9).

to recording precisely how a town or city was captured, see vi. 3. 10
n. *ui*, found first in Zr, is an obviously correct emendation of **N**'s *ut*;
for a similar corruption see Woodman and Martin on Tac. *ann.* iii.
12. 2. Siesbye, *ap*. Madvig (1877) 233, suggested deleting *ac*; but all
the ablatives go with *adortus*, and this proposal would spoil the progression *primo, dein, demum*.

2. postquam ea parum procedebant is an instance of standard
Livian phrasing; cf. esp. (because the contexts are similar) i. 57. 3
'temptata res est, si primo impetu capi Ardea posset: ubi id parum
processit, obsidione munitionibusque coepti premi hostes' and
xxxviii. 7. 6 (during the siege of Ambracia) 'itaque cum aperta ui
parum procederet consuli res, cuniculum occultum . . . instituit'.
Note also xxv. 22. 14, xxxvi. 25. 5, and xliv. 12. 5 (still in the context
of an assault on a town, the last example without *parum*); comparable
too but less close are xxiii. 35. 2, xxxi. 21. 11, and 36. 2 (this last
without *parum*). The expression is used about eight times by other
writers; to the instances cited at *TLL* x. 2. 1506. 62–5, 67–8, and
1507. 11–12, add Frontin. *strat.* i. 8. 8 and Front., p. 81. 23–4.

iniunctis: *iniungere* 'attach' is used regularly by L. in this context
but not by other writers; cf. e.g. [x] iv. 9. 14 'consul muro Ardeae
brachium iniunxerat', v. 7. 2 (of *uineae*, as here), xxvii. 41. 3, xxxvii.
26. 8 (of *uineae*), and xliii. 19. 11. See *TLL* vii. 1. 1665. 48–53.

ab hora quarta usque ad octauam fere horam: for the historians'
recording the duration of battles, see viii. 38. 10 n. For the repetition
hora . . . horam, cf. xliv. 37. 6 'ab hora secunda usque ad quartam
horam noctis'; contrast viii. 38. 10 and xxxv. 1. 5, where *horam* is
omitted.

**3. Samnitium caesi tria milia ducenti, capti quattuor milia
septingenti:** for the figure for enemy captured, see 14. 21 n.; for
general discussion of casualty figures, see vii. 17. 9 n.

septingenti: see 29. 18 n.

praeter praedam aliam: the coupling of *praeter* and *alius* seems to
be quite rare, but cf. i. 57. 2 'praeter aliam superbiam regno infestos
quod . . .', Quint. iv. 2. 25, and xi. 3. 74.

4. Feritrum is the reading of PZb¹Zt, the concidence of which must
point to Π; MZbᶜλ have or had *fertrum*, which must have stood in **N**;
U has *fertorum*; and Zs *Ferentinum*. Most editors adopt the reading
of PZb¹Zt, but, since the place is otherwise unknown, we have no
particular reason to think that it was called Feritrum rather than

Fertrum. More elaborate emendations, neither of which has any probability, are Gronovius' *Treuentinum* (which Alschefski improved to *Treuentum*, but *Teruentum*, the normal name for the *municipium* [modern Trivento], would have been even better) and Alschefski's tentative *Tifernum*. Nevertheless, Alschefski's final eloquent judgement deserves to be quoted: 'sed in re dubia, quo maior coniecturis faciendis locus datus est, in una antiquissimorum librorum auctoritate videtur standum, praesertim cum et in aliis Italiae partibus et in Samnio tot oppida a Livio commemorata videamus, quorum nulla ab aliis scriptoribus mentio facta sit'. Nevertheless, scholars have continued to speculate about the site of Fer(i)trum: for example, La Regina (1989: 399) has suggested that it lay in the Val Roveto. Agnosticism is the only prudent position.

ferri agique: expressions of this kind are used of the transportation (often, although not here, by plundering) of easily removed property: *ferri* refers to carrying by hand or on back, *agi* to the driving of animals. For this particular coupling cf. iii. 37. 7 'hi ferre agere plebem plebisque ⟨cum⟩ res tum fortunas', xxii. 3. 7, xxxiii. 13. 10, xxxviii. 15. 10, 18. 15, and xl. 49. 1; L. may be responsible for a deliberate calque on ἄγειν καὶ φέρειν (see L–S–J *s.u.* ἄγω 3). For an analogous expression see viii. 38. 13, xxxviii. 18. 15, and see further *TLL* i. 1369. 11–15 and vi. 556. 28–30.

per auersam portam: see viii. 26. 4 n.

5. compositus instructusque: for this coupling, cf. [x] xxxiv. 16. 2 (an interpolated passage) and xl. 28. 1. Although the participles qualify *consul*, they apply more logically to his army; W–M (on iii. 27. 6 'non itineri magis apti quam proelio . . . dictator . . . magister equitum') well compared xxvi. 5. 3 and Tac. *hist.* iv. 35. 2 'compositus inuadit'.

6. silentium uastum: a powerful expression, suggestive of broad, open, silent streets, and of the emptiness which had come from the enemy's removing its portable possessions (for *uastus* in the sense 'devastated', see 12. 8, *OLD s.u.* 1[c]). No writer exploited the resonances of *uastus* as effectively as Tacitus, and this expression made so potent an impression on him that he reproduced it at *Agr.* 38. 2, *hist.* iii. 13. 2, and *ann.* iv. 50. 4 (note also *ann.* iii. 4. 1 'dies . . . per silentium uastus'). *per uasta silentia* is found at Luc. v. 508.

nec arma nec uiros: see viii. 5. 3 n.

turribus: these towers, like those mentioned at 43. 7, almost certainly come from the imagination of L. or one of his sources. However, it is perhaps worth noting that, though towers are extremely rare on Samnite and other Italic fortified centres, they have been found at the Civitavecchia (Le Tre Torrette) of Campochiaro; for plans see conveniently Coarelli and La Regina (1984) 208–9 or Oakley (1995) 112–13.

occultam . . . fraudem: to the copious collection of Livian (iii. 18. 6, 25. 4, xxiv. 38. 3) and other parallels for this collocation listed at *TLL* vi. 1. 1272. 83–1273. 1 add xxxix. 14. 4.

7. turmas: see viii. 7. 1 n.

portam unam alteramque . . . patentes: see *addendum* to vi. 25. 7 n.

circumequitare is unique to L., being attested elsewhere [*] only at xxix. 7. 5 'circumequitabat urbem'. On his liking for compounds in *circum-*, see ix. 40. 13 n.; on his use of the rare cognate compound *obequitare* see vi. 13. 5 n.

unam alteramque: for this coupling see vii. 10. 10 n.

8. sensim: see viii. 8. 11 n.

ex tuto: 'from a position of safety' (see *OLD s.u. tutus* 4[c]); the phrase is to be taken with *conspiciunt*.

rectis itineribus: since the streets were straight, there was less danger from ambushes or unwelcome surprises. For *iter* with the meaning 'street', cf. e.g. xxvii. 16. 2, Tac. *hist.* i. 81. 2, *ann.* iii. 4. 1, and Suet. *Iul.* 84. 1; for *rectus* coupled with *iter*, *uia* or the like, see *OLD s.u.* 2, esp. (a).

strage: see vii. 23. 10 n.

trepidatione nocturna: for night's inducing fear, see ix. 24. 8 n.

passim: the final position of this word emphasizes the chaotic departure of the Samnites.

10. silentium ac solitudinem: for this coupling, cf. [x] xxxiv. 20. 8; also Curt. x. 5. 7 and, perhaps, Tac. *hist.* iii. 84. 4 'terret solitudo et tacentes loci'.

11. cohortes: see vii. 39. 7 n.

12. graues aetate: see vii. 39. 1 n.

migratu: the transitive use of *migrare*, to which our passage provides a virtual equivalent, is very rare in pre-Antonine Latin. Cicero employs the verb several times in the sense *transgredi* (e.g. *off.* i. 31); but the first parallels to our passage, in which it is equivalent to *transportare*, seem to be Sil. vii. 431–2 'num migrantur Rhoeteia regna | in Libyam superis?' (figurative) and Gell. ii. 29. 16. See further *TLL* viii. 938. 20–46.

13. direpta: see vi. 4. 9 n.
aliquot circa urbes: see vi. 15. 7, ix. 15. 1 nn.
conscisse fugam: cf. [x] v. 53. 5, xxxiii. 48. 10, and Tac. *hist.* iii. 9. 2.

35. 1–36. 19. *The battle at Luceria and the return of Regulus to Rome.* The successes of Postumius Megellus just recounted (34. 1–14 n.) contrast with the renewed difficulties of Regulus at Luceria. Here once again L. chooses an unusual theme, the fear which each side had of the other; and around this he has created a very expansive account. The initial, inconclusive battle in which the Romans come off worse is dispatched quickly (35. 1–2), as L. is more interested in dilating on the psychological states of the two armies in its aftermath. The information that neither side wishes to fight (35. 3–4) allows the reader to take an ironical view of the ensuing narrative. As the Samnites advance, hoping to march safely past the Roman camp (35. 4), the Roman officers desperately try to rouse their men, who are already frightened of a Samnite attack (§ 3). There follows an inconclusive dialogue in *oratio obliqua* between the consul and his men (§§ 8–11): the consul, by stating that the troops will have to fight the Samnites within their camp, returns to the theme of 32. 6–33. 6 (which connection, however, L. does not point explicitly); the men refuse to fight, an action that is quite extraordinary for Roman troops who are not being mistreated by their commander. The dialogue is interrupted by a glance at the advancing Samnites; and the short sentence *inter haec appropinquabat agmen* (§ 12) adds to the tension. The consul now turns to direct speech (§ 14),[1] and eventually the Roman troops march out; but this in turn disheartens the Samnites, who were fearful lest the Romans should wish to fight them (§ 18; cf. §§ 4, 17). Eventually, after the Samnites have deposited their baggage (36. 1), a paradoxical and half-hearted battle is joined (note *segnis* at 36. 3, with which cf. 35. 17). Then, when an attempt by the consul to make a decisive move has failed (36. 4–5), the Romans flee. The turning-point of the action has now been reached and, characteristically, L. leads into it with an inverted *cum*-clause (36. 6–7). The consul, standing firm and given another brief burst of direct speech (36. 8), threatens to kill anyone who flees and makes a vow to Jupiter Stator

---

[1] For the technique of turning from indirect to direct speech, see vol. i, pp. 119–20.

(36. 11). And the god makes a swift response: for the Romans now stand firm. Their final, whole-hearted effort is shown by 36. 12 *omnes undique adnisi ad restituendam pugnam, duces milites, peditum equitumque uis*; and victory is the reward of their commitment. Some of the Samnites try to defend their baggage (a good example of how L. makes a seemingly casual detail tell later in the narrative), and around it they are cut to pieces. This Roman victory compensates for the defeat described at 35. 1–2.[1] As a brief and unadorned pendant to this long passage L. then records how Regulus defeated the Samnites at Interamna and returned to Rome. See further Bruckmann (1936) 48–9.

35. 1. **Luceriam:** see ix. 2. 3 n.
hostis obuius fuit: for the expression see vi. 31. 6 n.
ira uires aequauit: Foster translates 'rage made their [i.e. the Samnites'] strength as great as his': the Samnites would not normally have been the equal of the Romans, but on this occasion their anger made them so; this equality is reflected in the following *proelium uarium et anceps fuit*.

2. **proelium . . . anceps:** see vi. 22. 3 n.
tristius tamen . . . caedis fuisset: see ix. 38. 8 n.
insueti erant uinci: for the idea, cf. iv. 31. 4 'maesta ciuitas fuit uinci insueta', xxxix. 31. 2 'insueta ignominia milite Romano accenso'; also Stat. *Theb.* iv. 837–8.
quantum . . . plus: the coupling of a comparative with an adverbial accusative rather than an ablative (e.g. *quantum* for *quanto*) is rare before L., who rather affects the usage; cf. e.g. iii. 15. 2 'quantum iuniores patrum plebi se magis insinuabant', xliv. 7. 6 'quantum procederet longius a Thessalia' and see W–M on v. 21. 14, Krebs and Schmalz (1905–7) ii. 445–6, K–S i. 402, and H–S 136–7. Therefore there is no need to emend to *quanto* with Wesenberg (1870/1: 40).
uolnerum ac caedis: for the coupling, cf. [x] i. 13. 3, iv. 28. 7, xli. 3. 3, and Tac. *hist.* iii. 26. 3.

3. **iam inuasurum:** for *iam* with the future participle, cf. e.g. v. 39. 6 'iam in urbem futurus . . . impetus', xxxvii. 21. 2, and see *TLL* vii. 1. 106. 67–80.

4. **hostes . . . hostes:** used first of the Samnites, then of the Romans.

---

[1] For this technique see vol. i, p. 97 and vol. iii, p. 36.

qua ingressi: many *recentiores* have *quam* for *qua*, a reading championed by H. J. Müller (1889*c*: 48–9) and easily paralleled (see e.g. iii. 17. 6 'iube hanc ingredi uiam' and *TLL* vii. 1. 1567. 77–1568. 21). However, although the paradosis cannot be paralleled precisely (at Cic. *Cael*. 41 'natura . . . multas uias adulescentiae lubricas ostendit quibus illa insistere aut ingredi sine casu aliquo ac prolapsione uix posset' *insistere* demands *quibus*), good analogies for it may be found at *TLL* 1574. 1–11 (see e.g. Hirt. *Gall*. viii. 20. 1 'recentibus proeli uestigiis ingressus Caesar'), and it may stand. Translate: 'along which moving forward'. For a similar problem see Powell on Cic. *Cato* 6.

5. consul arma capere milites iubet: see ix. 37. 5 n.
legatis, tribunis, praefectis sociorum: see viii. 36. 6 n.
quod . . . facto opus est: see vi. 19. 4 n.
apud quemque suggests 'in the quarter where each commanded' (J. Walker [1822] 89). There is therefore no need for Crévier's *cuique*.

6. iacere animos: for the expression cf. e.g. Cic. *Lael*. 59, Ov. *Pont*. i. 3. 27, Sen. *Tro*. 1022, and see *TLL* vii. 1. 28. 60–5.

7. pudore: see vi. 24. 7 n.
pro uictis: see viii. 1. 5 n.

8. sibimet ipsi circumeundos adloquendosque milites ratus: annalistic or Livian reconstruction based on the regular practice of Roman commanders; see viii. 39. 4 n. For L.'s phrasing, see ix. 13. 1 n.
cunctantes arma capere: see ix. 37. 5 n.

9. fugae . . . patere uiam: see 5. 11 n. and cf. esp. the passage of Justin cited there.

10. nudus atque inermis contrasts with *armatis ac dimicantibus*; for the coupling (much favoured by L.), cf. [x] iii. 23. 5, xxiii. 19. 6, xxv. 17. 2, xxix. 4. 7, xxx. 44. 10, xxxvi. 5. 5, Curt. ix. 3. 5, Sen. *epist*. 95. 33, and Tac. *hist*. iv. 64. 1. Madvig, *ap.* Madvig and Ussing², pronounced favourably on *iners*, a conjecture for *inermis* found by Gebhardus in two Palatine mss; it would make a good contrast with *dimicantibus*, but the parallels support the paradosis.
hostem maneat: see 17. 6.

12. certiora: see vi. 1. 3 n.
portare: see viii. 7. 13 n.

13. indignum facinus esse: see vi. 14. 12 n.

ignauissimo . . . hoste: a regular term of abuse; cf. ii. 46. 5 'adeo ignauissimos hostes magis timetis quam Iouem . . .?', iii. 67. 4, v. 28. 8, and Tac. *hist.* v. 16. 2; note also viii. 2. 10 'ignauissimis populis' and ix. 4. 8 'ab ignauissimo ad opera ac muniendum hoste' (n.). See further Opelt (1965) 183.

14. fame . . . ferro: for this contrast, and the implication that death *fame* was less virtuous than death *ferro*, cf. vii. 35. 8, xxii. 39. 14 'plures fame quam ferro absumpti', Sall. *hist.* iii. 93 'sin uis obsistat, ferro quam fame aequius perituros', Nep. *Ham.* 2. 4 'plures fame quam ferro interirent', and Amm. xxv. 7. 4 'miles ferro properans quam fame ignauissimo genere mortis absumi'. For the coupling of *fames* and *ferrum*, see also xxiii. 19. 17, xxvi. 6. 16, xxxviii. 15. 5, *per.* xcv, and the passages cited by Wölfflin (1881) 54–5 = (1933) 258–9 and at *TLL* vi. 1. 232. 72–3. For dishonour coming from death by starvation, see also Polyaen. i. 38. 2; for honourable death, see ix. 3. 3 n.

di bene uerterent, facerent[que] quod . . .: to follow **N** in coupling *uerterent* and *facerent* would spoil the idiom illustrated below, make the gods subject of *facerent*, and leave the ensuing *quod*-clause without a governing verb. Duker's deletion of -*que* (which could have arisen from a dittography of *quod*) provides a very simple remedy. M. Müller, citing ii. 12. 9 and xxiii. 9. 2, proposed either *facerent ⟨paterentur⟩que quod* or *facerent ⟨ferrent⟩que quod*; but neither supplement is convincing, and neither passage is close to ours. Walters and Conway (1918: 114–15) argued for Drakenborch's *facer-ent—quod di bene uerterent—quod . . .*; but the corruption would be harder to explain, and the repetition of *quod* inelegant.

   di bene uertant is one of a number of expressions (note also *quod bene [feliciter] eueniat* and *quod bonum faustum felix sit* [viii. 25. 10 n.]) used by the Romans to ask for divine approval of an action which has just been, or is just about to be, proposed; it is attested most often in colloquial Latin and hence is common in comedy: cf. e.g. Plaut. *aul.* 175, 257, and *Pseud.* 646. The idiom is found in many variant forms, several of which occur in L. Closest to our passage is xxxiv. 34. 2 'bene uertat . . . obsideamus Lacedaemonem, quando ita placet' (where, as here, the hope that the action will turn out well comes before a jussive subjunctive). Note also the pattern *quod bene uertat* (*uel sim.*) found at i. 28. 1, iii. 26. 9, 35. 8, 62. 5 (observe the clustering), vii. 39. 13, and viii. 5. 6. One interesting variant not employed by L. is the negative; see e.g. Ter. *ad.* 191 'quae res tibi uortat male' and Virg. *ecl.* 9. 6 'quod nec uertat bene'. See further Appel (1909) 171–4, *TLL* ii. 2121. 72–83, and *OLD s.u. uerto* 18, and Hickson (1993) 73–6.

se dignum . . . ducerent: for the idea of Romans acting (or being told to act) in a manner worthy of themselves, cf. Cic. *Sest.* 87 'quid se dignum esset . . . cogitabat', *diu.* ii. 6; also xlv. 42. 10 and Sall. *Cat.* 51. 6 (both of the senate).

15. consulem M. Atilium: this is the equivalent in *oratio obliqua* of the grandiloquent combination of first person and proper noun, on which see vii. 30. 6 n. A consul wished his magistracy to be remembered for great and no shameful deeds; contrast iii. 67. 1 'hoc posteris memoriae traditum iri Aequos et Volscos . . . T. Quinctio quartum consule ad moenia urbis Romae impune armatos uenisse!' (in which *T. Quinctio quartum consule* is analogous to *consulem M. Atilium*) with Cicero's *o fortunatam natam me consule Romam*.

16–36. 4. turmae equitum . . . turmas: see viii. 7. 1 n.

17. pudore: see vi. 24. 7 n.
segniter arma capit, segniter e castris egreditur: for the idea, cf. vi. 7. 2 'turbatas militum mentes esse, segniter arma capta, cunctabundosque et restitantes egressos castris esse'. Since *segniter arma capit* is omitted by both M and λ, a case could be made for holding that the words did not stand in **N**, and indeed they were deleted by Alschefski and Scheibe (1848: 558). Nevertheless, the clause makes good sense; *arma capit* picks up § 8 'arma capere' and § 10 'nudus atque inermis'; the anaphora of *segniter* is very much in L.'s style; there is no motive for interpolation; and the same corruption could easily have occurred in both M and λ through *saut du même au même*. See Weissenborn (1843) 271 and Ogilvie (1957) 74.
longo agmine nec continenti: i.e. they did not come out in line of battle and there were many gaps in their formation; for the coupling, cf. e.g. iii. 28. 2, xxxv. 27. 15, xxxvii. 23. 8, 29. 8, xliii. 10. 4, and Caes. *Gall.* v. 31. 6.

19. nullam . . . ne . . . quidem: see ix. 36. 1 n.
stratis: see vii. 24. 5 n.
per corpora eorum euadendum: for the expression see ix. 39. 8 n.

36. 1. in medium sarcinas coniciunt: for this τόπος of Livian battle-scenes, see viii. 11. 11 n. with *addendum*.

medium is the younger Gronovius' conjecture for **N**'s *medio*. Although *conicere* is found sometimes with *in* and the ablative, none of the passages cited for this usage at *TLL* iv. 306. 74–80 is like ours (the earliest is in Scribonius Largus), and elsewhere L. always uses the expression *in medium sarcinas conicere* (see 36. 13, xxviii. 2. 3, xxxi. 27. 7). Note also similar instances of *sarcinas conicere* with *in* and the accusative at iii. 28. 1, viii. 11. 11, xxix. 7. 5, xli. 12. 6, and *in medium conicere* at Virg. *georg.* iv. 25–6 'in medium . . . | transuersas salices et grandia conice saxa'; analogous too is the instance of *sarcinas referre* with *in medium* at Curt. vi. 6. 14.

2. stabant exspectantes . . . clamor inciperet: for hesitation before fighting, see ix. 32. 5 n.

3. integri atque intacti: see 14. 20 n.
cedenti instaturum alterum timuissent: for the expression cf. Ov. *met.* xii. 134 'cedentique sequens instat'. Woodman and Martin on Tac. *ann.* iii. 21. 4 'ubi instaretur cedens' may be correct to suggest that our passage is a reversal of Sall. *Iug.* 36. 2 '(Iugurtha) cedere instanti', which Tacitus too may echo. For the accusative and infinitive after a verb denoting fear, see vii. 39. 4 n.
clamore incerto: for the feeble shout see viii. 38. 10 n., for the expression xxi. 31. 12, xxxvii. 29. 4, and Tac. *hist.* ii. 41. 3.
uestigio: for *uestigium* used of stance or position in the line of battle, see e.g. xxii. 49. 4 'cum uicti mori in uestigio mallent quam fugere', Vell. ii. 55. 3, Stat. *Theb.* ix. 676, Tac. *hist.* iv. 60. 2, and Amm. xvi. 12. 20.

4. extra ordinem: i.e. they were detached from the main body of the cavalry; cf. iii. 62. 7 'duo extra ordinem milia quae in sinistrum cornu Romanorum . . . impressionem facerent tenuere'.
quorum cum plerique delapsi ex equis essent et alii turbati, et . . .: this, the punctuation of e.g. W–M, should be adopted. Walters placed the comma after *essent*, but *delapsi* and *turbati* balance each other in the same *cum*-clause. Drakenborch reports the omission (whether by accident or conjecture there is no knowing) of the first *et* by B.L. Burn. 201. 2, a reading on which Walters looked with some favour. It would avoid the possibility of confusion with the ensuing *et . . . et*, and could therefore be right. For *quorum plerique*, see ix. 46. 12 n.
delapsi ex equis essent: a hazard of fighting on horseback before the mediaeval invention of the stirrup; cf. xxi. 46. 6 'multis laben-

tibus ex equis', xxv. 18. 13, xxxv. 11. 8 (where the Numidians do it deliberately), xxxvii. 34. 6, and Just. xxxiii. 2. 1.

5. inritata pugna est: for the expression cf. xxviii. 33. 5 'leuibus telis, quae inritare magis quam decernere pugnam poterant'.
impigre magis: see 14. 2 n.
proculcauit: *proculcare* is found first here in prose (in verse at Lucr. v. 1235 and then Virg. *Aen.* xii. 534), and only here in L.; it is used regularly of trampling by horses; cf. e.g. Virg. loc. cit. and Ov. *met.* xii. 374.

6. iamque in terga fugientium pugnabant: for the expression cf. xxvii. 48. 14 'mox in terga iam pugnarent'.
praeuectus: see ix. 35. 7 n.

7. edictoque: see vi. 25. 5 n.
pro hoste haberent: for the idea, cf. vi. 24. 6. Since Regulus was issuing orders to the *equites* rather than pronouncing upon his own intentions, *haberent* (Πλ) is much to be preferred to *haberet* (M). All witnesses to χ have the easy conjecture *haberetur* (*-eretur* > *-eret* > *-erent*): this allows the same subject to be kept throughout *siue ille . . . haberetur*, but the paradosis is easy enough to understand and there is probably no need to emend.
ipse is to be taken with *obstitit* and underlines the contrast between the behaviour of the consul and that of his troops. It is a certain correction found in D for **N**'s *ipsa*, which adds pointless emphasis to *haec*.
profuse tendentibus: *profuse* is found only here in L., and is attested nowhere else in Latin in the sense 'in a stream'. Hence Madvig (1860: 194) first suggested *prope fuse tendentibus*, Weissenborn (*Komm.*³) *effuse tendentibus*, and Wesenberg (1870/1: 40), anticipating the second thoughts of Madvig (1877: 233), *prope effuse tendentibus*. Gundermann (1888: 365–6) espoused a different approach: arguing that Frontin. *strat.* ii. 8. 11 'M. Atilius consul bello Samnitico ex acie refugientibus in castra militibus aciem suorum opposuit' and Frontin. (?) *strat.* iv. 1. 29 'Atilius Regulus, cum ex Samnio in Luceriam transgrederetur exercitusque eius obuiis hostibus auersus esset, opposita cohorte iussit fugientes pro desertoribus caedi' derive ultimately from our passage, he proposed *refugientibus* for *profuse tendentibus*, suggesting that the corruption occurred as a result of perseveration from the earlier *tenderet*. The conjectures of Weissenborn and Gundermann give good sense, but Walters vindicated the para-

dosis by citing Caes. *ciu.* iii. 93. 3 'omnisque multitudo sagittariorum se profudit', to which may be added the other passages (all post-Livian) cited at *OLD s.u. profundo* 5 and *TLL* x. 2. 1742. 12–16 (the paradosis is rejected at 1745. 63–6).

8. 'quo pergis . . . pugnare malis': the short and dramatic speech uttered by the Roman commander is a characteristic feature of Livian battle-scenes; see vol. i, p. 119.
arma et uiros: i.e. hostile weapons and men prepared to use them against the fleeing Romans.
proinde: see vii. 30. 23 n.
cum ciue an hoste: for this contrast, see vii. 36. 2 n.

9. equites . . . peditem: this variation is regular in L.; cf. 41. 11, xxxv. 40. 6, and xlv. 34. 5. See further the notes of Briscoe and esp. Drakenborch on xxxv. 40. 6 (where numerous analogies are cited).
infestis cuspidibus: for the coupling, see viii. 7. 9 n.; here, however, *infestis* is not redundant.
circumagendi signa: see vi. 24. 7 n.
uirtus . . . fors: see vii. 34. 6 n.
consulis is the reading of MUTRD; P and L have (different) abbreviations; and Zt has *consulem*, which was conjectured independently by Gruter. This last has some attractions, but the paradosis (if one may write of a paradosis when L. may very well have written an ambiguous abbreviation such as *cons*) is more pointed. For the sentiment and the use of *adiuuare* without object expressed, cf. vii. 23. 8 'praeter uirtutem locus quoque superior adiuuit'. Further parallels are cited by Walters and Conway (1918: 115–16).

10. ab signiferis rapta signa: when a maniple advanced its *signa* went first (viii. 11. 7 n.); for the *signa* being used to rally the troops, see vi. 8. 1–4 n.

11. manus ad caelum attollens: this expression cannot be paralleled precisely in L.; but for *manus* and *ad caelum* with (*a*) *tollens* cf. v. 21. 15 and xxiv. 16. 10 (and note also x. 19. 17 'manibus ad caelum sublatis'); (*b*) *porrigens* cf. xxx. 21. 7; and (*c*) the more usual *tendens* cf. vi. 20. 10 (this passage does not have *ad caelum*), xxv. 37. 9, xxvi. 9. 8, xxxv. 31. 13, and xl. 4. 12. All these passages refer to prayers or invocations of gods: for the meaning of the gesture, see vi. 20. 10 n.
uoce clara, ita ut exaudiretur: for L.'s phrasing here, cf. i. 27. 8 'equitem clara increpans uoce ut hostes exaudirent'. Here his point

does not seem to be that Atilius spoke loudly just so that his men would be roused to action. Rather, a firmly voiced prayer was more likely to be heard by a deity; cf. Hom. *Il.* i. 450, Hor. *epist.* i. 16. 59, Pers. 2. 8, Stat. *Theb.* xi. 503, and Suet. *Nero* 37. 3 'et in auspicando opere Isthmi magna frequentia clare ut sibi ac populo Romano bene res uerteret optauit'. See further Appel (1909) 209–10 (with discussion also of occasions on which quiet prayers were appropriate).

templum Ioui Statori uouet: see vii. 28. 4 n. with *addendum* for the practice of vowing temples in battle, x. 37. 15 n. for this temple.

redintegratoque proelio: see vi. 24. 4 n.

12. numen . . . nomen: for the play on these two words cf. e.g. i. 23. 4 'magnum . . . deorum numen ab ipso capite orsum in omne nomen Albanum expetiturum poenas dictitans', Acc. *trag.* 646, 691–2, Manil. ii. 899, and Plin. *nat.* ii. 154.

respexisse: 'showed concern for'. *respicere*, like ἐφορᾶν, is used regularly of divine protection and is found particularly often in prayers (in which gods are often asked to cast a protective eye on a person or nation); cf. e.g. xxii. 49. 7 'L. Aemili, quem unum insontem . . . dei respicere debent . . .', Ter. *Andr.* 642 'Charine, et me et te imprudens, nisi quid di respiciunt, perdidi', Cic. *Att.* i. 16. 6 'rei publicae statum . . . nisi quis nos deus respexerit, elapsum scito esse', and Virg. *Aen.* v. 688–9. See further Nisbet and Hubbard on Hor. *carm.* i. 2. 36, Tarrant on Sen. *Ag.* 407, Friis Johansen and Whittle on Aesch. *suppl.* 1, and *OLD s.u.* 8(b).

inclinata res est: see vi. 8. 7 n.

13. sarcinarum cumulo . . . medium: see viii. 11. 11 n.

14. caesi captique: for the disjunctive *-que* see ix. 19. 3 n.

captiuorum . . . octingentos: for figures of enemy killed and captured, see vii. 17. 9 n. That the two figures recorded here and the third recorded in § 15 should all end in 800 may be merely an odd coincidence, but scribal error cannot be ruled out.

14–15. octingentorum . . . octingentorum was conjectured in both places by Drakenborch for *accc* or the like in the primary mss. For the first he was anticipated by A^c (note also *septingentorum* in Ricc. 485, which Drakenborch also considered in order to account for *acc* in some of his corrupt *recentiores*). For a similar corruption see 14. 21 n.

sub iugum missi: see ix. 4. 3 n.

15. ne Romanis quidem laeta uictoria fuit: see vii. 8. 7 n.

16–18. For the theme of a seemingly successful enemy army running into a Roman army which defeats it, Plathner (1934: 14) compared iii. 5 and 8. 7–10; but the similarities with our passage are at only a very general level.

16. dum haec . . . gerebantur: see ix. 32. 1 n.
altero exercitu: see 32. 2.
Interamnam: for Interamna Lirenas see ix. 28. 8 n.
uia Latina: the Via Latina led from Rome to Capua down the valleys of the Sacco and Liri. The date of its construction is uncertain and, indeed, whether it ever was formally constructed: probably there had always been a route down these valleys, and it would not be surprising if the quality of this road was enhanced in the late fourth century, when Latin colonies on it were established at Cales (334 [viii. 16. 13–14 (nn).]), Fregellae (328 [viii. 22. 1–2 (nn.)]), and Interamna Lirenas (312 [ix. 28. 8 (n.)]).

    H. J. Müller (1889*b*) conjectured ⟨*ad*⟩ *uia*⟨*m*⟩ *Latina*⟨*m*⟩, but in defence of the paradosis Walters well cited xxii. 1. 12 'signum Martis Appia uia'.

17. praedam . . . hominum atque pecudum: see vi. 31. 8. n.
longo atque impedito agmine incompositi: for the expression cf. xxxv. 1. 6 'longum et impeditum turba pecorum agmen'. For *agmine incompositi* see ix. 43. 11 n.

18. edicto dominis ad suas res noscendas recipiendasque reuocatis: see 20. 15 n.
comitiorum causa Romam est profectus: for L.'s phrasing here, see viii. 20. 1 n.

19. et ob amissa tot milia militum: for the reluctance of the senate to grant triumphs to those who had incurred heavy losses, see Val. Max. ii. 8. 1 (implicit) and Brennan (1996: 318 and n. 20), who cites instances of commanders who failed to gain a triumph, perhaps for this reason. He notes an annalistic or Dionysian retrojection of the idea at D.H. ix. 26. 9; compare also D.H. v. 47. 4, where a consul is said to have gained an ovation and not a triumph because of an earlier reverse. How far this attitude went back beyond the second century into earlier Roman history is doubtful: the proconsuls of 254 celebrated a triumph despite a naval disaster.

quod captiuos sine pactione sub iugum misisset: *sine pactione* perhaps suggests criticism of Regulus because he had not brought the campaign to a proper and formal conclusion. For the dismissing of enemy troops after they had been sent under the yoke one thinks in the first place of the Caudine Forks; but in other respects our passage does not recall that infamous Roman defeat.

37. 1–5. *Fighting in Etruria and the triumph of Postumius Megellus.* L. here returns to Postumius Megellus, describing his campaigning in Etruria (§§ 1–5) and his triumph (§§ 6–12). His account of the fighting is brief and unadorned, and the omission of parts of *esse* after *caesi, traductus, uastati, expugnatum, capta,* and *caesa* may suggest the style of the military communiqué (see vol. i, p. 139 n. 146). The triumph, however, and the political squabbles which preceded it, draw from him a more expansive narrative. Especially effective is the use of a brief passage of direct speech (§ 8) to emphasize the justified pride of the consul in his office and his achievements; noteworthy too is the splendid periodic sentence in §§ 6–7, to which the opening sentence of this speech comes as the climax. The episode is rounded off with one plain sentence describing the triumph (§ 12).

37. 1. materia belli, the meaning of which embraces both 'opportunity for war' and 'object of war', is an expression uncommon outside L.; cf. ii. 3. 5 (where, however, *materia* means 'wherewithal'), xxviii. 2. 13, xxxvii. 60. 2, and xxxix. 1. 8; also Tac. *hist.* i. 89. 2 and Flor. ii. 7(iii. 19). 3 (with dative *bello*).
⟨in⟩ **Etruriam:** like other writers, L. omits *in* before the names of towns, cities, and islands, but (*pace* Drakenborch) nowhere else before a word like *Etruriam* that denotes a region or province. The supplement, found in Zr and perhaps in some *recentiores*, restores regular idiom; cf. e.g. xxiii. 29. 16, xxix. 5. 9, and xxxviii. 36. 1.
peruastauerat: see vi. 4. 8 n.
Volsiniensium: see vii. 3. 7 n.

2. haud procul moenibus: for the omission of *a(b)*, see vi. 16. 6 n.
duo milia octingenti Etruscorum caesi: see vii. 17. 9 n.

3. Rusellanum: see 4. 5 n.
traductus is the spelling offered by the mss here after *transducto* in § 1; since it is impossible to be sure which L. is likely to have used and there is no certainty that he did not vary his spelling in the same paragraph, I have not tried to standardize; see also 46. 5 n.

capta ... caesa: see 14. 21 n. for the figure for enemy captured, vii. 17. 9 n. for general discussion of casualty figures.

4. pax ... indutias ... impetrauerunt: since *indutiae* and *pax* are generally contrasted, *pax* is perhaps used loosely by L. See further see ix. 41. 6–7 n.
Perusia: see ix. 37. 12 n.
Arretium: see ix. 37. 12 n.

5. et uestimentis ... pacti: see ix. 41. 6–7 n.
ut mitti Romam oratores liceret: for enemy ambassadors' being sent to Rome see viii. 36. 12 n.
multa: the first reference to an indemnity in L.'s account of the Roman conquest of Italy. Rome very regularly used indemnities to punish defeated foes during her conquest of the Mediterranean.

37. 6–12. *The triumph of Postumius Megellus.* The constitutional issues involved in the decision of Megellus to triumph without the authority of senate and people are discussed at vi. 42. 8 n. According to D.H. xvii/xviii. 5. 3, he triumphed without permission during his third consulate of 291. Since it is unlikely that he did this twice, we must choose between the rival dates of the two authors. Despite the difficulties which L.'s account for this year presents, it is perhaps to be preferred: although the detail in it may be the product of annalistic invention (modelled on debates concerning requests for triumphs in the later third, second, and first centuries, in which precedents were often cited), it is conceivable that for this comparatively recent year L. had good evidence for how the tribunes were divided. By contrast, D.H.'s narrative is rather vague. See further Henderson (1957) 84–5, Hölkeskamp (1987) 187–8, Loreto (1991*b*) 72–3, and Chaplin (2000) 140–56 (for triumphal debates in L.); for the stormy career and arrogance of Megellus, see ix. 44. 2 n.

6–8. A period with some striking internal balance; note the *cum*-clause with two main verbs positioned chiastically (*petisset uideret-que*), the further chiastic balance inside the first part of this clause (*moris magis causa quam spe impetrandi*), *alios ... alios*, and *partim ... partim*. For the periodic sentence introducing *oratio recta*, see vol. i, p. 135.

6. hasce: see ix. 10. 9 n.

7. alios quod . . . ab urbe exissent: if L.'s main narrative is correct as regards the distribution of provinces (see 32. 1–37. 16 n.), and if he has dated the triumph of Megellus correctly, then conceivably this passage rests on authentic testimony. In later years triumphs were sometimes denied on the ground that a (pro-)magistrate was fighting outside his province (see xxviii. 9. 10, xxxiv. 10. 5); but the alleged implication of Postumius' opponents, that it was incorrect for a consul to leave the province which the senate had assigned to him, can hardly have reflected the strict constitutional position: on such matters consular *imperium* did not have to subject itself to senatorial control (the implication of 18. 7 reflects the practice of the late Republic). Indeed, the famous march to the Metaurus of C. Claudius Nero in 207 shows clearly that a consul was free to leave his province (xxvii. 43. 6). There is no other evidence for a triumph being denied because a magistrate had set out late for war. See further Versnel (1970) 178–9.

8. non . . . obliuiscar: a quite similar remark of Megellus is found at D.H. xvii/xviii. 4. 5 ὑπερηφάνους καὶ τυραννικὰς ἔδωκεν ἀποκρίσεις, οὐ τὴν βουλὴν ἄρχειν ἑαυτοῦ φήσας, ἕως ἐστὶν ὕπατος, ἀλλ᾽ αὐτὸν τῆς βουλῆς and Dio fr. 36. 22 (similar to D.H.), both in the context of his third consulship of 291. Probably this was an anecdote not attached securely to any particular year.

uestrae maiestatis: see vi. 40. 3 n.

ut me consulem esse obliuiscar: in status-conscious Rome men were expected to be mindful of both their rank and their own or their families' repute; cf. xxvi. 31. 1 'non adeo maiestatis . . . populi Romani imperiique huius oblitus sum . . . ut . . . consul dicturus causam accusantibus Graecis fuerim', Cic. *IIVerr.* ii. 73 'Minucius, qui Syracusis sic negotiaretur ut sui iuris dignitatisque meminisset', *Phil.* ii. 70 'et consul et Antonius', iii. 8 (on D. Brutus) 'ciuem . . . memorem sui nominis', and Sulp. *ap.* Cic. *fam.* iv. 5. 5 'denique noli te obliuisci Ciceronem esse'; for criticism of those who were not so mindful see ix. 26. 13 'iam famae magis quam imperii memor', and Cic. *Phil.* iii. 20 'ampli quidam homines, sed immemores dignitatis suae'. One may compare also approving (or disapproving) comment on the behaviour of foreigners in this respect: xxiii. 4. 2 'senatores omissa dignitatis libertatisque memoria plebem adulari', xxx. 15. 6 'memor patris imperatoris patriaeque et duorum regum quibus nupta fuisset'. For similar ideas cf. vi. 27. 8 'si sit animus plebi memor patrum libertatis', viii. 21. 1 'magis condicionis in qua natus esset quam praesentis necessitatis memor', 28. 4 'ingenuitatis magis

quam praesentis condicionis memorem', Nep. *Han.* 12. 5, and, per-
haps, Virg. *Aen.* iii. 628–9 'nec talia passus Vlixes | oblitusue sui est
Ithacus discrimine tanto'. With our passage, cf. also Cic. *S. Rosc.* 53
'ut denique patrem esse sese obliuisceretur'.

**bellis feliciter gestis, Samnio atque Etruria subactis, uictoria
et pace parta:** at least since the late third century successive ablatives absolute seem to have been regular for summarizing a magistrate's achievements; cf. e.g. xxxviii. 50. 3 (the older senators argue
that that Manlius Vulso should triumph) 'qui deuictis perduellibus,
confecta prouincia exercitum reportasset', xli. 28. 9 (the *tabula* of
Gracchus) 're publica felicissime gesta atque liberatis ⟨sociis⟩ uecti-
galibus restitutis, exercitum saluum . . . reportauit',[1] *ILLRP* 122,
and Plaut. *Pers.* 753–6 (parodic of the style). L.'s Hannibal adopts
the style when listing Scipio's achievements (xxx. 30. 14): 'consul
creatus, cum ceteris ad tutandam Italiam parum animi esset, trans-
gressus in Africam duobus hic exercitibus caesis, binis eadem hora
captis simul incensisque castris, Syphace potentissimo rege capto,
tot urbibus regni eius, tot nostri imperii ereptis, me sextum decimum
iam annum haerentem in possessione Italiae dextraxisti'; comparable
too in tone and style to these ablatives absolute is *tantis rebus gestis* in
the famous utterance ascribed to Caesar at Suet. *Iul.* 30. 4 'tantis
rebus gestis Gaius Caesar condemnatus essem, nisi ab exercitu auxilium petissem.' By summarizing his achievements in the manner of a
triumphator, Postumius emphasizes his right to triumph.

9. inter tribunos plebis contentio orta: the question of whether or
not a commander should triumph was one on which the tribunes of
the plebs often exercised themselves, and we regularly read of actual
or threatened tribunician intercession. The most famous example of
this concerns the controversial triumph of Ap. Claudius Pulcher in
143 (for the sources see *MRR* i. 471), but see also e.g. xxxii. 7. 4,
xxxiii. 22. 1–10, xxxv. 8. 9, xxxviii. 47. 1 (generalizing comment by
L.'s Manlius Vulso), xxxix. 4. 3, and Brennan (1996) 316. For the
tribunes as guardians of the constitution, see ix. 33. 5 n.

nouo exemplo: the dominating ideology of Roman politics was
normally conservative, in which it was deemed important that
actions should have precedents. Therefore to describe someone as
acting *nouo exemplo* (for which cf. e.g. vii. 16. 7 'legem nouo exemplo ad Sutrium in castris . . . tulit', xlv. 21. 4, Cic. *IVerr.* 53, Caes. *ciu.*
i. 7. 2, Sall. *Cat.* 51. 27, and the Livian passages cited at the end of

---

[1] Sigonius' supplement is not certain.

this paragraph) had virtually the same derogatory connotations as to describe him as acting *nullo exemplo* (for which see Cic. *IIVerr.* iii. 116, *prou.* 45); see Cic. *IIVerr.* ii. 93 'nouo modo nullo exemplo';[1] for a paradoxical argument for the contrary point of view see Cicero in pro-Pompeian vein at *imp. Pomp.* 62–3. Here, however, Postumius is able to cite precedents for his proposed course of action. For citation of precedent in discussion of whether a commander should be allowed to triumph, cf. xxxi. 20. 3–5, 48. 2–3, xxxviii. 50. 3, xxxix. 29. 5, and see Brennan (1996) 317. See further Kornhardt (1936) 65–74, esp. 69–70.

10. iactata res ad populum est: for the expression cf. iii. 10. 3 'iactata per aliquot dies cum in senatu res tum apud populum est', xxii. 23. 7 'saepe iactata in senatu re', and see *TLL* vii. 1. 56. 17–23.
uocatus: see vi. 36. 10 n.
M. Horatium L. Valerium consules: respectively (8) and (304). The pro-plebeian sympathies of Horatius and Valerius had made them deeply unpopular with their aristocratic peers during their consulship in 449; for their triumph see vi. 42. 8 n.
C. Marcium Rutilum: see vii. 16. 1 n.; Marcius triumphed in 356 (vi. 42. 8 n.).
nuper: for the contrast between older and more recent precedents, and the use of *nuper* to point the contrast, see ix. 34. 14 n. To use *nuper* in 294 of an event that happened in 356 may be thought to involve special pleading, but the adverb is found elsewhere referring to events sixty years earlier; see Holford-Strevens (2003) 16 n. 26.
patrem eius qui tunc censor esset: for the younger Marcius Rutilus, see ix. 33. 1 n.; his censorship has not yet been mentioned by L., but see 47. 2 (n.).
ad: Ruperti suggested insertion of *id* before *ad*; but the paradosis is intelligible without emendation.

11. mancipia nobilium: cf. v. 11. 2 'cooptatos tribunos plebis non suffragiis populi sed imperio patriciorum'; such comments perhaps reflect the more stable political conditions of the early and middle second century rather than those of the fourth or early third century (thus e.g. Brunt [1966] 8 = Finley [1974] 80, but see below, § 12 n.). For *mancipium* as a term of abuse, cf. e.g. Sen. *suas.* 6. 12 (on Cicero, subservient to Pompey and Caesar) 'ueteranum mancipium uidetis',

---

[1] An analogous manner of thinking is found in passages like Cic. *IIVerr.* iii. 16 'qua in re primum illud reprehendo et accuso, cur in re tam uetere, tam usitata, quicquam noui feceris'.

7. 6, Curt. x. 8. 3, and see *TLL* viii. 256. 54–64 and Opelt (1965) index *s.u.* For the term *nobiles*, see vi. 37. 11 n.

uoluntatem . . . ac fauorem consentientis populi: that Postumius did not imagine this popular enthusiasm is shown by *celebrante populo* in § 12. *consentientis* contrasts with *aduersus . . . consensum senatus* in § 12.

esse ac futura: for the polyptoton, see vi. 26. 5 n. with *addendum*.

12. auxilio tribunorum plebis trium aduersus intercessionem septem tribunorum: details of this kind seem often to have been invented by L. or his annalistic sources (see vi. 35. 6, ix. 34. 26 nn.), but there is a chance that a notice referring to the events of 294 BC is sound. If so, this would be the first secure instance of a patrician appealing to the tribunes of the plebs: see Badian (1990: 458; also 1996: 212), who rightly argues that earlier instances reported by L. are almost certainly invented (he cites iii. 13. 6, 56. 5–57. 6, viii. 33. 6–35. 9 [discussed at viii. 33. 8 n.], ix. 26. 10, 16 [n.]; add ix. 34. 26 [n.]). If Badian is right, then he must also be right to observe that our passage shows the extent to which by 294 the tribunate had been institutionalized.

37. 13–16. *Variant versions of events.* For discussion of these variants, see above, pp. 345–9.

13. et huius anni parum constans memoria: L. reports discrepant information in his sources more often in book x than in book ix (see vol. i, pp. 14–15 with *addendum*); many of these discrepancies relate to confusion as to which magistrate commanded in which province (see vol. i, pp. 67–72). For his use of *constare* in reporting the views of his sources, see vi. 16. 4 n.

Claudius: see vi. 42. 5 n.

Apulia: sense can just about be extracted from **N**'s *Apuliam*, but this conjecture, found first in U (for whose innovations see vol. i, p. 299 with *addendum*) is preferable: *in Apulia* contrasts with *in Samnio*.

fusum fugatumque . . . compulsum: see ix. 42. 6 n.

14. Fabius: for Fabius Pictor see viii. 30. 9 n. That L.'s summary of Pictor continues to *uotam* is obvious; §§ 15–16 'ut Romulus . . . uenit' may also record what was found in Fabius but could be L.'s own comment.

adi[e]cit: the reading of Πλ (M has a wider omission here) would not be impossible here if interpreted as a past tense, but there would be no parallel in L. for it in this context. By contrast, the present follows better after *scribit* and is very regular; cf. e.g. 30. 6, ii. 17. 3, vii. 22. 3 'quidam Caesonem, alii Gaium praenomen Quinctio adiciunt', ix. 28. 6 'qui captae decus Nolae ad consulem trahunt, adiciunt Atinam et Calatiam ab eodem captas', xxiii. 47. 8, xxxiii. 30. 10, xl. 29. 8. Therefore one should either interpret the reading of Πλ as a present (see 8. 3 n.) or emend as in the lemma. Madvig (1860: 190 = 1877: 227) first suggested emendation but favoured the spelling *adiicit*.

15. Iouis Statoris aedem uotam, ut Romulus ante uouerat: the precise site of the temple of Jupiter Stator is disputed (see esp. Ziolkowski and Coarelli), but it was certainly on the Sacra Via and near the Porta Mugonia (themselves of disputed location) (D.H. ii. 50. 3, Plut. *Cic.* 16. 3) and near the forum (App. *ciu.* ii. 11. 40); it is not to be confused with that dedicated by Metellus Macedonicus in the Circus Flaminius. Romulus was said to have made his earlier vow during the famous battle in the forum against the Sabines of Titus Tatius (see e.g. i. 12. 3–7, D.H. ii. 50. 3, Ov. *fast.* vi. 793–4). L. may be correct to state that already in 294 there was on this site a *fanum* associated in myth with Romulus. However, it is quite possible that the existence of this previous *fanum* was invented at the same time as the vow of Romulus: the vow required the invention of a corresponding temple, and the alleged *fanum* would have been a way of sidestepping the difficulty that the temple of Jupiter Stator was dedicated only in 294. Wiseman (1995a: 127) suggests the 290s as a likely period for this part of the myth of Romulus to have been created, perhaps under the influence of the events of this year. For temples of Jupiter Stator elsewhere in Italy, see *CIL* ix. 3923 (Scurcola), 4534 (Nursia), and x. 5904 (Anagnia); but these are not very likely to have an origin independent of the Roman cult. See further Thulin, *RE* x. 1133, Platner and Ashby (1929) 303–4, Coarelli (1983–5) i. 26–33 and in Steinby (1993–2000) iii. 155–7, Ziolkowski (1989) and (1992) 87–91, L. Richardson (1992) 224, and Weigel (1998) 123.

fanum: L.'s definition of *fanum* is unusual (in his day the word was used regularly as an equivalent indifferently of *aedes* or *templum*); it may perhaps be supported by Fest. 476. 14–16 'sistere fana cum in urbe condenda dicitur, significat loca in oppido futurorum fanorum constituere', but otherwise seems to be unparalleled. See further Samter, *RE* vi. 1995–6 and Linderski (1985) 212–13 = (1995) 501–2. **templo:** see viii. 14. 12 n.

effatus: the technical word for inaugurating a *templum*; cf. e.g. Fest. 146 'itaque templum est locus ita effatus aut ita saeptus, ut . . .', Serv. *auct. Aen.* i. 446 '. . . ita templa faciebant, ut prius per augures locus liberaretur effareturque' and iii. 463 '"effatus" ergo uerbo augurali usus est, quia scit loca sacra, id est ab auguribus inaugurata "effata" dici', and the other passages cited at *TLL* v. 2. 199. 23–44. See also Wissowa (1912) 472 n. 3.

For *effatus* in Π(=PZ[*aff*- Zt¹]; U is defective)Tᶜ, λ(= T¹θ) had *effatus sacratus*, and M has *ia sacratus effatus*. Plainly *sacratus* is a gloss on *effatus* which has crept into the text, and Heraeus (1933: esp. 315–16) first elucidated *ia* as *in alio*, that is a pointer to a variant reading, which, like the variant itself, has intruded into the text. Π preserves the truth, either from a sensible emendation or from a correct choice from variant readings in **N**. For variants of this kind see further vol. i, pp. 316–20 and Ogilvie (1957) 76.[1]

16. ceterum: see viii. 3. 8 n.

uoti damnata: see vii. 28. 4 n.

re[s] publica: the nominative offered by the paradosis was defended by Drakenborch and F. C. Wolff (1826: 13–14), but the ablative, conjectured by Gronovius but found earlier in Aᶜ, is more stylish and supported by the parallel cited in the next note.

in religionem uenit: for the expression cf. xxii. 33. 7 'in religionem etiam uenit aedem Concordiae, quam per seditionem militarem biennio ante L. Manlius praetor in Gallia uouisset, locatam ad id tempus non esse'; also Cic. *nat.* ii. 10.

293 BC

38. 1–46. 16. *Aquilonia and Cominium and their aftermath*

SUMMARY OF L.'S ACCOUNT

With the wars of 293, for which these chapters are by far our most important source, L. brings the second pentad to its final climax. Making no attempt to keep his readers in suspense as to the outcome of the campaigning, he states at 38. 1 that this year brought a great victory to the consul L. Papirius Cursor, a foreshadowing designed to awaken the reader's curiosity. The diversity of the fighting precluded

---

[1] For *ut . . . fuerat* Ruperti very improbably conjectured *hanc Romulus ante uouerat, sed fanum tantum[, id est locus effatus] fuerat hactenus.*

the composition of one unified episode; instead, we are presented with a series of ten interlocking scenes, which take the narrative from the special levy of the Samnites to the triumph of Cursor's colleague, Sp. Carvilius Maximus. They may be analysed as follows.[1]

(*a*) 38. 1: introduction.

(*b*) 38. 2–13: the Samnites effect a special levy of 'consecrated' troops, who assemble at Aquilonia.

(*c*) 39. 1–42. 7: the battle of Aquilonia. Sp. Carvilius is the earlier of the consuls to leave Rome. Taking command of the troops which M. Atilius Regulus has left in the territory of Interamna Lirenas (39. 1), he captures Amiternum from the Samnites (39. 2), and then marches on Cominium (39. 5), ravaging the territory of Atina on the way. In the meantime, Papirius Cursor has captured Duronia (39. 4) and is marching on Aquilonia (39. 5), again ravaging the territory of Atina on the way. L. states that Aquilonia and Cominium were only 20 Roman miles apart (39. 7); hence the consuls are able to communicate with each other and plan to attack the two towns on the same day. Papirius defeats the 'consecrated' troops with the help of a stratagem and compels the Samnites to abandon Aquilonia, from which many Samnites flee to Bovianum.

(*d*) 43. 1–8: Cominium is captured by Carvilius.

(*e*) 43. 9–15: a detachment of Samnites, sent too late from Aquilonia to Cominium, is put to flight.

(*f*) 44. 1–9: the consuls reward their troops and decide to continue their campaign in Samnium by storming individual towns.

(*g*) 45. 1–8: news reaches Rome of the victories in Samnium at almost the same time as news that the Etruscans have rebelled and, in conjunction with Falerii, have raided the territory of Rome's allies.

(*h*) 45. 9–11: Carvilius captures Velia, Palumbinum, and Herculaneum, and then marches to Etruria.

(*i*) 45. 12–46. 9: Papirius Cursor captures Saepinum and triumphs. Then he leaves his army in the territory of Vescia.

(*j*) 46. 10–16: Carvilius captures Troilum and five other fortified sites, forcing the Falisci to sue for peace. He then returns to Rome and triumphs.

---

[1] See further the individual notes to each of the longer sections. This scheme is not the only way to analyse L.'s narrative: for instance, one may prefer to break chapter 38 into §§ 1–4 (an introduction to the events of the year) and §§ 5–13 (a digression on what happened at Aquilonia); note the framing *quod roboris* in § 4 and 13, and that analysis in this way is more compatible with modern conventions of paragraphing (see e.g. Walters's text). Furthermore, the breaks at 43. 15 and 45. 11 are not very pronounced. However, this scheme offers a convenient basis for discussion.

Throughout (*a*)–(*c*) religion is a dominant theme: despite Samnite attempts to use the divine, their rituals are hateful to the gods, who are shown to be on the side of the Romans and their pious consul, L. Papirius Cursor (see esp. 39. 1–42. 7 n.). Another feature of the whole episode is L.'s alternation between the activities of the two consuls. However, he places far more stress on Cursor and Aquilonia: he is introduced at 38. 1, Carvilius only at 39. 1; the graphic description of 38. 1–13 shows that the more powerful Samnite army was facing Cursor; Carvilius is said to have been more concerned about what was happening at Aquilonia than at Cominium (39. 7); and L.'s most elaborate and powerful writing is to be found in his account of the battle at Aquilonia, whereas the capture of Cominium is recounted much more briefly.

For discussion of the literary themes of this episode see Saulnier (1981) 107–9, Lipovsky (1981) 164–7, Feldherr (1991) 154–70 and (1998) 55–63, and Levene (1993) 237–9.

OTHER SOURCES

L.'s reporting of the two triumphs resembles his description of later triumphs (46. 2–8 n.), and is not to be doubted; it is supported by *F.T.*:

> Sp. Caruilius C. f. C. n. Maximus a. CDLX
> co(n)s(ul) de Samnitibus idibus Ian.
> [L. Papiriu]s L. f. Sp. n. Cursor an. CDLX
> [co(n)s(ul) de Sam]nitibus idibus Febr.

Since *F.T.* record the actual dates of the triumphs, it is tempting to follow them when they invert the order of the two triumphs; on the other hand, when they fail to notice the Etruscan campaign of Carvilius, they are likely to be in error.

More extensive material is provided by Dio fr. 36. 29 (a brief account of the Samnite oath which corresponds closely to 38. 2–13, esp. § 10):

ὅτι οἱ Σαυνῖται ἀγανακτήσαντες ἐπὶ τοῖς γεγονόσι [sc. their defeat in 294 BC, as too in Zonaras quoted below] καὶ ἀπαξιώσαντες ἐπὶ πολὺ ἡττᾶσθαι, πρὸς ἀποκινδύνευσιν καὶ πρὸς ἀπόνοιαν ὡς ἤτοι κρατήσοντες ἢ παντελῶς ἀπολούμενοι ὥρμησαν, καὶ τήν τε ἡλικίαν πᾶσαν ἐπελέξαντο, θάνατόν τε προειπόντες ὅστις ἂν αὐτῶν οἴκοι καταμένῃ, καὶ ὅρκοις σφᾶς φρικώδεσι πιστωσάμενοι μήτ' αὐτόν τινα ἐκ μάχης φεύξεσθαι καὶ τὸν ἐπιχειρήσοντα τοῦτο ποιῆσαι φονεύσειν

and esp. by Zon. viii. 1. 8–9:

Σαυνῖται δὲ ἐπὶ τοῖς γεγονόσιν ἀγανακτήσαντες πρὸς ἀπόνοιαν ὥρμησαν, ὡς ἢ
κρατήσοντες ἢ παντελῶς ἀπολούμενοι, θάνατον ἀπειλήσαντες τῷ οἴκοι
μενοῦντι. καὶ οἱ μὲν ἐς τὴν Καμπανίαν ἐνέβαλον, οἱ δ' ὕπατοι ἔρημον ὂν
στρατιωτῶν τὸ Σαύνιον ἐπόρθουν καὶ πόλεις εἷλόν τινας. (§ 9) ὅθεν οἱ Σαυνῖται
τὴν Καμπανίαν λιπόντες εἰς τὴν οἰκείαν ἠπείχθησαν, καὶ τῷ ἑνὶ τῶν ὑπάτων
συμμίξαντες ἔκ τινος ἥττηντο στρατηγήματος, καὶ φεύγοντες δεινῶς ἔπταισαν,
καὶ τὸ στρατόπεδον ἀπέβαλον, πρὸς δὲ καὶ τὸ πόλισμα, ᾧ ἐπεβοήθουν. ὁ
δὲ ὕπατος τά τε ἐπινίκια ἔπεμψε καὶ τὰ ἀθροισθέντα ἐκ τῶν λαφύρων
ἐδημοσίωσεν. ὁ δ' ἕτερος ὕπατος κατὰ τῶν Τυρσηνῶν ἐστρατεύσας, καὶ
καταστήσας αὐτοὺς δι' ὀλίγου, σῖτόν τε καὶ χρήματα παρ' αὐτῶν εἰσπράξας,
τὰ μὲν τοῖς στρατιώταις διέδωκε, τὰ δ' εἰσήνεγκεν εἰς τοὺς θησαυρούς.

As usual, Zonaras' account is derived from Dio.[1] Much of it, however, reads like an abbreviation of L., who also describes the capture
of eight Samnite sites, the stratagem (40. 8 and 41. 5–7), the capture
of the Samnite camp (41. 12), the abandonment of Aquilonia (42. 4),
the triumph of Papirius Cursor (46. 2–8), the placing of all the money
captured by Cursor into the *aerarium* (46. 5–6), the campaign of
Carvilius against the Etruscans (46. 10–16), his extraction of *stipendium* from the Faliscans (46. 11), and his greater generosity towards
his troops (46. 15). Nevertheless, Dio is unlikely to have derived his
account from L., who records neither an initial Samnite attack on
Campania (although there is an oblique allusion to it at 46. 9) nor that
Carvilius extracted *frumentum* from Falerii.[2] It follows that Dio and
L. used very similar sources, but that L. has virtually suppressed the
initial Samnite attack on Campania, perhaps in the interests of focus-
ing attention on Aquilonia.[3]

Pliny, *nat.* xxxiv. 43, makes a passing reference to the victory of
Carvilius:

fecit et Sp. Caruilius Iouem, qui est in Capitolio, uictis Samnitibus sacrata
lege pugnantibus e pectoralibus eorum ocreisque et galeis. amplitudo tanta
est ut conspiciatur a Latiari Ioue. e reliquiis limae suam statuam fecit, quae
est ante pedes simulacri eius.

This differs from the information provided by L., who implies that
the elite Samnite troops faced Papirius and not Carvilius.

---

[1] *Σαυνῖται . . . μενοῦντι* is derived from fr. 36. 29, of which it has several verbal echoes.

[2] Thus, rightly, Klinger (1884) 70.

[3] Since Zonaras alludes only to the fighting at Aquilonia and not to that at Cominium, one
may argue that Dio did not mention Cominium; but, given the extreme brevity of Zonaras,
such an inference would be dangerous.

THE SAMNITE WAR

From L.'s narrative of the Samnite Wars, only his account of the Roman disaster in the Caudine Forks surpasses in fame the tale of the battles of Aquilonia and Cominium; and for no other year in this period does he provide so much topographical information. However, the internal inconsistencies of this information and the difficulty of harmonizing it with evidence derived from other sources has made interpretation extremely controversial; and no matter is disputed more than the question of whether Aquilonia and Cominium are to be sought in northern or southern Samnium.[1]

Scholars agree that there was a town called Aquilonia in the territory of the Hirpini: it is mentioned at Plin. *nat.* iii. 105 and Ptol. *geog.* iii. 1. 71; and the Peutinger Table and the Ravenna Cosmography allow us to locate it at Lacedonia (or Lacedogna) near the Ofanto valley, where several Latin inscriptions survive (*CIL* ix. 968, 6255–67).[2] Our sources mention no other Aquilonia, and therefore, all other matters being equal, one would expect L. to be referring to this site.[3]

Cominium is mentioned at D.H. xvii/xviii. 4. 6 and 5. 1, where we are told that in 291 Postumius Megellus besieged and captured it before his successful assault on Venusia.[4] Later L. (xxv. 14. 14) refers to a Cominium Ocritum, which appears to have been situated close to Beneventum. Since a site to the east of Beneventum might plausibly be captured in an advance on Venusia, it is very tempting to regard Cominium Ocritum as the same as the Cominium of L. and

---

[1] On available evidence the question cannot be resolved. I expound at length the case for placing the battle of Aquilonia in southern Samnium not because I believe that it can be established with certainty but because, with the exception of Tullio (1989), it has been unfairly neglected by recent interpreters. Similarly, I present at length evidence against the views of La Regina, not because I am certain that they are wrong but because they are far more speculative than has sometimes been realized.

[2] The issue should not be blurred by reference to the modern village of Aquilonia, which lies just 8 km from Lacedonia: this was called Carbonara until 14 Dec. 1862.

[3] That the Aquilonia of 293 was Hirpinian was accepted in the past by e.g. De Sanctis (1907–64: ii. 361 n. 1) and Beloch (1926: 447–8) and recently by Tullio (1989). Likewise Buglione (1929: 55–82) had no doubts that Aquilonia was to be sought in these parts, and held that it was to be found at the church of the Incoronata of Monteverde (a village only 12 km from Lacedonia), where polygonal walls survive (see also Oakley [1995] 68–9). The identification is possible; but, even if Aquilonia lay in this part of Samnium, there may once have been a fortified centre rather closer to Lacedonia than the Incoronata.

[4] Beloch (1926: 448) and La Regina (1989: 402) object that the Cominium of 293 and that of 291 cannot be the same since Carvilius destroyed Cominium in 293; but (*a*) L.'s notice (44. 1–2) of the town's being burnt may be no more than annalistic colouring; (*b*) its houses and defences could have been restored by 291; (*c*) other towns changed hands more than once in the Samnite Wars (e.g. Sora [vii. 28. 6 n.] and Allifae [viii. 25. 4 n.]).

D.H.;[1] but, even if this argument is rejected, Lacedonia and Venusia are quite close to each other, and a town near Lacedonia might very easily have been captured in an advance on Venusia. There is a strong case, therefore, for holding that Cominium too lay in Hirpinian territory, in or near the Ofanto valley.[2] However, it should be noted that Pliny (*nat.* iii. 108) refers to a Cominium in the territory of the Aequiculi,[3] and that some modern scholars (see below) have argued that the name Val di Comino given to-day to the valley between Sora and Atina comes from a Cominium that once lay in the valley.

If Aquilonia and Cominium were Hirpinian, then the principal action of 293 may be viewed as part of a sequence of fighting on the southern borders of Samnium. Such campaigns are attested certainly for 297 (14. 1–15. 6 n.), 294 (32. 1–37. 16 n.), and 291 (D.H. loc. cit.), and may be inferred plausibly for 296 (16. 1–21. 12) and 292 (Zon. viii. 1. 10–14 and D.H.). In this context we should consider L.'s reference to the capture of Velia (or whatever site lies behind the references in L.'s mss to Velia, Vella, Veletia, Volana: see 44. 9 n.), Palumbinum, and Herculaneum by Carvilius (44. 9, 45. 9–11). Sceptical scholars have sometimes argued that these notices have no place in the events of 293 (see below); but the very obscurity of Palumbinum guarantees the authenticity of the reference to it and makes it quite likely that the references to Velia (*uel sim.*) and Herculaneum are likewise sound. If Roman armies were operating to the south of Samnium, and if the site to which L. refers was called Velia (both admittedly very far from certain), then L.'s Velia and Herculaneum may just conceivably have been the well-known towns on the Tyrrhenian coast: although Velia enjoyed a favourable treaty with Rome (Cic. *Balb.* 55), L.'s account (45. 9) does not rule out the possibility of surrender before capture; and, although no fighting in the area of Vesuvius has been mentioned since 308 (ix. 41. 3), Oscan Herculaneum may have seen this as a good opportunity to rebel. Palumbinum, the third site which L. mentions in this context, will then have been an unidentifiable settlement somewhere on the coast between Velia and Herculaneum; and it follows that Duronia may also have been Hirpinian.[4] However, it is not unlikely that Velia (*uel*

---

[1] As far as D.H. is concerned this is accepted by Bruno (1906: 70 n. 2). Salmon (1967: 275), who believed that the Cominium captured in 293 was a town on the northern borders of Samnium, stated that Cominium Ocritum (i.e. a different place) was captured in 291; but D.H. does not use the word Ocritum, and an unprejudiced reading of x. 38–46 and D.H. would lead one to the conclusion that both authors refer to the same town.

[2] See also Tullio (1989) 88.

[3] The reference to Cominian olives (ibid. xv. 20) does not help topographical discussion.

[4] One may also hazard the suggestion that the Atina of 39. 5 is not the well-known Volscian

sim.) and Herculaneum are otherwise unidentified sites bearing the same name as more famous sites.

Nevertheless, the view that the principal fighting took place on the southern borders of Samnium poses three major difficulties:[1] first, Samnite fugitives from Aquilonia and Cominium are said to have fled to Bovianum, but Bovianum is far from Lacedonia; second, Papirius Cursor is said to have captured Saepinum after Aquilonia, but Saepinum is hardly less far from Lacedonia than Bovianum; and, third, it is hard to see why Carvilius should first have advanced on Sabine Amiternum if the territory of the Hirpini was to be his ultimate destination.[2] These difficulties are serious, but perhaps not insurmountable. L.'s battle-scenes are full of elaboration and plausible reconstruction; and, while it is hard to doubt that the Romans really did capture Aquilonia in this year, it is most improbable that L. had authority for everything that he writes about the campaign.[3] For example, the capture of Bovianum seems often to have been invented by the annalists to colour their accounts (see ix. 24. 1–28. 2 n.), and the motif of flight to this town, even from a site quite far away, would have been well within their inventive capabilities.[4] Likewise, L.'s information about the capture of Saepinum almost certainly derives ultimately from reliable records; but at 44. 9 he does not state explicitly that Papirius Cursor had only a short distance to march there from Aquilonia; nor, if he had made such a statement, should we necessarily have to believe him: for the telescoping of distance is a regular feature of his account of the Samnite Wars.[5] It is quite easy to imagine Cursor marching through Samnium for several days before he reached his destination, and before reaching Saepinum he may have captured other strongholds, for whose fall L. had no notice.[6] If Bovianum really was captured in this year, then it too could have been captured in the same campaign that led to the capture of Saepinum. The reference to Amiternum is much less easy

town but the obscure Hirpinian Atina (Plin. *nat.* iii. 105). However, the difficulties of such an argument are obvious.

[1] See also Salmon (1967) 271 n. 3.

[2] One may add that conventional wisdom holds that the legend **Akudunniad** on certain Oscan coins (for which see Rutter [2001] 74) refers to Aquilonia, and that these coins have been found only in north Samnium at Agnone and Pietrabbondante; but, since the interpretation of the legend is insecure, this argument loses force.

[3] See below for fuller discussion of this matter.

[4] Thus Beloch (1926) 447.

[5] Three examples: at ix. 13. 4 the Samnites flee from Caudium to Luceria; at ix. 23. 2–3 Sora and the pass ad Lautulas appear to be in close proximity; and at ix. 28. 1 the Romans move from Caudium to Bovianum.

[6] Again, Beloch (1926: 448) has trenchant remarks on this matter.

to explain away,[1] but perhaps Carvilius may have fought a brief campaign against the Sabines before turning his attention to Samnium; and this reference is only marginally less problematic for those who locate Aquilonia and Cominium in central or northern Samnium.

Most modern scholars, however, have rejected the view that Aquilonia and Cominium were Hirpinian and have preferred to look for a site nearer to Bovianum. Such an approach undoubtedly makes it easier to understand how the fugitives could flee to that town and why Papirius Cursor decided to attack Saepinum (which is only 12 km in direct line from Bovianum); but this support for the possibly unreliable details of a Livian battle-scene against hard, external topographical evidence, involves a heavy price.[2] Instead of accepting the claims of an Aquilonia whose location is certainly known and a Cominium whose approximate location is known, one has to postulate the existence of other sites bearing the same names. Furthermore, if Cominium is to be placed in north Samnium, we have the spectacle of Carvilius marching down to the Campanian and Lucanian coast and then in a diametrically opposed direction to Etruria.[3] Consequently scholars who adopt this approach to the problem are forced to argue either that the references to Velia, Palumbinum, and Herculaneum are a retrojection from the campaigns undertaken by Carvilius in his second consulship of 272,[4] or that these three places are to be sought in central Samnium. This second alternative has proved attractive,[5] but it involves postulating not only a second Aquilonia and a second Cominium but also a second Herculaneum and a second Velia. The phenomenon of two ancient Italian sites bearing the same name is not especially rare;[6] but it seems dangerous confidently to accept an explanation of the events of 293 which postulates four otherwise unattested instances of the phenomenon. Nor does this relocation of Aquilonia much help in the

[1] Unless one is prepared to espouse one of the radical approaches to L.'s evidence discussed below.

[2] The following argument was adumbrated very briefly by De Sanctis (1907–64: 361 n. 1); Beloch (1926: 447), despite his radical views on Cominium, was scathing about attempts to find an Aquilonia in north Samnium.

[3] The logistical difficulties of L.'s account are well posed by Bruno (1906: 68–9).

[4] Thus Beloch (1926: 431) and Adcock (1928: 614); Beloch thought that Herculaneum was a reference to Heraclea. See also Bruno (1906) 72 n. 1.

[5] Thus Salmon (1967: 273 n. 1), with an array of arguments including the statement 'anyone who has watched the turtle doves rising from the meadows beside the Sangro will not be suprised to learn that there was once a town called Palumbinum in the vicinity'. *palumbes* is indeed the Latin for a species of dove, but a site in central Samnium is likely to have borne an Oscan name.

[6] Consider e.g. Interamna Lirenas and Interamna Nahars, Longula (ix. 39. 1 n.), and Atina (noted above).

elucidation of the reference to Amiternum, since Bovianum and its territory are still far from Sabine lands.

Although most scholars now believe that Aquilonia and Cominium are to be sought in northern Samnium, they do not agree as to which locations in that area are most probable. The most influential approach to the problem has been propounded by La Regina:[1] he hypothesized that Aquilonia must have been a large Samnite hill-fort near Bovianum,[2] and, after considering most of the known fortified sites in the area north of Bovianum and finding that Monte Vairano (in the *comune* of Busso) was the largest, he argued that it must have been the site of Aquilonia.[3] Even if one grants that Aquilonia was close to Bovianum, this approach involves difficulties: (*a*) some hill-forts have vanished without trace, and Aquilonia may have been amongst these; (*b*) L. states that Aquilonia was the place where the Samnites consecrated themselves and that it was well fortified, but does not imply that it was especially large: therefore many medium-sized sites in the area (e.g. Ferrazzano, Gildone) cannot be excluded; (*c*) if one interprets the notion of proximity to Bovianum more elastic-ally, then sites in the Trigno valley such as the large fortified centre at Carovilli and the medium-sized sites at Duronia and Pietrabbon-dante become possibilities;[4] (*d*) even if one grants that Aquilonia is likely to have been a large site, it need not have been the largest in the area, and Frosolone and Monte Saraceno of Cercemaggiore each have strong claims; and (*e*) if one holds that Aquilonia was indeed the largest site in the area, we now know that Monte S. Paolo of Colli

---

[1] La Regina put forward his hypothesis first at (1975) 281, and its fullest development may be found at (1989) 401–23. See also his comments in Cianfarani *et al.* (1978) ii. 402, AA.VV. (1980) 39–40, and Coarelli and La Regina (1984) 280–3. La Regina's views have won wide-spread acceptance among those concerned with the Samnites; see e.g. De Benedittis (1988) 15 and in *Sannio* (1980) 323–4.

[2] He also hypothesized (1989: 305) that for the period around 293 Aquilonia usurped the position of Bovianum as the capital of the Samnite Pentri, but none of his three arguments is cogent: that the Samnites chose to muster at Aquilonia and not at Bovianum may have been because they did not wish to let the Romans march unimpeded to their capital at Bovianum; that the Romans chose to attack Aquilonia and not Bovianum proves only that there was an important Samnite force there; and that Aquilonia (perhaps) issued coins does not prove that the coins were issued on behalf of the Pentri (if so, one would have expected them to bear the collective legend of the Pentri or the Samnites). See further the sensible counter-arguments of Capini (1992: 40–1).

[3] On Monte Vairano see conveniently Oakley (1995) 113–16, with further bibliography. The most important work on the site has been supervised by De Benedittis: see esp. De Benedittis (1974) and (1988).

[4] Garrucci (1885: 99–100) did indeed hold that Aquilonia was at Duronia (called Civita-vecchia in his day); but in his day it was believed that there were two Boviana, one at at Boiano, the other, Bovianum Vetus, at Pietrabbondante, which is very near modern Duronia. On the problem of the site of Bovianum see ix. 28. 1 n.

al Volturno was larger (although somewhat further away from Bovianum). In sum, if there was a northern Aquilonia, it may have been at Monte Vairano; but La Regina's method of argument allows the same conclusion to be reached for several other sites.[1]

Another approach has been to make use of modern toponyms, and in particular that of the Valle di Comino (that is the upper valley of the Melfa). Hülsen, *RE* ii. 332 and iv. 607, and Costanzi (1919: 177–9) placed Cominium in this valley, and argued that Aquilonia lay in the mountains which form the watershed of the Volturno and Sangro. Salmon (1967: 26 and 271 n. 3), arguing for this view with more precision, held that Aquilonia is to be sought at modern Montaquila, and Cominium near Alvito in the Val di Comino. If one grants the premise that the details of L.'s narrative are to be taken seriously, then these guesses are not absurd: Alvito is very close, and Montaquila quite close, to Atina, the territory of which the consuls pillaged before advancing on Aquilonia and Cominium; and Montaquila is reasonably close to Bovianum, and Alvito is about twenty Roman miles distant from it. Moreover, the discovery at Monte S. Paolo between Montaquila and Colli al Volturno of the largest of all Samnite fortified centres has given added strength to Salmon's case, and Capini (1992: 38–42) has now argued that this was the site of Aquilonia. Although it may be agreed that, if Aquilonia lay in northern Samnium, Monte S. Paolo is a more likely site than anywhere else, it should be remembered that the identification is only a little less speculative than any other. As for Cominium, Salmon failed to tie it to known ancient remains and did not observe that communication between the Volturno valley at Montaquila and the Valle di Comino involves crossing a high range

---

[1] If the identification of Aquilonia as Monte Vairano is insecure, it follows that La Regina's other hypothetical identifications consequential upon it are even less certain. Thus, even though Pietrabbondante is about twenty Roman miles from Monte Vairano, there is no compelling reason to regard that great Samnite site as Cominium (for the suggestion see La Regina in AA.VV. [1980] 40, [1989] 420–2 and Coarelli [1996] 15). Nor is there any reason to accept his alternative suggestions that Frosolone was Cominium (Coarelli and La Regina [1984] 282) and Pietrabbondante Herculaneum ([1975] 281 and in AA.VV. loc. cit.). Later (1989: 422–3) he argued that Herculaneum was at Campochiaro. Since the sanctuary at this site may perhaps correspond to the *fanum Herculis Rani* of the Peutinger Table, this idea is more plausible; but the very multiplicity of rival suggestions shows just how fraught with danger is this whole procedure. Equally hazardous is a minute reconstruction of the battle of Aquilonia: La Regina now (Coarelli and La Regina, loc. cit. and 1989, 419–20) holds that the battle was fought on the plain north-west of Campobasso, between S. Maria di Fuori and the Costa di Oratino, and that the name of the so-called Porta Vittoria at Monte Vairano reflects the point at which Scipio Barbatus broke into the city. Quite apart from its other frailties, such a reconstruction takes no account of the nature of annalistic elaboration.

of mountains. By contrast, Capini acquiesces in La Regina's speculative identification of the site with Pietrabbondante.

Jacobelli (1970: 15–65) suggested that both Aquilonia and Cominium lay in the Valle di Comino: Aquilonia at the Rocca degli Alberi
of Picinisco (where there are no polygonal walls), and Cominium at
Vicalvi (where there was indeed a fortified centre); but, since both
sites are far from Bovianum, this view hardly takes L.'s evidence
seriously. Likewise, the suggestion of Nissen (1883–1902: ii. 789)
that Aquilonia was the large and well known hill-fort at the Curino of
Alfedena and of Giannetti (1973) that it was the almost equally large
hill-fort at Colle Marena-Falascosa on Monte Sambucaro founder
because they are based neither on L. nor on any of our other topographical evidence.[1]

Radical hypotheses have been propounded to eliminate the
difficulties posed by L.'s reference to Amiternum. Some scholars
have argued that there was a second, otherwise unknown site of this
name in or near Samnium: Nissen (1883–1902: ii. 679) and Salmon
(1967: 270 n. 4) wished to place this at S. Elia Fiume Rapido (near
Cassino), while La Regina (1989: 399) tentatively considered
Roccasecca; but it is more economical to accept the difficulties of L.'s
text than to resort to invention of this kind. Beloch (1904/5: 273–5;
1926: 430–1, 447–8) and Bruno (1906: 71–3) argued that Carvilius
fought against the Sabines and not against the Samnites and hence
could easily have captured Amiternum; that the reference to Interamna which L. found in his sources and recorded at 39. 1 was not to
Interamna Lirenas but to Umbrian Interamna Nahars, a town much
closer to Amiternum and from which it would not have been difficult
for Carvilius to cross into Etruria; and that, since D.H. shows that
Samnite Cominium was taken first in 291, the Cominium captured in
293 must have been the Aequan town. Bruno (1906: 72) suggested
that Velia, Herculaneum, and Palumbinum should be sought in this
area; Beloch, as we have already seen, preferred to regard them as
retrojections from the second consulate of Carvilius in 272. The
strength of this hypothesis lies in its explanation of how Carvilius
could have fought at Amiternum. Its weakness is that it rejects much
of L.'s narrative: even if Aquilonia and Cominium were not as close
as L. implies (39. 7),[2] it is hard to doubt that the annalistic tradition

---

[1] However, Nissen too thought that Pietrabbondante was called Bovianum Vetus; since
Alfedena is reasonably close to Pietrabbondante, his hypothesis did not then seem as absurd as
it may now do.

[2] Bruno (1906: 70) rejects the notion that the consuls cooperated closely: 'il racconto di Livio
. . . ha un carattere molto più romanzesco che storico'.

recorded a joint drive by the consuls into Samnium. Nor is the double capture of Cominium a major difficulty: many towns must have changed hands several times during the Samnite Wars,[1] and there is no reason why Cominium should not have been reconstructed after its capture by Carvilius, only to be taken again in 291. As for the introduction of Interamna Nahars, while L.'s sources may have confused the two Interamnae, this hypothesis also involves revision of part of L.'s account for 294 (36. 16–19). Again, it is easier to believe that Carvilius campaigned in rather diverse areas than to accept such major revision.[2]

To conclude: without new discoveries the location of neither Aquilonia nor Cominium can be established beyond reasonable doubt.

THE DETAILS OF LIVY'S ACCOUNT

Since the battles of Aquilonia and Cominium took place only a generation before Fabius Pictor was born, there is in principle no reason why a fairly accurate memory of what happened in 293 should not have survived for use by the earliest historians of Rome. Therefore one may be tempted to argue that details such as the stratagem involving Sp. Nautius (40. 8, 41. 5–7) and the parts played by L. Cornelius Scipio and L. Volumnius Flamma in the capture of Aquilonia (41. 12–14) rest upon authentic information. And, if L. was correct to place Aquilonia and Cominium only twenty Roman miles from each other, then other details too may be believed: for instance, the close co-operation between the consuls, the simultaneous battle at Aquilonia and attack on Cominium, and the defeat of the Samnite contingent stranded between the two sites. Such a position cannot be disproved on our available evidence. It would be extraordinary, however, if L. and his annalistic predecessors had resisted the temptation to embroider their accounts of these famous campaigns, and the sensational story about the *pullarius* (40. 2–4, 9–14) suggests that the temptation was not resisted. Furthermore, L.'s uncertainty (41. 5) whether Octavius Maecius or Sp. Nautius was responsible for supervising the stratagem shows that not all his detailed information was reliable. The only prudent course is to regard all details of the battles themselves as suspect.

Noting that at Plin. *nat.* xxxiv. 43 (quoted above) Carvilius is

---

[1] Consider the fates of Allifae (viii. 25. 4 n.) and Sora (vii. 28. 6 n.).

[2] For fuller consideration of Beloch's hypothesis that in this period Rome was engaged in a Sabine War, see above, pp. 30–4.

credited with taking spoil from a Samnite army fighting *sacrata lege*, a passage which can hardly refer to any other year but this, and that Papirius Cursor and his nephew are very prominent in L.'s account, Sordi (1976: 162–4) argued that the detail of the tradition has been perverted by Papirian family traditions; but both Carvilius and Papirius may have fought against an army recruited *sacrata lege*, and the consul and his nephew (who may have been his closest living male relative) are likely enough to have been prominent in the fighting at Aquilonia.

The accounts of the triumphs are another matter: these resemble similar notices in books xxi–xlv and are likely to be sound (46. 2–8 n.). Likewise the notice that the army of Papirius wintered at Vescia is probably to be trusted: in the previous year a Roman army had wintered at Interamna Lirenas (36. 18, 39. 1).

THE ETRUSCAN WAR

Despite the peace made in 294 with the powerful cities of Volsinii, Perusia, and Arretium, Roman armies once again fought in Etruria. L. mentions fighting against Falerii and the otherwise unknown Troilum (46. 10 n.); his narrative is supported by Zonaras (see above, pp. 381–2). Since the Faliscans had last rebelled as long ago as 351 and—if L. (14. 3) is reliable—had been loyal as recently as 297,[1] it is unclear why they now decided to fight; but perhaps, like the Hernici in 307–306, they felt that the time had come to make a stand against the ever-increasing might of Rome, or perhaps they did not feel that from the general peace of 294 they had derived the benefits which their loyalty had deserved. L. records that the campaign of Carvilius resulted in *indutiae* for one year (46. 12), but the agreement seems not to have lasted that long, and in 292 the new consul D. Junius Brutus Scaeva had to effect a more lasting settlement (Zon. viii. 1. 10).[2] That held until 241, when in the aftermath of the First Punic War Falerii made her final bid for freedom; and ill-timed and unhappy though that was, it earned her the distinction of being the last state in peninsular Italy to fight Rome before the Hannibalic War.

See further Bruno (1906) 74–6, De Sanctis (1907–64) ii. 361–2, Münzer, *RE* iii. 1630, Costanzi (1919) 202–6, Beloch (1926) 445–6, Adcock (1928) 614, and Harris (1971) 76–8.

---

[1] Beloch's view that they had in fact been supporting the Etruscans since 298 is improbable.

[2] Costanzi shows that there is no good reason to follow Bruno in arguing that L.'s account of the Faliscan War should be placed in 292, when Carvilius served under Brutus Scaeva. Adcock later adopted a position similar to Bruno's, but no more successfully.

38. 1. INTRODUCTION

sequitur hunc annum et consul insignis . . . uictoriaque: see viii. 22. 1 n.

L. Papirius Cursor: (53). L. Papirius L. f. Sp. n. Cursor is best known from L.'s account of his victory and triumph over the Samnites in this year. He appears for the first time, however, in the muddled account of the aedilician elections for 299 (9. 10–13 n.). His later career included a praetorship in 292 (47. 5) and a second consulship in 272, when he and Sp. Carvilius Maximus (again his colleague) triumphed over the Tarentines, Samnites, Lucanians, and Bruttians (*per.* xiv, *F.T.*, and Zon. viii. 6. 12–13). For L., Papirius and Carvilius constituted one of Rome's great consular pairs: describing the unusual enthusiasm which greeted the accession to the magistracy of Fabius Verrucosus (for the fourth time) and M. Marcellus (for the third time) in 214, he writes (xxiv. 9. 7–8): 'multis enim annis tale consulum par non fuerat. referebant senes sic Maximum Rullum cum P. Decio ad bellum Gallicum, sic postea Papirium Caruiliumque aduersus Samnites Bruttiosque et Lucanum cum Tarentino populum consules declaratos'. The loss of his narrative of 272 is much to be regretted. See further viii. 12. 2 n. for Cursor's father, x. 40. 9 n. for his nephew, and ix. 16. 12–19 n. for the similar stories told about both father and son.

L.'s attention is so taken by the appearance of the younger Cursor that he fails to mention until 39. 1 (n.) that Sp. Carvilius Maximus was the other consul.

qua paterna qua sua: L. shows that Cursor lived up to his father's reputation; for this theme see vii. 10. 3 n. with *addendum*. In general 'fathers and sons' are an important theme in books vi–x: one thinks of Manlius Torquatus and his son (esp. vii. 9–10 and viii. 7), the *deuotiones* of the two Decii Mures, and the support to Fabius Rullianus given by his father (viii. 33–5). For *qua . . . qua* see ix. 3. 4 n.

38. 2–13. THE SAMNITE LEVY

Literary analysis. After the initial introductory sentence L. moves swiftly into his famous description of the gruesome Samnite levy, which forms a distinct short episode of its own inside the account of the events of the year.[1] He suggests that the revival of the old rituals used at the time of the capture of Capua was designed to bring help

---

[1] For an alternative analysis, see above, p. 380.

from the gods (38. 2); and, were the battle of Aquilonia to have a successful outcome for the Samnites, it could be seen as legitimizing both these rituals and the capture of Capua.[1] However, before L. ends this section with a matter-of-fact final sentence, he has introduced us to oaths taken under compulsion (§ 8), secrecy (§§ 8–9), men brought to altars more like victims than participants in a ritual (§ 9), an oath involving a *dirum carmen* (§ 10), a threat to the families of those participating (§ 10), the promise of citizen to kill citizen (§ 10), the gruesome murder of innocent soldiers, and the public view of their dead bodies (§ 11). Moreover, § 2 'initiatis' hints at initiation into a mystery cult (see n., with reference to other places in the episode where L.'s language anticipates his account of the Bacchanalia in book xxxix), hardly something of which conventional Roman opinion would have approved. Even if the description of this recruiting by Papirius Cursor at 39. 16 ('tum si qua coniectura mentis diuinae sit, nulli umquam exercitui fuisse infestiores quam qui nefando sacro mixta hominum pecudumque caede respersus, ancipiti deum irae deuotus . . . inuitus iurauerit') be viewed as partisan and exaggerated, the matter-of-fact voice of the narrator at 39. 2 'dum hostes operati superstitionibus concilia secreta agunt' confirms that a deep shadow lies over these rites. L. has created a picture of a very un-Roman scene, a perversion of a real sacrifice; and for this reason, given the principles on which his history operates, these rites are most unlikely to prove efficacious.[2]

Lex sacrata *and* legio linteata. L.'s distinction between the various rituals and procedures used by the Samnites in their levy is not entirely clear. He refers to four:

(*a*) an old *ritus sacramenti* used in the initial summons to Aquilonia (§ 2 'ritu quodam sacramenti uetusto uelut initiatis militibus');

(*b*) the new rule employed in the initial summons to Aquilonia, that whoever absented himself should be regarded as *sacer* to Jupiter (§ 3);

(*c*) the sacrifice performed by Ovius Paccius and the ensuing oath taken by the Samnite leaders (§§ 5–12);

(*d*) the injunction that ten of the men who had taken this oath should recruit others, *ut uir uirum legerent*, until a total of 16,000 had been reached (§ 12).

The reference to initiation shows that (*a*) must look forward at least to (*c*); but it may look forward also to (*d*), which follows closely on (*c*)

---

[1] Thus Feldherr (1998) 56.
[2] See further Sordi (1976) 161–2.

and could perhaps be regarded as part of the same ceremony (for further links between the two, see below).[1] It is possible that (*b*) too should be regarded as part of the *ritus sacramenti uetustus*, as it is introduced in an ablative absolute that follows immediately on the ablative absolute in which the *ritus* is introduced; but the contrast between *noua* in § 3 and *uetusto* and *uetere* in §§ 2 and 6 tells against this. However, the reference to it certainly enhances the impression given by this passage of a Samnite nation obsessed by rituals.

Nowhere does L. explicitly state that the Samnites recruited by means of a *lex sacrata* in this year. However, there are three reasons for thinking that this was the impression which he intended to give. First, note that *sacer* and its cognates occur regularly: § 2 'sacramenti', § 6 'sacrum', § 8 'sacri', § 9 'sacri', and § 12 'sacrata nobilitas'. Secondly, ritual (*d*) should be compared with four passages in which L. or Florus refer to warriors from one of the Italic peoples being recruited by means of a *lex sacrata*: iv. 26. 3 (the Aequi and Volsci in 431 BC) 'lege sacrata, quae maxima apud eos uis cogendae militiae erat, dilectu habito', ix. 39. 5 (310/9 BC) 'Etrusci lege sacrata coacto exercitu, cum uir uirum legisset, quantis numquam alias ante simul copiis simul animis dimicarunt', xxxvi. 38. 1 (191 BC) 'Ligures, lege sacrata coacto exercitu', and Flor. i. 11(16). 7 (in a general comment on the Samnites, perhaps derived ultimately from our passage) 'gentem . . . sacratis legibus humanisque hostiis in exitium urbis agitatam'. Note in particular the similarity between § 12 'primoribus Samnitium ea detestatione obstrictis, decem nominati sunt ab imperatore; eis dictum, ut uir uirum legerent donec sedecim milium numerum confecissent' and ix. 39. 5. Thirdly, Pliny (*nat.* xxxiv. 43 [quoted on p. 382]) refers to a victory of Sp. Carvilius over a Samnite army recruited in this way, by which he must mean that at Aquilonia and Cominium; Pliny's testimony is particularly valuable because it is independent of L. and points to the material that L. is likely to have found in his sources.

The similarity between § 12 and ix. 39. 5 leaves no doubt that the selection and binding of one man by another was an ancient and fundamental part of recruiting *lege sacrata*.[2] It may seem strange that

---

[1] For a different approach to these problems see Tondo (1963) 80–6; he argued (p. 85) that '*lex sacrata, ritus sacramenti* e *uir uirum legere* rappresentano tre istituti concettualmente autonomi'.

[2] Something similar to this Italic practice seems to have been used also at Rome. Frederiksen (1968*a*: 227) cited Plb. iii. 71. 8, Cic. *Mil.* 21, and Tac. *hist.* i. 18 (Cic. *Mil.* 21, which he also adduced, seems less pertinent); note too Augustus' use of this method of recruiting in a senatorial *lectio* (Suet. *Aug.* 35. 1 'quo uir uirum legit').

in our passage the Samnites started with only ten men (§ 12) when their ultimate target was 16,000 (especially as the process of doubling from one will not lead one to a figure anywhere close to it), and the same difficulty must have been faced by any nation recruiting in this way; but L. does state (§ 4) that the whole army was already at Aquilonia when the process began.[1]

As its name implies, oaths are likely to have been a part of the *lex sacrata*: L.'s statements at § 10 (cf. 41. 3 below) that the Samnite soldiers swore either to die fighting or to return victorious, and that, if they fled, they made themselves liable to be killed by their compatriots and called down a curse on themselves and their family, are exaggerated for literary effect but perhaps reflect the kind of oath taken by those recruited *lege sacrata*.[2] However, we should probably not imagine that when elsewhere L. refers to such recruiting he had in mind our gruesome ritual (*c*): for in §§ 2 and 6 he implies that this was reworked especially for 293 BC, and we shall see that several aspects of it better fit another context.[3]

L. does not make it entirely clear how the special arms and armour that some Samnite forces are said to have carried relate to the rituals described here. § 12 'ea legio linteata ab integumento consaepti, in quo sacrata nobilitas erat, appellata est; his arma insignia data et cristatae galeae, ut inter ceteros eminerent' and ix. 40. 9 (quoted above) perhaps suggest that L. believed that troops recruited according to the rituals described in §§ 5–12 were given special arms. However, at § 2 he could be taken to imply that all the Samnites who came to Aquilonia, and not just those who in §§ 5–12 were initiated into the *legio linteata*, were equipped with special arms; in § 13 he reports that the rest of the army too was armed in a similar manner to the *legio linteata* (but see n. on 'dispar'); and in ix. 40, as well as describing the Samnite force that consisted of *sacrati*, he mentions another force armed with golden arms. That the connection between

---

[1] However, if the ultimate source of some of L.'s information was an account of a Samnite attack on Capua (see below), this detail would fit well with such an account.

[2] The reference to these oaths at Dio fr. 36. 29 does not affect the argument: if at this point Dio is independent of L. (which is possible), his independence serves only to push the idea of the oath back to the late annalists.

[3] Likewise, despite § 3 'sacraretur', it seems unlikely that ritual (*b*) should be regarded as a standard part of the *lex sacrata*, for the reasons given above. At ix. 40. 9 (310/9 BC) 'sacratos more Samnitium milites eoque candida ueste et paribus candore armis insignes' L. may also refer to this style of recruiting. In which case *sacratos* most probably refers to an oath which they had sworn (in this passage from book ix L. seems to regard the Samnites as performing a ritual akin to Roman *deuotio*: see further the n. ad loc.) but could perhaps allude also to the system of recruiting in which one man recruits another.

special recruiting and special arms has a historical reality is possible but far from certain.[1]

The passages cited above show that the Roman historical tradition believed that the pre-Roman inhabitants of Italy occasionally held levies in this way. Given the similarity of these levies to recruiting for a *uer sacrum*,[2] it is tempting to connect the custom particularly with the Samnites and the peoples of central and southern Italy related to them. However, L. clearly saw nothing strange in ascribing the practice to the Etruscans and Ligurians; and there is good evidence for *leges sacratae* at Rome: Festus (p. 422) defines them ('sacratae leges sunt, quibus sanctum est qui quid aduersus eas fecerit, sacer alicui deorum †sicut† familia pecuniaque. sunt qui esse dicant sacratas, quas plebes in monte Sacro sciuerit'), and the plebeians bound themselves by a *lex sacrata* which gave sacrosanctity to their leaders (ii. 33. 1, iii. 55. 8, D.H. vi. 89. 2–4, Fest. loc. cit.; cf. Cic. *Tull.* 47). Indeed, the secessions of the plebeians had a military aspect (iii. 50. 11–16, D.S. xii. 24–5, D.H. xi. 43. 4–6), and their first tribunes of the plebs may be viewed as the equivalents of those Samnites in our passage who administered the oath.[3]

Since the possibility of Livian or annalistic invention can never be discounted, it is impossible certainly to establish the specific historicity of any of the passages which refer to recruiting *lege sacrata*; but there is no obvious reason why such a levy should not have been held in 293.[4] Which is not to say that it certainly was held, or that all that L. writes should be believed: Salmon in particular has argued that many of the details of his account are suspect, including the details of the taking of the oath in the tent (discussed below),[5] the reference to linen books (standard in the context of old rituals: see further § 6 n.), and even the name Ovius Paccius (which could be no more than a typical Oscan name invented for the occasion: again, see § 6 n.); others have held that much of the description has been borrowed from a report of another occasion (see below); and one may add that L. has put his own literary stamp on the whole chapter (see above).

---

[1] At Plin. *nat.* xxxiv. 43, where Pliny refers to the dedication by Carvilius of armour taken from a Samnite army recruited by means of a *lex sacrata*, the conjunction of *sacrata lege* and armour may be significant; but Pliny does not state that the armour was unusual.

[2] See conveniently Salmon (1967) 35–6.

[3] See further Altheim (1940) 29; but for speculation concerning an Oscan origin for the Roman *lex sacrata*, see Altheim, pp. 23–4.

[4] But see below for Coarelli's view that levies of this kind were not unusual.

[5] However, Salmon's notion (p. 185 n. 5), that a model was provided by the alleged oath taken by the Catilinarian conspirators (which involved the drinking of human blood [Sall. *Cat.* 22. 1, Min. Fel. 30. 5; cf. Dio xxxvii. 30. 3]), seems far-fetched.

L. (§ 12) and Paul. Fest. 102 'LEGIO Samnitium linteata appellata est, quod Samnites intrantes singuli ad aram uelis linteis circumdatam non cessuros se Romano militi iurauerant' (which probably derives ultimately from a source similar to that behind this chapter of L.) state that the *legio linteata* of §§ 5–12 took its name from the tent in which some of its members were enrolled. However, ix. 40. 3 'tunicae . . . argentatis linteae candidae' (part of a description of the 'sacred' silver legion) suggests a much more natural derivation: the legion was named after the linen tunics which its members wore.[1]

Three other difficulties in L.'s account of the rituals of §§ 5–12 may have a bearing on the origin of the information which he provides: first, secrecy in recruiting (§ 9) was not only unnecessary but actually a hindrance to the effective enrolling of an army; second, there is no good reason why the ritual had to be carried out in a tent (§ 6); and, third, it is curious that the oath was not administered to the whole legion together, but initially was forced only on the aristocrats. To these may be added the problem, already discussed, of understanding how one man recruited another. For all these difficulties the explanation adumbrated by Latte and later refined by Altheim and Cornell seems the most satisfactory. Developing the hint given by L. himself in § 6, they have argued that L. or his sources have added colour to an account of a Samnite levy conducted by means of a *lex sacrata* by combining it with details derived from the clandestine oaths sworn, or imagined by later historians to have been sworn, at the time of the Samnite capture of Capua (§ 6 n.), an operation for which secrecy was appropriate, and in which comparatively small numbers will have been involved. Such a combination would help to explain why it is so hard to interpret the rituals to which L. refers in this chapter.[2]

---

[1] For the (unconvincing) view that the legion was called *linteata* because of the general connection of linen with rituals, see e.g. Tondo (1963) 79–80.

[2] Other explanations of the origin of the scene described by L. have been propounded by Sordi, Saulnier, and Coarelli. Sordi (esp. pp. 164–8) argued that much of the detail of L.'s account is a reflection of the propaganda of the Social War; but, although the Italian insurgents bound themselves with oaths and treaties which Romans could regard as detestable (see e.g. D.S. xxxvii. 11 [the oath of loyalty to Drusus] and Flor. ii. 6[iii. 18]. 9 'hoc fuit impii belli sacramentum'), and although Roman hostility to the Samnites must have been rekindled by the Social War, there is no close correspondence in detail between L.'s account and our evidence for the Social War. Perhaps Sordi's best parallel (p. 165) is the promise of the insurgents not to spare the life of their kinsmen unless it be for the advantage of Drusus (D.S. xxxvii. 11), which may be compared to the threat to families reported by L. at 38. 10; but the circumstances are not very similar. Saulnier (1981: 109–13) argues that our text combines the reporting of an exceptional (because in her view the Samnites did not often assemble large armies) Samnite levy and of the consecration of a *corps d'élite* by means of a ritual akin to *deuotio*; the derogatory colour of L.'s account, she argues (esp., pp. 113–18), comes in part from the fact that the

Although L.'s immediate sources for this Samnite levy were almost certainly annalistic, it is quite likely, as Coarelli (pp. 12 and 14) has argued, that the ultimate source of this unusual material was an antiquarian writer.[1]

See further Latte (1936) 69 = (1968) 350, Altheim (1940), Tondo (1963) 71–103, Salmon (1967) 182–6, Frederiksen (1968a) 227, Cornell (1974) 199–202, Sordi (1976), Saulnier (1981) and (1983) 89–95, and Coarelli (1996).

38. 2–4. et forte eodem conatu apparatuque omni opulentia insignium armorum bellum adornauerant, et deorum etiam adhibuerunt opes, ritu quodam sacramenti uetusto uelut initiatis militibus, (3) dilectu per omne Samnium habito noua lege, ut qui iuniorum non conuenisset ad imperatorum edictum quique iniussu abisset caput Ioui sacraretur. tum exercitus omnis Aquiloniam est indictus: (4) ad sexaginta milia militum quod roboris in Samnio erat conuenerunt: the text and punctuation of this passage are disputed. For *sacraretur* the mss have *sacratum erat*, most having heavy punctuation after *erat* (Walters's apparatus is very misleading on this point). This was accepted by Alschefski but is ungrammatical, since *ut* introduces an indicative (*sacratum erat*) when a subjunctive is required. Before the mid-nineteenth century most editors tried to restore sense by emending *sacratum erat* to *sacratum esset*, a reading found by Sigonius in a ms.; but since the imperfect rather than the pluperfect subjunctive is required, either *sacraretur* (Weissenborn [1843] 266–7) or *sacrum esset* (Cobet, *ap*. Bisschop *et al.* [1852] 97: cf. iii. 55. 7 'sanciendo ut qui tribunis plebis, aedilibus, iudicibus decemuiris nocuisset, eius

Romans associated the Campanians with secret conspiracies, such as the capture of cities (see above) and the Bacchanalian affair, which originated in Campania; but the separation of consecration from recruitment is unconvincing. More interestingly, Coarelli argues that Samnite sanctuaries suggest that they served as places of assembly akin to Latin *comitia*; that, rather than Aquilonia, Pietrabbondante, the largest known Samnite sanctuary, is likely to have been the Samnite place of assembly in 293; and that levies of this kind, in which the rituals were initiatory, were more common than L. and our other sources allow. All these propositions are possible but none is certain: Samnite sanctuaries (in addition to Pietrabbondante, Coarelli cites the sanctuaries at Fonte Romita and San Giovanni in Galdo) would indeed have been suitable places in which to hold levies, but there is no clear proof that this happened; the Samnites may have found it convenient to hold a levy away from a major settlement, but we cannot be certain that they did not recruit at Aquilonia; Pietrabbondante is likely to have been important *c*.293 BC but we know little for certain about the site in this period; and, although it is attractive to argue that the rituals which L. describes were initiatory and that levies of this kind may have been commoner than he allows, that does not mean that the Samnites did not make a special effort in 293.

[1] Frederiksen tentatively suggested a Greek ethnographical source, which is also possible.

caput Ioui sacrum esset') is preferable. Despite the excellent parallel for Cobet's conjecture, Weissenborn's is probably easier, since *sacraretur* is more likely to have been corrupted into *sacratum erat* (corruption to *sacratum* and then insertion of *erat*).

Several scholars have punctuated with a full stop after *militibus*, the case for this being expounded most fully by Madvig (1860: 194–5 = 1877: 233–4), who argued that after *et deorum . . . militibus*, which provides a general comment on the Samnites' turning to the gods, the specific detail of what they did starts a new sentence. To this punctuation there are two principal objections: (*a*) *tum* is awkward at the beginning of the main clause; (*b*) it is easier to take the two ablatives absolute and their dependent constructions (*ritu . . . militibus* and *dilectu . . . sacraretur*) as co-ordinate, both illustrating *deorum etiam adhibuerunt opes*. Madvig countered the first objection by deleting *tum*, but the temporal indication which it gives is pointed: first the new-style levy was held throughout Samnium, then (*tum*) the troops recruited in this way assembled at Aquilonia. Freudenberg (1854–62: ii. 15), by contrast, retained *tum* but also retained *sacratum erat* and emended *ut* to *et*. However, the resulting sentence *dilectu per omne Samnium habito noua lege et qui iuniorum non conuenisset ad imperatorum edictum quique iniussu abisset caput Ioui sacratum erat, tum exercitus omnis Aquiloniam est indictus*, although grammatical, is awkward in expression, as it provides no explanation of what the *noua lex* was. The second objection has been ignored by critics who favour this punctuation. Walters understood the passage properly, but I have altered his punctuation in three minor particulars, removing a semi-colon after *adornauerant*, inserting a comma after *opes*, and putting a colon rather than a full stop after *indictus*.

Other textual matters that need discussion do not affect the general sense of the passage. Walters was right against e.g. Madvig and Ussing and W–M to prefer the perfect *adhibuerunt* (MPUZs) to the pluperfect *adhibuerant* (ZbZtλ): it has better ms. authority; it helps to explain the corruption in other mss (perseveration in λ from *adornauerant*); and, above all, it gives better sense (first the Samnites assembled their arms, then they invoked the help of the gods). Luterbacher proposed ⟨*eius*⟩ *caput* on the basis of the parallel at iii. 55. 7, and Foster, who, like M. Müller, printed this conjecture, adduced in addition ii. 8. 2 '. . . sacrandoque cum bonis capite eius qui regni occupandi consilia inisset'; but in our passage it is not difficult to understand *eius*: see Pettersson (1930) 31.[1]

---

[1] *qui[q]ue* (Kiehl, *ap*. Bisschop *et al.* [1852] 97) may be briskly dismissed: for disjunctive *-que* see ix. 19. 3 n.

conatu apparatuque: for this precise coupling cf. xxxv. 46. 2 and Cic. *fam.* x. 10. 1. Analogous expressions include *conatus* coupled with *paratus* (Sen. *dial.* iii. 20. 8); *conatus* used in close proximity to *apparare* (iv. 23. 6); and *conatus* used in close proximity to *parare* (e.g. viii. 25. 2, xxviii. 5. 2). For L.'s fondness for *conatu* see vii. 6. 9 n.
insignium armorum: see ix. 40. 1–17 n.
deorum . . . opes: see vii. 28. 4 n.
uelut initiatis militibus: with these words L. encourages comparisons between the rituals of the Samnites and religious mysteries into which worshippers were initiated. In this context note esp. the linguistic parallels with L.'s account of the Bacchanalian conspiracy in book xxxix (see 7–9, 10, 11 nn.), showing that L. viewed the rituals of both in a similar light. The comparison is developed fully by Tondo (1963: 87–94).

3. qui . . . abisset: L. gives the Samnite officials very Roman language; see vi. 26. 5 with *addendum*, vii. 23. 3, viii. 34. 10 nn. For *ut qui* see vii. 5. 9 n.
imperatorum: the plural is used here and in § 10 in generalizing contexts, the singular in § 7 and § 12 with specific reference to the commander at Aquilonia; see further Tondo (1963) 75 n. 9.

4. ad quadraginta milia militum: *quadraginta* is the reading of MUL; Π(= PZ)λ(= TRD) had *sexaginta*. If one were to try to solve this *crux* solely by weight of ms. authority, then one would probably follow Walters in adopting *sexaginta*. However, M can stand alone in the truth (here the support of U and L is of no consequence whatsoever, since their readings are eliminated by the agreement of their closest relatives), and its reading squares better with the evidence of §§ 12–13, where we are told that the assembled Samnites were divided into two forces, one of 16,000 men, the other of a little over 20,000.
quod roboris . . . erat: see ix. 39. 11 n.

6. ex libro uetere linteo sacrificatum, lecto sacerdote Ovio Paccio: 'the sacrifice was performed in accordance with an old linen book, after Ovius Paccius had been chosen as priest . . .'. *sacrificatum lecto* is a conjecture for **N**'s *lecto sacrificatum*; for faulty word-order in **N** see vol. i, p. 165. If *ex libro uetere linteo lecto* is sound, it must be translated 'in accordance with an old linen book that had been read'; but, as Madvig (1877: 234) first pointed out, *lecto* is awkward ('quasi ex non lecto sacrificari potuerint' was his sarcastic objection). His own *tecto* hardly convinces: L. was not concerned with how the book was covered. M. Müller's ⟨*a*⟩ *lecto* (or ⟨*a de*⟩*lecto*) ⟨*ad id*⟩ gives reasonable sense but is diplomatically uneconomical. Luterbacher's *nocte*, by contrast, gives even better sense, and the corruption of one dissyllabic word into another also containing -*ct*- is easy enough to postulate; but nowhere else does L. mentions the night. Professor Watt once suggested to me deletion of *lecto* 'as a gloss due to someone who thought that the meaning of *ex* was "(reading) from", instead of "in accordance with"'; this too gives excellent sense, but the motive for the interpolation is not strong. With the conjecture adopted it is perhaps a difficulty that L. would be stating that the priest was selected only after other preparations had been made; but this could be the implication of the paradosis too.[1]

For books made of linen cf. the famous *libri lintei* of Licinius Macer (discussed at vol. i, pp. 27–8), Aurel. *ap.* Front. p. 60. 9 'multi libri lintei, quod ad sacra attinet', *SHA* xxvi. 1. 7, and the passages cited at *TLL* vii. 2. 1468. 53–60.

Ovio Paccio: (8). This man's name, even if invented by L. or his annalistic sources, is authentically Oscan, being, like Pacuvius, a Latinized form of **Pakis**, for which see e.g. Vetter (1953) nos. 5, 6, and 72e.

cum adimendae Etruscis Capuae clandestinum cepissent consilium: for the gerundive after *consilium capere* see vi. 2. 1 n., Krebs and Schmalz (1905–7) i. 340, and K–S i. 743.

Our sources for the fifth and fourth centuries quite often refer to the raiding or invasion of coastal or low-lying areas by the peoples of the Apennines. The Aequan, Sabine, and Volscian attacks on Rome and Latium are part of this phenomenon, as are attacks by Samnites, Lucanians, and other Oscan-speakers on the peoples of central and southern Italy. Lying just below the mountains of central Samnium, Capua and Campania were particularly exposed to such raiding. After the fall of Capua the Samnites seized control of Etruscan Cumae (see iv. 44. 12 [420 BC Varronian], D.S. xii. 76. 4 [*ol.* 89. 4 = 420 BC = 428 BC Varronian], D.H. xv. 6. 4, Stb. v. 4. 4 [C 243], and the discussion at vol. ii, p. 633) and partly infiltrated Greek Neapolis (vol. ii, p. 636), and, although our sources are silent, there is no doubt they seized the other towns of Campania, such as Nola. The same fate befell almost all the Greek colonies on the Tyrrhenian coast, and by the time of the Roman conquest in the late fourth and early third

---

[1] I have also considered ⟨*neg*⟩*lecto*, but it is not obvious why the old book should have been neglected.

centuries only Velia and Neapolis remained Greek. For this process see ix. 13. 7 n., Heurgon (1970) 81–5, and Cornell (1974) 193–5.

For the Samnite capture of Capua see also iv. 37. 1 (423 BC Varronian): 'peregrina res, sed memoria digna traditur eo anno facta, Volturnum, Etruscorum urbem, quae nunc Capua est, ab Samnitibus captam, Capuamque ab duce eorum Capye uel, quod propius uero est, a campestri agro appellatam. cepere autem, prius bello fatigatis Etruscis, in societatem urbis agrorumque accepti, deinde festo die graues somno epulisque incolas ueteres noui coloni nocturna caede adorti', vii. 38. 5 (on the Roman mutineers of 342 BC) 'inibanturque consilia in hibernis eodem scelere adimendae Campanis Capuae per quod illi eam antiquis cultoribus ademissent', xxviii. 28. 6 (very brief allusion), D.S. xii. 31. 1 (*ol.* 85. 3 = 437 BC = 445 BC Varronian) κατὰ μὲν τὴν Ἰταλίαν τὸ ἔθνος τῶν Καμπανῶν συνέστη καὶ ταύτης ἔτυχε τῆς προσηγορίας ἀπὸ τῆς ἀρετῆς τοῦ πλησίον κειμένου πεδίου, D.H. xv. 3. 7 (from a speech attributed to the mutineers of 342 BC, in which they state that in seizing Capua from the Campani they would be doing nothing which the Campani themselves had not done) τί δὴ καὶ δράσομεν δεινόν, ἐὰν Καμπανοὺς ἐκβαλόντες τὰς ἐκείνων πόλεις κατάσχωμεν; οὗτοι γὰρ αὐτοὶ πρότερον οὐκ ἐκ τοῦ δικαίου κτησάμενοι τὴν γῆν κατέσχον, ἀλλ' ἐπιξενωθέντες Τυρρηνοῖς τοῖς κατοικοῦσιν αὐτὴν καὶ τοὺς ἄνδρας ἅπαντας διαφθείραντες τάς τε γυναῖκας αὐτῶν καὶ τοὺς βίους καὶ τὰς πόλεις καὶ τὴν περιμάχητον χώραν παρέλαβον· ὥστε σὺν δίκῃ πείσονται πᾶν ὅ τι ἂν πάθωσιν αὐτοὶ τῆς παρανομίας κατάρξαντες καθ' ἑτέρων, and Stb. v. 4. 3 (C 242) (a chronologically vague report of how the Samnites succeeded the Etruscans as possessors of Campania). Although the details in L. and D.H. of how the Samnites captured Capua may have been invented by an earlier historian, they are quite plausible: gradual Samnite settlement and encroachment on Campanian land is very likely; and seizure of political control of Capua itself could have followed this encroachment. Some scholars (e.g. Ogilvie [1968] 332 and [1970] 784, Heurgon [1970] 88, Rutter [1971] 60, Frederiksen [1984] 138) have related τὸ ἔθνος τῶν Καμπανῶν συνέστη in D.S. to this earlier settlement reported by L., but Cornell (1974: 198–9) is probably right to hold that both sources refer to the same event. The allusion in both authors to the derivation of Campania from *campus* suggests this; nor need the chronological discrepancy tell against it: such discrepancies are quite common between the accounts of the history of the fifth century in L. and D.S. and may usually be explained by their following different immediate sources. In which case either L. or D.S. must have the wrong date. Beloch (1890: 299) argued that

L.'s is less likely, since it is placed only three years before the Samnite capture of Cumae, which one would not have expected to follow so quickly; but this is hardly conclusive.

Our sources often mention the Campani in the context of the violent captures of cities: they captured Cumae in 421 or 420 (see above: of the sources Strabo particularly stesses their violence), Campanian mercenaries hired by Agathocles seized Messana in the 270s (Plb. i. 7. 2–4, with Walbank's note on 7. 2, D.H. xx. 4. 1, 4, Fest. p. 150 [a rather different account deriving from Alfius]); and a Campanian detachment serving in the Roman army seized Rhegium in 282 or 280 (*per.* xii, *per.* xv, xxviii. 28. 2–4, Plb. i. 7. 6–13 [with Walbank's notes], D.H. xx. 4. 1–5. 5, 16. 1–2, Oros. iv. 3. 3–6) and then Caulonia (a reasonable inference from Paus. vi. 3. 12). Hence some scholars (e.g. Beloch [1890: 299], Salmon [1967: 39], and Heurgon [1970: 94–5]; see also Saulnier [1981: 103–6]) have argued that the references in L. and D.H. to a violent and clandestine capture of Capua are an unreliable invention based on a stereotype of Campanian behaviour that had evolved by the third century, influenced in particular by the capture of Messana. However, in the matter of the capture of cities the behaviour of the Samnites was hardly worse than that of other ancient peoples (e.g. the Romans), and there is no obvious reason why L. and D.H. should not be believed.

The derivation of Campania from *campus*, to which both L. and D.S. allude, will work only in Latin and not in Greek. Cornell, developing the views of earlier scholars (see e.g. Ogilvie on iv. 29. 8 and Rutter [1971] 58) has argued that the notices in L. and D.S. concerning the Samnite capture of Capua and Cumae and also the account of the ritual found in our chapter (for the oddities of which see §§ 2–13 n.) go back ultimately to Cato's *origines*, from which they were taken into the annalistic tradition: since Cato's account was not annalistic, different annalists may have incorporated the information in different years, which would explain the discrepancies between L. and D.S. If this is right, Cato may well have derived his material, false etymology apart, from Greek historians of Campania.[1]

For the Samnite capture of Capua see further Beloch (1890) 297–9, Salmon (1967) 38–9, Frederiksen (1968b) 4 and (1984) 134–40, Heurgon (1970) 85–96, Rutter (1971), and Cornell (1974).

---

[1] Heurgon (1970: 94) suggests that the information on the capture of Capua in our passage comes from Varro; but it is not readily detached from its context, and it is easier to believe that it found its way into the annalistic tradition at an earlier date.

7. uiatorem: as so often, L. uses a Roman term to describe a foreign official; cf. xxxiii. 46. 5 (*uiatores* at Carthage) and [Caes.] *Afr.* 57. 2 (King Juba). See vi. 26. 5 n. with *addendum*.

7–9. singuli introducebantur . . . magis ut uictima: for the image cf. xxxix. 10. 7 'ut quisquis introductus est, uelut uictimam tradi sacerdotibus' (of youths being initiated into the Bacchic rites).

8. perfundere religione animum: for the figurative use of *perfundere* see ix. 16. 18 n.

loco circa omni contecto: 'in a place that was covered all around'.

arae: Paul. Fest. p. 102 (quoted above) mentions just one altar. For this reason Ruperti conjectured *ara*, but L. and Paulus may not have envisaged the scene in quite the same way.

uictimaeque circa caesae: L. refers to the more or less conventional sacrifices carried out in § 6; the mixture of these with the blood of murdered humans becomes a powerful motif in the story; cf. § 11 'iacentes . . . inter stragem uictimarum', 39. 16 '(exercitus) nefando sacro mixta hominum pecudumque caede respersus', and 41. 3 'promiscua hominum pecudumque strages et respersae fando nefandoque sanguine arae'.

centuriones: again L. uses a Latin technical term to describe Samnite officials; at 41. 3 he more appropriately calls these men *armati sacerdotes*.

9. admouebatur: the subject has to be inferred from § 7 'nobilissimum quemque genere factisque'; the passive verb brings out the fact that the men did not come to the altars of their own free will. W–M rightly say that § 8 can be viewed as a parenthesis; more importantly, it evokes the perspective of the *nobilissimus quisque* and the terrifying scene which confronts him as he is brought forward.

adigebaturque is a certain and uncontroversial correction in D^c and Zr (*-banturque* in Zs) for *adic(i)ebatur* in the other primary witnesses. For *adigere* in the context of oaths, in which it generally (as here) suggests compulsion, see *TLL* i. 678. 72–679. 23.

10. dein, the authenticity of which was championed forcefully by Welz (1852: 13), is omitted in M^1 and P^1, whose coincidence almost certainly points to a reading in **N**. However, the coincidence of P^{c}GrZ (*deinde* in Z) and λ could also point to a reading of **N**, and this suggests that **N** may have had variants, *dein* originally being omitted but then supplied as a correction (whether from another ms. or by conjecture, one cannot say). With hesitation (because the reading of MP[1] perhaps has better authority),[1] I have kept *dein*, since in L.'s regular manner (vol. i, p. 127) it points to the next stage of the ritual.

diro quodam carmine: cf. 41. 3 'dira exsecratio'. *dirus* is used regularly of curses and imprecations (*TLL* v. 1. 1269. 50–68); in this context its use of sinister omens (*TLL* 1268. 67–1269. 49) is also felt, emphasizing that these Samnite rituals will not be propitious. Compare also the *carmen* of the Bacchanals (xxxix. 18. 3).

exsecrationem: regularly used of curses that will become operative on failure to keep an oath or promise: see *TLL* v. 2. 1836. 37–1837. 12 and *OLD s.u.* 2. For such curses see Briscoe on xxxi. 17. 9.

quo is an easy correction in P[c]GrZT[c] for **N**'s nonsensical *quod*.

11. id primo quidam abnuentes iuraturos se obtruncati circa altaria sunt: so also the Bacchanals kill those who do not partake in their rituals (xxxix. 13. 11, 13). *primo* modifies *obtruncati sunt* (not *abnuentes*), as *deinde* modifies *documento . . . fuere*.

obtruncati: see vii. 26. 5 n.

iacentes inter stragem uictimarum: see § 8 n.; for *stragem*, see vii. 23. 10 n.

12. primoribus Samnitium ea detestatione obstrictis decem nominati s⟨unt⟩ ab imperatore; eis dictum ut . . .: Walters accepts the reading of **N**, punctuating thus: *primoribus Samnitium ea detestatione obstrictis, decem nominatis ab imperatore, eis dictum ut . . .*; but the two successive ablatives absolute read awkwardly, and, strictly speaking, the use of *eis* with reference to the ten men mentioned in the second ablative absolute is ungrammatical. Therefore A. Perizonius (followed by W–M) conjectured *nominati*, Drakenborch (tentatively) *edictum* for *eis dictum*, and Alschefski *nominati s⟨unt⟩*. With all these there would be just one ablative absolute (*primoribus . . . obstrictis*), the relationship of which to the main clause would be much easier; with Drakenborch's conjecture *decem nominatis* would be dative, dependent on *edictum*. The objection of Walters, that *ex* is needed before *primoribus*, is not valid: its presence would indeed make the Latin easier still, but there is no difficulty in interpreting the ablative absolute. All three conjectures make good sense. I have adopted that of Alschefski because it postulates the corruption that perhaps may be explained most easily (the -*s* arising from an abbreviation for *sunt*). However, it is scarcely less easy to

---

[1] If *dein* comes direct from T into P[c] and from P[c] to Gr, and if the Z mss have *deinde* because of contamination from Λ/λ, then λ is the only authority for it.

argue that *nominati* was corrupted to *nominatis* under the influence of the preceding ablative absolute, nor is the corruption postulated by Drakenborch difficult.

primoribus: see vi. 13. 8 n.

ut uir uirum legerent: the procedure is discussed above (pp. 394–5);[1] *uir . . . legerent* is a very easy example of illogical apposition: see K–S i. 249–50.

ea legio linteata ab integumento consaepti . . . appellata est: for discussion of this derivation see above.

⟨**in**⟩ **quo:** since the required sense 'in which' is not easily got out of *quo*, the supplement of Freudenberg (1854–62: ii. 15) is hard to resist; the preceding -*i* may have caused the omission of *in*.

arma insignia: see ix. 40. 1–17 n.

cristatae galeae: for these helmets see ix. 40. 3 n.

13. alius: 'the rest of', as often: see *TLL* i. 1647. 47–1648. 69 and *OLD s.u.* 6(a).

dispar: Conway's support for *par* (Gr and u, showing that the reading stood in U, for the innovations of which see vol. i, p. 299 with *addendum*) was not absurd, since one might have expected the force recruited by means of the *lex sacrata* to have been distinguished by special armour. However, L. does not in fact make this distinction (see §§ 1–2 and the discussion at p. 395 above), and *par* would give a very limp end to a chapter in which the potency of the Samnite army is stressed.

hic hominum numerus, quod roboris erat, ⟨ad⟩ Aquiloniam consedit: Weissenborn (*Komm.*) tentatively proposed deletion of *quod roboris erat*, on the ground that it was an interpolation from §§ 3–4 'tum exercitus omnis Aquiloniam est indictus. ad quadraginta milia militum quod roboris in Samnio erat conuenerunt'; but iteration of this kind is common in L. (vol. i, pp. 725–7), and it would be better to consider deletion of the whole sentence, which is otiose and adds nothing to §§ 3–4 and 39. 5 'Aquiloniam, ubi summa rei Samnitium erat'. However, L. probably wrote this sentence formally to round off, by ring-composition, his section (or digression) on the special Samnite levy.

quod roboris erat: see ix. 39. 11 n.

⟨**ad**⟩ **Aquiloniam:** *ad* is necessary to restore sense. It is restored by conjecture already in Zt and Zr.

---

[1] Virg. *Aen.* xi. 632 'legitque uirum uir' is different (on the field of battle one man finds another on the other side).

39. 1–42. 7. THE BATTLE OF AQUILONIA

This section, in which L. recounts the battle of Aquilonia, is the longest part of his narrative of the campaigns of 293. As in the previous section religion provides the dominant theme: the correct piety of the consul Papirius Cursor contrasts with the lack of piety exhibited by both the Samnites earlier and the consul's own *pullarius*. The episode is paradigmatic for the contrast between true Roman religion and foreign superstition, and for the attitude which a consul ought to take towards the auspices.

After describing the Samnite levy, L. turns to the response of the Roman consuls. Their initial campaigning is told swiftly and without adornment: he is saving his elaboration for the account of the fighting at Aquilonia and Cominium, and by § 5 he has brought Carvilius to Cominium and Papirius to Aquilonia. Unlike the Samnites, who waste their time on superstitious rituals (§ 2 'dum hostes operati superstitionibus'), we see that a Roman consul acts effectively. The following sentences (§§ 6–11) describe the close co-operation of the consuls, a theme which recurs in the narrative and helps to give it unity (cf. 40. 6, 43. 2, 44. 1–2, 44. 6–8, 45. 11; and note the gentle rivalry at 41. 7). When L. makes Papirius comment in § 8 that he intends to fight on the following day 'si per auspicia liceret', he deftly places a detail that later will become important.

With Papirius' long speech in *oratio obliqua* (§§ 11–17) L. returns to the religious theme established at 38. 1–13 and 39. 2. For anyone in doubt as to whether or not the special rituals of the Samnites were likely to win the favour of the gods, Papirius delivers a crushing answer in the negative: he contemptuously dismisses their new armour as mere show and argues that their rituals had made their army peculiarly loathsome to the gods, who were present on the Roman side (§ 15 'adesse'). As it moves towards its close, his speech becomes increasingly powerful: after the anaphora of *totiens* in § 15, there is a weighty final period in §§ 16–17, which includes a tricolon organized around the participles *respersus, deuotus,* and *horrens,* anaphora of *hinc,* and a final asyndetic tricolon—*inuitus iurauerit, oderit sacramentum, uno tempore deos, ciues, hostes metuat,* itself incorporating a three-member asyndeton in the final colon that introduces a theme which will be important later. These remarks dispel any foreboding which ch. 38 may have induced in readers: the battle may now be viewed as a contest, not just between Roman and Samnite but between the interpretations of the Samnite rituals offered by

Samnites and by Papirius,[1] and there is the clear expectation that Papirius will be proved right.

The Romans' eagerness to fight after they have heard this speech is reflected in the sentence-structure: note the short, incisive sentences in 40. 1–3, the series of historic presents, and the prominent initial position of § 1 'paenitet'. This response of the Romans makes a notable contrast to the fear which Papirius had claimed was present among the Samnites.

When Papirius takes the auspices at 40. 2–5, an event fore-shadowed at 39. 8, the religious theme returns, and L. reinforces it by deploying numerous technical or semi-technical terms; see § 2 'silentio', 'surgit', 'pullarium', § 4 'qui auspicio intererant', 'pascerentur', 'auspicium mentiri', 'tripudium solstimum', § 5 'laetus', 'auspicium egregium esse' (nn.).[2] The scrupulous behaviour of the consul, who plays his part in the taking of the auspices correctly, contrasts with that of the *pullarius*, who being impatient of any delay feigns good auspices and hence encourages the consul to fight without good omens. The battle is on the point of beginning (§§ 6–7), and, by leaving this tension unresolved, L. adds suspense to his narrative.

In § 6, as Papirius is about to bring his forces out of his camp, he is told about the twenty cohorts of Samnites who have left Aquilonia for Cominium. L. makes him send a message to his colleague: by this device not only does L. reinforce the impression of close co-operation between the consuls but he also provides a link between the fighting at Aquilonia and the next two scenes—(*d*) and (*e*) in the scheme at 38. 1–46. 16 n.—in this extended episode.[3]

Next (§§ 7–8) the careful delineation of the dispositions of Papirius reinforces the good impression which his care has already made, and once more provides suspense, as we are left waiting to see whether the five subordinates who are mentioned will return to the narrative. Eventually our expectations will be fulfilled: Nautius (in charge of a stratagem) reappears at 41. 5, Trebonius and Caedicius (in charge of the cavalry) at 41. 8, and Volumnius (in charge of the right wing) and Scipio (in charge of the left wing) at 41. 12.

The central importance of the religious theme to the tale of Aquilonia becomes particularly clear at 40. 9–14, where the death of the offending *pullarius* is recounted. Some cavalrymen hear the *pullarii* disputing whether the auspices of the day had been correctly reported and inform Sp. Papirius, the nephew of the consul. He in

---

[1] See further Feldherr (1998) 59–60.
[2] See further Linderski (1993) 60 = (1995) 615.
[3] For the technique see vol. i, p. 126 with *addendum*.

turn tells his uncle, who appears remarkably unconcerned, ordering the offending *pullarius* to be placed in the front line. Awaiting the fate of the *pullarius*, the reader's attention is diverted to the advance of the Samnites (40. 12), the impressiveness of which is emphasized by short sentences and verbs both in the historic present and in initial position (*promouent* and *insequitur*). Before the battle proper has begun the *pullarius* is promptly killed by a stray Samnite javelin. The consul declares that this is a good omen and that the gods are present in the battle (by implication on the Roman side); and he is supported by the simultaneous cry of a raven, which he interprets as a further good omen (§ 14): 'adfirmans nunquam humanis rebus magis praesentes interfuisse deos'. All this confirms the consul's prediction at 39. 15. L. underlines the moral of the episode by pointing out explicitly (§ 10) that the young Papirius was a *iuuenis ante doctrinam deos spernentem natus* and by employing direct speech—for the only time in his whole account of the events of 293—for the utterances of the consul in §§ 10 and 13. Given the standard Livian and Roman view that Rome will be successful when it has established peace with the gods, these two omens prepare the reader for Roman victories.

The theology of this episode has been discussed interestingly by Linderski (1993: 60–1 = 1995: 615–16). He argues that it mattered less to the Romans whether the auspices were actually good or bad than whether they were reported to the holder of *imperium* as good or bad and whether the holder of *imperium* acted in a manner appropriate to the announcement. Hence Papirius can argue (§ 13) that as far as he and the army are concerned the *auspicium* is *egregium*, but if the *pullarius* has in fact lied he will draw the wrath of Jupiter on himself; and events prove him correct. As an analogy Linderski cites Cicero's remarks on Antony: Cicero alleges that, even though the *uitium* in the auspices was falsified by Antony, it still had to be obeyed (*Phil.* ii. 88), but that by his mendacity Antony is likely to bring disaster on himself and, Cicero hopes, not to the state (*Phil.* ii. 83). This passage is like ours in that the auspices are reported incorrectly. Another analogy is provided by L.'s account (xli. 17. 8–18. 16) of the death of the consul Q. Petillius in the Ligurian War of 176: he seems[1] to have fought despite the fact that the *pullarius* had told him that there was a flaw in his auspices, and his punishment was his own death and not the defeat of his army.[2] Here the *pullarius* behaves

---

[1] There is a lacuna after xli. 18. 14.

[2] This episode is well discussed by Linderski (1986: 2173–5). Liebeschuetz (1979: 24) may be correct to link the behaviour of the consul in our passage with the principle that evil omens need not affect those who declare at the outset that they take no notice of them (on which see

properly but not the holder of *imperium*, and the latter is duly punished. These passages show that on occasions the Romans could indeed think in this way; but Linderski does not make clear that they did not always do so: for example, the defeat of P. Clodius Pulcher at Drepanum in 249, in which the fleet was defeated but the guilty consul survived, was not susceptible to interpretation of this kind.

An excessive religiosity could be regarded as a manifestation of *superstitio* (39. 2 n.); very Roman, therefore, was the relaxed attitude of the consul, who, in the knowledge that he had paid his dues to the gods, made no special fuss (cf. L.'s comment at 42. 7).

In the initial description of the fighting itself (41. 1–4) religion is again central, and produces a contrast and a paradox. The contrast is between the Romans, who supported by their good omens charge into battle led by anger, hope, and passion, and the Samnites, who, under the influence of *necessitas* and *religio*, cannot advance but can only resist. The paradox is found in the behaviour of the Samnites, who fear their own side more than the enemy (41. 2–3) and are too frightened to flee. L.'s style supports the content of his narrative: in § 1 the contrast between the Romans and the Samnites is brought out by each being placed at the head of a clause; the excitement of the Romans is underlined by the asyndeton *ira spes ardor*; the fears of the Samnites are brought out by the massive polysyndeton in § 3; the exciting development of the battle is enhanced by the use of the historic infinitive in § 4 (*instare, caedere*) and by the prominent position of the verbs *instare* and *repugnatur* in the first place in their sentences.

The paradoxical deadlock produced by an enemy too frightened to flee is broken by the stratagem involving Nautius, which introduces a peripeteia (41. 5 [n.]),[1] and by the generalship of Papirius Cursor, who tricks both sides into thinking that Roman reinforcements have arrived (41. 6–7) and effects plans that he had made earlier (note § 9 'ad nutum omnia, ut ex ante praeparato'). These were a cavalry charge (41. 8–9), at the head of which Caedicius and Trebonius make their reappearance, and, in a sentence (§ 9) made forceful by its trenchant brevity and its historic presents ('instant Volumnius et Scipio et perculsos sternunt'), the advance of the infantry under

Plin. *nat.* xxviii. 17); but Papirius does not so much ignore the faulty omen as argue that it is applicable only to the *pullarius*.

[1] It may seem strange that at this decisive moment L. introduces the parenthesis *Octauium Maecium quidam eum tradunt*; but, quite apart from the fact that the ancients could not use footnotes to register variants of this kind, this comment serves to draw further attention to the climax.

Scipio and Volumnius, who also make their reappearance. These tactics are decisive: *tum* in 41. 10 marks the final climax of the battle: the Samnites turn to flight and fear no one except the enemy (41. 10): 'pariter iurati iniuratique fugiunt nec quemquam praeter hostes metuunt'.

The capture of the enemy camp and of Aquilonia soon follows (41. 11–42. 4). L. carefully builds his narrative around the figures of Volumnius, Scipio, and the consul himself. In their eagerness to destroy the Samnites the wings of Volumnius and Scipio are in friendly rivalry and take initiatives beyond what the consul had expected: Volumnius and the right wing swiftly capture the camp (§ 12), in response to which Scipio successfully urges the left wing to break into the town (§§ 12–14). However, being few in number, they do not advance beyond the walls. The consul has not been mentioned since § 8, where he was on horseback; and in 42. 1–4 L. shows how he came to understand that his plans had been even more successful than he had hoped: at first (§ 1) he plans to call his troops back, as this was the conventional and normally sensible thing to do as dusk was falling; then (§ 2), moving forwards, he sees on his right that the enemy camp has been captured and hears on his left the noise from the fighting at the gates of the town ('et tum forte certamen ad portam erat' shows that this is simultaneous with 41. 12–13); then (§ 3), advancing still further (we learn that he is still on horseback), he actually sees on the left his troops on the walls of Aquilonia. Then (§§ 3–4) he takes decisive action and orders the troops who were with him to move into the town at the nearest point to them; the enemy soon abandon it.

Again L.'s sentence structure enhances the vividness of his narrative: between 41. 8 and 41. 14 the exciting climax to the battle produces no fewer than nineteen verbs in the historic present, a plethora of short sentences, and some verbs prominently positioned at the front of their clause (*panduntur, prouolat, instant*).

In the course of the fighting the prediction of Papirius with regard to the state of mind of the Samnites is proved correct: at 41. 3 the description of how their minds were haunted by memory of the rituals of ch. 38 recalls the words of Papirius at 39. 16; and 41. 2 'metus', 41. 4 'metu', and 41. 10 'metuunt' look back to 39. 17 'metuat'. Furthermore, the acquisition of booty to be displayed at Rome and elsewhere (46. 8) confirms the earlier comments of Papirius (39. 13–14), that collecting Samnite armour of this kind was a special prerogative of his family.[1]

[1] See further Feldherr (1998) 59.

Throughout the scene L. allows his readers to place events at the right time of day: at 39. 8 we look forward to the following day as the day of battle; at 39. 10 (only a little later than § 8) the messenger goes out and returns in the night; at 40. 2, when the messenger has returned Papirius orders the *pullarius* to attend to the auspices *tertia uigilia noctis*; then the battle begins (at dawn we presume, as in most battles); between 42. 1 and 42. 4 dusk advances; and at 42. 4 the city is abandoned *nocte* by the enemy.

In his summing up of the battle (42. 5–7) L. returns once more to religion, describing Papirius' humorous vow to Jupiter, and the fact that no general had been *laetior* in the line of battle. The adjective *laetus*, regular in religious contexts, has appeared already at 40. 5 (n.) and 40. 14, and *laetitia* will be used at 44. 1 and 45. 1; the idea may be viewed as a *Leitmotiv* of the tale.

39. 1. consules profecti ab urbe: prior Sp. Caruilius, cui ueteres legiones, quas M. Atilius superioris anni consul in agro Interamnati reliquerat, decretae erant, cum eis in Samnium profectus . . . Amiternum oppidum de Samnitibus ui cepit: the standard punctuation of this passage is to place a comma after *urbe* and a full stop after *erant*. However, short initial sentences elsewhere in L. (e.g. xxxiii. 36. 4 'consules in prouinciam profecti sunt' and xxxix. 54. 1 'dum haec in Macedonia geruntur, consules in prouincias profecti') encourage that adopted in the lemma. For the general sentiment cf. xxvii. 12. 1–2 'transactis omnibus quae Romae agenda erant consules ad bellum profecti. prior Fuluius praegressus Capuam; post paucos dies consecutus Fabius, qui . . .'.

profecti ab urbe: see vii. 32. 2 n.

Sp. Caruilius: (9). Unless L. (9. 12 [n.]) is mistaken in calling the Sp. Carvilius who was aedile in 299 *Q. f.*, this is the first appearance in Roman history of Sp. Carvilius C. f. C. n. Maximus (the filiation is given by *F.C.* for 272). After his successful campaigning and triumph in this year, Carvilius served as legate to Brutus Scaeva, the consul of 292, during his Faliscan campaign (Zon. viii. 1. 10), thus reversing the roles of the two men in this year. According to Velleius (ii. 128. 2), whose testimony on this matter at least we have no reason to doubt, he was a censor, and 289 is the only plausible year for him to have held this office (see *MRR* i. 184–5). In 272 he crowned his career by sharing another consulship with L. Papirius Cursor, for which see 38. 1 n.

The only earlier Carvilii recorded by our sources are the quaestor who allegedly made allegations against Camillus, presumably in 391 (Plin. *nat.* xxxiv. 13), and Sp. Carvilius Q. f. Maximus, the curule aedile of 299 (9. 12 n.). Sp. Carvilius Sp. f. C. n. Maximus Ruga, *cos.* I 234, II 228 and famous as the first Roman to divorce his wife for infertility (see D.H. ii. 25. 7 [231 BC], Val. Max. ii. 1. 4 [where the mss mention AVC 150, but the text must be corrupt], Plut. *comp. Thes. Rom.* 6. 4, Gell. iv. 3. 2 [227 BC, the date implied by Gellius' reference to the consuls; he himself gives AVC 523], xvii. 21. 44 [AVC 519 Varronian = 235 BC]; cf. also Plut. *comp. Lyc. Num.* 3. 2), may have been a son born to our Carvilius in old age.[1]

On Carvilius and his family, see further Syme (1956) 262–4 = (1979–91) i. 310–13 and Vishnia (1996) 437–40. For the *cognomen* Maximus see ix. 46. 15 n.

cui ... decretae erant: the legions of Atilius were mentioned last at 36. 18. For notices of this kind see ix. 24. 1 n. and *addendum* to vol. i, p. 62.

2. operati: used regularly in the same sense as *occupatus*, and particularly in the context of *res sacrae* (and hence not by itself pejorative in sense here); cf. e.g. 'operatum his sacris', xxi. 62. 6 'aliis (*sc.* prodigiis) procurandis prope tota ciuitas operata fuit', Hor. *carm.* iii. 14. 6, Tib. ii. 1. 9, Ov. *fast.* iii. 261, and see further *TLL* ix. 690. 7–31.

superstitionibus: the term *superstitio* could describe, *inter alia*, either the adoption of foreign rituals or an excessive attention to *religio*. Here the former meaning is plainly dominant (the killing of humans being the most un-Roman of rituals), but there is a hint of the latter. The former sense predominates too at iv. 30. 8–11 (in response to a drought and plague new and foreign methods of sacrifice are used) and xxxix. 16. 10 (the consuls warn the people *ne qua superstitio agitaret animos uestros* when they dismantle the bacchic rites). On the other five occasions on which L. uses *superstitio* and the related adjective *superstitiosus* the latter sense predominates: see i. 31. 6 (on Tullus Hostilius in old age) 'qui nihil ante ratus esset minus regium quam sacris dedere animum, repente omnibus magnis paruisque superstitionibus obnoxius degeret', vi. 5. 6 'in ciuitate plena religionum, tunc etiam ab recenti clade superstitiosis principibus', vii. 2. 3 (after a *lectisternium* has failed to end a plague) 'uictis superstitione animis ludi quoque scaenici . . . inter alia caelestis irae placamina instituti

---

[1] However, there are fifty-nine years between the first consulates of the two men. Hence Münzer, *RE* iii. 1630, thought that he was born too late to be son of our Carvilius, and Syme (1956: 262 = 1979–91: i. 311) wondered if he was his great-nephew.

dicuntur' (here, in addition to the use of ritual after ritual, it may be relevant that scenic games came from abroad), xxvi. 19. 4 (on Scipio Africanus claiming to receive visitations from the gods) 'siue et ipse capti quadam superstitione animi, siue ut imperia ... sine cunctatione exsequerentur', and xxix. 14. 2 (excessive interest in prodigies). A characteristic quite regularly ascribed to *superstitio* is that it is said to make those in its grip fear the gods: see Varr. *ap.* Augustin. *ciu.* vi. 9, Cic. *nat.* i. 117, 'superstitionem ... in qua inest timor inanis deorum', Serv. *Aen.* viii. 187, xii. 817; so too in this episode the Samnites fear the gods (§ 17, 41. 2–3, 10). On *superstitio* see further Grodzynski (1974), Janssen (1979), and Beard *et al.* (1998) i. 214–27.

Amiternum, the most important ancient site in the upper Aterno valley, was one of the major centres of the Sabines and the *patria* of the historian Sallust; the remains of the republican and imperial *municipium* may still be seen at the Campo S. Maria of S. Vittorino, 8 km from L'Aquila. Varro (*ling.* v. 28) derived its name from the river Aterno. If one discounts passing references at D.H. i. 14. 6 (from Varro) and ii. 49. 2 (= Cato, *orig.* fr. 50) to the role of Amiternum in imaginary prehistory, our passage is the first and only direct evidence for the history of the site in the period before the Hannibalic War. However, we may presume that along with the other Sabines it was given the citizenship, first *sine suffragio* and then *optimo iure* (see above, pp. 30–1 and vol. ii, p. 558). Even for the period after 219 most references to Amiternum are no more than passing comments (see e.g. xxi. 62. 5, xxiv. 44. 8, xxvi. 11. 10–11 [the view of Coelius Antipater (fr. 28) that Hannibal marched through Sabine territory], xxviii. 45. 19, xxxv. 21. 4, and xxxvi. 37. 3). Fortified centres in the territory of Amiternum which conceivably may have played a role in the campaign of 293 are known from Collimento and Colle Munito of Lucoli; see La Regina (1970) 195–6 and Segenni (1985) 208–9. General discussions of the history and archaeology of Amiternum include Hülsen, *RE* i. 1840–1, Coarelli and La Regina (1984) 17–24, and Segenni (1985), esp. 45–56. For attempts to postulate the existence of a second (Samnite) Amiternum, see above, p. 389.

ui cepit: see vi. 3. 10 n.

3–4. caesa ibi milia hominum duo ferme atque octingenti, capta milia ducenti septuaginta ... minus quam collega cepit hominum, plus aliquanto occidit: for the figure for enemy captured, see 14. 21 n.; for general discussion of casualty figures vii. 17. 9 n.; and for the neuter *caesa* below, 46. 12 n.

4. ita enim decretum erat: see 32. 3 n.

Duroniam: the site of Duronia is unknown. The modern village of this name, near Bagnoli in the valley of the Trigno, was called Civitavecchia until 1875, but, despite the presence of polygonal fortifications on the imposing hill known as the Civita, the identification with our site is entirely speculative, and in recent scholarship has been accepted only by Verrecchia (1953: 95–8). Other guesses have not been lacking: for example, Nissen (1883–1902: ii. 679) placed Duronia at Roccasecca in the middle Liri valley; Salmon (1967: 271 n. 2) at Cerasuolo, near the Mainarde, and La Regina (1989: 399) at Monte S. Croce of S. Biagio Saracinisco in the upper Melfa valley. As usual, such speculation is fruitless.

5. consules ... Caruilius ... Papirius ... peruenit: see vi. 2. 8 n. for the construction.

Atinate: see ix. 28. 6 n.

summa rei: see vi. 22. 9 n.

6. nauiter: 'with great effort'. L. employs the adverb for the first time here, and then at xxiv. 23. 9, xxx. 4. 5, and xliii. 7. 3; among other authors it is neither common, nor especially rare.

dies perhaps refers to several days, and not just to the day on which Papirius Cursor arrived at Aquilonia.

7. Quodcum⟨que⟩ inciperetur remittereturque, omnium rerum etiam paruarum euentus perferebatur in [dies] altera Romana castra, quae uiginti milium spatio aberant; et absentis collegae consilia omnibus gerendis intererant rebus, ...: translate: 'No matter what ⟨enterprise⟩ was begun or deferred, its outcome (even if it was an action of slight importance) was conveyed to the other Roman camp, which was twenty miles distant; and the plans of the absent consul [i.e. Carvilius] were of importance for all actions which had to be undertaken ...'. This text and interpretation differ from the paradosis in several particulars (highlighted by underlining): *quod cum inciperetur remittereturque, omnium rerum etiam paruarum euentus proferebatur in dies. altera Romana castra, quae uiginti milium spatio aberant, et absentis collegae consilia omnibus gerendis intererant rebus, ...* The various problems have been expounded best by Madvig (1877: 234–6), whose treatment I have generally followed.

(*a*) Long ago it was seen that the paradosis implies that both the *consilia* and, absurdly, the *castra* of Carvilius were influencing decisions taken by Papirius Cursor; therefore most editors before Madvig accepted the omission of *quae* in the Paris edition of 1510.

(*b*) Madvig, persuaded by Forchhammer that *proferebatur* should be changed to *perferebatur* (reported by Drakenborch from Leiden, Voss. Lat. F. 20), pointed out that *omnium rerum euentum proferre* is meaningless and that *etiam paruarum* has no real point. *perferebatur*, by contrast, is excellent: the outcome of even small events was not postponed but reported (*sc.* to the other consul).

(*c*) However, with this interpretation *in dies* is problematic (one would expect *quotidie*, which Madvig once considered). Madvig saw that it could be emended to *inde in*,[1] a conjecture which has the great merit of allowing one to punctuate as in the lemma above, and to retain *quae*. But neat though this conjecture is, *inde* is rather awkward, and better sense is given by the deletion of *dies* with H. J. Müller (1889c: 49). This proposal is diplomatically harder, but Müller may have been correct to postulate perseveration from *dies* in § 6.

(*d*) At the beginning of the sentence *quod* refers back most strangely to the previous sentence, and Madvig's *quodcum⟨que⟩* must be right.[2]

inciperetur: *pace* W–M, L. also employs a passive form of this verb at xlii. 30. 9. Like *remitteretur* it is a subjunctive of repeated action (vi. 8. 6 n.).

quo: 'in proportion as' (*OLD s.u. quo*² 2).

⟨in⟩ maiore discrimine res uertebatur: 'events there were in a greater crisis'. The supplement of Madvig (1877: 236) is very easy and must be correct; cf. vi. 36. 7 'in maiore discrimine domi res uertebantur', xxvi. 5. 12 'in summo discrimine rem uerti', and xxix. 7. 1 'in maiore discrimine Locris rem uerti'; for *uerti* with *in* and the ablative, cf. also e.g. iv. 31. 4 'in eo uerti spes ciuitatis', viii. 27. 4, and xxxv. 18. 8.

8. per omnia: 'in every respect'. The expression is found first in L.; cf. e.g. i. 34. 12 'per omnia expertus', Vell. ii. 33. 1 'per omnia laudabilis' (and often elsewhere), Quint. x. 1. 28, and see Wölfflin (1887) 147, (1888), K–S i. 558, and Woodman on Vell. ii. 100. 3.

---

[1] u already has *in dies ad*.

[2] Conway suggested *quodcum⟨que Comini⟩* or ⟨*ad Cominium*⟩, and Walters printed the former; but these conjectures would imply that the *altera castra* and the *consilia* below were those of Papirius Cursor, and *intentiorque Caruilius . . . in Aquiloniam quam ad Cominium quod obsidebat erat* then reads strangely. That L.'s emphasis is on Papirius' regular consultation of Carvilius (and not vice versa, though that is naturally implicit) is shown by §§ 9–10 below. For the sake of completeness I record an earlier proposal of Freudenberg (1854–62: ii. 16), who wished to delete *et*, change *intererant* to *inserebant*, and construe *consilia* as an accusative.

9. quanta maxima ui posset: see ix. 10. 10 n.
laxamenti: see ix. 41. 12 n.

10. diem does not mean 'Tag und Nacht' (W–M) but contrasts with the following *nocte. ad proficiscendum* means not 'for setting out' but 'for making the journey there'; see *TLL* x. 2. 1704. 42–5.
consulta: 'plans'; cf. e.g. Virg. *Aen.* xi. 410, Sil. vii. 34–5 (Cilnius addresses Hannibal) 'non cum Flaminio tibi res, nec feruida Gracchi | in manibus consulta . . .', and Tac. *hist.* ii. 4. 2. For understanding the different shades of meaning of the word *OLD s.u. consultum* is better organized than *TLL* iv. 586. 58–587. 39.

11. de uniuerso genere belli: for the expression cf. e.g. xxi. 40. 5 'ne genus belli neue hostem ignoretis, cum iis est uobis, milites, pugnandum, quos terra marique priore bello uicistis', xxii. 39. 8 'aut ego rem militarem, belli hoc genus, hostem hunc ignoro, aut nobilior alius Trasumennus locus nostris cladibus erit', Cic. *imp. Pomp.* 6 'primum mihi uidetur de genere belli . . . dicendum. genus est eius belli quod maxime uestros animos excitare atque inflammare ad persequendi studium debeat', *Phil.* ii. 59 'nihil de genere belli dicam', and Tac. *hist.* ii. 32. 1 'tunc Suetonius Paulinus dignum fama sua ratus . . . de toto genere belli censere'; also Cic. *imp. Pomp.* 17, 20, 28, *Balb.* 9, *Deiot.* 12, *Phil.* v. 43, and Caes. *ciu.* iii. 50. 1.
uana . . . specie: rightly explained by W–M as *qui uana specie esset.*

12. For the theme that fancy armour does not help one fight and is soon besmirched with blood, see ix. 40. 4–6 n.
cristas: see ix. 40. 3 n.
picta atque aureata scuta: see ix. 40. 2 n.

13. auream . . . fuisse: another explicit allusion to ix. 40. 1–17.
occidione occisum: see ix. 38. 3 n.

14. datum hoc forsan nomini familiaeque: see 28. 13 n. *forsan,* perhaps to be read at Ter. *eun.* 197 but first certainly attested at Lucr. vi. 729, was employed frequently by the poets, as the following comparative figures with *forsitan* indicate:[1] [*] Lucretius (*forsan* 1 :

---

[1] Throughout this note figures are not provided for writers earlier than Lucretius; likewise, no account has been taken of the expressions *forsit* and *fors fuat an,* whose existence does not affect the evidence for the tone of *forsan.* Neither *forsan* nor *forsitan* is found in Catullus, Caesar, Varro, Vitruvius, Grattius, Germanicus, Phaedrus, Mela, Celsus, Persius, the elder Pliny, or Suetonius.

forsitan 4), Virgil (3 : 4), Horace (1 : 0), Propertius (0 : 4), Tibullus (0 : 1), Ovid (8 : 94),[1] Manilius (0 : 2), Seneca (11 : 10), Lucan (7 : 6), Valerius Flaccus (7 : 2), Statius (11 : 8), Silius (9 : 1), Martial (6 : 9), and Juvenal (2 : 6). These show *forsan* becoming markedly more common in the middle of the first century AD, and in particular being adopted by the epic poets. By contrast, it fares badly beside *forsitan* in prose: Cicero (0 : 43), ps.-Caesar (1 : 3), Sallustian *corpus* (0 : 2), L. (2 : 30), Valerius Maximus (0 : 1), Curtius (0 : 16), Scribonius Largus (2 : 0), Seneca the Younger (0 : 11), Columella (0 : 3), Petronius (0 : 9), Quintilian (2 : 9), Frontinus (0 : 1), Pliny the Younger (0 : 1), Trajan (0 : 1), and Tacitus (0 : 3); particularly revealing is the figure for Seneca, as it may be contrasted with that for his verse. It is in fact found elsewhere only at iii. 47. 5, [Caes.] *Afr.* 45. 2, Scrib. Larg. *praef.* 7, 38, Quint. i. 5. 6, xii. 1. 31, and Quint. (?) *decl. min.* 368. 7 (in a spurious passage),[2] and must have been a poeticism for L.[3] See further K–S i. 810–12 and *TLL* vi. 1. 1136. 61–1140. 62.

insignia publicis etiam locis decorandis essent: for one such instance, from which one may suspect Papirius of generalizing, see ix. 40. 16 n.

15. deos immortales adesse propter totiens petita foedera, totiens rupta; tum si qua . . .:

Madvig (1860: 195 n. 1) held that the text was corrupt, though he had no emendation to offer; in particular he thought that *adesse* was intelligible only if *deos* was qualified by some word like *iratos*, and that *tum* was impossible, since 'neque enim noui quicquam (*praeterea*) additur'. In his wake numerous conjectures have been proposed: Seyffert (1861: 76) suggested *deos ⟨eis⟩ immortales abesse propter totiens petita foedera, totiens rupta: iam si qua* . . ., Wesenberg (1870/1: 40) *deos immortales adesse propter totiens petita foedera, totiens rupta ⟨iratos⟩; [tum] si qua* . . . (the same conjecture proposed again, most tentatively, by Madvig himself [1877: 236 n. 1]), Novák (reported by H. J. Müller [1884] 105) *deos immortales odisse propter totiens petita foedera, totiens rupta ⟨hos⟩tem; si qua* . . ., H. J. Müller (W–M) *deos immortales ⟨cum iratos⟩ adesse propter totiens petita foedera, totiens rupta; tum si qua* . . ., Luterbacher *deos immortales adesse propter totiens petita foedera, totiens rupta; tum [si]*

---

[1] The frequency of *forsitan* in Ovid is a notable idiosyncrasy.

[2] At *TLL* vi. 1. 1136. 77 an illusory instance—taken over by Ogilvie on iii. 47. 5—is claimed for Col. iii. 9. 1, where *forsitan* is found.

[3] Both *forsan* and *forsitan* are claimed as poetical at Char. *gramm. Lat.* i. 185. 16 and Cledon. ibid. v. 66. 30; but though *forsitan* is very common in poetry, the massive figure for Cicero refutes this judgement.

qua . . ., and M. Müller, citing esp. v. 15. 9 'iratos deos Veienti populo', *deos immortales ⟨cum Samniti populo iratos⟩, adesse propter totiens petita foedera, totiens rupta; tum si qua* . . . Yet the paradosis is sound: after commenting that the armour of the Samnites will become Roman spoil, Papirius Cursor states that the gods are on the Roman side because of the treaties broken by the Samnites (this is the obvious interpretation of *adesse*, and it is borne out by the parallels cited at vii. 26. 4 n.); and then, in a further development of this thought (*tum* = 'in addition' [*OLD s.u.* 9] and introduces the climactic development of the *oratio obliqua*), he states that the gods have never been more hostile to an army. Walters likewise retained *tum* but preferred to see it as equivalent to *nunc* in *oratio recta*; this seems more awkward.

totiens petita foedera, totiens rupta: L. refers to treaties between Rome and the Samnites at vii. 19. 4, viii. 2. 1–4, 37. 2, ix. 20. 1–3, and 45. 4; for his partisan account of the outbreak of the Third Samnite War, see 11. 11–12. 3.

16. coniectura is regular in divinatory contexts; cf. e.g. Cic. *diu.* i. 34, 78, 128, and see *TLL* iv. 316. 27–59.

mentis diuinae: a common expression, often used by Cicero; see e.g. Merguet (1887–94) i. 742.

nulli unquam: see ix. 32. 9 n.

quam qui: if the text is sound, *quam qui* must stand for *quam ei, qui* (thus W–M), which does not seem difficult; but it was not absurd of Novák (1894: 119) to conjecture *quam illi, qui*.

qui . . . respersus: see 38. 8 n. The omission of *respersus* by PGr gives acceptable sense, and Walters wondered whether it could be right; but the coincidence against it of of MZλ suggests that it is most unlikely to be what L. wrote.

deuotus: for the meaning of this word, see vol. ii, p. 481.

hinc . . . hinc: see vi. 2. 2 n.

foederum cum Romanis ictorum testes deos: for the idea, see vi. 29. 2 n.

17. ciues: a reference back to 38. 10.

40. 1. diuinae humanaeque spei pleni: for the expression see vi. 12. 8 n. The Romans blend the human and the divine, the Samnites (39. 16) the human and the bestial.

clamore consentienti: for the approval shown by the soldiers after the speech of their commander in a *contio* before battle, see vii. 33. 4

with *addendum*; for the expression here cf. esp. xl. 27. 14 'ad haec consentiens reddebatur clamor'; also (in a different context) v. 47. 10 'consentiente clamore militum'.

moram diei noctisque oderunt: for the idea cf. iii. 2. 10 'longam uenire noctem ratus quae moram certamini faceret'.

2. silentio: for this technical expression see viii. 23. 15 n.

surgit: for *surgere* in the context of an official rising at night to take the auspices, cf. Vel. Long. *gramm. Lat.* vii. 74. 18–19 (cited at viii. 23. 15 n.); *silentio surgere* is restored with some plausibility as a lemma at Fest. 474.

pullarium: see vi. 41. 8, viii. 30. 2, ix. 14. 4 nn.

in auspicium mittit: this expression seems to be unparalleled.

3. dux militum, miles ducis ardorem spectabat: Watt (1991: 219) argued that if one follows Foster in translating *spectabat* 'could see', then the sense is 'impossibly feeble'; he therefore proposed *excitabat*, comparing xxvi. 19. 2 and xl. 31. 7 for *ardorem excitare*. Although I have no parallel with which to support the paradosis, I do not share Watt's view that the sense is feeble (translate *spectabat* as 'observed').

4. qui auspicio intererant seems to be a characteristically Livian variation on the technical expression *in auspicio erant*, for which see Cic. *Att.* ii. 12. 1, *rep.* ii. 16 'qui sibi (i.e. Romulus) essent in auspiciis' (where Mai's ⟨*ad*⟩*essent*, adopted by Ziegler, is unnecessary), *diu.* ii. 71 'Q. Fabi, te mihi in auspicio esse uolo', *leg.* iii. 43 'eos quos in auspicio esse iusserit', and Messalla, *ap.* Gell. xiii. 15. 4. See further Linderski (1993) 60 = (1995) 615.

auspicium mentiri: since *ementiri* is the usual verb in this context (see e.g. xxi. 63. 5 'auspiciis ementiendis', Cic. *diu.* i. 29, *Phil.* ii. 83, 88, iii. 9, and *TLL* v. 2. 468. 64–9) and this use of *mentiri* is unparalleled, it is very tempting to emend to ⟨*e*⟩*mentiri*; but L. may deliberately have chosen to vary the compound verb with the uncompounded.

tripudium solistimum: another technical expression: see vi. 41. 8 n.

5. laetus is very regular after a propitious omen: see vii. 26. 4 n. and Linderski (1993) 60 = (1995) 615 n. 24 and (1995) 679.

auspicium egregium esse: see viii. 9. 1 n.

deis auctoribus: see vi. 12. 8 n.

signum pugnae proposuit: see vi. 12. 7 n.

6. iam forte: this coupling is found elsewhere in L. only at xxi. 51. 4.
signa proferri: see ix. 32. 5 n.
ocius: see vii. 26. 6 n.

7. subsidia[que]: the deletion of Madvig (1860: 195–6 = 1877: 236) is hard to avoid: *subsidia . . . adtribuerat* most naturally goes with what follows, but the *-que* in the paradosis links it to *signa ocius proferri iubet*. M's *quae[que]* below suggests that the corruption arose from *-que*'s being omitted and then inserted in the wrong place.

    The ability to draw up the *subsidia* correctly was considered to be one of the most important attributes of a Roman general: see ix. 17. 15 n.
cornu: for the dative in *-u*, see vii. 2. 6 n.
L. Volumnium: see ix. 17. 8 n.
L. Scipionem: see 11. 10 n.
C. Caedicium: (2). Otherwise unknown, apart from his brief reappearance at 41. 8. This legateship, however, may be the first indication of the rise of the *gens*, which was to bring Q. Caedicius Noctua to the consulship of 289 and the censorship of 283, and his son, also Quintus, to the consulship of 256. Note also that a Q. Caedicius, conceivably identical with the consul of 256, was said by Cato (*orig.* fr. 83 = Gell. iii. 7. 1–20) to be the military tribune who rescued the Roman army in Sicily in 258 (for discussion see vii. 34. 1–37. 3 n.). Earlier Caedicii mentioned by our sources are Lucius, the tribune of the plebs in 475 (ii. 52. 6, D.H. ix. 28. 1, 4), Marcus, who was alleged to have heard the supernatural voice on the Via Nova in 390 (v. 32. 6, Plut. *Cam.* 14. 2–4), and Quintus, the centurion who took command of the Roman forces at Veii (v. 45. 7, 46. 6). Both the authenticity of these notices and the relationship of these men to the third-century family are uncertain; but, if the notices are authentic, they may show that already in the early fourth century the Caedicii were a prominent plebeian family. See further Vishnia (1996) 435 n. 10; there is an eccentric treatment of the family in Basanoff (1950a), (1950b), and associated articles in the same volume of *Latomus*.
⟨T.⟩ **Trebonio:** (13). Otherwise unknown. The context shows that a *praenomen* is necessary, and the obvious supplement was made by Weissenborn (ed.). Earlier Trebonii mentioned by our sources include M. Trebonius, *cos. tr.* 383 (vi. 21. 1 n.), and various tribunes; their relationship to our man is unclear.

8. Sp. Nautium: (4). Otherwise unknown, but quite possibly the son of the consul of 316 (ix. 21. 1 n.); some of L.'s sources held that this stratagem was carried out by Octavius Maecius (see 41. 5).

clitellis: 'pack-saddles'; *clitellae* are defined by Ps.-Acro *ad* Hor. *serm.* i. 5. 47 as 'sarcinas siue sellas, alii instrumenta quibus animalia sternuntur, alii uncinos ligneos quibus onera imponuntur', and they are illustrated at Daremberg and Saglio i. 2. 1260. Adams (1993: 40–5) has demonstrated that female mules were preferred for the transport of humans, castrated males as pack-animals; and so we find the masculine *mulus* regularly used in the context of *clitellae* (as here); cf. e.g. Plaut. *most.* 780 'mulos clitellarios', Cic. *top.* 36 'mulus clitellarius', Col. vi. 37. 11 'clitellis aptior mulus', and see *TLL* iii. 1355. 72–6.

cum ⟨tribus⟩ cohortibus: the awkward phrasing of the paradosis suggests that some supplement is necessary. Besides, Gundemann (1888: 363–4) noted that Frontin. *strat.* ii. 4. 1 'Papirius Cursor . . . ignorantibus suis praecepit Sp. Nautio, ut pauci alares et agasones mulis insidentes ramosque per terram trahentes a colle transuerso magno tumultu decurrerent' must derive from L. and that *pauci* ought to be a generalization characteristic of Frontinus for a more precise number in his source (he compared ii. 7. 7 'paucos leuissimae operae domos remisit' with Liv. xxi. 23. 6 'supra septem milia hominum domos remisit', and iii. 9. 3 'paucos centuriones' with Sall. *Iug.* 93. 8 'quattuor centuriones'). *tribus* is due to Hertz, and *iii* could easily have fallen out after *-m* (on the same principle, however, *duabus* is also possible). Walters's notion that the supplement would be 'fort. melius post *cohortibus*' is diplomatically less probable, and goes against the word-order found at 43. 3 'decem cohortibus alariis'.

maxime: see ix. 10. 10 n.

moto puluere se: in the hot campaigning seasons of the Mediterranean the movement of troops tended to be accompanied by the dispersal of a cloud of dust; and such a cloud was the classic sign that an armed force was approaching (to the numerous passages cited by Friis Johansen and Whittle on Aesch. *suppl.* 180, add e.g. xlii. 58. 3, Hom. *Il.* iii. 13–14, Caes. *ciu.* ii. 43. 2, [*Afr.*] 12. 1, Virg. *Aen.* ix. 33, Luc. vi. 247, and Tac. *hist.* ii. 68. 3).[1] For the stratagem of raising dust to make an army seem larger, see Frontin. (?) *strat.* iv. 7. 20 'Ptolomaeus aduersus Perdiccam exercitu praeualentem, ipse inualidus, omne pecudum genus, religatis ad tergum quae traherent sarmentis, agendum per paucos curauit equites: ipse praegressus cum copiis quas habebat effecit, ut puluis, quem pecora excitauerant, speciem magni sequentis exercitus moueret, cuius exspectatione

[1] Statius, employing a type of metonymy regular in post-Virgilian poetic style, actually makes *puluis* stand for fighting (*Theb.* x. 484).

territum uicit hostem', Polyaen. iv. 19 and viii. 23. 12.[1] For dust, see also Echols (1951/2); for other stratagems involving the use of retainers dressed up as soldiers, see vii. 14. 6 n.

This reading is the conjecture of Madvig (1877: 236–7) for *moto puluere* (M) or *motu pulueres* (Πλ). Some editors (e.g. Luterbacher and W–M) acquiesce in M's reading, supplying *mulos* as the object of *ostendere*; but the resulting sense is not pointed (why specify that Nautius was to display the mules, which it was important for the enemy not to recognize?), and the reflexive pronoun supplied by Madvig is very desirable; cf. e.g. 14. 14 'auersoque hosti ab tergo repente se ostendere' and xxii. 29. 3 'Fabiana se acies repente uelut caelo demissa ad auxilium ostendit'. Walters conjectured *motu pulueris se*: this is based on the reading of Πλ and is as elegant as Madvig's conjecture; but it accounts rather less well for the two ms. readings.

9. Sp. Papirio, fratris filio consulis: (26). Otherwise unknown, apart from the further reference to him at 44. 3. Since there are numerous embellishments in the tale of Aquilonia and Cominium, the role played here by Sp. Papirius may have been invented by L. or his annalistic sources; but there is no strong reason for believing that the very existence of this young man is an invention.

10. ante doctrinam deos spernentem natus: for similarly disapproving comments on the morals of L.'s own day, see vi. 12. 5 n.
incompertum: see ix. 26. 15 n.
deferret . . . detulit: intermediate between the senses 'report' and 'bring an accusation against'; for this latter sense (from which the notorious *delatores* derived their name), cf. (from countless examples) e.g. iv. 14. 3 and see *TLL* v. 1. 316. 44–317. 74 and *OLD s.u.* 9.

11. macte uirtute diligentia esto: see vii. 10. 4 n.
religionem: see vii. 3. 9 n.
mihi quidem tripudium nuntiatum; populo Romano exercituique egregium auspicium est: punctuate thus. Walters substituted a comma for the semi-colon and placed another comma after *auspicium*; but there is no difficulty in the omission of *est* after *nuntiatum*, which may be paralleled hundreds of times in L. and which is far less awkward than Walters's separation of *nuntiatum* and *est*.

---

[1] Caesar (*Gall.* iv. 32. 1) states that a larger than usual cloud of dust allowed a planned enemy ambush on his own troops to be detected.

tripudium: cf. § 4, and see vi. 41. 8 n.
egregium auspicium est: see viii. 9. 1 n.

12. prima signa: see viii. 11. 7 n.
ut hostibus quoque magnificum spectaculum esset: 'with the result that even to their enemy [i.e. the Romans] it was a splendid sight'. *hostibus* is Glareanus' conjecture for **N**'s *hostium*; for the identical corruption, see ix. 37. 3 n. The paradosis is retained by Foster, who translates '—a splendid spectacle, though composed of enemies'; but the sense is much less pointed. *hosti* (Madvig [1860] 196 = [1877] 237) is hardly inferior to Glareanus' conjecture.

13. quod ubi . . . nuntiatum est: see vii. 6. 10 n.
ante signa: see ix. 32. 9 n.

13–14. Forsythe (1999: 89) observes that this is one of only six marvels in the whole of the first decade that have not been qualified by *dicitur* or the like (he compares i. 56. 4, ii. 42. 10–11, v. 15. 1–16. 11 [two marvels], and 32. 6–7).
clamor . . . clamorem: see viii. 38. 10 n.
'di in proelio sunt' . . . praesentes interfuisse deos: see vii. 26. 5 n.

14. coruus: for the raven in augury, see vii. 26. 3 n.
occinuit: for this technical verb see vi. 41. 8 n.
quo laetus augurio: see vii. 26. 4 n.
praesentes . . . deos: see vii. 26. 7 n.
signa canere . . . iussit: see 19. 12 n.

41. 1. proelium . . . atrox: see vii. 26. 6 n.
ira: see ix. 13. 3 n.
spes: see 40. 1.
ardor certaminis: for the expression cf. xxiv. 39. 6, Curt. viii. 14. 15, and Sil. ix. 8; for the *ardor* of the troops see 40. 3.
auidos hostium sanguinis: see ix. 1. 9 n.
magnam partem: for the other Samnites who had not sworn the oath, see 38. 12.
cogit, positioned at the same point in its clause as *rapit*, makes a strong contrast with that verb, and helps to point the difference in the morale of the two sides.

2. primum clamorem atque impetum: for the coupling, see vi. 4. 9 n.; for *clamorem*, viii. 38. 10 n.

per aliquot iam annos uinci adsueti: see ix. 39. 6 n.
insidens: see viii. 6. 12 n.

3. omnis . . . compositum: the massive polysyndeton of six nouns
and their epithets adds great emphasis to L.'s expression of the
superstitious fears of the Samnites. They now view their ritual in the
same way as the Roman consul (cf. 39. 16–17).
omnis ille occulti ⟨ap⟩paratus sacri: the poetical *paratus* makes
sense and is not certainly wrong; for the coupling with *sacri* the analogous Arnob. iii. 15 'reliquo caerimoniarum paratu' is cited at *TLL*
x. 1. 323. 28–33. However, before Tacitus it is attested elsewhere in
prose only at Cic. *fin.* v. 53, Sall. *hist.* i. 88, and thrice in Seneca. By
contrast, *apparatus*, reported by Drakenborch from several *recentiores*, is very common in prose (according to Breimeier's figures at
TLL x. 1. 322. 7–9, it is found ninety-five times in L., thirty-eight
times in Cicero, and twenty-seven times in the prose of the younger
Seneca, and it is attested in numerous other authors), and is coupled
with *sacri*, *sacrorum* or *sacrificii* at 38. 8, xxv. 1. 10, and Tac. *hist.* iii.
55. 1. Therefore it is safer to emend (thus Wesenberg [1870/1] 40;
contra F. Walter [1892] 624). For the word-order see viii. 32. 5 n.
armati sacerdotes: perhaps L. refers back to the armed *centuriones*
of 38. 8 (n.).
promiscua . . . arae: in general see 38. 10 n.; for the *arae* see 38. 8.
strages: see vii. 23. 10 n.
fando nefandoque: see vi. 14. 10 n.
dira . . . composito: see 38. 10 'diro quodam carmine, in exsecrationem capitis familiaeque et stirpis composito', where see n. on *diro*.
exsecratio . . . detestandae: for the coupling of *exsecrari* (*-atio*)
and *detestari*, cf. e.g. v. 11. 16 'qui . . . caput domum fortunasque L.
Vergini ac M'. Sergi sit exsecratus detestatusque', xxxi. 44. 6, Sen.
Phaedr. 566, and Apul. *met.* ix. 26. 1. For *detestor* in the sense 'curse',
see *TLL* v. 1. 810. 11–73 and *OLD s.u.* 1.
iis uinculis [fugae] obstricti: the objective genitive *fugae* is
extremely awkward. Walters was one of the few editors or commen-
tators who tried to explain it, citing 13. 14 'uinculum . . . ingens
immodicae cupiditatis iniectum est'; but the parallel is not close, and
in that passage the text is probably corrupt (see n. ad loc.). In the
absence of a satisfactory parallel, it is best to follow Gemoll (1890–8:
ii. 19) in deleting the word.
ciuem: again see 38. 10.

4. attonitos: see vii. 17. 3 n.

quos timor moraretur a fuga: a nice paradox.

5. iam . . . cum: for the inverted *cum*-clause introducing peripeteia, see vi. 24. 4–5 n.
ad signa: see viii. 11. 7 n.
puluis: see 40. 8 n.
Sp. Nautius: see 40. 8 n.
Octauium . . . tradunt: for this kind of parenthesis, and for *tradunt*, cf. ix. 36. 2 (n.).
Octauium Maecium: (1). Otherwise unknown.
dux ⟨cum⟩ alariis cohortibus ⟨ad⟩erat is the conjecture of Watt (1991: 219–20); **N**, followed by e.g. Walters, read *dux alaribus cohortibus erat*. However, even if the dative could stand as an equivalent to *alarium cohortium* (which is most doubtful) and one could translate 'was the leader of the auxiliary cohorts', *erat* remains feeble, since a verb meaning 'had arrived' would be preferable to one meaning 'was' or 'it was'. Wesenberg (1870/1: 40) conjectured *alarium cohortium* for *alariis cohortibus*, but *erat* remains difficult. Koch (1861: 8) conjectured *[dux]* ⟨*cum*⟩ *alaribus cohortibus erat*;[1] but, although the introduction of *cum* is desirable (cf. 40. 8 'cum ⟨tribus⟩ cohortibus alariis'), *erat* remains untouched, and, as Madvig (1877: 237) was the first to point out, the form *alaris* is not used by L. Madvig therefore proposed *cum auxiliaribus cohortibus erat*; but this clever proposal still leaves *erat*. Watt's conjecture gives a text without difficulty: ⟨*ad*⟩*erat* removes *erat*; *dux* ⟨*cum*⟩ is perhaps an easier corruption to explain than that postulated by Koch; and *alariis* for *alaribus* restores the usual form (cf. 40. 8, 43. 3, xxxv. 5. 8, 10, and xl. 40. 9; the corruption could have arisen as an anticipation of *cohortibus*). However, it would be as economical to combine the proposals of Madvig and Watt and suggest *cum auxiliaribus cohortibus* ⟨*ad*⟩*erat*.

6. puluerem: see 40. 8 n.
maiorem pro numero: see vii. 7. 5 n.
turbidam: see 33. 5 n.
in primo: see 14. 17 n.
speciem . . . dabat: 'gave the impression'; cf. e.g. Cic. *leg*. iii. 39, Hor. *epist*. ii. 2. 124 'ludentis speciem dabit', Quint. ii. 17. 19 'Hannibal . . . speciem hosti abeuntis exercitus dedit', and see *TLL* v. 1. 1685. 54–5.

---

[1] The conjecture is misreported by Walters. His own tentative suggestion that *alaribus cohortibus* is a gloss is improbable.

cogentium agmen: 'bringing up the rear'; to the parallels listed at *TLL* i. 1345. 84–1346. 7 add e.g. xxxiv. 28. 10, xxxvi. 44. 4, xlii. 64. 5, and xliv. 4. 12.

7. clamitans inter prima signa: see 19. 17, viii. 11. 7 nn.
uox etiam ad hostes accideret: see viii. 24. 11 n.
adniterentur uincere: see ix. 26. 15 n.
priusquam gloria alterius exercitus esset: see ix. 40. 8–11 n.

8. equitibus . . . equites: for cavalry-charges in L.'s battle-narratives, see vi. 29. 2 n.
Trebonio Caedicioque: see 40. 7 nn.
cuspidem erectam: for signals of this kind, cf. e.g. Plut. *Lys.* 11. 2–4, Polyaen. i. 45. 2, and ii. 5. 2 ἔνθα δὴ Γοργίδας κράνος ἐπὶ δόρατος ἀνατείνας σημεῖον ἔδωκεν ἀναστροφῆς.
quatientem: see vii. 26. 1 n.

9. ut ex praeparato: see viii. 30. 8 n.
panduntur inter ordines uiae: for the gaps between maniples see viii. 8. 5 n., for the expression 5. 11 n.
prouolat: see vii. 7. 8 n.
infestis cuspidibus: see viii. 7. 9 n.
impetum dedit: see ix. 43. 15 n.
sternunt: see vii. 24. 5 n.

10. tum iam deorum hominumque uicta uis; funduntur linteatae cohortes; pariter iurati iniuratique fugiunt nec quemquam praeter hostes metuunt: so I should punctuate, retaining *uicta uis* (Mλ) and making all three presents (*funduntur*, *fugiunt*, and *metuunt*) expand it: the double threat to the Romans from both the Samnites (who were not fleeing) and the Samnites' gods (who prevented them from fleeing) is overcome. *tum* regularly introduces the climax of a battle (vii. 33. 15 n.), and its coupling with *iam* is no impediment to this interpretation, since it is found elsewhere in L., with shades of meaning varying from 'now' to 'by this time': cf. vii. 31. 7, xxvii. 14. 10 'tum iam non unus manipulus, sed pro se quisque miles qui modo adsequi agmen fugientium elephantorum poterat, pila conicere', and xliv. 36. 6. Walters and Foster accepted PU's *uicta ui* (Π[= PUZbZtZsᶜ (*uicta* Zs¹)]), Walters separating *tum* from *iam* with a comma; but (*a*) this reading has less authority, and (*b*) it suggests that *pariter . . . metuunt* depends on *funduntur . . . cohortes*. Madvig (1860: 196–7 = 1877: 237–8) suggested *uictae ui*, on the ground that the gods were on Rome's side (cf. 40. 13); but a reference to the terrible oath to the nether gods seems more pointed.

iurati iniuratique: only a portion of the Samnite army swore the oath; see 38. 12–13.

nec quemquam praeter hostes metuunt: the members of the *legio linteata* had sworn to kill any Samnite whom they saw fleeing.

11. peditum agmen: Walters glossed Gronovius' deletion of *agmen* as *fort. recte*; but the word is quite innocuous (it suggests that the Samnites fled in a column), and this coupling is regular in L. (see Packard [1968] i. 296, iii. 829).

quod superfuit pugnae: see viii. 11. 5 n.

Bouianum is a certain correction, found in e.g. A and u, for **N**'s *uobianum* (or *-nium*) (an anagrammatic corruption). For Bovianum see ix. 28. 1 n.

equitesque . . . equites eques sequitur: with *peditem pedes* following, L.'s prose would have been more balanced had he written *equitem eques* (reported by Drakenborch from Holkham 345 and the *codex Portugallicus*) rather than *equites eques*; but for variation of this kind see 36. 9 n. For the Samnite cavalry see ix. 22. 6 n.

diuersa cornua dextrum . . . laeuum . . . tendit: for the construction see vi. 2. 8 n.

12. est: in 'classical' Latin *non quia* is regularly followed by the subjunctive when the rejected reason, in addition to not being the reason, is not even true; the indicative is used only when the writer vouches for the reality of the notion expressed in the causal clause (as at vii. 30. 13 [quoted below]). Hence Gronovius proposed *esset* and Allen (1864–74: i. 25) *sit* (thereby anticipating Wesenberg [1870/1: 32]). L.'s mss, however, offer breaches of this rule in other passages (viii. 19. 3 'ualuitque ea legatio, non tam quia pacem uolebant Samnites quam quia nondum parati erant ad bellum', xxi. 40. 6 'nec nunc illi quia audent sed quia necesse est pugnaturi sunt', xxxiii. 27. 6, and xl. 33. 2), and the phenomenon is found also in the mss of contemporary poets and later writers of prose. Although our passage and the two from the fourth decade may be emended with ease (see Briscoe's apparatus), viii. 19. 3 is more resistant to conjecture, and in general there are too many instances of the construction for it safely to be emended out of our texts. See further Riemann (1885) 291–2, K–S ii. 386–7, and H–S 588.

sed: it may be right to emend to *sed quia*. When an author uses the pattern *non quia . . . sed*, and when *sed* introduces a clause,[1] the word following *sed* is overwhelmingly likely to be a second *quia*; from L. note iv. 57. 3, vii. 30. 13 'nec enim nunc, quia dolent iniuriam acceptam Samnites sed quia gaudent oblatam sibi esse causam, oppugnatum nos ueniunt', xxi. 40. 6 (quoted above), xxviii. 42. 20, xxxi. 48. 10, xxxiii. 27. 6, xxxv. 40. 1, xxxviii. 33. 11, xl. 33. 2, and xlii. 25. 10.[2] However, there are some other passages in which the 'rule' is not followed, most of them in either Tacitus or Servius/Servius auctus, who affect this construction; see Cic. *Tusc.* i. 9 'hoc mihi Latinis litteris inlustrandum putaui, non quia philosophia Graecis et litteris et doctoribus percipi non posset, sed meum semper iudicium fuit omnia aut inuenisse per se sapientius quam Graecos aut . . .', Tac. *Agr.* 46. 3, *hist.* i. 15. 2 'sed Augustus in domo successorem quaesiuit, ego in re publica, non quia propinquos aut socios belli non habeam, sed neque ipse imperium ambitione accepi, et iudicii mei documentum sit non meae tantum necessitudines . . . sed et tuae', and iii. 80. 2 'aequioribus animis accepti sunt qui ad Antonium uenerant, non quia modestior miles, sed duci plus auctoritatis', Serv. *Aen.* iv. 209 'CAECIQVE IGNES non quia non uidentur, sed quorum origo non apparet', vi. 354, ix. 678, Serv. *auct. georg.* iv. 19 'et "inanes doli" non quia inanes sunt, sed inanes eos facies, si adhibueris uim', *Aen.* xi. 32; perhaps add Tac. *dial* 37. 6. It is unlikely that in all these passages the paradosis is corrupt.

13. colligerentur animi: 'their minds had regained their composure'; cf. e.g. iii. 60. 11, xxxvii. 11. 7, xlii. 60. 3, and see *TLL* iii. 1614. 52–63.
ab altero cornu: for the rivalry see ix. 40. 8–11 n.

14. ipse is omitted by F. Walters glossed this 'fort. recte'; but F has no authority, and *ipse* emphasizes the decisive action taken by Scipio himself.
scuto super caput elato: for the similar action of Scipio's most illustrious descendant, cf. xxvi. 44. 6–7 'Scipio . . . trium prae se iuuenum ualidorum scutis oppositis—ingens enim iam uis omnis generis telorum e muris uolabat—ad urbem succedit'.
testudine: the 'tortoise' (so-called because the animal protects itself under its shell) was a formation in which the troops raised their shields and locked them together, so as to leave no aperture through

---

[1] Contrast e.g. Sen. *contr.* vii. 1. 26, Sen. *dial.* vii. 26. 5 and *epist.* 86. 1.
[2] Occasionally *sed* introduces not a causal clause but a final clause introduced by *ut* or *ne* (e.g. Sen. *ben.* vi. 25. 1).

which hostile projectiles might intrude. It was used particularly often in attacking a heavily defended site (with our passage cf. 43. 5 and xxxi. 40. 3) but also on the battlefield as a defensive measure (29. 6, 12, xxxii. 17. 13, Curt. v. 3. 9). The classic description is Dio xlix. 30. 1–4, where both the defensive and aggressive possibilities of the formation are noted. It is not to be confused with the so-called 'ram tortoise', for which see Briscoe on xxxvii. 26. 8. See further Lammert, *RE* vA. 1062.

penetrare in interiora urbis is the reading of λ; *in* is omitted in MΠ(= PGrZ). It is perhaps possible that L. here used *penetrare* transitively (the usage is attested first at Lucr. ii. 539 and Cic. *Tusc.* i. 43: see *TLL* x. 1. 1071. 14–22); but, since he almost invariably uses the verb with *in*, *intra*, or *ad* and the accusative (from twenty-five instances only xxxiv. 29. 8 and xxxix. 9. 1 prove exceptions, neither passage being parallel to ours), λ's reading is probably right. Λ/λ is rarely right against the combined testimony of M and Π (see vol. i, p. 323), but here *in* could easily have been omitted coincidentally in two different branches of the tradition by haplography.

For the partitive gentive see vi. 32. 5 n.

42. 1. praeceps in occasum sol erat: *praeceps* is regular of the setting of planets; cf. e.g. Virg. *georg*. i. 365–6 'stellas . . . praecipitis caelo labi' and *TLL* x. 2. 416. 71–417. 2.
appetens nox: see viii. 38. 3 n.

2. clamorem perhaps suggests the traditional τόπος of the shout at the capture of a city; see esp. xxxvi. 24. 6 'clamor, index capti oppidi'; also ii. 33. 8, v. 21. 11, Virg. *Aen*. ii. 487–8, and Quint. viii. 3. 68.
mixtum pugnantium ac pauentium fremitu: cf. ii. 33. 8 'clamor . . . mixtus muliebri puerilique ploratu', xxii. 5. 4 (quoted below), and xxxviii. 22. 8 'clamor permixtus mulierum atque puerorum ploratibus'. L. rather affects this use of the genitive plurals of present participles; cf. v. 21. 11 'clamor omnia uariis terrentium ac pauentium uocibus . . . complet', xxii. 5. 4 'mixtos strepentium pauentiumque clamores', 29. 1, xxv. 24. 5, xxxv. 30. 5, and xxxvii. 42. 6.

3. temeritate: normally *temeritas* has negative connotations in L.; see vi. 22. 6 n.
integri . . . quicquam: for the neuter partitive genitive, cf. xxix. 8. 10 'nihil . . . integri', xxxvi. 7. 6, Cic. *Balb*. 17, and Sen. *clem*. i. 22. 1, and see *TLL* vii. 1. 2072. 84–2073. 3; at xxx. 12. 20 P's *ne quid relin-*

queret integri is probably right against the Spirensian reading *ne quid relinqueretur integrum.*

4. nox appropinquabat: *appropinquare* is quite regularly used in this way to express the passing of time; cf. v. 39. 8 'lux appropinquans', xliv. 43. 2, xlv. 6. 6, and see *TLL* ii. 315. 46–9.

5. capta tria milia octingenti [et] septuaginta, signa militaria nonaginta septem: see 14. 21 n. (for the figure of enemy captured), vii. 37. 16 n. (for enemy standards); also vii. 17. 9 n. *et* before *septuaginta* is unparalleled in L. and was rightly deleted by Wesenberg (1870/1: 40). λ inserts *et* before *signa*, but the agreement of MΠ makes it likely that the text printed is what L. wrote. The asyndeton is quite in his manner; cf. e.g. 14. 21 'tria milia et quadringenti caesi, capti octingenti ferme et triginta; signa militaria capta tria et uiginti', xxxi. 49. 7, and xlii. 66. 9.

6. non ferme alium: see vii. 33. 1 n.
laetiorem in acie: for the *laetitia* of a general before battle, cf. vi. 12. 7 and xxx. 32. 11 '(Scipio) celsus haec corpore uoltuque ita laeto ut uicisse iam crederes dicebat'; note also Tac. *Agr.* 33. 1 (of the troops) and Claud. i. 113 (of a general, but at the end of a battle). This attitude is generally linked closely to the knowledge of propitious omens, and this must be implied here too, even though in the following phrases introduced by *seu* L. gives other reasons.
suopte ingenio: see 16. 6 and vi. 15. 12 nn.

7. quo templa deis immortalibus uoueri mos erat: see vii. 28. 4 n. with *addendum.*
Ioui Victori: see 29. 14 n. for the vowing of the temple of Jupiter Victor.
pocillum . . . facturum: Cursor's vow is mentioned also at Plin. *nat.* xiv. 91 'L. Papirius imperator aduersus Samnites dimicaturus uotum fecit, si uicisset, Ioui pocillum uini'.
    This vow has given scholars needless difficulty.[1] *mulsum* was a beverage made out of honey and wine; in later antiquity the term was applied occasionally to a mixture of honey and water. The drink was popular at Rome, and it seems to have been customary for soldiers to drink it at a triumph (Plaut. *Bacch.* 972, 1074, and, perhaps, D.H. ii. 34. 2): see further *TLL* viii. 1579. 44–1580. 17 and Hug, *RE* xvi.

---

[1] Note the remarks of Orlin (1997: 30–1).

513–14. That it was traditional to vow *mulsum* to a god is shown by a neglected parallel, Plaut. *aul.* 620–2 'ibo hinc intro, perscrutabor fanum, si inueniam uspiam | aurum, dum hic est occupatus. sed si repperero, o Fides, | mulsi congialem plenam faciam tibi fideliam'; compare too offerings of wine, for which see e.g. Cato, *agr.* 132. 1–2, Virg. *Aen.* iii. 525–9, and passages which refer to the dedication by Aeneas or Ascanius or the Latins of a *uindemia* to Jupiter (D.H. i. 65. 2, Ov. *fast.* iv. 893–4, Plut. *quaest. Rom.* 45 = *mor.* 275e, Fest. 322, *Fast. Praen.* for 23 April [*I.I.* xiii. 2, pp. 130–1]; cf. Cato, *orig.* fr. 12). Therefore Papirius surprises not so much because he vows an offering of alcohol to the god, as in having so much confidence in Jupiter's favour that he vows him *mulsum* (a small reward, albeit associated with a triumph) rather than a large reward, such as the now customary temple. Schilling (1982: 143) and Ziolkowski (1992: 245) have argued that L. (or, perhaps one should say, his source[s]) has misunderstood what Papirius (or, if the tale is untrue, the inventor of the story) meant by his vow, on the ground that in 293 wine would have been seen as a valuable offering to a god; but with temples vowed to gods in 295 and 294 this seems unlikely.

temetum: an archaic equivalent of *uinum*, from which the more common adjective *temulentus* derives: see Plin. *nat.* xiv. 90 'hoc (i.e. in the time of the elder Cato) tum nomen uino erat', and (for full discussion of the word's distribution) Brink on Hor. *epist.* ii. 2. 163.

facturum: *facere* is regularly used as an equivalent of *sacrificare*; cf. e.g. xxii. 10. 3–5, xxvii. 25. 9, Cato *agr.* 134. 1 'porcam (*sc.* Cereri) . . . hoc modo fieri oportet', and see further *TLL* vi. 1. 97. 19–67.

cordi fuit: see vi. 9. 3 n.

43. 1–8. THE CAPTURE OF COMINIUM

After describing the capture of Aquilonia L. turns to simultaneous events at Cominium; the comparative brevity of his narrative emphasizes that this second battle was of rather less importance. We may note how, as in the previous scene, L. sets the time of day clearly (§ 1 'prima luce'); how, as earlier with Papirius Cursor, the delineation of Carvilius' dispositions throughout §§ 1–5 shows his skill as a general; how the messenger from his colleague (§ 2) provides a dramatic interruption (note 'iam dantem signum') and serves to link this scene with the previous one; and how the long and complex period in §§ 5–7 (*Samnites . . . fortunam*) very well reflects the struggle on the walls of the town. As so often the scene is rounded off with an account of casualties (§ 8).

43. 1. ad moenia . . . admotis: see vi. 10. 4 n.
corona: see vii. 27. 1 n.

2. nuntius . . . trepidus: see vi. 31. 3 n.

3. D. Brutum Scaeuam: (61). Scaeva was elected to the consulship of 292 (47. 5), when he fought against the Faliscans with Sp. Carvilius Maximus as his legate (Zon. viii. 1. 10). He was probably the son of the consul of 325/4 (viii. 12. 13 n.).
cum prima legione: see 18. 3–4 n.

4. manum . . . conferret: see ix. 5. 10 n.

5. testudine: see 41. 14 n.
simul et . . . et: L. much affected this construction, to introduce both clauses and phrases. To the instances listed by W–M on xxxii. 18. 3, add e.g. v. 26. 10 'ni Fortuna imperatori Romano simul et cognitae rebus bellicis uirtutis specimen et maturam uictoriam dedisset', xxviii. 26. 13, xxxii. 24. 3–4, xxxix. 47. 3; also Tac. *Agr.* 5. 1. See K–S ii. 34.
uis . . . fiebat: see vii. 31. 2 n.
satis animi . . . ad prohibendos . . . hostes: see 32. 8 n.

6. ex interuallo: i.e. *eminus*; add xxx. 18. 7 and xxxviii. 21. 4 to the passages cited at *TLL* vii. 1. 2296. 73–8 to illustrate the expression.
loco . . . uicto: for *uincere* used in the sense 'mastering' impersonal objects, see *OLD s.u.* 7; Virg. *Aen.* vi. 687–8 'tuaque exspectata parenti | uicit iter durum pietas' is closer to the sense here than the passages cited by W–M.

7. turribus: see 34. 6 n.
paulisper temptauerunt extremam pugnae fortunam is difficult: W–M gloss 'd.h. sie boten die letzte Kraft auf, um der Schlacht eine glückliche Wendung zu geben', and Foster translates 'they . . . made there one brief attempt to redeem the day', neither of which does justice to L.'s pregnant expression. The coupling with the genitive and with *temptauerunt* suggests that *fortunam* must have the meaning 'chance' or 'hazard'; see *OLD s.u.* 5 and cf. the analogous xxii. 60. 4 'nullam fortunam certaminis experti', xxv. 27. 8, and xxxviii. 28. 5 'belli fortunam experiri'. However, since the Samnites have not yet bothered to fight properly, and since *fortuna extrema* regularly has connotations of desperate circumstances (at *TLL* v. 2.

2004. 17–20 our passage is rightly cited with Cic. *Mur*. 34, Caes. *Gall*. vii. 40. 7, and *ciu*. ii. 32. 8), he must also imply that joining battle at this point reflected their desperation. Translate: 'as a last resort they briefly tried the hazard of battle'.

8. abiectis armis: see vi. 8. 10 n.
ad undecim . . . octoginta: see 14. 21 n. for the figure for enemy captured, and vii. 17. 9 n. for a general discussion of casualty figures.
in fidem: i.e. they made a formal *deditio*; for such appeals to the *fides* of a commander, see vol. ii, pp. 287–8.

43. 9–15. THE DEFEAT OF THE TWENTY COHORTS

Ever since 40. 6 we have been waiting to hear about the fate of the twenty cohorts, and their swift demise in this section, as they are recalled too late to Aquilonia, is in some respects anticlimactic. Yet the feebleness of their organization and tactics serves to sum up the general feebleness of the Samnites' military performance in the events of this year. L. skilfully uses this section to look back to what has happened before (esp. 41. 12–42. 4), referring both to the Samnite camp and to Aquilonia, previously viewed from the perspective of Papirius Cursor, now from that of these cohorts. Again, he carefully sets the time of day (§ 10 'primis tenebris', § 12 'noctis', 'lucem', § 13 'prima luce').

9. sic . . . sic . . .: see ix. 17. 11 n.
septem milia: see ix. 44. 8 n.

10. clamor . . . accidens: see viii. 24. 11 n.

11. incensa erat: see ix. 43. 15 n.
fusa is the equivalent of *diffusa*; cf. xxxiv. 39. 11, Sen. *nat*. i. 15. 1 'cum late fusus sit ignis', and see *TLL* vi. 1. 1570. 78–9.
certioris cladis indicio: there is no difficulty in regarding *certioris* as an instance of transferred epithet (for the figure see ix. 19. 2 n.); the younger Gronovius' *certiori* (better -*e*) is therefore unnecessary.

12. eo ipso loco temere: thus M: *eo ipso loco te prope mere* P¹: *eo ipso loco prope timore* PᶜTᶜ: *eo ipso loco prope temere* GrT¹: *prope eo ipso loco temere* θ. *prope* appears in three different positions in P and λ (although the readings of PᶜTᶜ and θ may be secondary developments); but it is not found in M, and no sense can be made of it in any position. Cornelissen (1889: 192) therefore emended to *forte temere*, an expression that L. uses five times elsewhere (add xxxix. 15. 11 to his parallels) and that makes reasonable sense here; but the phenomenon of variants in **N** is well attested, and it is probably easier to argue that *prope* and *temere* were originally variants in **N** for each other, even though it is not easy to see why one should have been corrupted into the other. In which case, M excised *prope*, Π and λ perhaps left it as a variant, which found its way into different parts of the text. There can be little doubt that M has what L. wrote; translate '⟨staying⟩ at the place in which they were, and having thrown themselves without thought on the ground still clad in their fighting-gear, they spent the whole sleepless night in waiting—and fearing—for dawn'. See also Madvig (1860) 19–21 = (1877) 21–2 and Winkler (1890–2) ii. 23.

sub armis: see ix. 37. 4 n.

inquietum omne tempus noctis: for the coupling of *inquietus* with *nox* and similar words, cf. v. 42. 6, Val. Max. viii. 14. *ext.* 1, and other passages cited at *TLL* vii. 1. 1805. 42–52.

13. in fugam consternantur: for the expression cf. xxxviii. 46. 4 and Gell. xv. 22. 6 (note too Tac. *hist.* iii. 79. 2 'ceteri foeda fuga consternantur'). *consternantur* is a conjecture for **N**'s *consternuntur*, found first in Dᶜ. Frigell (1875: 30–1) tried to defend the paradosis by citing xxviii. 15. 9, xl. 45. 3, and Caes. *Gall.* ii. 24. 2; but none of these passages offers any support for this use of *consternere*, and the regular *consternare* is required. See further vii. 42. 3 n.

conspecti: Madvig (1860: 197–8 = 1877: 238–9) argued that *conspecti* is otiose with *uiderant* following, and was interpolated under the influence of *et* in § 14 'conspecta et'. Walters and Conway (1918: 116–18) showed that *conspecta et* picks up *conspecti*.[1]

14. signa militaria duodeuiginti: see vii. 37. 16 n.

15. ut ex tanta trepidatione: see viii. 30. 8 n.
Bouianum: see ix. 28. 1 n.

44. 1–9. THE CONTINUATION OF THE SAMNITE CAMPAIGN

This chapter provides a transition between the account of the capture of Aquilonia and Cominium and the continued fighting in Samnium described at 45. 9–14. Since L. has placed events with

---

[1] Doujat's improbable conjecture *conspecti⟨s⟩* substitutes, in the words of Walters and Conway, 'the less for the more important side of the incident'.

regard to the time of day so clearly earlier in the episode, it is easy to infer that § 2 'eodemque die' refers to the day after the battle (cf. 'prima luce' at 43. 13). Once again the theme of the mutual co-operation of the two consuls is to the fore: see esp. §§ 1–2 and 6–8. Although at the end of this section L. will turn to events at Rome, which occupy 45. 1–8, the references in § 9 to Saepinum and Velia serve to make the reader wonder what will happen next in Samnium.

44. 3–5. in conspectu ... donat: for the *contio* after a battle, see vii. 10. 14 n. with *addendum*.

3. Sp. Nautium: see 40. 8 n.
Sp. Papirium: see 40. 9 n.
manipulum hastatorum: see viii. 8. 3–14 nn.

3–5. armillis ... armillisque argenteis: the *armilla* or bracelet was a minor military *donum*, which, according to Plin. *nat.* xxxiii. 37, could be awarded only to citizens and not to allies. Apart from texts relating to the legendary L. Siccius Dentatus, who is said to have been awarded 160 *armillae* (D.H. x. 37. 3, Val. Max. iii. 2. 24, Plin. *nat.* vii. 102, Gell. ii. 11. 2), the only other notice of its award in the Republic is Val. Max. viii. 14. 5 '... Scipionem dona militaria iis qui strenuam operam ediderant diuidentem T. Labienus ut forti equiti aureas armillas tribueret admonuit, eoque se negante id facturum, ne castrensis honos in eo qui paulo ante seruisset, uiolaretur, ipse ex praeda Gallica aurum equiti largitus est. nec tacite id Scipio tulit: namque equiti "habebis" inquit "donum uiri diuitis". quod ubi ille accepit, proiecto ante pedes Labieni auro uultum demisit. idem, ut audiit Scipionem dicentem "imperator te argenteis armillis donat", alacer gaudio abiit.' This somewhat obscure passage seems both to bear out the view of Pliny (the brave cavalryman had only recently become a citizen) and to reinforce the impression gained from § 5, that the silver *armilla* was an inferior award.[1] In the principate *armillae* were never awarded to anyone above the rank of centurion. See further von Domaszewski, *RE* ii. 1189, *TLL* ii. 615. 65–616. 20 (with extensive citation of imperial inscriptions), Steiner (1906) 26–9, and Maxfield (1981) 89–91.

3. aureisque coronis: see vii. 10. 14 n.

---

[1] L. does not actually state in § 3 that the *armillae* were golden, but this seems a legitimate deduction.

4. nauatam operam: see vii. 16. 4 n.

qua 'in which' or 'by means of which' is the reading of M and is more pointed than *quia* (Zλ) 'because', championed by Pettersson (1930: 19 n. 1); *qui* (PGr) makes no sense. If **N** read *qui* with an *a* written above the *i*, and if the Z mss are contaminated from Λ/λ, all the variant readings would be explained. For M alone in the truth see vol. i, pp. 321–4.

5. corniculis: the award of the *corniculum* is attested securely elsewhere only at *uir. ill.* 72. 3 (to Aemilius Scaurus in the late second century BC).[1] Unfortunately its representation has not been securely identified on tomb-stones and therefore we can only speculate as to what it looked like. See further Fiebiger, *RE* iv. 1604–5, *TLL* iv. 959. 9–13, Büttner (1957) 177–80, and Maxfield (1981) 97–9.

6. consilium inde habitum: see ix. 2. 15 and *addendum* to vii. 10. 14 nn.

iamne tempus esset . . . : *iamne* is Conway's conjecture, printed by Walters: MΠ(=PGrZ) have or had *cum iam*, λ *cum iamnec*. If one takes *cum* as concessive and places a full stop before it, the reading of MΠ gives quite good sense: although it was time to leave Samnium because wintry weather was arriving (cf. 45. 11 'frigoris iam' and 46. 1 'niues iam'), the consuls decided that at least one army should remain there. To be sure, *cum iam nunc* (Pettersson [1930] 179), which gives virtually identical sense, would account better for the *nec* in λ (the emphatic coupling *iam nunc* is found eight times in L.: cf. e.g. ii. 54. 5, iii. 40. 12 and see Packard [1968] ii. 925). Conway's conjecture postulates a more complex corruption (the intrusion of *cum* as a dittography after -*tum*, the omission of -*ne* in **N**[1], and its restoration in **N**[c], whence λ's *nec* [another dittographic corruption]). However, since it gives sense that is better still, allowing a clause which records what was deliberated to follow *habitum* (cf. e.g. ix. 15. 1 'dimissa contione consilium habitum omnibusne copiis Luceriam premerent an . . .' and xxxvii. 13. 5 'consilium habitum utrum extemplo decernerent an Rhodiam exspectarent classem'),[2] I have adopted it. It requires strong punctuation after the following *alterius*.

ab Samnio: Weissenborn (*Komm.*[3]) observed that the use of *ab*

---

[1] It may be attested also at Suet. *gramm.* 9. 1 'L. Orbilius Pupillus . . . in Macedonia corniculo, mox equo meruit', for the doubtful interpretation of which see Kaster's note.

[2] Conway's approach to the passage was anticipated by Weissenborn (*Komm.*), who once suggested *num* for *cum*; but *num* is found only rarely in L. outside direct speech, and is not a word lightly to be introduced by conjecture.

rather than *ex* is 'ungewöhnlich', and Madvig (1877: 239) then proposed *de* for *ab*, which would give a more regular construction after *deducere*. Nevertheless, I hesitate to change the paradosis in view of ii. 13. 4 'exercitum ab Ianiculo deduxit Porsenna', xxi. 41. 9 'praesidium deduxit ab Eryce', and xxxvii. 5. 4 'ab Heraclea . . . exercitus eo deductus': although these passages refer to towns or small localities rather than regions, they do suggest that here too L. could have used *ab*. See also K–S i. 368–9.

aut . . . aut certe: see ix. 37. 4 n.

8. signis conlatis: see viii. 17. 10 n.
pro aris ac focis: see ix. 12. 6 n.

9–45. 1. litteris . . . litterae: see viii. 30. 10 n.

44. 9. Saepinum: see 45. 12 n.
Veliam: the spelling of this settlement varies in the mss. Here **N** had *uellam* (but *uolonam* Zs and *ueleciam* R, both influenced by 45. 9). For its first occurrence in 45. 9 **N** had *ueletiam* (thus MPTD: *uellam etiam* [Gr], *ueliam* [Zb], *uel iam* [Zt], *uolanam* [Zs], *ueleciam* [R], and *uel eciam* [L] are all eliminable); for its second, for which PGru are defective, MZbZtλ (= TRL) had *ueliam* (*-ia* Zt), Zs *uolanam*, and D *uel etiam*. This divergence does not allow the correct spelling to be established beyond doubt, since Velia, Veletia, and Vella could all be extracted from the ms. evidence. For the possibility that L. refers to the Greek colony of Velia, see above, p. 384.

45. 1–8. *The Etruscan rebellion.* L. needed to interrupt his account of the Samnite War at this point in order to motivate the decision of the consuls that Carvilius should cross into Etruria (45. 11). The *litterae* of 45. 1 help to effect the transition from Samnium to Rome, and at 45. 6 the minor peripeteia with *ni*, which reveals that the Faliscans had also revolted, serves to increase the sense of danger facing Rome.

45. 1. et in curia et in contione: in the middle and late Republic letters from commanders were sent to the senate (see e.g. Cic. *Pis.* 44) and read out first there and then to an assembly (xxvii. 50. 11 'in senatu primum, deinde in contione litterae recitatae sunt', 51. 5–6, and xxxiii. 24. 4). Likewise legates (e.g. xxvii. 7. 2–4, xxx. 40. 1–3, xxxvii. 52. 2) and returning commanders (e.g. xxxvii. 58. 6) reported first to the senate and then to the people. Already by 293 this procedure is likely to have been established; but whether our passage goes back to an accurate memory or rests rather on (sensible) annalistic or Livian inference, there is no knowing.

quatridui supplicatione: for celebratory *supplicationes* see viii. 33. 10 n.; there is no particular reason to follow Bruno (1906: 73 n. 1) in thinking that this *supplicatio* was also propitiatory and occasioned by fear at the Faliscan uprising.

2. per idem forte tempus: see vii. 18. 2 n.

3. animum: the collective *animus* of the *populus*, unless L. has moved from considering the *populus* as a whole to the thoughts of individuals.

quonam ... habuisset: W–M were doubtless correct to regard this report of Roman worries as greatly exaggerated, and it almost certainly derives from the imagination of L. or one of his sources rather than authentically remembered or recorded evidence. Nevertheless, the resurgence of the Etruscan War can hardly have been welcomed at Rome.

coniuratione is taken by W–M to mean little more than 'concerted rebellion'; but there must be a reference also to the ritual described at 38. 5–13.

occupationem populi Romani pro occasione: for the contrast between *occupatio* and *occasio* cf. Sen. *epist.* 107. 1 'serui occupationes tuas occasionem fugae putauerunt'. Here GrZλ preserve the truth (but *occavi-* for *occasione* in Zs), which has been corrupted in M to *occupationemque pro occasione* and in P to *occupationem p.r. pro occupatione*.

4. legationes ... introductae: see vii. 30. 1 n.
sociorum: Bruno (1906: 76 n. 1) noted that in Ocriculum Rome had an ally near Falerii (see ix. 41. 20 [n.]).
M. Atilio: for Atilius, see 32. 1 n.; for the practice of holding the praetorship in the year after one's consulship, see 22. 9 n.; for the praetor presiding in the senate, see 22. 7 n.
uri ac uastari: for this coupling cf. [x] xxxiv. 9. 13, Curt. viii. 1. 26, Tac. *hist.* ii. 12. 2, and *ann.* iv. 48. 1; also Liv. xxviii. 44. 14.

5. ui atque iniuria: see vii. 31. 3 n.

6. quod ad ... attinebat: see vi. 6. 10 n.
ni: see vii. 15. 1 n.
Faliscos: see vi. 4. 4 n.

7. acuit curam: see viii. 6. 15 n.

fetiales mittendos . . . bellum Faliscis indictum est: see vi. 22. 4 and vii. 32. 1–2 nn.

8. iussique consules . . . transiret: normally we meet sortition for provinces at the beginning of the year (vi. 30. 3 n. with *addendum*). However, its use here was perfectly natural: a new war had broken out; both consuls were together; and there was no obvious reason why one rather than the other should cross from Samnium to Etruria.

45. 9–11. CARVILIUS CAPTURES VELIA, PALUMBINUM, AND HERCULANEUM

The narrative continues from 44. 9, where Carvilius was left leading his troops to Velia. *iam* (§ 1), the pluperfect *ceperat* (§ 1), and the reference to the capture of not only Velia but also Palumbinum and Herculaneum show that some time has passed; we should therefore view § 8 'iam'–§ 11 'caperentur' as happening simultaneously with events at Rome described in the previous section. Then with § 11 'sortientibus', the narrative moves forward: we infer that the views of the senate recorded in § 8 have reached the consuls, and Carvilius moves to Etruria. By recounting Carvilius' campaign first, L. allows himself the possibility of recounting in one unbroken stretch the final activities of Papirius Cursor in 293. His style is here plain and matter-of-fact.

9. Veliam . . . Veliam: see 44. 9 n.

Palumbinum: the location of this settlement is unknown. For the speculations of scholars see above, pp. 384–6.

Herculaneum: if this is a reference to the town on the Bay of Naples buried after the eruption of Vesuvius in AD 79 and made famous by excavations in the eighteenth and nineteenth centuries (which is just conceivable but not very likely), then it needs no note. If it refers to a Samnite settlement of this name, then we do not know its location; for La Regina's suggestion that it refers to the large sanctuary at Campochiaro (probably the *fanum Herculis Rani* of the Peutinger Table), see above, p. 388.

intra paucos dies . . . eodem quo ad muros accessit: since the Romans so carefully enumerated other aspects of campaigns (for the duration of a campaign and the number of towns captured, see ix. 45. 17 nn.) one would have expected them to have recorded the duration

of sieges. However, to compare with our passage I have found only
xxxvi. 23. 6 (which derives from Polybius) and Cic. *Att.* v. 20. 1
'Saturnalibus mane se mihi Pindenissitae dediderunt, septimo et
quinquagesimo die postquam oppugnare eos coepimus'. For *ad
muros accedere*, see ix. 40. 19 n.

10. signis conlatis: see viii. 17. 9 n.

11. capta . . . caperentur: see 14. 21 n. for the figures for enemy
captured, vii. 17. 9 n. for a general discussion of casualty figures.
euenit: see vii. 6. 8 n.
uim frigoris: central Samnium experiences heavy snow in winter,
and the higher mountains are sometimes clad in snow from late
October until April.

45. 12–46. 9. PAPIRIUS CURSOR CAPTURES SAEPINUM AND
TRIUMPHS

L. returns to Papirius Cursor, who at 44. 9 had been left marching to
Saepinum, and describes his last activities in 293 in an unbroken
stretch of narrative. From § 12 'Papirio ad Saepinum maior uis
hostium restitit' it may be inferred both that Papirius was detained
at Saepinum while Carvilius was capturing the three settlements
mentioned in §§ 8–10 and that it was at Saepinum that the consuls
drew lots. The reference to the winter (46. 1) at the end of the
description of the fighting in Samnium parallels the earlier reference
to the winter at the end of the description of Carvilius' campaign (45.
11). Apart from the anaphora of *saepe* (introducing an expanding
tricolon) and *nec* in § 12, his style remains unadorned.

12–14. *The capture of Saepinum.* L.'s comments are regularly quoted
by local antiquarians as good evidence for the nature of the fighting
at Saepinum; but, though it is possible that they are reliable, it is very
much more likely that they rest on no more authority than annalistic
inference and reconstruction.

12. Saepinum: for once in L.'s account of the events of 293 a place-
name may be linked securely to topographical and archaeological
evidence. The very extensive remains of the Roman *municipium* at
Saepinum may still be seen at Altilia in the *comune* of Sepino. The
Samnite stronghold, however, was situated some 3 km to the south-
west, on the hill known to-day as Terravecchia (953 m.). Here, inter-

FIG. 7 The so-called 'Postierla del Matese' at Saepinum

spersed with the ruins of mediaeval occupation, lie some splendid fortifications; and the quality of these, combined with L.'s account of the heroic Samnite resistance to Rome, has led to Terravecchia becoming the most celebrated of all Samnite fortified sites. It stands between the Matese and the south-eastern extremity of the Boiano–Sepino plain, the most fertile part of the Samnite heartland; its steep slopes offered refuge to the dwellers on this plain. From its summit there is a commanding view over the upper Tammaro valley, and in particular towards the neighbouring fortifications of the Rocca of Monteverde and Monte Saraceno of Cercemaggiore. The fortified circuit is best preserved on the south-western flank of the hill (i.e. that which faces the Matese), and the so-called Postierla del Matese (see FIG. 7) is a particularly well-preserved postern. See further Maiuri (1926) 250–1, Colonna (1962), Salmon (1967) pl. 5, Coarelli and La Regina (1984) 226–8, and Oakley (1995) 69–71 (the last two with plan of fortifications).

saepe . . . pugnatum: for the anaphora and the phrasing cf. Vell. ii. 47. 1 'pugnatum saepe derecta acie, saepe in agminibus, saepe eruptionibus'.

acie: formal pitched battle (see vii. 11. 10 n.), to which one would not have expected the Samnites to have exposed themselves. For a not dissimilar comment, cf. xxi. 8. 7 'nihil tumultuariae pugnae simile erat, quales in oppugnationibus urbium per occasionem partis alterius conseri solent, sed iustae acies uelut patenti campo inter ruinas muri . . . constiterant'.

in agmine: 'on the march'. Notoriously, it was harder to fend off attackers when marching; for a well-known example, see Sall. *Iug.* 97. 3–99. 3.

obsidio nec is the reading of P(= PGrZ), championed powerfully by Stroth; λ had *obsidioni nec*; M, followed by most editors, has *obsidio sed*. If M were right, L. would be stating that, as a result of the attacks by the Samnites on the Romans (*a*) in formal pitched battles, (*b*) when they (the Romans) were marching, and (*c*) in the form of sallies from the town, the campaign was not a siege but a war fought on the level (or 'on equal terms': see next n.). This gives reasonable sense, is stemmatically possible (for M alone in the truth see vol. i, pp. 321–4 with *addendum*), and postulates an easy corruption in Pλ (*sed* replaced by *nec* because of perseveration from the preceding *nec*).

Nevertheless, the reading of P (of which that of λ seems to be a corruption) gives better sense, namely that the campaign was neither a siege nor a war fought on the level (or 'on equal terms'). The preceding 'aduersus eruptiones hostium' and the following 'non enim muris magis', both of which make clear that some of the time the enemy were retreating behind their walls, show that the campaign was not entirely *ex aequo* and was sometimes an *obsidio*. This interpretation is confirmed by § 13 'obsidionem iustam': *iustam* has much more point if the proper siege that Papirius finally enforces is contrasted not with *bellum ex aequo* but with the whole *nec obsidio nec bellum ex aequo*.

ex aequo probably means 'on the level': the following sentence introduced by *non enim* shows that the enemy sometimes left their fortifications and ceased to fight from a superior position; cf. 43. 6 'ex aequo pugnabant', vii. 23. 8, and esp. *pan.* vi. 19. 6 '. . . ut sibi non murum scandere sed ex aequo congredi uiderentur'; also xliv. 31. 7–8 where fighting from behind walls is contrasted with fighting *loco aequo*. *ex aequo* can mean 'on level terms' (see e.g. xxxix. 36. 1), but, despite L.'s approval (see next n.), he is unlikely to have regarded the Samnite force as the equal of the Roman.

non enim muris magis se quam armis ac uiris moenia tutabantur: L. speaks approvingly; for comments of this kind, see ix. 23. 11 n.

13. tandem . . . expugnauit: for *ui atque operibus* and *obsidionem
. . . obsidendoque*, see respectively vi. 3. 10 and 32. 8 nn.

14. ira: see ix. 13. 3 n.
septem . . . hominum: see 14. 21 n. for the figure for enemy captured, and vii. 17. 9 nn. for general discussion of casualty figures.
praeda . . . militi concessa est: for this practice see vi. 2. 12 n. with
addendum; for the stock language see vi. 13. 6 n.

46. 1. niues: see 45. 11 n.

2–8. *The triumph of Papirius Cursor.* In his account of the triumphs
of Papirius Cursor and Carvilius Maximus (§§ 13–15 below) L.'s
reporting of the ceremony for the first time becomes more expansive
and closer in style to similar passages in the later books. Among
previous descriptions of triumphs detail of this kind is anticipated
only at 30. 10 'data ex praeda militibus aeris octogeni bini sagaque et
tunicae', where L. reports the donative given by Fabius Rullianus to
his troops in 295. In the later books triumphs and ovations are
reported in meticulous detail, and in a fixed pattern which paralleled
the nature of the ceremonies themselves. The account of the triumph
of C. Cornelius Cethegus in 197, selected because of its comparative
brevity, exemplifies this (xxxiii. 23. 4–7):[1]

C. Cornelius de Insubribus Cenomanisque in magistratu triumphauit.
multa signa militaria tulit. multa Gallica spolia captiuis carpentis trans-
uexit, multi nobiles Galli ante currum ducti, inter quos quidam Hamil-
carem ducem Poenorum fuisse auctores sunt; ceterum magis in se conuertit
oculos Cremonensium Placentinorumque colonorum turba, pilleatorum
currum sequentium. aeris tulit in triumpho ducenta triginta septem milia
quingentos, argenti bigati undeoctoginta milia; septuageni aeris militibus
diuisi, duplex equiti centurionique.

We should note the careful enumeration of several standard features
and the regular order in which they are listed: military standards,
spoil, captives, rescued allies, bronze, silver, and the donative. So
also in our passage, after a reference to the troops and their decorations which is not present at xxxiii. 23. 4–7, we find the spoil (§ 4 n.),
the captives (§ 4 n.), the bronze (§ 5 n.), the silver (§ 5 n.), and the

---

[1] The formulaic nature of L.'s later notices of triumphs and ovations has been analysed by
Phillips (1974*b*); she lists these notices at pp. 266–7, but unfortunately does not provide a full
discussion of the principal matter with which we shall be most concerned, that is the standard
features in the accounts of the triumphal procession itself.

(absence of) a donative; the order is identical. The account of the triumph of Carvilius is briefer, but note again the references to the quantity of bronze brought into the *aerarium* and to the donative (§ 15 n.). In both passages, and at 30. 10, the references to the precise amounts of bronze, and in ours to the precise amount of silver, are particularly significant. This suggests that for the first time in his narrative of 295, and then again of this year, L. had access to, or chose to use, detailed information about a triumph which went back to official records (the existence of such records is attested explicitly at Cic. *IIVerr*. i. 57 and is an obvious inference from triumphal notices in L. and others). This view is further supported by other details or expressions with parallels in L.'s description of later triumphs; see on *omnium consensu* (§ 2), *triumphauit* (§ 2), *in magistratu* (§ 2), *transiere ac transuecti sunt* (§ 3), *tulit in aerarium* (§ 14), and *militibus ex praeda . . . diuisit* (§ 15).[1]

2. omnium consensu: for this kind of comment on a triumph, cf. e.g. iii. 10. 2, vi. 42. 8, viii. 13. 9, xxxiii. 23. 1, 37. 10, xxxvii. 46. 2, 58. 3, and xxxix. 42. 2; conversely note 37. 12 and iii. 63. 8 'ubi cum ingenti consensu patrum negaretur triumphus . . .'. Such remarks reflect the fact that the award of a triumph might be disputed (see 37. 6–12 n.). L. was rather prone to making generalizations like *omnium consensu*: for the period after 219 he will often have had good evidence as to whether or not triumphs were controversial; but it is unlikely that his statements for the fifth and fourth centuries rest on authentic testimony. Our passage stands between the two classes, but, since the award of a triumph to Papirius can hardly have been controversial, it is only an academic question whether or not L. here had good evidence for his statement. It contrasts with the disputed triumph of Postumius Megellus in the previous year (37. 6–12 n.).

triumphauit . . . insigni triumpho: for the pattern of *triumphauit* introducing the description of the triumph proper after L.'s account of the preliminary debate on whether or not to allow the triumph, cf. iii. 10. 4, xxxi. 49. 2, xxxiii. 37. 10, xxxvii. 58. 4, 59. 2, xxxix. 5. 13, and xli. 13. 7. For the *figura etymologica* here see ix. 15. 10 n.

in magistratu: for this comment, cf. xxxi. 49. 2, xxxiii. 23. 4, 37. 10, xli. 13. 7; note also xxxvii. 59. 6 'triumphauit anno fere post quam consulatu abiit'. These remarks in the later books probably go back to

---

[1] Although the schematic pattern found in L.'s later triumphal reports may owe something to the work of the annalists (note the interest taken by Valerius Antias in these matters [xlv. 40. 1, 43. 8]), and although some details in them may be invented (see Briscoe on xxxvii. 46. 3 and 59. 6), most of the material that he presents probably goes back to authentic testimony.

official records: by the second century, when wars tended to be fought far from Rome, the early republican norm of consuls' triumphing in their magistracy had become increasingly rare, and hence the triumph of the pro-magistrate was very common; cf. xxxvi. 39. 10 (the views of P. Sempronius Blaesus) 'proconsulem P. Cornelium, multorum exemplo qui in magistratu non triumphauerunt, triumphaturum esse'. Our passage may reflect the fact that already by 293 the principle of proroguing commands had been established (viii. 23. 12 n.). It too may go back to official records at Rome, but, if so, it is slightly surprising that the fact that Papirius triumphed in his magistracy was thought worthy of record, since before 293 only one proconsul had triumphed (Q. Publilius Philo in 326 [viii. 27. 7]). See further J. S. Richardson (1975) 50–2.

ut illorum temporum: see 30. 10 n.

3. insignes donis: at a triumph the troops displayed their *dona* in front of them as they marched: see xxxix. 7. 3, Prop. iv. 3. 68, and Val. Max. iii. 2. 24. For the numerous troops decorated by Papirius see also 44. 3–5.

transiere ac transuecti s⟨unt⟩: verbs compounded in *trans-* are regular in L.'s triumphal notices (although *transiere* cannot be paralleled, *tra(ns)uehere* is used also at § 5, xxxiii. 23. 4, 37. 11, xxxvi. 40. 11, xxxix. 7. 2). Phillips (1974*a*) may have been correct to argue that this refers to the ritual crossing of the *pomerium*; but *trans-* could mean just 'past the eyes of the onlookers', as in the *transuectio equitum* (see *OLD s.uu. transuectio* 2 and *transueho* 3). Πλ had *transuecti*, which makes sense and could be right (note the ellipse of the auxiliary in the following sentence). However, if L. did not write *transuecti sunt* (found first in some *recentiores* reported by Drakenborch), it is hard to explain why M, our most 'honest' ms., has *transuectis*.

multae . . . conspectae: for the civic and mural crowns, see vi. 20. 7 nn. The *corona uallaris* was awarded for being the first on the rampart of the enemy camp. References to it in our sources for the Republic are rare (see Val. Max. i. 8. 6 and, perhaps, Liv. xxx. 28. 6), and it may even have been introduced after 293. See further Gell. v. 6. 17 and Paul. Fest. 49 (who both call it the *corona castrensis*), Steiner (1906) 34–5, Fiebiger, *RE* iv. 1641, and Maxfield (1981) 79–80.

4. spolia: for the display of captured spoil at a triumph, cf. e.g. iv. 10. 7, xxxiii. 23. 4, 23. 8, 37. 11, xxxiv. 52. 4–7, xxxvi. 40. 11, xxxix. 5. 15,

7. 2, xlv. 43. 3; its paradoxical absence is noted at xxxi. 49. 3 and xlv. 42. 2.

frequenti publicorum ornatu locorum: for one such instance see ix. 40. 16 n.

nobiles aliquot . . . ducti: captives were paraded at triumphs in front of the victor's chariot: see e.g. vi. 4. 2, 16. 5, and vii. 27. 8. Naturally important captives aroused particular interest: see e.g. iii. 29. 4, iv. 10. 7, xxx. 45. 4–5, xxxiii. 23. 5, xxxiv. 52. 9, xxxvi. 40. 11, xxxvii. 59. 5, xxxix. 5. 16, 7. 2, xl. 34. 8, xlv. 40. 6, 43. 6, Hor. *carm.* i. 37. 31–2, Prop. iv. 6. 66, Tac. *ann.* xii. 36. 1–37. 4, and Eutrop. vi. 16. (The absence of captives is noted at xxxi. 49. 3, xl. 38. 9, and xlv. 42. 2.)

For *aliquot* in Zλ, which gives the required sense, MP¹ have *aliquos* and PᶜGr *aliqui* (the last reading is probably a progressive corruption of the second; the Z-witnesses perhaps have the first by contamination, as the agreement against them of MP¹ suggests). Either there were variants in **N** or λ made a correct conjecture; for λ alone, or almost alone, in the truth, add this passage to those cited at vol. i, p. 323.

clari suis patrumque factis: for the expression see ix. 7. 2 n.

5. aeris . . . triginta: the enumeration of the amount of money brought in by a returning general is an almost ubiquitous feature of L.'s later triumphal notices; cf. § 14, xxx. 45. 3, xxxi. 49. 2, xxxiii. 23. 7, 23. 9, xxxiv. 52. 4–7, xxxvi. 40. 12, xl. 16. 11, 34. 8, xlv. 40. 1, and 43. 5. This passage and § 14 are the first precise reports in our sources of the sum of money brought back by a general for the treasury; the next such notice (at D.H. xix. 16. 3) concerns the campaign of Fabricius in 282 (400 talents).

trauecta: see § 3 n. After offering *transuecti* at § 3, the mss here provide *trauecta*. Both spellings are well attested by the mss elsewhere, and there is no rational way of deciding which L. is likely to have written. Indeed, since we cannot be certain that he did not vary his spelling within the same paragraph, I have not tried to standardize. See also 37. 3 n.

quingenti is Gelenius' restoration for *a* in **N** (for the corruption see 14. 21 n.). Gelenius comments 'syncera lectio', which is ambiguous as to whether the reading derives from a ms. or from his own divination. For this problem see vol. i, pp. 174–9.

id aes redactum ex captiuis dicebatur: see vi. 2. 12, vii. 27. 8 nn.

pondo mille is Alschefski's conjecture for p̄ (Πλ) or p̄ *co.* (M). *mille* accounts for *co.* in M, which may be a corruption of cIɔ, the regular abbreviation for *mille*. For similar corruptions elsewhere in the text of L. see McDonald (1965) p. xvii. *pondo* expands the $\bar{p}$ found in all the mss.

octingenti is Alschefski's conjecture for **N**'s *accc*; for the corruption see again 14. 21 n.

6. aucta . . . potuisset: this notice about the refusal of Cursor to pay a donative or alleviate the burden of *tributum* is perhaps to be explained by § 5 'id aes redactum ex captiuis dicebatur': Cursor had allowed the troops to keep booty at Saepinum (45. 14), but there and elsewhere he may have made an exception with regard to the captives, who were often retained by the commander himself. L. perhaps implies that he did not give a donative to the troops because it would have come from money that was not generally (or always) given to them.

There is no obvious motive for the fabrication of the notice, and it is probably sound. As Rome was in the middle of the most extensive (and doubtless expensive) war in which she had ever been engaged, Cursor may have felt that the replenishment of the treasury was an urgent priority; and that may also explain why the money was saved rather than used to pay *tributum*. It may be significant that in 293 the patrician consul showed concern for the treasury, the plebeian for his troops. For the meanness of some commanders towards their troops in our sources for early Roman history, and for some other matters discussed in this n., see vi. 2. 12 n. with *addendum*; for *stipendium* and *tributum* see vi. 31. 4 n.

ad plebem: see vi. 34. 4 n.

gloria . . . captiuae pecuniae in aerarium inlatae: for the *ab urbe condita* construction see vi. 2. 9, ix. 40. 21 nn.

et militi ⟨do⟩num dari ex praeda et stipendium militare praestari potuisset is the text advocated by Madvig (1860: 198 = 1877: 239–40) for **N**'s *et militi tum dari ex praeda et stipendium militare praestare potuisset*. Exception has been taken to the paradosis on three counts: the switch from passive infinitive (*dari*) to active (*praestare*) (this is the gravest objection), the weak sense of *tum* (which must either be correlative to *si* [*OLD s.u.* 5(b)] or mean 'then, at the end of the campaign'), and the absence of a subject of *dari*. The easiest way of removing the first fault and of restoring some meaning is to read *dare* with P¹ for *dari* ('and then he would have been able to give to the soldiers out of the booty and to furnish military pay'). However, since *tum* remains weak and the absence of an object for *dare* is extremely awkward, most critics have preferred other remedies. All read *praestare* for *praestari* with F^c and other secondary mss, and most eliminate *tum*, replacing it with a noun or pronoun that may serve as subject for *dari*. For *tum* Weissenborn (*Komm.*[3]) proposed *munus* (which is excellent in sense but postulates an improbable corruption), Koch (1861: 8) *aliquantum* (which is rather weak),[1] and F. Walter (1918: 933–4) *debi⟨tum⟩* (which is rather strong and gives a substantivized participle that L. does not use elsewhere). However, Madvig's conjecture in the lemma is as apt in sense as Weissenborn's and diplomatically as easy as, or easier than, all the others. A different approach was taken by Watt (2002: 184–5), who would delete *tum* as a dittographic corruption of *-ti* and understand *aliquid* from the preceding *nihil* (for the phenomenon he cited H–S 825); this too is attractive. Walters alone retained *tum*, adapting Madvig's proposal by reading *tum ⟨donum⟩ dari*: diplomatically this is the easiest conjecture of all, and it supplies a subject for *dari*, but it leaves *tum* untouched. Another possibility is to read *dare* and retain *praestare* with Madvig's *donum* or any of the other emendations of *tum* listed above, except Watt's.

praestari: for *praesto* in the context of *stipendium*, cf. e.g. v. 32. 5 'Volsiniensibus . . . ut . . . stipendium . . . eius anni exercitui praestarent . . . indutiae datae', xxviii. 34. 11, and xlii. 6. 6; it is also found in the more general context of reparations after war (e.g. ii. 18. 11, xxxvii. 35. 4).

7. aedem Quirini: for this dedication cf. Plin. *nat.* vii. 213 'princeps solarium horologium statuisse ante XII annos quam cum Pyrrho bellatum est ad aedem Quirini L. Papirius Cursor, cum eam dedicaret a patre suo uotam, a Fabio Vestale proditur. sed neque facti horologii rationem uel artificem significat nec unde translatum sit aut apud quem scriptum id inuenerit. M. Varro primum statutum in publico secundum Rostra in columna tradit bello Punico primo . . .'.[2] Quirinus was an old Roman deity (viii. 9. 6 n.), and the Romans believed that his cult on the Quirinal long preceded the construction of this temple (see e.g. iv. 21. 9 [a reference to the senate meeting in the temple in 435], Cic. *rep.* ii. 20, *leg.* i. 3, Ov. *fast.* ii. 511–12, Plin. *nat.* xv. 120 'inter antiquissima namque delubra habetur Quirini'); therefore it is almost certain that the temple dedicated by Cursor

---

[1] Koch anticipated Harant (1880: 68).

[2] Since the Pyrrhic War is generally held to have begun in 280, when Laevinus was defeated at Heraclea, the figure *XII* is awkward. Bruno (1906: 67 n. 4) therefore wondered whether Papirius made his dedication as praetor in 292; but it is easier either to emend to *XIII* or, better, to argue that Vestalis/Pliny thought that the Pyrrhic War began in 281, when Pyrrhus arrived in Italy.

replaced an earlier temple on the same site (Servius [*Aen*. i. 292] states that there was only one temple of Quirinus in the city itself). The day of dedication was almost certainly the Quirinalia (17 February): see Degrassi, *I.I*. xiii. 2. pp. 411–12 (*fast. Ant. Mai.*) and Ov. *fast*. ii. 475–512. Wiseman (1995*a*: 127) suggests that the dedication of this new temple points to this epoch as the time when Romulus is likely to have been equated with Quirinus. Although Pliny at *nat*. vii. 213 appears to be drawing attention to a discrepancy between Fabius Vestalis and Varro over when and where Rome's first sun-dial was set up, there is no obvious motive for Vestalis or his source(s) to invent the notion that Cursor affixed a sundial to the temple of Quirinus. The temple was hit by lightning in 206 (xxviii. 11. 4) and burnt in 49 (Dio xli. 14. 3), after which it seems to have been swiftly restored (an inference from Dio xliii. 45. 3). Its precise site on the Quirinal is disputed. See further Platner and Ashby (1929) 438–9, Degrassi, loc. cit. and pp. 303–4, L. Richardson (1992) 326–7, and F. Coarelli in Steinby (1993–2000) iv. 185–7 (with large bibliography and further ancient references to the temple; he favours a site east of the Via delle Quattro Fontane).

quam . . . potuisset: the weight of the clause falls on *ueterem*, as L. elegantly exposes a late annalistic fiction: one of his sources seems to have written an account of the battle in which Cursor was actually made to vow the temple.

in ipsa dimicatione: rather Cursor vowed his *mulsum* (42. 7).

hercule: see vii. 11. 1 n.

ab dictatore patre uotam filius consul dedicauit: when the elder Cursor made his vow is not known. For a son dedicating a temple vowed by his father see 1. 9 n.

dedicauit was deleted in the Aldine edn.; but the sentence starts again after the parenthesis and the repetition of the word is harmless.[1] For the rules governing dedication see ix. 46. 6–7 n.; see also Weigel (1998) 122.

exornauitque hostium spoliis: see vi. 4. 2–3 n.

8. sed . . . diuiderentur: for the practice of Roman commanders' sharing spoil among allied towns and colonies, cf. xliii. 4. 6–7, *ILLRP* 321 (L. Quinctius Flamininus), 321a (M'. Acilius Glabrio), 322 (M. Fulvius Nobilior), 326 (Scipio Aemilianus), 327–31 (L. Mummius), 332 (Ser. Fulvius Flaccus), and 335 (C. Sempronius Tuditanus), Cic. *IIVerr*. i. 55, ii. 3, and Vitr. v. 5. 8. All this evidence

---

[1] As Profesor Woodman points out to me, one could also delete the first instance of *dedicauit*.

relates to gifts and dedications made, or public works commissioned, by victorious generals a century or more after Aquilonia, but the practice seems to be the same as that mentioned here.

colon⟨i⟩isque: Madvig (1860: 198 = 1877: 240) argued that a reference to colonies as opposed to colonists should be spelt thus; later the reading was found in u and Aᵛ, neither a witness of any authority. However, it is not certain that L. would have spelt the dative or ablative plural of *colonia* with a double *i* (see 21. 9 n.), and I adopt this spelling simply to conform to modern convention.

9. infesta ab: see vi. 5. 3 n.

46. 10–16. THE ETRUSCAN CAMPAIGN AND TRIUMPH OF CARVILIUS

L. now turns to the final activities of Carvilius in 293; his style remains unadorned.

10. inter haec: see ix. 12. 5 n.
Troilum: Cluverius' identification of this otherwise unknown place with Trossulum, a site nine Roman miles south of Volsinii and known only because it was captured by the Roman cavalry without the assistance of the footsoldiers (Plin. *nat.* xxxiii. 35, Paul. Fest. 505, Σ Pers. 1. 82), has met with the approval of e.g. Ruperti and Harris (1971: 76 n. 7); but Volsinii had made peace the previous year (37. 4), and otherwise unrecorded hostilities between her and Rome are not very probable. The identification is rejected by e.g. Dennis (1907: i. 524–5) and De Sanctis (1907–64: ii. 362 n. 2).
pecunia grandi: as the testimony of the Romance languages proclaims, *grandis* came to triumph over *magnus*. Perhaps because of its popularity in the spoken language, many writers of elevated prose show a certain restraint in using it. Although Cicero shows less restraint than some, it is notable that in fifteen out of thirty-six instances in his speeches it qualifies *pecunia* (as it does in our passage). Caesar uses it four times, thrice in *Gall.* vii, a total surpassed by the author of the *bellum Africum*, whose seven instances reveal his less fastidious taste. Among the historians, L. uses it on only four other occasions, twice with *pecunia* (xxvii. 20. 7, xxxii. 40. 8), once of a large animal (xxv. 9. 13), and once with *periculum* (xxi. 50. 10); Sallust on five occasions, once with *pecunia* (*Cat.* 49. 3), twice with *aes alienum* (*Cat.* 14. 2, 24. 3), once of a ship (*hist.* iii fr. 8), and once of a tree (*Iug.* 93. 4); Curtius never; and Tacitus, perhaps

(somewhat surprisingly) influenced by the advance of the adjective in the spoken language during the principate, on fifteen occasions. Note too that Sisenna (fr. 105) uses it of a ship. In addition to *TLL* vi. 2179. 26–2188. 36, see Löfstedt (1911) 73 and Adams (forthcoming).

11. ceteram multitudinem: see ix. 24. 14 n.
ui cepit: see vi. 3. 10 n.

12. caesa ibi hostium duo milia quadringenti, minus duo milia capti: for the figure for enemy captured and for general discussion of casualty figures, see, respectively, 14. 21 and vii. 17. 9 nn. *caesa* and *capti* are somewhat irregular, for when L. gives a fraction of a thousand, he usually uses the masculine, and when he does not, he usually uses the neuter. Therefore *capta* (read by several of the *recentiores* cited by Drakenborch [including X] and commended by Wesenberg [1870/1: 41]) could be right; but *minus* perhaps encouraged L. to assimilate the gender to the masculine required for a number below 2,000, and there are analogies for a masculine following on from the neuter *milia*: see xxi. 21. 13 'quattuor milia conscripta . . . praesidium eosdem et obsides' and xliv. 42. 7 'ad sex ⟨milia⟩, qui Pydnam ex acie perfugerant, uiui in potestatem peruenerunt, et uagi ex fuga quinque milia hominum capta'. *caesi*, too, could be right, but cf. 43. 8 'caesa ad quattuor milia octingenti octoginta'. See further K–S i. 26.
pacem . . . militibus: see ix. 41. 6–7 n.

13. ad triumphum decessit: see viii. 19. 9 n.
ut . . . aequatum: for similar comments on the relative splendour of the triumphs of one year, cf. xxviii. 9. 11–18 (on Claudius Nero and Livius Salinator), xxxiii. 23. 8 (Minucius and Cethegus) 'is triumphus ut loco et fama rerum gestarum et quod sumptum non erogatum ex aerario omnes sciebant inhonoratior fuit, ita signis carpentisque et spoliis ferme aequabat', xlv. 43. 1–4 (Anicius and Aemilius Paullus), and D.H. v. 47. 2 (a triumph compared with an ovation [on which see *addendum* to vii. 11. 9 n.]). For other passages commenting on the degree of splendour of a triumph, cf. xxx. 45. 2 'triumpho . . . omnium clarissimo', xxxvii. 59. 2–6 'qui triumphus spectaculo oculorum maior quam Africani fratris eius fuit, recordatione rerum et aestimatione periculi certaminisque non magis comparandus quam si imperatorem imperatori aut Antiochum ducem Hannibali conferres', xl. 59. 1, D.H. ii. 55. 5 (where the idea is retrojected to the regal period), Tac. *ann.* xii. 38. 1, and see vii. 15. 8 n.

cumulo Etrusci belli: *cumulus* is regular in the sense *augmentum*; for the explanatory genitive see *TLL* iv. 1388. 6–36.

14. tulit in aerarium: a regular expression in descriptions of triumphs; cf. e.g. xxviii. 9. 16, xxx. 45. 3, xxxi. 49. 2, xxxiv. 10. 4, and xli. 28. 7 (also xxviii. 38. 5 and xxxii. 7. 4, in which commanders return to Rome but do not triumph). The plain *tulit* is also regular in descriptions of triumphs; cf. e.g. vi. 29. 8 'triumphansque signum Praeneste deuectum Iouis Imperatoris in Capitolium tulit', xxxiii. 23. 7, xxxiv. 46. 2, xli. 13. 7. See further vi. 2. 12 n. with *addendum* and Phillips (1974*b*) 271–2.

reliquo aere is distributed by *de manubiis* and *ex praeda*, as W–M noted.

aedem ... locauit: for the financing out of one's spoil of a building which might serve as a memorial to oneself, see viii. 30. 9 n.; for *locatio*, see ix. 43. 25 n.

Fortis Fortunae ... prope aedem eius deae ab rege Ser. Tullio dedicatam: the etymology of Fors Fortuna is disputed but the double formation should probably be compared with names of gods like Aius Locutius and Ops Opifera. For the festival of the goddess, see Ov. *fast.* vi. 773–86; for her special connection with the plebs and slaves, see ll. 781–4. In the decision of Carvilius to build this temple, it is tempting to see some rivalry with his consular colleague, who had just dedicated the temple of Quirinus. The choice of deity also had ideological significance: Fortuna, the goddess who raised lowly plebeians to the heights of the consulship and a triumph was a very appropriate deity for him to adopt; and, if already at this date the myth of Servius Tullius had developed, Carvilius was making a pointed recall of a dedication by Rome's lowliest-born king. The choice of deity almost certainly reflects the influence of Greek Τύχη and therefore provides a good example of the influence of Greek thought on Rome's religious life in this period (see above, p. 22). See further Champeaux (1982–7) i. 207–47 and ii. 69–72.

 Servius Tullius is said to have built his temple of Fors Fortuna on the right bank of the Tiber outside the city (Varr. *ling.* vi. 17, D.H. iv. 27. 7); its day of dedication was 24 June (Varro loc. cit., Ov. *fast.* loc. cit., *Fast. Esquilin.*, *Fast. Mag. Vic.*, and *Fast. Amitern.* [*I.I.* xiii. 2, pp. 88–9, 92, 187]), and, even if Servius Tullius himself did not exist, there is no need to doubt that there was an archaic temple of Fors Fortuna. However, the *Fasti* refer to two temples of Fors Fortuna, both on the Via Portuensis and both dedicated on 24 June, one near the first milestone, the other near the sixth. It is tempting to argue that L.'s *prope* is wrong and to equate the more distant of the temples mentioned by the *Fasti* with that of Carvilius (thus Latte [1960a] 124, Champeaux [1982–7] i. 202, and Ziolkowski); note that *CIL* i². 977 = *ILS* 9253 = *ILLRP* 96 (late republican) refers to two freedmen Carvilii among others worshipping Fors Fortuna there. However, Ovid (1. 784) mentions *templa propinqua*, and, unless he is using a poetic plural to refer to the temple of Servius alone, he presumably means two temples near to each other, which are most obviously understood as those of Servius and Carvilius (for all that Ovid, if he did intend a genuine plural, refers both to Servius). Since five miles does not constitute proximity, the question cannot be settled on available evidence.[1] In AD 17 Tiberius dedicated another temple, also on the right bank of the river, in the gardens of Julius Caesar (Tac. *ann.* ii. 41. 1), to which Plut. *Brut.* 20. 3 probably refers. The phenomenon of there being three or four temples of Fors Fortuna on the right bank of the Tiber is most odd, and would become odder still were the ascription of a temple of Fors Fortuna to Ancus Marcius at Plut. *mor.* 318e–f = *fort. Rom.* 5 not a mistake for Servius Tullius. See further Platner and Ashby (1929) 212–14, Syme (1956) 261–5 = (1979–91) i. 310–13, Degrassi, *I.I.* xiii. 2, pp. 472–3, Goodyear on Tac. loc. cit., Champeaux (1982–7) i. 199–207, L. Richardson (1992) 154–5, and Ziolkowski (1992) 38–9.

de manubiis: already by the second century AD the precise definition of *manubiae* was disputed (as Gell. xiii. 25 shows), and this uncertainty is reflected in modern discussions. Favorinus, whose views are reported by Gellius (esp. §§ 1–7, 28–32), demonstrated, what common sense dictates, that *manubiae* were not synonymous with *praeda* and held that (§ 29) they were 'pecunia per quaestorem populi Romani ex praeda uendita contracta'; but ps.-Asconius writes (p. 254) 'manubiae sunt autem praeda imperatoris pro portione de hostibus capta' and (p. 255) 'spolia quaesita de uiuo hoste nobili per deditionem manubias ueteres dicebant, et erat imperatorum haec praeda, ex qua quod uellent facerent' (with these passages compare also some glosses cited by Churchill [1999: 88]). Favorinus' view has been championed by several scholars (e.g. Mommsen [1887–8] i. 241 and Vogel, *RE* xxii. 1207) and finds its best support in Cato, *ORF* 203 'numquam ego praedam neque quod de hostibus captum esset neque manubias inter pauculos amicos meos diuisi', where explanation of the contrast between *quod de hostibus captum esset* and *manubi-*

---

[1] Ruperti tried to solve the problem by emendation, cleverly but very improbably proposing *prolapsa aede eidem* for *prope aedem eiusdem*.

ae as a contrast between portable plunder and plunder turned to cash is attractive; but against it, and in support of most of what ps.-Asconius says, are (*a*) passages which refer to the selling of *manubiae* (Cic. *agr.* i. fr. 4, ii. 53) and (*b*) the fact that dedications *de manubiis* were always made by men who had held *imperium*. It is therefore best to regard *manubiae* as that portion of booty that was reserved for the use of the commander: see e.g. Shatzman (1972) 179–88 and Churchill (1999) 87–93 (who argue [pp. 184 and 92] that the passage of Cato can also be explained as a contrast between the booty which was divided among the troops and that which was customarily reserved for the commander). The argument of Orlin (1997: 117–22), that *manubiae* were never precisely defined and that both definitions were current in republican times, is less attractive. Churchill may be right further to argue that *manubiae* was booty reserved by the commander during the campaign rather than after his triumph, but our evidence, which includes Vell. ii. 40. 3, does not allow this finally to be established. The reference to *de uiuo hoste* in ps.-Asconius may perhaps go back to the definition of *manubiae* in the early Republic. Whether ps.-Asconius was right to hold that a general could do what he liked with his *manubiae* is disputed: for the view that he could, see Shatzman (1972) 188–205; *contra* Churchill (1999) 188–205, who argues that *manubiae* had to be used for public works.

The expression *de manubiis* (or its rather less common variant *ex manubiis*) is used regularly to explain how a building or dedication was financed. For literary or epigraphic sources recording that work in Rome was financed in this way cf. e.g. xxxiii. 27. 4 'et de manubiis duos fornices in foro bouario . . . fecit', *ILLRP* 429, 431, and Suet. *Iul.* 26. 2. For many further parallels (including several from works financed outside Rome) see *TLL* viii. 336. 24–46 and Trisciuoglio (1998) 132–4.

Surprisingly few Romans are attested as having built temples *de manubiis*, but D. Junius Brutus (Val. Max. viii. 14. 2), Marius (*ILS* 59 = *I.I.* xiii. 3. 83), and Tiberius (Suet. *Tib.* 20) certainly join Carvilius; to their number may be added C. Papirius Maso and L. Licinius Lucullus on plausible interpretations of, respectively, Cic. *nat.* iii. 52 and Dio fr. 76. 2. See further Orlin (1997) 127–35, who shows that neither Marcellus nor Fulvius Nobilior financed his temple in this way (as Plut. *Marc.* 28. 2 states for the former and modern scholars have deduced from Cic. *Arch.* 27 for the latter).

faciendam: see vi. 32. 1 n.

15. militibus . . . diuisit: for the donative to the troops at the time of a triumph, cf. e.g. 30. 10, xxviii. 9. 17, xxx. 45. 3, xxxi. 20. 7, xl. 34. 8 (with no reference to variations in the size of the donative). For the double donative to centurions and cavalry, cf. xxxiii. 23. 7 and 23. 9; on one occasion (xxxiii. 37. 12) we meet a triple donative to both classes; but more frequently centurions were given a double donative, and cavalry a triple donative (xxxiv. 46. 3,[1] 52. 11, xxxvi. 40. 13, xxxvii. 59. 6, xxxix. 5. 17, 7. 2, xl. 43. 7, 59. 2, xli. 7. 3, 13. 7, xlv. 40. 5 [*e coni.*], 43. 7).[2] These passages show that before 194 (xxxiv. 46. 3), when the pattern of a double donative to centurions and a triple to cavalry began to become standard, various permutations were deemed acceptable. Although L. does not here use the word *duplex* (so regular in his later notices), our passage is of interest for showing gradations in the donative operating at an early date; and the equal amount which it records for centurions and cavalry should be used to reinforce Briscoe's arguments (on xxxiii. 23. 7) against emendation of xxxiii. 23. 7 and 37. 12. Special rewards for *equites* are found also in the payment of *stipendium* (vii. 41. 8 n.) and, occasionally, in the distribution of land (xxxv. 9. 8, 40. 6). On donatives see further Brunt (1971) 394.

militibus ex praeda . . . diuisit is the first instance of what was to become quite a regular expression in L.; cf. xxx. 45. 3 'militibus ex praeda quadringenos aeris diuisit', xxxi. 20. 7, xxxiv. 46. 3, and xxxix. 5. 17; at § 5 and 30. 10 L. varies the expression with *dare* for *diuidere*. L. regularly uses *diuidere* in the context of triumphal donatives; cf. also e.g. xxxvi. 40. 13, xl. 34. 8, and 59. 2.

alterum tantum: see viii. 8. 14 n.

malignitate: for *malignitas* in the distribution of the booty derived from war, cf. ii. 42. 1 'malignitate patrum, qui . . . militem praeda fraudauere' and v. 20. 2 'malignitate praedae partitae'.

16. L. Postumium: i.e. L. Postumius Megellus, the consul of 294, for whom see ix. 44. 2 n., where prosecutions of him are discussed.

dicta die: perhaps on account of his conflict with several tribunes of the plebs whilst triumphing (37. 9–12). For tribunician prosecutions in this period, see *addendum* to vi. 1. 6 n.

---

[1] The mss read 'in singulos ducenos septuagenos aeris, triplex equiti'; but there is no parallel for a special donative being given to the cavalry and not to the centurions, and Gronovius was probably correct to insert *duplex centurioni* before *triplex*. *Contra* Briscoe ad loc.

[2] For similar gradations in the donative at a naval triumph, see xlv. 42. 3. Note too that *socii* are explicitly recorded as having been given as much as Romans at xl. 43. 7, xli. 7. 3, and xlv. 43. 7, but only half as much at xli. 13. 8.

M. Scantio: (1). Otherwise unknown. The only other known Scantius is mentioned in the Oxyrhynchus epitome of book l; a Scantia is mentioned at Tac. *ann.* iv. 16. 4.

in legatione[m]: there seems to have been a principle at Rome that someone who was absent on public service should not be prosecuted; see Suet. *Iul.* 23. 1, and note Caesar's offer of a legateship to Cicero in 59 (Cic. *Att.* ii. 18. 3, *prou.* 41–2). For an attempt to get round the principle see xli. 6. 2–3 (rightly interpreted by Bleicken [1955] 123–4).

The accusative is impossible (despite Allen [1864–74] i. 25, who cited Cic. *Tusc.* v. 109, which is not parallel). Available conjectures are *in legatione* (thus F and, independently, A. Perizonius), *legatione* (an alternative proposal of Perizonius), *per legationem* (Ruperti), and *enim legatione* (Weissenborn [ed.²]). The first conjecture is diplomatically easiest and is supported by xlv. 31. 5 'partis eius fautores . . . soli in legationibus erant' and 32. 6 'qui in legationibus fuerant'. The second and third are possible but less economical; the last is barely intelligible.

populi iudicium is the regular expression for trials before the *populus* or plebs (cf. e.g. iii. 56. 5, vii. 28. 9, xxix. 22. 9) but is not technical for any particular kind of trial and can be used of any verdict of the people (cf. e.g. viii. 37. 8). See further Lintott (1972) 247, improving on Mommsen (1887–8) iii. 351 n. 2.

iactari: see 37. 10 n.

47. 1–7. *Annalistic notices*

47. 1. THE ELECTION OF NEW TRIBUNES OF THE PLEBS

hisque: Wesenberg (1870/1: 41) may have been right to commend θ's *iisque*: see ix. 15. 4 n.

uitio creati erant: for this expression see vi. 27. 4–5 n. For a parallel in the election of plebeian magistrates, see xxx. 39. 8, where plebeian aediles are said to have been *uitio creati* and hence to have resigned (albeit after holding their games and without the election of suffects as replacements). For the implications of these passages for the question of whether or not tribunes of the plebs had the right to take the auspices, see *addendum* to vi. 41. 5. See further ix. 44. 15 n. (on suffects) and Mommsen (1887–8) iii. 364–5 (putting a different emphasis on the evidence).

47. 2. THE CENSUS

P. Cornelio Aruina C. Marcio Rutilo censoribus: on this censorship see Cram (1940) 84, *MRR* i. 179, and Suolahti (1963) 238–40; for Cornelius Arvina see ix. 42. 10 n., for Marcius Rutilus ix. 33. 1 n. Rutilus became censor again in 265, a unique achievement (cf. Val. Max. iv. 1. 3, Plut. *Cor.* 1. 1); if he was responsible for the erection of a statue of Marsyas at Rome (see ix. 33. 1 n.), this is the year in which he may have done it.

lustrum conditum eo anno est . . . censores uicesimi sexti a primis censoribus, lustrum undeuicesimum fuit: for the expression *lustrum condere*, cf. 9. 14, i. 44. 2, iii. 24. 10, xxvii. 36. 6, xxix. 37. 5–6, xxxv. 9. 2, xl. 46. 8, xlii. 10. 1, Varr. *ling.* vi. 87, Cic. *de or.* ii. 268, and Fest. 144; further instances from writers of the first and second centuries AD are collected at *TLL* iv. 152. 27–39. Although this expression almost certainly refers to a purificatory ritual, its precise meaning is unclear; for a discussion of diverse interpretations, see Ogilvie (1961), who himself thought that it meant 'to assemble or store the purifying agent'. The ceremony was performed by only one of the two censors (see e.g. p. 12 and Suolahti [1963] 31).

The Romans recorded and enumerated the successful completion of *lustra*, and evidence from these records found its way into the works of writers like L. who drew on annalistic sources. It will be convenient to discuss first the evidence for the censorship and completion of the *lustrum* in the period covered by books vi–x, then the similarities between our notice and those found in L.'s later books.

The number recorded here for the censorship differs from that for the *lustrum* because (*a*) *lustra* were completed, or allegedly completed, by kings and consuls before the censorship was instituted, and (*b*) not all censorial pairs completed their *lustrum* (L. mentions abortive censorships at vi. 27. 4 [380 BC] and vii. 1. 8 [360], *F.C.* one for 319). Since we know the names and/or dates of only nineteen censorial colleges (our evidence is tabulated at vol. i, pp. 48–9), it follows that six have disappeared without trace. The evidence for completed *lustra* assembled below shows that at least one of these colleges fell in the period between 419 and 404 and at least one between 362 and 319. It shows too that not all these missing colleges completed their *lustra*.

As regards the counting of successfully completed *lustra*, the computations of the annalists and antiquarians are reflected in (*a*) *F.C.*, which seem originally to have recorded all *lustra*, although their extant remains now provide evidence only for nos. 8 (474 BC), 16

(403), 20 (363), 25 (318), 26 (312), 27 (307), 30 (294), 32 (280), 33 (275), 34 (269), 35 (265), and some *lustra* following the First Punic War; (*b*) L., who mentions the first *lustrum* at i. 44. 2, the tenth at iii. 24. 10 (459 BC), and a *lustrum* in 465, which he does not number but which must have been the ninth (iii. 3. 9); and (*c*) Valerius Maximus, who tells us (iii. 4. 3) that Servius Tullius completed the first four *lustra*. However, in reconstructing the years in which the annalists believed that early *lustra* were completed this material may be supplemented by important evidence in D.H.: unlike L., he regularly records the consular censuses of the sixth and fifth centuries; see v. 20 (508) (where he states that the census had never been taken under Tarquinius Superbus), 75. 3–4 (498), vi. 96. 4 (493), ix. 36. 3 (474), and xi. 63 (459).

If one combines this evidence from D.H. with (*a*) the evidence for the numbering of *lustra* that is given by L., *F.C.*, and Valerius Maximus and (*b*) the evidence for censorships carried out by censors in 443 (the year in which censors were in office for the first time: iv. 8. 1–7), 435, 430, 418, 403, 393, 378, 366, and 363,[1] then one may calculate the date of the *lustra* down to 363 as follows: 1–4: under Servius Tullius, 5: 508, 6: 498, 7: 493, 8: 474, 9: 465, 10: 459, 11: 443, 12: 435, 13: 430, 14: 418, 16: 403, 17: 393, 18: 378, 19: 366, and 20: 363. Only the date of the fifteenth *lustrum*, between 419 and 404, remains unclear.

For the period between 362 and 318, the year for which *F.C.* record the completion of the twenty-fifth *lustrum*, the evidence for completed *lustra* cannot be harmonized with our evidence for censorships: five more *lustra* were completed, but we know of only four censorial colleges, of which that of 319 is unlikely to have completed the *lustrum*.

For the period 317–293, the evidence provided by *F.C.* may be combined with other sources which reveal when censors were in office, and this allows one to calculate the dates for the following completed *lustra*: 26: 312, 27: 307, 28: 304, 29: 300, and 30: 293.

N's reading *lustrum undeuicesimum fuit* tallies with our other evidence only if *a primis censoribus* is taken with it, and if L. is counting exclusively, even though normal Roman practice was to count inclusively. Since both conditions cause no difficulty (exclusive counting is easily paralleled in L.; see e.g. xxxiv. 53. 7, xxxvi. 36. 6, xl. 52. 1, and Briscoe on xxxi. 1. 3), there is need neither to follow Huschke (1838: 520 n. 12) and Mommsen (1866 = 1905–13: vii. 161–2) in

---

[1] The censorship of 380 was abortive; see vi. 27. 4.

championing the conjecture *inde uicesimum*, found in three *recentiores* reported by Drakenborch, diplomatically neat though it is, nor to adopt *illud uicesimum* (Weissenborn [ed.²]); see Zumpt (1871) 9–11 and Leuze (1912) 43–5. Yet it is odd that, unlike *F.C.* and L.'s own earlier practice, **N**'s text does not enumerate *lustra* from the first *lustrum*. For this reason it is tempting to adopt Ruperti's *tricesimum* and to interpret the sentence as *censores uicesimi sexti a primis censoribus, lustrum tricesimum* (sc. *a primo lustro*) *fuit*; but mss normally write *xuiiii* and not *xix*.

For the period after 293 the evidence of the *periochae* (there are notices of completed *lustra* in those for books xi, xiii, xiv, xvi, xviii, xix, and xx) may be combined with the fragments of *F.C.* to allow further enumeration of *lustra*: 31: 290(?), 32: 280, 33: 275, 34: 269, 35: 265, etc.[1] In books xxi–xlv L. records the completion of the *lustrum* (without, however, numbering the *lustra*) at xxvii. 36. 6, xxix. 37. 5–6, xxxv. 9. 2, xxxviii. 36. 10, xlii. 10. 1; note too references to it in *periochae* of later books. At xxiv. 43. 4 he records that the death of a censor precluded the completion of the *lustrum*.

The notices of the successful completion of the *lustrum* for both the censorships of book x provide a good example of the way in which the 'annalistic' information provided by L. gets fuller in this book. Of the two notices, our passage is the more interesting, since its form, in which the notice of the completion is followed by a figure for the number of persons registered, closely resembles that found in all the passages from books xxi–xlv cited above.

The fact that the estimations for the period before 293 listed above can be made shows that L., *F.C.*, D.H., and Valerius Maximus all drew on sources which calculated censorships and completed *lustra* in the same way. Although these sources were not necessarily free of invention (witness the four *lustra* ascribed to Servius Tullius), the notices for the period after 318, at least, are likely to be sound. In general L., as was his wont, selected from the official information available to him, in both books i–x (cf. vol. i, p. 39) and books xxi–xlv (in which, although he records all censorships, he does not bother to record all completed *lustra*; see e.g. xxxii. 7. 1–3); D.H. was more thorough than L. (albeit recording censuses, not *lustra*) but omitted the census in which the ninth *lustrum* was completed.

See further Berve, *RE* xii. 2047–50 and Leuze (1912) 45–8; also Zumpt (1871) 35–8 and Klinger (1884) 51–2.

---

[1] See further *MRR* i. 184–5, 188, 191, 196, 198, 199, and 202.

censa capitum milia ducenta sexaginta duo trecenta uiginti unum: see ix. 19. 2 n.

47. 3. THE *LUDI ROMANI*

coronati primum ob res bello bene gestas ludos Romanos spectarunt: for the *ludi Romani* see viii. 40. 2 n. This is the only passage in books vi–x properly to anticipate the notices concerning the *ludi Romani*, which are very common in the later 'annalistic' sections of L.'s work: see e.g. xxiii. 30. 16, xxv. 2. 8, xxvii. 6. 19, 21. 9, 36. 8, xxix. 38. 8, and xxxi. 50. 2; also 23. 13 (n.) on the plebeian games. For L.'s reporting of an innovation at the games cf. esp. vii. 2. 3–13 (nn.), xxiv. 43. 7, and xxxiv. 54. 4 'horum aedilium ludos Romanos primum senatus a populo secretus spectauit'; note too that the innovations recorded at viii. 20. 2 (n.) affected the games. For his reporting of games enlivened by recent success in war cf. xxxiii. 25. 1 'ludi Romani . . . laetius propter res bello bene gestas'.

Among its other connotations, the garland was a symbol of victory given to the winners of sporting contests (see e.g. Ganszyniec, *RE* xi. 1598–9). For the practice of the whole populace's wearing garlands at the *ludi*, see esp. xxv. 12. 15 (the games of Apollo) 'populus coronatus spectauit' and Serv. *Aen.* v. 71 'CINGITE TEMPORA RAMIS: ex Romano more. nam festis ludis omnis aetas coronata spectabat'. Analogous was the practice of wearing garlands at *supplicationes*, both celebratory (for which see Cato *de re militari* fr. 2 [= Gell. vi. 4. 5 and Fest. 400; Cato is punning on the double meaning of *corona*: 'garland' or being sold *sub corona*] 'ut populus sua opera potius ob rem bene gestam coronatus supplicatum eat, quam re male gesta coronatus ueneat' and Val. Max. i. 8. 6 [after a victory in 278 BC in which Mars was said to have appeared to the Romans] 'itaque Fabrici edicto supplicatio Marti est habita et a laureatis militibus magna cum animorum laetitia oblati auxilii testimonium ei est redditum', referring to events only fifteen years after those described in this passage [however Valerius, perhaps mistakenly, refers only to soldiers wearing garlands]) and expiatory (for which see xxxiv. 55. 4, xxxvi. 37. 5, xl. 37. 3, and xliii. 13. 8, all of which refer to garlands being worn by the *populus*). The passages of Cato and Valerius Maximus allow one to infer that watching the games was a ritual akin to a *supplicatio*. Servius implies that the Romans were always garlanded when they watched the games, but *ob rem bene gestam* in the passage of Cato suggests that they did so only in a year in which the games followed a victory. This would seem to be the import of *primum* and *ob res bello bene gestas* in our passage (implying that garlands were not worn in years in which there was no such success); it goes well with xxv. 12. 15 (note the preceding 'uictoriae'); and it is the better interpretation of republican practice. However, since there were Roman victories in many years of the Republic, Servius' comment may not be very misleading.

In an attempt to illustrate and explain our passage W–M cited Plb. vi. 39. 9, where we are told that those who had won *dona militaria* were alone allowed to wear crowns in festal processions in the city, and several similar privileges may also be adduced.[1] However, this phenomenon is somewhat different: these men could always advertise their honour at the games and in procession, the whole populace only at times when a victory had been won.

Like the presentation of *palmae* (see below), the custom of wearing garlands was taken over from the Greeks, who associated it with Νίκη; we therefore have further evidence for the Roman adoption of the ideology of victory in this period (see further 29. 14 n. and Weinstock [1957] 217). Both these Hellenizing innovations were celebrated on the silver coinage of the early third century: see Crawford (1974) 138–40, 714, and pl. I.

primum ... primum: see vii. 5. 9 n.

palmaeque tum primum translato e Graeco more uictoribus datae: presumably the victors had previously been adorned with garlands, but, when the whole populace had taken to wearing garlands, an extra symbol of victory was needed. For both emblems being given to victors in the games, cf. Vitr. ix. *pr.* 1 and 3 (with reference to Greek games), Plin. *nat.* viii. 161 (an anachronistic retrojection: for the context of the tale see the discussion of Ratumenna at 23. 12 n.), *CIL* vi. 2065. ii. 37–8, 2075. ii. 25–6, 2080. 44, and 2086. 46; the combination of the two is nicely illustrated by a money-box on which there is a depiction of a charioteer both adorned with a garland and carrying a palm-branch (for illustration see Thédenat, in Daremberg and Saglio iii. 2. 1293, and Graeven [1901] 185); see also Varr. *ling.* v. 62, Sen. *epist.* 78. 16. For the carrying of the palm branch see also Paus. viii. 48. 2 ἐς δὲ τὴν δεξιάν ἐστι καὶ πανταχοῦ τῷ νικῶντι ἐστιθέμενος φοῖνιξ.

The palm branch became such a common symbol of victory (see e.g. [Cic.] *Her.* iv. 51, Matius fr. 3 (B and C), Hor. *carm.* i. 1. 5, Virg. *Aen.* v. 339, 472, Sen. *Phoen.* 638, Plin. *nat.* x. 47, Juv. 8. 58–9, and *TLL* x. 1. 143. 60–147. 43), that it is surprising to learn that it is not

---

[1] See Mommsen (1887–8) i. 437–41 and Weinstock (1971) 107–9.

attested in the Greek world before *c*.400 BC, the *floruit* of Eumolpus of Sicyon, who is said to have painted a picture of a victor in an athletic contest holding it (Plin. *nat.* xxxv. 75). See further Plut. *quaest. conu.* vii. 4 = *mor.* 723a–724f, Tarbell (1908), and Wolters (1924) 16–17.

47. 4. OTHER AEDILICIAN ACTIVITY

aedilibus curulibus qui eos ludos fecerunt: on aediles and the games see 23. 11–13, vii. 1. 6 nn.
pecuariis: see 23. 13 n.
uia . . . silice . . . perstrata est: the surfacing of this stretch of the Via Appia continued work commissioned in 295 (23. 12). For the high cost of road-works, see ix. 29. 6 n.; note that L. here records how the work was financed. The intensifying *persternere* is attested elsewhere [*] only at Vitr. vii. 1. 7 and Ambr. *in Luc.* 9. 11 (*PL* xv. 1887). For *sternere* used of paving or surfacing a road, see viii. 15. 8 n. For *silex* (Italian *selce*), its use in paving, and the sites near Rome from which it was quarried, see Laurence (2004).
ad Bouillas: Bovillae was a small town which lay close to the twelfth milestone of the Appia; it had been one of the original thirty Latin cities, but had long been absorbed by Rome. The *gens Iulia* performed family sacrifices there. See further Hülsen, *RE* iii. 798–9, Weinstock (1971) 5–7, De Rossi (1979), and Coarelli (1981) 70–2.
a Martis: for the temple of Mars, see vii. 23. 3 n. Among writers prior to L. the ellipse of *templum* or *aedes*, common after *ad*, is paralleled after *a* only at Cic. *fam.* xiv. 2. 2 'a Vestae'. See Wölfflin (1885) 369–70 and K–S i. 232.

47. 5. ELECTIONS

According to Zon. viii. 1. 10 the Romans τοὺς ὑπάτους οὐ κατ' ἀρετὴν ᾕρηντο, and this, together with the continuing pestilence, impelled the Samnites and Faliscans to war in 292. All this may be doubted.
Q. Fabium Maximi filium Gurgitem: for Gurges see 14. 10 n., where anecdotes in Valerius Maximus and Polyaenus which may possibly relate to this election are discussed. W–M (on iv. 16. 7 'L. Quinctium Cincinnati filium') well note that when L. refers to the son of a famous man he sometimes uses the *cognomen* and not the *praenomen* in filiation; cf. also iv. 43. 1 'T. Quinctio Capitolini filio Capitolino' and 45. 5.
D. Iunium Brutum Scaeuam: see 43. 3 n.

ipse Papirius praetor factus: for the practice of following a consulship with a praetorship, see 22. 9 n.; for the unusual phenomenon of
a magistrate presiding over his own election, see vii. 25. 2 n. with
addendum.

47. 6–7. THE PESTILENCE AND AESCULAPIUS

6. pestilentiae: Val. Max. i. 8. 2 states that this pestilence lasted for
three years. L. mentions a pestilence also for 295 (31. 8) but not for
294. Zon. viii. 1. 10 refers to a pestilence only for 293/2.
urentis: I have not been able to find a precise parallel for this use of
urere, but not dissimilar passages are listed at *OLD s.u.* 5(a) and 9.
urbem atque agros: for the expression cf. v. 14. 4 'pestilentiam
agris urbique inlatam', xxvii. 23. 6 'eo anno pestilentia grauis incidit
in urbem agrosque', xxxviii. 44. 7, and xl. 19. 3. L.'s phrasing is not
just conventional but emphasizes the scale of the pestilence.
libri aditi: see 31. 8 and vii. 27. 1 n. with *addendum.*
quinam finis aut quod remedium: for the expression cf. v. 13. 5
'cuius insanabili perniciei quando nec causa nec finis inueniebatur,
libri Sibyllini ex senatus consulto aditi sunt'.

7. Aesculapium . . . arcessendum: in 292 Q. Ogulnius Gallus (6. 3
n.) was sent at the head of an embassy of ten to bring the god
Aesculapius from Epidaurus to Rome; later legend had it that a snake,
representing the god, had spontaneously carried itself on to the
Roman ship and then established itself on the Isola Tiberina, where
the temple of Aesculapius was subsequently erected. Numerous
writers tell or allude to the tale: see e.g. *per.* xi, xxix. 11. 1, Ov. *met.* xv.
622–744, Val. Max. i. 8. 2, Plin. *nat.* xxix. 16, Plut. *quaest. Rom.* 94 =
mor. 286d, Lact. *inst. diu.* ii. 7. 13, Oros. iii. 22. 5, *uir. ill.* 22. 1–2, and
other passages cited at D'Ippolito (1988) 161 n. 7. The temple was
built swiftly and dedicated on 1 January 291 (Ov. *fast.* i. 291–4,
Degrassi, *I.I.* xiii. 2, p. 388). The size of the embassy, recorded by *uir.
ill.*, seems to point to the seriousness with which Rome took the whole
operation (see ix. 36. 14 n.). Orlin speculates, quite attractively, that
an important motive for the establishment of the cult was that Rome
had now begun to have more dealings with the cities of Magna
Graecia and wished to show that she could partake of their religious
beliefs.
    A close parallel for the response of the Sibylline books is found in
their pronouncement in 205 that the Magna Mater should be
brought to Rome (*MRR* i. 304); and just as here their response led

ultimately to the construction of a temple to Aesculapius, so also in
217 it led to the vowing of a temple to Venus Erycina and Mars (xxii.
9. 10, Ov. *fast.* iv. 875–6) and in 114 to Venus Verticordia (Ov. *fast.*
iv. 157–60).

For the possibility that the practice of Greek medicine was introduced to Rome with the cult of Aesculapius, see e.g. Langslow (1999)
204–5.

See further Wissowa (1912) 307–8, Altheim (1938*b*) 283, Latte
(1960*a*) 225–6, D'Ippolito (1988) 160–5, Orlin (1997) 23, 106–8, and
Weigel (1998) 138.

Epidauro: for the cult of Asclepios (Romanized as Aesculapius) at
Epidaurus, see conveniently Kern, *RE* vi. 50; Paus. ii. 26. 8–9 attests
how the cult spread around the Greek world from Epidaurus.

supplicatio: for *supplicationes* see vii. 28. 8 n. Since Aesculapius did
not yet have a temple at Rome, he must have been supplicated in the
temple of another god, perhaps Apollo.

Appendices

APPENDIX 1
FURTHER CONJECTURES IN BOOK X

2. 8. et dulcedine: *dulcedine* Weissenborn (ed.²).

2. 15. monumentum: *in monimentum* (Ruperti), *monumento* (Novák).[1]

8. 1. amplissimi: *ampli* Alschefski.

8. 4. parte uirili: *uirili parte* (Wex [1852] 316).

8. 9. militiaeque: *militiaeque habere* Novák (1894) 115.

10. 12. adiecti: *adiecta* (Allen [1864–74] i. 24).

11. 1. qui uixdum ingressus hostium fines, cum exerceretur: *qui cum uixdum ingressus hostium fines exerceretur* (Weissenborn [ed.²]).

14. 11. unquam: *del.* Cobet, *ap.* Bisschop *et al.* (1852) 96.

14. 20. maxime territos: *maximeque terruit eos* (Weissenborn ed.²]); Weissenborn also wondered if the text might be defective after the following *opprimerentur.*

15. 6. pugnantes: Walters thought that this word might have been a gloss; but he was misled by his erroneous belief that variation in word-order in our mss tends to indicate a gloss; here P has reversed the order of *pugnantes ferme* simply because it has made a mistake.

21. 14. exercitum: *uim* (Allen [1864–74] ii. 11).

22. 1. primo: *iure* Kiel, *ap.* Bisschop *et al.* (1852) 97.

25. 12. maius: *maius ⟨uisum⟩* (Koch [1861] 7–8).

25. 8. terroremque: *stuporemque* Shackleton Bailey (1986) 322 (but cf. § 5 'metu').

25. 18. belli: *bellum* (Allen [1864–74] ii. 11).

29. 12. equites: *equos* (Allen [1864–74] ii. 11). The coupling *ala equitum* is common in L.; see Packard (1968) i. 314–15 and 346.

35. 13. tunc: Wesenberg (1870/1: 40) conjectured *tum*, but see Packard (1968) iv. 1055.

37. 5. frumentoque: 'exciditne ... mensium numerus?' (Wesenberg [1870/1] 40); but among the passages cited at ix. 41. 6–7 n., ii. 54. 1 and ix. 41. 5 are similar.

40. 4. omnium etiam: *etiam* (Conway).

41. 8. ipse: *ipsi* (Weissenborn [ed.²]).

---

[1] Reported by H. J. Müller (1891: 186) from his note on i. 2. 6 in his 1890 Prague edn. of books i–ii, which I have not seen.

41. 13. lentiorem: *lentiorem* ⟨*rem*⟩ (Allen [1864–74] i. 25, very tentatively).
42. 7. pocillum: *pocillo* (Ruperti).
43. 9. in medio: *inde medio* (Weissenborn [ed.²]).
44. 7. infestius: *intentius* (Cornelissen [1889] 192).
47. 3. ludos Romanos: *ludi Romani* (Ruperti).
47. 6. quod: Allen (1864–74: i. 25) appears to advocate deletion of this word.

APPENDIX 2
ANNALISTIC EVIDENCE FOR THE WORKINGS OF
THE SENATE

In their accounts of the Roman conquest of Italy, and esp. for the period of the Second and Third Samnite Wars, L. and our other sources often record discussions in the senate, decisions of the senate, and communications between the senate and (pro-)magistrates. Since this evidence has been used by Loreto (1991–2: 268–84) in his reconstruction of the relationship between senate and magistrates in the period of the Roman conquest of Italy, it is important to determine how likely it is to be sound. What follows is a selection from it.

For the senate's making decisions on provinces see vii. 19. 7 (353) 'censuit igitur senatus neutram neglegendam rem esse; utroque legiones scribi consulesque sortiri prouincias iussit', ix. 41. 12 (308) 'itaque legati ad Fabium consulem missi sunt, ut si quid laxamenti a bello Samnitium esset, in Vmbriam propere exercitum duceret', 42. 4 (307) 'cum collegae (*sc.* L. Volumnio) . . . Sallentini hostes decernerentur', 43. 1–2 (306) 'itaque eo P. Cornelius cum exercitu missus. Marcio noui hostes . . . decernuntur', 44. 6 (305) 'ambo consules in Samnium missi', x. 16. 1 (296) 'ueteres consules iussi bellum in Samnio gerere prorogato in sex menses imperio', 18. 3 (296) 'Ap. Claudium primo quoque tempore in Etruriam ire placuit', 32. 1 (294) 'Samnium ambobus (*sc.* consulibus) decreta prouincia est', and Eutrop. ii. 9. 3 (290) 'deinde P. Cornelius Rufinus M'. Curius Dentatus, ambo consules, contra Samnitas missi'.

For instructions from the senate to magistrates in the field see vii. 26. 10 (349) 'consul . . . iussus ab senatu bellum maritimum curare', viii. 23. 13 (327) 'L. Cornelio, quia ne eum quidem in Samnium iam ingressum reuocari ab impetu belli placebat, litterae missae ut dictatorem comitiorum causa diceret', ix. 36. 14, 38. 11–14 (the two embassies from the senate to Fabius Rullianus recorded for 310/9), 41. 12 (308) (cited above), 42. 10 (306) 'iussique eam integram rem noui consules . . . ad senatum referre' (here it is not quite certain whether the new consuls were 'ordered' by the old consuls or by the senate), and D.H. xvii/xviii. 4. 5 (the embassy to Postumius Megellus in 291).

For other instructions from the senate to magistrates see viii. 5. 4 (340) 'Torquatus missus ab senatu ad dimittendos legatos'.

For reports from Rome's allies concerning developments in Italy being considered in the senate see x. 11. 7–8 (299), 14. 3 (297), 45. 2–4 (293). For the senate's reacting to rumours of war or of danger to Rome or to other reports see ix. 26. 6 (314), 29. 1–3 (312), and 38. 9 (310/9).

For allusions to senatorial debate see viii. 29. 2–3 (325/4) (debate on war against Vestini), ix. 26. 2–3 (314) (discussion of fate of Luceria), x. 21. 3–10 (296) (debates on Roman security), 25. 13–26. 1 (debate on Fabius Rullianus' conduct of the war), 45. 4–7 (293) (discussion of embassy from Rome's allies), Oros. iii. 22. 6 (on Fabius Gurges' conduct of the Samnite War in 292), and D.H. xix. 6. 1–3 (282) (debate on eve of Tarentine War).

For other reports of senatorial activity see e.g. viii. 19. 2–3 (330) 'missi tum ab senatu legati denuntiatumque Samnitibus . . .'.

For letters to the senate from consuls or other magistrates see vi. 22. 3 (382), vii. 19. 8 (353), viii. 23. 1 (327), 30. 10 (325/4), x. 21. 5 (296), 21. 11 (296), 24. 18 (295), 44. 9 (293)

If these notices were all reliable, they would show that already by the time of the Second and Third Samnite Wars the relationship between senate and magistrates was much the same as it is revealed to be by L.'s more detailed evidence in books xxi–xlv.

Now some of this evidence, especially that from book x, is almost certainly reliable. In his account of 296 BC L. writes (21. 7–9): 'tum de praesidio regionis depopulatae ab Samnitibus agitari coeptum; itaque placuit ut duae coloniae circa Vescinum et Falernum agrum deducerentur . . . (9) tribunis plebis negotium datum est, ut plebei scito iuberetur P. Sempronius praetor triumuiros in ea loca colonis deducendis creare', in which *placuit* must refer to the senate, mentioned earlier in § 3. Although it is just conceivable that this information about how the colonies of Minturnae and Sinuessa were founded was invented by an annalist who was aware that the consuls were away at war and that Sempronius was praetor in this year, it is extremely unlikely.

However, the difficulty of knowing what is reliable and what is not is well brought out by an earlier sentence in the same chapter (§ 3): 'his nuntiis senatus conterritus iustitium indici, dilectum omnis generis hominum haberi iussit'. There is no particular reason to doubt that a *iustitium* was decreed, and it is quite possible that authentic information survived about the manner in which this decision was made in the senate; but it would have been very easy for an annalist, looking to make his history plausibly detailed, to conjecture the part played by the senate; and, unfortunately, conjecture of this kind could have affected most of our other evidence listed above.

In addition to this consideration, there are two other grounds for scepticism. First, some similar notices are found for the period before 390: see e.g. (from a large body of passages that could be adduced) ii. 30. 8 (494) 'oratores Latinorum ab senatu petebant . . .', iii. 5. 15 (464) 'cohortes inde Latinae Hernicaeque ab senatu gratiis ob impigram militiam actis remissae domos', iv. 44. 7 (420) 'mentio in senatu de agris diuidendis inlata est', 48. 16 (416) 'gratiae intercessoribus ab senatu actae', and v. 20. 2 (396) (a letter from Camillus to the senate). That the majority of these could rest on secure testimony is incredible, and their existence virtually proves that the annalists were capable of invention of this kind. Secondly, there are other reasons for doubting the information offered by L. at viii. 5. 4, 30. 10, ix. 26. 2–3, 26. 6, 29. 1–3, 36. 14, 38. 9, 38. 11–14, and x. 24. 18: see nn. ad locc.

In the absence of the narratives of Fabius Pictor, Cassius Hemina, Piso, Cn. Gellius, and the later annalists, the survival of which would have allowed us to see whether information of this kind was introduced into the tradition at a late stage, it is impossible to argue with any confidence whether any of the information cited above is true or false. My suspicion is that the information from book x, with the exception of that which pertains to Ap. Claudius Caecus and Fabius Rullianus, is more reliable than that from the earlier books (although passages like viii. 23. 13 may offer examples of genuine survivals).[1]

From this it follows that Loreto's conclusions (he detects an increasingly important role for the senate in directing Roman strategy and suggests a model not dissimilar to that familiar from the end of the third century), although plausible, cannot be regarded as entirely secure.

APPENDIX 3
LEGISLATION BY CURULE MAGISTRATES, 366–c.287 BC

Sandberg (1993, 2000, and 2001) has proposed the extreme thesis that before Sulla (who changed the nature of Roman politics by curbing the power of the tribunate and further encouraging the recent tendency of the consuls to stay in Rome for their year of office) all legislation, except legislation dealing with military matters and declarations of war passed through the *comitia centuriata*, was promulgated by tribunes.[2] His argument may be summarized as follows:

(*a*) that the *comitia curiata* was the natural legislative body of the patricians (see Sandberg [1993] 88, 95–6);

(*b*) that after 366 it was replaced by the *concilium plebis*, largely because tribunician intercession had made the legislative powers of curule magistrates redundant (see Sandberg [2000] 138–40, [2001] 135–7);

(*c*) that the modern view that in the early and middle Republic the *comi-*

---

[1] For these considerations see also vol. i, pp. 100–2.

[2] For consideration of Sandberg's thesis see also Crawford (2004), who concerns himself mostly with the period from the Hannibalic War to Sulla. I quote one of his most telling points: 'the attempt to write out of the story such consular legislation as is attested reveals S.'s desperation; it is simply bizarre to describe the lex Licinia Mucia of 95 BC, which deprived of citizenship men who believed that they possessed it, and the Lex Julia of 90 BC, which more than doubled the size of the citizen body, as "pertaining to foreign relations" (p. 101 n. 16; p. 142)'.

tia centuriata was often used for legislation which did not pertain to military matters is unfounded (Sandberg [1993] 81–8, [2001] 119–131);

(*d*) that there was no *comitia tributa populi Romani* and that curule magistrates could not preside in the *concilium plebis* (Sandberg [1993] 76–81);

(*e*) that legislation said to have been passed by curule magistrates was in fact passed by tribunes: in other words *ferre* was not technical (Sandberg [1993] 90–2, [2001] 97–103);

(*f*) for the period before Sulla only tribunes are said *promulgare* or *rogare* laws (Sandberg [2000] 128–9).

Some parts of this thesis are acceptable: (*a*) could be right, although our poor evidence for the *comitia curiata* in all periods does not allow us to ascertain whether it is, and (*c*), on which see also Paananen (1993), is attractive: there is, *pace* Rotondi (1912) *passim*, virtually no positive evidence for laws' being passed through the *comitia centuriata* (on the other hand, the absence of direct evidence may be delusive, and the fact that in 339 [viii. 12. 15 (n.)] Publilius Philo felt the need to legislate on the use of *patrum auctoritas* and the *comitia centuriata* seems to show that this assembly was not at this date without legislative significance).

As for the rest, the evidence does not allow a decisive refutation of Sandberg's ideas, but it is possible to interpret it in a manner very different from his. Although (*b*) is not entirely without force—the possibility of tribunician intercession does explain the courteous terms in which the senate asked the tribunes to introduce legislation (see above, p. 17)—it seems improbable, for three main reasons.

(i) It is scarcely credible that the Romans evolved a constitutional practice in which the chief magistrates of the state could command armies but not legislate on civil matters: even if tribunes were the prime instrument for introducing legislation, the potential inconvenience was huge.

(ii) Once the Struggle of the Orders was over, tribunician intercession need not have been more of a threat to legislation by curule magistrates than it was to be to legislation promulgated by the tribunes themselves in the period covered by books xxi–xlv: increasingly integrated into the governing class, most tribunes had no motive to intercede arising from conflict with the patricians.

(iii) Our sources do record some legislation passed by curule magistrates (this is the most important objection). For the period of the Samnite Wars note:

357	Cn. Manlius Capitolinus, consul (vii. 16. 7–8; a tax on manumission)
356	C. Marcius Rutilus, dictator (vii. 17. 7; on expenses for war)
342	M. Valerius Corvus, dictator (vii. 41. 3; various laws on military matters, including *ne cui militum fraudi secessio fuit*)
339	Q. Publilius Philo, dictator (viii. 12. 13–17; on plebiscites, *patrum auctoritas*, and elections to the censorship)
332	L. Papirius Crassus, praetor (viii. 17. 12; grant of *ciuitas sine suffragio* to Acerrae)

326   C. Poetelius Libo Visolus, L. Papirius, consuls (viii. 28. 1–9; aboli-
      tion of *nexum*)
313   C. Poetelius Libo Visolus, dictator (Varr. *ling*. vii. 105; an alternative
      date for the legislation recorded by L. under 326)
300   M. Valerius Corvus (or Maximus), consul (x. 9. 3–6; on *prouocatio*)
287   Q. Hortensius, dictator (*per*. xi and *MRR* i. 185). On plebiscites
      being binding for the whole community.[1]

Even if one argues that the laws of 356, 342, and 332 (the first two certainly on military matters) were passed through the *comitia centuriata*, or
even the *comitia curiata*, this total is not much smaller than the number of
tribunician laws known to have been passed in the period 366–287.

Against (*d*) see *addendum* to vii. 16. 7–8 n. (*e*) is purely speculative, and is
forced on Sandberg to account for passages like xxiii. 30. 14 'senatus
decreuit ut Ti. Sempronius, consul designatus, cum †ibo† inisset, ad populum ferret'[2] and the laws just listed, for all of which L. uses *ferre*; but in the
case of the passage just quoted, why did the senate have to wait until
Sempronius was in office if all that was required was a request to the
tribunes, which could have been conveyed by the *praetor peregrinus*?[3] (*f*) is
correct, but has significance only if (*e*) is established.

Sandberg (2001: 103) looks with some favour on the suggestion of
Paananen (1993: 70) that a dictatorial law may have been closer to an edict
than a *lex rogata* but is still forced to accept that dictators may not fit in with
his thesis. However, once an exception is made for them, the rest of his
argument becomes weaker.

---

[1] As one would expect, Sandberg is aware of these laws; for his discussion of them see (2001)
85–96, esp. 94–6.
[2] The corruption in P (plainly *ibo* should be replaced by *magistratum* or the like) does not
affect the argument.
[3] If this praetor (for whom see xxii. 55. 1) was not available, then the senate could easily have
found someone else to convey the request to the tribunes.

Addenda and Corrigenda

THE following *addenda* and *corrigenda* reflect most of what I have learnt since 1997–8 about topics discussed in volumes i–ii of this commentary; a few relate to volume iii. They include correction of errors, citation of further bibliography on, or parallels for, phenomena discussed, and some entirely new notes on topics that I should not have ignored. I am grateful to Mr J. W. Rich and the late Professor W. S. Watt for pointing out several mistakes. I have not noted typographical errors except where they may mislead; some have been corrected in the paperback reprint of vol. i.

My dissatisfaction is greatest with chapter 3 of the Introduction (vol. i, pp. 21–108, 'The Annalistic Tradition'), which was conceived first in the early 1980s and thereafter received less revision than some other sections of vols i and ii. Although I still believe most of the arguments advanced in it, I regret in particular two weaknesses. First, I should have cited more of the very extensive relevant bibliography, especially on the *annales maximi*. Second, my determination to escape from undue speculation about the content of the works of Valerius Antias and the sources whom L. cites in books vi–x (Fabius Pictor, Piso, Claudius Quadrigarius, Licinius Macer, and Aelius Tubero), and my concern above all with the question of whether or not the information transmitted by these annalists was 'reliable', led me to give only a very cursory outline on pp. 72–4 of the development of the annalistic tradition before Livy. Full correction of these faults would require the rewriting of the whole chapter (and perhaps also the chapter 'Livy and his sources'), which it is inappropriate to do; but in what follows there is some discussion of the development of the tradition.

VOLUME I

INTRODUCTION

Ch. 1. *The Nature of Ancient Historical Writing*

p. 3 n. 2. The best general treatment of ancient historiography is now Marincola (1997).
p. 4. Some further bibliography should have been given on the marvellous in historiography: see, for example, the discussion of travellers' tales at Wiseman (1993) 131–2.
pp. 6 and 76–9. *Plausible reconstruction.* Reviewing this volume, Luce

(1999: 76) well points out that a weakness of the view that L., D.H., and their annalistic sources strove for plausible reconstruction is that some of the stories that they tell are full of contradictions and therefore implausible; as an example of this he points to the story of the downfall of M. Manlius Capitolinus (vi. 11. 1–20. 16). My argument, therefore, needs to be recast: in their reconstructions the annalists regularly added details to give verisimilitude to their inventions but did not always manage, or even try, to eliminate errors and contradictions.

p. 6. Plb. iii. 33. 17–18 is discussed from a point of view similar to that adopted here by Wiseman (1993: 141–2).

p. 6 n. 11. For history and tragedy see also Wiseman (1993: 132–5).

Ch. 2. *Livy and his Sources*

p. 15. To the list of L.'s references to his sources add vi. 4. 3 *constat*, 16. 4 *satis constat*, vii. 2. 3 *dicuntur*, 2. 8 *dicitur*, 3. 6 *ferunt*, 10. 5 *quoniam id memoria dignum antiquis uisum est*, 18. 2 *ut scripsere quidam*, 18. 10 *in quibusdam annalibus . . . inuenio*, 21. 6 *meriti aequitate curaque sunt ut per omnium annalium monumenta celebres nominibus essent* (not certainly a reference to L.'s sources), 22. 3 *quidam Caesonem, alii Gaium praenomen Quinctio adiciunt*, 25. 8 *dicuntur*, viii. 3. 6 *constat*, 12. 1 *constat*, 24. 1 *proditum*, 30. 4 *uocant*, ix. 7. 2 *dicitur*, 27. 14 *proditum memoriae est*, 29. 10 *traditur*, 36. 7 *dicuntur*, 40. 16 *dicitur*, 42. 3 *in quibusdam annalibus inuenio*, 44. 7–8 *alii . . . tradunt, alii . . .*, 46. 15 *ferunt*, x. 21. 8 *dicitur*, and 26. 7 *constare*. All these passages, and similar passages from book i–v, may be found at Forsythe (1999) 22–39.

pp. 17–18. Northwood (2000) has provided the fullest critique of the view that L. did not consult second-century annalists at first hand; he shows that it rests on no good evidence. On L.'s awareness of the potentially greater authority of earlier writers add xxii. 7. 4 'Fabium, *aequalem* temporibus huiusce belli, potissimum auctorem habui' (with which contrast viii. 40. 5 'nec quisquam *aequalis* temporibus illis scriptor exstat quo satis certo auctore stetur') and see now Forsythe (1999) 59–64.

p. 18 n. 17. For *ueteres auctores* or the like add ii. 18. 5.

p. 19 n. 23. The most extensive attempt to ascertain which sources L. used in books vi–x was made for book x by Klinger (1884), who argued that in general L. drew on Licinius Macer and Valerius Antias. Klinger makes many acute observations about L.'s literary and historical techniques and rightly draws attention to the appearance of various similar or stock motifs in different parts of L.'s narrative. However, I do not share the confidence with which he assigns passages in book x to these authors; quite apart from the considerations adduced at vol. i, pp. 16–19, his argument that the reappearance of these motifs in different parts of L.'s narrative suggests that L. used the same source in those different parts is logically flawed: the appearance of similar material in L. and D.H. shows that different authors can use the same motifs.

p. 19. Val. Max. ii. 2. 9 provides one piece of information (*trabeatos*) about

the *transuectio equitum* which cannot come from ix. 46. 15 (unless L.'s paradosis be emended); but, since his other remarks relating to the censorship of
304 seem to derive from ix. 46, he may have added this from his own knowledge of the ritual.

For the knowledge of L. which Plutarch exhibits in lives other than
Camillus see conveniently Pelling (1997) 263 n. 36.

p. 20. For the relationship of Dio and Zonaras to L. see also Klinger (1884)
65–70. Note too that Dio fr. 36. 29 and Zon. viii. 1. 8–9 show some independence from 38. 1–46. 16 (n.).

p. 20. For the relationship of the author of the *de uiris illustribus* to L. see
also Klinger (1884) 60–2. Other passages in which he provides information
not found in L. are 27. 3, where he mentions a detail about the *deuotio* of
Decius at Sentinum (for discussion see above, pp. 270–1); 32. 3 where he
provides information on the *transuectio equitum* not found at ix. 46. 15 (n.);
and 34. 5 where he mentions that Ap. Claudius Caecus defeated the Sabines
(for discussion see above, pp. 198–201).

Ch. 3. *The Annalistic Tradition*

For another discussion of the reliability of the annalistic tradition, see
Loreto (1993: 7–33), who makes many pertinent observations but under-
estimates the extent to which the annalists were capable of inventing plausible details. Of particular interest is his attempt (p. 29 n. 88) to distinguish
between battle-scenes that are schematic and likely to have been invented
and those that have unique features and for that reason are less likely to have
been invented. However, some of the battle-scenes that are unusual may be
unusual because the annalists were trying to invent something out of the
ordinary.

pp. 22–4. *Fabius Pictor, personal testimony, and oral tradition.* My words
(p. 22), 'Though later writers must have had access to new material, their
task was largely to react to a narrative whose outlines had already been
shaped; but Pictor had to create that narrative without the help of a continuous written history of Rome', need qualification in various respects.

(*a*) Those in the third and early second centuries BC concerned with presenting Rome's past in a reasonably coherent and accessible form had to
assemble the evidence available from somewhere, and I assumed that Pictor
consulted a variety of primary sources directly.[1] However, I failed to discuss
the hypothesis that Fabius found a developed chronicle in the alleged
pontifical *liber annalis*. See now *addendum* to pp. 24–7.

(*b*) I assumed without argument that Pictor wrote his account of the
period 509–265 annalistically, that is, he noted the magistrate for each year
and, when something of note happened in a year, he made comment on it;
but the assumption needs justification, since it has been argued that Pictor

---

[1] For similar views, emphasizing the plurality of Pictor's sources, see Jacoby (1949) 285 and
397–8 and Frier (1999) 255–84.

did not write thus (see e.g. Gelzer [1934] = [1962–4] iii. 93–103 and Walt [1997] 133–4), and that Piso was the first writer to compose the history of this period in this way (e.g. Rawson [1976] 704 = [1991] 259 [cautious], Wiseman [1979] 12–19, and Forsythe [1994] 38–52).

As regards Pictor, the meagre surviving evidence does not allow a resolution of the problem. I incline to the view that he wrote annalistically largely because annalistic writing was regular among ancient historians (note the example of Thucydides and Xenophon) and was the most convenient method by which to structure a narrative, but also because it is easiest to envisage fr. 19 (= Liv. x. 37. 14) as part of such an annalistic narrative. That Fabius used it for the period after 264 is generally agreed, and may receive some confirmation from ll. 304–8 of Ennius' *annales*, which introduce P. Tuditanus and M. Cethegus, probably as the consuls of 204 (but perhaps as censors in 209), if Ennius made use of his work. It would receive confirmation also from Cato, *orig.* fr. 77 = Gell. ii. 28. 6 'non lubet scribere quod in tabula apud pontificem maximum est, quotiens annona cara, quotiens lunae aut solis lumine caligo aut quid obstiterit', if one could be certain that Cato was criticizing earlier Roman historians. It is quite possible too that Cassius Hemina wrote annalistically; note Plin. *nat.* xiii. 84 'Cassius Hemina, uetustissimus auctor annalium' (but *annalium* here could be a synonym for *historiarum*).

The counter-arguments of Gelzer (1934: 343–4 = 1962–4: iii. 105–6), that D.H.'s reference (i. 6. 2) to Pictor narrating the period between the foundation and the First Punic War only κεφαλαιωδῶς excludes a full list of magistrates, and Forysthe (p. 44), that L. never cites Pictor in disputes over the names of magistracies, do not seem in any way decisive.[1]

The main positive reasons for believing that Piso created the annalistic tradition as we find it in L. are that he himself demonstrably wrote annalistically (see frr. 26 and 28) and that, on Mommsen's theory, the pontifical tables had been published by Scaevola shortly before he began his work and therefore provided an incentive for him to use this format (but for weaknesses in Mommsen's view see vol. i, p. 26 and below). A further argument from silence is that no fragments that prove the use of the annalistic format for this period survive from an earlier writer.

It is worth considering the implications of ix. 44. 3–4 = Pis. fr. 26, in which L. states that Piso omitted the years 307 and 306 from his narrative. The events said to have happened in these years include the defeat of the Hernici, the *locatio* of the temple of Salus, the start of work on the Via Valeria, and the renewal of the treaty with Carthage. There is no good reason to reject any of these. However, were Piso the first annalist, it would mean that these events did not enter the historical tradition, at least in a

---

[1] For the view that Fabius Pictor wrote annalistically see e.g. Walbank (1945) 1–3, 15–18 = (1985) 77–80, 94–8, Bung (1950) esp. 199–201, Perl (1964) 217–18, and Frier (1999) 270–8; many earlier scholars, seduced by Mommsen's erroneous view that Pictor was the source of Diodorus (on which see vol. i, p. 107), assumed unquestioningly that he was an annalist. For the contrary view see, in addition to Gelzer and Forsythe, Laqueur, *RE* xix. 2183.

proper chronological context, until after his time. It is easier to believe that some at least of them were there already in Fabius Pictor, and hence later annalists were able easily to correct Piso's mistake.

If my argument concerning Pictor (and, to a lesser extent, Hemina) is wrong, the consequences for our understanding of the process by which material came into the annalistic tradition need not be very great, since Pictor must have placed events in chronological order and therefore established a basic framework for his successors. However, it would follow that more credit should be given to Piso for his part in the formation of the tradition.

(c) I should have made more explicit the process by which I envisaged the arrival of new material in histories of Rome. Such material could have arrived either through invention (whether by the annalists [see vol. i, pp. 72–104] or in oral tradition [see below]) or from the discovery of new evidence. As for new evidence, all or most of the documentary sources, and doubtless also some oral tradition, available to Pictor were potentially available also to his successors; and, since it is very improbable that he exploited all of them, it is unsurprising that others were able to add material to the body that he had assembled. However, one should not see the process simply as one of accretion: L. himself ignored both fact and fiction in his sources in which he was not interested (see p. 39 for fact), and doubtless his sources and predecessors did the same.[1]

The loss of virtually all Roman historical writing before Sallust makes it very hard to determine exactly when new material entered the tradition. We have seen that there are difficulties with the hypotheses that the *annales maximi* were first published when Scaevola was *pontifex maximus* and that Piso was the first annalist. Nevertheless, if these hypotheses are true, much material would have entered the tradition first *c*.120, and there is indeed some evidence that the tradition expanded around this time. By comparing xxiv. 43. 5–44. 10, in which L. narrates the election of the younger Fabius and Gracchus as consuls for 213, the games of 214, the entry of the consuls into office, the distribution of provinces and armies, the expiation of prodigies, the departure of the consuls for their provinces, and finally the famous anecdote in which Fabius makes his illustrious father dismount, with Quadr. fr. 57 = Gell. ii. 2. 13, which begins 'deinde facti consules Sempronius Gracchus iterum Q. Fabius Maximus, filius eius qui priore anno erat consul. ei consuli pater proconsul obuiam in equo uehens uenit neque descendere uoluit, quod pater erat' and then continues with the well-known anecdote, Rich (1997) argues that Quadrigarius cannot regularly have included in his history the standard yearly material that is normally thought to be typical of all writers belonging to the late annalistic tradition. He therefore suggests that it was introduced first either by Cn. Gellius (in which case Quadrigarius would have ignored what was already in one of his predecessors; that it was not found already in other second-century

---

[1] For very helpful remarks on this process see Forsythe (1994) 71–2.

annalists, e.g. Piso, is suggested by the modest scale of their work) or (more probably) by Valerius Antias. Rich's argument with regard to Quadrigarius could be controverted if one were prepared to argue that Quadrigarius told the anecdote immediately after mentioning the election of the younger Fabius and that he then returned to the annalistic material; but the run of the fragment does not suggest that he wrote in this way. Therefore the only way to escape from the conclusion that quite a large body of important and largely sound material found its way into the tradition at a surprisingly late stage (unlike Rich, I should prefer Gellius to Antias as originator, as it would help to explain the size of his work) is to argue that Quadrigarius was ruthlessly selecting from the material available to him.

Oral tradition. My analysis of the influence of oral tradition on the annalistic tradition ignored both family tradition (the aristocratic funerals described at vol. i, pp. 28–9 took place in public) and, more importantly, the role of drama, the importance of which has been emphasized in recent years above all by Wiseman (1989 = 1994: 23–36, 124–7; 1991: 119–20; 1994: 1–22; 1998: esp. 1–16).

The titles of about fifteen *fabulae praetextae*, that is plays on a Roman historical theme, are known.[1] Some of these—which do not need consideration here—relate to contemporary or recent events, an equally large number (Naevius' *Romulus*, *Lupus*, and *Alimonium Remi et Romuli*, Ennius' *Sabinae*, Accius' *Brutus*, and Pomponius Secundus' *Aeneas*) to the regal period and to the first years of the Republic. All this is hardly surprising: recent events had obvious attractions for dramatists, and the regal period and early Republic were treated expansively in Rome's mythical and historical tradition (vol. i, p. 24). However, we know that Accius wrote an *Aeneadae*, also known as *Decius*, which dealt with the events of 295. And for the student of Livy books vi–x, this is important, since it suggests that among the scores of lost *praetextae* there were other plays that dramatized episodes in the history of the Republic prior to 264 BC. Such plays would have influenced annalists who had seen them or read them or heard others talk about them. And when L. himself writes (i. 46. 3) 'tulit enim et Romana regia sceleris tragici exemplum' and (v. 20. 8–9) 'inseritur huic loco fabula . . . haec ad ostentationem scaenae gaudentis miraculis aptiora quam ad fidem' it is hard not to believe that he was thinking of real plays on Roman themes.[2]

If the Roman historical and antiquarian tradition was correct that drama in its classical form came to Rome only with Livius Andronicus (see vii. 2. 3–13 n.), then *praetextae* as such will not have been composed before the

---

[1] They are listed conveniently at Wiseman (1998) 2–3. For the occasions on which they were performed, see esp. Flower (1995), who, however, may underestimate the number of such plays that were once put on.

[2] Nevertheless, attempts to detect the patterns of drama in the tales of early Roman history and hence to postulate lost plays on which the annalistic tradition drew are made problematic by the certain fact that ever since Herodotus historians had been incorporating dramatic incidents and style into their narrative (see vol. i, p. 5). Thus, rightly, Flower (1995) 174.

mid-third century. However, the Romans themselves dated the introduction of *ludi scaenici* to 364 BC, and Wiseman's view that at these early shows myths and tales relating to Rome's own history had been enacted before the *populus*, which by watching them celebrated its own past and present exploits, is very attractive. Such enacting and celebration would have constituted a lively oral tradition and could have played a very important role in the development of a national consensus on the interpretation of important episodes from earlier Roman history.

Oral culture could also have had a more profound effect than I allowed on the details of episodes described by the annalists: for some of the details with which scenes of battles and politics in L. and D.H. are expanded may owe their origin not to the pen of an annalist (as I have tended to assume throughout the commentary) but to either oral or written drama; in books vi–x the stories concerning Camillus, Manlius Capitolinus, the Lacus Curtius, and perhaps even the Caudine Forks could all have been subjects for the stage.

However, I see no reason to withdraw my sceptical view on p. 24 that oral tradition could have provided a channel through which many 'reliable facts' concerning the early Republic were transmitted to Fabius Pictor and later historians, at least before the period covered by books ix and x:[1] work on oral tradition in other cultures has shown how ineffective it is for conveying information of this kind.[2]

pp. 24–7. *The pontifical tables.* This section was too brief and did not do justice to the extensive scholarship on the *tabulae pontificum* and the *annales maximi*. To the bibliography at p. 24 n. 15 add e.g. Mommsen (1859) 137, 209–10, (1894–5) ii. 102–6, Seeck (1885) esp. 57–99, C. Cichorius, *RE* i. 2248–55 (the best introduction to the subject), Enmann (1902), Peter (1906–14) i. iii–xxix, Kornemann (1911), (1912), Bauman (1983) 91–3 and 290–8, Petzold (1993), Rüpke (1993), and Frier (1999) vi–xix.

Nowhere did I discuss why the *pontifices* should have kept records. It is easiest to suggest that, since the pontiffs were concerned with important matters such as sacrifices, procurations, and festivals, their records—which are likely to have been linked with the calendar, of which they had oversight—showed what rituals and words were needed on such occasions; and from this they developed the practice of recording all important events.[3]

Nor did I delineate with sufficient clarity some of the other major problems in the interpretation of the evidence relating to the *annales maximi*.

(*a*) *When did the* pontifex maximus *start to record information on his* tabulae? My remark (p. 25) 'it is noteworthy that the Romans believed that they went back to the beginnings of the Republic' is somewhat misleading, since

---

[1] On the proximity of the events of the late fourth and early third century to the time of the annalists, see also Loreto (1993) 16.

[2] For Greece this conclusion emerges very clearly from Thomas (1989).

[3] See Seeck (1885) *passim* (note the title of his book), Cichorius, *RE* i. 2249–51, and Petzold (1993) 159. Rüpke (1993) also links the development of pontifical record-keeping closely to their priestly function.

Cic. *de or*. ii. 52 refers to *ab initio rerum Romanarum*. However, vi. 1. 2 does indeed provide powerful testimony for the ancient view that these records started early, as does D.H. i. 74. 3 (mentioning a πίναξ, which must be equivalent to *tabula*, in the context of the foundation date of Rome); and L. refers to the *commentarii pontificum* also at iv. 3. 3. As for the other Livian passages cited in n. 17, it is easiest to believe that he refers to the *annales maximi* but just conceivable that he makes anachronistic references to historiography. The reference to Plut. *Num*. 1. 2 should be deleted (see below on vi. 1. 1–3; the passage is mentioned in the right context at vol. i, p. 30 n. 41)).

I still incline to think that this ancient view is likely to be right:[1] the less good evidence for Roman history in the period 500–350 can be explained by the failure of many records to survive. Cic. *rep*. i. 25, where it is stated that the eclipse of 400 was the first to be recorded by the *annales maximi* and that earlier eclipses were calculated from it, does not allow a decisive resolution of the problem: it shows that some records survived from the late fifth century but perhaps suggests that they did not go back much further. L. (vi. 1. 1–3) squares the view that the records started early with the poor evidence for the period before 390 by arguing that many of the records were destroyed in the Gallic Sack; but, since the quality of our evidence for the years immediately after 390 is not obviously better than that for the years before, it may be doubted whether he is right. Those who think that he is right tend to argue that in the aftermath of the Sack the pontiffs and others were able to replace some of the record of events in the previous generation, including the eclipse. For further discussion see *addendum* to vi. 1. 1–3 n.

My brief dismissal on p. 25 of Beloch's view does not do justice to the possibility that the years around 300 BC were important in the development of the pontifical chronicle. The strongest evidence for this view comes from the fact, amply documented at vol. i, pp. 38–72, that for the period covered by book x our evidence for Roman history becomes fuller and more reliable than for the period covered by books ii–ix. One may then connect this fact with the reorganization of the pontificate after the Ogulnian rogation of 300 BC (x. 6. 3–9. 2 n.). However, from all this one should not necessarily conclude that reliable records started only *c*.300 BC, since (i) there is no reason to doubt that some reliable 'annalistic' material appears in books ii–ix, (ii) the evidence offered by L. and others for the period after 300 may be more reliable simply because it relates to events closer in time to the annalists, and (iii) although the rise of the plebeians in the years around 300 may well have led to an interest being taken in Rome's past (see above, p. 23), there is no particular reason to think that a patricio-plebeian college kept records differently from an entirely patrician one.

The theory that the years around 300 were important for the development of the pontifical chronicle has been put forward in various forms.

(i) Several scholars (see vol. iii, p. 613) have argued that the publication of

---

[1] Thus also e.g. Seeck (1885) 73, who held that decisions about intercalation made by the pontiffs must have been posted, and therefore their records were as old as intercalation.

the *fasti* by Cn. Flavius involved publication also of the consular list: although this theory is possible, our sources refer only to the publication of the calendar by Flavius; the view is rejected briskly by Frier (1999: 146 n. 27).

(ii) Alföldi (1965: 167–8) argued that Flavius also published other more extensive historical materials: this is even more speculative than (i). (He argued too [1966: 721] that it was Flavius who introduced *cognomina* into the consular and other lists.)

(iii) Combining the testimony of vii. 3. 6 with that of Plin. *nat.* xxxiii. 19 (quoted at vol. iii, pp. 602–3), scholars have argued that the aedileship of Flavius was important for Roman calculations of the chronology of their early history. For a blunt statement of this view, see Alföldi (1965: 351) 'The year 509 B.C. . . . was fixed as the first year of the Republic when the aedile Cn. Flavius counted 204 annual nails in the wall of the *cella Iouis*'. This statement may be correct, but is very far from certain, since we do not know (*a*) whether or not Flavius was the first Roman to use a *post Capitolinam dedicatam* date, and (*b*) how he calculated this date.[1]

(iv) Beloch (1922: 119–26 and 1926: 86–95) argued that the pontifical records were published (and hence available for use by later annalists) first in 296, when the Ogulnii were aediles. However, most of the evidence which he adduced in support of this theory is frail.[2]

By contrast, Rüpke (1993) returns to the view of Enmann, that Ti. Coruncanius was responsible for the creation of the *annales maximi*. Although he is right to note that L.'s narrative in books i–x, the account of the Ogulnian rogation apart, shows little knowledge of the activity of the pontiffs[3] and has none of the notices recording succession in the office that we find in books xxi–xlv, there is very little positive evidence in favour of

---

[1] This is not to deny that the date of the dedication of the Capitoline temple may have been important in computations of Roman chronology. For an early argument for its importance see Mommsen (1859) 198–201.

[2] He argued (*a*) that the presence of prodigies in the annalistic tradition for 296 and 295 (see vol. i, pp. 59–60) shows that in these years material of this kind was being recorded in the pontifical chronicle. This argument is uncontroversial. (*b*) That the eclipse mentioned by Enn. *ann.* 153 = Cic. *rep.* i. 25 relates not to the eclipse of 400 BC but to that of 288. Although this argument is just conceivable if one is prepared to emend the text of Cicero (for consideration of it, see vol. iii, p. 612), it is very far from certain. (*c*) That the failure of the eclipses of 310 and 297 to appear in L. shows that they were not recorded in the pontifical tables, and that 297 is a *terminus post quem* for the start of the chronicle. This argument is insecure, since L. is highly selective in his reporting of annalistic material (see vol. i, pp. 38–72 *passim*) and since he mentions prodigies, which Beloch has to reject as invented, also in books ii–ix (vol. i, pp. 59–60). (*d*) That the material in *F.T.* becomes reliable first after 295: but it is not clear that the character of the material in *F.T.* changes so suddenly (see also vol. i, pp. 56–7). (*e*) That the use of the pontifical table after 296 was connected with the reform of the pontifical college by the Ogulnii; but Beloch's belief that they introduced this as aediles in 296 and not as tribunes in 300 is quite arbitrary. (He held that plebiscites had no validity before the *lex Hortensia* of 287; but several plebiscites which date from before this year seem to have been adopted by the whole state: see viii. 12. 15 n. with *addendum*.)

[3] Compare also Mommsen's argument about prodigies, discussed below, p. 490.

this position. Rüpke suggests that the Secular Games of 249 provided a spur.[1]

(*b*) *What was the character of the eighty-book edition mentioned by Servius* auctus *and its relationship to the* tabulae? The character of the eighty-book edition is revealed best by the fragments of the *annales maximi* with book-numbers that are quoted from Gell. iv. 5. 1–7 and *orig. gent. Rom.* 17. 3, 17. 5, 18. 3. Since the first three describe the fictitious history of the regal period and the fourth has all the trappings of the antiquarianism of the late Republic or early empire, there is agreement among scholars that this edition must have had a great deal of material added to whatever survived from the *tabulae*.

(*c*) *When was the eighty-book edition published?* I stated that the long-standard view that P. Mucius Scaevola published the *annales maximi* was 'demolished' by Frier.[2] This phrasing now seems to me to be too strong: Frier performed the great service of drawing attention to the fact that Mommsen's hypothesis was not based on any statement in the sources. Nevertheless, it is not an absurd deduction from Cic. *de or.* ii. 52; it has the merit of explaining the size of Gellius' history; and it is conceivable that this kind of material could have been developed *c.*120 BC:[3] for we know virtually nothing about Latin prose literature—Cato's *de agricultura* apart—before Cicero, and the rediscovery of Cn. Gellius' *annales* might transform our thinking about Roman historiography and antiquarianism in the late second century.[4] For this last reason I am not quite so certain of the strength of Frier's case that this edition was published in Augustan times,[5] even though many may feel more comfortable in ascribing the material reported by Aulus Gellius from the *annales maximi* to the Augustan Age, by which time Varro had developed Roman antiquarianism. All that is certain is that Verrius Flaccus, mentioned in the fragment cited by Gellius, provides a *terminus ante quem*.[6] A defect of Frier's position is that it must follow

---

[1] In this he was anticipated by Bernays (1857). Rüpke's argument that L.'s inability to verify the view that Fabius Verrucosus was an augur for sixty-two years shows that records were not in existence for the 260s is very weak: (*a*) L. himself was not much given to verification of this kind; (*b*) he refers to Fabius' augurate and not his pontificate; and (*c*) we do have evidence that evidence relating to the augurs survived for this period (see vol. i, pp. 53–4, in the *addendum* to which there is further discussion of Rüpke's views).

[2] For this view I cited on p. 26 only recent scholars writing in English; it goes back to Mommsen (e.g. 1894–5: iv. 248). I should have noted the brief remark of Henderson (1962: 278), anticipating Frier. For criticism of Frier's views see e.g. Petzold (1993) esp. 151–4 and Walt (1997) 128 n. 585.

[3] Mommsen's position has been reasserted recently by Petzold (1993: esp. 151–4).

[4] Those who believe that Piso was the first annalist (see above) are able to argue that it explains the annalistic form and content of his history.

[5] My sentence 'Frier (1979: 27–67) has made a very strong case for believing that Verrius Flaccus published it [the 80-book edition of the pontifical chronicle] in the Augustan age' misrepresents Frier's position; he argues that Verrius cited a work produced in his own time.

[6] Seeck (1885: 89–90) interestingly notes that in the late Republic and early Principate the *annales maximi* seem to have been consulted at first hand by almost no one apart from Cicero (who may owe his knowledge to Atticus) and Verrius Flaccus (who, Seeck held, was in a posi-

from it that, although Cicero and Servius auctus both use the term *annales maximi*, they mean different things by it.[1]

(*d*) *Was there an earlier transcription of the* tabulae? That there was such a transcription has been believed by various scholars. The best positive evidence for it is provided by Cic. *leg*. i. 6 'nam post annales pontificum maximorum, quibus nihil potest ieiunius (*Ursinus*: iocundius *codd*.), si aut ad Fabium aut . . . Catonem . . . uenias': *post* almost certainly implies that Fabius wrote after the *annales*, and it is awkward to have *annales* referring just to the *tabula(e)*. Those such as Frier who believe that the eighty-book edition was published after 91 BC are free to argue that *mandabat litteris* at Cic. *de or*. ii. 52 provides further evidence;[2] and, if this did happen, we should not have to postulate either that piles of old wooden *alba* were kept for years in the *regia* or that Fabius Pictor and other early Roman writers or their slaves spent much time rummaging around these piles.

Mommsen, locc. citt., developed a theory refined by others in the first years of the twentieth century (see esp. Enmann and Kornemann locc. citt.),[3] that Fabius Pictor was able to make use of a written source, the so-called *liber annalis*, an unattested chronicle hypothesized as a precursor of the later published *annales maximi*. Though now disregarded, this hypothesis has some real merits. It makes it possible to argue that the chronicle was not just an assemblage of odd facts but explains the fundamental unity of Roman accounts of their early history (something that does need explanation); and this in turn would mean that a Fabius could not be held to have shaped Rome's past according to his own whims. Various dates were suggested for the time at which this putative chronicle was written down: Mommsen, for example, suggested the era of the final Latin and the Samnite Wars, Kornemann that of the Pyrrhic War, and Enmann and Rüpke (1993: 167–70, arguing from a rather different perspective) the First Punic War, when Tiberius Coruncanius was *pontifex maximus*.[4]

The hypothesis should nevertheless be rejected. Its main weakness is that as the prime agent for assembling the facts about the early Republic it replaces a well-attested source (Fabius Pictor) with one that is unattested (*liber annalis*) and in doing so does no more than push the problem back a

tion to study Atticus' books); but he goes too far when he suggests that they were never formally published.

[1] This point was made clearly by Crake (1940: 377). This will be a problem for any theory that postulates the publication of the 80-book edition after 91 BC, the dramatic date of the *de oratore*. It is not a problem for any date between *c*.120 and 91.

[2] Note the argument of Rüpke (1993: 172–6), based on this passage of Cicero and supported by Liv. i. 32. 2 (quoted below), that the commentary of the *pontifex maximus* was the primary document and the *tabula* was a selection from it; but in Cicero *litteris* may refer simply to the *tabulae*, and Servius auctus (quoted at vol. i, p. 25) supports the conventional interpretation.

[3] There are helpful discussions of the various champions of this theory by Perl (1964: 187–8), Frier (1999: 11–14), and Walt (1997: 120–38).

[4] See also *addendum* to p. 25, on the development of the chronicle around 300, where Rüpke's view are discussed.

generation or two.[1] In all this it comes close to sharing the fallacy beloved of source-critics that in antiquity only lost or unknown works could innovate. Nor does the fundamental unity of our accounts of early Roman history have to be explained by the existence of such a work: the past may already have been shaped in outline, if not in detail, by oral tradition (see above).

In the revised form in which it is presented by Frier, in which a transcription of the pontifical tables was just one of many sources used by Fabius, this theory has much more to commend it, and I still think that it may be right.[2] Nevertheless, the view that Fabius and others did their own research among the *tabulae* has been held by reputable scholars and is defensible.[3]

p. 24. At Cic. *de or.* ii. 52 *referebat* is Lambinus' conjecture for *efferebat*; I now agree with e.g. Rüpke (1993: 174) that Liv. i. 32. 2 'omnia ex commentariis regiis pontificem in album elata proponere in publico iubet' protects the paradosis.

pp. 26–7. I should have made clear that in the passages quoted Cicero refers more to style than content; but the two are not easily separated, and it is hard to think that the early annalists could have imitated the style of the *tabulae* without familiarizing themselves to some degree with their contents. Nevertheless, I am now less confident that the passages of Cicero cited make it 'almost certain' that the early annalists used the pontifical tables. Cicero may have known very little about how Fabius Pictor and his successors worked, and his views in these passages may be no more than a schematic reconstruction, like that offered by our sources for the origins of Roman drama (on which see vii. 2. 4–13 n.); see Gelzer (1934) 53–5 = (1962–4) iii. 100–2 and Frier (1999) 275–7.

p. 27. For the *libri lintei* see now Forsythe (1994: 309) (who accepts their existence but with good reason doubts the ability of Licinius Macer accurately to interpret them) and Walt (1997: 75–85) (who takes an optimistic view of their reliability that I find unpersuasive). I omitted to document my statement 'It has been argued that the books were fabricated by Macer': see e.g. Mommsen (1859) 92–8 and Klotz (1937) 218–19, (1940–1) 295. Since Moneta was the goddess of memory and measurement (*addendum* to vi. 20. 13 n.), Meadows and Williams (2001: 29–30, 36–7) note the appropriateness of her temple as the repository of the *libri*.

p. 28. Further evidence for the existence of early lists of consuls is provided by the stone mentioned by Festus (190), which seems to have recorded the

---

[1] This point is made with exemplary sharpness by Perl (1964: 213). Other strong critics of the *liber annalis* theory include Crake (1940), Jacoby (1949: 61–5, with extensive notes) and Frier (1999: *passim*).

[2] However, my sentence 'As to the mechanics of the recording, it is preferable to believe that the contents of the *alba* were transcribed at an early date into a chronicle, rather than that piles of wood remained stacked up in the back of the office of the *pontifex maximus*' was written loosely, since it is rash to assume that transcription of *tabulae* took the form of a chronicle, rather than a commentary of the kind found in the *acta* of the Arval Bethren.

[3] The view of Bucher's mentioned at vol. i, pp. 25–6 is a compromise.

names of early consuls. For discussion see e.g. Forsythe (1994) 308.

pp. 28–9. Flower (1996), a full and comprehensive study, is now the standard treatment of *imagines*; she discusses family trees at pp. 211–17.

Further evidence for Roman families' recording the exploits of their ancestors is provided by Plin. *nat.* xxxv. 12 (quoted above, p. 221), where it is said that Ap. Claudius Caecus displayed *tituli* relating to his ancestors in his temple of Bellona. Although Pliny may make a mistake in dating Appius (see discussion of the text at p. 221), there is no reason to doubt his statement, and later in the Republic these *tituli* may have been used by those writing about Roman history.

p. 30 n. 42. The passage of Cicero is discussed well by Münzer (1999: 126–7).

p. 31. On legendary genealogies see now Hölkeskamp (1999) = (2004) 199–217.

p. 31. A possible example of an attempt by a family to claim for itself an exploit that was not its own is found on the *denarii* of 60 BC of P. Plautius Hypsaeus, in which he commemorates the capture of Privernum. That he was related to C. Plautius Decianus who captured Privernum in 329 is doubtful. See Crawford (1974) 444–5 with pl. li and Hölkeskamp (1999) 16–17 = (2004) 212–15.

pp. 31–2. My conclusions are in accord with those of Badian (1990: 216), who interestingly emphasizes the positive role that family records may have played in the creation of the Roman historical tradition.

pp. 32–3. The considerable familiarity with the gentile history of the Papirii which Cicero displays in his well-known letter to Paetus (*fam.* ix. 21) may derive from perusal of Atticus' writings. Even if it does not, it shows what information on families was available to the diligent researcher in the midfirst century BC.

p. 33. In one case the filiation preserved in *F.C.* can be confirmed by other inscriptional evidence. Under e.g. 260 and 259 we learn that Cn. Cornelius Scipio Asina and L. Cornelius Scipio were both *L. f. Cn. n.* This shows that they were the sons of L. Scipio Barbatus, *cos.* 298 (x. 11. 10. n.), and the grandsons of a probably otherwise unknown Gnaeus. That Barbatus' father was Gnaeus is confirmed by his *elogium* (*ILLRP* 309 = FIGS 4 and 5).

Against the reliability of family records may be set those passages where L. has difficulty in finding out the true *cognomen* of a consul and hence his real identity, or where another source disagrees with L. on a *cognomen* (e.g. viii. 18. 1, 22. 1, 23. 17 nn.). This may have been caused by the absence of *cognomina* from official documents until quite late in the Republic; and such was the fluidity of *cognomina* in the fourth century (see *addendum* to viii. 23. 17 n.) that one may have sympathy for later family historians who sometimes struggled on this matter.

However, the extensive use of *cognomina* in *F.C.*, *F.T.*, and our narrative sources for early Roman history should not be regarded as a sign of the unreliability of this evidence. It is true that some *cognomina* may have been backdated from later to earlier members of a family (ix. 16. 13 n.) and that the few *cognomina* that derive from conquered peoples have been regarded with suspicion (see below); but there is no evidence for widespread invention of these names, and there is little doubt that they, and especially those belonging to classes represented by e.g. Brutus, Bubulcus, Capitolinus (*addendum* to vi. 11. 1–20. 16 n.), Maximus (ix. 46. 15 n.), and Philo (vii. 21. 6, ix. 33. 5 nn.) were in use in the fourth century (see Alföldi [1966]). As for the names derived from conquered peoples, no one doubts that after his success in Sicily in 263 M'. Valerius Maximus was called Messalla. Much less certainly authentic are Calenus used of M. Atilius Regulus, *cos.* 335 (viii. 16. 5 n.), Privernas of L. Aemilius Mamercus, *cos.* II in 329 (vii. 39. 17 n.), and Caudinus of L. Cornelius Lentulus, *cos.* 275 (*F.C.* note *qui postea Caudinus appellatus est*). It is awkward that rival traditions suggest that the successes of 335 and 329 were won by the other consul. At worst these names are invented on the basis of known successes (Lentulus) or represent a claim to success (Aemilius, Regulus); but it is far from certain that the rival traditions are right and conceivable that these names represent early examples of a type that became fashionable only after the successes of Scipio Africanus.

pp. 35–7. Paintings in temples are another class of monument that may have provided a source for the earliest annalists. Note esp. Fest. 228 (quoted at x. 7. 9 n.) on the depiction in the temples of Consus and Vertumnus of the triumphs of, respectively, L. Papirius Cursor in 272 and M. Fulvius Flaccus in 264. See Coarelli (1996) 13.

p. 36 n. 79. The final comments of this footnote are replaced by viii. 13. 9 n. and *addendum*, where a less sceptical attitude is taken to the equestrian statues of 338.

p. 38. I ought to have noted that the battle of Sentinum was mentioned by the third-century Greek historian Duris (see above, p. 268), although one cannot be certain that any Roman historian had read his work.

pp. 41–4. If the argument of this section is mistaken and our evidence for the dictatorship is even less good than I have suggested, then a possible explanation has been provided by Badian (1990: 216), namely that most dictatorships were not recorded in the pontifical records.

p. 47. My reasons for holding that the *interregnum* recorded by L. at x. 11. 10 is authentic were anticipated by some earlier scholars, e.g. Lejay (1920: 104).

p. 47 *et alibi*. A parallel to L.'s selectivity in using material available to him in official records may be found in the way in which he sometimes alludes to earlier episodes in Roman history that he had not himself recounted (or fully recounted): see e.g. ix. 12. 5 (n.), the speech made by M. Antistius at the time of the defection of Satricum, mentioned by L. at xxvi. 33. 10; ix. 34. 20 (nn.), on co-option to the censorship in 392; and x. 46. 7, the temple to Quirinus vowed by the elder Papirius Cursor. See further Ridley (1991) 214–17. Badian (1996: 187–90) notes L.'s selectivity in his later books in reporting tribunician activity.

p. 50. For a list of known or conjecturable praetors between 366 and 49 BC see now Brennan (2000) 725–57.

pp. 51–2. Two other men are attested as having held the curule aedileship at some point before the First Punic War. *ILLRP* 309 reveals that L. Cornelius Scipio Barbatus held the office, probably before his consulship in 298. Cicero (*fam.* ix. 21. 2) mentions a L. Papirius Maso who was younger than the elder of the two Papirii Cursores who defeated the Samnites, was the ancestor of later Masones, and was an *aedilicius*. Therefore he was probably the grandfather (conceivably the great-grandfather) of C. Papirius C. f. L. n. Maso, *cos.* 231 (the filiation is given by *F.C.* and *F.T.*): see Münzer (1999) 106.

p. 52 n. 124. I am no longer so confident that Piso is correct: see x. 9. 10–13 n.

pp. 53–4. The view that *ILS* 9338 points to the existence of an augural archive is argued fully by Vaahtera (2003). On priestly archives see also Beard (1998). Rüpke (1993: 160–5) observes that the information preserved on augurs contrasts sharply with what we are told about pontiffs: L. and D.H. mention the names of several pontiffs but not in contexts that suggest the use of an archival source. He argues that both these names and the notices of the death of Ser. Sulpicius, the *curio maximus*, in 463 (iii. 7. 7) and of Ser. Cornelius, the *flamen Quirinalis*, in 453 (iii. 32. 3) are invented, the invention being due largely to Licinius Macer. However, the case against iii. 7. 7 and 32. 3 is weak, and the suggested role of Macer is no more than speculation.

p. 55 n. 134. For legates see also Loreto (1991–2) 284–7.

p. 56–7. It would have been useful to list the evidence for triumphs in the period covered by books vi–x. For the period down to 368, for which *F.T.* are not extant, L. refers to triumphs in:

389	M. Furius Camillus (vi. 4. 1–3)
385	A. Cornelius Cossus (vi. 16. 5)
380	T. Quinctius Capitolinus (vi. 29. 8–10)

For the period after 368, *F.T.* are almost entirely extant from 360–291, and in addition there are small fragments which are ascribed to 367 and 361. For this period L. and *F.T.* agree in recording the following triumphs:

360	C. Poetelius Balbus (vii. 11. 9)
360	M. Fabius Ambustus (an ovation) (vii. 11. 9, on which see *addendum* below)
358	C. Sulpicius Peticus (vii. 15. 8)
357	C. Marcius Rutilus (vii. 16. 6)
356	C. Marcius Rutilus (vii. 17. 9)
354	M. Fabius Ambustus (thus *F.T.*; L. [vii. 19. 2] does not specify the names of the consul or consuls who triumphed)
350	M. Popillius Laenas (vii. 25. 1)
346	M. Valerius Corvus (vii. 27. 8)
343	A. Cornelius Cossus and M. Valerius Corvus (vii. 38. 3)
339	Q. Publilius Philo (viii. 12. 9)
338	L. Furius Camillus and C. Maenius (viii. 13. 9)

335   M. Valerius Corvus (viii. 16. 11)
329   C. Plautius (viii. 20. 7)
326   Q. Publilius Philo (viii. 26. 7)
325/4 L. Papirius Cursor (viii. 37. 1)
310/9 L. Papirius Cursor and Q. Fabius Rullianus (ix. 40. 15 and 20; *F.T.*
       place the triumphs in the dictator-year 309)
306   Q. Marcius Tremulus (ix. 43. 22)
302/1 C. Junius Bubulcus and M. Valerius Corvus (x. 1. 9, 5. 12; *F.T.*
       ascribe the second triumph to the dictator-year 301)
298   Cn. Fulvius Maximus (x. 13. 1)
295   Q. Fabius Maximus Rullianus (x. 30. 8)
293   Sp. Carvilius Maximus and L. Papirius Cursor (x. 46. 2–6, 13–15)

Nevertheless, there are some discrepancies in years for which both L. and
F.T. record triumphs:

322   *F.T.* give triumphs to the consuls, Fabius Rullianus and Fulvius
      Curvus, a version known also to L. (viii. 40. 1). However, in his
      main version L. gives a triumph to the dictator A. Cornelius Arvina
319   *F.T.* and L.'s preferred version of events ascribe a triumph to L.
      Papirius Cursor; some of L.'s sources ascribed the triumph to the
      dictator Lentulus (ix. 15. 9–10, 16. 11)
305   *F.T.* give a triumph to the suffect consul M. Fulvius Curvus; L. (ix.
      44. 14) gives triumphs to L. Postumius Megellus and Ti. Minucius,
      whom Fulvius had replaced in office, but his reference to Fulvius,
      although vague on the matter of the triumph, does imply that some
      of his source(s) recorded information similar to that found in *F.T.*
304   *F.T.* give both consuls triumphs, Sempronius Sophus over the
      Aequi and Sulpicius Saverrio over the Samnites; L. (45. 18) states
      merely that there was a triumph over the Aequi, without mentioning
      the name of the consul(s) (however, earlier he had implied that
      Sempronius was in Samnium)
294   *F.T.* make both L. Postumius Megellus and M. Atilius Regulus tri-
      umph: L. narrates the triumph of Postumius (x. 37. 6–12) but states
      (37. 13) that Claudius Quadrigarius ascribed it to Atilius

In addition, *F.T.* record some triumphs not recorded by L.:

367   M. Furius Camillus (if *Degrassi, I.I.* xiii. 1, pp. 539–40, is right to
      restore *F.T.* in this way: but none of our other sources [see vol. i, p.
      716] records a triumph for Camillus in this year)
361   C. Sulpicius Peticus and T. Quinctius Pennus Capitolinus (if
      Degrassi, p. 540) is right to restore *F.T.* in this way; there is no other
      evidence for a triumph in this year, but for Sulpicius see *addendum*
      to vol. ii, p. 3)
358   C. Plautius Proculus
340   T. Manlius Torquatus

329 L. Aemilius Mamercinus
314 C. Sulpicius Longus
312 M. Valerius Maximus
311 Q. Aemilius Barbula and C. Junius Bubulcus
299 M. Fulvius Paetinus

None of these notices is supported by other sources.

For only one year does another source record a triumph found in neither L. nor *F.T.*:

312 P. Decius Mus (*uir. ill.* 27. 1)

Some of these discrepancies will be due to L.'s and *F.T.*'s using different sources (see esp. L.'s own comments), and I still see no reason to believe that the compilers of *F.T.* had access to better material than L. However, it is striking that, cases discussed by L. apart, *F.T.* omit no triumph recorded by L., but L. omits several triumphs recorded by *F.T.* Although some of these triumphs in *F.T.* may have been invented (for suspicious instances see ix. 29. 1–5 [312 BC], 31. 1–32. 10 [311 BC] nn.; one may add that the instance recorded for 312 at *uir. ill.* 27. 1 is unlikely to be sound: again see ix. 29. 1–5 n.), it is likely that rather more were omitted by L., whether deliberately or not (that of T. Manlius Torquatus in 340 is the most conspicuous example). His failure to record these triumphs is another good example of his selectivity in using the official information available to him: he was writing a history and not an official list, and probably did not see the need dutifully to record every triumph; and, on some occasions, he may have omitted triumphs because he found nothing to justify them in his sources.

The case for the view that triumphs were recorded in official records may be strengthened somewhat by referring to Asellio's polemic against the annalists (quoted at vol. i, pp. 73–4), in which he notes that annalists recorded *quis triumphans introierit*. However, it is not certain that Asellio refers to narratives of the period 509–293 rather than to those of his own day; and second-century annalists were probably as capable of inventing early Roman triumphs as their first-century successors.

p. 57. On the question of dates in *F.T.* Seeck (1885: 91–6) had taken the opposite view to Beloch: he held that almost all were likely to be right, the oddness of some both being explained by distortions in the calendar and making it unlikely that they were invented.

pp. 57–8. We also know from xxvii. 6. 8 that as *interrex* in 292/1 L. Postumius Megellus presided at the consular elections.

p. 59. The discussion of games is muddled. The paragraph should be replaced with the following: 'The *ludi Romani* are mentioned at vi. 42. 12 (367 BC), viii. 40. 2 (322 BC; see n. ad loc. and cf. ix. 34. 12), and x. 47. 3 (293 BC: see n. ad loc.), the *ludi plebeii* at x. 23. 13 (n.); these last two passages resemble the later "annalistic" sections of L.'s work. *Votive games* are mentioned throughout the decade (see viii. 40. 2 n., with *addendum*, below, pp. 586–7).'

pp. 59–60. That prodigies were a regular feature of annalistic narrative is implied by L. at xliii. 13. 1.

The prodigies reported at vii. 28. 7–8 include an eclipse, that is one of the items on whose presence in the *annales* Cato remarks (see vol. i, p. 24). For another eclipse in the early annalistic record, see Enn. *ann*. 153 = Cic. *rep*. i. 25. The observation that in book x L.'s reporting of prodigies begins to resemble what is found in books xxi–xlv could have been reinforced by citing Oros. iv. 4. 1–4 (269 BC) and 5. 1 (265 BC), passages which derive from L. and relate to a period of the Roman conquest of Italy for which L. is now lost.[1]

pp. 60–1. I omitted to record certain information relating to temples: that of Castor was vowed in 499 (ii. 20. 12), that of Ceres, Liber, and Libera was vowed in 496 and dedicated in 493 (D.H. vi. 17. 2 [cf. Tac. *ann*. ii. 49. 1] and 94. 3), that of Salus was vowed probably in 311 and had its *locatio* in 306 (see ix. 31. 1–16, 43. 25 nn.).

p. 62. For the later period we also have more precise notices of Roman troop-disposition and Roman casualties: see ix. 24. 1, x. 29. 18 nn.

p. 62. Although the statement 'the triumphs of 293 (x. 46. 2–6, 13–15) are the first to be described in a way that looks forward to later years' is basically correct, I should have noted (*a*) that the reference to the size of the donative in L.'s description of the triumph of Fabius Rullianus in 295 (30. 8–10) anticipates the notices of 293; (*b*) that the reference to the presence of troops at Fabius' triumph may be paralleled in L.'s later books; and (*c*) that the extended description (x. 37. 6–12) of the difficulties experienced by L. Postumius Megellus when he triumphed in 294 may also be paralleled in later books (see nn. ad loc.). Although there is some doubt about the triumph of 294, these passages provide further evidence for the quality of the material available to L. when he wrote book x.

p. 63. For the argument that obscure place-names in L. are likely to be authentic, see also e.g. Harris (1971) 60.

p. 69. Replace 'ix. 15. 9–10' with 'ix. 15. 9–10, 16. 11'.

pp. 72–3. In addition to the works of Badian and Wiseman cited, essential modern bibliography on the development of the annalistic tradition includes e.g. Timpe (1979), Petzold (1993), and Walt (1997) 119–42.

p. 73. In writing 'Valerius Antias wrote at least seventy-five books, but it is impossible to work out their distribution', I failed to take account of the fact that the mss at Gell. vi. 9. 2 show him referring to the events of 136 in book xxii (fr. 57). For Forsythe's view that this fragment comes from Antias' Caudine narrative, see vol. iii, p. 6 n. 1.

pp. 73–4. My brief comments on frr. 1 and 2 of Asellio give no indication that they are controversial and have generated a very large bibliography, for

---

[1] Since Obsequens records prodigies only from 249 BC onwards, Mommsen (*ap*. O. Jahn [1853] p. xx) held that they were first recorded systematically from this year. It would follow that there was no reliable recording of prodigies in the period covered by L.'s early books. However, it is quite unclear why Obsequens starts his work in this year, and Mommsen's thesis was rightly rejected by e.g. Klinger (1884: 45–6).

much of which see Cavazza (1988) 36–7 (adding Walbank [1945] 15–18 = [1985] 94–8). The controversy concerns both text (in fr. 2 I followed Mommsen in reading *bello gesta sint [iterare id fabulas] non praedicare* but did not signal the deletion) and interpretation (there has been much discussion of what Asellio means by *annales*). Schäublin (1983: 153–5) observes that no earlier historian could have produced a work quite so devoid of useful material as Asellio claims; he therefore follows Gelzer (1934: 47, 1954: 347–8 = 1962–4: iii. 94–5, 109–10) in arguing that Asellio must have been criticizing the *annales maximi* and not his predecessors. Even if this view is right, it is still possible to use these fragments as illustrative of attitudes that may have encouraged the expansion of the annalistic narrative of early Rome. However, Schäublin is far too literal-minded: Asellio is criticizing his historical predecessors by producing a caricature of their work.

D.S. xxx. 15. 1, a comment on how history ought to be written, has many similarities with these fragments of Asellio; it too stresses how moral improvement may come from reading a properly written history.

pp. 75–6. *The need for detail.* For a similar point of view to that expressed in this section see Wiseman (1993) 141–6.

p. 77 n. 206. For political bias in historians and claims to be free from it, see also Wiseman (1993) 126–8 and esp. Marincola (1997) 158–74.

pp. 76–9. See on p. 6.

pp. 83–5. When I wrote these pages, I was not aware that in the course of his analysis of book x Klinger (1884) regularly points out standard motifs in L. and D.H.; see further *addendum* to p. 19 n. 23.

pp. 89–91. I have not demonstrated, as Mr Rich points out to me, that some of the fictions in Antias could not have originated with a predecessor, e.g. Cn. Gellius. However, if they were found in a predecessor of Antias, they were more likely to have found their way into the other sources used by L. On p. 91 I should have observed that the case against the decree on Numa's books is far from certain.

p. 89. Münzer (1891) is not listed in the bibliography, but see that for vol. ii.

p. 90. Read 'Tappulus' for 'Tapulus'.

p. 92. My statement 'Macer certainly invented pro-plebeian activity for the Licinii' needs a little qualification, since the evidence which I adduce shows only that Macer invented activity for them. That he also invented pro-plebeian activity is a probable conjecture; see further *addendum* to vii. 9. 10 n.

p. 93. The story which Tubero (fr. 8) tells of Regulus' fight against the serpent was recounted also by L. (*per.* xviii, fr. 9 = Val. Max. i. 8 *ext.* 19) and various other authors (e.g. Sen. *epist.* 82. 24, Plin. *nat.* viii. 37 'nota est in Punicis bellis ad flumen Bagradam a Regulo imperatore ballistis tormentisque, ut oppidum aliquod, expugnata serpens CXX pedum longitudinis; pellis eius maxillaeque usque ad bellum Numantinum durauere Romae in templo', Sil. vi. 141–293, Zon. viii. 13. 2, Joh. Dam. *mir.* i, p. 472 A–B [like Zonaras, derived from Dio]). Although it is conceivable that Tubero invented this tale, the abundance of other testimony does not make this likely. If there is any truth in Pliny's statement that relics of this serpent survived in a temple until the time of the Numantine War, then these relics (which could have been of any exotic African animal) could have provided a starting-point for the story. It remains valid to use the story to illustrate Tubero's love of the sensational. It is possible, but far from certain, that in book xviii L. used Tubero as (one of) his source(s) for this story.

pp. 94–6. The story of Regulus and the serpent (see above, on p. 93) should have been cited in the context of the sensational in L.

p. 97. For the invention of victories to compensate for defeats note too x. 26. 7–13 (the defeat at Camerinum or Clusium in 295), discussed at x. 24. 1–31. 15 n.

p. 97. I quoted x. 30. 4–7 from Walters's text without making clear that *sexiens centena milia* was his conjecture: see now the n. ad loc.

p. 98. 'Antias and Quadrigarius produce Roman letters to Pyrrhus': in fact fr. 21, a summary by Gellius, only refers to such a letter and does not quote from it. We cannot know whether Antias himself quoted the letter.

pp. 98–9. As Kraus (1998: 269–72) makes clear, the role of stock family characteristics in L.'s history is dynamic rather than static. When different members of a family behave in a similar way, or perform similar exploits, we are being invited to compare and contrast them, the single combats of the two Manlii (vii. 9–10, viii. 7) being the most obvious example.

p. 102. For doublets in L. see also Kraus (1998) 273–4.

pp. 104–6. *Chronology.* I should have made clear that here and elsewhere in the commentary 'a year' in the context of Roman history means a consular year and not a calendar year, whether Roman or modern.

p. 107. Ruschenbusch (1997) argues that throughout his history D.S. used only Greek sources, claiming that this proposition is supported by numerous verbal similarities between writers whom D.S. is known to have used as a source (principally Polybius) and other Greek writers. Much of the evidence is worthless, since (*a*) the verbal similarities often turn out to be not close at all; (*b*) several are from D.H. and Plutarch, who admit to using Latin sources. Ruschenbush is unaware of the evidence adduced by Triemal for D.S's misunderstanding of a Latin source (see vol. iii, p. 530).

p. 108. The chronological compression that appears from time to time in D.S.'s Roman narrative appears also in other parts of his work (see e.g. xi. 54. 1–4, 60. 1–62. 3, and esp. 64. 4 and 67. 1). Given the nature of the history which D.S. was writing the technique was convenient, even if it causes difficulty for modern scholars trying to reconstruct a precise chronology.

Ch. 5. *The Style and Literary Techniques of Livy*

pp. 114–17. *Moralizing and the desire to instruct.* Chaplin (2000) now replaces Chaplin (1993). The conclusions which she reaches show that the account of Livian *exempla* given here is too static. By analysing the use which characters in L.'s history make of *exempla*, she shows that their role in his work is more dynamic. For instance, differing lessons may be learned from the same events, of which one is sometimes better than another (see vi. 27. 3–29. 10 n. [where Chaplin (2000) 73–4 should replace the reference to Chaplin (1993) 110]) and the discussion at ix. 1. 1–16. 19 n. of the use made later in L.'s history of the Caudine Forks), and more recent *exempla* may be more potent than those more distant (see ix. 34. 14 n.).

Moralizing in L.'s early books is discussed by Forsythe (1999: 65–73).

p. 115. On *exempla* see further Leigh (1997) 160–72.

p. 117. In the context of L.'s desire to instruct note also (*a*) his use of remarks like *ut fit* and *ut solet* to draw attention to standard patterns of action or behaviour (see vi. 34. 5 n. with *addendum*) and (*b*) his praise or criticism of individuals, a practice expected of an ancient historian (see *addendum* to vii. 21. 6 n.).

pp. 117–20. *Speeches.* See also Forsythe (1999: 74–86), who well remarks on L.'s caution in the inclusion of speeches, particularly in books i–iii.

pp. 122–5. *The annalistic framework.* See now Levene (1993) 38–125 and esp. Rich (1997), who show that L.'s handling of this material is subtler than has sometimes been believed.

p. 122 n. 72. That L. took over this annalistic framework from Quadrigarius is doubtful: see above, pp. 477–8.

p. 126. For further examples of links between episodes or scenes see x. 20. 1–16 and 39. 1–42. 7 nn.

p. 127. For episodes built around speeches note also x. 24. 1–18, discussed above, p. 271. For episodes ending with the notice of a triumph, note also ix. 16. 11, 40. 15, 45. 18, and x. 5. 13.

p. 128. For an episode ending with the report of an institution established because of the result of that episode, add ix. 40. 16–17 (the institution of gladiators called *Samnites*). With episodes that end with the return of troops to Rome compare also those that end with the return of troops to a base in a province (e.g. xxxv. 1. 11 and xli. 5. 12).

p. 132. For another good example of a (short) period with strained syntax, see ix. 35. 7 n.

p. 135 n. 130. For another periodic sentence introducing a speech, add ix. 33. 6–7.

p. 137. For the technique of splitting a group into its component parts, see also ix. 5. 8.

p. 140. U. Walter (2001: 253) well notes how in the sentence quoted from vi. 40. 3 *mihi* and *familiae nostrae* are balanced by *ego* and *Claudiae genti*.

p. 148. Imprecise use of technical terms; see ix. 38. 15 (*diem diffindere*), 41. 3 (*interpellare*), 45. 14 (*gradu*) nn. For words found only in speeches add *addendum* to vi. 37. 2 n. (*atqui*).

p. 148 n. 1. For colloquialisms in L.'s speeches, see also ix. 10. 5 (*en umquam*) and 24. 9 (*pro uestram fidem*) nn.

p. 148 n. 198. For expressions with an interesting distribution, see also nn. on ix. 20. 3 (*per aliquot dies*) and 42. 3 (*interpellare*).

p. 149. For variation in L.'s use of connecting conjunctions see also e.g. ix. 45. 1 (on *ultro citro*).

p. 149 n. 204. See also ix. 46. 7 (*ex auctoritate latum ad populum est*).

p. 149 n. 206. Delete the reference both to *rem perdere* and the n. on it at ix. 2. 13: the expression is found twice in Sallust and Florus, thrice in Tacitus.

p. 150 n. 207. For clustering see also ix. 45. 2 (on *ad id locorum*).

p. 150 n. 210. For L.'s development of the predicative dative, see ix. 41. 6 n.

Ch. 6. *The Manuscripts*

My main dissatisfaction with this chapter is that I drew my evidence for the readings of the *recentiores* largely from collation of three passages in books vi and vii. Although these passages (chosen after inspection of Drakenborch's edn. had suggested that they would provide sufficient errors of diagnostic significance) have proved very useful in furnishing readings that allow classification of mss that have no changes of exemplar in their ancestry, they do not help in the classification of the first part of the text of mss which switched exemplars before book vi (nor of a defective ms. like Geneva BPU 176). I now regret that I did not collate several pages from *praef.* onwards but have not thought the gains to be made by doing this to be of such importance that I should revisit all the mss, a task that would prove costly in terms of travel.

pp. 152–3. Since 1997 Professor Reeve has kindly alerted me to the existence of three more mss that include all or part of the first decade: Halle, Universitäts- und Landesbibliothek 22 E 14, Leipzig, Universitätsbibliothek 3470, and fragments of iii. 22. 4–6 in the binding of a copy of the Marcolini 1539 Venice edition of Petrarch's *Sonetti et Canzoni*, now in the Beinecke Library at Yale (see Babcock 1994: 312, 316). The textual affiliations of the first two I discuss below (p. 496). Of the third Professor Babcock kindly sent me a photograph, which reveals that too little of the text survives for any comment to be made on its affiliations; inspecting it, Professor de la Mare saw no reason why it should not have been written in the Veneto in the middle or second half of s. xv.

Of the two fragmentary mss (Modena, Arch. Cap. O II 8 and Ambr. D 542 inf. pastedown) about which I knew nothing in 1997, I still know nothing about the Modena palimpsest (reports of which suggest that little is legible for inspection), but discuss the Ambrosian pastedown below.

The article by Reeve cited in vol. i as forthcoming is cited here as Reeve (1996).

p. 158. On V see also Marchi (1996) 91–2.

p. 159. On Zb and its set see P. Supino Martini, in Buonocore (1996) 494–9 and fig. 518, with illustration of f. 1ʳ. On Zp see also AA.VV. (2003) 94 with plate 23 (of f. 1ʳ).

p. 165 n. 28. Add x. 38. 6 n.

p. 180. De la Mare (2000: 77) argued that Bergamo MA 299 (Δ. 9. 17) was written by Giacomo Curlo (she forgot to record that the attribution was suggested earlier to her [and to me] by Professor Reeve) and that some decoration was added to the ms. in the Veneto *c*.1470.

On Florence, Naz. B.R. 34 see now G. Lazzi, in Buonocore (1996) 387–91 and fig. 380, with illustration of f. 1^r.

p. 182. For x. 18. 3 read x. 18. 13. Further good readings in χ (all doubtless conjectures) are discussed at ix. 3. 10, 19. 7, x. 7. 9, 8. 6, and 31. 5 nn.

pp. 182–4. Further evidence for the derivation of χ from M^{1+c} is provided by the following readings at x. 20. 5: *excipiant* Πλ (certainly correct; see n.): *incipiant* M^1: *intercipiant* $M^c\chi$ (a progressive corruption of the error found in M^1).

p. 191. For a nice further illustration of the dependence of X and other mss on T^{1+c}, see x. 14. 21, where T^1, with most of the older mss, has *accc* (for the interpretation of which see n. ad loc.), T^c has *adccc*, and *ad trecentos* is reported by Drakenborch from X and various *recentiores*.

p. 203. (On Vatican, Chig. H VI 190) For ownership of this ms. by Giovannantonio Campano and Agostino Patrizi, see Avesani (1964) 48–9.

(On Vat. lat. 11604) Professor Reeve has now studied the text of Florus in this ms.; he kindly tells me that it is related closely to that in Vat. lat. 1861 and Brescia, Bibl. Quer. A VI 27 and that the whole group belongs to the region of Brescia and Milan. See further Reeve (1991) 472.

p. 207 n. 179. For p. 182 read pp. 182–3.

p. 214. (On New College 277) A plausible explanation is available for the appearance of errors from the family of Y (which is fundamentally north Italian) as 'corrections' in the Florentine mss New College 277 and 278:[1] the mss were corrected by Thomas Candour, who is known to have been in Florence in 1442 and in Padua in 1446. De la Mare (cited in vol. i, p. 258) suggested that the whole set, like other New College mss, was owned by Andrew Holes (or Hollis) of New College, who is known to have been in Florence from 1439 to 1442 and to have given at least one Florentine ms. to his college. If this were right, then Candour (who must have known Holes) could have borrowed the set from him; but Dr David Rundle kindly tells me that there is no evidence that Holes ever owned the set. For Candour and mss copied or corrected by him see de la Mare in Hunt and de la Mare (1970) 18–19 and 32–5 (where his hand is identified as belonging to a 'Thomas S.') and in de la Mare and Barker-Benfield (1980) 95–6 (with corrected identification).

(On Campano's edn.) Since Campano owned Chig. H VI 190, it is conceivable that this was the φ-ms. by which the text of the exemplar for his edn. was contaminated.

p. 221 n. 223. On Arch. S. Pietro C 132 see P. Supino Martini, in Buonocore (1996) 297–9 and figs 245 and 246, with illustration of ff. 65^r and 107^r.

p. 221 n. 224. On Giacomo Curlo see now de la Mare (2000), with discussion of Chig. H VIII 254 at pp. 83–4. She argues that the ms. was produced in Rome.

---

[1] There are corrections also to New College 279; but Y did not include the fourth decade. The only other ms. known to have been written by the scribe of this set is London, B.L. Add. 16980 (Cicero, *oratt.*); see A. C. de la Mare, *ap.* Rizzo (1983) 67.

Addenda *and* corrigenda

On Verona, Cap. CXXX (123) see now Marchi (1996) 220.

pp. 242–7. Leipzig, Universitätsbibliothek (Haenel) 3470 (*membr. saec.* xiii) is another ms. that derives from D/D^1.[1] Before correction it shared all the errors of D/D^1 listed on p. 218, with the possible exception of that at vi. 15. 4 (where, however, it has probably been corrected). It seems to be independent of all other witnesses: note, for example, that it avoids the transposition of Q^1 at vi. 39. 10, the omission of A^1 at vi. 27. 6, the errors of Rome, Bibl. Naz. Sess. 43 listed on p. 244, and the errors of Vat. lat. 1844 listed on p. 242 (unfortunately, it is defective at the beginning of book i, and so it cannot be consulted for the errors that I cite from Vat. lat. 1840 or the other errors that I cite from Sess. 43). It avoids all the errors that I cite as characteristic of mss deriving from D^{1+c}, with the exception of that at x. 41. 13 (however, before correction it may have had also that at vii. 39. 8). The presence of the error at x. 41. 13 shows that some slight contamination has influenced its original text. The ms. has been corrected very heavily indeed (by this correction all the errors that I cite as diagnostic of D/D^1 have been removed); the introduction of vi. 38. 4 *fauore legum ipsarum latorumque*] *legum ipsarum latorumque fauore* suggests that the ms. from which the corrections were taken derives from Y^{1+c} (for this error see vol. i, p. 197).

p. 246. Halle 22 E 14 needs to be discussed with Laur. Ashburnham 288, which probably derives from it. The two mss inherit the same errors from D (the Halle ms. also has that at vii. 1. 9, for which Ashb. is now defective) and avoid the errors of D^c. In the portions which I collate Ashb. 288 shares all the uncorrected errors of the Halle ms :

vi. 8. 6 *[ceteram]*, 8. 7 *[et] longa*, 8. 10 *esse animi*] *animi esse* (also Chig. H VIII 254), 9. 6 *depo[po]scit*, 38. 8 *emouerent*] *amouerent* (also other mss), 38. 9 *pro dictatore quid*] *quid pro dictatore*, 39. 5 *accenderent*] *accendant*, 39. 10 *tribun[ici]os*, 39. 11 *ferri*] *fore* (also other mss), 40. 1 *[Crassus]* (also almost all descendants of Y), 40. 3 *nunc ego quoque*] *quoque nunc ego*, vii. 5. 1 *criminum*] *-inis*

and—significantly—some of the errors introduced by Halle^c:

vi. 8. 9 *Satrici*] *satricis* Halle^1 (and many other mss): *satriciis* Halle^c, Ashb., 38. 6 *adero*] *aderem* (?) Halle^1: *uestrae adero* (also several other mss), 38. 7 *si C.*] *sicut* θ, Halle^1: *si* Halle^c, Ashb. (also Bergamo, MA 570, perhaps coincidentally), and 40. 1 *[inde]* (also Vat. lat. 11604^c).

The failure of Halle^1 to share more errors of D^1 than Ashb. 288 shows that the contamination in the ancestry of the two mss goes back beyond Halle^c. Professor de la Mare kindly inspected my microfilm of the Halle ms. (on its precise provenance she felt unable to offer an opinion beyond suggesting that it was written in northern Italy in *saec.* xv^1) and Ashb. 288 *in situ* (she suggested that it was written in Verona; she noted too that the colophon has the date 1465, of which the '5' may not be original).

pp. 248–9. On Paris lat. 5690 see now F. Avril, in Buonocore (1996) 262–3

[1] In 1998 Professor Reeve kindly collated this ms. for me in all the three portions of text for which I collated most *recentiores*, and in 2004 I was able to inspect it myself.

and fig. 185, with illustration of f. 201ʳ. For 'among other writings' in the text read Florus and Dictys Cretensis. This ms. appears to have no descendants in any of the decades of Livy, but Reeve (1991: 460) has suggested progeny for Florus, and four mss of Dictys (Bergamo, Civ. MA 336, Modena, Est. lat. 1070, Parma, Pal. 257, Schaffhausen, Stadtbibl. Min. 118) are likely to derive from it. Why this should have happened, it is hard to say: for although Livy circulated more profusely in *s*. xiv in northern Italy, neither Florus nor Dictys was rare there.

pp. 249–53. The pastedown of Ambr. D 542 inf., which Professor Reeve kindly collated on my behalf, should be added to this first group of mss which derive from D¹⁺ᶜ (for its text, see below). I should have observed that (*a*) Ambr. D 542 inf. itself was written by Iohannes de Regio at Modena and (*b*) Pächt and Alexander (1966–73: ii. 64) suggest Verona as the provenance of Oxford, Bodl. Laud lat. 112, which coincides quite nicely with the northeast Italian provenance of several other members of the group (Verona is not quite north-eastern, but it is not far distant from Modena, and we shall see that the text of this ms. presents some difficulties which make a related, but slightly different, provenance not entirely unwelcome). On Vat. Urb. lat. 423–5 see now P. Piacentini, in Buonocore (1996) 428–9 and fig. 444 (with illustration of f. 1ʳ of 423), who suggests that the set was illuminated in Ferrara.

I have now seen Toledo 51. 2, from the decoration of which I surmise that, like Ambr. D 542 inf., Urb. lat. 423 and some other members of the group, it must have been written in north-eastern Italy. Whether Urb. lat. 423 is a direct copy of it I have not been able to determine: if it is, then this would provide further decisive textual evidence, to support that from the illumination, that it was one of the mss produced locally for the Urbino library and not provided by Vespasiano da Bisticci from Florence; even if it is not a direct copy, the textual evidence still suggests, although not so decisively, that it was produced locally.

pp. 250–1. The text of the pastedown of Ambr. D 542 inf. covers ii. 35. 3 'non patrum'–37. 9 'coetu quodam'.

The errors which it shares with all or most of e.g. D (I have not thought it worthwhile to collate HXRL to ascertain which of D's errors go back to θ, T/Xθ, and Λ), Esc. g I 8, Ambr. D 542 inf., Bergamo MA 570, Paris, BNF 5737, and doubtless a host of other mss deriving from D (those shared also with Laud lat. 112, for the text of which see below, marked with an asterisk) include:

*ii. 35. 7 *is tum*] *iste*, *36. 2 *ludi[s]*, 36. 5 *eat*] *ea* (not Paris), 36. 5 *praesentior res erat*] *praesenserat* D (*quia praesens erat* Laud): *praescripserat* Paris, Esc., Ambr. and pastedown, Berg., 36. 6 *consilio⟨que⟩* (not Paris¹), *36. 6 *repraesentatas*] *-ntatis* (not Paris), *36. 6 *lectica defertur*] *lecto affertur*.

There are no significant uncorrected errors of D which the other mss, Laud 112 apart, do not share or progressively corrupt: those at 36. 5 and 6, avoided by Paris 5737, could easily have been corrected.

Addenda *and* corrigenda

It shares the following errors with Esc. g I 8, Ambr. D 542 inf., Bergamo MA 570, Paris 5737 (and doubtless other members of the family, which I have not thought it worthwhile to inspect):

*ii. 36. 1 *instaurandi⟨s⟩*, 36. 2 *Latin[i]o*, 36. 5 (see the progressive corruption noted earlier).

The other four mss share no errors against it.

Errors which it shares just with all or most of Esc. g I 8, Ambr. D 542 inf., and Bergamo MA 570 are:

*ii.36. 2 ⟨*sibi*⟩ *displicuisse*, 36. 2 *[consulibus]*, 36. 4 *satin'*] *statim*, 37. 5 *quippe qui⟨n⟩*, 37. 8 *sub*] *cum*, *37. 9 *discurren[te]s* (not Bergamo), and *37. 9 *oborta*] *aborta* (not Bergamo).

Again, the other mss share no errors against it, and Esc., which I have argued to be the source of the other witnesses, has no errors in the passage other than those mentioned already.

Errors which it shares with Ambr. D 542 inf. and (for the most part) with Bergamo MA 570 are:

ii. 36. 1 *furca⟨m⟩* (not Bergamo), 36. 2 ⟨*per*⟩ *somnium*, 36. 3 *uerecundia⟨m⟩*, 36. 3 *timor[em]*, 36. 7 *consulum*] -*ulis*, 37. 3 *sequius*] *sequi ius*, 37. 5 *nostro*] *uestro* (not Ambr.ᶜ), *37. 5 *simus*] *sumus*, 37. 8 *cum (ad patres)*] *tum* (not Ambr.ᶜ), 37. 8 *omnes eos*] *eos omnes*.

Ambr., which I have argued to be the source of Berg., has no errors in the passage other than those mentioned already.

Errors unique to itself against all these witnesses are:

ii. 35. 8 *exacerbarentur*] *exarcebatur* (*exercebantur* Laud), *36. 1 *Romae*] *ratione*, 36. 4 *illa*] *ista*, 36. 7 *illa*] *ista*.

Since the pastedown has all the errors of Ambr. D 542 inf. and more of its own, and since the two *istas* could be the result of misunderstanding the script of Ambr. D 542 inf., in which *illa* is abbreviated to just *i* with an *a* placed above it, it is tempting to argue (somewhat paradoxically—for one might have expected the reverse) that the pastedown derives from the ms. itself; but Professor Reeve, who observed these phenomena in collating, cautions me that the script of the pastedown seems to be older. In which case, both mss will derive independently from Esc. g I 8.

The failure of Bergamo, Civ. MA 570 to share some of these errors does not seem to constitute an argument against its derivation from Ambr. D 542 inf.: the errors in question could easily have been removed by conjecture. Since it does not have the two *istas*, it cannot derive from the pastedown.

Plainly Laud lat. 112 cannot here derive from this family. Since it shares iii. 3. 7 *ab altero consule res gesta egregie est; [qui, quam uenturum hostem sciebat, grauem praeda eoque impeditiore agmine incedentem adgressus,] funestam populationem fecit* with Arch. S. Pietro C 132¹ and Leipzig, Rep. I. 1 (the error may be found too in other mss related to these two which I have not checked), it may be right to conclude that it derives from D^1 via Q and α; such a derivation would work well for a ms. produced in Verona, since the text of α belongs fundamentally to northern Italy.[1]

Laud lat. 112 begins to derive from Ambr. D 542 inf. after v. 43. 6 on the divide of its fo. $37^{r/v}$, which is marked as a new chapter both in Ambr. and in some α-mss. After this point it shares all the uncorrected errors of Ambr. (the first are 43. 6 *experiendam] aperiendam* 44. 1 (*res*) *ac] ac*, and 44. 3 *autem] enim*) and also errors freshly introduced by Ambr.^{c} (the first is 44. 1 *eguit mea] in ea* Ambr.^{1}: *in ea egit* Ambr.^{c}, Laud). Before this point it avoids many errors of Ambr., of which the last are 43. 3 *Gallos; ut] gallicos et* and 43. 4 *urbe⟨m⟩*. It shares 43. 1 *tecta] -tis* with Leipzig, Rep. 1. 1. By a happy chance after 43. 1 'deditionem' the scribe of Laud lat. 112^1 interpolates 43. 6 'proficiscentes . . . quam sua' (later correcting his error), the text of which he presents with several errors (e.g. ⟨*in talibus*⟩ *experiendam*) but not that cited above from Ambr. However, when it comes to the correct point for transcribing this passage, it has, as we have just seen, the text found in Ambr. This both confirms the point at which exemplars were changed and makes it virtually certain that the scribe of Laud lat. 112, and not an ancestor, made the change.

p. 250 n. 294. I did not record this omission for Toledo 51. 2. Either I have been careless in collation, or a correction in Paris lat. 5737 is obscured on my microfilm, or at the very beginning of the text the *Toletanus* cannot derive in so straightforward a manner from the *Parisinus* (the evidence cited at vol. i, p. 252 shows that it must derive from the *Parisinus* from iii. 8. 8 at the latest).

p. 250 n. 295. My prediction that Toledo 51. 2 would not have the long omission at viii. 23. 6–7 has proved correct: like Paris lat. 5737^c it omits *se*.

p. 283. In line 9 read 'X against D' for 'X against T'.

pp. 296–8. Many more errors shared by P^c and U could have been cited; a notable instance is ix. 39. 4 ⟨*Interea res in Etruria gestae*⟩ *nam et cum* . . . I have come increasingly to share the view of Reeve (1996: 84–6) that U derives from P^{1+c}, with some errors of P eliminated by contamination. For a reading that is almost certainly a conflation of those of P^1 and P^c see x. 5. 8 *ea] ex* P^1: *hec* P^c: *hec ex* U (see further n. ad loc.). My statement (p. 298) '[t]he hypothesis of contamination, however, is not wholly satisfactory: for whoever effected the contamination would have done a very poor job, failing to correct from μ or Λ numerous passages where U shares errors with P or PEOZ' does not do justice to Reeve's position. He argues that the absence of significant agreements in error between U and μ or Λ suggests that the contamination must have come from another member of Π. This suggestion may be corroborated by another argument: the failure of U to eliminate

---

[1] A *caveat*: for the early part of the decade contamination among the north-eastern Italian mss makes the families of T and D hard to define (see vol. i, p. 212), and I have no proof that Arch. S. Pietro C 132 and Leipzig, Rep. I. 1 derive from α before v. 39. 3 (which is not to say that they do not).

errors of P¹⁺ᶜE or P¹⁺ᶜOZ/P¹⁺ᶜO/P¹⁺ᶜZ (E not extant) suggests that U cannot have inherited any readings either from Λ independently of Pᶜ or from μ. Reeve cites two readings in which U agrees in error with either EO or O (E not extant) against other witnesses. Add the reading of UZbZt cited at ix. 26. 7 (n.) (the failure of O to share this reading proves nothing: it could have been contaminated from Λ) and ix. 5. 4 *consules*] *consules praefecti* (*prof-* Zt) UOZbZtZs (the corruption arises probably from *saltus oculi* to 5. 1 'consules profecti' rather than from a scribe imagining that the Romans had prefects trapped in the Caudine Forks. It could have occurred independently in U and E, from which OZbZtZs must derive, but in view of the other readings shared by U and E, it would be unwise to think that it did). For probably true innovations in UOZ see x. 12. 6, 13. 1 nn.

Reeve notes that U shares with FB the omission of *Idibus Mais* at ii. 21. 7, and therefore raises the possibility that it derives from P¹⁺ᶜ via the same copy as that from which F and B derive. Beyond observing that the conflation of P¹ and Pᶜ cited above is found also in F (but with the following *ipsa* corrupted into *posita*) I have no evidence to cite for or against this hypothesis.

I have continued to cite U in the commentary, partly for consistency's sake. However a very strong case can be made that future editors should ignore it, except where it has a true or plausible conjecture.

p. 299. For other probably true readings of U see ix. 7. 3 *animi* U: *animo* **N**, 27. 1 *spes* U: *spe* **N**, 28. 5 *habita⟨ba⟩tur*, 34. 14 *quo⟨d⟩*, 37. 13 *Apulia[m]*, with nn. ad locc.; also *addendum* to vii. 3. 5. An interesting innovation is found at x. 38. 13 (n.). In the comment on ix. 18. 12 read Π for P.

p. 311. For another error shared by M and P against other witnesses see x. 25. 14 n.

pp. 315–16. In writing this summary of Reeve's findings with regard to the descendants of P I omitted to mention that I had seen all the mss in question except B, Darmstadt 4303, and Esc. g. I 13. I have since seen the *Scorialensis*: as one would expect of a descendant of Paris B.N.F. 5736¹⁺ᶜ, it does not share the errors at either i. 24. 5 or ix. 42. 5. I have now collated the whole family of Geneva 53 and Paris 5736 for i. 24. 1–26. 12 and ii. 8. 8–10. 10, and my findings confirm Reeve's stemma. The Darmstadt fragment has been discussed by Schneider (1998), who sees that it is derived from P; but his ignorance of mss and ms. readings other than those cited in editions, and also of Reeve (1996), means that he does not place it as accurately as it can be placed.

p. 319. Other readings which point to variants in **N** may be found at ix. 41. 17 *ante concentum*] *deinde ante concentum* (*-tu* M¹) M: *deinde concentu* (*uel sim.*) Πλ and 44. 13 *fama* MᶜUZsᶜ: *fama fame* M¹: *famae* P: *fame* OZbZtZs¹λ (here *fama* and *fame* may have stood as variants).

p. 320. To the list of ms. readings at the top of the page add x. 29. 7 *raris* Hertz: *uerarisque rutis* Mλ: *uerutis* (*-erru-* P) PUZ (with *scuta plerisque* in ZbZt for the preceding *plerisque in scuta*).

pp. 321–4. Increasing experience in the investigation of the transmission of

The manuscripts

Latin texts makes me more inclined to favour Reeve's view of the stemma; but the problem could be solved finally only by the discovery of part of **N**.
pp. 321–2. Other passages where M may be alone in the truth or may have a reading closer to the truth than that found in Πλ are ix. 13. 10 *obsessis* M: *et obsessis* Πλ, 24. 14 *et infandae* M: *infandae* Πλ, 43. 5 *gloria: gloriae* Πλ, x. 2. 15 *in flumine oppidi medio* M: *flumine in oppidi medio* λ: *in oppidi medio* Π (but *in oppidi medi medio* P¹; *in oppido medio* O or Oᶜ), 24. 14 *cum dimicatio* Zr, Ricc. 485: *tum dimicatio* M: *dimicatio* Πλ, and 38. 4 *quadraginta milia* MUL (but the support of UL is of no consequence): *sexaginta milia* Πλ. I no longer believe that M is right at x. 45. 12. See further nn. ad locc.
p. 321. For '*quia* Λ' read '*quia* Zλ'.
p. 322. Other passages where Π may be alone in the truth are ix. 7. 2, where *A. Calauius* may be correct: see n. ad loc., 19. 8 *quacumque*] *quasc-* Mλ, and 42. 6 *Q. Fabius*] *fabius* Mλ.
p. 323. Other passages, none of much significance, where λ is, or may be, alone in the truth are ix. 45. 17 *quadraginta* (*triginta* MΠ), x. 45. 3 *occupationem populi Romani pro occasione* (also Z) (*occupationemque pro occasione* M: *occupationem populi Romani pro occupatione* P) and 46. 4 *aliquot* (also Z) (*aliquos* MP¹: *aliqui* PᶜGr).

BOOK VI

Historical Introduction

p. 332. n. 4. For 'Cornell (1985)' read 'Cornell (1995)'.
p. 335. Beloch's interpretation of the quotation from Priscian was anticipated by Seeck (1882: 17), who states that it had been adopted 'längst'.
p. 339 n. 25. For *conubium* see Treggiari (1991) 43–9.
pp. 341–2. References from D.H. to the foundation of colonies were omitted; see iv. 63. 1 (Signia and Circeii), vi. 43. 1 (Velitrae in 494), vii. 13. 1–5 (Velitrae and Norba in 492), ix. 59. 1–3 (Antium in 467).
pp. 342–3. Weigel (1983: 194–6) challenges Salmon's view in a different way, arguing that Fest. 276 'PRISCAE LATINAE COLONIAE appellatae sunt, ut distinguerent a nouis, quae postea a populo dabatur' makes a distinction not between colonial foundations organized by the Latins and later ones organized by Rome but between foundations approved by the *populus* and earlier ones which were not. He himself dates this change between 312 and 296 (see 21. 5 n. with *addendum*). One may wonder, however, whether any colonies were founded by Rome without the approval of an assembly. As for Weigel's date, it is awkward to place Cales, Fregellae, Suessa, Interamna, and Saticula in a class different from e.g. Sora and Alba Fucens.
p. 345. For Mommsen '(1874–5: i. 430–1)' read '(1894–5: i. 430–1)'.
p. 347. For '416' read '426'.
p. 350. For the rebellion against Rome in the aftermath of the Gallic Sack I should have cited Varr. *ling.* vi. 18 'Dies Poplifuga uidetur nominatus, quod

eo die tumultu repente fugerit populus: non multo enim post hic dies quam decessus Gallorum ex urbe, et qui tum sub Vrbe populi, ut Ficuleates ac Fidenates et finitimi alii, contra nos coniurarunt'. If Fidenae and Ficulea rebelled, then the effect of the Gallic Sack was perhaps greater than I allowed; but it is far from clear that Varro's testimony is sound.

pp. 357–8. On the fighting against Tusculum see also Seeck (1882) 15–25. He speculated that the lists of Latin states given at D.H. v. 61. 1–3 and at Cato, *orig.* fr. 58, in which Tusculans are found as leaders of the Latins, should be ascribed to the wars of this time and are wrongly ascribed by D.H. to the beginnings of the Republic. He suggested that the story of Camillus' oddly peaceful campaign against Tusculum was invented by a late republican annalist who did not understand that the incorporation of a fellow city-state with Roman citizenship was an aggressive act and not a generous gesture.

p. 358. The authenticity of the campaign of T. Quinctius in 380 is also accepted by Forsythe (1994: 238). His suggestion that the annalistic account of campaigns conducted by the Quinctii in 464 and 458 was modelled on this campaign is possible but far from certain.

p. 362. The view that the account of the Gallic campaigns in Polybius is not certainly to be preferred to that found in writers dependent on the later annalistic tradition may be supported by his evidence for the fighting in the mid-280s (ii. 19. 7–20. 10), which several scholars plausibly regard as inferior to that provided by other sources: for a full discussion of the problem see Morgan (1972).

p. 365. To the bibliography on the Struggle of the Orders add Bunse (1998), who lucidly expounds a radical thesis (see below).

pp. 367–76. *The consular tribunate.* I omitted to cite Richard (1990), an important essay, fundamentally conservative in its approach to the sources, that is as good an introduction to the problems of the consular tribunate as any. Among Richard's interesting observations are the following: that the uncertain start of the consular tribunate in the years around 444 was probably due to political tensions in this period that are now irrecoverable; that the office was abandoned and a return made to the consulate when magistrates with full *imperium* were desired; that the non-patricians who held the office in its earlier days may not have been plebeians but *conscripti* (the address *patres conscripti* to senators may reflect a state of affairs in which some were patricians who took their place in the assembly by virtue of their descent, others had been enrolled for other reasons);[1] and that the demands of the Veientine War and other campaigns in the late fifth century forced the Romans to recruit more widely—hence the expansion of the *classis*, the introduction of *stipendium* and *tributum*, and the admission of some plebeians (e.g. the Licinii Calvi) to the consular tribunate *c*.400.

Since the publication of vol. i there has been further discussion of the

---

[1] My remarks on p. 366 were too brief to do justice to the explicative power of Momigliano's theory concerning the significance of terms like *conscripti*.

consular tribunate by e.g. Walt (1997: 313–18), Bunse (1998), Stewart (1998: 52–94), and Brennan (2000: 49–54).

Following Boddington (1959: 362–3), Stewart (pp. 56–71) emphasizes that our sources for the period between 405 (when a college of six consular tribunes became the standard chief magistracy at Rome, interrupted only by the consulships of 392 and 391) and 367 (when the office of consular tribune was abolished) regularly show the consular tribunes operating in pairs:

402	v. 8. 7–9. 3	Sergius and Verginius mentioned together in the context of defeat at Veii
401	v. 12. 5–6	Aemilius and Fabius command at Veii
397	v. 16. 5	Postumius and Julius command against the Etruscans
396	v. 18. 7–12	Titinius and Genucius command against Capena and Falerii
395	v. 24. 1–2	The two Cornelii command against Falerii, Valerius and Servilius against Capena
394	v. 26. 3, 28. 5	Aemilius and Postumius command against the Aequi
391	v. 32. 1–2	Lucretius and Aemilius command against the Volsinienses, Agrippa Furius and Sulpicius against the Sappinates
386	vi. 6. 12, 9. 6	Camillus and P. Valerius in command at Antium, later replaced by Quinctius and Horatius
382	vi. 22. 1	The two Papirii command at Velitrae
381	vi. 22. 5–6	Camillus and L. Furius command against the Volsci
379	vi. 30. 2	The Manlii command against the Volsci
378	vi. 31. 5	Furius and Horatius lead an army to Antium, Q. Servilius and Geganius to Ecetra
377	vi. 32. 4–5, 8	Three armies are said to have been conscripted (allowing for the possibility that two consular tribunes took charge of each); Aemilius and Valerius are said to have commanded together at Satricum, L. Quinctius and Sulpicius at Tusculum

This is a striking pattern—all the more so since L. and his sources may not have recorded all the information available to them, since in 387 and 384 there were no wars, and since 374–371 inclusive are years in the so-called anarchy for which L. is silent. Because it is not easy to see why a pattern of this kind should have been invented by L. or the annalists, it may be authentic, and Stewart may be right to argue that the consular tribunes were expected to operate in pairs.

There are some exceptions to this pattern:

| 403 | v. 2. 13 | Ap. Claudius remains at Rome while his colleagues fight at Veii |
| 401 | v. 12. 5–6 | L. mentions individual commands for Camillus (at Falerii), Cornelius (at Capena), and Valerius (at Anxur) |

Addenda *and* corrigenda

398	v. 14. 7	L. mentions indvidual commands for Valerius Poti-tus at Falerii and for Camillus at Capena
394	v. 26. 3, 28. 5	Camillus has sole command at Falerii

Since the notice for 394 concerns the legendary figure of Camillus, it is easy to argue with Stewart (p. 77) that L. and other sources have suppressed the part played by a colleague with whom he was working; but it is more doubtful whether she is right to discount the campaigns at Capena and Falerii in 401 and 398. Nevertheless, this evidence hardly outweighs the striking pattern outlined above.

Stewart argues that the use of the lot to determine which consular tribunes took which provinces and operated together served to lessen the power of the grander *gentes*. It made it less likely that two of their number could operate together (thus integrating the *gentes* further into the state and discouraging the notion that warfare should be conducted on a clan-basis) and it put members of lesser *gentes* on a par with those from more powerful *gentes*. This interesting thesis provides a new way of viewing the consular tribunate. However, it rests very heavily on the assumption that very substantial power was still wielded at Rome by the great patrician *gentes*.

In support of this assumption Stewart points out how office-holding in the period of the consular tribunate was dominated by a surprisingly small number of *gentes* (pp. 72–4):

According to the *Fasti*, members of the same *gens* held office together on eighteen occasions from 444–367: two Cornelii in 406, 404, 395, 369, and 367; two Furii in 398, 394, 391, and 381; two Manlii in 379; two Papirii in 382; two Postumii in 381; two Quinctii in 405 and 385; two Servilii in 402; two Valerii in 398, 380, and 370 . . . there is no evidence in the fifth century of limits on the number of relatives who might hold office in any given year or on the number of times particular individuals might hold office.

The *Fasti* show that these families dominated the magistracies, gaining among themselves more than half the curule posts (consuls, suffect consuls, and military tribunes) in the years 444–367. The Cornelii garnered thirty-four offices; the Furii, twenty-nine; and the Manlii and Servilii seventeen each. The Quinctii gained twenty-two offices; the Valerii, twenty-six; and the Papirii, nineteen. Moreover, while the increase in the magistracy in 406 in theory increased access to office, in practice seven families gained one half of the offices: the Cornelii, twenty-five; the Furii, nineteen; the Manlii, fourteen; the Quinctii, twelve; the Valerii, twenty-one; the Servilii, eleven; the Sulpicii, fourteen.

She notes also the frequency with which certain individuals held office in this period: e.g. L. Furius Medullinus (*cos.* 413, 409, *cos. tr.* 407, 405, 398, 397, 395, 394, 391), Ser. Cornelius Maluginensis (vi. 6. 3 n.), Q. Servilius Fidenas (vi. 4. 7 n.), P. Valerius Potitus (vi. 6. 3), and L. Valerius Potitus (*cos.* 393, 392; *cos. tr.* 403, 401, 398), to which one may add the name of Camillus himself. She argues that, although it is generally held that around 400 BC the importance of *gentes* in comparison with that of indvdual families had lessened or was lessening, these statistics provide some evidence that the power of *gentes*, led by the charismatic figures whose tenure of office was often repeated, still remained significant. The argument is not unattractive.

Bunse, building on some existing ideas,[1] puts forward a radical hypothesis:[2] that after the end of the monarchy the leading magistrate at Rome was called *praetor maximus* (vii. 3. 5 n. with *addendum*), that there were two other praetors (hence *maximus*), with each praetor at the head of one of the three primitive tribes (for which see x. 6. 3 n.);[3] that this state of affairs continued until the Licinio-Sextian rogations of 367/6; that the consular tribunate provided no interruption to it, since the three praetors remained in office; that our sources record four, five, or six consular tribunes because they have included supplementary military tribunes who were elected by the people (hence their appearance in lists of magistrates) to assist the praetors at war but who did not have *imperium*, the right to triumph, or to take the auspices; that since patrician claims to exclusivity with regard to the auspices are unintelligible if plebeians had already been at the head of the state, it follows that the plebeians recorded in our sources as consular tribunes were not praetors but merely these supplementary tribunes; that the variations in our sources with regard to the name of the consular tribunate (vi. 1. 1 n. with *addendum*) suggests that there was no secure tradition as to what it was called (in particular, those ancient terms for the office that included consul or proconsul are anachronistic);[4] that the supplementary military tribunes were the precursors of the tribunes regularly elected from 362 onwards; that neither the size of the state nor the complexity of Rome's wars required the steady increase in the number of magistrates with *imperium* from three to four to six (Bunse rejects both the ancient 'political' and 'military' explanations of the consular tribunate); that, if the number of chief magistrates had increased to six, a decrease to three in 366 would be inexplicable and would have been unacceptable to the patricians; that the praetorship after 366 was not originally inferior as a magistracy to the consulship, and that the plebeian success in 367/6 was the right to hold one of the three leading magistracies of the state; that, if L.'s view that the praetorship was introduced originally in 366 as an inferior magistracy was correct, it would be strange that the title of the old chief magistracy was chosen for it; that this view explains why praetors needed a *lex curiata* (ix. 38. 15 n.) when the equivalent law for censors was passed in the *comitia centuriata*: the praetorship dated back to a time when the *comitia curiata* was dominant, but the censorship was introduced only after the rise of the *comitia centuriata*; that the name *consul* came into being only after 366; that the concept of collegiality and the veto inherent in it were introduced in response to the plebeians' winning the right to hold one of the three chief magistracies; that gradually after 366 a distinction in the function of the

---

[1] Such as those of Sohlberg (1991).

[2] For his views on the consular tribunate see esp. pp. 82–181; for his views on the effect of the Licinio-Sextian rogations see pp. 182–201.

[3] See also Sohlberg (1991) 259–61.

[4] On this point see also ibid. 259.

three chief magistrates developed: two were normally expected to take command of armies, and the name *consul* became attached to them, whereas the third, who continued to be called *praetor*, became responsible primarily for Rome's legal system; and that the delay in the plebeians' capturing the praetorship (first in 337 [viii. 15. 9]) is odd on the standard understanding of the office, since they had reached the dictatorship and censorship twenty years previously, but explicable on this theory: the breakthrough of the plebeians in 337 was to capture two of the three leading magistracies.

Although the uncertainties of our sources make it very difficult securely to establish any radical interpretation that rejects the views of L., this is as lucidly argued as any reinterpretation and has the merit of removing several difficulties in our evidence for both the consular tribunate and the praetorship. Its weaknesses are threefold. First, although Bunse argues against the need to increase the number of chief magistrates in the later fifth century, he adopts the somewhat contradictory position that the demands of the wars with Veii may have led to the election of his supernumerary military tribunes. Second, Bunse does not give a satisfactory account of our evidence for 393 and 392 BC when consuls and not six consular tribunes are recorded as the chief magistrates. Third, for the years 400, 399, and 396, in which our sources record a majority of names in the colleges of six consular tribunes that are not obviously patrician (see vol. i, p. 372), Bunse has to resort rather lamely to claiming that some names may have been patrician.

p. 373 n. 143. For the political explanation add Pompon. *dig.* i. 2. 2. 25 and Zon. vii. 19. 3–5.

p. 373 n. 144. For '36. 4–37. 1' read '35. 4–37. 1'.

p. 375. Walt surveys the arguments for and against the ancient 'military' and 'political' explanations. Bunse (1998: 100–10) rejects both as inadequate (the view that I took); he adds (p. 106) a further argument against the military explanation: Rome's wars were not so far away or so complicated that she needed six commanders.

p. 375 n. 149. Add iv. 31. 2.

pp. 376–9. *Camillus.* Recent treatments include U. Walter (2000) and Bruun (2000*a*), both emphasizing the legendary elements in the tales told by our sources. Bruun, in a wide-ranging and interesting study, denies the historicity of Camillus, arguing that he was created by grafting the legendary Italic figure Marce Camitlnas depicted in the François tomb on to the careers of contemporary Furii Medullini. I should not wish to take scepticism so far.

Commentary

1. 1–3. Following Frier, I assumed that Plut. *Num.* 1 refers to the pontifical records; Crawford (1998) shows that it refers to stemmata. However, at *Cam.* 24. 2 (perhaps derived from our passage) Plutarch does refer to the destruction of records. For 390 as the starting-point of Quadrigarius' history see also Klotz (1937) 219. Much more bibliography could have been cited on the problem of whether the Gauls destroyed all or most of Rome's records: for example, Seeck (1885: 74), Cichorius, *RE* i. 2252, and Enmann (1902: 520) held that they did, De Sanctis (1907–64: i. 5) that they did not; Petzold (1993: 158) is cautiously agnostic. Roberts (1918) shows that writers of the late Republic and principate were able to cite quite a large number of documents that (they implicitly held) dated from before the Gallic Sack; but he followed L. in believing that the pontifical records were lost. Mommsen (1894–5: ii. 101) argued that, although their records were destroyed by the Gauls, the pontiffs were able to supplement their list of magistrates for the period before 390 from records kept in the Capitoline temple of Jupiter; but it is not certain either that there was a complete record of consuls in the temple of Jupiter or that the Roman belief that the Gauls never sacked the Capitol is true. Others (e.g. Seeck, Cichorius, Petzold) have argued that the pontiffs were able to recover (from memory) only some records from years immediately preceding the Sack.[1] If Rome did have records that were destroyed in the Sack, it is indeed a reasonable inference that an attempt was made to reconstitute them after the Sack; L. himself implies something similar in § 10, although it is doubtful whether he had any good evidence for this.

My reference to pp. 21–108 should have included a more precise reference to p. 39.

1. 1. tribunis consularibus: the various terms used by L. to describe these magistrates are helpfully listed by Bunse (1998: 225–6); I should have noted that Gellius refers to them as *tribuni militares qui pro consulibus fuissent* (xiv. 7. 5, paraphrasing Varro) and *tribuni militares consulari imperio* (xvii. 21. 19). On the powers of the consular tribunes see also Badian (1990: 469), Richard (1990: 778–88), Bunse (1998: 113–22), and Brennan (2000: 51–4). Bunse holds that those consular tribunes who on his view were praetors (see above, p. 505) enjoyed full magisterial powers. By contrast, Richard holds that their *imperium* had suffered a *deminutio* (see e.g. p. 786), and Badian and Brennan suggest that they did not have *imperium* at all, Brennan observing that *imperium* (whatever precisely that may mean) is ascribed to them only thrice (at iv. 7. 2, *ILS* 212 [Claudius], and Gell. loc. cit.). Although one should not place much weight on any of these three passages, it may be observed (*a*) that among our defective testimony for the consular tribunate they constitute a not negligible body of evidence, and (*b*) that, if the consular tribunes did not hold *imperium*, then we should have the improbable state of affairs in which for a generation before 367 *imperium* was held only when a dictator was in office. That the consular tribunes possessed the right to take the *auspicia* is generally accepted, but Brennan (p. 52) wonders whether their inability to triumph shows that their *auspicia* were impaired *militiae*. Given the poor quality of our evidence for the consular tribunate, these matters cannot be resolved.

---

[1] Hence—it is often held—the unreliability of the information transmitted from antiquity about Roman magistrates in the period 509–390; see e.g. Seeck (1885) 76–82 for an exposition characteristic of his time.

1. 2. [paruae et] rarae: at x. 2. 10 (*paruis* **N**: *raris* Heraeus) the conjecture of Heraeus, if right, would involve a corruption similar to that suggested here in an ancestor of **N**.

cum . . . tum quod: for further parallels for this construction see e.g. Cic. *fam.* xiii. 63. 1 and *Att.* vi. 1. 3.

uetustate nimia obscuras: for the difficulty in divining the truth about old stories add v. 21. 9 'sed in rebus tam antiquis si quae similia ueris sint pro ueris accipiantur, satis habeam' and D.S. xiii. 90. 7 to the passages cited. For full discussion of L.'s doubts about the reliability of old stories see Forsythe (1999: 40–51), who rightly stresses his caution.

per eadem tempora: since the emphasis given by *eadem* is surprising, since parts of *is* are often corrupted into parts of *idem*, and since the sequence *eatem* makes the corruption easy, Watt (2002: 179) may have been right to conjecture *ea* for *eadem*; but the paradosis is not certainly wrong.

1. 4. adminiculo . . . innixa: for the idea of the Roman state's needing a human prop, there is a very good parallel at Lact. *inst.* vii. 15. 14 = Sen. mai., *HRR*, fr. 1 'amissa enim libertate, quam Bruto duce et auctore defend-erat, ita consenuit, tamquam sustentare se ipsa non ualeret, nisi adminiculo regentium niteretur'. This passage also illustrates the coupling of *admin-iculo* and *niti*, which is analogous to the coupling of *adminiculo* and *inniti* found in our passage. For a similar use of *niti* cf. Cic. *Mil.* 19 'ei uiro (*sc.* 'Pompeio') autem mors parabatur, cuius in uita nitebatur salus ciuitatis'.

1. 4. principe: there should have been a cross-reference to the discussion at (vol. i) pp. 377–9.

1. 5. comitia . . . res ad interregnum rediit: I should have cited Linderski (1990) 38 = (1995) 564: 'Now if the auspices "return" to the *patres*, this must mean that normally, when the magistrates are in office, the *patres* (qua *patres*) do not have those auspices; they hold them solely in the period running from the moment the last "patrician" magistracy had been vacated to the appointment of the first *interrex*.'

Linderski (1993: 69 = 1995: 624) discusses all the passages mentioned in the second paragraph of this note. He helpfully distinguishes the expres-sions *auspicia renouare* (relevant to our passage) and *auspicia repetere* (for which see viii. 30. 2 n., where the same distinction is made).

The basic information on *interregna* is presented lucidly by Bunse (1998: 139–44). See also Brennan (2000) 15–18.

1. 6. ab Cn. Marcio tribuno plebis dicta dies est: in the middle Republic prosecutions by tribunes for *perduellio* and other charges which may some-what loosely be termed 'political' (often involving behaviour while holding a magistracy) are a regular feature of Roman constitutional practice; they are to be contrasted with prosecutions by aediles, which were generally for lesser, non-political offences (see x. 23. 11–13 n.). For a list and discussion of tribunician prosecutions known from the period after the passing of the *lex Hortensia* in 287, see Bleicken (1955) 120–31.

The prosecutions to which our sources refer for the period between the Decemvirate and the *lex Hortensia* are listed in the accompanying table.

date	source	nature of prosecution
449	iii. 56. 1–58. 6	conviction of Ap. Claudius by L. Verginius for crimes committed when *xuir*
449	iii. 58. 7–9	conviction of Sp. Oppius by Numitorius for crimes committed when *xuir*
449	iii. 58. 10	conviction of M. Claudius by L. Verginius for crimes committed on behalf of Ap. Claudius
436	iv. 21. 3–4	unsuccessful prosecution of L. Minucius by Sp. Maelius for giving false testimony against (the famous) Sp. Maelius
423	iv. 40. 4–41. 11	conviction of M. Postumius and unsuccessful prosecution of T. Quinctius, both *cos. tr.* 426, by C. Junius and other tribunes on charge of maladministration of the war at Veii
422	iv. 42. 3–9	unsuccessful prosecution of C. Sempronius, *cos.* 423, by L. Hortensius on charge of maladministration of war
420	iv. 44. 6–10	conviction of C. Sempronius by A. Antistius, M. Canuleius, and a colleague on same charge
401	v. 11. 4–16	conviction of M'. Sergius and L. Verginius, *cos. tr.* 402, by P. Curiatius, M. Metilius, and M. Minucius on charge of maladministration of war
393	v. 29. 6–10	conviction of A. Verginius and Q. Pomponius, *tr. pl.* 395–394, for interceding against a plebiscite. (L. does not specifically mention prosecution by tribunes, but that he was referring to such a prosecution may be inferred.)
391	v. 32. 8–9, Plut. *Cam.* 12. 1–13. 1	conviction of Camillus by L. Appuleius for appropriating to himself booty at Veii in 396
389	vi. 1. 6	conviction of Q. Fabius by Cn. Marcius for fighting against the Gauls at Clusium in 391 when a *legatus*
384	vi. 19. 5–20. 16	(for other sources see 11. 1–20. 16 n.) conviction of M. Manlius Capitolinus by M. Menenius and Q. Publilius on charge of *regnum*
362	vii. 4. 1–5. 9	(for other sources see n.) unsuccessful prosecution of L. Manlius Imperiosus by M. Pomponius on charge of unlawful conduct as dictator
323	viii. 37. 8–12, Val. Max. ix. 10. 1	unsuccessful prosecution of all (?) Tusculani by M. Flavius, on the ground of having helped Velitrae and Privernum to fight Rome
c.313	D.H. xvi. 4. 1–3, Val. Max. vi. 1. 11	conviction of M. Laetorius Mergus by Cominius for *stuprum*
293	x. 46. 16	prosecution of L. Postumius Megellus on unspecified charge, aborted because of his service as *legatus*
291	*per.* xi, D.H. xvii/xviii. 5. 4	prosecution of L. Postumius Megellus by two tribunes for employing troops on his own land

To these one may add numerous prosecutions which are said to have taken place in the period before the Decemvirate (listed by Ogilvie on ii. 35. 5). In all the prosecutions listed for which a Latin source (i.e. L. or Valerius

Maximus) survives, except that of Sp. Oppius and that of Postumius Megellus in 291, the expression *diem dicere* is used. Since this was the regular expression for *iudicia populi* brought about by tribunician, aedilician, and other prosecution, L., Valerius Maximus, and their sources seem to have imagined that these prosecutions were like those with which they were familiar from the middle Republic and their own day.

However, their historicity and constitutional status (if historical) are difficult to gauge. Since before 366 the tribunes were officials only of the plebs and not of the whole state, Ogilvie rejects all accounts of tribunician involvement in prosecutions before that year but suggests that some of the trials may actually have happened, with annalists later converting them into the tribunician prosecutions familiar from their own day. This is conceivable, but it is also possible that L. or the annalists have converted into proper trials accounts of rather summary justice administered against patricians by the tribunes in the *concilium plebis*.

When one examines the trials listed here, many are connected with much embroidered episodes in Roman legend and must be considered very doubtful: note those of 449 (connected with the Decemvirate), 436 (connected with story of Maelius), 391 (connected with Camillus and Sack of Rome), 389 (connected with Sack of Rome), and 384 (M. Manlius Capitolinus). Since it is unlikely that the early tribunes interceded on behalf of the patricians, the convictions of 393 also look unlikely. It is easier to conceive that some truth underlies the notices referring to 423, 420, and 401, but on this subject it is almost impossible to find a sure criterion for distinguishing between prosecutions that are total inventions and those behind which some grain of truth may lie.

The period between 366 and 287 saw the gradual integration of the tribunate into the regular system of government (see introduction to book x, above pp. 16–17). Since some tribunician legislation seems to have been accepted by the whole state before the passing of the *lex Hortensia*, it is possible that the later practice of prosecuting for *perduellio* and related charges originated in this period. Therefore the notices for 293 and 291, and perhaps also that for *c.*313, may be sound; in particular those for 293 and 291 look like early examples of what was to become regular tribunician behaviour in the middle Republic. That for 362, connected with a legend concerning the youth of the great Torquatus, is much more doubtful. Whether the prosecution of the Tusculans by M. Flavius should be considered in this context is also doubtful; and our understanding of the episode is so limited that little useful can be said about it (see viii. 37. 8–12 n.).

If many of these notices are to be rejected outright, it follows that L. or his sources have invented the names of the prosecuting tribunes. For the general difficulty posed by the names of early tribunes, see vol. i, pp. 54–5.

In addition to Ogilvie see Jones (1972) 30–9.

1. 7. mors . . . subtraxit: for the suicide of those threatened with conviction see also Griffin (1986) 193.

1. 8. creat: see vol. ii, pp. 21–2 with *addendum*.

1. 9. nulla . . . consuluere: for the sacral rituals at the beginning of the year see also App. *ciu*. iii. 50. 202.

1. 10. quae autem . . . animos suppressa: for the tradition of patrician and pontifical secretiveness with regard to the law, see also D.H. x. 1. 4 (referring, however, to the period before the Decemvirate). Before 'see ix. 46. 1–15 n.' insert 'for some examples of pontifical control'.

1. 11. quo die ad Cremeram Fabii caesi, quo deinde ad Alliam foede pugnatum: for the habit of remembering on which day a disaster occurred cf. Suet. *Aug*. 23. 2 (on the defeat of Quintilius Varus) 'diemque cladis quotannis maestum habuerit ac lugubrem'.

For the *dies Alliensis* see now Rüpke (1995: 567–9), who notes how the Romans liked to observe that defeats, victories, or other notable events occurred on the same date. As a parallel for the defeats at the Cremera and the Allia being linked in this way he cites Ov. *fast*. vi. 563–8 (referring to the defeat by the Marsi at the Tolenus in 90 BC and the death, otherwise unattested, of T. Didius on the same day in 89 BC). For successes he cites *I.I*. xiii. 2. 191 (*fast. Amit*. for 2 August) (Caesar victorious in Spain and Pontus) and Hor. *carm*. iv. 14. 34–8 (Augustus enters Alexandria in 30 and returns to Rome in 15 on the same date).

The reference to ix. 38. 16 n. should have been a more general reference to ix. 38. 15–16, with accompanying nn. As Rüpke makes clear, this passage in book ix offers an analogous phenomenon: L. states not that the defeats at the Allia in 390 and in the Caudine Forks in 321 happened on the same day but that the same *curia* had the *principium* when the *lex curiata de imperio* for those years was passed, and that Macer said that this *curia* also had the *principium* in the year of the Cremera.

1. 11. diebus religiosis: the information given at xxxvii. 33. 6 is not entirely reliable: Plb. xxi. 13. 12 shows that throughout March the Salii were forbidden to move.

quo die: for the repetition of the antecedent see further Landgraf on Cic. *S. Rosc*. 8.

†insignemque rei nullius† publice priuatimque agendae fecerunt: as Watt (2002: 179) observed, I failed to notice that Walters had proposed *diemque* for *insignemque*, and this is a better conjecture than Weissenborn's *indicemque*. For the dependent genitive Watt cited xxii. 25. 16 'rogationis ferendae dies'.

1. 12. quod . . . religio esset: for *dies atri* see now Rüpke (1995) 570–5.

2. 2. hinc . . . factam: on Etruscan *principes* add a reference to e.g. ix. 36. 5 (where it is unclear whether L. refers to Etruscans, or Umbrians, or both) and 12, and see also Scullard (1967) 226.

2. 3. Hernicorum: in the list of passages cited from D.H. insert 'vi' before '5. 3'.

2. 6. indicto: see vii. 6. 12 n.

seniores: see *addendum* to 6. 14 n.

2. 9. tantum Camillus auditus imperator terroris intulerat: for the idea add Dio lxii. 19. 1 (the announcement of Corbulo as commander frightens the Parthians) to the parallels cited; for a related τόπος see x. 11. 5 n.; and for *Camillus auditus imperator* cf. the parallels cited by Heubner on Tac. *hist.* i. 76. 2. For the *ab urbe condita* construction see also x. 31. 14 n.

2. 10. quod ubi animaduertit: this particular collocation is found first here in L.; cf. also xxiii. 44. 7, xxviii. 3. 8, xxxv. 5. 8; also xxi. 50. 4. From other authors note e.g. Dict. iii. 8 and many instances in Caesar.

2. 11. in castra Volscorum: I now doubt whether the arguments adduced against this phrase are of sufficient weight to justify deletion.

2. 12. praedam . . . gratiorem: the first paragraph of this n. down to 'would be most usual' on the first line of p. 410 contains some statements that, although not certainly wrong, are potentially misleading; it also fails to record some information important for understanding the subject. It should be replaced by the following three new paragraphs.

A Roman commander had the power to decide when and where troops could plunder (indiscriminate plundering was not allowed, even in a *direptio* [vi. 4. 9 n.]) and how booty that came into their possession was to be distributed. Although it was technically possible for him to deny his troops any share of spoil, this would have been both inexpedient and against custom (for one alleged tradition note Tac. *hist.* iii. 19. 2 'expugnatae urbis praedam ad militem, deditae ad duces pertinere'). Sometimes our sources seem to suggest that all plunder from ravaging or the capture of a camp or city was granted to the troops: with our passage compare ii. 60. 2, iii. 29. 1, iv. 47. 4, vii. 37. 17, ix. 31. 5, x. 19. 22, 45. 14, xxvii. 1. 2, and xli. 11. 7–8, Caes. *Gall.* vii. 11. 9, D.H. vi. 29. 4, ix. 16. 8, and xvii/xviii. 5. 3. However, it was not unusual for a commander to specify that certain items of plunder were not to be distributed to the troops. Most often, he would retain captives (see e.g. 13. 6, v. 22. 1 [by implication], vii. 27. 8, x. 31. 3, xxiii. 37. 13, xxiv. 16. 5, xxvii. 19. 2, xliii. 19. 2, Cic. *Att.* v. 20. 5 [if Wesenberg's conjecture is correct], D.H. ix. 56. 5, and Tac. *ann.* xiii. 39. 4), but we also read of him retaining slaves (D.H. x. 21. 6), gold and silver (ix. 37. 10 [by implication captives were granted to the troops], D.H. x. 21. 6), the treasury of the enemy (Plut. *Luc.* 29. 3), and animals which could be identified by their owners (xxiv. 16. 5). He could also decree that some items were not to be plundered at all (xxvii. 16. 8, Plut. *Marc.* 21. 5). Although there is no clear attestation of the fact in our sources, the evidence for the dedication by commanders in temples of works of art taken from the enemy (see x. 46. 7 n.) suggests that large items of spoil were generally not given to the troops.

The distribution of plunder usually happened immediately after a battle or the capture of a camp or city (explicit or implicit in virtually all the passages cited above): at least by the time of Polybius (x. 16. 2–9), and perhaps much earlier, the Romans had a system in which plunder was brought to the military tribunes and then divided by them fairly among the troops. Sometimes troops would be forced to sell this booty because it was impeding the effectiveness of the fighting force (see x. 17. 6–8 and 20. 16, passages which doubtless reflect the practice of historical times). A further distribution might be made at the time of a triumph (see x. 46. 15 n.).

Booty retained by the commander might be displayed in his triumph (x. 46. 2–8 n.), handed over to the *aerarium* (x. 46. 14 n.), given as a reward to senior officers, friends, and relatives who had fought in the campaign, or used for public works (see x. 46. 8 and 14 nn. and Trisciuoglio [1998] 132–4). Whether all such booty was called *manubiae* or only what was left in a commander's possession after his triumph, and whether a commander could do what he wished with *manubiae*, are both disputed: see x. 46. 14 n.

In the rest of the paragraph the first reference to xxvi. 40. 13 should be deleted and the following items added to the bibliography: Vogel, *RE* xxii. 1200–13 and Churchill (1999) (both with full citation of earlier bibliography).

With regard to the second paragraph, a further example of patrician concern for the treasury may be found at iii. 10. 1; further examples of generosity by early commanders may be found at ii. 60. 2, vii. 37. 17, x. 19. 22, and D.H. ix. 16. 8; and Fabricius in 282 was another early Roman commander who struck a judicious balance between the needs of the treasury and of his own troops: see D.H. xix. 16. 3. The role of booty in the politics and economics of the period is discussed by Loreto (1993) 89–91.

2. 14. Aequos: for the alternative form Aequiculi see x. 13. 1 n. The Aequi are mentioned first as foes of Rome not in 488 as stated in this n. but in 494 (ii. 30. 8–31. 6, D.H. vi. 42. 1–3).

3. 2. Sutrium, socios: for this figure cf. also x. 2. 9 'Patauium . . . eos' and xliv. 30. 8 (with W–M's note).

3. 5. nullam stationem ante moenia, patentes portas: for *stationes* in front of gates the n. on viii. 8. 1 in these *addenda* replaces the information given in the n. on this passage.

considere . . . iubet: see ix. 24. 5 n.

3. 8. ab desperatione: note two further parallels for a general's trying to prevent the enemy fighting more bravely from desperation: (*a*) in the version of the battle of Mantinea (419 BC) recounted by D.S. (xii. 79. 6) the Spartans left open a way of escape for 1,000 Argives who were obstinately prepared to fight to the death and were killing many of their own number; (*b*) Veg. *mil.* iv. 25. 4–5 'obsidentes portas ciuitatis aperire consuerunt, ut resistere desinant fugiendi potestate concessa. necessitas enim quaedam uirtutis est desperatio'.

3. 10. quia non ui captum sed traditum per condiciones fuerat: the Greek text of *CIL* iii. 14147⁵. 3 (the monument of Gallus) illustrates particularly well the manner in which Roman commanders distinguished between different methods of capture of a town: πέν[τε τε πό]λεις τὰς μὲν ἐξ ἐφόδου, τὰς δὲ ἐκ πολιορκί[ας] καταλαβόμενος (curiously the Latin text has just 'quinque urbium expugnator'). On the capture of a town *primo impetu* see Veg. *mil.* iv. 12. 1–4, where the dangers posed by this first charge are discussed.

4. 2–3. tantum aeris . . . positas fuisse: for the dedication of spoil in temples, add D.S. xiii. 34. 5 to the passages cited by Jackson. For Roman temples see esp. the discussion of Orlin (1997: 131–9), who draws particular attention to the works of art placed by Marcellus in his temple of Honos and Virtus (see xxv. 40. 2, Cic. *II Verr.* iv. 121, *rep.* i. 21); see also Dio fr. 76. 2.

4. 3. tres paterae aureae: see x. 23. 13 n.

5. 6. superstitiosis: for the meaning of the word see x. 39. 2 n.

5. 7. magistratum occepere: *occipere* is found often in the translation of 'Dictys' by Septimius, an author who—as will be noted several times in these *addenda*—affected the vocabulary of the classical historians: see e.g. ii. 35, 37, 50, iii. 10 (*bis*), 15, 22, and vi. 5.

5. 8. duumuiro sacris faciendis: for *iiuiri aedi locandae* and *aedi dedicandae* see further Orlin (1997) 147–58 and 172–8.

6. 3. collegae additi: this expression goes back at least as far as Ennius: see *ann.* 304–6 'additur orator Cornelius suauiloquenti | ore Cethegus Marcus Tuditano collega | Marci filius' (probably referring to elections to the consulship of 204 BC: see Skutsch's note).

6. 3. Ser. Cornelius Maluginensis: the reference to the sixth consular tribunate of Maluginensis in 370 (36. 3) was accidentally omitted. I also failed to note a late mastership of the horse recorded for 361 BC (vii. 9. 3, *F.C.*).

6. 7. uiro uno: see further ix. 16. 19 n.

6. 9. certantem secum ipsum: for the idea of competing with oneself, cf. also Plin. *epist.* viii. 24. 8 and Arr. *an.* vii. 1. 4.

6. 13. patre . . . dignum: see esp. *addendum* to vii. 10. 3 n.

6. 14. senioribus: those who had passed their forty-sixth birthday were called *seniores*, were classified separately in the *comitia centuriata* (see e.g. Liv. i. 43. 1–2, 4, 5, D.H. iv. 16. 2, 3, 5, 17. 1, 2, 3, 4), and were normally exempt from military service: see xliii. 14. 6, Plb. vi. 19. 2, Tub. fr. 4 = Gell. x. 28. 1, and D.H. iv. 16. 3. However, in their descriptions of the Servian census both L. (i. 43. 2) and D.H. (loc. cit.) explicitly mention that *seniores* could be called up in an emergency. Both passages mention that *seniores* were expected to garrison the city itself, a role mentioned in this passage; cf. also v. 10. 4, x. 21. 4, and D.H. v. 45. 3. Other passages in which we read of *seniores* are vi. 2. 6, xl. 26. 7, xlii. 31. 4, 33. 4, and App. *ciu.* ii. 150. 627. (All but the first and last of these passages refer to the enlistment of men up to fifty years of age; but their contexts show that this recruiting was abnormal, and they do not demonstrate that fifty was in fact the age at which people ceased to be eligible for military service.)

alia belli: for Reiz's conjecture see also Haupt (1850) 103 = (1875–6) i. 306.

6. 15. huius publici consilii: *publicum consilium* is a regular term for the senate and for its deliberations. To the large number of passages cited by Mommsen (1887–8: iii. 1028 n. 1) add e.g. Cic. *Cat.* iii. 7 and *Vat.* 35.

6. 18. parere atque imperare simul paratos: the idea that it is a virtue that men should be willing both to command and to obey goes back to Greek political thought, in which it is found in various miscellaneous political contexts (Soph. *Ant.* 669, Plat. *leg.* 643e), as well as being connected specifically with the Spartan Agesilaus (Xen. *Ages.* 2. 16, Plut. *apopth. Lac.* 41 = *mor.* 211c, *Ages.* 20. 2) and with democracy (Aristot. *pol.* 1259$^{a–b}$, 1317^{b} ἐλευθερίας

Book VI

δὲ ἐν μὲν τὸ ἐν μέρει ἄρχεσθαι καὶ ἄρχειν, Plut. *sen. ger. resp.* 1 = *mor.* 783d). See further Brunt (1988) 312 n. 69 and Shipley on Plut. *Ages.* 1. 5. It is likely that the idea was taken from Greek into Roman thought.

It is found twice in D.H.: iv. 36. 3 (Servius Tullius' explanation of why he is prepared to hand back his kingdom to the people) ὅτι καὶ ἄρχειν ἐπίσταμαι καλῶς καὶ ἄρχεσθαι δύναμαι σωφρόνως and 74. 3 (on the establishment of the Roman Republic, with a reference to Athens in the previous sentence) τὸ γὰρ ἐν μέρει τὸν αὐτὸν ἄρχειν τε καὶ ἄρχεσθαι καὶ πρὸ τοῦ διαφθαρῆναι τὴν διάνοιαν ἀφίστασθαι τῆς ἐξουσίας συστέλλει τὰς αὐθάδεις φύσεις καὶ οὐκ ἐᾷ μεθύσκεσθαι ταῖς ἐξουσίαις τὰ ἤθη. Whether D.H. took the idea from his Greek education or from the Roman annalistic tradition, it is not possible to say.

7. 1. indicto: see vii. 6. 12 n.

7. 3–6. My comments on the *cohortatio* apply to this passage but are perhaps not apt for the other passages from L. cited in this n. In all of these the commander seems to be addressing his troops at a *contio* before the *praetorium* in his camp (see *addendum* to vii. 10. 14 n.); the troops are not spread out in line of battle, and therefore it may have been possible for the voice of the commander to have been heard.

7. 3. quae tristitia . . . haec: for the word-order cf. also xxiv. 31. 3 'qui mos ille . . .?'.

tristitia: as K. notes, a general sought good omens before battle, and *laetus/laetitia* are regular in the context of such omens (vii. 26. 4 n.); *tristitia* is the opposite of *laetitia* and of what a general would desire in this situation.

hostem an me an uos ignoratis?: as K. again notes, this summarizes what is to follow, and Camillus proceeds to discuss each of the enemy, himself, and his troops, but in the order enemy, troops, himself.

8. 1–4. For the hurling of a standard into the ranks of the enemy, see also xli. 4. 1–2 and D.H. viii. 65. 5 (another good instance of the motif's being retrojected into early Roman history). For the conventional wisdom that a good general should not expose himself to danger, see also Don. *ad* Ter. *Eun.* 783 'poeta . . . ostendit officium imperatoris hoc esse, ne se in periculum proiciat'. For further discussion of the reasons why generals sometimes fought in the front line and of the dangers which they faced, see Rosenstein (1990) 117–21 and Goldsworthy (1996) 154–63.

8. 1. desilit: according to Massa-Pairault (1995) 48 'Cet acte tout politique, s'appelle en réalité d'un règlement archaïque, qui interdisait au *magister populi* de monter à cheval, parce qu'il devait être le meilleur de la phalange.' So she sees at vii. 7. 8 'consulto prius dictatore equites, permissu deinde eius relictis equis . . . prouolant ante signa' a reflex of the old idea that the commands of the cavalry and the infantry were two separate domains, which should not be crossed by the cavalry choosing to fight on foot (p. 49). However, this interpretation leaves the appearance of Camillus on horseback unexplained, and it is easier to argue that here L. (or whichever annalist first invented this detail) had no thought for the old rule and that at vii. 7. 8 the cavalry asked the permission of the dictator because he was the commanding officer of the Roman army.

arreptum . . . rapit: for this figure see x. 24. 14 n.

8. 2. uadentem: *uado* is another of the words affected by the historians that is employed by 'Dictys'; cf. e.g. iii. 12 'uaderent'.

8. 6. conspectu suo proelium restituit: cf. also Dict. iii. 8 'ita praesentia eius (*sc.* Hectoris) animi tolluntur'.

9. 2. ualida: I should have observed that I comment on this adjective because it occurs here for the first time in books vi–x and that, because of the frequency with which L. uses it, I have not supplied cross-references back to this n.

9. 9. non tam a: of the parallels which I cited for *a(b)* in the sense 'because of', the best is xxvii. 17. 5, but only if the reading which I adopted is sound. For *a spe* is found only in the *codex Spirensis* (now lost but reported by Rhenanus). *ea spe*, though rejected by editors, is found in both the *Puteaneus* and the Italian relatives of the *Spirensis* and therefore may have better ms. authority; it gives reasonable sense, and could conceivably be what L. wrote.

10. 8. terrorem . . . quam pestem: for the use of the relative pronoun see x. 31. 9 n.

11. 1–20. 16. *The sedition and death of M. Manlius Capitolinus*

p. 476. The *cognomen* Capitolinus is discussed at length by Valvo (1984). As he observes, in addition to Manlii and Quinctii Capitolini, in early Roman history we meet Sp. Tarpeius Montanus Capitolinus (*F.C.* for 454) and P. Maelius Capitolinus (*F.C.* for 400 and 396); the name is therefore comparable to Esquilinus and Caeliomontanus found among the Verginii and Aventinensis found among the Genucii (see further *addendum* to vii. 1. 7 n., Alföldi [1966] 720). Valvo argues quite attractively that it fell into disuse in the later fourth century (the last patrician known to have held it is Cn. Quinctius, *dict.* 331 [viii. 18. 13 n.]), and that this reflects the ban, reported by L. (20. 13), on patricians living on the Capitol, the authenticity of which is confirmed by the onomastic evidence.

p. 478. For the theme of *unus* in the digression see further ix. 16. 19 n.

p. 479. For the visual symbolism of the curule chair, of which ancient depictions are conveniently reproduced by Schäfer (1989), see also e.g. Ov. *fast.* i. 82 'et noua *conspicuum* pondera sentit *ebur*' and Plut. *quaest. Rom.* 81 (= *mor.* 283b). Note also ix. 10. 8 'tribunal' (with ix. 10. 6–12. 4 n.).

pp. 480–1. Forsythe (1999: 84) well observes that L.'s uncertainty as to whether Manlius aimed at tyranny is reflected in the indeterminate close to his speech at 18. 5–15 (note the vague *maiora*).

pp. 483–4. For further Catilinarian allusions see *addenda* to 14. 11, 18. 3, 18. 5, 18. 14, 19. 2 nn. That some Catilinarian allusions in L. and D.H. originated with Tubero was argued by Klotz (1938: 43–7, 1940–1: 296).

p. 493. To the bibliography add Mustakallio (1994) 48–58 and Forsythe (1999) 82–6 (with a good discussion of the Catilinarian allusions). Jaeger (1993) is reprinted and updated in Jaeger (1997) 57–93.

11. 1. patriciae gentis uiro: my note illustrates the use of the genitive but offers no comment on the use of *gentis* in the context of a patrician: see now x. 8. 9 n.

11. 2. inclitae: *inclitus* is another word found in 'Dictys' (see e.g. iii. 15, 16, iv. 1, v. 15).

11. 3. nimius animi: if at Sen. *ben.* v. 6. 1 the untranslatable *minus animis* (of Alexander the Great) is emended with the early editors to *nimius animi*, as it should be, then this passage is a better parallel than any of those which I cited.

solum . . . solum: on the autocratic implications of *solus* I should have followed K. in citing Vell. ii. 33. 3 (on Pompey) 'in quibus rebus primus esse debebat, solus esse cupiebat'.

esse: I remain unconvinced that the paradosis is corrupt; but, if it is, then *posse*, proposed by Watt (2002: 180), improves on the conjectures of Madvig and Koch.

11. 5. illius gloriae pars uirilis apud omnes milites sit: for a commander's having to share his glory with his troops, cf. also Dio lxxii. 11. 1 (on L. Maximus). For the related idea that commanders stole glory that belonged by right to the troops, cf. esp. Eur. *Andr.* 693–8, verses which Clitus is said (Curt. viii. 1. 28–9, Plut. *Al.* 51. 8) to have recalled during his fatal quarrel with Alexander the Great. In his note on this passage, Stevens cites Dem. xxiii. 198 and Aeschin. iii. 183 and 185, in which it is noted that glory rightly accrued not to generals but to the whole populace.

11. 7. plebem iam aura . . . famaeque magnae malle quam bonae: the argument that L. alludes to Sall. *Cat.* 54. 6 may be developed. In his second n. on Cic. *off.* i. 65 'uera autem et sapiens animi magnitudo honestum illud quod maxime natura sequitur in factis positum, non in gloria iudicat, principemque se esse mauult quam uideri. etenim qui ex errore imperitiae multitudinis pendet, hic in magnis uiris non est habendus' Dyck plausibly argues that the Sallustian passage is part of a sustained allusion to Cicero. If this is right, then L., by referring to the *aura popularis*, alludes to both Sallust and his source.

11. 9. et erat: for *et* introducing a parenthesis see also K–S ii. 26.

re damnosissima etiam diuitibus, aedificando: there is comment, sometimes only implicit, on the dangerously high cost of building also at Cic. *off.* i. 140, Vitr. x. *pr.* 1–3, Plut. *Cic.* 10. 5, and Dio lxii. 25. 3.

12. 1. postero cum auspicato prodisset hostiaque caesa pacem deum adorasset: for this sequence see ix. 14. 4 n.

12. 5. aut innumerabilem . . . uindicant: for ancient praise of the healthy population of a city, Brunt (1971: 4–5) cites four passages missed in my note: Plin. *epist.* vii. 32. 1 'cupio enim patriam nostram omnibus quidem rebus augeri, maxime tamen ciuium numero: id enim oppidis firmissimum ornamentum' and Dio lvi. 7. 4–8. 1 illustrate praise of a healthy population; Plb. iii. 89. 9 ἦν δὲ τὰ προτερήματα Ῥωμαίων ἀκατάτριπτα χορήγια καὶ χειρῶν πλῆθος and Liv. ix. 17. 3 'plurimum in bello pollere uidentur militum copia et uirtus . . .', the importance of a large population for war. Cf. also e.g. D.S.

xiii. 44. 3 and Liban. *progymn.* vii (*loci communes*) 1. 5 πολυανθρωπία φοβερὰ μὲν τοῖς ἐναντίοις, τοὐναντίον δὲ λίαν εὐκαταφρόνητον.

12. 7. propositum pugnae signum: see also Fischer (1914) 102.

luce prima: see ix. 32. 3 n.

processit: the *contio* took place before the *praetorium*; see *addendum* to vii. 10. 14 n.

12. 8. pilis ante pedes positis: the role of the infantryman in Roman battles has been reconsidered recently by Goldsworthy (1996: 171–227), Zhmodikov (2000), and Sabin (2000). The standard view of scholars has been that in Roman battles the initial exchange of javelins and other projectiles was relatively unimportant and that most of the fighting took place with swords. Zhmodikov has argued that the use of projectiles was much more common than is generally realized. His arguments include the following.

(*a*) That our sources provide numerous references to Romans' being hit by projectiles in battle (e.g. vii. 24. 3, viii. 9. 12, 10. 10, x. 28. 18, xxii. 49. 12, xxiv. 42. 2, xxv. 19. 16, xli. 18. 11).

(*b*) 'In the course of a battle against the Romans, after long fighting, Hannibal moved his elephants on the Romans, but the Roman infantrymen drove them away using *pila* [xxvii. 14. 6–10] . . . It is difficult to understand how the elephants could pass through fighting infantry and how the Romans could use their *pila* if the long preceding battle had been a fight with swords' (p. 70).

(*c*) It is unlikely that intense hand-to-hand fighting could have been sustained throughout the long duration of Roman battles (for the length of Roman battles see viii. 38. 10 with *addendum*).

(*d*) Many of Rome's opponents are described as fighting with projectiles.

(*e*) Lines of maniples, in Zhmodikov's view, could not have replaced one another during intense hand-to-hand fighting.

(*f*) At ix. 19. 7 L. himself stresses the importance of the *pilum* as a weapon.

(*g*) In some of Caesar's descriptions of battles there is extensive fighting with javelins (e.g. *Gall.* ii. 25. 1, *ciu.* i. 46. 1).

With regard to (*a*) and (*d*) better evidence would be provided if the Romans themselves were said to have thrown the javelins, but for this Zhmodikov cites only Plut. *Pyrrh.* 21. 13 (Ausculum) and *Aem.* 19. 9 (Pydna); with regard to (*e*) there seems to be no reason why well-trained units could not have done what Zhmodikov thinks impossible. With regard to (*f*) this passage is not a reliable account of what went on in a battle. Although Zhmodikov seems to have demonstrated that the use of projectiles was more common than has been realized, he has not demonstrated that the Romans did not spend much time fighting with swords, as here and in the other passages cited in the n. For this reason it seems better to accept the model of Sabin (2000: 14–17), in which hand-to-hand combat was mixed with the hurling of projectiles from a distance.

12. 10. terrorem equestrem: cf. also xxx. 33. 16.

13. 1. multitudo hostium nulli rei praeterquam numero freta: for the enemy's despising the numerical inferiority of the Romans, see also D.H. ix. 70. 1 (of the Volsci). For the idea of the Romans being superior in virtue, the enemy in numbers, see also Caes. *Gall*. vii. 50. 1.

13. 2. To illustrate the phenomenon of troops being unable to withstand the *uultus* of their opponents I ought to have made a clearer cross-reference to vii. 33. 17 n. (on which see also below, p. 564).

13. 3. suum terrorem: the use of *suus* (= 'characteristic of him/her/them', 'proper') found here is well illustrated at *OLD s.u.* 11. Add e.g. Luc. iii. 580 'inrita tela suas peragunt in gurgite caedes'. I should not have cited iii. 10. 3, which has a slightly different sense and belongs rather with the passages cited at ix. 6. 6 n. and *OLD s.u.* 12.

fluctuanti: for the danger posed by a line of battle which has become out of shape and training undertaken by the Romans to prevent this happening, see Veg. *mil*. i. 26. 4.

13. 5. obequitando: see also x. 34. 7 n. on L.'s use of *circumequitare*.

13. 6. omnibus contumeliis eludent: for this mocking cf. also Veg. *mil*. iii. 11. 6.

13. 7. principes . . . iuuentutis: see ix. 14. 16 n.

14. 9. unius hominis esset: for Greek analogies for the genitive see Kühner and Gerth (1898–1904) i. 372–3 and Diggle on Theophr. *char*. 26. 4.

14. 11 and 18. 3. noctuque: I ought to have made clear that Cic. *Cat*. i. 8–9 and Sall. *Cat*. 20. 1 refer specifically to the Catilinarians' meeting at night. No passage reveals Roman distrust of unofficial assemblies and of meeting at night better than xxxix. 15. 11–12 (part of a speech invented by L., but still indicative of Roman attitudes) 'maiores uestri ne uos quidem, nisi cum aut uexillo in arce posito comitiorum causa exercitus eductus esset, aut plebei concilium tribuni edixissent, aut aliquis ex magistratibus ad contionem uocasset, forte temere coire uoluerunt; et ubicumque multitudo esset, ibi et legitimum rectorem multitudinis censebant debere esse. quales primum nocturnos coetus, deinde promiscuos mulierum ac uirorum esse creditis?' Other references to meeting at night in our sources for the suppression of the Bacchic rites in and after 186 may be found at xxxix. 8. 4, 8. 6, 12. 4, 13. 10, 14. 4, 14. 6, 14. 10, 15. 6, 16. 4, 16. 11, 16. 13. For this suspicion in another period cf. also Cic. *agr*. ii. 12. For criticism of Christians for (allegedly) meeting at night, see Min. Fel. 8. 4 and 9. 4. For ancient suspicion of meetings in a private house, see also Aen. Tact. 10. 4.

14. 11. inter quos [cum] omisso discrimine uera an uana iaceret, thesauros Gallici auri occultari a patribus iecit nec iam possidendis publicis agris contentos esse: instead of deleting *cum* Watt (2002: 180) suggested emending it to *iam*, a conjecture which I should now adopt; as he notes, L. uses *iam* before *omisso* at 15. 8 and xxvii. 48. 2.

14. 12. paucorum: I should have made the obvious point that the Latin use of *paucus* in politics is closely analogous to Greek ὀλίγος (for which cf. e.g. Aristot. *pol*. 1290^{b}).

14. 13. differenteque et tempore suo se indicaturum dicente ceteris

omissis eo uersae erant omnium curae: to my argument that **N**'s *differentique* and *dicenti* should be emended as in the lemma, Watt made three objections: (*a*) that the ablatives absolute do not go easily with the pluperfect; (*b*) that *-que* tacked on to a short final *-e* is rare; and (*c*) that the this involves a double change to the paradosis. If these objections (of which [*a*] is the strongest) are cogent, then his proposal to insert a verb such as *instabant* after *omissis* and to punctuate with a full stop after it is a plausible solution to the *crux*. Alternatively, one could emend *uersae erant* to *uertebantur*, but the corruption would be hard to explain.

15. 1. hominum: i.e. senators; see ix. 8. 11 n.

uiatorem: for *uiatores* see also Purcell (1983) esp. 152–4.

15. 2. agmine ingenti: for crowds following politicians see also Bell (1997) 9.

15. 7. totiens hostis: to the bibliography add H–S 58–9, Williams on Stat. *Theb.* x. 3, and Goodyear on Tac. *ann.* ii. 60. 3.

in arma agant: the expression is discussed by Fletcher (1945: 18), who cites xxx. 14. 10, Luc. ii. 254, Stat. *Theb.* v. 676–7, and Tac. *hist.* iii. 53. 1.

15. 10. sed quid ego: on this expression see Adams (1999: 102), who notes the formulaic quality of *quid ego haec* (found in books vi–x at viii. 32. 5).

conspectior: the comparative is used first by L. (also ii. 5. 5, vii. 7. 6, and xxii. 40. 5): see *TLL* iv. 497. 26–34.

15. 12. nam quod attinet: see also vi. 6. 10 n.

16. 2. Iuppiter . . . incolitis: it was natural for a person threatened with violence to appeal to an appropriate divinity; for a Greek instance see Ar. *Ach.* 55.

16. 3. nec . . . audebant: the discussion of the relationship of *prouocatio* to the dictatorship needs modification. The following remarks should be read in conjunction with x. 9. 3–6 n.

If *prouocatio* gained statutory recognition in 449, then it is attractive to argue that the dictatorship was initially exempt from it and made subject to it only in 300 (thus Mommsen op. cit., followed by e.g. Bauman [1973] and Humbert [1988: 488]). In which case, the patricians, and later the patricio-plebeian nobility, would have had to be careful that the appointment of a dictator was justified by the circumstances and did not provoke civil unrest.[1] This would explain the annalistic view that the office was not subject to *prouocatio* (to the passages cited in the n. add D.H. vi. 58. 2, Pompon. *dig.* i. 2. 2. 18; perhaps also D.H. v. 73. 1 and Lyd. *mag.* i. 37), and indeed no dictators in the period covered by books ii–x or the extant books of D.H. would have been subject to *prouocatio*.

It would help to explain too the virtual disappearance of the *dictator rei gerundae causa* after 302/1.[2] In the period 300–218 dictatorships are certainly attested only for the following years:

[1] That they did not always do this is shown by the disturbances at many elections between 366 and 343, over several of which a dictator presided (see vol. ii, p. 22).

[2] The double dictatorship of 302/1 and a possible oddity concerning the dictatorship for this year may conceivably have helped in the demise of the office, see x. 1. 7–5. 13, 5. 14 nn.

287 Q. Hortensius was appointed at the time of the Third Secession of
the Plebs
280 Cn. Domitius appointed to hold the elections
257 Q. Ogulnius Gallus appointed to celebrate the Latin festival
246 Ti. Corucanius appointed to hold the elections
231 C. Duilius appointed to hold the elections
224 L. Caecilius Metellus appointed to hold the elections.

In addition, dictatorships are attested for Ap. Claudius Caecus (see his
elogium, quoted at vol. iii, p. 352), M. Aemilius Barbula (see his *elogium* [*I.I.*
xiii. 3. 68], but the man is otherwise unknown), P. Cornelius Rufinus (an
ex-dictator when expelled from the senate in 275: see D.H. xx. 13. 1, Val.
Max. ii. 9. 4), and Q. Fabius Maximus Verrucosus (his appointment to the
dictatorship in 217 was his second: see xxii. 9. 7, Val. Max. i. 1. 5, *I.I.* xiii.
3. 80). Of these dictatorships only that for 287, the first, must have been *rei
gerundae causa*, and the political circumstances of the time and the obscurity
of the dictator make it unusual. The next certain *dictator rei gerundae causa*
was Q. Fabius Verrucosus, whose famous dictatorship of 217 was highly
abnormal: it was created by the *populus* (xxii. 8. 6), and during it the dictator suffered the indignity of having his *magister equitum* given powers equal
to his own (xxii. 25. 1–27. 11). If legislation intended to curb its powers had
been passed, the office of dictator may have seemed less attractive to the
patres, not least as the new institution of prorogation now allowed the
appointment of more commanders.[1]

This theory may also explain Fest. 216 'OPTIMA LEX [. . .] in magistro
populi faciundo, qui uulgo dictator appellatur, quam plenissimum posset
ius eius esse significabatur, ut fuit Mani Valerii M. f. †Volusuinae gentis†,
qui primus magister a populo creatus est. postquam uero prouocatio ab eo
magistratu ad populum data est, quae ante non erat, desitum adici "ut optima lege", ut pote imminuto iure priorum magistrorum'. If this notice is
accurate, 300 BC could be the year in which dictators ceased to be appointed
optima lege, and the dictators appointed to oversee elections or the Latin
festivals would be good examples of those appointed *imminuto iure*.

However, if *prouocatio* gained statutory recognition only with the *lex
Valeria* of 300 BC, then the fact that the office of *dictator rei gerundae causa*
almost disappears after 302/1 makes it almost certain that it too was made
subject to *prouocatio* by this law. In which case, as regards *prouocatio*, the
standing of the office would never have been any different from that of
the consulship: just like a consul, a dictator too would have had to deal with
the protests of the tribunes and plebs, some of which he might not have been
able to surmount (for clashes between dictators and tribunes see vi. 38.
4–10, vii. 3. 9, viii. 34. 1, 5–7). This view of the position of the dictatorship

---

[1] L.'s comment (x. 11. 4) that the *patres* considered nominating M. Valerius Corvus dictator for 299 does not contradict this view. Even if it did, it is easy to argue that it derives from
either annalistic or his own invention.

in the fifth and fourth centuries has been championed by Staveley (1954: 427–8).[1]

For recent discussion see Lintott (1999: 111–12), who thinks that in the middle Republic it was disputed as to whether or not a dictator was subject to *prouocatio*.[2]

attollere oculos: on downcast eyes see also Diggle on Theophr. *char.* 24. 8. Just as unwillingness to raise one's eyes may indicate shame and modesty, so raising them to meet someone's glance may indicate brazenness: see Olson on Ar. *Ach.* 292.

17. 1. exprobranti multitudini: the criticism of the plebs for their failure to support their champions has an analogy at [Sen.] *Oct.* 877–95, where, however, the poet stresses more the fickleness of both fortune and popular support.

17. 4. noctis . . . quae paene ultima atque aeterna: perhaps cf. also Virg. *Aen.* vi. 513–14 'namque ut supremam falsa inter gaudia noctem | egerimus, nosti', where *supremam* suggests the moment of destruction.

17. 5. uno omnibus . . . multus uni: for the juxtaposition of a part of *unus* with a part of *multus*, compare the Greek passages cited by Fraenkel on Aesch. *Ag.* 1455.

18. 5. 'quo usque tandem ignorabitis . . .': for Manlius's using words spoken by Cicero against Catiline see also *addendum* to 18. 14.

quas natura ne beluas quidem ignorare uoluit: Forsythe (1999: 83–4) observes that the juxtaposition of *natura* and *beluas* recalls Sall. *Cat.* 1. 1 'pecora quae natura prona', another indication of the extent to which this episode is permeated with Catilinarian allusions.

18. 7. ostendite modo bellum; pacem habebitis: for *ostendite* in '*ostendite* serves as the protasis of a conditional clause', read *ostendite modo bellum*. For the construction see also x. 7. 7 n.

18. 14. ego me patronum profiteor plebis: K. adduces Cic. *Cat.* ii. 11 'huic *ego me* bello ducem *profiteor*, Quirites', of which L. repeats three words. This therefore is a second occasion on which L. gives his Manlius words spoken by Cicero against Catiline. However, this instance, in which the echo may or may not be deliberate, is less complicated than that discussed at 18. 5, where a passage of Sallust is also in play.

For the use of the first-person pronoun towards the end of a speech see x. 8. 12 n.

19. 2. unius iactura ciuis finiat intestinum bellum: a similar idea is found at Cic. *Cat.* ii. 7 'uno me hercule Catilina exhausto leuata mihi et recreata res publica uidetur', adduced by K. This may constitute another

---

[1] However, his view that the annalistic doctrine on the dictatorship was a reconstruction based on a view of the dictatorship similar to that found in the passage of Festus quoted above is unconvincing. Lovisi (1999: 202–3) argues that the dictatorship was restricted later in the third century; her reasons for rejecting the position adopted here are not entirely clear.

[2] But his view that the story of the quarrel between Papirius Cursor and Fabius Rullianus was designed to show that the dictator was subject to *prouocatio* cannot be right, at least for L.'s version, in which the tribunes and people finally submit to the *imperium* of Papirius.

Catilinarian motif in this tale. K. cites additionally Liv. ii. 35. 3 'sed adeo infensa erat coorta plebs ut unius poena defungendum esset patribus', which is rather less close.

19. 7 diem dicere: the matters alluded to in the final sentence of this n. are discussed in the *addendum* to 1. 6 n.

20. 2. sordidatum: for additional parallels, see Kübler, *RE* xiii. 1698–70. I ought to have referred to the *capilli passi* of women in mourning, for which i. 13. 1, vii. 40. 12, xxvi. 9. 7, and Petron. 111. 2 may be added to the passages cited by Kübler.

20. 4. apud neminem auctorem inuenio: add a reference to ix. 23. 5.

20. 7. decora . . . belli: see further Yardley (2003) 55.

20. 8. nudasse pectus insigne cicatricibus bello acceptis: for display of scars in the law-courts, cf. also Petron. 1. 1 'declamatores . . . qui clamant: "haec uulnera pro libertate publica excepi, hunc oculum pro uobis impendi"'. Note also that Licinius Regulus, irked by threatened expulsion from the senate, made an appeal to the *patres* in which he revealed his scars (Dio liv. 14. 2–3). The idea is parodied at Cic. *IIVerr.* v. 32. I should have pointed out that *insigne* is paralleled in the passages cited from book xlv and Pliny; note also Tac. *ann.* ii. 9. 1 'Flauus insignis fide et amisso per uulnus oculo'.

20. 10. manus tendens . . . auertisset: for pointing to a place to help one's speech, cf. also Val. Max. iv. 2. 5 'qui (*sc.* P. Clodius Pulcher) incesti crimine a tribus Lentulis accusatus unum ex his ambitus reum patrocinio suo protexit, atque in animum induxit et iudices et praetorem et Vestae aedem intuens amicum Lentulo agere, inter quae ille salutem eius foedo crimine obruere cupiens, hostili uoce perorauerat'.

20. 11. in Petelinum lucum: for a grove as a place of assembly of the Roman people see also vii. 41. 3 (342 BC; again the *lucus Petelinus*) and Plin. *nat.* xvi. 37 (287 BC) 'Q. Hortensius dictator, cum plebes secessisset in Ianiculum, legem in Aesculeto tulit, ut quod ea iussisset omnes Quirites teneret'. Since both the Lucus Petelinus and the Aesculetum were outside the *pomerium*, it was probably the *comitia centuriata* which was convened in both 342 and 287. See further Vaahtera (1993) 103–7.

20. 12. locusque idem: for the paradox of the same man in the same place at the height of his glory and at the time of his death, cf. Dio lxiv. 20. 2 (on Vitellius) κατήγαγον ἐκ τοῦ παλατίου τὸν Καίσαρα τὸν ἐν αὐτῷ ἐντρυφήσαντα, καὶ διὰ τῆς ἱερᾶς ὁδοῦ ἔσυραν τὸν αὐτοκράτορα τὸν ἐν τῷ βασιλικῷ δίφρῳ πολλάκις σοβήσαντα, ἔς τε τὴν ἀγορὰν ἐσεκόμισαν τὸν Αὔγουστον ἐν ᾗ πολλάκις ἐδημηγόρησε and Just. xxii. 7. 7–8 'Bomilcar . . . in medio foro . . . patibulo suffixus est, ut idem locus monumentum suppliciorum eius esset, qui ante fuerat ornamentum honorum' (very close in phrasing to our passage, as Yardley [2003: 57] observes). For the paradox of someone's dying or lying dead in the place where he had performed a notable deed, cf. Val. Max. i. 1. 19 (on Turullius, a partisan of Mark Antony, who cut down part of a grove sacred to Aesculapius and was killed by troops of Octavian in the same grove; cf. Dio li. 8. 2–3, where the paradox is recounted less sharply) and

Dio xliv. 49. 3 (Caesar's body lies in the forum, where he had often spoken and through which he had passed on his triumphal processions). Perhaps one should compare too Ovid's Astyanax dying at a place made famous by his father (*met.* xiii. 415–17): 'mittitur Astyanax illis de turribus, unde | pugnantem pro se proauitaque regna tuentem | saepe uidere patrem monstratum a matre solebat'. For *idem* used to point a paradox compare in addition to Just. loc. cit. Suet. *Iul.* 89 (on Caesar's assassins) 'nonnulli semet *eodem* illo pugione, quo Caesarem uiolauerant, interemerant'.

20. 13. publica . . . habitaret: note also that there is an enigmatic reference to the destruction of a house at Paul. Fest. 117 'MANCINA TIFATA appellabatur, quod Mancinus habuit insignem domum, quae publicata est eo interfecto'. Technically, *s.c. de Cn. Pisone* ll. 105–8 cited in the n. shows that Piso was guilty of *inaedificatio* (see Eck *et al.* [1996] 207–8); but it is hard not to think that the destruction of his property had important symbolic significance. The symbolic associations which a house had in Roman politics are well brought out at Cic. *off.* i. 138–9.

20. 13. Monetae: for Juno Moneta as the goddess of memory see Meadows and Williams (2001) *passim*.

20. 13. latum ad populum est ne quis patricius in arce aut Capitolio habitaret: Lange (1863–76: ii. 620) held that this law is likely to have been a plebiscite. However, it is conceivable that the patricians themselves could have instigated a resolution of this kind, no longer wishing to see some of their number live on the Capitoline hill.

21. 1. multiplex bellum: Yardley (2003: 61–2) adds Just. xxvi. 2. 1.

L. Lucretio ⟨tertium⟩: replace 'Contrast ix. 7. 15 n.' with 'See also ix. 7. 15 n.'.

21. 4. creauerunt: on these matters see also Weigel (1983), who likewise believes that there may have been a change in practice between 312 and 296 BC. I still think that this view may be right; but at ix. 28. 8 'insequentes consules M. Valerius P. Decius' L. may have meant merely 'in the following year' and not that the consuls themselves arranged the matter (with or without consultation of a legislative assembly). Similarly, in our passage *creauerunt* may not mean that the *patres* appointed *uuiri* and *iiiuiri* without consultation of a legislative assembly. On the increasing use of tribunes to introduce legislation see the Historical Introduction to book x (above, p. 16).

21. 5. nequiquam dissuadentibus tribunis plebis: Pabst (1969: 178) rightly notes that in many of L.'s reports of plebeians' blocking the levy there is a tone of explicit or implicit criticism; he cites iii. 22. 2, 25. 9, iv. 55. 1, and vi. 27. 10.

21. 7. ni priuato, ut fit, periculo publicum implicitum esset: for the contrast between public and private danger Yardley (2003: 61) adds Just. xxvi. 1. 9.

21. 9. fama exorta: the final paragraph of this n. should be read with ix. 38. 9 n., which amplifies and corrects it.

22. 5. L. Furius: since Furius is Sp. f. L. n., he cannot be the son of the L. Furius L. f. Sp. n. Medullinus, *cos.* 413 and *tr. cos.* 407, 405, 398, 397, 394, and 391. He may be mentioned in Cn. Gell. fr. 27, if the military tribune L. Furius whom the senate asked to establish a temple of Saturn was our man (the aftermath of the Gallic Sack provides a plausible but far from certain context).

22. 6–27. 1, p. 580. In general on the legendary elements in this scene see Bruun (2000*a*) 64–5. For the contrast between Camillus and the rest of the army, see further ix. 16. 19 n.

22. 9. in aciem procedunt: for humiliation coming from not accepting a challenge to battle, cf. also Tac. *ann.* vi. 34. 1; for confidence being given to the other side when a challenge is not accepted, see xxxiv. 46. 8 and Caes. *Gall.* iii. 24. 5. See also Goldsworthy (1996) 144–5.

23. 2. ex incertissimo: *incertissimus* is found elsewhere only at viii. 20. 12, in four passages each of Cicero and the younger Seneca, at Val. Max. vi. 9. *ext.* 7, and at Stat. *Theb.* xi. 391; only at Sen. *ben.* vii. 26. 5 is it used as here as a substantive. This usage is a development of the substantivized use of *incertum*.

For the ablative neuter singular of an adjective or a past participle with *ex* (which L. affects more than earlier writers of prose), see W–M on ii. 37. 8, Riemann (1885) 100, K–S i. 506–7, and esp. *TLL* v. 2. 1124. 3–1125. 23. *ex incerto*, from which the usage in our passage doubtless arose, is attested earlier at Plaut. *Pseud.* 965, later at ix. 24. 8, Sen. *epist.* 13. 9, and Tac. *ann.* iv. 62. 3. For *ex insperato* at ix. 7. 10 see also i. 25. 9, ii. 35. 1, v. 23. 2, xxviii. 39. 9, xxx. 10. 20, xlii. 65. 11, xliv. 5. 9, Vell. ii. 112. 6, Val. Max. i. 5. *ext.* 2, and Plin. *nat.* xxv. 17.

23. 3. ferox: on the tone of this adjective see Skard (1933) 32–3.

23. 5. rapere: in post-Augustan Latin *rapere* comes to mean 'to do something quickly': see Langen's notes on Val. Fl. ii. 255 and iii. 341. Among his illustrations of the idiom is Luc. vi. 268–9 'castella . . . rapit', which is parallel to our passage.

23. 7. cum uitae satis tum gloriae esse: in accounts of early Roman history this idea also occurs in the speech of Servius Tullius at D.H. iv. 11. 6. That it finds itself in our passage via the mediation of Tubero was argued by Klotz (1938: 45, 1940–1: 296).

23. 8. actumque de ciue non de hoste: perhaps compare also xxiii. 10. 8 (Decius Magius speaking) 'ite obuiam Hannibali, exornate urbem diemque aduentus eius consecrate, ut hunc triumphum de ciue uestro spectetis'.

24. 10. tradi equos: for cavalry fighting on foot, cf. also ix. 22. 10 n.

25. 7. non cultus agrorum intermissus; patentibus portis urbis: the continued cultivation of the land with the gates of a town left open suggests security; cf. esp. Sall. *hist.* i. fr. 14, Hor. *carm.* iii. 5. 23–4 'portasque non clausas et arua | Marte coli populata nostro'; also Hor. *ars* 199 'apertis otia portis' (with ps.-Acro and Brink ad loc.), and Sil. xvi. 694. Therefore, as our passage shows, leaving the gates open was a sign of friendliness; see also xxv. 31. 2, xl. 50. 1, Caes. *ciu.* i. 18. 2, 20. 5, iii. 11. 5, and Curt. ix. 1. 21. By contrast, closed gates were a symbol of war (Virg. *Aen.* viii. 385–6): for if a town did not wish to welcome or submit to an approaching army, it would close its gates (the most vulnerable point of the fortified circuit), thereby forcing the opponent to assault it, besiege it, or pass it by; see e.g. vii. 9. 1, xxvi. 31. 3, xxxi. 40. 3, xxxiii. 20. 5, xliii. 22. 2, Val. Max. ii. 7. 7 (of a camp rather than a town), Dio Chr. xxxvi. 16, Hld. vii. 1. 1, and ps.-Call. ii. 6. 2; also Frontin. *strat*. iii. 16. 5. It is a sign of the carelessness of L.'s Romans after their defeat at the Allia that they do not bother even to close the gates of the city (v. 38. 10). It is a sign of the stupidity of Gentius that he makes a sortie from Scodra against the Romans, leaving its gates open and the city exposed (xliv. 31. 7). At ix. 25. 6 the Auruncans adopt an intermediate position: 'nec claudentes portas Romanis, ne arcessant bellum, et obstinatos claudere si exercitus admoueatur'. At x. 34. 7 the open gates of Feritrum are a sign that its inhabitants have fled.

26. 4. armati paratique: for the coupling see ix. 32. 5 n.

26. 5. plebis nostrae: for L.'s describing foreign states in Roman terms, see, in addition to vi. 26. 3 n., x. 18. 8, 20. 15, 38. 3, 38. 7 nn. For a good example in a famous passage of another author cf. Cato, *orig*. fr. 86 = Gell. x. 24. 7 'igitur dictatorem (*sc*. Hannibalem) Carthaginiensium magister equitum (*sc*. Maharbal) monuit'.

fuit eritque: for the polyptoton cf. also x. 13. 12. The phenomenon has now received its most penetrating discussion from Wills (1996: 298–302).

26. 6. haec mens nostra est, di immortales faciant tam felix quam pia: Professor Watt pointed out to me that my explanation of this passage is faulty. Rather, punctuating as in the revised lemma given above and supplying *futura* with *tam felix* and *est* with *quam pia*, translate: 'Such is our resolution; may the gods grant that it will be no less fortunate than it is loyal' (cf. Foster's version). For easier examples of a wish for the future tacked on to a sentence, cf. Cic. *Phil*. ii. 113 'eripiet et extorquebit tibi ista populus Romanus, utinam saluis nobis!' and Virg. *Aen*. iii. 497–9 'effigiem Xanthi Troiamque uidetis | quam uestrae fecere manus, melioribus, opto, | auspiciis, et quae fuerit minus obuia Grais'. The construction in our passage is also comparable to that found at Luc. vii. 435–6 (of *Libertas*) 'nec respicit ultra | Ausoniam, uellem populis incognita nostris', where a wish expressed by a participle is tacked on to a preceding noun (but in our passage the participle itself has to be supplied).

27. 3–29. 10, pp. 607–8. For discussion of the return to the Allia in the context of repeated scenes in L.'s history, see Kraus (1998) 267–8.

27. 3 adgrauantibus summam eius inuidiosius tribunis plebis: for Reiz's conjecture see also Haupt (1850) 103 = (1875–6) i. 306.

fide magis quam fortuna debentium: see *addendum* to vii. 21. 8 n.

27. 4–5. religio erat . . . uitio creati: on *uitium* in elections see further the very helpful discussion of Linderski (1986: 2162–73). On the refusal to elect suffect censors see ix. 34. 20–1 nn.

27. 4. tabulas publicas: the theme found here and in § 3, that a census was needed to reveal the precise extent of indebtedness, has a parallel at vii. 22. 6 'quia solutio aeris alieni multarum rerum mutauerat dominos, census agi placuit'.

27. 7. passim iam . . . agentem: for the motif of patricians' deliberately keeping the plebeians under arms, see also Pabst (1969) 178–9.

27. 9–11. For L.'s implication that the blocking of the levy was irresponsible, see the *addendum* to 21. 5 n.

28. 3. in muros atque ⟨ad⟩ portas: Dr N. Holmes (to whom most of the substance of this n. is owed) kindly points out to me that I was almost certainly wrong to prefer Gronovius' *adque* to *atque ad*, since in classical Latin there is no entirely secure instance of *adque = et ad*. The most promising is *ILLRP* 528 = *CIL* i². 1529 '(L. Betilienus Vaarus) lacum ad portam, aquam in opidum adqu(e) arduom pedes CCCXL fornicesq(ue) fecit', where *adqu* is found on the inscription, and Mommsen may have been right to regard it as equivalent to *atque*, even though most recent interpreters follow Ritschl (1862: 105 = 1866–79: iv. 164 n.), who observed that *adque* for *atque* is not attested epigraphically before the Augustan age. At Varr. i. 2. 8 'mente captus est adque agnatos et gentiles est deducendus' inspection of Politian's collation of the archetype (Paris B.N.F., Rés. S. 439) reveals that it had *adque*, but the early conjecture *atque ad* is easy and attractive. In two other passages we have a corruption similar to that found here, in that the paradosis presents us with a corrupt *atque*: at Sis. fr. 125, where the mss of Nonius offer 'Marius ostio Liris euehitur atque Aenariam suos continuatur' Peter adopted Mercier's *adque* but Müller's *atque ad* is only a little less easy; however, since Aenaria is a small island Sisenna may have omitted *ad* before it. At Val. Max. iii. 7. 3 'C. Curiatius . . . productos in contionem consules compellebat ut de frumento emendo atque id negotium explicandum mittendis legatis in curia referrent' Briscoe adopts *adque* with Aᶜ, but Novák's *atque ⟨ad⟩*, which Briscoe terms *fort. recte*, is again only a little less easy. In all three passages I should read *atque ad*. The other instances of *adque* cited at *TLL* i. 473. 7–11 (Enn. fr. inc. xiv V = Courtney fr. 41 and *carm. epigr.* 1111. 10) disappear on proper interpretation of the texts. Dr Holmes notes that in our passage one could also emend to *ad[que]*, but the asyndeton reads somewhat less attractively.

28. 9. ne quis . . . perferret: that the idea of no one's surviving even to report a disaster was a commonplace is shown particularly well by D.S. xi. 23. 2 καὶ τὸ δὴ λεγόμενον μηδὲ ἄγγελον εἰς τὴν Καρχηδόνα διασωθῆναι (on Gelon's great victory over the Carthaginians at Himera). Cf. also D.S. xiii. 21. 3.

29. 3. praeter castra: for comment on troops' abandoning their camp in their flight from the field of battle, cf. also Nep. *Milt.* 5. 5.

29. 8. binis castris hostium captis: on the significance of the capture of a camp, cf. also xliv. 39. 3 (Aemilius Paullus speaking) '. . . quod qui castris exutus erat, etiamsi pugnando acie uicisset, pro uicto haberetur'. For the capture of the enemy's camp featuring in annalistic narrative, see also D.H. vi. 46. 5.

29. 8. signum Praeneste deuectum Iouis Imperatoris: the Roman practice of taking statuary and other works of art from defeated enemies began long before any of the wars against Greek states. Other examples

Addenda *and* corrigenda

from the period before the Hannibalic War are the famous *euocatio* of Juno from Veii and removal of her statue (v. 22. 3–7), and the removal of statues from Tarentum (Flor. i. 13[18]. 27), Volsinii (Prop. iv. 2. 3–6 [the statue of Vertumnus, which may be presumed to have been removed in this year] and Plin. *nat.* xxxiv. 34 [Metrodorus Scepsius held that Rome took 2,000 statues]), and Falerii (Ov. *fast.* iii. 835–44 and Serv. *Aen.* vii. 607). See further Gruen (1992) 86–90.

imperator is attested as an epithet for Jupiter only at Cic. *IIVerr.* iv. 129 (for the connection of this passage with ours, see vol. i, p. 608).

29. 9. fixa: for this use of *figere* cf. also x. 2. 14.

30. 3. sine sorte, sine comparatione, extra ordinem: the first paragraph of my n. on this passage is not entirely adequate as a basis for discussion of x. 24. 10, and publications on the subject subsequent to 1997 render it obsolete. I have found it easiest to recast and greatly extend this whole paragraph rather than present some supplementary material at x. 24. 10. I should now write as follows.

L. refers to the three possible ways of determining in which province a republican magistrate should command. Since prowess in war was a main qualification for office, and since a victorious campaign was the easiest way to make a success of one's magistracy, a magistrate, and esp. a consul, did not normally wish of his own free will to relinquish a command, or the more desirable of two commands. Hence throughout republican history recourse was often had to the lot. For the period covered by books xxi–xlv the phenomenon is so common that it hardly needs illustration (but see Bunse, p. 417). For the period before 367 L. states that consuls drew lots for provinces in 423 and 420 (iv. 37. 6, 43. 1) and consular tribunes in 395 and 381 (v. 24. 2, vi. 22. 6). For the period 366–293 L. states that consuls drew lots for provinces in 362 (vii. 6. 7), 342 (vii. 38. 8), 325/4 (viii. 29. 6), 323 (viii. 37. 3), 311 (ix. 31. 1), and 299 (x. 11. 1).

At x. 24. 10 L. makes the younger Decius claim that all consuls before those of 295 had drawn lots for provinces. The claim is tendentious (something that is hardly surprising in a speech) and ignores the other two methods of determining provinces that are mentioned in our passage, although we shall see that a convincing parallel for the assignment of a province *extra ordinem* is not easily found. Since one province or command was often more desirable than the other, *comparatio*, the agreeing of provinces without the drawing of lots, was always rarer than sortition. For the period before 293 L. states or implies that the consuls agreed provinces (*comparatio*) without the drawing of lots in 329 (viii. 20. 3) and 327 (viii. 22. 9); for the period after 218 see Bunse, p. 426.

For 487 (ii. 40. 14), 474 (ii. 54. 1), 471 (ii. 58. 4), 461 (iii. 10. 9), 449 (iii. 57. 9), 360 (vii. 11. 2), 358 (vii. 12. 6), 357 (vii. 16. 2), 353 (vii. 19. 8), 320 (ix. 12. 9), 308 (ix. 41. 2), and 298 (x. 12. 3) L.'s language leaves it unclear whether he envisaged *sortitio* or *comparatio* as having been used.[1]

[1] The presence of *euenire* and *obuenire* in all but iii. 10. 9 and ix. 12. 9 does not necessarily

Book VI

In the period after 218 the senate (or people) did on occasion try to insist that a province be given *extra ordinem* (or *extra sortem*) to one of the consuls without *sortitio* or *comparatio*; see e.g. xxvi. 29. 1–8, xxviii. 40. 1, 45. 1, xxxvii. 1. 7–10 (with Briscoe's discussion of L.'s probable unreliability), xlii. 32. 1–4, Cic. *prou. cons.* 19, Sall. *Iug.* 114. 3, and App. *Lib.* 112 (province determined by populace). This procedure, however, was highly abnormal, as the Livian passages show; hence expressions like *consules . . . comparare inter se prouincias iussi* (viii. 20. 3; cf. e.g. xxxvii. 1. 7, xxxviii. 35. 9) or *censuerunt patres ut consules inter se compararent sortirenturue* (xxx. 1. 2; cf. e.g. xxx. 40. 12, xxxv. 20. 2, etc.). However, most of our evidence for provinces being given *extra ordinem* comes from the early books of L.; in addition to our passage see iii. 2. 2 (with Ogilvie's n.) (465), iv. 45. 8 (418), vi. 22. 6 (381), vii. 23. 2 (350), 25. 12 (349), viii. 16. 5 (335), x. 24. 3, 10, 12, and 18 (295). Loreto tentatively adds also ix. 43. 1–2 (306) (but L. does not actually use the expression *extra ordinem*), D.H. xvii/xviii. 4. 2 (291) (a plausible inference, but *comparatio* cannot be excluded entirely) and Zon. viii. 3. 3 (280) (but the language of Zonaras could in fact point to any of the three methods of assigning a province).

For many years in the period covered by books vii–x (and for that covered by his earlier books, whose evidence I ignore) L. makes no reference to the division of provinces, perhaps because the consuls fought together or in the same district (e.g. in 321 [ix. 1. 1], 317 [ix. 20. 7–9], 314 [ix. 24. 1], 305 [ix. 44. 6], 304 [ix. 45. 9], 294 [x. 32. 1], 293 [38. 1]) or because a dictator was appointed to take charge of a campaign (e.g. in 322 [viii. 38. 1], 316 [ix. 21. 1], 315 [ix. 22. 1], 313 [ix. 28. 1–2]); but sometimes he makes reference to neither of these factors (e.g. for 356 [vii. 17. 1–2], 330 [viii. 19. 5], 326 [viii. 25. 2], 319 [ix. 16. 1–2], 310/9 [ix. 33. 1–2], 307 [ix. 42. 4], and 306 [ix. 43. 1]).

Bunse and Stewart take contrasting views of the trustworthiness of the evidence for sortition provided by the earlier books of L. Stewart accepts virtually all L.'s evidence as authentic; but, although the result of sortition could have been recorded in the Pontifical Tables or other official records, there are two reasons for caution before accepting this body of material. First, our evidence for the division of provinces between the consuls is notoriously bad for the period of the Samnite Wars (see vol. i, pp. 67–72). Second, since L. and the annalists knew by what methods provinces and commands were determined, it would have been very easy for them to colour their accounts with references to these processes. Therefore all such details in books i–vi, and many of those in books vii–ix, should be viewed with grave suspicion. With regard to the references to the assignment of a province *extra ordinem*, it seems most unlikely that the instances from books

point to the lot, since (*a*) L.'s writing can be loose, (*b*) *euenire* is found at viii. 20. 3 and 22. 9 in the context of *comparatio* (on these passages see further Stewart [1998] 148). However, ix. 42. 1 'sortis', admittedly at the end of the narrative for the year, does suggest that L. thought that the lot was used in 308. Stewart vainly seeks further evidence for *comparatio* in the phenomenon of the re-election of the same consular college: see ix. 1. 1 n.

iii–vi are sound; and one may be sceptical about viii. 16. 5, where the other consul allegedly asked that the war against Cales be entrusted to Valerius Corvus. However, since at vii. 23. 2 and 25. 12 the other consul is said, respectively, to have been ill and to have died, L.'s evidence is perhaps to be trusted.

It follows that Stewart's attempt to use the evidence assembled above to interpret the politics of the late fourth and early third centuries is hazardous. While her view that the method of assigning consular provinces and other official duties by *comparatio* emerged in the late fourth and early third century is not in itself implausible (many of the institutions of the classical Republic developed at this time), it rests largely on speculation and, as the lists above show, there is little positive evidence in favour of it. When one considers the frailty of L.'s evidence in books iv–vi on all political matters, the absence of evidence for *comparatio* amongst the consular tribunes is of little consequence.

Bunse (pp. 421–2) interestingly argues that sortition was introduced after the Licinio-Sextian reforms of 367/6 in response to plebeian demands for full parity with the patricians, but perhaps assumes too easily that there would have been no disputes over commands (and hence no need for sortition) when there were consular tribunes or pairs of patricians in office. Nevertheless, his argument that the practice of sortition was encouraged by the rise of the plebeians is quite attractive: a powerful analogy is provided by *per.* xiii (280/79 BC) 'Cn. Domitius censor primus ex plebe lustrum condidit', since we know that sortition was later used to determine which censor should perform this important ritual act (xxxviii. 36. 10, Varr. *ling.* vi. 87).

See further Mommsen (1887–8) i. 52–7, Loreto (1991–2) 271–8 (with particular reference to the role of the senate in the assignment of provinces), Stewart (1998) *passim*, and Bunse (2002).

30. 5. caedunt caedunturque: cf. also esp. App. *ciu.* iv. 128. 533 ἔκοπτόν τε καὶ ἐκόπτοντο; note too D. H. iii. 19. 4, Tac. *ann.* vi. 35. 1, Hld. i. 22. 5, and v. 32. 3; also Hegemon of Thasos, fr. 1. 8–9 (parodying Hom. *Il.* iv. 450–1 and viii. 64–5), and Basil, *serm. gen.* ii. 4. 7. Analogous too (but with different verbs in the two parts of the formulation) is D.S. xiii. 16. 2.

30. 6. militum . . . uirtus: for the contrast between poor commanders and the bravery of the troops, I should have drawn attention to xxxv. 6. 8 (quoted on the next page). For stress on the bravery of Rome's troops cf., in addition to the two passages cited in the n., xxxvii. 30. 6, Plaut. *Amph.* 191 (parodying Roman attitudes), Caes. *Gall.* v. 43. 4, and Sall. *Iug.* 52. 2; for references to it in narrative see also viii. 38. 4; for credit given to it in speeches see iii. 62. 2 (the credit shared with the *consilium* of the commander), xxvi. 41. 5, xxviii. 25. 6 (the soldiers themselves speaking), xxxviii. 12. 3, and Cic. *Phil.* xiv. 35 and 38 (for other references to it in speeches see vii. 13. 5, 34. 6, xl. 27. 11). At viii. 13. 11, xxxiv. 38. 2, and Caes. *Gall.* v. 52. 6 the speaker divides the credit for success between the gods and the bravery of the troops. See further Rosenstein (1990) 94 (to whom most of these passages are owed).

30. 7. nescire eos uictoria et tempore uti: delete the reference to ix. 3. 12 n., where the usage of *nescire* illustrated is different from that found here.

31. 1. P. Cloelio: for the Cloelii see Münzer (1999) 413.

31. 6. populatio itaque . . . latrocinii . . . ab iusto exercitu iusta ira facta: for the contrast between brigandage and warfare note also Fronto, p. 206. 1–2 'nationes quae rapinis et direptionibus clades ediderunt, latronum potiusquam hostium numero duco'.

32. 1. murum: for the view that this fourth-century wall was the first ever to surround all of Rome, see e.g. Smith (1996) 152–8. I should have observed that the need to raise public money to build these defences is hardly surprising: all construction was expensive (see 11. 9 n. with *addendum*), and in antiquity the cost of defences could draw special comment (Liban. *progymn.* xiii. 2. 9).

a censoribus: for censors' overseeing construction, see vol. iii, pp. 355–6.

32. 5. subita belli: for the analogous *reliqua belli* cf. also fr. 22 line 32.

32. 8. turbauit; turbatis: for two other, excellent discussions of this figure see Landgraf on Cic. *S. Rosc.* 32 (particularly good on passages in which the participle varies the preceding main verb) and Wills (1996) 311–25 (much more comprehensive and penetrating than my note). Wills notes that it is not common outside L. and Ovid and suggests that L. may have affected it as a mild archaism. He also notes how often L. uses the figure with *capere*. For the participle varying the preceding main verb see also ix. 24. 3 'duci . . . deductus' (the variation only slight) and 30. 9 'sopiunt . . somno uinctos'. This and related figures are occasionally found in Greek: they were affected by Herodotus (e.g. ix. 15. 4, 20); for another good instance see Plut. *Demetr.* 1. 2.

ut semel inclinauit pugna: *ut semel* is used by L. also at ix. 39. 10, xxx. 34. 4, xxxi. 35. 5, and xxxv. 16. 10, of which only the last does not come in the description of a battle. With our passage Klinger (1884: 24 n. 1) compares D.H. vi. 33. 2 ὡς δ' ἅπαξ ἀνεκόπησαν οἱ βάρβαροι; the implication of his argument, that L. and D.H. express themselves in the same way because they are drawing on the same annalist (albeit in different parts of their work), is possible but far from certain.

33. 1. [ex]spectarent: for the corruption cf. also ix. 18. 2 (*spect-* **N**: *exspect-* T¹), Sen. *nat.* vii. 1. 4, Curt. vii. 11. 15, Veg. *mil.* iii. 14. 4, and see Hartel (1868–71) index *s.u. spectare* and Diercks (1972) 162. As Dr Holford-Strevens points out to me, the pronunciation in Romance of both *spect-* and *exspect-* as *espett-* or the like made this particular corruption especially easy.

33. 11. If **excipitur** is retained, one should probably read *maiore* (= 'by a louder shout') with the Froben (Basle) edn. of 1531: a scribe misunderstanding the ablative could easily have changed *maiore* to the nominative. *excipere* is here used in the sense illustrated at *OLD s.u.* 15 'to take up in turn'; cf. Virg. *Aen.* ix. 54 'clamorem excipiunt socii' (cited in *OLD*).

Addenda *and* corrigenda

34. 1–42. 14. *The Licinio-Sextian rogations and the reforms of 367–366*

pp. 648–9. On the origin of the praetorship I failed to cite Pompon. *dig.* i. 2. 2. 27 (quoted on vii. 3. 5 n.) and observe that it is plainly a deduction made on the basis of the later development of the praetorship: see e.g. Bunse (1998) 164–5.

My dismissal of L.'s account of the creation of the praetorship was a little too confident. Brennan (2000: 63–5) makes a not unreasonable case for holding that it was the result of a bargain struck between the patricians and the plebeians: plebeians were to be allowed to hold the consulship, but the disadvantage to the career structure of the patricians was lessened by the creation of the praetorship. Mommsen (1887–8: ii. 204) had challenged L.'s view (vi. 42 11, vii. 1. 1, 1. 5) that the praetorship was originally open only to patricians, but Brennan (p. 64) likewise makes a reasonable case that 'the praetorship was originally (and legally) the preserve of the patricians' and that this changed only with the election of Q. Publilius Philo to the office in 336. However, L. and his annalistic sources may have reached their view about the creation of the praetorship by inference rather than through the survival of sources that gave an accurate account of any bargain struck between the patricians and plebeians.

Bunse's radical views have been outlined above (pp. 505–6). Brennan's thesis must be wrong if Bunse's is right, and vice versa.[1]

p. 651. 366 (in discussion of the dictatorship of P. Manlius Capitolinus) is a typographical error for 368.

p. 654. Against the view of the *lex Genucia* taken here see Bunse (1998) 187; but the fact that the law was a plebiscite need not be a problem: see viii. 12. 15 n. with *addendum*.

p. 658. In the quotation from Cato an important sentence was omitted. After *multa esto* supply 'si quis plus quingenta iugera habere uoluerit, tanta poena esto'. Then the quotation continues with *si quis maiorem*.

p. 659. To the bibliography on the agrarian law add Bunse (1998: 182–3), who takes a sceptical view of L.'s evidence.

pp. 659–61. On measures taken in the fourth century to alleviate the burden of debt see Storchi Marino (1993), esp. 239–50. On the rogation of 367/6 see Bunse (1998: 182–3), who again takes a sceptical view of L.'s evidence.

p. 661. For the view that the *lex Marcia* was carried by the younger C. Marcius Rutilus, see Coarelli (1983–5) ii. 105; for the view that it was carried by his father, see Storchi Marino (1993) 237–8. See further ix. 33. 1 n.

34. 5. ut plerumque solet: expressions of this kind are discussed by

---

[1] For Bunse's very different approach to the problem of the reduction in the number of magistracies available to patricians, see esp. his pp. 161–3. However, on the matter of plebeian eligibility for the praetorship he reaches (p. 220) a conclusion similar to Brennan's, despite the divergence in perspective.

Haehling (1989: 25–7). By drawing attention to what is a regular or standard occurrence they enhance the didactic content of L.'s history.

34. 6. forem, ut mos est, uirga percuteret: for lictors preceding their magistrate see also x. 25. 5 n.

risui: the predicative dative, perhaps unique to L. in this word, should have been discussed; see now ix. 41. 6 n.

34. 11. strenuo: for the connotations of this word in popular and plebeian ideology, see x. 8. 3 n.

35. 1. uim aeris alieni, cuius . . . mali: for the use of the relative pronoun see x. 31. 9 n.

35. 3. si uideatur: for this polite form of address see further Henderson (1957) 85 and esp. Mommsen (1887–8) iii. 1027.

35. 5. tertiam, ne tribunorum militum comitia fierent consulumque utique alter ex plebe crearetur: Richard (1999: 317–18) shows that the interpretation of *utique* suggested in the n. is wrong and that it must be translated by something like 'at least' (thus W–M and K.); he cites decisive parallels: 37. 4 'nisi alterum consulem utique ex plebe fieri necesse sit, neminem fore', viii. 12. 16 'tertiam, ut alter utique ex plebe . . . censor crearetur', and D.S. xii. 25. 3 . . . τῶν δὲ κατ' ἐνιαυτὸν γιγνομένων ὑπάτων τὸν μὲν ἕνα ἐκ τῶν πατρικίων αἱρεῖσθαι καὶ τὸν μὲν ἕνα πάντως [reflecting *utique* in a Latin source] ἀπὸ τοῦ πλήθους καθίστασθαι . . . There is no difficulty in supplying *ut* from the preceding *ne*.

35. 6. nullo remedio alio . . . comparauerunt: I should have made clear that Badian's argument on tribunician intercession refers only to the generation before Ti. Gracchus; at p. 699 he notes some instances of intercession earlier in the second century. For the tribunician veto in L.'s account of the political struggles of early Rome, add a reference to x. 9. 1, where it should probably be associated with a Claudius (see x. 7. 1). As this passage from book x is later than most of the others cited in the n., it is less certain that it is invented (for discussion see x. 6. 3–9. 2 n.).

35. 7. stipati patrum praesidiis: for crowds of supporters in late republican politics, see also Nicolet (1980) 358–9. For D.H. x. 5. 2 read x. 4. 4–5. 2.

36. 6. For **his** Alschefski conjectured *iis*; see ix. 15. 4 n.

36. 8. capti et stupentes animi: perhaps the force of *animi* is felt also with *capti*, cf. Tac. *hist.* iii. 73. 1 'captus animi'. For the locative *animi* see also ix. 6. 11 'abiectiores animi' (n.) and Sen. *ben.* v. 6. 1 (cited in *addendum* to 11. 3 n.).

36. 12. [ni] potius quam: I wrote that the interpolation of *ni* is surprising; but it could have arisen from a dittography of *-m*.

37. 2. atqui, a continuative and usually adversative particle, deserved a longer note. L. uses it fourteen times but only in speeches. With regard to the instances in book vi–x, at vii. 35. 10 and viii. 6. 4 it introduces 'a statement contrary, but not contradictory, to what precedes' (*OLD s.u.* 2[a]); at ix. 9. 7 '"di meliora", inquis. atqui non indignitas rerum sponsionis uinculum leuat' it introduces 'an answer to an imagined objection' (*OLD s.u.* 1[b]). In our passage it mixes both functions: it responds to the interruption of the plebs but does not necessarily have an adversative function: 'and what is more'. The *si*-clause that follows *atqui* at vii. 35. 10 is paralleled at xxii. 39. 8 and xl. 8. 3.

37. 2. custodem: for the assocations of this word see Woodman on Vell. ii. 104. 2.

37. 8. socordius: *socors* is used also by Dictys (iii. 1), another instance of his aping the vocabulary of the classical historians.

38. 3–13. *The dictatorship of Camillus.* See also above, *addendum* of pp. 376–9.

p. 686. For 'L.'s own attempt' read 'the attempt of some of L.'s sources'.

38. 3. summum imperium: for this expression used of the dictatorship cf. viii. 32. 3 and xxii. 27. 6; note also *summa potestas* at Pompon. *dig.* i. 2. 2. 18. In iv. 1. 4 and v. 14. 1 it is used in a different context.

38. 5. primae tribus: the reference to Mommsen should read (1887–8: iii. 397). For 'if not always at elections' it would be safer to say 'if not at elections'. Plut. *Mar.* 43. 4 (where three or four tribes are said to have voted for the recall of Marius from exile before he entered the city) should also have been cited. There is a good summary of the evidence and arguments at Taylor (1966) 128–30.

38. 7. patricium magistratum: see ix. 33. 3 n.

38. 8. qui de medio plebem emouerent: in my note I discussed the verb *emouere* but failed to observe that in these contexts the regular verb is *summouere* (see viii. 33. 4 n.); an analogous variation is found at Tac. *hist.* iii. 80. 2 'occiditur proximus lictor, dimouere turbam ausus'. Nor did I point out that removing people from the path of a magistrate was a regular task for a lictor (again see viii. 33. 4 n., but add references to e.g. xlv. 7. 4, Tac. *hist.* iii. 80. 2 [cited above], Mommsen [1887–8] i. 376–7, Fischer [1914] 165–6 [for lictors in the camp], and Kübler, *RE* xiii. 511).

38. 13. et quod usque ad memoriam nostram tribuniciis consularibusque certatum uiribus est, dictaturae semper altius fastigium fuit: Professor Watt (*per litteras*) rejected my defence of the paradosis, arguing that the passages which I cite are not parallel. Although I should have referred to parataxis rather than hypotaxis and although 23. 7 is not parallel, it is not clear to me that I was wrong either to defend the paradosis or to cite ii. 12. 2. Watt (2002: 181) suggested that the insertion of *cum* before *certatum* is the easiest conjecture, on which Dr Holford-Strevens (whom I thank for discussion of the problem) comments: 'to be sure the sense "when there have been conflicts between tribunes and consuls, the dictatorship has been left unscathed", which is implied by your word "hypotaxis", requires Watt's *cum* or some similar conjunction; but it is not the sense we want, since it requires (*a*) that tribunes carried on their traditional war with consuls even when there was a dictator, (*b*) that they would never quarrel with a dictator if they were not in conflict with the consuls.'

39. 3. C. Licinio: the alternative to believing that the Calvus who was consul in either 364 or 361 was the first plebeian master of the horse is to argue that L. has made a mistake here, and should have written *P. Licinio*, a reference to the consular tribune of 396 (who would now be very old, though no more so than Camillus). I should have noted that Münzer's reasoning, which depended largely on his own tendentious interpretation of the politics of the years 366–361, does not withstand close scrutiny. He held that in these years a fragile peace was brokered by a moderate faction of patricians and plebeians, who shared the consulship between them, keeping Licinius Stolo, a notorious trouble-maker, out of the consulship until 361, after which year the fragile peace broke down. Macer, in his view, wished to place the responsibility for the breakdown on the patrician Sulpicius (see vii. 9. 3–5) and therefore switched the consulships of Calvus and Stolo around: the absence of the trouble-maker from the consulship of 361 would make it seem all the more likely that the patrician was responsible. There is no evidence either for Münzer's agreement between moderate factions or for his interpretation of the character of Stolo. See Walt (1997) 271.

The problem of how to distinguish Stolo from Calvus would be solved if Scaramella (1897: 160) was right to argue that they were the same man, who bore two *cognomina*. This bold suggestion cannot be proved wrong, but it is probably easier to hold that there were two Licinii whose identities the annalists found hard to separate.

39. 5. continuari: add ix. 34. 2 to the parallels cited.

40. 1–41. 12. *The speech of Ap. Claudius Crassus.* For a good analysis of the arguments used by Ap. Claudius, see Walter (2001). He well brings out how dominant in the speech is the theme of the tyranny of the tribunes and how the argumentative strategy of Appius depends on *reductio ad absurdum* and great exaggeration (note esp. 40. 12, 40. 17). Throughout one may note the skill with which Appius tries to dissociate himself from his Claudian heritage (40. 3, 6, 13) and to identify himself with the humblest in the crowd and his suffering (40. 5, 10 [note the repetition of *unus* in these passages], 12).

40. 2. Ap. Claudius Crassus: on L.'s portrayal of Ap. Crassus in books iv and v see also Vasaly (1987) 222–5.

dicitur: see also x. 19. 17 n.

40. 3. patrum maiestate: for the *maiestas* of a consul, see further ix. 5. 14 n.; for that of a dictator, see also ix. 26. 19.

40. 4. auspiciis . . . omnia geri: for the idea cf. too Cic. *diu.* i. 3 'exactis regibus nihil publice sine auspiciis nec domi nec militiae gerebatur' and Serv. *Aen.* iv. 340 'maiores omnia auspicato gerebant'; also Serv. *Aen.* i. 346 'Romanos . . . qui nihil nisi captatis faciebant auguriis'.

40. 7. licentiae: for the contrast between *libertas* and *licentia* see Wiseman (2000*a*) 266 and n. 8.

40. 8. inquit: U. Walter (2001: 254–5) well describes §§ 7–19 as being like a dialogue between the tribunes and a humble plebeian.

40. 10. regnant and **40. 10. Tarquinii tribuni plebis:** for another comparison to Tarquin in speech invented for a character in early Roman history, cf. D.H. xi. 5. 2.

40. 11. non licebit . . . tu: K., who interprets the sentence as I do, well glosses 'the second half of the sentence . . . is focalized by Appius, who cannot stay out of his own *sermocinatio*'.

L. Sextium atque hunc C. Licinium consules uideas: for disgust at having to look up to someone holding office, cf. also Plin. *nat.* xxxvii. 81 'Nonius senator, filius Strumae Noni eius, quem Catullus poeta in sella curuli uisum indigne tulit, auusque Seruili Noniani, quem consulem uidimus'. The importance of visual image and imagery in late republican politics is emphasized by Bell (1997), who disappointingly takes no note of the idea illustrated by this passage and those parallel to it. For the general importance of how one is viewed in a 'shame-culture' see also ix. 8. 9 n.

40. 18. parum est si . . . ni: for *parum est* followed by a *ni*(*si*)-clause cf. Sall. *Iug.* 31. 22, Curt. vi. 10. 30, Sen. *ben.* v. 16. 1, vi. 11. 3, vii. 14. 5, *epist.* 86. 13, 89. 20, Plin. *nat.* ix. 105, and Plin. *pan.* 60. 1; also, with *parumne . . .?*, Plaut. *merc.* 692–3, Ter. *Phorm.* 546–7, Cic. *II Verr.* v. 157, *diu.* ii. 95, and Vulg. *gen.* 30. 15. In this usage *parum est* behaves in a similar manner to *paenitet*; note too that like *paenitet* at ix. 34. 18–19 (n.) it can be used with a *quod*-clause as subject and following *ni*-clause; see Pac. *trag.* 277–8 and Vulg. *num.* 16. 12 (for the *quod*-clause alone cf. xxi. 44. 7 and Cic. *Sest.* 32). For other analogies and bibliography see Landgraf on Cic. *S. Rosc.* 49.

41. 2. est aliquis qui se inspici, aestimari fastidiat . . .?: against Bayet's punctuation, which I tentatively recommended, Watt (2002: 181) argued that the answer to the question (namely Licinius and Sextius) is only too obvious. I should now adopt his elegant conjecture *est aliquis ⟨ciuilis⟩ qui . . .?*, which restores excellent sense and makes our passage look back to 40. 15.

According to *TLL* vi. 311. 68–9 *fastidire* governs an accusative and infinitive only here. See further x. 8. 6 n.

41. 3. sit: Professor Watt persuaded me that *erit* is probably correct. It would allow *uolueritis* and *nolueritis* to be parallel future perfects, and the corruption could have been caused by omission of the initial *e*- after *necesse*.
tam humilis: for the meaning of *humilis* see ix. 46. 1 n.

41. 4. auspiciis hanc urbem conditam esse: this idea and the echo of Ennius (often, however, with *auspiciis* or the like substituted for *augurio*) is found also at iii. 61. 5, xxviii. 28. 11, Cic. *rep.* ii. 5, 16, 51, *diu.* i. 3, ii. 70, *leg.* ii. 33, Cens. *nat.* 17. 15, and Nepotian. i. 4. *praef.* 'urbem Romam auspiciis conditam certum est'. See further Vaahtera (2001) 96 n. 12.

41. 5. nam plebeius quidem magistratus nullus auspicato creatur: the note on this passage is rather simplistic and should be replaced by the following paragraphs.

Here the primary meaning of Appius is that no plebeian magistrates (i.e. tribunes of the plebs and plebeian aediles) were created with the auspices; however, he may imply also that no plebeian holder of what had been hitherto a patrician magistracy could truly be created with the auspices. Similar views are found elsewhere in the annalistic tradition in speeches by patricians: see vii. 6. 11 (where the patricians claim that the *lex Licinia* was *inauspicata* and that plebeian consuls were defiling the auspices) and esp.

D.H. x. 4. 3 (the plebeians avoid various religious rituals, including taking the auspices). With regard to the lack of precision in L.'s thought in our passage and at vii. 6. 11, Badian argues that L. is confused; this is likely enough, but the evidence of D.H. suggests that the confusion goes back to the annalistic tradition; and, however poorly the annalists may have understood the issues, patrician claims to exclusive control of the auspices are likely to have been an important issue in the Struggle of the Orders, especially before 367.

Our sources are divided on the question of whether the auspices were ever taken in the *concilium plebis*. At D.H. ix. 49. 5 there is a particularly clear statement concerning their absence at the elections of plebeian magistrates: ἀπ᾽ ἐκείνου τοῦ χρόνου τὰ τῶν δημάρχων καὶ ἀγορανόμων ἀρχαιρέσια μέχρι τοῦ καθ᾽ ἡμᾶς χρόνου δίχα οἰωνῶν τε καὶ τῆς ἄλλης ὀττείας ἁπάσης αἱ φυλετικαὶ ψηφοφοροῦσιν ἐκκλησίαι. However, the contrary view may be implied at Cic. *ap*. Ascon. *Corn*. 60 (on the first tribunes) 'itaque auspicato postero anno [i.e. 493] tr. pl. comitiis curiatis creati sunt' (but this may mean no more than that the patricians made sure that the first tribunes were elected in the proper manner) and at Zon. vii. 19. 1 οἱ εὐπατρίδαι . . . τοὺς δημάρχους οἰωνοσκοπίᾳ ἐν συλλόγοις χρῆσθαι δεδώκασιν· ὃ λόγῳ μὲν τιμὴν αὐτοῖς ἔφερε καὶ ἀξίωμα (μόνοις γὰρ τοῦτο ἐκ τοῦ πάνυ ἀρχαίου τοῖς εὐπατρίδαις ἐπετέτραπτο), ἔργῳ δὲ κώλυμα ἦν, ἵνα μὴ ῥᾳδίως οἱ δήμαρχοι καὶ τὸ πλῆθος ὅσα βούλοιντο πράττοιεν, ἀλλὰ προφάσει τῆς οἰωνοσκοπίας ἔστιν οὗ ἐμποδίζοιντο. Resolution of this discrepant testimony is not easy, not least because between the fifth and first centuries Roman attitudes to the taking of auspices in the *concilium plebis* may have changed.

Many scholars (e.g. Niccolini, Drummond, Bleicken, Linderski) have agreed with D.H., arguing that the evidence of Cicero is an antiquarian construct designed to make the office of tribune of the plebs seems a natural constitutional development and that that of Zonaras, an author of no great authority, may be dismissed as (at best) a garbled reference to the right of *obnuntiatio* which by the late Republic tribunes undoubtedly had come to possess.

Others (e.g. Lange, Badian, and Vaahtera) side with Zonaras, in whose support the following evidence may be cited.

(*a*) The tribunes conferred in a *templum* (see ii. 56. 10, iii. 17. 1, passages which must reflect tribunician practice in the time of the annalists if not in the fifth century), addressed the plebs from the *rostra*, which were a *templum* (viii. 14. 12 n.), and held *concilia* in a *templum* (Cic. *Sest*. 62, 75, 85, and other evidence adduced by Badian). As Badian argues, 'it seems difficult to believe that meetings would take place in a *templum* without any auspication'.

(*b*) Cicero (*leg*. ii. 31) says that augurs could dismiss *concilia*.

(*c*) in the late Republic tribunician laws could be annulled if passed *contra auspicia* (from the evidence adduced by Mommsen [1887–8: iii. 367] note e.g. Ascon. *Corn*. 55 [on the laws of Livius Drusus] 'decretum est enim contra auspicia esse latas').

(*d*) L. (x. 47. 1 [n.] and xxx. 39. 8) reports that plebeian magistrates had to resign because they were *uitio creati*. Since the expression *uitio creatus* or the like is used elsewhere in the context of magistrates with the right to take the auspices,[1] these two passages, adduced by Lange, not entirely convincingly dismissed by e.g. Niccolini and Bleicken as instances of *obnuntiatio*, and neglected by those writing on this subject in the last thirty years, constitute powerful evidence in support of Zonaras.

Against the argument that this evidence applies only to oblative auspices and does not prove that the tribunes had the right to take the auspices, Badian (p. 201) well observes, 'I do not see how tribunes could have been forced to accept an augur in a purely obstructive function at their assemblies.' He argued that these rights were established after the passing of the *lex Hortensia* in 287 and that previously tribunician legislation had been brought under favourable auspices when *patrum auctoritas* was granted. However, x. 47. 1 may suggest that these rights must have been acquired earlier, and Lange argued acutely that the involvement of the augurs in the *concilium plebis* would have provided a powerful motive for the Ogulnian plebiscite, which brought plebeian admission to this college.

See further Lange (1863–76) ii. 52, 90, 444–6, Niccolini (1932) 132–3, Bleicken (1955) 22 n. 5 and 26 n. 1, Ogilvie on ii. 58. 1, Drummond (1989) 228, Linderski (1990) 41–8 (esp. 41 n. 22), Badian (1996) 197–202, and Vaahtera (2001) 160–4.

41. 5–6. plebeius . . . magistratus . . . patricios magistratus: see ix. 33. 3 n.

41. 6. nobis . . . habent: I ought to have noted that the view that private auspices once belonged to the patricians has been held by several scholars, for instance Ogilvie (see his note on iv. 2. 5).

41. 8. si pulli non pascentur: for the taking of the auspices before battle see also ix. 14. 4 n.

sed parua . . . fecerunt: the reference to Miles (1988) should have been to pp. 186–93 = (1995) 111–19.

maiores uestri. The rhetorical strategy of the reference to ancestors deserved more illustration. For similar appeals or references in speeches to the Roman people cf. e.g. iv. 3. 13, v. 53. 9, xxxiv. 2. 11, 3. 1, xxxix. 15. 2, 15. 11, and xlv. 39. 10, Cic. *imp. Pomp.* 6, and *Phil.* iv. 13 (note too numerous references in Cicero's speeches before juries, beginning with *Quinct.* 51). All these passages illustrate the respect for ancestral precedent shown by Roman republican politicians (at least in theory, if not always in practice), whose style of arguing L. doubtless imitates. However, Miles locc. citt. is right to point out that L. often places such appeals in the context of highly partisan political debate.

41. 9. sacrificuli reges: the statement that *rex sacrorum* was the more usual

---

[1] This conclusion emerges from the discussion of *uitium* by Linderski (1986: 2159–73); Linderski himself does not believe that the tribunes had the right to take the auspices (p. 2166) but does not discuss these passages. For instances of the expression *uitio creatus* see vi. 27. 4–5 n.

title is not accurate; in the passages cited it is found only at Cic. *dom*. 38; see further ix. 34. 12 n. The statement that even after the Struggle of the Orders all *reges sacrificuli* were patrician takes no account of the M. Marcius whose death L. records at xxvi. 6. 16: for discussion see above, p. 85.

41. 10. tamquam Romulus ac Tatius . . . regnent: Appius chooses the *exemplum* because Licinius and Sextius were a pair and, of Rome's kings, only these two ruled as a pair. Although Appius criticizes the tribunes for behaving like kings, Appius need not mean that Romulus and Tatius behaved like tyrants. Since the joint rule of Romulus and Tatius was productive for the Roman state, and since the events of 367–366 were to mark a new beginning for the Romans, Kraus sees the *exemplum* as unstable, and as revealing more than Appius intended.

41. 11. For other epiphonemata see e.g. Theophr. *char*. 8. 11 οὕτως καὶ καταπονοῦσι ταῖς ψευδολογίαις (part of an interpolated passage) and Dio lxii. 13. 3 τοιαῦτα μὲν ὁ Νέρων ἠσχημόνει.

41. 11. dulcedo: for L.'s use of this word see ix. 38. 2 n.

42. 2. decemuiris sacrorum: on these priests see also Szemler (1972) 26–7.

42. 4. T. Quinctium Poenum: the second paragraph of this n. is rendered incoherent by a slip in the first line of p. 718. Read 'with the consul of 351' instead of 'with the consul of 354'. In the first paragraph reading 'most modern scholars' for 'modern scholars' would make the argument easier to follow.

42. 8. consensu patrum plebisque triumphus decretus: on the rules for triumphs and on the triumph on the Alban Mount, see also Brennan (1996) 316–20. For L.'s interest in triumphs see Chaplin (2000) 140–56.

42. 10. prope secessionem: according to Ampel. 25. 4 'quarta secessio, in foro propter magistratus "ut plebei consules fierent", quam Sulpicius Stolo concitauit' there was a secession. (Ampelius has confused Licinius Stolo with his wife's brother-in-law: see 34. 5.)

42. 11. de praetore uno qui ius in urbe diceret: for the possible anachronism in L.'s language see x. 22. 7 n.

42. 12. in concordiam redactis ordinibus: Pabst (1969: 182–4) notes that L. often views *concordia ordinum* and *discordia* from a perspective similar to that of late republican *optimates*; he cites ii. 54. 2, iv. 47. 8, and vii. 22. 7.

merito . . . deum immortalium: in addition to the two passages from Virgil, numerous other analogies for *meritus* used in the context of a reward earned by the gods may be cited: cf. e.g. xxiii. 11. 3, xlv. 39. 11, Ov. *fast*. iii. 268, iv. 898, v. 596, and see *TLL* viii. 811. 61–74, 812. 21, 823. 53–59 and Bömer on Ov. *fast*. iv. 898.

42. 13–14. aedilibus plebis . . . duumuiros aediles: the Roman historical tradition held that the office of plebeian aedile was established in 493 after the First Secession of the Plebs: see D.H. vi. 90. 2–3, Gell. xvii. 21. 11, Paul. Fest. 259, and Zon. vii. 15. 10. The name *aedilis* suggests that originally their duties were associated with buldings or temples (presumably the plebeian temple of Ceres, Liber, and Libera in particular); but D.H. states that they were more extensive: assisting the tribunes of the plebs; taking charge of some prosecutions delegated to the aediles by the tribunes (for these prosecutions see x. 23. 11–13 n.); and having special responsibility for matters to do with temples and the forum. Zonaras additionally states that the aediles acted especially as scribes of the tribunes. None of these sources mentions the oversight of the *ludi plebeii*, one of their most important tasks (x. 23. 13 [with 11–13 n.]), nor their activities with regard to the corn-supply (see Plin. *nat.* xviii. 15). The plebeian aediles were sacrosanct (iii. 55. 9, xxix. 20. 11, Fest. 422, D.H. vii. 35. 3).

In our sources for Roman history before 366 the plebeian aediles are mentioned at D.H. vii. 14. 2–17. 6 (492); D.H. vii. 26. 3, 27. 2, 35. 3, and Plut. *Cor.* 18. 3–4 (491); Liv. iii. 6. 9 (463); Liv. iii. 31. 5, D.H. x. 48. 3–4 (454); Liv. iv. 30. 11 (428); and vi. 4. 6 (389). Most of these notices are of very doubtful historicity (D.H.'s account of the First Secession and the ensuing saga of Coriolanus is very unreliable, and it is most unlikely that in 463, 428, or 389 plebeian aediles would have been entrusted with administration on behalf of the state: see Mommsen [1887–8 ii. 477 n. 2]); the least likely to be invented are those that relate to 454. In books vii–x L. refers for certain to the plebeian aediles only at x. 23. 13. It is unclear whether the references at vii. 28. 9 and x. 13. 14 are to the plebeian or (more likely) the curule aediles.

The newly created curule aediles provide a unique example of a patrician magistracy that was modelled on an existing plebeian office. In addition to their responsibility for the *ludi Romani* (on which see also ix. 40. 16 n.), the curule aediles too undertook prosecutions (x. 23. 11–13 n.) and, by the late third century at the latest, had responsibility for the corn-supply (x. 11. 9 n.). Our sources make it hard to distinguish between the two offices. L. usually refers to the actions of the curule aediles before those of the plebeian aediles, and the curule aedileship seems to have become the more important magistracy.

For a succinct treatment of the two magistracies see Lintott (1999) 129–33; also Garofalo (1989).

Appendices

pp. 725–7. *Iteration.* For the repetition of a word in a different sense add ix. 17. 14–15 *unus* (thrice), 19. 2–4 *omnis* (thrice), 32. 6–8 *inclinare* (twice), 37. 7 *quod* (twice), 39. 1 *ad* (twice), x. 2. 9 *altera . . . altera . . . altero*, 24. 5–6 *legere* (twice). For the repetition of a word in the same sense add ix. 37. 11 *tam* (twice), 41. 3–5 *subigere* (twice), 41. 4 *is* (twice), 43. 11–19 *ut qui* (twice), 44. 8–10 *et ipsos . . . et ipsum*, 44. 10 *ducere* (twice), 44. 13–14 *capere* (thrice), x. 2. 9 *autem* (twice in parentheses), 6. 3–4 *undique* (twice), 17. 7 *admouere* (twice), 19. 17 *ita* (twice), 24. 2 *inter se* (twice), 25. 1–9 *pro se quisque* (twice), 26. 5–6 *certaminum . . . quae exposui . . . certamina exponere* (see n.), 27. 2–28. 14 *in aciem descendere* (twice), 28. 2–5 *quam* (thrice), 31. 1–3 *rebellare* (twice), 38. 8 *circa* (twice).

Volume I: Appendices

p. 729. *Anaphora.* Add the following examples ix. 37. 10 *non signum certum, non ducem sequentes,* 37. 10 *ad castra, ad siluas diuersi tendebant,* x. 19. 21 *per uallum, per fossas.*

p. 730. *Verbal hyperbaton.* Add the following examples: ix. 31. 7 *expeditae ducerentur legiones,* 32. 1 *ingens orsi bellum,* 33. 8 *ad causam pertinere suam,* 37. 9 *stratos passim inuadit hostes,* 37. 10 *tutius dedere refugium,* 39. 3 *suis diffidentes uiribus,* x. 20. 13 *memorandum deinde edidere facinus,* 29. 1 *nouam de integro uelle instaurare pugnam,* 29. 2 *uana in cassum iactare tela,* 29. 12 *Gallicam inuadere aciem.* From speeches note x. 25. 3 *multis rem geram militibus,* 25. 18 *quantisque administrandum copiis.*

VOLUME II

BOOK VII

Historical Introduction

p. 3. The triumph recorded in *F.T.* for 361 needs more comment. The spacing of *F.T.* suggests that it recorded two triumphs in this year: that one was celebrated by C. Sulpicius Peticus is made likely by the fact that *F.T.* record his triumph of 358 as his second. Before 358 Peticus had held the consulship in 364, for which year L. records no fighting, and 361, for which L. states that one or both of the consuls won successes against the Hernici.

pp. 18–27. *Internal affairs 366–342 BC.* An initial footnote should have signalled that the most penetrating discussion of the politics of these years is that of Hölkeskamp (1987: 62–90). In general, my interpretation of the evidence is very similar to his, but I regret not drawing attention to several good points made by him. See below.

pp. 19–22. I treated *interregna* and dictatorships *comitiorum habendorum causa* separately. However, as Hölkeskamp (1987: 62) observes, if one adds together dictatorships and *interregna,* the number of years in this period (356/5, 353/2, 352/1, 351/0, 350/49, 349/8, 344/3, 341/0) in which a consul did not take charge of the elections is extraordinary. From this (and also from L.'s stories of political conflict, although L. himself does not make this point) it is a probable deduction that the patricians had conceded that a plebeian could be elected consul but had not acquiesced in a plebeian's taking charge of the elections, and that this was often a point at issue (following Hölkeskamp, pp. 62–72 and Bunse [1998] 149–50 I should now make this point more strongly than I did on pp. 20–1).

Although I accepted Rilinger's thesis that the consul named first by our sources normally had the right to hold the elections, I offered no comment on the cases of L. Genucius (365), M. Popillius Laenas (359), and C. Marcius Rutilus (357), all of whom on Rilinger's principles were elected first: perhaps, in the aftermath of the plebeian successes of 367/6, they were persuaded not to press their claims, and only in the more heated political

Addenda *and* corrigenda

atmosphere of the years following 356 (see below) did the issue become contentious. If this is wrong and these men did hold the elections, then the thesis of Rilinger and Hölkeskamp is much less likely to be right.[1]

It is attractive to argue that the struggles of these years were sparked by the dictatorship of C. Marcius Rutilus in 356. He was perhaps nominated by a plebeian (conceivably the first time that a plebeian consul had nominated a dictator, a fact of some significance for the handling of the auspices)[2] and, more certainly and more controversially, was the first plebeian dictator and triumphed against the wishes of the patricians. The patricians responded by letting the year end in an *interregnum* and forcing the election, for the first time since 366, of two patrician consuls.

p. 20. For 'college of pontiffs' read 'colleges of pontiffs and augurs'.

pp. 21–2. On the question of how elections in an *interregnum* worked, I should have followed Ogilvie on iii. 8. 2 in citing other texts which suggest that the *interrex* oversaw the election of both consuls (or of consular tribunes): v. 31. 9, vi. 1. 8, viii. 3. 5 (for the text see n.), 23. 17, ix. 7. 17, x. 11. 10. All these, like the passages cited on pp. 21–2 (with the exception of vii. 21. 4, on which I should now place less weight) are instances of *creare* used of an *interrex*. Ogilvie followed Staveley, Hölkeskamp (1987: 67–8) Jahn. Hölkeskamp is prepared to dismiss all the passages that tell against Jahn's thesis, because it explains so clearly why patricians stood to gain from *interregna*. However, they stood to gain by the mere fact that an *interregnum* meant that a plebeian could not take the auspices at election time, and I still do not believe that a clear resolution of the problem is possible.

p. 22. The argument that patricians liked to use dictators *comitiorum habendorum causa* because they believed that they were more likely to effect the election of two patricians is vulnerable to the objection that only in 350 did dictators achieve this: in 353 and 352 they could not hold the elections and *interregna* resulted, and in 351, 349, and 348 they presided over the election of mixed colleges; see further Walt (1997) 270. Therefore it is desirable to give at least as much weight to the argument that the patricians were trying to avoid plebeian presidency at the elections (all these dictators were patrician). This view of dictators *comitiorum habendorum causa* would be undermined were Macer right to have argued that in 361 C. Licinius Calvus nominated T. Quinctius Poenus for this reason (see 9. 3–5). For then we should have a plebeian consul nominating a patrician dictator of his own

---

[1] Hölkeskamp (1987: 63) may have been right to argue that the dictatorships of 352 and 348 were occasioned by a patrician desire to stop, respectively, Marcius Rutilus and Popillius Laenas holding the elections; certainly they had more prestige than their patrician colleagues, even though there is no strong evidence that they were elected first.

[2] L. does not explicitly state this: it is Hölkeskamp's deduction from 17. 6–9; in arguing that Marcius was the first dictator to be nominated by a plebeian he has to reject Macer's view (fr. 16 = 9. 3–5) that Quinctius Poenus was nominated by C. Licinius Calvus in 361 to hold the elections and L.'s statement (12. 9) that C. Sulpicius Peticus was nominated by the plebeian Plautius in 358. Since L. himself gives reasons for rejecting Macer's views (see below), it is easy for a modern to follow. Hölkeskamp may also be right as regards Peticus, but this is an obvious weakness in his argument.

free will (again see Walt, loc. cit.). However, as L. observes, none of his other sources knew of this reason for Quinctius' appointment, and therefore the notion is likely to be an invention of Macer's.

On the development of the dictatorship *comitiorum habendorum causa* from a device to avoid plebeian consuls being entrusted with oversight of the elections to a practical solution of the problem of what to do when both consuls were at war, see Hölkeskamp (1988*b*) 285 = (2004) 59 and Bunse (1998) 208.

pp. 23–5. To the bibliography on iteration of the consulship cited in the footnotes add Develin (1985) 105–18, Loreto (1993) 55–60, and Brennan (2000) 65–7, 647–52.

The point that in the period 366–342 excessive iteration by some had thwarted the ambitions of others, and that this explains the restrictions on iteration which came into force in 342, is well made by Hölkeskamp (1993: 22–3 = 2004: 23).

The rule on iteration laid down by the *lex Genucia* was broken more often by patricians than plebeians: see Hölkeskamp (1987: 127 n. 5), who observes that the patrician holding the consulship broke the rule in 340 (T. Manlius Torquatus), 335 (M. Valerius Corvus), 320 (L. Papirius Cursor), 319 (L. Papirius Cursor), 315 (L. Papirius Cursor), 313 (L. Papirius Cursor), 311 (Q. Aemilius Barbula), 308 (Q. Fabius Rullianus), 299 (M. Valerius Corvus as *cos. suff.*), 295 (Q. Fabius Rullianus), 291 (L. Postumius Megellus), the plebeian in 320 (Q. Publilius Philo), 319 (Q. Aulius Cerretanus), 315 (Q. Publilius Philo), 313 (C. Junius Bubulcus), 311 (C. Junius Bubulcus), 308 (P. Decius Mus), and 295 (P. Decius Mus). However, since the rule was violated by plebeians as well as patricians, and since patricians allowed themselves to be bound by other plebiscites in this period, the view that the Genucian plebiscites were regarded as binding only by plebeians is not attractive. *Contra* Stewart (1998) 151, 173 and Brennan (2000) 65–7.

Brennan argues that by 330 the *lex Genucia* had lapsed and challenges the standard view that it was efficacious except in times of extreme emergency. His statistical argument (p. 649), that 63 per cent of iterations break the law (only 55 per cent if one accepts the 'dictator-years'), has considerable force, but the standard view remains defensible.

The implications of the *lex Genucia* for the holding of the praetorship are discussed at ix. 41. 1 n.

pp. 26–7. Hölkeskamp (1987: 72) rejects Münzer's views, noting that it is highly unlikely that mixed patricio-plebeian factions would have come into being at a time when the plebeians were struggling for electoral parity and against the burden of debt. Poma (1995) too rejects Münzer's hypothesis, arguing for rivalry between C. Marcius Rutilus and M. Fabius Ambustus in these years. She notes (pp. 79–89), for example, that, according to L., Marcius came to the dictatorship of 356 after a not wholly successful campaign of Fabius (vii. 17. 1–6) which contrasted sharply with Marcius' successes in the previous year; that the patricians forced an *interregnum* at the end of Marcius' dictatorship, something that suited their electoral purposes, as it led to the return for the first time since 366 of an all-patrician college; and that Fabius, despite being too preoccupied to hold the elections (17. 10), was able to return to Rome within five days to be an *interrex*. These observations are of considerable interest, although their cogency depends to a large extent on the accuracy of the details supplied by L., about which one may have doubts.

Commentary

1. 1. annus . . . insignis . . . insignis: Yardley (2003: 34) notes that this expression is found thrice in Justin (v. 8. 7, vi. 6. 5, xxxii. 4. 9), perhaps under Livian influence.

1. 2. L. Aemilius Mamercus: for brief comment on variation between Mamercus and Mamercinus and analogous phenomena see Alföldi (1966) 720–1.

1. 5. tres patricios magistratus: see ix. 33. 3 n.

curulibus sellis praetextatos: for simultaneous reference to the *sella curulis* and the *toga praetexta* see x. 7. 9 n.

uno plebeio . . . sibi sumpsisset: the converse of plebeian criticism of the number of patrician magistracies is patrician desire to have more such magistracies; see iv. 8. 5.

sibi: for the position of the pronoun see *addendum* to vii. 33. 17 n.

1. 6. praetorem . . . collegam consulibus atque iisdem auspiciis creatum: Brennan (2000) is the fullest ever study of the praetorship after 366 and supersedes all previous treatments of the subject.

For the notion of a praetor being a colleague of the consuls, in addition to the two Livian parallels, cf. Cic. *Att.* ix. 9. 3 'praetores . . . conlegae consulibus', Messalla *ap*. Gell. xiii. 15. 4 'conlegae non sunt censores consulum aut praetorum, praetores consulum sunt . . . praetor, etsi conlega consulis est', Gell. ibid. § 6 'sed et conlegam esse praetorem consuli docet (*sc.* Messalla), quod eodem auspicio creantur', Plin. *pan.* 77. 4 (Trajan as consul refers to the praetors as *conlegae*). This collegiality is reflected in the high status of the praetorship before 242: see ix. 41. 1, x. 22. 9 nn.

Bunse and Stewart, though arguing from different perspectives, both hold that in the immediate aftermath of the passing of the Licinio-Sextian rogations the *imperium* of a praetor was equal to that of a consul. That they are right is quite possible but far from certain. However, the passages of Cicero and Messalla (and others not cited) make clear that in the late Republic a consul had *imperium* which was greater than a praetor's. Therefore it may be preferable to stress with Brennan (pp. 34–59) that the introduction of a new magistracy with *imperium* that was *minus* than that of the consuls was an important development in Roman constitutional thought and practice, even if anticipated in some respects by the dictatorship, censorship, and consular tribunate. Brennan argues (p. 59) that the new system of two consuls and a praetorship was 'a rationalized consular tribunate of three members'; but, unless that office had become a sinecure for some of the six consular tribunes by 367, or unless the curule aediles took over functions that had previously been undertaken by consular tribunes, it is not entirely clear how the administration of the state was adapted to cope with the reduction in the number of senior magistrates.[1]

The idea that praetors were created with the same auspices as consuls, for which see the passages of L. quoted in the note and Gell. § 6, may arise from the fact that originally elections to the praetorship were held on the same day as elections to the consulship (see x. 21. 13–22. 9, from which it is probably reasonable to generalize). However, probably by 209 (xxvii. 21. 5), and certainly by 197 (xxxiii. 24. 2), the elections for the (by then enlarged) praetorship were held one or more days later than that for the consulship.

See further Mommsen (1887–8) ii. 193–4, Richard (1982), Stewart (1998) 97–111 (on the expression *iisdem auspiciis*), Bunse (1998) *passim*, and Brennan (2000) (esp. 29–30 and 58–9 on the relationship of the praetor to the consuls).

uerecundia ... promiscu⟨u⟩m fuit: the end of the discussion of the alternation between patricians and plebeians in the 290s is vitiated by two mistakes. Replace all from 'In the 290s . . .' to the end of the paragraph with the following.

In the 290s we have patricians for 295 and plebeians for 296. The variants recorded by L. for 299 do not allow us to determine who was curule aedile in that year (see x. 9. 10–12 n.): if Macer and Tubero were right in naming patricians, the pattern would be maintained; if Piso, or L.'s report of Piso, was right in naming plebeians, it would be broken. However, this is not a certain argument against Piso, since (*a*) there are reasons for doubting what Macer says (again see n.); (*b*) L. makes Cn. Flavius curule aedile in 304 (ix. 46. 1–15 n.), a year which ought to have been 'patrician', since 301 is one of the dictator-years that did not exist; and (*c*) in the light of (*b*) it is just conceivable either that the pattern exhibited by 296 and 295 was not stable in the 290s or that the arrangement involving alternation came into being *c*.296. (However, it is possible too that Flavius' aedileship was placed by L. in the wrong year.) If our scanty testimony (for which see vol. i, p. 51) for earlier in the fourth century is reliable, it shows that the arrangement can have come in place only after 331, since there were patrician aediles in 331 and 328. See further vii. 16. 9 n., Mommsen (1864–79) i. 97–102, (1887–8) ii. 480–3, and Forsythe (1994: 348–9).[2]

1. 7. L. Genucio: *the cognomen* probably shows that the family resided, or once resided, on the Aventine; cf. Capitolinus, used amongst others by the Manlii and Quinctii (vol. i, p. 476 with *addendum*).

---

[1] But on Bunse's thesis, discussed above, pp. 505–6, there would have been no such reduction.

[2] Forsythe makes the interesting suggestion that the seemingly random placing of the dictator years may have been an attempt to solve this problem of the aedilician *fasti*; but this would have been a drastic solution to a minor problem.

ne . . . uacarent: final clauses of this kind, in which the *uoluntas fati* is expressed, are discussed fully by R. G. Nisbet (1923); see also H–S 642 (with further bibliography). For other examples see x. 6. 3 'tamen ne undique tranquillae res essent' and 24. 2.

1. 10. titulo tantae gloriae: there is an analogy for this expression at Pont. (?) *uit. Cypr.* 5. 2 'indignum se titulo tanti honoris existimans'; for *titulo* see *addendum* to viii. 40. 4 n.

2. 1. C. Sulpicio Petico: on the probable triumph of Peticus in 361 see *addendum* to vol. ii, p. 3 above.

2. 2. tertium tum post conditam urbem lectisternium fuit: Forsythe (1994: 313) suggests that the second *lectisternium*, not noticed by L., 'could have been observed in 384 when Livy briefly mentions a plague' (see vi. 20. 15–21. 1). On *lectisternia* see also Latte (1960*b*) 12–14 = (1968) 844–5.

2. 3. superstitione: see x. 39. 2 n.

2. 4–13. *Digression on the origins of the* ludi scaenici *at Rome*

p. 51. L. does not say at which festival *ludi scaenici* were first performed. At [Cypr.] *spect.* 4 we are told that they were put on first at the Liberalia, but it is doubtful whether this evidence is reliable. For Varro's views on the Liberalia see vol. ii, p. 46.

pp. 55–8. Wiseman (2000*a*), esp. 267–86, uses iconographic and other evidence to make a strong case for Dionysiac rituals and drama having been common in archaic Italy. This drama can be linked with L.'s *satura*.

2. 4. quoque: to the emendations listed add *modo* (Watt [2002] 181–2).

2. 8. Liuius: for discussion of his career see also Wachter (1987) 328–30.

argumento fabulam serere: *OLD* classifies our passage under *sero*² 2(a) 'to join in a series, string together'. This seems better than the view expressed in my note, that *serere* is an instance of *sero*¹.

2. 10. inde ad manum cantari histrionibus coeptum: Watt (2002: 182) suggests supplying *tacentibus* after *histrionibus*: 'thereafter the singing began to be done (*cantari* passive impersonal) to the accompaniment of gestures, the actors being silent, and only the spoken parts were left for their own delivery'. This is the most attractive conjecture yet proposed in this passage.

2. 12. ut actores . . . faciant: on the disrepute of actors note also the ban instituted by the *lex Julia* of 18 BC on marriage between them or their children and *senatorii* (see Paul. *dig.* xxiii. 2. 44. *pr.* and the discussion by Treggiari [1991: 61–2]).

2. 13. in hanc insaniam: Wiseman (2000*b*: 82–3) suggests that L. may have been thinking of riots at the games; he notes that Val. Max. ii. 4. 1 refers to the theatre as *urbana castra* and that the pantomime-artist Pylades 'was recalled 'in 18 B.C. after having been exiled for stasis (Dio 54.17.4)'.

opulentis regnis: to the parallels cited add e.g. Plaut. *Bacch.* 647, Val. Max. iv. 3. 2, *pan.* vi(vii). 15. 1, and Porph. *carm.* i. 1. 12 'ATTALICIS CONDICIONIBVS: id est, regiis opibus'.

Book VII

3. 5–8. *Digression on the dictatorship* claui figendi causa

pp. 75–6. I wrote: 'He [i.e. L.] states that the annual ritual became defunct, and that when it was revived in the emergency of 363 a dictator took over duties which had been performed first by the praetor maximus and then by the consuls.' However, L. (§ 8) in fact places *intermisso deinde more* after he has referred to the transfer of the ritual from consuls to dictator. I should now prefer to argue (with Bunse [1998: 52], following the lead of Mommsen [1887–8: ii. 75]) that with *qui praetor maximus sit* L. may not have had in mind a magistracy called *praetor maximus*. Rather, he may have understood 'the chief commander in the state' (unlike modern scholars working from the evidence L. presents here, L. himself knew nothing of praetors as early republican magistrates; and since the dictatorship on his view was established after the consulship and was superior to it, and since in the fourth and third centuries the ritual of fixing the nail was performed by dictators, it was not unnatural for him to believe that the ritual was transferred to dictators). Bunse suggests that L. forgot that the dictatorship was not an annual magistracy, whereas the ritual which he had just described was; but it is just conceivable that he thought that dictators were appointed for the purpose, as they were (on an admittedly much less regular basis) in the fourth and third centuries. The ensuing explanation of the ritual that I offered still seems possible, although it would need modification if Bunse is right (see above, pp. 505–6) that the title *consul* came into use only after 366.

Bunse (pp. 208–12) argues that a dictator may have been appointed to hammer in the nail because the ritual required someone with supreme *imperium* (which a dictator had) and (on his thesis) there had been no such person since 366, when the old office of *praetor maximus* had become defunct. He notes an analogous idea at xxii. 10. 10 (217) 'Veneri Erycinae aedem Q. Fabius Maximus dictator uouit, quia ita ex fatalibus libris editum erat ut is uoueret cuius maximum imperium in ciuitate esset' (however, Fabius had already been appointed dictator for military reasons).

3. 5. praetor maximus: to the bibliography add Sohlberg (1991) 260–5 and Bunse (1998), *passim* but esp. 44–61 (and note p. 78 n. 2 for sensible dismissal of the evidence allegedly found by Augustus that relates to Cossus). For Sohlberg's and Bunse's thesis that Rome's chief magistrates were called *praetor* until 366 see *addendum* to vol. i, pp. 367–76. For *praetor* as the name of the Roman Republic's first chief official add ps.-Ascon. p. 234. 5–8 (analogous to Paul. Fest. 249 cited in the note). As evidence for this use of *praetor* in the fifth century Bunse (1998: 76–9) cites further references to the praetor in our sources for the XII Tables (i. 12 = Gai. *inst*. iv. 17, i. 19 = Gell. xi. 18. 8, iii. 5= Gell. xx. 1. 47, viii. 5 = Plin. *nat*. xviii. 12 [Crawford (1996), 602, 613, 625, 684]); these are usually regarded as reflecting Roman society after 366, when the praetor (as conventionally understood) was responsible for administering Rome's laws, but are compatible with Bunse's thesis.

ea parte qua is a conjecture in U for **N**'s *ea qua parte*, which gives no sense. The transposition postulated is diplomatically as easy a conjecture as any (vol. i, p. 165), and this word-order is paralleled at Sen. *dial.* ii. 6. 3, Col. iii. 18. 5, v. 11. 3, xii. 52. 5, and Frontin. *strat.* i. 5. 21. L. too in nine other passages has *ea parte* followed by *qua* or the relative pronoun (see Packard [1968] ii. 9), and it need not tell against the reading that *ab*, *ex*, or (occasionally) *in* precedes *ea* in all. For true or plausible readings found first in U see vol. i, p. 299. Alternative conjectures are *ex qua parte* (Gronovius) (this is diplomatically as easy as the reading of U, and in its support he cited 12. 6 'Tarquinienses fines Romanos, maxime qua ex parte Etruriam adiacent, peragrauere'; but there motion is implicit—L. is saying from which quarter the Etruscans are attacking—, as it is more obviously at ix. 23. 6 'quoque tempore et qua ex parte hostem adgrederetur', and it is not clear that this meaning is welcome here), *qua parte* (Walters) (this gives as good sense as U's conjecture but is diplomatically harder [Walters suggests that H's *.ea. qua parte* shows that H intended *ea* to be deleted; but, even if this be correct, H's isolated testimony is of little authority]), and *a qua parte* (Shackleton Bailey [1986] 321) (this has the same disadvantage as Gronovius' conjecture, and L. never uses *a qua parte*).

3. 8. et lege⟨m et⟩ templum . . . dedicauit: I should have observed that with Madvig's conjecture *dedicauit* picks up *dicatam* in § 6. Sohlberg (1991: 263 n. 31) conjectures *ea lege ⟨clauum primum fixit et⟩ templum . . . dedicauit.* This meets some of Madvig's objections to other emendations but is a less elegant solution to the *crux*.

4. 1. dies Manlio dicitur a M. Pomponio tribuno plebis: for tribunician prosecutions see *addendum* to vi. 1. 8 n.

4. 2. acerbitas in dilectu, non damno modo ciuium sed etiam laceratione corporum †lata†: for *acerbitas* ('harshness') in conducting the levy cf. xxi. 11. 13 'populi dilectus acerbitate consternati' and Suet. *Cal.* 43 'dilectibus ubique acerbissime actis'. This second passage suggests that *acto* is a possible emendation of *lata*, albeit lacking diplomatic probability.

4. 7. uita agresti et rustico cultu inter pecudes: for the expression and idea Yardley (2003: 77) compares Just. xliii. 2. 6 'inter greges pecorum agresti uita nutriuit', for *uita agrestis* (generally regarded as bestial and inhuman) also Cic. *de or.* i. 33, *leg.* ii. 36, Vitr. ii. 1. 6, and Sen. *dial.* v. 2. 1.

5. 3. a porta domum: to the parallels cited add Cic. *IIVerr.* i. 23 'quae cum Verrem a porta subito ad iudicium retraxisset' and Val. Max. vi. 2. 3 'P. Africanum . . . ab ipsa paene porta in rostra perductum'. Clearly expressions of this kind were an idiomatic way of saying 'as soon as he arrived in the city, he went [or 'was taken' etc.] to . . .'.

5. 6 subactum se incepto destitisse: the use of the infinitive after *subigere* should have been discussed: see now ix. 41. 5 n.

5. 9. eo anno primum: among the Livian parallels I should have cited x. 47. 3; for notices of 'firsts' in L.'s predecessors, see also Hemina fr. 21 and Macer fr. 9.

placuisset: a measure restricting the freedom of choice enjoyed by consuls is likely to have been a plebiscite.

procul: to the parallels add [Quint.] *decl.* 13. 2 (relevant esp. to 39. 12).

6. 6. fabula: for the contrast between *fabula* and *historia* add Serv. *Aen.* i. 235 '. . . quod fabula est dicta res contra naturam, siue facta siue non facta, ut de Pasiphae, historia est quicquid secundum naturam dicitur, siue factum siue non factum, ut de Phaedra'; to the bibliography add Wiseman (1993) 128–31.

6. 7–8. 7. Ferenczy (1965: 367–8; 1976: 125–6) defended the authenticity of the dictatorship of Ap. Claudius Inregillensis in 362, using arguments similar to those put forward in this note.

6. 11. inauspicatam legem: if plebeian magistrates were not elected with the auspices and did not have the right to take the auspices, then these facts would explain this expression (see Linderski [1990] 41); but both points have been challenged: see further vi. 41. 5 n. (with *addendum*).

turbato iure gentium: for *ius gentium* add a reference to iv. 4. 4. For *turbare* in this context cf. Cic. *leg.* iii. 21 (on Clodius' adoption by Fonteius) 'gentes . . . perturbandas'. Cicero uses *perturbatio* in the context of the auspices at *ad Brut.* 13. 4.

6. 12. Ap. Claudium . . . dictatorem dicit: on L.'s failure to name a *magister equitum* see below, *addendum* to viii. 22. 1 n.

7. 6. conspectior: see *addendum* to vi. 15. 10 n.

7. 8. consulto prius dictatore: for *prius* in ablatives absolute see x. 2. 10 n. For consultation of the dictator see *addendum* to vi. 8. 1 n.

prouolant: this verb is attested also at Quadr. fr. 19.

8. 3 clamore renouato: see ix. 35. 6 n. as well as viii. 38. 10 n.

8. 6. Sign⟨in⟩is: for this conjecture see also Reiz, *ap.* Haupt (1850: 103 = 1875–6: i. 307).

palatum est: see also ix. 31. 15 n. (on the coupling of *palari* with *inermis* and *semiermis*).

8. 7. nec Romanis incruenta uictoria fuit: on this expression see also Yardley (2003) 51.

9. 1. portas clausere: see *addendum* to vi. 25. 7 n.

9. 4. Macer Licinius: I stated that it cannot be proved that Macer's history was pro-plebeian. This is true but probably too cautious. I agree with many scholars that it was: it would be quite astonishing if the *popularis* tribune of 73 were not responsible for some of the pro-plebeian narratives in L. and D.H., all the more so when in the speech which Sallust gives him he alludes to the travails of the early plebs. For an early exponent of this view see Scaramella (1897), for a recent Wiseman (2002c) 297–301. Too cautious on this last point, Walt (1997) offers a full treatment of all other aspects of Macer's work.

9. 6–10. 14. *The duel between Manlius Torquatus and the Gaul*

p. 114. To the bibliography add Courtney (1999) 144–50.

p. 119. With regard to the structure of the episode, note also how L. introduces both the Gaul (9. 8) and Manlius (10. 2) with parallel *tum*s: see Albrecht (1989) 100.

pp. 119–20. For the emotions of those watching a battle cf. also D.S. xiii. 16. 7, 98. 5, and Dict. iv. 6 (as here, a single combat). The whole topic is studied, with special reference to theories of *enargeia*, by A. D. Walker (1993).

p. 121. Replace 'no hyperbaton' with 'virtually no hyperbaton', noting Quadr. § 9 'pugnae facta pausa est'.

p. 121 n. 4. For the juxtaposition of verbs see also x. 28. 10 (discussed above, p. 277).

9. 6. tumultus Gallici: in the discussion of *iustitia* a reference is needed to ix. 7. 8 n., where *iustitia* in times of mourning are discussed. My argument against Cicero at p. 126 n. 2 is wrong, since the *lex colonia Genetiuae* (see Crawford loc. cit.) refers to both an Italian and a Gallic tumult. Replace: 'Another feature of such a crisis is the disposition of guards around the city (iii. 3. 5, 5. 4, 15. 8, iv. 31. 9, vi. 6. 14, x. 4. 1, 21. 4, and, perhaps, vi. 6. 14' with 'A *iustitium* is often said to have been accompanied by the disposition of guards around the city; see iii. 3. 5, 5. 4, iv. 31. 9, and x. 4. 1–2 (n.). For the placing of guards without reference to a *iustitium* see iii. 15. 8 and vii. 12. 3; perhaps also x. 21. 4.'

9. 7. [e]rumpentibus: conceivably perseveration from *erat* could have caused the corruption to *erumpentibus*.

9. 8. 'quem nunc . . . utra gens bello sit melior': for another example of a specific challenge to single combat, see Dict. iv. 6.

10. 2. statione: see *addendum* to viii. 8. 1 n.

iniussu tuo: for soldiers banned from breaking ranks and fighting without permission cf. also Tac. *ann*. xi. 18. 2 (Corbulo enforcing old standards). On the requirement that a soldier who wished to fight in single combat should gain the permission of his commanding officer, see also Fischer (1914) 137–8.

10. 3. me ex ea familia ortum: the whole topic of the desire of Romans to emulate their forebears and of the stock characteristics of families has now received its fullest discussion from Treggiari (2003), who draws her evidence mostly from Cicero. Here I cite a few of the same passages and add others from other authors.

For the desire of children to emulate their parents or forebears, see Cic. *off*. i. 116 'quorum uero patres aut maiores aliqua gloria praestiterunt, ii student plerumque eodem in genere laudis excellere, ut Q. Mucius P. f. in iure ciuili, Paulli filius Africanus in re militari. quidam autem ad eas laudes quas a patribus acceperunt addunt aliquam suam, ut hic idem Africanus eloquentia cumulauit bellicam gloriam'. For pressure on them to do this see also Cic. *IVerr*. 51–2, *off*. i. 78 (with reference to Cicero's own son), 121 (with reference to the failure of the elder Africanus' son to do this), Flower (1996) 150–4, 220–1, Cooley (1998) 205–7, and Treggiari, pp. 155–7. For

Greek analogies see e.g. Griffith (1998) 30–5. For a good example of rivalry with ancestors see [Tib.] iii. 7 (*pan. Mess.*) 28–32 'nam quamquam antiquae gentis superant tibi laudes, | non tua maiorum contenta est gloria fama, | nec quaeris quid quaque index sub imagine dicat, | sed generis priscos contendis uincere honores, | quam tibi maiores maius decus ipse futuris'. For the importance of domestic *exempla* see e.g. Cic. *Phil.* xiii. 15 and Treggiari, pp. 157–62; a good example of an aristocrat imitating the actions of an earlier member of his family may be found at Dio xxxviii. 7. 1 (Metellus Celer citing his distant cousin Metellus Numidicus as an example for refusing to obey a law). For the fact that a man lived up to or surpassed his ancestors as a τόπος of praise, or failed to live up to his ancestors as a τόπος of blame, see [Cic.] *Her.* iii. 13; and for the implication that the younger Papirius Cursor lived up to his father's glory, see x. 38. 1 n. The pressure on sons to live up to their parents explains terms of approbation such as *similis patri* (*uel sim.*) (of the examples cited by Eck, Caballos, and Fernández [1996: 213–14], the most relevant are Cic. *Phil.* v. 39, Ov. *Pont.* ii. 8. 31–2, Vell. i. 12. 3, *CIL* xi. 1421. 13; but add Cic. *IIVerr.* iii. 160, v. 30 [both ironical], *Att.* x. 1. 1, *off.* i. 121 [most pertinent of all], and *Phil.* xiii. 29; and note *dissimillumum* at *s.c. de Cn. Pisone patre* 97) and *dignus parente* (*uel sim.*) (see iv. 17. 9, vi. 6. 13 [n.], x. 13. 13; contrast Val. Max. v. 8. 3 'domo mea indignum'; and see further Treggiari, pp. 150–2). This idea also explains the notion that families had stock behavioural characteristics (for which see Quint. v. 10. 24 and Treggiari, pp. 152–5), exploited by the annalists in the manner illustrated at vol. i, pp. 98–9.

10. 5–7. habili . . . armis habilibus: for the idea cf. also Ampel. 15. 16 'arma habiliore pondere'.

10. 5, p. 137. As Millar (1964: 43–4) demonstrates, Dio is particularly concerned with the dignity of his history, to the extent that he avoids dates throughout most of his work and many precise details (e.g. of Caesar's legislation at xxxviii. 7. 6). The two most striking examples are the passage on Domitian that I cited and lxxii. 18. 3 (where, after reporting how Commodus himself killed innumerable beasts in the arena, the historian defends himself μή μέ τις κηλιδοῦν τὸν τῆς ἱστορίας ὄγκον . . . νομίσῃ). Many centuries earlier Xenophon had wondered whether certain ἀποφθέγματα that he recorded were ἀξιόλογα. In the related genre of biography Nepos (*praef.* 1) noted that some would find some of his subject matter unworthy of those whose lives he was writing.

pp. 138–9. For historians' commenting that subject matter is not worthy of mention or elaboration, see also e.g. xxxii. 9. 5, xlii. 26. 1, D.S. xiii. 104. 8, Dio lxv. 3. 1, lxvii. 8. 1. Lucian (*hist. consc.* 56) recommended that the budding historian should avoid the trivial. At xliii. 13. 2 L. defends his decision to include reports of prodigies, stating explicitly that, since earlier generations of Romans had recorded them, he regarded them as worthy of a place in his annals.

10. 7. uersicolori may also emphasize the barbarian elements in L.'s description of the Gaul: see ix. 40. 3 n.

militaris statura: for this idea cf. also Sen. *dial*. vi. 24. 1 'adulescens statura, †pulchritudine†, certo corporis robore castris natus'.

10. 8. non cantus, non exsultatio armorumque agitatio uana: for the noise made by Gauls cf. also Sis. fr. 72.

discrimen . . . certaminis is paralleled at Val. Max. iii. 8. 2 and Just. xxii. 7. 7; see Yardley (2003) 57.

10. 10. in spatium ingens ruentem porrexit hostem: for the τόπος of the dead warrior occupying a huge space, cf. also Ov. *fast*. iv. 895–6.

10. 12. statione: see *addendum* to viii. 8. 1 n.

10. 14. pro contione: this n. should be supplemented with the following observations on *contiones* in books vi–x. (*a*) The regular position for the *contio* seems to have been in front of the *praetorium*; see vi. 12. 7, ix. 13. 1, and xxvii. 13. 9–13 (where this position is implicit in *aderant*). (*b*) The *contio* before battle usually took place on the day of the battle; see vii. 16. 4, ix. 13. 1, 23. 9–13, xxvi. 43. 2, and xli. 18. 10. Sometimes, for obvious reasons, it took place the day before; see ix. 37. 5–6, x. 39. 11, xxv. 38. 1–23. (*c*) Often a *contio* was coupled with a meeting of the commander's *consilium*. At e.g. ix. 15. 1, x. 44. 6–8, xliv. 2. 1–3 the *contio* precedes; at e.g. xxv. 25. 7 and xxviii. 26. 1–3 it follows. (*d*) In the *contio* after the battle those whose bravery deserved to be commended were praised before *dona* were distributed; with *laudibus* in this passage cf. e.g. x. 44. 3, xxv. 18. 15, xxvi. 48. 14, xxx. 15. 11, 13, xxxviii. 23. 11, xxxix. 31. 17, xlii. 60. 10, Caes. *Gall*. v. 52. 4, [*Afr*.] 86. 3, Plb. vi. 39. 2, and D.H. vi. 94. 1. Only in our passage is there a reference to the *dona* before the *laudatio*. In all the Latin passages *laudare* or a cognate is used to denote this praise. See further Fischer (1914) 156–9 (to whom most of this material is owed).

11. 4. dictatorem: for discussion of the triumph of the consul in a year in which a dictator was appointed, see Brennan (2000) 39–40.

ludos magnos uouit: see also *addendum* to viii. 40. 2 n.

11. 6. in conspectu parentum coniugumque ac liberorum: for this encouragement to troops cf. also D.S. xiii. 15. 5 and 60. 4. For the motif of τειχοσκοπία see Nisbet and Rudd on Hor. *carm*. iii. 2. 6–8 and Tarrant on Sen. *Ag*. 622.

11. 7. magna utrimque . . . caede: Yardley (2003: 42) adds Just. xii. 1. 9.

11. 8 proeliis . . . pugna: for a passage where *proelium* and *pugna* seem hardly to be distinguished, see ix. 41. 4 'cum Samnitibus acie dimicatum . . . neque eius pugnae memoria tradita foret, ni Marsi eo primum proelio cum Romanis bellassent'.

11. 9. ouans: the *ouatio* of Fabius, recorded also in *F.T.*, deserves comment. In previous Roman history *ouationes* are attested for 503 (D.H. v. 47. 2–4, *F.T.*, Plin. *nat*. xv. 125), 487 (D.H. viii. 67. 10), 474 (D.H. ix. 36. 3; *ouans* restored in *F.T.*), 462 (iii. 10. 4; *ouans* restored in *F.T.*), 421 (iv. 43. 2), 410 (iv. 53. 11), and 392 (v. 31. 4). After our passage the only *ouatio* attested before that of Marcellus in 211 is that of M'. Curius Dentatus in 283 (*uir. ill*. 33. 4 'tertio de Lucanis ouans urbem introiit'). There is no reason to doubt that, even though some of the earlier instances may be invented, the institution of the *ouatio* existed in early Rome. That of Fabius is the last in this phase of its history (that of Curius Dentatus, if genuine, comes some seventy years later). The institution was to be revived by Marcellus, who set the pattern for later *ouationes*. See further Richardson (1975) 54–6, Brennan (1996) 324, and esp. Rohde, *RE* xviii. 2. 1889–1903.

12. 2. subita res et nocturnus pauor: for this combination of ideas cf. xxv. 38. 1 'subita res et nocturnus terror'.

12. 3. portae stationibus murique praesidiis: the discussion of *stationes* is now superseded by the *addendum* to viii. 8. 1 n.

12. 11. iis corporibus . . . languesceret mora: for Celtic lack of staying-power, cf. also Caes. *Gall.* iii. 19. 6 'nam ut ad bella suscipienda Gallorum alacer ac promptus est animus, sic mollis ac minime resistens ad calamitates perferendas mens eorum est' and Sil. viii. 16–18 'quin etiam ingenio fluxi, sed prima feroces, | uaniloquum Celtae genus ac mutabile mentis, | respectare domos' and xv. 715–19 (both cited by Ash [1999: 128], who notes that the τόπος is used occasionally of other nations). For their dislike of heat cf. also D.S. xiv. 113. 3, Tac. *hist.* ii. 32. 1 'Germanos . . . tracto in aestatem bello fluxis corporibus mutationem soli caelique haud toleraturos', and Flor. i. 20(ii. 4). 1–2 (cited by Ash). At Vitr. vi. 1. 3–4 the idea is explained with reference to ancient views of the effect of climate on physignomy.

Related to the idea illustrated in the n., that the Gauls and Germans tended to expend their energy in their first onslaught, is the notion that they attacked without reflection; see Vitr. vi. 1. 10.

12. 12. stationibus uigiliisque: see *addendum* to viii. 8. 1 n.

12. 14. in principiis: rather than a brief reference to the *uia principalis*, for which see further x. 33. 1 n., I should have noted that the *principia* are mentioned at xxviii. 24. 10, 13, 25. 5 (quoted in n. on *circulis*), xxxvii. 17. 9 'ibi in principiis sermo . . . oritur', Val. Max. ii. 7. 9, Tac. *hist.* i. 54. 1, Hyg. *mun.* 14, and Macer, *dig.* xlvix. 16. 12. 2 'officium tribunorum est . . . principiis frequenter interesse', and other passages listed at *TLL* x. 2. 1318. 1–46. The term denoted that part of the *uia principalis* outside the *praetorium* and the tents of the *tribuni* which was the centre of the life of the camp. In three of the five passages in which he mentions the *principia* L. refers to gossiping there; this corresponds to Plb. vi. 33. 4 τὴν γὰρ διατριβὴν ἐν ταῖς καθημερείαις οἱ πλεῖστοι τῶν Ῥωμαίων ἐν ταύτῃ ποιοῦνται τῇ πλατείᾳ· διόπερ ἀεὶ σπουδάζουσι περὶ ταύτης, ὡς ῥαίνηται καὶ καλλύνηται σφίσιν ἐπιμελῶς and to Tacitus and Macer locc. citt. In the fifth (xxviii. 24. 10) he mentions that this was the place where the tribunes carried out their jurisdiction. See further Fischer (1914) 40 and Zevi (1996).

12. 14. circulis: for *circuli* and élite suspicion of them, see O'Neill (2003) esp. 137–43.

13. 5. uirtute: see *addendum* to vi. 30. 6 n.

13. 10. tuum sequentes currum: for this practice see x. 30. 8 n.

13. 11. ut signum daret, ut capere arma iuberet: see ix. 37. 5 n.

14. 1. †cernebat censebat tamen facturum quod milites uellent se

recepit†: Watt (2002: 182) may have been right to tackle the difficulties of this passage by more drastic emendation. He suggested *faciendum* for *facturum* and a supplement like ⟨*itaque in praetorium*⟩ *se recepit*.

15. 1. dextrum: for confusion between left and right in accounts of battles, see Ridley (1991) 218–19, discussing evidence adduced by J. Perizonius.

15. 5. For the ellipse with *clamor . . . ortus* cf. ix. 37. 4 'clamor repente circa duces ortus, ut . . .'.

15. 9. inconsulte: for *inconsulte* in a military context cf. e.g. Veg. *mil.* iii. 26. 16.

15. 11. ludi uotiui, quos M. Furius dictator uouerat: if Camillus made his vow in battle, there is a later parallel in the games vowed by Q. Fulvius Flaccus in 180 (xl. 40. 10, xlii. 10. 5). However, although there is no reason to think that the notice of the games is invented, the report of Camillus' vowing them may be an annalistic reconstruction or invention.

16. 1. C. Marcio: on Marcius see Hölkeskamp (1987) 73, Storchi Marino (1993) 230–9, and Poma (1995) esp. 76–8, who point out how in each of his consulships and in his dictatorship the indebtedness of the plebeians was an issue. In this year a law on interest was passed and Marcius allowed the troops to keep their booty (§ 4), in 352 *uuiri mensarii* were appointed (21. 5), in 344 *faeneratores* were prosecuted (28. 9), and in 342 there was the agitation on debt connected with the Genucian plebiscites. Note too that in 351, a year in which the assessment of the extent of indebtedness was important, Marcius was elected the first plebeian censor (22. 6–10). To these may perhaps be added the *lex Marcia* on debt (discussed at vol. i, p. 661), which ought to have been mentioned in the n. on this passage.

16. 3. integrum pace longinqua: for the idea cf. also Just. v. 5. 2 'agros longa pace diuites'.

16. 4. uocatis ad contionem militibus: see *addendum* to vii. 10. 14 n.

16. 7–8. *The tribal assembly at Sutrium.* My statement of the evidence for a curule magistrates presiding over the tribes needs to be refined. In addition to the eccentric assembly described in this passage, it comprises (in legislative contexts) *lex Gabinia Calpurnia de insula Delo* (Crawford [1996] no. 22) l. 3 (58 BC: the reference to the temple of Castor shows that the consuls must have called a tribal assembly), Frontin. *aq.* 129 = *lex Quinctia* (Crawford [1996] no. 63) ll. 1–4 (9 BC: a clear reference to the tribes) and (in electoral or quasi-electoral contexts) x. 24. 18 (295 BC: a difficult and disputed passage; see n. ad loc.) and the evidence adduced for the election of curule aediles by the tribes (to which add ix. 46. 2, Pis. fr. 27 = Gell. vii. 9. 3 [where the paradosis suggests that an aedile presides, but see vol. iii, p. 601], and esp. Varr. *rust.* iii. 2. 2 [showing that a consul was presiding]). I should not now place any weight on Caes. *ciu.* iii. 1. 4.

Sandberg (1993: esp. 76–81, 2000: esp. 132–6, and 2001: esp. 105–10), noting that in this passage alone of our sources for the period before Sulla's reforms a curule magistrate is said to pass a measure through the tribes, has argued forcefully for the view that before Sulla there was no *comitia tributa* presided over by curule magistrates and that the tribes met only under the presidency of tribunes in the *concilium plebis*. Even if one grants (which one should not certainly do) (*a*) that x. 24. 18 is too difficult a passage to provide useful evidence, (*b*) that our direct evidence for consular presidency at aedilician elections is post-Sullan, and (*c*) that Sandberg's question (2001: 108) 'Why should the election of minor officials of minimal political import-ance not be entrusted to the plebeians?' disposes of the evidence from the election of quaestors, the argument does not convince, largely because Sandberg himself has shown that for the period after 366 there is very little evidence for the *comitia centuriata* being used to pass measures that do not pertain in some degree to war. However, several laws are attested as having been passed by consuls or dictators, and Sandberg's attempt to argue that in reality they were passed by tribunes is implausible. That tribunes of the plebs normally presided over the tribes is uncontroversial; but that dicta-tors, consuls, and praetors were debarred from doing so seems an odd restriction to have imposed on the chief magistrates of the state. See further Appendix 3 to the commentary on book x, above, pp. 470–2.

16. 7. nouo exemplo: see x. 37. 9 n.

17. 3. uelut lymphati et attoniti: *attonitus* has a parallel in Greek ἐμβρόντητος. To the passages cited by L–S–J add e.g. Men. *dysc.* 441. For *uelut* toning down expressions of this kind cf. x. 29. 2 'uelut alienata mente' (n.).

17. 6. ad salinas: for discussion of these salt-beds and of their importance in early Roman history, see Smith (1996) 179–80.

dictator primus de plebe dictus: I should have observed that L.'s account of this very important plebeian breakthrough is surprisingly low-key.

17. 7. omnique . . . parareturue: in addition to Mommsen, see Hölkeskamp (1987) 66–7.

17. 9. octo milibus hostium captis: for enemy casualty figures in our sources for early Roman history, add Val. Max. i. 8. 6 (on the victory of Fabricius over the Lucanians and Bruttians in 282 BC) 'uiginti enim milia caesa, quinque cum Statio Statilio duce utriusque gentis et tribus atque uiginti militaribus signis capta sunt'.

17. 12. in duodecim tabulis legem esse: although the notion that the Twelve Tables contained such a law may be bogus, something similar to the sentiment of *quodcumque postremum populus iussisset, id ius ratumque esset* may well have been expressed at elections in the middle Republic. See also next *addendum*.

id ius ratumque esset: for parallels to this expression see ix. 33. 9 n. For the idea that a later measure of the people can supersede an earlier one, see Cic. *Att.* iii. 23. 2 and Cic. *Balb.* 33 'tamen id esset quod postea populus iussisset ratum'. That the sentiment of our passage is expressed in connec-tion with an election is interesting, since ideas similar to it are found in annalistic reports of elections in the middle Republic; see xxv. 2. 7 (in response to protests that he is too young to be elected curule aedile L. makes Scipio say *si me . . . omnes Quirites aedilem facere uolunt, satis annorum habeo*

Addenda *and* corrigenda

[however, at this date there was no formal *lex* regulating age of election])
and App. *Lib.* 112. 529–34 (the populace, who wish to see the under-age
Scipio Aemilianus elected consul, claim that at elections they can annul any
law which they wish); note too the occasional pressure on the tribunes to
relax the rules governing eligibility for election (see x. 13. 9 n.). Badian
(1990: 397; 1996: 211) argues that the provision mentioned in our passage
was a device for settling conflicts between laws; however, on neither of the
two occasions on which L. refers to it is there a conflict between laws. See
also Lintott (1999) 63.

18. 3–10. Since there is an honorific reference to Licinius Stolo at § 5, and
since the late republican motifs found in this passage are pro-plebeian,
Wiseman (2000*b*: 82) may be right to suggest that the elaboration of the
scene is largely the work of Licinius Macer.

18. 9. uicit: Professor Watt pointed out to me that, if Gelenius' *uictae* is
what L. wrote, the corruption to *uicta* could have been caused by assimila-
tion to the case of *perseuerantia*.

18. 12. memoria ex annalibus repetita: the reference must be to the
annales maximi; see vol. i, p. 25 n. 17.

19. 4. res . . . accepti: Rome's treaty with the Samnites is mentioned also at
D.S. xvi. 45. 8. Although L. can use terms such as *amicitia* and *societas*
loosely and sometimes interchangeably, I ought to have noted that in this
passage and at x. 3. 1 the additional reference to the treaty serves to define
the nature of the *amicitia*, as also at vii. 27. 2 and ix. 45. 18. On these matters
see also ix. 20. 7–8 n.

20. 5. florentem . . . afflicti: these words are quite commonly found contrasting with each other. To the passages cited by Landgraf on Cic. *S. Rosc.*
24 and Martin and Woodman on Tac. *ann.* iv. 68. 3 add this passage, xxviii.
41. 17, Cic. *Flacc.* 16, and *fam.* xiv. 4. 5. Martin and Woodman suggest that
the image suggests a plant once thriving but now laid low.

20. 8. ut maleficii quam beneficii potius immemores essent: I might
have cited some passages where people are said to be *memor beneficii* (*uel
sim.*): e.g. Val. Max. v. 2. 1 and v. 2. *ext.* 3.

21. 4. L. Cornelium Scipionem: Ryan (1998) points out that amongst
known *interreges* Scipio is unique in not being attested as having previously
held a curule magistracy. He suggests that he had either held the praetorship or the curule aedileship or that he was censor in 358. If he was not
censor in 358, then he is likely to have been censor in 340 (thus vol. i, p. 49),
and Ryan suggests that the appearance of two brothers in the censorship of
340 may have encouraged the restrictions of the *lex Publilia* of 339 (for
which see viii. 12. 16 n.).

21. 5–8. *The quinqueuiri mensarii.* See also Andreau (1987) 221–46 (with
discussion of *mensarius* and related terms) and, above all, the very full discussion of this episode by Storchi Marino (1993). I ought to have pointed
out that Nicolet regarded the episode as a retrojection of the episode from
216 mentioned at § 5 n.

21. 6. meriti aequitate curaque sunt, ut . . . celebres nominibus

essent: historians were expected to single out individuals for praise or blame: see Plb. i. 14. 5, ii. 61. 5–6, Cic. *fam.* v. 12. 8, D.S. xi. 38. 6, 46. 1, xv. 1. 1, and D.H. *Pomp.* 5, Scheller (1911) 48–50, Marincola (1997) 158–74, and Chaplin (2000) 10 (all with further references to ancient texts and modern bibliography). For praise of an individual cf. xxviii. 12. 2–5 (Hannibal), D.S. xi. 38. 5–6 (on Gelo), xi. 46. 1–4 (Pausanias criticized, Aristides praised), xi. 58. 4–59. 4 (Themistocles praised), and Dio lxiii (lxiv). 6. 4–5 (Dio explains that he is mentioning the centurion Sempronius Densus by name because of his loyalty to Galba). For criticism see e.g. i. 53. 4, D.S. xi. 46. 2–3, xiii. 103. 2, and 106. 10. Seneca the Elder (*suas.* 6. 22) thought L. a very fair judge.

per omnium annalium monumenta: with this expression L. suggests that his sources were unanimous and that the *uuiri* deserved posthumous fame and, although *monumentum* can refer to a literary work, he hints too at the public records that lay behind the annalistic tradition. See further Storchi Marino (1993) 216–17.

21. 6. Q. Publilius: on the career of Q. Publilius Philo see also Garzetti (1947) 184–6 = (1996) 28–30, Develin (1985) 59–63, and Stewart (1998) 154–5. For his Greek-sounding *cognomen* see ix. 33. 5 n.

21. 8. inertia debitorum quam facultatibus: for *inertia* cf. Cic. *Cat.* ii. 21 (some are in debt through *inertia*). Storchi Marino (1993: 218) interprets the word as referring to an absence of economic opportunity; however, this sense is not established, and the standard translation 'idleness' works well in both passages and suits the social views of both L. and Cicero. Analogous with our passage is vi. 27. 3 'quibus fide magis quam fortuna debentium laborare creditum uideri expediebat', where, however, the failure to remove debt is put down to bad faith rather than idleness.

22. 6. censum agi placuit: see *addendum* to vi. 27. 4 n.

23. 3. portam Capenam: for the *porta Capena* as a point of departure for the Roman army, see Stewart (1998) 125.

praetore: most of the duties of a praetor concerned jurisdiction and other matters in the city (from books vi–x of L. see viii. 2. 1, 17. 12, 40. 2, ix. 20. 5, x. 21. 9, 45. 4), but, since a praetor had *imperium* similar to that of a consul, there is no reason why he should not have commanded an army. Here the praetor is said to command because a consul is ill, but stays behind to defend the city. A praetor was left in charge of the city also in 296 (x. 21. 4: P. Sempronius Sophus) and perhaps in 280 (Q. Marcius Philippus: for the doubtful evidence for this praetorship see *MRR* i. 191). At vii. 25. 12 (349) and x. 31. 3–5 and 8 (295) we read of a praetor commanding an army in the field after the death of a consul. In 242 the praetor Q. Valerius Falto was sent to Sicily after the *pontifex maximus* had forbidden the consul A. Postumius Albinus to go there (for the sources see *MRR* i. 218–19). Rather differently, because we have no knowledge of the unavailability of a consul, L. Caecilius Metellus and A. Atilius Caiatinus commanded as praetors in, respectively, 283 and 257 (see *MRR* i. 188, 208). See further Stewart (1998) 117–22.

23. 5–7. *The fortification of the Roman camp.* For the technique of the general's ordering the *triarii* to fortify the camp while the rest of the army faces the enemy, cf. esp. xxxv. 4. 6 and Caes. *ciu.* i. 41. 3–6; perhaps also v. 26. 7. For Roman theory on the subject, see Veg. *mil.* i. 25 and iii. 8. 14. See also Fischer (1914) 93–4.

23. 8. stragem: Yardley (2003: 42) observes that Justin uses *strages* six times.

23. 9. quibus . . . scuta: for projectiles sticking in shields see also x. 29. 7.

24. 3. cesserat parumper: for this expression, cf. xxvi. 44. 3 'Romani duce ipso praecipiente parumper cessere', [Caes.] *Afr.* 52. 2 'equites Caesariani ui uniuersae subitaeque hostium multitudinis pulsi parumper cesserunt', and *Hisp.* 23. 3 'hic tum, ut ait Ennius [fr. 480], "nostri parumper cessere"'. The passage from the *bellum Hispaniense* reveals that this is an Ennian tag; quite why Ennius' use of what does not seem a very remarkable expression should have made such an impression on three different authors, it is hard to say. In general, *parumper* is more choice than *paulisper* but was quite acceptable in prose; for statistics see *TLL* x. 1. 545. 70–80.

24. 4. non cum Latino Sabinoque hoste res est, quem . . .: for another good parallel cf. Quint. (?) *decl. min.* 339. 11 'non enim nobis cum hoste ⟨ex⟩ Graecia res erat, ubi . . .'.

25. 2. ut se ipse consulem dictator crearet: among the instances from the first century of a consul's presiding over his own election an interesting example is recorded at *per.* lxxxiii 'L. Cinna et Cn. Papirius Carbo a se ipsis consules per biennium creati', the first instance of a consular pair presiding over their own re-election. For discussion of this passage see Badian (1962) 58 = (1964) 233 n. 12.

25. 3–26. 15. *The duel of Valerius Corvus*

p. 231 n. 2. The case that Gell. ix. 11. 1–10 derives from Valerius Antias is made as strongly as it reasonably can be by Holford-Strevens (2003: 251).

25. 8–10. decem legiones scriptae . . . quem nunc nouum exercitum . . . Camillum, cui unico consuli: for the use of the relative pronoun in these passages see x. 31. 9 n.

26. 2. M. erat Valerius: for arguments (not entirely compelling) that Corvus did not hold magistracies in his old age, see Bruno (1906) 10–12.

26. 4. laetus: for further instances of *laetus* in religious contexts see Linderski (1993) 60 n. 24 = (1995) 615 n. 24.

26. 6. quietae utrimque stationes fuere: see *addendum* to viii. 8. 1 n.

26. 9. Further instances of polar error include xxx. 16. 3 *seniorum*] *iuniorum* Florence, Laur. Conv. Soppr. 263, Cic. *S. Rosc.* 12 *maleficia*] *beneficia* Naples IV B 17, 15 *nobilitate*] *humilitate* Madrid Nac. 10119[1] (the scribe then correcting his own mistake), *Mur.* 73 *diligentiam*] *negligentiam* Venice, Marc. lat. xi. 39 (3929), *Mur.* 75 *reprehendere*] *defendere* Vat. lat. 10660, Cic. *Sest.* 10 *puerilis*] *uirilis* H and other mss (e.g. Oxford, New College 249), Varro, *rust.* ii. 1. 4 *descendisse*] *ascendisse* several related mss (including e.g.

Paris lat. 11213, Vat. lat. 1524 and 3310), Ov. *fast.* i. 308 *summa* UMω: *ima* A, ii. 636 *larga* AUω: *parca* Zꞩ, Pont. iii. 9. 23 *magis*] *minus* BC, and *s.c. de Cn. Pisone patre* 34 and 35 *maius* (twice) copy A: *minus* (twice) copy B. Confusion between *maior* and *minor* is discussed by Josephson (1955: 99) (with reference to the mss of Columella) and by Watt (2001: 102). Professor Reeve kindly tells me of a marginal comment on f. 17ᵛ of El Escorial N II 23: *abicienda est pro honore mors* (where *uita* should have been written for *mors*).

26. 10. decem bubus: as a parallel to the probable Livian or annalistic invention in our passage, I ought to have noted that a similar reward for bravery was said to have been made to Coriolanus; see Val. Max. iv. 3. 4 (cf., but less close, D.H. vi. 94. 1–2, Plut. *Cor.* 10. 1–4, and *uir. ill.* 19. 1). The award of thirty oxen to Laelius is mentioned also at Sil. xv. 258–9.

26. 12. absentem: this n. needs modification in four respects.

(*a*) For elections to the consulship in absence add those of Marius for 103 and 101 (*per.* lxvii, lxviii, Plut. *Mar.* 12. 1, 14. 9, *ILS* 59 = *I.I.* xiii. 3. 83 [in this last *absens*, of the third consulship, plainly shows how election in absence could be viewed as honorific]), of Crassus and Pompey for 70 (to be inferred from the fact that they celebrated, respectively, an *ouatio* and a triumph before entering office: see App. *ciu.* i. 121. 560–1), and of Pompey for 52 (*per.* cvii). Other elections in absence include Scipio Nasica as *pontifex maximus* (Vell. ii. 3. 1 'primus omnium absens pontifex maximus factus est'); on elections to the priestly colleges see also Cic. *Att.* ii. 5. 2 (where he seems to imply that the absence of Metellus Nepos debarred him from election to the augurate) and *ad Brut.* 13 (i. 5). 3 (where Cicero discusses the subject at length, and mentions the election of Marius *absens* as augur).

(*b*) A passage which nicely illustrates the honour of election *in absentia* is Petron. 71. 12 'C. Pompeius Trimalchio Maecenatianus hic requiescit. huic seuiratus absenti decretus est'; see also Cic. *Lucull.* 1 and Vell. loc. cit.

(*c*) That *absens* may mean no more than absent from the electoral assembly is suggested very strongly by D.H. ix. 42. 3 (odd though the absence of a member of the senate from the Campus Martius would have been, unless it was caused by illness). Although this passage is based on annalistic or Dionysian reconstruction, there is no reason to think that it falsifies Roman electoral terminology. If this is correct, it allows explanation of x. 22. 9, which otherwise would seem very odd (see n.), and of several of the passages questioned by Rich, especially xxvi. 22. 13 (Marcellus may have been present at Rome but not at the electoral assembly).[1]

(*d*) Election in absence is discussed by Balsdon (1962: 140–1), who cites some of the passages noted above. He offers a plausible explanation of Cic. *agr.* ii. 24: in his bill Rullus proposed that no one should ever be given dispensation to be elected in absence to his commission; in denying that this

---

[1] As Dr Briscoe points out to me, the difficulties of this passage could be solved by emending *absentes* to *absentem*.

state of affairs pertained for regular magistracies Cicero was ignoring the fact that to be elected in absence one needed special permission.

26. 15. ea tempestate: for another instance of this expression, in an author who affected the language of the historians, see Dict. vi. 7.

27. 1. libros Sibyllinos inspicerent: for a full study of the Sibylline books see Orlin (1997) 76–115. The import of the expressions *libros adire* and *inspicere* is stated better at x. 31. 8 n.

27. 2. The treaty with Carthage

p. 256. On Polybius' reference to these consuls see the sensible remarks of Kornemann (1912: 56).

pp. 258–62. Note the good arguments of Eckstein (1987: 77–8) against the existence of the treaty of Philinus; he suggests that the failure of the alleged violations of the alleged treaty to have any repercussions at the time when they happened is a powerful indication that no treaty was violated.

27. 4. tributo ac dilectu: Brunt (1971: 636) cites the passages which I quote and additionally passages in which the levy and tribute are seen as evils imposed by the Romans on subject peoples: Tac. *Agr.* 13. 1, *hist.* iv. 26. 1, Amm. xvii. 13. 3; cf. too the analogous xxvii. 9. 2 and 13 and Tac. *Agr.* 31. 1.

27. 9. sunt qui . . . uenisse: for the view adopted see also Forsythe (1999) 68.

28. 4. ultro bellum intulerant: for the expression see Woodman on Vell. ii. 120. 1.

28. 4–6. Iunoni Monetae . . . Monetae: according to Val. Max. i. 8. 3 the temple of Juno Moneta was founded by the great Camillus in 396; I am more inclined than Meadows and Williams (2001: 31) to regard this as a slip.

The vowing and dedication of the temple are discussed by Johner (1990), who notes certain similarities with the story of the death of M. Manlius Capitolinus in 385 and 384 (vi. 11. 1–20. 16 n.) (most notably the involvement of a Manlius and Camillus in the events of the year, the connection with Juno [who featured in the life of the elder Camillus with the famous *euocatio* at Veii (v. 21. 3, 22. 3–7) and when Manlius saved the Capitol (v. 47. 4)], and the prodigies that may be compared with the pestilence that broke out after Manlius' death [vi. 20. 15–16]), and suggests that the building of the temple on the site of Manlius' house evoked ill-omened memories of the death of Manlius. However, these similarities may all be coincidental.

28. 4. uouit: note too that L. Papirius Cursor dedicated a temple to Consus (vowed presumably when he was consul in 272) and M. Fulvius Flaccus to Vertumnus (vowed almost certainly at the time of his capture of Volsinii in 264): see Fest. 228; but it is not absolutely certain that either vowed his temple on the field of battle. Likewise a temple to Summanus was vowed in the Pyrrhic War (Ov. *fast.* vi. 731–2), but again we are not told that the vow was made on the field of battle. Some temples seem to have been vowed after victory had come to the Romans, perhaps as a thank-offering to the god concerned: see ii. 20. 12, x. 29. 14, xl. 40. 10, and Orlin (1997) 29–30. To the bibliography add Orlin (1997) 35–75.

28. 5. For *area* used of the space left after a house had been pulled down or had fallen down, cf. iv. 16. 1 'domum (*sc*. Sp. Maelii) deinde, ut monumento area esset oppressae nefariae spei, dirui extemplo iussit', Val. Max. vi. 3. 1c (also of the house of Maelius), Sen. *ben*. vii. 31. 5, Traj. *ap*. Plin. *epist*. x. 71, and Paul. *dig*. xx. 1. 29. 2 (all cited at *TLL* ii. 497. 32–6).

28. 7. namque et lapidibus pluit et nox interdiu uisa intendit: for prodigies introduced in this way cf. also xxii. 36. 7 and Oros. iv. 13. 12. Luterbacher loc. cit. shows that L. more often introduces prodigies with asyndeton.

Since the temple of Juno was dedicated on the Kalends of June, and since in a lunar calendar solar eclipses can occur only on the Kalends of a month, this passage provides evidence that in 344 Rome was using a largely lunar calendar; see the discussion at vol. iii, p. 612. For further discussion of these prodigies see Mazzarino (1966) ii. 272 (tentatively but improbably suggesting an eruption of the Alban Mount) and Brind'Amour (1983) 187–92, who notes that there were eclipses on 22 April 351, 6 October 350, 19 February 348, and 14 July 337 (Julian chronology) and favours equation of our eclipse with the last of these. Dr Holford-Strevens points out that in the republican calendar all that is needed for one solar eclipse to take place on *Non. Iun.* = 21 June 400 (the date to which Enn. *ann.* 153 = Cic. *rep.* i. 25 is generally held to refer) and another on *K. Iun.* = 14 July 337 is that 30 intercalations, 21 of 22 days and 9 of 23 days, be made over 63 years, which is not in the least implausible. That subtraction of the four dictator-years will not bring the year conventionally known as 344 down to 337 raises problems to which there is no easy solution: either Roman chronology is more seriously wrong than scholars other than Sordi and her followers (for whom see vol. iii, pp. 651–2) are prepared to admit; or the notice here about the eclipse is placed in the wrong year or invented. Brind'Amour further suggests that it was the conjunction of the two prodigies with the dedication of the temple which drew such an alarmed response from the Romans.

28. 7. dictatorem feriarum constituendarum causa: for dictators appointed to hold games note also that, according to *F.C.*, Q. Ogulnius Gallus was appointed in 257, *Latinarum feriarum caussa*.

28. 8. finitimos . . . populos: for the request for a supplication over territory beyond the *ager Romanus*, cf. xl. 19. 5 (181 BC) 'eorum (*sc*. decemuirorum) decreto supplicatio circa omnia puluinaria Romae in diem unum indicta est. iisdem auctoribus et senatus censuit et consules edixerunt ut per totam Italiam triduum supplicatio et feriae essent.'

28. 9. iudicia . . . populi: see x. 46. 16 n.

29. 2. quotiens . . . imperium posset: for the image of Rome's collapsing in the civil wars because it could not sustain its own weight, cf. also Lact. *inst*. vii. 15. 4 = Sen. *mai*. (*HRR*) fr. 1. The idea is taken up by Ben Jonson, *Catiline* i. 531–44.

29. 3–31. 12. *Rome and Capua.* For a state's being received into Rome's *fides* see also x. 11. 13.

29. 4. Campanis: for Capua as an Etruscan city see also Serv. *Aen.* x. 145.

29. 5. duratis usu armorum: for the image, in both Greek and Latin literature, of the Samnites as hardy, see also Dench (1998) esp. 134–46.

molem omnem belli: see further Yardley (2003) 65, adducing further parallels.

29. 6. quadrato agmine is used by L. also at fr. 22 line 80.

30. 4. omni ope diuina humanaque: see x. 29. 1 n.

30. 6. Campani . . . uenimus: for two further instances of this idiom in *oratio obliqua* see x. 35. 15 and n.

30. 12. conflagrassent: L. often uses *conflagrare* of those who have been injured or ruined: Baur (1864: 7) cites xxiv. 26. 3, xxx. 13. 12, xxxix. 6. 4, xl. 15. 9. On his liking for metaphors of fire see ibid. 6–8.

30. 18. umbra uestri auxilii . . . tegi possumus: cf. also *pan. Lat.* vi(vii). 15. 5 'ille . . . uestro laetus tegitur umbraculo', where the language is similar to that found in our passage but the sense slightly different (Diocletian is glad to be 'covered' [which has connotations of being both put in the shade and protected] by the growing glory of Constantine, whom he himself established). For other metaphorical examples in L. of *umbra* see Baur (1864) 3.

30. 19. conditorum, parentium, deorum immortalium numero nobis eritis: for the general sentiment cf. Cic. *Quir.* 11 'P. Lentulus consul, parens, deus, salus nostrae uitae'; for the divinity of those who had saved a state, cf. Cic. *rep.* i. 12 'neque enim est ulla res in qua propius ad deorum numen uirtus accedat humana quam ciuitatis aut condere nouas aut conseruare conditas'. For praise of someone as a *pater* or *parens* of a city see Nisbet and Rudd on Hor. *carm.* iii. 24. 27.

30. 21. frequentia . . . prosequente: for the escort of (a) departing ambassador(s) cf. Cic. *Phil.* ix. 30. 21; for large numbers escorting persons about to embark on a journey or an expedition, cf. e.g. D.S. xiii. 2. 3 (the Athenian fleet departing for Sicily from the Piraeus), Xen. Eph. i. 10. 6 πᾶν μὲν τὸ Ἐφεσίων ⟨πλῆθος⟩ παρῆν παραπεμπόντων and 12. 3, and *hist. Apoll.* 11 (in all redactions but esp. B and C); for an individual escorting another cf. *hist. Apoll.* 25 and Hld. vi. 11. 2; for the escorting of (a) foreigner(s) to the edge of the state (what we find at ix. 6. 10) cf. esp. Hdt. viii. 124. 3 προέπεμψαν ἀπιόντα τριηκόσιοι Σπαρτιητέων λογάδες, οὗτοι οἵ περ ἱππέες καλέονται, μέχρι οὔρων τῶν Τεγεητικῶν. μοῦνον δὲ τοῦτον πάντων ἀνθρώπων τῶν ἡμεῖς ἴδμεν Σπαρτιῆται προέπεμψαν (whence Plut. *Them.* 15. 3) Parthen. *erot. path.* 8. 8, and Charit. v. 1. 8; also Lucian, *uer. hist.* i. 27. Sometimes an important person might be accompanied for a very long way: Augustus escorted Tiberius, who was setting out for Illyricum, to Beneventum (Vell. ii. 123. 1, Suet. *Aug.* 97. 3), Marcus Aurelius escorted Verus, who was setting out for Parthia, to Capua (*SHA* iv. 8. 10, v. 6. 7). In each case it is noteworthy that the *princeps* himself provided the escort; see Halfmann (1986) 113. See also Hld. x. 1. 1

31. 10. denuntiaret Samnitibus populi Romani senatusque uerbis: for the expression cf. Sall. *Iug.* 21. 4 'tres adulescentes in Africam legantur qui

ambos reges adeant, senatus populique Romani uerbis nuntient uelle et
censere eos ab armis discedere'. Mommsen (1887–8: iii. 1026) argues, perhaps correctly, that in formulations of this kind the reference to the senate
was a late development.

32. 1–2. fetialibus . . . iussuque populi: the *fetiales* are mentioned also at
D.H. xv. 7. 6. To the bibliography add Loreto (1991–2) 198–219.

32. 2. ab urbe profecti: for the ritual departure of a Roman magistrate for
war see also x. 7. 6 n. (where many of the passages cited to illustrate the
taking of vows on the Capitol, and esp. xlii. 49. 1–2, refer also to other
aspects of the ritual of departure), Varr. *ling.* vii. 37 'paluda a paludamentis.
haec insignia atque ornamenta militaria: ideo ad bellum cum exit imperator
ac lictores mutarunt uestem et signa incinuerunt, paludatus dicitur
proficisci' (where note *proficisci*), Magdelain (1968) 40–2, and Briscoe on
xxxi. 14. 1.

32. 10–33. 3. Raimondi (1995a) argues that the similarities between L.'s
Corvus and Sallust's Marius are to be explained by the politics of the years
of the Cimbric War, in which opponents of Marius contrasted the span over
which Corvus held his five consulships with Marius' continuation in the
office; see esp. Plut. *Mar.* 28. 9. That gave annalists the opportunity to turn
Marian slogans against Marius by applying them to Corvus. Similarly,
Wiseman (2000b: 82) suggests that the appearance of the slogans of late
republican *noui homines* in the speech of Valerius Corvus may be explained
by the hypothesis that they were present already in a similar speech in
Valerius Antias, who may have wished to portray the Valerii as friends of
the people. Both arguments are quite attractive, but L.'s immediate debt to
Sallust should not be underestimated.

**32. 11. intueri cuius ductu auspicioque ineunda pugna sit, utrum qui
audiendus dumtaxat magnificus adhortator sit, uerbis tantum
ferox, operum militarium expers, an qui . . .:** 'they should examine
under whose auspices and leadership the battle was going to be joined,
whether he was someone fit only to be heard, a great exhorter, fierce only
with words but ignorant of military matters, or someone who . . .'. Thus I
understand the passage. Watt (2002: 182) preferred to emend to ⟨ut⟩
magnificus ('someone who deserved hearing only as a great exhorter, fierce
only with words . . .').

32. 12. facta mea, non dicta: for the contrast between words and deeds cf.
also ix. 45. 2.

32. 14. nec generis, ut ante, sed uirtutis est praemium: in L.'s account
of the Struggle of the Orders this idea is found also at x. 24. 9.

32. 16. colo atque colui: Wills (1996: 300–1) cites similar instances of
polyptoton involving *colere* at Hor. *saec.* 2–3 and Ov. *met.* viii. 350. As both
these instances involve cult, it is possible (as he observes) that this was a
formula used in cult; in which case Valerius may be implying that he
worshipped the plebs like a priest performing his ritual duties.

**33. 2. in ludo praeterea militari, cum uelocitatis uiriumque inter se
aequales certamina ineunt:** for these *certamina* cf. also *pan. Mess.*

([Tib.] iii. 7) 88–97 'laudis ut adsiduo uigeat certamine miles | quis tardamue sudem melius celeremue sagittam | iecerit aut lento perfregerit obuia pilo, | aut quis equum celeremque arto compescere freno | possit et effusas tardo permittere habenas | inque uicem modo derecto contendere passu, | seu libeat, curuo breuius conuertere gyro, | quis parma, seu dextra uelit seu laeua, tueri | siue hac siue illac ueniat grauis impetus hastae, | aptior, aut signata cita loca tangere funda'.

comis ac facilis: on the coupling of these ideas cf. also Cic. *Mur.* 66 and *Lael.* 66 and see also Treggiari (1991) 242.

33. 3. quibus artibus petierat magistratus, iisdem gerebat: for failure of magistrates and others to live up to promises made when seeking office or power see also Dio xli. 16. 1–3.

33. 4. incredibili alacritate: that a commander should discover the mood of his troops is enjoined at Veg. *mil.* iii. 12. 1 'ipsa die, qua certaturi sunt milites, quid sentiant diligenter explora'. Elsewhere *assensus* and its cognates are used quite often to denote the approval of the troops: in addition to 35. 2 and 37. 3 (where similar language is used of a *contio* after a battle) note e.g. xxiv. 14. 9 and xxxviii. 12. 5. Note also *clamor consentiens* at x. 40. 1 and xl. 27. 14.

33. 5. ut quod maxime umquam: to the examples of this idiom cited ad loc. and in K–S, add Plin. *epist.* ix. 22. 2 'amat ut qui uerissume, dolet ut qui impatientissime, laudat ut qui benignissime, ludit ut qui facetissime' and Gell. xv. 28. 1 'Cornelius Nepos . . . M. Ciceronis ut qui maxime amicus familiaris fuit'.

33. 15. nox uictoriam magis quam proelium diremit: a parallel not noted at *TLL* v. 1. 1260. 1–24 is Dares 19 'nox proelium diremit'.

That the idea of night stopping a battle was a τόπος of annalistic narrative was established by Klinger (1884: 18–19). For the idea of the revelation of the victors in a battle (which the previous evening had appeared drawn) by the retreat of one side on the following day, add D.H. ix. 13. 2.

33. 17. oculos sibi Romanorum ardere uisos aiebant: for the importance of the face in combat, see also Curt. vii. 9. 13, Veg. *mil.* iii. 21. 5 'animus semel territus non tam tela hostium cupit declinare quam uultum'; for the eyes in battle see also Eur. *Hcld.* 687 and 684 Ιο. οὐδεὶς ἔμ' ἐχθρῶν προσβλέπων ἀνέξεται. | Th. οὐκ ἔστ' ἐν ὄψει τραῦμα μὴ δρώσης χερός (for the reordering of the lines necessary here see Wilkins's note on 683–91) and Flor. i. 11(16). 12 'et in congressu arsisse omnium oculos hostis auctor fuit' (for which Florus probably takes his theme from our passage [note *hostis auctor fuit*], despite the fact that he places this comment after his description of the surrender in the Caudine Forks); for the idea of eyes on fire in other contexts, contrast e.g. Stat. *Ach.* i. 164 'tranquillaeque faces oculis' (the young Achilles does not yet have fire in his eyes).

sibi strikingly splits the constituent *oculos Romanorum* and is at some distance from *uisos*, on which it depends. For another, though less striking, example involving *sibi* and *uisos* see ix. 6. 11 'uocati . . . in curiam percontantibus maioribus natu multo sibi maestiores et abiectiores animi uisos referrent', in which *sibi* splits *multo maestiores*. In both passages *sibi* is in second place in its colon, but Adams (1994) argues that this position is explained better by postulating that weak, unstressed personal pronouns had a tendency to attach themselves enclitically on 'focused' hosts (in these passages, respectively, *oculos* and *multo*) than by the operation of 'Wackernagel's law'. Indeed, Adams (p. 104) uses our passage to start his discussion. For other instances involving *multo* cf. Cic. *IIVerr.* v. 1, *Att.* i. 13. 5, *fam.* xii. 30. 3, Catull. 45. 15, and Ov. *met.* vi. 196 (in each of these passages the pronoun splits *multo* from the adjective or adverb which it modifies). Other such hosts include demonstratives (Adams, pp. 122–4, 134), as is illustrated by vii. 1. 1 'hos sibi patricii quaesiuere honores pro concesso plebi altero consulatu' (where note the emphasizing hyperbaton). And after a demonstrative a nominative personal pronoun, often formally redundant, may behave as a weak enclitic, serving to 'focus' its demonstrative; to the passages adduced by Adams, pp. 141–51, add e.g. iii. 67. 2 'hanc ego ignominiam . . . uitassem', v. 18. 5 'hunc ego institutum disciplina mea . . . do', x. 23. 7 'hanc ego aram . . . Pudicitiae Plebeiae dedico', xxxvii. 53. 8 'hanc ego maximam hereditatem a patre accepi', and xxxviii. 55. 8 'has ego summas auri et argenti relatas apud Antiatem inuenio', Plaut. *Cas.* 224, *cist.* 204, *Pers.* 455, Cic. *Mur.* 34, *Sest.* 100, 128, *dom.* 5, 63, 145, *Vat.* 32, *fam.* iii. 8. 7, vii. 3. 3, 17. 2, *Phil.* iii. 33 (I cite some from many passages in which the pronoun splits a constituent; even more can be found in which the pronoun follows a demonstrative without splitting a constituent).

34. 1–37. 3. *The army of A. Cornelius is rescued by P. Decius Mus*

pp. 332–4. Jaeger (1999: 183–93) reads the episode in terms of the guiding image or idea of the labyrinth; the attractions of such a reading are very much diminished by L.'s failure to use any Latin equivalent of 'labyrinth'. See also Pelling (1999: 339–43), who notes several surprising aspects of Decius' behaviour (for example, Romans do not normally operate at night) and how L. enhances the drama of the episode by declining to finish it at several points at which one might have expected closure (see esp. 36. 4 and 10).

34. 6. uirtus: see *addendum* to vi. 30. 6 n.

35. 1. tesseram: for the *tessera* see also Fischer (1914) 117–20; he observes that in this passage, vii. 36. 7, and ix. 32. 4 it is easier to think of a command that was oral rather than one committed to writing.

ubi secundae uigiliae bucina datum signum esset: for this *signum* cf. also xxiv. 46. 2. For general discussion see also Fischer (1914) 188–9.

35. 2. militari adsensu: see also *addendum* to 33. 4.

35. 10. atqui: see *addendum* to vi. 37. 2 n.

sicut est: 'as indeed it is'. For this idiom, in which *sicut est* (or *erat*), *ut est* (or *erat*), *uel sim.* confirms the reality of a statement that might otherwise seem hypothetical or improbable or mistaken, add e.g. i. 45. 5, ii. 28. 2, 30. 1 (all instances of *ut erat*: note the clustering), xlv. 7. 1 'secundam eam

Paullus, sicut erat, uictoriam ratus', Cic. *rep*. iii. 4 (an instance of both *ut est* and *sicut est*), *par*. 35, *off*. i. 153, Ov. *met*. xii. 204–5 (pointing the reality of the metamorphosis of Caenis into a man) 'poteratque uiri uox illa uideri | sicut erat', Plin. *epist*. v. 14. 2 'sit licet (sicut est) ab omni ambitione longe remotus, debet tamen ei iucundus honor esse ultro datus' to the passages cited by Krebs and Schmalz (1905–7: ii. 702) and by Landgraf on Cic. *S. Rosc*. 22.

35. 11. per corpora . . . uadetis: see also ix. 39. 8 n.

36. 9. ad praetorium: see ix. 2. 12 n.

36. 11. iussae legiones arma capere: see ix. 37. 5 n.

36. 12. palati . . . inermes: see ix. 31. 15 n.

37. 2. gramineam coronam obsidi⟨on⟩alem: for this *corona* see also Fischer (1914) 159 and Weinstock (1971) 148–52.

37. 3. immolauit: in the Cimbric War, after saving his detachment by performing an exploit similar to that of Decius, Cn. Petreius Atinas is also said to have sacrificed: see Plin. *nat*. xxii. 11 'inuenio apud auctores eundem praeter hunc honorem adstantibus Mario et Catulo cos. praetextatum immolasse ad tibicinem foculo posito'. Despite his mistaken belief that the passage just quoted refers to M. Calpurnius Flamma, Versnel (1970: 375–6) has an interesting discussion of the implications of a soldier's carrying out a sacrifice that would normally have been performed by a bearer of *imperium*.

37. 3. ingenti alacritate . . . assensus: see *addendum* to 33. 4 n.

37. 9. fremere is found quite often as an historic infinitive at the head of its clause; cf. e.g. i. 17. 7, iv. 58. 9, and see Yardley (2003) 43.

37. 10. rerum omnium inopia: the expression is found also at fr. 22 line 50.

37. 11. quantum . . . attulissent: for other instances of troops carrying large amounts of food see xliv. 2. 4 'menstruum iusso milite secum ferre' and *per*. lvii 'militem . . . triginta dierum frumentum . . . ferre cogebat'. See further Fischer (1914) 11.

37. 16. signa militaria ad centum septuaginta: for references to military standards captured from the enemy in our sources for early Roman history, add Val. Max. i. 8. 6 (quoted in the *addendum* to 17. 9 n.).

38. 3. sequente Decio insigni cum laude donisque: for legates and military tribunes following behind the triumphal chariot of their commanding officers, cf. xxxi. 49. 10, Cic. *Pis*. 60, App. *Mithr*. 117. 578. For the display in the triumphal procession of *dona* won on campaign cf. App. *Lib*. 66. 299. Both phenomena are illustrated by some of our sources for the legendary L. Siccius Dentatus (Val. Max. iii. 2. 24, Plin. *nat*. vii. 102). In general, see Ehlers, *RE* viiA. 509.

38. 3. incondito militari ioco: I should have stated that revelry, both in the procession itself and in the watching crowd, was a hallmark of the triumph; see esp. App. *Lib*. 66. 299 (a full description of the triumph over Carthage of the elder Scipio Africanus).

38. 4–42. 7. *The mutiny at Capua and the Genucian plebiscites.* Scardigli (1997) compares L.'s account with those in other sources, esp. Appian. She concludes that the tale found in L.'s first version and in Appian, with its praise of Valerius Corvus, derives from Valerius Antias (so also others; see p. 363 n. 2) and that that found in L.'s second version, with its stress on impoverishment and the spontaneous settlement imposed by the troops of both sides, derives from Licinius Macer. These speculations could be right but cannot be confirmed (for difficulties in positing Antias as a source of all pro-Valerian stories, see vol. i, pp. 89–92). She argues too that the version in which Corvus is praised contrasts him with Sulla; and certainly these tales are redolent of the civil wars of the Sullan epoch and in some respects provide a striking contrast to them (see p. 365).

Wiseman (2000*b*: 82), by contrast, points out that the appearance of C. Manlius in L.'s second version of the mutiny of 342 may suggest an origin for the tale in the years after the Catilinarian conspiracy (C. Manlius recruited troops for Catiline); if this is correct, then, as Wiseman notes, Tubero may have been responsible for it. However, a difficulty should be noted: L. (42. 3) claims to have found the tale in more than one source, but of his known sources only Tubero certainly wrote after 63 BC.

p. 362. Scardigli (1997: 405–6) remarks that the recruiting of slaves mentioned by D.H. and Appian could have been suggested by the behaviour of Marius on his return from exile (see Plut. *Mar.* 41. 3, Exup. 27, Σ Gron. *ad* Cic. *Cat.* iii. 24, p. 286). It could also have been suggested by Manlius and Catiline in 63–62.

38. 5. consilia . . . adimendae . . . Capuae: the cross-references given are to notes which illustrate this use of the gerundive. For the Samnite capture of Capua, see x. 38. 6 n.

38. 9. comperta: this verb is regular in the context of both formal (ix. 16. 10 n.) and semi-formal (Cic. *Cat.* i. 10, 27) inquiries into real or alleged conspiracies.

39. 1. dicendo: for a gerund as equivalent to a present participle, see also W–M on ii. 32. 4.

39. 17. L. Aemilium Mamercum: on the problem posed by the *cognomen* Privernas see *addendum* to vol. i, p. 33.

40. 3. omnes . . . ciues . . . complexus: for the idea and metaphor cf. esp. Cic. *Mil.* 72 'quia nimis amplecti plebem uidebatur' and Tac. *ann.* ii. 82. 2 'populum Romanum aequo iure complecti' (with Goodyear's note).

40. 4. ab urbe proficiscens: see also the *addendum* to 32. 2 n.

40. 5. inter uota nuncupanda: the n. on the taking of vows as part of the rituals performed by a magistrate departing to war, now written for x. 7. 6, might have been placed here and linked to the discussion of *ab urbe proficisci* at 32. 2 n.

40. 9. signa canent: for the distribution of *signa canere* and related expressions (e.g. *tubae canunt*), which Skard (1933: 28) regarded as poetical, see *TLL* iii. 266. 18–28. Before the late first century AD they are found in prose only in L. (thirteen times), Sallust (thrice), at Varr. *ling.* v. 99 'ut tuba ac cornu . . . canere dicuntur', and in one passage of Cicero written in a figurative style (*rep.* i. 3. 5), in verse at Plaut. *Amph.* 227 'tubae utrimque canunt' (a passage written in the high style), Acc. *trag.* 385, Virg. *Aen.* x. 310, Prop. iv. 11. 9, and Luc. vi. 130. This distribution, in which the absence of attestation in Caesar is notable, shows Skard's judgement to be possible but not certain. See also x. 19. 12 n.

40. 12. crinibus passis: see *addendum* on vi. 20. 2 n.

41. 3. dictator equo citato: a dictator, originally *magister populi*, was formally debarred from riding a horse (hence the appointment of a *magister equitum*) but could request permission to do so (xxiii. 14. 2, Plut. *Fab.* 4. 1–2, Zon. vii. 13. 13). In campaigns any distance from Rome this must have been a great inconvenience, and as L. loc. cit. implies (*ut solet*) the granting of permission to ride must have been absolutely standard. In accounts of early Rome a dictator is found on horseback also at iii. 28. 1 and D.H. x. 24. 2. Either L. and D.H. (or their annalistic sources) forgot this rule or they assumed that permission had been granted at the time of the appointment. See further Mommsen (1887–8) ii. 159 and Weinstock (1971) 327–8.

ne cui . . . exprobraret: one is reminded of the Greek concept of μὴ μνησικακεῖν and amnesty, for which see e.g. Andoc. i. 81, Dittenberger (1915–24) ii, nos. 588 and 633, and *SEG* xxix. 1130*bis*. If the information which L. gives is accurate, the idea may have come to Rome from Greek practice (although it could also have arisen spontaneously at Rome). If it is invented, the invention could have arisen from knowledge of Greek practice.

42. 6. permixtos . . . lacrimantes: Scardigli (1997: 406) suggests that the fraternization between the two armies is modelled on what probably occurred between the armies of Sulla and L. Scipio in 83 (Sall. *hist.* i. 34, App. *ciu.* i. 85. 385–7). Neither passage cited presents a scene quite like that here or at 40. 2, but, if Scardigli is right to detect this echo, then the contrast with the behaviour of Sulla would strengthen her case (see above) for viewing this whole tale as anti-Sullan.

BOOK VIII

1. 3. agri partes duae ademptae: I should have made clear that in this note I listed only passages where our sources state explicitly that Rome took land from conquered foes; the confiscation of land from many other cities and tribes may legitimately be conjectured from the later presence of colonies or *ager publicus*. Add D.H. xx. 17. 2 (on confiscation of Samnite land in 270–269 BC), Flor. i. 10(15). 3 and other sources cited by Frank (1911: 370) for the conquest of land from the Sabines in 290 (about which Frank is too sceptical), Eutrop. ii. 28 (supporting the testimony of Zonaras, cited in the n., with regard to Falerii in 241), and, perhaps, Plb. ii. 19. 11, a doubtfully reliable notice (see *addendum* to vol. i, p. 362), which refers to the Roman control of all the territory of the Senones.

1. 6 armorum . . . dixit: the burning of the spoil at Sentinum (x. 29. 18) is mentioned also in the parallel narrative of Zon. viii. 1. 7.

1. 6. Luae matri: for *Matri* see viii. 9. 6, x. 29. 4 nn.

2. 1. cum . . . praetor senatum consuluisset: for the praetor's presiding in the senate see x. 22. 7 n.

3. 6. Alexandrum Epiri regem: this note, and that at 24. 1–18, is awkward to use, since I should have given dates BC both according to modern retro-jected Julian calendar years (= J) and according to the chronology conven-tionally used in modern writing on Roman history, that is the Varronian sequence of consular and dictator-years (= V), the dictator years being 333, 324, 309, 301 V. D.S. refers to the installation of Alexander of Epirus at xvi. 72. 1 (342/1 J = 346 V) and to the wedding of Alexander at xvi. 91. 4 (336/5 J = 340 V). L.'s date for the crossing of Alexander of Epirus is either 341 V = 337/6 J or 340V = 336/5 J; his date for his battle at Paestum is 332V = 329/8 J; and his date for his death is 327V = 324/3 J. The real date for his death was the winter of 331/0 J = 335V. For a remark alleged to have been made by Alexander when he was dying, see ix. 19. 11 n. For L.'s unreliable synchronism of the affairs of Rome with those of the two Alexanders, see Forsythe (1999) 104–6. To the bibliography add Berve (1926) ii. 19–21 and Urso (1998) 23–51.

4. 2. foederis aequi: see ix. 20. 7–8 n.

4. 8. qui . . . dabant: for the Latins' being granted (or not granted) permis-sion to fight see also D.H. ix. 60. 3 and 67. 4–6.

6. 4. atqui: see *addendum* to vi. 37. 2 n.

6. 5. est caeleste numen; es, magne Iuppiter: for affirmation that the gods exist cf. also T. Williams (1971), who makes a good case for the view that εἰσὶ τρίχες at anon. *anth. Pal.* xii. 39. 4 is a parody of the exclamation εἰσὶ θεοί, and Howell on Mart. i. 12. 12 (a text which alludes to the idea found in our passage, although its phrasing is different). Other passages which they cite include Hom. *Od.* xvii. 475–6 ἀλλ' εἴ που πτωχῶν γε θεοὶ καὶ ἐρινύες εἰσίν, | Ἀντίνοον πρὸ γάμοιο τέλος θανάτοιο κιχείη (where the formulation is found in a conditional clause), Ar. *Thes.* 672 φήσει δ' εἶναί τε θεοὺς φανερῶς (where it is found in indirect statement), Athen. *deipn.* viii. 42, p. 350 D (on the wit of Stratonicus) δοκοῦ δέ ποτε καταπεσούσης καὶ ἀποκτείνασης ἕνα τῶν πονηρῶν "ἄνδρες", ἔφη, "δοκῶ εἰσι θεοί· εἰ δὲ μή εἰσι, δοκοί εἰσιν", and Mart. ii. 91. 1–2 'rerum certa salus, terrarum gloria, Caesar | sospite quo magnos credimus esse deos' (where again it is found in indirect statement). For a denial that some gods exist see Athen. *deipn.* vi. 62–3, p. 253 C and E θεοὶ | ἢ οὐκ ἔχουσιν ὦτα | ἢ οὐκ εἰσίν. For a denial of the efficacy of the gods parallel in content to other passages cited but different in form, cf. Acc. *trag.* 142–3 'iam iam neque di regunt | neque profecto deum summus rex hominibus curat'. For analogous expressions of the kind θεοὺς νομίζω see Collard on Eur. *suppl.* 732 with further bibliography.

6. 9. uiri maioris quam pro humano habitu augustiorisque: for the portrayal of gods larger than men cf. also e.g. Ov. *met.* xiii. 895 (Acis becomes larger at deification), Val. Max. i. 8. 6 (an *eximiae magnitudinis iuuenis* helps the Romans in battle; the youth disappears, and they realize that he was Mars), and Dio lxviii. 25. 5 (Trajan escorted from the earthquake at Antioch προσελθόντος αὐτῷ μείζονός τινος ἢ κατὰ ἄνθρωπον). For greater size and majesty associated with the divine, cf. Sen. *epist*. 115. 4 'hanc faciem altiorem fulgentioremque quam cerni inter humana consueuit'. For an apparition of abnormal size in a dream or vision, cf. Suet. *Claud*. 1. 2 and Dio lv. 1. 3–4 (Drusus dissuaded from further advances in Germany by a 'species barbarae mulieris humana amplior'), Xen. Eph. i. 12. 4, and Pont. *uit. Cypr.* 12. 3 (showing that this idea persisted in early Christian thought). See further Hopkinson on Call. *hymn*. 6. 58.

6. 14. in consilio: see ix. 2. 15 n.

7. 1–22. Schäublin (1996), noting the echoes of Ennius found elsewhere in this episode (§ 16 n.), argued that the description of the single combat, which has epic touches (§ 9 n.), goes back to his account of the same event, which is reflected too in Virgil's account of the death of Mezentius (*Aen.* x. 833–908). Although this cannot be established, Schäublin (pp. 152–3) is right to note that Homeric duels tend to be fought on foot (my 'the detail is reminiscent of epic' at § 10 n. is a little misleading, although the parallels cited are just), and it is quite attractive to suggest that Ennius had a famous account of a duel on horseback.

7. 2. uir cum genere inter suos tum factis clarus: for *inter suos* cf. e.g. xxiii. 1. 2 'Compsanus erat Trebius nobilis inter suos', Cic. *S. Rosc.* 16 'ipse honestissimus inter suos numerabatur', *Planc*. 32 'princeps inter suos', and other parallels cited by Landgraf on Cic. *S. Rosc.* loc. cit.; Landgraf notes that the expression is similar to *domi nobilis*, for which see 19. 4 n. (with *addendum*). For *clarus* with *genere* and *factis* see ix. 7. 2 n. (a note which could have been placed here).

7. 8. seu . . . seu . . .: for the alternative explanations cf. also ix. 14. 6 n.

7. 12. ad praetorium: see ix. 2. 12 n.

7. 14. classico: see further Fischer (1914) 164.

7. 19. i, lictor: for the command to the lictor, and in particular for its emotional resonances amongst onlookers, see Marshall (1984: 131).

8. 1. custodiae uigiliaeque et ordo stationum: this is the only passage in books vi–x in which L. uses together the terms *custodiae*, *uigiliae*, and *statio*. Although Latin writers sometimes use these terms loosely (as L. perhaps uses *stationum* loosely here), it is generally possible to distinguish between *uigiliae* and *custodiae* on the one hand and *stationes* on the other.

From several passages it is clear that, in the context of the Roman camp, the *uigiles* were the troops who guarded the rampart and that *uigiliae* is an abstract noun used to denote the activity of the *uigiles*: see xxii. 1. 8, xxv. 7. 7, xli. 26. 2. This makes it likely that in other places where one of these terms is used, in several of which it is coupled with *stationes*, it has this meaning: as well as this passage see e.g. iii. 28. 4, iv. 27. 11 (used of Rome's enemy), vii. 12. 12, xxv. 38. 16 (of the enemy), Sall. *hist*. ii. 89, iii. 96B, Tac. *ann.* i. 32. 3, xi. 18. 3, and xiii. 35. 1. However, *custodes* and *custodiae* could be used too of guards on the rampart: see xxv. 39. 2 (of the enemy, but with explicit reference to the rampart); also v. 15. 4 and 44. 6 (of the enemy). If the two terms are to be distinguished, it is likely that *uigiliae*, which can also denote the watches into which the night was divided, was used more particularly of guarding at night, and *custodiae* of guarding by day (but note xxiv. 46. 4, quoted below); see xxiv. 37. 4 'itaque nocte ⟨dieque⟩ iuxta parata instructaque omnia custodiis ac uigiliis erant' (where *iuxta* guarantees either this supplement of Zr or Weissenborn's *nocte ac die* or Hertz's *die ac nocte*). At ix. 45. 15 (of the enemy) there is a reference to *stationes* and to troops guarding the rampart, but neither of these terms is used.

Likewise, several passages show that a *statio* was the detachment that guarded the gate of a camp: see x. 32. 7, xxv. 39. 2 (of the enemy), xxxi. 38. 5 (of the enemy), xxxiv. 15. 7 (of the enemy), xli. 26. 2, Caes. *Gall.* iv. 32. 1, and Tac. *ann.* i. 25. 1. Doubtless this is the meaning of the word in most passages where it is used without explicit reference to a gate: see e.g. iii. 28. 4, iv. 27. 11 (of the enemy), v. 44. 6 (of the enemy), vii. 12. 12, 26. 6, ix. 22. 3, x. 10. 1, xxi. 52. 10 (of the enemy), xxii. 22. 15, xxiv. 47. 12, xxv. 26. 3, 38. 16 (of the enemy), xxviii. 14. 8, 16. 1, 22. 12, xxx. 8. 3 (of the enemy), 11. 6, xxxviii. 18. 5, xlv. 26. 9, Sall. *hist.* ii. 89, iii. 96B, Tac. *ann.* i. 32. 3 (of the enemy), xi. 18. 3, and xiii. 35. 1. From several passages it is clear that *stationes* could be placed some way in front of a gate: see e.g. vii. 10. 6, 12, xxiii. 47. 2, xxv. 34. 4, xli. 2. 3, and xlii. 64. 4. This meant that they were particularly exposed to skirmishing: see xxx. 8. 3–4, 11. 6, and xxxii. 10. 9; hence, by contrast, the expression *quietae stationes* found at vii. 26. 6 and xxv. 26. 3. At ix. 37. 4 the withdrawal of Roman *stationes* is taken by the enemy as a sign of fear, at xlii. 57. 11 as a sign of unwillingness to fight. For either *uigiles* or *stationes* escorting inside people who had arrived at the camp, see ix. 24. 3 n.

However, in some passages the terms are used more loosely: for instance, in ours *ordo stationum* may mean no more than 'turns at sentry-duty' and may include duty on the walls as well as at the gates (cf. xxv. 38. 16 'uigiliarum ordinem'); at xxiv. 46. 4 'imber ab nocte media coortus custodes uigilesque dilapsos e stationibus subfugere in tecta coegit' and Tac. *hist.* i. 23. 1 *stationibus* must mean 'posts'; at ix. 24. 5 we read 'ut minus intentae in custodiam urbis diurnae stationes ac nocturnae uigiliae essent', and xxxviii. 5. 5 'eruptionibus nocturnis in custodias operum et diurnis in stationes', *stationes* (in both passages), *uigiliae*, and *custodias* are likely to have a more general reference; and at Tac. *ann.* i. 28. 4 'uigiliis stationibus custodiis portarum' the genitive *portarum* explains why *stationibus* and *custodiis* are inverted.

Note also that these terms can be used of the guarding of a town: see esp. iii. 5. 4, 42. 6, iv. 40. 2, vii. 3. 3, and x. 4. 2 (all of Rome). In the first four of these passages there is a reference to *stationes* before the gates, but in the last these guards are called *custodiae*. In the first two and the last there is a reference to *uigiliae*, but by this watches throughout the city are meant (so also at e.g. Sall. *Cat.* 30. 7 and 32. 1).

For fuller discussion see Fischer (1914) 168–91 (to whom much of the material assembled here is owed).

8. 3–14. *Digression on the structure of the Roman legion*

p. 452. Central to the manipular tactics described by L. and others was the keeping of fresh troops in reserve; see ix. 32. 9 n.

p. 454 n. 1. Another very useful survey of scholarly opinion on the 'Servian' reforms is Thomsen (1980) 144–89.

pp. 454–5. I should have stated explicitly that Last, like Fraccaro, dated the splitting of the legion to the beginning of the Republic. Others who have taken this view include Staveley (1956: 80) and Sealey (1959: 526). De Sanctis (1933) and Bunse (1998: 195–6) argue strongly for 366.

p. 458. In line four read 'ten maniples' for 'twenty maniples'.

p. 464. For 'Veg. *mil.* ii. 16, iii. 14' read 'Veg. *mil.* i. 20. 14, ii. 16. 1, 17. 1, and iii. 14. 17'.

p. 465. At x. 25. 2, a most unreliable passage, Fabius Rullianus states that he proposes to take with him 4,000 men; presumably this number is meant to be equivalent to a legion.

8. 10. haud secus quam uallo saepta ut horreret acies: for the spears of a line of battle compared to the stakes of a palisade, cf. xxxi. 39. 10, xxxii. 17. 14, xxxv. 30. 6, xxxvi. 18. 6, and Plut. *Aem.* 20. 6. See Fischer (1914) 22.

8. 14. scribebantur autem quattuor fere legiones: for the number of legions in the mid-republican consular army see ix. 30. 3 n.

8. 14. equitibus in singulos legiones trecenis: in the footnote x. 25. 2 should have been cited, where Fabius Rullianus states that he plans to take 600 cavalry with his 4,000 troops.

8. 16. strenuus uir: see x. 8. 3 n.

8. 19–11. 1. *The battle of the Veseris and the* deuotio *of Decius*

p. 482. Saulnier (1981: 110–13; 1983: 99–100) also connects *deuotio* with Samnite ritual, arguing that it was introduced at Sentinum by P. Decius Mus, who knew about the rituals because of his Campanian origin and was also a *pontifex* at Rome and hence well placed to make such an introduction. But the similarities with Samnite ritual can be explained by the common heritage of Italy, and against a Campanian origin for Decius see vii. 21. 6 n.

p. 486. To the general bibliography on *deuotio* add Saulnier (1981: 110–13).

9. 1. immolauerunt: see ix. 14. 4 n.

9. 5. uelato capite: for the Roman practice of covering the head during a religious ceremony, see x. 7. 10 n.

9. 6. Mars pater: for further discussion of epithets of this kind see x. 29. 4 n.
Diui Nouensiles: Forsythe (1994: 330–5) suggests that the reference to these gods at Pis. fr. 45, comes from a Decian context, such as ours. He notes that Piso quoted the pontifical formula on rekindling Vesta's fire, and thus it is possible that he could have quoted the formula for *deuotio*.

9. 8. mecum and *secum* are used in a similar context at x. 28. 13 and 29. 4.
9. 9. cinctu: Koesters (1893: sent. controv. III) proposed *ritu*; but the

paradosis is protected by the passages with *cinctu* cited in my n.

10. 1. audito euentu collegae: cf. x. 29. 12 'audita morte collegae' (from the same point in the battle of Sentinum).

10. 8. eius pugnae memoriam: cf. ix. 41. 4 'eius pugnae memoria' (n.) and the parallels there cited.

10. 10. Decii corpus . . . factum est: so also L. records that at Sentinum Fabius Rullianus sent men to look for the body of the younger Decius.

10. 11. consuli dictatorique et praetori: on the use of -*que . . . et* here see ix. 42. 11 n.

10. 12. uideri: the phrase 'formal and legal contexts' should have been more precise. *uideri* is used in this way in the pronouncements of judges (see e.g. Cic. *IIVerr*. ii. 93 'iste pronuntiat STHENIVM LITTERAS PVBLICAS CORRVPISSE VIDERI', *Luc*. 146, and Plin. *nat*. xiv. 90), the senate (xxx. 42. 9, xxxviii. 44. 6, and xxxix. 4. 9), augurs (see 23. 14 [n.]), pontiffs (Cic. *dom*. 136 and *Att*. iv. 2. 3), and others in formal contexts (with our passage cf. e.g. 32. 18). The discussion of the usage by Daube (1956: 73–7) does not quite bring out its full range; but he well compares the pronouncements of augurs, and (one may add) pontiffs, to that of judges and notes that this style enhances the claims of judges and augurs (we may add the senate and others) to be impartial and to have investigated diligently.

11. 1. noua peregrinaque omnia priscis ac patriis praeferendo: L.'s view that Roman institutions declined under foreign influence appears first by implication at *praef*. 11 'immigrauerint'. For the appearance of this influence already in the extant books, see Luce (1977) 250–75.

11. 11. sarcinis . . . in aceruum coniectis: the normal Roman practice, when time permitted, was to construct a camp in which the baggage could be protected: see e.g. xliv. 36. 6. In other passages L. describes how the baggage was removed away from the scene of immediate fighting: see viii. 38. 8 'impedimentis ex agmine remotis' and x. 14. 7 'impedimentis in locum tutum remotis praesidioque modico imposito'. Note too that Philopoemen in his study of generalship is said to have devoted much thought to the placing of baggage: see xxxv. 28. 4. See further Fischer (1914) 93–5.

11. 16. monumentoque ut esset: the use of *monumentum* in the predicative dative, unique to L., should have been discussed; see now ix. 41. 6 n.

12. 2. Ostiensem: for the idea that Ostia was a regal foundation see further the coins of C. Marcius Censorinus (with the discussion of Crawford [1974: 361]) and e.g. Enn. *ann*. 128–9, Plin. *nat*. iii. 56 ' in principio est Ostia colonia ab Romano rege deducta', Fest. 214 'OSTIAM urbem ad exitum Tiberis in mare fluentis Ancus Marcius rex condidisse et feminino appellasse uocabulo fertur; quod siue ad urbem siue ad coloniam, quae postea condita est, refertur [quod] neutrum certe plura . . .', and *CIL* xiv suppl. 4338 (a fragmentary inscription in which a reference to Marcius and to a *colonia* can be discerned). The last three also provide evidence that Ostia was regarded as a colony (a status denied to it unconvincingly by Pohl [1983]), as does xxvii. 38. 3–4, and the passage of Festus shows that the later foundation was regarded as distinct from any regal foundation which may have existed. The existence of the earlier settlement is denied by many scholars, including e.g. Alföldi (1965: 290–1), and the absence of archaeological testimony for it has forced those who believe in it to argue that it was not on precisely the same spot as the Roman colony. Alföldi and others before him have suggested that the legend of the foundation of Ostia by Ancus Marcius reflects the fact that C. Marcius Rutilus established the Roman colony, perhaps in 356 when he was active in the area (vii. 17. 6–9). This argument is quite attractive. L.'s narrative of the Second Punic War shows that by then Ostia was established as a Roman naval base (see xxii. 11. 6, xxiii. 38. 8, xxv. 20. 3). See also Pavolini (1988) esp. 20–1.

12. 13. Aemilius . . . collegam dictatorem dixit: the nomination of a consul to a dictatorship by his colleague is attested also for T. Larcius in 501 (ii. 18. 4–11) or 498 (D.H. v. 72. 3), A. Postumius Albus in 496 (D.H. vi. 2. 3; but some sources placed this dictatorship in 499: see Liv. ii. 21. 3–4), and M. Livius Salinator in 207 (xxviii. 10. 1). See further Mommsen (1887–8) i. 514 n. 1.

cuius tum fasces erant: see ix. 8. 2 n.

12. 15. unam . . . tenerent, pp. 524–5. A possible alternative to the view that even before 339 plebiscites were binding on the whole community if they received the *patrum auctoritas* is that, if a plebiscite received strong backing from the plebs, individual patricians would not have contravened it, for fear of action being taken against them by the tribunes of the plebs.

Two other tribunician measures accepted by the *patres* from the period between 339 and 287 are the law on dedications recorded for 304 (ix. 46. 7 'itaque ex auctoritate senatus latum ad populum est . . .' [n.]) and the Ovinian plebiscite which regulated composition of the senate (the date of its passing is likely to have been between 339 and 287: see ix. 30. 1 n.).

Among plebiscites passed before 339 the Poetelian plebiscite *de ambitu* of 358 was singled out in the n. because we are told that it was passed with patrician approval; probably one should add the Canuleian plebiscite of 445 (iv. 1. 1–6. 4) (at 6. 3 L. comments 'uicti tandem patres ut de conubio ferretur') and both the Licinio-Sextian rogations of 367/6 (*patrum auctoritas* is mentioned at vi. 42. 9–10) and the earlier decision to reform the *iiuiri sacris faciundis* so as to admit plebeians (vi. 42. 1), even though the patricians' acquiescence in these measures may have been grudging.

Other plebiscites with regard to which L. makes no reference to patrician assent are nevertheless likely to have been binding on the whole community for one of the two reasons given above. Those mentioned in books vi–viii are the Duillian and Menenian plebiscite of 357 *de unciario fenore* (vii. 16. 1 n.), the plebiscite of 357 banning the calling of assemblies outside Rome (vii. 16. 8), and the Genucian plebiscites of 342 (vii. 42. 1–2). For other possible plebiscites see *addenda* to vi. 20. 13 and vii. 5. 9 nn.

For the tribunate of the plebs losing its revolutionary character, see also the Historical Introduction to book x, above, pp. 16–17.

Further bibliography on the problem of the standing of plebiscites before 287 includes Siber (1936) esp. 39–50, Maddox (1984) (who somewhat improbably argues that the *lex Publilia* merely ratified 'certain plebiscites previously carried'), and Humbert (1988) 472–8.

13. 1. L. Furio Camillo: in the last sentence of this n. read 'Furius' for 'Camillus'.

13. 5. crudeliter consulere: for the expression cf. iii. 36. 7, Just. i. 7. 10, v. 3. 6, and xlii. 5. 4, and see Yardley (2003) 25.

13. 6. aeque prospero: for the coupling of *aeque* and *prosperus* see x. 2. 10 n.

13. 9. statuae equestres: Gruen (1992: 90–1) and Tanner (2000: 29) also argue that this notice, and that at ix. 43. 22 (n.), are reliable. Note esp. Tanner's argument at his n. 53: 'the use of column statues conceivably (if one accepts the authenticity of the columna Maenia) and rostrate columns without question in public honorific monuments were Roman innovations, and it would not be surprising if Rome also took the lead in equestrian monuments, eschewed until the Hellenistic period in the more egalitarian Greek poleis'.

13. 11–18. *The speech of Camillus.* For a parallel to the humane sentiments of this speech from elsewhere in the annalistic tradition, see Larcius' speech at D.H. vi. 19. 1–4. That they both derive ultimately from the pen of the same annalist is possible.

13. 11. id iam deum benignitate ac uirtute militum: for credit being shared between the gods and the *uirtus militum*, see *addendum* to vi. 30. 6 n.

13. 15. uastas inde solitudines facere: this passage, and the surrounding context, is recalled also at Curt. viii. 8. 10–12; note esp. 'ueni in Asiam, non ut funditus euerterem gentes nec ut dimidiam partem terrarum solitudinem facerem . . . non est diuturna possessio, in quam gladio inducimur; beneficiorum gratia sempiterna est'.

13. 16. 6. uoltis . . . suppeditat: for the idea add D.H. vi. 19. 4.

13. 16. id firmissimum imperium est quo oboedientes gaudent: for this idea cf. also D.S. xiii. 22. 1–5 and D.H. vi. 19. 4.

14. 1–12. *The settlement after the Latin War*

p. 550. I am now less certain that the Trebula mentioned at x. 1. 3 is the Aequan or Sabine site at Ciciliano: see n. ad loc.

p. 552 n. 6. On prefectures and the local autonomy of *ciuitates sine suffragio* see also the good discussion of Knapp (1980).

p. 553. '[I]n the period after the Second Punic War' is written loosely. Read rather 'at some point after the establishment of the Roman colonies at Volturnum, Liternum, and Puteoli in 194 BC (xxxiv. 45. 1)'. See Knapp (1980) 26.

p. 557. For civil discord in Campania during the Hannibalic War, see also Sil. xi. 44–50.

p. 558. For aristocratic support for Rome in Italian towns, see also ix. 25. 4–8 (*principes iuuentutis* in Auruncan towns support Rome) and Zon. viii. 24. 4 (the older and wealthier Tarentine citizens favour peace with Rome in

281; for factions in Tarentum at this time see also Plut. *Pyrrh.* 13. 4–5). At ix. 16. 2–10 L. refers to two factions at Satricum, one of which supported Rome, but does not state that the aristocracy belonged to this faction. In this context Bandelli (2002: 65) adduces the betrayal of Nequinum in 299 by two *oppidani* (x. 10. 1–5), but it is not certain that the *oppidani* represented a pro-Roman faction. See further Urso (1999), who, however, accepts Sordi's speculative revised chronology of events in the late fourth century (see vol. iii, pp. 651–2).

14. 3. Aricini Nomentanique et Pedani: on the use of -*que* . . . *et* here see ix. 42. 11 n.

14. 12. rostrisque earum suggestum in foro exstructum adornari placuit: for the display of Antiate *rostra* see also Schol. Gron. on Cic. *imp. Pomp.* 55 (p. 321) 'primum populus Romanus contra Antiates bellum gessit et duodecim captiuis nauium rostris forum ornauit, non, ut imperiti dicunt, Carthaginiensium nauibus'. For the wider phenomenon of the display of *rostra* see also Dio li. 19. 2 (Octavian allowed to display the beaks of Cleopatra's ships).

templum: for the distinction between *aedes* and *templum* see esp. Gell. xiv. 7. 7.

15. 8. uiam stratam: for *uiam sternere* see also Humm (1996) 698–700.

15. 9. Q. Publilius Philo praetor primum de plebe: for Philo see vii. 21. 6 n. (with *addendum*); for patrician monopoly of the praetorship see *addendum* to vi. 34. 1–42. 14 n.; for this election see Brennan (2000) 67–9.

16. 5. M. Atilius Regulus: the possibility that the consul of 294 (M. Atilius M. f. M. n. Regulus) was a grandson of our man ought to have been mentioned: note the thirty-seven-year gap (dictator-years excluded) between 335 and 294. It is possible too that the famous M. Atilius M. f. L. n. Regulus (*cos.* I 267) was the great-grandson of our man rather than the grandson of his putative brother. The filiation of C. Atilius M. f. M. n. Regulus (*cos.* I 257, II 250) suggests that he was the son or (less probably) the grandson of the consul of 294. A. Atilius A. f. C. n. Caiatinus (or Calatinus: no decisive resolution of this famous *crux* is possible) (*cos.* I 258, II 254) is harder to place on the family tree: he cannot descend from the consul of 294 and could descend from the consul of 335 only if the C. Atilius who was his grandfather was the son of the consul of 335.

If there is any truth in the anecdote told by Valerius Maximus (viii. 1. *absol.* 9; quoted at vol. iii, p. 557) about an A. (or M.) Caiatinus (or Calatinus) being involved in a defection of Sora, and if the anecdote is to be dated to 306, then the man must have been at least twenty in that year. If the mss of Valerius Maximus are right and his *praenomen* was Aulus, then he could be the father of the famous Caiatinus, who is likely to have been born *c*.300–295. If Vat. lat. 4929, the archetype for the *epitome* of Julius Paris, is right, as it quite often is, and his *praenomen* was Marcus, then he either is otherwise unknown (perhaps an uncle of the famous Caiatinus) or may be equated with the consul of 294 (the *cognomen* Caiatinus being substituted for Regulus: for this possibility see x. 32. 1 n.). On the *cognomen* Calenus see further *addendum* to vol. i, p. 33. How the family acquired the name Caiatinus is uncertain.

On the Reguli see also Ridley (1991) 234–5, discussing the views of Perizonius.

16. 9. cum per neglegentiam custodum die festo: for the dangers of festivals in a besieged town, see e.g. Aen. Tact. 4. 8, 17. 1–4, 29. 3. For the importance of those in a besieged town making sure that their guard is reliable during a festival, see Aen. Tact. 22. 16.

16. 12. T. Veturius: on the plebeian status of Veturius see now Bunse (1998) 188–9 (more sceptical of it than I should be), Stewart (1998) 154. For discussion of the Veturii see Münzer (1999) 116–26; his view (p. 126) that this Veturius transferred to the plebs so as to curtail plebeian rights is improbable.

Sp. Postumius: for better discussion of the *cognomen* bestowed on Postumius by *F.C.* for 332, see vol. iii, p. 11 (with further bibliography).

17. 5. Cn. Domitius: if Plin. *nat.* xxxiii. 17 is correct, then 'or grandson' should be deleted.

18. 1–13. *The trial for poisoning*

p. 595. Replace 'by a specially appointed commission chaired by a magistrate' with 'by a magistrate, in later times normally chairing a specially appointed commission, in earlier times with the help of his own *consilium*'.

p. 596. Note that at ix. 26. 20 L. states that the consuls, on the instruction of the senate, took over the *quaestio* of 314 after the resignation of C. Maenius from his dictatorship.

18. 11. prodigii ea res loco habita captisque magis mentibus quam conscaeleratis similis uisa: for the *comparatio compendiaria* see ix. 18. 11 n.

19. 1. L. Plautius Venox: for the *cognomen* see ix. 20. 1 n.

Lucani: La Regina (1989: 393) argues that there was a Volscian Luca, at the Monte dei Fichi (where polygonal walling survives) near Boville Ernica.

19. 3. uolebant: for the use of the indicative see x. 41. 12 n.

19. 4. Vitruuius Vaccus: on Vaccus and his punishment see also Mustakallio (1994) 59–64.

domi . . . clarus: expressions of this kind are much more widely diffused than my n. suggests: see e.g. Cic. *IIVerr*. i. 45, ii. 35, 128, and the other passages cited by Landgraf on Cic. *S. Rosc.* 16. Therefore it is probably wrong to draw particular attention to the parallel in Sallust. For the comparsion between a man's repute at Rome and at home, cf. Cic. *Flacc.* 52 'homines apud nos noti, inter suos nobiles'. See also *addendum* to 7. 2.

19. 5. Setinum Norbanumque et Coranum: on the use of -*que* . . . *et* here see ix. 42. 11 n.

20. 2. carceres eo anno in circo primum statuti: for the layout and development of the Circus Maximus, see the brief remarks of Wiseman (1974: 4).

20. 3. eo ipso die, Kalendis Quintilibus, quo magistratum inierunt: to the bibliography cited add *MRR* ii. 637–9.

20. 4. opificum quoque uolgus: for the low status of craftsmen see also D.S. i. 28. 5 (where D.S., perhaps projecting Greek attitudes on to the Egyptians, claims that they are not suitable for fighting) and Sen. *epist.* 88. 21 'quattuor ait esse artium Posidonius genera: sunt uulgares et sordidae . . . uulgares opificum, quae manu constant et ad instruendam uitam occupatae sunt, in quibus nulla decoris, nulla honesti simulatio est.'

20. 7. Vitruuium in carcere adseruari iussit quoad consul redisset, tum uerberatum necari: for the killing of enemy leaders at the end of the festivities of a triumph, cf. xxvi. 13. 15, Cic. *IIVerr.* v. 77, and Marquardt (1881–5) ii. 581.

21. 6. uiri . . . mansurum: for a parallel to these sentiments see D.H. vi. 19. 3.

21. 6. uiri et liberi: there is a good parallel at Petron. 81. 6 'nam aut uir ego liberque non sum, aut noxio sanguine parentabo iniuriae meae'. The expression may have been more common than the evidence of surviving Latin suggests. For the shape of the expression cf. *uir ac Romanus*, illustrated at vii. 13. 9 n.

21. 9. eos demum qui nihil praeterquam de libertate cogitent dignos esse qui Romani fiant: for the idea of liberty as a particular characteristic of the Romans, cf. Cic. *Phil.* iii. 36 and vi. 19 and see Mouritsen (2001) 11–12.

21. 10. ex auctoritate patrum latum ad populum est: the stock phrasing of this passage should have been illustrated; see now the parallels listed at ix. 46. 7 n.

22. 1. P. Cornelio Scapula: this note is seriously misleading and is in need of various corrections and modifications.

(*a*) It ignores *ILLRP* 1274a *P. Cornelio(s) P. f. Scapola pont(ifex) max(imus)* on a sarcophagus found at Rome in the Via Cristoforo Colombo. The discovery of this inscription guaranteed the existence of Cornelii Scapulae, something that was previously uncertain, since L.'s testimony here may be wrong and since the true reading of *F.C.* for 362 is uncertain. The *pontifex maximus* may very well have been our man. The old view that he is to be equated also with the P. Cornelius Scipio whom L. (ix. 44. 1) makes dictator in 306 and the Cornelius Barbatus whom L. (ix. 46. 6) makes *pontifex maximus* in 304 has been argued skilfully by Etcheto (2003: 447–54); quite apart from the fact that Barbatus and Scapula were both *pontifex maximus*, it is likely that the dictator of 306 was a senior man. Etcheto well notes the fluidity of *cognomina* in this period: Ap. Claudius Caecus originally bore the family *cognomen* Crassus (vol. iii, p. 351); L. Papirius Cursor seems originally to have been a Mugillanus (viii. 23. 17 n.); and P. Cornelius Arvina (ix. 42. 10 n.) seems to have shed the old family *cognomen* of his father A. Cornelius Cossus Arvina (vii. 19. 10 n.). Therefore it is conceivable that one man could have been known as both Scapula and (Scipio) Barbatus.

(*b*) *F.C.* for 362, heavily abraded and damaged, now reveal only *SCA* and

LA. Since there is space for eight letters, the original reading can have been *SCAPVLA* only if there was a gap in the engraving between *SCAPV* and *LA* (for which there is no real parallel in *F.C.*, unless one counts the spelling *AVENTIN ENSIS*, which is found three times but seems rather different) or if the *cognomen* was spelt *SCAPVLLA* (which is unparalleled). See Degrassi (1947) 104.

In a full review of the evidence Ridley (1997) argues that one should read *SCA[EVO]LA* with Bartolommeo Marliani, one of the first scholars to view the stone. From an epigraphic point of view this may be the best reading, but Mucii Scaevolae are unattested in our evidence for Roman history between 486 and 215.

(*c*) *F.C.* for 362 cannot be elucidated from L., since (uniquely) he fails to tell us who was *magister equitum* to Ap. Claudius Crassus in this year.

22. 2. populo uisceratio data: on *uisceratio* see now the long discussion of Kajava (1998). He points out that the passages of Servius quoted are the only direct evidence for the view that the meat shared out came from sacrificial victims (my 'e.g.' is misleading), and he makes a good case against it (the logistical difficulties of conducting so many sacrifices would have been huge). For an instance of a *uisceratio* at a funeral in a *municipium* see *ILLRP* 588 (with l. 8, which is presented in corrupt form by Degrassi) as interpreted by Kajava, p. 114 n. 17. The feeding of a whole city finds parallels in Greek history; cf. D.S. xiii. 84. 1 (on Tellias of Acragas providing a banquet at his daughter's marriage). Flamininus died in 174 not 173.

22. 3. aedilibus: on aedilician prosecutions see further x. 23. 11–13 n.

22. 4. tribunusque plebei: as attractive as Zingerle's *tribunusque* for *tribunatuque* is *tribunorumque*, which Professor Watt suggested to me (*per litteras*).

22. 5. haud procul inde ubi nunc Neapolis sita est: for the expression cf. xxxix. 22. 6 'haud procul inde ubi nunc Aquileia est locum oppido condendo ceperunt'. The note on *haud procul inde* at ix. 26. 2 should have been placed here.

22. 7–27. 11. *Foreign affairs in 328–326 BC*. On the factions in Naples at this time see further Urso (1999) 137–41.

22. 8. gente lingua magis strenua quam factis: for L.'s view of the Greeks see also Rostagni (1934) = (1955–6) ii. 2. 222–48; also ix. 18. 6 n. For *strenua* see x. 8. 3 n.

23. 1. Publilius duo milia Nolanorum . . . recepta Palaepoli miserat; †Romae compertum† Cornelius dilectum indictum . . .: Watt (2002: 182–3) suggests that *Romae* alone should be deleted, that *compertum* should be taken as object of *miserat*, and *duo . . . Palaepoli* as an indirect statement dependent on *compertum*. This is more economical than Sigonius' conjecture.

23. 2. Priuernatem Fundanumque et Formianum: on the use of -*que* . . . *et* here see ix. 42. 11 n.

23. 12. *The prorogation of the consular* imperium *of Q. Publilius Philo*. The discussion of *priuati cum imperio* in this note is inadequate, since it does not distinguish between those appointed by the senate and people (for which see x. 26. 15 n.) and those appointed by magistrates with *imperium* (for which see x. 29. 3). For L.'s omitting to record a vote of the people see ix. 46. 6–7 n. To the bibliography add Lintott (1999) 113–15 and Brennan (2000) 73–5 (rightly stressing the need for senatorial resolutions to be backed up with a popular vote).

23. 12. actum cum tribunis est ad populum ferrent ut: for discussion of this expression see Sandberg (1993) 90–1 and (2000) 129. The role of the tribunes is discussed further in the Historical Introduction to book x (above, p. 16) and in Appendix 3.

pro consule: by late antiquity there was doubt as to whether it was correct to use *pro consule* and *pro praetore* or the declinable nouns *proconsul* or *propraetor* (for the views of grammarians see *TLL* x. 2. 1542. 38–43). However, the evidence of inscriptions shows that *pro consule* and *pro praetore* were the norm in the late Republic and early principate; only in apposition to nouns in the dative singular do writers seem to have had scruples about using them.

As for L.'s primary mss, inconsistencies in their spelling and their descent from exemplars in which words were not divided (there is inconsistency in the placing of a space after *pro*) render their evidence of limited value and make it very hard to be confident about his usage. In books i–x he uses one or other of these expressions at iii. 4. 10, iv. 41. 10, ix. 42. 6, x. 16. 2*, 18. 8, 25. 11, 26. 12*, 26. 15*, 27. 11*, 29. 3, 30. 1*, 30. 6, 31. 5. Only in the five asterisked passages do any of Conway, Walters, or Ogilvie print the noun: in all these passages this decision makes the text easier to read for a modern, but it is far from certain that L. himself used the nouns. There is little to be gained from presenting here the large number of variations in abbreviation that the mss contain; but inspection of all their testimony in all the passages listed above leads to the conclusion that they never unambiguously suggest that L. used the noun *propraetor* and that they point to his having used the noun *proconsul* only at x. 27. 11 (*proconsule* MPUZtRLD: *pro consule* Zs: om. Zb), where indeed he may have done. However, note also iv. 41. 10 *proconsule* MPUEXRLD: *proconsul& H* (but *proconsul* ought to have been in the nominative and therefore L. must have written *pro consule*) and x. 30. 6 (*proconsule* MPUT [*-lae* T¹L]: *proconsulem* ZsRD: *pro consule* ZbZt (where *pro consule* has most support but *proconsulem* is not impossible), and 31. 5 *proconsule* MPZtTR¹: *pro consule* UZbL: *proconsul* ZsRᶜ (where *pro consule* must be right for the same reason as at iv. 41. 10)—all passages that show how little ms. evidence is to be valued on this matter. See further Briscoe (1980) 323–5, Walsh (1986) p. x, Hajdú (1999) and in *TLL* x. 2. 1542. 17–1545. 57.

23. 13–17. *The dictatorship of M. Claudius Marcellus and subsequent* interregna. This episode is discussed by Linderski (1986: 2172–3), who well brings out the augural language used by L. He rightly argues that this language does not prove the authenticity of the episode, which he rejects, following Münzer in regarding it as a retrojection of the events of 215; but he takes no account of the arguments in favour of authenticity that are listed in the first paragraph of my note.

23. 14. consulti augures: the augurs generally worked by responding to consultation by a magistrate or the senate: cf. iv. 31. 4, xxiii. 31. 13, xlv. 12. 10, and Cic. *Phil.* ii. 83. For further evidence and bibliography see Linderski (1986) 2159–62.

23. 15. consul oriens nocte silentio diceret dictatorem: on *silentium* see also Fest. 476. 31–4. The practice of nominating a dictator at night explains why his first action as dictator is sometimes introduced by L. with the phrase *postero die* or *luce prima*: see iii. 27. 1, iv. 14. 1, 22. 1 and Magdelain (1968) 29 n. 2 (but iv. 17. 12, 32. 10, vi. 12. 7, and viii. 38. 3, also adduced by Magdelain, are not parallel).

23. 16. sedentes: many more parallels for *sedere* used of augurs are cited by Linderski (1989: 92 = 1995: 529 n. 2); see also Skutsch on Enn. *ann.* 74–5 and Vaahtera (2001) 100.

quid . . . uitii obuenisset: for *obuenire* in the context of augury or the auspices, Linderski (1986: 2173 n. 94) cites Cic. *diu.* ii. 77 and *Phil.* ii. 83 'id igitur obuenit uitium'.

23. 17. L. Papirium Mugillanum: Münzer's argument is supported strongly by Etcheto (2003: 461–2); it improves on earlier views (for example, Mommsen [1859: 112 n. 195] had argued that for no obvious reason the engraver of *F.C.* had substituted *Mugillanus* for *Cursor*).

24. 1–18. *The foundation of Alexandria and the death of Alexander of Epirus*

p. 667. 'Oscans' is potentially misleading; read 'Lucanians and Samnites'.

p. 667 n. 1. Nissen's suggestion is rejected also by Urso (1998: 29 n. 20).

24. 11. incerto uado: for the expression cf. Tac. *hist.* v. 14. 2 and *ann.* xii. 33.

24. 16. unius may be defended as reiterating the point made by *una* in § 15; but if *illius* (Shackleton Bailey [1986] 16) had stood in **N**, it would never have been questioned.

25. 4. Rufrium: for variation in the spelling of Italian place-names add the examples of Ostia (treated both as a feminine singular and neuter plural: for the evidence see Skutsch on Enn. *ann.* 128) and Tarentum (for which a form in *-us* is attested: see Housman [1907] 233 = [1972] 714).

25. 6. indigna iam ⟨in⟩ liberis quoque ac coniugibus . . . patiebantur: Watt (2002: 183) rightly observes that *cum* would give better sense than *in* and could have been omitted after *iam*.

25. 7, p. 681 n. 1: my statement 'the alliance of Greek and Oscan proved surprisingly enduring' is not based on good evidence. Although Tarentum may indeed have helped the Samnites against Rome in 326, it is not likely that her relations with her old foes, the Lucanians, were entirely harmonious between 326 and the events involving Cleonymus (above, pp. 48–52); see De Sanctis (1907–64) ii. 303 and Giannelli (1974) 354–5.

For the view that the treaty between Rome and Tarentum recorded by

Addenda *and* corrigenda

Appian should be dated to the time of the expedition of Cleonymus, see also De Sanctis (1907–64) ii. 347, Beloch (1912–27) iv. 1. 202, Giannelli (1974) 363, and Braccesi (1990) 19.

For general discussion of Rome's relations with Tarentum and Tarentine foreign policy, see also Giannelli (1974) 353–64 and Raaflaub *et al.* (1992) 15–23.

26. 3. multitudine semet impediente: for this idea see also Caes. *Gall.* vii. 70. 3 'hostes in fugam coiecti se ipsi multitudine impediunt' and Dict. ii. 43 'tum magna uis barbarorum trepida impeditaque inter se caesa extinctaque'.

26. 4. foedus Neapolitanum: Naples is first attested as furnishing ships for Rome in 264 BC, when the Roman army needed to be transported over the Straits of Messina (Plb. i. 20. 14). This episode is also the first appearance of Naples in our sources for Roman history after the events described by L. here.

27. 1–11. *Tarentum and the defection of the Lucani.* The view that an alliance was agreed between Rome and the Lucani and then rescinded is adopted by De Sanctis (1907–64: ii. 303) and Giannelli (1974: 355).

27. 4. nec eam ipsam satis ualidam: for the idiom see ix. 18. 9 n.

28. 1–9. *The violation of C. Publilius.* For discussion of the sources see also Münzer (1999) 117–18. The revised heading more accurately reflects L.'s text.

29. 1–37. 2. *Fighting against the Vestini and Samnites.* Forsythe (1999: 60–1) takes a view of the manner in which L. has used his sources broadly similar to that taken on p. 697.

29. 2. quae res: see x. 29. 1 n.

sermonibus magis passim hominum: for some speculation on the role of public opinion at Rome in this period see Loreto (1993) 170–1; but it is doubtful whether the information which L. gives here goes back to reliable sources.

29. 5. uicit tamen: in addition to the eight instances of this expression in L., it is found at Cic. *de or.* ii. 54, Sall. *Iug.* 16. 1, 25. 8, 34. 1, Curt. viii. 3. 15, Sen. *epist.* 66. 1, Quint. ix. 4. 44, and (without a strong pause preceding) at Ov. *am.* iii. 2. 17. This raises the possibility that L. was influenced by Sallust's usage, and Curtius by L.'s. I should also have noted that *uincit tamen* is found at xxv. 14. 1 (and Cic. *Caecin.* 92, where however the preceding pause is not strong).

30. 1–36. 12. *The dispute between Papirius Cursor and Fabius Rullianus.* There is an extended discussion of this episode by Chaplin (2000: 108–13); she stresses the precedents cited by both Cursor and Rullianus' father.

30. 1. incertis . . . auspiciis: for discussion of *certus* and *incertus* in augural law, see Linderski (1986: 2292): 'the interpretation of *signa incerta* was a delicate matter for it could happen that *aliquod signum dubie datum pro certo sit acceptum* (Cic. de div. 1. 124)'.

non in belli euentum: the intimate link, in both L. and Roman thought in general, between successful taking of the auspices and victory in battle

582

needs a more extended discussion. See esp. Linderski (1993: 69 = 1995: 624 n. 29), who illustrates it with numerous good examples, such as v. 21. 1, vi. 12. 7, ix. 14. 3–4, and x. 40. 2–14. The doctrine is also illustrated by the defeat of the *magister equitum* of 302/1 (x. 3. 6–7), who fought while his dictator had returned to Rome *auspiciorum repetendorum causa*. That is what one might have expected to have happened in our passage.

Linderski (1993: 62–3 = 1995: 617–18) thinks L.'s explanation (§ 1 'cuius rei uitium non in belli euentum, quod prospere gestum est, sed in rabiem atque iras imperatorum uertit') of why no military disaster befell Fabius when he fought *incertis auspiciis* is lame; but perhaps a quarrel that takes six chapters to recount is a sufficient calamity. Note that at xxvii. 23. 4 'in capita consulum re publica incolumi exitiabilis prodigiorum euentus uertit' L. says something very similar: the failure to propitiate the gods leads not to a major military reverse but to a disaster that affects the consuls (in this later passage their death, rather than a quarrel).

Linderski prefers to suggest that Fabius was successful because the auspices were only 'ambiguous—not adverse. It was risky and foolhardy to engage the enemy, but the result was open. L. in his rhetorical zeal put into the mouth of the enraged dictator one phrase too much: *aduersus numen deorum*, high ringing but doctrinally unsound' (the passage quoted is from 32. 6). Perhaps Linderski does not place enough stress on the fact that the *incerta auspicia* were themselves a warning; but, if he is right and Papirius does exaggerate, then this may be regarded as part of L.'s characterization of Papirius.

30. 2. pullario: for the taking of the auspices before battle see ix. 14. 4 n.

ad auspicium repetendum Romam proficisceretur: for the expression *auspicium (-ia) repetere* cf. also *CIL* 1², p. 192 *elog.* 8. I ought to have made more clear that the auspices were those taken by a commander at the time of his departure from the city. In this context note Flaminius' alleged departure from Rome in 217, and in particular the view put in the mouths of unspecified Roman opponents that these auspices could be taken only on Roman soil (xxii. 1. 7 'nec priuatum auspicia sequi nec sine auspiciis profectum in externo ea solo noua atque integra concipere posse'). For Roman generals returning to the city *ad auspicium repetendum* one should perhaps cite the return of Fabius Verrucosus to Rome in 217 (xxii. 18. 8, Plb. iii. 94. 9, Sil. vii. 381–408, Plut. *Fab.* 8. 1, App. *Han.* 12. 52); although the rituals and sacrifices to which Fabius had to attend are specified by no source, he is likely to have had to seek favourable auspices.

To the modern mind it may seem odd that generals should have left Rome with uncertain auspices, when this was likely to necessitate their return or their recall; but perhaps the nature of their auspices became clear (whether to the generals themselves or to others in the city) only after they had left. Or unsatisfactory campaigning may have made them wonder about their auspices; see Serv. *Aen.* ii. 178: 'et respexit Romanum morem. nam si egressi male pugnassent, reuertebantur ad captanda rursus auguria'. Servius auctus (who does not respect the distinction between *auspicia repetere* and *a. renouare* outlined in the n.) adds the information that when the Romans were fighting outside Italy a piece of land was termed 'Roman' for the purposes of taking the auspices.

On this whole subject see further Wissowa, *RE* ii. 2582–3, Magdelain (1968) 43 and 52, Linderski (1993) 69 = (1995) 624, and Vaahtera (2001) 25–6.

30. 3. per exploratores: for this detail in L.'s early battle narratives see also x. 14. 6 n.

30. 9. Fabio auctori: the question whether Fabius was the first Roman annalist is considered in more detail above, pp. 475–8. To the general bibliography on Pictor add Gelzer (1933) (the most important development of the view, contested by Momigliano but remaining very plausible, that an important part of Pictor's purposes was to present Rome in a good light to the Greeks), (1934), and (1954) = (1962–4) iii. 51–110, Bung (1950), and Petzold (1993) 161–9.

nomenque ibi inscriberet: for *nomen* in the context of self-advertisement add e.g. Lucr. iii. 78 'intereunt partim statuarum et nominis ergo'. I ought to have made clear that in passages such as Prop. iii. 2. 25–6 'at non ingenio quaesitum nomen ab aeuo | excidet: ingenio stat sine morte decus' and Ov. *met.* xv. 876 'nomenque erit indelebile nostrum' there is a more or less explicit contrast with *nomina* written on stones, which can perish. Even more explicit is Auson. xiii (*epigr.*). 37. 10 'mors etiam saxis nominibusque uenit'.

Dio (xxxvii. 44. 1) remarks that in 62 BC Julius Caesar tried to get the *nomen* of Catulus removed from the Capitoline temple of Jupiter. For another attempt to obliterate someone's *nomen*, see [Sen.] *Oct.* 609–12 'saeuit in nomen ferus | matris tyrannus, obrui meritum cupit, | simulacra, titulos destruit mortis metu | totum per orbem'.

31. 1. ductu auspicioque: amongst the parallels for this expression I should have cited x. 7. 7 'ductu et auspicio'; but the reference to x. 19. 14 should be removed.

32. 3. summum imperium: see *addendum* to vi. 38. 3 n.

consules, regia potestas: I ought to have cited the view of Polybius (vi. 11. 12, 12. 9) that the power of the consuls constitutes τὸ βασιλικόν in the constitution: on the origin of this idea, see e.g. Rawson (1975) 151 = (1991) 175. For the idea that consular *potestas* was related to that of the kings, see also Cic. *leg.* iii. 8 and Ampel. 50. 2 'nam et regiam potestatem consules habent'.

32. 5. sed quid ego haec: see also *addendum* to vi. 15. 10 n.

32. 6. qui tu: in the parallel quoted from ix. 10. 7, one should probably read *adducis*; see n. ad loc.

32. 11. tumultum ⟨ultima⟩ iam in contione miscentes: there is a good parallel for *ultima contio* at Ascon. 48 'lapidesque etiam ex ultima contione in consulem iacti'.

33. 2. prae strepitu: for this combination see x. 13. 9 n.

33. 4. summouentium: see also the *addendum* to vi. 38. 8 n.

33. 8. tribunos plebis appello et prouoco ad populum: quite apart from the difficulties involved in having a patrician appealing to the tribunes, I should have observed that the model of *prouocatio* behind this passage and those cited from books ii and iii (all of which involve the Roman crowd, and to which ii. 27. 11–13, esp. § 12 should be added) may be based only on annalistic reconstruction: see the full discussion at x. 9. 3–6 n.

Cloud (1998: 40–1) interestingly suggests that Fabius may have fled to Rome (33. 3) because L. and his sources knew that there was no *prouocatio* outside Rome until the second century. He also suggests that in this passage L. combines two models of *prouocatio* (both discussed at x. 9. 3–6 n.), that found in the story of Horatius in which the people are final arbiters of life and death and that found in the passages cited from books ii and iii, in which an appeal is made to the crowd to resist magisterial coercion.

In addition to Lintott (cited in the note) and Cloud, this passage is discussed by Heuss (1944: 113) and Bleicken (1959: 332–3).

34. 10 ordines seruent: see ix. 19. 7 n.

36. 1. praeposito in urbe: on the *praefecti urbi* see now Brennan (2000) 34–8. He argues that these officials did not have *imperium* in their own right but derived it by delegation from the consuls.

36. 4. ita instruxit aciem †loco ac subsidiis† ita omni arte bellica firmauit: in my note I provided a cross-reference to ix. 17. 15 n., where numerous parallels are cited. However, that passage does not refer specifically to the skill of drawing up a line of battle in the correct position; this is illustrated by Frontin. *strat.* ii. 2, a chapter entitled *de loco ad pugnam eligendo*.

36. 9. nullam uim nec apertam nec ex insidiis expertus: for the contrast between *uim apertam* and *ex insidiis* cf. also Sen. *Oed.* 275 'aperto Marte an insidiis iacet?'

37. 2. arrecti . . . animi sunt: for this particular expression see Skard (1933) 24–5.

37. 7. nec auctor nec causa: this n. is superseded by the material assembled at ix. 10. 1 n.

37. 8. populi . . . iudicium: see x. 46. 16 n.

37. 11. sententia: see x. 11. 4 n.

38. 1–40. 5. *Foreign affairs.* Brennan (2000: 40) rejects the idea of the appointment of a dictator to hold the games as an 'absurd notion'; but he does not attempt to answer the arguments put forward in the note or in the sensible discussion of Forsythe (1999: 68–70).

38. 1. L. Fuluio: C. Fulvius Curvus, *aed. pl.* 296 (x. 23. 13 n.), is perhaps another son of this Fulvius.

38. 4. militum uirtuti: see *addendum* to vi. 30. 6 n.

ignibus crebris relictis qui conspectum hostium frustrarentur: for the use of fires to hide a retreat, cf. D.S. xiii. 111. 2; for the practice of calculating the size of enemy forces from the number of their fires, see also Curt. vii. 8. 2; for the kindling of fires to give a false impression of the size of one's own force, see also Curt. ix. 4. 24; for the possibility of fires giving away the position of troops, see also Aen. Tact. 23. 1.

38. 8. impedimentis ex agmine remotis: see *addendum* to viii. 11. 11 n.

38. 10. ab hora diei tertia ad octauam: for information about the duration of a battle given in this format add xl. 50. 2 'a prima luce ad sextam horam diei'. Other passages in which the length of battles is recorded include: xxii. 6. 1 (three hours), xxiii. 40. 9 (four hours), xxiv. 15. 3 (over four hours), 42. 2 (four hours), xxv. 19. 15 (two hours), xxxvi. 38. 3 (over two hours), xlii. 7. 5 (more than three hours), and Caes. *ciu.* i. 46. 1 (five hours). There are vaguer notices at ix. 44. 11 'proelium in multum diei processisset', x. 12. 5 'pugnatum maiore parte diei', 29. 8 'Fabius . . . extraxerat diem', xxvii. 12. 10 (until nightfall), 14. 6 'diu', App. *Ib.* 27. 106 δι' ὅλης ἡμέρας, 40. 164 (fighting until evening), 77. 328 τὴν ἡμέραν ὅλην ἠγωνίζοντο. This evidence is important, because if, as it suggests, battles involving Roman armies were regularly of four hours' duration or longer, it is hard to imagine that all this time was spent in hand-to-hand fighting with swords. See further *addendum* to vi. 12. 8 n., Sabin (2000) 4–5, and Zhmodikov (2000) 71.[1]

38. 12. auiditate praedae: see ix. 37. 2 n.

39. 4. tum . . . uocare: for troops being encouraged in this way by generals see also D.H. viii. 65. 5 (another good instance of the τόπος being applied to early Roman history), App. *ciu.* iv. 125. 523, and Rosenstein (1990) 119; for *appellare* cf. also Caes. *Gall.* v. 33. 2; and for a general calling on troops by name, cf. also Dict. iii. 5.

39. 5. nouato clamore: see ix. 35. 6 n.

40. 1. quidam auctores sunt: one of the expressions which L. uses regularly for reporting variants in his sources; cf. i. 48. 9 (on Servius Tullius) 'id ipsum tam mite ac tam moderatum imperium tamen quia unius esset deponere eum in animo habuisse quidam auctores sunt, ni scelus intestinum liberandae patriae consilia agitanti interuenisset', ix. 37. 11, 44. 15, x. 26. 10, and about a dozen instances from later decades.

40. 2. ludis Romanis: this note should be supplemented with various observations: (*a*) the games, and esp. the Roman and plebeian games, were a very important part of the Roman social and religious calendar, as is revealed to us by L. more than any other author; (*b*) Ritschl's demonstration works only for L.'s usage (in all three of the passages cited in the previous parenthesis the *ludi Romani* are called *magni* or *maximi*); (*c*) the following reference to curule aediles makes it probable that vi. 42. 12 refers to the *ludi Romani*; (*d*) the *ludi plebeii* need discussion (see now x. 23. 13 n.); (*e*) in the later Republic the *ludi Romani*, *ludi plebeii*, and special votive games were joined by special funeral games (a practice attested first in 264 BC [for the evidence see ix. 40. 17 n.] at the funeral of M. Junius Pera, but almost certainly started many years earlier), the *ludi Megalenses*, and the *ludi Florales*; (*f*) v. 19. 6 and vii. 11. 4 are parallel to each other, in that in both a dictator vows *ludi magni* before setting out on campaign (compare also xxxi.

---

[1] Most of the evidence adduced above comes from Zhmodikov, but he should not have cited xxv. 15. 14, xxxiv. 28. 11, xl. 32. 6, App. *Ib.* 45, which are too vague to be of much value.

9. 5–10 and see further Orlin [1997: 41–2]); (*g*) a reference to ix. 34. 12 (which, however, probably refers to our passage) should be added in the second paragraph of the n.; and (*h*) Taylor (1937) (on the *ludi Romani*) should be cited.

40. 3. signum mittendis quadrigis daret: for the role of the praetor (or consul or dictator or other official) in starting off the chariot race at the games, see xlv. 1. 6 'C. Licinio consuli ad quadrigas mittendas escendenti', Enn. *ann.* 79–81 'expectant ueluti consul quom mittere signum | uolt, omnes auidi spectant ad carceris oras | quam mox emittat pictos e faucibus currus', Mart. xii. 28. 9–10 'cretatam praetor cum uellet mittere mappam | praetori mappam surpuit Hermogenes', Suet. *Nero* 22. 2 'aliquo liberto mittente mappam unde magistratus solent', *act. frat. Aru.* (p. 36) '(magister) supra carceres escendit et signum quadrigis et desultoribus misit'. The passages of Martial and Suetonius suggest that by the first century AD the sign given was a white handkerchief dropped from above the *carceres* (cf. also Quint. i. 5. 57 '"mappam" circo quoque usitatam nomen'). For *mittere* used of starting the chariots at the games, cf. xliv. 9. 4, xlv. 1. 6–7, and other passages cited at *TLL* viii. 1174. 40–54. See further Mommsen (1887–8) i. 413 n. 2 and Skutsch on Enn. loc. cit (to which this note owes much).

40. 4. imaginum titulis: 'The *imagines* were housed in the *atrium* in special cupboards called *armaria* . . . Each cupboard was labeled with a *titulus* recording the name of the ancestor and probably the most basic outline of his career as reflected by the offices he had held' (Flower [1996] 206–7). For *tituli* mentioned in connection with *imagines* see x. 7. 11, xxii. 31. 11, Hor. *serm.* i. 6. 17, *pan. Mess.* 27–36, Val. Max. v. 8. 3, and Tac. *dial.* 8. 4.

40. 5. nec . . . stetur: for L.'s awareness of the greater authority of older writers, and especially those contemporary with the events which they were describing, see vol. i, pp. 17–18 with *addendum*.

Appendices

p. 780. *Roman relations with Tarentum.* These relations are discussed at length by Urso (1998: esp. 53–67); but his views are rendered very speculative because of his adoption of chronological rearrangements in the manner of Sordi (on which see vol. iii, pp. 651–2).

VOLUME III

BOOK IX

15. 8. mutatione subita rerum: for the expression, which is paralleled precisely at Just. xi. 1. 5, see Yardley (2003) 39.

19. 4. fractos bello: for the expression Yardley (2003: 66) compares xxxix. 42. 1, Virg. *Aen.* ii. 13, Luc. vii. 684, Sil. xvi. 272, and Just. xxx. 4. 17.

20. 3. fatigasset . . . precibus: a regular expression in L., who uses it five times. It is found thrice in Justin and thrice elsewhere. See further Yardley (2003) 25.

20. 5. discordia intestina: see also Yardley (2003) 55.

20. 7. C. Iunium Bubulcum: for the part played by Bubulcus in the creation of the myth of Brutus the first consul (but one may prefer to believe that the *cognomen* Brutus originated with the historical rather than the legendary figure), and for the possible influence of this campaign on the mythical Brutus, son of Daunus, see Wiseman (2003) esp. 32–8.

29. 3. reliquias belli persequente: this expression is found also at Just. xxii. 8. 15 and xlii. 4. 5. See Yardley (2003) 58.

29. 5–11. *The censorship of Ap. Claudius Caecus.* On Appius see also Campanile (2002), esp. 31–8.

29. 11. sed censorem . . . captum: on the basis of Non. p. 720L 'CAECVM non solum oculis captum, sed et insidiosum et occulte malum et tacitum uel latens quid dicendum ueteres aestimauerunt', Campanile (2002: 39–46) argues that the *cognomen* Caecus was first given to Appius to denote his slippery political behaviour and that later generations misunderstood this. It is easier to believe that he was blind in old age.

34. 22. in contemptu deorum hominumque: Yardley (2003: 32) notes that the expression is paralleled at Quint. (?) *decl.* 377. 1 and Just. iii. 7. 2.

35. 1–40. 21. *Foreign affairs*

p. 460. The view that L. ought to have referred to Clusium rather than Camerinum is argued forcefully by Firpo (2002: 99–109), with full bibliography of others who have so held. Firpo holds that Roman involvement with Camerinum would have been strategically useless. That is an exaggeration: although less useful than an alliance with a major Etruscan city, an alliance with Camerinum was of value to Rome as she began to expand northwards.

36. 6. armorum habitus: 'character of their weapons'; for the expression cf. xxii. 18. 3, xxiv. 30. 14, Sil. xvii. 443, Just. xx. 3. 8, and see Yardley (2003) 54.

38. 2. dulcedine . . . praedae: see also Yardley (2003: 33–4), who adds Just. xxxii. 3. 12.

46. 3. triumuiratibusque, nocturno altero, altero coloniae deducendae: on the *iiiuiri capitales* see Cascione (1999), who argues (pp. 1–24) that they were preceded by officials who could have been known as *iiiuiri nocturni*. If this view is correct, then Macer is not certainly guilty of anachronism; but the texts cited in its support (Pompon. *dig.* i. 2. 2. 30, Lyd. *mag.* i. 50, Σ Vet. Juv. 13. 157) add up to little, and Mommsen's view still seems right.

Bibliography

Only works cited in this book are listed here. For full bibliographies of writing on Livy, see Engelmann and Preuss (1880–2) ii. 368–91 (for the period 1700–1878), Klussmann (1909–13) ii. 513–46 (for 1878–96), Lambrino (1951) 350–7 (for 1896–1914), Marouzeau (1927–8) i. 220–4 (for 1914–24), Kissel (1982) (for 1933–78), and *L'Année philologique* (for 1924–). There are extensive bibliographies of writing on early Roman history in Hölkeskamp (1987) 259–76, Walbank *et al.* (1989) 673–771, and Eder (1990) 562–86.

Periodicals are abbreviated for the most part according to the practice of Lambrino (1951) and *L'Année philologique*.

AA.VV. (1976). *Padova preromana* (Padua).

AA.VV. (1977). *Padua before Rome* (Padua) [an abbreviated translation of AA.VV. 1977].

AA.VV. (1980). *Sannio: Pentri e Frentani dal vi al i secolo a.C.* (Rome).

AA.VV. (1984). Sodalitas: *scritti in onore di Antonio Guarino* (Naples).

AA.VV. (1993). Senatus Populusque Romanus: *studies in Roman republican legislation* [Acta Instituti Romani Finlandiae xiii] (Helsinki).

AA.VV. (2003). *I manoscritti datati della Sicilia* (Florence).

Adams, J. N. (1993). 'The generic use of *mula* and the status and employment of female mules in the Roman world', *RhM* n.s. cxxxvi. 35–61.

——(1994a). 'Wackernagel's law and the position of unstressed personal pronouns in classical Latin', *Transactions of the Philological Society* xcii. 103–78.

——(1994b). *Wackernagel's law and the placement of the copula* esse *in classical Latin* [PCPhS Suppl. xviii] (Cambridge).

——(1999). 'Nominative personal pronouns and some patterns of speech in republican and Augustan poetry', in J. N. Adams and R. G. Mayer (edd.), *Aspects of the language of Latin poetry* (Oxford), 97–133.

——(2003). *Bilingualism and the Latin language* (Cambridge).

——(forthcoming). 'The *bellum Africum*'.

Adcock, F. E. (1928). 'The conquest of central Italy', in S. A. Cook, F. E. Adcock, and M. P. Charlesworth (edd.), *The Hellenistic monarchies and the rise of Rome* [The Cambridge Ancient History vii] (Cambridge).

Afzelius, A. (1942). *Die römische Eroberung Italiens (340–264 v. Chr.)* [Acta Jutlandica xiv. 3] (Copenhagen).

Albrecht, M. von (1989). *Masters of Roman prose from Cato to Apuleius* [trans. N. Adkin from *Die Meister römischer Prosa von Cato bis Apuleius*] (Leeds).

Alföldi, A. (1965). *Early Rome and the Latins* (Ann Arbor).

——(1966). 'Les *cognomina* des magistrats de la République romaine', in R. Chevalier (ed.), *Mélanges d'archéologie et d'histoire offerts à André Piganiol* (Paris), 709–22.

Allen, H. E. (Alanus). (1864–74). *Emendationes Livianae* (Dublin).

Altheim, F. (1938*a*). 'The first Roman silver coinage', in J. Allan, H. Mattingly, and E. S. G. Robinson (edd.), *Transactions of the International Numismatic Congress organized and held in London by the Royal Numismatic Society June 30–July 3, 1936, on the occasion of its centenary* (London), 137–50.

——(1938*b*). *A history of Roman religion* [trans. by H. Mattingly from an expanded version of *Römische Religionsgeschichte*] (London).

——(1940). Lex Sacrata: *die Anfänge der plebeischen Organisation* [Albae Vigiliae i] (Amsterdam).

Amirante, L. (1983). 'Sulla provocatio ad populum fino al 300', *Iura* xxxiv. 1–27.

Andreau, J. (1987). *La Vie financière dans le monde romain* [BEFAR cclxv] (Rome).

Andrén, A. (1960). 'Origine e formazione dell'architettura templare etrusco-italica', *RPAA* xxxii. 21–59.

Appel, G. (1909). *De Romanorum precationibus* [Religionsgeschichtliche Versuche und Vorarbeiten vii] (Giessen).

Ash, R. (1999). 'An exemplary conflict: Tacitus' Parthian battle narrative (*annals* 6. 34–5)', *Phoenix* liii. 114–35.

Astin, A. E. (1978). *Cato the Censor* (Oxford).

Austin, R. G. (1964). *P. Vergili Maronis* Aeneidos *liber secundus* (Oxford).

——(1971). *P. Vergili Maronis* Aeneidos *liber primus* (Oxford).

Avesani, R. (1964). 'Per la biblioteca di Agostino Patrizi Piccolomini', *Studi e testi* ccxxxvi (= *Mélanges E. Tisserant* vi) 1–87.

Babcock, R. G. (1994). 'Manuscripts of the classical authors in the bindings of sixteenth-century Venetian books', *S&C* xviii. 309–24.

Backmund, — (1874). '*Praerogativa* oder *praerogativae*', *BBG* x. 231–4.

Badian, E. (1962). 'Waiting for Sulla', *JRS* lii. 47–61 = (1964) 206–34.

——(1964). *Studies in Greek and Roman history* (Oxford).

——(1966). 'The early historians', in T. A. Dorey (ed.), *The Latin historians* (London), 1–38.

——(1968). 'Sulla's augurate', *Arethusa* i. 26–46.

——(1971). 'The family and early career of T. Quinctius Flamininus', *JRS* lxi. 102–11.

——(1980/1). 'Notes on the *laudatio* of Agrippa', *CJ* lxxvi. 97–109.

——(1990). 'Diskussion' and 'Kommentar', in Eder (1990), 396–7 and 458–75.

——(1996). '*Tribuni plebis* and *res publica*', in Linderski (1996) 187–213.

Bibliography

Baehrens, W. A. (1913). 'Vermischtes über lateinischen Sprachgebrauch', *Glotta* iv. 265–80.

Balsdon, J. P. V. D. (1962). 'Roman history, 65–50 B.C.: five problems', *JRS* lii. 134–41.

Balzano, V. (1923). *Aufidena Caracenorum* (Rome).

Bandel, F. (1910). *Die römischen Diktaturen* (Diss. Breslau).

Bandelli, G. (2002). 'Roma e l'Italia centrale dalla battaglia del Sentino (295 a.C.) al plebiscito di Gaio Flaminio (232 a.C.)', in Poli (2002), 63–80.

Bardt, C. (1871). *Die Priester der vier großen Collegien aus römisch-republikanischer Zeit* [Progr. K. Wilhelms-Gymnasium] (Berlin).

Basanoff, V. (1950a). 'Les Caedicius dans la tradition romaine', *Latomus* ix. 263–4.

——(1950b). 'Caius Caedicius, legatus à Aquilonia', *Latomus* ix. 265–72.

Bauman, R. A. (1973). 'The lex Valeria de prouocatione of 300 B.C.', *Historia* xxii. 34–47.

——(1974). 'Criminal prosecutions by the aediles', *Latomus* xxxiii. 245–64.

——(1983). *Lawyers in Roman republican politics: a study of the Roman jurists in their political setting, 316–82 BC* [Münchener Beiträge zur Papyrusforschung und antiken Rechtsgeschichte lxxv] (Munich).

Baur, F. A. (1864). *Aliquot translationum quae dicuntur Livianarum genera collecta* (Augsburg).

Bayet, J. (1962). 'L'étrange "omen" de Sentinum et le celtisme en Italie', in M. Renard (ed.), *Hommages à Albert Grenier* [Collection Latomus lviii] (Brussels), i. 244–56.

Beard, W. M. (1998). 'Documenting Roman religion', in AA.VV., *La Mémoire perdue: recherches sur l'administration romaine* [CEFR ccxliii], 75–101.

——North, J. A., and Price, S. R. F. (1998). *Religions of Rome* (Cambridge).

Bell, A. J. E. (1997). 'Cicero and the spectacle of power', *JRS* lxxxvii. 1–22.

Beloch, K. J. (1890). *Campanien²* (Breslau).

——(1904/5). 'La conquista romana della regione Sabina', *RSA* ix. 269–77.

——(1912–27). *Griechische Geschichte²* (Berlin and Leipzig).

——(1922). 'Die Sonnenfinsternis des Ennius und der vorjulianische Kalender', *Hermes* lvii. 119–33.

——(1926). *Römische Geschichte bis zum Beginn der punischen Kriege* (Berlin and Leipzig).

Bernays, J. (1857). 'Vergleichung der Wunder in den römischen Annalen', *RhM* n.s. xii. 436–8.

Berve, H. (1926). *Das Alexanderreich auf prosopographischer Grundlage* (Munich).

Bickerman, E. J. (1969). 'Some reflections on early Roman history', *RFIC* xcvii. 393–408.

Bispham, E. (1997). 'The end of the *tabula Heracleensis*: a poor man's *sanctio*?', *Epigraphica* lix. 125–56.

Bisschop, W., Blanchenay, W. J. C., Cobet, C. G., du Rieu, W. N., Kiehl,

E. J., Mehler, E., and Naber, S. A. (1852). 'Verbeteringen op Livius', *Mnemosyne* i. 94–101.

Bleicken, J. (1955). *Das Volkstribunat der klassischen Republik* [Zetemata xiii] (Munich).

——(1957). 'Oberpontifex und Pontifikalkollegium: eine Studie zur römischen Sakralverfassung', *Hermes* lxxxv. 345–66.

——(1959). 'Ursprung und Bedeutung der Provocation', *ZSS* lxxvi. 324–77.

Boddington, A. (1959). 'The original nature of the consular tribunate', *Historia* viii. 356–64.

Bömer, F. (1957–8). *P. Ovidius Naso:* die Fasten (Heidelberg).

——(1969–86). *P. Ovidius Naso:* die Metamorphosen (Heidelberg).

Bonnefond-Coudry, M. (1989). *Le Sénat de la république romaine* [BEFAR cclxiii] (Rome).

Botsford, G. W. (1909). *The Roman assemblies from their origin to the age of Augustus* (New York).

Bowersock, G. W. (1965). *Augustus and the Greek world* (Oxford).

Braccesi, L. (1990). *L'avventura di Cleonimo (a Venezia prima di Venezia)* (Padua).

Bradley, G. J. (2000). *Ancient Umbria: state, culture, and identity in central Italy from the Iron Age to the Augustan era* (Oxford).

Brakman, C. (1928). 'Liviana V', *Mnemosyne*, ser. 2, lvi. 60–9.

Braund, D. C., and Gill, C. (edd.) (2003). *Myth, history and culture in republican Rome: studies in honour of T. P. Wiseman* (Exeter).

Brecht, C. H. (1939). 'Zum römischen Komitialverfahren', *ZSS* lix. 261–316.

Bremer, F. P. (1896–1901). *Iurisprudentiae antehadrianae quae supersunt* (Leipzig).

Brennan, T. C. (1996). '*Triumphus in Monte Albano*', in Wallace and Harris (1996) 315–37.

——(2000). *The praetorship in the Roman republic* (New York).

Brind'Amour, P. (1983). *Le calendrier romain: recherches chronologiques* (Ottawa).

Briquel, D., and Thuillier, J. P. (edd.) (2001). *Le Censeur et les Samnites. Sur Tite-Live, livre IX* (Paris).

Briscoe, J. (1973). *A commentary on Livy books xxxi–xxxiii* (Oxford).

——(1980). 'Notes on the manuscripts of Livy's fourth decade', *Bulletin of the John Rylands University Library* lxii. 311–27.

——(1981). *A commentary on Livy books xxxiv–xxxvii* (Oxford).

——(1991). *Titi Livi* ab urbe condita *libri xxxi–xl* (Stuttgart).

Bruckmann, H. (1936). *Die römischen Niederlagen im Geschichtswerk des T. Livius* (Diss. Münster).

Bruno, B. (1906). *La terza guerra sannitica* (Rome).

Brunt, P. A. (1964). Review of Kunkel (1962), *Tijdschrift voor Rechtsgeschiednis* lxxxii. 440–9.

Bibliography

——(1966). 'The Roman mob', *Past and Present* xxxv. 3–27 = M. I. Finley (ed.), *Studies in ancient society* (London, Henley, and Boston, 1974) 74–102.

——(1969). 'The enfranchisement of the Sabines', in J. Bibauw (ed.), *Hommages à Marcel Renard* [Collection Latomus cii] (Brussels), ii. 121–9.

——(1971). *Italian manpower 225 B.C.–A.D. 14* (Oxford).

——(1974). Review of Jones (1972), *CR* n.s. xxiv. 265–7.

——(1980). 'Free labour and public works at Rome', *JRS* lxx. 81–100.

——(1982). '*Nobilitas* and *novitas*', *JRS* lxxii. 1–17.

——(1988). *The fall of the Roman Republic and related essays* (Oxford).

Bruun, C. (2000a). '"What every man in the street used to know": M. Furius Camillus, Italic legends and Roman historiography', in id. (2000b) 41–68.

——(ed.). (2000b). *The Roman middle Republic: politics, religion, and historiography c.400–133 B.C.* [Acta Instituti Romani Finlandiae xxiii] (Rome).

Buglione, V. (1929). *Monteverde* (Melfi).

Bung, P. (1950). *Q. Fabius Pictor, der erste römische Annalist* (Diss. Cologne).

Bunse, R. (1998). *Das römische Oberamt in der früheren Republik und das Problem der 'Konsulartribunen'* [Bochumer altertumswissenschaftliches Colloquium xxxi] (Trier).

——(2002). 'Entstehung und Funktion der Losung (*sortitio*) unter den *magistratus maiores* der römischen Republik', *Hermes* cxxx. 416–32.

Buonocore, M. (ed.) (1996). *Vedere i classici* (Rome).

Büttner, A. (1957). 'Untersuchungen über Ursprung und Entwicklung von Auszeichnungen im römischen Heer', *BJ* clvii. 127–80.

Büttner, F. (1819). *Observationes Livianae* (Prenzlau).

Campanile, M. D. (2002). 'Osservazioni sulla fortuna di Appio Claudio e un'ipotesi sulla sua cecità', in Poli (2002), 31–46.

Capini, S. (1992). 'L'insediamento di Monte San Paolo a Colli a Volturno e la guerra nel Sannio nel 293 a.C.', *BCAR* xvi–xviii. 33–42.

—— and Di Niro, A. (edd.) (1991). *Samnium: archeologia del Molise* (Rome).

Carcopino, J. (1925). *La Louve du Capitole* (Paris).

Cartledge, P. A., and Spawforth, A. (1989). *Hellenistic and Roman Sparta: a tale of two cities* (London and New York).

Cascione, C. (1999). *Tresviri capitales: storia di una magistratura minore* (Naples).

Cavallaro, M. A. (1976). 'Duride, i *Fasti Cap.* e la tradizione storiografica sulle *devotiones* dei Decii', *ASAA* n.s. xxxviii. 261–316.

Cavazza, F. (1988). 'Sempronius Asellio fr. 2 Peter', *Orpheus* ix. 21–37.

Champeaux, J. (1982–7). *Fortuna: recherches sur le culte de la Fortune à Rome et dans le monde romain des origines à la mort de César* [CEFR lxiv] (Rome).

Chaplin, J. D. (2000). *Livy's exemplary history* (Oxford).

Chouquer, G., Clavel-Lévêque, M., Favory, F., and Vallat, J.-P. (1987). *Structures agraires en Italie centro-méridionale* [CEFR c] (Rome).

Churchill, J. B. (1999). '*Ex qua quod uellent facerent*: Roman magistrates' authority over *praeda* and *manubiae*', *TAPhA* cxxix. 85–116.

Cianfarani, V., Dell'Orto, L. F., and La Regina, A. (1978). *Culture adriatiche antiche d'Abruzzo e di Molise* (Rome).

Cloud, J. D. (1984). '"Prouocatio": two cases of possible fabrication in the annalistic sources', in AA.VV. (1984), iii. 1365–76.

——(1998). 'The origin of *provocatio*', *RPh* lxxii. 25–48.

Coarelli, F. (1965–7). 'Il tempio di Bellona', *BCAR* lxxx (1965–7) 37–72.

——(1981). *Dintorni di Roma* [Guide archeologiche Laterza vii] (Rome and Bari).

——(1982). *Lazio* [Guide archeologiche Laterza v] (Rome and Bari).

——(1983–5). *Il foro Romano* (Rome).

——(1988). *Il foro boario dalle origini alle fine della repubblica* (Rome).

——(1996). '*Legio linteata*: l'iniziazione militare nel Sannio', in Del Tutto Palma (1996) 3–16.

——and La Regina, A. (1984). *Abruzzo, Molise* [Guide archeologiche Laterza ix] (Rome and Bari).

Cobet, G. C. (1882). 'De locis nonnullis apud Livium', *Mnemosyne*, ser. 2, x. 97–121.

Coleman, K. M. (1990). 'Fatal charades: Roman executions staged as mythological enactments', *JRS* lxxx. 44–73.

——(1993). 'Launching into history: aquatic displays in the early Empire', *JRS* lxxxiii. 48–74.

Colonna, G. (1962). 'Saepinum', *ArchClass* xiv. 80–107.

Conway, R. S. (1901). *Livy book II* (Cambridge).

Cooley, A. (1998). 'The moralizing message of the *senatus consultum de Cn. Pisone patre*', *GR* xlv. 199–212.

Cornelissen, J. J. (1889). 'Ad Livi decadem primam', *Mnemosyne*, ser. 2, xvii. 175–92.

Cornell, T. J. (1974). 'Notes on the sources for Campanian history', *MusHelv* xxxi. 193–208.

——(1989). 'The recovery of Rome' and 'The conquest of Italy', in Walbank *et al.*, 309–419.

——(1995). *The beginnings of Rome: Italy and Rome from the Bronze Age to the Punic Wars (c.1000–264 B.C.)* (London and New York).

Costanzi, V. (1919). 'Osservazioni sulla terza guerra sannitica', *RFIC* xlvii. 161–215.

Courtney, E. J. (1980). *A commentary on the satires of Juvenal* (London).

——(1999). *Archaic Latin prose* (Atlanta, GA).

Crake, J. E. A. (1940). 'The annals of the pontifex maximus', *CPh* xxxv. 375-86.

Cram, R. V. (1940). 'The Roman censors', *HSCPh* li. 71–110.

Bibliography

Crawford, M. H. (1974). *Roman republican coinage* (Cambridge).

——(1996). *Roman statutes* [BICS Suppl. lxiv] (London).

——(1998). 'Numa and the antiquarians', *Faventia* xx. 37–8.

——(2003). 'Land and people in republican Italy', in Braund and Gill (2003) 56–72.

——(2004). Review of Sandberg (2001), *CR* n.s. liv. 141–2.

Curti, E. (2000). 'From Concordia to the Quirinal: notes on religion and politics in mid-republican/Hellenistic Rome', in E. Bispham and C. J. Smith (edd.), *Religion in archaic and republican Rome and Italy* (Edinburgh), 77–91.

Daube, D. (1956). *Forms of Roman legislation* (Oxford).

David, E. (1981). *Sparta between empire and revolution (404–243 B.C.): internal problems and their impact on contemporary Greek consciousness* (Salem, NH).

De Benedittis, G. (1974). *Il centro sannitico di Monte Vairano presso Campobasso* [Documenti di antichità italiche e romane v] (Campobasso).

——(1988). *Monte Vairano: la casa di 'LN'* (Campobasso).

Dell, H. J. (1967). 'The origin and nature of Illyrian piracy', *Historia* xvi. 344–58.

Del Tutto Palma, L. (ed.) (1996). *La tavola di Agnone nel contesto italico: convegno di studi, Agnone 13–15 aprile 1994* (Florence).

Delz, J. (1987). *Sili Italici* Punica (Stuttgart).

De Martino, F. (1953). 'La gens, lo stato e le classi in Roma antica', in AA.VV., *Studi in onore di Vincenzo Arangio-Ruiz* (Naples), 25–49 = (1979) 51–74.

——(1972–90). *Storia della costituzione romana*² (Naples).

——(1979). *Diritto e società nell'antica Roma* (Rome).

Dench, E. (1998). 'Austerity, excess, success, and failure in Hellenistic and early imperial Italy', in M. del C. Wyke (ed.), *Parchments of gender: deciphering the bodies of antiquity* (Oxford), 121–46.

Dennis, G. (1907). *The cities and cemeteries of Etruria*² (ed. W. M. Lindsay) (London).

De Rossi, G. M. (1979). *Bovillae* [Forma Italiae i. 15] (Florence).

De Sanctis, G. (1907–64). *Storia dei romani* (Turin).

——(1910). 'La leggenda della lupa e dei gemelli', *RFIC* xxxviii. 71–85.

——(1933). 'Le origini dell'ordinamento centuriato', *RFIC* xi. 289–98.

Deubner, L. (1934). 'Die Tracht des römischen Triumphators', *Hermes* lxix. 316–23.

Develin, R. (1978). '*Provocatio* and plebiscites', *Mnemosyne*, ser. 4, xxxi. 45–60.

——(1978–9). 'Religion and politics at Rome during the third century B.C.', *JRH* x. 3–19.

——(1985). *The practice of politics at Rome 366–177 B.C.* [Collection Latomus clxxxviii] (Brussels).

Diercks, G. F. (1972). *Novatiani* opera [Corpus Christianorum Series Latina iv] (Turnhout).

Dieterich, A. (1900). 'Die Widmungselegie des letzten Buches des Propertius', *RhM* n.s. lv. 191–221.

Diggle, J. (1981). *Studies on the text of Euripides* (Oxford).

——(2004). *Theophrastus* characters (Cambridge).

D'Ippolito, F. (1986). *Giuristi e sapienti in Roma arcaica* (Rome and Bari).

——(1988). 'Gli Ogulnii e il serpente di Esculapio', in G. Franciosi (ed.), *Ricerche sulla organizzazione gentilizia romana* (Naples, 1984–95), ii. 155–65.

Dittenberger, W. (1915–24). *Sylloge inscriptionum Graecarum*[3] (Leipzig).

Drummond, A. (1989). 'Rome in the fifth century', in Walbank *et al.*, 113–242.

Dulière, C. (1979). *Lupa Romana: recherche d'iconographie et essai d'interprétation* (Brussels and Rome).

Du Ruyt, F. (1982). *Alba Fucens III* (Brussels and Rome).

Dyck, A. R. (1996). *A commentary on Cicero, de officiis* (Ann Arbor).

Echols, E. (1951/2). 'Military Dust', *CJ* xlvii. 285–8.

Eck, W., Caballos, A., and Fernández, F. (1996). *Das* senatus consultum de Cn. Pisone patre [Vestigia xlviii] (Munich).

Eckstein, A. M. (1987). *Senate and general: individual decision-making and Roman foreign relations, 264–194 B.C.* (Berkeley, Los Angeles, and London).

Eder, W. (ed.) (1990). *Staat und Staatlichkeit in der frühen römischen Republik* (Stuttgart).

Elter, A. (1891). 'Vaticanum', *RhM* n.s. xlvi. 112–38.

Engelmann, W., and Preuss, S. (1880–2). *Bibliotheca scriptorum classicorum*[8] (Leipzig).

Enmann, A. (1902). 'Die älteste Redaction der Pontificalannalen', *RhM* n.s. lvii. 517–33.

Etcheto, H. (2003). '*Cognomen* et appartenance familiale dans l'aristocratie médio-républicaine: à propos de l'identité du consul patricien de 328 av. J.-C.', *Athenaeum* xci. 445–68.

Evans Grubbs, J. (1995). *Law and family in late antiquity: the emperor Constantine's marriage legislation* (Oxford).

Fabricius, E. (1932). 'Some notes on Polybius's description of Roman camps', *JRS* xxii. 78–87.

Farrell, J. (1986). 'The distinction between *comitia* and *concilium*', *Athenaeum* n.s. lxiv. 407–38.

Favuzzi, A. (1999). 'Su due frammenti storici adespoti della Suda', *AFLB* xlii. 119–27.

Fay, E. W. (1920). 'Scipionic forgeries', *CQ* xiv. 163–71.

Feldherr, A. M. (1991). *Spectacle and society in Livy's* history (Diss. Berkeley).

——(1998). *Spectacle and society in Livy's* history (Berkeley, Los Angeles, and London).

Ferenczy, E. (1965). 'La carrière d'Appius Claudius Caecus jusqu'à la censure', *Acta Antiqua* xiii. 379–404.

Bibliography

——(1976). *From the patrician to the patricio-plebeian state* (Amsterdam).

Firpo, G. (2002). 'Quale Sentino?', in Poli (2002), 95–126.

Fischer, W. (1914). *Das römische Lager insbesondere nach Livius* (Leipzig).

Fletcher, G. B. A. (1945). 'Notes on Tacitus', *AJPh* lxvi. 13–33.

——(1964). *Annotations on Tacitus* [Collection Latomus lxxi] (Brussels).

Flower, H. I. (1995). '*Fabulae praetextae* in context: when were plays on contemporary subjects performed in republican Rome?', *CQ* n.s. xlv. 170–90.

——(1996). *Ancestor masks and aristocratic power in Roman culture* (Oxford).

Fordyce, C. J. (1961). *Catullus: a commentary* (Oxford).

——(1977). *P. Vergili Maronis* Aeneidos *libri vii–viii* (Oxford).

Forni, G. (1953). 'Manio Curio Dentato uomo democratico', *Athenaeum* n.s. xxxi. 170–240.

Forsythe, G. (1994). *The historian L. Calpurnius Piso Frugi and the Roman annalistic tradition* (Lanham, MD).

——(1999). *Livy and early Rome: a study in historical method and judgement* [Historia Einzelschriften cxxxii] (Stuttgart).

Fraenkel, E. D. M. (1950). *Aeschylus* Agamemnon (Oxford).

Franco, C. (2002). 'Duride di Samo e la battaglia del Sentino', in Poli (2002), 47–62.

Frank, T. (1911). 'On Rome's conquest of Sabinum, Picenum, and Etruria', *Klio* xi. 367–81.

——(1921). 'The Scipionic inscriptions', *CQ* xv. 169–71.

Frayn, J. M. (1984). *Sheep-rearing and the wool trade* (Liverpool).

Frederiksen, M. W. (1968a). Review of Salmon (1967), *JRS* lviii. 224–9.

——(1968b). 'Campanian cavalry: a question of origins', *DdA* ii. 3–31.

——(1984). *Campania* (London).

Freudenberg, J. (1854–62). *Observationes Livianae* (Progr. Bonn).

Frier, B. W. (1999). Libri annales pontificum maximorum: *the origins of the annalistic tradition*² (Michigan).

Frigell, A. (1875). *Livianorum librorum primae decadis emendandae ratio* (Diss. Uppsala).

Friis Johansen, H., and Whittle, G. W. (1980). *Aeschylus:* the suppliants (Copenhagen).

Gagé, J. (1960). *Matronalia* [Collection Latomus lx] (Brussels).

Gaggiotti, M., Manconi, D., Mercando, L., and Verzár, M. (1980). *Umbria, Marche* [Guide archeologiche Laterza iv] (Rome and Bari).

Gardner, J. F. (1986). *Women in Roman law and society* (London and Sydney).

Garofalo, L. (1989). *Il processo edilizio* [Pubblicazioni della Facoltà di Giurisprudenza dell'Università di Padova cxii] (Padua).

Garrucci, R. (1885). *Le monete dell'Italia antica* (Roma).

Garzetti, A. (1947). 'Appio Claudio Cieco nella storia politica del suo tempo', *Athenaeum* n.s. xxv. 175–224 = (1996) 19–62.

——(1996). *Scritti di storia repubblicana e augustea* (Rome).

Bibliography

Gatti, S., and Onorati, M. T. (1991). 'Carsioli: annotazioni topografiche', in AA.VV., *Il Fucino e le aree limitrofe nell'antichità* (Rome), 442–7.

Geist, [H.] (1877). 'Livius ix, 45, 13', 'Livius ix, 13, 9', 'Livius x, 16, 6', 'Livius x, 19, 18', *BBG* xiii. 257–9.

Gelzer, M. (1933). 'Römische Politik bei Fabius Pictor', *Hermes* lxviii. 129–66 = (1962–4) iii. 51–92.

——(1934). 'Der Anfang römischer Geschichtsschreibung', *Hermes* lxix. 46–55 = (1962–4) iii. 93–103.

——(1954). 'Nochmals über den Anfang der römischen Geschichtsschreibung', *Hermes* lxxxii. 342–8 = (1962–4) 104–10.

——(1962–4). *Kleine Schriften* (edd. H. Strasburger and C. Meier) (Wiesbaden).

Gemoll, W. (1890–8). *Kritische Bemerkungen zu lateinischen Schriftstellern* (Progr. Liegnitz).

Giannelli, C. A. (1974). 'Gli interventi di Cleonimo e di Agatocle in Magna Grecia', *CS* xi. 353–80.

Giannetti, A. (1973). 'Mura ciclopiche in S. Vittore del Lazio (Colle Marena-Falascosa): probabile identificazione del sito dell'antica Aquilonia', *RAL* xxviii. 101–12.

Giers, A. (1862). *Observationes Livianae* (Diss. Bonn).

Giuffrè, V. (1970). '"Plebeii gentes non habent"', *Labeo* xvi. 329–34.

Goldsworthy, A. K. (1996). *The Roman army at war 100 BC–AD 200* (Oxford).

González, J. (1986). 'The lex Irnitana: a new copy of the Flavian municipal law', *JRS* lxxvi. 147–243.

Goodyear, F. R. D. (1981). *The annals of Tacitus books 1–6, volume II: annals 1. 55–81 and annals 2* (Cambridge).

Gow, A. S. F., and Page, D. L. (1965). *The Greek anthology: Hellenistic epigrams* (Cambridge).

Graeven, H. (1901). 'Die thönerne Sparbüchse im Altertum', *Jahrbuch des Kaiserlich Deutschen Archäologischen Instituts* xvi. 160–89.

Griffin, M. T. (1986). 'Philosophy, Cato, and Roman suicide: II', *GR* xxxiii. 192–202.

Griffith, M. (1998). 'The king and the eye: the rule of the father in Greek tragedy', *PCPhS* xliv. 20–84.

Grodzynski, D. (1974). '*Superstitio*', *REA* lxxvi. 36–60.

Grossi, G. (1984). *Insediamenti italici nel Cicolano: territorio della 'res publica Aequicolanorum'* (L'Aquila).

Gruen, E. S. (1992). *Culture and national identity in republican Rome* (Ithaca, NY, and London).

Guarino, A. (1975). *La rivoluzione della plebe* (Napoli).

Gudeman, A. (1914). *P. Cornelii Taciti dialogus de oratoribus²* (Leipzig).

Gundermann, G. (1888). 'Quaestiones de Iuli Frontini strategematon libris', *NJPhP* Suppl. xvi. 315–71.

Haehling, R. von (1989). *Zeitbezüge des T. Livius in der ersten Dekade seines*

Geschichtswerkes: nec vitia nostra nec remedia pati possumus [Historia Einzelschriften lxi] (Stuttgart).

Häggström, F. W. (1874). *Excerpta Liviana* (Uppsala).

Hajdú, I. (1999). *'pro consule* oder *proconsul?'*, *MusHelv* lvi. 119–27.

Halfmann, H. (1986). Itinera principum*: Geschichte und Typologie der Kaiserreisen im römischen Reich* [Heidelberger althistorische Beiträge und epigraphische Studien ii] (Stuttgart).

Halkin, L. (1953). *La Supplication d'action de grâces chez les Romains* [Publ. Fac. Philos. Univ. de Liège cxxviii] (Paris).

Harant, A. (1880). *Emendationes et adnotationes ad Titum Livium* (Paris).

Harris, W. V. (1971). *Rome in Etruria and Umbria* (Oxford).

——(1979). *War and imperialism in republican Rome 327–70 B.C.* (Oxford).

——(1990). 'Roman warfare in the economic and social context of the fourth century B.C.', in Eder (1990) 494–510.

Hartel, G. (1868–71). *S. Thasci Caeciliani Cypriani* opera omnia [Corpus Scriptorum Ecclesiasticorum Latinorum iii] (Vienna).

Haupt, M. (1842). 'Livius', *RhM* n.s. i. 474.

——(1850). 'Verbesserungen zum Livius aus Randbemerkungen von Reiz mitgetheilt', *Berichte sächs. Gesellschaft der Wissenschaften*, phil.-hist. Klasse ii. 101–5 = (1875–6) i. 305–9.

——(1875–6). *Opuscula* (Leipzig).

Häussler, R. (1965). *Tacitus und das historische Bewußtsein* (Heidelberg).

Hell, N. (1870). *Observationes Livianae* (Diss. Marburg).

Hellegouarc'h, J. (1963). *Le Vocabulaire latin des relations et des partis politiques sous la république* (Paris).

Henderson, M. I. (1957). *'Potestas regia'*, *JRS* xlvii. 82–7.

——(1962). Review of P. G. Walsh, *Livy: his historical aims and methods*, *JRS* li. 277–8.

Henzen, W. (1874). *Acta fratrum Arvalium quae supersunt* (Berlin).

Heraeus, (K.) W. (1885). *Quaestiones criticae et palaeographicae de vetustissimis codicibus Livianis* (Diss. Berlin).

——(1893). Review of Luterbacher's edns of Livy books ix and x, *WKlPh* x. 77–9.

——(1901). Review of M. Müller's edition of books vii–x, *WKlPh* xviii. 375–8.

——(1933). 'Ein Textproblem in einem Zwölftafelgesetz', *RhM* n.s. lxxxii. 315–24.

Herzog, E. (1884–91). *Geschichte und System der römischen Staatsverfassung* (Leipzig).

Heubner, H. (1963–84). *P. Cornelius Tacitus* Die Historien (Heidelberg).

Heurgon, J. (1964). *Daily life of the Etruscans* [trans. J. Kirkup from *La Vie quotidienne chez les Étrusques*] (London).

——(1970). *Recherches sur l'histoire, la religion et la civilisation de Capoue préromaine*² (Paris).

Heuss, A. (1944). 'Zur Entwicklung des Imperiums der römischen

Oberbeamten', *ZSS* lxiv. 57–133.

Hickson, F. V. (1993). *Roman prayer language: Livy and the* Aeneid *of Vergil* [Beiträge zur Altertumskunde xxx] (Stuttgart).

Hofmann, J. B. (1951). *Lateinische Umgangssprache*[3] (Heidelberg).

Holford-Strevens, L. A. (2003). *Aulus Gellius: an Antonine scholar and his achievement*, rev. edn. (Oxford).

Hölkeskamp, K.-J. (1987). *Die Entstehung der Nobilität* (Stuttgart).

——(1988*a*). 'Das *plebiscitum Ogulnium de sacerdotibus*: Überlegungen zu Authentizät und Interpretation der livianischen Überlieferung', *RhM* n.s. cxxxi. 51–67.

——(1988*b*). 'Die Entstehung der Nobilität und der Funktionswandel des Volkstribunats: die historische Bedeutung der *lex Hortensia de plebiscitis*', *Archiv für Kulturgeschichte* lxx. 271–312 = (2004) 49–83.

——(1993). 'Conquest, competition, and consensus: Roman expansion in Italy and the rise of the *nobilitas*', *Historia* xlii. 12–39 = (2004) 11–48.

——(1999). 'Römische gentes und griechische Genealogien', in G. Vogt-Spira and B. Rommel (edd.), *Rezeption und Identität* (Stuttgart), 3–21.

——(2004). *Senatus populusque Romanus: die politische Kultur der Republik — Dimensionen und Deutungen* (Stuttgart).

Hollemann, A. W. J. (1987). 'The Ogulnii monument at Rome', *Mnemosyne*, ser. 4, xl. 427–9.

Holzapfel, L. (1902). 'Die drei ältesten römischen Tribus', *Klio* i. 228–55.

Hopkinson, N. (1984). *Callimachus* Hymn to Demeter (Cambridge).

Horden, P., and Purcell, N. (2000). *The corrupting sea* (Oxford and Malden, MA).

Housman, A. E. (1907). 'Corrections and explanations of Martial', *JPh* xxx. 229–65 = (1972) ii. 711–39.

——(1972). *Classical papers*, ed. J. Diggle and F. R. D. Goodyear (Cambridge).

Howell, P. (1980). *A commentary on book 1 of the epigrams of Martial* (London).

Hubeaux, J. (1950). 'Ratumena', *BAB* (5ᵉ Série) xxxvi. 341–53.

Humbert, M. (1978). Municipium *et* civitas sine suffragio*: l'organisation de la conquête jusqu'à la guerre sociale* [CEFR xxxvi] (Rome).

——(1988). 'Le tribunat de la plèbe et le tribunal du peuple: remarques sur l'histoire de la *prouocatio ad populum*', *MEFRA* c. 431–503.

Humm, M. (1996). 'Appius Claudius Caecus et la construction de la *Via Appia*', *MEFRA* cviii. 693–746.

——(1999). 'Le comitium du forum romain et la réforme des tribus d'Appius Claudius Caecus', *MEFRA* cxi. 625–94.

——(2001). 'Le figure d'Appius Claudius Caecus chez Tite-Live', in Briquel and Thuillier (2001), 65–96.

Hunt, R. W., and Mare, A. C. de la (1970). *Duke Humfrey and English humanism: catalogue of an exhibition held in the Bodleian Library* (Oxford).

Huschke, G. P. E. (1838). *Die Verfassung des Königs Servius Tullius* (Heidelberg).

Ihm, M. (1898). 'Die arretinischen Töpfereien', *BJ* cii. 106–26.

Innocenti Prosdocimi, E. (1980/1). 'Sull'elogio di Scipione Barbato', *AISF* ii. 1–23.

Jacobelli, M. (1970). *La valle di Comino* (Rome).

Jacoby, F. (1949). *Atthis: the local chronicles of ancient Athens* (Oxford).

Jaeger, M. K. (1997). *Livy's written Rome* (Ann Arbor).

——(1999). 'Guiding metaphor and narrative point of view in Livy's *ab urbe condita*', in Kraus (1999) 169–95.

Jahn, J. (1970). *Interregnum und Wahldiktatur* [Frankfurter Althistorische Studien iii].

Jahn, O. (1853). *T. Livi ab urbe condita librorum cxlii periochae. Iulii Obsequentis ab anno urbis conditae DV prodigiorum liber* (Leipzig).

Janssen, L. F. (1979). '*Superstitio* and persecution', *VigChrist* xxxiii. 131–59.

Jashemski, W. F. (1950). 'The origins and history of the proconsular and propraetorian imperium to 27 B.C.' (Diss. Chicago).

Johner, A. (1990). 'Camille, Manlius et la fondation de Juno Moneta chez Tite-Live: légende de temple et doublet symbolique au livre vii', *Ktèma* xv. 217–23.

Jolowicz, H. F., and Nicholas, B. (1972). *Historical introduction to the study of Roman law*[3] (Cambridge).

Jones, A. H. M. (1972). *The criminal courts of the Roman Republic and Principate* (Oxford).

Josephson, A. (1955). *Die Columella-Handschriften* (Uppsala and Wiesbaden).

Kajava, M. (1998). 'Visceratio', *Arctos* xxxii. 109–31.

Kaster, R. A. (1995). *Suetonius de grammaticis et rhetoribus* (Oxford).

Kenney, E. J. (1971). *Lucretius de rerum natura book iii* (Cambridge).

Keppie, L. J. F. (1984). *The making of the Roman army: from Republic to Empire* (London).

Kiepert, H. (1894–1910). *Forma orbis antiqui* (Berlin).

Kissel, W. (1982). 'Livius 1933–78: eine Gesamtbibliographie', *ANRW* xxx. 2. 899–997.

Klinger, G. (1884). *De decimi Livii libri fontibus* (Diss. Leipzig).

Kloft, H. (1977). *Prorogation und außerordentliche Imperien 326–81 v. Chr.: Untersuchung zur Verfassung der römischen Republik* [Beiträge zur Klassischen Philologie lxxxiv] (Meisenheim am Glan).

Klotz, A. (1937). 'Diodors römische Annalen', *RhM* n.s. lxxxvi. 206–24.

——(1938). 'Zu den Quellen der Archaiologia des Dionysios von Halikarnassos', *RhM* n.s. lxxxvii. 32–50.

——(1940–1). *Livius und seiner Vorgänger* (Leipzig and Berlin).

Klussmann, R. (1909–13). *Bibliotheca scriptorum classicorum et Graecorum et Latinorum* (Leipzig).

Bibliography

Knapp, R. C. (1980). 'Festus 262L and *praefecturae* in Italy', *Athenaeum* n.s. lviii. 14–38.

Koch, A. (1861). *Emendationum Livianarum pars altera* (Progr. Brandenburg).

Koehler, U. (1860). *Qua ratione T. Livii annalibus usi sint historici Latini atque Graeci* (Diss. Göttingen).

Koesters, H. (1893). *Quaestiones metricae et prosodiacae ad Valerium Flaccum pertinentes* (Diss. Marburg).

Kornemann, E. (1911). 'Die älteste Form der Pontifikalannalen', *Klio* xi. 245–57.

——(1912). *Der Priestercodex in der Regia und die Entstehung der altrömischen Pseudogeschichte* (Tübingen).

Kornhardt, H. (1936). Exemplum: *eine bedeutungsgeschichtliche Studie* (Diss. Göttingen).

Kraus, C. S. (1992). 'How (not) to end a sentence: the problem of *-que*', *HSCPh* xciv. 321–9.

——(1998). 'Repetition and empire in the *ab urbe condita*', in P. E. Knox and C. Foss (edd.), *Style and tradition: studies in honor of Wendell Clausen* (Stuttgart and Leipzig), 264–83.

——(ed.) (1999). *The limits of historiography: genre and narrative in ancient historical texts* [Mnemosyne Suppl. cxci] (Leiden, Boston, and Cologne).

Krauss, F. B. (1930). *An interpretation of the omens, portents, and prodigies recorded by Livy, Tacitus, and Suetonius* (Diss. Philadelphia).

Krebs, J. P., and Schmalz, J. H. (1905–7). *Antibarbarus der lateinischen Sprache*[7] (Basle and Stuttgart).

Kromayer, J., and Veith, G. (1928). *Heerwesen und Kriegführung der Griechen und Römer* (Munich).

Kühnast, L. (1872). *Die Hauptpunkte der livianischen Syntax* (Berlin).

Kühner, R., and Gerth, B. (1898–1904). *Ausführliche Grammatik der griechischen Sprache*[3] (Hanover and Leipzig).

Kunkel, W. (1962). *Untersuchungen zur Entwicklung des römischen Kriminalverfahrens in vorsullanischer Zeit* (Munich).

Lachmann, F. (1822–8). *De fontibus historiarum T. Livii* (Göttingen).

Lambrino, S. (1951). *Bibliographie de l'antiquité classique* (Paris).

Landgraf, G. (1914). *Kommentar zu Ciceros Rede* pro Sex. Roscio Amerino[2] (Leipzig and Berlin).

Lange, L. (1863–76). *Römische Alterthümer* (vols. i[3], ii–iii[2]) (Berlin).

Langen, P. (1896–7). *C. Valeri Flacci Setini Balbi Argonauticon libri octo* (Berlin).

Langslow, D. R. (1999). 'The language of poetry and the language of science: the Latin poets and medical Latin', in J. N. Adams and R. G. Mayer (edd.), *Aspects of the language of Latin poetry* [*PBA* xciii] (Oxford), 183–226.

La Regina, A. (1968). 'L'elogio di Scipione Barbato', *DdA* ii. 173–90.

——(1975). 'Centri fortificati preromani nei territori sabellici dell'Italia centrale adriatica', *Posebna izdanja*, 24. 271–82.

——(1989). 'I Sanniti', in C. Ampolo *et al.*, *Italia* (Milan), 301–432.

Last, H. M. (1949). 'Rome and the druids: a note', *JRS* xxxix. 1–5.

Latte, K. (1936). 'Zwei Excurse zum römischen Staatsrecht', *NGG* n.s. 1. 59–77 = (1968) 341–58.

——(1960a). *Römische Religionsgeschichte* (Munich).

——(1960b). 'Der Historiker L. Calpurnius Frugi', *SDAWB* vii. 1–16 = (1968) 837–47.

——(1968). *Kleine Schriften zu Religion, Recht, Literatur und Sprache der Griechen und Römer* (Munich).

Laurence, R. M. (2004). 'The economic exploitation of geological resources in the Tiber valley: road building', in H. Patterson (ed.), *Bridging the Tiber: approaches to regional archaeology in the middle Tiber valley* [Archaeological Monographs of the British School at Rome xiii] (London), 285–95.

Lease, E. B. (1928). 'The ablative absolute limited by conjunctions', *AJPh* xlix. 348–53.

Le Bonniec, H. (1958). *Le Culte de Cérès à Rome des origines à la fin de la République* (Paris).

Leigh, M. (1997). *Lucan: spectacle and engagement* (Oxford).

Lejay, P. (1920). 'Appius Claudius Caecus', *RPh* xiv. 92–141.

Leumann, M. (1977). *Lateinische Laut- und Formenlehre* (Munich).

Leutsch, E. von (1855). 'Zu Livius', *Philologus* x. 125.

Leuze, O. (1912). *Zur Geschichte der römischen Censur* (Halle).

Levene, D. S. (1993). *Religion in Livy* [Mnemosyne Suppl. cxxvii] (Leiden).

Liebeschuetz, J. H. W. G. (1979). *Continuity and change in Roman religion* (Oxford).

Linders, T. (1987). 'Gods, gifts, society', in T. Linders and G. Nordquist (edd.), *Gifts to the gods* (Uppsala), 115–22.

Linderski, J. (1985). 'The *libri reconditi*', *HSCPh* lxxxix. 207–34 = (1995) 496–23.

——(1986). 'The augural law', *ANRW* II. 16. 3. 2146–312.

——(1989). 'Sannio and Remus', *Mnemosyne*, ser. 4, xlii. 90–3 = (1995) 527–30.

——(1990). 'The auspices and the Struggle of the Orders', in Eder (1990) 34–48 = (1995) 560–74.

——(1993). 'Roman religion in Livy', in W. Schuller (ed.) *Livius: Aspekte seines Werkes* [Xenia xxxi] (Konstanz, 1993) 53–70 = (1995) 608–25.

——(1995). *Roman questions: selected papers* (Stuttgart).

——(ed.) (1996). Imperium sine fine: *T. R. S. Broughton and the Roman Republic* [Historia Einzelschriften cv (Stuttgart)].

Lintott, A. W. (1968). *Violence in the Roman Republic* (Oxford).

——(1972). 'Provocatio', *ANRW* i. 2. 226–67.

——(1992). *Judicial reform and land reform in the Roman Republic* (Cambridge).

Bibliography

Lintott, A. W. (1999). *The constitution of the Roman Republic* (Oxford).

Lipovsky, J. P. (1981). *A historiographical study of Livy books vi–x* (New York).

Löfstedt, E. (1911). *Philologischer Kommentar zur* peregrinatio Aetheriae*: Untersuchungen zur Geschichte der lateinischen Sprache* (Uppsala).

Loreto, L. (1989–90). 'La riforma romana della leva a partire dal 318 a.C.', *BIDR* xcii–xciii. 617–24.

——(1991*a*). 'Due note di storia romana medio-repubblicana', *AFLS* xii. 281–92.

——(1991*b*). 'Sui meccanismi della lotta politica a Roma tra il 314 e il 294 a.C.', *AFLM* xxiv. 61–76.

——(1991–2). 'È scoppiata la guerra coi Romani: i meccanismi delle decisioni di politica internazionale e delle decisioni militari a Roma nella media repubblica (327–265 a.C.)', *BIDR* xciv–xcv. 197–287.

——(1992–3). 'Aspetti dell'ideologia del ceto magistratuale-senatorio a Roma tra il 326 e il 264 a.C.', *Annali della Facoltà di Lettere e Filosofia dell'Università di Macerata* xxv–xxvi. 329–59.

——(1993). *Un'epoca di buon senso: decisione, consenso e stato a Roma tra il 326 e il 264 a.C.* (Amsterdam).

Lovisi, C. (1999). *Contribution à l'étude de la peine de mort sous la République romaine (509–149 av. J.-C.)* (Paris).

Lübtow, U. von (1955). *Das römische Volk: sein Staat und sein Recht* (Frankfurt am Main).

Luce, T. J. (1977). *Livy: the composition of his history* (Princeton).

——(1999). Review of vol. i of this commentary, *CR* n.s. xlix. 74–6.

Luterbacher, F. (1904). *Der Prodigienglaube und Prodigienstil der Römer*[2] (Burgdorf).

MacBain, B. (1980). 'Appius Claudius Caecus and the Via Appia', *CQ* n.s. xxx. 356–72.

McDonald, A. H. (1965). *Titi Livi* ab urbe condita *libri xxxi–xxxv* (Oxford).

Maddox, G. (1984). 'The binding plebiscite', in AA.VV. (1984), i. 85–95.

Madvig, J. N. (1860). *Emendationes Livianae* (Copenhagen).

——(1871–84). *Adversaria critica* (Copenhagen).

——(1877). *Emendationes Livianae*[2] (Copenhagen).

Magdelain, A. (1968). *Recherches sur l'"imperium": la loi curiate et les auspices d'investiture* (Paris).

——(1990). *Jus Imperium Auctoritas: études de droit romain* [CEFR cxxxiii] (Rome).

Maggiani, A. (1986). 'Cilnium genus', *SE* liv. 171–96.

Maiuri, A. (1926). 'Saepinum', *NSc*, ser. 6, ii. 244–51.

Malcovati, H. (1975). *Oratorum Romanorum fragmenta*[4] (Turin).

Maltby, R. (1991). *A lexicon of ancient Latin etymologies* [ARCA xxv] (Leeds).

Mancini, G. (1921). 'Regione I', *NSc*, ser. 5, 73–141.

Mangani, E., Rebecchi, F., and Strazzulla, M. J. (1981). *Emilia, Venezie* [Guide archeologiche Laterza ii] (Rome and Bari).

Bibliography

Marasco, G. (1980). *Sparta agli inizi dell'età ellenistica: il regno di Areo I (309/8—265/4 a.C.)* (Florence).

——(2002). 'La terza guerra sannitica e la Magna Grecia', in Poli (2002) 127–38.

Marchio, S. (ed.) (1996). *I manoscritti della Biblioteca Capitolare di Verona: catalogo descrittivo redatto da don Antonio Spagnolo* (Verona).

Marcotte, D. (1985). '*Lucaniae*: considérations sur l'*Éloge de Scipion Barbatus*', *Latomus* xliv. 721–42.

Mare, A. C. de la (2000). 'A Livy copied by Giacomo Curlo dismembered by Otto Ege', in L. C. Brownrigg and M. M. Smith (edd.), *Interpreting and collecting fragments of medieval books* (Los Altos Hills, CA, and London), 57–76.

—— and Barker-Benfield, B. C. (1980). *Manuscripts at Oxford: an exhibition in memory of Richard William Hunt (1908–1979)* (Oxford).

Marincola, J. (1997). *Authority and tradition in ancient historiography* (Cambridge).

Marouzeau, J. (1927–8). *Dix années de bibliographie classique* (Paris).

Marquardt, J. (1881–5). *Römische Staatsverwaltung*² (Leipzig).

——(1886). *Das Privatleben der Römer*² (revised by A. Mau) (Leipzig).

Marshall, A. J. (1984). 'Symbols and showmanship in Roman public life: the fasces', *Phoenix* xxxviii. 120–41.

Martin, J. (1970). 'Die Provokation in der klassischen und späten Republik', *Hermes* xcviii. 72–96.

Martin, R. H., and Woodman, A. J. (1989). *Tacitus* annals *iv* (Cambridge).

Massa-Pairault, F.-H. (1995). '"Eques Romanus — eques Latinus" (v^e–ive siècle)', *MEFRA* cvii. 33–70.

——(2001). 'Relations d'Appius Claudius Caecus avec l'Étrurie et la Campanie', in Briquel and Thuillier (2001), 97–116.

Matthaei, L. E. (1908). 'The place of arbitration and mediation in the ancient systems of international ethics', *CQ* ii. 241–64.

Mattingly, H. (1945). 'The first age of Roman coinage', *JRS* xxxv. 65–77.

—— *et al.* (1923–). *The Roman imperial coinage* (London).

Maxfield, V. A. (1981). *The military decorations of the Roman army* (London).

Mazzarino, S. (1966). *Il pensiero storico* (Bari).

Meadows, A., and Williams, J. H. C. (2001). 'Moneta and the monuments: coinage and politics in republican Rome', *JRS* xci. 27–49.

Merguet, H. (1887–94). *Lexicon zu den philosophischen Schriften des Cicero* (Jena).

Mertens, J. (1969). *Alba Fucens I–II* (Brussels and Rome).

Miles, G. B. (1988). '*Maiores, conditores*, and Livy's perspective on the past', *TAPhA* cxviii. 185–208 = (1995) 110–36.

——(1995). *Livy: reconstructing early Rome* (Ithaca and London).

Millar, F. G. B. (1964). *A study of Cassius Dio* (Oxford).

——(1989). 'Political power in mid-republican Rome: curia or comitium?', *JRS* lxxix. 138–50 = (2002) 85–108.

Bibliography

Millar, F. G. B. (2002). *The Roman Republic and the Augustan Revolution* (Chapel Hill and London).

Momigliano, A. D. (1963). 'An interim report on the origins of Rome', *JRS* liii. 95–121 = (1966a) 545–98 = (1989b) 73–113.

——(1966a). *Terzo contributo alla storia degli studi classici e del mondo antico* (Rome).

——(1966b). 'Procum patricium', *JRS* lvi. 16–24 = (1969) 377–94 = (1989b) 73–113.

——(1969). *Quarto contributo alla storia degli studi classici e del mondo antico* (Rome).

——(1984). *Settimo contributo alla storia degli studi classici e del mondo antico* (Rome).

——(1989a). 'The origins of Rome', in Walbank *et al.* (1989) 52–112 = (1984) 379–436.

——(1989b). *Roma arcaica* (Florence).

Mommsen, T. (1857). 'Zu Festus', *RhM* n.s. xii. 467–70 and 633–4 = (1904–13) vii. 280–2.

——(1859). *Die römische Chronologie*² (Berlin).

——(1860). 'Die römischen Eigennamen', *RhM* n.s. xv. 169–210 = (1864–79) i. 1–68.

——(1864–79). *Römische Forschungen* (Berlin).

——(1866). 'Zu Livius', *Hermes* i. 129–30 = (1905–13) vii. 161–2.

——(1868). 'Heroldstab von Thurii', *Hermes* iii. 298–9.

——(1887–8). *Römisches Staatsrecht*³ (Leipzig).

——(1894–5). *The history of Rome*² [trans. W. P. Dickson from *Römische Geschichte*] (London).

——(1899). *Römisches Strafrecht* (Leipzig).

——(1905–13). *Gesammelte Schriften* (Berlin).

Moore, T. J. (1989). *Artistry and ideology: Livy's vocabulary of virtue* [Beiträge zur klassischen Philologie cxcii] (1989).

Morgan, M. G. (1972). 'The defeat of L. Metellus Denter at Arretium', *CQ* n.s. xxii. 309–25.

Mouritsen, H. (2001). *Plebs and politics in the late Roman Republic* (Cambridge).

Müller, C. F. W. (1865). Review of F. Neue, *Formenlehre der lateinischen Sprache*, *NJPhP* xci. 45–54.

Müller, H. J. (1884). 'Livius', *JPhV* x. 80–109.

——(1889a). 'Zu Livius', *ZGW* xliii. 434–6.

——(1889b). 'Zu Livius', *ZGW* xliii. 256.

——(1889c). 'Livius', *JPhV* xv. 1–64.

——(1890). 'Livius', *JPhV* xvi. 153–236.

——(1891). 'Livius', *JPhV* xvii. 160–91.

——(1899). 'Livius', *JPhV* xxv. 1–28.

Munro, H. A. J. (1866). *T. Lucreti Cari de rerum natura libri sex*² (Cambridge).

Münzer, F. (1891). *De gente Valeria* (Diss. Berlin).
——(1999). *Roman aristocratic parties and families* [trans. T. Ridley from *Römische Adelsparteien und Adelsfamilien*] (Baltimore and London).
Mustakallio, K. (1994). *Death and disgrace: capital penalties with* post mortem *sanctions in early Roman historiography* (Helsinki).
Mynors, R. A. B. (1990). *Virgil georgics* (Oxford).
Naso, A. (2000). *I Piceni* (Milan).
Nettleship, H. (1889). *Contributions to Latin lexicography* (Oxford).
Neue, F., and Wagener, C. (1892–1905). *Formenlehre der lateinischen Sprache³* (Leipzig).
Niccolini, G. (1932). *Il tribunato della plebe* (Milan).
——(1934). *I fasti dei tribuni della plebe* (Milan).
Nicolet, C. (1980). *The world of the citizen in republican Rome* [trans. P. S. Falla from *Le Métier de citoyen dans la Rome républicaine* (1976)] (London).
Niebuhr, B. G. (1837–44). *The history of Rome* [trans. J. C. Hare, C. Thirlwall, W. Smith, and L. Schmitz from *Römische Geschichte*] (London).
Niemeyer, H. J. (1890). 'Zu Livius', *NJPhP* cxli. 707–12.
Nisbet, R. G. (1923). '*Voluntas fati* in Latin syntax', *AJPh* xliv. 27–43.
——(1939). *M. Tulli Ciceronis de domo sua ad pontifices oratio* (Oxford).
Nisbet, R. G. M. (1978). '*Felicitas* at Surrentum (Statius, *silvae* 2. 2)', *JRS* lxviii. 1–11 5 = (1995) 29–46.
——(1995). *Collected papers on Latin literature* (Oxford).
——and Hubbard, M. E. (1970). *A commentary on Horace:* odes book I (Oxford).
————(1978). *A commentary on Horace:* odes book II (Oxford).
——and Rudd, N. (2004). *A commentary on Horace,* odes book III (Oxford).
Nissen, H. (1883–1902). *Italische Landeskunde* (Berlin).
North, J. A. (1981). 'The development of Roman imperialism', *JRS* lxxi. 1–9.
Northwood, S. J. (2000). 'Livy and the early annalists', in C. Deroux (ed.), *Studies in Latin literature and Roman history x* [Collection Latomus ccliv] (Brussels), 45–55.
Novák, R. (1894). *Mluvnicko-kritická studia k Liviovi* (Prague).
Oakley, S. P. (1983). Review of P. G. Walsh (ed.), *T. Livius, libri xxvi–xxvii, CR* n.s. xxxiii. 215–18.
——(1985). 'Single combat in the Roman Republic', *CQ* n.s. xxxv. 392–410.
——(1993). 'The Roman conquest of Italy', in J. W. Rich and G. Shipley (edd.), *War and society in the Roman world* (London and New York), 9–37.
——(1995). *The hill-forts of the Samnites* [Archaeological Monographs of the British School at Rome x] (London).
Ogilvie, R. M. (1957). 'The manuscript tradition of Livy's first decade', *CQ* n.s. vii. 68–81.

Bibliography

Ogilvie, R. M. (1961). 'Lustrum condere', *JRS* li. 31–9.

——(1965). *A commentary on Livy books 1–5* (Oxford).

——(1968). Review of Salmon (1967), *CR* n.s. xviii. 330–2.

——(1970). 'Addenda' to (1965) (pp. 775–86).

Olson, S. D. (2002). *Aristophanes* Acharnians (Oxford).

O'Neill, 'Going round in circles: popular speech in ancient Rome', *ClassAnt* xxii. 135–65.

Opelt, I. (1965). *Die lateinischen Schimpfwörter und verwandte sprachliche Erscheinungen* (Heidelberg).

Orlin, E. M. (1997). *Temples, religion and politics in the Roman Republic* [Mnemosyne Suppl. clxiv] (Leiden, New York, and Cologne).

Ormerod, H. A. (1924). *Piracy in the ancient world: an essay in Mediterranean history* (Liverpool and London).

Otto, A. (1890). *Die Sprichwörter und sprichwörtlichen Redensarten der Römer* (Leipzig).

Paananen, U. (1993). 'Legislation in the *comitia centuriata*', in AA.VV. (1993), 9–73.

Pabst, W. (1969). *Quellenkritische Studien zur inneren römischen Geschichte der älteren Zeit bei T. Livius und Dionys von Halikarnass* (Diss. Innsbruck).

Pächt, O., and Alexander, J. J. G. (1966–73). *Illuminated manuscripts in the Bodleian Library, Oxford* (Oxford).

Packard, D. W. (1968). *A concordance to Livy* (Cambridge, MA).

Pais, E. (1908). *Ricerche storiche e geografiche sull'Italia antica* (Turin).

Palmer, R. E. A. (1974). 'Roman shrines of female chastity from the caste struggle to the papacy of Innocent I', *RSA* iv. 113–59.

——(1990). Review of Coarelli (1988), *JRA* iii. 234–44.

Pasqualini, A. (1966). 'Isernia', *Quaderni dell'Istituto di Topografia Antica* ii. 79—84.

Patterson, J. R. (1985). 'A city called Samnium?', in R. Hodges and J. Mitchell (edd.), *San Vincenzo al Volturno: the archaeology, art and territory of an early medieval monastry* [BAR International Series cclii] (Oxford), 185–99.

——(1988). *Sanniti, Liguri e Romani/Samnites, Ligurians and Romans* (Circello).

Paul, G. M. (1984). *A historical commentary on Sallust's* bellum Jugurthinum (Liverpool).

Pavolini, C. (1988). *Ostia* [Guide archeologiche Laterza viii] (Rome and Bari).

Pease, A. S. (1920–3). *M. Tulli Ciceronis* de divinatione [University of Illinois Studies in Language and Literature vi. 2, 3; viii. 2, 3] (Urbana).

Pelling, C. B. R. (1997). *Plutarco:* Filopemene, Tito Flaminino (Milan).

——(1999). 'Epilogue', in Kraus (1999) 325–57.

Perl, G. (1964). 'Der Anfang der römischen Geschichtsschreibung', *F&F* xxxviii. 185–9, 213–18.

Perthes, H. (1863). *Quaestiones Livianae* (Bonn).

Peter, H. (1906–14). *Historicorum Romanorum reliquiae* [vol. i, 2nd edn.] (Leipzig).

Petersen, E. (1908). 'Lupa capitolina', *Klio* viii. 440–56.

——(1909). 'Lupa capitolina II', *Klio* ix. 29–47.

Pettersson, O. (1930). *Commentationes Livianae* (Uppsala).

Petzold, G. (1993). 'Zur Geschichte der römischen Annalistik', in Schuller (1993) 151–88.

Pfeiffer, G. J., and Ashby, T. (1905). 'Carsioli: a description of the site and the Roman remains, with historical notes and a bibliography', *Supplementary Papers of the American School at Rome* i. 108–40.

Pfiffig, A. J. (1968). 'Das Verhalten Etruriens im Samniterkrieg und nachher bis zum 1. Punischen Krieg', *Historia* xvii. 307–50.

Phillips, J. E. (1974*a*). 'Verbs compounded with *trans*- in Livy's triumph reports', *CPh* lxix. 54–5.

——(1974*b*). 'Form and language in Livy's triumph notices', *CPh* lxix. 265–73.

Plathner, H. G. (1934). *Die Schlachtschilderungen bei Livius* (Diss. Breslau).

Platner, S. B., and Ashby, T. (1929). *A topographical dictionary of ancient Rome* (Oxford).

Pohl, I. (1983). 'Was early Ostia a colony or a fort?', *PP* xxxviii. 123–30.

Poli, D. (ed.) (2002). *La battaglia del Sentino: scontro fra nazioni e incontro in una nazione* [Quaderni linguistici e filologici xiv] (Rome).

Poma, G. (1995). 'Su Livio vii, 17, 6: dictator primus e plebe', *RSA* xxv. 71–90.

Poucet, J. (1967). *Recherches sur la légende sabine des origines de Rome* (Kinshasa).

Powell, J. G. F. (1988). *Cicero:* Cato maior de senectute (Cambridge).

Purcell, N. (1983). 'The *apparitores*: a study in social mobility', *PBSR* n.s. xxxviii. 125–73.

Raaflaub, K. A. (1996). 'Born to be wolves? Origins of Roman imperialism', in Wallace and Harris (1996), 273–314.

—— Richard, J. D., and Samons, S. J. (1992). 'Rome, Italy and Appius Claudius Caecus before the Pyrrhic Wars', in T. Hackens, N. D. Holloway, R. R. Holloway, and G. Moucharte (edd.), *The age of Pyrrhus* [Archeologia Transatlantica xi] (Providence and Louvain-la-Neuve), 13–50.

Radin, M. (1914). 'Gens, familia, stirps', *CPh* ix. 235–47.

Radke, G. (1991). 'Beobachtungen zum Elogium auf L. Cornelius Scipio Barbatus', *RhM* n.s. cxxxiv. 69–79.

Raimondi, M. (1995*a*). 'I discorsi di Caio Mario nel 107 a.C. (Sall. *Jug.* 85) e di M. Valerio Corvino nel 343 v (Liv. VII 32)', *Aevum* lxix. 95–100.

——(1995*b*). 'Fabio Rulliano in Liv. 10, 13: *legem recitari iussit, qua intra decem annos eundem consulem refici non liceret*', *InvLuc* xvii. 149–58.

Rawson, E. D. (1975). 'Caesar's heritage: Hellenistic kings and their Roman equals', *JRS* lxv. 148–59 = (1991) 169–88.

Rawson, E. D. (1976). 'The first Latin annalists', *Latomus* xxxv. 689–717 = (1991) 245–71.

——(1981). 'Chariot-racing in the Roman Republic', *PBSR* xlix. 1–16 = (1991) 389–407.

——(1990). 'The antiquarian tradition: spoils and representations of foreign armour', in Eder (1990) 158–73 = (1991) 582–98.

——(1991). *Roman culture and society* (Oxford).

Rayet, O. (ed.) (1884). *Monuments de l'art antique* (Paris).

Reeve, M. D. (1991). 'The transmission of Florus and the *periochae* again', *CQ* n.s. xli. 453–83.

——(1996). 'The place of P in the stemma of Livy 1–10', in C. A. Chavannes-Mazel and M. M. Smith (edd.), *Medieval manuscripts of the Latin classics: production and use* (Los Altos Hills, CA, and London), 74–90.

Reid, J. S. (1899). Review of F. F. Abbott, *Selected letters of Cicero*, *CR* xiii. 310–13.

——(1916). 'Roman ideas of deity', *JRS* vi. 170–84.

Ribbeck, O. (1887–1892). *Geschichte der römischen Dichtung* (Stuttgart).

Rich, J. W. (1997). 'Structuring Roman history: the consular year and the Roman historical tradition', in *Histos* i (http://www.dur.ac.uk/Classics/histos/1997/rich1.html).

Richard, J.-C. (1978). *Les Origines de la plèbe romaine: essai sur la formation du dualisme patricio-plébéien* [BEFAR ccxxxii] (Rome).

——(1982). '*Praetor collega consulis est*: contribution à l'histoire de la préture', *RPh* lvi. 19–31.

——(1990). 'Réflexions sur le tribunat consulaire', *MEFRA* cii. 767–99.

——(1999). Review of vols i and ii of this commentary, *REL* lxxvii. 316–18.

Richardson, J. S. (1975). 'The triumph, the praetors, and the senate in the early second century B.C.', *JRS* lxv. 50–63.

Richardson, L. (1992). *A new topographical dictionary of ancient Rome* (Baltimore and London).

Rickman, G. E. (1980). *The corn supply of ancient Rome* (Oxford).

Ridley, R. T. (1986). 'The "consular tribunate": the testimony of Livy', *Klio* lxviii. 444–65.

——(1991). 'The historical observations of Jacob Perizonius', *MAL* xxxii. 181–298.

——(1997). 'The missing magister equitum', *ZPE* cxvi. 157–60.

Riemann, O. (1885). *Études sur la langue et la grammaire de Tite-Live*[2] (Paris).

Ritschl, F. (1859). 'Teretina Tribus', *RhM* n.s. xiv. 637 = (1866–79) iv. 760–1.

——(1862). *Priscae Latinitatis monumenta epigraphica* (Berlin).

——(1866–79). *Opuscula* (Leipzig).

Rizzo, S. (1983). *Catalogo dei codici della* pro Cluentio *ciceroniana* (Genoa).

Roberts, L. G. (1918). 'The Gallic fire and Roman archives', *MAAR* ii. 55–65.

Bibliography

Robinson, O. F. (1995). *The criminal law of ancient Rome* (London).

Rosenstein, N. (1990). Imperatores victi: *military defeat and competition in the middle and late Republic* (Berkeley, Los Angeles, and Oxford).

Rospatt, J. J. (1856). 'Kleonymus von Sparta in Italien', *Philologus* xxiii. 72–80.

Rostagni, A. (1934). 'Roma e la Grecia in Tito Livio', in AA.VV., *Studi Liviani* (Rome), 185–207 = (1955–6) ii. 2. 222–48.

——(1955–6). *Scritti minori* (Turin).

Rotondi, G. (1912). *Leges publicae populi Romani* (Milan).

Rüpke, J. (1990). Domi militiae: *Die religiöse Konstruktion des Krieges in Rom* (Stuttgart).

——(1993). 'Livius, Priesternamen und die *annales maximi*', *Klio* lxxv. 155–79.

——(1995). *Kalendar und Öffentlichkeit: die Geschichte der Repräsentation und religiösen Qualifikation von Zeit in Rom* (Berlin and New York).

Ruschenbusch, E. (1997). 'Die Sprache der Vorlagen Diodors für die römische Geschichte', *Historia* xlvi. 185–95.

Rutter, N. K. (1971). 'Campanian chronology in the fifth century B.C.', *CQ* n.s. xxi. 55–61.

——(2001) (ed.). Historia numorum: *Italy* (London).

Ryan, F. X. (1998). 'The interrex L. Cornelius Scipio', *Athenaeum* n.s. lxxx. 244–51.

Sabin, P. (2000). 'The face of Roman battle', *JRS* xc. 1–17.

Säflund, G. (1935). 'Ancient Latin cities of the hills and plains', *OA* i. 64–85.

Salmon, E. T. (1967). *Samnium and the Samnites* (Cambridge).

——(1982). *The making of Roman Italy* (London).

Sandberg, K. (1993). 'The *concilium plebis* as a legislative body during the Republic', in AA.VV. (1993) 74–96.

——(2000). 'Tribunician and non-tribunician legislation in mid-republican Rome', in Bruun (2000*b*) 122–40.

——(2001). *Magistrates and assemblies: a study of legislative practice in republican Rome* [Acta Instituti Romani Finlandiae xxiv] (Rome).

Santoro L'hoir, F. (1990). 'Heroic epithets and recurrent themes in *ab urbe condita*', *TAPhA* cxx. 221–41.

Saulnier, C. (1981). 'La *Coniuratio clandestina*: une interprétation livienne de traditions campanienne et samnite', *REL* lix. 102–20.

——(1983). *L'Armée et la guerre chez les peuples samnites (viie–ive s.)* (Paris).

Scaramella, G. (1897). 'I più antichi Licini e l'annalista C. Licinio Macro', *ANSP* xii. 5–30.

Scardigli, B. (1997). 'Una marcia su Roma nel 342 a.C.? A proposito di Appiano, *Samn.* fr. 1', in L. B. P. Doria (ed.), *L' incidenza dell'antico: studi in memoria di Ettore Lepore II* (Naples), 403–10.

Schäfer, T. (1989). Imperii insignia: sella curulis *und* fasces: *zur Repräsentation römischer Magistrate* (Mainz).

Bibliography

Schäublin, C. (1983). 'Sempronius Asellio fr. 2', *WJA* ix. 147–55.

——(1996). 'Ennius, Vergil—und Livius', *MusHelv* liii. 148–55.

Scheibe, K. (1848). 'Interpolationen im Livius', *Philologus* iii. 555–61.

Scheller, P. (1911). *De Hellenistica historiae conscribendae arte* (Diss. Leipzig).

Schilling, R. (1982). *La Religion romaine de Vénus depuis les origines jusqu'au temps d'Auguste²* (Paris).

Schneider, W. C. (1998). 'Ein neu entdecktes Fragment einer Livius-Handschrift in Darmstadt', *Philologus* cxlii. 185–7.

Schönberger, O. (1960). 'Motivierung und Quellenbenützung in der Deciusepisode des Livius (10,24–30)', *Hermes* lxxxviii. 217–30.

Scullard, H. H. (1967). *The Etruscan cities and Rome* (London).

Sealey, R. (1959). 'Consular tribunes once more', *Latomus* xviii. 521–30.

Seeck, O. (1882). 'Urkundstudien zur älteren römischen Geschichte', *RhM* n.s. xxxvii. 1–25.

——(1885). *Die Kalendertafel der Pontifices* (Berlin).

Segenni, S. (1985). *Amiternum e il suo territorio in età romana* (Pisa).

Seyffert, M. (1861). 'Emendationes Livianae', *NJPhP* vii. 63–80 and 823–43.

Shackleton Bailey, D. R. (1956). *Propertiana* (Cambridge).

——(1965–70). *Cicero's letters to Atticus* (Cambridge).

——(1986). 'Liviana', *RFIC* cxiv. 320–32.

Shatzman, I. (1972). 'The Roman general's authority over booty', *Historia* xxi. 177–205.

Shipley, D. R. (1997). *A commentary on Plutarch's* Life of Agesilaos (Oxford).

Siber, H. (1936). *Die plebejischen Magistraturen bis zur Lex Hortensia* (Leipzig).

Silvestri, D. (1978). 'Taurasia Cisauna e il nome antico del Sannio', *PP* xxxiii. 167–180.

Skard, E. (1933). *Ennius und Sallustius: eine sprachliche Untersuchung* (Oslo).

Skutsch, O. (1985). *The* annals *of Q. Ennius* (Oxford).

Smith, C. J. (1996). *Early Rome and Latium: economy and society* c.*1000– 500 BC* (Oxford).

Sohlberg, D. (1991). 'Militärtribunen und verwandte Probleme der frühen römischen Republik', *Historia* xl. 257–74.

Soltau, W. (1894). 'Der Annalist Tubero', *Hermes* xxxix. 631–3.

——(1909). 'Die Entstehung der Romuluslegende', *ARW* xii. 101–25.

Sommella, P. (1967). *Antichi campi di battaglia in Italia* [Quaderni dell'Istituto di topografia antica della Università di Roma] (Rome).

Sordi, M. (1976). 'Il giuramento della *legio linteata* e la guerra sociale', in ead. (ed.) *I canali della propaganda nel mondo antico* [Contributi dell'Istituto di Storia Antica iv] (Milan, 1976) 160–8.

Starr, C. G. (1980). *The beginnings of imperial Rome: Rome in the middle Republic* (Ann Arbor).

Staveley, E. S. (1954). 'Prouocatio during the fifth and fourth centuries B.C.', *Historia* iii. 412–28.

——(1956). 'The constitution of the Roman Republic', *Historia* v. 74–112.

——(1972). *Greek and Roman voting and elections* (London).

Stein, E. (1927). *Der römische Ritterstand* [Münchener Beiträge zur Papyrusforschung und antiken Rechtsgeschichte x] (Munich).

Steinbauer, D. (1998). 'Zur Grabinschrift der Larthi Cilnei aus Aritim/Arretium/Arezzo', *ZPE* cxxi. 263–81.

Steinby, E. M. (ed.) (1993–2000). *Lexicon topographicum urbis Romae* (Rome).

Steiner, P. (1906). 'Die dona militaria', *BJ* cxiv. 1–98.

Stevens, P. T. (1971). *Euripides* Andromache (Oxford).

Stewart, R. (1998). *Public office in early Rome: ritual procedure and political practice* (Ann Arbor).

Storchi Marino, A. (1993). '*Quinqueuiri mensarii*: censo e debiti nel iv secolo', *Athenaeum* n.s. lxxxi. 213–50.

Suolahti, J. (1963). *The Roman censors* [Annales Academiae Scientiarum Fennicae cxvii] (Helsinki).

Sydenham, E. A. (1952). *The coinage of the Roman Republic* (London).

Syme, R. (1956). 'Seianus on the Aventine', *Hermes* lxxxiv. 257–66 = (1979–91) i. 305–14.

——(1979–91). *Roman papers* (Oxford).

Szemler, G. J. (1972). *The priests of the Roman republic: a study of interaction between priesthoods and magistracies* [Collection Latomus cxxvii] (Brussels).

——(1974). 'The dual priests of the Republic', *RhM* n.s. cxvii. 72–86.

Tanner, J. J. (2000). 'Portraits, power, and patronage in the late Roman Republic', *JRS* xc. 18–50.

Tarbell, F. B. (1908). 'The palm of victory', *CPh* iii. 264–72.

Tarrant, R. J. (1976). *Seneca:* Agamemnon (Cambridge).

Taylor, L. R. (1937). 'The opportunities for dramatic performance in the time of Plautus and Terence', *TAPhA* lxviii. 284–304.

——(1956). 'Trebula Suffenas and the Plautii Silvani', *MAAR* xxiv. 9–30.

——(1957). 'The centuriate assembly before and after the reform', *AJPh* lxxviii. 337–54.

——(1960). *The voting districts of the Roman Republic* [PMAAR xx] (Rome).

——(1966). *Roman voting assemblies* (Ann Arbor).

Terzani, C. (1991*a*). 'La colonia latina di Aesernia', in Capino and Di Niro (1991) 111–12.

——(1991*b*). 'Aesernia', in Capini and Di Niro (1991) 225–8.

——(1996). 'L'ambiente latino: Isernia', in Del Tutto Palma (1996) 147–53.

Thenn, A. (1877). 'Zu Livius', *BBG* xiii. 440–6.

Thomas, R. (1989). *Oral tradition and written record in classical Athens* (Cambridge).

Thomsen, R. (1980). *King Servius Tullius: a synthesis* [Humanitas v] (Copenhagen).

Till, R. (1970). 'Die Scipionenelogien', in D. Ableitinger and H. Gugel (edd.), *Festschrift Karl Vretska* (Heidelberg), 276–89.

Tillyard, H. J. W. (1908). *Agathocles* (Cambridge).

Timpe, D. (1979). 'Erwägungen zur jüngeren Annalistik', *A&A* xxv. 97–110.

Tondo, S. (1963). 'Il "sacramentum militiae" nell'ambiente culturale romano-italico', *SDHI* xxix. 1–123.

Torelli, M. (1975). *Elogia Tarquiniensia* (Florence).

——(1982). *Etruria*² [Guide archeologiche Laterza iii] (Rome and Bari).

Toynbee, A. J. (1965). *Hannibal's legacy* (London).

Tränkle, H. (1968). 'Beobachtungen und Erwägungen zum Wandel der livianischen Sprache', *WS* n.s. ii. 103–52.

Treggiari, S. (1991). *Roman marriage: iusti coniuges from the time of Cicero to the time of Ulpian* (Oxford).

——(2003). 'Ancestral virtues and vices: Cicero on nature, nurture, and presentation', in Braund and Gill (2003) 139–64.

Trisciuoglio, A. (1998). *'Sarta tecta, ultrotributa, opus publicum faciendum locare': sugli appalti relativi alle opere pubbliche nell'età repubblicana e augustea* [Università di Torino: Memorie del Dipartimento di Scienze Giuridiche. Serie v. 7] (Naples).

Tullio, R. (1989). 'Aquilonia e Monte Vairano', *A&R* n.s. xxxiv. 87–96.

Ullmann, R. (1927). *La Technique des discours dans Salluste, Tite-Live et Tacite: la matière et la composition* (Oslo).

Unger, G. F. (1891). 'Die Glaubwürdigkeit der capitolinischen Consuln-tafel', *NJPhP* cxliii. (1891) 289–321.

Urso, G. (1998). *Taranto e gli xenikoì strategoí* (Rome).

——(1999). 'Le fazioni filoromane in Magna Grecia dalle guerre sannitiche alla spedizione di Pirro', in M. Sordi (ed.), *Fazioni e congiure nel mondo antico* [Contributi dell'Istituto di Storia Antica xxv] (Milan), 135–50.

Vaahtera, J. (1993). 'On the religious nature of the place of assembly', in AA.VV. (1993) 97–116.

——(2001). *Roman augural law in Greek historiography: a study of the theory and terminology* [Historia Einzelschriften clvi] (Stuttgart).

——(2003). 'Livy and the priestly records: à propos ILS 9338', *Hermes* cxxx. 100–8.

Vahlen, J. (1907–8). *Opuscula academica* (Leipzig).

Valente, F. (1982). *Isernia: origine e crescita di una città* (Campobasso).

Valeton, I. M. J. (1891). 'De inaugurationibus Romanis caerimoniarum et sacerdotum', *Mnemosyne*, ser. 2, xix. 405–60.

Valvo, A. (1984). 'Il "cognomen Capitolinus" in età repubblicana e il sorgere dell'area sacra sull'arce e il Campidoglio', in M. Sordi (ed.), *I santuari e la guerra nel mondo antico* [Contributi dell'Istituto di Storia Antica x] (Milan), 92–106.

Bibliography

Vasaly, A. (1987). 'Personality and power: Livy's depiction of the Appii Claudii in the fiirst pentad', *TAPhA* cxvii. 203–26.

Verrecchia, G. (1953). 'Pagine non chiare di Tito Livio sulle guerre sannitiche?', *Samnium* xxxi. 93–108.

Versnel, H. S. (1970). *Triumphus* (Leiden).

Vetter, E. (1953). *Handbuch der italischen Dialekte* (Heidelberg).

Vishnia, R. F. (1996). 'The Carvilii Maximi of the Republic', *Athenaeum* n.s. lxxxiv. 433–56.

Viti, A. (1982). *Res Publica Aeserninorum* (Isernia).

Wachendorf, H. (1864). *Observationes Livianae* (Diss. Bonn).

Wachter, R. (1987). *Altlateinische Inschriften: sprachliche und epigraphische Untersuchungen zu den Dokumenten bis etwa 150 v. Chr.* (Bern, Frankfurt am Main, New York, and Paris).

Walbank, F. W. (1945). 'Polybius, Philinus, and the First Punic War', *CQ* xxxix. 1–18 = (1985) 77–98.

——(1957–79). *A historical commentary on Polybius* (Oxford).

——(1985). *Selected papers: studies in Greek and Roman history and historiography* (Cambridge).

——Astin, A. E., Frederiksen, M. W., Ogilvie, R. M., and Drummond, A. (edd.) (1989). *The rise of Rome to 220 B.C.* [The Cambridge Ancient History² vii. 2] (Cambridge).

Walch, G. L. (1815). *Emendationes Livianae* (Berlin).

Walker, A. D. (1993). '*Enargeia* and the spectator in Greek historiography', *TAPhA* cxxiii. 353–77.

Walker, J. (1822). *Supplementary annotations on Livy* (London).

Wallace, R. W. (1990). 'Hellenization and Roman society in the late fourth century B.C.: a methodological critique', in Eder (1990) 278–92.

——and Harris, E. M. (1996). *Transitions to empire: essays in Greco-Roman history, 360–146 B.C., in honor of E. Badian* (Norman, OK, and London).

Walsh, P. G. (1986). *Titi Livi ab urbe condita libri xxviii–xxx* (Leipzig).

——(1999). *Titi Livi ab urbe condita libri xxxvi–xl* (Oxford).

Walt, S. (1997). *Der Historiker C. Licinius Macer: Einleitung, Fragmente, Kommentar* [Beiträge zur Altertumskunde ciii] (Stuttgart and Leipzig).

Walter, F. (1892). Review of Luterbacher, *BBG* xxviii. 624–5.

——(1918). 'Zu Livius und Curtius', *BPhW* xxxviii. 933–6.

Walter, U. (2000). 'Marcus Furius Camillus — die schattenhafte Lichtgestalt', in K.-J. Hölkeskamp and E. Stein-Hölkeskamp (edd.), *Von Romulus zu Augustus: große Gestalten der römischen Republik* (Munich), 58–68.

——(2001). 'Rollentausch und Übersetzung ins Absurde: zur rhetorischen Strategie in der Rede des Ap. Claudius Crassus (Liv. 6,40,3–41)', *Hermes* cxxix. 251–8.

Walters, C. F., and Conway, R. S. (1918). 'Restorations and emendations in Livy vi–x', *CQ* xii. 1–14, 98–105, and 113–19.

Warde Fowler, W. (1916). 'Jupiter and the triumphator', *CR* xxx. 153–7.

Ward-Perkins, J. B. (1964). *Landscape and History in central Italy* [The Second J. L. Myres Memorial Lecture] (Oxford).

Warren, L. B. (1970). 'Roman triumphs and Etruscan kings: the changing face of the triumph', *JRS* lx. 49–66.

Watson, W. A. J. (1974). *'Enuptio gentis'*, in Watson (ed.), *Daube noster: essays in legal history for David Daube* (Edinburgh), 331–41.

Watt, W. S. (1991). 'Notes on Livy 6–10', *C&M* xlii. 213–20.

——(2001). 'Textual notes on Nepos, Florus, Justin', *Philologus* cxlv. 100–7.

——(2002). 'Notes on Livy 6–10', *Prometheus* xxviii. 179–85.

Weigel, R. D. (1983). 'Roman colonization and the tribal assembly', *PP* xxxviii. 191–6.

——(1998). 'Roman generals and the vowing of temples, 500–100 B.C.', *C&M* xlix. 119–42.

Weinstock, S. (1957). 'Victor and Invictus', *HThR* l. 211–47.

——(1971). *Divus Julius* (Oxford).

Weissenborn, W. (1843). Review of Alschefski's edn. of books vi–x, *NJPhP* xiii. 243–83.

Welz, E. (1852). *Adnotationes criticae in quosdam locos Livianos* (Progr. Leobschütz).

Werner, R. (1963). *Der Beginn der römischen Republik* (Munich and Vienna).

Wesenberg, A. S. (1870/1). 'Emendatiunculae Livianae', *Tidskrift for Philologi og Pædagogik* ix. 1–41, 81–111, 275–302.

Wex, F. C. (1852). *C. Cornelii Taciti de vita et moribus Cn. Iulii Agricolae liber* (Brunswick).

Wiedemann, T. E. J. (1992). *Emperors and gladiators* (London and New York).

Williams, G. W. (1958). 'Some aspects of Roman marriage ceremonies and ideals', *JRS* xlviii. 16–29.

Williams, J. H. C. (2001). *Beyond the Rubicon: Romans and Gauls in republican Italy* (Oxford).

Williams, T. (1971). 'Gr. Anth. 12, 39 (anon.) and Greek folk humour', *Hermes* xcix. 423–8.

Wills, J. (1996). *Repetition in Latin poetry* (Oxford).

Winkler, L. (1890–2). *Die Dittographien in den nikomachianischen Codices des Livius* (Progr. des Leopoldstädter Communal-, Real- und Obergymnasiums in Wien).

Wiseman, T. P. (1971). *New men in the Roman Senate 139 B.C.–A.D. 14* (Oxford).

——(1974). 'The Circus Flaminius', *PBSR* xlii. 3–26.

——(1979). *Clio's Cosmetics* (Leicester).

——(1981). 'The temple of Victory on the Palatine', *Antiquaries Journal* lxi. 35–52 = (1987) 187–204.

——(1987). *Roman studies literary and historical* (Liverpool).

——(1989). 'Roman legend and oral tradition', *JRS* lxxix. 129–37 = (1994) 23–36, 124–7.

——(1991). 'Democracy and myth: the life and death of Remus', *LCM* xvi. 115–24.

——(1993). 'Lying historians: seven types of mendacity', in C. Gill and T. P. Wiseman (edd.), *Lies and fiction in the ancient world* (Exeter), 122–46.

——(1994). *Historiography and imagination: eight essays on Roman culture* (Exeter).

——(1995a). *Remus: a Roman myth* (Cambridge).

——(1995b). 'The god of the Lupercal', *JRS* lxxxv. 1–22.

——(1996). 'The Minucii and their monument', in Linderski (1996) 57–74 = Wiseman (1998) 90–105, 201–6.

——(1998). *Roman drama and Roman history* (Exeter).

——(2000a). 'Liber: myth, drama and ideology in republican Rome', in Bruun (2000b) 265–99.

——(2000b). Review of volume ii of this commentary, *CR* n.s. l. 81–3.

——(2002c). 'Roman history and the ideological vacuum', in id. (ed.), *Classics in progress* (Oxford), 285–310.

——(2003). 'The legend of Lucius Brutus', in M. Citroni (ed.), *Memoria e identità: la cultura Romana costruisce la sua immagine* (Florence), 21–38.

Wissowa, G. (1897). *Analecta Romana topographica* (Progr. Halle) = (1904) 253–79.

——(1904). *Gesammelte Abhandlungen zur römischen Religions- und Stadtgeschichte* (Munich).

——(1912). *Religion und Kultus der Römer*² (Munich).

Wolff, E. (1896). Review of C. Haupt's commentary on books viii–x, *WKlPh* xiii (1896), 1225–9.

Wolff, F. C. (1826). *Observationes et emendationes Livianae* (Flensburg).

Wölfflin, E. von (1864). *Livianische Kritik und livianischer Sprachgebrauch* (Progr. Winterthur [Berlin]) = (1933) 1–21.

——(1881). 'Über die allitierenden Verbindungen der lateinischen Sprache', *SBBA* 1–94 = (1933) 224–81.

——(1885). 'Genetiv mit Ellipse des regierenden Substantivs', *ALL* ii. 365–71.

——(1887). 'Ex toto, in totum', *ALL* iv. 144–7.

——(1888). 'Per omnia', *ALL* v. 144.

——(1890). 'De Scipionum elogiis', *RPh* xiv. 113–22.

——(1933). *Ausgewählte Schriften* (ed. G. Meyer) (Leipzig).

Wolters, H. (1924). 'Das älteste Bild der Römer', in AA.VV., *Festschrift Heinrich Wölfflin: Beiträge zur Kunst- und Geistesgeschichte* (Munich), 9–18.

Woodman, A. J. (1977). *Velleius Paterculus: the Tiberian narrative (2. 94–131)* (Cambridge).

——(1983). *Velleius Paterculus: the Caesarian and Augustan narrative (2. 41–93)* (Cambridge).

Woodman, A. J., and Martin, R. H. (1996). *The* annals *of Tacitus: book 3* (Cambridge).

Wuilleumier, P. (1939). *Tarente: des origines à la conquête romaine* (Paris).

Yardley, J. C. (2003). *Justin and Pompeius Trogus: a study of the language of Justin's* epitome *of Pompeius Trogus* [Phoenix Suppl. xli] (Toronto).

Zevi, F. (1996). 'Sulle fasi più antiche di Ostia', in A. G. Zevi and A. Claridge (edd.), *'Roman Ostia' revisited* (London), 69–89.

Zhmodikov, A. (2000). 'Roman republic heavy infantrymen in battle (iv–ii centuries BC)', *Historia* xlix. 67–78.

Zingerle, A. (1889). 'Zu Livius', *ZöG* xl. 983–8.

Ziolkowski, A. (1989). 'The *sacra via* and the temple of Juppiter Stator', *ORom* xvii. 224–39.

——(1992). *The temples of mid-republican Rome and their historical and topographical context* [Saggi di Storia Antica iv] (Rome).

Zumpt, A. W. (1871). 'Über die lustra der Römer', *RhM* n.s. xxvi. 1–38.

Indexes

For all ancient persons, including mythological figures (but with the exception of Livy), one should look in the index of ancient persons. It has not been possible to compile an index of passages cited, but some references to authors whose views are discussed may be found in the index of ancient persons: Latin authors are listed under their full Roman name, Greek under the name by which they are generally known. In both the index of ancient persons and the general index **bold** has sometimes been used, and particularly in long entries, to point out a general or principal discussion of a person, place, or phenomenon. Latin has been placed in the index of Latin, where the reference is to a discussion of Livian or Latin usage, in the general index where the reference is to a discussion that is not concerned primarily with linguistic usage (e.g. of political and rhetorical terms). All Greek words are listed separately in the index of Greek. Attention should be drawn to the long entries LIVY, MANUSCRIPTS, τόποι AND OTHER COMMONPLACE IDEAS, and TRIUMPHS. The Samnites are mentioned *passim* in the commentary, and full indexing of all references to them would be pointless: events in which they were involved in any particular year can be found easily by using the headings in the commentary. Some entries in the index are to notes that merely provide a cross-reference to earlier volumes of this commentary: the inclusion of these entries seemed more helpful than their exclusion.

I. ANCIENT PERSONS

Roman magistrates are generally identified by the year in which they first held the consulship or consular tribunate. If they did not hold either of these offices, then they are identified by the most important office which they are known to have held. When a magistrate held a dictatorship some years before a consulship or consular tribunate, the dictatorship is sometimes noted as well.

Sp. Postumius Albus Regillensis (*cos.* 464)
54
Sp. Postumius Albus Regillensis (*cos. tr.*
394) 503
L. Postumius Megellus (*cos.* I 305): as
aedile (date uncertain) 260, 358;
breaches *lex Genucia* 543; first Roman
known to have spoken Greek 22;
military service in 290s BC 10;
prepared to go against *consensus* of
peers 15–16; relationship to other
Postumii unknown 14; utterances of
374; in 305 BC (as consul) 292, 488
(possible triumph); in 295 BC (as
propraetor) 274, 275, 282, 288, 289,
292–3, 305, 311–12, 313; in 294 BC (as
consul) 346, 348, 349, 350, 357, 358,
362, 372, 373, 374, 375, 488; in 293 BC
(as legate and threatened prosecution)
10, 456; in 292/1 BC (as *interrex*) 489;
in 291 BC (as consul) 188, 373, 374,
383, 543; prosecutions of 509
Potitii, religious rituals of 115
Ps.-Asconius, on *manubiae* 455
Ptolemy Philadelphus, Roman embassy to
87, 188
Publicii, claim descent from seer 119
Publicius (seer) 119
C. Publilius (victim of L. Papirius),
violation of 582
Q. Publilius (*tr. pl.* 384) 509
T. Publilius (*aug.* 300) 120
Volero Publilius (*tr. pl.* I 472) 124
Q. Publilius Philo (*cos.* I 339) **557**; breaches
lex Genucia 543; perhaps father of T.
Publilius 120; in 339 BC (as consul and
dictator) 471, 487; in 336 BC (as first
plebeian praetor) 12, 112, 532, 576; in
326 BC (as proconsul) 9, 446, 488
(triumph), 579–80
Pudicitia: general 248; Patricia 116, 247,
248, 249; Plebeia 245, 247, 250;
possible statue of 248–9; temple on Via
Latina 248
Pylades (pantomime artist) 546
Pyrrhus 55, 74, 104, 116, 117, 291
Pythagoras, statue of 22–3

Quinctii: in annalistic tradition 502;
Quinctii Capitolini 516
L. Quinctius Cincinnatus (*cos. tr.* I 386)
503
T. Quinctius Cincinnatus Capitolinus (*cos.
tr.* I 388, *dict.* 380): campaign in 380 BC
502; triumph in 380 BC 487
Quinctii Flaminini 118

L. Quinctius Flamininus (*cos.* 192) 75, 450
T. Quinctius Flamininus (*cos.* 198): perhaps
younger than L. Flamininus 75; death
of 579
T. Quinctius Flamininus (*iiiuir mon.* 126)
118
T. Quinctius Poenus Captolinus Crispinus
(*dict.* 361; *cos.* I 354): possible triumph
in 361 BC 488; said by Macer to have
been appointed *comitiorum habendorum
causa* in 361 BC 542–3
T. Quinctius Poenus Cincinnatus (*cos.* I
431), prosecution of 509
Quirinus 449–50; temples of 449–50, 486

C. Rabirius, trial of 121, 123
Ratumenna 262–3
Remus, *see* Romulus
Romulus (first king of Rome): and augurate
89, 90; as *conditor* 317; as mythological
and antiquarian construct 94–5; co-
regent with T. Tatius 111, 539; creates
tribes 93–4; origin of myth 247, 378;
equated with Quirinus 450; in Tubero
147; statue of Romulus and Remus
beneath she-wolf 263, 264–5; tribe
Ramnes supposedly named after 92,
93; vow to Jupiter Stator 378
Rumina 264

C. Sallustius Crispus (*pr.* 46 and historian):
alludes to Cicero 517; imitates
Thucydides 148; origin of 414; echoed
by Livy and/or Tacitus 367, 517; on
Licinius Macer 549
Salus: cult of 22; temple of 476, 490;
dedication of temple 45, 59
Q. Salvidienus Rufus (*pro pr.* or *pro cos.*
41–40) 314
Saturnus, temple of 525
Scantia 457
Scantius (mentioned in *epit. Oxy.* book l)
457
M. Scantius (*tr. pl.* 293) 457
Scribonii Curiones 118
C. Scribonius Curio (*pr.* 193) 118
Sempronii, term *gens* applied to 115
Sempronius Asellio (historian): on *annales
maximi* and predecessors 490–1;
recording of triumphs 489
C. Sempronius Atratinus (*cos.* 423),
prosecutions of 509
P. Sempronius Blaesus (*tr. pl.* 191) 446
Sempronius Densus 557
C. Sempronius Gracchus (*tr. pl.* I 123) 233,
354

II. GENERAL

ablative absolute: in enumeration of commander's achievements 375; modified by *quamquam* 169; by *ut* 73

Abruzzo 35, 46, 228; tribes of 23, 330

ab urbe condita construction 345, 512

accents, non-standard 76–7

accusative, adverbial, used with comparative 363

Acerrae 4

Actium, battle of 65

actors, rules for marriage 546

adjectives: of quantity acting as 'host' to auxiliary 220; neuter, substantival use 81

Adriatic Sea 25, 30, 35, 49, 61, 293, 294

Aeclanum 208

aediles, general: and games 259; building of 260–1; later dedicate temples vowed in aedileship 358; notices of activities provided by Livy 182, 245, 259–61; oversight of corn supply 160; prosecute in pairs 261; prosecutions by 122, 123, 182, 187, 259–61, 341–2, 508, 579

curule: general 7; alternation of office between patricians and plebeians 140, 545; did not have presidency over assemblies 554; our deficient records for 13

plebeian 7, 267, 539–40; fining by 267; *uitio creati* 538

Aegina, ox taken from 251

Aenaria 527

Aequi **177–8**, **513**; and Alba 37; and Cominium 384; and *lex sacrata* 394; territory of 35, 37–8

Aequan Wars: general: 25–6, 35, 205, 328; in 463 BC 73; in 394 BC 503; in 304 BC 31, 488; in 302/1 BC 44–6, 50; in 300 BC 137; in 299 BC 151

Aequicoli **177–8**

aerarium 382, 513

aes multaticium, see *pecunia multaticia*

Aesculetum 523

Aesernia (Isernia) **335–6**; colonization of 25, 335; geographical position of 183, 228, 292; road from to Aufidena and Sulmo 177; in 295 BC 281, 292, 336

ager publicus: infringement of rules for use of 182, 260, 261, 266; originates in

Roman conquest and confiscation 568

ager Romanus: size of 3; distance of Latin colonies from 35

ager Stellas 281, 292, 337

ager Vaticanus, see Vatican

Agnone 385

Agrigentum (Greek Acragas, now Agrigento) 579

A(ha)rna (Civitella d'Arno) 27, **303**

Alba Fucens (Albe) **37–8**; colonization of 26, 35, 44

Alban Mount 539, 561

Aletrium (Alatri) 36, 40

Alfedena 177, 389

Allia: *dies Alliensis* 511; Romans behave in unRoman manner during and after defeat 72, 526

allies: numbers of serving with legions 213, 214; report enemy activity to Romans 469; Roman use of allied manpower 214

Allifae 24, 25, 228, 383

allotment, viritane 310

Altilia (Sepino) 441

Alvito 388

ambassadors: enemy, sent to Rome 372; escorting of 562

Ameria (Amelia) 27

amicitia 556

Amiternum 30–1, 33, 34, 380, 385, 387, 389

amnesties 568

anachronism 238–9

anacoluthon 109

Anagnia 378

anaphora 104, 366, 407, 441, 442, 541

ancestry, invented 23

anger 339

Anglesey 64

Aniene, river 25, 30, 45, 151

annales maximi **479–84**; and Atticus 482–3; and Cicero 482; and P. Mucius Scaevola 476, 477, 482–3; and Ti. Coruncanius 481, 482; and Verrius Flaccus 482–3; character of eighty-book edn. 482; not mentioned at beginning of Plutarch's *Numa* 506; perhaps did not record dictatorships 486; perhaps did not record division of

632

LIVY

Indexes

General

III. LATIN

Indexes

paenitere, with negative 99
palari 549
pandere, uiam pandere 79
par, modified by *haudquaquam* 179
parare, used with *conatus* 400
paratus 425
pars: used without previous distributive word 63–4; *ea parte qua* 548; *parte alia* 335
partus, with *labor* dependent 155
parum, modifying *procedere* 359; modifying *proficere* 189
 parum est + ni(si) clause 536; with *quod*-clause as subject 536
parumper, modifying *cedere* 558
paruus, of ships 62
Pater, as epithet of gods 323, 572
pati, ferre ac pati 168–9
patricius, suggested derivation from *patrem ciere* 116
paucus: pauci in political contexts 519
paulisper 558
pauor, governed by *offundere* 78
pax, used loosely 373; *pace deum (uel sim.)* 108–9
pecunia, qualified by *grandis* 451
pedes, peditum agmen 428
per omnia, 'in every respect' 416
perdere, archaic forms of 222
perfundere, figurative use 404
pergere: used as substitute for *ire* 217; coupled with *persequi* 356
perlaetus 233
perlicere, coupled with *societas* 168
persequi: coupled with *pergere* 356; *reliquias belli persequi* 588
pertinere, ad famam pertinere 300
peruincere, 'gain one's object' 297; with final clause 297
pestilentia, qualified by *grauis* 339
plerique, with genitive 367
ponere, in context of assertions about veracity of information 216
populatio, qualified by *effusus* 62
populus Romanus, consul populi Romani 216
porrigere, manus ad caelum porrigere 369
porta, a porta domum (uel sim.) 548
potestas, contrasted with *arbitrium* 297
prae strepitu 180
praeceps, of setting of planets 430
praeda, dependent on *dulcedo* 588; on *trahere* 227
praedator, qualified by *uagus* 228
praedicere, in cross-references 186
praescribere and *praescriptum* 244
praeses, with genitive or dative 243

praesidium, qualified by *modicus* 185
praestare, in context of reparations 449
praestituere, praestituta die 231
praeter, used with *alius* 359
precatio, qualified by *sollemnis* 321
premere, with *caligo* as subject 353
prex, precibus fatigare 588
primus: qualifying *signa* 221; *primo quoque tempore* 214; *primum* as equivalent of *prima acies* 191
princeps: of founder of family's nobility 111; with dative 111
prius, modifying ablatives absolute 63
pro: used near to *de* 206; *pro consule* and *pro praetore* 580
procedere: modified by *lente* 77; by *parum* 359
procella, qualified by *equestris* 78
proceres 319
proconsul 580
proculcare 368
proelium, with *integrare* or *profligare* 230
proferre, with *castra* as object 357
proficere, modified by *parum* 189
proficisci: 'make journey' 417; of ritual departure for war 563
profligare, with *bellum* or *proelium* 230
prope esse ut, with *iam* 215
propraetor 580
prorogatum in annum imperium est (uel sim.) 245
prosperus, modified by *aeque* 63
prouocare, 'challenge' 124
prouolare 549
publicum consilium, of senate 514
pudicitia, in close proximity to *sanctus/-titas* 258
pugna, object of *irritare* 368
pugnare, with *in terga* 368

quadratus, qualifying *agmen* 562
quae res, = quod 322
quam mallem and *quam uellem*, at opening of speech 219
quam pro 193
quamquam, modifying ablative absolute 169
-que: after short final *-e* 520; disjunctive 218, 370, 399; with ellipse of *ceteri (uel sim.)* 300; *-que . . . et* 576, 577, 579; probably not used after *ad* 527
quia, quia-clauses, rules for mood of verb in 428; *non quia . . . sed (quia)* 428–9
quicquam, with partitive genitive 430–1
quid: sed quid ego (uel sim.) 520; *quid ego haec (uel sim.)* 520
quidam auctores sunt 586

656

IV. GREEK